History
of
CUMBERLAND COUNTY

Pennsylvania

CONTAINING HISTORY OF THE COUNTIES, THEIR TOWNSHIPS, TOWNS, VILLAGES, SCHOOLS, CHURCHES, INDUSTRIES, ETC.; PORTRAITS OF EARLY SETTLERS AND PROMINENT MEN; BIOGRAPHIES; HISTORY OF PENNSYLVANIA, STATISTICAL AND MISCELLANEOUS MATTER, ETC., ETC.

— ILLUSTRATED —

P. A. Durand and *J. Fraise Richard*

HERITAGE BOOKS
2008

HERITAGE BOOKS
AN IMPRINT OF HERITAGE BOOKS, INC.

Books, CDs, and more—Worldwide

For our listing of thousands of titles see our website
at
www.HeritageBooks.com

A Facsimile Reprint
Published 2008 by
HERITAGE BOOKS, INC.
Publishing Division
100 Railroad Ave. #104
Westminster, Maryland 21157

Originally published 1886

— Publisher's Notice —
In reprints such as this, it is often not possible to remove blemishes from the original. We feel the contents of this book warrant its reissue despite these blemishes and hope you will agree and read it with pleasure.

International Standard Book Numbers
Paperbound: 978-1-58549-396-8
Clothbound: 978-0-7884-7559-7

CONTENTS.

PORTRAITS

Ahl, C. W. ... 123	Miller, Capt. W. E. ... 163
Ahl, Daniel V. ... 263	Moore, James ... 365
Ahl, John A. ... 133	Moore, J. A. ... 193
Ahl, Peter A. ... 253	Moser, Hon. H. G. ... Part I, 45
Ahl, Thomas W. ... 213	Mullin, A. F. ... 203
Bosler, Abraham ... 43	Niesley, C. B. ... 153
Clever, George ... 293	Paxton, George W. ... 313
Coyle, James ... 233	Plank, A. W. ... 173
Dale, William W., M. D. ... 83	Pratt, Capt. R. H. ... 183
Gorgas, S. P. ... 53	Rea, J. D. ... 223
Gorgas, Hon. William R. ... 23	Sadler, Hon. W. F. ... 2
Hemminger, George, M. D. ... 73	Sibbet, R. Lowry, M. D. ... 93
Herman, A. J., M. D. ... 103	Snyder, Simon ... 303
Hutton, John ... 283	Stewart, Alex., M. D. ... 33
Kauffman, Levi ... 273	Thomas, R. H. ... 143
Kieffer, S. B., A. M., M. D. ... 63	Wherry, Hon. Samuel ... Part I, 79
Manning, H. ... 243	Wing, Rev. Conway P. ... 13
Mickey, Robert ... 113	

BIOGRAPHICAL SKETCHES

Carlisle, Borough of ... 367	Middlesex Township ... 498
Mechanicsburg, Borough of ... 405	Mifflin Township ... 502
Newville, Borough of ... 447	Monroe Township ... 506
Shippensburg, Borough of ... 442	Newton Township ... 517
Shiremanstown, Borough of ... 456	North Middleton Township ... 525
Cook Township ... 458	Penn Township ... 526
Dickinson Township ... 459	Silver Spring Township ... 535
East Pennsborough Township and Borough of Camp Hill ... 465	Southampton Township ... 545
Frankford Township ... 476	South Middleton Township and Borough of Mount Holly Springs ... 549
Hampden Township ... 479	Upper Allen Township ... 562
Hopewell Township and Borough of Newburg ... 485	West Pennsborough Township ... 574
Lower Allen Township and Borough of New Cumberland ... 492	

HISTORY OF CUMBERLAND COUNTY.

CHAPTER I.—DESCRIPTIVE ... 3-7
Geography—Geology—Topography, etc.

CHAPTER II.—PIONEERS ... 7-40
"Louther Manor," etc.—Taxes paid from 1736 to 1749—Earliest List of Taxables in Cumberland County—First Settlers in the North Valley—Taxables in the County in 1762—Early Settlers—Wild Animals and Fish—Customs and Habits—Formation of Townships and Boroughs—Lands.

CHAPTER III.—INDIAN HISTORY ... 41-66
French and Indian War—Pontiac's War.

CHAPTER IV.—COUNTY ORGANIZATION ... 66-77
Location of the County Seat—Division of the County into Townships—County Buildings—Population—Postoffices in 1885—Internal Improvements—Public Roads—Railroads.

CHAPTER V.—MILITARY ... 77-108

CONTENTS.

Cumberland County in the Revolution—The Whisky Insurrection—The War of 1812—The Mexican War. ... PAGE

CHAPTER VI.—MILITARY (Continued)......109-130
Carlisle Barracks—Cumberland County in the War of the Rebellion.

CHAPTER VII.—COURTS............130-138
County Officials—Members of Congress, Senators and Assemblymen.

CHAPTER VIII.—BENCH AND BAR............138-170
Provincial Period—From the Revolution Until the Adoption of the Constitution of 1790—Constitutional Period.

CHAPTER IX.—MEDICAL............170-187
Biographical—Physicians in Cumberland County since 1879—Physicians in Cumberland County Registered in Office of Prothonotary at Carlisle—Cumberland County Medical Society.

CHAPTER X.—THE PRESS............188-195
Of Carlisle—Of Shippensburg—Of Mechanicsburg—Of Newville—Of Mount Holly.

CHAPTER XI.—EDUCATIONAL............195-206
Legal History—Early Schools—Dickinson College—Metzgar Female Institute—Indian Industrial School—Cumberland Valley State Normal School—Teachers' Institute—County Superintendents.

CHAPTER XII.—RELIGIOUS............207-220
Presbyterian Church—Episcopal Church—Methodist Church—Roman Catholic Church—German Reformed Church—Lutheran Church—Church of God—German Baptists—United Brethren—The Mennonites—Evangelical Association.

CHAPTER XIII.—POLITICAL............221-222
Slavery in Cumberland County, etc.

CHAPTER XIV.—AGRICULTURAL............225-228
Cumberland County Agricultural Society—Grangers' Picnic-Exhibition, Williams' Grove.

CHAPTER XV.—THE FORMATION OF TOWNSHIPS, ETC............228-229
The First Proprietary Manor—Formation of Townships—Organization of Boroughs.

CHAPTER XVI.—BOROUGH OF CARLISLE....229-248
Its Inception — Survey — First Things—Meeting of Captives—Revolutionary Period—War of 1812—Growth of the Town, etc.—The Borough in 1846—McClintock Riot—War of the Rebellion—Situation, Public Buildings, etc. — Churches — Cemeteries — Schools, Institutes and College—Newspapers—Manufacturing Establishments, etc.—Gas and Water Company—Societies—Conclusion.

CHAPTER XVII.—BOROUGH OF MECHANICSBURG............249-256
Its Beginning—Growth — William Armstrong—Population—War of the Rebellion — Schools and Educational Institutes — Churches — Newspapers — Public Hall and Market House—Banking Institutions—Gas and Water Company—Societies—Conclusion.

CHAPTER XVIII.—BOROUGH OF SHIPPENSBURG............257-268
Its First Settlement—Early Reminiscences—List of Original Land Purchasers—Early Hotels in Shippensburg—Churches—Cemeteries — Schools — Newspapers — Bank — Societies.

CHAPTER XIX. — BOROUGH OF SHIREMANSTOWN............268-269
Locality—Origin of Name—Churches—Societies—Miscellaneous.

CHAPTER XX.—COOK TOWNSHIP............269-270
Formation — Topography — Roads — Pine Grove Furnace and Laurel Forge—George Stevenson—Postoffice and Railroad.

CHAPTER XXI.—DICKINSON TOWNSHIP....270-275
Formation — Topography — Railroads—Original Settlers, Early Land-Owners and Settlers—Negro Kidnaping—Hotel, etc.—Churches—Schools, etc.

CHAPTER XXII. — EAST PENNSBOROUGH TOWNSHIP AND BOROUGH OF CAMP HILL............275-278
Origin—Name—Boundary—Early History—Villages — Miscellaneous — BOROUGH OF CAMP HILL—Location, etc.—Name, etc.—Church and Cemetery.

CHAPTER XXIII.—FRANKFORD TOWNSHIP............278-286
Formation — Boundary — Topography — Earliest Settlers—The Butler Family—Village.

CHAPTER XXIV.—HAMPDEN TOWNSHIP..286-290
Formation — Boundary — Topography — Early Settlers—Mills, Bridges, etc.—The Indians—Paxton Manor in Hampden—Churches—Hamlets—Miscellaneous.

CHAPTER XXV.—HOPEWELL TOWNSHIP AND BOROUGH OF NEWBURG............290-298
Formation — Topography — Early Settlement—The Bradys—Hopewell Academy—Miscellaneous—BOROUGH OF NEWBURG—Location—The Village in 1819, 1845 and 1886—"The Sunny Side Female Seminary."

CHAPTER XXVI.—LOWER ALLEN TOWNSHIP AND BOROUGH OF NEW CUMBERLAND...298-305
Formation, Locality, Boundary, etc.—Indians—Early Settlers—Character of Soil, etc.—Lisburn — Milltown — Churches — Cemeteries — Schools — Miscellaneous—BOROUGH OF NEW CUMBERLAND—Location—Origin—Early Incidents and Industries—Incorporation—Railroads, etc.—New Cumberland of To-day—Churches—Miscellaneous.

CHAPTER XXVII.—MIDDLESEX TOWNSHIP............305-307
Formation, Boundary and Topography—Railroad—Early Settlers—Middlesex—Carlisle Springs—Miscellaneous.

CHAPTER XXVIII.—MIFFLIN TOWNSHIP..307-312
Formation, Boundary and Topography—Indian Trail and Village—First Settlement—The Williamson Massacre and Other Early Incidents — Block Houses — Capt. Samuel Brady—First Settlers Along Big Run—Early Roads, Viewers, etc.—Sulphur Springs, etc.—Churches—Miscellaneous.

CHAPTER XXIX.—MONROE TOWNSHIP.....315-317
Formation — Boundary — Topography — First Settlers—Churches and Cemetery—Schools, Industries, etc.—Villages.

CHAPTER XXX.—NEWTON TOWNSHIP AND BOROUGH OF NEWVILLE............317-327
Formation — Boundary — Topography — General Description—Indian Pack Trail—Fort Carnahan—Early Settlers—The Sharp Family—Other Pioneers—Villages—Miscellaneous—BOROUGH OF NEWVILLE—Location — Incorporation — First Settlement—First Sale of Lots—First Hotels, Stores, etc. Incorporation, etc.—An Historical Character—Churches—Cemetery—Educational Institutions—Newspapers—Banks—Fire Department—Societies.

CHAPTER XXXI.—NORTH MIDDLETON TOWNSHIP............328-332
Origin — Boundary — Description — Early Settlers—"Heads of Families"—The Cave—Meeting House Springs—The Grave-yard at Meeting House Springs—Miscellaneous.

iv

CONTENTS.

CHAPTER XXXII.—PENN TOWNSHIP.......333–335
Formation — Boundary — Physical Features—The Yellow Breeches Creek—Industries—Land-Owners—Pioneer Settlers—Villages—Churches—Schools—Miscellaneous.

CHAPTER XXXIII.—SILVER SPRING TOWNSHIP..336–343
Formation — Boundary, etc.—Origin of Name—Conodoguinet Creek—Early Settlement and Road—Original Settlers—Some Early Events—Hogestown—New Kingston—First Covenanters' Communion in America—Silver Spring Church and Cemetery—"Silver Spring" (a Poem)—Miscellaneous.

CHAPTER XXXIV.—SOUTHAMPTON TOWNSHIP..343–347
Boundary — Formation—Erection—Character of Soil, etc.—Earliest Settlers—Villages—Middle Spring Church and Grave-yard—Middle Spring Church Lands—Miscellaneous.

CHAPTER XXXV. — SOUTH MIDDLETON TOWNSHIP AND BOROUGH OF MOUNT HOLLY SPRINGS..............................347–356
Origin—Boundary—Topography—Roads and Streams—Early Settlements—Some Early Reminiscences—Schools—Railroads and Postoffices—Boiling Springs—BOROUGH OF MOUNT HOLLY SPRINGS—Location, etc.—Early Reminiscences—Early Settlement and Industries—War of the Rebellion—Incorporation, etc.—Churches, Schools and Newspaper—Hotels—Societies.

CHAPTER XXXVI.—UPPER ALLEN TOWNSHIP...356–360
Formation — Boundary — Early Settlers, Mills, Mines, etc. — Villages — Churches, Burial Places, etc.—Schools—Miscellaneous.

CHAPTER XXXVII.—WEST PENNSBOROUGH TOWNSHIP...................................360–364
Its Origin—First Settlements, etc.—Villages—Miscellaneous.

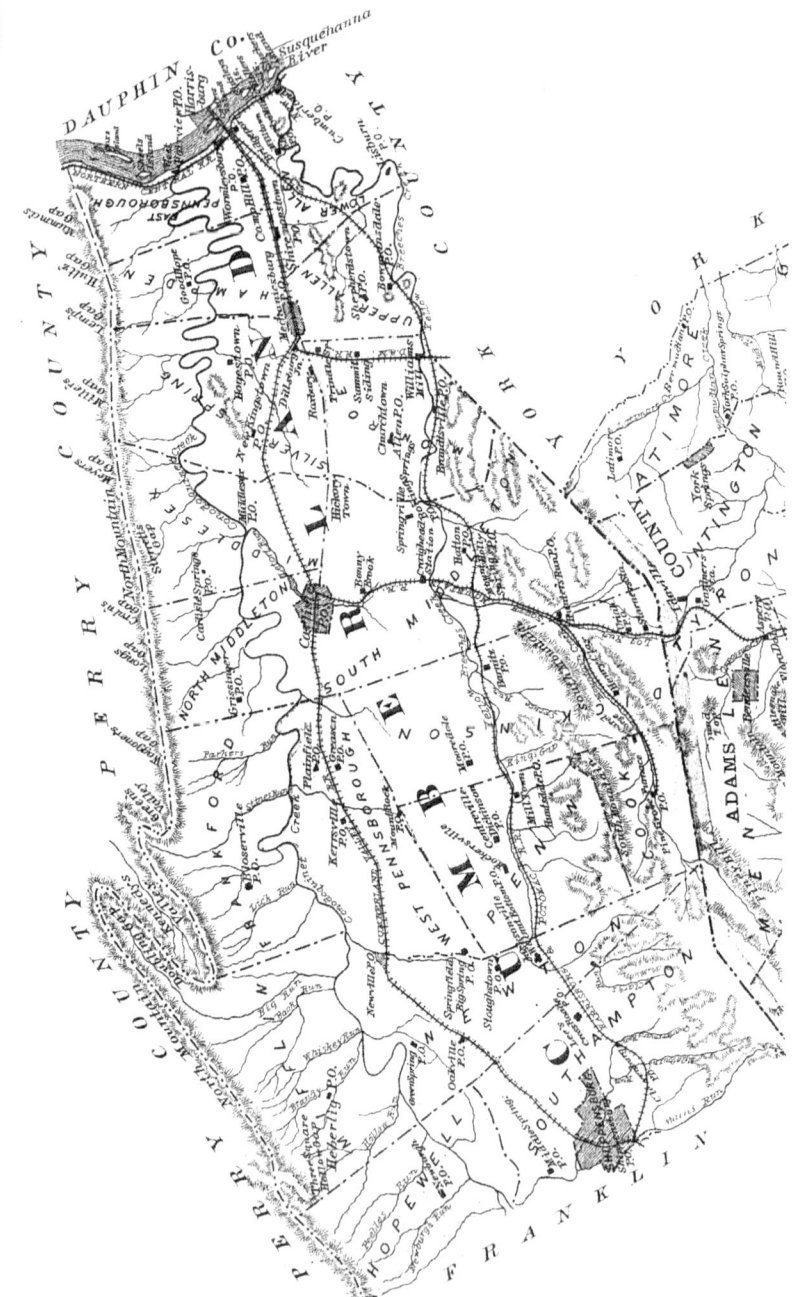

HISTORY OF CUMBERLAND COUNTY.

CHAPTER I.

DESCRIPTIVE.

GEOGRAPHY—GEOLOGY—TOPOGRAPHY, ETC.

CUMBERLAND COUNTY, although extending into the mountains along its northern and southern boundaries, lies mostly in the picturesque valley between the two great ridges. The North Mountain was called by the Indians *Kau-ta-tin-chunk,* signifying "endless mountains," or, as some authorities give it, main or principal mountain. It extends in a long, smooth-topped ridge from northeast to southwest, broken only by occasional gaps through which highways have been constructed leading into the counties to the northward of Cumberland. The South Mountain trends in the same general direction as its neighbor on the north, but its surface is far more uneven. Both are covered with a thick growth of timber and shrubbery, in which appear such varieties as pine, oak, ash, willow, maple, poplar, chestnut, spruce, elm, cedar, alder, sumac, etc. The timber in the valley was never a heavy growth, and consisted mainly of a few varieties of oak. A thick brush grew in portions of the valley, and was easily cleared away; it was therefore a comparatively light task to prepare the soil for cultivation.

Probably nowhere in the State are the colors of autumn brought out with more pleasing effect than in the South Mountain region of the county of Cumberland. A writer upon the subject has given the following fine description: "In the dry, burning summer month—a month in which it is hard to believe there are any nights—the leaf, panting, as it were, in the furnace, knows not any repose. It is a continual and rapid play of aspiration and respiration; a too-powerful sun excites it. In August, sometimes even in July, it begins to turn yellow. It will not wait for autumn. On the tops of the mountains yonder, where it works less rapidly, it travels more slowly toward its goal; but it will arrive there. When September has ended, and the nights lengthen, the wearied trees grow dreamy; the leaf sinks from fatigue. If the light did but succor it still! But the light itself has grown weaker. The dews fall abundantly, and in the morning the sun no longer cares to drink them up. It looks toward other horizons, and is already far away. The leaves blush a marvelous scarlet in their anger. The sun is, as it were, an evening sun. Its long, oblique rays are protruded through the black trunks, and create under the woods some luminous and still genial tracks of light. The landscape is illuminated. The forests around and above, on the hills, on the flanks of the mountains, seem to be on fire. The light abandons us, and we are tempted to think that it wishes to rest in the leaf and to concentrate within it all its rays. Summer is comparatively monotonous; it wears always the same verdure. Autumn is a fairy spectacle. Where the trees huddle close together, every tone of color is intermingled—pale, golden tints with glowing or slightly burnished gold, scarlet, and crimson, and every hue of blushing carnation. Every leaf shows color. The vivacity of the maple contrasts sharply with the gloom of the pine; lower down this hill, the rusty hues of the oaks; lower still, and all around, the drooping and fallen brambles and wild vines blend their glowing reds with the wan yellow of the grasses. It is the festival of the foliage.''

The valley in which Cumberland County is located is, with exceptional instances, slightly rolling, and in places nearly level. The lands along the Conodoguinet and other streams are more or less broken, and there is sufficient variety to make the landscape very attractive from almost any point of view.

The principal and largest stream in the county is the Conodoguinet Creek, which rises in Franklin County and flows through Cumberland in a winding course, which grows exceedingly tortuous as it approaches the Susquehanna River, into which it empties at West Fairview, near the center of the eastern boundary of the county. The Conodoguinet affords abundant water-power, which is utilized in various places for driving the machinery of mills. Next in size is the Yellow Breeches (called by the Indians Callapasscinker), forming in part of its course the boundary line between Cumberland and York Counties. Its head is in the mountains in the southwest portion of Cumberland County, and it is a clear and very rapid stream, fed by many springs and very rarely freezing over in winter. Considering the size of the stream the power it affords is wonderful; upon it and its various branches are mills, forges and furnaces.

Tributary to the Conodoguinet, Main's Run is the chief from the South. It rises at the foot of South Mountain, flows northward and forms the boundary line along its course (eight miles) between Cumberland and Franklin Counties, passing through Shippensburg, and emptying into the Conodoguinet a few miles north of that place. Other streams of more or less importance in the county are Newburgh Run, Peebles Run, Hollow Run, Brandy Run, Whiskey Run, Back Run, Big Run, Lick Run, Stine's Run, Parker's Run, and others, all discharging into the Conodoguinet from the North; Milesburn's Run, Quartersman's Run, Big Spring, Green Spring, Letort Creek, and others from the South, besides Cedar Run, Log Run, Mountain Creek, Spruce Run, Clark's Run, and many smaller ones. A number of the streams in the county have their sources in large springs, some of them furnishing excellent water-power, notably one which rises at Springfield, south of Newville, Letort's, Silver Spring, Big Spring, etc. At Mount Rock, seven miles west of Carlisle, a stream issues from a large spring in the limestone, sinks into the earth after a short course, passes under a hill and reappears on the other side. Springs in various places are strongly impregnated with sulphur and other mineral substances. Carlisle Springs, in Middlesex Township, four miles northeast of Carlisle, was at one time a favorite summer resort, and a hotel was erected for the accommodation of guests; but the building was burned and the business of the Springs declined.

The agricultural resources of the county are very great, "equal," says Dr. Egle, "to any other county of the same population in the State. The farms are highly cultivated and produce large crops of corn, wheat, oats, etc, while fruits, of most kinds grown in the latitude, are generally abundant. The mineral belt of the county lies principally in the South Mountain region, where great quantities of iron ore exist. It has been the source of much wealth, and numerous furnaces and forges have turned out a vast product of pig metal and forged iron from the ores close at hand.

HISTORY OF CUMBERLAND COUNTY.

Geological.—While not of great variety, the geological formations which appear in Cumberland County are very interesting, from the fact that they tell of an early period in the history of the earth as we now see it. Leaving the red sandstone of York and Adams Counties, with its soft, crumbling shales and beautiful conglomerates, a bed of primary rock is found in the long ridge of the South Mountain, and overlying it is a "hard, white, compact sandstone, almost purely silicious, and sometimes exhibiting evidence of the heating agency of the rocks beneath by its excessive hardness, its ringing sound when struck, its splintery fracture, and occasional discoloration."* Next above this sandstone, in regular order, and extending from the northern base of the South Mountain more than half way across the valley to the northward, is a belt of limestone, the presence of which gives to the soil of the region its agricultural value. It is easily traced in a continuous line from the Delaware River westward and southwestward into Maryland and Virginia. It has generally a bluish color, is very hard and sometimes is grayish or nearly black. It is largely used as ballast along the line of the Cumberland Valley Railroad, being broken into fragments for the purpose, and forming a solid road-bed. For the most part it is quite pure, and when burned yields excellent lime; but in places it contains sand, clay and oxide of iron easily discernible. There are also, sometimes met with in this formation, bands and nodules of chert, or flint, usually of a dark color; and fossil shells and zoöphytes peculiar to the era in which the rock was laid down are found plentifully in some localities. It is a well-known fact that upon a limestone soil the agriculturist meets with excellent reward for his labors, and such is the case here, some of the finest agricultural districts in Pennsylvania lying along this formation in the beautiful Cumberland Valley.

Above this limestone, however, in a district which in Cumberland County is included in a strip extending southward from the base of the North, or Kittatinny Mountain, is a black or bluish slate, sometimes varying in color to gray, olive or yellowish. The lands where this exists are colder and not so valuable for farming purposes as those lying upon the limestone, though in the latter it is often necessary to blast and quarry away outcropping ridges of the rock in order that the plans of cultivation may be more easily carried out. The slate lands are made fairly productive by the use of lime and other manures. A peculiar feature is a dyke or seam of trap rock, or greenstone, which extends entirely across the valley east of the center of the county, and which doubtless forms a continuation of the same ridge seen both to the south and north of this county, penetrating the mountains in both directions. It is of igneous origin, and was forced upward from the intensely heated interior, through the overlying formations, to the surface. The contiguous rocks were so discolored and hardened by the upheaval of the trap that in some places they bear little resemblance to the body of the rock of which they really form a part.

Along the border of the limestone district, or in the soil above it, are valuable beds of iron ore, which in some localities have been and are being extensively worked. In Penn Township, Cumberland County, on Mountain Creek, a detached bed of limestone appears, surrounded by the white or mountain sandstone. Growing on the latter, in an extremely thin soil, is timber which affords fuel for the furnaces. Connected with this isolated limestone district is a deposit of brown argillaceous and hematite iron ore, which has been worked since a very early period in the history of the county. "Along the northern side of the South Mountain, near the contact of the white sandstone

---
*Trego's Geography of Pennsylvania, 1843.

with the limestone, iron ore is abundant and is extensively mined for the supply of furnaces. Further north and wholly within the limestone formation, pipe ore and other varieties of excellent quality may be obtained in many places."*

The rocks of the NorthMountain are coarse gray and reddish sandstone, valuable neither for building nor mineral purposes. Like the South Mountain they are covered with a dense growth of the varieties of timber which flourish in the region. Of the ores which occur in the limestone formations of the valley, a valued writer speaks as follows: "Beneath the surface are inexhaustible deposits of magnetic iron, conveniently near to valuable beds of hematite, which lie either in fissures, between the rocky strata, or over them in a highly ferruginous loam. This hematite is of every possible variety, and in immense quantities. When it has a columnar stalactite structure, it is known under the name of pipe ore, and it is found abundantly along the slopes of the valley of the Yellow Beeches. It usually yields a superior iron, and at the same time is easily and profitably smelted. It generally produces at least 50 per cent of metallic iron. The beds are frequently of extraordinary extent, and the actual depth to which they reach has not been determined. Over a space of ten acres a number of holes have been opened, from sixteen to forty-two feet in depth, without going through the vein. Together with the magnetic ore these hematite beds, many of which remain untouched, are sufficient for supplying a large part of the manufacture of the United States. But in the valley there are traces, also, of sulphuret of copper (the blue vitriol of commerce), red and yellow ochre and chrome ores, alum earth, copperas ores, porcelain earth, and clay for stone-ware, common glazed ware and fire bricks; also epsom salts, shell lime, marl, manganese, and valuable marbles. * * * In every part of the limestone region tho earth resounds under the tread of the traveler, and numerous sink holes communicate with caverns or running streams beneath them. These constitute a natural drainage, which is amply sufficient for all the ordinary demands of the highest culture. Two or three caves have been discovered and entered, which have been esteemed as curiosities. The most wonderful of these is on the bank of the Conodoguinet, about a mile north from Carlisle. It is under a small limestone cliff, not more than thirty feet high above the surface of the creek; but through a semi-circular arched entrance, from seven to ten feet high and ten in width, it descends gradually to an antechamber of considerable size. From this a vaulted passage large enough to allow one to walk erect extends 270 feet, to a point where it branches off in three directions. One on the right is somewhat difficult on account of the water which percolates through the rocks on every side, but leads to a large chamber of great length. The central one is narrow and crooked, and has never been completely explored on account of a deep perpendicular precipice which prevents all progress beyond about thirty feet. The other passage is smaller and has but little interest. In different parts are pools of water, supposed by some to be springs, but as they have no outflow they are more probably formed from drippings from the surrounding rocks. Human bones have been found in it, and no doubt it has been used as a place of refuge or temporary lodgment by the Indians. No such articles as are usually deposited with their dead have yet been discovered."†

Another cave has been discovered on the bank of the Conodoguinet, in the township of West Pennsborough, about one and a half miles north of Greason. The opening is about 10 feet wide and 6 feet high, extending back about 10

---
*Trego.
†Rev. C. P. Wing in "History of Cumberland County," 1879.

feet; then 3 feet wide and 16 feet high for a distance of 38 feet. Then another room is reached 10x10 feet, and 15 feet high, from which a passage leads to a similar room not so large, but with a high ceiling; thence a long narrow passage opens into a room 40 feet in circumference and the same height as the others, and from this another small passage leads to near the place of entrance. This cave abounds in stalactites and many curious shapes.

It is said that the white men who first came to the valley were greatly impressed with its beauty and the natural productions of the soil. The grass was rich and luxuriant, wild fruits were abundant, and there was a great variety of trees in places, including numerous species of oak, black and white walnut (butternut), hickory, white, red and sugar maple, cherry, locust, sassafras, chestnut, ash, elm, linden, beech, white pine and scrub pine. There was also a shrub growth of laurel, plum, juniper, persimmon, hazel, wild currant, gooseberry, blackberry, raspberry, spice-bush and sumach, while in the open country the strawberry, dewberry and wintergreen made a luscious carpeting and furnished to the Indians in their season a tempting and welcome partial supply of food.

CHAPTER II.

PIONEERS—"LOUTHER MANOR," ETC.—TAXES PAID FROM 1736 TO 1749—EARLIEST LIST OF TAXABLES IN CUMBERLAND COUNTY—FIRST SETTLERS IN THE NORTH VALLEY—TAXABLES IN THE COUNTY IN 1762—EARLY SETTLERS—WILD ANIMALS AND FISH—CUSTOMS AND HABITS—FORMATION OF TOWNSHIPS AND BOROUGHS—LANDS.

BEFORE any attempts at permanent settlement were made in the valley the region was known to and explored by traders among the Indians, who had posts in various places on the frontier. Some of these traders were in reality emissaries of the French Government, sent among the Indians for the purpose of seducing them from their allegiance to the English, and the proprietary government regarded them with watchful jealousy. On the 22d of July, 1707, Gov. Evans laid before the council at Philadelphia an account of his journey among the Susquehanna Indians, in which he mentions Martines Chartieres as being located at Pequehan (now Pequea), at the mouth of the creek of the same name in Lancaster County, where was an Indian town also bearing the name. Nicole Godin was a trader near Peixtan, and he was decoyed and captured during the journey, put on a horse with his legs tied under the animal's belly, and taken to Philadelphia and imprisoned. Peter Bezallion, who had a license, resided near the mouth of Peixtan or Paxton Creek, and James Le Tort was also a trader in the region. Bezallion and Le Tort were both in prison in 1709 for sundry offenses. Chartieres was known as "Martin Chartieres, the French glover of Philadelphia."* Other traders were in the neighborhood. The post of Chartieres, or as it is more commonly given, Chartier, was on the east bank of the Susquehanna, about three miles below Columbia, Lancaster County, and the Penns gave him a large tract of land on Turkey Hill, in that county. He died, in April, 1718, much esteemed. His son, Peter Chartier,

*Notes on Lancaster County in Day's Hist. Coll., p. 391.

after living a few years at his father's place, moved to the neighborhood of New Cumberland, in the southeast corner of Cumberland County, where he established a trading post. He subsequently removed to a point on the Ohio River below Pittsburgh, where a creek now bears his name. He was all his life an Indian trader, and finally becoming a resident among the Indians, took sides with them against the English.* Peter Chartier was not, however, one of the first actual settlers in this county, for it was not until 1740 that he purchased 600 acres of land lying in the southeast corner of what is now Lower Allen Township, bounded east by the Susquehanna, and south by the Yellow Breeches.

James Le Tort (now written Letort) was a French-Swiss, who acted as an Indian interpreter and messenger to the government. He was also a trader, and very early built a cabin at the spring at the head of the run which now bears his name. His first cabin is said to have been burnt by the Indians. It was built as early as 1720. So far as known, he was the first white man to have an abode, even temporarily, in what is now Cumberland County. His location was near Carlisle, at a place since known as Beaver Pond. Letort was a man of excellent reputation. He received £12 annually from the government for his services.

Before the Indian title to the lands west of the Susquehanna had been extinguished, the Government authorized Samuel Blunston, of Lancaster County, to issue to the settlers licenses allowing them to go and improve the land, a title to which should be granted as soon as the land office should be opened. These documents were known as "Blunston's licenses," and many of the earlier settlers held them previous to 1736.

Andrew Ralston.—Authentic information points to the fact that this person settled at the "Big Spring," either in Newton or West Pennsborough Township, in 1728. Ralston was a native of County Armagh, Ireland, and upon applying at the land office for a warrant, soon after it was opened, he stated that he had occupied the land "ye past eight years." The following is a verbatim copy of the license directed to be issued to him at that time.†

LANCASTER COUNTY, ss.
  By Order of the Proprietary:
  These are to license and allow Andrew Ralston to Continue to Improve and Dwell on a Tract of Two Hundred acres of land on the Great Spring, a branch of Conedogwainet, Joyning to the Upper Side of a Tract Granted to Randel Chambers for the use of his son, James Chambers; To be hereafter surveyed to the s'd Ralston on the Comon Terms Other Lands in those parts are sold, provided the same has not been already Granted to any other person, and So much can be had without Prejudice to other Tracts before Granted. Given under my hand this third day of January, Ano: Dom: 1736-7.   SA: BLUNSTON.
PENSILVANIA, ss.
  Indorsed: License to Andrew Ralston, 200 acres.

The land was subsequently surveyed to him by Samuel Blunston, surveyor of Lancaster County, of which it was then a part. Mr. Ralston had two daughters, who married a Hayes and a Dickey, and a son, David, who remained at Big Spring for many years, but finally removed to Westmoreland County, and died about 1810.

Tobias Hendricks located in the valley before Andrew Ralston, possibly previous to 1725. He was a son of Tobias Hendricks, of Donegal. It is positively certain he was west of the Susquehanna in 1727, for in a letter to John Harris, dated May 13 that year, he speaks of his father "at Donegal," and requests Mr. Harris to forward a letter to him. He also alludes to "a trader" at the Potomac of whom he purchased skins, and also of the "grate numbers

*Samuel Evans, in Notes and Queries, Part I. p. 17.
†Notes and Queries, Part I, p. 19.—Dr. H. W. Egle.

coming this side of ye Sasquahannah." The Scotch-Irish emigration had then begun and the valley was being rapidly settled.* Whether Hendricks became a permanent settler is not stated.

The Chambers Brothers.—Four brothers, James, Robert, Joseph and Benjamin Chambers, from County Antrim, Ireland, were among the very first to cross the Susquehanna and settle upon lands in the North Valley. They landed at Philadelphia in 1726, and pushing westward located at the mouth of Fishing Creek, on the east bank of the Susquehanna, a few miles above Harris' ferry, where they built a mill which was a great convenience for the settlers over a large tract of country. Benjamin, the youngest, was but eighteen years of age when the brothers came to this country, and he died February 17, 1788, aged eighty years. Not long after their settlement at Fishing Creek the brothers became attracted by the prospect for procuring fine farms west of the river, and in or before 1730 crossed over and settled at different places: "James at the head of Green Spring, near Newville; Robert at the head of Middle Spring, near Shippensburg; and Joseph and Benjamin near the confluence of Falling Spring and the Conococheague, where Chambersburg now stands." Joseph soon returned to Fishing Creek; the others remained where they had settled and became prominent and influential citizens in many respects.

It would appear that the land included in the Louther Manor, in the eastern part of the county, was very early the home of white settlers. That tract, being first laid out as a hunting ground for the Delawares and Shawnees, three men were appointed to visit the Indians whither they had gone upon the branches of the Ohio, and induce them to return. They had left this region partly on account of the encroachments of white settlers upon their lands, and partly through the efforts of emmissaries of the French in the guise of traders. The three persons mentioned indited a document as follows:

PESHTANK,† Nov. ye 19th, 1731.

Ffriend Peter Chartiere, This is to Acquaint Thee that By the Comisioners' and the Governour's order We are now Going over Susquehanna, To Lay out a Tract of Land between Conegogwainet & The Shaawna‡ Creeks five or six miles back from the River, in order to accomodate the Shaawna Indians or such others as may see fit to Settle there, To Defend them from Incroachments, And we have also orders to Dispossess all Persons Settled on that side of the River, That Those woods may Remain free to ye Indians for Planting & Hunting, And We Desire thee to Comunicate this to the Indians who Live About Allegening. We conclude

Thy Assured Ff'ds,

JOHN WRIGHT,
TOBIAS HENDRICKS,
SAM'L BLUNSTON.§

As seen elsewhere the Indians did not return; the above simply shows that white persons had settled in the eastern part of the county as early as 1731, and probably earlier. Peter Chartier had been appointed a trader by the court at Lancaster, and he married a Shawanese squaw. His subsequent desertion to the French has been noted.

"The influx of immigrants into North or Kittatinny Valley," says Mr. Rupp, "increased fast after 1734. In 1748 the number of taxables was about 800, and the population rising to 3,000. As early as 1735 a road was laid out from Harris' Ferry toward the Potomac river. November 4, 1735, the court at Lancaster appointed Randle Chambers, Jacob Peat, James Silvers, Thomas Eastland, John Lawrence and Abram Endless, to lay out said road. These

---
*Notes and Quries, Part I, p. 18.
†Peshtank, Pejtank or Pehtank was the original name of the manor.
‡Yellow Breeches, or Callapasskinker, or Callapasseink—Indian name of stream, Delaware language.
§From article on Louther Manor, by Dr. J. A. Murray, of Carlisle, in Carlisle *Herald*, 1885.

gentlemen made a report February 3, 1736, of their views of the road, which was opposed 'by a considerable number of the inhabitants on the west side of the Susquehanna in those parts,' and praying for a review. The court then ordered that William Rennick, Richard Hough, James Armstrong, Thomas Mayes, Samuel Montgomery and Benjamin Chambers view the road, and to make such alterations in it as to them may seem necessary for the public good, and report their proceedings to next court. They made the following report, May 4, 1736: 'That they had reviewed the eastern most part of the said road, and find it very crooked and hurtful to the inhabitants, etc., and therefore have altered the said road and marked it in the manner following, to-wit : From the said ferry, near to a southwest course about two miles; thence a westerly course to James Silvers', then westward to John Hogg's meadow; then westward to a fording place on Le Tort's spring, a little to the northward of John Davison's; thence west northerly to the first marked road in a certain hollow; thence about southwest a little to the south of Robert Duning's, to the former marked road; thence along the same to the Great Spring head, being as far as any review or alteration to them appeared necessary,' which so altered as above said, and altered from the return to go by James Silvers' house, was allowed to be recorded."

The North Valley (now constituting Cumberland and Franklin Counties) was divided in 1735 into two townships, called Pennsborough and Hopewell, and the line dividing them was thus described: "That a line running northerly from the Hills to the southward of Yellow Breeches (crossing in a direct line by the Great Spring) to Kightotinning Mountain, be the division line; and that the easternmost township be called Pennsborough and the western Hopewell." Hopewell was divided in 1741 "by a line beginning at the North Hill, at Benjamin Moor's; thence to Widow Hewre's and Samuel Jamison's, and on a straight line to the South Hill, and that the western division be called Antrim, and the eastern Hopewell." This was before the organization of Cumberland County.

Taxes and Collectors.—Table of taxes paid, and names of collectors in townships in what is now Cumberland County, from 1736 to 1749:

1736—Pennsborough, £13 17s. 6d.; James Silvers, collector. Hopewell, £5 2s.

1737—Pennsborough, £13 9s. 9d. East part of Hopewell, £3 2s.: west part of Hopewell, £2 19s.

1738—Pennsborough, £20 14s. 0d. East part of Hopewell, £10 0s. 3d.; west part of Hopewell, £7 7s. 9d.

1739—Pennsborough, £23 16s. 8d.; William Tremble, collector. South part of Hopewell, £11 8s. 1d.; Jacob Snebly, collector. North part of Hopewell, £6 11s. 6d.; Abraham Endless, collector.

1740—West part of Pennsborough, £11 4s. 7d.; Robert Dennin, collector. East part of Pennsborough, £14 18s. 7d.; John Walt, collector. East Hopewell, £4 0s. 2d.; James Laughlin, collector. West Hopewell, £4 19s. 3d.; Philip Davis, collector.

1741—Pennsborough, £17 15s. 10d.; Robert Redock, collector. Hopewell, £3 8s. 9d.; James Montgomery, collector.

1742—West end of Pennsborough, £7 19s. 2d.; William Weakly, collector. East end of Pennsborough, £16 7s. 8d.; John Swansey, collector. Hopewell, £5 11s. 4d.; David Herren, collector.

1743—East end of Pennsborough, £9 0s. 6d.; John Semple, collector; West end of Pennsborough, £10 7s. 3d.; Robert Miller, collector. Hopewell, £6 16s. 11d.; Henry Hallan, collector.

HISTORY OF CUMBERLAND COUNTY. 11

1744—West end of Pennsborough, £22 4s.; John Mitchell, collector; east end of Pennsborough, £17 12s. 7d.; Thomas Fisher, collector. Hopewell, £10 16s. 2d.; Thomas Montgomery, collector.

1745—West Pennsborough, £23 1s. 11d.; James Chambers, collector; East Pennsborough, £13 4s.; John McCrackin, collector. Hopewell, £12 10s. 4d.; William Thompson, collector.

1746—East Pennsborough, £10 5s.; John Rankin, collector; West Pennsborough, £13 4s. 8d.; James McFarlin, collector. Hopewell, £9 17s. 9d.; John Erwin, collector.

1747—East Pennsborough, £10 12s.; Joseph Green, collector; West Pennsborough, £13 18s. 6d.; Patrick Davis, collector. Hopewell, £12 7s. 7d.; John Currey, collector.

1748—East Pennsborough, £12 2s.; Christopher Huston, collector; West Pennsborough, £14 14s. 6d.; William Dunbar, collector. Hopewell, £13 13s. 6d.; James Walker, collector.

1749—East Pennsborough, £23 16s. 6d.; Tobias Hendricks, collector; West Pennsborough, £28 8s. 9d.; Archibald McAllister, collector. Hopewell, £43 3s. 9d.; John Kirkpatrick, collector.

Antrim Township we do not give as it was outside the present limits of Cumberland County, being in Franklin.

Earliest List of Taxables.—The earliest list of taxables in Cumberland County, as given by Mr. Rupp in the history of Dauphin, Cumberland and other counties, is as follows:

East Pennsborough, 1750.—Tobias Hendricks, Widow Jane Woods, Samuel Calhoon, Thomas Spray, Thomas Kenny, James Shannon, James Dickey, John Bigham, Samuel Chambers, William Barrohill, William Noble, William Crawford, William McChesney, Richard Fulton, John McClellan, William Rose, Adam Calhoun, William Shannon, John Semple, Charles West, Christopher Hewston, Walker Buchanan, David Reed, James Armstrong, Hugh Wharton, Edward Eliot, Francis McGuire, William Findley, Josias McMeans, Hugh Mahool, Robert Carrithers, William Ross, Henry Quigly, William Morton, John Armstrong, John Buchanan, Nathaniel Nelson, John Nailer, Andrew Armstrong, Thomas McCormick, John Dickey, John McCracken, Widow Clark, Widow McMeans, Robert Eliot, Robert Eliot, Jr., James Corrithers, William Gray, Alexander Lamferty, John Willey, Robert Duning, Joseph Junkin, William Walker, Alex Armstrong, Moses Star, James Crawford, Roger Cook, Hugh Cook, William Miller, John McCormick, Jamer Silvers, John Stevenson, James Coleman, David Wason, John Hunter, William Douglas, John Mitchel, Andrew Milekin, John Milekin, Patrick Holmes, James Finley, Peter Shaver (Shaver was a trader among the Indians and was employed by Gov. Thomas, in 1744, to carry letters to the Shawanese Indians on the Ohio inviting them to come to Philadelphia), John Erwin, William Carrithers, Widow Quigly, Samuel Martin, William Hamilton, Robert Samuels, John Waugh, Thomas Rankin, Richard Rankin, John Clendenin, Joseph Waugh, Widow Roberts, Thomas Henderson, William Hamilton, William Marshal, William Miller, Wilson Thomas, Alex Crocket, Widow Branan, Thomas Calvert, William Griffith, Robert Bell, William Orr, James McConnel, John Bowan, Robert McKinley, Samuel Fisher, Titus Hollinger, Samuel McCormick, Rowland Chambers, Robert Kelton, Isaac Rutlidge, Rowland McDonald, Walter Gregory, Widow Stewart, James McTeer, Peter Leester, Peter Title, Joseph Willie, Anthony McCue, James Beaty, William Crocket, Andrew Miller, Robert Roseborough, Joseph Green, James Douglas, Widow Steel, Widow McKee, Joseph Reynolds, Jr. *Freemen*—William Hogg, George Crogham, Esq., Jonathan Hogg, Samuel Huston, John Willie

HISTORY OF CUMBERLAND COUNTY.

son, Robert Airs, Abraham Hendricks, Archibald Armstrong, Joseph Ferret, Clime Horal, Daniel Campbell, William McDonald, Matthew Lindham, J. Armstrong, Cornelius Brown, Hugh Shannon, Robert Walker, Nathaniel Wilson, Matthew Brown (two silversmiths at William McChesney's), John Adams, David Kenworthy, James Gaily, William McTeer, Edward Ward, Arthur Erwin, James Clark, William Cranula—total 190,

West Pennsborough 1751.—William Queery, William Lamont, Archibald McAllister, William Carithers, John Davison, Allen Leeper, Neal McFaul, John McClure (the less), William Logan, John Atchison, Thomas McCoy, Charles Gillgore, Andrew Griffin, William Dunbar, William Harkness, William Patton, Samuel McClure, Robert Walker, James Kirkpatrick, John Swansy, Arthur Clark, Adam Hays, James McMeans, John Deniston, John McIntire, James McFarland, William Laughlin, Robert Brevard, Robert McQueston, James Peebles, John McClure (mountain), Alex McClure, John Langley, John Gordon, William Livingston, Robert Guthrie, William Anderson, John Glass, John Logan, William Duglass, Alex Erwin, Alex Logan, William Townsley, William Parker, Margaret Parker, Andrew Forbush, John Morrison, David Kollogh, George Brown, Francis Cunningham, Alex Robb, Anthony Gillgore, Jacob Peebles, Samuel Wilson, Allen Scroggs, David Kenedy, Mary Dunning, William Carithers, John Carithers, John Chestnut, Thomas Patton, Andrew Ralston, John McClung, Ezekiel Dunning, James Lea, John Lusk, Alex McBride, James McNaught, William Blackstock, James Crutchlow, William Dunlap, Thomas Evans, Steven Cesna, James Weakly, David Hunter, Josh Cornelius, Alex Weyly, Lewis Hutton, James Warnock, David Dunbar, David Miller, John Wilson, Josh Thomson, Josh Dempsay, Samuel Lindsay, Paul Piercy, Owen McCool, Pat Robeson, Thomas Parker. *Freemen*—Samuel Wilson, James McMunagle, David McCurdy, Pat Reynolds, Andrew McAdams, John McCurdy—total 95.

Middleton, 1751.—William Trent, Thomas Wilson, John Elder, John Chambers, Robert McNutt, James Long, John Mahafy, James Reed, John Moor, John Craighead, James Dunlop, Patrick Hawson, Walter Denny, James Gillgore, Patrick Davison, Thomas Elder, Henry Dinsmore, John Mitchell, Samuel Lamb, James Williams, James Matthews, Alexander Sanderson, James Henderson, Matthew Miller, John Davis, William Graham, William Campbell, William Parkeson, Francis McNichley, John McKnaught, John Calhoun, William Peterson, John Robb, Robert Graham, Samuel McLucass, Daniel Williams, George Sanderson, Alexander Sanderson, Joseph Clark, John McClure, Jonathan Holmes, James Chambers, Thomas Armstrong, William Waddel, James McConnell, Richard Nicholson, John Neely, John McCrea, John Stuart, Archibald Kenedy, John Jordan, William Jordan, George Templeton, James Stuart, Richard Venable, Widow Wilson, David Dreanan, John Dinsmore, Samuel Gauy, William Davison, Samuel Bigger, Thomas Gibson, John Brown, John McKinley, Robert Campbell, John Kinkead, Samuel Wilson, Robert Patterson, John Reed, Robert Reed, James Reed, William Reed, William Armstrong, James Young, Robert Miller, William Gillachan, Josh Davies, William Fleming, John Gilbreath, Richard Coulter, Richard Kilpatrick, Andrew Gregg, Robert Thomson, John Dicky, James Brannan, John McClure, John Buyers, Arthur Foster, Harmanus Alrichs,[*] John Armstrong, John Smith, William Buchanan, William Blyth, John McAllister, William Montgomery, John Patterson, Robert Kilpatrick, Archibald McCurdy, William Whiteside, John Woodle, William Dillwood, William Huston, Thomas Lock-

---

[*] Some give this Hermanus Alricks, but Harmanus Alrichs is the way it appears in his own handwriting on the old records at the court house.

Conway P. Wing.

ward, Thomas Henderson, Joseph Thornton, James Dunning, William Moor, George Davison, Alexander Patterson, John McBride, Robert Robb, Dennis Swansy, Daniel Lorrance, Jonathan Hogg, Oliver Wallace, John Bell, Arthur Buchanan, Robert Guthrie, Berry Cackel, Cornelius McAdams, Andrew McIntire, Alexander Roddy, Josh Price, Hugh Laird, William Ferguson, Widow Duglas, Abraham Sanford, Moses Moor, Joseph Gaylie, Charles Mahaufy, William Kerr, Hugh Creanor, William Guilford, William Stuart, William Chadwick. *Freemen in Middleton and Carlisle*—Andrew Holmes, Jonathan Kearney, Francis Hamilton, Jonathan Donnel, William Wilson, Patrick Long, Robert Patterson, William Kinaird, George Crisp, Hugh Laird, William Braidy, James Tait, Patrick Kearney, Arthur Foster, James Pollock, Thomas Elmore, Robert Mauhiny, Jonathan Hains, William Rainiston, James Gambel, John Woods, David Hains, Henry Hains—total, 158.

Hopewell Township, 1751.—Robert Gibson, David Heron, Moses Donald, Thomas Donald, Francis Ignue, Daniel McDonald, John Eliott, Alexander McClintock, James McFarland, Joshua McClintock, Hugh Terrance, Hugh Thomson, Josh Thomson, Josh Thomson, Jr., Robert McDowell, James McDowell, Robert Rusk, John Scrogs, William Walker, William Cornahan, Thomas Gawlt, James Hamilton, John Laughler, Josh Gair, Samuel Williamson, Samuel Smith, David Kidd, John Hodge, Robert McCombs, Thomas Micky, John Wray, Richard Nicholson, Andrew McIlvain, George Hamilton, John Thomson, William Gambel, Samuel Montgomery, Robert Simson, John Brown, Allen Nisbit, John Nesbit, Jr., John Nesbit, Sr., James Wallace, Andrew Peeble, John Anderson, Patrick Hannah, John Tremble, Moses Stuart, William Reigny, John Moorhead, James Pollock, Samuel Stuart, Robert Robinson, David Newell, James McCormick, Charles Murray, Joseph Boggs, John Lysee, Andrew Leckey, John Montgomery, John Beaty, James Walker, William Smyley, James Chambers, Robert Meek, Dr. William McGofreek, James Jack, James Quigly, Robert Simonton, John McCune, Charles Cumins, Samuel Wier, John McCune, Jr., Josh Martin, James Carrahan, Allen Kollogh, James Young, Francis Newell, John Quigly, Robert Stuart, Samuel Montgomery, Daniel Mickey, Andrew Jack, Robert Mickey, Hugh Braidy, Robert Chambers, William Thomson, Edward Leasy, Alexander Scrogg, John Jack, James Laughlin, John Laughlin, Jr., Robert Dinney, David Simrel, Samuel Walker, Abraham Walker, James Paxton, James Uxley, Samuel Cellar, W. McClean, James Culbertson, James McKessan, John Miller, Daniel O'Cain, John Edmonson, Isaac Miller, David McGaw [Magaw—Ed.] John Reynolds, Francis Camble, William Anderson, Thomas Edmonson, James Dunlop, John Reynolds, Jr., William Dunlop, Widow Piper, George Cumins, Thomas Finley, Alexander Fairbairn, John Mason, James Dysert, William Gibson, Horace Brattan, John Carothers, Patrick Mullan, James Blair, Peter Walker, John Stevenson, John Aiger, John Ignue. *Freemen*—John Hanch, Josh Edmonson, John Callwell, John Richison (skinner), P. Miller—total, 134.

First Settlers.—The first settlers in the North Valley and the region to the northward, embraced in what was Cumberland County, were mostly Scotch-Irish, a fearless and aggressive people who were impatient at the delays of the land-office, and began as early as 1740–42 to settle on lands to which the Indian title had not been fully extinguished. A few Germans were also among them, and the settlements were made principally on the Juniata River, Shearman's Creek, Tuscarora Path (or Path Valley), in the little and big caves formed by the Kittatinny and Tuscarora Mountains and by the Big and Little Conolloways. The Indians very naturally regarded them no intruders, and in 1750 threatened to settle matters in their own way if the Government failed to put a stop to the proceedings. Measures were promptly adopted. "The secretary of the province, Mr. Richard Peters, and the interpreter. Mr. Conrad Weiser, were directed to proceed to the county of Cumberland, in which the new settlements lay, and to expel the intruders. They were joined by the magistrates of the county, the delegates from the Six Nations, a chief of the Mohawks, and Andrew Montour, an interpreter from Ohio. The commissioners met with little resistance in the execution of their duty, a few only of the settlers, under an apprehension of imprisonment, making a show of opposition. All readily entered into recognizance for their appearance at the next sessions, and many aided to reduce their own habitations to ashes in the presence of the magistrates and attendant Indians."*

Following is the report of the proceedings made to the governor by Mr. Peters, under date of July 2, 1750:

To JAMES HAMILTON, ESQ., GOVERNOR OF PENNSYLVANIA,

May it please Your Honor:—Mr. Weiser, having received your Honor's orders to give information to the proper magistrates against all such as had presumed to settle and remain on the lands beyond the Kittochtinny Mountains, not purchased of the Indians, in contempt of the laws repeatedly signified by proclamations, and particularly by your Honor's last one, and bring them to a legal conviction, lest for want of their removal a breach should ensue between the Six Nations of Indians and this province, we set out on Tuesday, the 15th of May, 1750, for the new county of Cumberland, where the places on which the trespassers had settled lay.

At Mr. Croghan's we met with five Indians, three from Shamokin, two of which are sons of the late Schickcalamy, who transacted the business of the Six Nations with the Government; two were just arrived from Allegheny, viz.: one of the Mohock's Nation, called Aaron, and Andrew Montour, the interpreter at Ohio. Mr. Montour, telling us he had a message from the Ohio Indians and Twightwees to this Government, and desiring a conference, one was held on the 18th of May last, in the presence of James Galbreth, George Croghan, William Wilson and Hermanus Alricks, Esq., justices of the county of Cumberland; and when Mr. Montour's business was done, we, with the advice of the other justices, imparted to the Indians the design we were assembled upon, at which they expressed great satisfaction.

Another conference was held at the instance of the Indians, in the presence of Mr. Galbreth and Mr. Croghan, before mentioned, wherein they expressed themselves as follows:

"Brethren, we have thought a great deal of what you imparted to us, that ye were come to turn the people off who were settled over the hills; we are pleased to see you on this occasion, and as the council of Onondago has this affair exceedingly at heart, and it was particularly recommended to us by the deputies of the Six Nations, when they parted from us last summer, we desire to accompany you, but we are afraid, notwithstanding the care of the Governor, that this may prove like many former attempts; the people will be put off now, and next year come again, and if so, the Six Nations will no longer bear it but do themselves justice. To prevent this, therefore, when you shall have turned the people off, we recommend it to the Governor to place two or three faithful persons over the mountains who may be agreeable to him and us, with commissions empowering them immediately to remove every one who may presume after this to settle themselves until after the Six Nations shall agree to make sale of their land."

To enforce this they gave a string of wampum and received one in return from the magistrates, with the strongest assurances that they would do their duty.

On Tuesday, the 22d of May, Matthew Dill, George Croghan, Benjamin Chambers, Thomas Wilson, John Finley and James Galbreath, Esqs., justices of the said county of Cumberland, attended by the under sheriff, came to Big Juniata, situate at the distance of twenty miles from the mouth thereof and about ten miles north from the Blue Hills, a place much esteemed by the Indians for some of their best hunting ground, and there they found five cabins or log houses, one possessed by William White, another by George Cahoon, another, not yet quite finished in possession of David Hiddleston, another possessed by George and William Galloway, and another by Andrew Lycon. Of these persons, William White and George and William Galloway, David Hiddleston and George Cahoon appeared before the magistrates, and being asked by what right or authority they had possessed themselves of those lands and erected cabins thereon, they replied by no right or authority, but that the land belonged to the proprietaries of Pennsylvania. They then were asked whether they did not know they were acting against the law, and in contempt of frequent notices given them by the Governor's proclamation. They said they had seen

---
*Rupp's Cumberland, etc., p. 378.

one such proclamation, and had nothing to say for themselves, but craved mercy. Hereupon the said William White, George and William Galloway, David Hiddleston and George Cahoon, being convicted by said justices on their view, the under sheriff was charged with them and he took William White, David Hiddleston and George Cahoon into custody; but George and William Galloway resisted, and having got at some distance from the under sheriff, they called to us: "You may take our lands and houses and do what you please with them: we deliver them to you with all our hearts, but we will not be carried to jail."

The next morning being Wednesday, the 23d of May, the said justices went to the log house or cabin of Andrew Lycon, and finding none there but children, and hearing that the father and mother were expected soon, and William White and others offering to become security, jointly and severally, and to enter into recognizance as well for Andrew's appearance and immediate removal as for their own, this proposal was accepted, and William White, David Hiddleston and George Cahoon entered into a recognizance of one hundred pounds, and executed bonds to the proprietaries in the sum of five hundred pounds, reciting that they were trespassers and had no manner of right, and had delivered possession to me for the proprietaries. When the magistrates went to the cabin or log house of George and William Galloway (which they had delivered up as aforesaid the day before, after they were convicted and were flying from the sheriff), all the goods belonging to the said George and William were taken out, and the cabin being quite empty, I took possession thereof for the proprietaries. And then a conference was held, what should be done with the empty cabin; and after great deliberation all agreed that if some cabins were not destroyed they would tempt the trespassers to return again, or encourage others to come there should these trespassers go away, and so what was doing would signify nothing, since the possession of them was at such a distance from the inhabitants could not be kept from the proprietaries, and Mr. Weiser also giving it as his opinion that if all the cabins were left standing the Indians would conceive such a contemptible opinion of the government that they would come themselves in the winter, murder the people and set their houses on fire. On these considerations, the cabin, by my order, was burnt by the under sheriff and company.

Then the company went to the house possessed by David Hiddleston, who had entered into bond as aforesaid, and he having voluntarily taken out all the things which were in the cabin, and left me in possession, that empty and unfurnished cabin was likewise set on fire by the under sheriff by my order.

The next day being the 24th of May, Mr. Weiser and Mr. Galbreath, with the under sheriff and myself, on our way to the mouth of the Juniata called at Andrew Lycon's with the intent only to inform him that his neighbors were bound for his appearance and immediate removal, and to caution him not to bring himself or them into trouble by a refusal. But he presented a loaded gun to the magistrates and sheriff; said he would shoot the first man that dared to come nigher. On this he was disarmed, convicted, and committed to the custody of the sheriff. This whole transaction happened in sight of a tribe of Indians who by accident had in the night time fixed their tent on that plantation; and Lycon's behavior giving them great offense, the Shickcalamies insisted on our burning the cabin or they would do it themselves. Whereupon, when everything was taken out of it (Andrew Lycon all the while assisting) and possession being delivered to me, the empty cabin was set on fire by the under sheriff and Lycon was carried to jail.

Mr. Benjamin Chambers and Mr. George Croghan had about an hour before separated from us, and on my meeting them again in Cumberland County they reported to me they had been at Sheerman's Creek, or Little Juniata, situate about six miles over the Blue Mountain, and found there James Parker, Thomas Parker, Owen McKeib, John McClare, Richard Kirkpatrick, James Murray, John Scott, Henry Gass, John Cowan, Simon Girtee and John Kilough, who had settled lands and erected cabins or log houses thereon; and having convicted them of the trespass on their view, they had bound them in recognizances of the penalty of one hundred pounds to appear and answer for their trespasses on the first day of the next county court of Cumberland, to be held at Shippensburg, and that the said trespassers had likewise entered into bonds to the proprietaries in five hundred pounds penalty to remove off immediately, with all their servants, cattle and effects, and had delivered possession of their houses to Mr. George Stevenson for the proprietaries' use; and that Mr. Stevenson had ordered some of the meanest of those cabins to be set on fire, where the families were not large nor the improvements considerable.

On Monday, the 28th of May, we were met at Shippensburg by Samuel Smith, William Maxwell, George Croghan, Benjamin Chambers, Robert Chambers, William Allison, William Trent, John Finley, John Miller, Hermanus Alricks, and James Galbreth, Esqs., justices of Cumberland County, who, informing us that the people in the Tuscarora Path, in Big Cove, and at Aucquick would submit, Mr. Weiser most earnestly pressed that he might be excused any further attendance, having abundance of necessary business to do at home; and the other magistrates, though with much reluctance, at last consenting, he left us.

On Wednesday, the 30th of May, the magistrates and company, being detained two days by rains, proceeded over the Kittochtinny Mountains and entered into the Tuscarora

HISTORY OF CUMBERLAND COUNTY.

Path, or Path Valley, through which the road to Alleghany lies. Many settlements were formed in this valley, and all the people were sent for and the following persons appeared, viz.: Abraham Slack, James Blair, Moses Moore, Arthur Dunlap, Alexander McCartie, David Lewis, Adam McCartie, Felix Doyle, Andrew Dunlap, Robert Wilson, Jacob Pyatt, Jacob Pyatt, Jr., William Ramage, Reynolds Alexander, Samuel Patterson. Robert Baker, John Armstrong and John Potts, who were all convicted by their own confession to the magistrates of the like trespasses with those at Shearman's Creek, and were bound in the like recognizances to appear at court, and bonds to the proprietaries to remove with all their families, servants, cattle, and effects, and having all voluntarily given possession of their houses to me, some ordinary log houses to the number of eleven were burnt to the ground, the trespassers, most of them cheerfully and a very few of them with reluctance, carrying out all their goods. Some had been deserted before and lay waste.

At Aucquick, Peter Falconer, Nicholas De Long, Samuel Perry and John Charleton were convicted on the view of the magistrates, having entered into the like recognizances and executed the like bonds. Charlton's cabin was burned and fire set to another that was just begun, consisting only of a few logs piled and fastened to one another.

The like proceedings at Big Cove (now within Bedford County) against Andrew Donnaldson, John Macclelland, Charles Stewart, James Downy, John Macmean, Robert Kendell, Samuel Brown, William Shepperd, Roger Murphy, Robert Smith, William Dickey, William Millican, William Macconnell, Alexander Macconnell, James Campbell, William Carrell, John Martin, John Jamison, Hans Patter, John Maccollin, James Wilson and John Wilson, who, coming before the magistrates, were convicted on their own confession of the like trespasses in former cases, and were all bound over in like recognizances and executed the like bond to the proprietaries. Three waste cabins of no value were burned at the north end of the cove by the persons that claimed a right to them.

The Little Cove (in Franklin County) and the Big and Little Connolloways being the only places remaining to be visited, as this was on the borders of Maryland the magistrates declined going there and departed for their homes.

About the year 1740 or 1741 one Frederic Star, a German, with two or three more of his countrymen, made some settlements at the very place where we found William White, the Galloways and Andrew Lycon (on Big Juniata situate at the distance of twenty miles from the north thereof and about ten miles north of the Blue Hills, a place much esteemed by the Indians for some of their best hunting ground.—(*Votes Assem. Vol. IV. p.* 138,) which (German settlers) were discovered by the Delawares at Shamokin to the deputie of the Six Nations as they came down to Philadelphia in the year 1742 to hold a treaty with this government; and they were so disturbed as to inquire with a peculiar warmth of Governor Thomas if these people had come there by the orders or with the privity of the government, alleging that if it was so this was a breach of the treaties subsisting between the Six Nations and the proprietor, William Penn, who in the most solemn manner engaged to them not to suffer any of the people to settle lands until they had purchased them from the council of the Six Nations. The Governor, as he might, with great truth, disowned any knowledge of these persons' settlements, and on the Indians requesting that they should immediately be thrown over the mountains, he promised to issue his proclamation and if this had no effect to put the laws in execution against them. The Indians, in the same treaty publicly expressed some very severe threats against the inhabitants of Maryland for settling lands for which they received no satisfaction, and said if they would not do them justice they would do justice to themselves; and would certainly have committed hostilities if a treaty had not been on foot between Maryland and the Six Nations under the mediation of Governor Thomas, at which the Indians consented to sell lands and receive a valuable consideration for them, which put an end to the danger.

The proprietaries were then in England, but observing, on perusing the treaty, with what asperity they had expressed themselves against Maryland, and that the Indians had just cause to complain of the settlements at Juniata, so near Shamokin, they wrote to their governor in very pressing terms, to cause those trespassers to be immediately removed; and both the proprietaries and Governor laid their commands on me to see this done, which I accordingly did in June, 1743, the Governor having first given them notice by a proclamation served on them.

At that time none had presumed to settle at a place called Big Cove—having this name from its being enclosed in the form of a basin by the southernmost range of the Kittochtinny Hills and Tuscarora Hills, which last end here and lose themselves in other hills. This Big Cove is about five miles north of the temporary line and not far west of the place where the line terminated. Between the Big Cove and the temporary line lies the Little Cove, so-called from being likewise encircled with hills: and to the west of the Little Cove, toward Potowmec, lie two other places called the Big and Little Conollaways, all of them situated on the temporary line, was it to be extended toward Potowmec.

In the year 1741 or 1742 information was likewise given that people were beginning to settle in those places, some from Maryland and some from this province. But as the two governments were then not on very good terms, the Governor did not think proper to take any other notice of these settlements than to send the sheriff to serve his proclamation on them, and thought it ample occasion to lament the vast inconveniencies which attend unsettled boundaries. After this the French war came on, and the people in these parts, taking advantage of the confusion of the times, by little and little stole into the Great Cove; so that at the end of the war it was said thirty families had settled there—not, however, without frequent prohibitions on the part of the government, and admonitions of the great danger they ran of being cut off by the Indians, as these settlements were on lands not purchased of them. At the close of the war Mr. Maxwell, one of the justices of Lancaster County, delivered a particular message from this government to them, ordering their removal, that they might not occasion a breach with the Indians; but it had no effect.

These were, to the best of my remembrance, all the places settled by Pennsylvanians in the unpurchased part of the province till about three years ago, when some persons had the presumption to go into Path Valley or Tuscarora Gap, lying to the east of Big Cove and onto a place called Aucquick, lying to the northward of it; and likewise into a place called Shearman's creek, lying all along the waters of Juniata, and is situate east of the Path Valley through which the present road goes from Harris' Ferry to Allegheny; and lastly they extended their settlements to Big Juniata, the Indians all this while repeatedly complaining that their hunting ground was every day more and more taken from them, and that there must infallibly arise quarrels between their warriors and these settlers which would in the end break the chain of friendship, and pressing in the most importunate terms their speedy removal. The government in 1748 sent the sheriff and three magistrates with Mr. Weiser unto these places to warn the people; but they, notwithstanding, continued their settlements in opposition to all this, and as if those people were prompted by a desire to make mischief, setiled lands no better—nay not so good—as many vacant lands within the purchased parts of the province.

The bulk of the settlements were made during the administration of President Palmer; and it is well known to your Honor, though then in England, that his attention to the safety of the city and lower counties would not permit him to extend more care to places so remote.

Finding such a general submission, except the two Galloways and Andrew Lycon, and vainly believing the evil would be effectually taken away, there was no kindness in my power which I did not do for the offenders. I gave them money where they were poor, and telling them they might go directly on any part of the two millions of acres lately purchased of the Indians; and where the families were large, as I happened to have several of my own plantations vacant, I offered them to stay on them rent free till they could provide for themselves. Then I told them that if, after this lenity and good usage, they would dare to stay after the time limited for their departure, no mercy would be shewed them, but that they would feel the rigor of the law.

It may be proper to add that the cabins or log houses which were burnt were of no considerable value, being such as the country people erect in a day or two and cost only the charge of an entertainment.

After the close of Pontiac's war, the valley, which had been so sadly devastated, soon began to wear an air of great prosperity. When it became a positive assurance that the savages, in fear of whom the people had lived for years, were to trouble them no longer, the joy of the afflicted was great, being tempered, however, by the recollections of the awful scenes through which they had so lately passed. The inhabitants who had left their homes to seek safety in the older settled counties to the east now returned to their homes in the valley, and many immigrants of a desirable class also came in and took advantage of the chances offered to them in the new country. In 1762 of 141,000 acres of land in the county, 72,000 acres had been patented and warranted by actual settlers. About the same time (1761-62) a few Germans had settled in the eastern part of the county, near the Susquehanna. Louther Manor was resurveyed and opened for settlement (1764-65), and two years later it was again surveyed and divided into twenty-eight lots or parcels, containing from 150 to 500 acres each, which lots were purchased principally by Scotch-Irish in Lancaster and Cumberland Counties, though some were sold to Germans. Robert Whitehill is said to have erected the first stone house on the manor. Among purchasers of manor lands who were of Scotch-Irish nativity were Isaac Hendricks, Capt. John Stewart, John Boggs, John Armstrong, James Wilson, Robert Whitehill, Moses Wallace, John Wilson, Samuel Wallace, James McCurdy, David Moore, Rev. William Thompson (Episcopal minister at Carlisle), Alex Young, Jonas Seely. Among the Germans were John Mish, Conrad Reinninger, Caspar Weaver, Christopher Gramlich, Philip Kimmel, Andrew Kreutzer.

Prominent settlers about the same time in various parts of the county were Ephraim Blaine, who built a grist-mill in 1764 on the Conodoguinet about a mile north of Carlisle; Robert Collander, who also built a mill near the confluence of the Conodoguinet and Letort's Spring, in Middlesex Township; William Thompson, a captain in the Indian war, and later a general in the Revolution; William Lyon, justice, judge and military officer; John Holmes, elected sheriff October 5, 1765; William McCoskry, coroner in 1764; Stephen Duncan, Rev. George Duffield (pastor of a Presbyterian Church as early as 1768); John Montgomery, Esq., Dr. Jonathan Kearsley, Robert Miller, Rev. John Steel (captain in the Indian war)—all at Carlisle; George Armstrong, member of the Assembly, and Walter Gregory, both in Allen. James Carothers, Esq., James Galbraith, Esq., James and Matthew London,* in East Pennsborough; George Brown, Ezekiel Dunning (sheriff in 1764). John Byers, an extensive farmer near Alexander Spring and subsequently a member of Council, all of West Pennsborough; William Buchanan, James Blaine, John McKnight (judge), Thomas Wilson (judge)—all of Middleton.

Shippensburg, the oldest town in the county, had become a prosperous settlement also. A company of twelve persons had settled there in June, 1730, and were soon joined by others. Hopewell Township, which was formed as a part of Lancaster County in 1735, had settlements outside of Shippensburg (then in its limits) as early as 1731. And it is easy to see that upon the breaking out of the war of the Revolution the number of residents in the territory now included in Cumberland County was quite considerable.

The following interesting sketch, written by Thomas Craighead, Jr., of Whitehill, December 16, 1845, and published in Rupp's History of Dauphin, Cumberland and other counties, is worthy of insertion in this connection, and will doubtless be new to many:

* * * The facts, incidents, etc., I communicate, I record as they occur to my mind. I will confine myself to my youthful neighborhood and such facts as I heard related by those who have, by reason of age, gone beyond the bourne whence none return. I need not inform you that the first settlers of new countries have to encounter trials, hardships and dangers. These my ancestors, in common with others, experienced on their first coming into this county. Nothwithstanding their multiplied trials and difficulties, they had ever in mind the fear and worship of one common Creator. An ancestor of mine, who early immigrated to America, was a student of theology under the Rev. Tuckney, of Boston, who had been a member of the General Assembly at Westminster. You will find, on consulting the history of the Presbyterian Church of this county, that the name of Craighead appears at an early period. In establishing churches in this county, Craighead appears as one of the first ministers. The first sermon preached west of the Susquehanna was delivered by the Rev. Thomas Craighead, then residing, as I believe, in Donegal Township, Lancaster County. Soon after, these congregations were organized in what is now Cumberland and Franklin, viz.: One in the lower settlement, near Carlisle; one at Big Spring, near Newville, and one in the Conogocheague settlement. Thomas Craighead preached at Big Spring. When divine service was first held, the settlers went with their guns to hear preaching. These defensives were then deemed necessary to deter the Indians from attacking them. However, the peaceful disposition of the true Christian had its salutary influence upon the untutored Indian—the Indian feared and respected the consistent professor of religion. Religious influence was felt—at Big Spring protracted meetings were held for public worship. So powerful, it is said, were the influences of the Spirit, that the worshippers felt loth, even after having exhausted their stores of provisions, to disperse. I have heard it from the lips of those present, when Thomas Craighead delivered one of his parting discourses, that his flow of eloquence seemed supernatural—

---

*Matthew and James Loudon had come from Scotland and settled first in Shearman's Valley, but were driven out by the Indians, and relocated on land near Hogestown, southeast of Carlisle. James returned to Shearman's Valley after peace was declared with the Indians. His son, Archibald, born on shipboard during the passage from Scotland, afterward became postmaster at Carlisle, and also published several volumes, one of which was descriptive of outrages during the Indian wars, and has been much quoted.

HISTORY OF CUMBERLAND COUNTY.   21

he continued in bursts of eloquence, while his audience was melted to tears—himself however exhausted, hurried to pronounce the blessing, waving his hand, and as he pronounced the words, "farewell, farewell," he sank down, expiring without a groan or struggle. His remains rest where the church now stands as the only monument to his memory.

John Craighead, a son of Thomas, settled at an early date on Yellow Breeches Creek, near Carlisle. His son John officiated a short time as pastor at Big Spring. He then removed to Conegocheague, and was there placed as pastor. When the Revolution was the absorbing question of the day, he was an ardent Whig, and fearless of consequences; the Government had an eye on him, but the people were with him. He preached liberty or death from the pulpit; the young men's bosoms swelled with enthusiasm for military glory—they marched to the tented field, and several were killed. Still he urged them not to be daunted. On one occasion he brought all his eloquence to bear on the subject, until the congregation arose to their feet as if ready to march. An old lady who had just lost a son in battle, hallooed out: "Stop, Mr. Craighead! I just want to tell ye agin you loss such a purty boy as I have in the war, ye will na be so keen for fighting. Quit talking and gang yersel to the war. Ye're always preaching to the boys about it, but I dinna think ye'd be very likely to gang yersel. Jist go and try it!" He did try it, and the next day, he and Mr. Cooper—I think—a preacher also, set about to raise a company. They did raise one, of the choicest spirits that ever did live; marched in short order, and joined the army under Washington, in the Jerseys. He fought and preached alternately, breasted all danger, relying on his God and the justice of his cause for protection.

One day, going to battle, a cannon ball struck a tree near him, a splinter of which nearly knocked him down. "God bless me," says Mr. Cooper, "you were nearly knocked to staves." "Oh, yes," says he very cooly, "though you are a cooper you could not have set me up." He was a great humorist.   *   *   *   When he marched his company they encamped near where I am now writing, at the Hon. Robert Whitehill's, who opened his cellar, which was well stored with provisions and barrels of apple brandy. Col. Hendrick's daughters assisted in preparing victuals for them. They fared sumptuously with this brave man. They next encamped at Boyd's, in Lancaster County; he fell in love with Jennie Boyd and married her. He died of a cancer on his breast, leaving no children. His father, John, had been educated in Europe for the ministry, but on his return he found preaching a poor business to live by. He stopped at Philadelphia, took to tailoring, took good care when he went into good company to tie up his forefinger, for fear of his being discovered, but being a handsome little man and having a good education he was courted by the *elite* of the day. He fell in with an English heiress, of the name of Montgomery, I think, married her, and spent the fortune all but a few webs of linen, with which he purchased from the proprietor 500 acres of land on Yellow Breeches.   *   *   *   *

His other two sons, Thomas and James, were farmers; they had great difficulty in paying the balance due on their land. They took their produce to Annapolis (no business done in Baltimore then); prices got dull; they stored it; the merchant broke; all seemed gone; they applied for more time; built a saw-mill. They had made the money, but the war came on. Thomas was drafted; his son John, thirteen years old, and my father drove the baggage wagon. It took the money to equip and bear their expenses while going to and in camp. Thomas took the camp fever and his son the small-pox. Gen. Washington gave them a furlough to return home. A younger son, James, met them below Lancaster, and drove the team home. He often stopped and looked into the wagon to see if they were still living, but he got them home, and they both recovered. By some mistake in recording their furlough, there was a fine imposed on Thomas for leaving camp a few days before his time was up. When the bailiff came to collect it he was up on a barrack building wheat. The officer was on horseback. He told him he would come down and pay him. He came down, took a hickory withe that happened to lie near, caught his little horse by the tail, and whipped the officer, asking him if he was paid, until he said he was paid. That settled the fine. He was paid off with Congress money; broke up again with a chest full of money. By this time things began to go up; all prospered. John Craighead, his father, had been an active member of the Stony Ridge convention, which met to petition parliament for redress of grievances. He was closely watched by the Tories, and one Pollock was very near having him apprehended as a rebel, but the plot was found out and Pollock had to leave the county. Near the place where this convention met, at the stony ridge, one Samuel Lamb lived on his land. There was a block-house, where the neighbors flew for shelter from hostile Indians.   *   *   *   Lamb was a stone mason, built stone chimneys for the rich farmers who became able to hew logs and put up what was called a square log house. They used to say he plumbed his corners with spittle—that is, he spit down the corner to see if it was plumb. Indeed, many chimneys are standing to this day and look like it; but he had a patriotic family. When the army rendezvoused at Little York, four of his sons were in the army—two officers and two common soldiers. His daughters had a web of woolen in the loom; they colored the woof with sumach berries, and made it as red as they could, for all war habiliments were dyed red as possible; made coats by guess for their brothers, put them in a tow cloth wallet, along it upon their young brother, Samuel, to take to camp. He hesitated, the country being nearly all forest and full of wolves, bears, etc. One of them, Peggy, asked him: "What are you afraid of? Go on! Sooner come home a corpse than a coward!" He did go on, and enlisted during the war; came home, married Miss Trindle, of Trindle Spring, removed to Kentucky, raised a large family. * * * It seems as if there was something in the blood, as one of his sons in the last war* was a mounted volunteer in Gen. Harrison's army. At the battle of Tippecanoe he rode a very spirited horse, and on reining him to keep him in the ranks, his bridle bit broke. Being an athletic, long-legged young fellow, and his horse running at full speed toward the ranks of the enemy, he brandished his sword, hallooing: "Clear the way, I am coming!" The ranks opened, let him through, and he escaped safe and got back to his camp.† Peggy Lamb deserves a notice. She afterward married Capt. William Scott, who was a prisoner on Long Island, and she now (1845) enjoys a captain's half pay; lives in Mechanicsburg, near her native place, a venerable old lady in full strength of intellect, though more than four-score years have passed over her. She well deserves the little boon her country bestows upon her. The first horse I remember to ride alone was one taken in the Revolution by William Gilson, who then lived on the Conodoguinet Creek, where Hurlacher's mill now is. He was one of Hindman's riflemen, and after the battle of Trenton, he being wounded in the leg, two of his brother soldiers were helping him off the field; they were pursued by three British Light Horsemen across an old field and must be taken. They determined to sell themselves as dearly as possible. Gilson reached the fence, and propped himself against it. "Now," says he, "man for man; I take the foremost." He shot him down, the next was also shot, the third was missed. The two horses pursued their courses, and were caught by Gilson and his companions and brought into camp. His blue dun lived to a great age. Gilson was offered £1,500 for him. Gilson removed to Westmoreland County. His wife was also a Trindle. He left a numerous and respectable family. I wish I was able to do those families more justice for their patriotism and integrity to their country. They have left a long line of offspring, who are now scattered far and wide over the Union. If they would but all take their forefathers for examples! I come now within my own remembrance of Cumberland County. I have seen many a pack-horse loaded with nail rods at Ege's Forge to carry out to Somerset County and the forks of Youghelgany and Red Stone Fort, to make nails for their log cabins, etc. I have seen my father's team loading slit iron to go to Fort Pitt. John Rowan drove the team. I have known the farmer's team to haul iron from the same forge to Virginia; load back corn for feed at the forge. All the grain in the county was not enough for its own consumption. I have known fodder so scarce that some farmers were obliged to feed the thatch that was on their barns to keep their cattle alive. James Lamb bought land in Sherman's Valley, and he and his neighbors had to pack straw on horses across the mountain. He was on the top of the mountain waiting until those going over would get up, as they could not pass on the path. He hallooed out: "Have they any more corn in Egypt?" I saw the first mail stage that passed through Carlisle to Pittsburgh. It was a great wonder; the people said the proprietor was a fool. I think his name was Slough. I happened a short time ago to visit a friend, Jacob Ritner, son of that great and good man, ex-Gov. Ritner, who now owns Capt. Denny's farm, who was killed during the Revolutionary war. The house had been a tavern, and in repairing it Mr. Ritner found some books, etc., which are a curiosity. Charge, breakfast, £20; dinner, horse-feed, £30; some charges still more extravagant. But we know it was paid with Congress money. The poor soldier on his return had poor money, but the rich boon, liberty, was a prize to him far more valuable. As late as 1808 I hauled some materials to Oliver Evans' saw-mill at Pittsburgh. I was astonished to see a mill going without water. Mr. Evans satisfied my curiosity by showing and explaining everything he could to me. He looked earnestly at me and said: "You may live to see your wagons coming out here by steam." The words were so impressed that I have always remembered them. I have lived to see them go through Cumberland County, and it seems to me that I may see them go through to Pittsburgh; but I have seen Mr. Evans' prophecy fulfilled beyond what I thought possible at that time. But things have progressed at a rate much faster than the most gigantic minds imagined, and we are onward still. * * * * Yours, truly, etc., THOMAS CRAIGHEAD, JR.

In truth, could Mr. Craighead now peep at the region he knew for so many years, he would be even more greatly surprised. The "steam wagons" have reached Pittsburgh and gone beyond it to the shores of the distant Pacific Ocean, over mountains beside which the Alleghenies would be but pigmy foothills. Side by side is the great telegraph, and even the human voice, by means of the delicate instrument known as the telephone, can be heard almost across the continent. The most wonderful strides toward the perfection of civilization have been taken since Mr. Craighead was laid to rest, and the end is not yet.

---

*War of 1812.
†Pretty tough story. [Ed.]

Yours Truly
Wm R. Gorgas

HISTORY OF CUMBERLAND COUNTY.   25

In a pamphlet history of the United Presbyterian Church of Big Spring, at Newville, Cumberland County, published in 1878 by James B. Scouller, occur the following passages:

"The first known settlements in Cumberland County were made in 1730, and at no great distance from the river. But new settlers came in very rapidly and passed up the North Valley, or the Kittochtinny Valley as then called, following the Conodoguinet and Yellow Breeches Creeks, and locating also upon Silver Spring, Letort Spring, Big Spring, Mean's Spring, Middle Spring, Falling Spring, Rocky Spring and the different branches of the Conococheague, until in 1736 a line of settlements extended from the Susquehanna clear through to the western part of the province of Maryland. In 1748 there were 800 taxables in the valley, and in 1751 the number had increased to 1,100 indicating a population of at least 5,000 inhabitants. These, with the exception of about fifty German families in Franklin County, were immigrants from Ireland and Scotland, and the descendants of those who had taken root in Lancaster County. In 1751 a sudden and large increase in the flow of immigration commenced, which ministered greatly to the rapid settlement of the county. This tidal wave owed its origin to a very unusual and novel cause. In 1730 Secretary Logan* wrote thus: 'I must own from my own experience in the land office that the settlement of five families from Ireland gives me more trouble than fifty of any other people. Before we were broke in upon ancient friends and first settlers lived happily, but now the case is quite altered.' The quick temper and belligerent character of this people, which kept them generally in a kind of chronic broil with their German neighbors, did not seem to improve with time, for in 1743 Secretary Peters wrote in very much the same strain as had done his predecessor, and even the Quaker forbearance of the Proprietaries finally became exhausted, so that in or about 1750, the year in which Cumberland County was organized, positive orders were issued to all the agents to sell no more land in either York or Lancaster County to the Irish, and to make very advantageous offers to those of them who would remove from these counties to the North Valley. These offers were so liberal that large numbers accepted, and built their huts among the wigwams of the native inhabitants, whom they found to be peaceful but by no means non-resistant."

A pamphlet containing an historical sketch of Carlisle, together with the charter of the borough and published in 1841, also says: "In the year 1755 instructions were given by the proprietaries to their agents that they should take especial care to encourage the immigration of Irishmen to Cumberland County. It was their desire to people York with Germans and Cumberland with Irish. The mingling of the two nations in Lancaster County had produced serious riots at elections.†"

In the year 1749 the total revenue from taxation in the county of Cumberland was only £117 7s. 8d., and the amount of excise collected in the county for the year ending June 1, 1753, was £55. In 1762 the county contained 896 taxables, 37,820 acres of warranted land, 21,500 acres of unwarranted land, 19,304 acres of patented land, 201 town lots, and there was paid £726 in rents and £4,641 10s. in taxes. "The proprietaries were the owners of land estimated at 5,167 acres in Middleton Township, near Carlisle, and 7,000 in

---
*Logan was himself an Irishman, but had been so long in the confidence and pay of the proprietaries that he was at this time, probably, somewhat prejudiced even against his own people.
†The same authorities relate, concerning the manner of settling election difficulties, that, "in 1756, when William Allen was returned a member of the Assembly for two counties, Cumberland and Northampton, he was merely requested by the speaker to name the county for which he would sit, as he could not serve for both. He chose Cumberland, and a new election was ordered for Northampton." Elections were somewhat irregular because of the sparse population.

East Pennsborough, of which 1,000 had been given up to Peter Chartier (and now in the hands of his assigns) and Tobias Hendricks, who took care of the whole manor. They also were the owners of sixty-four lots in Carlisle, eight of which were rated at £100 and the remainder at £15 each. The manor lands were valued for taxes, 3,000 of those in Middleton at £100 per hundred, and those in East Pennsborough at £75 per hundred, on which they paid a tax of 6s. on the pound. Before 1755 the proprietary estates had not been included in any general land-tax bill, but in that year the proprietaries had yielded the point and consented to be taxed on all really taxable property (that is, appropriated lands, all real estate except unsurveyed waste land, lots in town and rents of all kinds), and on equal terms with the other owners. There was, however, so much dispute on various points connected with this matter, that no collections were made on the proprietaries, but in consideration of the dangers of the province they had made a donation of £5,000.* In 1759, therefore, when the tax was levied, it was made retrospective for the five years (1755–59) inclusive, which had been in dispute, allowing them credit for the £5,000 which had been given.†"

Taxables in 1762.—The following is a list of the taxables in the county in 1762:

East Pennsborough Township, 1762.—James Armstrong, Andrew Armstrong, Samuel Anderson, James Armstrong, Samuel Adams, Samuel Bell, William Brians, William Beard, John Beard, Walter Buchanan, William Bell, David Bell, John Buchanan, John Biggar, James Carothers, Esq., William Chestnut, Thomas Clark, William Carothers, Thomas Culvert, Samuel Chambers, John Clendening, Adam Calhoon, Samuel Calhoon, Robert Carothers, John Crosier, John Chambers, William Culbertson, William Cronicle, John Carson, Thomas Donallson, Robert Denny, William Duglas, John Dickey, James Dickey, Andrew Ervin, William Ervin, James Ervin, John Ervin, John Edwards, John Fulton, James Galbreath, James Gattis, John German, William Gray, Samuel Gaily, Samuel Hustin, Tobias Hendricks, John Hickson, William Harris, Patrick Holmes, John Hamilton, Widow Henderson, Clement Horril, Jonathan Hogg, David Hogg, Joseph Junkin, Robert Jones, James Kerr, James Kile, Widow Keny, Brian Kelly, Matthew Loudon, Alex Laverty, Widow McClure, William Martial, Edward Morton, John Morton, Robert McKinly, James McConall, Samuel McCormick, John McCormick, Francis Maguire, James McCormick, Thomas McCormick, Matthew McCaskie, James McKinstry, William Mateer, William Millar, Edward Morton, Andrew Milligan, John McTeer, Thomas Murray, Shedrick Muchmore, James McConnell, Jr., Brian McColgan, James Nealer, Nathaniel Nilson, Nathaniel Nilson (again), William Noble, John Orr, William Orr, William Oliver, William Parkison, James Purdy, William Plunket, John Quigley, David Rees, William Ross, James Reed, Nathaniel Reaves, Archibald Stuart, Robert Steel, John Semple, Francis Silvers, David Semple, Robert Samuels, John Shaw, Mr. Seely, William Speedy, Thomas Spray, Henry Taylor, Henry Thornton, John Trimble, Benjamin Vernon, John Williams, William Walker, George Wood, John Wood, John Waugh, James Waugh, John Willey, Henry Warton, Samuel Williamson—126.

Carlisle, 1762.—John Armstrong, Esq., Samuel Allen, Harmanus Alricks, Nicolas Albert, William Armstrong, Thomas Armstrong, John Anderson, John Andrews, Widow Andrews, Mary Buchanan, Widow Buchanan, Thomas Bell, William Blyth, James Bell, William Bennet, William Blair, James Barclay, William Brown, Thomas Blair, Joseph Boyd, Charles Boyle, Isaac Burns, James Brandon, John Chapman (wagoner), John Crawford, Henry

*See Indian History.
†Dr. Wing, p. 64.

HISTORY OF CUMBERLAND COUNTY.

Creighton, William Crocket, Robert Crunkelton, Roger Connor, William Caldwell, George Crocket, Samuel Coulter, Andrew Colhoon, James Crocket, Simon Callins, Robert Callender, William Christy, John Chapman, William Clark, John Craig, Thomas Copling, Jacob Cart, Thomas Christy, Widow Colhoon, Michael Dill, George Davidson, James Duncan, Samuel Davidson (not of age), Thomas Duncan, Ezekiel Dunning, Thomas Donallan, William Devinport, William Denny, Widow Dunning, Adam Duglas, Stephen Duncan, Denis Dougherty, Rev. George Duffield, James Eckles, James Earl, David Franks, Stephen Foulk, John Fortner, James Ferguson, James Fleming, Thomas Fleming, Mary Gallahan, William Gray, Joseph Galbreath, James Gregg, William German, John Gamble, Daniel Gorman, Robert Gorral, Robert Gibson, Robert Guthrie, Abraham Holmes, Adam Hoops, Barnabas Hughes, Joseph Hunter, Jacob Hewick, Jacob Houseman, John Hastings, George Hook, John Huston, John Hunter, Joseph Jeffreys, Thomas Jeffreys, John Kennedy, John Kelly, Benjamin Kid, Andrew Kinkaid, John Kerr, John Kinkaid, John Kearsley, Robert Little, Agnes Leeth, William Lyon, William McCurdy, William Main, David McCurdy, John McCurdy, Widow McIntyre, Robert Miller, James McCurdy, John Montgomery, Esq., Hugh McCormick, William McCoskry, James McGill, John Mordough, Widow Miller, John McKnight, Esq., Hans Morrison, Patrick McWade, William Murphy, John Mather, Widow Miller, John McCay, Hugh McCurd, William Miller, Robert McWhiney, Andrew Murphy, Philip Nutart, Joseph Nilson, Culbert Nickelson, John Orr, Thomas Parker, William Parker, Philip Pendergrass, John Pattison, Charles Pattison, William Plunket, William Patterson, James Taylor Pollock, James Parker, James Pollock, Thomas Patton, John Pollock, William Reaney, William Roseberry, William Rusk, Mary Rogers, John Robison, Robert Robb, James Robb, William Rodeman, Widow Ross, Henry Smith, Ezekiel Smith, John Scott, Robert Smith, William Sharp, Widow Steveson, Charles Smith, Widow Sulavan, James Stakepole, John Starret, John Steel, John Smith, William Spear, Timothy Shaw, Peter Smith, Rev. John Steel, Joseph Smith, Rowland Smith, William Spear, for court house, James Thompson, Samuel Thompson, Wilson Thompson, James Thomas, James Templeton, William White, William Ward, Roger Walton, Samuel ——, William Watson, William Wadle, Edward Ward, Francis West, William Whiteside, Widow Welch, Thomas Walker, Abraham Wood, William Wallace, John Welch, James Woods, Nathaniel Wallace, Widow Vahan, John Van Lear, James Young—190.

Allen Township, 1762.—John Anderson, James Atkison, George Armstrong, Alex Armstrong, William Abernathy, George Armstrong, James Brown, William Boyls, James Beatty, Robert Bryson, William Boyd, William Crocket, George Crocket, John Clark, Roger Cook, James Crawford, Rowland Chambers, Samuel Cunningham, Philip Cuff, James Crocket, William Crosby, Thomas Davis, William Dickey, John Dunlap, William Elliott, Widow Frazer, Henry Free, John Glass, Walter Gregory, John Grindle, Richard Gilson, John Gilkison, James Gregory, John Gibson, John Giles, William Hamersly, Robert Hannah, Thomas Hamersly, Isaac Hendricks, Charles Inhuff, Nicholas King, James Long, Henry Longstaff, Hugh Laird, James McTeer, John McTeer, William McCormick, William Martin, John McMain, Rowland McDonald, Widow McCurdy, Anthony McCue, Hugh McHool, Andrew Miller, John McNail, Samuel Martin, Thomas McGee, John Nailer, Richard Peters, Richard Peters, Esq., Henry Quigley, Richard Rankin, Thomas Rankin, John Rutlidge, Robert Rosebary, Isaac Rutledge, John Sands, Widow Steel, Thomas Stewart, James Semple, Charles Shoaltz, Moses Starr, Peter Titlo, William Tidule,

Alex Trindle, David Willson, John Willson (weaver), John Willson, Alex Work, Ralph Whiteside, George Wingler—81.

West Pennsborough Township, 1762.—John Armstrong, Esq., Jacob Arthur, Peter Ancle, Laurence Allport, John Byers, Robert Bevard, George Brown, Thomas Butler, James Brown, Widow Bratton, William Blackstock, James Bevard, William Bevard, John Buras, William Carothers, James Carothers, William Clark, John Campbell, Widow Crutchlow, David Cronister, Matthew Cralley, John Denny, Ezekiel Dunning, William Dunbar, William Dunlap, John Dunlap, John Dunbar, James Dunning, John Dunning, George Davidson, John Dunning, William Dillwood, Robert Erwin, William Eakin, Thomas Eakin, Thomas Evans, William Ervin, John Ervin, Alex Erwin, William Ewing (at Three Springs), Thomas Ewing, William Ewing, Andrew Forbes, Alex Fullerton, Andrew Giffin, James Graham, Rob Guthrie, James Gordon, William Gattis, Thomas Gray, Samuel Henry, John Hodge, Adam Hays, William Harkness, James Hunter, Joseph Hasteen, Thomas Holmes, Barney Hanley, David Hall, Henry Hauwart, Joseph Kilgore, John Kerr, Matthew Kerr, Charles Kilgore, Samuel Kilgore, John Kenner, William Lemmon, William Laughlin, Allen Leeper, William Leviston, William Logan, George Little,' George Leavelan, William Little, Samuel Lindsay, John Lusk, William Leich, John McClung, Robert Meek, James McFarlane, William McFarlane, Robert McFarlane, John McFarlane, Andrew McFarlane, David McNair, John McClure, Edward McMurray, John McGeary, Patrick McClure, Robert McClure, John McCune, Robert McQuiston, James McQuiston, James McCay, Thomas McKay, Daniel McAllister, Archibald McAllister, James McNaught, Alex McBride, Samuel McCullough, David McAllister, John Miller, Robert McCullough, John McIntyre, John McNair, David McNair, Alex McCormick, William McMahan, Daniel Morrison, Matthew McCleares, James McAllister, Francis Newell, John Newell, Herman Newman, Alex Officer, Richard Peters, Esq., William Parsons, Proprietaries' Manor (700 acres patented), William Dutton, Paul Pears, Richard Parker, William Parker, Widow Parker, Joseph Peoples, Jacob Peoples, Michael Pears, John Patton, Thomas Parker, William Quiry, David Ralston, Matthew Russell, Robert Rogers, William Robison, Archibald Robison, John Robison, Samuel Reagh, Patrick Robison, Singleton's Place, Robert Stuart, John Scroggs, Allen Scroggs, John Smily, James Sea, Robert Swaney, John Swaney, David Stevenson, Thomas Stewart, Robert Stewart, William Scarlet, William Stewart, James Smith (attorney), Anthony White, Widow Willson, Samuel Willson, Samuel Wilson, James Weakley, Robert Walker, William Woods, James White, Robert Welsh, Alex Young—164.

Middleton Township, 1762.—Nathan Andrew, William Armstrong, James Alcorn, Adam Armwick, John Beatty, John Bigham, William Beatty, William Brown, John Beard, William Buchanan, John Brownlee, James Blair, Richard Coulter, Widow Clark, William Campbell, John Crennar, Robert Caldwell, Charles Caldwell, John Craighead, James Chambers, John Davis, George Douglass, John Dinsmore, David Drennan, William Dunbar, John Dickey, Walter Denny, David Dunbar, James Dunlap, Widow Davies, William Davison, Jr., James Eliot, Robert Eliot, Jr., John Elder ("Disputed Land," 150 acres), James Eliot, Jr., Andrew Eliot, William Forgison, William Fleming, Joseph Fleming, Ann Fleming, Arthur Foster, John Forgy, Thomas Freeman, John Gregg, Samuel Guay, Widow Guliford, Andrew Gregg, Robert Gibson, Lodwick Ginger, Joseph Gaily, Joseph Goudin, Thomas Gibson, Nicholas Hughs, Samuel Harper, William Henderson, Thomas Holt, William Hood, Jonathan Holmes, Humphrey's land, Hamilton's land, Patrick Hason, Andrew Holmes,

HISTORY OF CUMBERLAND COUNTY. 29

Thomas Johnston, John Johnston, Archibald Kenedy, James Keny, Matthew Kenny, John Kincaid, George Kinkaid, James Kinkaid, Richard Kilpatrick, William Leer, Robert Little, John Little, George Leslie, Samuel Lamb, David McClure, William McKnitt, Andrew McBath, William McClellan, Hugh McBride, John McCrea, David McBride, "Meeting-house land," Hugh McCormick, James McCullough, Matthew Miller, James Matthews, James McAllister, Francis McNickle, John McKnight, Esq., James Moore, William Moore, James McManus, Guain McHaffy, John McHaffy, Thomas McHaffy, Samuel McCrackin, John Mitchell, Widow McIntyre, John Neely, Matthew Neely, John Patton, William Parkison, James Pollack, Robert Patterson, William Patterson, Richard Peters' land, John Patterson, William Riddle, Archibald Ross, James Robison, John Reed, Robert Reed, William Reed, John Reed, Jr., John Robb, Adam Ritchy, David Reed, James Reed, William Riggs, George Riggs, Jacob Stanford, Abraham Stanford, John Stuart (weaver), James Stuart, William Smith, John Stinson, George Sanderson, Sr., Robert Sanderson, Jean Sanderson, George Sanderson, Jr., James Sharon, John Smith, Alex Sanderson, Andrew Simison, Randles Slack, William Shaw, James Smith, William Stewart, Robert Stinson, Ezekiel Smith, John Stewart, James Smith, Widow Templeton, Robert Urie, Patrick Vance, Solomon Walker, Daniel Williams, Samuel Willson, John Waddell, Widow Williamson, Francis West, John Welsh, Thomas Wilson, Esq., Samuel White, Thomas Woods, James Woods—159.

Hopewell Township, 1762.—Thomas Alexander, John Anderson, Widow Andrews, Hugh Brady, Samuel Brown, Benjamin Blyth, William Bricer, Joseph Brady, John Brady, Samuel Bratin, Hugh Brady, Jr., William Crunkelton, John Coff, James Chambers, George Clark, James Chambers, William Carnahan, James Carnahan, George Cunningham, Robert Chambers, Francis Campble, Robert Campble, William Duncan, Thomas Duncan, Daniel Duncan, John Daizert, James Daizert, Moses Donally, Widow Donally, Philip Dusky, Henry Davies, John Eager, John Egnew, Joseph Eager, John Eliot, James Eliot, Robert Fryer, Clement Finley, Thomas Finley, William Gibson, Ann Gibson, Andrew Gibson, Samuel Gibson, Widow Gibbs, Robert Gibbs, William Gamble, Samuel Gamble, John Hanah, Josiah Hanah, Samuel Hindman, John Hunter, William Hodg, James Hamilton, George Hamilton, John W. Hamilton, John Taylor Hamilton, David Herrin, John Hannah, William Hunter, John Jack, Joseph Irvin, James Jack, James Kilgore, Thomas Lyon, James Long, Edward Leasy, John Laughlin, James Laughlin, James Little, Andrew Lucky, John Laughlin, Widow Leasin, Josiah Martin, Daniel McDowel, James McFarlan, John McFarlan, John McClintock, James McGaffog, Andrew Mankelwain, Samuel Morrow, Patrick McGee, Robert McComb, Samuel Montgomery, Thomas Montgomery, James Mahan, John Moorhead, James McCormick, George McCormick, John Montgomery, James Montgomery, John McCune, Jr., John McCune, Robert McCune, John McClean, Daniel Mickey, Robert Mickey, John S. Miller, Samuel Montgomery, David McGaw, Philip Millar, Isaac Miller, James McAnay, John Millar, James McCall, John Meason, Nail McClean, George McCully, John McIntire, Samuel Moor, Andrew Mankelwain, John Morris, William McGaffog, Widow Myers, William Moorhead, Samuel Mitchel, Samuel Mackelhing, John Montgomery, David McCurdy, Patrick McFarlan, John McDowel, Robert McDowel, Thomas McKiny, James Mankelwain, Samuel McGready, Samuel Neaves, John Nisbet, Richard Nickelson, William Nickelson, James Nesbit, John Nisbet, William Plumstead, Richard Peters, William Piper, Samuel Perry, Nathaniel Peoples, James Pollock, William Powell, John Porter, Thomas Pordon, John Porterfield, James Quigly, John Quigly, John Robison, William Reynolds, John Redman,

James Reynolds, Samuel Smith, George Sheets, Samuel Stewart, David Simiral, William Stitt, Robert Simonton, Edward Shipper, Alex Scroggs, John Stinston, Samuel Sellars, Nathaniel Scruchfield, Samuel Sorre, Hugh Torrins, John Thompson, William Thompson, John Trimble, Widow Trimble, Joseph Thompson, David Thompson, Widow Thompson, John Thompson, Joseph Woods, John Wodden, William Walker, Robert Walker, Samuel Walker, James Williamson, Samuel Wier, Samuel Williamson, James Work, William Walker, James Walker, James Wallas, James Jocky Williamson, West & Smith, James Young.

More Early Settlers.—Dr. Wing, at pages 24 and 25 of his History of Cumberland County, mentions the following early settlers:

George Croghan, five miles from the Susquehanna River, on the north side of the Conodoguinet, also owned lands in various parts of the county, and in 1748 was the owner of 800 acres, which extended nearly to the mouth of Silvers' Run, on the Conodoguinet. Part of it had been taken up by Robert Buchanan, in 1743, and part by William Walker, who sold to William Trent. Mr. Croghan also owned a large tract in Hopewell, north of Shippensburg. He was a trader with the Indians, did not cultivate his land, and changed his residence frequently to suit the convenience of trade. He was originally from Dublin, and lived afterward at Aughwick, in what is now Huntingdon County. He was greatly trusted by Sir William Johnson as an agent among the Indians.

Robert Buchanan, above mentioned, sold his first claim and removed farther up the creek with his brother Walter, living in East Pennsborough. William Buchanan kept an inn at Carlisle in 1753, and another Buchanan was a resident of Hopewell Township in 1748, adjoining the Kilpatrick settlement. James Laws lived next to Croghan, opposite to the mouth of Silvers' Run. At a spring adjoining on the south was James Silvers, from whom the stream and spring were named. He had settled there with his wife, Hannah, before 1733, and owned 500 acres of land or more; was public-spirited and honorable; has no descendants bearing his name. Within ten or fifteen years from the time he settled there located around him James Pollock, who built a gristmill at or near the confluence of the Conodoguinet and the stream which issues from Silvers' Spring, John Scott, Robert and James Robb, Samuel Thompson, Thomas Fisher, Henry Quigley and William Berryhill. Andrew and John Galbreath owned land adjoining them on the east, and William Walker on the west.

John Hoge settled very early on the site of Hogestown, and had numerous distinguished descendants. Two brothers, named Orr, coming from Ireland before 1738, settled near him. William Trindle, John Walt, Robert Redock, John Swanzey, John McCracken, Thomas Fisher, Joseph Green and John Rankin owned land in Pennsborough, and were at different times tax collectors before 1747. John Oliver, Thomas McCormick and William Douglas had farms in Hoge's vicinity, John Carothers at the mouth of Hoge's Run, and William Douglas west of and opposite him up the Conodoguinet. In the same neighborhood were John and Abraham Mitchell, John Armstrong, Samuel Anderson, Samuel Calhoun, Hugh Parker, Robert Dunning, John Hunter (near Dirty Spring), Samuel Chambers, James Shannon, William Crawford, Edward Morton, Robert Fulton, Thomas Spray, John Callen, John Watts, Michael Kilpatrick, Joseph Thompson, Francis Maguire and James Mateer. James Armstrong lived farther west, and on the ridge back of the present site of Kingston was the residence of Joseph Junkin, who early settled upon a large tract. Robert Bell lived near Stony Ridge, and south of him were

Samuel Lamb, "a stone mason and an ardent patriot," John Trindle, near Trindle's Spring, James Irvine, Mathew Miller, John Forney and David Denny. At Boiling Spring there settled early Dr. Robert Thompson, formerly of Lancaster, Joseph Graley, Patrick Hassen, Andrew, William, James and George Crocket, David Reed and John Dickey. Charles Pippin settled on "Pippin's Tract," on Yellow Breeches, in or before 1742. West of him, on the same stream, were John Campbell, who had a mill, Roger Cook, David Wilson, John Collins, James McPherson, Andrew Campbell, Andrew and John Miller, Robert Patrick, J. Crawford, William Fear, John Gronow, Charles McConnel, Alexander Frazier, Peter Title (or Tittle, as sometimes given), Arthur Stewart, Thomas Brandon, Abraham Endless, John Craighead, the last earlier than 1746 on lands extending along the creek eastward from the Baltimore Turnpike. Adjoining him on the southwest was James Moore, who had a mill which is still in existence. On the Letort, near Middlesex, James Davison lived in 1736, a little south of the fording place where the road from Harris' Ferry crossed the run. The land in this vicinity is said to have been thickly settled before Carlisle was laid out. Patrick and William Davison, William Gillingham, James Gillgore (or Kilgore), Joseph Clark, Peter Wilkie and John McClure owned land near the proposed site of Carlisle, part of which the proprietaries bought back for the purpose of laying out the town upon it. Richard lived two miles southwest. "William Armstrong's settlement" was on the Conodoguinet just below Meeting-house Springs. "David Williams, a wealthy land-holder and the earliest known elder in the congregation of Upper Pennsborough, James Young and Robert Sanderson were probably included in this settlement." Thomas Wilson was farther east, near the present Henderson mill; next east was James Smith, and south, Jonathan Holmes, "another elder and an eminently good man," who lived near the Spring on land more recently owned by Mrs. Parker, just northeast of Carlisle. Rowland Chambers lived near the mouth of the Letort on the State road, and below or back of him on Conodoguinet was a settlement where the first mill in the county was claimed to have been erected. North and on the north side of the creek were Joseph Clark and Robert Elliott, who came from Ireland about 1737. Abraham Lamberton came soon after, also Thomas Kenny. East of them were John Semple, Patrick Maguire, Christopher Huston and Josiah McMeans. "On the glebe belonging to the congregation of Upper Pennsborough, about two miles northwest from Carlisle, was the Rev. Samuel Thompson (1738), near which were lands belonging to John Davis, Esq.; and farther up the creek were William Dunbar and Andrew Forbes, near whom a mill was afterward erected by William Thompson." About four miles west of Carlisle Archibald McCallister had an extensive purchase, the upper part of which was sold to John Byers, Esq., as early as 1742. Samuel Alexander was on Mount Pleasant, and east of him on and near the road to Carlisle were David Line, Andrew McBeath, James Given, John Roads, M. Gibbons, Jacob Medill, Stephen Colis and Samuel Blyth. Farther south, near the present Walnut Bottom road, were John Huston and two brothers, from Donegal, Lancaster County, Samuel and William Woods. Between them and the South Mountain, as early as 1749, were James McKnight, William Dunlap, Robert Walker and James Weakley, and in the same vicinity were James L. Fuller, John McKnight, Esq., William Campbell, John Galbreath, Hugh Craner, John Wilson, James Peoples, Robert Queston, Thomas Armstrong, William Parkinson and John Elder.

"In the settlement commenced by James Chambers (whose residence was about three miles southwest of Newville) was one of the most numerous clusters of inhabitants in the valley. It was very early (1738) strong enough to form a religious congregation, which offered to pledge itself to the support of a pastor. In each direction from the Big Spring the land was almost entirely taken up before 1750; so that the people there presented strong claims to the county seat. Among the earliest of these settlers was Andrew Ralston [see page 8, this Part], on the road westward from the Spring; Robert Patterson the Walnut Bottom road; James McKehan, who came from Gap Station, Lancaster County, and was for many years a much respected elder in the church of Big Spring; John Carson, John Erwin, Richard Fulton, Samuel McCullough and Samuel Boyd. On the ground now occupied by the town of Newville were families of the name of Atchison and McLaughlin, and near them were others of the name of Sterrett, Blair, Finley, Jacobs, and many whose locations are not known to the writer.*

The third brother of the Chambers family, who located near Middle Spring (north of Shippensburg at the county line) soon had a numerous settlement around him. A history of the Middle Spring Presbyterian Church in 1876, by Rev. S. S. Wylie, then its pastor, has the following: "There is good evidence for the statement that at that time (1738) this section of this valley, between Shippensburg and the North Mountain, was as thickly settled as almost any other portion of it. It is a matter of history that the first land in this valley taken up under the 'Samuel Blunston license' was by Benjamin Furley, and afterward occupied by the Herrons, McCombs and Irwins, a large tract lying along the Conodoguinet, in the direction of and in the neighborhood of Orrstown. At the house of Widow Piper, in Shippensburg, as early as 1735, a number of persons from along the Conodoguinet and Middle Spring met to remonstrate against the road which was then being made from the Susquehanna to the Potomac, passing through 'the barrens,' but wanted it to be made through the Conodoguinet settlement, which was more thickly settled. This indicates that at this time a number of people lived in this vicinity. I give the names of some of them, on or before the year 1738: Robert Chambers, Herrons, McCombs, Youngs (three families), McNutts (three families), Mahans (three families), Scotts, Sterretts and Pipers; soon after the Brady family, McCunes, Wherrys, Mitchells, Strains, Morrows and others. It was such pioneers as these who, with their children, made Shippensburg the most prominent town of this valley prior to the year 1750. Many of the names given above constituted some of the most prominent and worthy members of Middle Spring Church." Dr. Wing gives names in this settlement as follows: Hugh and David Herron, Robert McComb, Alex and James Young, Alex McNutt, Archibald, John and Robert Machan, James Scott, Alex Sterrett, William and John Piper, Hugh and Joseph Brady, John and Robert McCune and Charles Morrow. The twelve persons who, in June, 1730, made the first settlement at Shippensburg, were Alex Steen, John McCall, Richard Morrow, Gavin Morrow, John Culbertson, Hugh Rippey, John Rippey, John Strain, Alex Askey, John McAllister, David Magaw, John Johnston.

Wild Animals and Fish.—Dr. Wing says, in his general work on Cumberland County: "These fields and forests were full of wild animals, which had multiplied to an unusual degree with the diminution of their enemies—the Indians. Deer were especially numerous, particularly on the mountains; but bears, wolves, panthers, wildcats, squirrels, turkeys and other game were everywhere plentiful. Along the creeks and smaller streams the otter, muskrat and other amphibious animals were taken, and their skins constituted no small part of the trade with the Indians and early hunters. Fish of all kinds

*Dr. Wing's History, pp. 24-5.

were caught in the streams, and large quantities even of shad are said to have come up the Susquehanna and to have frequented the Conodoguinet in the Eastern part of the county. Many of these were taken in the rude nets and seines called "brushnets," made of boughs or branches of trees. Most of these wild animals and fish have now disappeared, but the accounts of the early settlers are filled with tales of their contests with each other, the Indians and themselves." The same facts are substantially given in Rupp's History of Dauphin and other counties.

Customs and Habits.—Wearing apparel was "home-spun and home-made," and the men went about dressed in this, and in hunting shirts and moccasins. Carpets were unknown. Floors were of the "puncheon" variety—logs split and hewed, with the smooth surface uppermost. Benches made of the same material with legs in them answered in the place of chairs. Instead of crockery and china-ware the table furniture consisted of plates, spoons, bowls, trenchers, and noggins made of wood, or of gourds and hard-shell squashes; though in the families in better circumstances pewter took the place of wood, and there was nothing finer. The border settlers who could eat their meals from pewter dishes were rich indeed. Says Rupp: "Iron pots, knives and forks, especially the latter, were never seen of different sizes and sets in the same kitchen."

The few sheep, cows and calves possessed by the first settlers were for some years a prey to wolves, unless securely protected and watched. The ravenous wolves were bold in their marauding expeditions, and many a time they came prowling around the houses at night, poked their noses into the openings and looked in through the crevices in the log dwellings upon the families within, while the discordant howling sounded like the yelling of demons and made the darkness appalling. Woe be then to the domestic animal that was not securely housed or penned, for in the morning only its glistening bones would be left to tell that it ever existed. The country lying between the Conodoguinet and the Yellow Breeches, for a distance of ten or twelve miles westward from the Susquehanna, was a barren, or tract devoid of timber, and across this deer were occasionally seen in a race for life with a pack of snarling and hungry wolves at their heels. These cadaverous and cunning animals were seldom taken in steel traps; a better plan offered for their capture was the log pen, with sloping exterior, open at the top, with retreating inner walls. The wolf could easily climb up the outside, and get at the bait within—generally the carcass of a sheep which had previously furnished a wolf a meal—but once inside they could not get out, and were at the mercy of the settlers. Many were destroyed in this way, yet it was forty years or more before they ceased to be very troublesome.

The pioneers were a "rude race and strong," or they never could have withstood the terrible hardships and privations of life in a border region, with wild beasts and wilder men continually harrassing them and making their lot desperate indeed. There is that in the Anglo-Saxon blood which appears to court difficulty and danger, and the resources of the race in time of trial are wonderful beyond comparison. In this broad and beautiful valley, in the days when the colonists were going through experiences which should finally cause their separation from the mother country and the upbuilding of a magnificent Republic, there were hours, months and years of extremest peril, of which he who reads at this late day can hardly have conception.

Necessarily the buildings erected by the first settlers were simple and unpretending, whether for dwellings, places for worship or schools. Their supplies must be brought on horseback from Philadelphia, and across the Susquehanna in canoes or simple boats. It may, therefore, readily be understood that they did not make pretensions to style, though there was a degree of uniformity about their buildings, dress, furniture and mode of living, which their isolation brought about as a matter of course. Lumber was not to be had for any price; wooden pins took the place of nails; oiled paper answered for glass in the windows. Says Dr. Wing: "They could dispense for a time with almost everything to which they had been accustomed, provided they could look forward with confidence to a future supply. Their cabins were soon erected, and they did not scorn to receive suggestions from the rude savages whose skill had so long been tasked in similar circumstances. The same forests and fields and streams were open to them, and the Indian did not grudge his white brother his knowledge of their secrets. These buildings were constructed of the logs to be had off the banks of the streams or from the neighboring hills; the combined strength of a few neighbors was sufficient to put them in position and small skill was needful to put them together, to fill up the interstices between them, and to roof them with rude shingles, thatched straw or the bark of trees, and in a little while the same ingenuity would split and carve out of timber, and fashion the floors, benches, tables and bedsteads which were wanted for immediate use. As the number of settlers increased, these dwellings became of a better order. More skilled workmen began to be employed, and better materials and furniture were introduced, but for the first twenty years the people were contented with the most humble conveniencies. A few houses were constructed of stone, but these were not common. The first stone dwelling on Louther Manor, or in the eastern part of the county, was said to have been put up by Robert Whitehill, after his removal over the river, in 1772. The houses for schools and for public worship may have been of a better quality, for they were not usually erected under such extreme emergency, but they were of like materials and by the same workmen. Those, however, who know the buoyancy of hopes which ordinarily characterize the pioneers of a new country will not be surprised to learn that these were a happy people. The rude buildings in which they slept soundly, studied diligently, and worshiped devoutly, were quite as good for them, and were afterward remembered as pleasantly as were the more costly edifices of their father-land."

Flour was an article not easily obtained until after the erection of mills to grind the wheat raised in the valley. The latter was found to flourish on the soil of the region, easily cleared of the bushes which grew upon it, and "as soon as it could be carried to market it became the most important article of trade." Maize, or Indian corn, was for some time more abundant, and afforded a good source of food supply. The Indians raised it and none was exported, and the process of preparing it for eating was simple.

Buckskins were made into breeches and jackets of great durability, though the working classes more commonly wore garments of hempen or flaxen tow, or woolen. The men had wool hats, cowhide shoes, linsey frocks, and sometimes deer-skin aprons, while the women had frocks of similar materials, and occasionally sun-bonnets. They managed to have a little better dress for Sunday, or for social meetings, in which they indulged for "amusement and good cheer." In out-of-door sports the Indians often came in for a share in the exercises.

After the long French and Indian war, and the subsequent war precipitated by Pontiac, there was a greater feeling of relief than had been experienced since the settlements began, and prosperity became more general. Some families had by that time become possessed of considerable wealth, and were enabled to maintain a style of living which those less fortunate could not indulge in. This style was naturally modeled after English customs. Dr. Wing, who quotes as authority "'Watson's Annals of Philadelphia,'" continues: "To have a house in town for winter and another on a plantation for summer was not very unusual, and in the proper season a large hospitality was indulged in. In many families slaves were possessed, and even where a more ordinary style of servitude prevailed there were not a few forms of aristocratic life. Some slaves were found even on the smaller farms, but the great majority of servants were German or Irish 'redemptioners.'* As their term of service was commonly not more than four or five years, and the price not more than the hire of laborers for a less term, many farmers found this an advantageous method of obtaining help. As they were not much distinguishable from their employers and afterward received good wages, they soon became proprietors of the soil, and their children, being educated, passed into better society. In such a state of affairs there was a perpetual tendency to a uniformity of conditions and of social life. The great body of the people were moral, and all marked distinctions among them were discountenanced, but those who followed rough trades were not unwilling to be recognized. A style of dress and manners prevailed to which our later American habits are generally averse, and which plainly distinguished between them and professional men and persons of independent means. Each class had its special privileges, which amply compensated for inferiority of position. The long established relations which thus grew up were the sources of mutual benefits and pleasures. The dress of those who aspired to be fashionable was in many respects the reverse of what it now is. Men wore three-square or cocked hats and wigs; coats with large cuffs, big skirts lined and stiffened with buckram; breeches closely fitted, thickly lined and coming down to the knee, of broadcloth for winter or silk camlet for summer. Cotton fabrics were almost unknown. linen being more common, the hose especially being of worsted or silk. Shoes were of calfskin for gentlemen, while ordinary people contented themselves with a coarser neat's leather. Ladies wore immense dresses expanded by hoops or stiff stays, curiously plaited hair or enormous caps, high-heeled shoes with white silk or thread stockings, and large bonnets, universally of a dark color. The dresses of the laboring classes were different from these principally in the materials used. Buckskin breeches, checked shirts, red flannel jackets and often leather aprons were the ordinary wear. While at their work in the fields the appearance of the men and women continued much as we have described it at an earlier period. Before the Revolution Watson tells us that 'the wives and daughters of tradesmen throughout the provinces' all wore short gowns, often of green baize but generally of domestic fabric, with caps and kerchiefs on their heads, for a bare head was seldom seen except with laborers at their work. Carriages were not common and were of a cumbrous description. People usually rode horseback, and good riding was cultivated as an accomplishment. At the country churches on the Sabbath not unfrequently the horses on the outside were nearly as numerous as the people inside the buildings. Stores in town were places of resort, and did a more extensive business than they have done since the cities have been so accessible. Newspapers were rare, published generally only once a week and reaching subscribers in this county nearly a week after date. Eight weekly newspapers and one semi-weekly had been started in Philadelphia, but as the post went into the interior only once a week, the latter was of little advantage to our people. The sheets on which they were printed were small, and the amount of news would now be considered very meager. The death of a sovereign about this time was not proclaimed in the province until nearly six weeks after the occurrence, and Thompson's history and treaty with the Indians were not

---

*Emigrants hired out until their passage money, which had been advanced to them, should be repaid.

known in Carlisle until between three and four weeks from those events. Visitors to Philadelphia usually went in their own two-wheeled chaises or on horseback, occupying two or three weeks in the journey. The numerous courts and transactions in land, as well as the lively social intercourse, made such journeys frequent. The transportation of goods both ways rendered needful trains of heavily loaded wagons (since called by the name of Conestoga or Pennsylvania), with four, five or six horses. As the woods westward and over the mountains would not allow of this method, either at Shippensburg or Smiths (Mercersburg), the goods had to be transferred to pack-horses. 'It was no uncommon thing at one of these points to see from fifty to 100 packhorses in a row, one person to each string of five or six horses, tethered together, starting off for the Monongahela country, laden with salt, iron, hatchets, powder, clothing and whatever was needed by the Indians and frontier inhabitants.'"

In the days of pack-trains, time about 1770-80, there were seen at one time in Carlisle as many as 500 pack-horses, going thence to Shippensburg, Fort London and other western points, loaded with merchandise, salt, iron, etc. Bars of iron were carried by first being bent over and around the bodies of the horses. Col. Snyder, an early blacksmith of Chambersburg, once told (1845) that he "cleared many a day from six to eight dollars in crooking, or bending iron, and shoeing horses for Western carriers." [Rupp's History of Cumberland and other counties, p. 376.] The same authority says: "The pack horses were generally led in divisions of about twelve or fifteen horses, carrying about two hundred weight each, all going single file and being managed by two men, one going before as the leader, and the other at the tail to see after the safety of the packs. When the bridle road passed along declivities or over hills, the path was, in some places, washed out so deep that the packs, or burdens, came in contact with the ground, or other impeding obstacles, and were frequently displaced. However, as the carriers usually traveled in companies, the packs were soon adjusted and no great delay occasioned. The pack horses were generally furnished with bells, which were kept from ringing during the day drive, but were let loose at night when the horses were set free and permitted to feed and browse. The bells were intended as guides to direct their whereabouts in the morning. When wagons were first introduced, the carriers considered that mode of transportation an invasion of their rights. Their indignation was more excited and they manifested greater rancor than did the regular teamsters when the line of single teams was started, some thirty [now seventy] years ago."

Formation of Townships and Boroughs.—The townships, as they now exist in the County of Cumberland, were formed at dates as follows:

Cook, from a part of Penn, June 18, 1872; Dickinson, April 17, 1785; East Pennsborough, 1745 (originally Pennsborough, 1735); Frankford, 1795; Hampden, January 23, 1845; Hopewell, 1735; Lower Allen, 1849, (originally Allen, 1766); Middlesex, 1859; Mifflin, 1797; Monroe, 1825; Newton, 1767; North Middleton, 1810 (originally Middleton, 1750); Penn, from part of Dickinson, October 23, 1860; Shippensburg, 1784; Silver Spring, 1787; Southampton, 1791;* South Middleton, 1810, (originally Middleton, 1750); Upper Allen, 1849 (originally Allen, 1766); West Pennsborough, 1745, to present limits in 1785, part of original township of Pennsborough, 1735; Carlisle Borough, 1782, new charter, 1814; Camp Hill Borough, November 10, 1885; Mechanicsburg Borough, 1828; Mount Holly Springs Borough, 1873; Newburg Borough, 1861; New Cumberland Borough, 1831; Newville Borough, February 26, 1817, township in 1828, borough in 1869. Shippensburg Borough, 1819; Shiremanstown Borough, 1874 or 1875.

*One authority says before 1782, but we have found no record to that effect.

HISTORY OF CUMBERLAND COUNTY. 39

Lands.—The lands in this region at the time of the early settlements were of two classes: those to which the Indian title had not yet been extinguished, and upon which white people were not allowed to settle until the government should purchase them and open an office for their sale; and the proprietary lands "sometimes surveyed into manors and reserved for special purposes and sometimes held open for private purchase," but belonging to them (the proprietaries) in fee simple. Purchasers of land from the proprietaries, who had surveyed and divided them into lots, paid very low prices, sometimes as low as one shilling sterling per acre, and even down to a merely nominal valuation according to location. These purchasers often had to borrow money to pay even the small sums required, and gave mortgages upon the lands for security. They were generally able to meet their obligations in a few years. Every acre of land sold by the proprietaries was also subject to an annual rental, from one penny down, and sometimes a diminutive quantity of wheat or corn, or perhaps poultry.*

It was not until the treaty of October, 1736, that the Indian title to lands in Cumberland County was extinguished and vested in the heirs, successors and assigns of Thomas and Richard Penn. Paxton Manor had been set off in 1731-32 by Thomas Penn as an inducement to the Shawanees to settle here and live at peace with the whites; the title to it was, however, acquired in 1736 with the other lands included in the deed, and it was then laid out.† Its limits were described as follows in the return, May 16, 1765, of the warrant for its resurvey, issued December 26, 1764: "On the west side of the Susquehannah River, opposite to John Harris' ferry, and bounded to the eastward by the said river; to the northward by Conodogwinet Creek; to the southward by the Yellow Breeches Creek, and to the westward by a line drawn north, a little westerly from the said Yellow Breeches to Conodogwinet Creek aforesaid, containing 7,507 acres, or upward." The survey showed it to contain 7,551 acres. It embraced all the land between the two creeks, according to reliable authority, extending westward to "the road leading from the Conodogwinet to the Yellow Breeches, past the Stone Church or Frieden's Kirch, and immediately below Shiremanstown." Its first survey had been made very early (1731-32). John Armstrong surveyed it in 1765, and divided it into twenty portions, and in 1767 John Lukens surveyed it and divided it into twenty-eight tracts or plantations of various sizes, aggregating about the original quantity of land in the manor. These tracts were sold originally to the following persons: No. 1, 530 acres, to Capt. John Stewart; No. 2, 267½ acres, to John Boggs; 300 acres to Casper Weber; 256 acres to Col. John Armstrong; 227 acres to James Wilson; 227 acres to Robert Whitehill (including site of town of Whitehill); No. 3, 200 acres; No. 4, 206 acres, to Moses Wallace; No. 5, 200 acres, to John Wilson; Nos. 6 (267 acres) and 7 (283 acres), to John Mish; No. 8, 275 acres, to Richard Rogers; No. 9, 195 acres, Conrad Renninger; No. 10, 183 acres, to Casper Weaver; No. 11, 134 acres, to Casper Weaver; No. 12, 181 acres, to William Brooks; No. 13, 184 acres, to Samuel Wallace; No. 14, 153 acres, Christopher Gramlich; No. 15, 205 acres, James McCurdey; No. 16, 237 acres, Isaac Hendrix; No. 17, 213 acres, Robert Whitehill; No. 18, 311 acres, Philip Kimmel; No. 19, 267 acres, Andrew Kreutzer; No. 20, 281 acres, David Moore; Nos. 21 and 22, 536 acres, Edmund Physick; No. 23, 282 acres, Edmund

---
*The annual quit rent was placed at 1 shilling per 100 acres, payable in lawful money forever. Its collection was very difficult, however, for the people deemed it preposterous that they should have to pay it even though it exempted them from all other proprietary taxes. Some were paid in Cumberland County though, until some time after the Revolutionary War. The amount was payable to the heirs of William Penn. Gold and silver was very scarce and the province issued paper money, which depreciated to half its face value. Many farmers had their farms through having to pay mortgages, looking at the third time their earlier payments and improvements.

†Dr. J. A. Murray in article upon Louther Manor, in Carlisle *Herald*, early in 1885.

Physick; No. 24, 287 acres, Rev. William Thompson; No. 25. 150 acres, Alex Young; No. 26, 209 acres, Jonas Seely; Nos. 27 (243 acres) and 28 (180 acres), Jacob Miller. The manor included portions of Hampden, East Pennsborough and Lower Allen Townships, as at present existing, and the western boundary would pass just east of Shiremanstown. Within its area are now situated the towns and settlements of New Cumberland, Milltown (or Eberly's Mills), Bridgeport, Wormleysburg, Camp Hill and Whitehill Station.

The troubles between the proprietors of Pennsylvania and Maryland over the boundary between the two provinces, with their final settlement by the running of "Mason and Dixon's Line," are set forth in Chapter X of the history of Pennsylvania in this volume, and it is unnecessary to repeat them here.

At one time during the Revolutionary period, when the titles of lands in Cumberland County were examined with a view to taxation, it was discovered that a large quantity of land was yet vested in the proprietary family and no revenue was derived from it. "The following tracts," says Dr. Wing, "were described as belonging to them: in East Pennsborough a tract called Lowther (formerly Paxton) Manor, containing 7,551 acres; in West Pennsborough these tracts are called Jericho, containing 807 acres and 40 perches, another of 828 acres, and another of 770 acres and 20 perches; a tract adjoining the mountains of 988 acres; one composed of several fragments, originally 6,921 acres and 23 perches, and including the borough of Carlisle and then in the vicinity of the town; one adjoining the North Mountain, 3,600 acres; another near the Kittatinny Mountains of 55 acres; two tracts in Hopewell Township, most if not all of which are probably now in Franklin County, 4,045 acres and 120 perches, and 980 acres—making in all 26,536 acres. Much of the land which had been sold had been subjected by the terms of sale to a perpetual quit rent. During the war none of these quit rents had been collected, no further sales could be effected, and no tax could be collected from this large amount of property. Many persons, too, had settled upon such proprietary lands as were unoccupied without the form of any title, and were making improvements on them. November 27, 1779, the Assembly passed resolutions annulling the royal charter, and granting to the Penn family as a compensation for the rights of which this deprived them £130,000. This, however, did not affect their ownership of lands and quit rents as private persons, so that they still remain the largest land owners in the State. On a subsequent occasion (1780) these private estates were forfeited and vested in the commonwealth, by which act the State government became possessed of a large amount of land which it bestowed upon officers and soldiers, or sold to private settlers for the profit of the State."

We have seen a copy of an original draft of a "proprietary manor southwest of the borough of Carlisle, in Middleton Township, Cumberland County, containing in the whole 1,927 acres, 34 perches, and an allowance of six acres per cent for roads, etc. Resurveyed the 6th, 7th and 8th days of January, 1791. Pr. Samuel Lyon, D. S." This joined Carlisle on the southwest, being bounded north by Gillanghan's tract, Armstrong's tract, Richard Peters' tract and Richard Coulter's tract; east by lands belonging to Patrick and William Davidson, Banton & Co., Stephen Foulk, Joseph Thornburgh and William Patterson; south by James Lyon's and the heirs of George Lyre's land; west by Lyre's heirs, William Reaney and John Carver. It was quite irregular in form.

CHAPTER III.

INDIAN HISTORY—FRENCH AND INDIAN WAR—PONTIAC'S WAR.

IN this connection it will not be necessary to enter into an extended history of the Indian nations who at various periods claimed power over this region. It will be sufficient to state that when the Cumberland Valley first became known to the European races, and was looked upon as a place of future colonization, it was virtually in possession of the aggregation of tribes known as the Six Nations. It has been said that at the opening of the seventeenth century "the lower valley of the Susquehanna appears to have been a vast, uninhabited highway, through which hordes of hostile savages were constantly roaming between the northern and southern waters, and where they often met in bloody encounters. The Six Nations were acknowledged as the sovereigns of the Susquehanna, and they regarded with jealousy and permitted with reluctance the settlement of other tribes upon its margin."*

The Six Nations—originally the Five Nations until the Tuscaroras of North Carolina joined them in 1712—were the Onondagas, Cayugas, Oneidas, Senecas, Mohawks and Tuscaroras. They were termed the "Iroquois" by the French. The "Lenni Lenape," or the "original people," commonly called the Delaware Nation, were divided into three grand divisions—the Unamis, or Turtle tribes; the Unalachtgos, or Turkeys, and the Monseys, or Wolf tribes. The first two occupied the territory along the coast and between the sea and the Kittatinny or Blue Mountains, with settlements reaching from the Hudson on the east to the Potomac on the west. The Monseys, a fierce, active and warlike people, occupied the mountainous country between the Kittatinny and the sources of the Susquehanna and Delaware Rivers. These three divisions were subdivided into various subordinate classes bearing distinguishing names. The Lenni Lenape tribes occupying this region soon after the first settlement of Pennsylvania were the Tuteloes and Nantecokes, formerly in Maryland and Virginia. The Shawanos, or Shawanese, a fierce and restless tribe which was threatened with extermination by a more powerful tribe in the south, sought protection from the northern tribes whose language was similar to their own, and a portion of them settled near the forks of the Delaware and on the flats below Philadelphia. Becoming troublesome they were removed by either the Delawares or Six Nations to the Susquehanna Valley, and during the Revolution and the war of 1812 their terrible deeds became matters of historic record. From them sprang the renowned chieftain Tecumseh (or Tecumthe). The historian Bancroft, in speaking of the Shawanese, says: "It was about the year 1698 that three or four score of their families, with the consent of the government of Pennsylvania, removed from Carolina and planted themselves on the Susquehanna. Sad were the fruits of that hospitality. Others followed; and when, in 1732, the number of Indian fighting men in Pennsylvania was estimated to be 700, one-half of them were Shawanee emigrants. So desolate was the wilderness that a vagabond tribe could wander undisturbed from Cumberland down to the Alabama, from the head waters of the Santee to the Susquehanna." Some historians believe the Shawanese came north in 1678. They

---
*Day's Historical Collection of Pennsylvania, pp. 388, 389.

had a village in Lancaster County, at the mouth of Pequea (or Pequehan) Creek, and their chief's name was Opessah, and there were several Indian towns along both sides of the Susquehanna. Those who had settled at Pequea removed a quarter of a century later to lands on the Conodoquinet, within the present limits of Cumberland County, with also a village at the mouth of the Yellow Breeches Creek. They deserted the villages about 1725, when the whites began to look to it for homes, and removed westward to the Ohio. The lands on the Conodoquinet were surveyed for the use of the Indians upon a treaty of purchase being made by the proprietaries for their lands on the Susquehanna, at the mouth of the Conestoga and elsewhere. "The intrusion of the white settlers upon their hunting ground," says Conyngham, "proved a fresh source of grievance; they remonstrated to the governor and to the Assembly, and finally withdrew and placed themselves under the protection of the French. Big Beaver, a Shawanee chief, at the treaty of Carlisle in 1753, referred to a promise made by William Penn, at Shackamaxon, of hunting grounds forever." The treaty mentioned was one "of amity and friendship," made at Carlisle in October, 1753, with the Ohio Indians, by Benjamin Franklin, Isaac Morris and William Peters, commissioners. The expense thereof, including presents to the Indians, was £1,400.

Treaties.—Says Dr. Wing (pp. 14-15 History of Cumberland County): "For one or two generations at least the land of Penn was never stained by an Indian with the blood of a white man. Deeds were obtained on several different occasions during the years 1682-1700 for lands lying between the Delaware and the Potomac, and south of the South Mountain. In 1696 a purchase was effected through Gov. Dongan, of New York, in consideration of one hundred pounds sterling, 'of all that tract of land lying on both sides of the river Susquehanna and the lakes adjacent in or near the province of Pennsylvania.' As the right of the Six Nations to sell this territory was not acknowledged by the various tribes living on the Susquehanna, Conestoga and Potomac Rivers, other treaties were entered into with the sachems of those tribes (September 30, 1700, and April 23, 1701), by which their sale was expressly confirmed. So vague, however, was the language used in these deeds that a question arose whether the phrases 'lands on both sides of the Susquehanna and adjoining the same,' would give any rights beyond that river, and it was thought best to effect another purchase before any settlement should be allowed on that territory. Accordingly the chiefs of the Six Nations met October 11, 1736, in Philadelphia, when they revived all past treaties of friendship and executed a deed conveying to John, Thomas and Richard Penn and their heirs 'all the said river Susquehanna, with the lands lying on both sides thereof, to extend eastward as far as the heads of the branches or springs which run into the said Susquehanna, and all the land lying on the west side of the said river to the setting of the sun, and to extend from the mouth of the said river northward up the same to the hills or mountains called in the language of said nations Tayamentasachta, and by the Delaware Indians the Kekachtannin* hills.' This deed included all the lands comprised in the present county of Cumberland, but was not executed until a few years after settlements had been commenced there."

Previous to the purchase of 1736, a number of unauthorized settlements had been made upon the Conodoguinet and Conococheague, mostly by persons from the north of Ireland, and after the purchase, but before the lands were surveyed, these settlements were encouraged for the purpose of preventing intruders coming in under Lord Baltimore's title. "These settlements," says Day, "gave rise to the complaints of the Shawanese."

*By other authority Kekachtanamin.

After Franklin's treaty with the Indians at Carlisle, in 1753, a dispute arose between the governor and Council, and the Assembly, over a complaint made by the Shawanese, "that the proprietary government had surveyed all the land on the Conodoguinet into a manor, and driven them from their hunting ground without a purchase and contrary to treaty." The remarks made by Big Beaver at said treaty have been mentioned. They were mentioned by the Assembly in the dispute, but "by the governor and Council it was alleged that no such thing had occurred, and that a treaty held in 1754, the same Shawanee chiefs who were at Carlisle the year before made the strongest professions of their friendship, without any complaint on account of the same tract of land. They alleged, too, that the Shawanese never had any claim to the Conodoguinet lands; for that they were southern Indians who, being rendered uneasy by their neighbors, had settled on these lands in 1698, with the permission of the Susquehanna Indians and the proprietary, William Penn." However, no compensation being made to the Shawanese, they removed as stated and put themselves under the protection of the French and became a source of terror to the colonists because of their hostility during the great French and Indian war of 1753–60.

Indians belonging to various tribes were met with by the early settlers. Among them were the Shawanese, Delawares, Susquehannas (of which people but a remnant was left, the tribe having been swept away by wars and smallpox), Manticokes, Mingoes, Tuteloes, etc. A Mingo village is said to have existed on Letort Run, in the neighborhood of Carlisle and the famous Logan, whose residences were many, if all tradition be true, is said to have once occupied a cabin on the Beaver Pond, at the head of Letort Spring. The Shawanees were not so numerous as in former years, as many of them had removed westward. They had professed that the lands, being barren, or devoid of large trees were not suitable for a hunting ground, and for that reason they had left, but indiscretion on the part of some of their young men, who had in drunken frolics given offense to the Delawares, had undoubtedly been a greater reason. although both the Delawares and the Six Nations made investigations, forgave their offenses, and invited them to return, which they would not do. Even the proprietary, Thomas Penn, upon his arrival in 1732, extended the same invitation and assigned them a large tract of the land they had previously occupied provided they would return. A few of them did so, and lived peaceably with the settlers. In order to prevent whites from locating upon the land given to the Shawanese, a tract containing 7,551 acres was surveyed in 1732 and erected into a manor called Paxton. The Indians were finally found unwilling to occupy this land, and it was surveyed December 26, 1764, and given the name "Louther Manor," in honor of a sister of William Penn, who married a nobleman of that name. The order for the resurvey was given December 6, 1764, and returned May 16, 1765, the quantity being found as above—7,551 acres. The bounds are described as follows: "Bounded on the east by the Susquehanna, opposite John Harris' ferry; north by the Conodoguinet; south by the Yellow Breeches Creek, and on the west by a line drawn a little westerly from the said Yellow Breeches to Conodoguinet Creek, containing 7,507 acres or upward."

The state of mind the Shawanese were in over their pretended wrongs, and the bargaining away of their land by the Six Nations with little regard for their welfare, rendered them easy to win from their friendship to the English. "More than once," says Dr. Wing, "when messengers were sent to them by the Governor and the Six Nations, they confessed that they had been mistaken, and promised that they would return, or at least live in peace where they were;

but every year it became more and more evident that their friendship was forced, and lasted only while they were in expectation of some benefits, and that their hostility might be counted upon whenever an opportunity of vengeance should occur. The Delawares had not as extensively gone beyond the mountains; the main body adhered to their chiefs, and were almost supported by the government, but an increasing number of them were wandering off and were making common cause with the Shawanees. The 'Indian Walk,' by which a portion of their lands had been acquired, seemed at least sharp practice, but the injustice had been more than compensated by subsequent dealings."

The use of liquor among the Indians was the cause of much trouble between themselves, and to a certain extent between them and the whites. They knew not how to govern their appetites, and more than once Indian murders occurred which could be directly traced as the effects of the liquor the perpetrators had swallowed. It burned any humanity out of them and made their naturally savage dispositions wilder and fiercer. It is known that Sassoonan, king of the Delawares, in 1731 killed his nephew while in a drunken frenzy, and was overcome with remorse and shame when he became sober, and yet he could not bring himself to ask that the sale of the poison to the Indians be entirely prohibited, but only that it might be kept from his people, *except as it was asked for by themselves.*

The French began their work of alienating the Shawanese from the English as early as 1730, desiring to secure their influence in the furtherance of their own purposes. The following, from a message by Gov. Gordon to the Provincial Assembly, August 4, 1731, as given in the provincial record, shows "that by advices lately brought to him by several traders (from Ohio) in those parts, it appears that the French have been using endeavors to gain over those Indians (Shawanese) to their interest, and for this end a French gentleman had come among them some years since, sent, as it was believed, from the governor of Montreal, and at his departure last year carried with him some of the Shawanese chiefs to that government, with whom they at their return appeared to be highly pleased. That the same French gentleman, with five or six others in company with him, had this last spring again come among the said Indians and brought with him a Shawanese interpreter, and was well received by them." [Rupp's History of Cumberland and other counties, page 351. The same authority says that "Hetaquantagechty, a distinguished chief, said, in a council held at Philadelphia, August 25, 1732, that last fall (1731) the French interpreter, Cahichtodo, came to the Ohio River (or Allegheny) to build houses there, and to supply the Indians with goods, etc."]

Settlements by the Scotch-Irish upon unpurchased lands about the Juniata assisted in fanning the flame of Indian hostility. Yet, in what is now Cumberland County, these settlements must have been as stated by Mr. Rupp, made "by permission from the Indians, whom the first settlers conciliated," for there were no outbreaks here for more than thirty years after the pioneer locations had been made. Yet it was evident that a crisis was impending. The provincial government was hard pressed to provide presents for the Indians, in order to keep them peaceable and to maintain a line of frontier defense against French incursions. Finally war was declared between France and England,* and the storm, which had for so many years been gathering force, broke with deadly fury upon the mountain region, and sad were the experiences of the colonists before morning dawned upon a peaceful horizon.

Matters began to look dark for the settlers upon this declaration of hostil-

---
*Open hostility was declared in March, 1744, although the actual strife in Pennsylvania did not break out until 1753, when the French established posts to connect the lakes with the Ohio.

ities. The French had encroached upon territory claimed by the English, and the Six Nations were silent when messages were sent them concerning the other tribes they had previously held in check. Chartier, the Indian trader, formerly located at the mouth of the Yellow Breeches, had made his home with the Shawanese and accepted a commission in the French Army. He was a half-breed with Shawanese blood in his veins, and had great influence over that tribe. A conference was held with the Six Nations at Lancaster June 24, 1744, when the latter pledged themselves to remain at peace and to do all in their power to prevent the tribes which owed them allegiance from indulging in hostile forays. But as a large portion of the Shawanees and Delawares had gone beyond their jurisdiction, the treaty could not reach them, and it became the inhabitants to cast about for means of security and defense. The foolish differences between the governor and the Assembly for years prevented steps being taken sufficient to allay fear. Finally, through the sagacity of Benjamin Franklin, aided by James Logan, 10,000 volunteer militiamen were formed into 120 companies throughout the provinces, and the expense was met by voluntary subscriptions. The regiments thus raised were called "Association regiments," and this was the beginning of a system which continued on into the Revolutionary war. Bancroft states on the authority of Logan that "the women were so zealous that they furnished ten pairs of silk colors wrought with various mottoes." The inhabitants of Lancaster County, for Cumberland was not yet formed, being largely Scotch-Irish and naturally warlike and aggressive, entered heartily into the military spirit. A number of companies was formed in the valley, the officers being chosen by the soldiers and commissioned by the governor. The several militia captains in the county were sent letters, dated December 15, 1745, stating that news had been received that "the French and their Indian allies were preparing to march during the winter to the frontiers of Pennsylvania under the conduct of Peter Chartier, who would not fail to do them all the mischief in his power. The news served to stir up the people, as may well be imagined, but the alarm proved groundless. March 29, 1748, a list of officers in an Associated regiment, raised in "that part of Lancaster which lay between the river Susquehanna and the lines of this province," was presented to the provincial council. The officers had been chosen by the men in their commands and commissioned by the governor, and were as follows: Colonel—Benjamin Chambers, of Chambersburg; lieutenant-colonel—Robert Dunning, of East Pennsborough; major—William Maxwell, of Peters; captains—Richard O'Cain, Robert Chambers, of Hopewell; James Carnaghan, of Hopewell; John Chambers, of Middleton; James Silvers, of East Pennsborough; Charles Morrow, of Hopewell; George Brown, of West Pennsborough; James Woods, of Middleton; James McTeer, of East Pennsborough, and Matthew Dill; lieutenants—William Smith, of Peters; Andrew Finley, of Lurgan; James Jack, of Hopewell; Jonathan Holmes of Middleton; Tobias Hendricks, of East Pennsborough; James Dysart, of Hopewell; John Potter, of Antrim; John McCormick, of East Pennsborough; William Trindle, of East Pennsborough; Andrew Miller, of East Pennsborough; Charles McGill, of Guilford; John Winton, of Peters; John Mitchell, of East Pennsborough; ensigns—John Lesan, John Thompson, of Hopewell; Walter Davis, of Middleton; Joseph Irwin, of Hopewell; John Anderson, of East Pennsborough; John Randalls, of Antrim; Samuel Fisher, of East Pennsborough; Moses Starr, of East Pennsborough; George Brenan, Robert Meek, of Hopewell; James Wilkey, of Peters, and Adam Hayes, of West Pennsborough. No invasions of which is now Cumberland County occurred, and no murders of citizens of this immediate valley are recorded during this period.

The home government were in doubt about the legality and expediency of these associated organizations, but their doubts were easily removed, and the council, in a letter to the proprietaries dated July 30, 1748, said: "The zeal and industry, the skill and regularity of the officers have surprised every one, though it has been for them a hard service. The whole has been attended by such expense, care and fatigue as would not have been borne or undertaken by any who were not warm and sincere friends of the government, and true lovers of their country. In short, we have by this means, in the opinion of most strangers, the best militia in America; so that, had the war continued, we should have been in little pain about any future enterprises of our enemies. Whatever opinion lawyers or others not fully acquainted with our unhappy circumstances may entertain of it, it is in our opinion one of the wisest and most useful measures that was ever undertaken in any country." The peace of Aix-la-Chapelle, in October, 1748, did not affect the American colonies, for the French continued to erect forts and take other steps until war was precipitated in 1753.

In what is at present Cumberland County, forts—in some instances mere trading-houses—were erected at various times from 1753 to 1764, and so far as now known were as follows: Fort Le Tort, a trading house near Carlisle, 1753; Fort Louther, at Carlisle, 1753; Fort Croghan, a trading-house, eight miles up the Conodoguinet from Harris' ferry, where the veteran trader, George Croghan, resided; Fort Franklin, at Shippensburg, said to have been commenced in 1755; Fort Morris, at Shippensburg, 1755; Forts Dickey, Ferguson and McAllister, all in 1764. (These are on authority of an historical map of Pennsylvania issued by the Pennsylvania Historical Society.) The defeat of Gen. Braddock on the Monongahela, July 9, 1755, left the frontier in a greatly exposed condition, and the people were quick to apprehend their danger. Gov. Morris visited Carlisle July 10, 1755, for the purpose of sending on supplies to Braddock and encouraging the people in the midst of their panic over various Indian depredations and the removal of troops for their protection from the valley, and while there learned of the disastrous end of Braddock's expedition. The troops in Pennsylvania were sent north, and the province was left to take care of itself as best it could. Large quantities of provisions had been accumulated at Shippensburg, Carlisle and other points, which the retreating army had no pressing need for, and it was well for the inhabitants of the valley. Work on the military road, elsewhere described, was abandoned, and the people looked to the future with dire forebodings. "News of contemplated attacks upon the settlements along the frontier from the Delaware to the Maryland and Virginia line came upon the people in quick succession, and some actual massacres, burnings and captivities were reported from the south, west and north. Even before Braddock's defeat, and when that general with his army had gone only thirty miles from Fort Cumberland, a party of 100 Indians, under the notorious Shingas, came to the Big Cove and to the Conoloways (creeks on the border of Maryland in what is now Fulton County) and killed and took prisoners about thirty people, and drove the remainder from their homes."[*] The fugitives spread the news, and terror and consternation resulted among the inhabitants of the region, not lessened when warning was given that an attack had been planned against Shearman's Valley and the settlements here. "John Potter," says Wing, "the sheriff of Cumberland County, who resided in the vicinity which had been ravaged, gathered some companies to resist the assailants, but it was only to witness the burning buildings, bury the dead and form a gathering of the fugitives; the nimble foe was

---

[*]By Dr. Wing, from Pennsylvania Archives, Vol. II, p. 375.

always at a distance on some other depredations before the pursuers reached any point where they had been. James Smith (a brother-in-law of William Smith, the justice and commissioner on the road), a youth of eighteen, had been captured with several others while engaged in conveying provisions along the road, and a still larger number up the river Susquehanna was slain and driven in. Twenty-seven plantations were reported as utterly desolated in the southwestern part of this valley and vicinity, and no prospect seemed to be before the people but that of being given up to the will of the savages."

When Gov. Morris learned in Carlisle of Braddock's defeat he was importuned by the people to take some steps for their protection. He issued writs to summon to a meeting on the 23d of July at Philadelphia, to devise means to defend the frontier and provide for the expense; and upon request of the people laid out ground for wooden forts at Carlisle and Shippensburg, and gave orders to have them built and supplied with arms and ammunition. He at the same time encouraged the inhabitants to form associations for their own defense, and they scarcely needed a second bidding. Four companies of militia were formed and supplied with powder and lead. John Armstrong and William Buchanan, of Carlisle, Justice William Maxwell, of Peters, Alexander Culbertson, of Lurgan, and Joseph Armstrong, of Hamilton Townships, received supplies to distribute among the inhabitants. There was great danger from the enemy at the upper end of the valley, though no locality was safe. Petitions were sent to the governor by numerous citizens in the valley, showing their inability to provide adequate protection for themselves, and calling upon him for assistance. The people at Shippensburg offered to finish a fort begun under the late governor if they might be allowed men and ammunition to defend it.

Dr. Egle in his History of Pennsylvania (pp. 89-90), says: "The consternation at Braddock's defeat was very great in Pennsylvania. The retreat of Dunbar left the whole frontier uncovered; whilst the inhabitants, unarmed and undisciplined, were compelled hastily to seek the means of defense or of flight. In describing the exposed state of the province and the miseries which threatened it, the governor had occasion to be entirely satisfied with his own eloquence; and had his resolution to defend it equaled the earnestness of his appeal to the Assembly, the people might have been spared much suffering. The Assembly immediately voted £50,000 to the King's use, to be raised by a tax of 12 pence per pound, and 20 shillings per head, yearly, for two years, on all estates, real and personal, throughout the province, the proprietary estate not excepted. This was not in accordance with the proprietary instructions, and therefore returned by the governor. In the long discussions which ensued between the two branches of government, the people began to become alarmed, as they beheld with dread the procrastination of the measures for defense, and earnestly demanded arms and ammunition. The enemy, long restrained by fear of another attack, and scarcely crediting his senses when he discovered the defenseless state of the frontiers, now roamed unmolested and fearlessly along the western lines of Virginia, Maryland and Pennsylvania, committing the most appalling outrages and wanton cruelties which the cupidity and ferocity of the savage could dictate. The first inroads into Pennsylvania were in Cumberland County, whence they were soon extended to the Susquehanna. The inhabitants, dwelling at the distance of from one to three miles apart, fell unresistingly, were captured or fled in terror to the interior settlements. The main body of the enemy encamped on the Susquehanna, thirty miles above Harris' ferry, whence they extended themselves on both sides the river, below the Kittatinny Mountains. The settlements at the Great Cove in Cumberland County, now Fulton, were destroyed, and many of the inhabitants slaughtered or made captives, and the same fate fell upon Tulpehocken, upon Mahanoy and Gnadenhutten."

As an illustration of the desperate strait the people were in, the following letter, written to the governor by John Harris, of Harris' ferry, October 29, 1755, is quoted: "We expect the enemy upon us every day, and the inhabitants are abandoning their plantations, being greatly discouraged at the approach of such a number of cruel savages, and no sign of assistance. The Indians are cutting us off every day, and I had a certain account of about 1,500 Indians, besides French, being on their march against us and Virginia, and now close on our borders, their scouts scalping our families on our frontiers daily. Andrew Montour and others at Shamokin desired me to take care; that there was forty Indians out many days, and intended to burn my house and destroy my family. I have this day cut holes in my house, and it is determined to hold out to the last extremity if I can get some men to stand by me, few of which I yet can at present, every one being in fear of their own families being cut off every hour; such is our situation. I am informed that a French officer was expected at Shamokin this week with a party of Delawares and Shawnese, no doubt to take possession of our river; and, as to the state of the Susquehanna Indians, a great part of them are actually in the French interest; but if we should raise such a number of men immediately as would be able to take possession of some convenient place up the Susquehanna, and build a strong fort in spite of French or Indians, perhaps some Indians may join us, but it is trusting to uncertainty to depend upon them, in my opinion. We ought to insist on the Indians declaring either for or against us. As soon as we are prepared for them, we must bid up for scalps and keep the woods full of our own people hunting them, or they will ruin our province, for they are a dreadful enemy. We impatiently look for assistance. I have sent out two Indian spies to Shamokin. They are Mohawks, and I expect they will return in a day or two. Consider our situation, and rouse your people downward, and do not let about 1,500 villains distress such a number of inhabitants as is in Pennsylvania, which actually they will, if they possess our provisions and frontier long, as they now have many thousands of bushels of our corn and wheat in possession already, for the inhabitants goes off and leaves all."*

Gov. Morris, moved by the sad tidings from the frontier, summoned the Assembly to meet November 3, (1755), when he demanded money and a militia law, after laying before the body an account of the proceedings of the enemy. Petitions were constantly coming in for arms and ammunition, and asking for the taking of such steps as should carry out the Governor's ideas and afford protection to the inhabitants. With the Indians committing depredations on the south side of the Blue Mountains, the obstinate Assembly "fooled along" as if there were no necessity for action. The proprietaries made a donation of £5,000, and the Assembly finally passed a bill for the issuance of £30,000 in bills of credit, based upon the excise, which was approved by the Governor. The people held public meetings in various places to devise means to bring the Assembly to its senses, and the dead and mangled bodies of some of the victims of savage cruelty were sent to Philadelphia and hauled about the streets, with placards announcing that they were victims of the "Quaker policy of non-resistance." The province of Pennsylvania erected a chain of forts and block-houses along the Kittatinny Hills, from the Delaware to the Maryland line, and garrisoned them with twenty to seventy-five men each. The whole expense was £85,000, and the principal mountain

*Egle's History of Pennsylvania, pp. 90-91.

passes were guarded by them. Benjamin Franklin and his son William were leading spirits and raised 500 men, with whom they marched to the frontier and assisted in garrisoning the forts.

October 30, 1755, about eighteen citizens met at the residence of Mr. Shippen, of Shippensburg, pursuant to a call by Sheriff John Potter, and resolved to build five forts: one at Carlisle, Shippensburg, Benjamin Chambers', Steel's meeting-house and William Allison's, respectively. Fort Louther at Carlisle, had existed in an uncompleted state since 1753, and Fort Franklin, which stood in the northeastern part of Shippensburg, was begun as early as 1740. The latter was a log structure, and its ruins were torn down about 1790. Fort Morris, commenced after the meeting of citizens above alluded to, was not finished until the 17th of December following, although 100 men worked upon it "with heart and hand" every day. It was built on a rocky hill at the western end of town, of small stones, the walls being two feet thick and laid in mortar. A portion of this fort was in existence until 1836, when it was torn down. Its construction was carried on during an exciting period. Fort Franklin, the log structure, was enlarged by the addition of several sections, and in 1755 had a garrison of fifty men. Edward Shippen, writing to William Allen June 30, 1755, tells of murders committed by the Indians "near our fort."

Twenty-five companies of militia, numbering altogether 1,400 men, were raised and equipped for the defense of the frontier. The second battalion, comprising 700 men, and stationed west of the Susquehanna, was commanded by Col. John Armstrong, of Carlisle. His subordinates were, captains, Hans Hamilton, John Potter, Hugh Mercer, George Armstrong, Edward Ward, Joseph Armstrong and Robert Callender; lieutenants, William Thompson, James Hayes, James Hogg, William Armstrong and James Holliday; ensigns, James Potter, John Prentice, Thomas Smallman, William Lyon and Nathaniel Cartland.

Four forts were built by the province west of the Susquehanna, viz.: Fort Lyttleton, in the northern part of what is now Fulton County; Fort Shirley at Augharich, the residence of George Croghan, where Shirleysburg now is, in Huntingdon County; Fort Granville, near the confluence of the Juniata and Kishicoquillas, in Mifflin County, and Pomfret Castle on the Mahantango Creek, nearly midway between Fort Granville and Fort Augusta (Sunbury), on the south line of Snyder County. Capt. Hans Hamilton commanded Fort Lyttleton; Capt. Hugh Mercer, Fort Shirley, subsequent to the resignation of Capt. George Croghan; Col. James Burd, Fort Granville, and Col. James Patterson, Pomfret Castle. These forts were too far from considerable settlements to be effectual, and in 1756 John Armstrong advised the building of another line along the Cumberland Valley, with one at Carlisle. The old fort (Fort Louther) at Carlisle was simply a stockade of logs, with loop-holes for muskets, and swivel guns at each corner of the fort. In 1755 it was garrisoned by fifty men; it probably received its name in 1756. Other forts were erected in the valley outside of what is now Cumberland County, and Col. John Armstrong was at the head of the military operations. In 1757 breastworks were erected by Col. Stanwix, northeast of Carlisle, near the present Indian school (old United States barracks). Col. Stanwix wrote to Secretary Peters, July 25, 1757, as follows: "Am at work at my intrenchment, but as I send out such large and frequent parties, with other neccessary duties, can only spare about seventy workingmen a day, and these have very often been interrupted by frequent and violent gusts, so that we make but a small figure yet; and the first month was entirely taken up in clearing the ground, which was full of monstrous stumps. Have built myself a hut in camp, where the captains and I live together." *

An early writer (1757) upon the mode of warfare adopted by the Indians thus describes their maneuvres: "They come within a little way of that part they intend to strike, and encamp in the most remote place they can find to be quite free from discovery; the next day they send one, or sometimes two, of their nimble young fellows down to different places to view the situation of the town, the number of people at each house, the places the people most frequent, and to observe at each house whether there are most men or women. They will lie about a house several days and nights watching like a wolf. As soon as these spies return they march in the night in small parties of two, three, four or five, each party having a house for attack, and each being more than sufficient for the purpose intended. They arrive at their different destinations long before day, and make their attack about day-break, and seldom fail to kill or make prisoners of the whole family, as the people know nothing of the matter until they are thus labyrinthed. It is agreed that the moment each party has executed its part they shall retreat with their prisoners and scalps to the remote place of rendezvous which they left the night before. As soon as they are thus assembled they march all that day (and perhaps the next night, in a body if apprehensive of being pursued) directly for the Ohio. Perhaps at some of these houses thus attacked some of the people may be fortunate enough to escape; these as soon as the Indians are gone, alarm the forts and the country around, when a detachment, if possible, propose to pursue the enemy. But as the whole or the chief part of the day is spent in assembling, taking counsel, and setting out on the expedition, the Indians, having eight or ten hours the start, cannot be overtaken, and they return much fatigued and obliged to put up with their loss. Upon this the chief part of inhabitants adjacent to the place fly, leaving their habitations and all they have, while perhaps a few determine to stay, choosing rather to take the chance of dying by the enemy than to starve by leaving their all. These must be constantly on the watch, and cannot apply themselves to any industry, but live as long as they can upon what they have got. The Indians avoid coming nigh that place for some time, and will make their next attack at a considerable distance, where the people are not thinking of danger. By and by the people who had fled from the first place, hearing of no encroachments in that quarter, are obliged, through necessity, to return to their habitations again and live in their former security. Then in due time the Indians will give them a second stroke with as much success as the first."

The autumn of 1755 was fraught with terror to the citizens of Carlisle and vicinity. November 2, John Armstrong wrote Gov. Morris: "I am of the opinion that no other means than a chain of block-houses along or near the south side of the Kittatinny Mountain, from Susquehanna to the temporary line, can secure the lives and properties of the old inhabitants of this county; the new settlements being all fled except those in Shearman's Valley, who, if God do not preserve them, we fear will suffer very soon." Armstrong wrote the same day to Richard Peters as follows:

CARLISLE, Sunday night, November 2, 1755.

Dear Sir:—Inclosed to Mr. Allen, by the last post, I send you a letter from Harris'; but I believe forgot, through that day's confusion, to direct it.

You will see our melancholy circumstances by the Governer's letter, and my opinion of the method of keeping the inhabitants in this country, which will require all possible despatch. If we had immediate assurance of relief a great number would stay, and the inhabitants should be advertised not to drive off nor waste their beef cattle, etc. I have

---
*By a letter from Col. Armstrong dated June 30, 1757, it is known that Col. Stanwix had begun these intrenchments shortly previous to that date.

S. P. Gorgas

not so much as sent off my wife, fearing an ill precedent, but must do it now, I believe, together with the public papers and your own.
There are no inhabitants on Juniata nor on Tuscarora by this time, my brother William being just come in. Montour and Monaghatootha are going to the Governor. The former is greatly suspected of being an enemy in his heart—'tis hard to tell—you can compare what they say to the Governor with what I have wrote. I have no notion of a large army, but of great danger from scouting parties.

January 15–22, 1756, another Indian treaty of amity was held at Carlisle, when Gov. Morris, Richard Peters, James Hamilton, William Logan, Joseph Fox (a commissioner from the Assembly) and George Croghan (interpreter) were present. But seven Indians only were present, including one chief from the Six Nations and one or two from a portion of the Delawares. Nevertheless, it was found that the hostile savages were confined to the Delawares and Shawanese tribes, and even among them there was a considerable minority opposed to the war. After taking all matters into consideration it was decided by the Governor to issue a declaration of war against the Delawares, the Shawanese not being included, because it was hoped they might be brought back to their former homes. Therefore, on the 14th of April, 1756, a proclamation of war was published against the Delaware Indians and all who were in confederacy with them, excepting a few who had come within the border and were living in peace. By advice of the Assembly's commissioners, who deemed any steps, however extreme, wise when the punishment of the savages and the cessation of hostilities was the object, rewards were offered as follows, as shown by the colonial records: "For every male Indian enemy above twelve years of age, who shall be taken prisoner and be delivered at any fort garrisoned by the troops in the pay of this province, or at any of the county towns to the keepers of the common jails, there shall be paid the sum of one hundred and fifty Spanish dollars or pieces of eight; for the scalp of every male Indian enemy above the age of twelve years, produced as evidence of their being killed, the sum of one hundred and thirty pieces of eight; for every female Indian taken prisoner and brought in as aforesaid, and for every male Indian prisoner under the age of twelve years, taken and brought in as aforesaid, one hundred and thirty pieces of eight; for the scalp of every Indian woman, produced as evidence of their being killed, the sum of fifty pieces of eight, and for every English subject that has been taken and carried from this province into captivity that shall be recovered and brought in, and delivered at the city of Philadelphia to the governor of this province, the sum of one hundred and fifty pieces of eight, but nothing for their scalps, and that there shall be paid to every officer or soldier as are or shall be in the pay of this province, who shall redeem and deliver any English subject carried into captivity as aforesaid, or shall take, bring in and produce any enemy, prisoner or scalp as aforesaid, one-half of the said several and respective premiums and bounties." Very few rewards were claimed under this proclamation, and it was not considered probable that any Indians were killed for the sake of procuring the bounty.

The proclamation issued in May, 1756, subsequent to that against the Delawares, declaring war against France, was hardly necessary so far as the American territory was concerned, for, nothwithstanding the treaty of Aix-la-Chapelle in 1748, the French had kept up their movements in this country, building forts and inciting the Indians to commit outrages upon the English settlements, and winning the savages over to their own standards by arts well plied.

The year 1756 was a dark one for the colonists, to whom the terrible experiences of Indian warfare were nothing new. Murders were committed in what was then Cumberland County, but now Bedford, Union, Franklin, Dauphin, Perry and others, the leading spirits among the Indians being Shingas and Capt. Jacobs. Samuel Bell, residing on the Stony Ridge, five miles below Carlisle, had a lively experience, which is thus told by Loudon: "Some time after Gen. Braddock's defeat, he and his brother, James Bell, agreed to go into Shearman's Valley to hunt for deer, and were to meet at Croghan's (now Sterret's) Gap, on the Blue Mountain. By some means or other they did not meet, and Samuel slept all night in a cabin belonging to Mr. Patton, on Shearman's Creek. In the morning he had not traveled far before he spied three Indians. who at the same time saw him. They all fired at each other; he wounded one of the Indians, but received no damage except through his clothes by the balls. Several shots were fired on both sides, as each took a tree. He took out his tomahawk and stuck it into the tree behind which he stood, so that should they approach he might be prepared; the tree was grazed with the Indians' balls, and he had thoughts of making his escape by flight, but on reflection had doubts of his being able to outrun them. After some time the two Indians took the wounded one and put him over a fence, and one took one course and the other another, taking a compass, so that he could no longer screen himself by the tree; but by trying to ensnare him thay had to expose themselves, by which means he had the good fortune to shoot one of them dead. The other ran and took the dead Indian on his back, one leg over each shoulder. By this time Bell's gun was again loaded. He then ran after the Indian until he came within about four yards from him, fired and shot through the dead Indian and lodged his ball in the other, who dropped the dead man and ran off. On his return, coming past the fence where the wounded Indian was, he dispatched him but did not know that he had killed the third Indian until his bones were found afterward."

February 15, 1756, William Trent, in writing from Carlisle, stated that "several murders or captures and house burnings had taken place under Parnell's Knob, and that all the people between Carlisle and the North Mountain had fled from their homes and come to town, or were gathered into the little forts, that the people in Shippensburg were moving their families and effects, and that everybody was preparing to fly."* Shingas kept the upper end of the county in a state of terror, and fresh outrages were reported daily. The Indians killed, indiscriminately, men, women and children, and received rewards from the French for their scalps; they boasted that they killed fifty white people for each Indian slain by the English. Inhabitants of the Great Cove fled from their homes in November, with the crackling of their burning roofs and the yells of the Indians ringing in their ears. John Potter, formerly sheriff, sheltered at his house one night 100 fleeing women and children. The cries of the widows and fatherless children were pitiful, and those who had fortunately escaped with their lives had neither food, bedding nor clothing to cover their nakedness, everything having been consumed in their burning dwellings. "Fifty persons," so it is recorded, "were killed or taken prisoners. One woman, over ninety years of age, was found lying dead with her breasts torn off and a stake driven through her body. The infuriated savages caught up little children and dashed their brains out against the door-posts in presence of their shrieking mothers, or cut off their heads and drank their warm blood. Wives and mothers were tied to trees that they might witness the tortures and death of their husbands and children, and then were carried into a captivity from which few ever returned. Twenty-seven houses were burned, a great number of cattle were killed or driven off, and out of the ninety-three families settled in the two coves and by the Conolloway's, members of forty-seven fam-

*Dr. Wing, from Pennsylvania Archives.

ilies were either killed or captured and the remainder fled, so that these settlements were entirely broken up." Small wonder that such circumstances excited the people of the Cumberland Valley! Preparations were made at Shippensburg and Carlisle, where the people flocked in such numbers as to crowd the houses, to give the enemy a warm reception, and 400 men (of whom 200 were from this part of the valley) marched under the command of Hans Hamilton, sheriff of York County, to McDowell's Mill, in Franklin County, a few miles from the scene of the slaughter, but the Indians had retreated. Rev. John Steel, pastor of the "Old White Church," of Upper West Conococheague, raised a company among his parishioners for defense of their church and individual property in 1755, and was commissioned captain. The church was afterward burned, the congregation scattered, and Mr. Steel removed to Carlisle in 1758.

April 2, 1756, a body of Indians attacked and burned McCord's fort, on the Conococheague, in what is now Franklin County, killing and capturing a total of twenty-seven persons. The alarm extended to Shippensburg, and three companies were raised in various parts of the valley, for the pursuit and punishment of the marauders, commanded respectively by Capts. Culbertson, Chambers and Hamilton. Capt. Alex Culbertson's company with nineteen men from the other two, overtook the Indians west of Sideling Hill and a fight ensued which lasted two hours. The Indians, from the report made by one of their number who was captured, lost seventeen killed and twenty-one wounded. The whites suffered severely. Among those killed were Capt. Culbertson, John Reynolds (ensign of Capt. Chambers' company), William Kerr, James Blair, John Leason, William Denny, Francis Scott, William Boyd, Jacob Paynter, Jacob Jones, Robert Kerr and William Chambers; wounded, Francis Campbell, Abraham Jones, William Reynolds, John Barnet, Benjamin Blyth, John McDonald and Isaac Miller.

Another party, commanded by Ensign Jamison, from Fort Granville, under Capt. Hamilton, in pursuit of the same Indians, had about the same experience, losing Daniel McCoy, James Robinson, James Peace, John Blair, Henry Jones, John McCarty and John Kelly, killed; and Ensign Jamison, James Robinson, William Hunter, Matthias Ganshorn, William Swails and James Louder, wounded—the latter afterward died of his wounds. Most of these men were from the oldest and most respectable families in Cumberland County.

All around the settlements in this county outrages were frequent and the number of lives taken was appalling, considering the sparsely settled condition of the country. Bands of Indians even ventured within a few miles of Carlisle. The military were employed in protecting men harvesting their crops in 1756, and it was necessary for all persons to be ever on the alert to guard against surprise and attack. In June, 1756, a Mr. Dean, living about a mile east of Shippensburg, was found murdered in his cabin, his skull cleft with a tomahawk. It was supposed a couple of Indians seen in the neighborhood the day before had committed the deed. On the 6th of the same month, a short distance east of where Burd's Run crosses the road leading from Shippensburg to the Middlespring church, a party of Indians killed John McKean and John Agnew and captured Hugh Black, William Carson, Andrew Brown, James Ellis and Alex McBride. A party of citizens from Shippensburg pursued the Indians through McAllister's Gap into Path Valley, and on the morning of the third day out met all the prisoners except James Ellis. and on their return home, they having escaped. Ellis was never afterward heard from. The pursuers returned with the men who had escaped, further pursuit being useless.

Many other instances of murders and kindred outrages by the Indians might be mentioned, for the history of that dread time teems with them, but it is not necessary to recount them. Enough has been said to show the terrible state the region was in, and the horrid tales are dropped to tell of an expedition in which the whites took the initiative.*

Gov. Morris was superseded on the 20th of August, 1756, by Gov. William Denny, but before the latter's arrival he (Morris), in view of the constant cries for help from the frontier, and especially from East Pennsborough Township, Cumberland County, and the upper portion of the county, whose inhabitants sent in urgent petitions for aid, had arranged with Col. Armstrong for a movement against the Indian town of Kittanning, on the Allegheny River, about twenty miles above Fort DuQuesne, in what is now Armstrong County. The place was the chief stronghold of the red men, was the base of their operations eastward and toward the Ohio, and was the home of both Shingas and Capt. Jacobs.† There were also held a considerable number of white prisoners. A small army was organized under the command of Lieut.-Col. John Armstrong, consisting of seven companies,‡ whose captains were John Armstrong, Hans Hamilton, Dr. Hugh Mercer, Edward Ward, Joseph Armstrong, John Potter, and Rev. John Steel. The command set out in August, 1756, and at the dawn of the 7th (8th?) of September made the attack on the Indian town, which was totally destroyed, together with large quantities of ammunition. Capt. Jacobs and his nephew were killed, and few, if any, escaped the avenging hand of the officer, whose rapid march and well executed plans won for him the approval of his people. The corporation of Philadelphia voted him a medal for his exploit.§ This disaster to the Indians led them to remove to the Muskingum, in Ohio, but served only for a short time to check their operations in Pennsylvania. The year 1757 was fraught with unabated horrors. Cumberland County, with others, was kept in a state of continual alarm, although in May of that year another conference was held with the Indians at Lancaster to try and bring about peace. The western Indians,

---

*At one period (1750-55) there was a noted person in the valley who figured conspicuously in movements against the Indians. He was known as "Captain Jack," "the black hunter," "the black rifle," "the wild hunter of the Juniata," "the black hunter of the forest," etc. He was a white man, an early comer to the region, and happy and contented in his occupations of fishing and hunting, until the Indians, one day when he was absent, burned his cabin and murdered his wife and children. Then he became imbued with a spirit of revenge, and his exploits rendered him famous. He was a dead shot with the rifle, a terror to the Indians, and greatly respected and appreciated by the scattered settlers, whose lives and property he was more than once the means of saving. It is said of him that "he never shot without good cause. His look was as unerring as his aim. He formed an association to defend the settlers against savage aggressions. On a given signal they would unite. Their exploits were heard of in 1756 on the Conococheague and Juniata."—[Egle's Hist. of Pa., p. 616.] He was also sometimes called the "Half Indian." Through Col. Croghan he proffered his aid to Gen. Braddock, in the latter's disastrous campaign, and Croghan, in recommending him to the General, said; "He will march with his hunters; they are dressed in hunting shirts, moccasins, etc., are well armed, and are equally regardless of heat or cold. They require no shelter for the night, they ask no pay." This character, it appears, in a letter written from Carlisle in 1754, as well as one the previous year by John O'Neal to Gov. Hamilton, was also known as "Captain Joel." He was given a captain's commission in 1753. The movements of himself and his band of rangers were very rapid, and the mention of his name, like those of Brady, Boone, Logston, Kenton and others, struck terror to the hearts of his painted foemen.

†Capt. Jacobs was a large man, very powerful and exceedingly cruel. Shingas was not as large, but made up for his stature in ferocity. Capt. Jacobs' nephew, who with him was killed in Armstrong's attack upon Kittanning, was said to be seven feet tall.

‡Most authorities place the total number of men at 300; some give it 280.

§From Col. Armstrong's report of the affair to Gov. Denny it is learned that the casualties among the volunteers were as follows: *From his own company—Killed*, Thos. Power, John McCormick; *wounded*, Lieut.-Col. Armstrong (in the shoulder by a musket ball), James Carothers, James Strickland, Thomas Foster. *Capt. Hamilton's company—Killed*, John Kelly. *Capt. Mercer's company—Killed*, John Baker, John McCartney, Patrick Muller, Cornelius McGinnis, Theophilus Thompson, Dennis Kilpatrick, Bryan Croghan; *wounded*, Richard Fitzgibbons; *missing*, Capt. Hugh Mercer (wounded, but found to have been carried away safely by his men), Ensign John Scott, Emanuel Menisky, John Taylor, John ——, Francis Philips, Robert Morrow, Thomas Burke, Philip Pendergrass. *Capt. Armstrong's company—Killed*, Lieut James Hogg, James Anderson, Holdcraft Stringer, Edward O'Brian, James Higgins, John Leeson; *wounded*, William Fridley, Robert Robinson, John Ferrol, Thomas Camplin, Charles O'Neill; *missing*, John Lewis, William Hunter, William Baker, George Appleby, Anthony Grissy, Thomas Swan. *Capt. Ward's company—Killed*, William Welsh; *wounded*, Ephraim Bratton; *missing*, Patrick Myers, Laurence Donnahan, Samuel Chambers. *Capt. Potter's company—Wounded*, Ensign James Potter, Andrew Douglass. *Capt. Steel's company—Missing*, Terrence Cannabery. Total—killed 17; wounded 13; missing 19—49 in all. Seven captives were recovered and a number of Indians taken prisoners. Thirty or forty warriors were slain.

however, would hear to nothing, and it became evident that subduing them by force of arms was the only sure method. Col. Stanwix was at Carlisle building intrenchments, and Col. Armstrong had two companies, part stationed at Carlisle and part at Shippensburg. These two officers did all in their power to protect the citizens and punish the savages, but they were handicapped in numerous regards. Murders were frequent in the upper part of Cumberland (now Franklin) County, and the lower portion was not without its visitations of bloodshed. May 13, 1757, William Walker and another man were killed near a private fort called McCormick's, on the Conodoguinet, in East Pennsborough; two men were killed and five taken prisoners near Shippensburg on the 6th of June; Joseph Mitchell, James Mitchell, William Mitchell, John Finlay, Robert Steenson, Andrew Enslow, John Wiley, Allen Henderson, William Gibson and an Indian were killed in a harvest field near Shippensburg, July 19, and Jane McCommon, Mary Minor, Janet Harper and a son of John Finlay were captured or missing at the same time; four men were killed July 11 near Tobias Hendricks', who lived on and had charge of Louther Manor, six miles from the Susquehanna, in East Pennsborough, and two men were killed or carried off near the same place September 8, while out hunting horses. July 18, in a harvest field a mile east of Shippensburg, belonging to John Cesna, Dennis O'Neiden and John Kirkpatrick were killed, and Mr. Cesna, his two grandsons, and a son of Kirkpatrick were made prisoners and carried off. Others working in the field happened to be concealed from the view of the Indians, and escaped without injury. There was little rest from anxiety until after the expeditions of 1758 and the capture of Fort DuQuesne, with the building upon its ruins of Fort Pitt, which remained under English rule while the mother country had jurisdiction over the American colonies. The troops were mostly disbanded in 1759 by act of Assembly, which body imagined the war was ended. Practically for this region it was so, although the two powers met in conflict afterward on the northern frontier.

The inhabitants enjoyed for a brief period immunity from danger and rejoiced that peace smiled upon the valley. A worthless Delaware Indian called "Doctor John" who had for two years lived in a cabin near the Conodoguinet and not far from Carlisle, was killed in February, 1760, together with his wife and two children, by whites; and though he had talked contemptuously about the soldiers, and boasted of having killed sixty white people with his own arm the event was looked upon as untoward by the inhabitants of the region, who feared the vengeance of the tribe and steps were taken to apprehend and punish the murderers. Several arrests were made, but the more guilty parties fled and were not found, while the others were released as they could scarcely be convicted on hearsay evidence. Very likely the people were glad the Indians were out of the way, for they had no pleasing recollections of their fiendish fellows.

Presently, however, came the dread news that a more desperate war was to be waged under the leadership of the wonderful western chieftain, Pontiac, and close upon the heels of the alarm followed actual invasion of the country bordering the valley, with a renewal of the horrid scenes of previous years. July 5, 1763, a gentleman wrote from Carlisle to Secretary Peters as follows: "On the morning of yesterday horsemen were seen rapidly passing through Carlisle. One man rather fatigued, who stopped to get some water, hastily replied to the question, 'What news?' 'Bad enough! Presque Isle, Le Beuf and Venango have been captured, their garrisons massacred, with the exception of one officer and seven men who fortunately made their escape from Le Beuf. Fort Pitt was briskly attacked on the 9th of June, but succeeded in repelling the assailants.' Thus saying he put spurs to his horse and was soon out of sight. From others I have accounts that the Bedford militia have succeeded in saving Fort Ligonier. Nothing could exceed the terror which prevailed from house to house, from town to town. The road was nearly covered with women and children flying to Lancaster and Philadelphia. Rev. Thomson, pastor of the Episcopal Church, went at the head of his congregation to protect and encourage them on the way. A few retired to the breastworks for safety. The alarm once given could not be appeased. We have done all that men can do to prevent disorder. All our hopes are turned upon Bouquet."

The following extracts of letters written from Carlisle in July, 1763, and published at the time in the *Pennsylvania Gazette* at Philadelphia, will also serve to show the condition of affairs then existing in the valley:*

CARLISLE, July 12, 1763.

I embrace this first leisure since yesterday morning to transmit you a brief account of our present state of affairs here, which indeed is very distressing, every day almost affording some fresh object to awaken the compassion, alarm the fears, or kindle into resentment and vengeance every sensible breast; while flying families, obliged to abandon house and possession to save their lives by a hasty escape; mourning widows, bewailing their husbands, surprised and massacred by savage rage; tender parents, lamenting the fruit of their own bodies, cropped in the very bloom of life by a barbarous hand, with relations and acquaintance pouring out sorrow for murdered neighbors and friends, present a varied scene of mingled distress.

When, for some time after striking at Bedford the Indians appeared quiet, nor struck any other part of our frontiers, it became the prevailing opinion that our forts and communication were so peculiarly the object of their attention; that, till at least after harvest, there was little prospect of danger to our inhabitants over the hills, and to dissent from this generally received sentiment was political heresy, and attributed to timidity rather than judgment, till too early conviction has decided the point in the following manner:

On Sunday morning, the 10th instant, about 9 or 10 o'clock, at the house of one William White, on Juniata, between thirty and forty miles hence, there being in said house four men and a lad, the Indians came rushing upon and shot White at the door, just stepping out to see what the noise meant. Our people then pulled in White, and shut the door; but observing through a window the Indians setting fire to the house, they attempted to force their way out at the door. But the first that stepped out being shot down, they drew him in and again shut the door, after which one attempting an escape out of a window on the loft was shot through the head, and the lad wounded in the arm. The only one now remaining—William Riddle—broke a hole through the roof of the house, and an Indian, who saw him looking out, alleged he was about to fire on him, withdrew, which afforded Riddle an opportunity to make his escape. The house, with the other four in it, was burned down, as one McMachen informs, who was coming to it, not suspecting Indians, and was by them fired at and shot through the shoulder, but made his escape.

The same day about dinner time, at about a mile and a half from said White's, at the house of Robert Campbell, six men being in the house, as they were dining three Indians rushed in at the door, and after firing among them and wounding some they tomahawked in an instant one of the men, whereupon one George Dodds, one of the company, sprang back into the room, took down a rifle, shot an Indian through the body who was just presenting his piece to shoot him. The Indian being mortally wounded staggered, and letting his gun fall was carried off by three more. Dodds, with one or two more, getting upon the loft, broke the roof in order to escape, and looking out saw one of the company, Stephen Jeffries, running, but very slowly by reason of a wound in the breast, and an Indian pursuing, and it is thought he could not escape, nor have we heard of him since, so that it is past dispute he also is murdered. The first that attempted getting out of the loft was fired at and drew back. Another attempting was shot dead, and of the six Dodds was the only one who made his escape. The same day about dusk, about six or seven miles up Tuscarora and about twenty-eight or thirty miles hence, they murdered one William Anderson, together with a boy and girl, all in one house. At White's were seen at least five, some say eight or ten Indians, and at Campbell's about the same number. On Monday, the 11th, a party of about twenty-four went over from the upper part of Shearman's Valley to see how matters were. Another party of twelve or thirteen went over from the upper part of said valley, and Col. John Armstrong, with Thomas Wilson, Esq., and a party of between thirty and forty from this town, to reconnoitre and assist in bringing in the dead.

Of the first and third parties we have heard nothing yet, but of the party of twelve six are come in, and inform that they passed through the several places in Tuscarora and saw the houses in flames or burnt entirely down. That the grain that had been reaped the

---

*See Rupp's History of Cumberland and other Counties, pp. 139-143.

Indians burnt in shocks, and had set the fences on fire where the grain was unreaped; that the hogs had fallen upon and mangled several of the dead bodies; that the said company of twelve, suspecting danger, durst not stay to bury the dead; that after they had returned over the Tuscarora Mountain, about one or two miles this side of it and about eighteen or twenty from hence (Carlisle, Penn.), they were fired on by a large party of Indians, supposed about thirty, and were obliged to fly; that two, viz., William Robinson and John Graham, are certainly killed, and four more are missing, who it is thought have fallen into the hands of the enemy, as they appeared slow in flight, most probably wounded, and the savages pursued with violence. What further mischief has been done we have not heard, but expect every day and hour some more messages of melancholy news.

In hearing of the above defeat we sent out another party of thirty or upward, commanded by our high sheriff, Mr. Dunning, and Mr. William Lyon, to go in quest of the enemy or fall in with and reinforce our other parties. There are also a number gone out from about three miles below this, so that we now have over the hills upward of eighty or ninety volunteers scouring the woods. The inhabitants of Shearman's Valley, Tuscarora, etc., are all come over, and the people of this valley, near the mountain, are beginning to move in, so that in a few days there will be scarcely a house inhabited north of Carlisle. Many of our people are greatly distressed through want of arms and ammunition, and numbers of those beat off their places have hardly money enough to purchase a pound of powder.

Our women and children I suppose must move downward if the enemy proceeds. To-day a British vengeance begins to rise in the breasts of our men. One of them that fell from among the twelve, as he was just expiring, said to one of his fellows: "Here, take my gun and kill the first Indian you see, and all shall be well."

Another letter dated at Carlisle July 13, has the following: "Last night Col. Armstrong returned. He left the party who pursued further, and found several dead, whom they buried in the best manner they could, and are now all returned in. From what appears the Indians are traveling from one place to another along the valley, burning the farms and destroying all the people they meet with. This day gives an account of six more being killed in the valley, so that since last Sunday morning to this day, twelve o'clock, we have a pretty authentic account of the number slain being twenty-five, and four or five wounded. The Colonel, Mr. Wilson and Mr. Alricks are now on the parade endeavoring to raise another party to go out and succor the sheriff and his party, consisting of fifty men, which marched yesterday, and I hope they will be able to send off immediately twenty good men. The people here, I assure you, want nothing but a good leader and a little encouragement to make a very good defense."

July 28, 1763, the editor of the *Pennsylvania Gazette* printed the following: "Our advices from Carlisle are as follows, viz. That the party under the sheriff, Mr. Dunning, mentioned in our last, fell in with the enemy at the house of one Alexander Logan, in Shearman's Valley, supposed to be about fifteen or upward, who had murdered the said Logan, his son and another man, about two miles from said house, and mortally wounded a fourth who is since dead; and that at the time of their being discovered they were rifling the house and shooting down the cattle, and it is thought about to return home with the spoil they had got. That our men, on seeing them, immediately spread themselves from right to left with a design to surround them, and engaged the savages with great courage, but from their eagerness rather too soon, as some of the party had not got up when the skirmish began; that the enemy returned our first fire very briskly, but our people, regardless of that, rushed upon them, when they fled and were pursued a considerable way till thickets secured their escape, four or five of them, it was thought, being mortally wounded; that our parties had brought in with them what cattle they could collect, but that great numbers were killed by the Indians, and many of the horses that were in the valleys carried off; that on the 21st, the morning, news was brought of three Indians being seen about 10 o'clock in the morning; one Pummeroy and his wife, and the wife of one Johnson, were surprised in a house between Shippensburg and the North Mountain and left there for dead; but that one of the women, when found, showing some signs of life, was brought to Shippensburg, where she lived some hours in a most miserable condition, being scalped, one of her arms broken, and her skull fractured with the stroke of a tomahawk; and that since the 10th inst., there was an account of fifty-four persons being killed by the enemy!

"That the Indians had set fire to houses, barns, corn, wheat, rye, and hay—in short, to everything combustible—so that the whole country seemed to be in one general blaze; that the miseries and distress of the poor people were really shocking to humanity, and beyond the power of language to describe; that Carlisle was becoming the barrier, not a single inhabitant being beyond it; that every stable and hovel in the town was crowded with miserable refugees, who were reduced to a state of beggary and despair, their houses, cattle and harvest destroyed, and from a plentiful, independent people they were become real objects of charity and commiseration; that it was most dismal to see the streets filled with people in whose countenances might be discovered a mixture of grief, madness and despair; and to hear now and then the sighs and groans of men, the disconsolate lamentations of women, and the screams of children, who had lost their nearest and dearest relations; and that on both sides of the Susquehanna, for some miles, the woods were filled with poor families and their cattle, who made fires and lived like savages, exposed to the inclemencies of the weather."

Letter dated at Carlisle July 30, 1763: "On the 25th a considerable number of the inhabitants of Shearman's Valley went over, with a party of soldiers to guard them, to attempt saving as much of their grain as might be standing, and it is hoped a considerable quantity will yet be preserved. A party of volunteers, between twenty and thirty, went to the farther side of the valley, next to the Tuscarora Mountain, to see what appearance there might be of the Indians, as it was thought they would most probably be there if anywhere in the settlement—to search for and bury the dead at Buffalo Creek, and to assist the inhabitants that lived along or near the foot of the mountain in bringing off what they could, which services they accordingly performed, burying the remains of three persons, but saw no marks of Indians having lately been there, excepting one track, supposed to be about two or three days old, near the narrows of Buffalo Creek Hill, and heard some hallooing and firing of a gun at another place. A number of the inhabitants of Tuscarora Valley go over the mountain to-morrow, with a party of soldiers, to endeavor to save part of the crops. Five Indians were seen last Sunday, about sixteen or seventeen miles from Carlisle, up the valley toward the North Mountain, and two the day before yesterday, about five or six miles from Shippensburg, who fired at a young man but missed him.

"On the 25th of July there were in Shippensburg 1,384 of our poor, distressed back inhabitants, viz.: men, 301; women, 345; children, 738, many of whom were obliged to lie in barns, stables, cellars and under old leaky sheds, the dwelling-houses being all crowded."

Indians were also occasionally seen in the valley after Bouquet had left, and occasionally some of the inhabitants were fired upon within a few miles of Carlisle. Where is the wonder that the stricken people looked so eagerly to Bouquet for deliverance, or that they suspected and mistrusted every being in the shape of an Indian, whether professedly friendly or otherwise! Such terrible experiences were sufficient to foster all the fiendishness of revenge in the breasts of the afflicted, and the great wonder at the present day is that they did not resolve upon and enter into a war of extermination of the red race.

S. B. Kieffer A.M, M.D.

HISTORY OF CUMBERLAND COUNTY. 65

Upon the outbreak of the savages the Assembly had ordered the raising of 700 men to protect the frontier during the harvest, but almost without effect. The safety of the garrison at Fort Pitt was the cause of anxiety, and finally Col. Henry Bouquet was ordered to march to its relief. This he did with barely 500 men, the remnants of two shattered regiments of regulars—the Forty-second and Seventy-second—lately returned from the West Indies in a debilitated condition, together with 200 rangers (six companies) raised in Lancaster and Cumberland Counties. Although depending so greatly upon him, the inhabitants of Carlisle and vicinity were in such a state of terror and utter consternation that they had taken no steps to prepare provisions for him and his little army, and they arrived at Carlisle to find matters there and along the line of march in a desperate condition, though several quite heavy contributions had been raised by various congregations in Philadelphia and sent for their relief. Instead, therefore, of the inhabitants being able to lend him aid, they were dependent upon him, and he was forced to lie at Carlisle eighteen days until supplies could be sent for and received. By this time the people had regained courage and confidence in themselves, although the appearance of Bouquet's army led them to expect little from its expedition. Most happily were they disappointed, however, for the Colonel's successful march, his relief of Fort Ligonier, his terrible thirty-six hours fight at Bushy Run with the Indians, who were defeated and driven from the field, his relief of Fort Pitt, and his subsequent expedition against the Indians in Ohio, with the treaty on terms of his own dictation, and the release of many white prisoners who were returned to their homes, are all matters of history. Bouquet became the savior of the region, and to his memory let all honor be accorded. The Indians committed outrages along the frontier in 1764, but an army of 1,000 men was raised, of which a battalion of eight companies of 380 men, mostly from Cumberland County—commanded by Lieut.-Col. John Armstrong, with Capts. William Armstrong, Samuel Lindsey, James Piper, Joseph Armstrong, John Brady, William Piper, Christopher Line and Timothy Green, with a few under Lieut. Finley—was sent against them under Col. Bouquet, who pierced to the very heart of their western stronghold, and compelled them to accede the terms above mentioned. The battalion of provincial troops from this county was paid off and mustered out of service, the arms were delivered to the authorities, and the long and dreadful Indian war, with all its attendant sickening horrors, was at an end.

The people had little confidence, however, in the Indians, and were not disposed to place in their hands any weapons or materials which would give them the slightest advantage over the whites, at least until their new relations had time to become fixed. It had been agreed that trade should be opened with the Indians, and large quantities of goods were gathered in places for the purpose before the governor issued his proclamation authorizing trading. This led to the destruction of a large quantity of goods in which Capt. Robert Collender, a flouring-mill proprietor near Carlisle, was part owner, the goods having been started westward. A party under James Smith, who had done service under Braddock, Forbes and Bouquet, waylaid them near Sideling Hill, killed a number of horses, made the escort turn back, burned sixty-three loads, and made matters exceedingly lively, when a squad was sent out to capture the rioters. Smith afterward acknowledged himself too hasty. He was subsequently arrested on suspicion of murder and lodged in jail at Carlisle in 1769. An attempt was made to rescue him, but he dissuaded the party, and upon his trial was acquitted. He became a distinguished Revolutionary officer and member of the Legislature.

Another occurrence, which might have resulted seriously for the settlers, was the murder of ten friendly Indians in the lower part of Shearman's Valley, on Middle Creek, in January, 1768, by Frederick Stump and an employe of his named Hans Eisenhauer (John Ironcutter). The authorities captured the murderers and placed them in jail in Carlisle, although the warrant for their arrest charged that they be brought before the chief justice at Philadelphia. That step the people of Cumberland County resisted, claiming it was encroaching upon their rights to try the men in the county where the crime was committed. They were detained at Carlisle until the pleasure of the authorities at Philadelphia could be ascertained, and were rescued by a large armed party on the morning of the 29th of January, four days after their arrest. The prisoners were carried away over the mountains and were never afterward found, though it was the opinion that they got away and took refuge in Virginia. The matter was finally dropped after the heat of the affair was over.

CHAPTER IV.

COUNTY ORGANIZATION—LOCATION OF COUNTY SEAT—DIVISION OF COUNTY INTO TOWNSHIPS—COUNTY BUILDINGS—POPULATION—POSTOFFICES IN 1885—INTERNAL IMPROVEMENTS—PUBLIC ROADS—RAILROADS.

CUMBERLAND COUNTY was named after a maritime county in England, bordering on Scotland. I. Daniel Rupp, in a sketch of this county in Egle's History of Pennsylvania, published in 1876, says: "The name is derived from the Keltic, Kimbriland. The Kimbrie, or Keltic races, once inhabited the county of Cumberland, in England," but we are inclined to think that the word Cumberland signifies "land of hollows," from the Anglo Saxon word "comb," a valley or low place.

In the matter of pedigree Cumberland is the sixth county formed in Pennsylvania; Philadelphia, Bucks and Chester were established in 1682, Lancaster in 1729 and York in 1749. Petitions having been presented to the Assembly by numerous inhabitants of the North or Cumberland Valley, among whom were James Silvers and William Magaw, in behalf of the inhabitants of the North Valley, on the ground of their remoteness from the county seat, Lancaster, and the difficulty which the sober and the quiet part of the valley experienced in securing itself against the thefts of certain idle and dissolute persons (who easily avoided the courts, the officers and the jail of so distant a county town), praying for the establishment of a new county, an act was passed to that effect on the 27th of January, 1750. Robert McCoy, of Peters Township, Benjamin Chambers, of Antrim, David Magaw, of Hopewell, James McIntire and John McCormick, both of East Pennsborough, were appointed commissioners to carry out the provisions of the act. The territory embraced in Cumberland County was set off from Lancaster, and its ample limits were thus described: "That all and singular the lands lying within the province of Pennsylvania, to the westward of the Susquehanna, and northward and westward of the county of York, be erected into a county, to be called Cumberland; bounded northward and westward with the line of the provinces; eastward partly by the Susquehanna and partly by said county of York; and southward in part by the line dividing said province from that of Maryland."

HISTORY OF CUMBERLAND COUNTY.

It was also further enacted, in order to better ascertain the boundary between Cumberland and York Counties, that commissioners should be appointed on the part of the latter to act in conjunction with those of the former for that purpose. The York County commissioners were Thomas Cox, Michael Tanner, George Swope, Nathan Hussey and John Wright, Jr. The commissioners of the two counties disagreed when they met to fix the boundary line. Those from Cumberland wished the line to commence opposite the mouth of Swatara Creek and run thence along the ridge of the South Mountain (or Trent Hills, or Priest Hills); but to this the York County commissioners would not listen; they wished the Yellow Breeches, or Callapasscinker Creek, to form a portion of the boundary. The difficulty was finally settled by the Assembly in an act passed February 9, 1751, which says: "But for as much as the ridge of mountains called the South Mountain.—along which the lines, dividing the said counties of York and Cumberland, were directed to be run by the several hereinbefore mentioned acts, before the river Susquehannah, to the mouth of a run of water called Dogwood Run,—is discontinued, much broken, and not easily to be distinguished, whereby great differences have arisen between the trustees of the said counties concerning the matter of running said lines; by which means the boundaries of said counties, between the river Susquehanna and the mouth of aforesaid run of water called Dogwood Run, are altogether unsettled and so likely to continue to the great injury of the said counties, and to the frustrating the good purposes by the hereinbefore mentioned acts of Assembly intended for the preventing hereof, it is hereby enacted, that the creek called Yellow Breeches Creek, from the mouth thereof where it empties into the Susquehanna aforesaid, up the several courses thereof, to the mouth of a run of water called Dogwood Run, and from thence on one continued straight line, to be run to the ridge of mountains called the South Mountain, until it intersects the Maryland line, shall be and is hereby declared to be the boundary line between said counties of York and Cumberland."

Previous to this legislation a petition from the commissioners appointed on the part of Cumberland County to run the line had been presented to the Assembly setting forth facts as follows: "That the York commissioners, refusing to run the line agreeable to the act of Assembly, the petitioners conceived it their duty to do it themselves, and accordingly began opposite to the mouth of the Swahatara [now Swatara—Ed.], on Susquehanna River, and then took the courses and distances along the highest ridge of the mountain, without crossing any running water, till they struck the middle of the main body of the South Mountain, at James Caruther's plantation; a true draught whereof is annexed to the petition. That the draught of the line and places adjacent, laid before the house by the York commissioners, as far as relates to the waters and courses, is altogether imaginary, and grounded on no actual survey; those commissioners having no surveyor with them, nor so much as attempting to chain any part of it. That the petitioners would willingly agree to the proposal of making Yellow Breeches Creek the boundary, if that draught had any truth in it; but as it is altogether false, and the making that creek the line would actually cut off a great part of the north valley, reduce it to a point on the Susquehanna, and make the county quite irregular, the petitioners pray that the line in the draught to their petition annexed may be confirmed, or a straight line granted from the mouth of Swahatara to the middle of the South Mountain." This petition was read and ordered to lie on the table.—[*Votes Assem.*, IV, 154, 8th mo., 18th, 1750, as quoted by Rupp.]

Had the line been established as prayed by this petition, the eastern end of the county, as now existing, would have been about the same in extent as the western; wheareas now it is much less—or narrower. Mr. Chambers, one of the Cumberland County commissioners, on the establishment of the line had written as follows to Richard Peters, secretary, but all to no avail:

CUMBERLAND COUNTY, October 8th, 1750.

Sir: I received your letter in which you enclosed the draughts of the line run by the commissioners of York County and ours; and if the branches of the Yellow Britches and Great Conewago interlocked in the South Mountain, as laid down in the aforesaid draught, I would be of opinion with the Assembly that a line consisting of such a variety of courses could not be a good boundary between two counties. I can assure you that the courses that we, the commissioners of Cumberland, run, we chained, and have returned by course and distance the ridge of the mountain, and can send our deposition that we crossed no running water above ground, and that we have run it past Capt. Dills, till we are in the middle of the mountains, as laid down in the *red line* in their draughts; so that our draughts will show you that theirs is but an imaginary of the waters, done by some friends of York County who had no regard for our country's welfare; for we sent our return to be laid before the Assembly at the same time that York County laid this one before them that your Honor was pleased to send me. But our messenger did not deliver our return to the House, or if he had, I suppose they would not have troubled his Honor, the Governor, to send any further instructions to us, for I humbly suppose that there cannot be any better boundary than the ridge of the mountain; for, were there a line run to cross the heads of the waters of both sides and the marks grown old, it would be hard for a hunter to tell which county the wolf was killed in, but he may easily tell whether it was killed on the descent of the North or South Valley waters. Likewise, a sheriff, when he goes to any house where he is not acquainted and enquires at the house whether that water falls into the North or South Valley, can tell whether they live in his county or not, which he could not tell by a line crossing the heads of the waters of both sides till he made himself acquainted with said line; so that if you will give yourself the trouble to enquire at any of the authors of that draft that was laid before the Assembly, you will find that they never chained any part of their line to know the distance, and therefore cannot be capable to lay down the heads of the waters.

Sir, I hope you will send me a few lines to let me know if our return be confirmed, or we must run it over again. But you may believe that the ridge of the mountain and heads of the waters are as laid down in our return; and we run it at the time we went with you to Mr. Croghan's, and did not expect to have any further trouble; and I yet think that his Honor, the Governor,* will confirm our return, or order them to disapprove of it by course and distance.

Sir, I am your Honor's most humble servant,

BENJAMIN CHAMBERS.

Location of County Seat.—In the act organizing the county of Cumberland the same persons appointed to run the boundary line, or any three of them, were authorized to purchase a site for county court house and prison, subject to approval by the governor. It was at the same time the desire of the proprietaries to lay out a town at the same place. The matter of selecting a suitable site was very difficult, as no less than four locations were offered. At length Thomas Cookson, Esq., the deputy surveyor at Lancaster, was sent to examine the different places and report to the governor, after hearing the arguments in favor of each. He reported mainly as follows:

LANCASTER, March 1, 1749.

Honored Sir:—In pursuance of your directions I have viewed the several places spoken of as commodious situations for the town in the county of Cumberland, and also the several passes through the Kittochtinny and Tuscarora Mountains, for the convenience of the traders to Allegheny. I shall take the liberty of making some observations on the several places recommended, as the inhabitants of the different parts of the county are generally partial to the advantages that would arise from a county town in their own neighborhood. And first, the inhabitants about the river recommended the Manor, that being a considerable body of the propietaries' land, well timbered, and likely to be rendered valuable should the town be fixed there; but the body of the county cry loudly against that location as lying in a distant corner of the county, and would be a perpetual inconvenience to the inhabitants attending public business, and a great charge of mileage to the respective officers employed in it. The next situation is on Le Tort's Spring. This place is convenient to the new path to Allegheny now mostly used, being at the distance of four miles from the gap in the Kittochtinny Mountain. There is a fine stream of water

*Gov. James Hamilton.

and a body of good land on each side, from the head down to Conodogwainet Creek, and the lands on both sides of the Conodogwainet are thickly settled. As these lands are settled, if it should be thought a proper situation for the town, the people possessed of them are willing to sell their improvements on reasonable terms, or exchange them for other lands of the honorable proprietors'. There is a tract of about 2,000 acres of tolerably well timbered land, without water, adjoining the settlements on Le Tort's Spring, which may be serviceable to accommodate the town, and lies as marked in the plan.

If this place should not be central enough, the next situation is the Big Spring. It rises a mile and a half to the northwest of the great road, five miles from Dunnings, and seven from Shippensburg; runs into the Conodogwainet in about three miles, and has good land on each side and on the Conodogwainet, and a great quantity of land to the southward, which is tolerably well timbered, but has no water. The honorable proprietaries have a tract of 4,000 acres on the north side of the Conodogwainet, opposite to the spring, and there is a gap in the mountain called McClure's Gap, convenient for bringing the road from Allegheny to this place; and, with the purchase of two or three small improvements, the proprietaries might be accommodated with a sufficient quantity of land for that purpose.

As to Shippensburg, I have no occasion to say anything, the lands being granted; and, indeed, if that were not the case, the lands about it are unsettled, for the want of water, which must be a sufficient objection.

The next place proposed was on the Conococheague Creek, where the road crosses it. The lands to the eastward of it are vacant, the settlements being chiefly on the sides of the creek. The situation is very good, and there is enough vacant land, as only the plantations on the creek would need to be purchased. This place was proposed as more convenient for the Indian trade, and opened a shorter and better passage through the mountains. It is true a tolerable passage may be had, but it must be by various turnings. Upon the whole, the choice appears to me to lie between the two situations of Le Tort's Spring and the Big Spring.

Upon fixing the spot, directions will be necessary for a plan of the town, the breadth of the streets, the lots to be reserved and those to be allotted for the public buildings. In the execution of which or any other service for the honorable proprietaries committed to me I shall take great pleasure.

I am, honored sir, your most obedient, humble servant,
THOMAS COOKSON.

The site upon Le Tort's Spring was finally determined upon, and Carlisle sprang into existence; though, even after the courts were removed from Shippensburg, there was considerable effort made to have the county seat located elsewhere than on the Le Tort, various reasons being urged why other locations were better adapted for the purpose. The place was laid out in 1751, and as late as May 27, 1753, it contained but five dwellings.

Division of County into Townships.—The records of the court of quarter sessions of Lancaster County for November, 1735, contain the following: "On the petition of many of the inhabitants of the North Valley on the west side of the Susquehanna River, opposite to Paxton, praying that the parts settled between the said River and Potomac River, on Conodogwainet, Yellow Britches and Conegochegue Creeks may be divided into townships and constables appointed in them, it was ordered by court that a line running northerly from the Hills to the southward of Yellow Britches (crossing a direct line by the Great Spring) to Kightotining Mountain, be the division line, and the easternmost township be called Pennsborough and the western Hopewell." In 1741 Hopewell was divided "by a line beginning at the North Hill at Benjamin Moor's; thence to Widow Hewres' and Samuel Jamison's and in a straight line to the South Hill," the western division to be called Antrim (in what is now Franklin County) and the eastern retaining the name of Hopewell. In 1745 Pennsborough seems to have been divided, as the returns are then first made from East Pennsborough and West Pennsborough. Dickinson was formed from a portion of West Pennsborough in 1785; Silvers' Spring (now Silver Spring) from part of East Pennsborough in 1787, and Middleton was divided into North and South Middleton in 1810, the original township of Middleton having been formed as early as 1750, when the county was organized. [See Chapter III.]

The first courts at Carlisle were held in a temporary log building on the northeast corner of the Public Square, where St. John's Church now stands. About 1766 a small brick court house was erected in the southwest quarter of the Square. March 3, 1801, the county commissioners advertised for proposals to build "a house for the safe keeping of the public records of the county," which are known to have been nearly completed December 22, 1802. It was a building also of brick, adjoining the court house. In 1809 a cupola and bell were placed upon the court house. An incendiary fire on the morning of Monday, March 24, 1845, destroyed these buildings, with the fire company's apparatus in a building close by. The county records were mostly saved through the efforts of the citizens. The court house bell, which fell and was melted in the fire, was a gift from some of the members of the old Penn family and had been greatly prized. Steps were at once taken to erect a new court house, and the present substantial fire-proof brick building was completed in 1846, having cost $48,419. It is 70x90 feet with a row of fine Corinthian columns in front, and is surmounted by a belfry in which are a clock and bell.

A stone jail was built about 1754, on the northwest corner of High and Bedford Streets and was enlarged in 1790. A petition to the Assembly for aid to complete it in 1755 met with no response. Stocks and a pillory were also erected on the Public Square in 1754, and it was many years before their use and the custom of cropping the ears of culprits were abolished. The present massive jail, with a brown stone front and an appearance like that of an ancient feudal castle, with battlemented towers, was built in 1853-54 at a cost of $42,960. It stands on the site of the old one and has a yard in the rear surrounded by a high and solid stone wall. The sheriff resides in the front part of the building.

The poor of the county were for many years either "collected near the dwelling of some one appointed to have charge of them, or farmed out to those who for a compensation were willing to board them." It was not until about 1830 that an alms-house was erected and then after much "consultation and negotiation" the fine farm and residence of Edward J. Stiles, about two miles east of Carlisle, in Middlesex Township, were purchased for the purpose, and additional buildings have since been erected. Mr. Stiles was paid $13,250 for his property. In 1873, at a cost of $33,284, a building was erected especially for the accommodation of the insane and idiotic. Many improvements have been made on the farm and it is a credit to the county.

From the territory originally embraced in Cumberland County Bedford was formed in 1771; Northumberland in 1772; Franklin in 1784; Mifflin in 1789 and Perry in 1820. These have been in turn subdivided until now, 1886, the same territory embraces about forty counties, with wondrous resources, great wealth and extensive agricultural, mining, stock and manufacturing interests. Cumberland County as now existing includes a tract thirty-four miles long and from eight to sixteen miles in width. Of its total area, 239,784 acres are improved.

Population.—By the United States census for each year it has been taken, the population of Cumberland County is shown to have been as follows: In 1790, 18,243; in 1800, 25,386; in 1810, 26,757; in 1820, 23,606; in 1830, 29,226; in 1840, 30,953; in 1850, 34,327; in 1860, 40,098; in 1870, 43,912; in 1880, 45,997.

The following table gives the population by townships and boroughs from 1830 to 1870, except for the year 1840:

HISTORY OF CUMBERLAND COUNTY. 71

Township or Borough.	1830.	1850.	1860.	1870.
Dickinson Township	2,505	3,094	3,446	1,617
East Pennsborough Township	2,186	1,605	1,845	2,719
Frankford Township	1,282	1,241	1,401	1,369
Hampden Township		1,273	1,229	1,199
Hopewell Township	901	1,053	1,326	977
Newburg Borough				392
Lower Allen Township	2,336	1,184	1,383	1,336
Middlesex Township			1,520	1,417
Mifflin Township	1,431	1,574	1,460	1,455
Monroe Township	1,562	1,772	1,849	1,833
Newton Township	1,349	1,666	1,978	2,345
Newville Borough	530	885	715	907
North Middleton Township	1,933	2,235	1,046	1,223
Carlisle Borough	3,708	4,581	5,664	6,650
Carlisle, East Ward			2,913	3,379
Carlisle, West Ward			2,751	2,271
Penn Township				1,888
Shippensburg Township	180	198	277	381
Shippensburg Borough	1,608	1,568	1,843	2,065
Silver Spring Township	1,792	2,308	2,301	2,259
Mechanicsburg Borough	554	882	1,939	2,569
Southampton Township	1,484	1,651	1,985	2,050
South Middleton Township	2,072	2,262	2,873	3,226
Upper Allen Township		1,220	1,275	1,341
New Cumberland Borough		315	394	515
West Pennsborough Township	1,732	2,040	2,175	2,180

By the census of 1840 the county made the following showing: Number furnaces in the county, 6, producing 2,830 tons cast iron; hands employed in furnaces and forges, 400; capital invested, $110,000. Number horses and mules in the county, 9,247; neat cattle, 24,204; sheep, 23,930; swine, 47,235; value of poultry (estimated), $12,671. Bushels of wheat raised, 567,654; barley, 11,104; oats, 654,477; rye, 247,239; buckwheat, 13,772; Indian corn, 645,056. Other productions: Pounds wool, 47,133; hops, 4,812; beeswax, 680; bushels potatoes, 121,641; tons hay, 24,423; tons hemp, 11¾; cords wood sold, 14,849; value of dairy products, $100,753; orchard products, $18,860; value of home-made or fancy goods, $24,660. Number tanneries, 31, which tanned 12,970 sides of sole leather, 10,777 of upper, and employed 64 men on a capital of $89,175. Soap manufactured. 230,218 pounds; candles, 45,060 pounds. Number of distilleries, 28, producing 252,305 gallons "alcoholic beverages;" breweries, 3, producing 12,000 gallons beer. Fulling-mills, 12; woolen factories, 9, making $26,800 worth of goods and employ 61 persons; 1 cotton factory; 1 paper-mill; 54 flouring-mills, making 71,652 barrels flour; 8 grist-mills; 63 saw-mills; 1 oil-mill. Total capital invested in manufactories, $390,601.

The census for 1880 shows the following exhibit for Cumberland County: White population, 43,807; colored, 2,167; Japanese, 3. Of the colored population Carlisle had 1,117, and of the total inhabitants in the county 45,322 were natives and 655 foreign born. Number farms in county, 2,983; acres improved land, 232,093; value of farms, including land, fences and buildings, $19,776,-980; value farming implements and machinery, $727,411; value live-stock on farms, $1,358,224; cost of building and repairing fences in 1879, $86,166; costs of fertilizers purchased in 1879, $52,042; estimated value of farm products sold and on hand for 1879, $2,509,572; bushels barley raised in 1880, 2,553; buckwheat, 1,242; Indian corn, 1,219,107; oats, 937,166; rye, 33,055; wheat, 884,517; value of orchard products, $16,554; tons hay raised, 52,284; bushels Irish potatoes, 144,418; bushels sweet potatoes, 9,510; pounds tobacco, 448,114;

number horses, 10,737; mules and asses, 652; working oxen, 4; milch cows, 12,614; other cattle, 13,442; sheep, 8,772; swine, 32,773; pounds wool, 53,816; gallons milk, 121,619; pounds butter, 960,516; pounds cheese, 2,352; number manufacturing establishments, 308; capital invested, $2,266,409; total hands employed, 1,892; wages paid, $535,008; materials used, $1,727,681; value of products, $2,850,640; assessed value of real estate, $12,223,355; value of personal property, $2,054,110; total taxation for 1880, with the exception of one or more townships from which no reports were received, $185,480; indebtedness of county, bonded and floating, $142,106.

In 1778, when the townships in the county were Allen, East and West Pennsborough, Hopewell, Middleton and Newton, besides the borough of Carlisle, there were 111,055 acres of patented and warranted lands, 512 acres of proprietary manor lands, and 206 lots in Carlisle, upon all of which the total taxation was £120 3s. 4d.

The population of Cumberland County, by townships and boroughs in 1880, was as follows, according to the United States census report:

Carlisle Borough, 6,209 (comprising Ward No. 1, 1,714; Ward No. 2, 1,202; Ward No. 3, 1,613; Ward No. 4, 1,680); Cook Township, 417; Dickinson Township, 1,741; East Pennsborough Township, 3,084; Frankford Township, 1,514; Hampden Township, 1,000; Hopewell Township, 1,069; Lower Allen Township, 972; Mechanicsburg Borough, 3,018 (comprising Ward No. 1, 1,153; Ward No. 2, 763; Ward No. 3, 543; Ward No. 4, 559); Middlesex Township, 1,466; Mifflin Township, 1,507; Monroe Township, 1,905; Mount Holly Springs Borough 1,256; Newbury Borough, 433; New Cumberland Borough, 569; Newton Township, 1,843; Newville Borough, 1,547; North Middleton Township, 1,115; Penn Township, 1,521; Shippensburg Borough, 2,213; Shippensburg Township, 494; Shiremanstown Borough, 404; Silver Spring Township, 2,263; Southhampton Township, 1,992; South Middleton Township, 2,864; Upper Allen Township, 1,400; West Pennsborough Township, 2,161.

In November, 1885, the county contained the following postoffices: Allen, Barnitz, Big Spring, Bloserville, Boiling Springs, Bowmansdale, Brandtsville, Camp Hill, Carlisle*, Carlisle Springs, Cleversburgh, Dickinson, Eberly's Mill, Good Hope, Greason, Green Spring, Grissinger, Hatton, Heberlig, Hoguestown, Hunter's Run, Huntsdale, Kerrsville, Lee's Cross Roads, Lisburn, Mooredale, Mechanicsburgh*, Middlesex, Middle Spring, Mount Holly Springs, Mount Rock, Newburgh, New Cumberland, New Kingstown, Newlin, Newville*, Oakville, Pine Grove Furnace, Plainfield, Shepherdstown, Shippensburgh*, Shiremanstown, Stoughstown, Walnut Bottom, West Fairview, Williams Mill, Wormleysburgh—total 47.

INTERNAL IMPROVEMENTS.

Public Road, 1735.—The first public road in the "Kittochtenny" (or Cumberland) Valley west of the Susquehanna River, was laid out in 1735, by order of the court of Lancaster, from Harris' ferry on the Susquehanna to Williams' ferry on the Potomac. (See pioneer chapter for further items concerning the road.) The commissioners to lay out this road, appointed November 4, 1735, were Randle Chambers, Jacob Peat, James Silvers, Thomas Eastland, John Lawrence and Abraham Endless. It was not finished beyond Shippensburg for a number of years, and even at the time of Braddock's expedition (1755) "a tolerable road" was said to exist "as far as Shippensburg." Indian trails were the first highways, and some of them were nearly on the routes of subsequent public roads.

---

*Money order offices.

George Hemminger M.D.

HISTORY OF CUMBERLAND COUNTY.

Military road, 1755.—This was in no part in the present county of Cumberland, though at the time it was Cumberland. It extended from McDowell's mill, near Chambersburg, "over the mountains to Raystown (Bedford) by the forks of the Youghiogheny, to intersect the Virginia road somewhere on the Monongahela," being supposed indispensable for the supply of Braddock's troops on the route to Fort DuQuesne, and after their arrival. The commissioners appointed to lay it out were principally from Cumberland County: among them were George Croghan, the Indian trader; John Armstrong, who had come from Ireland about 1748, and was then (when appointed commissioner) a justice of the peace; Capt. James Burd; William Buchanan, of Carlisle, and Adam Hoops, of Antrim. A route was surveyed from a gap in the mountain near Shippensburg over an old Indian trail to Raystown. Armstrong and Buchanan were called from the work by other duties, and William Smith, Francis West and John Byers were appointed in their places. The road was from 10 to 30 feet wide, according to work necessary to construct it. 200 men from Cumberland County worked on the road, the whole cost being nearly £2,000. The road was completed to Raystown in the latter part of June. Braddock's defeat rendered further work unnecessary and Indian troubles caused a cessation of labor upon the roads.

The Harrisburg & Chambersburg Turnpike, passing through Hogestown, Kingston, Middlesex, Carlisle and Shippensburg was begun by an incorporated company in 1816, and was extensively traveled before the completion of the Cumberland Valley Railroad.

The Hanover & Carlisle Turnpike,* running southeast from Carlisle by way of Petersburg in Adams County, to Hanover and thence to Baltimore, was begun in 1812, and the Harrisburg & York Turnpike was built along the west side of the Susquehanna.

The State road leading from Harrisburg to Gettysburg and crossing the southeast portion of Cumberland County, was laid out in 1810. It is said that "it met with much opposition at first, even from those who were appointed to locate it. They directed it over hills that were almost impassable, hoping thus to effect its abandonment, but its usefulness has since been so thoroughly demonstrated that these hills have been either graded or avoided."

Among other very early roads were one from Hoge's Spring to the Susquehanna River opposite Cox's town, laid out in October, 1759, and another from Trindle's spring to Kelso's ferry in January, 1792.

Cumberland Valley Railroad. Looking back over the past fifty years, the half century's horizon includes the sum total of that almost fairy story of magic that we find in the development of our entire system of railroads to their present marvellous perfection. The crude and simple beginnings; the old strap rails that would so playfully curl up through the car and sometimes through a passenger; the quaint, little, old engines that the passengers had to shoulder the wheels on an up-grade, where they would "stall" so often with five of the little cars attached to them; the still more curious coaches, built and finished inside after the style of the olden-time stage coaches, where passengers sat face to face, creeping along over the country—what a wonder and marvel they were then to the world, and now in the swift half century what a curiosity they are as relics of the past. The railroad forced the coming of the telegraph, the telephone, the electric light,—the most wonderful onward sweep of civilization that has yet shed its sunshine and sweetness upon the world in this brief-told story of fifty years.

---
*The company to build this road was incorporated March 23, 1809, but work was not begun until 1812. The portion between Carlisle and the York County line was built upon a public road laid out in 1793 and known as "the public road from Carlisle through Trent's Gap to the York County line."

The history of the Cumberland Valley Railroad spans the entire period of railroad existence in this country. The first charter is dated in April, 1831. The active promoters were, among others, Judge Frederick Watts, Samuel Alexander, Charles B. Penrose, William Biddle, Thomas G. McCullough, Thomas Chambers, Philip Berlin and Lewis Harlan. The designated termini were Carlisle and the bank of the river opposite Harrisburg. In 1836 a supplemented charter authorized the construction of a bridge at Harrisburg. Surveyors completed the location of the line in 1835; the road was at once contracted for and the work actively commenced in the spring of 1836. In August, 1837, it was "partially and generally" opened for business. At first, passengers and freight were transported across the river by horse-power, and but a small force of this kind could do all the business easily. In 1835 an act was passed extending the line of the road to Chambersburg.

In 1856 the Cumberland Valley Road was authorized, by the authority of the States of Pennsylvania and Maryland, to purchase the Franklin Railroad, which also was one of the early-built roads of the country. It was then a completed road from Chambersburg to Hagerstown. The consolidation of the two lines was effected fully in 1864, and at once the line was completed to the Potomac—Martinsburg—the present Cumberland Valley Railroad; a distance of 94 miles from Harrisburg to Martinsburg. An extension is now contemplated of twenty-two miles from Martinsburg to Winchester, which opens the way for this road to the tempting marts and traffic of the South and West. The first president was Hon. Thomas G. McCullough, elected June 27, 1835. His executive abilities and ripe judgment—for he had no precedents then to follow, so he had to evolve a system for the young and awkward giant from his own brain—show that he was the right man in the right place. In 1840, Hon. Charles B. Penrose became the president. He resigned in 1841, having been appointed solicitor of the treasury, when Judge Frederick Watts, now of Carlisle, became the president, and filled the position ably and acceptably until 1873, when he resigned to become the commissioner of agriculture, by the appointment of President Grant, where he remained six years and retired to private life, though still an efficient and active member of the board of directors of the railroad.

Thomas B. Kenedy, the present incumbent, was elected to the position on the retirement of Judge Watts. He resides in Chambersburg, which has been his home since early boyhood. The history of the other general officers of the road is told wholly in the long life's labor of General E. M. Biddle, who is now the secretary and treasurer, and who has filled the place so ably and well since 1839. What a wonderful panorama in the world's swift changes since 1839, has unfolded itself and has been a part of the official life of General Biddle! He owes now one great duty to this generation and to future mankind, and that is to tell the story of what he saw and was a part of—the particulars of the little crude commencement of railroads and the steps leading to their present greatness and boundless capabilities. A sleeping car was put on this road in 1839—a historical fact of great interest because it was the first of the kind in the world. They were upholstered boards, three-deckers, held by leather straps, and in the day were folded back against the wall, very simple and plain in construction, but comfortable.

The Dillsburg & Mechanicsburg Railroad is a branch of the Cumberland Valley Railroad, extending from the towns indicated in its name. The length is eight miles. It was organized September 2, 1871, and completed the following year. It has been a paying property from the first, and adds much to the comfort and well-being of the people of the country it taps.

The financial affairs of the road are fully explained in the following:

First preferred stock	$241,900 00
Second preferred stock	248,000 00
Common preferred stock	1,292,950 00
First Mortgage Bonds, due 1904	161,000 00
Second Mortgage Bonds, due 1908	109,500 00
Dividends and Interest due	41,313 70
Profit and loss	704,871 91
Total	$2,794,535 61

Harrisburg & Potomac Railroad. The original, active promoters, the organizers and builders of this road were the Ahl brothers, Daniel V. and Peter A. Ahl, of Newville. They procured the charter, furnished the money for the preliminary work, cashed the bonds to a large extent, and contracted and built the original road. The road was chartered June 27, 1870, as the Meramar Iron & Railroad Company, its name explaining the original purposes of the enterprise. The officers elected June 20, 1870, were Daniel V. Ahl, president; Asbury Derland, secretary; William Gracey, treasurer; William H. Miller, solicitor. The road was built from Chambersburg to Richmond. The project was then expanded, and the road built from Chambersburg to Waynesboro, via Mount Alto. The charter members: Daniel V. Ahl, John Evans, Asbury Derland, John Moore, W. H. Langsdorf, George Clever, Samuel N. Bailey, Alexander Underwood and James Bosler. A branch road was surveyed and built from the main line to Dillsburg. When the construction of the line was about completed the concern fell into great financial difficulties, when the almost omnipotent Pennsylvania Road gathered it quietly to its fold and shaped its destinies into the present line of road, and it took its present name, The Harrisburg & Potomac Railroad.

The Northern Central Railroad passes along the shore of the Susquehanna, crossing the eastern end of Cumberland County in which it has about nine miles of road.

The South Mountain Railroad, built or completed in 1869, by the South Mountain Iron Company extending from Carlisle to Pine Grove Furnace, is seventeen and one-half miles long.

CHAPTER V.

MILITARY—CUMBERLAND COUNTY IN THE REVOLUTION—THE WHISKEY INSURRECTION—THE WAR OF 1812.

FOR more than ten years after the close of the Indian wars the inhabitants of the county gave their attention to peaceful pursuits. Agriculture flourished and the population increased. Great Britain finally attempted to force her American colonies to comply with all her outrageous demands without giving them any voice in the Government. They naturally objected. The famous "Boston port bill" roused their ire. This county had few citizens who stood by the mother country in such proceedings. July 12, 1774, a public meeting was called, of which the following are the minutes:

"At a respectable gathering of the freeholders and freemen from several townships of Cumberland County in the province of Pennsylvania, held at

Carlisle, in the said county, on Tuesday, the 12th day of July, 1774, John Montgomery, Esq., in the chair—

1. *Resolved*, That the late act of the Parliament of Great Britain, by which the port of Boston is shut up, is oppressive to that town and subversive of the rights and liberties of the colony of Massachusetts Bay; that the principle upon which the act is founded is not more subversive of the rights and liberties of that colony than it is of all other British colonies in North America; and, therefore, the inhabitants of Boston are suffering in the common cause of all these colonies.

2. That every vigorous and prudent measure ought speedily and unanimously to be adopted by these colonies for obtaining redress of the grievances under which the inhabitants of Boston are now laboring; and security from grievance of the same or of a still more severe nature under which they and the other inhabitants may, by a further operation of the same principle, hereafter labor.

3. That a congress of deputies from all the colonies will be one proper method for obtaining these purposes.

4. That the same purpose will, in the opinion of this meeting, be promoted by an agreement of all the colonies not to import any merchandise from nor export any merchandise to Great Britain, Ireland, or the British West Indies, nor to use any such merchandise so imported, nor tea imported from any place whatever, till these purposes be obtained; but that the inhabitants of this country will join any restriction of that agreement which the general Congress may think it necessary for the colonies to confine themselves to.

5. That the inhabitants of this county will contribute to the relief of their suffering brethren in Boston at any time when they shall receive intimation that such relief will be most seasonable.

6. That a committee be immediately appointed for this county to correspond with the commitee of this province or of the other provinces upon the great objects of the public attention; and to co-operate in every measure conducing to the general welfare of British America.

7. That the committee consist of the following persons, viz.: James Wilson, John Armstrong, John Montgomery, William Irvine, Robert Callender, William Thompson, John Calhoon, Jonathan Hoge, Robert Magaw, Ephraim Blane, John Allison, John Harris and Robert Miller, or any five of them.

8. That James Wilson, Robert Magaw and William Irvine be the deputies appointed to meet the deputies from other counties of this province at Philadelphia on Friday next, in order to concert measures praparatory to the General Congress.

JOHN MONTGOMERY, *Chairman*.

This meeting was held in the Presbyterian Church at Carlisle, and the chairman (Montgomery) was an elder in the church. The meeting was called on receipt of a letter from the Assembly, under action of June 30, calling upon each county to provide arms and ammunition and men to use them from out their associated companies, also to assess real and personal estates to defray expenses. The Assembly encouraged military organizations, and promised to see that officers and men called into service were paid. We quote Dr. Wing's notes upon the men composing the committee:

"James Wilson was born in 1742 in Scotland; had received a finished education at St. Andrews, Edinburgh and Glasgow, under Dr. Blair in rhetoric and Dr. Watts in logic, and in 1766 had come to reside in Philadelphia, where he studied law with John Dickinson, from whom he doubtless acquired something of the spirit which then distinguished that eminent patriot. When admitted to practice he took up his residence in Carlisle. In an important land case, which had recently been tried between the proprietaries and Samuel Wallace, he had gained the admiration of the most eminent lawyers in the province, and at once had taken rank second to none at the Pennsylvania bar. At the meeting of the people now held in Carlisle, he made a speech which drew forth the most rapturous applause. Robert Magaw was a native of Cumberland County, belonging to a family which had early settled in Hopewell Township, and was also a lawyer of some distinction in Carlisle. The career on which he was now entering was one in which he was to become known to the American people as one of their purest and bravest officers. William Irvine was a native of Ireland from the neighborhood of Enniskillen; had been classically educated at the University of Dublin, and had early evinced a fondness for military life, but had been induced by his parents to devote himself to the medical and surgical profession. On receiving his diploma he had been appointed a surgeon in the British Navy, where he continued until the close of the French war (1754–63), when he resigned his place, removed to America and settled in Carlisle, where he acquired a high reputation and an extensive practice as a physician. William Thompson had served as a captain of horse in the expeditions against the Indians (1759–60), had been appointed a justice of the peace in Hopewell Township, and had lately been active in the relief of the inhabitants in the western part of the province in their difficulties with Virginia on the boundary question. Jonathan Hoge and John Calhoon had been justices of the peace and judges in the county, and belonged to two of the oldest and most respectable familes in the vicinity of Silvers' Spring. Ephriam Blaine we have known for his brave defense of a fort at Ligonier, and was now the proprietor of a large property and mills on the Conodoguinet, near the cave, about a mile north of Carlisle. John Allison, of Tyrone Township; John Harris, a lawyer of Carlisle, and Robert Miller, living about a mile northeast of Carlisle in Middleton Township; John Montgomery, a member of the Assembly, and Robert Callender, formerly an extensive trader with the Indians, a commissary for victualing the troops on the western campaign and the owner of mills at the confluence of the Letort with the Conodoguinet, were all of them active as justices, judges and commissioners for the county."

The three delegates from Cumberland County were at Philadelphia a few days later, when the delegates from the various counties of the province assembled, and James Wilson was one of the committee of eleven which brought in a paper of "Instructions on the present situation of public affairs to the representatives who were to meet in the Colonial Assembly next week." The proceedings of this meeting, the subsequent steps of the Assembly, and all the proceedings up to the opening of hostilities, are matters of record not necessary to introduce here. The committee of thirteen which had been appointed at Carlisle, July 12, 1774, kept busy, and through their efforts a "committee of observation" was chosen by the people who had general oversight of civil affairs, and few counties were more fortunate than Cumberland in their choice of men. About this time the terms "whig" and "tory" began to be heard, and the bitterness the two partisan factions held toward each other after the declaration by the colonies of their independence, was extreme, leading to atrocious crimes and terrible murders by the tories when they could strike like cowards, knowing their strength. "Few such," says Dr. Wing, "were found among the native population of this valley. There were indeed some both in civil and in ecclesiastical life who questioned whether they had a right to break the oath or vow of allegiance which they had taken on assuming some official station. Even these were seldom prepared to go so far as to give actual aid and comfort to the enemy, or to make positive resistance to the efforts of the patriots. They usually contented themselves with a negative withdrawal from all participation in efforts at independence. Many of them were earnest supporters of all movements for redress of grievances, and paused only when they were asked to support what they looked upon as rebellion. These hardly deserved the name of "tories," since they were not the friends of extreme royal prerogative, and only doubted whether the colonies were authorized by what they had suffered to break entirely away from the crown to which they had sworn allegiance, and whether the people were yet able to maintain this separate position. Among these who deserved rather to be ranked as non-jurors were one of the first judges of the county, who had recently removed over the mountain to what is now Perry County, and two clergymen who held commissions as missionaries of the 'Venerable Society in England for the Propagation of Religion in Foreign Parts.'"

James Wilson, of Cumberland County, was in December, 1774, appointed one of nine delegates to a second Congress to be held the next year in Philadelphia, and held the position until 1777. Both he and Robert Magaw were members from this county of the provincial convention which met at Philadelphia January 23, 1775, and continued in session six days, during which time much business of great importance was transacted.

Upon receipt of the news of the battle of Lexington (April 19, 1775), Congress resolved to raise an army, and the quota of Pennsylvania was figured at 4,300. Word was sent to the committee of Cumberland County, and they proceeded at once to organize companies of "associators," many of which were already formed on the old plan in use since the days of the Indian troubles. A letter from this county dated May 6, 1775, said: "Yesterday the county committee met from nineteen townships, on the short notice they had. About 3,000 men have already associated. The arms returned amount to about 1,500. The committee have voted 500 effective men, besides commissioned officers, to be immediately drafted, taken into pay, armed and disciplined to march on the first emergency; to be paid and supported as long as necessary, by a tax on all estates real and personal in the county; the returns to be taken by the township committees, and the tax laid by the commissioners and the assessors; the pay of the officers and men as in times past. This morning we met again at 8 o'clock; among other subjects of inquiry the mode of drafting or taking into pay, arming and victualing immediately the men, and the choice of field and other officers, will among other matters be the subjects of deliberation. The strength or spirit of this county perhaps may appear small if judged by the number of men proposed, but when it is considered that we are ready to raise 1,500 or 2,000, should we have support from the province, and that independently and in uncertain expectation of support we have voluntarily drawn upon this county a debt of about £27,000 per annum, I hope we shall not appear contemptible. We make great improvement in military discipline. It is yet uncertain who may go."

From July 3, 1775, to July 22, 1776, John Montgomery, Esq., of Carlisle, was an active and a prominent member of a committee of safety, consisting of twenty-five men from different parts of the province, sitting permanently at Philadelphia, and having management of the entire military affairs of the province. The first troops sent out from Cumberland County, were under the call of Congress in May, 1775, and were from the association companies, the call by the committee of safety not being made until some months later. To furnish arms and ammunition for the soldiers was the greatest difficulty, especially in Cumberland County. "Each person in the possession of arms was called upon to deliver them up at a fair valuation, if he could not himself enlist with them. Rifles, muskets, and other fire-arms were thus obtained to the amount of several hundred, and an armory was established for the repairing and altering of these, in Carlisle. On hearing that a quantity of arms and accoutrements had been left at the close of the Indian war at the house of Mr. Carson, in Paxtang Township, and had remained there without notice or care, the commissioners of Cumberland County, regarding them as public property, sent for them and found about sixty or seventy muskets or rifles which were capable of being put to use, and these were brought to Carlisle, repaired and distributed. Three hundred pounds were also paid for such arms and equipments as were collected from individuals who could not themselves come forward as soldiers. All persons who were not associated, and yet were of the age and ability for effective service, were to be reported by the assessors to the county commissioners and assessed, in addition to the regular tax, £2 10s. annually, in lieu of the time which others spent in military training. The only persons excepted were ministers of the gospel and servants purchased for a valuable consideration of any kind. It was assumed that those who had conscientious scruples about personally bearing arms ought not to hesitate to contribute a reasonable share of the expense for the protection they received."

The first troops going out from Cumberland made up eight companies of, generally, 100 each, and nearly all from the county. The regiment, which became the First Rifle Regiment of Pennsylvania, was formed of men already associated, and therefore the more easily organized for immediate service. It was formed within ten days after the news of the battle of Bunker Hill had been received. The companies rendezvoused at Reading, where the regiment was fully organized by the election of officers as follows: Col. William Thompson, a surveyor who lived near Carlisle and had served with distinction as an officer in the Indian war; Lieut.-Col. Edward Hand, of Lancaster; Maj. Robert Magaw, of Carlisle. The captains of the several companies were James Chambers, of Loudon Forge, near Chambersburg; Robert Cluggage, of Hamilton Township; Michael Doudel, William Hendricks, of East Pennsborough; John Loudon, James Ross, Matthew Smith and George Nagle. Surgeon—Dr. William Magaw, of Mercersburg, a brother to Robert. Chaplain —Rev. Samuel Blair. The regiment marched directly to Boston, reaching camp at Cambridge in the beginning of August, 1775, when it consisted of 3 field officers, 9 Captains, 27 lieutenants, 1 adjutant, 1 quartermaster, 1 surgeon, 1 surgeon's mate, 29 sergeants, 13 drummers and 713 privates fit for duty, or 798 men all told. The officers were commissioned to date from June 25, 1775; term of enlistment, one year. This was the first regiment from west of the Hudson to reach the camp, and received particular attention. They were thus described by a contemporary: "They are remarkably stout and vigorous men, many of them exceeding six feet in hight. They are dressed in white frocks or rifle shirts and round hats. They are remarkable for the accuracy of their aim, striking a mark with great certainty at 200 yards distance. At a review a company of them, while on a quick advance, fired their balls into objects of seven inches in diameter at a distance of 250 yards. They are stationed in our outlines, and their shots have frequently proved fatal to British officers and soldiers who exposed themselves to view even at more than double the distance of a common musket shot." Col. Thompson, with two of his companies under Capts. Smith and Hendricks, went with the expedition to Canada, being probably part of the troops who went on the eastern route with Arnold. December 31, 1775, they were in the assault on Quebec, carried the barriers, and for three hours held out against a greatly superior force, being finally compelled to retire. Of the body to which this regiment belonged, Gen. Richard Montgomery said: "It is an exceedingly fine corps, inured to fatigue and well accustomed to common shot, having served at Cambridge. There is a style of discipline amongst them much superior to what I have been accustomed to see in this campaign."

By subsequent promotions Col. Thompson became a brigadier-general; Lieut.-Col. Hand succeeded to the command of the regiment; Capt. Chambers became lieutenant-colonel, and James Armstrong Wilson, of Carlisle, major, in place of Robert Magaw, transferred. Part of the regiment was captured at

Trois Rivieres and taken to New York, while Col. Hand barely escaped with the balance. Gen. Thompson was finally paroled and sent home to his family in 1777, but was not exchanged until October 26, 1780, when he and others were exchanged for Maj.-Gen. De Reidesel, of the Brunswick troops. He died on his farm near Carlisle September 3, 1781, aged forty-five years, and his death was undoubtedly hastened by exposure while in a military prison.

Upon the expiration of the term of enlistment of this regiment, June 30, 1776, most of the officers and men re-enlisted "for three years or during the war," under Col. Hand, and the battalion became the first regiment of the Continental line. The two separated parts of the regiment, one from Cambridge and the other from Canada, were reunited at New York, though some of its officers, like Magaw, were transferred by promotion to other portions of the army. It was at Long Island, White Plains, Trenton and Princeton under Hand. In April, 1777, Hand was made a brigadier, and James Chambers became the colonel. Under him the regiment fought at Brandywine, Germantown, Monmouth and in every other battle and skirmish of the main army until he retired from the service, January 1, 1781, and was succeeded by Col. Daniel Broadhead May 26, 1781. With him the first regiment left York, Penn., with five others into which the line was consolidated under the command of Gen. Wayne, and joined Lafayette at Raccoon Ford on the Rappahannock June 10; fought at Green Springs on July 6, and opened the second parallel at Yorktown, which Gen. Steuben said he considered the most important part of the siege. After the surrender the regiment went southward with Gen. Wayne, fought the last battle of the war at Sharon, Ga., May 24, 1782, entered Savannah in triumph on the 11th of July, Charleston on the 14th of December, 1782; was in camp on James Island, S. C., on the 11th of May, 1783, and only when the news of the cessation of hostilities reached that point was embarked for Philadelphia. In its services it traversed every one of the original thirteen States of the Union. Capt. Hendricks fell during the campaign in Canada. A few of the original members of the regiment were with it through all the various scenes of the eight years of service. Col. Chambers and Maj. Wilson both retired from the service because of wounds which incapacitated them from duty. The regiment had a splendid record.

Additional regiments from Pennsylvania were called for by Congress in the latter part of 1775, and the Second, Third and Fourth Battalions were raised and placed under the command of Cols. Arthur St. Clair, John Shea and Anthony Wayne. The Fifth Battalion was commanded by Robert Magaw, who had been major in the First, and was composed of companies principally from Cumberland County. It was recruited in December, 1775, and January, 1776, and in February, 1776, some of its companies were in Philadelphia, though the main body of the regiment left Cumberland County in March. It departed from Carlisle March 17, 1776, on which occasion Rev. William Linn, who had been licensed to preach by the Presbytery of Carlisle, and had been appointed Chaplain of the Fifth and Sixth Battalions of Pennsylvania militia, delivered a stirring patriotic sermon, which has been preserved in print to the present day. The command proceeded to Long Island, assisted in the construction of defenses, and upon the retreat assisted other Pennsylvania regiments in covering the retreat. They were afterward placed in Fort Washington at the head of Manhattan Island, with other Pennsylvania troops, commanded by such officers as Cols. Cadwallader, Atlee, Swope, Frederick Watts (of Carlisle) and John Montgomery, the whole commanded by Col. Robert Magaw. Gen. Howe demanded the surrender of the fort, threatening dire consequences if it had to be carried by assault. Col. Magaw replied that "he doubted

HISTORY OF CUMBERLAND COUNTY.

whether a threat so unworthy of the General and of the British nation would be executed." "But," said he, "give me leave to assure your excellency that, actuated by the most glorious cause that mankind ever fought in, I am determined to defend this post to the very last extremity." And that he did, Washington witnessing part of the operations from the opposite side of the Hudson. Finally, however, November 19, 1776, the gallant Colonel was compelled to capitulate, and the strong position, with 2,818 men, fell into the hands of the British. Col. Magaw remained a prisoner on parole until October 25, 1780, when, with Gens. Thompson and Laurens he was exchanged for the British major-general, De Reidesel. Many of Magaw's men suffered greatly in the British prisons, but they refused all temptations held out to induce them to desert and enlist in the royal service. A few were exchanged in 1777, but most remained prisoners until nearly the close of the war.

The committee of correspondence for Cumberland County wrote to Congress about the middle of August, 1775: "The twelfth company of our militia has marched to-day, which companies contain in the whole, 833 privates; with officers, nearly 900 men. Six companies more are collecting arms, and are preparing to march." This committee of correspondence included, among others, John Armstrong, John Byers, Robert Miller, John Agnew and James Pollock; all but Byers residents of Carlisle. (Mr. Miller, in 1768 until 1782, and later, according to the records, owned a tan-yard, and he also is said to have been a merchant. He was an elder in the church and held numerous offices. His daughter, Margaret, married Maj. James Armstrong Wilson.) The committee reported in December, to the committee of safety, that they expected to be able to raise an entire battalion in the county, and hoped they might be allowed to do so, in order to do away with the discords generally prevalent among bodies of men promiscuously recruited. They recommended as officers for such a regiment, colonel, William Irvine; lieutenant-colonel, Ephraim Blaine; major, James Dunlap; captains, James Byers, S. Hay, W. Alexander, J. Talbott, J. Wilson, J. Armstrong, A. Galbreath and R. Adams; lieutenants, A. Parker, W. Bratton, G. Alexander, P. Jack, S. McClay, S. McKenney, R. White and J. McDonald. The Sixth Regiment was accordingly organized, and William Irvine received his commission as colonel, January 9, 1776. Changes were made in the other officers, and they were as follows: lieutenant-colonel, Thomas Hartley, of York; major, James Dunlap, who lived near Newburg; adjutant, John Brooks; captains, Samuel Hay, Robert Adams, Abraham Smith (of Lurgan), William Rippey (resided near Shippensburg), James A. Wilson, David Grier, Moses McLean and Jeremiah Talbott (of Chambersburg). The regiment marched in three months after Col. Irvine was commissioned, and joined the army before Quebec, in Canada. It was brigaded with the First, Second and Fourth Regiments; the brigade being commanded first by Gen. Thomas, and after his death, by Gen. Sullivan. The latter sent Col. Irvine and Gen. Thompson on the disastrous Trois Rivieres campaign, when, June 8, 1776, so many of the men were captured, together with the commanders. The portion of the regiment that escaped capture fell back to Lake Champlain and wintered under command of Lieut.-Col. Hartley. Most of the men re-enlisted after their original term of service had expired (January 1, 1777), and the broken Sixth and Seventh Regiments were consolidated into a new one under the command of Col. David Greer. Col. Irvine, like the others on parol, was exchanged May 6, 1777, and appointed colonel of the Second Pennsylvania Regiment. May 12, 1779, he was made a brigadier-general, and served one or two years under Gen. Wayne. In 1781 he was stationed at Fort Pitt. He died at Philadelphia July 29, 1804. Capt. Rippey, who was captured at Trois Rivieres, succeeded in making his escape. After the war he resided at Shippensburg, where he kept a hotel.

May 15, 1776, Congress passed a resolution recommending "to the respective assemblies and conventions of the United Colonies, where no government sufficient to the exigencies of their affairs has been hitherto established, to adopt such government as shall, in the opinion of the representatives of the people, best conduce to the happiness and safety of their constituents in particular and America in general." On the 3d of June, that body also devised measures for raising a new kind of troops, constituting them the "flying camp," intermediate between militia and regulars, to consist of 10,000 men from the States of Pennsylvania, Maryland and Delaware. The quota of Pennsylvania was 6,000 men, but as 1,500 had already been sent into the field, the immediate demand was for 4,500, and it was finally settled that the quota of Cumberland County was 334, as so many had already been sent out from said county. Meantime, the Assembly having dissolved, and the committee of safety declining to act, it became necessary for the people to organize some form of government, and on recommendation the several county committees met and sent delegates, for that purpose, to a meeting held at Carpenter's Hall, Philadelphia, June 18, 1776. Cumberland County was represented by James McLane, of Antrim Township; John McClay, of Lurgan; William Elliot, Col. William Clark and Dr. John Calhoon, of East Pennsborough; John Creigh and John Harris, of Carlisle; Hugh McCormick and Hugh Alexander, of Middle Spring. This conference continued in session one week, approved the resolutions of Congress, declared the existing government in the province incompetent, and appointed the 15th of July as the date for holding a convention at Philadelphia to frame a new government based upon the authority of the people. Voting places for delegates from Cumberland County, were established at Carlisle, with Robert Miller and James Gregory, of that town, and Benjamin Blyth, of Middle Spring, as judges of election; at Chambersburg, with John Allison and James Maxwell and John Baird as judges; at Robert Campbell's, in Hamilton Township, with William Brown, Alex Morrow and James Taylor as judges. The election was held July 8, and William Harris, then practicing law at Carlisle, William Clark, William Duffield (near Loudon); Hugh Alexander, of Middle Spring; Jonathan Hoge and Robert Whitehill, of East Pennsborough; James Brown, of Carlisle, and James McLane, of Antrim, were chosen delegates. The convention met per appointment, July 15, and adopted a constitution, which in spite of some informalities, was acquiesced in by the people for a number of years. Among other acts of the convention it appointed a council of safety, of which William Lyon was a member from Cumberland County.

George Chambers, in an excellent work upon the "Irish and Scotch and Early Settlers of Pennsylvania," published at Chambersburg in 1856, says of the period at which we have now arrived: "The progress of the war and the oppressive exactions of the British Government after a few months unsettled public opinion on this question [that of separation from the mother country. Ed.] and the necessity and policy of independence became a debatable question with the colonists in their social meetings. At this time there were no newspapers published in Pennsylvania, we believe, west of York. The freemen of the County of Cumberland, in this province, were amongst the first to form the opinion that the safety and welfare of the colonies did render separation from the mother country necessary. The first public expression of that sentiment and its embodiment in a memorial emanated from the freemen and inhabitants of that county to the assembly of the province and is among the national archives." Mr. Chambers in further speaking of this memorial says: "The me-

HISTORY OF CUMBERLAND COUNTY.   87

morial from Cumberland County bears evidence that the inhabitants of that county were in advance of their representatives in the Assembly and in Congress, on the subject of independence. The considerations suggested to them had their influence on the Assembly, who adopted the petition of the memorialists and withdrew the instructions that had been given to the delegates in Congress in opposition to independence. As the Cumberland memorial was presented to the Assembly on the 23d* of May, 1776, it probably had occupied the attention and consideration of the inhabitants of the Cumberland Valley early in that month. As there was no remonstrance from this district by any dissatisfied with the purposes of the memorial we are to suppose that it expressed the public sentiment of that large, respectable and influential district of the province which had then many officers and men in the ranks of the Continental Army."

When in Congress the motion for independence was finally acted upon, the vote of Pennsylvania was carried for it by the deciding vote of James Wilson, of Cumberland County, and of him Bancroft says (History of the United States Vol. VIII, pp. 456-459): "He had at an early day foreseen independence as the probable, though not the intended result of the contest; he had uniformly declared in his place that he never would vote for it contrary to his instructions; nay, that he regarded it as something more than presumption to take a step of such importance without express instructions and authority. 'For' said he, 'ought this act to be the act of four or five individuals, or should it be the act of the people of Pennsylvania?' But now that their authority was communicated by the conference of committees he stood on very different ground." Mr. Chambers says: "The majority of the Pennsylvania delegates remained inflexible in their unwillingness to vote for the measure, at the head of which opposition was the distinguished patriot, John Dickinson, who opposed the measure not as bad or uncalled for, but as premature. But when on the 4th of July the subject came up for final action, two of the Pennsylvania delegates, Dickinson and Morris, who voted in the negative, absented themselves, and the vote of Pennsylvania was carried by the votes of Franklin, Wilson and Morton against the votes of Willing and Humphreys. The men who voted in opposition to this measure were esteemed honest and patriotic men but were too timid for the crisis. They faltered and shrank from responsibility and danger when they should have been firm and brave." The Declaration of Independence though adopted on the 4th of July was not signed until August 16 following. The name of James Wilson was affixed to the document with those of the other delegates, and Cumberland County has the satisfaction of knowing that her citizens and foremost men had an important voice in the formation of the Republic which is now so dear to more than 50,000,000 people.

After this step had been taken by the colonies there was no way of honorable retreat from the ground they had taken. The struggle was upon them, and many were the dark and trying hours before it closed in their favor and the nation was firmly established. It was with difficulty the ranks were kept full. Many had enlisted for only one year, and some as emergency soldiers for as short a period as three months. The appeals of the recruiting officers are described as most stirring, and the county of Cumberland, like others, was kept in a constant state of excitement. By strenuous efforts the flagging energy of the people was renewed. October 16, 1776, William Lyon, who that day took his seat as member from Cumberland County of the council of safety, proposed to the board of war to continue a larger force in the State, to protect it both against British troops and "the growing party of disaffected persons which unhappily exists at this time," also to carry on the necessary

---
*Other authority says May 28.

works of defense. It was resolved to raise four battalions of 500 men each (for the immediate defense of the State), of militia from the counties of York, Cumberland, Lancaster and Berks—one battalion for each county. The news from Trenton (December 3, 1776) and Princton (January 3, 1777) encouraged the people and recruiting became more lively. July 4. 1776. a military convention representing the fifty-three associated battalions of Pennsylvania, met at Lancaster and chose two brigadier-generals to command the battalions and forces of Pensylvania (Daniel Robardeau, of Philadelphia, and James Ewing, of York). Cumberland County was represented at this convention by Col. John Armstrong; Lieut.-Cols. William Blair, William Clark and Frederick Watts, Maj. James McCalmont; Capts. Rev. John Steel, Thomas McClelland, John Davis, James McFarlane and George Robinson, and privates David Hoge, Ephraim Steel, Smith, Pauling, Brown, Sterrett, Hamilton, Read, Finley, and Vance. When the "Flying Camp" was formed, two regiments had been organized in Cumberland County under Cols. Frederick Watts and John Montgomery, of Carlisle, and sent to Washington at Long Island; they were captured with others at Fort Washington, but the officers were soon exchanged and later commanded regiments under a new arrangement. We quote at considerable length from Dr. Wing:

"When Gen. Howe appeared to be about crossing New Jersey to get possession of Philadelphia by land (June 14, 1776), messengers were dispatched to the counties to give orders that the second class of the associated militia should march as speedily as possible to the place to which the first class had been ordered, and that the third class should be got in readiness to march at a moment's notice. These orders were at once complied with, but before the companies from this county had started, the order was countermanded on account of the return of the British troops to New York. It soon, however, became known that the approach to Philadelphia was to be by transports up Chesapeake Bay and Delaware River, and a requisition was made upon the State for 4,000 militia in addition to those already in the field. One class, therefore, was again ordered from the county. On the 5th of October, 1776, the council of safety resolved to throw into the new continental establishment two of the three Pennsylvania battalions, before in that service, to serve during the war, and the third was to be retained in the service of the State until the 1st of January, 1778, unless sooner discharged, and to consist of ten companies of 100 men each, including officers. The privates of the three battalions were to continue in the service of the State, the officers according to seniority to have the choice of entering into either, and the two battalions to be recruited to their full complement of men as speedily as possible. By this new arrangement Pennsylvania was to keep twelve battalions complete in the Continental service." Of course this broke up all previous organizations, and renders it difficult to trace the course of the old companies. We have seen that on the 16th of August thirteen companies fully officered and equipped had left the county for the seat of war, and six others were preparing to go. The regiments of Cols. Thompson. Irvine and Magaw, we have noticed, and two or three others must have been in existence about this time. One of these was commanded by Col. Frederick Watts and Maj. David Mitchell, and another by John Montgomery, who after the dissolution of the committee of safety. July 22, 1776, appears to have taken charge of a regiment. Both of these regiments were at the taking of Fort Washington and were then captured. One of the volunteer companies under Col. Watts, after the latter had been set at liberty and been put again at the head of a regiment, was commanded by Capt. Jonathan Robinson, of Sherman's Valley. the son of George Robinson, who suffered so much in the

Indian war, and who now, though above fifty years of age, had entered the patriot army. This company was in the battle of Princeton, and was for some time stationed at that town to guard against the British and to act as scouts to intercept their foraging parties. Near the close of the year 1776, or the beginning of 1777, battalions began to be designated by numbers in their respective counties and are made of the First, Second, Third, etc., of Cumberland County. This was under the new organization of the militia of the State. The first was organized in January, 1777, when 'Col. Ephraim Blaine of the First Battalion of Cumberland County militia is directed to hold an election for field officers in the said battalion, if two-thirds of the battalion, now marched and marching to camp, require the same.' Accordingly the Colonel was furnished with blank commissions to fill when the officers should be chosen. Capts. Samuel Postlethwaite, Matthias Selers, John Steel, William Chambers and John Boggs are mentioned in the minutes of the council of safety as connected with this regiment. Col. Blaine's connection with the regiment must have been brief, for he was soon transferred to the commissary department, and we find it under the command of Col. James Dunlap (from near Newburg, and a ruling elder in the congregation of Middle Spring), Lieut.-Col. Robert Culbertson, and connected with three companies from what is now Franklin County, viz.: those of Capts. Noah Abraham of Path Valley, Patrick Jack of Hamilton Township and Charles McClay of Lurgan. The Second Battalion was at first under the command of Col. John Allison, a justice of the peace in Tyrone Township, over the mountains, and a judge of the county, but after his retirement (for he was now past middle life) it was for awhile under the command of Col. James Murray, and still later we find it under John Davis, of Middleton, near the Conodoguinet. Under him were the companies of Capts. William Huston, Charles Leeper (of the Middle Spring congregation), James Crawford, Patrick Jack (sometimes credited to this regiment), Samuel Royal and Lieut. George Wallace. While this regiment was under marching orders for Amboy, near January 1, 1777, they took from such persons as were not associated, in Antrim and Peters Township, whatever arms were found in their possession, to be paid for according to appraisement by the Government. The Fourth Battalion was under Col. Samuel Lyon, and had in it the companies of Capts. John Purdy, of East Pennsborough; James McConnel, of Letterkenny, and, in 1778, of Jonathan Robinson, of Sherman's Valley; Stephen Stevenson, who was at first a lieutenant but afterward became a captain. The Fifth Battalion was commanded by Col. Joseph Armstrong, a veteran of the Indian war and of the expedition to Kittanning, and in 1756-57, a member of the Colonial Assembly. Most of this regiment was raised in Hamilton, Letterkenny and Lurgan Townships, and its companies at different times were under Capts. John Andrew, Robert Culbertson (for a time), Samuel Patton, John McConnel, Conrad Snider, William Thompson, Charles McClay (at one period), James McKee, James Gibson, John Rea, Jonathan Robinson, George Matthews and John Boggs. John Murphy was a lieutenant and John Martin ensign. Capt. McClay's men are said to have been over six feet in height and to have numbered 100, and the whole regiment was remarkable for its vigor and high spirit. It suffered severely at the battle of "Crooked Billet," in Berks County, May 4, 1778, when Gen. Lacy was surprised and many of his men were butchered without mercy. The Sixth Battalion was commanded by Col. Samuel Culbertson, who had been a lieutenant-colonel in the First but was promoted to the command of the Sixth. John Work was the lieutenant-colonel; James McCammont, major; John Wilson, adjutant; Samuel Finley, quartermaster, and Richard Brownson, surgeon, and Patrick Jack, Samuel Patton, James Patterson, Joseph Culbertson, William Huston, Robert McCoy and John McConnel were at some periods captains.

"As the period for which the enlistments about this time, when the invasion of Pennsylvania was imminent, was usually limited to six months and sometimes even to three and two months, we need not be surprised to find that at different times the same men and officers served in two or three different regiments. As an instance J. Robinson says that he entered the service a number of times on short enlistments of two or three months, and was placed in different regiments and brigades. The Seventh Battalion is believed to have consisted of remnants of the old Fifth and Sixth Continental Regiments, and was commanded by Col. William Irvine. These soldiers re-entered the service as the Seventh Battalion in March, 1777, and were under the command of its major, David Grier, until the release of Irvine from his parole as a prisoner of war (May 6, 1777). In 1779 Col. Irvine was commissioned a brigadier, and served under Gen. Wayne, but before this (July 5, 1777) Abraham Smith, of Lurgan Township, was elected colonel. Among the captains were William Rippey; Samuel Montgomery, who became captain of Smith's company when the latter was promoted; John Alexander, before a lieutenant in Smith's company; Alexander Parker; Jeremiah Talbott, who in the latter part of the year 1777 was promoted a major in the Sixth, and served in that position until the close of the war. He was the first sheriff of Franklin County (October, 1784) and was twice re-elected. The Eighth Battalion was commanded by Abraham Smith, who was chosen July 6, 1777, probably from Lurgan, and a member of the congregation of Middle Spring. Its officers were largely taken from a single remarkable family in Antrim Township. The head of this family had settled very early, about 1735, two and a half miles east of where Greencastle now is, and had died near 1755, leaving a large property and four sons. Each of these sons entered the army. The eldest, James, was a lieutenant-colonel of the Eighth Battalion, but afterward was the colonel of a battalion during a campaign in New Jersey. John, the youngest, was the major, and Thomas, the second son, was adjutant, and was present at the slaughter at Paoli, September 20, 1777, but survived to be promoted to a colonelcy and lived till about 1819. Dr. Robert, the other brother, was a surgeon in Col. Irvine's regiment, was in the South during the latter years of the war, was at the surrender of Yorktown, in October, 1781, and in 1790 was an excise collector for Franklin County. Terrence Campbell was the quartermaster. The captains were Samuel Roger, John Jack, James Poe and John Rea, who afterward became a brigadier-general.

"Besides these we have notices of several companies, regiments and officers, whose number and position in the service is not given in any account we have seen. Early in the war James Wilson and John Montgomery were appointed colonels, and in the battalion of the former are mentioned the companies of Capts. Thomas Clarke and Thomas Turbitt. Montgomery was in the army at New York in 1776, and was at the surrender of Fort Washington, but both he and Wilson were soon called into the civil department of the service, and do not appear in the army after that year. Besides them were Cols. Robert Callender, of Middlesex, now in advanced life, whose death early in the war deprived his country of his valuable services; James Armstrong, Robert Peoples, James Gregory, Arthur Buchanan, Benjamin Blythe, Abraham Smith, Isaac Miller and William Scott. Among the captains, whom we are unable to locate in any particular regiment, at least for any considerable time, were Joseph Brady, Thomas Beale, Matthew Henderson, Samuel McCune (under Col. William Clarke for awhile, and at Ticonderoga), Isaac Miller, David Mc-

HISTORY OF CUMBERLAND COUNTY.   91

Knight, Alexander Trindle, Robert Quigley, William Strain, Samuel Kearsley, Samuel Blythe, Samuel Walker, William Blaine, Joseph Martin, James Adams, Samuel Erwin and Peter Withington. One of the companies which were early mustered into the service was that of Capt. William Peebles. The officers' commissions were dated somewhere between the 9th and the 15th of March, near the time at which Magaw's regiment left the county. The company was in Philadelphia August 17, and was then said to consist of eighty-one riflemen. It was in the battle of Long Island, August 27, when a portion was captured, and the remainder were in the engagements at White Plains, Trenton and Princeton. On his return from the war Capt. Peebles resided on Peebles' Run, a little distance from Newburg, and was for many years an elder in the congregation at Middle Spring. He was promoted to be a colonel September 23, 1776. Matthew Scott was the first-lieutenant, and among the captured at Long Island, but he was exchanged December 8, 1776, and promoted captain April 18, 1777. He married Peggy, the daughter of Samuel Lamb, a stonemason near Stony Ridge, who long survived him and was living in Mechanicsburg in 1845. The family of Mr. Lamb was distinguished for its ardent patriotism. The second lieutenant was Robert Burns, promoted to be a captain in Col. Hazen's regiment December 21, 1776. The third lieutenant was Robert Campble, also promoted to be a captain at the same time in the same regiment, and when wounded was transferred to an invalid regiment under Lewis Nichola. The sergeants were Samuel Kenny, William McCracken, Patrick Highland (captured), and Joseph Collier. James Carson, drummer, and Edward Lee, fifer, were also captured at Long Island August 27, 1776. The privates were William Adams, Zachariah Archer, William Armstrong, James Atchison (captured), Thomas Beatty, Henry Bourke, William Boyd, Daniel Boyle (enlisted for two years, discharged at Valley Forge July 1, 1778, and in 1824 resided in Armstrong County), James Brattin, John Brown, Robert Campble, John Carrigan, William Carson, William Cavan, Henry Dibbins, Pat Dixon, Samuel Dixon (captured), Barnabas Dougherty, James Dowds, John Elliott, Charles Fargner, Daniel Finley, Pat Flynn, James Galbreath, Thomas Gilmore, Dagwell Hawn, John Hodge, Charles Holder, Jacob Hove, John Jacobs, John Justice, John Keating, John Lane, Peter Lane, Samuel Logan, Robert McClintock, Alexander McCurdy, Hugh McKegney, Andrew McKinsey, Charles McKowen, Niel McMullen, Alex. Mitchell, John Mitchell (justice of the peace in Cumberland County in 1821), Laurence Morgan, Samuel Montgomery, William Montgomery, David Moore, James Moore, John Moore, James Mortimer, Robert Mullady, Patrick Murdaugh, John Niel, James Nickleson, Robert Nugent, Richard Orput, John Paxton, Robert Pealing, James Pollock, Hans Potts, Patrick Quigley, John Quinn, Andrew Ralston, James Reily, Thomas Rogers (captured on Long Island, died in New Jersey, leaving a widow, who resided in Chester County), James Scroggs, Andrew Sharpe, Thomas Sheerer, John Shields, John Skuse, Thomas Townsend, Patten Viney, John Walker, John Wallace, Thomas Wallace, William Weatherspoon (captain), Peter Weaver, Robert Wilson and Hugh Woods. Total of officers ten, and of privates, eighty.

"A company of rangers from the borders of this county, who had been accustomed in the Indian wars to act under James Smith, also deserves notice. He had now removed to the western part of the State, and was a member of the Assembly from Westmoreland. While attending on that body early in 1777, he saw in the streets of the city some of his former companions in forest adventure, from this region, and they immediately formed themselves into a company under him as their commander. Obtaining leave of absence for a short time from the Assembly, he went with them to the army in New Jersey, attacked about 200 of the British, at Rocky Hill, and, with only thirty-six men, drove them from their position; and on another occasion took twenty-two Hessians with their officers' baggage-wagons, and a number of our Continental prisoners they were guarding. In a few days they took more of the British than there were of their own party. Being taken with the camp fever Smith returned to the city, and the party was commanded by Maj. McCammont, of Strasburg. He then applied to Gen. Washington for permission to raise a battalion of riflemen, all expert marksmen, and accustomed to the Indian method of fighting. The council of safety strongly recommended the project, but the General thought it not best to introduce such an irregular element into the army, and only offered him a major's commission in a regular regiment. Not fancying the officer under whom he was to serve, he declined this, and remained for a time with his companions in the militia. In 1778 he received a colonel's commission, and served with credit till the end of the war, principally on the western frontier.

"Another partisan leader was Samuel Brady, originally from near Shippensburg, and among those who went first to Boston. Though but sixteen years of age when he enlisted, in 1775, in a company of riflemen, he was one of the boldest and hardiest of that remarkable company. At the battle of Monmouth he was made captain; at Princeton he was near being taken prisoner, but succeeded in effecting an escape for himself and his colonel, and in many places displayed an astonishing coolness and steadiness of courage. He so often acted on special commissions to obtain intelligence that he became distinguished as the 'captain of the spies.' In 1778 his brother, and in 1779 his father were cruelly killed by the Indians, and from that time it was said of him, 'this made him an Indian killer, and he never changed his business. The red man never had a more implacable foe or a more relentless tracker. Being as well skilled in woodcraft as any Indian of them all, he would trail them to their very lairs with all the fierceness and tenacity of the sleuth hound.' During the whole sanguinary war with the Indians he gave up his whole time to lone vigils, solitary wanderings and terrible revenges. He commenced his scouting service in 1780, when he was but twenty-one years old, and became a terror to the savages and a security to a large body of settlers. He did not marry until about 1786, when he spent some years at West Liberty, in West Virginia, where he probably died about 1800. [See McKnight's "Western Border," pp. 426–442.]

"The Patrick Jack, who is mentioned more than once above as connected at different times with several regiments, was probably the same man who afterward became famous as the 'Wild Hunter, or Juniata Jack the Indian Killer.' He was from Hamilton Township, and is said by George Croghan in 1755 to have been at the head of a company of hunter rangers, expert in Indian warfare, and clad, like their leader, in Indian attire. They were therefore proposed to Gen. Braddock as proper persons to act as scouts, provided they were allowed to dress, march and fight as they pleased. 'They are well armed,' said Croghan, 'and are equally regardless of heat and cold. They require no shelter for the night and ask no pay.' It is said of him as of Brady that he became a bitter enemy of the Indians by finding his cabin one evening, on his return from hunting, 'a heap of smoldering ruins, and the blackened corpses of his murdered family scattered around.' From that time he became a rancorous Indian hater and slayer. When the Revolutionary war began he was among the first to enlist, and he afterward enlisted several times on short terms in various companies. He was of large size and stature, dark almost as an Indian, and stern and relentless to his foes. John Armstrong in his ac-

count of the Kittanning expedition, calls him 'the half Indian,' but he could have had no Indian blood in his veins. His monument may be seen at Chambersburg, with this inscription: 'Colonel Patrick Jack, an officer of the Colonial and Revolutionary Wars—died January 25, 1821, aged ninety-one years.'"

We shall now give a few of the important events of the war as relating to Cumberland County without going further into details. In 1778 George Stevenson, John Boggs, Joseph Brady and Alexander McGehan were appointed a committee to attend to estates forfeited for treason, and the commissioners for the county, James Pollock and Samuel Laird, were required to collect from non-associators the amounts they owed the State as a fair equivalent for military services, also to collect such arms and ammunition as may be found in their possession. In September, 1777, information had been given of plots by "tories" to destroy public stores at York, Lancaster, Carlisle and other points, and several prominent persons in the region were implicated. "By a proclamation of the Supreme Executive Council, June 15, 1778, John Wilson, wheel-wright and husbandman, and Andrew Fursner, laborer, both of Allen Township; Lawrence Kelley, cooper; William Curlan, laborer; John M. Cart, distiller and laborer, and Francis Irwin, carter, of East Pennsborough; George Croghan, Alexander McKee, Simon Girty and Matthew Elliott, Indian traders, were said severally to have aided and assisted the enemy by having joined the British Army, and were therefore attainted of high treason and subject to the penalties and forfeitures which were by law attached to their crime. The committee on forfeited estates rendered an account of several hundred pounds which they had handed over to the proper officers to be used in the purchase of arms, provisions, etc., from which it would appear that some persons had been found guilty of treason in the county. The names which have come down to us either by tradition or documentary evidence were usually of persons of no prominence, or of such as were then residing beyond the limits of the present county of Cumberland."—[*Wing.*]

An act of the Supreme Executive Council passed March 17, 1777, provided for the appointment of one or more lieutenants of militia in each city or county, also of sub-lieutenants, with duties which the act prescribed. John Armstrong and Ephraim Blaine were successively appointed lieutenants for Cumberland County, but both declined for sufficient reasons. April 10, 1777, James Galbreath, of East Pennsborough Township, was appointed, and finally accepted the position and performed its duties faithfully. He was succeeded by John Carothers, and he by Col. James Dunlap, in October, 1779. Abraham Smith held the office in April, 1780. The sub-lieutenants were Col. James Gregory, of Allen Township; Col. Benjamin Blythe, near Middle Spring; George Sharpe, near Big Spring; Col. Robert McCoy (died in May, 1777); John Harris, of Carlisle; George Stewart, James McDowell, of Peters Township (in place of Col. McCoy), all appointed in 1777, and Col. Frederick Watts, Col. Arthur Buchanan, Thomas Buchanan, John Trindle, Col. Abraham Smith and Thomas Turbitt appointed in 1780.

In June, 1777, the Supreme Executive Council appointed an entirely new board of justices for Cumberland County, as some of the old ones had failed to take the oath of allegiance required of them and several of the positions were vacant. Those newly appointed were John Rannels (Reynolds), James Maxwell, James Oliver, John Holmes, John Agnew, John McClay, Samuel Lyon, William Brown, John Harris, Samuel Royer, John Anderson, John Creigh, Hugh Laird, Andrew McBeath, Thomas Kenny, Alexandria Laughlin, Samuel McClure, Patrick Vance, George Matthews, William McClure, Samuel Culbertson, James Armstrong, John Work, John Trindle, Stephen Duncan, Ephraim Steel, William Brown (Carlisle), Robert Peebles, Henry Taylor, James Taylor, Charles Leeper, John Scouller, Matthew Wilson and David McClure. November 5, 1777, John Agnew, on the nomination of these justices, was appointed a clerk of the peace, and February 20, 1779, a commissioner for the exchange of money. These justices were required to "administer the oath of allegiance to every person who should vote for officers or enter upon any office either under the State government or under the Continental Congress." From 1777 to 1779 Col. William Clark was paymaster of troops in Cumberland County. In 1777 he reported concerning the destitute condition of the militia, and a committee was appointed consisting of John Boggs, Abraham Smith, John Andrew, William McClure, Samuel Williamson, James Purdy and William Blair "to collect without delay from such as have not taken the oath of allegiance and abjuration, or who have aided or assisted the enemy with arms or accoutrements, blankets, linen and linsey-wolsey cloth, shoes and stockings for the army." Besides this committee, George Stevens, John Boggs and Joseph Brady were appointed commissioners "to seize upon the personal estates of all who have abandoned their families or habitations, joined the army of the enemy, or resorted to any city, town or place within the commonwealth in possession of the enemy, or supplied provisions, intelligence or aid for the enemy, or shall hereafter do such things; and they shall as speedily as possible dispose of all the perishable part thereof, and hold possession of all the remainder subject to the future disposition of the Legislature."

Large numbers of wagons and teams and teamsters were employed to transport the great quantities of stores and supplies from place to place as necessary, and a special department was maintained for the organization and management of this service. Cumberland County was required to furnish a large proportion of supplies, wagons and teams, and sent out at one time 200, at another 800, and at various times smaller numbers of wagons. Hugh McCormick was appointed wagon-master in 1777, Matthew Gregg in 1778 and Robert Culbertson in 1780. Dr. Wing states: "In November, 1777, the assessment was upon East Pennsborough, Peters and Antrim Townships, each for twelve wagons and teams; Allen for eleven, Middleton, West Pennsborough, Newton, Hopewell, Lurgan, Letterkenny, Guilford and Hamilton each for ten. Each wagon was to be accompanied by four horses, a good harness and one attendant, and the owner was paid thirty shillings in specie or forty in currency, according to the exchange agreed upon by Congress."

Early in 1776 a number of British prisoners captured on the northern frontier and in the east were confined at Lancaster, but by order of Congress they were removed in March, half to York and half to Carlisle. At that time Lieuts. Andre, Despard and Anstruther were taken to Carlisle; and, as stated by early writers, were confined in a stone building which stood on the east side of Hanover Street, on Lot 161. These prisoners were exchanged in the latter part of the same year, most of them being sent to New York, November 28, "under the escort of Lieut.-Col. John Creigh and Ephraim Steel, two members of the committee of inspection, with their servants and their servants' wives and their baggage, by way of Reading and Trenton to the nearest camp of the United States in New Jersey." With the subsequent fate of Andre, promoted to captain and then to major, everybody is familiar. A large number of the Hessians captured at Trenton, December 25, 1776, were sent to Carlisle, and while here were set at work building barracks, which became noted in later years as a school for cavalry training and in other ways, and stood on the site now occupied by the Indian school.

"About the 1st of August, 1777," says Dr. Wing, "John Penn, James Hamilton, Benjamin Chew, and about thirty others who had been officers under the royal and proprietary government, and declined to take the oath of allegiance to the new government, were arrested in Philadelphia, received by the sheriff of Reading and by the sheriff of Cumberland County, and escorted through this valley to Staunton, Va., where they were detained until near the conclusion of the war."

In April, 1777, Gen. Armstrong, of Carlisle, was placed in command of the militia of the State; resigning his position as first brigadier-general in the Continental Army, he was appointed first brigadier-general and a month afterward major-general of the State of Pennsylvania. Though advanced in years he entered vigorously upon the work of protecting the State against the enemy, and erected and maintained defensive works along the Delaware River. Portions of his command did splendid service at Brandywine and Germantown. Five hundred men or more enlisted and went to the fort from Cumberland County early in 1778. The county was nearly bereft of men to carry on necessary business or to guard the prisoners which from time to time were sent to Carlisle. It was difficult to provide arms and ammunition until France came to the aid of the colonies in 1778. "Hence the efforts in the beginning of the conflict to establish at every available town shops for the manufacture of rifles, muskets and even cannon. Old arms were repaired and altered so that even fowling-pieces could be used for deadlier purposes, and bayonets were prepared. Armories are spoken of in Carlisle and Shippensburg at which hundreds of rifles were got in readiness at one time. A foundry was started at Mount Holly and perhaps at Boiling Springs, at which cannon were cast, and at which William Denning [Deming?] was known to have worked at his inventions. Aware of the many failures which had followed all previous attempts, under the most favorable conditions, to make cannon of wrought iron; he is said to have persevered until he constructed at least two of such uniform quality and of such size and calibre as to have done good service in the American Army. One of them is reported to have been taken by the British at the battle of Brandywine, and now kept as a trophy in the Tower of London, and another to have been for a long time and perhaps to be now, at the barracks near Carlisle. (William Denning was a resident of Chester County when the war broke out; enlisted in a company and was its second lieutenant for nine months; was a blacksmith by trade, and very ingenious; was placed at head of a band of artificers at Philadelphia, but removed to Carlisle upon the approach of the British Army; iron from the South Mountain was made into gun-barrels, bayonets, etc., and Denning had a chance to exercise his ingenuity to his greatest desire. In welding the heavy bars of iron for bands and hoops to his wrought iron guns, few could be induced to assist him on account of the great heat. He made four and six-pounders and attempted a twelve-pounder, but never completed it. He resided at Big Spring after the war, and died December 19, 1830, aged ninety-four years). So great was the destitution of lead for bullets, that the council of safety requested all families possessing plates, weights for clocks or windows, or any other articles made of lead, to give them up to the collectors appointed to demand them, with the promise that they should be replaced by substitutes of iron. Payments were acknowledged for considerable quantities of lead thus collected in this county. Every part of the county was explored to obtain sulphur and other substances in sufficient quanties for the manufacture of gunpowder. Jonathan Kearsley, of Carlisle, was for some months employed in learning the art and in the attempt to manufacture saltpetre out of earths impregnated with nitrous particles in

Dauphin County. After nearly three months of experiments he wrote that the amount obtained was not sufficient to warrant his continuance at the work in that vicinity. Common salt finally became so scarce that Congress took upon itself the business of supplying the people as well as the soldiers. Before the construction of those vast establishments which have since been created for the manufacture of these articles, the whole population was dependent on foreign countries, and now were cut off from all importation of it. Near the close of 1776 a law was passed against those who endeavored to monopolize the sale of salt, and a large purchase of it was made by Congress itself. A certain quota was assigned to each State, and then to each county under the direction of the State authorities. The proportion which fell to Cumberland County (November 23, 1776) was eighty bushels. On its arrival a certain portion was delivered to each householder who applied for it with an order from the county committee, 'on his paying the prime cost of 15 shillings a bushel, expenses of carriage only added.'"

August 17, 1776, by authority of a resolution of the Assembly passed a month previous, the committee of inspection and observation for Cumberland County drew an order on the council of safety for £200 for the relief of the poor families of associators called into service. The greater part of the grain raised in the county was sent away for supplies or distilled into liquor, and the men were so scarce it was difficult to harvest and thresh the grain. Gen. Armstrong, noting this condition of affairs, wrote on the 17th of February, 1777: "From the best information that I can get, the rye in both this and the county of York is almost all distilled, as is also considerable quantities of wheat, and larger still of the latter bought up for the same purpose; nor can we doubt that Lancaster and other counties are going on in the same destructive way, so that in a few months Pennsylvania may be scarce of bread for her own inhabitants. Liquor is already 10 shillings per gallon, wheat will immediately be the same per bushel, and if the complicated demon of avarice and infatuation is not suddenly changed or cast out, he will raise them each to twenty!"

To Col. Ephraim Blaine, of Cumberland County, as assistant quartermaster-general, under Gen. Greene, quartermaster-general, was due great praise and much credit for his aid in times of financial depression during the war. His flouring-mill on the Conodoguinet, near Carlisle, was enlarged and kept in operation to its utmost capacity for the benefit of the suffering army and without profit to himself. His extensive fortune was ever at the disposal of his country, and by his earnest and careful management he kept the soldiers from actual starvation, more than once in the face of pronounced opposition to his measures. His name became dear to his countrymen. The schemes of Congress to provide money led to disastrous results, and many inhabitants of Cumberland County were very seriously embarrassed or completely broken up financially for years. Many dark days were experienced by the people of the struggling republic during the war, and at times even mutiny and violence were advocated or attempted; the Indian troubles of 1778 and succeeding years brought to mind the terrible scenes of days gone by, and soldiers from the county were sent with others for the punishment of the marauding murderers. The sad end of the expedition of Col. Crawford, in 1782 against the western Indians, called numbers into the service for vengeance, for Crawford was known and loved in the valley, but the British recalled their Indian allies from the frontiers of the northwest, and the troops organized to march against them under Gens. Irvine and Potter were disbanded. The peace of 1783 brought relief to the land, and the war cloud was lifted.

HISTORY OF CUMBERLAND COUNTY.

March 3, 1781, Samuel Laird and William Lyon were appointed auditors of depreciated accounts, "to settle with officers and soldiers in the county the amount which should be allowed on their pay for the depreciated value of the notes paid them." Gen. William Irvine, of Carlisle, was made one of the board of censors October 20, 1783, from Cumberland County, as was also James McLene, of Chambersburg. The only meeting was at Philadelphia November 10, 1783, for the new constitution (1790) abolished it.

The Whiskey Insurrection, 1794.—When it became evident that some source of revenue must be looked to besides the duties on imported goods, and Congress decided to levy a tax (of 4 pence per gallon) on distilled spirits (March 3, 1791), believing that article to be of the least necessity, the tax was violently opposed by people in the interior and western parts of Pennsylvania, where it bore with most severity. There had been no market for the great quantities of grain raised, and it was largely used to fatten cattle and hogs upon. When distilled it was more easily transported over the mountains and found a ready market, and in numerous sections every fifth or sixth farmer had a still-house. [The consumption was not all away from home, either.—Ed.] The excise law was felt to be oppressive, as most of the money brought into the region was sent out in the shape of excise duties. The people hoped the law would be unexecuted and finally repealed, and the collectors were often threatened, intimidated, and as in the instance of Pittsburgh, roughly handled and their property destroyed. The excitement spread and the fury grew by the aid of mass meetings, pole raisings, and the like, and steps were taken for an armed resistance to the authorities should a force be sent against the disturbers. Braddock's Field, ten miles east of Pittsburgh, was designated as a place of rendezvous for the rebellious troops. The general sympathy of even the most prominent men was with those who openly opposed the law, but they did not, as the end shows, believe in a resort to arms. President Washington issued proclamations, September 15, 1792, and August 7, 1793, requiring insurgents to disperse and directing that troops should be raised to march at a moment's warning before the 15th of September in the latter year. Those who had been opposed to the law, but hoped a few trials of aggressors would lead to its repeal, now joined hands with the Government. An army of 12,900 men was called for from the four States most interested, and the quota of Pennsylvania was 5,200. Gen. William Irvine, of Carlisle, was one of a number of commissioners appointed to confer with such deputies as the deputies might appoint, but they returned with an adverse or unfavorable report, though they were followed by commissioners from the insurgents who were more reasonable than those with whom they had conferred. The army was put in motion and finally reached Carlisle. The softened commissioners met the President and commander-in-chief at that point October 10, 1794, and assured him that it was unnecessary to send the military to obtain submission and order, but he declined to stay the march of the army, though promising that no violence would be offered if the people would return to their allegiance. Carlisle was the place of rendezvous for the army. Cumberland County furnished 363 men and officers who were brigaded with others from York, Lancaster and Franklin Counties, under Brig.-Gen. James Chambers, of Franklin County. They encamped on "an extensive common near the town (Carlisle) said to be admirably fitted for the purpose."

A large number of distilleries then undoubtedly existed in Cumberland County, where those opposed to the law had not been over-cautious in making remarks or in demonstrations of disfavor. A liberty pole had been erected in the Public Square on the night of September 8, 1794, with the words,

"Liberty and No Excise, & Whisky," thereon. A few friends of law and order cut it down the next morning, and the excitement was great. A large number of country people, some bearing arms, came in a few days later, one afternoon, and put up a large pole with the words, "Liberty and Equality." They were mostly of the poorer class, although the county treasurer was a leader among them and distributed money to buy whisky. Deeds of violence were offered occasionally, the insurgents patroling the town to prevent the pole being taken down. Col. Ephraim Blaine was pursued and fired upon by three of them while conducting his sister, Mrs. Lyon, out of town, but fortunately without injury. Threats were made against the militia should they turn out, and affairs were rather desperate. Gen. Irvine, as commissioner, attended strictly to the business of his office, saying, "I make a rule of doing what I think is right, and trust to events for consequences." The presence of troops in Carlisle brought the people to their senses. Gov. Mifflin arrived on the 1st of October, and in the evening delivered a stirring address in the Presbyterian Church. His arrival was in advance of the army, which reached Carlisle October 3. A writer says "the beloved Washington" approached in a traveling dress, attended by his secretary, Alexander Hamilton, and proceeds: "As he passed our troops he pulled off his hat and, in the most respectful manner, bowed to the officers and men, and in this manner passed the line, who were (as you may suppose) affected by the sight of their chief, for whom each individual seemed to show the affectionate regard that would have been paid to an honored parent. As he entered the town the inhabitants seemed anxious to see this very great and good man; crowds were assembled in the streets, but their admiration was silent. The President passed to the front of the camp, where the troops were assembled in front of the tents; the line of artillery, horse and infantry appeared in the most perfect order; the greatest silence was observed. The spectacle was grand, interesting and affecting; every man as he passed along poured forth his wishes for the preservation of this most valuable of their fellow-citizens. Here you might see the aged veteran, the mature soldier and the zealous youth assembled in defense of that government which must (in turn) prove the protection of their persons, family and property." The court house was illuminated in the evening, and a transparency was prepared, bearing the inscriptions: "Washington is ever triumphant." "The reign of the laws," and "Woe to Anarchists." President Washington while here was the guest of Col. Ephraim Blaine. A number of the principal inhabitants presented him the following address on Monday of the week following:

CARLISLE, October 17, 1794.

To GEORGE WASHINGTON, ESQ., PRESIDENT OF THE UNITED STATES:

Sir: We, the subscribers, inhabitants of this borough, on behalf of ourselves, our fellow-citizens, friends to good order, government and the laws, approach you at this time to express our sincere admiration of those virtues which have been uniformly exerted with so much success for the happiness of America, and which at this critical period of impending foreign and domestic troubles have been manifested with distinguished lustre.

Though we deplore the cause which has collected in this borough all classes of virtuous citizens, yet it affords us the most heartfelt satisfaction to meet the father of our country and brethren in arms, distinguished for their patriotism, their love of order and attachment to the constitution and laws; and while on the one hand we regret the occasion which has brought from their homes men of all situations, who have made sacrifices unequaled in any other country of their private interests to the public good, yet we are consoled by the consideration that the citizens of the United States have evinced to our enemies abroad and the foes of our happy constitution at home that they not only have the will but possess the power to repel all foreign invaders and to crush all domestic traitors.

The history of the world affords us too many instances of the destruction of free governments by factious and unprincipled men. Yet the present insurrection and opposition to government is exceeded by none, either for its causeless origin or for the extreme malignity and wickedness with which it has been executed.

The unexampled clemency of our councils in their endeavors to bring to a sense of duty the western insurgents, and the ungrateful returns which have been made by that deluded people, have united all good men in one common effort to restore order and obedience to the laws, and to punish those who have neglected to avail themselves of and have spurned at the most tender and humane offers that have ever been made to rebels and traitors.

We have viewed with pain the great industry, art and misrepresentations which have been practiced to delude our fellow-citizens. We trust that the efforts of the General Government, the combination of the good and virtuous against the vicious and factious, will cover with confusion the malevolent disturbers of the public peace, and afford to the well-disposed the certainty of protection to their persons and property. The sword of justice in the hands of our beloved President can only be considered an object of terror by the wicked, and will be looked up to by the good and virtuous as their safegard and protection.

We bless that Providence which has preserved a life so valuable through so many important scenes, and we pray that He will continue to direct and prosper the measures adopted by you for the security of our internal peace and the stability of our Government, and that after a life of continued usefulness and glory you may be rewarded with eternal felicity.

There was no doubt of the sincerity of the foregoing address, and Washington, whom it could not fail to touch with a feeling of pleasure, responded as follows:

GENTLEMEN: I thank you sincerely for your affectionate address. I feel as I ought what is personal to me, and I can not but be particularly pleased with the enlightened and patriotic attachment which is manifested towards our happy constitution and the laws.

When we look around and behold the universally acknowledged prosperity which blesses every part of the United States, facts no less unequivocal than those which are the lamented occasion of our present meeting were necessary to persuade us that any portion of our fellow-citizens could be so deficient in discernment or virtue as to attempt to disturb a situation which, instead of murmurs and tumults, calls for our warmest gratitude to heaven, and our earnest endeavors to preserve and prolong so favored a lot.

Let us hope that the delusion cannot be lasting, that reason will speedily regain her empire, and the laws their just authority where they have lost it. Let the wise and the virtuous unite their efforts to reclaim the misguided, and to detect and defeat the arts of the factious. The union of good men is a basis on which the security of our internal peace and the stability of our government may safely rest. It will always prove an adequate rampart against the vicious and disorderly.

In any case in which it may be indispensable to raise the sword of justice against obstinate offenders, I shall deprecate the necessity of deviating from a favorite aim, to establish the authority of the laws in the affections rather than in the fears of any.

GEORGE WASHINGTON.

Before Washington arrived at Carlisle, the accidental discharge of a soldier's pistol killed the brother of a man whom a party of soldiers were pursuing because of his action in conjunction with the insurgents, and another countryman was killed in a quarrel with a soldier. The circumstances were regretted by the President and his secretary (Gen. Hamilton). Several who had acted with the insurrectionists were arrested and lodged in jail at Carlisle, but they appeared to be little concerned at the consequences of their proceedings.

Andrew Holmes, Esq., a member of a company from Carlisle, in the command of Gen. Chambers, kept a private journal in which he recorded the movement of the troops, and under date of Sunday, October 11, 1794, 2 o'clock P. M., he wrote as follows: "The Carlisle Light Infantry, together with from 3,000 to 4,000 troops, cavalry, rifle and infantry, marched from Carlisle to Mount Rock. The officers of the Carlisle Infantry were as follows: Captain, George Stevenson; first-lieutenant, Robert Miller; second-lieutenant, William Miller; ensign, Thomas Creigh; orderly sergeant, William Armor; sergeant-major, George Hackett; drum-major, James Holmes; and fifty-two privates, among whom were Thomas Duncan, David Watts, Robert Duncan,

John Lyon, Nathaniel Weakley, George Pattison, Charles Pattison, William Andrew, Abraham Holmes, Archibald Ramsey, Joseph Clark, William Dunbar, Archibald McAllister, William Crane, Jacob Fetter, Archibald Loudon, Thomas Foster, Jacob Housenet, George Wright, Thomas Wallace, Francis Gibson, Joseph and Michael Egolf, Robert McClure and William Levis. At Sideling Hill Capt. Stevenson was made a major, and William Levis, quartermaster."

The following brigade order, December 4, 1794, is from the same journal:

The General congratulates the troops which he has the honor to command, on their arrival at Strasburg,* and feelingly anticipates the pleasure which the worthy citizen soldiers and himself shall have in the company of their nearest connections. He also has the pleasure of announcing to the brigade the entire approbation of the commander-in-chief for their orderly conduct and strict discipline, which reflects the highest honor on both officers and soldiers. He is likewise happy in assuring his fellow-citizens that their soldierly behavior during the whole campaign has merited his highest acknowledgments and as they have supported the laws of their country he rests assured that they will, when they have retired to private life, support civil society in every point of view. As the worthy men who stepped forward in support of the happiness of their country and the support of the Constitution of the Federal Government are to deposit their arms in this town to-morrow, the commanding officers of the regiments composing the brigade will see that fair inventories of every article are made to Mr. Samuel Riddle, brigade quartermaster, who is to give receipts for such delivery. And the quartermaster of the brigade is to detain a sufficient number of wagons to transport the arms to the place pointed out in the orders of the commander-in-chief of the 17th ult. The officers commanding the several corps will meet tomorrow morning to certify to the men as to their time of service and the balance due and to become due, agreeable to General Irvine's orders of the 30th of November.

By order of   GEN. CHAMBERS.
WILLIAM ROSS, *Adjutant.*

The company of Carlisle infantry was mustered out of service and arrived at home December 5, 1794. Thus ended the famous "Whiskey Insurrection of 1794."

The following account of Washington's visit is from a recent account published by George R. Prowell in the *Gettysburg Compiler:*

"Much has been written that is inaccurate concerning the visit of Gen. Washington to western Pennsylvania for the purpose of quelling the so-called Whisky Insurrection in that section of our State in 1794. An original record of the facts and incidents of that famous trip having lately come into my possession, and in a condensed form, I feel a pleasure in hereby furnishing them to the readers of the *Compiler.*

"President Washington, accompanied by a portion of his cabinet, left Philadelphia, then the capital of the United States, for the west via Reading, on Wednesday, October 1, 1794. He reached Harrisburg on the afternoon of Friday, October 3, when he was presented with an address by the burgesses, to which he replied the next morning. He reached Carlisle at 12 o'clock, noon, October 4. The town was the place of rendezvous for the Pennsylvania and New Jersey troops, and he remained in Carlisle from Saturday, October 4, to Saturday, October 11, reviewing the troops. On the last named date he left for the West, dined at Shippensburg and reached Chambersburg the same evening. At this place tradition says he stopped and spent Sunday with Dr. Robert Johnson, a surgeon of the Pennsylvania line during the Revolution. He passed through Chambersburg, and arrived at Williamsport, Maryland, on the evening of October 13, Monday. Early the next morning he set out for Fort Cumberland, where he arrived on Thursday, October 16, and the next day reviewed the Virginia and Maryland troops under command of Gen. Lee.

"On Sunday, October 19, Gen. Washington arrived at Bedford, where he remained until Tuesday, October 21. The approach of the armed troops soon

---

*A village ten miles northwest of Chambersburg, where the troops were then encamped.

caused a cessation of hostilities. On the last named date he set out on his return, spending the night of Friday, October 24, at Shippensburg, and the following night (Saturday) with Gen. Michael Simpson, in Fairview Township, York County, who then owned the ferry across the river and what is now known as the "Haldeman property" below New Cumberland. At this place he is supposed to have spent a quiet Sunday, as he arrived in Philadelphia on the following Tuesday morning.

"One time in the history of this great man's life he crossed the southern border of Adams County. The facts of this trip I will be pleased to furnish at some future time, giving exact facts and data from original documents, which are the only true sources of history."

In the Northwestern Indian wars of 1790-94, under Gens. Harmar, St. Clair and Wayne, Cumberland County was represented by a number of daring men, though no companies were raised or called for in Pennsylvania except west of the Allegheny Mountains. Dr. William McCoskry, then of Carlisle but afterward of Detroit, served as surgeon in the expeditions of St. Clair and Wayne; and Robert McClellan, son of a pioneer in East Pennsborough, distinguished himself as a scout, winning the title "Fleet Ranger" by his exploits and daring.

In 1798, when a war with France was threatened, companies of militia were by order of Gov. Mifflin held in readiness for immediate service, and quite a speck of war cloud was visible above the horizon. Some of the people sympathized with the French, and affairs might have become very serious but for the accession of Napoleon Bonaparte to power in France, by which event the aspect was changed and France withdrew from her offensive attitude. To meet any emergency the Tenth Regiment of Pennsylvania troops was organized under Thomas L. More, of Philadelphia, as colonel, and William Henderson and George Stevenson, of Cumberland County as majors. These men had been active in the Revolution. Maj. Stevenson had command of the recruiting service in that portion of the State west of the Allegheny Mountains. Alexander McComb—afterward a major-general and noted in the war of 1812-15—was an ensign in this Tenth Regiment, and Hugh Brady, also a general afterward, was a lieutenant.

War of 1812-15.—Upon the call of the President for troops at the breaking out of the second war with Great Britian in June, 1812, Pennsylvania responded quickly, and Cumberland County hastened to furnish her quota of soldiers. There was little opposition to the war in the county, and four full companies were speedily mustered and equipped at Carlisle, generally for six months' service, ready to march wherever ordered.

Principal among these was the "Carlisle Light Infantry," which, as seen, took part in the campaign against the whisky insurrectionists in 1794. It was originally organized in 1784, by soldiers who had served in the Revolution, and after its service in the second war it continued to exist until some time in 1854. From its organization its commanders were Capts. Magaw, George Stevenson, Robert Miller, William Miller, William Alexander (who was captain when the second war began, and had been, since July 1, 1802, printer and editor of the Carlisle *Herald*, established that year), Lindsey, Thompson, Spottswood, Edward Armor (1823), George D. Foulke (1827), John McCartney (1829), William Sterrett Ramsey (1835), William Moudy (1839), Jacob Rehrar (1840), George Sanderson (1842) and Samuel Crop (from November 24, 1845, to 1854).

Two small companies of riflemen—one from Carlisle commanded by Capt. George Hendall, and the other from Mechanicsburg under Capt. Coover—were united into one company. George Hendall was chosen captain, and they went with the Light Infantry to the Niagara frontier in 1814. It is said of them: "Both companies participated in most of the battles and sorties of that hard fought campaign. In the battle of Chippewa they were a part of the detachment of 250 Pennsylvanians under the command of Col. Bull, of Perry County, who were sent with fifty or sixty regulars and 300 Indians, into the woods to strike the Chippewa Creek about a half mile above the British works. Here they were attacked by a party of 200 militia with some Indians, but so impetuous was the charge with which our troops met them that they were compelled to give way in every direction and were pursued with great slaughter up to the very guns of the fort. This little band of Pennsylvanians here found themselves forsaken by the Indians, and in the face of the enemy's main force and assailed by four companies on the left and flank. They were of course compelled to retire, but having gone about 300 yards they reformed and kept up a heavy fire for about ten minutes, when, being raked by a cannon on the right, outflanked and almost surrounded by the entire four companies now brought against them they were obliged to retreat. They had depended on and every moment expected a support from the main army, but as this was not given them in season they retired in good order and keeping up a fire upon their assailants. They had fought more than an hour, had chased their enemies a mile and a half, and when exhausted by their exertions and extreme heat they rejoined their regiment, which they met entering the field under Col. Fenton. They then re-entered the field and bore their part as if they had been fresh from their tents. Not more than twelve men (and these on account of extreme exhaustion) were absent from this second encounter. Eight of their men had been killed in the woods and the number of their wounded was in the usual proportion. One hundred and fifty of the enemy's militia and Indians were left dead on the field. Col. Bull was treacherously shot down by the enemy after his surrender, and Maj. Galloway and Capt. White were taken prisoners. These two officers on their return home were received by their former companions with great rejoicings. The time of enlistment for these companies was short, being not over six or nine months, but whether they continued during another term we are not informed."

Besides these Cumberland County troops there were other men from the county connected with the regular army on the same (Niagara) frontier. Among them were George McFeely and Willis D. Foulke. The former became a lieutenant-colonel in the Twenty-second United States Infantry, July 6, 1812, and colonel of the Twenty-fifth April 15, 1814. He had in the early part of 1812 been in charge of the recruiting service at the Carlisle Barracks. He left that place October 5, 1812, and proceeded to the Niagara frontier, with 200 men of the Twenty-second Regiment. With his men he was sent to the old Fort Niagara to relieve Col. Winder in the command of that station, arriving November 14. In the artillery duel with Fort George on the 21st the British had the worst of the game. May 27, 1813, Lieut. Col. Winfield Scott ("to whom he yielded precedence") invited him to lead the vanguard in the movement into Canada. Col. McFeely was second in command in that expedition and had about 650 men under him. They routed a superior force of the enemy and captured Fort George, and subsequently suffered greatly during the campaign. Lieut.-Col. McFeely was sent to Lake Champlain later, and in June, 1814, was promoted to colonel, to rank from April previous. Reported to Maj.-Gen. Jacob Brown on the Niagara frontier again, and joined his new regiment under Gen. Scott. Held several responsible commands until close of war. "He was an excellent disciplinarian, had his troops under admirable control, and was remarkable for his coolness under the enemy's fire and his patient hardihood under the severest sufferings."

The "Patriotic Blues" was another company, commanded by Capt. Jacob Squier; first lieutenant, Samuel McKeehan; second lieutenant, Frederick Fogle; and ensign, Stephen Kerr. The company was sent to Baltimore to assist in repelling the British attack upon that city, and was attached to the Forty-ninth Maryland Militia under Lieut. Col. Veazy. Took an important part in the actions of September 12-15, 1814, and on the 16th, danger being apparently over, left for home with the assurance that they had performed their duty honorably and well.

"There were other companies," says Dr. Wing, "which went to Baltimore from the eastern towns in the county, and from what is now Perry County. It is said that these were in the detachment which was sent to lie in ambush by the route on which the British troops were expected to advance on its way to Baltimore. As Gen. Ross, the commander of these troops, was riding by the spot where they were concealed, it is said that two sharpshooters raised their pieces and were about to fire. An order was given them to desist, but before one of them, whose name was Kirkpatrick, from over the mountains, could understand the order, he fired his gun and the British general fell. The result was that a tremendous volley was fired into the thicket where they were concealed; but confusion was thrown into the plans of the invading party by the loss of their commander, and the idea of occupying Baltimore was given up."

In order to protect Philadelphia from possible violence at the hands of an invading force, a large body of troops was massed at that point, and among them was a company known as the "Carlisle Guards," who marched under Capt. Joseph Halbert early in September, 1814, and were encamped on Bush Hill, near Philadelphia, for nearly a month, drilling, constructing intrenchments, etc. They saw no enemy, but were subjected to as strict dicipline as troops at the front. Capt. Halbert, on the 3d of August, 1811, had been commissioned by Gov. Snider, a major of the Second Battalion, Twelfth Regiment Pennsylvania Militia, in First Brigade, Second Division, including militia of Cumberland and Franklin Counties. His commission was for four years from that date.

THE MEXICAN WAR.

When the Mexican war broke out Carlisle Barracks was in command of Capt. J. M. Washington, Battery D, Fourth United States Artillery. This company of light artillery received recruits from various portions of the country, and finally left Carlisle for the seat of war June 23, 1846. The organization was as follows: Captain, J. M. Washington; first lieutenant, J. P. J. O'Brien; second lieutenant, Henry L. Whiting; acting assistant quartermaster, Thos. L. Brent; surgeon, C. M. Hitchcock.

The company did valiant service with Taylor's army in Mexico. At the battle of Buena Vista the battery was divided into sections, one of which, consisting of three guns, under charge of Lieut. O'Brien, was captured, but not till every man was shot down and every horse killed. Lieut. O'Brien was wounded, but continued steadfast at his post till the last. In this engagement the casualties to the section were as follows: Killed, privates, Edwin Holley, Green, Weakley, Rinks and Doughty. Wounded: first lieutenant, J. P. J. O'Brien; sergeant, Queen; lance sergeant, Pratt; privates, Hannams, Puffer, Beagle, Berrin, Floyd, Hannon, Baker, Brown, Birch, Butler, Clark and Robbins.

On the 18th of January, 1847, an election of officers for an independent company of volunteers occurred at Carlisle, resulting as follows: Captain, John F. Hunter; first lieutenant, Marshall Hannon; second lieutenant, Wm. H. Gray; third lieutenant, Geo. L. Reighter.

This company, organized by Capt. Hunter under what was known as "the ten regiments' bill," embraced recruits from Cumberland, Perry and Franklin Counties, and probably some from others. They were enlisted to serve during the war, and were rendezvoused at Carlisle Barracks. The company required sixty-six men, but left Carlisle with some forty-six, additions having been made to it *en route* for Mexico. It was known as Company G, Eleventh Infantry.

The following is the roster of enlisted men as it left Carlisle: first sergeant, E. G. Heck; second sergeant, Wm. Blaine; third sergeant, Alex. F. Meck; fourth sergeant, F. O. Baker; first corporal, S. W. Hannon; second corporal, Wm. Hipple; third corporal, Jacob Bender; fourth corporal, John Thompson; drummer, George King; fifer, Archibald Rowe; privates, Applegate, John Brannon, George Boyer, Samuel Baxter, Wm. Biceline, Crell, James Carey, Culp, Deung, John Evinger, Joseph Faust, James Gallagan, Graham, John Gill, Samuel Gnysinger, George Hikes, Higbee, Wm. Hudson, Leonard Hoffman, Wm. Hollinger, Hetrich Wm. James, Kunkle, Casper Kline, George Lamison, McCracken, Wm. Moore, McIntire, Wm. McDonald, Misinger, Samuel Peck, Lafayette Searcy, Amos Steffey, Scheime, Samuel Swigert, Stein, George Shatto, Emanuel Weirich, Lewis Weaver, Wilde, Samuel Zell.

This company was first under command of Capt. Hunter, but on reaching the field he was promoted to be major of the Eleventh Infantry, and Lewis Carr, of Philadelphia, was chosen captain. Lieut. Gray finally became commander of Capt. Waddel's company, Eleventh Infantry.

The company left Carlisle Barracks on Monday morning, March 29, 1847, for the field. Marching to town it was halted in front of the court house, where the men were addressed by L. G. Brandeberry, Esq., in a few appropriate and well-timed remarks. They were then presented, each with a new testament, by Mr. Samuel Ensminger, after which they marched to the cars to the tune of "The Girl I left Behind Me." Going by rail to Harrisburg, the company proceeded thence by canal-boat to Pittsburgh, whence it sailed by boat to New Orleans, and thence to the mouth of Rio Grande River via Brazos Island. After a time it sailed for Vera Cruz, but after eighteen days' detention on the Gulf, it was compelled to stop at Tampico, where it lost about one-third of its number by yellow fever and other forms of disease. The company, from no fault of its own, never reached Vera Cruz, and did not fight.

Other companies were organized in Cumberland County and their services tendered to the Government, but not accepted. In this list is found a company of young men organized, in May, 1847, with the following officers: Capt. R. M. Henderson; Lieuts. Hampton R. Lemer, Robert McCord.

In June, 1846, Capt. Samuel Crop tendered a company with full complement of men known as Carlisle Light Infantry.

Edward Watts, formerly a student of West Point, established a recruiting station at Winrot's Hotel (now Mansion House) for a company of infantry. This was in June, 1847.

Capt. R. C. Smead, Fourth United States Artillery, superintended recruiting service at the barracks during several months in 1847.

From the time Capt. Washington relinquished command of the barracks (June 23, 1846) George M. Sanno, barrack master, had charge of the public property until the return of Col. A. C. May, August 25, 1847.

CHAPTER VI.

MILITARY CONTINUED—CARLISLE BARRACKS—CUMBERLAND COUNTY IN THE WAR OF THE REBELLION.

IN 1777, by the aid of the Hessian prisoners captured by Gen. Washington at Trenton, New Jersey, certain buildings were erected in the edge of Carlisle, and known thereafter as "Carlisle Barracks." Of the buildings thus constructed, one, situated at the main entrance to the ground and known as the "Guard House" still remains. These buildings, increased as necessity demanded, were used for military purposes afterward till they were diverted to their present purpose for the Indian Industrial School. The officials who, from time to time were stationed at the Barracks, constituted an active element of Carlisle society, and subsequently figured conspicuously in the war of the Rebellion.

The following officers served as commanders of Carlisle Barracks from 1838 to the commencement of the Rebellion, the facts being obtained from the War Department at Washington:

Capt. E. V. Sumner, Capt. R. S. Dix, Second Lieut. A. J. Smith and First Lieut. R. H. West, First Dragoons; First Lieut. W. H. Saunders, Second Dragoons; Maj. C. Wharton, First Dragoons; Capt. J. M. Washington, First Lieut J. W. Phelps and Lieut. Col. M. M. Payne, Fourth Artillery; Capt. Chas. A. May and First Lieut. A. Pleasonton, Second Dragoons; First Lieut. R. C. W. Radford, First Dragoons; Lieut.-Col. P. St. G. Cooke and First Lieut. R. H. Anderson, Second Dragoons; Capt. A. J. Smith, First Dragoons; Capt. Chas. F. Ruff, Mounted Rifles; Col. E. A. Hitchcock, Capt. Geo. W. Patten, Capt. D. Davidson, Capt. C. S. Lovell, Capt. S. P. Heintzelman and Capt. H. W. Wessells, Second Infantry; Lieut.-Col. C. F. Smith and Col. E. B. Alexander, Tenth Infantry; Lieut.-Col. G. B. Crittenden and First Lieut. Julian May, R. M. Rifles; Capt. R. H. Anderson, Second Dragoons; First Lieut. D. H. Maury, R. M. Rifles; First Lieut. K. Garrard, Second Cavalry; First Lieut. Alfred Gibbs, R. M. Rifles; Maj. L. P. Graham, Second Dragoons.

Of the foregoing, it will be observed that Sumner, A. J. Smith, Pleasonton and Heintzelman were major-generals during the Rebellion, and held prominent positions in the Union Army; R. H. Anderson was a major-general in the Confederate service, and commanded a division of Hill's Corps at the Battle of Gettysburg.

Cumberland County, like other portions of the Cumberland Valley and the Keystone State, always responded to any call which sought to defend the Nation against any foes, external or internal. When the wires announced that a portion of this country had raised the puny arm of revolt, and that the National flag had been insulted by those whom it had previously protected and honored, its citizens were fired with indignation, and responded, with patriotic alacrity, to the call of President Lincoln, but recently installed as the legally elected President of this great commonwealth, for 75,000 men to protect public property and maintain the supremacy of the Federal Union. The firing on Fort Sumter in April, 1861, and the surrender of Gen. Anderson to overwhelming forces of secessionists, stirred the patriotic heart of the country. In response to the President's call for 75,000 men to serve for three months, some three companies proffered their services within a week from the issuing of the proclamation. One of these companies, with 100 brave men, started from Carlisle Saturday, April 13, and reached Harrisburg, the place of rendezvous, to be mustered, on the 23d instant. Three other companies in Carlisle and one in Mechanicsburg were awaiting orders to march to the front in a short time. By the 9th of June, they were mustered into reserve regiments, and shortly participated in the severest engagements of that early period of the Rebellion.

Sumner Rifles.—The first company was the Sumner Rifles with the following organization: Captain, Christian Kuhns; first lieutenant, Augustus Zug; second lieutenant, John B. Alexander; sergeants, John S. Lyne, Barnet Shafer, John W. Keeney and John S. Low; corporals, Charles F. Sanno, Charles H. Foulk, Thomas D. Caldwell and John T. Sheaffer. It became Company C of the Ninth Regiment of Pennsylvania Volunteers, under the command of Col. Henry C. Longnecker, of Allentown.

Eleven days after its muster into service, viz., May 4, this regiment was sent for drill purposes to West Chester, where it remained in Camp Wayne till the 26th, when it was transferred to Wilmington, Del., to aid the loyal people of that State. Returning by way of Carlisle June 6, it was attached at Chambersburg to the Fourth Brigade of First Division, under Col. Dixon S. Miles. It performed faithful duty in West Virginia, in the region of Martinsburg, Falling Waters and Williamsport, till July 21, when its term of service having almost expired, it returned to Harrisburg to be mustered out. Many of its men re-entered the service for a longer period.

A second company of three months' men was that enlisted at Mechanicsburg with the following organization: Captain, Jacob Dorsheimer; first lieutenant, David H. Kimmell; second lieutenant, Isaac B. Kauffman; sergeants, George M. Parsons, Benjamin Dull, Samuel F. Swartz and David R. Mell; corporals, Theophilus Mountz, Wm. H. Crandall, John G. Bobb, and Levi M. Coover. It was designated Company C, and was attached to the Sixteenth Regiment, under Col. Thomas A. Zeigle of York. It also belonged to the Fourth Brigade under Col. Miles, and had the same experiences as the company from Carlisle. When its term of service had expired, it was the first company from the Keystone State to re-enlist.

RESERVE REGIMENTS.

First Reserve. On the 20th of April, 1861, Gov. And. G. Curtin recommended to the Special Legislature of Pennsylvania, "the immediate organization, disciplining and arming of at least fifteen regiments of cavalry and infantry, exclusive of those called into the service of the United States." In harmony with this suggestion, a law was passed, authorizing a body of soldiers known as the "Reserve Volunteers Corps of the Commonwealth," to consist of thirteen regiments of infantry and one each of cavalry and artillery, and to be mustered for three years or during the war, for State or National service.

Under this call, the Carlisle Light Infantry, in existence since 1784, was reorganized and mustered in June 8, 1861, with the following commissioned and non-commissioned officers: Captain, Robert McCartney; first lieutenant, Joseph Stuart; second lieutenant, Thomas P. Dwynn; sergeants, John A. Waggoner, Andrew J. Reighter, Robert McManus and Abram Heiser; corporals, John A. Blair, William Corbett, Frederick Deemer, Frederick K. Morrison and Daniel Askew.

HISTORY OF CUMBERLAND COUNTY.   111

Capt. McCartney resigning in August, 1861, his position was taken in October following by Lieut. Dwynn, who was killed at South Mountain September 14, 1862. His successor was F. B. McManus, who retained command till the company was mustered out, June 13, 1864. Lieut. Joseph Stuart was killed at Gaines' Mill, June 27, 1862, and was succeeded by John A. Crowl, who was promoted from the ranks through the intermediate grades.

The Carlisle Guards, a second organization, was mustered June 10, with the following officers: Captain, Lemuel Todd; first lieutenant, George W. Cropp; second lieutenant, Isaiah H. Graham; sergeants, Wm. B. Wolf, James Broderick, Robert B. Smiley, George A. Keller; corporals, T. B. Kauffman, Isaac Gorgas, J. T. Bailey and Levi H. Mullen.

These companies became Companies H and I respectively, of the Thirtieth Regiment, under the command of E. Biddle Roberts, colonel; H. M. McIntyre, lieutenant-colonel, and Lemuel Todd, major. The promotion of Capt. Todd to the majorship gave the position of captain to George W. Cropp. The place was subsequently filled, also, by T. B. Kauffman and Isaiah Graham. After the battle of Bull Run, the Thirtieth Regiment was ordered to Washington, but stopping at Annapolis, it performed such efficient service in guarding railroad communication and preventing the smuggling of supplies into the South, as to elicit special mention by Gen. John A. Dix. On August 30, the regiment was sent, via Washington, to Tennallytown, Md., where it united with other reserves under Gen. McCall. During the autumn and winter of 1861, it engaged in the Virginia campaign, near Dranesville, Manassas Junction and Fredericksburg. In the engagements at Mechanicsville and Gaines' Mill, during the Peninsular campaign of 1862, the command suffered heavily, losing some fourteen killed and about fifty wounded. Among the former was Lieut. Stuart of Company H. Subsequently, at Centreville and South Mountain, the regiment met its former foes and achieved new successes.

The same year it engaged in the severely contested battles of Antietam and Fredericksburg, and the following year was a part of the grand army which, at Gettysburg, turned the fate of the Confederacy July 1-3, 1863. Its services continued with the Army of the Potomac through the campaign of 1863 and early 1864 till June 13, when it was mustered out at Philadelphia. Its muster-rolls, originally, had 1,084 men. Of this number, 139 were lost by sickness and death on the field of battle, 233 were wounded, 258 were discharged for disability, and 148 re-enlisted as veterans.

Seventh Reserve.—A company known as the Carlisle Fencibles, was ready for service in April, 1861. With a beautiful satin flag, bearing the motto, "May God Defend the Right," the gift of Mrs. Samuel Alexander, granddaughter of Col. Ephraim Blaine, the company left Carlisle, on June 6, for Westchester, its organization consisting of the following officers: Captain, Robert M. Henderson; first lieutenant, James S. Colwell; second lieutenant, Erkwries Beatty; orderly sergeant, John D. Adair.

Capt. Henderson, wounded both at Charles City Cross Roads and Bull Run, was promoted to lieutenant-colonel, July 4, 1862, his position being filled by Lieut. J. S. Colwell. The latter being killed at Antietam, September 17, 1862, Lieut. Beatty became captain, Samuel V. Ruby and D. W. Burkholder became first and second lieutenants, respectively.

Almost simultaneous with the organization of this company, one was raised at Mechanicsburg, with Joseph Totten as captain; Jacob T. Zug, as first and Geo. W. Comfort as second lieutenant, and John W. Cook as first sergeant Capt. Totten was promoted to lieutenant-colonel soon after the departure of the company, and was followed by Henry I. Zinn, who, resigning November 30, was succeeded by Samuel King. The latter remained with the company till it was mustered out June 16, 1864. Jacob Zug lost an arm by a wound December 30, 1862, when he resigned as first lieutenant and was followed by Jacob Heffeltinger. George W. Comfort was killed at Fredericksburg, December 13, 1862.

These companies, on their arrival at Camp Wayne, became Companies A and H of the Seventh Regiment of Reserves, whose officers were: Colonel Elisha B. Harvey, of Wilkes Barre; lieutenant-colonel, Joseph Totten; major, Chauncey A. Lyman, of Lock Haven. The regiment was ordered to report to Washington, D. C., where on the 27th of July, it was mustered into the United States Service, and finally attached to the Brigade of Reserves under command of Gen. George G. Meade. Having spent the autumn and winter in northern Virginia, the regiment was given active service in the Peninsular campaign. At Gaines' Mill it was called upon to meet an impetuous attack on Butterfield's artillery. Though met by overwhelming numbers it saved the caissons, Capt. King, however, being taken prisoner with twenty of his men. The loss of the regiment was large, embracing about one-half of its effective force. In the succeeding seven days' fighting, June 26 to July 2, it was continually occupying posts of danger and death, the muster revealing the fact that the loss was 301, embracing, among the wounded, Capt. Henderson and Lieuts. Zug and Beatty, and that only about 200 of the men who started on the campaign were ready for duty. Promotions changed the stations of officers, and Capt. Henderson became lieutenant-colonel.

In August following this brigade was sent to the Rappahannock, and joined to the Army of Northern Virginia, commanded by Gen. Pope. At Groveton, after two days' severe skirmishing, the regiment was engaged in a spirited battle, with heavy loss and the wounding of Col. Henderson. It followed the Army of the Potomac again, under command of Gen. McClellan, the successor of Pope, to Washington; thence through western Maryland to South Mountain and Antietam. At the latter place (September 17), the Seventh took an important part, but suffered heavily in killed and wounded. The explosion of a shell either killed or wounded mortally, Capt. Colwell and Privates John Gallio, Leo Faller, David Spahr and Wm. Culp of Company A.

A few months later, viz., December 12, it participated in Gen. Burnside's unsuccessful attack upon the Rebels at Fredericksburg. Crossing the river in the face of the enemy, it was subjected to a galling fire from Stuart's battery; but moving up the height, leaping ditches, it penetrated Longstreet's lines, capturing and sending back more than 100 prisoners. Though finally repulsed, the captures by soldiers of Company A alone embraced the swords of three rebel captains and the battle-flag of a Georgia regiment. Corp. Cart was given a medal for capturing the colors. The losses to the regiment were heavy, embracing 6 killed, 72 wounded and 22 missing. After this sanguinary battle the regiment was called to perform duty around Washington, where it remained till the next spring, when it moved out on the Campaign to Richmond. In the Wilderness, near Chancellorsville, 272 officers and men, pursuing the enemy, were captured on the 2d of May, 1863. The soldiers were taken to Southern prisons, notably Andersonville and Florence, where many of them died under most pitiable circumstances. The officers, taken to Macon, were subsequently exposed to the fire of Federal guns at Charleston, to defend the city against attack. A fragment of the regiment not captured, increased by recruits furnished by Capt. King of Company H, participated in the Campaign against Richmond in 1864. At the expiration of its service it was mustered out June 16, 1864 at Philadelphia.

HISTORY OF CUMBERLAND COUNTY. 115

CAVALRY SERVICE.

In 1861, Cumberland County furnished two companies of cavalry at a time when this branch of the service was fully appreciated. One of these was known as Big Spring Adamantine Guards, and had had an organized existence for fifty years. It embraced 108 men, under command of Capt. S. Woodburn. After a year's service he was mustered out by special order August 28, 1862, when his position was filled by Wm. E. Miller, promoted from the second lieutenancy. The first lieutenants in order were Wm. Baughman and E. L. Cauffman. The second lieutenants in succession were Wm. E. Miller, Louis R. Stille and Elwood Davis. It became a part of the Third Cavalry under command for a time of Col. Wm. H. Young. Under the rigid discipline of Col. W. W. Averill, at Washington, it became highly efficient, and engaged in the movement southward in March, 1862, participating in the siege of Yorktown. With Averill it participated in the severe campaigns of McClellan near Richmond, at Harrison's Landing, and during the Maryland invasion at Antietam.

When Col. Averill was promoted to the rank of brigadier-general, the regiment was commanded (November, 1862) by Col. J. B. McIntosh, its operations being in Virginia mainly during the remainder of the year. When its term of service expired, a veteran battalion was formed, which participated with the Army of the Potomac in its active operations preceding, during and subsequent to the Battle of Gettysburg, where the regiment did such valiant service against Stuart's cavalry.

The second company recruited under authority of the War Department by Wm. B. Sipes, of Philadelphia, was formed in small part from Fayette, but mainly from Cumberland County. It was joined to the Seventh Cavalry with Geo. C. Wyncoop as colonel and Wm. B. Sipes as lieutenant-colonel. Of this company, David T. May, of West Fairview, was the first captain. After his death at Chickamauga, September 21, 1863, James G. Taylor became captain. His death ensuing, Wm. H. Collins assumed the place. Joseph G. Vale, of Carlisle, was first lieutenant, but in August, 1862, he was promoted captain of Company M of same regiment. This regiment was sent west to the Department of the Cumberland, where, in 1862-63, it did efficient service. It participated in the Chickamauga battle, in which Lieut. Vale was wounded. In 1864 most of the men re-enlisted at Huntsville, Ala. After various services in Georgia and other States, it was mustered out at Macon, Ga., August 13, 1865.

In 1862, two companies of cavalry were authorized by the Secretary of War to be organized for three years' service. They were known as H and I of the Ninth Pennsylvania Cavalry. Company H was recruited by David H. Kimmel, afterward promoted (May 22, 1863) to be major. Wm. H. Shriver, previously a first lieutenant in Company I succeeded him for half a year, when his resignation gave the position to Thomas W. Jordan. Company I was under the command of Capt. H. W. McCullough, who was killed at Moore's Hill, Ky., June 6, 1862, and was succeeded by Wm. H. Longsdorf, who, after two years of service, became major, his former position falling to O. B. McKnight.

The regiment bore the name of "Lochiel Cavalry," and was commanded successively by Edward C. Williams, Thomas C. James and Thomas J. Jordan. Its service was, during the first two years, mainly in Kentucky and Tennessee, but subsequently with Sherman in his "march to the sea."

The Anderson Troop was an independent company which was recruited at Carlisle Barracks during the closing part of 1861, from various parts of the United States. In it were some young men from Cumberland County. Of this number, Edward B. Inhoff, of Carlisle, was a representative, being appointed quartermaster-sergeant of the regiment. It operated in Kentucky and Tennessee, with Gens. Buell and Rosecrans, until by the latter it was ordered mustered out of service March 24, 1863.

NINE MONTHS' MEN—ONE HUNDRED AND THIRTIETH REGIMENT.

The notion was still entertained in 1862 that the war would not continue much longer, and that enlistments for a period of nine months would be sufficient. The One Hundred and Thirtieth Regiment, with five full companies and a part of another from Cumberland County, was organized on this supposition. In this regiment, organized August 17, 1862, were the following field officers: Colonel, Henry I. Zinn, Mechanicsburg; lieutenant-colonel, Levi Maish, York County; major, John Lee, Cumberland County.

Company A was made up at Carlisle early in the summer of 1862, and selected Wm. R. Porter as captain, which position he held during his term of service. First lieutenant was John R. Turner, who was subsequently chosen quartermaster of the regiment; second lieutenant, John Hays, finally becoming first lieutenant and then regimental adjutant (February 18, 1863). John O. Halbert was, at first, its orderly sergeant and then second lieutenant. He was succeeded by Alphonso B. Beissel March 1, 1863.

Company D, recruited in and near Shippensburg, had as officers: Captain, James Kelso; first lieutenant, Samuel Patchell; and second lieutenant, Daniel A. Harris.

Company E was formed at Newville with Wm. Laughlin as captain; Joshua W. Sharp, first lieutenant; and Henry Clay Marshall, second lieutenant. Capt. Laughlin was killed at Fredericksburg, December 13, 1862, and Lieut. Sharp succeeded him. He was succeeded as first lieutenant by John P. Wagner. Henry Clay Marshall was appointed regimental adjutant August 17, 1862. First Sergt. Joseph A. Ege was promoted to be second lieutenant in place of Wagner.

Company F, from Mechanicsburg, composed largely of three months' men, had the following organization: Henry I. Zinn, captain; John B. Zinn, first lieutenant; W. A. Givler, second lieutenant; Levi M. Haverstick, first sergeant. When Capt. Zinn was appointed colonel, August 17, Lieut. Zinn was promoted to be captain; resigning this place, March 19, 1863, he was succeeded by Haverstick. Michael W. French rose from a sergeancy to first lieutenancy. William A. Givler was killed at Antietam, and was succeeded by M. W. French, and he by Wm. E. Zinn.

Company G was formed in and around Carlisle, with John Lee, captain; John S. Lyne, first lieutenant; Thomas D. Caldwell, second lieutenant. Lee was promoted to major; but after his resignation, February 5, 1863, was succeeded by John S. Low.

Company H was secured by Capt. John C. Hoffaker, mainly at New Cumberland and West Fairview. The first lieutenant was George C. Marshall, and John K. McGann, second lieutenant. Capt. Hoffaker, resigning February 13, 1863, the lieutenants were regularly promoted, and Sergt. Chas. A. Hood became second lieutenant.

The day after the organization of the regiment it was sent to Washington, where it was assigned to French's division of Sumner's corps. Its first active service was in the battle of Antietam, where it lost forty killed and 256 wounded. Though new and undisciplined, its brave conduct elicited the strong commendation of Gen. French, its division commander. After camping for a time at Harper's Ferry, it moved to Fredericksburg, and engaged in that sanguinary struggle, losing sixty-two killed or wounded, a large per cent of its depleted ranks. Among the killed were Col. Zinn and Capt. Laughlin. Lieut. Haverstick was again wounded. Its next service was in the campaign around Chancellorsville, where Lieut.-Col. Maish and Lieut. John Hays were wounded. Its term of enlistment having expired, the regiment was mustered out at Harrisburg on the 21st of May, and its citizen-soldiers were welcomed home with great demonstration of feeling.

THREE YEARS' MEN.

The three months' men, already spoken of, who had served under Capts. Christian Kuhns and Jacob Dorsheimer, re-enlisted and were mustered for three years' service. Christian Kuhns was captain of the reorganized company, and remained with it till April 2, 1863, when he was succeeded by First Lieut. James Noble. The company was known as Company A, of the Eleventh Regiment, and served as an integral part of the Army of the Potomac in the Virginia campaigns. The second company, known as Company A, One Hundred and Seventh Regiment, of which Thomas A. Zeigle, of York, was colonel, was presided over by Capt. Dorsheimer for about a year, when he resigned, and was succeeded by Theodore K. Scheffer and Samuel Lyon. The regiment served also with the Army of the Potomac at Antietam, Chancellorsville, Gettysburg, and in the usual minor contests. These two Cumberland County companies, faithful from the beginning to the close of the war, having participated in the grand review at Washington May 23, 1865, were mustered out of service with richly earned honors.

A number of men went from the county into Company A, of the One Hundred and First Regiment, commanded at first by Capt. David M. Armour, and afterward by James Sheafer. Active service was seen in North Carolina, where some of the men were captured and compelled to undergo the horrors of Andersonville.

In 1861 a part of a company was enlisted in Cumberland County, and joined at Harrisburg with men from Cameron County, forming Company G, of the Eighty-fourth Regiment. The company officers consisted of Capt. Merrick Housler, First Lieut. James W. Ingram and Second Lieut. Daniel W. Taggart. It operated in West Virginia during the early part of 1862, but participated subsequently at Bull Run (second battle), Chancellorsville, Gettysburg, Wilderness and siege of Petersburg.

MILITIA OF 1862.

The terrible defeat of the Union Army at the second battle of Bull Run afforded grave apprehensions of the devastation of southern Pennsylvania by Lee's soldiers. Gov. Curtin summoned 50,000, to be mustered at Harrisburg at once, to serve as protectors for the border. Everywhere did the people respond cheerfully to the call. Two columns, one of 15,000 at Hagerstown, and another of 25,000 ready to march from Harrisburg, if needed, attested the patriotic spirit of the Keystone State. Of these troops, so quick to respond, Cumberland County furnished one regiment, which was held in service only two weeks, viz., September 11 to 25. Its officers consisted of Col. Henry McCormick, Lieut.-Col. Robt. A. Lamberton and Maj. Thos. B. Bryson. The alacrity with which these troops appeared on the scene of action called forth warm praise from both Gen. McClellan and the governor of Maryland.

COMPANIES OF 1863.

Toward the close of 1862, some companies were gathered in the county, but did not get into actual service till the early part of 1863. One of these was organized for nine months' service, with the following officers: Captain, Martin G. Hall; first lieutenant, Henry S. Crider; second lieutenant, Patrick G. McCoy. It became Company F, of the One Hundred Fifty-eighth Regiment, under Col. David B. McKibben, and with its regiment served in North Carolina, principally assisting in the recovery of a Union garrison at Washington from the clutches of Gen Hill; afterward it served with Gen. Meade in in the Army of the Potomac till Lee was driven across into Virginia. It was mustered out of service at Chambersburg August 12, 1863.

Company F, of the One Hundred and Sixty-second Regiment, Seventeenth Cavalry, was raised by Capt. Charles Lee, for three years. The regiment, colonels, Josiah H. Kellogg and James Q. Anderson, was in Devin's (Iron) Brigade, and served with Hooker at Chancellorsville, Buford at Gettysburg, in eastern Virginia next year, with Sheridan in the Shenandoah Valley, and with Army of Potomac when peace was declared.

Company B, of the One Hundred and Sixty-fifth Regiment of drafted militia, was formed in the eastern part of the county, with Abraham J. Rupp as captain, and Henry Lee as first lieutenant. It served from November, 1862, till it was mustered out July 28, 1863. There were also some men in the Eighteenth Cavalry (One Hundred and Sixty-fifth Regiment, Pennsylvania), whose record can not be given.

COMPANIES OF 1864.

Portions of the Two Hundredth and Two Hundred and First Regiments were recruited from Cumberland County, one from the towns of West Fairview and New Cumberland. Company K, of the Two Hundred and First Regiment was mustered into service, for one year, at Harrisburg, August 29, 1864. Its officers were: Captain, Alexander C. Landis; first lieutenant, Alexander Stewart; second lieutenant, John H. Snow; sergeants, Daniel F. Rohrer, John A. Witmer, S. G. Glauser, Henry G. Walters and Richard G. Moore; corporals, George Shields, Hiram C. Senseny, W. A. Clugh, Theo. Artz, Wm. H. Tritt J. O. M. Butts, Geo. McCormick and Thos. V. Baker; musicians, Wm. W. Snyder, Jos. H. Snyder, Henry Dumbaugh and Henry Graves. This company was formed from Shippensburg and vicinity. The two regiments operated largely in eastern Virginia, and performed meritorious service.

Companies G. H and part of Company D, of the One Hundred and Second Regiment were formed from the county, and were commanded, respectively, by Capts. David Gochenauer, John P. Wagner and S. C. Powell. The regiment guarded the Manassas Gap Railroad, to keep it open for carrying army supplies.

Companies A and F, of the Two Hundred and Ninth Regiment, were mustered September 16, 1864, under Capts. John B. Landis and Henry Lee. Its colonel, Tobias B. Kauffman, Capt. Lee and Lieut. Hendricks, with nineteen men, were captured November 17, while defending the picket line, and were held prisoners till the close of the war. The regiment remained in active service till the close of the Rebellion by Lee's surrender.

BUSINESS MEN IN THE ARMY.

The public men of the county took an active part in support of the Government during the war. Particularly was this true of the legal profession. Says Dr. Wing, in his History of Cumberland County, p. 137: "At the very first call, when the example of prominent men was of peculiar importance, a large number of these gentlemen promptly gave in their names and entered in most instances as privates until they were promoted to office. Ignorant as they all were of military drill, they at once submitted to the instruction of a sergeant at Carlisle Barracks, and as soon as possible left their pleasant homes for the severities of an ill-supplied and perilous service. In most cases this was at the sacrifice of health and sometimes of life, and they were intelligent enough to know beforehand what these sacrifices were likely to be. They were not alone, for they were accompanied by many in every walk of life. Among them were R. M. Henderson, John Lee, Lemuel Todd, A. Brady Sharpe, Christian P. Humrich, C. McGlaughlin, George S. Emig, C. P. Cornman, Joseph G. Vale, Wm. E. Miller, J. Brown Parker, Wm. M. Penrose, Joseph S. Colwell, S. V. Ruby, Wm. D. Halbert, D. N. Nevin, J. B. Landis, John Hays and J. M. Weakley. These took their places, not in some single company or regiment to which special eclat might be awarded, but wherever their lot happened to fall. As, however, the companies belonging to the One Hundred and Thirtieth were in process of formation at that time, most of them were connected with that regiment."

REPRESENTATIVES IN REGULAR ARMY.

Thus far the records have shown the work of men in volunteer service. Cumberland County had an honorable representation in the regular army, among whom we can specify the following only briefly:

Samuel Sturgis, born at Shippensburg in 1822, and graduated at West Point, served through the Mexican war with distinction, gave valuable aid afterward in suppressing hostile Indians, and with increasing and deserved promotions to the rank of brigadier-general, aided greatly in quelling the great Rebellion.

Washington L. Elliott, whose father, Com. Jesse D. Elliott, was second in command at the naval battle at Lake Erie September 10, 1813, was born at Carlisle in 1825. After three years' study in Dickinson College, he graduated at West Point in 1844. With the rank of second lieutenant he served efficiently in the Mexican war, and among the Indians with the rank of first lieutenant and captain. He served during the late Rebellion, with the ranks of major, colonel and brigadier-general, in both the Eastern and Western Armies. In all the stations to which he was assigned, he demonstrated himself to be an able and trustworthy commander.

John R. Smead was born in 1830 and graduated from West Point in 1851. When the war of the Rebellion began he was employed with Prof. Bache on the coast survey. He entered the artillery service, and as captain of a battery in the Fifth Artillery, he participated in the campaign around Richmond and in the second battle of Bull Run. At the latter place he was struck and killed by a ten-pound cannon ball, August 31, 1862.

Alexander Piper, graduate of West Point in 1851, and an associate of Smead, served through the Rebellion in various responsible positions, having attained the rank of captain and become Smead's successor after the battle of Bull Run. He died October 30, 1876.

LEE'S INVASION IN 1863.

The most exciting period of the war to the Cumberland Valley was that connected with the invasion of 1863. The devastating and demoralizing features of war were brought home to the citizen engaged in the lawful pursuits of every-day life. The advance of the enemy to the Potomac in the region of Williamsport or Harper's Ferry was always a signal for a stampede along the valley in the direction of Harrisburg. Money and other valuables were removed, horses and cattle were driven out of the country for their own safety and to prevent giving aid to the Rebels, and a general restlessness and anxiety took possession of the people. When in May, 1863, after the defeat of Hooker's army at Chancellorsville, Gen. R. E. Lee made requisition on the Confederate commissary department for rations for his hungry men, he was answered, "If the General wants provisions, let him go and look for them in Pennsylvania." He came. On the 20th of June, Gen. Ewell's corps began to cross the Potomac at Williamsport and commenced to move in the direction of Harrisburg. Chambersburg was reached by a portion of Ewell's corps on the 23d, Gen. R. S. Ewell himself arriving on the 24th.

Gradually the troops marched along the valley, occupying Shippensburg on the 25th, and reaching Carlisle on Saturday, the 27th.

When the alarm of the Rebel approach was first sounded, companies of civilians were organized by Capts. Martin Kuhn, John S. Low, A. Brady Sharpe, David Block and Robert Smiley. These companies embraced the best elements of the community, the pastors of the Episcopal and the Reformed Churches entering as privates. In connection with these militia companies, Capt. W. H. Boyd, First New York Cavalry, with 200 of his men, performed picket duty.

As Gen. A. G. Jenkins' advance of 400 cavalry came toward town, these companies fell back. Jenkins was met en route by Col. William M. Penrose and Robert Allison, assistant burgess, and was requested to make no dash upon the town lest a panic among the women and children might ensue. He entered in good order, his men being on the alert against surprise. He demanded of the place supplies for men and horses. The citizens responded generously, and the provisions were stored in the stalls of the market house. A good supply of corn was also obtained from the crib of John Noble.

In the afternoon of the same day (Saturday), Rodes' and Johnson's divisions of Ewell's corps arrived, Early's division having crossed the mountains, via Fayetteville, to York. The band at the head of the column played "Dixie," the men conducting themselves with much decorum notwithstanding their ragged condition. Gen. Ewell established his headquarters in the barracks, he occupying the dwelling of Capt. Hastings, while his staff took the adjacent buildings. The commanding general was well acquainted with the barracks and the town, having been stationed there in former years. In consequence of this acquaintanceship, he spared the public buildings from being burned on the eve of his departure.

He at once made a public demand for 1,500 barrels of flour, four cases of surgical instruments, quinine, chloroform and other medical supplies. They could not be furnished, however. Strict orders were issued against the selling of intoxicating drinks to soldiers, and the pillaging of private property by them.

Sunday and Monday were dreary days for the town. All communication with the loyal world was cut off. On the Lord's day, services were conducted at several of the churches by their own pastors. At the same time the chaplains of rebel regiments encamped in the college campus, and at the garrison conducted services for their troops with great fervor. Guards were stationed at the street corners, to preserve order and to receive any complaints made by citizens. Some spirited discussions between soldiers and citizens on moral and political questions were had, but with more courtesy and good feeling than generally characterize such controversies. All conversation with Southern officers and soldiers led the people to believe that their movement was directed toward Harrisburg and Philadelphia. On Monday evening, however, Johnson's division, encamped at McAlister's Run, began to move in the direction of Stoughstown, Shippensburg and Fayetteville, the march being characterized by a want of dicipline and the commission of heinous outrages upon unoffending people.

As early as 3 o'clock of Tuesday morning, the remaining troops from the college campus and the barracks, accompanied by Gen. Ewell, began to move along the pike in the direction of Mount Holly. The town was deserted by rebel forces except 200 cavalry, who continued till evening doing provost duty, when they also left. The pillaging around the barracks and the destruction of public and private property were performed by dissolute characters, some of whom proved to be deserters that afterward enlisted in the Union service. It has been said the town was largely deserted by rebel forces. This needs a little modification. About the time the people began to rejoice over the disappearance of the rebel forces, a body of cavalry, under command of Col. Cochran and numbering about 400, made its appearance at the gas works on the Dillstown road, and took possession of the streets. These men, intoxicated against orders, became unmanagable, and their stay in the town made citizens restless. Thus closes the condition of affairs in Carlisle Tuesday, June 30.

The incidents of the following day are so graphically and carefully presented by Dr. Wing that we give his account entire:

"Early on Wednesday morning, the town was gladdened by the return of Capt. Boyd with his 200 men of the First New York Cavalry. They had been at the extreme eastern part of the county, in the neighborhood of Fort Washington, and had had, on Sunday evening, a slight artillery skirmish at Oyster's Point, about three miles west of Harrisburg, with a small party of Gen. Jenkins' men. That general had spent a night at Mechanicsburg, and on Sunday advanced with a few men to reconnoitre the bridge over the Susquehanna; but on seeing the preparations there, had deemed it prudent to retire. This was the farthest point in the direction of Harrisburg to which the invading troops ventured to proceed. On hearing the rapid progress of the Union Army under Gen. Meade, in his rear, Gen. Lee at once perceived that he could not safely advance with such a force between him and the base of his operations, and that a great battle was inevitable in the neighborhood of Gettysburg. Both armies had mustered in unexpected strength and discipline, and neither could afford to dispense with any of its forces. Every regiment was called in, and summoned in haste to the expected field of conflict. But there were a few regiments in both armies near the river, to which the summons could not be sent in time, and which, therefore, were unaware of the movements of the main bodies. Early in the afternoon, Gen. W. F. (Baldy) Smith, who had taken command in this valley, reached town. There were then under him, two Philadelphia regiments, one militia battery from the same city, parts of two New York regiments, and a company of regular cavalry from Carlisle Barracks. While he was selecting a suitable place for his artillery, a body of rebel troops made its appearance near the east end of Main Street, at the junction of the Trindle Springs and York roads. One or two rebel horsemen rode nearly to the center of the town, but hastily returned to their companions, who sat in their saddles and gazed up the street at the Union infantry. A call to arms was at once made, and the companies which had been disbanded during the occupation of the town came together, and with other citizens armed themselves as best they could, and formed a line of skirmishers along the Letort. They kept up a desultory fire upon the advanced portion of the enemy and prevented them from penetrating our lines. Of course such an opposition was soon driven in and silenced; but for a while its true character could not be known. It was not long before the whizzing and explosions of shells in the air over and within the town, announced that a formidable en-

emy was at hand. No warning of this had been given, and it was soon accompanied by grape and canister, raking the principal streets and the central square.

"As twilight set in, a flag of truce was forwarded to Gen. Smith, informing him that Gen. Fitzhugh Lee, with a force of 3,000 cavalry, was ready for an assault and demanded an immediate and unconditional surrender. The offer was promptly declined, and was followed by the threat that the shelling of the town would be at once resumed. 'Shell away!' replied Gen. Smith; and scarcely had the bearer of the flag left, before a much fiercer bombardment commenced. And now began a general flight of the inhabitants into the country, into cellars, and behind anything which was strong enough to afford hope of protection. A stream of women and children and infirm people on foot was seen, with outcries and terrified countenances in every direction. Some of these fell down breathless or seriously injured by some accident, and lay in the barns or by the fences through the ensuing night. To add terror to the scene, the sky was lighted up by the flames of a wood-yard in the vicinity of the rebel encampment, and about 10 o'clock the barracks and the garrison were burned and added their lurid glare to the brightness. In the middle of the night there was another pause in the firing, and another call for a surrender was made, to which a rather uncourteous reply was made by Gen. Smith, and the shelling proceeded, but with diminished power and frequency. It is supposed that ammunition had become precious in the hostile camp."

Gen. Fitzhugh Lee, now governor of Virginia, in a letter to the writer under date of May 20, 1886, says of the attack on Carlisle: "On July 1, 1863, I was ordered to attack and occupy the place, by Gen. J. E. B. Stuart, commanding cavalry corps of the Confederate Army, and did attack it on my arrival late that evening—night put a stop to the fighting. At light next morning I intended to renew the attack, but during the night received information that the two contending armies were concentrating for a general battle at Gettysburg, and, in pursuance of orders, left the vicinity of Carlisle before daylight, on the 2d of July, marching for Gettysburg. Carlisle was at that time defended by Gen. William Smith, who commanded, I believe, the Pennsylvania Reserves; he was known in the old United States Army as 'Baldy' Smith."

The battle of Gettysburg was fought. In a few days, demand was made by the authorities for medical aid to be sent to wait upon the Union and rebel wounded at that terrible field of death and suffering. The claims of humanity prevailed, and Cumberland County responded generously. In addition to the aid sent much was given at home; for the maimed soldiery of both armies had to be cared for in the adjoining villages and cities. The college chapel and recitation rooms of Dickinson and one of the central churches were converted into regular hospitals, the latter being thus used for a considerable time.

THE SOLDIERS' MONUMENT.

Subsequent to the close of the war, the erection of a suitable monument to perpetuate the memory of the country's fallen heroes was agitated. The effort to do justice to the soldier had been made by several towns. This stimulated the desire to have a common monument centrally located. In 1868 a meeting of citizens was called, and a committee appointed to formulate a feasible plan for securing such a result. Subscriptions were taken and it was decided that the shaft should be located on the Public Square in Carlisle. The dimensions were, height thirty feet; base to stand on a mound four feet high, ten and one-half feet square. The base was to be of Gettysburg granite, three feet high and ten feet square, surmounted by a marble pedestal containing tablets

for the names of fallen heroes. The work was done by Richard Owens, Esq. of Carlisle, and cost about $5,000. The shaft was erected February 9, 1871, and with the iron fence which surrounds it is a place of much interest to pedestrians. The inscription is

IN HONOR OF THE SOLDIERS OF CUMBERLAND COUNTY
WHO FELL IN DEFENSE OF THE UNION
DURING THE GREAT REBELLION.

This Monument is erected by those who revere the Patriotism, and wish to perpetuate the Memory, of the Brave Men, who aided in saving the Nation and securing the Blessings of Liberty to all.

The "battle wreath" which encircles the shaft contains the names of the following engagements: Mechanicsville, Drainsville, Gainesville, New Market Cross Roads, Second Bull Run, South Mountain, Bethesda Church, Spottsylvania, Wilderness, Gettysburg, Vicksburg. Evidently the artist must have omitted Antietam and probably some other engagements.

NAMES OF FALLEN HEROES.

OFFICERS.

Col. Henry J. Biddle, Assistant Adjutant-General Pennsylvania Reserve Volunteer Corps.
Col. Henry I. Zinn, One Hundred and Thirtieth Pennsylvania Volunteers.
Capt. John R. Smead, Fifth United States Artillery.
Capt. Thomas P. Owen, Company H, First Pennsylvania Reserve Volunteer Corps.
Capt. James S. Colwell, Company A, Seventh Pennsylvania Reserve Volunteer Corps.
Capt. William Laughlin, Company E, One Hundred and Thirtieth Pennsylvania Volunteers.
Capt. D. G. May, Company K, Seventh Pennsylvania Cavalry.
Capt. Hugh W. McCullough, Ninth Pennsylvania Cavalry.
Lieut. Jos. Stuart, Company H, First Pennsylvania Reserve Volunteer Corps.
Lieut. Geo. W. Comfort, Company H, Seventh Pennsylvania Reserve Volunteer Corps.
Lieut. Wm. A. Givler, Company F. One Hundred and Thirtieth Pennsylvania Volunteers.
Lieut. I. B. Kauffman, Company H, Ninth Pennsylvania Cavalry.
Lieut. Theo. Mountz, Ninth Pennsylvania Cavalry.
Lieut. Alf. F. Lee, Company E, Seventeenth Pennsylvania Cavalry.
Lieut. Wm. B. Blaney, Second Iowa Cavalry.
Sub. John B. Goover, Sixth Pennsylvania Cavalry.
Asst. Eng. William E. Law, United States Navy.

SOLDIERS.

FIRST PENNSYLVANIA RESERVE VOLUNTEER CORPS.

COMPANY H.

Frank Hunt.
Joseph Ewing.
Wm. Watson.
John Sheafer.
John Black.
Saml. Baker.
John Clouser.
F. Morrison.

David Askew.
Wm. Donnelley.
Curtis Griffin.
G. Kauffman.
Fred Brown.
Wm. Quigley.
George Morton.

COMPANY I.

John Lusk.
Wm. Baxter.
John Baker.
Jos. Buttorf.
John Mathias.
John Shisler.

Frank Wilson.
Wm. Dunlap.
Wm. Spottswood.
Chas. F. Gould.
Levi Kennedy.

FIFTH PENNSYLVANIA RESERVE VOLUNTEER CORPS.

COMPANY G.

G. W. Savage.

SEVENTH PENNSYLVANIA RESERVE VOLUNTEER CORPS.

COMPANY A.

Wm. Culp.
Wm. R. Holmes.
G. W. Brechbill.
John Callio.
Fred K. Rieff.
Henry T. Green.
B. Haverstick.
R. H. Spottswood.
Geo. I. Wilders.
Jacob Landis.
John T. Cuddy.
Joseph U. Steele.
Chas. Jarmier.
J. Harvey Eby.
Patrick Brannon.
Wm. B. Sites.
J. A. Schlosser.

Wm. M. Henderson.
Geo. W. Wise.
Wm. A. Low.
John T. Adams.
Ed. T. Walker.
D. Haverstick.
Wm. Nevil.
Saml. E. Smith.
Wm. Zimmerman.
John B. Kenyon.
James Miller.
S. Heffelfinger.
Van Buren Eby.
Wm. McCleaf.
Leo W. Faller.
David H. Spahr.

COMPANY D.

Michael J. Foucht.

COMPANY H.

Michael Hess.
Levi A. Bowen.
Jac. A. Welty.
Daniel M. Hoover.
John Lininger.
John Anthony.
Jonas Blosser.
Frank A. Smith.
Jos. B. Mooney.
John Devlin.
G. Beaverson.
Isaiah Siders.
Saml. S. Gooms.
Wm. H. Kline.
J. Richey Clark.
Saml. Wesley.
Thos. J. Acker.
D. W. Conrad.
Milton Warner.
Geo. W. Smith.
Max. Barshal.
Benj. Baker.

ELEVENTH PENNSYLVANIA VOLUNTEERS.

COMPANY A.

Moses Boss.
Thos. Morgan.
Wm. Fielding.
Wilson Vanard.
John Spong.
Geo. L. Reighter.
J. Christman.
James Warden.
Thomas Conway.

FORTY-SIXTH PENNSYLVANIA VOLUNTEERS.

COMPANY F.
Thos. Lyne.

COMPANY H.
S. Kriner.

FORTY-NINTH PENNSYLVANIA VOLUNTEERS.

COMPANY A.
H. Strough.

FIFTY-FIFTH PENNSYLVANIA VOLUNTEERS.

COMPANY B.
Jas. Tyson.

COMPANY C.
Wm. H. Vance.

COMPANY E.
J. C. Filey.   Samuel Bear.

COMPANY F.
Geo. Sanno.   Fred Sanno.

SEVENTY-EIGHTH PENNSYLVANIA VOLUNTEERS.

COMPANY D.
Geo. Grove.   Geo. H. Coover.

EIGHTY-FOURTH PENNSYLVANIA VOLUNTEERS.

COMPANY C.

Samuel T. Kunkle
Richard Lilly.
John Ritson.
Adam Sheaffer.
Reuben Line.
Benj. H. Getz.
Benj. Hipple.
Thos. Snoddy.

EIGHTY-SEVENTH PENNSYLVANIA VOLUNTEERS.

COMPANY E.

Michael Ritta.
E. Beaverson.
Thomas Neely.
Charles Huber.
Henry Snyder.

NINETY-NINTH PENNSYLVANIA VOLUNTEERS.

COMPANY A.
Wm. H. Chapman.

ONE HUNDRED AND FIRST PENNSYLVANIA VOLUNTEERS.

COMPANY A.
Levi Kutz.
Chris. Rothe.

ONE HUNDRED AND SECOND PENNSYLVANIA VOLUNTEERS.

COMPANY H.
J. Fahnestock.

ONE HUNDRED AND SEVENTH PENNSYLVANIA VOLUNTEERS.

COMPANY D.
P. R. Pislee.

ONE HUNDRED AND FIFTEENTH PENNSYLVANIA VOLUNTEERS.

COMPANY G.
J. F. McMath.

ONE HUNDRED AND TWENTY-SEVENTH PENNSYLVANIA VOLUNTEERS.

COMPANY F.
E. Crandle.
Benj. Hoover.

ONE HUNDRED AND THIRTIETH PENNSYLVANIA VOLUNTEERS.

COMPANY A.
P. Faber.
Joseph P. Weaver.
Geo. W. Green.
Wm. E. Greason.
A. Bronswell.

COMPANY D.
N. Lenhard.
Henry Miller.
Joseph Matthews.
M. S. Carbaugh.
W. B. Grabill.
Geo. Brenizer.
Geo. J. McLean.

COMPANY E.
J. W. Crull.
Wm. P. Woods.
Jesse K. Allen.
J. A. Stickler.
Thad. McKeehan.
Wm. A. McCune.
David L. Miller.
Wm. Lockery.
Jos. Connery.

COMPANY F.
Geo. White.
P. Y. Kniseley.
Thos. English.
H. F. Lambert.
B. Barshinger.
John Fetzer.
Theo. R. Zinn.
Keller Bobb.

COMPANY G.
J. Barkley.
S. McMaughton.
Jas. Withrow.

HISTORY OF CUMBERLAND COUNTY.   127

COMPANY H.
J. B. Snavely.
D. B. Kauffman.

ONE HUNDRED AND FORTY-THIRD PENNSYLVANIA VOLUNTEERS.

COMPANY E.
J. Heiser.

ONE HUNDRED AND FORTY-EIGHTH PENNSYLVANIA VOLUNTEERS.

COMPANY A.
Isaac Bear.

ONE HUNDRED AND FORTY-NINTH PENNSYLVANIA VOLUNTEERS.

COMPANY A.
Levi Rupp.
Geo. Ensor.

ONE HUNDRED AND FIFTY-EIGHTH PENNSYLVANIA VOLUNTEERS.

COMPANY A.
H. Oatman.   David Barnhill.
J. Cunningham.   Jacob Bricker.
Abraham Myers.

COMPANY C.
John Sells.   Wm. Wetzel.
J. A. McNaskey.

COMPANY F.
Eli Ford.   D. A. Ziegler.
Zach. Ford   Andrew Fickes.
Samuel Mixell.   Joseph Stine.
Hugh Campbell.

ONE HUNDRED AND EIGHTY-FOURTH PENNSYLVANIA VOLUNTEERS.

COMPANY C.
J. C. Grant.

ONE HUNDRED AND EIGHTY-SEVENTH PENNSYLVANIA VOLUNTEERS.

COMPANY B.
F. Eschenbaugh.

COMPANY D.
Samuel Lutz.   Theo. K. Boyles.
Joseph A. Shaw.   McE. Fanchender.
H. Nonnemaker.   Uriah Stahl.
David Sheriff.   William P. Gensler.

ONE HUNDRED AND EIGHTY-EIGHTH PENNSYLVANIA VOLUNTEERS.

COMPANY I
William Sipe.
Joseph Millard.

ONE HUNDRED AND NINETY-FOURTH PENNSYLVANIA VOLUNTEERS.

COMPANY H.
D. Moore.

ONE HUNDRED AND NINETY-FIFTH PENNSYLVANIA VOLUNTEERS.

COMPANY F.
J. Plank.

TWO HUNDREDTH PENNSYLVANIA VOLUNTEERS.

COMPANY E.
George Wolf.   John Askew.
James Krall.   Lewis B. Fink.
D. Lenker.   Henry Yost.
Michael Smith.

COMPANY I.
Wm. W. Heacy.

TWO HUNDRED AND FIRST PENNSYLVANIA VOLUNTEERS.

COMPANY K.
R. C. Moore.

TWO HUNDRED AND SECOND PENNSYLVANIA VOLUNTEERS.

COMPANY G.
William Webb.   Robert Gracy.
J. Cockenauer.   S. J. Cockenauer.
Joseph Reese.   Jesse Swartz.
D. Hippensteel.

COMPANY H.
Alex. Fagan.   S. J. Orris.
J. Burkhart.   Daniel Stum.
J. Fahnestock.   James McGaw.

TWO HUNDRED AND NINTH PENNSYLVANIA VOLUNTEERS.

COMPANY A.
T. Hoerner.
John P. Leib.

COMPANY F.
E. Sykes.
S. Hollinger.

TWO HUNDRED AND TENTH PENNSYLVANIA VOLUNTEERS.

COMPANY A.
L. Matchett.

THIRD PENNSYLVANIA CAVALRY.

COMPANY G,
A. Bucher.

COMPANY H.

William Myers.
C. A. Holtzman.
Alex. Koser.
Edward Tarman.
George W. Trout.
Josh McCoy.
Samuel Golden.
Henry A. Martin.

William Ewing.
Abdil Trone.
Cul'n Koser.
C. Vanderbilt.
Z. McLaughlin.
J. Nicholson.
Frank Cramer.

COMPANY M.

James Gilbert

SEVENTH PENNSYLVANIA CAVALRY.
COMPANY K.

George W. Heck.
J. Livingston.
John Givler.

Arch. Mullen.
Hiram Gleaver.

EIGHTH PENNSYLVANIA CAVALRY.
COMPANY C.

H. Irvine.

COMPANY E.

E. Speece.

COMPANY H.

J. Bishop.
Jacob Day.

Jacob Agle.

COMPANY I.

J. C. Creps.
C. Liszman.
Robt. T. Laughlin.
Henry Shriver.
L. Keefauver.
S. McCullough.
H. L. Sennet.
Elijah Bittinger.

Joshua Dunan.
Wm. Bricker.
Jos. A. Shannon.
Chris. Felsinger.
Samuel A. Welsh.
Robt. T. Kelley.
David Woods.

COMPANY K.

S. Bowman.

ELEVENTH PENNSYLVANIA CAVALRY.
COMPANY K.

A. Y. Kniseley.

THIRTEENTH PENNSYLVANIA CAVALRY.
COMPANY F.

Joseph Rudy.
Anson Smith.
D. W. McKenny.
Jas. A. Kelso.
John Snyder.
John F. Gettys.
Wm. D. Kauffman.
Jas. Y. Stuart.

Geo. W. Graham.
D. F. Hoerner.
Wm. H. Miller.
Benj. D. Hehn.
P. Huntsberger.
J. F. Eigenower.
Geo. Forney.

COMPANY H.

Jacob Myers.

COMPANY L.

C. W. Nailor.

FIFTEENTH PENNSYLVANIA CAVALRY.
COMPANY H.

J. W. Buttorf.

SEVENTEENTH PENNSYLVANIA CAVALRY.
COMPANY B.

J. Conley.

COMPANY F.

David Kutz.
Thos. Speece.
M. F. Shoemaker.
Abner W. Zug.
S. C. Weakline.
Wm. H. Weaver.
D. E. Hollinger.
Solomon Sow.
John G. Burget.
Samuel Deardorf.
A. Herschberger.

J. W. Kauffman.
Geo. W. McGaw.
E. Stouffer.
Geo. W. Whitmore.
Wilson Seavers.
Lewis Ringwalt.
Eman. Smith.
Robt. Kelley.
David Carle.
C. Evilhock.

NINETEENTH PENNSYLVANIA CAVALRY.
COMPANY A.

Samuel Grier.

COMPANY C.

W. F. Miller.

TWENTIETH PENNSYLVANIA CAVALRY.
COMPANY A.

M. A Griffith.
F. F. Steese.

John M. Kunkle.

COMPANY B.

J. H. Christ.

COMPANY D.

Wm. Sheeley.

COMPANY F.

Wm. Balsley.
Andrew Bear.

Geo. W. Matthews.

TWENTY-SECOND PENNSYLVANIA CAVALRY.
COMPANY F.

J. Palm.

COMPANY M.

W. T. Fanus.

PENNSYLVANIA ARTILLERY.
FIRST REGIMENT.

Geo. W. Welsh.
R. M. Houston.

J. H. Baughman.

SECOND REGIMENT.

Fred Faber.

THIRD REGIMENT.

Peter Paul.
J. W. Christ.
Samuel Bortel.

Wm. Hawkes.
Wm. H. Albright.

TENTH UNITED STATES INFANTRY.
COMPANY C.

A. Webbert.

SEVENTEENTH PENNSYLTANIA CAVALRY.
COMPANY F.

W. B. Flinchbaugh.

HISTORY OF CUMBERLAND COUNTY.

GRAND ARMY POSTS.

One of the permanent organizations resulting from the late war is that of the Grand Army of the Republic. It is a patriotic institution, whose primary object is to watch carefully the rights and privileges of those who imperilled their lives and fortunes in behalf of their country, and to assure the widows and orphans of such fallen comrades that they shall not be forgotten. It is the organized society of America to see that the sacrifices of life and blood and treasure during the war shall not have been made in vain. Nearly every town of importance has such an organization named in honor of some fallen comrade. We give the list in Cumberland County.

Capt. Colwell Post, No. 201, at Carlisle—This post was organized in 1881, its charter bearing date February 24 of that year. Its charter members consisted of the following persons: J. T. Zug, Wm. E. Miller, Isaac Elliott, Wm. Vance, A. C. Ensminger, John S. Humor, J. B. Haverstick, John Albright, P. D. Beckford, Peter Monger, M. A. Hufner, John G. Bobb, J. L. Meloy, James Campbell, D. A. Sawyer, R. P. Henderson, J. P. Brindle, Smith McDonald, H. Linnehul, H. G. Carr, J. G. Vale and Wm. Bottengenbach.

The original corps of officers embraced W. E. Miller, C.; J. L. Meloy, S. V. C.; P. D. Beckford, J. V. C.; Jacob T. Zug, Q. M.; J. B. Haverstick, Adj.; J. S. Bender, Surg.; Joseph G. Vale, O. D.; J. P. Brindle, O. G.; A. C. Ensminger, S. M.; John S. Humor, Chaplain.

The present corps (1886) consists of J. P. Brindle, C.; Wm. Lippert, S. V. C.; H. G. Carr, J. V. C.; Wm. E. Carnes, Chaplain; B. K. Goodyear, Adj.; Wm. E. Miller, Q. M.; J. S. Bender, Surg.; Joseph Lider, O. D.; Lazarus Minnich, O. G.; J. M. Goodyear, Q. M. S.; D. A. Carbaugh, S. M. The post has an active membership of 105, and is in a prosperous condition.

Capt. James S. Colwell, after whom the post was named, was born near Shippensburg, Penn., August 19, 1813. His education in elementary subjects was received at home and at Chambersburg. He graduated finally from Princeton College, New Jersey, in 1839. Returning to his native county, he read law in the office of Wm. Biddle, Esq., at Carlisle, where he practiced, after being admitted to the bar, till he entered the Army. He was mustered as first lieutenant in Seventh Pennsylvania Reserves (Thirty-sixth Pennsylvania Volunteers) April 21, 1861, and as captain July 4, 1862. He engaged in the Peninsular campaign in 1862; was in the second battle of Bull Run of same year; the battle of South Mountain and finally in the battle of Antietam, where he was killed, September 17, 1862, by the explosion of a shell of the enemy. He was a brave soldier, a worthy citizen and a faithful husband and father. His widow still resides in Carlisle.

There is also a colored post at Carlisle, having a small membership, concerning which, however, no facts could be obtained.

Col. H. I. Zinn, Post No. 415, Mechanicsburg, was organized March 4, 1884, by Asst. Adj.-Gen. T. J. Stewart, aided by Post No. 58, of Harrisburg. It had forty-four charter members. Its first corps of officers embraced the following comrades: Col. Wm. Penn Lloyd, Com'dr; H. S. Mohler, S. V. C.; A. C. Koser, J. V. C.; S. B. King, Q. M.; L. F. Zollinger, Adj.; F. K. Ployer, Chap.; E. N. Mosser, Q. M. S.; A. Hauck, O. D.; A. F. Stahl, O. G.

The post is a live one, and has a membership at present of 132, and commands the confidence of the public. It was named in honor of Col. H. I. Zinn, who was born in Dover Township, York Co., Penn., December 8, 1834. He was the son of John and Anna Mary Zinn. On the 15th of September, 1855, he was married, by the Rev. J. C. Bucher, to Miss Mary Ann Clark, the ceremony being performed at Carlisle. As the result of this union three children were born, viz.: Elsie Myra, James Henry and George Arthur. The first two died in 1862, of measles and diphtheria, respectively. Col. Zinn was killed December 13, 1862, in the desperate battle of Fredericksburg, Va.

Corp. McLean Post, 423, at Shippensburg, was organized by Capt. Haverstick April 7, 1884, with thirty-nine charter members. In its first corps of officers were the following comrades: M. G. Hale, C.; Wm. Baughman, S. V. C.; John S. Shugars, J. V. C.; M. S. Taylor, Adj.; J. K. C. Mackey, Q. M. Since its organization Wm. Baughman and John Shugars have also held the position of commander. The membership has increased to seventy-one, rendering the post a flourishing one.

George Johnston McLean, whose name the post wears and reveres, was born at Shippensburg March 7, 1842. He was a member of Company D, One Hundred and Thirtieth Pennsylvania Volunteers, and was wounded in front of Marye's Hill, Fredericksburg, Va., December 13, 1862. From this wound he died nine days afterward in the hospital at Washington, D. C. He was unmarried at the time of his death.

Kennedy Post, 490, at Mount Holly Springs, was organized August 15, 1885. First members were Henry Wollet, C. A. Burkholder, Moses Waggoner, Philip Harman, Samuel Sadler, Silas Tower, N. J. Class, Joseph S. Early, B. F. Wollet, A. Adams, W. H. Brinn, James Cuddy, David A. Cornman, John Goodyear, Augustus Miller, David Taylor, Joseph Swords, Christ Harmon, Joseph Wise, David Newman, William Kennedy, William Hummelbough, J. N. Allen, John Snyder, J. E. Mandorf, Alex Noffsinger, David Noggle, A. T. Richwine, William Ricker, George Slosser, W. M. Still, Philip Snyder, Joseph K. Snyder, Eli B. Tower, John Ward, A. J. McGonnigal, G. W. Kinter, John Kauffman, William H. Hartz, Jacob Hoffert, John Bennett, Frank Stoner, A. P. Richwine, David Withrow and George Fair; present membership, sixty-eight. First officers were Henry Wollet, Commander; C. A. Burkholder, S. V. C.; Moses Wagner, J. V. C.; Joseph Early, Adj.; Alec Adams, Q. M. Present officers are Rev. J. G. Shannon, Commander; Samuel Sadler, S. V, C.; A. Miller, J. V. C.; Phil. Harman, Q. M.; William Goodyear, Adjt. The society meets every Saturday night in the hall of the I. O. O. F.

Private B. F. Eisenberger Post, at New Cumberland, organized in the early part of 1885. The original members were Henry and B. H. Eisenberger, John Robinson, Henry Drager, Capt. J. W. Fight, A. D. Repman, Henry Goriger, Frank Mathias, M. K. Brubaker, Frank Hager, Sr., Frank Hager, Jr., Wash. Shipe and Harry Free. Officers: John Kirk, Commander; B. F. Hager, Secy.; Jesse Oren, Adjutant.

CHAPTER VII.

COURTS—COUNTY OFFICIALS—MEMBERS OF CONGRESS, SENATORS AND ASSEMBLYMEN.

DURING nearly 100 years succeeding the settlement of Pennsylvania," says a writer in 1879, "few of our judges understood the principles of the law, or knew anything about its practice before their appointment. Our county courts were presided over by the justices of the peace of the respective counties, all of whom were *ex officio* judges of the courts of common pleas and quarter sessions of the peace, any three of whom were a quorum to transact business. At the same time the provincial council and the high court of errors and appeals, which was presided over by the governor of the province for the time being, very frequently had not a lawyer in it. And yet the business of that day was done, and well done, too. The judges were generally selected because of their well-known integrity of character, extended business experience and sound common sense, and by close observation and long experience became well acquainted with the duties of their positions and fitted to adjudicate the important interests committed to their charge. Nor was the bar inferior. Gentlemen, eminent for their legal abilities and oratorical powers, practiced before them, and by the gravity of their demeanor and respectful behavior shed lustre upon the proceedings and gave weight and influence to the decisions rendered. Great regard was had for the dignity of the court, and great reverence felt for forms and ceremonies; and woe to the unlucky wight who was caught in a 'contempt,' or convicted of speaking disrespectfully of the magistrate or of his sovereign lord—the king."

The usual form of record at the opening of court may be seen in the following:

At a Court of Common pleas held at Carlisle, for Cumberland County, the Twenty-third day of July, in the fifth year of the Reign of our Sovereign Lord, George the Third, by the Grace of God of Great Britain, France and Ireland, King, Defender of the Faith, &c., and in the Year of our Lord One Thousand Seven hundred & sixty-five, before John Armstrong, Esq., and his Associate Justices, &c., of the Same Court.

As a matter of necessity the first courts in Cumberland County were held at Shippensburg, it being then the only town in the valley (1750) and therefore the only place which could accomodate those who gathered at court. By a commission dated March 10, 1750, the following persons were appointed justices of the peace and of common pleas in Cumberland County: Samuel Smith, of Carlisle; William Maxwell, of Peters; George Croghan, of East Pennsborough; Robert Dunning, of West Pennsborough; Matthew Dill and Benj. Chambers, of Antrim; Wm. Trent, of Middleton; Wm. Allison, of Antrim; Hermanus Alricks, of Carlisle; John Miller, of West Pennsborough; Robert Chambers, of Hopewell; John Finley, of Lurgan; and Thomas Wilson, of Middleton. Samuel Smith was president of the court. He had previously been a member of the Assembly, sheriff and justice of the peace in Lancaster County. He was succeeded by Francis West in 1797.

The date of the first court held at Shippensburg was "the twenty-fourth day of July, in the twentieth year of the reign of his Majesty King George the Second, *Annoque Domini* 1750." The last at that place was held in April, 1751. John Potter, who had come to America in 1741 and settled "in the neighborhood of Shippen's farm," now Shippensburg, as early as 1746 or earlier, had been appointed sheriff,* and on the original organization of the county returned the writ of venire which had been directed to him with the panel annexed, and the following persons were sworn as grand jurors: Wm. Magaw, John Potter, John Mitchell, John Davison, Ezekiel Dunning, John Holliday, James Lindley, Adam Hoops, John Forsyth, Thomas Brown, George Brown, John Reynolds, Robert Harris, Thos. Urie, Charles Murray, James Brown and Robert Meek. The record of this first session of the court shows also that "Hermanus Alricks, Esq., produced to the court a commission under the hand of the Hon. James Hamilton, Esq., governor, and the great seal of the province, appointing him clerk of the peace of the county of Cumberland, and the same was read and allowed and ordered to be recorded." The beauti-

*Mr. Potter was twice sheriff, his commissions bearing date October 6, 1750, and October, 1754. His son, James, was a lieutenant in the militia, and a captain in Armstrong's Kittanning, expired in 1756. He removed to what is now Centre County in 1772, and became distinguished both in military and civil offices

ful penmanship of Mr. Alricks is as plain to-day on the old records as it was when written.

The first court of common pleas and the criminal courts were, by order of the Governor, first held at Carlisle, July 23, 1751, and under the above named justices, and were held at that place regularly afterward. "The orphans' court, however, for four or five years remained unfixed to any one place, and is said to have followed the persons of the judges." The justices were intended to be appointed at least one from each township, and out of the number some one was commissioned to act as president.

On account of some existing vacancies in the county, the Governor, in October, 1764, appointed a new board of justices, consisting of John Armstrong, James Galbreath, John Byers, Wm. Smith (superseded January 15, 1766, for participation in the affair at Fort Loudon), John McKnight, James Carothers, Hermanus Alricks, Adam Hoop, Francis Campbell, John Reynolds, Jonathan Hoge, Robt. Miller, Wm. Lyon, Robt. Callender, Andrew Calhoun, James Maxwell, Samuel Perry, John Holmes and John Allison. These were reappointed in 1769, together with some others outside the present limits of the county, except, perhaps, John Agnew and Turbutt Francis. John Holmes was appointed sheriff, and James Jack, coroner, in 1765, and in October, 1768, David Hoge was appointed sheriff, and William Denny, coroner (these appointments made by the Governor upon returns of election to him).

August 16, 1765, at a court of oyer and terminer, before Alex. Steadman, of the supreme court, and John Armstrong and James Galbreath, Esqs., John Money was tried and convicted of felony and the murder of Archibald Gray in March previous, and was not long after executed for his crime. One Warner was very early tried and executed for the robbery and murder of a man named Musselman, near New Kingston. The courts of the county have been called upon to try a number of murder cases, and several legal executions for murder have occurred in the county. A case in the first court held at Shippensburg was recorded as follows:

Dominus Rex vs. *Bridget Hagen.* Sur Indictmt. for Larceny, not guilty & now ye deft ret her pl and submits to ye Ct. and thereupon it is considered by the Court and adjudged that ye sd Bridget Hagen restore the sum of Six pounds seventeen shillings & six pence lawful money of Penna. unto Jacob Long ye owner and make fine to ye Governor in ye like sum and pay ye costs of prosecution & receive fifteen lashes on her bare back at ye Public Whipping post & stand committed till ye fine & fees are paid.

The whipping post was, with the stocks and pillory, on the square near the court house. Generally in the sentence where a culprit was to receive lashes they were to be "well laid on," as in the case of Wm. Anderson, convicted of felony at the January term in 1751. Whipping was the ordinary mode of punishment, and probably the executioner used his lash with telling effect.

In the court of quarter sessions for July, 1753, sixteen bills were presented to the grand jury against a number of persons "for conveying spurious liquor to the Indians out of the inhabited portion of this province." The jury ignored most of them. As a writer says: "To the noble red man civilization had already become a failure."

Cases of imprisonment for debt occupied the time and attention of the early courts and lawyers, as page after page of the common pleas record testifies. Entries like the following are by no means uncommon:

Upon reading the petition of A. B., a prisoner under execution in the public gaol of this county, to the court, it is therefore ordered by the Court that the petitioner notify his creditors to appear the —— day of —— next, and now (same date) the Court order the above petitioner to be brought into court; and now, being brought into court, the Court do thereupon remand him, the said A. B., to the public gaol.

BY THE COURT.

Sometimes it was so arranged that the prisoner was discharged, or occasionally sold or bound to some one to work out the amount of his indebtedness, the person having advanced the same to the creditors.

COUNTY OFFICIALS.

Clerks of Quarter Sessions.—1789, Samuel Postlethwaite; 1794, John Lyon; 1798, F. J. Haller; 1809, Charles Bovard.

Clerks Orphans' Court, Registers of Wills and Recorders of Deeds.—John Creigh, appointed April 7, 1777; resigned February 9, 1779, and succeeded February 13, by William Lyon, who was also appointed to receive subscriptions for the State loan. Mr. Lyon was also in 1777-79 Clerk of oyer and terminer, and prothonotary.

Clerks Orphans' Courts, Oyer and Terminer, and Prothonotaries.—1798, William Lyon; 1809, William Rumsey; 1816, Robert McCoy.

Prothonotaries.—1750-70, Hermanus Alricks, Turbutt Francis, John Agnew; 1777, Wm. Lyon; 1820, B. Aughinbaugh; 1823, John P. Helfenstein; 1826, R. McCoy; 1828, Willis Foulke; 1829, John Harper; 1835, George Fleming; 1839, George Sanderson; 1842, Thomas H. Criswell; 1845, William M. Beetem; 1848, James F. Lamberton; 1851, George Zinn, Jr.; 1854, Daniel K. Noell; 1857, Philip Quigley; 1860, Benjamin Duke; 1863, Samuel Shireman; 1866, John P. Brindle 1869, Wm. V. Cavanaugh; 1872, David W. Worst; 1875, John M. Wallace; 1878, Robert M. Graham; 1881, James A. Sibbet; 1884, Lewis Masonheimer.

Registers and Recorders.—1798, George Kline; 1804, Francis Gibson; 1809, George Kline; 1816, William Line; 1820, F. Sharretts; 1823-28, J. Hendell; 1829, John Irvine.

Registers (only).—1834, James G. Oliver; 1835,Wm. Line; 1839, Isaac Angney; 1842, Jacob Bretz; 1845, James McCulloch; 1848, Wm. Gould; 1851, A L. Sponsler; 1854, Wm. Lytle; 1857, Samuel M. Emminger; 1860, Ernest N. Brady; 1863, George W. North; 1866, Jacob Dorsheimer; 1869, Joseph Neely; 1872, John Reep; 1875, Martin Guswiler; 1878, J. M. Drawbaugh; 1881, C. Jacoby; 1884, Lemuel R. Spong.

Coroners.—1765-67, James Jack; 1768-70, William Denny; 1771-73, Samuel Laird; 1774-76, James Pollock; 1777, John Martin; 1778, William Rippey; 1779, William Holmes 1781,William Rippey; 1783, John Rea.

Clerks of Court.—1820, John McGinnis; 1823-26, John Irvine; 1828, F. Sharretts: 1829, R. Angney.

Clerks and Recorders.—1832, Reinneck Angney; 1834, John Irvine; 1836, Thos. Craighead; 1839, Willis Foulke; 1842, Robt. Wilson; 1845, John Goodyear; 1848, John Hyer; 1851, Samuel Martin; 1854, John M. Gregg; 1857, Daniel S. Croft; 1860, John B. Floyd; 1863, Ephraim Cornman; 1866, Samuel Bixler; 1869, George C. Sheaffer; 1872, George S. Emig; 1875, D. B. Stevick; 1878. John Sheaffer; 1881, D. B. Saxton; 1884, John Zinn.

Sheriffs.—1749, John Potter; 1750, Ezekiel Dunning; 1756, Wm. Parker; 1759, Ezekiel Smith; 1762. Ezekiel Dunning; 1765, John Holmes; 1768, David Hoge; 1771, Ephraim Blaine; 1774, Robt. Semple; 1777, James Johnson; 1780, John Hoge; 1783, Sam'l Postlethwaite; 1786, Chas. Leeper; 1789, Thos. Buchanan; 1792, James Wallace; 1795, Jacob Crever; 1798, John Carothers; 1801, Robt. Greyson; 1804, George Stroup; 1807, John Carothers; 1810, John Boden; 1813, John Rupley; 1816, Andrew Mitchell; 1819, Peter Ritney; 1822, James Neal; 1825, John Clippinger; 1828, Martin Dunlap; 1831, George Beelem, 1834, Michael Holcomb; 1837, John Myers; 1840, Paul Martin; 1843, Adam Longsdorf; 1846, James Hoffer; 1849, David Smith;

1852, Joseph McDarmond; 1855, Jacob Bowman; 1858, Robert McCartney; 1861, J. Thompson Rippey; 1864, John Jacobs; 1867, Joseph C. Thompson; 1870, James K. Foreman; 1873, Joseph Totten; 1876, David H. Gill; 1879, A. A. Thomson; 1882, George B. Eyster; 1885, James R. Dixon.

Treasurers.—1787, Stephen Duncan; 1789, Alex McKeehan; 1795, Robt. Miller; 1800, James Duncan; 1805, Hugh Boden; 1807, John Boden; 1810, Robert McCoy; 1813, John McGinnis; 1815, Andrew Boden; 1817, George McFeely; 1820, Jas. Thompson; 1824, Geo. McFeely; 1826, Alex. Nesbitt; 1829, Hendricks Weise; 1832, John Phillips; 1835, Jason W. Eby; 1838, Wm. S. Ramsey; 1839, Robt. Snodgrass; 1841, Wm. M. Mateer; 1843, Robt. Moore, Jr.; 1845, David N. Mahon; 1847, Robt. Moore, Jr.; 1849, Wm. M. Porter; 1851, William S. Cobean; 1853, N. Wilson Woods; 1855, Adam Senseman; 1857, Moses Bricker; 1859, Alfred L. Sponsler; 1861, John Gutshall; 1863, Henry S. Ritter; 1865, Levi Zeigler; 1867, Christian Mellinger; 1869, George Wetzel; 1871, George Bobb; 1873, Levan H. Orris; 1875, A. Agnew Thomson; 1878, John C. Eckels; 1881, W. H. Longsdorff; 1884, Jacob Hemminger.

District Attorneys.—1850, Wm. H. Miller; 1853 and 1858, Wm. J. Shearer; 1859 and 1864, J. W. D. Gillelen; 1865 and 1870, C. E. Maglaughlin; 1871, W. F. Sadler; 1874, F. E. Beltzhoover; 1877, George S. Ewing; 1880, John M. Wetzel; 1883, John T. Stuart.

County Commissioners.—1839, Alex. M. Kerr; 1840, Michael Mishler; 1841, Jacob Rehrar; 1842, Robt. Laird; 1843, Christian Titzel; 1844, Jefferson Worthington; 1845, David Sterrett; 1846, Daniel Coble; 1847, John Mell; 1848, James Kelso; 1849, John Sprout; 1850, Wm. H. Trout; 1851, James G. Cressler; 1852, John Bobb; 1853, James Armstrong; 1854, George M. Graham; 1855, Wm. M. Henderson; 1856, Andrew Kerr; 1857, Sam'l Magaw; 1858, Nath'l H. Eckels; 1859, James H. Waggoner; 1860, George Miller; 1861, Michael Kast; 1862, George Scobey; 1863, John McCoy, three years; Mitchell McClellan, two years; 1864, Henry Karns, John Harris; 1865, Alex. F. Meck; 1866, Michael G. Hale; 1867, Allen Floyd; 1869, Jacob Rhoads; 1870, David Deitz; 1871, J. C. Sample; 1872, Samuel Ernst; 1873, Jacob Barber; 1874, Joseph Bautz; 1875, Jacob Barber; 1878, Jacob Barber, Hugh Boyd; 1881, Hugh Boyd, Alfred B. Strock; 1884, James B. Brown, George Hauck.

President Judges.—1750-57, Samuel Smith; 1757, Francis West; 1791, Thos. Smith; 1794, Jas. Riddle; 1800, John Joseph Henry; 1806, James Hamilton; 1819, Chas. Smith; 1820, John Reed; 1838, Sam'l Hepburn; 1848, Fred'k Watts; 1851, James H. Graham; 1871, Benj. F. Junkin; 1875, Martin C. Herman; 1884, Wilbur F. Sadler.

Associate Judges.—1791, James Dunlap, John Jordan, Jonathan Hoge, Sam'l Laird; 1794. John Montgomery; 1800, Wm. Moore, John Creigh; 1813, Ephraim Steel; 1814, Jacob Hendel; 1818, Isaiah Graham; 1819, James Armstrong; 1828, Wm. Line; 1835, James Stewart, John LeFevre; 1842, T. C. Miller; 1847, John Clendenin; 1851, Sam'l Woodburn, John Rupp; 1856, Sam'l Woodburn, Michael Cochlin; 1861, Robt. Bryson; 1862, Hugh Stuart; 1866, Thos. P. Blair; 1871, John Clendenin, Robt. Montgomery; 1872, Henry G. Moser, Abram Witmer.

MEMBERS OF CONGRESS, SENATORS AND ASSEMBLYMEN.

Representatives in Congress.—1775-77, Col. James Wilson; 1778-80, Gen. John Armstrong; 1783 (to July 4), John Montgomery; 1797-1805, John A. Hanna; 1805-13, Robt. Whitehill; 1813-14, Wm. Crawford; 1815-21, Wm. P. Maclay; 1827-33, Wm. Ramsey; 1833 (unexpired term), C. T. H. Craw-

HISTORY OF CUMBERLAND COUNTY.

ford; 1835-37, Jesse Miller; 1838-40, Wm. Sterrett Ramsey; 1841-43, Amos Gustine; 1843-47, James Black; 1847-49, Jasper E. Brady; 1849-53, J. X. McLanahan; 1853-55, Wm. H. Kurtz; 1855-57, Lemuel Todd; 1857-59, John A. Ahl; 1859-61, Benj. F. Junkin; 1861-65, Joseph Bailey; 1865-69, Adam J. Glossbrenner; 1869-73, Richard J. Haldeman; 1873-75, John A. Magee, also Lemuel Todd at large; 1875-79, Levi Maish; 1879-81, Frank E. Beltzhoover; 1883, W. A. Duncan (died in office, and Dr. John A. Swope, of Gettysburg, elected to fill vacancy December 23, 1884; also re-elected in November, 1885).

State Senators.—1841-43, J. X. McLanahan; 1844-46, Wm. B. Anderson; 1847-49, Robt. C. Sterrett; 1850-52, Joseph Baily; 1853-55, Sam'l Wherry; 1856-58, Henry Fetter; 1859-61, Wm. B. Irwine; 1862-64, George H. Bucher; 1865-67, A. Heistand Glatz; 1868-70, Andrew G. Miller; 1871-74, James M. Weakley; 1875-78, James Chestnut; 1878, Isaac Hereter; 1882, Samuel C. Wagner.

Representatives in Assembly.—1779-80, Abraham Smith, Sam'l Cuthbertson, Fredk. Watts, Jona. Hoge, John Harris, Wm. McDowell, Ephraim Steel; 1780-81, S. Cuthbertson, Stephen Duncan, Wm. Brown, J. Hoge, John Andrew, John Harris, John Allison; 1781-82, James McLean, John Allison, Jas. Johnston, Wm. Brown, Robt. Magaw, John Montgomery, Stephen Duncan; 1782-83, S. Duncan, John Carothers, J. Johnston, Wm. Brown, Jas. McLene, J. Hoge, Patrick Maxwell; 1783-84, Wm. Brown, of Carlisle, F. Watts, Jas. Johnston, John Carothers, Abraham Smith, Wm. Brown, Robt. Whitehill; 1814, Jacob Alter, Samuel Fenton, Jas. Lowry, Andrew Boden and Wm. Anderson; 1815, Philip Peffer, Wm. Wallace and Solomon Gorgas; 1824, James Dunlap; 1829, Wm. Alexander, Peter Lobach; 1833, Michael Cochlin, Sam'l McKeehan; 1834, David Emmert; 1835, William Runsha (died suddenly in office), Chas. McClure; 1836-38, Wm. R. Gorgas, Jas. Woodburn; 1840, Abraham Smith McKinney, John Zimmerman; 1841, Wm. Barr, Joseph Culver; 1842, James Kennedy, Geo. Brindle; 1843, Francis Eckels; 1843-44, Jacob Heck; 1844, Geo. Brindle; 1845, Augustus H. Van Hoff, Joseph M. Means; 1846, James Mackey, Armstrong Noble; 1847, Jacob LeFevre; 1847-48, Abraham Lamberton; 1848, Geo. Rupley; 1849-50, Henry Church, Thos. E. Scouller; 1851, Ellis J. Bonham; 1851-52, Robt. M. Henderson; 1852-53, David J. McKee; 1853, Henry J. Moser; 1854, Montgomery Donaldson, Geo. W. Criswell; 1855-56, William Harper, James Anderson; 1857, Chas. C. Brandt; 1857-58, Hugh Stuart; 1858-59, John McCurdy; 1859, John Power; 1860, Wm. B. Irvine, Wm. Louther; 1861, Jesse Kennedy; 1861-62, John P. Rhoads; 1863-64, John D. Bowman; 1865-66, Philip Long; 1867-68, Theodore Cornman; 1869-70, John B. Leidig; 1871-72, Jacob Bomberger; 1873-74, Wm. B. Butler; 1874-75, G. M. Mumper; 1876-77, Sam'l W. Means; 1877-78, Samuel A. Bowers; 1878-80, Alfred M. Rhoads, Robt. M. Cochran, Jr.; 1882, Geo. M. D. Eckels. John Graham.

Representatives in Supreme Executive Council.—March 4, 1777, Jonathan Hoge; November 9, 1778 (from what is now Franklin County), James McLean; December 28, 1779, Robert Whitehill, of East Pennsborough; 1781-84, John Byers.

In the committee of safety John Montgomery was representative from Cumberland County during the life of the committee. William Lyon was a member of the Council of Safety until its close, December 4, 1777.

Commissioners in Assembly, etc.—From November, 1777, and later, William Duffield, James McLean, William Clark, James Brown, Robert Whitehill, John Harris. In 1777 John Andrew was commissioner of the county, while

James Lyon, William McClure, William Finley, James McKee, James Laird and George Robinson were assessors. William Piper was collector of excise in 1778, and Matthew Henderson in 1779, William Irvine in 1781, and John Buchanan in 1782. James Poe became commissioner of taxes October 22, 1783, and Stephen Duncan county treasurer. J. Agnew was at the same time clerk of the quarter sessions, over which court John Rannells, Esq., presided for some time subsequent to January 20, 1778, on which date the "Grand Inquest for the Commonwealth of Pennsylvania and the body of the County of Cumberland" presented the following: "That the public Court House of the County of Cumberland is now occupied by Capt. Coran and his men, who are employed in the service of the United States, as a laboratory and storehouse, and has been occupied by the people in the service of the United States for a considerable time past, so that the County of Cumberland can not have the use of the said Court House, but are obliged to hire other places for the county's use—they are of opinion that the United States ought to pay to the treasurer of the County of Cumberland, after the rate of £10 per month, monthly and every month Capt. Coran hath been possessed of said Court House, and for every month he or they may continue to occupy it, not exceeding the 20th day of April next; and of this they desire that Capt. Coran, or the commanding officer of the laboratory company, may have notice. Per Wm. Moore, foreman."

CHAPTER VIII.

BENCH AND BAR—PROVINCIAL PERIOD—FROM THE REVOLUTION UNTIL THE ADOPTION OF THE CONSTITUTION OF 1790—CONSTITUTIONAL PERIOD.

I.

PROVINCIAL PERIOD.

THE bar of Cumberland County had its birth in the colonial period of our history—in the days when Pennsylvania was a province, and when George II was the reigning king. Courts of justice had been established by the proprietaries in the settled portions of the province, at first under the laws of the Duke of York, and subsequently under the rules of the common law; but the necessity for them became greater as the population increased, as new sections were settled, and it was this necessity for the establishment of courts of justice nearer than Lancaster, in this newly settled portion of Pennsylvania, which was the principal reason for the formation of Cumberland County in 1750.

From this period begins the history of our bar. For nearly one hundred years succeeding the settlement of Pennsylvania, few of the justices knew anything of the theory or practice of law, until after they had received their commissions from the King. Even the "Provincial Council," which was the high court of appeal, and which was presided over by the governor of the province, had frequently no lawyer in it; but by the time of the formation of our county a race of lawyers had arisen in Pennsylvania, who "traveled upon the circuit"—many of whom became eminent in the State and nation—whose names will be found in the early annals of our bar.

HISTORY OF CUMBERLAND COUNTY.

COURTS AT SHIPPENSBURG.

The first courts in the Cumberland Valley were held at Shippensburg; four terms, dating from the 24th of July, 1750, to and including April, 1751. But when Carlisle (Letort's Spring, as it had been called) was laid out and chosen by the proprietaries as the county seat, they were removed to that place.

At the first term of court in Shippensburg Samuel Smith, who had been a member of the Colonial Assembly, and his associate justices presided; John Potter had been appointed the first sheriff, and Hermanus Alricks, of Carlisle, a grandson of Peter Alricks, who came from Holland in 1682 with dispatches to the Dutch on the Delaware, and who was himself, at this time (1749-50), the first representative of Cumberland County in the assembly, produced his commission from the governor of the province, under the great seal, as clerk of the peace for the said county, which was read and recorded.

FIRST COURTS AT CARLISLE.

The first court held at Carlisle was in the year immediately succeeding the formation of the county, and was "a court of general quarter sessions, held at Carlisle, for the county of Cumberland, the twenty-third day of July, 1751, in the twenty-fifth year of our Sovereign Lord, King George II, over Great Britain, etc. Before Samuel Smith, Esq., and his associate justices."

These first courts were probably held in "a temporary log building on the northeast corner of the public square." The court house was used during the Revolution, and as late as January, 1778, by Capt. Coran and a company of United States troops as a laboratory, so that the justices were compelled to hold courts at temporary places elsewhere.

THE EARLY COURTS.

The justices who presided were commissioned, through the governor of the province, by the King. The number of these justices varied from time to time. The courts of quarter sessions and common pleas were held four times each year, and private sessions, presided over often by the associate justices, irregularly, as occasion called for.

At the beginning of our history the public prosecutor was the Crown, and all criminal cases are entered accordingly in the name of the King, as: The King vs. John Smith. This is until the Revolution, when, about 1778, the form is changed to "Pennsylvania vs. ———," which is used until August, 1795, after which the form "*Respublica vs.* ———" is used until August, 1832, when the word "Commonwealth," which is now in use, appears.

The form of the pleadings at this early period may be considered curious:

THE KING }
    vs.   }   Sur Indictment for Assault and Battery.
CHARLES MURRAY. }

Being charged with avers he is not guilty as in the indictment is supposed, and upon this he puts himself upon the court and upon the King's attorney likewise.

But now the defendant comes into court and retracts his plea, not being willing to contend with our Sovereign Lord, the King. Protests his innocence and prays to be admitted to a small fine. Whereupon it is adjudged by the court that he pay the sum of two shillings, six pence. October term, 1751.

Besides the ordinary actions of trespass, debt, slander, assault and battery and the like, there were actions in the early courts against persons for settling on land unpurchased from the Indians, and quite a number "for selling liquor to the Indians without license." For the lighter offenses there were fines and imprisonments, and for the felonies the ignominious punishment of the whipping post and pillory.

This was then the ordinary method of punishment and the form of the sentence was, to take one of many instances, "that he [the culprit] receive twenty-one lashes well laid on his bare back, at the public whipping-post in Carlisle, to-morrow morning, between the hours of eleven and twelve o'clock, that he make restitution to Wm. Anderson in the sum of £18, 14 shillings and 6 pence. That he make fine to the Governor in the like sum, and stand committed until fine and fees be paid."—[January term, 1751.] "Twenty-one lashes" was the usual number, although in some few cases they were less. The whipping-post seems to have been abandoned during the Revolution, as we find the last mention of it in the records of our court in April, 1779. These records also show that the justices of the courts, who seem to have been *ex officio* justices of the peace, superintended the laying out of roads, granted licences, took acknowledgments of deeds and registered the private marks or brands of cattle. They exercised a paternal supervision over bond servants, regulated the length of their terms of service, and sometimes, at the request probably of the prisoners, sold them out of goal as servants for a term of years, in order that they might be able to pay the fines imposed. In short the cases in these early courts, which had distinct equity powers, seem to have been determined according to the suggestions of right reason, as well as by the fixed principles of law.

FOUNDATION OF THE COURTS.

In order that we may get some idea of the foundation of the courts in Cumberland County—of the authority, in the days of kings, from which their power was derived—it may be interesting to turn to the old commissions, in which the power of the early justices was more or less defined.

A commission issued in October, 1755, appointing Edward Shippen, Sr., George Stevenson and John Armstrong, justices, is as follows:

George II, by the Grace of God, of Great Britain, France and Ireland, King, Defender of the Faith, &c., to Edward Shippen, Senr., of the County of Lancaster, George Stevenson of the County of York, and John Armstrong of the County of Cumberland, in our said Province of Pennsylvania; Esqrs:

GREETING: Know ye that reposing special Trust and Confidence in your Loyalty, Integrity, Prudence and Ability, *We have* assigned you or any two of you our Justices to Enquire by The Oaths or affirmation of honest and Lawful men of the said Counties of York and Cumberland * * * of all Treasons, Murders and such other Crimes as are by the Laws of our said Province made Capital or felonies of death * * * to have and determine the said Treasons, Murders, etc., according to Law, and upon Conviction of any person or persons, Judgment or sentence to pronounce and execution thereupon to award as The Law doth or shall direct. And we have also appointed you, the said Edward Shippen, George Stevenson and John Armstrong, or any two of you, our justices, to deliver the Goals of York and Cumberland aforesaid of the prisoners in the same being for any crime or crimes, Capital or Felonies aforesaid, and therefore we command you that at certaint imes, which you or any two of you shall consider of, you meet together at the Court Houses of the said Counties of York and Cumberland, to deliver the said goals and Make diligent inquiry of and upon the premises, and hear and Determine all and singular the said premises, and do and accomplish these things in the form aforesaid, acting always therein as to Justice according to Law shall appertain. Saving to us the Amerceiments and other things to us thereof Belonging, for we have commanded the Sheriffs of the said Counties of York and Cumberland that at certain days, which you shall make known to them, to cause to come before you all of the prisoners of the Goals and their attachments, and also so many and such honest and Lawful men of their several Bailiwicks as may be necessary by whom the truth of the matters conccearning may be the better known and enquired. In testimony whereof we have caused the Great Seal of our Province to be hereunto affixed. Witness, Robert Turner Morris, Esq. (by virtue of a commission from Thomas Penn and Richard Penn, Esqs., true and absolute proprietaries of this Province), with our Royal approbation, Lieutenant-Governor and Commander-in-Chief of the Province aforesaid and counties of New Castel, Thrent and Sussex-on-Delaware. At Philadelphia, the ninth day of October, in the year of our Lord one thousand, seven hundred and fifty-five and in the twenty-ninth year of our reign. *Signed*, ROBERT T. MORRIS.

Another commission was issued April 5, 1757, to John Armstrong, appointing him a justice of the court of common pleas for the county of Cumberland. The powers of these provincial justices were much more extensive then than those which belong to the office of a justice now, and for some time the county of Cumberland, over which their jurisdiction extended, included nearly all of Pennsylvania west of the Susquehanna.

Many of the justices who were appointed never appear upon the bench. Not less than three presided at each term of court, one as the presiding justice and the others as associates. Sometimes only the name of the presiding justice is given; sometimes all are mentioned. They seem to have held various terms, and to have rotated without any discoverable rule of regularity. The justices who, with their associates, presided during the provincial period, until the breaking out of the revolution, were as follows:

JUSTICES DURING THE PROVINCIAL PERIOD.

Samuel Smith, from July, 1750, to October, 1757; Francis West, from October, 1757, to 1759; John Armstrong, Francis West and Hermanus Alricks, January, 1760; Francis West, July, 1760; John McKnight, October, 1760; John Armstrong, April, 1761; James Galbreath, October, 1761; John Armstrong, Jannary, 1762; James Galbreath, April, 1762; John Armstrong, July, 1762; Thomas Wilson, April, 1763; John Armstrong, from October, 1763, to April, 1776.

The above embraces the names of all the justices who presided prior to the Revolution, with the exception possibly of a few, who held but a single term of court. It will be seen that from October, 1757, the judges rotated irregularly at brief intervals until October, 1763, when John Armstrong occupied the bench for a period of nearly thirteen years.

Of these justices John McKnight was afterward a captain in the Revolution; Francis West was an Englishman who went to Ireland and then immigrated to America and settled in Carlisle in or before 1753. He was an educated man and a loyalist. His sister Ann became the wife of his friend and co-justice, Hermanus Alricks, and his daughter, of the same name, married Col. George Gibson, the father of John Bannister Gibson, who was afterward to become the chief justice of Pennsylvania. Francis West some time prior to the Revolution moved to Sherman's Valley, where he died in 1783.

Thomas Wilson lived near Carlisle.

James Galbreath, another of these justices, was born in 1703, in the north of Ireland. He was a man of note on the frontier, and the early provincial records of Pennsylvania contain frequent reference to him. He had been sheriff of Lancaster in 1742, and for many years a justice of that county. He had served in the Indian wars of 1755-63, and some time previous to 1762 had removed to Cumberland County. He died June 11, 1786, in what was then East Pennsborough Township.

Hermanus Alricks was the first clerk of the courts, from 1750 to 1770, and the first representative of Cumberland County in the Provincial Assembly. He was born about 1730 in Philadelphia. He settled in Carlisle about 1749 or 1750, and brought with him his bride, a young lady lately from Ireland, with her brother, Francis West, then about to settle in the same place. He was a man of mark and influence in the valley west of the Susquehanna. He died in Carlisle December 14, 1772.

But the greatest of these, and "the noblest Roman of them all." was Col. John Armstrong. He first appears as a surveyor under the proprietary government, and made the second survey of Carlisle in 1761. In 1755 we find him commissioned a justice of the courts by George II, and from 1763 until his duties as a major-general in the Revolution called him from the bench, we find him, for a period of nearly thirteen years, presiding over our courts. He was at this time already a colonel, and had already distinguished himself in the Indian war. In 1755 he had cleaned out the nest of savages at Kittanning, and had received a medal from the corporation of Philadelphia. When, later the Revolution broke out, we find him, in 1776, a brigadier-general of the Continental Army (commissioned March 1, 1776), and in the succeeding year a major-general in command of the Pennsylvania troops. He was a warm, personal friend of Washington. He was a member of Congress in 1778-80, and 1787-88. It was, probably, owing to his influence, in a great measure, that the earliest voice of indignant protest was raised in Carlisle against the action of Great Britain against the colonies. "He was a man of intelligence, integrity, resolute and brave, and, though living habitually in the fear of the Lord, he feared not the face of man."* He died March 9, 1795, aged seventy-five years. He was buried in the old grave-yard at Carlisle.

PROSECUTORS FOR THE CROWN.

In this provincial period these were our judges: George Ross, afterward a signer of the Declaration of Independence, was the public prosecutor for the Crown from 1751 to 1764; Robert Magaw follows in 1765–66, and Jasper Yeates in 1770; Benjamin Chew, who was a member of the Provincial Council, and afterward, during the Revolution, a Loyalist, was, at this time, 1759–68, attorney-general, and prosecuted many of the criminal cases, from 1759 to 1769, in our courts. He was, in 1777, with some others, received by the sheriff of this county, and held at Staunton, Va., till the conclusion of the war.

PRACTITIONERS.

The earliest practitioners at our bar, from 1759 to 1764, were George Ross, James Smith (afterward a signer of the Declaration of Independence), James Campbell, Samuel Johnston, Jasper Yeates and Robert Magaw.

From 1764 to 1770, George Stevenson, James Wilson (also a signer of the Declaration of Independence), James Hamilton (afterward judge), David Sample, David Grier, Wetzel, Morris, and Samuel Johnston, were the leading attorneys. Up to this time Magaw, Stevenson and Wilson had the largest practice. During this period, in 1770, Col. Turbutt Francis becomes clerk of the court, as successor of Hermanus Alricks; and from 1771 to 1774, Ephraim Blaine, afterward commissary in the Revolution, and the grandfather of the Hon. James G. Blaine, of Maine, was sheriff of the county.

THE BAR IN 1776.

During this first year of our independence the practitioners at the bar were John Steel (already in large practice), James Campbell, George Stevenson, James Wilson, Samuel Johnston, David Grier, Col. Thomas Hartley (of York), Jasper Yeates, James Smith, Edward Burd and Robert Galbreath. It is a noteworthy fact that two of the men who practiced in our courts in this memorable year were signers of the Declaration of Independence.

---

*Chamber's tribute to the Scotch-Irish settlers, p. 88.

Hon. George Ross, who, at the age of twenty-two, was the first public prosecutor for the Crown in our courts in Cumberland County, was the son of George Ross, an Episcopal minister, and was born in New Castle, Del., in 1730. He began the practice of law in Lancaster in 1751. He acted as prosecuting attorney for the Crown in our county from 1751 to 1764, and practiced in our courts until October, 1772. He was a member of the Colonial Assembly of Pennsylvania from 1768 to 1776, and when this body ceased, or was continued in the Legislature, he was a member of that body also. In 1774 he was one of the committee of seven who represented Pennsylvania in the Continental Congress, and remained a member until January, 1777. He was a signer of the Declaration of Independence. He died at Lancaster in July, 1779. In appearance George Ross was a very handsome man, with a high forehead, regular features, oval face, long hair, worn in the fashion of the day, and pleasing countenance.

Col. James Smith is one of the earliest names found as a practicioner, in this provincial period, at the bar of Cumberland County. There is a brief notice of him in Day's Historical Collections. He was an Irishman by birth, but came to this country when quite young. In Graydon's Memoirs it is stated that he was educated at the college in Philadelphia, was admitted to the bar, and afterward removed to the vicinity of Shippensburg, and there established himself as a lawyer. From there he removed to York, where he continued to reside until his death, July 11, 1806, at the age of about ninety-three years. He was a member of Congress in 1775–78. He was one of the signers of the Declaration of Independence. For a period of sixty years he had a large and lucrative practice in the eastern counties, from which he withdrew in about 1800. During the Revolution he commanded, as colonel, a regiment in the Pennsylvania line. A more extended notice of him can be found in Saunderson's or Lossings' Lives of the signers of the Declaration of Independence.

James Wilson LL. D. is another of these earliest practitioners at the bar. His name occurs on the records as early as 1763. He was a Scotchman by birth, born in 1742, and had received a finished education at St. Andrews, Edinburgh and Glasgow, under Dr. Blair in rhetoric, and Dr. Watts in logic. In 1766 he had come to reside in Philadelphia, where he studied law with John Dickinson, the colonial governor, and founder of Dickinson College. When admitted to practice he took up his residence in Carlisle, and at once forged to the foremost of our bar. At the meeting at Carlisle, in July, 1774, which protested against the action of Great Britain against the colonies, he, with Irvine and Magaw, was appointed a delegate to meet those of other counties of the State, as the initiatory step to a general convention of delegates from the different colonies. He was subsequently a signer of the Declaration of Independence, and when the motion for independence was finally acted upon in Congress, the vote of Pennsylvania was carried in its favor by the casting vote of James Wilson, of Cumberland County. "He had," says Bancroft, in his History of the United States, "at an early day foreseen independence as the probable, though not the intended result of the contest," and although he was not, at first, avowedly in favor of a severance from the mother country, he desired it when he had received definite instructions from his constituents, and when he saw that nearly the whole mass of the people were in favor of it. In 1776 he was a colonel in the Revolution. From 1779 to 1783 he held the position of advocate-general for the French nation, whose business it was to draw up plans for regulating the intercourse of that country with the United States, for which services he received a reward, from the French King, of 1,000 livres. He was at this time director of the Bank of North America.

He was one of the most prominent members in the convention of 1787 which formed the constitution of the United States. "Of the fifty-five delegates," says McMaster, in his History of the People of the United States, "he was undoubtedly the best prepared by deep and systematic study of the history and science of government, for the work that lay before him. The Marquis de Chastellux, himself a no mean student, had been struck with the wide range of his erudition, and had spoken in high terms of his library. 'There,' said he, 'are all our best writers on law and jurisprudence. The works of President Montesquieu and of Chancellor D'Aguesseau hold the first rank among them, and he makes them his daily study.' (Travels of Marquis de Chastellux in North America p. 109.) This learning Wilson had in times past turned to excellent use, and he now became one of the most active members of the convention. None, with the exception of Gouverneur Morris, was so often on his feet during the debates or spoke more to the purpose."* [McMaster's History Vol. I. p. 421.] By this time Wilson had removed from Carlisle and lived in Philadelphia. He was appointed, under the Federal Constitution, one of the first judges of the Supreme Court of the United States, by President Washington, in which office he continued until his death. In 1790 he was appointed professor of law in the legal college at Philadelphia, which, during his incumbency, was united with the university. He received the degree of LL.D., and delivered a course of lectures on jurisprudence which were published. He died August 26, 1798, aged fifty-six.

Col. Robert Magaw, was another practitioner at this early period. He was an Irishman by birth, and resided in Cumberland County, prior to the Revolution, in which war he served as colonel of the Fifth Pennsylvania Battalion. In 1774 he was one of the delegates from this county to a convention at Philadelphia for the purpose of concerting measures to call a general congress of delegates from all the colonies. He was a prominent member of the bar, a brave officer, and a trustee of Dickinson College from 1783 until his death. He had a very large practice prior to the Revolution. He died January 7, 1790.

The name of Jasper Yeates appears upon our records as early as 1763, and for a period of twenty-one years (1784) his name appears as a practitioner at our bar. He resided in Lancaster. He was an excellent lawyer and practiced over a large territory in the eastern counties of the State. On March 21, 1791, he was appointed by Gov. Mifflin one of the associate justices of the supreme court, which position he filled until the time of his death in 1817. In appearance he was tall, portly, with handsome countenance, florid complexion and blue eyes. He was the compiler of the early Pennsylvania reports which bear his name.

George Stevenson, LL.D., was a prominent member of the bar in 1776. His name appears upon the records as early as 1770. He was born in Dublin in 1718, educated at Trinity College, and emigrated to America about the middle of the century. He was appointed deputy surveyor-general under Nicholas Scull for the three lower counties on the Delaware, known as the "territories of Pennsylvania," which William Penn obtained from the Duke of York in 1682. He afterward removed to York and was appointed a justice under George II in 1755. [See commission, page 7.] In 1769 he moved to Carlisle and became a leading member of the bar. He died at this place in 1783. Some of his correspondence may be seen in the Colonial Records, and the Pennsylvania Archives. He married the widow of Thomas Cookson, a distinguished lawyer of Lancaster, who was instructed, in connection with Nicholas Scull, to lay out the town of Carlisle in 1751.

---

*As a matter of curiosity we may mention: number of speeches were Morris, 173; Wilson, 168; Madison, 161; Sherman, 138; Mason, 136; Elbridge Gerry, 119.

HISTORY OF CUMBERLAND COUNTY.   147

Capt. John Steel was a prominent member of our bar in 1776. He had been admitted, on motion of Col. Magaw, only three years previously, April term, 1773, and seems immediately to have come into a large practice. We find him having a large practice again from 1782 to 1785, shortly after which date his name disappears from the records. Capt. John Steel was the son of Rev. John Steel, known as the "fighting parson," and was born at Carlisle, July 15, 1744. Parson Steel led a company of men from Carlisle and acted as a chaplain in the Revolutionary Army, while his son, John Steel, the subject of our sketch, led, as a captain, a company of men from the same place, and joined the army of Washington after he had crossed the Delaware. He was the father of Amelia Steel, the mother of the late Robert Given, of Carlisle. He married Agnes Moore, a sister of Mrs. Jane Thompson, who was the mother of Elizabeth Bennett, the maternal grandmother of the writer. He died about 1812.

Col. Thomas Hartley, who appeared as a practitioner at our bar in 1776, was born in Berks County in 1748. He received the rudiments of a classical education at Reading, when he went to York at the age of eighteen, and studied law under Samuel Johnston. He commenced practice in 1769. He appears as a practitioner at our bar from April, 1771, to 1797. Col. Hartley became distinguished, both in the cabinet and the field. In 1774 he was elected member of the Provincial Meeting of deputies, which met in Philadelphia in July of that year. In the succeeding year he was a member of the Provincial Convention. In the beginning of the war he became a colonel in the Revolution. He served in 1778 in the Indian war on the west branch of the Susquehanna, and in the same year was elected a member of the Legislature from York County. In 1783 he was a member of the council of censors. In 1787 he was a member of the State Convention, which adopted the Federal Constitution. In 1788 he was elected to Congress and served for a period of twelve years. In 1800 he was commissioned by Gov. McKean major-general of the Fifth Division of Pennsylvania Militia. He was an excellent lawyer, a pleasant speaker, and had a large practice. He died in York December 21, 1800, aged fifty-two years.*

These were some of the men who practiced at our bar in the memorable year 1776, men who by their services in the forum and the field helped to lay broad and deep the foundations of the government which we enjoy.

II.

FROM THE REVOLUTION UNTIL THE ADOPTION OF THE CONSTITUTION OF 1790.

From the period of the Revolution, until the adoption of the constitution of 1790, the courts were presided over by the following justices:

John Rannalls and associates, from 1776 to January, 1785; Samuel Laird and associates, from January, 1785, to January, 1786; Thomas Beals and associates, April, 1786; John Jordan and associates, from July, 1786, till October, 1791.

Owing to the adoption of the Declaration, and the necessity of taking anew the oath, most of the attorneys were re-admitted in 1778. Among these were Jasper Yeates, James Smith, James Wilson, Edward Burd and David Grier. Thomas Hartley was re-admitted in July of the succeeding year.

James Hamilton, who afterward became the fourth judge under the Consti-

*Brief sketches of him will be found in Day's Historical Collections, and in "Dickinsoniana," p. 336, &c. Also in the Archives and Records.

tution was admitted to practice upon the motion of Col. Thomas Hartly in April, 1781.

Among the names of those who practiced during this period between the Revolution and the adoption of the Constitution of 1790, are the following:

Hon. Edward Shippen was admitted to our bar in October, 1778. He was the son of Edward Shippen, Sr., the founder of Shippensburg, and was born February 16, 1729. In 1748 he was sent to England to be educated at the Inns of Court. In 1771 he was a member of the "Proprietary and Governors' Council." He afterward rose rapidly and became chief justice of Pennsylvania. He was the father of the wife of Gen. Benedict Arnold. During the Revolution his sympathies were with England, but owing to the purity of his character and the impartiality with which he discharged his official duties, the new government restored him to the bench. His name appears upon our records as late as 1800.

James Hamilton was admitted in April, 1781. He afterward became the fourth president judge of our judicial district. He was an Irishman by birth, and was admitted to the bar in his native country, but immigrated to America before the Revolution, and first settled for a short time in Pittsburgh, then a small frontier settlement, but soon afterward removed to Carlisle, where he acquired a large practice.

Hon. Thomas Duncan's name is found as a practitioner as early as 1781;* The date of his admission to the bar is not known to us. He was of Scotch ancestry, and a native of Carlisle. He was educated, it is said, under Dr. Ramsey, the historian, and studied law in Lancaster, under Hon. Jasper Yeates, then one of the judges of the Supreme Court of Pennsylvania. On his admission to the bar he returned to his native place and began the practice of law; his rise was rapid, and in less than ten years from his admission he was the acknowledged leader of his profession in the midland counties of the State, and for nearly thirty years he continued to hold this eminent position. He had, during this period, perhaps, the largest practice of any lawyer in Pennsylvania outside of Philadelphia.

In 1817 he was appointed by Gov. Snyder to the bench of the supreme court, in place of Judge Yeates, deceased. He shortly after removed to Philadelphia where he resided until his death, which occurred on the 16th of November, 1827.

During the ten years he sat upon the bench, associated with Tilghman and Gibson, he contributed largely to our stock of judicial opinions, and the reports contain abundant memorials of his industry and learning. These opinions begin with the third volume of "Sergeant & Rawle," and end with the seventeenth volume of the same series.

For years preceding the beginning of the present century and under five of the judges after the adoption of the first constitution, namely: Smith, Riddle, Henry, Hamilton and Charles Smith, Thomas Duncan practiced at our bar. As a lawyer he was distinguished by acuteness of discernment, promptness of decision, an accurate knowledge of character and a ready recourse to the rich stores of his own mind and memory. He was an excellent land and criminal lawyer, "although," says one, "I think it could be shown by citations from his opinions that his taste inclined more strongly to special pleading than to real estate, and that his accuracy in that department was greater than in the law of property."†

---

*In Dr. Nevin's "Men of Mark" it is stated that he was educated at Dickinson College, which is evidently an error, as that institution was not founded until two years later.
†Porter, in speaking of Duncan, in his essay on Gibson.

He was enthusiastically devoted to his profession, "His habits of investigation," says Porter, in speaking of him as a judge, "were patient and systematic; his powers of discrimination cultivated by study and by intercourse with the acutest minds of his day; his style, both in speaking and writing, easy, natural, graceful and clear, and his acquirements quite equal to those of his predecessors on the bench."

In appearance Mr. Duncan was about five feet six inches high, of small, delicate frame, rather reserved in manners, had rather a shrill voice, wore powder in his hair, knee breeches and buckles, and was neat in dress.

Upon a small, unobtrusive-looking monument in the old grave-yard in Carlisle, is the following inscription:

"Near this spot is deposited all that was mortal of Thomas Duncan, Esq., LL. D.; born at Carlisle, 20th of November, 1760; died 16th of November, 1827. Called to the bar at an early age, he was rapidly borne by genius, perseverance and integrity to the pinnacle of his profession, and in the fulness of his fame was elevated to the bench of the supreme court of his native State, for which a sound judgment, boundless stores of legal science, and a profound reverence for the common law, had peculiarly fitted him. Of his judicial labors the reported cases of the period are the best eulogy. As a husband, indulgent; as a father, kind; as a friend, sincere; as a magistrate, incorruptible, and as a citizen, inestimable, he was honored by the wise and good, and wept by a large circle of relatives and friends. *Honesta quam splendida.*" A panegyric which leaves nothing to be said.

Stephen Chambers, who appears upon the records of the court occasionally about 1783, although re-admitted later, was from Lancaster, and was a brother-in law of John Joseph Henry, who was afterward appointed president judge of our judicial district in 1800.

James Armstrong Wilson, whose name appears occasionally after the Revolution as a practitioner at our bar, was the son of Thomas Wilson, who resided near Carlisle, and whom we have mentioned as a provincial justice. He was educated at Princeton, where he graduated about 1771. He studied law with Richard Stockton, and was admitted to the bar at Easton. He was a major in the Revolution. The earliest mention of his name in the records of our court is about 1778.

John Clark, who was from York, Penn., appears occasionally as a practitioner about 1784. He was a major in the Revolution, of large frame, fine personal appearance, witty, so that his society was much courted by many of the lawyers who rode the circuit with him in those days.

Ross Thompson, who had practiced in other courts, was admitted to our bar in 1784. He lived some time in Chambersburg, but removed to Carlisle, where he died at an early age.

John Wilkes Kittera, admitted in 1783, was from Philadelphia, but settled in Lancaster. He was admitted to the first term of court two years later, May, 1785, in Dauphin County.

Gen. John Andrew Hanna (1785), settled in Harrisburg at about the time of the organization of Dauphin County. He is noticed favorably in the narrative of the Duke de Rochefoucault, who visited the State capital in 1795. He says that Gen. Hanna was then "about thirty-six or thirty-eight years of age, and was brigadier-general of militia." He was a brother-in-law of Robert Harris, the father of George W. Harris, the compiler of the Pennsylvania Reports, and was an executor of the will of John Harris, the founder of Harrisburg. He was elected to Congress from his district in 1797, and served till 1805, in which year he died.

Ralph Bowie, from York, was admitted to our bar at October term, 1785, and practiced considerably in our courts from 1798 till after 1800. He was a Scotchman by birth and had probably been admitted to the bar in his native country. He was a well-read lawyer and much sought after in important cases of ejectment. He was of fine personal appearance, courtly and dignified in manner, and neat and particular in dress. He powdered his hair, wore short clothes in the fashion of the day, and had social qualities of the most attractive character.

Of James Riddle, Charles Smith, John Joseph Henry and Thomas Smith, all of whom became judges, we will speak later.

Thomas Creigh, who was admitted in 1790, was the son of Hon. John Creigh, who emigrated from Ireland and settled in Carlisle in 1761. John Creigh was an early justice, and one of the nine representatives who signed the first Declaration, June 24, 1776, for the colony of Pennsylvania. Thomas Creigh was born in Carlisle August 16, 1769. He graduated in the second class which left Dickinson College in 1788. He probably studied law under Thomas Duncan, upon whose motion he was admitted. He died in Carlisle October, 1809. One sister, Isabel, married Samuel Alexander, Esq., of Carlisle; Mary married Hon. John Kennedy, of the Supreme Court of Pennsylvania, and Elizabeth, Samuel Duncan, Esq., of Carlisle.

David Watts (1790), a son of Frederick Watts, who was a member of the early Provincial Council, was born in Cumberland County October 29, 1764. He graduated in the first class which left the then unpretentious halls of Dickinson College in 1787. He afterward read law in Philadelphia under the eminent jurist and advocate, William Lewis, LL.D., and was admitted to our bar in October, 1790. He soon acquired an immense practice, and became the acknowledged rival of Thomas Duncan, who had been for years the recognized leader on this circuit. He died September 25, 1819.

We have now given a brief sketch of our bar, from the earliest times down to the adoption of the constitution of 1790, when, in the following year, Thomas Smith, the first president judge of our judicial district, appears upon the bench.

III.

CONSTITUTIONAL PERIOD.

From the adoption of this first constitution until the present, the judges who have presided over our courts are as follows:

JUDGES.

Thomas Smith, 1791; James Riddle, 1794; John Joseph Henry, 1800; James Hamilton, 1806; Charles Smith, 1819; John Reed, 1820; Samuel Hepburn, 1838; Frederick Watts, 1848; James H. Graham, 1851; Benjamin F. Junkin, 1871; Martin C. Herman, 1875; Wilbur F. Sadler, 1885.

Hon. Thomas Smith first appeared upon the bench in the October term, 1791. He resided at Carlisle. He had been a deputy surveyor under the government in early life, and thus became well acquainted with the land system in Pennsylvania, then in process of formation. He was accounted a good common law lawyer and did a considerable business. He was commissioned president judge by Gov. Mifflin on the 20th of August, 1791. He continued in that position until his appointment as an associate judge of the supreme court, on the 31st of January, 1794. He was a small man, rather reserved in his manner, and of not very social proclivities. He died at an advanced age in the year 1809.

Owing to the necessity of being resworn, according to the provisions of the new constitution, the following attorneys "having taken the oath prescribed by law," were readmitted at this term of court: James Riddle, Andrew Dunlap, of Franklin; Thomas Hartley, of York; David Watts, Thomas Nesbitt, Ralph Bowie, Thomas Duncan, Thomas Creigh, Robert Duncan, James Hamilton and others.

Hon. James Riddle first appears upon the bench at the April term, 1794. He was born in Adams County, graduated with distinction at Princeton College, and subsequently read law at York. He was about thirty years of age when he was admitted to the bar. He had a large practice until his appointment as president judge of this judicial district, by Gov. Mifflin, in February, 179–. His legal abilities were very respectable, though he was not considered a great lawyer. He was well read in science, literature and the law; was a good advocate and very successful with the jury. He was a tall man, broad shouldered and lusty, with a noble face and profile and pleasing manner. Some time in 1804 he resigned his position of judge, because of the strong partisan feeling existing against him—he being an ardent Federalist—and returned to the practice of the law. He died in Chambersburg about 1837.

Hon. John Joseph Henry, of Lancaster, was born about the year 1758. He was the third president judge of our judicial district and the predecessor of Judge Hamilton. He was appointed in 1800. He had previously been the first president judge of Dauphin County in 1793. In 1775 young Henry, then a lad of about seventeen or eighteen years of age, entered the Revolutionary Army and joined the expedition against Quebec. He was in the company under Capt. Matthew Smith, of Lancaster. The whole command, amounting to about 1,000 men, was under the command of Gen. Benedict Arnold. Young Henry fought at the battle of Quebec and was taken prisoner. He subsequently published an account of the expedition. Judge Henry was a large man, probably over six feet in height. He died in Lancaster in 1810.

THE BAR IN 1800.

And now we have arrived at the dawn of a new century. Judge Henry was upon the bench. Watts and Duncan were unquestionably the leading lawyers. They were engaged in probably more than one-half the cases which were tried, and always on opposite sides. Hamilton came next, six years later, to be upon the bench. There also were Charles Smith, who was to succeed Hamilton; Bowie, of York, and Shippen, of Lancaster, with their queues and Continental dress, and the Duncan brothers, James and Samuel, and Thomas Creigh, all of them engaged in active practice at our bar at the beginning of the century. At this time the lawyers still traveled upon the circuit, and circuit courts were held also as will be seen by the following entry: "Circuit Court held at Carlisle for the County of Cumberland this 4th day of May, 1801, before the Hon. Jasper Yeates, and Hon. Hugh Henry Brackenridge, justices of the Supreme Court."

Among the prominent attorneys admitted to the bar during the time Judge Henry was upon the bench, were John Bannister Gibson, afterward chief justice of Pennsylvania, George Metzgar and Andrew Carothers. Gibson was admitted in March, 1803.

On the motion of Thomas Duncan, Esq., and the usual certificates filed stating that Alexander P. Lyon, John B. M. S. Gibson and James Carothers had studied law under his direction for the space of two years after they had respectively arrived at the age of twenty-one. Com. Ralph Bowie, Charles Smith and William Brown.

George Metzgar was born in 1782, and graduated at Dickinson College in 1798. He studied law with David Watts after he had arrived at the age of twenty-one, and was admitted in March, 1805. Afterward he served as prosecuting attorney, and was a member of the Legislature in 1813-14, and held a respectable position at the bar. He died in Carlisle June 10, 1879. He was the founder of the Metzgar Female Institute in Carlisle.

Andrew Carothers was born in Silver Spring, Cumberland County, about 1778. He learned the trade of a cabinet-maker, but when about nineteen years of age his father's family was poisoned, and Andrew, who survived, was crippled by its effects in his hands and limbs to such an extent that he was incapacitated for the trade which he had chosen. He had received but the education of the country school, and it was not until he had become unfitted for an occupation which required bodily labor, that he turned his attention to the law. He entered the office of David Watts, in Carlisle, and after three years' study, was admitted to the bar December, 1805. In the language of Judge Watts "He became an excellent practical and learned lawyer, and very soon took a high place at the bar of Cumberland County, which at that time ranked amongst its numbers some of the best lawyers of the State, Watts, Duncan, Alexander and Mahan were at different times his competitors, and amongst these he acquired a large and lucrative practice, which continued through his whole life. Mr. Carothers was remarkable for his amiability of temper, his purity of character, his unlimited disposition of charity and his love of justice."

On all public occasions and in courts of justice his addresses were delivered, by reason of his bodily infirmity, in a sitting posture. He was active in promoting the general interests of the community, and was for years one of the trustees of Dickinson College. He died July 26, 1836, aged fifty-eight years.

THE BAR UNDER HAMILTON.

Of James Hamilton, who appears upon the bench in 1806, we have before spoken. Watts and Duncan were still leaders of the bar under Judge Hamilton. Mr. Watts came to the bar some years later than Thomas Duncan, but both were admitted and the latter had practiced under the judges prior to the constitution; but from that time, 1790, both practiced, generally as opponents, and were leaders at the bar under the first five judges who presided after the constitution, until the appointment of Duncan to the supreme bench in 1817. David Watts died two years later.

Judge Hamilton was a student, but lacked self-confidence, and was more inclined, it is said, to take what he was told ruled the case than to trust to his own judgment, and there is a legend to the effect that a certain act, which can be found in the pamphlet laws of Pennsylvania, 1810, p. 136, forbidding the reading of English precedents subsequent to 1776, was passed at his instance to get rid of the multitudinous authorities with which Mr. Duncan was wont to confuse his judgment.

Mr. Watts was an impassioned, forcible and fluent speaker. He was a strong, powerful man. Mr. Duncan was a small and delicate looking man. The voice of Mr. Watts was strong and rather rough, that of Mr. Duncan was weak and sometimes shrill in pleading. In Mr. Brackenridge's "Recollections," he speaks of attending the courts in Carlisle, in about 1807, where there were two very able lawyers, Messrs. Watts and Duncan. "The former," says he, "was possessed of a powerful mind and was the most vehement speaker I ever heard. He seized his subject with a herculean grasp, at the same time throwing his herculean body and limbs into attitudes which would have de-

lighted a painter or a sculptor. He was a singular instance of the union of great strength of mind with bodily powers equally wonderful.

"Mr. Duncan was one of the best lawyers and advocates I have ever seen at a bar, and he was, perhaps, the best judge that ever sat on the supreme bench of the State. He was a very small man, with a large but well-formed head. There never was a lover more devoted to his mistress than Mr. Duncan was to the study of law. He perused Coke upon Littleton as a recreation, and read more books of reports than a young lady reads new novels. His education had not been very good, and his general reading was not remarkable. I was informed that he read frequently the plays of Shakespeare, and from that source derived that uncommon richness and variety of diction by which he was enabled to embellish the most abstruse subjects, although his language was occasionally marked by inacuracies, even violation of common grammar rules. Mr. Duncan reasoned with admirable clearness and method on all legal subjects, and at the same time displayed great knowledge of human nature in examination of witnesses and in his addresses to the jury. Mr. Watts selected merely the strong points of his case, and labored them with an earnestness and zeal approaching to fury; and perhaps his forcible manner sometimes produced a more certain effect than that of the subtle and wiley advocate opposed to him."

Among the attorneys admitted under Hamilton was Isaac Brown Parker, March, 1806, on motion of Charles Smith, Esq. Mr. Parker had read law under James Hamilton, just previous to the time of his appointment to the bench. His committee was Ralph Bowie, Charles Smith and James Duncan, Esqrs. Alexander Mahan, graduated at Dickinson College in 1805; August, 1808, read under Thomas Duncan; committee David Watts, John B. Gibson and Andrew Carothers, Esqrs....William Ramsey same date, instructor and committee.

In 1809 William Ramsey, Democrat, ran for sheriff of Cumberland County. The opposing candidate was John Carothers, Federalist. At this time, under the old constitution the governor appointed one of the two having the highest number of votes. Ramsey had the highest number of votes but Carothers was appointed. Gov. Snyder afterward appointed William Ramsey prothonotary, which office he held for many years. He had great influence in the Democratic party. About 1817 he began to practice his profession and acquired a very large practice. He died in 1831.

James Hamilton, Jr., was the son of Judge Hamilton. He was born in Carlisle, October 16, 1793. He graduated at Dickinson College in 1812. He read law with Isaac B. Parker, who was an uncle by marriage, and was admitted to the bar while his father was upon the bench in April, 1816. He was, from 1824 to 1833, a trustee of Dickinson College. For several years Mr. Hamilton followed his profession, but being in affluent circumstances he gradually retired from active practice. He died in Carlisle June 23, 1873.

John Williamson, was for many years a member of our bar. He was the brother-in-law of Hon. Samuel Hepburn, with whom he was for a long time associated. He was born in Mifflin Township, Cumberland County, September 14, 1789, and graduated at Dickinson College, Carlisle, in 1809. He was admitted to our bar at the August term, 1811. He previously read law with Luther Martin, of Baltimore, Md., who was one of the counsel for Aaron Burr, in his trial for high treason, at Richmond, Va. Luther Martin, the "Federal Bull-dog," as he was called, was a character altogether *sui generis*, with an unlimited capacity both for legal lore and liquor. In the former respect only his pupil somewhat (although in a less degree) resembled his preceptor. Mr. Williamson seems to have been exceedingly well versed in law, with an intimate knowledge of all the cases and distinctions, but the very depth or extensiveness of his learning seemed at times to confuse his judgment. He saw the case in every possible aspect in which it could be presented; but then which particular phase should, in the wise dispensation of an all-ruling Providence, happen to be the law, as afterward determined by the court, was a question often too difficult to decide. His aid as a counselor was valuable, and as such he was frequently employed. He died in Philadelphia, September 10, 1870.

John Duncan Mahan was admitted under Hamilton in April, 1817. He was born November 5, 1796; graduated at Dickinson College in 1814, and immediately began the study of law under the instruction of his uncle, Thomas Duncan. He became a leader of the bar of Carlisle at a brilliant period, until in 1833, when he removed to Pittsburgh and became a prominent member of the bar of that city, where he resided until his death July 3, 1861. When Mr. Mahan was admitted to the bar Watts and Duncan were at the zenith of their fame, and were retained in all great cases within the circuit of their practice. But this was near the end of their career, as competitors, for at that very time Duncan was appointed to the supreme bench, which he adorned during his life, and Watts died two years later. Judge Duncan transferred his whole practice to his then young student and nephew, John D. Mahan and his eminent success justified his preceptor's confidence. His first step was into the front rank of the profession.

Mr. Mahan was a man of rare endowments. What many learned by study and painful investigation he seemed to grasp intuitively. He had the gift, the power and the grace of the orator, and in addressing the passions, the sympathies, or the peculiarities of men he seldom made mistakes. "His every gesture," it has been said of him, "was graceful, his style of eloquence was the proper word in the proper place for the occasion, and his voice was music." He was affable in temper, brilliant in conversation and was among the leaders of our bar, under Hamilton, Smith and Reed, at a time when it had strong men, by whom his strength was tested and his talents tried.

A writer speaking from his recollections of the bar at about this period, says: "John D. Mahan was its bright, particular star; young, graceful, eloquent, and with a jury irresistible. Equal to him in general ability, and superior, perhaps, in legal acumen, was his contemporary and rival, Samuel Alexander. Then there was the vehement Andrew Carothers and young Frederick Watts, just admitted in time to reap the advantages of his father's reputation and create an enduring one of his own. And George Metzgar, with his treble voice and hand on his side, amusing the court and spectators with his not overly delicate *facetiæ*. And there was "Billy Ramsey with his queue," a man of many clients, and the *sine qua non* of the Democratic party.

Hon. Charles Smith was appointed to succeed Hamilton as the fifth president judge of our judicial district, in the year 1819. Mr. Charles Smith was born at Philadelphia, March 4, 1765. He received his degree B. A. at the first commencement of Washington College, Charleston, Md., March 14, 1783. His father, William Smith, D. D., was the founder, and at that time the provost of that institution. Charles Smith commenced the study of the law with his elder brother, William Moore Smith, who then resided at Easton, Penn. After his admission to the bar he opened his office in Sunbury, Northumberland County, where his industry and rising talents soon procured for him a large practice. He was elected delegate, with his colleague, Simon Snyder, to the convention which framed the first constitution for the State of Pennsylvania, and was looked on as a very distinguished member of that talented body of men. Although differing in the politics of that day from his colleague, yet Mr. Snyder for more than thirty years afterward remained the firm friend of Mr. Smith, and when the former became the governor of the State for three successive terms it is well known that Mr. Smith was his confidential adviser in many important matters. Mr. Smith was married in 1719 to a daughter of Jasper Yeates, one of the supreme court judges of the State, and soon removed from Sunbury to Lancaster, where Judge Yeates resided. Under the old circuit court system it was customary for most of the distinguished country lawyers to travel over the northern and western parts of the State with the judges, and hence Mr. Smith, in pursuing this practice, soon became associated with such eminent men as Thomas Duncan, David Watts, Charles Hall, John Woods, James Hamilton, and a host of luminaries of the middle bar. The settlement of land titles, at that period, became of vast importance to the people of the State, and the foundation of the law with regard to settlement rights, the rights of warrantees, the doctrine of surveys, and the proper construction of lines and corners, had to be laid. In the trial of ejectment cases the learning of the bar was best displayed, and Mr. Smith was soon looked on as an eminent land lawyer. In after years, when called on to revise the old publications of the laws of the State, and under the authority of the Legislature to frame a new compilation of the same (generally known as Smith's Laws of Pennsylvania) he gave to the public the result of his knowledge and experience on the subject of land law, in the very copious note on that subject, which may well be termed a treatise on the land laws of Pennsylvania. In the same work his note on the criminal law of the State is elaborate and instructive. Mr. Smith was, in 1819, appointed president judge of the district, comprising the counties of Cumberland and Franklin, where his official learning and judgment, and his habitual industry, rendered him a useful and highly popular judge.

On the erection of the District Court of Lancaster he became the first presiding judge, which office he held for several years. He finally removed to Philadelphia, where he spent the last years of his life, and died in that city in 1840, in the seventy-fifth year of his age.

Hon. John Reed, LL.D., appeared upon the bench in 1820. Judge Reed was born in what was then York, now Adams County, in 1786. He was the son of Gen. William Reed, of Revolutionary fame. He read law under William Maxwell, of Gettysburg. In 1809 he was admitted to the bar and commenced the practice of law in Westmoreland County. In the two last years of his professional career he performed the duties of deputy attorney-general. In 1815 Mr. Reed was elected to the State Senate, and on the 10th of July 1820, he was commissioned by Gov. Finley president judge of the Ninth Judicial District, then composed of the counties of Cumberland, Adams and Perry. When, in 1839, by a change in the constitution, his commission expired, he resumed his practice at the bar, and continued it until his death which occurred in Carlisle, on the 19th of January, 1850, when he was in the sixty-fourth year of his age. In 1839 the decree of LL.D. was conferred upon him by Washington College, Pennsylvania. In 1833 the new board of trustees of Dickinson College formed a professorship of law, and Judge Reed was elected professor of that department. The instructions consisted of lectures, and of a moot court of law, where legal questions were discussed, cases tried, and where the pleadings were drawn up in full—Reed being the supreme court. After a full course of study, this department conferred the decree of LL.B. Many were admitted to the bar during this period, most of whom practiced elsewhere, and many of whom afterward became eminent in their profession.

THE BAR UNDER JUDGE REED.

At this period, and later, the bar was particularly strong. Of the old veterans, David Watts was dead, and Duncan was upon the supreme bench. But among the practitioners of the time were such men as Carothers, Alexander, Mahan, Ramsey, Williamson, Metzgar, Lyon, William Irvine, William H. Brackenridge and Isaac Brown Parker; while among those admitted, and who were afterward to attain eminence on the bench or at the bar, were such men as Charles B. Penrose, Hugh Gaullagher, Frederick Watts, William M. Biddle, James H. Graham, Samuel Hepburn, William Sterritt Ramsey, S. Dunlap Adair and John Brown Parker—a galaxy of names such as has not since been equaled.

Gen. Samuel Alexander was practicing at our bar in 1820, when Judge Reed took the bench. He was the youngest son of Col. John Alexander, a Revolutionary officer, and was born in Carlisle September 20, 1792. He graduated at Dickinson College in 1812, after which he read law in Greensburg with his brother, Maj. John B. Alexander, and became a prominent lawyer in that part of the State. He afterward returned to Carlisle, and by the advice of Judge Duncan and David Watts was induced to become a member of our bar, at which he soon acquired a prominent position. In 1820 he married a daughter of Col. Ephraim Blaine, but left no sons to perpetuate his name.

As an advocate Mr. Alexander had but few, if any, superiors at the bar. In the early part of his career he was a diligent student and was in the habit of carefully digesting most of the reported cases. In addition to this he was possessed of a tenacious memory and seemed never to forget a case he had once read. He was always fully identified with the cause of his client, and possessed that thorough onesidedness so necessary to the successful advocate.

He possessed also great tact and an intuitive quickness of perception. In the management of a case he was apt, watchful and ingenious. If driven from one position, like a skillful general he was always quick to seize another. In this respect his talents, it is said, only brightened amid difficulties, and shone forth only the more resplendent as the battle became more hopeless. Nor was oratory, the crowning grace and the most necessary accomplishment of the advocate, wanting. He was a forcible speaker, with a large command of language, and with the happy faculty of nearly always finding the right word for the right place. His diction was choice, and in his matter, although sometimes diffusive, in his manner he was always bold, vigorous and aggressive. He had the power of sarcasm, was often ironical, and was a master in personal invective. In this he had no equal at the bar. In the examination of witnesses, also, he had no superior.

Mr. Alexander had a natural inclination for mechanics, and was passionately fond of anything pertaining to military life. He was for years at the head of a volunteer regiment of the county. He cared for this, strange as it may, appear, more than for his profession, which, toward the close of his life, seems to have become distasteful to him; at least with his abilities unimpaired, he appeared but seldom in the trial of a cause. He died in Carlisle in July, 1845, aged fifty-two.

Hugh Gaullagher, a practitioner at the bar under Reed, studied law with Hon. Richard Coulter of Greensburg, and shortly after his admission commenced the practice of law in Carlisle. This was about 1824, from which time he continued to practice until about the middle of the century.

He was eccentric, long limbed, awkward in his gait, and in his delivery with an Irish brogue, but he was well-read, particularly in history and in the elements of his profession. He was an affable man, an instructive companion, fond of conversation, with inherent humor and a love of fun, and was popular in the circle of his friends, of whom he had many. He was among the number of the old lawyers of our bar who were fond of a dinner and a song, however gravely they appear upon the page of history.

At the bar his position was more that of a counselor than of an advocate. He was fond of the old cases and would rather read an opinion of my Lord Mansfield, or Hale, or Coke, than the latest delivered by our own judges, "not that he disregarded the latter, but because he reverenced the former."

He is well remembered, often in connection with anecdotes, and is as frequently spoken of by survivors as any man who practiced at our bar so long ago. He died April 14, 1856.

Hon. Charles B. Penrose was born near Philadelphia October 6, 1798. He read law with Samuel Ewing, Esq., in Philadelphia, and immediately moved to Carlisle. He soon acquired a prominent position at the bar. He was elected to the State Senate in 1833, and at the expiration of his term was re-elected. In this capacity he achieved distinction even among the men of ability who were then chosen for this office. In 1841 he was appointed by President Harrison, solicitor of the treasury, which position he held until the close of President Tyler's administration. After practicing in Carlisle he moved first to Lancaster, then to Philadelphia, in both places successfully pursuing his profession. In 1856 he was again elected as a reform candidate to the State Senate, during which term he died of pneumonia at Harrisburg, April 6, 1857.

William M. Biddle was admitted under Reed in 1826. He was born in Philadelphia July 3, 1801, and died of heart disease in that city, where he had gone to place himself under the care of physicians, on the 28th of February, 1855. He was the great-great-grandson of Nicholas Scull, surveyor-general of Pennsylvania from 1748 to 1761, who, by direction of Gov. Hamilton, laid out the borough of Carlisle in 1751. Mr. Biddle was originally destined for mercantile pursuits, but the death of his cousin, Henry Sergeant, an East India trader, who had promised him a partnership in business, put an end to these plans and his attention was turned to the law. He went to Reading, Penn., and studied with his brother-in-law, Samuel Baird, Esq. In 1826, shortly after his admission to the bar, he moved to Carlisle, induced to do so by the advice of his brother-in-law, Charles B. Penrose, Esq., who had recently opened a law office there, and was then rising into a good practice. Located in Carlisle he soon acquired a large business and soon took a high position at the bar, which he retained to the day of his death, a period of twenty-nine years.

Mr. Biddle was an able lawyer and had a keen perception of the principles of law, which, when understood, reduce it to a science. He was endowed with a large fund of wit, in addition to which he was also an excellent mimic, and often indulged in these powers in his addresses to the jury. He was rather a large man, of fine personal presence, great affability, endowed with quick wit and high moral and intellectual qualities which made him a leader at the bar at a time when many brilliant men were among its members.

Gen. Edward M. Biddle was born in Philadelphia; graduated at Princeton College, and then removed to Carlisle, where he studied law under his brother-in-law, Hon. Chas. B. Penrose, and in 1830 was admitted to practice in the several courts of Cumberland County.

Hon. Charles McClure was admitted to the bar under Reed in August, 1826. He was born in Carlisle, graduated at Dickinson College, and afterward became a member of Congress, and still later, 1843-45, secretary of state of Pennsylvania. He was a son-in-law of Chief Justice Gibson. He did not practice extensively at the bar. He removed to Pittsburgh, where he died in 1846.

Hon. William Sterritt Ramsey, one of the most promising members of the bar admitted under Reed, was born in Carlisle June 16, 1810. He entered Dickinson College in the autumn of 1826, where he remained three years. In the summer of 1829 he was sent to Europe to complete his education and to restore, by active travel and change of scene, health to an already debilitated constitution. The same year he was appointed (by our minister to the court of St. James, Hon. Lewis McClane) an *attache* to the American Legation. He pursued his legal studies, visited the courts of Westminister, and the author of Waverly at Abbottsford, to whom he bore letters from Washington Irving. After the Revolution of three days in July, 1830, he was sent with dispatches to France, and spent much of his time, while there, at the hotel of Gen. Lafayette. In 1831 he returned to America and began the study of law under his father. In the month of September of this year his father died. He continued to study under Andrew Carothers, and in 1833 was admitted to the bar of Cumberland County.

In 1838 he was elected a member of Congress by the Democratic party, and at the expiration of his term was re-elected. He was at this time the youngest member of Congress in the House. He died, before being qualified a second time, by his own hand in Barnum's Hotel, Baltimore, October 22, 1840, aged only thirty years. An eloquent obituary notice was written on the occasion of his death by his friend, Hon. James Buchanan, afterward President of the United States, from which some of the above facts are taken.

S. Dunlap Adair was admitted under Reed in January, 1835. For fifteen years he was a practitioner at the bar. He was born March 26, 1810. While a youth he attended the classical school of Joseph Casey, Sr., the father of Hon. Joseph Casey, in Newville, and was among the brightest of his pupils. He was apt in acquiring knowledge and particularly in the facility of acquiring languages. He became a good Latin scholar, and, after his admission to the bar, made himself acquainted with the German, French and Italian languages. He was well read in English literature, and although not a graduate of any college, his attainments were as varied as those of any member of the bar. He studied law under Hon. Frederick Watts, and soon after his admission was appointed deputy attorney-general for the county. He was a candidate of his party in the district for Congress when William Ramsey, the younger, was elected. He had a chaste, clear style, and was a pleasant speaker. In stature he was below the medium height, delicately formed, near-sighted, and whether sitting or standing had a tendency to lean forward. He was of sanguine temperament, had auburn hair and a high forehead. He died of bronchial consumption in Carlisle, September 23, 1850.

John Brown Parker, Esq., was born in Carlisle October 5, 1816. He graduated at the University of Pennsylvania, at Philadelphia, in 1834. He read law with Hon. Frederick Watts for the period of one year, completing his course of study in the law school under Judge Reed, and was admitted to practice in April, 1838. He was for a time associated with his preceptor, Hon. Frederick Watts. He retired from practice in 1865, and moved to Philadelphia, where he resided for some years.

Capt. William M. Porter was born in Carlisle, this county, in 1808; read law under Samuel A. McCoskry, and was admitted to the Carlisle bar in 1835. He died in 1873.

In 1827 John Bannister Gibson, LL. D., was appointed chief justice of Pennsylvania.

He was born on the 8th of November, 1780, in Sherman's Valley, then Cumberland, now Perry, County, Pennsylvania. He was of Scotch-Irish descent, and the son of Col. George Gibson, who was killed at the defeat of St. Clair in 1791. In 1795 young Gibson studied in the preparatory school connected with Dickinson College, and subsequently in the collegiate department, when that institution was under Dr. Nesbitt, graduating at the age of eighteen, in the class of 1798.

During this period he was in the habit of frequenting the office of Dr. McCoskry—one of the oldest practitioners of medicine in the place—and there acquired a taste for the study of physic, which he never lost.

On the completion of his collegiate course, he entered on the study of law in Carlisle in the office of his kinsman, Thomas Duncan, with whom he was afterward to occupy a seat on the bench of the supreme court. He was admitted to the bar of Cumberland County in March, 1803.

He first opened his office in Carlisle, then removed to Beaver, then to Hagerstown, but shortly afterward returned to Carlisle. This was in 1805, and at this point is the beginning of a remarkable career.

From 1805 to 1812 Mr. Gibson seems to have had a reasonable share of the legal practice in Cumberland County, particularly when we consider that the field was occupied by such men as Duncan, Watts, Bowie of York, and Smith of Lancaster, who, at the time of which we speak, had but few equals in the State. Nevertheless it may well be doubted whether his qualifications were of such a character as would ever have fitted him to attain high eminence at the bar. His reputation, at this period, was not that of diligence in his profession, and it is quite probable that, at this time, he had no great liking for it. In fact, at this period, of his life Mr. Gibson seems to have been known rather as a fine musical connoisseur and art critic than as a successful lawyer. He was a good draughtsman, a judge of fine paintings, and a votary of the violin.

In 1810 Mr. Gibson was elected by the Democratic party of Cumberland County to the House of Representatives, and after the expiration of his term, in 1812, he was appointed president judge of the court of common pleas for the Eleventh Judicial District, composed of the counties of Tioga, Bradford, Susquehanna and Luzerne.

Justice Gibson's personal appearance at this time is within the recollection of men who are still living. He was a man of large proportions, a giant both in physique and intellect. He was considerably over six feet in height, with a muscular, well-proportioned frame, indicative of strength and energy, and a countenance expressing strong character and manly beauty.

"His face," says David Paul Brown, "was full of intellect and benevolence, and, of course, eminently handsome; his manners were remarkable for their simplicity, warmth, frankness and generosity. There never was a man more free from affectation or pretension of every sort."

Until the day of his death, says Porter, "although his bearing was mild and unostentatious, so striking was his personal appearance that few persons to whom he was unknown could have passed him by in the street without remark."

Upon the death of Judge Brackenridge in 1816, Judge Gibson was appointed by Gov. Snyder Associate Justice of the Supreme Court, where, as it has been said, if Tilghman was the Nestor, Gibson became the Ulysses of the bench.

This appointment of Gibson to the bench of the supreme court seems first to have awakened his intellect and stimulated his ambition. He partly withdrew himself from his former associates, and was thus delivered from numerous temptations to indolence and dissipation. He became more devoted to study, and for the first time perhaps in his life he seems to have formed a resolution to make himself master of the law as a science. Coke particularly seems to have been his favorite author, and his quaint, forcible and condensed style, together with the severity of his logic seem to have had no small influence in the development of Gibson's mind, and in implanting there the seeds of that love for the English common law, which was afterward everywhere so conspicuous in his writings.

It is pertinent here to remark that Judge Gibson, like Coke and Blackstone, seems never to have had any fondness for the civil law. Whether this was on account of the purely Anglo-Saxon of his mind, or on account of a want of opportunity in the means through which to become thoroughly acquainted with the most beautiful and symmetrical system of law which the world has ever known, we can not say, but certain it is that he seems to have cast ever and anon a suspicious glance at the efforts of a judge story, and writers of that school to infuse its principles in a still greater degree into our common law. We need but refer to the opinions delivered in Dyle vs. Richards, 9 Sergeant and Rawle, 322, and in Logan vs. Mason, 6 Watts and Sergeant 9, in proof of the existence of these views in the mind of their author.

In an old number of the "American Law Register" there is a review of Mr. Troubat's work on limited partnership by Gibson. It was the last essay he ever wrote, and in it he says: "The writer of this article is not a champion of the civil law; nor does he profess to have more than a superficial knowledge of it. He was bred in the school of Littleton and Coke, and he would be sorry to see any but common law doctrines taught in it." But here Gibson is speaking of the English law of real property, and he afterward says "The English law merchant, an imperishable monument to Lord Mansfield's fame, shows what a magnificent structure may be raised upon it where the ground is not preoccupied."

Hitherto the bench of the supreme court had consisted of but three judges, but under the act of April 8, 1826, the number was increased to five. But little more than one year elapsed before the death of Chief Justice Tilghman. Gibson was his successor. He received his commission on the 18th of May, 1827, and from this time forward the gradual and uniform progress of his mind, says Col. Porter, "may be traced in his opinions with a certainty and satisfaction which are perhaps not offered in the case of any other judge known to our annals. His original style, compared to that in which he now began to write, was like the sinews of a growing lad compared to the well-knit muscles of a man. No one who has carefully studied his opinions can have failed to remark the increased power and pith which distinguished them from this time forward." In the language of Hon. Thaddeus Stevens "he lived to an advanced age, his knowledge increasing with increasing years, while his great intellect remained unimpaired."

From 1827 he remained as the chief upon the bench, until 1851, when by a change in the constitution the judiciary became elective, and was elected the same year an associate justice of the court, being the only one of the former incumbents returned. But although "nominally superseded by another as the head of the court, his great learning, venerable character and over shadowing reputation still made him," in the language of his successor, Judge Black, "the only chief whom the hearts of the people would know.

"His accomplishments were very extraordinary. He was born a musician, and the natural talent was highly cultivated. He was a connoisseur in painting and sculpture. The whole round of English literature was familiar to him.* He was at home among the ancient classics. * * * He

---

*He was well read, we have seen it stated, in the British classics, fond of English drama, and familiar with the dramatists of the Restoration.

had studied medicine in his youth and understood it well. His mind absorbed all kinds of knowledge with scarcely an effort."*

In regard to his mental habits, he was a deep student, but not a close student; he worked most effectively, but he worked reluctantly. The concurrent testimony of all who knew him is that he seldom or never wrote, except when under the pressure of necessity, but when he once brought the powers of his mind to a focus and took up the pen, he wrote continuously and without erasure. When he once began to write an opinion he very rarely laid it aside until it was completed. This, with the broad grasp with which he took hold of his subject, has given to his opinions a consistency and unity otherwise difficult to have attained. He saw a case in all its varied relations, and the principles by which it was governed, rather by the intuitive insight of genius, than as the result of labor.

These opinions very seldom give a history of decided cases, but invariably put the decision upon some leading principle of law—referring to but few cases, by way of illustration, or to show exceptions to the rule. He was eminently self-reliant. He appeared at a time when the law of our commonwealth was in process of formation, and in its development his formulating power has been felt.

Of his style much has been said. Said Stevens "I do not know by whom it has been surpassed." It is a judicial style, at once compact, technical and exact. His writing can be made to convey just what he means to express and nothing more. His meaning is not always upon the surface, but when it is perceived it is certain and without ambiguity. [It may be interesting to state that Chief Justice Gibson often thought out his opinions while he was playing upon the violin. When a thought came to him he would lay down his instrument and write. As to his accuracy of language, he was in the habit of carrying with him a book of synonyms. These facts have been told to the writer by his son, Col. George Gibson, of the United States Army.]

It has been said that one "could pick out his opinions from others like gold coin from among copper." He was, for more than half his life, a chief or associate justice on the bench, and his opinions extend through no less than seventy volumes of our reports †—an imperishable monument to his memory.

Chief Justice Gibson died in Philadelphia May 3, 1853, in the seventy-third year of his age. He was buried two days afterward in Carlisle.

In the old grave-yard, upon the tall marble shaft which was erected over his tomb, we read the following beautiful inscription from the pen of Chief Justice Jeremiah S. Black:

> In the various knowledge
> Which forms the perfect SCHOLAR
> He had no superior.
> Independent, upright and able,
> He had all the highest qualities of a great JUDGE.
> In the difficult science of Jurisprudence,
> He mastered every Department,
> Discussed almost every question, and
> Touched no subject which he did not adorn.
> He won in early manhood,
> And retained to the close of a long life,
> The AFFECTION of his brethren on the Bench,
> The RESPECT of the Bar
> And the CONFIDENCE of the people.

Hon. John Kennedy, who had studied under the elder Hamilton and had been admitted to our bar under Riddle in 1798, was appointed to the bench

---
* Judge Black's Eulogy on Gibson.
† From 2 Sergeant and Rawle to 7 Harris.

of the supreme court in 1830. He was born in Cumberland County in June, 1774; graduated at Dickinson College in 1795, and after his admission to the bar, removed to a northern circuit, where he became the compeer of men like James Ross, John Lyon, Parker Campbell, and others scarcely less distinguished. He afterward removed to Pittsburgh, where his high reputation as a lawyer at once introduced him to a lucrative practice. From 1830 he remained upon the bench until his death, August 26, 1846. His opinions, extending through twenty-seven volumes of reports, are distinguished by lucid argumentation and laborious research. Judge Gibson, who had known him from boyhood, and who sat with him upon the bench for a period of over fifteen years, said: "His judicial labors were his recreations. He clung to the common law as a child to its nurse, and how much he drew from it may be seen in his opinions, which, by their elaborate minuteness, remind us of the overfullness of Lord Coke. Patient in investigation and slow in judgment, he seldom changed his opinion. A cooler head and a warmer heart never met together in the same person; and it is barely just to say that he has not left behind a more learned lawyer or a more upright man." In David Paul Brown's "Forum" we find the following: "It is recorded that Sergeant Maynard had such a relish for the old Year Books, that he carried one in his coach to divert his time in travel, and said he preferred it to a comedy. The late Judge Kennedy, of the supreme court, who was the most enthusiastic lover of the law we ever new, used to say that his greatest amusement consisted in reading the law; and indeed, he seemed to take almost equal pleasure in writing his legal opinions, in some of which, Reed vs. Patterson, for instance, he certainly combined the attractions of law and romance." He is buried in the old grave-yard at Carlisle.

Hon. Samuel Hepburn (seventh president judge), the successor of Judge Reed, first appears upon the bench in April, 1839. Judge Hepburn was born in 1807 in Williamsport, Penn., at which place he began the study of law under James Armstrong, who was afterward a judge on the supreme bench. He completed his legal studies at Dickinson College under Reed, and was admitted to the bar of Cumberland County in November, 1834. He was, at the time of his admission appointed adjunct professor of law in the Moot court of Dickinson College by Judge Reed. Before he had been at the bar five years, he was appointed by Gov. Porter, president judge of the Ninth Judicial District, then embracing Cumberland, Perry and Juniata, and he presided at times also, during his term in the civil courts of Dauphin. He was at this time the youngest judge in Pennsylvania to whom a president judge's commission had been ever offered. Among the important cases the McClintock trial took place while he was upon the bench. After the expiration of his term he resumed the practice of law in Carlisle, where he still resides. The degree of LL. D. was conferred upon Judge Hepburn by Washington College, Penn.

The most prominent practitioners admitted under Judge Hepburn were J. Ellis Bonham, Lemuel Todd, William H. Miller, Benjamin F. Junkin, William M. Penrose and Alexander Brady Sharpe.

J. Ellis Bonham, Esq., was among the ablest lawyers admitted under Judge Hepburn. He was born in Hunterdon County, N. J., March 31, 1816, graduated at Jefferson College, Penn., studied law in Dickinson College under Reed, and was admitted to the bar in August, 1839.

"He had no kindred here nor family influence. His pecuniary gains were small during the first few years of his professional career, and he had little or no aid outside of them, as his father was in moderate circumstances." He had not been long, however, at the bar before he was appointed deputy attorney-general for the county—a position which he filled with conspicious ability. He had a taste for literature and his library was large and choice. He had little fondness for the drudgery of his profession, but he had political ambition, and his political reading and knowledge were extensive. He wrote for the leading political journals of his party articles on many of the prominent questions of the day. "During his term in the Legislature he was the acknowledged leader of the House, as the Hon. Charles R. Buckalew was of the Senate; and they were not unlike in mental characteristics, and somewhat alike in personal appearance. They were decidedly the weakest men physically and the strongest mentally in either House."

After the expiration of his term he was nominated for Congress, and although he was in a district largely Democratic, eminently fitted for the position, and had, himself, great influence in the political organization, he was defeated by the sudden birth of a new party. He died shortly afterward of congestion of the lungs, March 19, 1855.

In personal appearance Mr. Bonham was rather under than above the medium height, delicately formed, with light hair and complexion. He was of nervous temperament. His countenance was handsome and refined. As an advocate he was eminently a graceful and polished speaker, attractive in his manner, with a poetic imagination and chaste and polished diction. His speeches, although they at times bore traces of laborious preparation, were effective, and on one occasion, we are told, many persons in the court were moved to tears.

He died before his talents had reached their prime, after having been at the bar for fifteen years and before he had attained the age of forty.

Hon. Lemuel Todd was born in Carlisle July 29, 1817. He graduated at Dickinson College in 1839, read law under Gen. Samuel Alexander and was admitted to practice in August, 1841. He was a partner of Gen. Alexander until the time of his death in 1843. He was elected to Congress from the Eighteenth District in 1854 on the Know-nothing ticket as against J. Ellis Bonham on the Democratic, and was elected congressman at large in 1875. He presided over the State conventions of the Republican party at Harrisburg that nominated David Wilmot for governor; at Pittsburgh that nominated Gov. Curtin; and at Philadelphia that advocated for President Gen. Grant.

Gen. Todd has practiced continuously at the bar except for a period during the late war, a portion of which time he acted as inspector-general of Pennsylvania troops under Gov. Curtin.

William H. Miller, for more than a quarter of a century, was an active practitioner at the bar of our county. He was a student of Judge Reed, and was admitted to the bar in August, 1842; William M. Biddle, S. Dunlap Adair and J. Ellis Bonham, Esqs., being his committee of examination. His initiate was difficult, but by perseverance and talent he succeeded in winning a large practice and an honorable position at the bar. As a speaker he was deliberate and dignified; as a man refined and amiable; scholarly in both his taste and in his appearance. As a lawyer he was cool and self-possessed, and with deliberate logic and tact he won, as a rule, the implicit confidence of a jury. He died suddenly of congestion of the brain in June, 1877.

William McFunn Penrose, was admitted under Hepburn. He was born in Carlisle March 29, 1825; graduated with honor at Dickinson College in 1844, and was admitted to the bar in November, 1846. He was the oldest son of Hon. Charles B. Penrose. As a lawyer he was eminently successful, learned, quick and accurate in his perceptions, cogent in argument, fluent but terse in a speaker, he seldom failed to convince a jury. He had a keen perception of distinctions in the cases, and of the principles which underlie them, and in all questions of practice was particularly at home. He served for a time as colonel of the Sixth Regiment at the beginning of the war. He died September 2, 1872, in the prime of life and in the midst of usefulness.

Hon. Robert M. Henderson, born near Carlisle March 11, 1827. Graduated at Dickinson College in 1845. Read law under Judge Reed, and was admitted to the bar in August, 1847. He was elected, by the Whig party, to the Legislature in 1851 and 1852. He served, by appointment in April, 1874, as additional judge of the Twelfth Judicial District, and was elected to that office in the same year. He became president judge of this district in January, 1882, resigned his position in March of the same year, and returned to his practice in Carlisle. He served as a colonel in the late war.

Alexander Brady Sharpe was born in Newton Township, Cumberland County, August 12, 1827. He graduated with honor at Jefferson College, Pennsylvania, in 1846. He read law under Robert M. Bard, Esq., of Chambersburg, and subsequently with Hon. Frederick Watts, of Carlisle. He was admitted to the bar in November 1848, since which time he has practiced, except during the period of the war, when he was in the service of his country, a portion of the time serving upon the staff of Gen. Ord.

Hon. Frederick Watts became judge of our courts in 1849. He was the son of David Watts, a distinguished member of the early bar, and was born in Carlisle May 9, 1801. He graduated at Dickinson College in 1819. Two years later he entered the office of Andrew Carothers, and was admitted to practice in August, 1824. He remained for a time in partnership with his preceptor and acquired a lucrative practice. During a period of forty-two years from the October term, 1827, to May term, 1869, in the Supreme Court, there is no volume of reports containing cases from the middle district (except for the three years when he was upon the bench) in which his name is not found. For fifteen years he was the reporter of the decisions of that court, from 1829; three volumes, "Watts & Penrose," ten volumes "Watts Reports," and nine "Watts & Sergeant." On March 9, 1849, he was commissioned by Gov. Johnston, president judge of the Ninth Judicial District, containing the counties of Cumberland, Perry and Juniata. He retired in 1852, when the judiciary became elective, and resumed his practice, from which after a long and honorable career, he gradually withdrew in about 1860–69. In August, 1871, he was appointed and served as commissioner of agriculture under Hayes. As a man he had great force of character, sterling integrity, and, as a lawyer, ability, dignity and confidence. He had great power with a jury from their implicit confidence in him. He was always firm, self-reliant, despised quirks and quibbles, and was a model of fairness in the trial of a cause. He is still living in honorable retirement in Carlisle at an advanced age, being now the oldest surviving member of the bar.

We have now brought the history of our bar with sketches, some of them dealing with living members, down to the time when Judge Graham appears upon the bench, which is within the recollection of the youngest lawyer. For the future we must for obvious reasons satisfy ourself with briefer mention.

Hon. James H. Graham, born September 10, 1807, in West Pennsborough Township, graduated at Dickinson College in 1827, studied law under Andrew Carothers, Esq., admitted to the bar in November, 1829. In 1839, after the election of Gov. Porter, he was appointed deputy attorney-general for Cumberland County, a position which he filled ably for six years. After the amendment of the Constitution making the judiciary elective, he received the nomination (Democratic) and was elected in October, 1851, president judge of the Ninth Judicial District, comprising the counties of Cumberland, Perry and Juniata. At the expiration of his term he was re-elected in 1861, serving another full term of ten years. After his retirement from the bench he returned again to the practice of law. He died in the fall of 1882. In 1862 his *alma mater* conferred upon him the degree of LL.D. Perhaps the highest eulogy we can pay is to say that for more than half a century at the bar or on the bench, there was never, in the language of Judge Watts, a breath of imputation against his character as a lawyer, or upon his honor as a judge."

Hon. Benjamin F. Junkin was admitted to the bar in August, 1844. He lived in Bloomfield and became, with the younger McIntyre, a leader of the bar of Perry County. In 1871, he was elected the tenth president judge of the Ninth Judicial District—then including the counties of Cumberland, Perry and Juniata. He was the last of the perambulatory judges. On the redistribution of the district under the constitution of 1874, he chose Perry and Juniata, and therefore, from that period, ceased to preside over the courts in Cumberland County.

Hon. Martin C. Herman, who succeeded Hon. Benjamin Junkin as the eleventh judge of our Judicial District, was born in Silver Spring Township, Cumberland County, February 14, 1841. He graduated at Dickinson College in 1862. He had registered as a student of law previous to this time with B. McIntyre & Son, Bloomfield, then with William H. Miller, of Carlisle, under whom he completed his studies. He was admitted to the bar in January, 1864. He was elected by the Democratic party president judge of the Ninth Judicial District, in 1874, taking the bench on the first Monday of January in the succeeding year, and serving for full term of ten years, and was nominated by acclamation in August, 1884.

Hon. Wilbur F. Sadler, twelfth and last judge, was born October 14, 1840; read law under Mr. Morrison at Williamsport, and afterward in Carlisle; was admitted to the Carlisle bar in 1864, and acquired a large clientage; was elected district attorney in 1871, and, in 1884, president judge of the Ninth Judicial District of Pennsylvania.

The present members of the bar, with the dates of their admission, are as follows:

J. E. Barnitz, August, 1877; Bennett Bellman, April, 1874; Hon. F. E. Beltzhoover, April, 1864; Edward W. Biddle, April, 1873; Theodore Cornman, 1870; Duncan M. Graham, November, 1876; John Hays, 1859; Hon. Samuel Hepburn, November, 1834; Samuel Hepburn, Jr., January, 1863; Hon. Martin C. Herman, January, 1864; Christian P. Humrich, November, 1854; W. A. Kramer, August, 1883; John B. Landis. 1881; Stewart M. Leidich, August, 1872; W. Penn Lloyd, April, 1865; John R. Miller, August, 1867; George Miller, January, 1873; Henry Newsham, April, 1859; Richard M. Parker, November, 1876; A. Brady Sharpe, November, 1848; William J. Shearer, January, 1852; John T. Stuart, November, 1876; Silas Stuart, April, 1881; J. L. Shelley, August, 1875; Alexander Bache Smead; Hon. Lemuel Todd, April, 1841; William E. Trickett*, August, 1875; Joseph G. Vale, April, 1871; Hon. Frederick Watts (retired), 1829; Edward B. Watts, August, 1875; Hon. J. Marion Weakley, January, 1861; John W. Wetzel, April, 1874; Muhlenburg Williams (Newville), November, 1860; Robert McCachran (Newville), 1857.

Among the early members of our bench and bar were men who fought

---

*William E. Trickett, formerly professor of metaphysics in Dickinson College, and author of "Liens in Pennsylvania."

and were distinguished in the Indian wars and in the Revolution. No less than three who practiced in our courts were signers of the Declaration of Independence, and two were members of the colonial convention at its inception. Three sat upon the supreme bench, one as Chief Justice, who has been justly called, in a legal sense, the "great glory of his native State." Since then many have become distinguished, in their day, on the bench, in the halls of legislation, or at the bar. In its prestige the bar of Cumberland County has been equal to any in the State, and its reputation has been won in many a well contested battle for a period of now more than a century and a quarter, so that, whatever it may be to-day, it may well pride itself upon its past, and stand, among the younger bars of our sister commonwealths, like a Douglas bonneted, and bow down to none.

CHAPTER IX.

MEDICAL—BIOGRAPHICAL—PHYSICIANS IN CUMBERLAND COUNTY SINCE 1879— PHYSICIANS IN CUMBERLAND COUNTY REGISTERED IN OFFICE OF PROTHONOTARY AT CARLISLE—CUMBERLAND COUNTY MEDICAL SOCIETY.

THE genesis of medical science, like that of chemistry, astronomy or government, is necessarily slow, and attended with much of empiricism. Observations, even if correctly made, are either imperfectly recorded or not recorded at all. The common people are destitute of scientific methods of investigation. Even if they were so disposed, they lack both the opportunity and the ability to note, scientifically, the nature and symptoms of disease together with their proper remedial agents.

It is not strange, therefore, that mothers and grandmothers of the olden time should insist, on applying, externally, skunk oil or goose fat for the curing of internal derangements. The day of herbs and salves as panaceas was not far removed from the period when special luck was supposed to attach to first seeing the moon over the right shoulder; when potatoes planted or shingles laid in the dark of the moon would fail to serve their purposes; when water-witches were deemed necessary to locate wells properly; and when bleeding the arm for the ailments of humanity was considered absolutely essential to health.

The superstition which sought cures in miraculous interferences in these various tricks of sleight-of-hand performances, and meaningless signs and tokens, would readily believe that the hair of the dog will cure his own bite; that the carrying, around the neck, of a spider imprisoned in a thimble will cause whooping-cough to disappear; that washing the face in water formed from the first snow of the season will remove freckles; that the weather of the first three days of December will presage the weather of the three following months; that the washing of the hands in stump water will cure warts; and that if the ground hog sees his shadow on the 2d day of February, he will retire to his den to endure a six weeks' cold siege.

The transition from these simple superstitions of the olden times to the patent medicine cure-all remedies of the present day was an easy one. He who imagined that warts could be removed or pain alleviated by the sorcerer's pow-wow, or that skunk fat would cure pleurisy or consumption, would not be slow to believe in the curative properties of some thorougly advertised patent nostrum. The statements in patent medicine circulars would receive full credence by those suffering the ills to which humanity is subject, and unknown and perhaps absolutely worthless remedies would be used assiduously until the system was thoroughly deranged. From the ravages of these patent nostrums, as well as from the ignorance of the human system prevailing among the masses, the medical profession had to save their patients. Everywhere people were perishing from a lack of knowledge of the physical organization which they were expected to preserve, and suffering humanity, racked with the pains of real or imaginary ills, was ready to seek relief in any direction. Hence the difficulty of placing medical science on a substantial basis in which its advocates could practice intelligently and conscientiously, and yet receive a proper reward for their labors. No class of pioneer citizens made greater sacrifices for humanity, or deserve stronger marks of recognition, than the genuine medical practitioners of a country. With the impetus given to the æsculapian art by their labors and sacrifices, it is safe to predict that the introduction of rudimentary science into the public schools, and especially the teaching of anatomy, physiology and hygiene, will finally usher in a period when the people shall obey the laws of their being, and physicians, instead of being migratory drug stores, shall be, as the term "doctor" literally implies, teachers of health principles.

In this chapter brief sketches of most of the medical practitioners of Cumberland County, more or less noted in their fields of labor, are given.

CARLISLE.

Among the early physicians who practiced in Carlisle before the Revolution was Dr. William Plunkett, but we know nothing more of him than that he resided in Carlisle and is spoken of as "a practitioner of physic in 1766."

The most noted of all the pre-Revolutionary practitioners of medicine in Carlisle was Dr. William Irvine. He was born near Enniskillen, Ireland, in 1740; was educated at the University of Dublin, studied medicine and surgery, and was appointed a surgeon in the British Navy. In 1763, he immigrated to America and settled in Carlisle, where he soon acquired a high reputation and a large practice as a surgeon and physician. In 1774 he took a conspicuous part in the politics of Cumberland County and was appointed as a delegate to the Provincial Convention. He had a strong leaning toward a military life, and was commissioned by Congress colonel of the Sixth Batallion and was ordered to Canada, where he was captured. He was afterward colonel of the Seventh Pennsylvania Batallion. In 1779 he was commissioned a brigadier-general and served under Wayne. In March, 1782, he was ordered to Fort Pitt, to which place he marched with a regiment to protect the northwestern frontier, then threatened with British and Indian invasion. He was engaged in allaying the trouble arising from disputed boundaries between Pennsylvania and Virginia. He was a member of the convention to form a constitution for the State of Pennsylvania, and was appointed commander-in-chief of the Pennsylvania troops to suppress the Whiskey Insurrection, and a commissioner to treat with the insurgents. Dr. Irvine married Anne Callender, the daughter of Robert Callender, of Middlssex, near Carlisle. He removed to Philadelphia in 1801, and died in July, 1804, aged sixty-three years. He was president of the celebrated society of the Cincinnati until his death.

Another pioneer physician was Dr. Samuel Allen McCoskry, who settled there in 1774. Others may have entered the valley in 1756, while in connection with the army, but we have no record of their having been engaged in a regular practice.

Dr. McCoskry, born in 1751, where or in what month is not known; practiced medicine in Carlisle until he had achieved eminence in his profession; and died September 4, 1818, and was buried in the old Borough Cemetery in Carlisle. From the inscription on a tombstone, we gather that his first wife, Ann Susannah McCoskry, died November 12, 1792, being thirty-eight years old. Dr. McCoskry was afterward married to Alison Nisbett, daughter of the first president of Dickinson College.

Dr. Lemuel Gustine, was born in Saybrook, Conn., in the year 1749; settled in the Wyoming Valley in 1769, or thereabouts; married the daughter of one Dr. Wm. Smith, to whom one daughter, Sarah, was born.

In the scenes attendant upon the Indian invasion and massacre in the Wyoming Valley, Dr. Gustine took a prominent part. He remained on the field of that bloody conflict until further resistance became useless, when, on the night following the capitulation of the "Forty Fort" to Maj. Butler, the commander of the Tory and Indian troops, with his daughter and a few friends as companions, he drifted down the Susquehanna to John Harris' Ferry (now Harrisburg), where he landed, and proceeded to Carlisle. Here he commenced the practice of medicine. He married Rebecca Parker soon afterward, and became the father of six children. He continued the practice of his profession to within a short time before his death, which occurred October 7, 1805. He was buried in the old cemetery in Carlisle.

Dr. James Gustine, son of preceding, graduated at Dickinson College in 1798; studied medicine with his father, and afterward received the degree of M. D. from the University of Pennsylvania. He commenced practice in Natchez, Miss., returned to Carlisle; and again went South, where he remained until his death.

Dr. Samuel Gustine, second son of Lemuel, studied medicine with his father, and went South with his brother James.

Dr. George Stevenson, son of Geo. Stevenson, LL.D. born in York, Penn., in 1759; attended classical academy at Carlisle; entered Patriot army in 1778, as first lieutenant of Chambers' regiment; served with distinction at Brandywine, and resigned commission to return to the aid of his family; studied medicine under Dr. McCoskry; re-entered the army as surgeon, and served until close, when he returned to his practice in Carlisle. He was commissioned captain of infantry in 1793; created major in following year; aided in suppression of famous Whiskey Insurrection in 1794, after settlement of which removed to Pittsburgh, where he commenced practice of medicine; commissioned major in Tenth United States Regiment, during the troubles with France; returned to practice in Pittsburgh, where he became distinguished for connection with many civil and political enterprises, in which he served in the following capacities: Trustee of Dickinson College; member first board of trustees of the Western University of Pennsylvania, member first board of directors of Branch Bank of Pennsylvania; president of United States Bank, at Pittsburgh; first director of United States Bank, at Cincinnati; and for a long time president of the city council of Pittsburgh. Dr. S. declined the presidency of the United States Bank at Cincinnati, and in 1825 removed to Wilmington, Del., where he died in 1829.

Dr. Samuel Fahnestock, a physician, practiced his profession in Carlisle, from 1800 to 1820, when he removed to Pittsburgh.

Dr. George Delap Foulke, born near Carlisle, November 12, 1780; graduated at Dickinson College in 1800; studied medicine under Dr. Potter, medical professor in the University of Maryland; married Mary Steel, daughter of Ephraim Steel, of Carlisle; practiced in Bedford, Penn., and afterward in

Carlisle, where he died August 14, 1849, and was buried in the old cemetery.

Dr. George Willis Foulke, son of preceding, born in Carlisle, October 8, 1822; graduated at Dickinson College in 1845; returned to commence practice in Carlisle, but died suddenly on March 5, 1850, in the springtime of his life.

Dr. Lewis W. Foulke, brother of preceding, born at Carlisle August 6, 1809; graduated at Dickinson College in 1829; studied medicine with his father, afterward receiving degree of M. D. from University of Maryland; commenced practice with his father at Carlisle, but afterward removed to Chillicothe, Ohio, where he continued in his profession.

Dr. James Armstrong. born at Carlisle in 1749; completed academic course at Nassau Hall, N. J.; studied medicine with Dr. John Morgan, of Philadelphia, afterward receiving the degree of M. D. from University of Pennsylvania; commenced practice in Winchester, Va., but becoming discouraged, went to Europe. where he prosecuted the study of his profession in London; returned to Carlisle, where he married Mary Stevenson, daughter of a prominent settler; removed to Kishacoquillas Valley, from which place he was elected congressman of the Third District of Pennsylvania; held the offices of trustee of Dickinson College, trustee of the old Presbyterian Church at Carlisle, associate judge of Cumberland County, and others of trust, which he filled with credit. He returned to Carlisle to reside in the old family mansion, in which he had been born, and from which he was called to rest in the year 1828. He was buried in the old cemetery at Carlisle.

Dr. John Armstrong, son of preceding, born in 1799; educated in Dickinson College and University of Pennsylvania; completed a medical course under his father's tuition; married in 1825; practiced in Dillsburg, Penn., and later returned to Cumberland; thence removed to Princeton, N. J., where he died in 1871.

Dr. Ephraim M. Blaine, grandson of Col. Ephraim Blaine, of Revolutionary renown, was born in Carlisle, September 24, 1796; graduated at Dickinson College in the class of 1814; received the degree of M. D. from University of Pennsylvania in 1827; practiced in Carlisle for a number of years, and finally entered the army as assistant surgeon, in which service he died March 13, 1835.

Dr. Adam Hays, born in Cumberland County, Penn., in 1792; educated at Dickinson College; studied medicine with Dr. McCoskry and in the University of Pennsylvania, where he took the degree of M. D.; practiced as surgeon in the army, at Chillicothe, Ohio, and at Carlisle; removed to Pittsburgh in 1829, where he died in 1857.

Dr. William Chestnut Chambers, born near Harrisburg in 1790; educated at Dickinson College; prepared for his profession in the University of Pennsylvania; practiced in Carlisle for a number of years, when he engaged in the iron and flour business; removed to Philadelphia in 1838, and died in 1857.

Dr. Alfred Foster, born in Carlisle in 1790; graduated at Dickinson College; prepared for the practice of medicine in the office of Dr. McCoskry; entered army, where he engaged in hospital work until the close of the war of 1812; returned to Carlisle, and commenced the duties of practitioner, in which labor he continued until his death in 1847. He was buried in the old cemetery of Carlisle.

Dr. John Creigh, born in Carlisle September 13, 1773; studied medicine under Dr. McCoskry and in the University of Pennsylvania, being also a graduate of Dickinson College; located as physician at Pittsburgh, but after changing his residence a number of times, finally settled at Carlisle, where he continued in his profession until his death, which occurred November 7, 1848. Dr. C. was a prominent citizen, and took great interest in the affairs of his county. He was buried in the old cemetery.

Dr. John Steel Given, born in Carlisle January 3, 1796; educated and took degree of M. D. in the University of Pennsylvania; settled at Carlisle, and was killed by the bursting of a cannon on July 4, 1825.

Dr. Theodore Myers, born in Baltimore, Md., May 27, 1802; took degree of M. D. at University of Maryland in 1823; settled in Carlisle and engaged in the practice of his profession; married Sarah A. Irwin, a lady of distinction. Dr. M. died February 20, 1839, being in the prime of life. He was buried in the old cemetery.

Dr. John Myers, brother of preceding, born in Baltimore January 23, 1806; graduated and received degree of M. D. in the University of Maryland; settled at Carlisle as druggist and physician; entered the army hospital service, and died in Winchester, Va.

Dr. John Elliot, born in Carlisle in 1797; educated at Dickinson College; studied medicine under Dr. McCoskry and in the University of Pennsylvania, taking the degree of M. D. from the latter; settled at Newville; returned to Carlisle, where, after practicing a few years, was called by death June 12, 1829.

Dr. David Nelson Mahon, born in Pittsburgh, Penn.; graduated at Dickinson College; studied medicine under Dr. Gustine, of Carlisle, and afterward was created an M. D. by the University of Pennsylvania; entered the navy service as assistant surgeon in 1821; took leave of the sea after three years' experience, and engaged in the practice of his profession at Carlisle, where he died and was buried in the Ashland Cemetery in 1876.

Dr. Jacob Johnston commenced to practice in Carlisle in 1825, and continued until his death in 1831.

Dr. John Paxton, born in 1796; received degree of M. D. from University of Pennsylvania, after which he practiced in Carlisle until shortly before his death, which took place in 1840, while he was visiting in Adams County, Penn.

Dr. William Boyd, a physician, settled in Carlisle in 1833, but removed after several years' residence.

Dr. Charles Cooper practiced in Carlisle a number of years, but afterward went West.

Dr. William Irvin, born in Centre County, Penn.; graduated in the University of Pennsylvania with degree of M. D.; practiced in Carlisle until 1846, when he left for China.

Dr. Stephen B. Kieffer, born in Franklin County, Penn.; graduated at Marshall College in 1848; entered the office of Dr. R. Parker Little, and in 1851 received the degree of M. D. from the University of Pennsylvania; received the degree of M. A. at the same time from his *alma mater*, Marshall College; married Kate E., daughter of George Keller, Esq., of Carlisle, where Dr. K. began the practice of his profession. He is a member of the County Medical Society; was at one time president of the State Medical Society, and in the centennial year was a member of the International Medical Congress which met at Philadelphia. Dr. Kieffer was elected a fellow of the American Academy of Medicine in 1877. He still resides at Carlisle, where he has established a large and remunerative practice.

Dr. R. Lowry Sibbet, now living and practicing medicine in Carlisle, was born near Shippensburg, Cumberland County, in the early half of the present century. His ancestry are of Scotch-Irish extraction. His grandfather, Samuel Sibbet, of Presbyterian and Republican proclivities, was deemed an unsafe man in his native country, Ireland, and hence a reward of 50 guineas was placed upon his head. Advised by Masonic friends of this movement, he set sail secretly for the United States, landing in Baltimore in May, 1800. After the lapse of a few months he was joined by his faithful wife and their children, James, Robert and Thomas. The Cumberland Valley, with its Scotch-Irish settlements, having been heard of, the family proceeded at once to the head of Big Spring, where they were heartily welcomed by warm friends who had preceded them. To the family were added Samuel, Margaret, Lowry and Hugh Montgomery.

Thomas, the third child, was born October 5, 1797. In due time he married Catherine Ryan, from which union sprang seven children, five of whom still remain, viz.: Rachel A., Robert L., Henry W., William R. and Anna M. The parents and the two children are buried in the Spring Hill Cemetery of Shippensburg.

The subject of this sketch graduated in 1856 from Pennsylvania College with the degree of A. B., and three years subsequent, obtained from his *alma mater* the degree of A. M. After several years teaching in a classical school, he studied medicine with Drs. Stewart and Holland, of Shippensburg. He attended the usual course of medical lectures, and graduated from the University of Pennsylvania in 1866. Having practiced for a time at Harrisburg and New Kingston, he visited Europe in 1870, spending some two years in its universities and hospitals, distributed as follows: Seven months in Paris during the siege; two in Berlin; ten in Vienna; two in London, and the remainder in Spain, Italy and Switzerland. After his return, the Doctor located at Carlisle, and began a series of correspondence, which resulted in the organization of the "American Academy of Medicine,"—an associated corps of men who have been regularly graduated from reputable institutions of learning. As a member of this association, together with the county and State medical societies, his labors have been given for the advancement of reforms in his profession, notably the registration of all practitioners and the necessity of medical men having both literary and professional diplomas. He is one of those persons who never practically accepted the doctrine that it is not good for man to be alone.

Dr. Alfred J. Herman, born in Montgomery County, Penn., studied medicine under Dr. Rutter, of Pottstown, Penn., and also received the degree of M. D. from the University of Pennsylvania, in 1846. Dr. Herman settled in the Cumberland Valley soon afterward, and eventually removed to Carlisle, where he continued the practice of his chosen profession.

Dr. William W. Dale was born in Lancaster, Penn.; graduated from Jefferson Medical College, Philadelphia, in 1838; moved to Carlisle in 1847.

Dr. Wm. H. Longsdorf was born in this county in 1834; graduated in 1856 from Jefferson Medical College, and, in 1857, from the Pennsylvania Dental School; first commenced practice in this county in 1857.

Dr. William H. Cooke, born near York Sulphur Springs, Penn.; educated in Chester County, Penn.; entered the office of Dr. Hiram Metcalfe, and afterward took the degree of M. D. from the Jefferson Medical College; engaged in public speaking in the Western country; returned in 1859 to Pennsylvania, and after marrying Elizabeth Richmond, settled at Carlisle, and commenced practicing his profession.

Dr. Eugene A. Grove, born in Cumberland County, Penn., was a descendant of Hans Graf, a noted Switzer. Dr. Grove received an education in the public schools of Carlisle; studied medicine under Dr. S. B. Kieffer, and took the degree of M. D. from the University of Pennsylvania, in 1870. He is engaged in the practice of his profession in Carlisle.

Dr. George Hemminger, born in Cumberland County, Penn.; educated in the county schools, a select school at Plainfield, and was a sophomore in Pennsylvania College when the war broke out, and he abandoned his studies to defend the Union. In 1862 he entered the One Hundred and Thirty-eighth Regiment of Pennsylvania Volunteers; served with distinction in many severe engagements; was captured and confined in Libby prison in 1865; was exchanged and rejoined his regiment, in which he served until the close of the war. Dr. Hemminger, after his return, entered the office of Dr. J. J. Gitzer, of Carlisle, and after studying some time, entered the Detroit Medical College, and graduated there in 1869, with the degree of M. D. He located first at Newville, Penn., but afterward returned to Carlisle, where he is engaged in a large practice.

Dr. Jacob S. Bender was born in Bendersville, this county, in 1834; graduated from Pennsylvania Homœopathic College of Medicine in 1862; commenced the practice of medicine, after close of the war, between Omaha and the Rocky Mountains, and there continued for four years; then came to Carlisle.

Dr. Wm. F. Reily, a native of Carlisle, born in 1851, graduated from the University of Pennsylvania, Philadelphia, in 1875; then located in Carlisle, where he has practiced ever since.

Dr. J. Simpson Musgrave was born in Ireland; attended lectures at the Toland Medical College, in San Francisco, Cal.; entered the University of Maryland, and finally graduated in the University Pennsylvania, with the degree M. D. Dr. Musgrave located in Carlisle in 1877, but remained only a short time.

MECHANICSBURG.

Dr. Asa Herring, born in New Jersey in 1792; moved to Mechanicsburg in 1815, where he engaged in the practice of medicine until 1828, when he removed to Elizabethtown, Penn.

Dr. James B. Herring, son of preceding; born at Hamilton, Penn., March 4, 1829; graduated from University of Pennsylvania, in 1851, receiving the degree of M. D.; commenced practice in Mechanicsburg; married Elizabeth Riegel; continued to practice, in partnership with Dr. Ira Day until his death, November 9, 1871. He was buried in Chestnut Hill Cemetery, near Mechanicsburg.

Dr. Jacob Weaver, practiced in Mechanicsburg between the years 1825 and 1840.

Dr. James G. Oliver, born in Cumberland County, December 6, 1801; educated at Dickinson College; graduated from Jefferson Medical College in 1828 with degree of M. D.; practiced first at Oyster's Point, afterward at Mechanicsburg, where he also owned a drug store: married Jane Carothers, and became father of three children; continued his practice until his death, May 31, 1836. He was buried in the Spring Hill Cemetery.

Dr. Ira Day, born in Royalton, Vt., in 1799; educated in Royalton Academy; taught select school in Harrisburg, at the same time studying medicine under Dr. Luther; graduated as M. D. from University of Vermont, in 1823; continued practicing medicine in Mechanicsburg; engaged in State and County Medical Associations; was elected trustee of Dickinson College in 1833; continued his practice until his death, in November, 1868. He is buried in the cemetery near Mechanicsburg.

Dr. George Fulmer, born in 1829, the oldest practicing physician in Mechanicsburg, and one of the oldest in the county, is a graduate of Jefferson Medical College, Philadelphia.

Drs. A. H. Van Hoff, W. A. Steigleman and Philip H. Long were practitioners of medicine in Mechanicsburg some forty years ago.

Dr. E. B. Brandt, born in Cumberland; educated in county schools; graduated from Jefferson Medical College in 1855; practiced in New Cumberland, Shiremanstown and Mechanicsburg; married Margaret Mateer in 1856; and is still engaged in his profession at Mechanicsburg.

Dr. Robert Graham Young was born in Louther Manor, Penn., December 6, 1809, and educated at Dickinson College. He studied medicine with Dr. John Paxton, and graduated at the University of Pennsylvania with the degree of M. D. He practiced in Louther Manor, Shiremanstown and Mechanicsburg. He married Annetta Culbertson and became father of five children. Dr. Young was one of the public-spirited and exemplary citizens of the community.

Dr. Martin B. Mosser was born in Upper Paxton, Dauphin Co., Penn. He studied medicine in the office of Dr. E. H. Coover, in New Cumberland. He graduated from Jefferson Medical College in 1862, and entered the army as assistant surgeon of the Fourth United States Artillery; was assigned to duty in the United States general hospital at Philadelphia. He resigned in 1865, and commenced civil practice at Shiremanstown. He married Rebecca Rupp, and became the father of two children; removed to Mechanicsburg, where he practices his profession.

Dr. Robert N. Short was born in Kentucky in 1831; graduated from the Southern Medical College in 1853, and from Miami Medical College in 1871; moved to Centerville, this county, in 1861, and there practiced medicine and surgery till 1865, when he came to Mechanicsburg, where he has ever since been in active practice.

Dr. L. P. O'Neale was born in Virginia in 1838; came to Mechanicsburg from York County, Penn., in 1870, and has here since been actively engaged in the practice of his profession.

Dr. Levi H. Lenher, a native of Lancaster County, Penn., born in 1822; graduated at Pennsylvania College, Philadelphia, in 1843; came to Churchtown, this county, in 1847, and there remained till 1872; then moved to Mechanicsburg; thence to Iowa; thence to Harrisburg, Penn., and finally again to Mechanicsburg.

Dr. Jacob H. Deardorff, born in Washington Township, York Co., Penn., in 1846; graduated from Hahnemann Medical College, Philadelphia, in 1876; located in Middletown, Penn., for two years and a half; then came to Mechanicsburg, where he has practiced medicine ever since.

CHURCHTOWN.

Dr. Charles Harrison Gibson, born in Perry County, Penn., graduated from the Miami Medical College, with the usual degree of M. D.; entered a Cincinnati hospital as resident physician; removed to Churchtown in 1875, and engaged in the duties of his profession.

HOGESTOWN.

Dr. Isaac Wayne Snowden, born in Harrisburg, Penn., on the 5th of March, 1794, being descended from an illustrious ancestry. He was educated in an academy, prepared for the medical profession in the office of Dr. Nathaniel Chapman, of Philadelphia; entered the army as assistant surgeon in 1816; served in the Seminole war, being an intimate friend of Gen. Jackson; resigned his position in 1823, and commenced the practice of his profession in Mifflin County, Penn.; married Margery B. Loudon, and removed to the lower part of

Cumberland Valley in 1832; established a practice here, in which he was engaged until his death, which took place in 1850.

Dr. Joseph Crain, born in Lancaster, Penn., December 25, 1803; educated at Dickinson College; studied medicine under Dr. Whiteside, of Harrisburg, and also graduated with the degree of M. D. at the University of Maryland; commenced practice in Hogestown in 1830; married Rebecca Wells, and became father of four children; afterward married Ellen Chambers, by whom one son was born. Dr. Crain continued in practice until his death, which occurred April 18, 1876. He was buried in the Silver Spring Cemetery.

LISBURN.

Dr. Lerew Lemer, born in Harrisburg, October 6, 1806; entered office of Dr. Luther Reily, and in 1832 took degree of M. D. from Yale College; commenced practice in New Cumberland; removed to Lisburn, where he lived until his death, in 1876.

Dr. J. W. Trimmer, born in Adams County, Penn., educated at Millersville Academy and Dickinson Seminary, studied medicine with Dr. A. D. Dill, of York Sulphur Springs; graduated from Rush Medical College in 1875; completed third course of lectures at Bellevue Hospital Medical College in 1876; commenced practice in Lisburn, where he is still engaged in a large and growing practice.

SHIPPENSBURG.

Dr. John Simpson, a physician, commenced practice in Shippensburg about 1778, and continued until February 17, 1826, when he died.

Dr. Robt. McCall practiced healing in Shippensburg up to 1799, when his death is recorded.

Dr. Alexander Stewart, born in Lancaster County, Penn.; practiced medicine in Shippensburg from 1795 to 1830, when he died.

Dr. John Ealy, born in Shippensburg in 1788; commenced practice there in 1809, and continued until his death, in 1831.

Dr. Elijah Ealy, son of preceding, also practiced in Shippensburg, but afterward moved to Dayton, Ohio, where he died in 1851.

Dr. William A. Findlay practiced in Shippensburg for a number of years after 1815. He afterward moved to Chambersburg.

Dr. William Rankin, born at Potter's Mills, Centre Co., Penn., in October, 1795; graduated at Washington College in 1814; studied medicine with Dr. Dean, of Chambersburg, Penn., and afterward, in 1819, received the degree of M. D. from University of Penn.; practiced in Campbellstown, but, in 1821, removed to Shippensburg; married Caroline Nevin, and became father of five children; practiced until his death, July 15, 1872.

Dr. David Nevin Rankin, son of preceding, born in Shippensburg; studied medicine with his father, and graduated with degree of M. D. from Jefferson Medical College, in 1854; practiced in partnership with his father until the war, when he entered, as assistant surgeon; after long and arduous service, settled at Allegheny City, where he still lives.

Dr. Alexander Stewart was born in Maryland, in 1809; graduated from Washington Medical College, Baltimore, Md., in 1831; same year commenced practice in Shippensburg, where he has since resided.

Dr. Thomas Greer and Dr. John N. Duncan practiced medicine in Shippensburg; the former from 1834 to 1839, when he died; the latter from 1841 to 1850, when he removed to Chambersburg.

Dr. William M. Witherspoon, a native of Franklin County, Penn., born in 1844; graduated from medical department of the University of Pennsylvania, in 1869, and has been in active practice in Shippensburg ever since.

HISTORY OF CUMBERLAND COUNTY.   181

SHIREMANSTOWN.

Dr. W. Scott Bruckhart, born in Lancaster Co., Penn.; graduated from Jefferson Medical College in 1870; practiced in Mountjoy Township, but removed to Shiremanstown in 1874, where he still practices.

Dr. Jacob Black and Dr. William Mateer practiced medicine in Shiremanstown some time near 1853.

NEWVILLE.

Dr. John Geddes, born in Cumberland County, August 16, 1776, studied medicine with Dr. McCoskry, of Carlisle. He settled in Newville as a practitioner in 1797, and died December 5, 1840.

Dr. John P. Geddes, son of the preceding, was born in Newville, October 10, 1799. He studied under his father, and graduated as M. D. from the University of New York; settled at Newville and practiced his profession until his death in October, 1837.

Dr. William M. Sharp, born at Green Spring, in 1798; graduated at Dickinson College in 1815. He studied medicine under Dr. McCoskry, and received the degree of M. D. from the University of Pennsylvania in 1819; practiced in Newville until his death August 20, 1835.

Dr. Alexander Sharp, son of Wm. M. Sharp, born in Newville in 1826; graduated from Jefferson Medical College in 1850. He practiced in Newville until he died December 13, 1860.

Dr. William S. Rutger was born December 13, 1782, in Germany. He studied medicine and embarked for America, landing at Baltimore in September, 1803; married Ann C. Afer in 1806, and practiced medicine in Baltimore, but removed to Newville in 1812, being known as the "Dutch Doctor." He removed to Illinois, where he died in 1847.

Dr. J. C. Claudy, grandson of the above, born in Cumberland County; studied medicine with Dr. David Ahl, of Newville, and afterward received degree of M. D. from Bellevue Hospital Medical College; entered army as assistant surgeon; returned to Newville to practice his profession; married Lucinda Blean, and still continues in his practice.

Dr. John Ahl, born in Bucks County, Penn.; educated in Baltimore; practiced medicine in Rockingham County, Va.; removed to Newville, where he died April 9, 1844.

Dr. John Alexander Ahl, son of preceding, was born in Strasburg, Penn.; studied under his father, and took his degree, M. D., from Washington Medical College, Baltimore; commenced practice in Centerville, Cumberland County; removed to Newville, where he engaged in various business enterprises, and from which place he was elected to the Thirty-fifth Congress. Died in 1882.

Dr. David Ahl, born in York County, Penn.; entered West Point as cadet; resigned in 1850, and entered office of Dr. Smith, of York, Penn.; graduated from University of Maryland as M. D. in 1853; moved to Newville, where, after practicing a number of years, he died April 8, 1878.

Dr. Joseph Hannon, a graduate of Jefferson Medical College, practiced in Newville from 1844 for about ten years.

Dr. Mathew F. Robinson, born near Greencastle, Penn., April 26, 1820; studied medicine under Dr. J. K. Davidson, of Greencastle, and took degree of M. D. from Washington Medical College, of Baltimore, in 1847; practiced in Mercersburg and later at Newville, where he died January 7, 1874.

Dr. John G. Barr, born in Newville in 1830; graduated at Washington, D. C., with degree of M. D., in 1858; practiced in Newville until the war, when he entered the army as surgeon, and died in 1863.

Dr. Samuel H. Brehm, born in Cumberland County, Penn.; received common and classical education; received degree of M. D. from Jefferson Medical College, in 1866; commenced and still continues practice in Newville.

NEWBURG.

Dr. David Smith was a resident practitioner of medicine in Newburg, where he resided about twenty-nine years. He died in 1863, and is buried in the cemetery near Newburg.

Dr. Alexander A. Thomson was born in Franklin County, Penn., in 1841; graduated from Jefferson Medical College, Philadelphia, in 1864; practiced several years in Newburg, this county; now resides in Carlisle.

NEW CUMBERLAND.

Dr. John Mosser was born in Lancaster County, June 20, 1777; married Elizabeth Neff, with whom he had eight children. He purchased property in the vicinity of New Cumberland in 1815, and engaged in the practice of medicine until his death, June 10, 1826. He is buried in Mount Olivet Cemetery, near New Cumberland.

OAKVILLE.

Dr. Israel Betz, born in Lancaster County, Penn.; studied under Dr. W. E. Swiler, of York County, Penn.; graduated with degree of M. D. from University of Pennsylvania; settled at Oakville, where he still continues in his practice.

BOILING SPRINGS.

Dr. Jacob Sawyer, born in Wilmington, Mass., December 26, 1794, educated in the village schools and also in Phillips Academy, Exeter, N. H.; studied for the practice of medicine in the office of Dr. Hill, and in the medical department of Howard University, where he attended lectures given by such distinguished physicians as Drs. Channing, Ingalls, and others; commenced the practice of his profession in Dillsburg, Penn., where he succeeded to the practice of his brother, Dr. Asa Sawyer; married Mary Ann McGowan, daughter of David McGowan, of Boiling Springs, in 1825; exchanged practices with Dr. Thomas Cathcart, of Bloomfield, Perry County, in 1833; purchased a farm near Boiling Springs, where he soon established a large country practice; removed to Carlisle some time in 1857, where he was taken away by death two years later. Dr. Sawyer had lived an active and eventful life, having served as surgeon to the fifth division of State militia and as resident practitioner in various parts of the State.

PLAINFIELD.

Dr. Joshua E. Van Camp, born in Perry County, Penn.; educated in Louisville Academy and Pennsylvania College; enlisted and served in One Hundred and Thirty-third Regiment, Pennsylvania Volunteers, in 1862; served until close of the war, having been promoted to sergeant; graduated from the University of Michigan in 1870, with degree of M. D.; practiced in Markelsville, and later in Plainfield, where he still resides.

OYSTER'S POINT.

Dr. Peter Fahnestock practiced at what is now called Oyster's Point about the beginning of the nineteenth century.

R H Pratt
Capt. 10th Cav'y U.S.A.

HISTORY OF CUMBERLAND COUNTY.   185

PHYSICIANS IN CUMBERLAND COUNTY SINCE ABOUT 1879.

Grove, Dr. George, Big Spring, born in Chambersburg, Franklin County, in 1811; graduated from Jefferson Medical College, Philadelphia, with honors, in 1836. He is to-day the oldest practicing physician in the Cumberland Valley.

Davis, Dr. J. C., Mount Holly Springs, was born in this county in 1848; graduated from Jefferson Medical College, in 1875; has here an extensive practice.

Koons, Philip R., born in Shippensburg; residence at Allen postoffice; graduated at Jefferson Medical College, March 12, 1879.

Smith, Jacob H., a native of Cumberland County; present residence Dickinson Township; graduated at Jefferson Medical College, 1880.

Leberknight, Dr. F. B., Newburg; graduated at Jefferson Medical College, Philadelphia, about 1873, with honors; also at Bellevue Hospital Medical College, New York, in 1879, since which date his practice has been uninterrupted in Newburg.

Cramer, David C., born in Newburg, Cumberland County, where he is located in the practice; received his degree of M. D. from Jefferson Medical College, 1880.

Fickel, James G., a native of Adams County; resides in Carlisle; graduate of Hahnemann Medical College, 1878.

Koser, John J., born in Shippensburg, where he resides; graduated in the University of Pennsylvania, 1881.

Marshall, J. Buchanan, a native of Adams County, resides in Shippensburg; graduated at Bellevue Hospital Medical College, N. Y., February, 1879.

Prowell, Robert S., a native of Cumberland County; resides in New Cumberland; graduated at College Physicians and Surgeons, Baltimore, March 3, 1880.

Smith, S. McKee, born in Perry County; resides in Heberlig; graduated at College of Physicians and Surgeons, Baltimore, 1880.

Conlyn, Edward S., born in Carlisle, where he resides; graduated at Hahnemann College, March, 1880; was in Ward's Island Hospital from April, 1880, to October, 1881.

Longsdorf, Harold H., born in Nebraska; resides in Dickinson; graduated at College of Physicians and Surgeons, Baltimore, March 1, 1882; received the degree of M. A. from Dickinson College, June 27, 1879.

Bowers, Moses K., a native of Mifflin, Penn.; resides in Boiling Springs; graduate of Jefferson Medical College, March 30, 1882.

Deshler, Joseph J., born in Armstrong, Centre County; resides at Shippensburg; graduated at College Physicians and Surgeons, Baltimore, March 3, 1880.

Polinger, Robert B., a native of Cumberland County; residence Carlisle; graduated at Columbus Medical College (Ohio) March 1, 1883.

Ayres, Wilmot, born in York County; resides in Middlesex; graduated at Baltimore Medical College, April 12, 1883.

Orr, James P., native of Westmoreland County; residence New Cumberland; graduated at Michigan University, March 6, 1879.

Kauffman, John H., born in Martinsburg, West Virginia; residence Newburg; graduated at New York University, March 11, 1884.

McGary, Robt. M., a native of Shiremanstown, where he resides; graduated at Jefferson Medical College, March 29, 1884.

Diven, S. L., born at Mount Holly Springs; residence Carlisle; graduated at University Pennsylvania May 1, 1884; received degree of A. B. and A. M., at Dickinson College, 1878-81.

Hobach, John U., a native of Perry County; residence Mechanicsburg; graduated at the University of Pennsylvania, May 1, 1884.

Bowman, Dr. John D., Camp Hill, was born in 1832; graduated from Jefferson Medical College, Philadelphia, about 1856, then commenced practice in Camp Hill, remaining over sixteen years; then removed to Harrisburg, and in 1885 returned to Camp Hill.

Lauck, David A., a native of Cumberland County; residence Mechanicsburg; graduated at University, Baltimore, March 3, 1885.

Rodgers, John R., born at Cumberland County; resides at Sterrett's Gap, graduated at Western Reserve University, February 25, 1885.

Eckels, Geo. M., born at Mechanicsburg, where he now resides; graduated at Pennsylvania University, May 1, 1885.

Casteel, D. T., of Allen, Cumberland County; born in Garrett County, Md.; graduated at University of Maryland, 1885.

Stouffer, Alvin, P., of Shippensburg; born Goodville, Lancaster County; graduated at Pulte Medical College, Cincinnati, March 4, 1885. His diploma was endorsed by Hahnemann Medical College.

Kasten, William J., of Boiling Springs; born in Baltimore; graduated at University of Maryland, March 17, 1886.

Spangler, Jacob B., of Mechanicsburg; born in Greencastle, Penn.; graduated at Jefferson Medical College, April 2, 1886.

PHYSICIANS IN THE COUNTY REGISTERED IN THE OFFICE OF THE PROTHONOTARY AT CARLISLE.

The following is a list of the physicians in Cumberland County, who, in compliance with law, have registered in the office of the prothonotary at Carlisle, their names occuring in the order of registration:

Isaac Young Reed, Leesburg.
John A. Morrett, New Kingston.
R. Lowry Sibbet, Carlisle.
Geo. W. Ziegler, Carlisle.
John C. Claudy, Newville.
Charles C. Hammel, Mechanicsburg.
L. H. Lenher, Mechanicsburg.
Ephraim N. Mosser, Mechanicsburg.
John W. Trimmer, Lisburn.
John W. Bowman, Camp Hill.
Levi Fulk, New Kingston.
Eli B. Brandt, Mechanicsburg.
Jacob W. Roop, New Cumberland.
George Grove, Big Spring.
Philip R. Koons, Allen.
R. M. Hays, Newville.
Jno. H. Sherman, Mount Holly Springs.
Wm. W. Dale, Carlisle.
Saml. P. Zeigler, Carlisle.
L. P. O'Neale, Mechanicsburg.
H. D. Cooper, Newville.
Adam B. Sechrist, Upper Allen Township.
Jacob H. Deardorff, Mechanicsburg.
Thos. J. Stevens, Mechanicsburg.
Z. D. Hartzell, Newburg.
C. W. Krise, Carlisle.
Jesse Laverty, Sr., East Pennsborough Tp.
A. A. Thomson, Carlisle.
Jacob H. Smith, Dickinson Township.
W. F. Reily, Carlisle.
Michael L. Hoover, Silver Spring Township.
Wm. H. Longsdorf, Carlisle.
A. J. Herman, Carlisle.

John L. Bacher, Leesburg.
Robert Graham Young, Mechanicsburg.
Thomas Stewart, Sr., Carlisle.
Thomas Stewart, Jr., Carlisle.
Wm. H. Lauman, Mount Holly Springs.
David C. Cramer, Newburg.
Robt. W. Ross, Shepherdstown.
Matthew B. Rodgers, Middlesex Township.
Wm. A. English, Shippensburg.
Mrs. Susie A. English, Shippensburg.
Austin Best. Shiremanstown.
Alvin I. Miller, Carlisle.
Theophilus L. Neff, Carlisle.
James G. Fleck, Carlisle.
Robt. N. Short, Mechanicsburg.
Wm. B. Reynolds, Newville.
Jno. J. Koser, Shippensburg.
Henry R. Williams, Hogestown.
Robt. P. Long, Mechanicsburg.
George Fulmer, Mechanicsburg.
Chas. H. Hepburn, Carlisle.
Geo. Hemminger, Carlisle.
Robt. C. Stewart, Shippensburg.
Jas. B. Marshall, Shippensburg.
Alex. Stewart, Shippensburg.
Wm. M. Witherspoon, Shippensburg.
David D. Hayes, Shippensburg.
Wm. G. Stewart, Newville.
Joshua E. Van Camp, Plainfield.
Saml. Myers, West Pennsborough Township.
Saml. H. Brehm, Newville.
Robt. S. Prowell, New Cumberland.
Saml. M. Smith, Heberlig.

Robt. C. Marshall, West Fairview.
S. H. C. Bixler, Bloserville.
M. M. Ritchie, Carlisle.
Henry W. Linebaugh, New Cumberland.
Jesse H. Houck, Boiling Springs.
Israel Betz, Oakville.
F. B. Leberknight, Newburg.
Austin W. Nichols, Camp Hill.
J. L. Schoch, Shippensburg.
David Coover, Upper Allen Township.
D. W. Bashore, West Fairview.
W. S. Bruckart, Shiremanstown.
Wm. E. Cornog, Mount Holly Springs.
Jacob S. Bender, Carlisle.
Finley E. Rodgers, Mechanicsburg.
Charles A. Howland, Shippensburg.
Jacob H. Boyer, Mechanicsburg.
Edward S. Conlyn, Carlisle.
Joseph T Hoover, Southampton Township.
Joseph H. Mowers, Shippensburg.
Fred. Hartzell, Churchtown.
Jacob R. Bixler, Carlisle.
Saml. N. Eckee, Jacksonville.
Joseph C. Davis, Mount Holly Springs.
H. H. Longsdorf, Dickinson.
Stephen B. Kieffer, Carlisle.
Levi Clay, West Pensborough Township.

B. P. Backus, Philadelphia.
Moses K. Bowers, Boiling Springs.
J. K. Bowers, Reading.
J. J. Deshler, Shippensburg.
Robt. B. Pollinger, Carlisle.
Wilmot Ayres, Middlesex.
J. P. Orr, New Cumberland.
Max Von Slutterheim, Newville.
Jno. C. McCoy, Harrisburg.
C. M. Fager, West Fairview.
John Logan, Harrisburg.
John H. Kauffman, Newburg.
Robt. M. McGary, Shiremanstown.
S. L. Diven, Carlisle.
John U. Hobach, Mechanicsburg.
Jacob Peters, Henry Clay.
M. J. Jackson, New York City.
David A. Lauck, Mechanicsburg.
Jno. R. Rodgers, Sterrett's Gap.
Geo. M. Eckels, Mechanicsburg.
C. J. Heckert, Wormleysburg.
D. T. E. Casteel, Allen.
G. S. Comstock, Bloserville.
A. P. Stauffer, Shippensburg.
W. J. Kasten, Boiling Springs.
Jacob B. Spangler, Mechanicsburg.
Eugene A. Grove, Carlisle.

CUMBERLAND COUNTY MEDICAL SOCIETY.

On the 17th of July, 1866, the Medical Society of Cumberland County was organized, by the following gentlemen:

Drs. W. W. Dale, Saml. P. Zeigler, S. B. Keiffer, J. J. Zitner, A. D. Schelling, A. J. Herman, E. K. Demme, Carlisle; James B. Herring, R. N. Short, Eli B. Brandt, Mechanicsburg; Joseph Crain, Richard M. Crain, Hogestown; M. B. Mosser, Shiremanstown; John D. Bowman, White Hall; E. H. Coover, New Cumberland; D. W. Bashore, West Fairview; R. C. Hays, W. W. Nevin, Shippensburg; W. G. Stewart, Middle Springs; W. H. Lowman, Mount Holly Springs; J. W. C. Cuddy, Mount Rock; David Ahl, M. F. Robinson, G. W. Haldeman, Newville.

The temporary officers elected were Dr. J. Crain, president; Dr. G. W. Haldeman, secretary.

A constitution and by-laws were adopted, consisting of fourteen articles in the former and seven in the latter. Article III of the constitution reads: "Any gentleman who is a resident of this county, having a good moral character, and in regular standing with the profession, shall be eligible to membership." The membership fee is fixed at $2. Meetings are held on first Tuesdays of January, May and September of each year.

As showing the nature of the topics discussed at regular meetings, the list of subjects for the meeting held at the Indian Industrial School on Thursday afternoon, June 24, 1886, is given: Obstetric Practice, Dr. Hiram Corson; Hospital Clinic, Dr. O. G. Given, Uterine Displacements; Dr. M. K. Bowers; Early Diagnosis and Treatment of Phthisis, Dr. S. H. Brehm; Luxations, Dr. R. R. Koons; Narcotics—Their Uses and Abuses, Dr. R. L. Sibbet.

The present corps of officers embraces the following well-known gentlemen: Dr. Geo. W. Zeigler, president; Drs. W. F. Reily and L. H. Lenher, vice-presidents; Dr. T. Stewart, Jr., recording secretary; Dr. R. L. Sibbet, corresponding secretary; Dr. S. P. Zeigler, treasurer; Drs. E. N. Mosser, J. J. Koser, J. C. Claudy, J. W. Bowman and W. H. Longsdorf, censors.

CHAPTER X.

THE PRESS—OF CARLISLE—OF SHIPPENSBURG—OF MECHANICSBURG—OF NEWVILLE—OF MOUNT HOLLY.

THE corner-stones of modern civilization are the family, the school, the church and the State. Each of these has its functions to perform and its mission to fill in the world's progress. In proportion as each one accomplishes its work successfully, will the succeeding organization be better supplied with competent agents and preparation to move forward to the accomplishment of its destined mission. If the preparation—the preparatory training—in each be made satisfactory, a race of men and women will ultimately be developed that will meet the demands of Holland's "Men for the Hour:"

"God give us men! a time like this demands
Strong minds, great hearts, true faith and ready hands;
Men whom the lust of office does not kill;
Men whom the spoils of office can not buy;
Men who possess opinions and a will;
Men who have honor—men who will not lie;
Men who can stand before a demagogue
And damn his treacherous flatteries without winking;
Tall men, sun-crowned, who live above the fog
In public duty and in private thinking."

The public press supplies the mental and moral pabulum for these four cardinal organizations. It is a sort of general text-book for this educational quartet—an *omnium gatherum* of this world's sayings and doings—a witches' kettle into which are thrown more heterogeneous elements than Shakspeare ever dreamed of—a sheet, not always let down from heaven, but containing all manner of beasts and birds and creeping things, clean and unclean. Such is the modern newspaper—the power greater than the throne. Formerly, the public speaker enlightened the people upon the great political and other questions of the day. Now he finds that the press has preceded him, and has found an audience in every household of the land. It is the source of information—the means of forming public sentiment. He can arouse enthusiasm, perhaps, and direct forces, but he can not enlighten as before.

The press of Cumberland County has exerted an important influence in its development. Regret is to be expressed that more complete files have not been preserved of the various papers issued, for they afford, when perfect, the fullest local history of a people to be had. From Dr. Wing's excellent history, as well as from a variety of other sources, the following facts are gleaned:

THE PRESS OF CARLISLE.

The Carlisle Weekly Gazette, a small four-paged sheet issued in July, 1785, on blue paper, by Kline and Reynolds, was the first publication of the kind in the county, and probably the first west of the Susquehanna. It continued till 1815, and files of it, more or less perfect, are still preserved. Its subscription price was 15 shillings ($2) per annum, or 6 cents per single copy. It advocated the doctrines of the Federalists.

The Carlisle Eagle, according to one account, began in October, 1799, and was published by John P. Thompson, deputy postmaster, until 1802, when he was succeeded by Archibald Loudon, who continued in that capacity for about two years, George Phillips acting as editor. In 1804, Capt. Wm. Alexander, afterward an officer in the war of 1812, assumed editorial management under the ownership of Mrs. Ann C. Phillips, and continued the same till about 1823-24, when the paper passed into the hands of Gen. E. M. Biddle and Geo. W. Hitner who changed the name to *Carlisle Herald and Expositor.* George Fleming, George M. Phillips, son of George Phillips, and Robert M. Middleton were successively its editors. Middleton, who was an able newspaperman, was succeeded by Capt. E. Beatty, who edited the sheet from 1843 to 1857. After this period its name was changed again to *Carlisle Herald,* and it was edited successively by A. R. Rheem and James Dunbar. By process of time it passed into the hands of Weakley & Wallace; and subsequently was published by a regular organization known as the "Carlisle Herald Publishing Company."

In March, 1881, a paper known as the *Mirror* was merged into into it; and for a time the *Herald* was issued semi-weekly under the name of *Herald and Mirror.* The editors under the company have been J. Marion Weakley, Esq., O. Haddock, Alfred H. Adams, William E. Trickell, Esq., and John Hays, Esq., present editor. It has been rigidly consistent in its political principles, being first Federal, then Whig, and ever since Republican.

The *Cumberland Register* was a small paper published by Archibald Loudon. The number dated June 22, 1814, is numbered No. 40, Vol. IX., showing that the paper must have been begun about 1804.

The *American Volunteer* was started in 1814, during the progress of the war with Great Britain, by Wm. B. and James Underwood, brothers, by whom it was conducted conjointly till one of them died and the other conducted it until 1836, when George Sanderson bought it for about $300. By Sanderson it was carried on till 1845, when Messrs. Bratton & Boyer purchased it. Boyer after a time withdrew and established a new paper, called *The American Democrat,* rival, J. B. Bratton continuing the *Volunteer.* He edited it in connection with his duties as postmaster during the administrations of Pierce and Buchanan, and up to 1865, when he associated Wm. B. Kennedy with him in the enterprise. Kennedy continued it till 1871, when he sold back to Bratton, who conducted the paper alone from 1871 to 1877. At that time (April, 1877) Mr. Bratton sold it to Hon. S. M. Wherry, a farmer in Southampton Township, near Shippensburg, and an intelligent citizen, graduate of Princeton, who owned it twenty months and then sold it (December, 1878) to Jacob Zeamer, the present manager. The paper has been Democratic from its origin, and still maintains its position.

In 1822, a paper known as the *Carlisle Gazette* was started by John McCartney. He continued it for three years when John Wightman seized the editorial quill, and ran it for a time. Its subsequent career is wrapped in mystery.

About the same time, religious journalism was represented by a weekly known as *The Religious Miscellany.* It was published on the press of Fleming & Geddes, and was announced as "containing information relative to the Church of Christ, together with interesting literary and political notices of events, which occur in the world." After struggling "with its evil star" for several years, it peacefully departed for the "sweet by and by."

In August, 1830, the *Messenger of Useful Knowledge* was issued from the same press. In pamphlet form, under the editorial control of Prof. Rogers, of Dickinson College. After one year's existence, it, too, quietly breathed its last and slept with its ancestors.

The Valley Sentinel (daily and weekly) was started April 22, 1861, in Shippensburg. The gathering clouds of the great civil war, the mustering squadrons, the response to the country's call to arms of the fathers and sons of the country were taking away from home so many of our people, that the citizens of this rich and beautiful valley felt that they must have a newspaper to bring them frequent and correct reports from the army of those who had gone away and left at home so many aching hearts. A meeting of prominent citizens was had, and a stock company organized, and twenty-eight subscribers to the stock secured $1,100 to purchase the material for the office. The material secured, William Kennedy, of Chambersburg, was placed in charge. The first issue was April 22, 1861, published weekly, Democratic in politics; and in this style was published until 1865, nearly 1,000 subscribers being on its books.

In 1865 Mr. Kennedy retired from the *Sentinel*, and in partnership with Mr. J. B. Bratton commenced the publication of the *American Volunteer*, in Carlisle, and the *Valley Sentinel* was put in charge of Joseph T. Rippey, a young man, a practical printer from Baltimore. Mr. Rippey, tired of the enterprise, left it November 3, 1866, closing the office and stopping the publication.

November 26, 1866, a meeting of the stockholders tendered the editorial charge to R. J. Coffey, of Cleversburg, who was then teaching school in Sidetown. After a suspension of one month Mr. Coffey revived the publication December 5, 1866. Within the next year it was twice enlarged, the old Washington hand-press replaced by a Cotterell & Babcock power-press, and steam-power introduced, new type, and it became a thirty-two column paper and flourished greatly. Mr. Coffey had in the meantime become chief owner of the stock, so that on and after July 4, 1869, he became sole proprietor and editor. President Johnson appointed Mr. Coffey United States revenue assessor. In April, 1869, the greater portion of the *Sentinel* office was destroyed by fire, and again in 1870 it had another fire visitation, but, phœnix-like, it quickly arose from the ashes, each time with equal or greater facilities added.

In 1871 Mr. Coffey sold the office and good-will of the *Valley Sentinel* to Mr. T. F. Singiser, of Mechanicsburg, for the sum of $4,372, reserving the collection of all outstanding dues to the office. At this time the circulation had reached 1,538 copies. Six months after the sale Mr. Coffey purchased back the paper, and published it until March 10, 1872, when the concern was forced into the bankrupt courts, and Mr. Coffey's connection with the paper ceased. By order of the United States Court it was sold in May, 1872, and George Bobb, A. H. Brinks, H. Manning and H. K. Peffer became the purchasers. Under the new management the publication was resumed May 30, 1872. Mr. Peffer in editorial charge. January 16, 1873, the firm becam Peffer, Brinks & Co., Mr. Manning retiring. In January, 1873, the *Sentinel* proprietors purchased the entire material of the *Democratic Safeguard*, a defunct newspaper that had a brief and troubled career in Shippensburg.

May 22, 1874, the office of the *Valley Sentinel* passed to the hands of the present owner, H. K. Peffer, and the office at once removed to its present home—Carlisle. Only missing one issue it appeared as an eight-page, forty-eight columns, and much improved every way. Sparkling, bright and newsy it then started upon a new career. Its prosperity was unexampled; in the spring of 1881 Rheem's Hall was purchased, and at once converted into a most commodious and elegant home for the newly arrived paper, where it now issues daily and weekly editions to its constituency of eager readers.

December 13, 1881, the proprietors made the bold venture of issuing a daily paper, commencing as a five-column folio. It was welcomed by many friends, but some feared it could not sustain itself. It has, though. Indeed, so popular and prosperous was the daily that it has not only sustained itself, but has been enlarged three times, the last improvement occurring August 17, 1886. It commenced a modest five column paper, and now it is a seven column, every inch of its space crowded with the latest news, vigorous editorials, choice literary and micellaneous matter and paying advertisements.

It must not be supposed that the foregoing list exhausts the products of the Carlisle press. In both the temporary and permanent form, publications have issued "thick as autumnal leaves in the valley of Vallambrosa." Some of the books issued were works of considerable merit.

THE PRESS OF SHIPPENSBURG.

For a brief period, during the early part of the present century, John McFarland, a politician of the Jacksonian school, published at Shippensburg a small paper, the name of which is not recalled.

April 10, 1833, the *Shippensburg Free Press* made its appearance under the watchful care of Augustus Fromm. On the 19th of the ensuing September David D. Clark and James Culbertson commenced the publication of a rival paper called *The Intelligencer*. November 14, of the same year, the two papers were consolidated under the title of *Free Press*, Fromm having sold his establishment to his rivals. After a brief existence the *Free Press* was permitted to die for the want of "the sinews of war."

In May, 1837, the first number of the *Shippensburg Herald* was launched by John F. Weishampel, and its existence guaranteed for about two years. After Weishampel's exit from the editorial tripod, Henry Claridge revived the *Herald* for a few weeks, and then allowed it "to sleep the sleep that knows no waking."

On the 1st of April, 1840, the *Cumberland and Franklin Gazette*, under the supervision of William M. Baxter, did obeisance to a patronizing public, and continued on the stage for more than a year, and then took an affectionate but final farewell.

Toward the close of 1841 *The Cumberland Valley*, directed by William A. Kinsloe, made its bid for public favor. On the 2d of November, 1842, its ownership was transferred by sale to Robert Koontz and John McCurdy. After about six months Mr. Koontz became sole owner. This relation continued for a short time, when Mr. Kinsloe secured the paper a second time. By him it was permitted to "depart in peace."

The Weekly News was born April 26, 1844, under the parentage of John L. Baker, by whom it was sold, in a few years, to Jacob Bomberger. In 1851 D. K. Wagner formed a partnership with Mr. Bomberger, and in 1856 sold out his interest. Mr. Bomberger sold his interest to Edward W. Curriden, who published it till 1863, when he disposed of it to Daniel W. Thrush, Esq. In 1867 it passed into the hands of D. K. and J. G. Wagner, its present owners.

In 1845–46 Messrs. Cooper & Dechert established a Democratic paper called *The Valley Spirit*, which they removed, in a year or two, to Chambersburg. It is now the Democratic organ of Franklin County.

The Shippensburg Chronicle was established on the 4th of February, 1875, by B. K. Goodyear and Samuel R. Murray; and was conducted by them until January, 1879, when Mr. D. A. Orr, now of the Chambersburg *Valley Spirit* became editor and proprietor. It remained in his possession until August, 15, 1879, when Messrs. Sanderson & Bro. became proprietors. These gentlemen conducted it until May 9, 1882, when it passed into the hands of Wolfe & McClelland, the former assuming editorial charge. Prof. Wolfe had been a teacher for several years, and resigned his position in the Cumberland Valley State Normal School to take full charge of the *Chronicle*. It is ably managed and circulates among a good, thrifty class of people.

Valley Sentinel.—[See account of this newspaper under " Press of Carlisle."]

THE PRESS OF MECHANICSBURG.

The first newspaper published in Mechanicsburg was called *The Microcosm*. It began in 1835 under the foster-care of Dr. Jacob Weaver, but yielded up its small-world spirit in a short time. The *School Visitor*, published a short time afterward by A. F. Cox, soon shared a similar fate. In due course of time (1843 or 1844) The *Independent Press* appeared under the direction of Mr. Sprigman. Its spirit was independent but its body was dependent on bread and butter, and hence its early decease.

In 1853 or 1854 the *Mechanicsburg Gleaner* was founded by John B. Flynn. It was issued with considerable regularity till 1856, when it was sold to Samuel Fernall, who, in turn, disposed of it, in 1858, to W. E. McLaughlin. He changed the name of the paper to *Weekly Gazette*. After a time he sold his interest to David J. Carmany, foreman of the office, who made some marked improvements, and changed the title to *The Cumberland Valley Journal*. He conducted it in the interest of the g. o. p. till January, 1871, when, owing to ill health, he sold the establishment to Joseph Ritner, grandson of the old governor of like name.

In March, 1868, a paper was started by a joint-stock company, and called *The Valley Democrat*. Capt. T. F. Singiser was chosen editor and publisher. In December, 1870, the *Democrat* was purchased by R. H. Thomas and E. C. Gardner, the latter having a third interest and acting as local editor. By them the name was changed to *The Valley Independent*. In September, 1872, Mr. Thomas purchased the *Cumberland Valley Journal* and consolidated it with his paper, naming the product *The Independent Journal*, by which title it is still known, and under which it advocates non-partisan, independent sentiments.

In 1873 Mr. Thomas purchased of Mr. Gardner his interest in the newspaper business, and then sold an interest to Maj. H. C. Deming, of Harrisburg. In January, 1874, Messrs. Thomas and Deming established *The Farmer's Friend and Grange Advocate*, a paper devoted to the interests of the Patrons of Husbandry in the Middle States. It soon secured a large circulation, and is now the oldest grange paper in the United States. In 1878 Mr. Deming sold his interest to Mr. Thomas, who continued to be its editor and publisher.

The *Saturday Journal* was established in October, 1878, by R. H. Thomas, Jr. It began and has continued as a Republican paper during political campaigns, but ordinarily is a newsy society paper.

Journalism in Mechanicsburg has suffered many reverses, newspaper men having suffered the following losses, as shown by the books: Mr. Flynn, $3,000; Messrs. Fernall and McLaughlin, $2,000; Mr. Singiser, $5,000; Mr. Carmany, $4,500; Mr. Ritner, $3,500; R. H. Thomas, before securing a good foothold $8,000.

About 1873, a paper called *The Republican* was started, but six months' terrestrial existence satisfied its desire for life. In June, 1877, J. J. Miller and J. N. Young, started the *Semi-Weekly Ledger*, a Republican journal. After the first year A. J. Houck was received as a partner, *vice* Young retired. The paper was changed to a weekly, but finally disappeared from the scene of earthly conflict.

HISTORY OF CUMBERLAND COUNTY.   195

Other ephemeral publications have issued from Mechanicsburg, but their names being legion, can not be recalled. At present the entire field is held by R. H. Thomas, proprietor of a mammoth publishing house, which has been developed by pluck and perseverance.

THE PRESS OF NEWVILLE.

The first effort to establish a newspaper in Newville, was made by a Mr. Baxter in 1843, by the transfer of *The Central Engine* from Newburg. The experiment proving unsuccessful, the enterprise continued but a few months. The next effort was made in 1858, when J. M. Miller began, in company with John C. Wagner, the publication of *The Star of the Valley*, a non-partisan weekly, which January 1, 1885, J. C. Fosnot bought, his son, George B. McC., conducting same for one year, when Mr. Fosnot united it with the *Enterprise*, under name of *Star and Enterprise*, the double paper achieving a rare success.

In December, 1874, the Fosnot Bros. brought from Oakville, where it had been established in May, 1871, a paper known as *The Enterprise*, commenced by J. C. Fosnot, which was amalgamated with *The Star of the Valley*.

About 1858, *The Weekly Native* was started by J. J. Herron; but its failure to secure a proper patronage gave it a permanent leave of absence from the field journalism.

In May, 1882, John W. Strohm began the publication of the *Plainfield Times*, at Plainfield, this county, in November, 1885, he removed to Newville, and called *The Newville Times*, having a large circulation. In August, 1883, Mr. Strohm started a matrimonial paper, called *Cupid's Corner*, which has proved a profitable venture.

THE PRESS OF MOUNT HOLLY.

Mount Holly has a paper known as the *Mountain Echo*, R. M. Earley, editor, publisher and proprietor.

CHAPTER XI.

EDUCATIONAL—LEGAL HISTORY—EARLY SCHOOLS—DICKINSON COLLEGE—METZGAR FEMALE INSTITUTE—INDIAN INDUSTRIAL SCHOOL—CUMBERLAND VALLEY STATE NORMAL SCHOOL—TEACHERS' INSTITUTE—COUNTY SUPERINTENDENTS.

LEGAL HISTORY.

THE history of education in Pennsylvania may be said to date from the beginning of Penn's colony on the banks of the Delaware.

In the first plan of government drawn up by Penn, in 1682, provision was made for the "governor and provincial council to erect and order all public schools, and reward the authors of useful sciences and laudable inventions in said provinces."

In the year following a school for the education of the young was founded by enactment of the provincial council; and, to further the design, it elected one Enoch Flower to conduct the school work. The branches taught were "reading, writing, and the casting of accounts." This was the first school established within the present boundaries of Pennsylvania.

In 1698 a school was organized by the Society of Friends in Philadelphia, in which all children and servants might be taught, and provision was made "for the instruction of the poor, gratis." Several charters were granted this school by Penn, the final one in 1711, extending the privileges and rights so as to form, in reality, a public school, the first in Pennsylvania.

The work thus begun was aided by private contributions, and it was as late as April, 1776, that the first school law was adopted, which provided that a "school or schools shall be established by the Legislature for the convenient instruction of youth, with such salaries to the masters paid by the public as will enable them to instruct youth at low prices," and which set apart 60,000 acres of land as a permanent endowment for said schools, the income from said land to be invested, and the said schools to be conducted by the Legislature as their discretion might dictate.

Thus it will be seen that the educational interest was left wholly at the mercy of men who had little, if any, experience in educational matters, and who were occupied with weightier affairs than the fostering of a young school system.

Even with State aid the schools were neglected, and had to be nourished by the bounty of benevolent persons who contributed to the support of the struggling interest. In 1788 a subscription of something near £40, signed by the leading citizens and containing the following agreement, was taken in Cumberland County: "WHEREAS, a number of children in the borough of Carlisle, from the extreme indigence of their parents, are brought up in the greatest ignorance; and, whereas, these people laboring under the unfortunate condition of slavery, are, from circumstances, generally debarred from acquiring a knowledge of the Holy Scriptures and the principles of morality; the subscribers being of the opinion that a free school and Sunday evening school, under proper regulations, would tend to the advancement of knowledge and of good order in society, agree to pay the sums annexed to their names for one year for the above benevolent purposes," etc., which may serve as an illustration of the dependence upon personal aid.

But an advance was made by the Constitution of 1790, which stated that "the Legislature should, as conveniently as might be, provide by law for the establishment of schools throughout the State, in such manner that the poor might be taught gratis." The same provision occurred in the law of 1809, which required the assessors to obtain the names of all children residing in their districts, between the ages of five and twelve years, whose parents were too poor to pay for their schooling, and to furnish each teacher a list of these names. It then became the teacher's duty to instruct all such children as applied for instruction, and to present the county commissioners with his account for the tuition of these same children. This drawing of distinction between rich and poor aroused violent opposition among the opponents of the measure, who termed it the "pauper system." The whole number of children entered in these schools during the year 1833, the last in which this law was in force, was only 17,467, and the expenditure, in their behalf, $48,466.25.

In 1834 a free school system was introduced throughout the whole State, which continues, with certain modifications and amendments, to be the school law of Pennsylvania. There were many opponents to the law, and, as its acceptance was made optional with each district, the first year in which the new law was in operation only ninety-three districts out of 900 were reported as having adopted it. The report of the State superintendent shows that in Cumberland County, in 1834, thirteen districts accepted, three rejected, and one not reported—certainly a good record, considering the general opposition where in the State.

In Carlisle, however, during the following year, there was "no school in operation—fund inadequate, and deemed prudent by the directors not to commence at present."

EARLY SCHOOLS.

As the first school had been started under Quaker control, the German settlers who subsequently entered the valley were compelled to submit their educational affairs largely to the schoolmaster who opened the private school. As a general rule, the school was conducted by the minister of the village church, and the building used was also devoted to religious worship. Many of the earliest schools were even conducted in barns, and very good schools they were thought, too. The early teachers in Shippensburg were Andrew Gibson, John Chambers, Jacob Steinman, John Morrison, Michael Hubbley, Robert McKean and Dr. Kernan, the latter's school being of a higher grade than the others. A select school was opened by two ladies named Mary Russell and Elizabeth Anderson, in 1824, which became very popular, and which continued, under the charge of Miss Eliza Russell, until the free school system was introduced, when it was closed, the proprietors taking charge of the district school.

In Carlisle Samuel Tate, Capt. Smith, Mrs. Shaw, and others not known of by the writer were the early teachers.

About the year 1809 a Methodist minister by the name of Boden conducted a school in Silver Spring Township, but he was shortly succeeded by a young Hessian named Henry De Lipkey, who, having been buffetted about by the fickle goddess, became soured on humanity, and dealt many a stroke upon the backs of refractory urchins. John Stevenson, Michael Boor, Arthur Moore, Adam Longsdorf and William Jameson, the latter said to have been a fine mathematician, were also known among the early teachers in the township.

A church, erected by general contribution, was used as a school in Allen Township, and was presided over by a Mr. McGlaughlin, William Kline, John Foster, James Methlin and Solomon Tate. Other early teachers in the township were Messrs. Bausman, Durborrow and Pittinger.

According to "Sypher's History of Pennsylvania," the first school of a higher grade was a classical school opened in Carlisle about the year 1760. It was in charge of one Robert McKinley, and continued until the war of the Revolution, when both principal and students enlisted in the patriot army.

Another classical school was in operation in Carlisle in the year 1781. It was at first a "grammar school," but was enlarged and chartered as an academy.

An institution known as the Carlisle Institute was opened in 1831, which acquired a large patronage. The date of its discontinuance is not known.

In Newburg, Hopewell Township, a school called "Hopewell Academy" was opened in 1812 by Mr. John Cooper, a linguist of no mean reputation, and numbered among its patrons such eminent men as Dr. Alfred Nevin, H. M. Watts, once United States minister to Austria, the Rev. Dr. Samuel McCoskry, and others of equal prominence. This institution was maintained until 1832, when the founder removed to Shippensburg.

Two classical schools were opened in Newville—one in 1832, by Joseph Casey, and the other in 1843, by Mr. French. The latter changed owners many times, and was finally converted into Big Spring Academy, under the charge of W. R. Linn and Rev. Robert McCachran, in whose hands it perished.

About the year 1840 a select school was opened in Mechanicsburg by F. T. Gillelen, and was continued by him with much success until 1853, when it was purchased by Rev. Joseph S. Loose, A. M. He immediately removed it to a better building, and termed it the Cumberland Valley Institute. This institution existed until recently, its various owners having been Mr. I. D. Rupp, Messrs. Lippincott, Mullin & Reese, Rev. O. Ege, and his son, A. Ege, A. M.

Irving Female College, at Irvington (East Mechanicsburg), was founded as a seminary for ladies by Solomon P. Gorgas, and was chartered as a college in 1857. It was conducted by Rev. A. G. Marlatt until his death in 1865, when Rev. T. P. Ege was elected. It was located in a comely brick building, capable of accommodating forty boarding, in addition to the day pupils.

Dr. R. Lowry Sibbet, a graduate of Pennsylvania College, commenced a private school in Centerville, Penn Township, in 1856. It was conducted by him for three sessions, during which he instructed in the Greek and Latin languages, higher mathematics and natural sciences. Dr. Sibbet severed his connection with this school, and was succeeded by Rev. George Hays and Mr. E. M. Hays, after which the school was discontinued.

Sometime about 1848 a classical school was opened in New Kingston by Mr. A. W. Lily, a graduate of Pennsylvania College. His successor, Rev. J. H. Cupp, did not continue long in the enterprise, and it was abandoned in 1850.

An institution called White Hall Academy, was opened in East Pennsborough Township in 1851, by Mr. David Denlinger, under whose charge it was operated until 1867, when it was changed to a Soldiers' Orphan School. It was then purchased by Capt. J. A. Moore and Mr. F. S. Dunn, and was conducted without change until 1875, when Messrs. Amos Smith and John Dunn took charge. Capt. Moore is the present able and popular principal.

In 1860 the Episcopal Church founded a seminary for young ladies, called the Mary Institute, in Carlisle. The principals have been Rev. Francis J. Clerc, Rev. William C. Leverett and Mary W. Dunbar. It has been discontinued for some time.

In 1858, the Sunny Side Female Seminary was opened in Newburg, with Mrs. Caroline Williams as principal. She married Rev. Daniel Williams, a few years after, and under his charge the school perished.

The Shippensburg Collegiate Institute, a reorganization of an old academy, was opened in Shippensburg, with Rev. James Colder as principal. He was succeeded by Dr. R. L. Sibbet (who retired to engage in the study of medicine), Rev. J. Y. Brown, ——Vaughan and Miss McKeehan.

DICKINSON COLLEGE.

The difficulties experienced by the early settlers of the Cumberland Valley in securing a liberal education for their sons, who had formerly been sent either to England or to the academies located in Philadelphia and in more remote places, led them to contemplate the establishment of an institution to combine all the advantages of the existing schools with that of being of much easier access. With this end in view, the friends of the movement secured a charter for a college in the borough of Carlisle, in which it says that "in memory of the great and important services rendered to his country by His Excellency, John Dickinson, Esq., president of the supreme executive council, and in commemoration of his very liberal donation to the institution, the said college shall be forever hereafter called and known by the name of Dickinson College." It was placed under the control of a board composed of forty trustees. The support was to be derived from the Presbyterian Church directly, and also from all friends of education who deemed fit to make donations.

Prominent among the founders and first trustees, were John Dickinson, first governor of Pennsylvania and first president of the board of trustees, and Dr. Benjamin Rush, of Philadelphia. The first meeting of the board was held in 1783, and in the following year a faculty was chosen, consisting of Rev. Charles Nisbett, D. D., of Montrose, Scotland, as president, and James Ross, author of the well-known Ross Latin Grammar, as professor of the Greek and Latin languages.

After much hesitation and correspondence, Dr. Nisbett was induced to accept the position offered, and arrived at Carlisle on July 4, 1785, being welcomed with the sound of cannon and bells. The following day saw the opening of the college in a small building, between Pomfret Street and Liberty Alley.

With such a beginning, the school grew rapidly into prominence, and was only retarded by the insufficiency of the funds. Strenuous efforts to increase the income were made by the friends of the institution, and in 1791 they succeeded in securing an appropriation from the Assembly of $7,500, which, with an additional donation of $3,000 given in 1798, served to place it upon a firm basis.

In 1802, when a new building had been completed on the new grounds purchased in 1798, and when everything was prepared for the reception of students, a spark carried by the wind from an ash pile far away, kindled a fire which destroyed nearly everything. Before the smoke had blown away, a new subscription list was in circulation, and on August 3, 1803, the first stone of the new building planned by the public architect at Washington, Mr. Latrobe, was laid.

The college was inspired with a new vigor, and for a number of years continued with increasing influence and prosperity. But troubles arose which led to a change in the controlling influence in 1833. The Baltimore Conference of the Methodist Episcopal Church, learning of the difficulties into which the institution had entered, made proposals to a committee of the board of trustees, and a final agreement was made by which the college and all connected with it passed into the control of the Methodist Episcopal Church.

Now the school revived. New departments were added, and the old ones strengthened, until Dickinson College was placed in the front rank of institution for higher education. The following are the departments of study maintained: (1) Moral science, (2) ancient languages and literature; (3) pure mathematics; (4) philosophy and English literature, including history and constitutional law, (5) physics and mixed mathematics, and the application of calculus to natural philosophy, astronomy and mechanics; (6) chemistry, and its application to agriculture and the arts; (7) physical geography, natural history, mineralogy and geology; (8) modern languages; (9) civil and mining engineering and metallurgy.

Those who wish to obtain the collegiate degrees are required to devote the earlier part of their course to the study of the classics and the pure mathematics, but during the latter half, the student is granted more freedom, and if he desires to complete any of the special courses provided, he has the liberty to do so, at the same time retaining his right to the degree of B. A. upon graduation equally with those who have remained in the regular classical course.

The institution is well provided with all apparatus for the elucidation of the principles of physical science; the libraries number about 28,000 volumes, many of them very rare and valuable; the permanent endowment exceeds $170,-000; and a valuable property, which is not productive at present, but which will add materially to the income of the school in the near future.

Within the last few years the course has been opened to the ladies, so that now students of both sexes have equal privileges.

The Tome Scientific Building, a long, handsome, fire-proof structure, of native limestone, with trimmings of gray stone, brought from the Cleveland quarries, facing on Louther Street, was finished in 1885, a donation of Col. Robert Tome, of Port Deposit, Md., from whom it derives its name. The last and most beautiful building added to the college in the near past is the Bosler Memorial Hall, a pressed brick building, with handsomely carved brown stone ornamentation, meant principally to contain the college library; begun in 1885 and finished in the succeeding year. It is a donation from the widow of the late James W. Bosler, of Carlisle.

Among the graduates of Dickinson College many have held responsible and honorable positions. One has been President of the United States, one has been Chief Justice of the Supreme Court of United States, one Justice of the Supreme Court, one Governor of a State, two United States Senators, ten Representatives in Congress, two district judges, three justices of the State Supreme Court, eleven presidents and sixteen professors of colleges, one bishop of the Protestant Episcopal Church, and sixty-eight ministers of the Gospel.

The following is a table of the officers and presidents of Dickinson College, with the periods of their service:

Presidents of Board of Trustees.—John Dickinson, LL.D., 1783-1808; Rev. John King, D.D., 1808-1808; James Armstrong, 1808-24; John B. Gibson, LL.D., 1824-29; Andrew Carothers, 1829-33.

Since 1833, the president of the college has been, *ex officio*, president of the board of trustees.

Secretaries.—Rev. William Linn, D.D., 1783-84; Thomas Duncan, 1784-92; Thomas Creigh, 1792-96; James Duncan, 1796-1806; Alex. P. Lyon, 1806-08; Andrew Carothers, 1808-14; Isaac B. Parker, 1814-20; James Hamilton, 1820-24; Frederick Watts, LL.D., 1824-28; Rev. S. A. McCoskry, D.D., 1828-31; William Biddle, 1831-33; James W. Marshall, 1850-54; Rev. Otis H. Tiffany, D.D., 1854-57; James W. Marshall, 1857-58; Rev. William L. Boswell, 1858-65; John K. Stayman, 1865-68; Charles F. Himes, 1868—.

Treasurers.—Samuel Laird, 1784-90; Samuel Postlethwaite, 1790-98; John Montgomery, 1798-1808; John Miller, 1808-21; And. McDowell, 1821-33; John J. Myers, M.D., 1833-41; William D. Seymour, 1841-54; James W. Marshall, 1854-61; Samuel D. Hellman, 1861-68; John K. Stayman, 1868; Charles F. Himes, 1868-82; J. W. Smiley, 1882-85; Henry C. Whitney, 1885—.

Librarians.—James Ross, 1784-92; William Thomson, 1792-1804; John Borland, 1804-05; John Hays, 1805-09; Henry R. Wilson, 1809-13; Joseph Shaw, 1813-15; Gerard E. Stack, 1815-16; Joseph Spencer, 1822-30; Charles D. Cleveland, 1830-32; Robert Emory, 1834-40; John McClintock, 1840-48; James W. Marshall, 1848-60; William L. Boswell, 1860-65, John K. Stayman, 1865-70; Henry M. Harman, 1870—.

College Presidents.—Charles Nisbett, D.D., 1785-1804; Robert Davidson, D.D., 1804-09; Jeremiah Atwater, D.D., 1809-15; John McKnight, D.D., 1815-16; John Mitchell Mason, D.D., 1821-24; William Neill, D.D., 1824-29; Samuel Blanchard Howe, D.D., 1830-31; John Price Durbin, D.D., 1833-45; Robert Emory, D.D., 1845-48; Jesse Truesdell Peck, D.D., 1848-52; Charles Collins, D.D., 1852-60; Herman Merrills Johnson, D.D., 1860-68; Robert Lawrenson Dashiell, D.D., 1868-72; James Andrew McCauley, D.D., LL.D., the present efficient and scholarly president.

HISTORY OF CUMBERLAND COUNTY. 201

METZGAR FEMALE INSTITUTE.

The Metzgar Female Insitute, occupying a beautiful and commodious brick structure, surrounded by pleasant shade trees and a rich variety of flowers, is one of the attractions of Carlisle, and reflects great honor upon the memory of the man whose funds supplied it, Mr. Metzgar, an honored member of the Cumberland County bar. It has attained a position among the educational institutions of the county, as is shown by its constantly increasing attendance. It was erected some five or six years ago.

INDIAN INDUSTRIAL SCHOOL.

The Indian Industrial School, at Carlisle, under the management of Capt. R. H. Pratt, Tenth Cavalry, is one of the pioneer institutions of the United States to attempt the civilization of a savage race.

By act of Congress dated June 17, 1879, the extensive grounds and buildings known as the Carlisle Barracks were appropriated for the Indian school. Sometime in 1876, Capt. Pratt conceived the idea that Indians could be educated and their labor and skill utilized. About that time, of the hundred prisoners at Fort Marion, Florida, captured from the Cheyennes, Arapahoes, Wichitas, etc., a number were taken to Hampton, Va., where they were organized into a school, thus originating the system of Indian industrial education in this country. Carlisle was next to be developed.

In addition to the extensive buildings secured from the Government at the time the school began, there have been erected, since, a chapel, 1879; hospital, 1881; new dining hall and laundry, 1885; and a new wing to old dining hall for printing office.

The first pupils received (eighty-four in number) arrived October 5, 1879, from the Rosebud and Pine Ridge agencies, Dakota. The fathers of those boys and girls were leaders in their tribes (the Sioux). On the 27th of October, fifty more came from the Poncas, Pawnees, Kiowas, Comanches, Wichitas, Cheyennes and Arapahoes; and on the 6th of November, eight children arrived from Green Bay agency, Wisconsin, and Sisseton agency, Minnesota.

The board of managers consists, at present, of Capt. R. H. Pratt, Tenth Cavalry, superintendent; A. J. Standing, assistant superintendent; O. G. Given, M. D., physician; S. H. Gould, chief clerk; Miss A. S. Ely and W. C. London, assistant clerks.

From the sixth annual report of the superintendent, dated August 18, 1885, the following facts are gleaned: Number of tribes represented, 38; number of boys in school, 344; number of girls in school, 150. Total, 494.

These children are classed in nine sections, properly graded, for school work, and study such subjects as are usually taught in public schools. Each section is under the guidance of a special teacher, whose whole time is given to its instruction and management. Every pupil is also given the choice of learning some trade, and is required to spend a certain length of time each day in the mastery of his trade. On the whole, the Indian school is a successful institution, and well merits careful study.

This labor of the Indian School, even as early as the annual report of 1881, amounted to $6,333.46, as governed by the regular contract prices of the Indian Department. The pupils are particularly apt in the ordinary English branches, while many display also a very considerable skill in the departments of practical mechanics. With such a record it is not surprising that this school should have attracted very considerable attention, and that representatives, both of the nobility and brains of England—the Duke of Sutherland and Edward H. Freeman, the celebrated English historian—should have been among its visitors, soon after it was established.

CUMBERLAND VALLEY STATE NORMAL SCHOOL.

This institution, located at Shippensburg, is the State school for the Seventh District, comprising the counties of Adams, Bedford, Blair, Cumberland, Fulton, Franklin and Huntington.

Its history is briefly this: An act of the Legislature, passed April 1, 1850, authorized the board of school directors at Carlisle to establish a normal school in these terms: "And said board also have power to establish a normal school of a superior grade in said district, provided no additional expense is thereby incurred over and above the necessary schools for said borough, and to admit scholars in said normal school from any part of the county, or elsewhere, on such terms and on such plans as said board may direct; and the board of directors in any other school district, in said county, may, if they think proper, make an agreement with the directors in Carlisle to contribute to the support of the same according to the number of scholars they may send to said normal school."

On the 16th of the said month a county convention was called, at which a plan for a normal school was submitted. Of this convention Judge Watts was chairman. The Carlisle school board issued a call to the other districts for a meeting of delegates on May 7, to mature plans for said school, and announced May 15 as the time for a three months' session to begin, tuition being fixed at $8 per pupil. The attendance of delegates was not sufficiently large to warrant the establishment of the school.

The previous agitation resulted, however, in a movement among the teachers at the county institute held at Newville December 23, 1856. The action was thus expressed: "*Resolved*, That a committee of one director from each township be appointed, to take into consideration the establishment of a normal school in Cumberland County." The committee met at Carlisle, January 13, 1857, and determined its location at Newville, it having guaranteed the necessary buildings. The management was vested in a board, consisting of the county superintendent and one director from each school district. The board agreed upon the opening of the school, April 3, 1857, with the following faculty: Daniel Shelly, county superintendent, principal; W. R. Linn, S. B. Heiges and D. E. Kast, instructors. George Swartz was chosen principal of the Model School, and J. H. Hostetter and Miss Mary Shelly, instructors.

A three months' term was held, with ninety-one pupils in the Normal School and 149 in the Model School. About $500 worth of school apparatus was provided by contributions from the citizens. The session of 1858 continued five months, but those of 1859 and 1860 only three months each, George Swartz being principal.

The attempt to secure a State Normal School for the Seventh District began at Newville November 2, 1865, when, during the county institute, the directors of the county instructed the county superintendent, George Swartz, to address a circular to the various school boards in the district, asking them to appoint delegates to meet in a general convention at Chambersburg January 10, 1866, to hear reports and take general steps for the establishment of such a State school. No definite results accrued from this movement, but in the spring of 1870 the preparatory steps for the location of the school at Shippensburg, its present site, were taken. A meeting was called and Hon. J. P. Wickersham, State superintendent, was invited to deliver an address. After several meetings, an application to the court for a charter was granted in April, 1870. Subscriptions to the amount of $24,000 had been secured. On the first Monday of May the first election for trustees was held, resulting in the choice of the following gentlemen: J. W. Craig, Dr. W. W. Nevin, C. L.

Shade, John Grabill, John E. Maclay, R. C. Himes, Robt. C. Hays and A. G. Miller. The capital stock was subsequently increased from $30,000 to $100,000.

The excavation for the foundation was begun in August, 1870, and the contract let for $74,000. The corner-stone was laid by the Masonic Order May 31, 1871. The entire cost of the structure, which is 225x170 feet, three stories high, together with grounds, heating apparatus, gas fixtures, etc., was $125,000, and of the furnishing about $25,000.

The property was accepted as a State institution in February, 1873, and the first session of the school began April 15, 1873, under the principalship of George P. Beard. A. M. He continued in his position until July, 1875, when he resigned. His successors have been Rev. I. N. Hays, B. S. Patten, S. B. Heiges and J. F. McCreary, present incumbent.

TEACHERS' INSTITUTE.

In no department of educational activity has so much improvement been shown as in the methods and philosophy of instruction. In the private schools, academies and colleges of the olden times, the great purpose was to secure the accumulation of facts—the storing of the mind with useful knowledge. In too many institutions is this false notion still entertained. The relationship between crude facts and the child's mind was not dreamed of. The "what" of knowledge, or the subject-matter, was all that the teacher sought. The "how," or the method of reaching and classifying these facts, was reserved, in the natural order of things, for development at a later day. In due course of time the subject of methods or the best way of doing certain things, began to attract the attention of the more thoughtful; and still later in educational progress, the "why," or the reason for certain processes, demanded consideration of the professional instructor. All this is evidence that the world moves—that progress is not confined to the domain of the material world.

In the securing of these progressive steps, the teachers' institute in its various forms had much to do. In associations of those of like calling, friction of minds never fail to secure beneficial results. At the convention of teachers and other friends of education, held in the court house at Carlisle December 19, 1835, Dr. Isaac Snowden was chosen president. Important questions were discussed, and arrangements were made to hold semi-annual meetings in the future. In the program for the session to be held June 25, 1836, are to be found these important subjects, which show that even at that early date the leaven of educational improvement had commenced to work:

"1. What is the best mode of securing a competent number of well qualified teachers of common schools to meet the exigencies of the county?

2. The influence of education on the character and stability of civil institutions, and the direction and modification which it gives the political relations.

3. The evils existing in our common schools, and appropriate remedies.

4. The influence of employing visible illustrations in imparting instruction to children.

5. Best mode of governing children, and of exciting their interest in their studies.

6. Importance of a uniformity of text-books, etc."

What was done at subsequent meetings does not appear, but the questions introduced at this session are living questions, and the impetus given to educational work in the county was manifest.

From the interesting article in Wing's History of Cumberland County, written by D. E. Kast, we quote: "At the call of the county superintendent, the directors and teachers generally assembled in Education Hall, Carlisle, on Saturday, the 2d day of September, 1854, for the purpose of holding a school teachers' convention, for devising more favorable means for the promotion of education generally in the common schools of Cumberland County. Ex-Gov. Ritner presided at this meeting, and Mr. Dieffenbach, deputy superintendent of common schools in Pennsylvania, was in attendance. A committee, appointed to prepare business for the meeting, reported a series of resolutions, the subject-matter of which engaged the attention of the assembly during its sessions. Provision was made for the permanent organization of a county institute, by appointment of a committee to report a constitution for its government."

On the 21st of the following December (1854), the "Cumberland County Teachers' Institute" was permanently organized, with ex-Gov. Ritner in the chair and an attendance of 94 teachers out of 160 at its first session. Among those present on that occasion, were Hon. Thomas H. Burrowes, who aided in its deliberations, and Dr. Collins, president of Dickinson College, who lectured. The subject of methods of teaching was freely and profitably discussed. The sentiment of the institute was expressed in the following characteristic resolution: "That as teachers and members of this institute we will cordially co-operate with our superintendent in his laudable efforts to elevate the standard of teaching and advance general education throughout the county."

Annual sessions from that time to the present have been held at some point in the county, the time between the holidays being usually preferred. The benefits to the county have been quite marked, justifying the wisdom of those who inaugurated the agency of professional culture.

COUNTY SUPERINTENDENTS.

School systems, like other activities, need efficient supervision and execution. The establishment of county superintendency met this want. At first it met with some opposition, as might be expected; but it has come to be accepted as an indispensable feature of the school system. The names of the officials who have filled this position are as follows:

Daniel Shelly, from 1854 to 1860, two terms. He was efficient in the performance of his duties, and succeeded in arousing general educational interest.

D. K. Noel, a prominent teacher of the county was elected, in May, 1860, as his successor; but ill health ensuing, he resigned in a few months, and was succeeded by Joseph Mifflin, who was appointed to fill his unexpired term. Mr. Mifflin was a teacher, but, prior and subsequent to his superintendency, had given attention to civil engineering. At the expiration of his term of office, he was followed, in 1863, by George Swartz, a teacher who, by self-exertion and perseverance, had attained honorable distinction in his calling. He held the position for six years, and performed its duties creditably. In 1869, owing to some legal difficulties connected with the election, W. A. Lindsey was appointed to the position, and continued to discharge its duties till 1872, when D. E. Kast was chosen to fill the place. He did this acceptably, and was re-elected in May, 1875, to serve the public three years longer, which he did till 1878, when Samuel B. Shearer was chosen for the position, and has satisfactorily discharged its duties ever since.

CHAPTER XII.

Religious—Presbyterian Church—Episcopal Church—Methodist Church—Roman Catholic Church—German Reformed Church—Lutheran Church—Church of God—German Baptists—United Brethren—The Mennonites—Evangelical Association.

THE religious sentiment was strongly developed in the primitive inhabitants of the Cumberland Valley. Its settlers made early and adequate provision for the preaching of the word of God. Family instruction in the inspired record was supplemented by the public proclamation of the gospel at such times and places as the sparsely settled condition of the country warranted. The simplicity of that primitive worship secured a religious fervor not seen in these days of costly edifices and fashionable services. The sacrifices made by both minister and people guaranteed a worship largely free from hypocrisy.

The log meeting-house, with its humble appointments, was, perhaps, more thoroughly consecrated to the worship of Him, who "prefers before all temples the upright heart and pure" than the stately structures of modern times are. Says Dr. Wing: "The period of religious indifference and unbelief had not yet arrived. In the countries from which the people had come, there were doubtless formalism and 'moderation,' but every family would have felt dishonored had they been found without the forms of public worship. And now, when these wanderers into the wilderness were far away from any place of worship, a sense of special desolation was felt by every one. A large part of their social as well as religious life was gone. With but few books or periodicals, the most probable occasion of hearing from the great world and the people they had left was through the letters and arrivals of others. It was in the Sabbath assembly that the sweetest and best enjoyments of the week might be hoped for. The deepest and most urgent longings of their hearts were toward the weekly assembly and what they called the 'house of God.' No sooner, therefore, were they sheltered from the weather, than they began to inquire for a place of worship.

"It would be interesting to have some account of the place where these godly men first met and sought the God of their fathers. We are not sure that we can make any near approach to the satisfaction [gratifying] of this desire. We have traced the settlements over a district of not less than twenty miles from east to west, and eight to ten from north to south. This could be traveled only on foot or on horses; for carriages were, for some time, out of the question. The first meetings must have been at private houses, in barns, or in the open air, and were perhaps confined to no one place."

PRESBYTERIAN CHURCH.

The early settlers of the Cumberland Valley having been Scotch-Irish, were identified with the Presbyterian Church. This condition of things existed for nearly thirty years, the first exception to this unity of church fellowship being the preparatory steps to establish an Episcopal congregation by Rev. William Thompson, an English missionary, as early as July, 1753.

All this region was, at first, under the spiritual watch care of the Presbytery of Donegal, which was organized about 1732, and whose limits extended as far west as did the boundaries of Lancaster County at that time. The nearest places for regular preaching at that early date were in Dauphin County, where several congregations enjoyed the pastoral care of Rev. William Bertram. On the 16th of October, 1734, it was "ordered that Alexander Craighead supply over the river two or three Sabbaths in November." Mental and moral light have always followed the direction of physical illumination. Though not regularly ordained to preach at that date, his ministrations were the only ones the "settlements over the river" (the region west of the "Long, Crooked River") enjoyed for a time. In April, 1735, however, Rev. John Thompson was appointed to aid Mr. Craighead in the instruction of "the people of Conodoguinet or beyond the Susquehanna," as the settlement near Carlisle was known. The site of this preaching is supposed to have been about two miles northwest of Carlisle, and since known as "Meeting House Springs." Though it is claimed by some that "Silvers' Spring" was the site of this first preaching, it is quite certain that the *Meeting House Springs* was the first congregation established west of the Susquehanna.

These two congregations, viz.: *Meeting House Springs* and *Silvers' Spring*, were subsequently known as "Upper and Lower Pennsborough," and must have had an existence as early as 1734. The following year, 1735, the people of Hopewell Township, just formed, applied for permission to erect a house of worship at a place called Big Spring (now Newville), but their request was not granted for a time on account of its being but eight miles from Pennsborough. Within a year or two, however, this place of worship was erected, and shortly after, if not simultaneous with it, another place of divine service was established about five miles north of the present site of Shippensburg, and known as the *Middle Spring Congregation.* Thus it will be seen that within eight or ten years after the first crossing of the Susquehanna (viz.: 1734 to 1744), some four regular congregations were established and supported within what is now Cumberland County, as follows: *Meeting House Springs, Silvers' Spring, Big Spring* and *Middle Spring.* These congregations sought from the presbytery to which they belonged, only ministers of the gospel, pledging and furnishing houses of worship and adequate support.

The first settled pastor was Rev. Thomas Craighead, father of Alexander, already mentioned. He was properly installed at Big Spring November 17, 1737, and preached also for Middle Spring. The second regular pastor was Rev. Samuel Thompson, who began his charge of Meeting House Springs and Silvers' Spring (Upper and Lower Pennsborough) November 14, 1739.

We shall present briefly the leading facts connected with these several congregations, commencing with

Silvers' Spring.—This was so called in honor of Mr. Silvers, one of the first settlers of that region. The first occasional preaching was by Rev. Alexander Craighead and then by Revs. Bertram, Thomas Craighead and Goldston. The regular preachers and pastors were: Rev. Samuel Thompson from 1739 to 1745. His resignation was on account of "bodily illness." He was recommended as "generous and industrious in preaching to the congregation, either on Sabbath-days or week-days, according to his convenience and their necessity." Rev. Samuel Caven, from 1745 to the time of his death, November 9, 1750, in the forty-ninth year of his age. Rev. John Steel, from 1764 to his death in 1779. He was employed at £150 per year, Silvers' Spring agreeing to pay half that sum. At first six men, and afterward forty-two men, signed a promissory note guaranteeing his pay. Rev. Samuel Waugh,

1782 to 1808; Rev. John Hayes, 1808 to 1814; Rev. Henry R. Wilson, 1814 to 1823; Rev. James Williamson, 1824 to 1838; Rev. George Morris, 1839 to 1860; Rev. W. H. Dinsmore, 1861 to 1865; Rev. W. G. Hillman, 1866-67; Rev. W. B. McKee, 1868 to 1870; Rev. R. P. Gibson, 1872 to 1875; Rev. T. J. Ferguson, 1878—.

The church edifice at Silvers' Spring, a substantial stone building, 45x58 feet, was erected in 1783 under the pastorate of Rev. Waugh. The original house, predecessor of the present one, was a small log building. The congregation was regularly incorporated by an act of the Assembly September 25, 1786, the trustees named being Andrew Galbreath, Samuel Wallace, Daniel Boyd, John Wather, Hugh Laird, Samuel Waugh, William Mateer, Francis Silvers and David Hoge.

Big Spring.—This congregation was originally known as "Hopewell." Its origin has already been given. The pastors in succession were: Rev. Thomas Craighead. 1737. He died in the act of pronouncing the benediction after a very eloquent discourse. As he enunciated the word "farewell" he sank to the floor and expired without a groan or a struggle. He was succeeded for a time by Rev. James Lyon, of Ireland. Rev. George Duffield, installed in 1759. He also gave a portion of his time to Carlisle. Rev. William Linn, successor, began probably about 1778, and continued till 1784, when he resigned to accept the principalship of Washington Academy, Somerset County, Md. After a vacancy of two years Rev. Samuel Wilson became pastor, which position, till his death, March, 1799, he filled acceptably. His call, dated "Big Spring, Cumberland County, 21st of March, 1786," and signed by 204 pew-holders, is an interesting document: "We, the subscribers of this paper, and members of the congregation of Big Spring, do hereby bind and oblige ourselves annually to pay Mr. Samuel Wilson, preacher of the gospel, on his being ordained to be our minister, and for his discharge of the duties of said office, the sum of £150, Pennsylvania currency, in specie, and allow him the use of the dwelling-house, barn and all the clear land on the glebe possessed by our former minister; also plenty of timber for rails and fire-wood; likewise a sufficient security for the payment of the above mentioned sums during his incumbency." April 14, 1802, Rev. Joshua Williams was installed on an annual salary of £200. He was a graduate of Dickinson College of the class of 1795, and began to preach in 1798, having pursued theological studies under Dr. Robert Cooper. With declining health he continued his labors at Big Spring till 1829, when he resigned. Rev. Robert McCachren, a native of Chester County, began his labors as pastor about 1830, and continued in such capacity till October, 1851, when he resigned. During his pastorate, 485 communicants were added to the congregation. Rev. J. S. Henderson, 1852 to 1862. Rev. P. Mowry, 1863 to 1868. Rev. E. Erskine, D. D., 1869, the present incumbent.

The first house of worship was built of logs about 1738, and stood in the southern part of the grave-yard. The present stone edifice was built about 1790, and remodeled in 1842.

Middle Spring.—John the Harbinger, as we learn from the inspired record "preached at Enon, near to Saline, because there was much water there." In the early history of the Cumberland Valley churches were located near living springs, for the accomodation of the vast concourse of people who assembled on occasions of divine worship. Middle Spring, so called probably from its intermediate position between Big Spring and Rocky Spring, has rather an uncertain origin. The congregation began probably about 1740. Some of the early church records mention the names of Allen Killough, John

McKee, David Herron and John Reynolds as elders in 1742; John Finley, William Anderson and Robert McComb, 1744; and John Maclay, 1747.

The names of its preachers can not be given with certainty. The following are some of them: Rev. Mr. Calls, of Ireland, and Rev. Mr. Clarke of Scotland, both labored with the congregation for a time. The first regular pastor, however, was Rev. John Blair, whose time and labors were divided equally between Rocky Spring, Middle Spring and Big Spring congregations from 1742 to 1749. He was a pious and learned man, and greatly endeared to his congregation. As proof of this witness the fact that he was presented with a deed for a farm of 250 acres lying near the church. When he resigned his position the farm was sold and he went to New York City.

From 1750 to 1760 little is known of the internal history of the congregation. In May, 1765, a call was extended to Rev. Robert Cooper, who accepted the same in the following October, £100 currency being pledged to him.

Dr. Cooper was a graduate of Princeton College. His first pastorate was that of Middle Spring, which he held from 1765 to the time of his resignation April 12, 1797.

Rev. John Moodey, a graduate of Princeton College, succeeded to the pastorate of Middle Spring, having been installed October 5, 1803. He continued his labors until 1854, a period of over half a century. In June, 1855, Rev. I. N. Hays began his pastoral services, and continued them fourteen years, when he removed to Chambersburg. He was succeeded in May, 1871, by Rev. D. K. Richardson, who officiated for about eighteen months, when he was followed, June 11, 1872, by Rev. S. S. Wylie.

The first house of worship was a log building thirty-five feet square, erected about the time of the organization of the congregation. This house proving insufficient for the increasing congregation, a second one, 48x58, was built in 1765. This was succeeded in 1781 by a stone structure, 58x68, two stories high. In 1847 a new brick structure was erected, which afterward was greatly remodeled and improved.

The following officers and soldiers of the Revolutionary war were members of this congregation, or attendants of this church: Colonels—Benjamin Blythe, Isaac Miller, Robert Peebles, William Scott, Abraham Smith; major—James Herron; captains—William Rippey, Matthew Henderson, Matthew Scott, David McKnight, John McKee, William Strain, Joseph Brady, Robert Quigley, Charles Leeper, Charles Maclay, Samuel Blythe, Samuel Walker, James Scott, Samuel McCune, Samuel Kearsley; lieutenant—Samuel Montgomery; soldiers—John Heap, Esq., Samuel Cox, Esq., Francis Campble, John Reynolds, Esq., Thomas McClelland, Joseph McKinney, James McKee, Robert Donavin, William Turner, Thomas McCombs, William Sterritt, John Woods, Esq., Wm. Anderson, John Maclay, James Dunlop, Esq., James Lowry, Esq., William Barr, Archibald Cambridge, John Herron, David Herron, David Duncan, John McKnight, James McCune, David Mahan, John Thompson, Jacob Porter, Isaac Jenkins, Samuel Dixon, John Grier.

Meeting-House Spring.—What has been said in a previous part of this chapter concerning this congregation need not be repeated. Dr. Nevin, in his "Churches of the Valley," says: "About the year 1736 the Presbyterians erected a log church on Conodoguinet Creek, about two miles north of Carlisle, or West Pennsborough, as it was then called, at a place known ever since as the 'Meeting-House Spring.' No vestige of this building now remains, nor are there any of the oldest surviving residents of the neighborhood who are able to give anything like a satisfactory account of it. The members of the large congregation which worhiped within its walls have long ago disappeared, and with them the memory of the venerable edifice, and the interesting incidents, which were doubtless associated with its history, have well-nigh perished."

Carlisle.—The borough of Carlisle was founded in 1751. Shortly after this event a Presbyterian congregation was organized in it, and a house of worship erected. Relative to this edifice the following letter from John Armstrong to Richard Peters will be of historic interest:

CARLISLE, 30 June, 1757.

To-morrow we begin to haul stones for the building of a meeting-house on the north side of the Square; there was no other convenient place. I have avoided the place you once pitched for a church. The stones are raised out of Col. Stanwix's entrenchment. We will want help in this political, as well as religious, work.

As a means of raising funds with which "to enable them to build a decent house for the worship of God," the managers of the enterprise, about the year 1760, obtained from Gov. Hamilton a license to inaugurate a lottery scheme, which subserved its purpose, however objectionable.

In 1759 Rev. George Duffield was called to take pastoral charge of the congregations at Carlisle and Big Spring, giving two-thirds of his time to the former. At the same time there seems to have been, probably as the result of a general division in the church throughout the synod, a rival Presbyterian Church in Carlisle. Says Rev. I. D. Rupp, in his History of Cumberland County: "A short time afterward (1761) the congregation in the country, then under the care of the Rev. Mr. Steel, constructed a two-story house of worship in town; and, some time before the Revolution, erected the present First Presbyterian Church, on the northwest corner of the Centre Square. Mr. Duffield's congregation erected a gallery in Mr. Steel's church, and the two parties worshiped separately." These two congregations, known as the "Old Lights" and "New Lights," were finally united, and in 1785 called Rev. Robert Davidson to be pastor. This relation continued till the time of his death, in 1812. He was assisted a portion of the time by Rev. Henry R. Wilson, professor in Dickinson College.

In 1816 Rev. George Duffield, a grandson of the first pastor, was called to Carlisle. His labors for many years were signally blessed. In 1832, however, his work on "Regeneration" created much dissension, and resulted in a trial by the presbytery of his orthodoxy. The decision was briefly: "*Resolved*, That presbytery at present do not censure him any further than warn him to guard against such speculations as may impugn the doctrines of our church, and that he study to maintain 'the unity of the spirit in the bond of peace.'" Dr. Duffield's relation with the church was severed, at his own request, in March, 1835.

Contemporaneous with Dr. Duffield's difficulties with the presbytery were serious troubles in the congregation. A petition, signed by Andrew Blair and seventy-seven others, sought a separation from the old organization and the formation of a new one. The request was granted, and the *Second Presbyterian Church* of Carlisle was organized in the town hall January 12, 1833, with the following officers taken from the old church: *Elders*—Andrew Blair, John McClure and Robert Clark; *deacons*—Peter B. Smith, Robert Irvine, John Proctor and Robert Giffin. Its *pastors* in succession have been Rev. Daniel McKinley, 1833–38; Dr. Alexander T. McGill, 1839–40; Dr. T. V. Moore, 1842–45; Rev. James Lillie, 1846–48; Rev. Mervin E. Johnston, 1849–54; Rev. W. W. Eels, 1854–62; Rev. John C. Bliss, 1862–67; and Rev. George Norcross, since 1869.

The pastors of the First Church after Dr. Duffield have been Rev. William T. Sprole, Rev. Ellis J. Newlin, Rev. Conway Phelps Wing and Rev. J. S. Vance, the present incumbent.

212   HISTORY OF CUMBERLAND COUNTY.

In Dickinson Township.—In 1810 application was made to presbytery by James Moore and Joseph Galbraith for preaching in Dickinson Township for a congregation known as *Walnut Bottom.* It was granted, and Rev. Henry R. Wilson, of Dickinson College, aided them. In 1823 a congregation was regularly organized by Rev. Messrs. Williams, Duffield and McClelland, with about twenty members. The early pastors in succession were Revs. McKnight Williamson, Charles P. Cummins and Oliver O. McLean. The building, brick structure, 45x56 feet, was erected in 1829 on ground given by William L. Weakley, Esq.

In Newville.—*First United Presbyterian Church of Newville* (formerly associate) was organized as early as 1760. Its pastors: John Rogers, 1772–81; John Jamieson, 1784–92; John Craig, 1793–94; James McConnel, 1798–1809; Alexander Sharp, D.D., 1824–57; Isaiah Faries, 1858–59; W. L. Wallace, 1861.

In Carlisle.—About 1796, a lot of ground in Carlisle was transferred by Thomas and John Penn, in consideration of £6, "to Wm Blair, Wm. Moore, John Smith and John McCoy, as trustees of the *Associate Presbyterian Congregation,* adhering to the subordination of the Associate Presbytery of Pennsylvania, of which the Rev. John Marshall and James Clarkson are members." Two years later an organization was established, and in 1802 a building was erected upon the lot. Rev. Francis Pringle was called to be the pastor. Gradually its members, never numerous, were absorbed by other churches, and the house became the property of the Bethel Church.

In Mechanicsburg.—The rapid growth of Mechanicsburg in consequence of the construction of the Cumberland Valley Railroad, rendered the erection of a house of worship at that place a necessity. This was consummated in 1858, and in October, 1860, a congregation was organized, deriving much of its strength from the Silvers' Spring congregation. Under the efficient administration of Rev. Samuel W. Reigart, who has been its pastor since 1868, this congregation has developed great power in the community and in the denomination to which it belongs.

EPISCOPAL CHURCH.

Mention was made in the first part of this sketch of the efforts of Rev. William Thompson, acting under the direction of an English missionary society, to preach the gospel and establish a congregation as early as 1753.

In Carlisle.—The church of Carlisle worshiped in a stone building till about 1825, when a new structure was raised on the site of the present one. This structure underwent several remodelings until the present neat and commodious one has been reached. Its vestry has always embraced men of prominence and worth in the community, embracing such individuals as Robert Callender, Francis West, George Croghan, Samuel Postlethwaite, David Watts, Stephen Foulke, Frederick Watts, John Baker, etc.

The rectors in regular succession have been the following named scholarly gentlemen: Rev. Dr. John Campbell, 1793–1819; Rev. J. V. E. Thorn, 1819–21; Rev. George Woodruff, 1821–22; Rev. Joshua Spencer, professor in Dickinson College, 1823–29; Rev. George E. Hare, D. D., 1830–34; Rev. John Goodman, 1835–38; Rev. Patrick H. Greenleaf, 1838–40; Rev. Wm. H. Norris, 1840–50; Rev. Jacob B. Morss, 1851–60; Rev. Francis J. Clerc, 1860–66. Since 1866 Rev. Wm. Leverett has held the position.

METHODIST CHURCH.

In Shippensburg.—The Hon. John McCurdy, in his historical sketch of Shippensburg, says: "In the year 1787 Methodism was introduced into this

HISTORY OF CUMBERLAND COUNTY. 215

part of the Cumberland Valley by Rev. John Hagerty and Nelson Reed. Up to that time there was no organization of that denomination of people here, and the congregation then formed was, it is said, the only one in the valley. The first church was built about the year 1790, on the northwestern end of the lot upon which the old brick church now stands. It was built of logs one-story in height, and was probably large enough to seat 200 persons. During its early years the congregation was small, but at the commencement of the present century it began to increase, and many of its members were amongst the most prominent men of the place. Among them were Rev. John Davis, John Scott, Esq., William Sturgis, William Brookins, Esq., William Devor, Esq , John Duncan, Robert Porter, Esq., William McKnight, Benjamin Hunt, Thomas and Caleb Atherton, with many others of equal standing and respectbility." "Their first camp-meeting was held in either 1810 or 1811, on the farm about a mile northwest of Shippensburg;" the second, in 1813; a Sunday-school was organized in 1815, but, proving lifeless, was suspended till 1834, when it took on vigorous life. In 1825 a new brick church was erected, and, after being used for half a century, was sold to the Colored Methodists, and a new one built, in 1875, on King Street.

In Carlisle.—The Methodist Church in Carlisle became a separate charge about 1823. A house of worship, the "old stone church," had been built, as early as 1802, on the corner of Pitt Street and Church Alley. In 1815, a second, a commodious brick structure, was erected on Church Alley. In course of time, a still larger and better one was erected on the corner of Pitt and High Streets, the site of the present house.

After Dickinson College passed from the hands of the Presbyterians into the hands of the Methodists, an unusual impetus was given to the church in and around Carlisle. Dr. John Price Durbin, president of Dickinson College from 1833 to 1845, was a popular pulpit orator, and drew large audiences at his monthly supplies of the Carlisle pulpit. He was ably supported by such ministers as the Revs. Henry Kepler, 1835; Geo. D. Cookman, 1836-37; T. C. Thornton, 1838-39; Henry Slicer, 1840-41; Henry Tarring, 1842-43; John Davis, 1844, and others.

In Newville.—The first Methodist Church in Newville was constructed of brick in 1826, and the present one in 1846. The first was erected largely through the agency of Nathan Reed and Robert McLaughlin.

In Mechanicsburg.—Though preaching was conducted at Mechanicsburg as early as 1819 by Revs. James Riley and John Tanneyhill, the church was not organized till 1827, when Rev. Oliver Ege, the only member in that locality, formed a temporary class. Two years later, however, a permanent class was formed at the house of George Webbert, still an honored citizen of the town. This class, Henry Shrom, leader, had, at first, but eighteen or twenty members, but the number increased to 200. The pastors in charge at the time of its organization were Revs. Thomas Megee and Thos. H. W. Monroe.

Preaching in the primitive times was conducted in private houses, then in the old Union Church on Main Street, next in the first edifice erected in 1830 and 1831 on the southeast corner of Arch and Locust Streets. The building is still standing and used for dwelling purposes. In 1853 a lot was procured and a new house erected on the corner of Main and Market Streets; this house was greatly improved by repairs in 1858 and 1885. Near the church is a commodious parsonage, the gift of Daniel Coffman, an honored member. The present membership of the church is 175; of the Sunday-school, under the supervision of Oliver Mordorf, 100.

The following pastors have served the congregation, viz.: Revs. James

Reiley, John Bowen, Thomas Megee, John Donohue, Elisha Butler, William O. Lumsden, Thomas Myers, Andrew I. Megee, Samuel Kepler, John Rhoads, James Watts, J. R. Wheeler, James Sanks, William McMullin, T. H. W. Monroe, William Guin, Cambridge Graham. S. B. Dunlap, Thomas McCartney, J. Wesley Black, Job A. Price, J. C. Clark, John Stine, Thomas Dougherty, J. H. McGarrah, J. M. Lantz, William Rink. P. F. Eyer, A. S. Bowman, John A. Woodcock, B. H. Mosser and B. F. Stevens, who is the present incumbent.

Other congregations exist in the county, viz.: *Mount Holly, New Cumberland, West Fairview, Rehoboth*, etc., which are of more recent origin, and whose history properly belongs to the townships in which they are located. These congregations are the aggressive ones of the county.

ROMAN CATHOLIC CHURCH.

St. Patrick's Church, Carlisle, was for a time a supply station of the Jesuits of Conowago, to whom it belonged. In 1807 the present brick structure was built, and somewhat enlarged in 1823. Its title became diocesan under the administration of Rt. Rev. Bishop Connell, and Rev. Diven became its first priest. In 1858 the house was destroyed by fire, but was rebuilt in a short time through the agency of Rev. Maher, of Harrisburg. Subsequent to his departure it was a dependency, for a time, on Chambersburg and Harrisburg; but in 1877 its separate existence was restored, and Rev. Louis J. McKenna became its pastor. At present it is under the care of Rev. Father McKenny.

GERMAN REFORMED CHURCH.

The Reformed Church, as it is now called in this country, had an early hold upon the people of Cumberland Valley, its accessions coming mainly from the large influx of German immigrants. For a time, meeting-houses were used conjointly with the Lutherans, who shared with them in religious watch-care over the rapidly increasing German settlements. Without attempting to arrange these congregations chronologically, we refer briefly to a few of the leading ones.

Some time prior to 1797 a congregation was formed in the lower part of the county, near Shiremanstown, known then as "Frieden's Kirche," "Salem, or Peace Church," but latterly as "The Old Stone Church," through the labors of Rev. Anthony Hautz. The first structure was wooden, and was used conjointly for church and school purposes.

The subscription paper for this house, now used for school purposes exclusively, was dated April 4, 1797, and contained the following names and amounts, "Fredrich Lang, £2 5s.; Jonas Rupp, £2 5s.; Johannes Schopp, £3; Johannes Schnevely, 15s.; George Wuermle, 15s.; George Wild, 7s. 6d.; Conrad Weber, 7s. 6d.; Martin Thomas. 3s.; Johannes Schwartz, 11s. 4d.; Philip Heck, 7s. 6d.; Adam Viehman, 7s. 6d.; Jacob Colp, £1 10s.; John Merkle, £3; Casper Swartz, 7s. 6d.; Christian Swartz, 7s. 6d.; Abraham Wolf, 7s. 6d.; Frederich Schweitzer, 7s. 6d.; Martin Hausser, £5; Johannes Eberly, £4 17s. 6d.; Elizabeth Lang (Wittfrau), 15s."

On the 26th of May, 1797, the congregation obtained deeds for the land connected with the schoolhouse from Henry Schnevely and Nicholas Kreutzer. In 1798 the stone church was erected, under the superintendence of the following building committee: Fred Lang, Jonas Rupp, Leonard Swartz and Rev. Anthony Hautz, the architects being Martin Rupp and Thomas Anderson.

May 18, 1806, a half interest in this church and school property was sold to a neighboring Lutheran congregation, known as Poplar Church, for £405 17s.

3d. The early pastors of this congregation were Revs. Anthony Hautz, J. G. Bucher, Thomas Apple, A. R. Kreamer, —— Fritchey and John Ault. On the 23d of June, 1866, this congregation held its last communion, most of its members uniting soon afterward with St. Paul's Reformed Church, of Mechanicsburg.

In Shippensburg.—A Reformed congregation was organized at Shippensburg about 1780. Somewhat later in the last century a lot for burial purposes was secured by the Reformed and Lutheran congregations on the southeast corner of Queen and Orange Streets. On this lot a log church edifice was erected, which was used till 1812. About the same time a brick edifice was built on the site of the present Reformed Church, and was used by the two congregations for a number of years. In 1823 Rev. John Habblestine becoming one of its pastors, preached doctrines not accordant with those of his people. The church doors were closed against him, when he withdrew, with certain followers, and organized the Church of God. Subsequently these two churches separated, each building an edifice of its own.

In Carlisle.—The Reformed Church in Carlisle was built in 1807. As a means of giving vitality to the cause in this portion of the State, a movement was inaugurated in 1817 to establish a theological seminary, a plan for the execution of which was not, however, developed till 1820. Some $30,000 were subscribed, conditionally, but never realized. Through the influence of the Carlisle Church and Dickinson College the institution was located in Carlisle, and maintained a doubtful existence for four years, the subscriptions not proving sound. In 1829 the seminary was removed to York, and in 1835 to Mercersburg.

LUTHERAN CHURCH.

Referring to the remarks made concerning the Reformed Church, it may be stated that the growth of this denomination has occurred largely during the present century.

In East Pennsborough.—David F. Eyster, in his account of East Pennsborough Township, for Wing's History, says: "The first church built in this end of the county is one mile north of Camp Hill and is called 'Hickory Wood Church.' It was built probably as early as 1765, by the Lutherans, of logs, and in two departments, the lower story being used for school purposes and the residence of the teacher, while the second story was kept exclusively for divine services. The old church has been removed and another one built, known as the 'Poplar Church.'"

The pastors of this congregation were Revs. Frederick Sanne, Benjamin Keller, Augustus Lochman, Edmund Keller, Augustus Babb, N. J. Stroh, A. Hight, C. F. Stover, J. R. Groff and H. N. Fegley. A new brick building, costing with bell included $9,104.91, was dedicated July 2, 1866.

In Newville.—The first Lutheran Church in Newville was built of brick in 1832; the second of brick in 1862. Names of pastors: Revs. D. P. Rosenmuller, 1832–40; John Heck, 1841–45; E. Breidenbaugh, four years; Sidney L. Harkey, two years; Joshua Evans, 1852–60; H. Baker, 1861–67; Harry McKnight, 1867–71; H. Fleck, 1871–72; J. A. Clutz, 1872–73; H. J. Watkins, 1874—.

In Shippensburg.—The church in Shippensburg is contemporaneous with that of the Reformed, dating back to the close of the last century. (See above.)

In Centerville.—The church in Centerville was built, in 1852, under the pastorate of Rev. Charles Klink. Its pastors: D. P. Rosenmuller, John Rosenberg, Christian Kunkle, Charles Klink, S. S. Link, J. Wefley, A. Babb, S. L. Guss, S. W. Owen, G. M. Garhart, G. D. Keedy, J. Deitrich, D. Swope.

In Carlisle.—The church in Carlisle was early blessed with the labors of strong men, among whom may be mentioned Jacob Goehring, George Butler, F. D. Schaeffer, A. H. Meyer, John Herbst. Commencing with 1816, the regular pastors were: Revs. Benjamin Keller, 1816–28; C. F. Heyer, C. F. Schaeffer, John Ulrich, J. N. Hoffman, Jacob Fry, S. P. Sprecher, Joel Swartz, D. D., C. S. Albert, ——Freas, and H. B. Wile, the present incumbent. On the 11th of March, 1851, the house of worship was consumed by fire. Though it was not insured, a large structure was immediately erected. This has been enlarged several times since, to meet the demands of the increasing congregation.

A number of other congregations exist in the county whose histories are referred to in their respective towns and townships.

CHURCH OF GOD.

This organization began about 1830, under the leadership of Rev. John Winebrenner, of Harrisburg. The first effort to establish a congregation in Cumberland County was made at Shippensburg, Rev. John Habblestine taking advantage of some dissension in the Reformed and Lutheran Churches to form a new organization, to be known as the "Union Christian Church." A constitution was adopted October 24, 1828, with John Heck, Jacob Dewalt and John Blymire as elders; David Wagner, Michael Ziegler, Henry Keefer and John Taughinbaugh as deacons, and Jacob Knisley and John Carey as trustees. They were subsequently under charge of Revs. Rebo, Dietrich Graves and James Mackey. About 1834 or 1835 the name was changed to the "Church of God."

The first house of worship was built in 1828; the next, a two-story brick, was erected in 1870, at a cost of $17,000. Congregations were organized in all parts of the county, and suitable houses of worship, called "Bethels," supplied as follows: *Milltown*, 1833, by Elder Winebrenner; *Walnut Grove Schoolhouse*, 1835, by Elder J. Keller; *Shiremanstown*, 1838, by Rev. Keller; *Newburg*, 1834, by Elder James Mackey; *Newville*, 1837, by Elder David Kyle; *Green Spring*, 1852, by Elder Kyle; *Plainfield*, 1854, by Elder Peter Klippinger; *Carlisle*, 1864, a congregation of eighteen members.

GERMAN BAPTISTS.

This denomination, which occupies such a conspicuous position in country places, had, for a time, no other place of worship than private houses, barns and schoolhouses. Its congregations were served by an unpaid ministry. We subjoin a sketch from notes prepared in 1878 by Elder Moses Miller: Adam and Martin Brandt's, in Monroe Township; Daniel Basehoar's, in East Pennsborough Township, and John Cochlin's, in Allen Township, were the first meeting places, and the first communion meeting was held at Adam Brandt's nearly eighty years ago. Adam Brandt was the first minister chosen, though he did not serve, and about 1820 John Zeigler and Michael Mishler were chosen, the former of whom removed to Ohio some years afterward. In 1823 Daniel Bollinger, from Juniata County, became the first ordained elder in Cumberland County, and gave the church a regular organization. He served some twenty-five years, and died in 1855 at Lebanon, Ohio, whither he had removed in 1848. Adam Steinberger was chosen about 1829, and Rudolph Mohler in 1832. Rev. Christopher Johnson came to Dickinson Township from Maryland in 1828. Daniel Hollinger and Samuel Etter were chosen about 1835, and David Horst in 1841.

About 1836 the church divided into two sections, known as "Upper Cumberland" and "Lower Cumberland," respectively, Baltimore Turnpike and the Long's Gap road being the dividing line. The ministers of the "Lower" Church have been Moses Miller, chosen in 1849, Adam Beelman, in 1851; David Niesley and A. L. Bowman, in 1863; Jacob Harnish, in 1865; Cyrus Brindle, in 1868; B. H. Nickey, in 1871. Rev. J. B. Garver came from Huntingdon County in 1874 to within the limits of this congregation.

The first minister and the first ordained elder of the "Upper" Church was Christopher Johnson, and David Ecker, from Adams County, was (1836) the second elder. John Eby was chosen in 1841; Joseph Sollenberger, in 1843; Allen Mohler, in 1846; Daniel Hollinger removed to the "Upper" Church from the "Lower" one in 1848; Daniel Keller, chosen in 1851; George Hollinger, about 1858; Daniel Demuth, in 1860; Daniel Hollinger, in 1868; Caspar Hosfelt, in 1873.

Until 1855 the Lower Congregation had no house of worship of its own, but had an allotment in union houses built in Mechanicsburg in 1825, at Shepherdstown and at Cochlin's, in some of which meetings are still held. In 1855 Baker's Meeting-House was built on the Lisburn road, in Monroe Township; Miller's a mile from Sterrett's Gap, in 1858, and Mohler's, in 1861, six miles southwest from Harrisburg, on the State road. In 1863 a good brick building was erected near Huntsville, and a few years later a union church was built in Frankford Township, one-third of which the German Baptists own, and in 1875 a house of worship was put up by them exclusively at Boiling Springs. Four miles north of Shippensburg is the Fogelsanger Meeting-House.

UNITED BRETHREN.

This aggressive denomination owes its organized form largely to the efforts of William Otterbein, "a pious and zealous preacher from Germany," and began about the opening of the present century. Its numbers have increased rapidly, and congregations may be found in all portions of the county. The following have been some of the members who have served as its preachers: Revs. H. A. Schlichter, W. O. Quigley, A. H. Rice, W. H. Wagner, J. C. Wiedler, J. German, J. P. Anthony, J. R. Atchinson, B. G. Huber, D. R. Burkholder.

In Mechanicsburg—The church in Mechanicsburg began, in 1846, in the labors of Rev. Jacob S. Kessler, who served three years. His successors in work were the following reverend gentlemen: Alexander Owen, J. C. Smith, Samuel Enterline, W. B. Wagner, William Owen, John Dickson, Daniel Eberly, W. B. Raber, J. Philip Bishop, S. A. Mowers, C. T. Stearnthen, H. A. Schlichter, J. T. Shaffer, J. B. Funk and J. R. Hutchinson, the present incumbent.

From 1846 to 1857 the congregation occupied the old Union Church. In the latter year a house was built by the congregation, and it answered all necessary purposes till 1874, when the present brick structure was erected at a cost of $6,000. The membership of the congregation is 220, and the pastor's salary $550.

In Shippensburg.—The congregation in Shippensburg began in 1866. In June, 1869, a good house of worship was dedicated. The congregation has been growing rapidly in numbers and influence.

THE MENNONITES.

This religious body began to appear in Cumberland County at the opening of the present century (*Cir.* 1803). The first effort to establish a congregation was made at Slate Hill, a mile south of Shiremanstown, under the labors of

George Rupp, Sr., and Henry Martin. In 1818 was erected a large brick building, which was reconstructed and improved in 1876. The congregation increased quite rapidly, enjoying the labors of Jacob Mumma and Henry Rupp.

About the same time preaching began about two miles east of Carlisle, resulting in the forming of a congregation which, in 1832, erected a building since known as the "Stone Church." Some of the preachers were John Erb and Christian Herr, and latterly Henry Weaver and Jacob Herr. Under the direction of such ministers as Messrs Rupp, Mumma, Martin, Abram Burgert, Martin Whistler, and others whose names are not recalled, preaching has been supplied, in German or English, at a number of places in the county: Martin's Schoolhouse (1828), Union Church near Michael Cochlin's (1848), Union House, at Jacob Herr's, near Boiling Springs, Diller's Mill, Union Church in Mechanicsburg.

The *Reformed Mennonites*, who claim to hold, in greater reverence, the doctrines and usages of the primitive church than those from whom they separated, have a number of congregations: One at Winding Hill, two miles and a half from Mechanicsburg; One near Middlesex, and one at Plainfield. Some of the early settlers, about 1825 or 1830, were Samuel Bear, Dietrich Steiner, Peter Miller, Christian Genrich, Samuel Newcomer and others. Most of their preachings have been conducted by men living without the limits of the Cumberland, George Keiser being a resident minister.

EVANGELICAL ASSOCIATION.

This society owes its commencement to Jacob Albright, who began to form societies about 1800. The first church organized in Cumberland County was in 1833, in the house of David Kutz, a mile or two east of Carlisle. Among the first members were John Kratzer, Christian Ruhl and David Kutz. Revs. J. Barber and J. Baumgartner were the first ministers. Letort Spring Church, where the first organization was made, is a building of no ordinary pretentions, and is attended by an influential congregation. There are several hundred communicants in the county, and there are church buildings at following named points: Carlisle, Cleversburg, Hickorytown, Leesburg, Letort Spring, McClure's Gap, Middlesex, Mifflin, Mount Holly, Mount Rock, New Kingston and Wagner's. The Carlisle congregation had its inception in a class of some dozen persons, which was formed in 1866, and for a time they held meetings at the house of Rev. J. Boas; in 1867 the meetings were held in Rheem's Hall. May 15, 1870, St. Paul's Evangelical Church, a substantial brick building on Louther Street, was dedicated. This congregation has been served by Revs. J. G. M. Swengel, J. H. Leas, H. B. Hartzler, J. M. Ettinger, J. M. Pines, H. A. Stoke, A. H. Irvine. The church is thriving and prosperous.

CHAPTER XIII.

POLITICAL—SLAVERY IN CUMBERLAND COUNTY, ETC.

THERE is little to say concerning the political leaning of the inhabitants of Cumberland County through the century and a quarter and more of its existence. We have followed its soldiery through several wars and learned how they fought and fell; we have seen that, with so few exceptions as hardly to be accounted, the people have been at all times arrayed on the side of home and country, and given of their means and of their life blood to attain their preservation. Where these motives are uppermost there is little need of asking what is the political belief of the citizens, for they can not go far in the wrong in any event. For many years the majority of the voters in Cumberland County have cast their ballots with the party of Jefferson and Jackson, the Democratic majority at the local election in the autumn of 1885 being over 1,000. At times, however, the popularity of candidates on the side of the Republican, or minority party, is sufficient to win for them responsible positions, as in the case of the present president judge, Wilbur F. Sadler.

SLAVERY IN CUMBERLAND COUNTY.

Many of the early residents of Cumberland County owned slaves, and on the old assessment records we find property holders taxed often with one or more "negroes," according to their position and means. One instance only is given, that of Carlisle, in 1768, when the following persons owned the number of negroes set opposite their respective names:

John Armstrong, Esq., two; Robert Gibson, one; John Kinkead, one; John Montgomery, Esq., two; Robert Miller, Esq., three; James Pollock, tavern-keeper, two; Charles Pattison, one; Rev. John Steel, two; Joseph Spear, two; Richard Tea. two—total, eighteen.

Even ministers, it is seen from the foregoing, adopted the common custom of owning slaves, as well as the people, yet the public feeling in the Colony—or State—was never in favor of that form of bondage, especially among the Quakers, the Scotch and Irish settlers looking at it more favorably and having numbers of negroes, then not exceedingly valuable in market. It is said that "slaves were generally allowed to share in all family and domestic comforts, from long residence in families they attained to much consideration and affection, and seldom were made the subjects of cruelty. In many respects their position in the families to which they belonged was preferable to that which was awarded to hirelings for only brief terms of service." The attention of the Assembly was called to the subject of slavery by the Supreme Executive Council, James McLene* at the time representing Cumberland County, that body referring to the matter February 15, 1779, in the following language: "We would also again bring into your view a plan for the gradual abolition of slavery, so disgraceful to any people and more especially to those who have been contending in the great cause of liberty themselves, and upon whom Providence has bestowed such eminent marks of its favor and protection. We

---
*Resided in Antrim Township, now Franklin County, and died March 13, 1806.

think we are loudly called on to evince our gratitude in making our fellow-men joint heirs with us of the same inestimable blessings, under such restrictions and regulations as will not injure the community and will imperceptibly enable them to relish and improve the station to which they will be advanced.' Honored will that State be in the annals of history which shall abolish this violation of the rights of mankind, and the memories of those will be held in grateful and everlasting rememberance who shall pass the law to restore and establish the rights of human nature in Pennsylvania. We feel ourselves so interested on this point as to go beyond what may be deemed by some the proper line of our duty, and acquaint you that we have reduced this plan to the form of a law, which if acceptable we shall in a few days communicate to you."

The Assembly did not act upon the matter at that meeting, but through the exertions of George Bryan, the author of the proposed law in the council, who subsequently become a representative in the Assembly, the bill was passed March 1, 1780, by a vote of 34 to 21, and slavery was abolished in Pennsylvania. The act provided for the registration of every negro or mulatto slave or servant for life, before the 1st of November, 1780, and that "no man or woman of any color or nation, except the negroes or mulattoes," so registered should thereafter, at any time, be held in the commonwealth other than as *free.* Exceptions were made in the servants of members of Congress, foreign ministers, and people passing through or not stopping longer than six months in the State. In 1790 Cumberland County had 223 slaves; in 1800, 228; in 1810, 307; in 1820, 17; in 1830, 7; in 1840, 24; and in 1850, none, those registered as such by the act of 1780, and so continuing through life, having passed away. Negroes were often advertised for sale in the early newspapers of Carlisle, showing up their desirable qualities; and such notices appeared as late as 1830.

During the exciting years last preceding the civil war of 1861-65 more than one fugitive from the terrors of slavery was assisted on his way to freedom and safety by sympathizing citizens of this county. The county was so near the border of a Slave State that it was an easy matter for kidnapers to make bold raids into it and carry off unsuspectingly colored persons over the border into slavery. One incident occurred in Dickinson Township worth mentioning: Some time in the spring of 1859 a mulatto named John Butler settled with his wife and child in a small house near Spruce Run. The child attended the Farmers' Academy and the parents worked at such employment as they could find. On the night of June 10 following they disappeared suddenly, under circumstances which pointed to a case of kidnaping. Measures were taken to secure the perpetrators of the crime and punish them. Emanuel Myers, of Maryland, a noted negro catcher, was apprehended by the sheriff soon after, while in Pennsylvania, and placed in jail at Carlisle. The people in Maryland and South became angry over the matter, claiming he was decoyed into Pennsylvania to be captured. The Northern papers united in demanding that Myers be tried and punished. His trial came off in August, the commonwealth being represented by A. Brady Sharpe, Esq., and Hon. Fredk. Watts, of Carlisle. Myers was found guilty, but promised to return Butler and his family if he himself might be set free. Sentence was suspended, he was released on his own recognizance to appear at a subsequent session of court, and soon after the colored family returned to Dickinson Township. The commonwealth practically dropped the case then. The war soon followed, and slavery was ended in the entire country.

CHAPTER XIV.

AGRICULTURAL — CUMBERLAND COUNTY AGRICULTURAL SOCIETY—GRANGERS' PICNIC-EXHIBITION, WILLIAMS' GROVE.

THE advancement of science has been seen in the improvements which characterize the cultivation of the soil, and the progress that has marked the introduction of agricultural implements. Farming, stock-raising, bee culture and fruit-growing were, formerly, largely matters of chance. Inherited knowledge sufficed for the average husbandman. He plowed and sowed and reaped as his ancestors did. Drainage, fertilization, the improvement of stock, the use of improved implements of husbandry—these subjects did not agitate his mind. Not so the intelligent modern farmer. He keeps abreast of his age, and reads the latest and best literature bearing on his chosen field of labor. A knowledge of physiology, botany, mineralogy, geology and vegetable chemistry seems to be a necessity for him. He realzes that his occupation affords a superior opportunity for making and recording observations that will be valuable, not only to him but others similarly engaged He rises above the narrow selfishness that too often characterizes his fellow-laborers, and becomes a philanthropic scientist whom the future will rise up and call blessed.

To this class belongs Hon. Frederick Watts of Carlisle, who, though engaged in the intricacies of the legal profession, always had both time and inclination to advance the true interests of the farming community. He was both a theoretical and a practical farmer, and to him more than to any other man in the Cumberland Valley may be attributed the improvements in agriculture in that region.

In June, 1839, Judge Watts was driving a carriage, containing himself and wife, from New York to Philadelphia, no railroad at that time connecting the two cities. Near Trenton, N. J., he was met on the road by Lieut. William Inman, of the United States Navy, and asked, "Watts, where are you going?" Being told, he took the Judge to his farm, on which was growing an excellent quality of wheat. It proved to be a Mediterranean variety, three bushels of which were brought by him a year or two previous from Italy, near Leghorn. He sent Judge Watts six barrels of the seed, which were sown on his farm near Carlisle. By these two men was introduced into the United States, and especially into the Cumberland Valley, this popular variety of wheat.

During the harvest of 1840 the first McCormick reaper ever used in Pennsylvania, was taken by Judge Watts into a twelve-acre field that would yield about thirty-five bushels of wheat per acre. It was a trial of the machine. There were present from 500 to 1,000 spectators to witness "Watts' folly," as it was called. The cutting of the wheat was rapid and perfect, but the general verdict was, that "one man could not rake off the grain with sufficient rapidity." A well-dressed stranger came up, and gave some suggestions which aided the raker somewhat; but even yet the team could not be driven more than ten or fifteen rods before a halt was called to ease up on the raker. Finally, the well-dressed gentleman stepped upon the machine, and raked off the wheat with perfect ease, compelling the spectators to reverse their somewhat hasty decision and say, "It can be done." The well-dressed man proved to be Cyrus H. McCormick, the inventor of the American reaper. This little episode marks the introduction of the reaper into the Cumberland Valley, and relieves "Watts' folly" from the odium which first attached to it.

Similar difficulties attended the introduction of the left-handed, steel mold-board plow. Farmers had been accustomed to use a right-handed, wooden mold-board implement, clumsy and burdensome, and were loth to make a change. Repeated trials, however, brought the better class of implements into favor, and thus introduced a higher order of agriculture into the county.

The County Agricultural Society, an account of which is given below, was the legitimate outgrowth of these public exhibitions. Judge Frederick Watts was its founder, and for many long years its president and chief patron. Whatever of good it has accomplished for the farming interests of the county may be ascribed largely to the efficiency which he imparted to its management.

CUMBERLAND COUNTY AGRICULTURAL SOCIETY.

This society was organized in 1854, through the instrumentality of Judge Watts. It has been a well managed and prosperous institution from its first existence to the present, holding its annual meetings (the only failures in this respect being one or two years during the late war), and the interest and good influences that have marked its career are plainly evidenced all over the county.

The society purchased the first lot of ground, containing six acres and six perches, August, 1855, and have at different times made additional purchases, until they now have enclosed and in a high state of improvement twenty-two acres, a fine half-mile driving track, amphitheater, boarding houses, halls, booths, pens and all other necessary buildings of a substantial and commodious kind are on the grounds. In short, everything necessary to conduct a first-class county fair has been prepared in an unstinted manner.

There are 200 life members, and the directors run the institute in a liberal and generous spirit, paying out on an average, each year, in premiums, from $2,000 to $2,500.

The following is a list of the officers of the society:

First corps of officers: President, Frederick Watts; vice-presidents, And. Frasier, Skiles Woodburn, Daniel Coble, Geo. H. Bucher, Thos. Bradley, W. M. Henderson; secretary, Richard Parker; treasurer, Geo. W. Stouffer; managers, Chas. Tetzel, Samuel Myers, Robert Laird, Geo. Brindle, John Paul, Jos. Culver, Wm. Schriver, Robert Bryan and Robert G. Young.

1855—President, Geo. H. Bucher; secretary, Robert Moore; treasurer, George W. Sheaffer.

1856—President, Thomas Paxton; secretary, Robert Moore; treasurer, Geo. W. Sheaffer.

1857—President, Thomas Galbraith; secretary, Robert Moore; treasurer, Geo. W. Sheaffer.

1858 to 1866 (inclusive)—President, F. Watts; secretary, D. S. Croft, treasurer, Geo. W. Sheaffer.

1867—President, Thomas Lee; secretary, W. F. Sadler; treasurer, Henry Saxton.

1868—Same as 1867.

1869—President, John Stuart; secretary, John Hays; treasurer, Ephraim Cornman.

1870—President, F. Watts; secretary, Lewis F. Lyne; treasurer, Henry Saxton.

1871—Same as 1870.
1872—President, Charles H. Miller; secretary, Lewis F. Lyne; treasurer, Henry Saxton.
1872 to 1886—The last-named officers have held their positions continuously, except Henry Saxton, who died in 1882, and was succeeded in 1883 by the present treasurer, Joshua P. Bixler.

GRANGER'S PICNIC-EXHIBITION, WILLIAMS' GROVE.

From the smallest beginnings in 1873, this has now became a National institution. A few individuals, farmers mostly, were led to give this beneficent institution their favorable attention by the efforts of Mr. R. H. Thomas, proprietor of the *Farmer's Friend and Grange Advocate*, of Mechanicsburg. Thirteen years ago the Patrons of Husbandry selected Williams' Grove as a place for holding social reunions, and held successful meetings at this point. Then others saw the possibilities that might be made to shape and grow out of these meetings; and with a view of bringing the farmer and manufacturer in closer relationship, the picnic of 1874 was appointed, and the manufacturers of the country were invited to bring the work of their shops and mills, and, with the farmers, side by side to display the products of the farm and factory. The beginning, of necessity, was small, because as wise as was its purposes it had to be advertised to the country. But it told its own story, its fame rapidly extended throughout all the States, and soon it reached proportions that may be called National. In 1885, without entering into dry details, there were over 300 car loads of agricultural implements and machinery displayed upon the grounds, and the people in attendance estimated at 150,000. Farmers were present from twenty-nine States of the Union, and the manufacturers had quite as extended a representation. Goods sold upon the grounds, and orders taken aggregated over $300,000, and over $1,000,000 worth of machinery was on exhibition.

R. H. Thomas, general manager, Mechanicsburg, opened the fair of 1886, on Monday August 30, with an unprecedented attendance and the widening interest evidently increasing and extending.

The grounds occupied are called the Williams' Grove picnic grounds. There are forty acres in the inclosure. These are leased by the picnic exhibition management; a co-lease is held by the D. & M. Railroad, and frequently the place under their management is used as picnic grounds. Two amphitheaters, a National Grange Hall, a two-story hotel, and quite a number of smaller buildings used by exhibitors and visitors. Williams' Grove is on an island in the Yellow Breeches Creek, on the D. & M. Railroad, thirteen miles southwest of Harrisburg. The constant addition of new improvements and spacious buildings, etc., make this the most elegant grounds in the country for these purposes, and the spot is surpassingly beautiful and inviting. One admirable and attractive feature of this inter-State exhibition is that it is a free show—no admittance charge, and back of it are no grasping board of directors or stockholders eager only to make money. It is run at a minimum of expense, and this is collected by a small fee from exhibitors, the booths and stands really paying the larger part of the expenses. Several of the large manufacturers are now about erecting permanent and spacious buildings upon the grounds, and still others are soon to follow this good example. A twenty acre field (wheat stubble) adjoining the grove has now been secured for trials of plows, harrows, rollers, drills, etc.

The inter-State picnic institution is unique in its arrangement, having no predecessor, and its success phenomenal. Away from the great cities, in the cool and grateful shades of the groves, in the quiet retreat of the rich and beautiful Cumberland Valley, here the real farmer and actual manufacturer meet and learn to know and appreciate each other, and certainly it is the beginning, already vast and extended in its proportions, of a happy fraternizing and of mutual benefits to these two most important classes of men in our Nation.

CHAPTER XV.

THE FORMATION OF TOWNSHIPS.

THE Cumberland (then known as the North) Valley was first divided into the townships of Pennsborough and Hopewell. This was in 1735, years before the formation of the county, which was then a portion of Lancaster. At this time the Indian title to the lands had not yet been extinguished, for it was in October of the following year that the Penns finally purchased their title. White settlers, by permission of the Indians, had come into the valley about the year 1730, but they were few in number, and Cumberland County was not formed until fifteen years after the formation of these two townships.

The First Proprietary Manor.—A small portion in the lower part of the North Valley, and which was afterward a portion of Pennsborough Township, was surveyed at a still earlier period (1732) into a "Proprietary Manor on Conodoguinette," the more effectually to keep off white settlers as opposed to the rights of the Indians, which had not yet been satisfactorily purchased. This manor was also called "Pastang" or "Paxton Manor," and after the formation of Cumberland County "Louther Manor," in compliment to a nobleman of that name who had married a sister of William Penn.

About sixty families of the Shawanese Indians, who had come from the south, settled there about 1698, by permission of the Susquehanna Indians, to which the first proprietory, William Penn, afterward agreed. In 1753, complaint is made "that they had not been paid for the lands, part of which had been surveyed into the Proprietory Manor on Conodoguinette."

This manor embraced all of what is now East Pennsborough, Lower Allen, and a corner of Hampden Townships. In other words, it was bounded on the east by the Susquehanna River, opposite John Harris' ferry, and included all the land lying between the Conodoguinet and Yellow Breeches Creeks, past the Stone Church or Frieden's Kirche, and immediately below Shiremanstown. It was surveyed by John Armstrong in 1765, and by John Lukens, Esq., surveyor-general under the Provincial Government, in 1767, at which time it was reported to contain 7,551 acres.

The two original townships, we have seen, were Pennsborough and Hopewell. Pennsborough, which lay on the east, at its formation included the whole of the territory which is now embraced in Cumberland County. Hopewell, which lay on the west, included most of the land which is now embraced in Franklin. Six years later (1741) the township of Hopewell was divided, and the western division was called Antrim, after the county in Ireland. This territory afterward became a portion or nearly the whole of what is now included in Franklin County.

Soon after the formation of Pennsborough Township, portions of it began to be called North and South, East and West Pennsborough, and in 1745, ten years after its formation, and five years before the formation of the county, it seems to have been definitely divided into East and West Pennsborough. In the years which have elapsed many townships have been formed, so that now one portion of this original township lies west of the center, and the other at the northeastern extremity of the county, separated by the many intervening townships which have been formed from them.

One other township, Middleton, also originally part of Pennsborough, was just before or coincident in its birth with the formation of Cumberland County, so that when the county was formed, its map, including only that portion of it which was known by the name of "North Valley," would have embraced East and West Pennsborough, Hopewell, Antrim and Middleton Townships. That is the map of this portion of Cumberland County at its formation in 1750.

The date of the formation of the succeeding townships is as follows: Allen, 1766; Newton, 1767; Southampton, 1783; Shippensburg, 1784; Dickinson, 1785; Silvers' Spring, 1787; Frankford, 1795; Mifflin, 1797; North and South Middleton, 1810; Monroe, 1825; Newville, 1828; Hampden, 1845; Upper and Lower Allen, 1849; Middlesex, 1859; Penn, 1859; Cook, 1872.

The organization of boroughs was as follows: Carlisle, 1782; Newville, 1817; Shippensburg, 1819; Mechanicsburg, 1828; New Cumberland, 1831; Newburg, 1861; Mount Holly Springs, 1873; Shiremanstown, 1874; Camp Hill, 1885.

CHAPTER XVI.

BOROUGH OF CARLISLE.

ITS INCEPTION—SURVEY—FIRST THINGS—MEETING OF CAPTIVES—REVOLUTIONARY PERIOD—WAR OF 1812—GROWTH OF THE TOWN, ETC.—THE BOROUGH IN 1846—MCCLINTOCK RIOT—WAR OF THE REBELLION—SITUATION, PUBLIC BUILDINGS, ETC.—CHURCHES—CEMETERIES—SCHOOLS, INSTITUTES AND COLLEGE — NEWSPAPERS — MANUFACTURING ESTABLISHMENTS, ETC.—GAS AND WATER COMPANY—SOCIETIES—CONCLUSION.

THE town of Carlisle was laid out in pursuance of a letter of instruction issued by the proprietary government to Nicholas Scull in 1751. With the exception of Shippensburg and York, it is the oldest town in Pennsylvania west of the Susquehanna River. It derives its name from Carlisle, in the county of Cumberland, in England. That Carlisle, near the border of Scotland, is the prototype of this. Like it, it is built with rectangular streets, from a center square, and is situated between two parallel ranges of lofty hills, which inclose the valley, watered by the Eden and the Calder, where it lies.* But, although the town of Carlisle was laid out according to the instructions of the commissioners as early as 1751, there were, of course, earlier settlers. One of these was James Le Tort, a French-Swiss, who was an Indian interpreter, and who erected and lived in a log cabin, probably as early as 1720, at the head of the stream which bears his name, and which flows through the eastern portion of the town. At some unknown period, also, be-

---
*Carlisle, in England, was originally a Roman station, and its name is often used in the early border ballads.

fore the founding of Carlisle, the Colonial Government had erected a stockade fort, occupying "two acres of ground square, with a block-house in each corner," which, two years after the town of Carlisle was laid out, had become a ruin, and given place to another of curious construction within the precincts of the town, which was known as Fort Lonther. It had loop-holes and swivel guns, and two years after (1755) a force of fifty men. It rendered important aid in defense of the earlier settlers against the Indians, whose savage cruelties and bloody massacres form such a striking feature in the early history of the Kittatinny Valley.

The first letter of instructions for a survey of the town was issued by Gov. Hamilton April 1, 1751. It was again surveyed by Col., afterward Gen. John Armstrong in 1762. When the town was first located it extended no further than the present North, South, East and West Streets, all the other part now within the borough being known as commons. The courts of justice were first held, for one year, at Shippensburg, but in the succeeding year, after the formation of the county, they were removed to Carlisle. Thus, just twenty-five years before the Declaration of Independence, before the imbecile King, George III, whose stubborn policy provoked the colonies to assert their rights, had yet ascended the throne of England, Carlisle was founded, in the reign of George II, as the county seat.

The first tax upon the citizens of Carlisle, of which we have any record, was laid in December, 1752, and amounted to £25 9s 6d.

A very pretty pen picture of the infant town of Carlisle in the summer of 1753 is as follows. It was written to Gov. Hamilton by John O'Neal, who had been sent to repair the fortifications, and is dated the 27th of May, 1753.

"The Garrison here consists only of twelve men. The stockade originally occupied two acres of ground square, with a block-house in each corner. These buildings are now in ruin. Carlisle has been recently laid out and is the established seat of justice. It is the general opinion that a number of log cabins will be erected during the ensuing summer. The nmber of dwelling houses is five. The court is at present held in a temporary log building, on the northeast corner of the centre square. If the lots were clear of brush wood it would give a different aspect to the town. The situation, however, is handsome, in the centre of a valley with a mountain bounding it on the North and South at a distance of seven miles. The wood consists principally of oaks and hickory. The limestone will be of great advantage to the future settlers, being in abundance. A lime kiln stands on the centre square, near what is called the deep quarry, from which is obtained good building stone. A large stream of water runs above two miles from the village, which may at a future period be rendered navigable. A fine spring runs to the east, called Le Tort, after the Indian interpreter who settled on its head about the year 1720. The Indian wigwams in the vicinity of Great Beaver Pond are to me an object of particular curiosity. A large number of the Delawares, Shawanese and Tuscaroras continue in this vicinity; the greater number have gone to the west." In October of this year, 1753, a treaty was held at Carlisle between Benjamin Franklin and the other commissioners, and the chiefs of the Six Nations and their allies of other Western tribes. The party of chiefs sat upon the floor of the court house, smoking, as was the custom, during the entire treaty. Conrad Weiser and Andrew Montour were interpreters. One complaint was that in exchange for their lands the white man had given them nothing but rum, and indictments at about this period are to be found in the old records of the court "for illegal sale of liquor to the Indians who live outside of the inhabited portion of this province." *In passing, we may mention that the whipping post and the pillory erected in 1754 were then and afterward the usual methods of punishment, and that they stood upon that portion of the Public Square upon which the Episcopal Church now stands.

Besides the stockade forts which we have mentioned, there were also, somewhat later (about 1757), breastworks or intrenchments erected northeast of the town by Col. Stanwix, and in this year also the first weekly post was established between Philadelphia, then the largest city in the country, and Carlisle, the better to enable his honor the Governor and the Assembly to communicate with his majesty's subjects on the frontier. In the history of the Indian wars at this period Carlisle holds a conspicuous place. In the autumn of 1755, particularly, the citizens were much alarmed in consequence of numerous massacres by the Indians. The defeat of Gen. Braddock at Fort DuQuesne in this year left the whole western frontier defenseless. In July of this year Gov. Morris, who had succeeded Gov. Hamilton (under whose instructions the town was laid out) came to Carlisle for the purpose of sending supplies to Gen. Braddock, and to encourage the people in the midst of their panic, and it was while he was there that he received the first tidings of the disastrous battle. It was then that Col. John Armstrong, of Carlisle (afterward a general in the Revolutionary Army and a friend of Gen. Washington) decided to take the aggressive and to attack the enemy in their own stronghold. It fell to the lot of the infant town of Carlisle—then only five years old—to turn the tide and to stay the current which threatened to sweep everything away. Col. Armstrong, with a party of 280 resolute men, started from that place, and by a rapid march of some 200 miles, over lofty and rugged mountains, discovered and destroyed the savages in their nest at Kittanning. For this gallant service medals and presents were voted to Col. Armstrong and his officers by the corporation of Philadelphia. The destruction of Kittanning by Col. Armstrong was in September, 1756.

Another Indian council was held at Carlisle on the 13th, 15th, 16th, 17th and 19th of January, 1756, preceding the Indian catastrophe at Kittanning, at which were present Hon. R. H. Morris, lieutenant-governor, Gov. James Hamilton and several other commissioners. It was held to arrive at an understanding as to the action of the Shawanese and Delawares, who had been under the control of the Six Nations, but who had joined the French. At this meeting, where many belts of wampum, etc., as was the custom, were exchanged, Conrad Weiser and George Croghan were interpreters. In May of the succeeding year (1757) a number of Cherokee warriors, who had come from the South, came to Carlisle to aid the English against the French and their savage allies. At this time it was often necessary that the farmers should be protected during the harvest, in order that they might gather their grain. August 20, 1756, Col. Armstrong writes: "Lyttleton, Shippensburg and Carlisle (the last two not finished) are the only forts, now built, that will, in my opinion be serviceable to the public. The duties of the harvest have not permitted me to finish Carlisle Fort with the soldiers; it should be done, otherwise the soldiers can not be so well governed, and may be absent, or without the gates, at a time of the greatest necessity."

At this time (June 30, 1757) Col. Stanwix had begun and was continuing to build his entrenchments on the "northeast part of this town and just adjoining it." In a letter headed "Camp, near Carlisle, July 25, 1757," he writes "I am at work at my entrenchments, but as I send out such large and frequent parties, with other necessary duties, I can only spare about seventy working

---

* The expenses of this treaty, including presents to the Indians, amounted to £1,400.

men a day, and these have been very often interrupted by frequent violent gusts, so that we make but a small figure yet, and the first month was entirely taken up in clearing the ground, which was all full of monstrous stumps, etc."

From these brief pictures, thus painted by contemporaries, we may form some idea of Carlisle at this early date. Le Tort's lonely cabin on the stream, if it still remained; the stockade fort which had given place to the one which was in ruins; the grass-grown streets; the number of dwelling houses (four years before) only five; the temporary log court house on the northeast corner of the center square; the entrenchments near the town; the Indian wigwams which were an object of particular curiosity; the "monstrous stumps" which told of the primeval forest which was for the first time felled by the hand of man—all point to a period recent in history, but fabulous, seemingly, already, and as strange as can be found.

In 1760 considerable excitement was caused by the murder of a friendly Delaware Indian, Dr. John and family, who had moved to Cumberland County in the winter of that year and lived in a log cabin on the Conodoguinet Creek, near Carlisle. News was immediately sent to Gov. Hamilton, and a reward of £100 was offered for the apprehension of the parties concerned. The excitement was intense, for it was feared that the Indians might seek to revenge the murder upon the settlers.

Another panic occurred about two years afterward. At noon, on the 4th of July, 1763, one of a party of horsemen rode rapidly into the town, and told of the capture of Presque Isle, Le Bœuf, and Venango by the French and Indians. The greatest alarm spread among the citizens of the town and neighboring country. The roads were crowded in a little while with women and children hastening to Lancaster for safety. The pastor of the Episcopal Church headed his congregation, encouraging them on the way. Some retired to the breastworks. Col. Bouquet writes, asking aid from the people of York in building a post here, on the plea that they were protected by Cumberland. Truly these were stirring times. The seed was sown and the harvest reaped under the fear of the tomahawk and rifle. The early history of Cumberland County is fraught with items of the deepest interest to all who hold in grateful remembrance the trials and dangers of the first settlers of this beautiful portion of our State.

We are now at about the close of the Indian war, but from the formation of Carlisle down until this period (1764), there was continued danger and depredations throughout the valley.

THE MEETING OF CAPTIVES.

In August of this year, Col. Bouquet, two regiments of royal troops, and one thousand provincials assembled at Carlisle. The Indians, who by this time had been thoroughily conquered, were compelled to bring back all prisoners whom they had captured. The incidents of the meeting of relatives who had been separated for year, which occurred upon the Public Square, has been graphically told. Some had forgotten their native tongue. Some had married with their captors, had grown to love their bondage, and refused to leave their lords. One German mother recognized her long lost child by singing to her the familiar hymn "Alone, yet not alone am I. Though in this solitude so drear," which she had sung to it in childhood. This incident happened December 31, 1764. (*Hallische Nacht, 1033.*)*

One of the most vivid panoramic pictures might be drawn of a scene

---

*Col. Bouquet had advertised for those who had lost children to come to Carlisle, "and look for them." Sup. Rupp's Hist. 402; which accounts, we suppose, for seeming discrepancy of dates.

which happened before the old jail in Carlisle, at about 10 o'clock on Friday morning, the 29th of January, 1768, when a large body of men, some of whom were armed with rifles and others with tomahawks, endeavored, against the earnest protests of Col. John Armstrong, Rev. John Steel, Robt. Miller, William Lyon and John Holmes, the sheriff, to rescue two prisoners, Frederick Stump and Hans Eisenhauer (known as "Ironcutter"), who were confessedly guilty of the brutal murder of several Indian families, from the jail, in order that the prisoners might not be sent for trial to Philadelphia; in which attempt at rescue the mob succeeded, much to the regret and alarm of the government, which was afraid it would awaken an outbreak of Indian retaliation.

REVOLUTIONARY PERIOD.

We approach the period of the Revolution. The encroachments of the Crown upon the rights of the colonists found ready resentment from the hardy settlers of this frontier. In July, 1774, at a public meeting in Carlisle, resolutions were adopted severely condemning the act of the English Parliament in closing the port of Boston, and urging vigorous remedies to correct the wrong. They also advocated a general congress of the colonies; non-importation of British goods; pledged contributions for the relief of Boston; and urged that "a committee be immediately appointed for this county, to correspond with the committee of this province upon the great objects of the public attention; and to co-operate in every measure conducing to the general welfare of British America." James Wilson, Robert Magaw, and William Irvine were appointed deputies to meet those from other counties of the province. The first was afterward a signer of the Declaration, the second a colonel, and the third a general in the Revolutionary Army.

After the battle of Lexington prompt and energetic action was taken; men were pledged, and in July following Col. Thompson's "battalion of riflemen" embraced the first companies south of the Hudson to arrive in Boston, and in January, 1776, this command became the "First Regiment" of the United Colonies, commanded by Gen. George Washington. John Steel, the elder, and his son John Steel, Jr., both led companies from Carlisle, the former acting as chaplain and the latter joining the army of Gen. Washington after he had crossed the Delaware. In short, from the beginning to the end of the Revolution, Carlisle was a central point of patriotic devotion and influence.

We may mention that the two most important facts connected with Carlisle at about this period was the building of the old barracks by the Hessians captured at Trenton, in 1777, and the founding of Dickinson College in 1783.

One year previous to this latter event (April 13, 1782) Carlisle had been incorporated by an act of the Assembly.*

Maj. Andre's Imprisonment.—The town, in consequence of its being seated on what was then the frontier and away from the theater of war, was used as a place of detention for military prisoners. Maj. Andre and Lieut. Despard† were confined here a portion of their time on parole of the town. While here, in 1776, they occupied a stone house on Lot No. 161, at the corner of South Hanover Street and Chapel Alley. They were on parole of honor of six miles, but were prohibited from going out of the town except in military dress.

The Whiskey Insurrection.—In 1794 Gen. Washington, accompanied by Secretary Hamilton, rendezvoused at Carlisle with his army of 4,000 men and six-

---

*A new charter was granted March 4, 1814.
†Lieut. Despard was an Irish officer, afterward a colonel. He served under Nelson, and had a high reputation for rash bravery. He carried back from America Democratic sentiments, and was executed for treason in 1803. Sir Walter Scott says: "Three distinguished heroes of this class have arisen in my time: Lord Edward Fitzgerald, Col. Despard and Capt. Thistlewood, and, with the contempt and abhorrence of all men, they died the death of infamy and guilt." See Dr. Wing's History of Cumberland County, p. 93, note.

teen pieces of artillery, on his way to quell the whiskey insurrection. He was enthusiastically received. The old court house was illuminated with transparencies, speeches were made, and troop of light-horse and a company of infantry promptly offered their services, and marched to Fort Pitt.

A Royal Exile.—In December, 1797, Louis Philippe, then twenty-four years of age, accompanied by his two brothers, the Duke of Montpensier and Count Beaujolais, passed through Carlisle on their way to New Orleans. An incident of their brief stay in that place is related in "Chambers' Miscellany." They arrived at Carlisle on Saturday, when the inhabitants of the neighboring country appeared to have entered the town for some purpose of business or pleasure, and drove up to a public house, near which was a trough for the reception of oats. The Duke of Montpensier sat in the wagon, when the horses became frightened and ran away, upsetting it and his highness, who was somewhat injured. Getting back to the tavern he there acted as his own surgeon, and performed the operation of letting out some of his royal blood in the presence of a number of bucolic admirers, who, believing him to be a physician, proposed that he should remain at Carlisle and begin there his professional career. At this time (1795), by the *Universal Gazetteer*, published in London, we find that Carlisle contained "about 1,500 inhabitants and 300 stone houses, a college and a court house."

WAR OF 1812.

In the war of 1812 four companies were raised in Carlisle; two of which, the "Carlisle Infantry," under Capt. William Alexander, and a "Rifle Company," under Capt. George Hendel, served for a term of six months on the northern frontier. Another, the "Carlisle Guards," under Capt. Joseph Halbert, marched to Philadelphia, and the fourth, the "Patriotic Blues," under Capt. Jacob Squier, served for a time in the entrenchments at Baltimore.

GROWTH OF THE TOWN, ETC.

The town continued steadily to increase. Its population in 1830 was 3,708. Ten years later it was 4,350, of which 2,046 were white males, 1,989 white females, 138 colored males, and 177 colored females.

The common schools first went into operation in Carlisle August 15, 1836. In 1837 the Cumberland Valley Railroad was built through High Street, at the request of some, though not without vigorous protest of other citizens of the town; and in the same year the old market-house, a low wooden structure in the form of the letter L, laid out upon the southeast section of the Public Square, was also erected. It was the third building of the kind, and occupied the site of the original "deep quarry" of 1753, where the present commodius brick structure now stands.

Dr. Crooks, in his "Life of Rev. John McClintock," writing long afterward, but thinking of these early days, gives the following, somewhat imaginative, picture of Carlisle in 1839:

"The valley in the midst of which Carlisle stands has often been compared by the imaginative mind to the happy vale of Rasselas. Encircled lovingly on either side by the Blue Mountain ridge, and enveloped in an atmosphere of crystal clearness, on which the play of light and shade produce every hour some new and stirring effect, it was in a measure withdrawn from the tumult of the world. The tumult might be heard in the distance, but did not come near enough to disturb the calm of studious pursuits."

"The town preserved the traditions of learned culture which has distinguished it from the beginning of the present century. Its population was not enterprising; manufacturing was but little, if at all, known to it. The rich soil of the valley poured out every year abundant harvests, and the borough was no more than the center of exchange and the market for supplies.

"The steady pace and even pulse of agricultural life seemed here to tone down the feverish excitement which is the usual condition under which American society exists."

Early on the morning of Monday, March 24, 1845, the court house which had been erected originally upon that square in 1765-66, and afterward extended in 1802, was destroyed by fire. The old bell, which had been a much valued gift from the Penn family, gave forth its last sounds as it struck the hour of one, ere it sank to silence in the flames below. This bell, it is said, was originally sent from England as a present to the Episcopal Church or Chapel, but was used, by general consent, for the court house, on condition that it should be returned to the church at some future time.

THE BOROUGH IN 1846.

The local statistics of the borough, January 1, 1846, are as follows: There are 3 printing offices and papers—the *Herald and Expositor* (weekly), edited by Mr. Beatty, and devoted to the cause of the Whigs; the *American Volunteer*, edited by Messrs. Boyers and Bratton, Democratic; the *Pennsylvania Statesman*, by J. S. Gitt, a Democratic semi-weekly paper. The first paper established in this county was edited and published by Mr. Kline in 1782, and was called *Kline's Carlisle Weekly Gazette*. There are 10 churches, 48 stores, a number of shops, 4 warehouses, 12 physicians, 3 foundries, common schools sufficient, Dickinson College, under the superintendence of the Methodist Episcopal Church; a new court house, 25 shoe establishments, 4 hatters, 18 tailors, 2 chandleries, 2 auction stores, 7 cabinet-makers, 16 carpenters, 2 coach-makers, 3 brick-makers, 20 bricklayers and masons, 2 bakeries, 5 cake bakers, 1 ropewalk, 1 grist-mill, 12 taverns, 3 distilleries, 5 tinners and coppersmiths, 5 tanners, 6 saddlers, 5 coopers, 2 breweries, 9 butchers, 6 painters, 3 chair-makers, 11 plasterers, 3 dyers, 5 weavers, 2 silver-platers, 1 locksmith, 2 gun-smiths, 1 lime burner, 3 wagon-makers, 3 stone-cutters, 14 blacksmiths, 5 watch-makers, 2 barbers, 3 dentists, 1 clock-maker, 3 jewelry shops, 1 mattrass-maker, 2 threshing-machine manufactories, 3 board-yards, 3 livery-stables, 2 bookbinderies, 2 spinning-wheel manufactories, 1 brush-maker, 2 pump-makers, 5 gardeners, 1 dairy, 1 stocking weaver, 2 cigar-makers, 9 mantua-makers, 6 milliners, 1 bird-stuffing establishment, 5 music-teachers, 4 justices of the peace, 12 male school-teachers, 5 female school-teachers, a large market-house, 15 lawyers, with a sufficient number of physicians, professors, and ministers of the gospel.

At this time (1846) the appearance of Carlisle was, as might be expected, very different from what it is to-day. The present jail had not been built, the present court house had been erected that year; the old open market-house, with its low roof and pillars, stood upon the square; the Episcopal Church stood where it now stands, but with its gothic steeple built at its eastern extremity, and with the square enclosed with iron chains, depending from heavy posts. To the west, upon the other square, was, of course, the venerable stone church, but without its modern tower; and beyond, where the house and grounds of Mrs. Robert Givin now are, the long, low line of buildings, the front one of which was used as a hotel. The pavements were of stone flags. The railroad, as we have mentioned, ran through the street, but the square was more open, and the town had a more rural and primitive appearance, more in keeping with the imaginative picture we have presented of it.

McCLINTOCK RIOT.

In June, 1847, occurred in Carlisle what is known as the McClintock riot. It was caused by the resistance made to the capture of three runaway slaves, and resulted in the death of one of the men who had come for them, and in the trial of a great number of negroes and of Dr. McClintock, who was, however, with some of the others, acquitted.*

We have now brought the history of Carlisle down to a period within the recollection of many of its inhabitants. It is a history which is full of interest; which embraces the early Indian days, the "Provincial" and the "Revolutionary" periods, down to the present; during which time a great government has been founded, and a great nation has sprung into existence. To preserve that nation, Carlisle also did its duty.

WAR OF THE REBELLION.

During the late war Cumberland County was prompt in furnishing its quota for the defense of the National Government. Six companies left Carlisle and participated bravely in a number of the most severely contested battles of the war.

During a great part of the struggle the inhabitants of the valley were kept in a state of constant alarm by reason of frequent threatened invasions of the enemy, and stampedes often from an imaginary foe. There was almost, therefore, a feeling of relief when the Confederate forces actually made their appearance in the summer of 1863.

The first alarm of the approach of the enemy was early in June, but the alarm subsided, and scarcely had the people begun to be lulled into a fatal security, when the news was received that the entire Rebel army was advancing down the valley. Two New York Regiments, the Eighth and Seventy-first, which had been stationed at Shippensburg, retreated to this place, and began making active preparations for defense. Militia were organized, pickets were thrown out, and rude breastworks were hastily constructed about a mile west of the town. On Wednesday, June 24, the home companies proceeded to the scene of the expected action on the turnpike. During the afternoon the cavalry pickets on the Shippensburg road were driven slowly in, and at evening reported the enemy to be within four miles of the town. A scene of excitement ensued, which lasted during the following day. College commencement was held at an early hour in the chapel, and the class graduated without much formality, troops were drawn up in the streets, and, altogether, the town wore quite a military and rather disturbed aspect. On Friday it was more than usually quiet, but on Saturday morning (June 27), the cavalry pickets fell back through the place and announced that the enemy was at hand. It was Jenkins' cavalry. They were met by several citizens and informed that the town was without troops and that no resistance would be made. Accordingly they advanced and entered the town quietly from the west, with their horses at a walk, but with their guns in position to be used at a moment's warning. A portion went to the garrison and the rest came back and stopped at the Market House Square. The hotels were filled with officers and the streets with soldiers. A requisition for 1,500 rations was made upon the town, and was immediately supplied by the citizens. At 5 o'clock in the afternoon the sound of music announced the arrival of Gen. Ewell's corps, which came by the way of the Walnut Bottom road, its bands playing "Dixie" as it marched through the streets of Carlisle. They presented a sorry appearance.

---

*A full account of this riot and the trial which followed can be found in Dr. Crook's Life of Rev. John McClintock.

BOROUGH OF CARLISLE. 239

Many of them were shoeless or hatless, most of them were ragged and dirty, and all were wearied with their long march. A brigade encamped upon the college grounds and others at the United States Garrison; guards were posted, and strict orders to permit no violence or outrage were issued, and so well enforced that scarcely a trace of occupation by a hostile force was visible after their departure.

Upon the failure of the authorities to comply with an extravagant requisition for supplies, squads of soldiers, accompanied by an officer, were commanded to help themselves from the stores and warehouses. On Monday, 29th, the force showed symptoms of retiring, and before the dawn of the next day the rumbling of the wagon train announced the movement of the army.

About 2 o'clock in the afternoon (Tuesday, June 30) some 400 of Col. Cochran's cavalry entered the town from the Dillsburg road, and were soon riding wildly through the streets, shouting, screaming and acting like madmen. During the night the entire force of the enemy left, after having destroyed the railroad bridge, and by Wednesday (July 1) the town was clear of the last band of rebels, when, amid the acclamations of the people, the Union troops entered with several batteries of artillery.*

The most exciting scene in this little drama was yet to come. At about 7 o'clock in the evening of this day (July 1, 1863), a large body of cavalry (under Gen. Fitzhugh Lee) made its appearance at the junction of the Trindle Spring and York roads, and at first were supposed to be a portion of our own forces. Their boldness was well calculated to produce such an impression. They came within 200 yards of the town, sat in their saddles, gazing up the street at the stacked arms of the infantry. After a few shots had been exchanged, they commenced shelling the town. The citizens were upon the streets at the time. The utmost alarm prevailed. For more than half an hour the bombardment was kept up, when they begun raking the town with grape. At about dusk they ceased firing and dispatched a flag of truce with a demand for the surrender of the town. This was indignantly refused. The bombardment was renewed with greater violence than before. The scene which followed it would be difficult to describe. Many persons began fleeing from their homes, some to seek protection in the open country, and others to find a refuge from the shells in the cellars of their dwellings. At about 10 o'clock a great sheet of flame spread over the sky in the northeast, and the angry crackling of the fire, as it mounted heavenward, could be heard amid the roar of the artillery. They had fired the barracks. Just when the scene was grandest the artillery ceased, and, in the silence which succeeded, another flag of truce was sent into the town, and another demand was made for its unconditional surrender. This was again refused. After shelling the town again, more feebly, however, than before, and destroying, in addition to the barracks, the gas works and some private property, the Confederate forces retired.

Gen. Fitzhugh Lee withdrew with his forces that night over the mountains, and in the afternoon of that ever memorable 2d of July, the people in Carlisle could hear the heavy thunder of the guns at Gettysburg.

In the light of subsequent events there is no doubt that Carlisle could have easily been captured, and that the shelling of the town was meant, in part at least, only to cover the retreat of these Confederate forces, who were already under the shadow of the great catastrophe which was to follow.

SITUATION, PUBLIC BUILDINGS, ETC.

The borough of Carlisle is situated in latitude 40° 12' north, longitude 77° 10' west, eighteen miles west of Harrisburg, in the Cumberland Valley, bounded

---
*At sunrise Col. Body's cavalry, and half past 6 o'clock Gen Smith, preceeded by three regiments.

upon either side by the long ranges of the Blue or Kittatinny Mountains. The town lies in the midst of a rolling country which is both beautiful and productive. The borough is laid out into wide and straight streets, rectangular, well macadamized, and with many trees which, particularly during the spring and summer months, add greatly to the beauty of the town. The two principal streets, High and Hanover, are eighty, and all the others sixty, feet in width. The Public Square in the center of the town, bisected by the two principal streets, is peculiarly attractive. It is handsomely laid out, ornamented with trees, and has the court house, market-house, First Presbyterian Church and St. John's Episcopal Church on its four corners.

A monument erected to the memory and inscribed with the names of the officers and men who fell during the Rebellion, stands upon the southwestern portion of the square. The court house, also upon the southwest corner of the square, was erected in 1846, the one previously erected in 1766 and extended in 1802, to which the cupola, containing a clock, was added in 1809, having been destroyed by fire. The present brick building has a massive portico somewhat after the Greek style, supported by heavy white pillars, and is surmounted by a cupola and clock for public uses. The commodious modern brick market-house, erected in 1878, occupies the whole of the southeastern section of the square. The county jail, on the corner of Main and Bedford Streets, is a large and imposing brown stone structure with high turreted front and round tower, and which might almost be mistaken for a Rhenish castle, if it stood on the green slopes of that romantic river. It was built in 1854, on the site of the old prison, which was erected just one century before, and which was enlarged in 1790. The county almshouse, beyond the eastern border of the town, is as large and commodious establishment, with farm attached. Beyond it, looking toward the town, to the right, and only about half a mile away are the large lawns and long lines of yellow buildings, known heretofore as the Carlisle Barracks. They were built by the Hessians captured at Trenton, in 1777. They have been occupied by troops, cavalry, artillery and infantry, or have been used as a recruiting station during most of the time since the Revolution. They have also been the home, at different times, of many of the officers, both Union and ex-Confederate, who were engaged in the late war. On the night of July 1, 1863, they were almost totally destroyed by the Confederate forces under Gen. Fitzhugh Lee, but they have since been thoroughly rebuilt, extended and beautified, and for the last five years have been used as a training school for the education of Indians.

CHURCHES.

There are many churches in Carlisle, so that almost every religious denomination is represented in the structures which they have erected, in which each individual can worship God according to his conscience. Of these, for its solid architectural beauty and its age, the old First Presbyterian stone church, on the northwest corner of the square, is particularly worthy of mention. Although built before the Revolution, two Presbyterian Churches had preceded it. The first church edifice erected in Carlisle by what was then known as the "old side," a two-story building, stood at the northeastern intersection of Hanover and Louther Streets, and was erected about 1758; and the church erected by the "new side" was at the southwestern intersection of Hanover and Pomfret Streets, and was probably erected about the same time. Rev. John Steel was pastor of the former, and George Duffield, D. D., was ordained pastor of the latter in 1761. The next church edifice erected by the old side —which is the present First Presbyterian Church—was begun in 1769 and probably finished in 1772, at which time Dr. Duffield removed to Philadelphia, and the two congregations were afterward, in May, 1786, united. The large additional stone tower was erected in 1873, but the main body of the building, with its solid masonry of grey limestone with marble trimmings, stands as it was first constructed.

St. John's Episcopal Church, on the northeast corner of the square, was built in 1825, near the site of its predecessor, erected about 1765, and is a very neat and tasteful Gothic building. The chapel was added in 1885.

The Second Presbyterian Church, on the southeast corner of Hanover and Pomfret Streets, is a fine specimen of the usual modern gothic type, and was erected in 1872, on the site of the former erected in 1834. (In 1833 a portion of the Presbyterian congregation, by reason of a doctrinal dispute, organized themselves into a separate congregation and worshiped in the county hall till 1834, when their first church was built.)

Methodist Episcopal Church.—After the Revolution the Methodists met in the market place, then in the court house, and subsequently in a small frame building on Pomfret Street, in which place they formed a small class in 1792–93. A few years afterward, in 1802, they built a small stone house on Lot 61, at the corner of Pitt Street and Church Alley, which was followed in 1815 by a more commodious building on Church Alley; and this, in turn, gave way to another of still larger proportions on the corner of Pitt and High Streets, where the present church now stands. This was taken down in 1876, and the present Centennial Church erected. In 1854 a portion of the members withdrew, and after worshiping for a time in the chapel of Dickinson College, erected the church edifice known as Emory Chapel, which, after the reunion of the congregations, was used as the preparatory department of the college.

English Lutheran.—The German Reformed and Lutheran congregations worshiped on alternate Sabbaths in the same church (which stood upon the present German Reformed burying-ground) until 1807, when each congregation erected a house of worship for its own use. The Lutherans built theirs near the corner of Louther and Bedford Streets, but it was burned down in the destructive fire of March, 1851.* It was immediately rebuilt. It is their present place of worship.

The German Reformed Church (built in 1807) was located on the lot afterward used as a preparatory school building of Dickinson College. Having sold it, they built, in 1827, a church at the corner of High and Pitt Streets, which they afterward sold to the Methodist Episcopal congregation, and, in 1835, erected the one which they now occupy on Louther Street. During the year 1866 they remodeled the church, greatly enlarged the building, which they surmounted with a spire 127 feet in height. The style is gothic, with stained windows and interior frescoed.

German Lutheran.—In 1853 the German portion of the Lutheran congregation separated from the English, and erected a neat church on the corner of Bedford and Pomfret Streets.

The Roman Catholic Church, on Pomfret Street, is built in the figure of a cross. It was erected in 1807, and enlarged in 1823. The lot upon which it stands was owned at an early day by the Jesuits of Conowago, who had upon it a small log church, in which the Roman Catholic congregation worshiped until the present one was built.

---

*On a windy night, the 13th of March, 1851, occurred one of the largest fires that has ever devastated the town. Some forty-two buildings were destroyed, and among them was the English Lutheran Church, near the corner of Bedford and Louther Streets. It was immediately rebuilt. On this occasion all the inmates of what was then the old jail, were liberated, necessity compelling the jailor to give them temporary freedom.

An Associated Presbyterian congregation was organized in 1798. They had bought, two years previously, a lot from the Penns, and on it they erected a stone church, on South West Street, in 1802, which was purchased and remodeled in 1866, and re-opened as the Church of God. It is now the Methodist African Zion Church.

The Evangelical Association has a very creditable church upon Louther Street, built in 1869. Besides these which we have mentioned, there are several African churches in the town, and a very beautiful gothic mission chapel, built in 1884, in the northeastern portion of the town, a donation of Mrs. Mary Biddle, of Philadelphia.

CEMETERIES.

The two principal burial places of the borough are the beautiful Ashland Cemetery—with its winding walks overshadowed by green trees—which was dedicated as a place of burial, on Sabbath afternoon, October 8, 1865; and the Old Graveyard, coincident with the borough in its birth, which contains the monuments of very many old families and noted names.

SCHOOLS, INSTITUTES AND COLLEGE.

The public school buildings of the borough, eight in number, are ample in size and well adapted to their purpose. (The common school system went into operation in Carlisle August 15, 1836. There were then 16 schools and 928 scholars. In 1879 there were 20 schools and 1,003 scholars, 481 being males and 522 females). The schools, now 21 in number, are judiciously graded, and the high school will compare favorably in grade and thoroughness of training with similar institutions elsewhere.

The importance of education was fully appreciated by the earlier settlers, and the church and the school were inseparable companions. A classical academy was in existence in Carlisle prior to the Revolutionary war.

An account of the "Metzgar Female Institute," "Indian Industrial School" and "Dickinson College" will be found in the Educational Chapter XI., page 195.

LIBRARIES.

The libraries in the borough consist of the Law Library, in the court house building, which, containing not only the various State reports, but the English reports also, and many text-books, is as complete as can be found in any town in the State; the College Library, and the libraries of the two societies belonging to the College; and the Hamilton Historical Library, for which a separate building, comparatively as yet without books, has been erected from funds left by its founder, James Hamilton, Esq.

NEWSPAPERS.

The first newspaper published in Carlisle was called *The Carlisle Weekly Gazette*, edited by Messrs. Kline & Reynolds. It was a small four page paper, the first number of which was issued in July, 1785. The present papers in Carlisle are the *Carlisle Herald*, the *American Volunteer* and the daily and weekly *Valley Sentinel*. The *Carlisle Eagle* (Federal) was commenced as early as 1799, and was the progenitor in a straight line of descent, of the present (Republican) paper. The *American Volunteer* was born September 15, 1814, and has always been consistently, or inconsistently, Democratic. The *Valley Sentinel* (Democratic) was started in April, 1861, at Shippensburg. It was purchased by Mr. H. K. Peffer, its present proprietor, in May, 1874, and removed to Carlisle. *The Daily Evening Sentinel* was first issued in December, 1881.

BOROUGH OF CARLISLE. 245

MANUFACTURING ESTABLISHMENTS, ETC.

Carlisle is still, as it always has been, chiefly the county seat and center of a rich agricultural district, but of late years, with the more developed resources, and more extended railroad facilities of the Cumberland Valley, it has grown with its growth and awakened to the importance of the manufacturing industries also. The most extensive industrial establishments are the shoe, carriage and large car factories, the chain and spoke works, machine-shops and foundry. The new car-works are very extensive buildings, erected in 1882, lying within the eastern boundary of the borough. There is, of course, the usual, or more than the usual, number of various mercantile establishments, banks, etc., of which the town seems always to have been well supplied.

GAS AND WATER COMPANY.

Carlisle is plentifully supplied with pure limestone water from the reservoir on the Conodoguinet Creek, and the streets of the town are also lighted with gas, both reservoirs being under the control of an incorporated stock company, started in 1853.

SOCIETIES.

The *Young Men's Christian Association*, of Carlisle, was organized March 21, 1859, by a number of leading Christian men in the town, when Mr. Joseph C. Hoffer was chosen president. The association opened a public reading room in Marion Hall on West High Street, on September 19, of the same year. They had a library of 405 volumes, the gift of the citizens, and in their rooms and upon their tables and files were found six daily newspapers, fifty weekly religious and secular papers, and magazines. The association also sustained a series of free lectures, which were largely attended, and it also maintained a union prayer meeting, which was held weekly under its auspices. The association did a good work for the community by its free reading-room and religious work. The records show 1,944 visits to the rooms from the 19th of September, 1859, to March 21, 1860. After some time the rooms were closed, but the religious work of the association was sustained, when, on Friday evening, August 2, 1867, pursuant to a notice given at the young men's prayer meeting, which was held on Monday evening, previous, a committee, consisting of a number of leading church members, was appointed to take into consideration the practicability of reorganizing the Young Men's Christian Association. The committee reporting favorably, the organization was at once effected, with Mr. Jacob C. Stock as president, who filled the office until January, 1868. Public reading-rooms were opened on the second floor of the Kramer building, on the corner of West High Street and Court House Avenue. A circulating library was again opened and six leading daily newspapers and eight monthly magazines were provided, besides a number of weekly papers. A daily morning meeting was instituted, cottage prayer meetings were carried on under the direction of the association, and monthly sermons were preached for the benefit of young men. Mr. H. K. Peffer was elected president for the year 1868. In the spring of 1869 the association vacated their rooms on West High Street, moving into the second-floor rooms, known as the "Halbert corner," on the southeast corner of North Hanover and Louther Streets. In connection with the other religious services of the association, open air meetings were conducted in different parts of the town on the Sabbath evening during the summer and early fall. Mr. John T. Green served the association as president during the years 1869 and 1870. In the spring of 1870 the young men vacated their rooms, sustaining a religious work of the association and holding their business meetings at the homes of members. Mr. J. C. Stock was again elected president, serving from 1871 to 1873 inclusive. The association instituted Sabbath afternoon meetings at the jail and also at the county almshouse, and a tract distributor was appointed for the town work. In the beginning of the year 1872, the association purchased the Mission Chapel located at the corner of North and East Streets, known as Dickinson Mission Chapel, the amount paid being $900. Mr. J. C. Stock was elected superintendent of the school, which numbered about thirty scholars. The State Convention of the Young Men's Christian Association of Pennsylvania was held at Carlisle September 10 and 12, 1872, with 150 delegates in attendance. Mr. John H. Wolf was elected and served as president of the association for the year 1874. Mr. Andrew Blair was president during the year 1875, he was also elected by the association as superintendent of the Mission Sunday-school. Mr. Samuel Coyle was elected and served the association as its president from 1876 until his death which occurred August 23, 1879, when Rev. William Halbert was chosen president serving until within a short time of his death, in March, 1881. In October, 1879, the association again rented and furnished rooms in the Patton building, northwest corner of West High and North Pitt Streets. The Mission Chapel was sold to Mr. Andrew Blair in December, 1880, for the sum of $500. In March, 1881, Mr. A. A. Line was elected president of the association, serving until January, 1883. In April, 1881, the association moved into the Given building, located on Church avenue, north of West High street. December 5, 1881, the following resolution was passed by the association: That Allan A. Line, president, Harry Wetzel, Levi Brenneman, Reuben Brubaker and Charles E. Eckels, members of the executive committee, and W. Scott Coyle, treasurer, and Mirvin McMillen, recording secretary, are hereby authorized and directed to sign the application of the court of common pleas for a charter of incorporation of this association under the corporate name of "The Young Men's Christian Association of Carlisle, Pennsylvania." The boys' work was established in the fall of 1882, when weekly entertainments were held for them, consisting of talks of travel, chemical experiments on scientific subjects, magic lantern entertainments, etc. In November, 1882, the association with the assistance of W. A. Bowen, assistant State secretary of Pennsylvania, raised a subscription of $1,000 to meet the current expenses of the association for the coming year, including the employment of a competent general secretary to have charge and oversight of the entire work of the association, the maintaining of a free reading-room, and the general enlargement of the work. Mr. David R. Thompson was elected president of the association for 1883. Prof. J. A. McKnight of Pennsylvania, was chosen as general secretary to the association, at a salary of $50 per month. He took charge of the association January 25, 1883.

The boys' branch was organized as a part of the association, which, in a short time, numbered forty members. Also the ladies' auxillary society was organized as part of the association. August 13, 1883, the association moved into Marion Hall building, on West High street, using the parlors on the first floor for daily and evening reading-rooms, and having control of the halls and rooms on the second floor front, also the large back building and spacious yard. Mr. D. D. Thompson was elected president of the association for the year 1884. In November, 1884, Prof. J. A. McKnight, the general secretary, was called to the Allentown Association, when Mr. F. M. Welsh, of Philadelphia, acted as general secretary for the Carlisle Association, until July, 1885, when J. F. Mohler, of Carlisle, served as general secretary until the following October, when Mr. A. B. Paul, assistant secretary of Columbus (Ohio) Association, was called to fill the position, and is general secretary at the present time. Mr. John C. Eckels, Jr., served as president of the association for the year 1885, when his successor, Dr. George Neidich, was called to the chair for the year 1886. The membership of the association has varied at different times throughout its history, numbering from thirty to sixty, while at the present writing it numbers 165, active, associate and sustaining. A decided step in advance was taken when the association employed a general secretary for the supervision of the work. Religious meetings are held for young men only on Sabbath afternoons, with an average attendance of thirty. A class for Bible study on Tuesday evenings. A meeting for boys semi-monthly on Friday evenings, when they are provided with practical talks, wonder lectures and entertainments. At stated times public receptions are held at the rooms for members and contributors, for clerks and mechanics, and during the winter of 1885–86 a course of lectures and entertainments was arranged for the public, which have given great satisfaction. The association, in its present appointment, is meeting the demands needed for the work among the youth and young men of the community. (*Communicated.*)

Temperance Societies.—The subject of temperance received early attention in Cumberland County. As early as 1829 a society, pledging its members to total abstinence from all intoxicating drinks, was formed in Carlisle, the first of the kind in the county. Distilleries were regarded then as legitimately necessary business enterprises, and the drinking of ardent spirits was not only approved by society, but a failure to do so was looked upon with disfavor. It may well be conjectured that moral heroism was required to join a total abstinence temperance organization at that time, when the Cumberland Valley had some eighty distilleries.

But the cause of temperance grew, and with it a public conscience on the subject. Men of position finally gave it their sanction and influence. Organizations in various parts of the county sprang up, whose meetings were largely attended. On Christmas Day, 1835, the annual meeting of a county organization was held, at which such men as Rev. Dr. Durbin, of Dickinson College, and John Reed, president-judge of the court of common pleas, participated, and succeeded in passing the following resolution: "*Resolved*, That the cause of temperance is the cause of humanity, of philanthropy and of religion; and that all laws licensing or in any way recognizing the traffic in, or sale of, ardent spirits, are erroneous in principle and injurious in practice."

Temperance has an unceasing warfare to wage. The conflict between the stomach and the brain is a severe one; and with the unthinking, who seek present gratification at the expense of personal and society welfare, victory usually declares in favor of the stomach. Hence the beneficent results expected by temperance advocates have not always been fully realized.

St. John's Commandery, No. 8, M. K. T. Number of present members, seventy-nine. Names of present officers: Rev. Jeremiah M. Carvell, E. C.; Samuel R. Cloudy, Genlo.; William R. Bailie, Capt. Gen.; Joshua P. Bitler, Treas.; John G. Bobb, Recorder.

St. John's Chapter, No. 171, R. A. M., organized August, 1853. Charter members: Dr. Charles E. Blumenthal, John Hyer, Dr. George Z. Bretz, Dr. O. H. Tiffany, John Gutshall, James M. Allen, S. M. L. Consor, Ephraim Cornman, George Weise. Present number of members, sixty seven. Present officers: Charles W. Strohm, M. E. H. P.; Rev. Jeremiah M. Carvell, K.; Edward J. Gardner, S.; John Hyer, Treasurer; John G. Bobb, Secretary.

Cumberland Star Lodge, No. 197, F. & A. M., organized November 6, 1894. Charter members: Willis Foulk, George Patterson, Jr., and John Lease. Present membership, ninety. Present officers: Niles M. Fissel, W. M.; E. J. Gardner, S. W.; John Olliver, J. W.; W. Vance, Treasurer; Theodore Cornman, Secretary.

St. John's Lodge, No. 260, F. & A. M. Organized April, 1852. Charter members: Dr. Blumenthal, John Hyer, Dr. Geo. L. Bretz, Dr. O. H. Tiffany, R. K. Burns, Michael G. Ege, Rev. Herman M. Johnson, William J. Collisshaw, H. J. Meck. Present number of members, eighty-two. Present officers: Chas. W. Strohm, W. M.; John A. Means, S. W.; Joseph L. Herman. J. W.; William H. Bretz, Treasurer; John G. Bobb, Secretary.

Carlisle Lodge, No. 91, I. O. O. F. Instituted December 22, 1843. Charter members: Edward P. Lyons, N. G.; Holmes Fernald, V. G.; Thomas Conlyn, Sec.; John C. Williams, Ass't Sec.; Peter Monyer, Treas. Present number of members, 119. Present officers: J. H. Gardner, N. G.; Dr. I. M. Bentz, V. G.; Theodore Cornman, Sec.; H. G. Beetem, Ass't Sec.; Robert Sheaffer, Treas.

Conodoquinet Tribe, No. 108, I. O. R. M. Established September 27, 1868. Charter members: F. C. Kramer, C. C. Faber, Levi Leeds, John Yaiser, L. Leidig, John Liszman, H. Gotverth, Wm. Elmer, P. Liszman, Peter Miller, John Doner, A. More, H. Linekhul, Fred A. Chel. Number of present members, 55. Present officers: Harry G. Beetem P.; Louis Klucker, S.; J. R. Brown, S. S.; Charles Faber, J. S.; A. B. Ewing, K. of W.; C. C. Faber, C. of R.

Knights of the Golden Eagle, Carlisle Castle, No. 110. Instituted in July, 1886. Present membership, 75. Present officers: J. E. Barnitz, N. C.; O. F. Conly. V. C.; William Vance, P. C.; —— Weltzel, H. P.

Patriotic Order Sons of America, Washington Camp, No. 171, was chartered June 18, 1886, with 43 names.

Sons of Veterans, Captain Beatty Camp, No. 35, was instituted January 30, 1883.

There was also instituted, in October, 1885, for social and insurance benefits, the *Improved Order of Heptasophs.*

CONCLUSION.

We have given briefly, in the foregoing pages, a general outline of the history of this old and historic borough. The town, until of late years, has been noted principally, not as a mercantile or manufacturing center, but as a place of homes. In it there are many handsome residences, built by those who have left the more busy scenes of active life, or those who have always lived retired lives, withdrawn, in a measure, from the tumult of the world. Its capital has often been idle, and it has been conservative in its business interests. On the other hand, the beneficial influences of its institutions of learning are clearly perceptible, while the social atmosphere of the place, although much changed since the days when it was a military post, makes it still a distinctive town in the Valley in this respect

CHAPTER XVII.

BOROUGH OF MECHANICSBURG.

Its Beginning—Growth—William Armstrong—Population—War of the Rebellion—Schools and Educational Institutes—Churches—Newspapers—Public Hall and Market House—Banking Institutions—Gas and Water Company—Societies—Conclusion.

MECHANICSBURG is the second town in population and importance in the county. It lies almost midway between Carlisle and Harrisburg, on the Cumberland Valley Railroad, and almost midway between the mountains north and south, in a rich and productive portion of the valley.

It dates its early history as a settlement, from nearly the beginning of the present century. In 1790 the woods or underbrush grew where the town now stands, and the deer and other animals could be seen. About this time, or shortly afterward, there were two houses built at what are now opposite ends of the town; the lower one an inn, built by one Frankenberger, and the upper one by some one now unknown. Even as late as 1806 the greater part of the site of the town was covered with underbrush or woods. A "few stragling houses were to be seen," of which only one or two remained in 1846.

Considering the date of the formation of the county, the town is therefore of comparatively recent origin. Its beginning was unpretentious. The first brick house was not built until after the war of 1812. This was a house built about 1816, in the western portion of the town, by Lewis Zearing.

For some time after the settlement, which had begun in 1805 or 1806, the place was known as Drytown, owing to the great scarcity, at times, of water, and as Stoufferstown after Henry Stouffer, who owned the land in what became afterward, the central portion of the town. The houses which existed up to 1820, had been built before any lots were regularly laid out and we have no evidence to show that the place was known as Mechanicsburg prior to this time. Up to this year, 1820, the number of houses, we are told, had increased to twenty-five or thirty; but about this time, or in the succeeding year, a number of lots were laid out in the eastern portion of what is now the town, upon which some six or eight houses were soon afterward erected. In 1828, Henry Stouffer laid out some lots upon his land in the central part of the town, and a number of dwellings were erected. In April (28th) of this year, it was incorporated as a borough, and a new impetus was given to the place. From this time it grew rapidly. Within the next three years some twenty or thirty houses were put up. In December, 1831, Maj. Henry Lease and David Brenizer bought eight or ten acres of land, on the south side of Main Street, from George Steinbring, which they laid out in lots. From that time forward, for the next fifteen years, the town gradually increased, until in the year 1845, it had, according to the description given of it by "Rupp," 133 comfortable dwellings, 41 of brick, 67 frame, 35 plastered; 4 churches: a Union, Methodist, Lutheran and Bethel; a commodious schoolhouse, in which three public schools were taught; 3 taverns; 3 warehouses on the railroad; a foundry and machine shop; a number of mechanics' shops and of mercantile houses, and a population rising to 800. After its incorporation in 1828, a burgess and town council were elected.

This was on the 16th of May. Henry Ford was the first burgess and Lewis Zearing the first president of the town council.

Nine years later (1837) the Cumberland Valley Railroad was finished through the town, and opened for travel and transportation, thus giving to it increased facilities for future growth. For a quarter of a century after its incorporation the town steadily improved, and from 1853 to the breaking out of the Rebellion, its progress was still more marked, both in population and in material development. During this period several new churches were erected, Cumberland Valley Institute and Irving Female College were built, two or three forwarding houses, a new town hall and engine house, and a large number of dwelling houses were put up, all adding greatly to the appearance and prosperity of the town. During the period of the war there was but little improvement, but after it was over the town started on what seemed to be an unexampled period of prosperity. Houses sprang up as if by magic, and the borough was extended. In one summer alone not less than 120 houses were erected, mostly by men of moderate means. Mechanicsburg threatened to outstrip her sister towns. But this period of rapid development was of short duration. She had grown too rapidly, and a reaction came. This, however, lasted only for a few years, since which time the town has continued steadily to improve. Within the last ten years new streets have been added, and many handsome residences and villas have been erected. Particularly is this true of the east and west ends, and the southern side of the town, where its rapid improvement has been most marked. The whole new portion of the town, south of Simpson Street, has been built up within the last quarter of a century, and many of the handsomest residences in Mechanicsburg have been erected within the last few years.

POPULATION.

The total population of Mechanicsburg, in the different years here given, was as follows: 1830, 554; 1840, 670; 1850, 882; 1860, 1,939; 1870, 2,569; 1881, 3,018.

In 1876 the population, in detail, was as follows: White male adults, 719; white female adults, 947; white male children, 645; white female children, 645; colored male adults, 29; colored female adults, 39; colored male children, 27; colored female children, 30. Total, 3,081.

WILLIAM ARMSTRONG.

In June, 1879, Mechanicsburg lost its oldest citizen in the death of William Armstrong. He was a native of the northern portion of Ireland, born April 6, 1779. When but three years of age his parents immigrated to this country, landing at Philadelphia, and taking up their residence at Harrisburg, in 1783, then but a small village. About the year 1792 Mr. Armstrong was indentured to Robert Harris, a grandson of John Harris, the founder of Harrisburg, and with whom he lived until he was about nineteen years of age, when he took French leave and landed in Carlisle, where he was soon afterward discovered by Mr. Harris, who used every effort to have him return with him to his old home, but without avail; so, for a valuable consideration, $40, Mr. Harris released the indentured lad, and "Uncle Billy" was a free man. Whilst in the service of Mr. Harris, Mr. Armstrong, in 1794, then but a lad of fifteen years, witnessed the father of his adopted country, George Washington, crossing the Susquehanna on his way to the western portion of the State, with a force of men to quell the Whiskey Insurrection that occurred in that year. Mr. Armstrong was married by the rector of the Protestant Episcopal Church of Carlisle, and soon after (1812) enlisted in the Carlisle Guards. He met

Kossuth, the Hungarian refugee, and heartily shook hands with the exiled patriot. In 1853 he came to Mechanicsburg and took up his residence with his nephew, Robert Wilson, and with him continued to live till his death, which occurred June 20, 1879, at the patriarchal age of one hundred years, two months and fourteen days. The deceased was never sick during his century of years, his death being the result, not of disease but old age. He was buried in the Trindle Spring grave-yard with the honors of war.

WAR OF THE REBELLION.

Mechanicsburg contributed many brave soldiers to the war of the Rebellion, and was among the towns of the valley invaded by the Confederate forces in 1863. Some 1,200 or 1,500 of Jenkins' cavalry entered the town at about 9:30 o'clock on Sunday morning on the 28th of June. They came in with a flag of truce, which is explained by stating that they mistook Chestnut Hill, where the new cemetery had just been laid out, for a fortification, and that they supposed Union troops were near. They soon found to the contrary; captured the flag that had been floating in the center of the town, which had been taken down and concealed; when they encamped below the town, the General making his headquarters at the Railroad Hotel. They then demanded rations, which were granted, and after having remained for about three days as uninvited guests they departed, without having done any injury either to individuals or property. By Wednesday morning on the 1st of July, the town was clear of the last band of Confederate troops, who went thence to Gettysburg.

SCHOOLS AND EDUCATIONAL INSTITUTES.

Mechanicsburg has twelve public schools, systematically graded, which are under the control of a competent body of directors. The schools are in buildings comparatively new, and are well furnished with all modern appliances. Besides the public schools, Mechanicsburg had, until within a few years, two other educational institutions—the Cumberland Valley Institute at the upper, and the Irving Female College at the lower end of the town. A brief history of them is as follows: Some time prior to 1853 a select school was opened by Mr. F. M. L. Gillelen, which passed into the hands of Rev. Joseph S. Loose, A. M., who removed it, in 1853, to a building erected for that purpose, which has since been known as the Cumberland Valley Institute. In 1857 it passed into the hands of Prof. I. D. Rupp, of local historic fame, and in 1855 into the possession of Messrs. Lippincott, Mullen and Reese, who conducted it until 1860, when it was purchased by Rev. O. Ege, who, in connection with his son, Alexander Ege, and several adjunct professors, conducted it until 1875, since which time it has not been open for the reception of students.

Irving Female College, situated at Irvington, a name given to the eastern end of the town, was founded by Solomon P. Gorgas, and incorporated as a college by an act of the Legislature in 1857. Its first principal was Rev. A. G. Marlatt, under whose management this institution for the education of young women attained considerable popularity and influence. At his death, in 1865, it passed into the hands of Rev. T. P. Ege, who conducted it until within the past few years, when, owing to the gradual diminution of patronage or want of financial support, the college was closed.

CHURCHES.

The churches of Mechanicsburg, ten in number, are as follows: Methodist Episcopal, Presbyterian, Reformed, St. Luke's Lutheran, Trinity Lutheran, United Brethren, Bethel, African Methodist Episcopal Zion, the old Union Church and a handsome Episcopal Chapel in the new portion of the town.

NEWSPAPERS.

There have been a number of newspapers published in Mechanicsburg, an account of which will be found elsewhere.

"*The Microcosm*," started by Dr. Jacob Weaver, in 1835, was the first paper published in the town. *The Independent Journal*, which was created by consolidation of *The Valley Democrat* and *The Cumberland Valley Journal*, by Robt. H. Thomas, in October, 1872, is the paper still in existence, and still edited by Mr. Thomas, who has also since (January, 1873) established the *Farmer's Friend*. As Mr. Thomas is the Principal founder of the State Grange of Pennsylvania he has made this paper the mouth-piece of that prominent organization. The *Saturday Evening Journal*, a small local sheet, is also published in the *Independent Journal* office, and furnished gratuitously to the subscribers of the latter paper.

PUBLIC HALL AND MARKET HOUSE.

Franklin Hall and Market House, on the Public Square, at the corner of Market and Main Streets, is a three-story brick edifice, surmounted by a tower and town clock. The building was begun in 1866 and completed in 1867. The hall was formally dedicated by a *soiree* under the auspices of Irving Female College, on the evening of December 24, 1866. The third story of the main building is used as a Masonic Hall; the second floor is the hall proper, with a seating capacity for 600 persons; while the side and the two-story rear extension on Market Street, are occupied by stores and the commodious market house. The first market in this building was held on the 3d of November, 1866.

BANKING INSTITUTIONS.

The first bank in Mechanicsburg was started in 1859 by Levi Merkel, Jacob Mumma and others, transacting business under the title of Merkle, Mumma & Co. This institution was incorporated by the Legislature in 1861 as the "Mechanicsburg Bank," and, a few years later, when the National banking system was inaugurated, it applied for and obtained a charter, in March, 1864, as "The First National Bank," under which title it commenced business in May following, with a capital of $100,000. Its first president was S. P. Gorgas; cashier, A. C. Brindle. It now occupies a handsome brick and brownstone building on West Main Street.

The Second National Bank was organized under the United States banking law, February 20, 1863, with a capital of $50,000. Thomas B. Bryson was its first president, and Levi Kauffman its first cashier. Both of the above banks have been successfully conducted and have been of great benefit to the business interests of the town.

GAS AND WATER COMPANY.

Mechanicsburg was first lighted with gas in September, 1868. The gas works are owned by an incorporated company, and are situated at the eastern limits of the borough. The town is also well supplied with water, from a reservoir located in Upper Allen Township. Both the gas and water are under the control of the same "Gas and Water Company," which was chartered in 1854. The water works were built in 1856.

SOCIETIES.

Eureka Chapter, No. 209. R. A. M., was organized July 3, 1866, with the following charter members: Robert H. Thomas, Samuel N. Eminger and George K. Mooney. Number of members, about thirty-five. Present officers: Josiah P. Wilbar, H. P.; J. Morris Miller, K.; Robert H. Thomas, Jr., S.; E. Rankin Huston, Treas.; George Bobb, Sec.

BOROUGH OF MECHANICSBURG. 255

Eureka Lodge, No. 302, F. & A. M., had its charter granted June 16, 1856. First officers: John Palmer, W. M.; Ira Day (now deceased), S. W.; Jacob Dorsheimer (now deceased), J. W. Number of members about 106. Present officers: Levere G. Firestine, W. M.; A. J. Loudon, S. W.; H. S. Mohler, J. W.; J. C. Miller, Sec.; S. F. Houston, Treas.

Mechanicsburg Lodge, No. 215, I. O. O. F., was organized December 21, 1846. Its first officers were Isaac Kinsey, N. G.; John Palmer, V. G.; Henry Carns, S.; John Emminger, A. S.; Samuel Eckels, T. Number of members, ninety-eight. The present officers are Martin Milleisen, N. G.; Thos. M. Mauk, V. N. G.; S. S. Diehl, T.; R. Senseman, S.

Wildey Encampment, No. 29, I. O. O. F., was organized at Carlisle, and a new charter obtained July 11, 1878, Geo. Bobb, John Webbert, J. A. Sibbet, Jos. Totton, Reuben Senseman, S. B. King, Christian Swartz and Simon S. Diehl being petitioners. Number of members, twenty-nine. The present officers are John Webbert, C. P.; W. H. Hench, H. P.; W. B. Railing, S. W.; J. N. Young, J. W.; R. Senseman, S.; S. S. Diehl, T.

Melita Lodge, No. 83, K. of P., obtained its charter June 4, 1868, charter members being, F. F. Singiser, William Matthews, J. S. Shopp, William Y. Johnson, J. R. West, D. H. Westfall, G. K. Mooney, George W. Titzell, and Henry F. Geyer. Has a membership of about seventy-five. Present officers are S. R. Miller, C. C.; Samuel Landis, V. C. C.; Samuel Kline, K. of R. & S.; G. S. Markley, M. of F.; Martin Arnold, M. of E.

Washington Camp of Patriotic Sons of America, No. 164, was organized June 5, 1872, the first officers being P. P., A. Z. Hade; P., P. B. Grable; M. of F. & C., J. J. Miller; Sec., S. J. Mountz; Treas., George W. Singiser. Number of members September 17, 1886, 106. Present officers are P. P., L. W. Pierce; P., W. M. Koller; V. P., H. R. Bowman; M. of F. & C., E. C. Rupp; Sec., E. C. Gardner; Treas., J. A. Hutton. (D. H. Barnhill of this camp is District President.)

Order of U. A. Mechanics, Integrity Council, No. 197, was organized March 18, 1869. Number of members, about eighty-three. Officers: E. E. Mountz, S. ex-C.; Daniel White, J. ex-C.; Henry Schriver, Councilor; S. A. King, V. Councilor; E. C. Gardner, Rec. Sec.; F. P. Hall, F. Sec.; S. M. Wagoner, Treas.

Knights of the Golden Eagle, Cumberland Valley Castle, No. 109, was organized July 3, 1886; membership about 100. Officers are H. H. Mercer, N. C.; T. M. Mauk, V. N. C.; Israel Flohr, P. C.; W. H. Coover, K. of E.; George Hullinger, C. of E.; John Felker, M. of R.

There have also been organized, for social and insurance benefits, *Royal Arcanum* and *Improved Order of Heptasophs*.

Allen & East Pennsborough Society for the Recovery of Stolen Horses and Mules and the Detection of Thieves, was originally organized October 22, 1836; revised and adopted June 7, 1854, and again January 7, 1865, and again February 22, 1873, and again February 22, 1886. Chartered November 14, 1870. To Dr. J. F. Stadiger belongs the credit of bringing together a number of the citizens of Allen and East Pennsborough Townships, at the public house of Frederick Kuster, in Shiremanstown, on the 24th day of September, 1836. The stealing of horses having become frequent, and the ordinary protection found insufficient, the community, impressed with these facts, met to form an association for mutual defense and assistance. Daniel Sherban was appointed president, and Levi Merkel, secretary of this meeting. A committee was appointed to draft a constitution and by-laws, consisting of Dr. J. L. Stadiger, Levi Merkel and William R. Gorgas, met October 29, 1836, agreeable to adjournment, at the house of Frederick Kuster, in Shiremanstown. Christian

Stayman was appointed president, and Levi Merkel, secretary, when Dr. Stadiger, chairman of the committee, presented a constitution and by-laws. In 1837, Samuel Shoop's horse was the first one reported stolen, and from that time up to the present, January 3, 1885, there have been only about forty stolen, less than one a year and all these recovered except six.

Officers of the Society: Dr. E. B. Brandt, president; J. O. Saxton, vice-president; C. B. Neisley, secretary; H. W. Pressel, assistant secretary; Martin Mumma, treasurer. Board of Managers: Henry Z. Zorger, 1 year; Jacob Kutz, 1 year; Martin Brinton, 1 year; John H. Bowman, 2 years; John Fought, 2 years; Samuel Mumper, 2 years. Past presidents, each elected for one year excepting where indicated: William R. Gorgas, October 22, 1836, to January 1837; Dr. J. F. Stadiger, elected January 1837; Jacob Shelly, 1838; William R. Gorgas, 1839; Michael Hoover, 1840; John Thompson, 1841 (2 years); Benjamin H. Mosser, 1843; George H. Bucher, 1844; Benjamin H. Mosser, 1845; Jacob Shelly, 1846; Christian Titzel, 1847; Benjamin H. Mosser, 1848; Lewis Hyer, 1849; Simon Oyster, 1850; Joseph Mosser, 1851; Jacob Shelly, 1852; Benjamin H. Mosser, 1853; Dr. Ira Day, 1854; Dr. R. G. Young, 1855; Levi Merkel, 1856; John C. Dunlap, 1857; George Sherbahn, 1858; Eli Grabil, 1859; John C. Dunlap, 1860; Dr. E. B. Brandt, 1861 (2 years); H. G. Moser, 1863; James Orr, 1864; J. O. Saxton, 1865; Henry R. Mosser, 1866 (2 years); William R. Gorgas, 1868; Dr. E. B. Brandt, 1869 (18 years).

Library and Literary Association.—At Mechanicsburg, in the autumn of 1871, steps were taken for the organization of "The Mechanicsburg Library and Literary Association;" and on April 4, 1872, a charter was obtained from the Legislature. Additions were made from time to time until several thousand choice volumes were secured, making it a well-spring of intellectual life to the community.

CONCLUSION.

Situated, as Mechanicsburg is, in the midst of a purely agricultural region, it is also one of the most enterprising industrial towns of its size in the State. It has become a productive center for certain kinds of manufactured goods. Among its leading industries may be mentioned the manufacture of agricultural implements; of carriages, particularly by the long-established firm of Schroeder; the iron foundry of Houck & Comstock, the inception of which dates back to 1847; and three spoke and wheel works, for the manufacture of wheels, spokes, hubs, etc., which has grown to be a distinctive industry of the town. One of these, that of Frederick Seidle, won medals at the Exposition at Philadelphia in 1876, at Paris in 1878, and at Atlanta in 1881, for superior workmanship and goods; while the shipment of any of these firms is not limited to our own country, but extends to France, Germany, Russia, England and Australia.

Mechanicsburg has, besides these industries, which we have mentioned, a planing-mill, wagon and plow works, tannery, two horse-net factories, boot and shoe factory, a brick-yard, a grain-fan factory, and a number of other industries of lesser note. It is a handsome town for residence, the center of a rich agricultural community, of growing importance as a manufacturing center, and, in every way, one of the most prosperous towns of its size in the State.

CHAPTER XVIII.

BOROUGH OF SHIPPENSBURG.

ITS FIRST SETTLEMENT—EARLY REMINISCENCES—LIST OF ORIGINAL LAND PURCHASERS — EARLY HOTELS IN SHIPPENSBURG — CHURCHES — CEMETERIES— SCHOOLS—NEWSPAPERS—BANK—SOCIETIES.

SHIPPENSBURG is the oldest town in the valley and, with the exception of York, the oldest town in the State west of the Susquehanna River. The first settlement at this place is said to have been made by twelve families in June, 1730.* In May, 1733, there were eighteen cabins in the settlement, which had, as yet, no name. These cabins were mostly at the eastern end of the town, which was the first to present the appearance of a village. "When the town was subsequently laid out by the proprietor, the point where Queen Street crosses King was selected as the centre."

The following letter, written in May, 1733, will serve to give some vivid idea of this settlement at that period:

MAY 21st, 1733.

Dear John: I wish you would see John Harris at the ferry and get him to write to the Governor to see if he can't get some guns for us; there's a good wheen of ingens about here, and I fear they intend to give us a good deal of troubbel and may do us a grate dale of harm. We was three days on our journey coming from Harrises ferry here. We could not make much speed on account of the childer; they could not get on as fast as Jane and me. I think we will like this part of the country when we get our cabbin built. I put it on a level peese of groun, near the road or path in the woods at the fut of a hill. There is a fine stream of watter that comes from a spring a half a mile south of where our cabbin is built. I would have put it near the watter but the land is lo and wet. John McCall, Alick Steen and John Rippey built there's near the stream. Hugh Rippey's daughter Mary [was] berried yesterday; this will be sad news to Andrew Simpson when he reaches Maguires bridge. He is to come over in the fall when they were to be married. Mary was a verry purty gerl; she died of a faver, and they berried her up on rising groun, north of the road or path where we made choice of a peese of groun for a graveyard. She was the furst berried there. Poor Hugh has none left now but his wife, Sam and little Isabel. There is plenty of timber south of us. We have eighteen cabbins bilt here now, and it looks [like] a town, but we have no name for it. I'll send this with John Simpson when he goes back to paxtan. Come up soon, our cabbin will be ready to go into in a week and you can go in till you get wan bilt; we have planted some corn and potatoes. Dan McGee, John Sloan and Robert More was here and left last week. * * * Tell Billy Parker to come up soon and bring Nancy with him. I know he will like the country. I forgot to tell you that Sally Brown was bit by a snaik, but she is out of danger. Come up soon. Yr. aft. brother

JAMES MAGAW.

In the year succeeding the Penn purchase of the land in the north valley, Edward Shippen obtained (in January and March, 1737) patents for two tracts of land, containing in all, 1,312 acres, on the first of which, west of the center and not far from the southeastern border stood the nucleus of the village, which thirteen years later, became, for a brief time, the county seat, and which, from that time until this has been known as Shippensburg.

Edward Shippen, the founder and proprietor of Shippensburg, was born in Boston July 9, 1703. He moved to Philadelphia, where he married Miss Mary

---

*Their names were Alexander Steen, John McCall, Richard Morrow, Garvin Morrow, John Culbertson Hugh Rippey, John Rippey, John Strain, Alexander Askey, John McAllister, David Magaw, John Johnston Soon after, Benjamin Blythe, John Campbell and Robert Caskey.

Plumley, in September, 1725. His fourth son, Edward (born February 16, 1729), became chief justice, and, by the marriage of his daughter Margaret, he was the father-in-law of Benedict Arnold. The elder Shippen removed from Philadelphia and lived in Lancaster. He died in 1781.

For some time after the buying of the land by Mr. Shippen, the population of the town seems to have increased rapidly. Three years after (1740) the first fort was built. The whites, seeing that the Indians were becoming alarmed at the rapid increase of population, met at the public house of the Widow Piper, and determined to erect a fort. A time was fixed, the people assembled, cut the logs, and erected the building on the northeastern side of the town. This was in the spring, and in the autumn of that year Gov. Thomas sent a garrison of twenty-two men to supply the fort. A well was afterward dug by soldiers and citizens within the outward inclosure of the fort, the traces of which are still visible on Burd Street, just outside of what is known as the "Fort Field." This log structure was named "Fort Franklin," probably in 1755, to distinguish it from Fort Morris, which was then in process of construction.

As early as 1740 or 1741 a log flouring-mill was built by William Leeper (then of Shippensburg) on the west bank of the stream, south of the town. In this year, 1740, the Campbells, Culbertsons, Duncans, Reynoldses, Rippeys, McCalls, Dunlaps, Pipers and Lowerys were among the leading families of the place.*

It is not certain when the town was first laid out, but it seems to have been as early as 1749. From the time of the Shippen purchase until February, 1763, the first inhabitants held their lots upon grants or permits issued by Mr. Shippen. In the above mentioned year deeds, or leases as they were then called, were issued by him, with the reservation of an annual quit-rent (of 1.66\frac{2}{3}$) on each lot of sixty-four feet four inches in breadth. After his death, in 1781, when the property descended to his sons, the quit-rent upon the remaining unsold lots was $4.

When the county of Cumberland was formed in January, 1750, the first courts of justice were held in Shippensburg. This was, indeed, "the only town in the valley," and, although it had not regularly been so appointed, it was regarded as the county seat. There were but four terms of court held in Shippensburg; the first on the 24th day of July, 1750, and the last April 24, 1751.† In this latter year the courts were removed to Carlisle (Letort's Spring), which had been chosen by the proprietors as the county seat, which action on their part caused great excitement and called forth a vigorous protest from the inhabitants of the upper end of the county. In what house the courts were held, in Shippensburg, is not known; there was, however, a public whipping post, which is said to have stood at or near the intersection of King and Queen Streets.

For some time after this period the growth of Shippensburg was slow. This was not owing to the removal of the courts, but to that terrible period of Indian depredation, which began in 1753, and ended in 1764.

Among the Indian depredations in 1757, near Shippensburg, are the following: "On the 6th of June, 1757, two men were murdered, and five taken

---

*Francis Campbell was a man of culture, a ready and forcible writer, and one of the first merchants in Shippensburg. He died in 1790. Daniel Duncan built a stone house on Lot 52, in which he kept a store and tavern. His son Stephen represented the county in the Colonial Legislature, and was at one time the heaviest tax-payer in the place. The others were names of prominence, but there is not a male descendant of any one remaining in Shippensburg to-day. See sketch by late Hon. John McCurdy.

†This date is, by an error in the records, marked 1730, which make the four terms at Shippensburg stand thus: July 24, 1750; October 23, 1750; January 22, 1750; April 24, 1750. But those of July and October are the first on the records, besides which the next regular term in Carlisle, July 23, 1751, follows naturally, if we correct the error.

prisoners, by a party of Indians, a short distance east of where Burd's Run crosses the road leading from Shippensburg to Middle Spring. The names of the killed were John McKean and John Agnew, and those of the captured, Hugh Black, William Carson, Andrew Brown, James Ellis and Alexander McBride. All but Ellis, it appears, made their escape. These escaped prisoners stated that Ellis was the only one who remained, as a white girl, whom this band had captured in Maryland, previously becoming exhausted, had been killed and scalped by them on the evening before they made their escape. On the 18th of July, 1757, a band of savages surprised a party who were harvesting in John Cessna's field, about a mile east of Shippensburg. They approached the field from the east through the woods, which bounded it on that side, and, when within short range, fired, killing Dennis O'Neiden and John Kirkpatrick; then rushing forward they captured Mr. Cessna, his two grandsons, and a son of John Kirkpatrick, and made their escape with their prisoners. There were other hands in the field at that time, but a thicket which stood between them and the Indians concealed them from view. The next day, in a field belonging to Joseph Steenson, nine persons were killed and four taken prisoners."

When the town was laid out, the old Indian path became the main road, and was chosen for the location of King Street. Three-fourths of the residents of the town, in 1751, lived upon that portion of this street, which lies between Washington Street and the top of the hill west of the toll-gate.

In the spring of 1755 the road-cutters were at work opening a road west. Braddock's army was in the field, and it was proposed to make Shippensburg the base of supplies.

On June 14, 1755, Charles Swain writes to Gov. Morris from Shippensburg: "I arrived at this place on Monday, and judge there are sufficient buildings for storing the provisions without erecting any; these will want but a small repair, except the fastings, and to be had on easy terms, as they are all left, to be possessed by any one who will inhabit them. The owners do not seem inclined to take any advantage of their being wanted on this occasion. I find not above two pastures here; these but mean as to grass, from drought; but there is a fine range of forage for upward of four miles in the woods, quite to the foot of the South Mountain; also a good run of water, that the cattle will be continually improving after they come here. I shall use the methods practiced here of keeping their beasts together; have a constant watch on them; daily see to them myself. I can find but little cellaring here for securing the pork, but have pitched on a shady and dry spot in the woods for making a cellar for what I can not store in such cellars as are in the town. There are no bricks here, and little lime at present, so the making of ovens would be difficult, and, if made of clay, then there would be some iron wanting. The principal expense which seems to attend the magazine here will be the hire of some person or persons to attend the cattle, also to watch the stores and pork, etc. * * The coopers in these parts have plantations, and they but occasionally work at their trades * * The mills, also, here have no bolting cloths, so that they make only a coarse flour." In another letter, dated July, 4, 1755 (just five days before Braddock's defeat), Mr. Shippen says: "I shall give orders to Mr. Burd's servant, a cooper, to take charge of some cattle, as Mr. Swain shall direct. The cattle are provided with a range of pasture. But the place which shall be agreed upon by the General (Braddock) for the magazine, ought to be protected by at least twenty or thirty soldiers; and there should be a blockade built, otherwise they (the Indians) may easily destroy the cattle, for they can march through the woods, undiscovered, within twenty miles of Shippensburg, and they may come these twenty miles one way on a path, leaving Jacob Pyatt's near Tuscarora Mountain, on the right hand and see but two houses till they are within two miles of my place."

Within a few days after the writing of this letter Braddock was defeated, and the ominous danger-cloud which had threatened the inhabitants of the valley, burst.

At Shippensburg they began immediately to erect another fort. This fort was called Fort Morris, after the Governor of the province. In a letter written by Charles Swain to him, July 30, 1755, he says: "A defeat is, I believe, beyond doubt. I suppose that the people will now come fast into these parts, and shall use all expedition in forwarding a fort. I have pitched on a piece of ground of Mr. Shippen's, and the timber about here is all his; therefore should be glad he was to write about it, if your Honor thought proper, that there may be no afterclaps on his part." On November 2, of this year (1755), James Bard writes to Edward Shippen, at Lancaster: "We are in great confusion here at present. * * * This town is full of people, they being all moving in with their families—five or six families in a house. We are in great want of ammunition; but with what we have we are determined to give the enemy as warm a reception as we can. Some of our people had been taken prisoners by this party, and have made their escape from them and come in to us this morning. * * * We have 100 men working at Fort Morris every day."

He also wishes that they would send guns—"great guns, small arms and ammunition"—from Philadelphia. This fort seems to have been completed in 1756.

"It stood," says Hon. John McCurdy, "on the rocky hill at the western end of the town. The brick schoolhouse now standing there, which was built some [forty-two] years ago, stands within the boundaries of the fort, the foundation of a part of which can still be traced." The walls were built of small stone, with mortar which became hard, and were about two feet in thickness. The roof and timbers of the building were removed before 1821, and the remaining portion of the walls were torn down in 1836.*

In the sudden unslaught of the Indians, and the panic which ensued, in 1763, there was, on the 25th of July, 1,384 of these fugitives in Shippensburg, of whom 301 were men, 345 women, and 738 children, many of whom were obliged to lie in barns, cellars and sheds, the dwelling houses being all crowded. Fort Franklin had, before this time, we are told, been enlarged with additions, and during the Indian troubles of this period the various sections were occupied by private families. It was afterward allowed to decay, and was torn down about 1790.

At the time of these Indian troubles in 1763, and previous to it, various parties, and, among others, those living around Shippensburg, sent piteous appeals to the Government for aid, but they seem often to have been powerless, or to have turned a deaf ear to the supplications of these border inhabitants.

In February, 1763, Mr. Shippen began to issue the first deeds or leases to purchasers, and to those who had previously settled upon the lots. The list of original purchasers, with the number of the lot is as follows:

*On the 19th of March, 1764, the Indians carried off five people from within nine miles of Shippensburg, and shot one man through the body. The enemy, supposed to be eleven in number, were pursued successfully by about 100 provincials The houses of John Stewart, Adam Simms, James McCammon, William Baird, James Kelley, Stephen Caldwell and John Boyd were burnt. These people lost all their grain, which they had threshed out with the intention to send it for sale further down among the inhabitants.—*Gordon's History of Pennsylvania*, p. 624.

BOROUGH OF SHIPPENSBURG.

1 Samuel Montgomery.
2 David Magaw.
3, 4 Francis Campble.
5 Peter Miller.
6, 7 William Piper.
8 John Cunningham.
9 Anthony Maule.
10, 11 Richard Long.
12, 13. 14 Francis Campble.
15 Alexander Sterrit.
16 William Cowan.
17 John Brady.
18 William Reynolds.
19, 20 James McCall.
21 Robert Chambers.
22 John Cesna.
23 William Hendricks.
24 George Ross.
25 Andrew Wilkins.
26, 27 William Barr.
28 Andrew Wilkins.
29 Thomas Finley.
30 Humphrey Montgomery.
31 Thomas Finley.
32 Daniel Duncan.
33 Isaac Miller.
34 John Montgomery.
35, 36 Samuel Perry.
37 John Corbet.
38 Daniel Duncan.
39 Blank.
40 Daniel Duncan.
41 Archibald Flemming.
42 James Lowery.
43 Andrew Keith.
44 James McClintock.
45 William Leeper.
46 Blank.
47 David McKnight.
48 William Barr.
49 William Sutherland.
50, 51 John Miller.
52 Martin Holderbaum.
53 Samuel Tate.
54 William Brookins.
55 Samuel Duncan.
56 Matthew Adams.
57 William McConnel.
58 Blank.
59, 60 Meeting-house, graveyard.
61 Richard Long.
62 Henry Davis.
63. 64 Edward Lacey.
65 Archibald Mahan.
66 James McKeeny.
67 Jacob Kiser.
68 Blank.
69 Dr. Robert McCall.
70 Blank.
71 George Taylor.
72, 73 Andrew McLean.
74 Church lot—free.
75 Benjamin Coppenheffer.
76 Robert Reed.
77 Joseph Campbell.
78 John Reynolds.
79 Jacob Milliron.
80 Valentine Haupt.
81 Simon Rice.
82 Adam Carnahan.
83 James Reynolds.
84 Robert Peebles.
85 Anthony Maule.
86 James Dunlap.
87 Gideon Miller.
88 Andrew Boyd.
89 Joseph Parks.
90 Tristram Miller.
91 John Redott.
92 Anthony Maule.
93 James Reynolds.
94 George Eiley.
95 William Duncan.
96 Anthony Maule.
97 John Mains.
98 Robert Brown.
99 John Heap. Meadow lot.
100, 101 Samuel Rippey.
102 Lucinda Piper.
103 Samuel Rippey.
104 Robert Peebles.
105 John Smith.
106 Anthony Maule.
107 Johnson Smith.
108 James Piper.
109 Samuel Rippey.
110 William Wilson.
111 Margaret McDaniel.
112, 113 Benjamin Kilgore.
114 Blank.
115 Anthony Maule.
116 William Campbell.
117, 118 James McCall.
119 George McCandless.
120, 121 Daniel Duncan.
122 Blank.
123 Blank.
124 David Ellis.
125 John Montgomery.
126 James Russell.
127 Blank.
128 John Montgomery.
129, 130, 131 Blank.
132 Thomas Atkinson.
133 Blank.
134 Robert Beatty.
135 Samuel Perry.
136 John Carnahan.
137 Samuel Perry.
138 John Cessna.
139 Alexander Askey.
140 John Mahan.
141 to (and including) 148 Blank.
149 Alexander Johnston.
150, 151 John Dietrick.
152 Abraham Beidleman.
153 Anthony Maule.
154 Jacob Lightner.
155 John Gregory.
156 George McCandless.
157 Jacob Kiser.
158 John Davenport.
159 Joseph Mitchel.
160 Thomas Moore.
161 John Dietrick.
162, 163 Frederick Chiploy.
164 John Stall.
165 Christian Gish

166 Andrew Patterson.
167, 168 Blank.
169 Casper Sallsgibber.
170 David Duncan.
171 Christian Gish.
172 Frederick Sheval.
173 Walter Welsh.

The place in early days was sometimes spoken of as "Shippen's Farm." As a specimen of the deeds, an indenture made on the 13th of March, 1764, "between Edward Shippen of the Borough of Lancaster, of the one part, & Archibald Machan, of the other," conveys, subject to the quit rent "a certain lot of ground Scituate within a certain new town called Shippensburg, in the county of Cumberland, containing in breadth sixty-four feet four inches, & in length 457, 4 inches. No 65, Bounded on the South by King Street & on the west by Lot No 60 granted or intended to be granted to James Mackeney, & on the east by Lot No 64 Granted to Edward Lacey & on the north by a fourteen foot alley, &c. (Signed) Edward Shippen."

In the Revolutionary war Shippensburg was prompt to respond to the call for men. Capt. Matthew Henderson, at the beginning of the war, raised a company of 104 men in Shippensburg, and another, but not a full one, was raised by Capt. Mathew Scott. It is said that at this time there "was scarcely an able bodied man in the place who was not enrolled in one or the other of these organizations."

In December, 1775, Capt. William Rippey, of Shippensburg, enlisted a company, of which he was commissioned captain January 9, 1776, which became one of the companies of the Sixth Regiment, commanded by Col. Irvine. With the brigade to which it shortly afterward belonged it was sent to Canada, where, at Trois Rivieres, Capt. Rippey with his colonel and most of the men were captured. Rippey made his escape, and after the war resumed keeping the Branch Hotel in Shippensburg—down to the time of his death in 1819.

Until 1790 there was no postoffice in Shippensburg. Previous to this time the people depended simply upon private carriers. But by an act of Congress in 1788, "posts" were established for the regular transportation of mails between Philadelphia and Pittsburgh by the route of Lancaster, York, Carlisle, Chambersburg and Bedford, from which mails were dispatched once in each fortnight. The first postmaster, at the establishment of the first "post" in Shippensburg, May 13, 1790, was Robert Peebles.

During the "Whiskey Insurrection" of 1794 Gen. Washington passed through Shippensburg, at which place he remained for some portion of the day. It is said the citizens gathered to pay him their respects, but others, a few days after his visit, in order to show their disapprobation of the use of a military force to suppress the insurrection, during the hours of night, erected a "liberty pole" on the corner where the council house now stands. This pole was afterward cut down at night by the opposite party—or by parties "to whom its presence was objectionable."

Although Shippensburg is the oldest town in the valley, it was not incorporated as a borough until January, 1819.

The population of the place at various times was as follows: In 1800, it contained less than 800 inhabitants; in 1810, 1,159; in 1820, 1,410; in 1830, 1,308; in 1840, 1,473; and at present about 2,500. Although it has not increased rapidly in population, the town in other respects has improved greatly within the last quarter of a century.

EARLY HOTELS IN SHIPPENSBURG.

The earliest public house in Shippensburg was, in all probability, that of "The Widow Piper." It existed as early as 1735, when a number of persons living in the vicinity met to protest against the new road running through

"the barrens."* Here, for many years, the public business was transacted, and in it, it is possible, the first courts were held.†

"A brewery was started at a very early day in the building now known as the Black Bear Hotel. This building was erected for that purpose, and the business of brewing was carried on there for a number of years; at first by Adam Carnahan, and afterward by James Brown. This house was subsequently converted into a tavern, and was first kept by a man named John Saylor, who was succeeded by Jacob Raum, he by John Snyder, and he, in 1821, by Jacob Hartzell. ‡ We find that this hotel was known as the "Black Bear" as early or prior to 1792; for in the records of the court, August, 1792, there is a petition for a "road from the sign of the Bear in King Street past Reynold's mill to Middle Spring Church," which was granted. And, among public papers owned lately by the late Jason Eby, kindly furnished to us by Christian Humrich, Esq., we find the original petition presented to the court in August, 1792, as follows: "The humble Petition of Jacob Rahm, of Shippensburg, Humbly Sheweth—That your Petitioner, having provided a Commodious House & accomodations for Travellers in the Town of Shippensburg, Humbly prays your Honorable Court to grant him a licence for the purpose of keeping a house of intertainment in the said town," etc. §

There was also a hotel in Shippensburg prior to 1792, known by the name of the "Black Horse." For in another petition to this term of court (August, 1792) from Patrick Cochran, we find "that the petitioner hath lately rented and now occupies the commodious and long accustomed public house known by the name of the Black Horse, in Shippensburg, where he is well provided with liquor and all other necessaries for a public house, and also has had many repairs made for the better acoommodation of travellers." There was also another hotel in Shippensburg, in and prior to 1792, know by the name of the "King of Prussia." The application is by Conrad Beamer, presented at the same term of court (August, 1792), who prays that "Whereas your petitioner continues to keep the old accustomed and commodious tavern known by the name of the 'King of Prussia,' in Shippensburg," that the court will recommend him to his Excellency the Governor for license to continue a publichouse in the said place. One other petition is made, also August, 1792, by George McCandless, who "hath kept a house of entertainment in the house where he now lives, the preceding year, and is desirious of continuing the same." And this is all we know of the "taverns" of ye Town of Shippensburg," before the beginning of this century.

Following the Indian moccasin, "when the days of the pack-horse had passed away, the Black Bear Hotel became the principal stopping place for wagons engaged in the transportation of merchandise to the West." Shippensburg was then lively with this traffic to and from Pittsburgh and Philadelphia. But the Conestoga teams, with their noise and bustle, have passed away. They have ceased "to collect nightly in groups around the house," and the recollection of them, even, has grown dim.‖

Sixty years ago there were six wagon-maker shops, each employing a number of hands, and nine blacksmith shops all busily employed.

---

* Historical Discourse (Middle Spring) by Rev. S. S. Wylie.
† There is, in the records a bill of sale from Jannet Piper, of Shippensburg, innkeeper, in 1755.
‡ Hon. John McCurdy's sketch in Wing.
§ The petitioner of this is recommended by John Heap, a handsome signature, Jacob Blocher, James Cissire,(?) Samuel Quigley, James Moore, Patrick Cochran and Samuel Rippey; the latter by John Scott, Thomas Wilson, Robert Colwell, Samuel Colwell, Alexander Beatty, William Beil, John White, Samuel Peebles, R. McCall, William Brookins, William Burr, John Heap and Samuel Mitchell, "residents of Shippen·burg and parts adjacent."
‖ Many of these wagons were made at Shippensburg and Loudon, and this was one of the most prominent industries of the place.

CHURCHES.

The Scotch Irish Presbyterians who settled at Shippensburg belonged to the church at Middle Spring, so that no church of that denomination was for some time erected. Mr. Shippen and his agents, and the Goverment employes at Forts Morris and Franklin, located at Shippensburg, were Episcopalians, and "an effort was made to establish an Episcopal Church. This scheme, however, never promised to be successful, and when the agents withdrew, was abandoned."*

In 1767 Lot 59 was conveyed by Mr. Shippen to Francis Campble in trust, for a *Presbyterian Church,* "with yearly rent of one penny sterling," and a log house was erected about 1768, but little used, and was turned into a schoolhouse, neglected, and finally torn down. The adjoining Lot 60 had previously been set apart and used for the burial of the dead. There was early a Reformed Associate Presbyterian Church in Shippensburg. "Lot 216 on the village plot was, June 2, 1794, deeded by the Shippen brothers to this church, and a stone meeting-house was erected on it about 1797, which was subsequently enlarged," and is still standing. Its pastors were Rev. James Walker, ordained September 4, 1799 (of congregations of Shippensburg and Chambersburg, giving to each half his time), resigned August 8, 1820. Rev. Thomas Strong, ordained (over the two churches) October 23, 1821. at which time a union was formed between his congregation in Shippensburg and the members of the church at Middle Spring, who resided in or near the village. On February 18, 1824, Rev. Henry R. Wilson, D. D., was installed and remained till October, 1839. He was born near Gettysburg in 1780; graduated at Dickinson College under Nesbit; was chosen professor of languages in that institution in 1806. He preached in the First Presbyterian Church at Carlisle, as colleague with Dr. Davidson. In 1814 accepted call at Silver's Spring, from which place he went to Shippensburg. He died in Philadelphia March 22, 1849.

He was followed by Rev. James Harper in 1840, who served till May 8, 1870, and was succeeded, in 1872, by Rev. W. W. Taylor, succeeded, in May, 1875, by Rev. W. A. McCarrell.

In April, 1839, a suit was brought for the exclusive right to the church property by a few Associate Reform members still remaining in the town, which was successful. The little society gradually dwindled away, and the church building was leased to the borough for school purposes for ninety-nine years, for $1,000. When this case was decided, the Presbyterian Congregation purchased a lot in another portion of the town and erected the neat brick edifice in which they worship. A new church is now being erected.

Methodist Church.—The first church was built in 1790. It was a log structure, one story high, and stood on the northwest end of the lot where the old brick church stands. At first the congregation was small, but it grew in strength and importance, and has included in its membership many of the most prominent residents of the town. In 1825, a new brick church was erected on the southwest end of the old lot. It was used about half a century. The present church, on King Street, was built in 1875.

German Reformed and Lutheran.—Some time during the latter part of the last century a lot located on the southeast corner of Orange and Queen Streets was selected as a place of burial by the Lutheran and Reformed denominations, and on it a log church was erected, which was used until about 1812.

---

*Until the (Presbyterian) organization was effected, the Episcopal element was, perhaps, dominant in the borough, through the influence of Mr. Shippen, the proprietor, who was connected with that denomination."—*Nevin's Churches of the Valley,* p. 155.

BOROUGH OF SHIPPENSBURG.

In about that year a brick church was erected, where the German Reformed Church now stands, and was at first used as a place of worship by both congregations. After some time the two congregations separated, each erecting a church edifice of its own.

A brick church was built by the denomination known as the *Church of God* about 1828, which was torn down in 1870, when the present one was erected.

In 1868 the *United Brethren* built their present church on North Penn Street.

CEMETERIES.

The burial places of Shippensburg having become full of the bodies of those who, during more than a century of its existence, had taken up their abode "in the dark house and narrow bed" in the various inclosures. A new burial place, known as the "Spring Hill Cemetery," was incorporated January 18, 1861, and twelve acres of land, which were purchased for that purpose, were laid out into lots. We may mention that the first burial in these grounds was that of Robert McFarland, who had contracted a fever in the army, and that of thirty-two soldiers who served in the late war are buried beneath its sod.

SCHOOLS.

There are nine public schools in Shippensburg, which are taught for eight months during the year; but the main educational institution is "The Cumberland Valley State Normal School," which was chartered in 1870 and opened on April 15, 1873, with a registered list of 300 pupils. Its cornerstone was laid on May 31, 1871. The building, which is about one-fourth of a mile north of town, is a handsome architectural design, and is situated on a commanding eminence, surrounded by beautiful and spacious grounds, tastefully laid out. It was erected at a cost of over $125,000.

NEWSPAPERS.

There have been ten papers published in Shippensburg since the formation of the town. One, the "*Valley Spirit*," was, about 1846, moved to Chambersburg, where it is still published. Another, the *Valley Sentinel*, was bought by Henry K. Peffer, Esq., who moved it to Carlisle, where it is still published. The present papers in Shippensburg are the Shippensburg *News*, established in 1844, and the Shippensburg *Chronicle*, started in 1875.

BANK.

There is one National Bank in Shippensburg, which was established under the title "The First National Bank of Shippensburg," in 1866.

SOCIETIES.

Cumberland Valley Lodge, No. 315, F. & A. M., was instituted February 18, 1858, with following named charter members: Rev. James Colder, Rev. F. A. Rupley, Henry Ruby, Sr., Jacob Heck, John S. Blair, John Wunderlich, R J. Lawton and Rev. D. A. Laverty. Present membership, twenty-nine. Present officers: John Wolf, W. M.; J. M. Gardner, S. W.; S. M. Houston, J. W.; S. C. Henderson. Treas.; W. M. Geesaman, Sec.

Lincoln Lodge, No. 38, A. Y. M. (colored), instituted in 1868; has about eighteen members. Present officers are Henry Johnston, W. M.; George A. Barnes, Jr., S. W.; Edward Arthur, J. W.; William A. Barnett, Sec.; Thomas Miller, Treas.

Valley Encampment, No. 34, I. O. O. F., was chartered June 22, 1846, with charter members William F. Carey, John C. Altick, William B. Cochran,

John Fisher, J. H. M. Peebles, John A. Clippinger and John Bender. Present membership thirty-eight. Present officers: G. F. Cressler, C. P.; G. S. Clark, H. P.; Elmer E. Shelley, S. W.; R. W. Hockersmith, J. W.; J. K. L. Mackey, Scribe; W. J. Angle, Treas.

Cumberland Lodge, No. 90, I. O. O. F., was organized December 12, 1843, the charter members being William F. Carey, B. F. Irvin, William H. Hoover, John McCurdy and John C. Altick. Present membership, seventy-two. Present officers: George W. Noftsker, N. G.; J. E. Wolfe, V. G.; John A. Fleming, Treas.; J. K. L. Mackey, Sec.

Mount Alto Lodge, G. U. O. F., No. 1941 (colored), was organized in 1879 with about twenty members. Discontinued working in 1885.

Royal Arcanum.—There was also organized, August 24, 1886, for social and insurance benefits, a council of the Royal Arcanum.

CHAPTER XIX.

BOROUGH OF SHIREMANSTOWN.

LOCALITY—ORIGIN OF NAME—CHURCHES—SOCIETIES—MISCELLANEOUS.

SHIREMANSTOWN is situated on the main road leading from Carlisle to New Cumberland, known as the Simpson Ferry Road, and within a short distance of the Cumberland Valley Railroad in a fertile and highly improved portion of the county.

It is twelve miles east of Carlisle and five miles west of Harrisburg. It derives its name from Daniel Shireman, one of the first residents and landowners of most of the place upon which the town is built, and who kept a hotel there for a period of some years. The first house was built by John Davis about 1812 or 1814. It was afterward used as a hotel, and still later as a store, which was the earliest one kept in the town.

Shiremanstown was incorporated as a borough in August, 1874.

CHURCHES.

There are three churches. The first was originally a frame building, one story high, erected as a union house of worship in 1838, but since enlarged and remodeled by the *Church of God*.

United Brethren.—This society erected their church in 1854. It is two stories high, the lower portion being built of limestone, and the upper part of brick.

Messiah's Church.—This is also two stories in height; was erected in 1867, and is the handsomest church edifice in the town. The seats and doors are made of polished chestnut. Its bell, cast in 1787, is the oldest one now in Cumberland County.

SOCIETIES.

Irene Lodge, No. 425, K. of P., instituted in March, 1874, has a membership of about fifty-seven. The officers are D. Y. Zimmerman, P. C.; D. C. Eberly, C. C.; William Welty, V. C.; John G. Bentz, P.; L. O Sheaffer, K. of R. and S.; W. H. Zearing, M. of F.; J. Morris Miller, M. of E.; J. E. Straining, M. of A.

COOK TOWNSHIP.

Beneficial Society of Shiremanstown was organized in 1841, with the following officers: William R. Gorgas, president; Dr. William Mateer, vice-president; Levi Merkel, treasurer; Daniel Shelley, secretary. Membership numbers about seventy. Present officers are Dr. W. S. Bruckart, president; Christian Stoner, vice-president ; David C. Mohler, secretary; Joseph A. Willis, treasurer; A. H. Dill, financial secretary.

MISCELLANEOUS.

The borough, besides its warehouses, wagon shops and stores, has also a large, commodious, brick schoolhouse, built in 1868 by Lower Allen Township before the borough was incorporated.

The Cumberland Valley Railroad passes through the borough from east to west, and does considerable business at this point.

CHAPTER XX.

COOK TOWNSHIP.

COOK TOWNSHIP, at present the youngest township in Cumberland County, was formed from the southern part of Pennsylvania in the year 1872. The whole of it is mountain land, well timbered, and containing at places large quantities of valuable iron ore. There are several streams in the township, the most important of which is the Mountain Creek, which, after being formed by the junction of two smaller streams near Pine Grove, flows in a slightly northeasterly direction through the mountainous portion of Dickinson Township; then almost north, through South Middleton, until it empties into the Yellow Breeches Creek.

The State road from Carlisle to Gettysburg passes through the wild and uncultivated mountain scenery of this township, as does also the Harrisburg & Gettysburg Railroad, which was originally built, in 1869–70, as the South Mountain Road, from Carlisle to Pine Grove, by the South Mountain Iron Company, for the development of their extensive property at that place. In 1883, under the name of the Gettysburg & Harrisburg Railroad, it was extended from Hunters Run, a station on the former road, to the celebrated "Round Top," on the battle-field, three miles beyond Gettysburg. It was opened for travel on April 21, 1884.* J. C. Fuller was the first president and William H. Woodward the first general superintendent, secretary and treasurer, a position which he still holds. The road has established a popular and pleasant park near Pine Grove Furnace, in the midst of the wild mountains, and which is one of the most attractive places of its kind which is to be found in the county.

The chief property, however, of the company, in the township, is the Pine Grove Furnace and the Laurel Forge, with about 25,000 acres of land, some small part of which, however, is in Adams County. These Pine Grove Iron Works are located on Mountain Creek about ten miles north of Mount Holly Springs. It is not known when the first furnace was erected at this place. The tract of about 150 acres was originally granted by Thomas and Richard

---

* In August of this first year, over 50,000 people were carried over the road in ten days to the encampment of the National Guards of Pennsylvania at Gettysburg.

Penn, in July, 1762, to Samuel Pope, and on the 7th of October of that year it was conveyed by him to George Stevenson, who was a partner at that time in the Carlisle Iron Works, at Boiling Springs. George Stevenson was born in Dublin in 1718, educated at Trinity College and came to America about the middle of the last century. He was a prominent man—a judge at one time of the counties of York and Cumberland by a commission in 1755 under the reign of George II. He was later a prominent lawyer at Carlisle. In connection with William Thompson (afterward a general), and George Ross, a signer of the Declaration of Independence, he became a large land-owner and manufacturer of iron, and erected, in 1764, a furnace and forge (known as Mary Ann Furnace) in York County. In 1769 he removed to Carlisle and engaged in the iron business at Mount Holly. He married Mary Cookson, the widow of Thomas Cookson, the deputy surveyor who laid out the town of Carlisle. In 1772 George Stevenson conveyed this Pine Grove property to Findlay McGrew, in which deed it is described "as being the same tract as was surveyed by William Lyon, Esq., and whereon the said Findlay McGrew hath lately erected a saw mill," etc.; and in the year following, McGrew conveyed said tract to Jacob Simons, who, in December, 1782, conveyed it, together with another tract which he had improved, to Michael Ege and the two Thornbergs, Thomas and Joseph. It is in this deed that the property is called the Pine Grove Iron-works—a name by which it has been known ever since. Michael Ege continued to own this property until his death in 1815, after which it was confirmed, by proceedings in partition, to his son Peter Ege, since which time it has passed through various hands, until it came into the possession of the present owners.

The only postoffice in the township is called Pine Grove Furnace, and the only iron way is the South Mountain Railroad, spoken of fully above.

CHAPTER XXI.

DICKINSON TOWNSHIP.

DICKINSON TOWNSHIP was formed from a portion of West Pennsborough Township, April 17, 1785. At its formation it included the townships of Penn and Cook, and in all probability extended from South Middleton on the east to Newton on the west; and from the "great road leading from Harrisburg to Chambersburg on the north," to the Adams County line on the south. It is a rectangular township, now bounded by South Middleton (east), Penn (west), West Pennsborough (north), Adams County (south), and is about twelve miles long, north and south, and about five miles wide. The character of its soil is, in the north, undulating limestone land, which portion is covered with fine farms in a high state of cultivation. The southern portion, beginning at the Yellow Breeches Creek, is sand and gravel land, which industry has made productive; while the extreme southern section of the township is a mountain region, covered with a light growth of oak, chestnut and yellow pine. The Gettysburg & Harrisburg Railroad and the South Mountain branch, also the Mountain Creek pass through this southern section, while the Harrisburg & Potomac Railroad, running almost parallel with the Yellow Breeches Creek, passes through the center of the township.

DICKINSON TOWNSHIP.

The original settlers of this township were Scotch-Irish. They seemed to have settled first upon the Yellow Breeches Creek, upon which stream they purchased from the Proprietaries large tracts of land. Many of the descendants of these original settlers still live upon those lands.

One of the earliest land-owners in this section was Michael Ege, the elder, who came into Cumberland County at a very early period. He owned a tract which extended from somewhere about Boiling Springs, to what is now Hay's Station, on the Harrisburg & Potomac Railroad, a distance of about twelve miles. The bulk of this land lay between what is known as the first and second range of hills along the the South Mountain, which, in Dickinson, extend down on the north side of the mountain a considerable distance into the valley, at some places as far north as the Yellow Breeches Creek. This property was distributed among his children, but, with the exception of the Carlisle Ironworks, the whole of it passed out of their hands in the first generation. A large portion of this Ege tract, perhaps all of that which went to Mrs. Wilson, a daughter of Michael Ege, a considerable time after her death, and after much of it had been improved and made into farms by the purchasers, was claimed by Mrs. Wilson's heirs. This claim gave rise to very protracted litigation. It involved the title to perhaps a hundred farms or pieces of property in what is now Penn Township. After various conflicting decisions it was finally decided in favor of the purchasers and against the Wilson heirs.

Among the early settlers of the township were the Houcks, or two families of Houcks. They owned what was known as the Salome Forge. The Galbreaths were an old family, as were also the Weakleys and the Lees. The Weakleys probably settled in this section as early as 1732, and owned large tracts of land four generations ago, including that now known as Barnitz Mill. Another branch of the Weakley family settled just above the Cumberland Furnace, and owned the land about Spring Mills, now called Huntsdale, and considerable farm land north, extending to the Dickinson Presbyterian Church, which is built upon land donated for that purpose by (William L. Weakley) one of the family.

Three generations ago the Lees, *(four brothers, Warren, Thomas, Holiday and George), lived on the Walnut Bottom Road. The easternmost of these farms was afterwards owned by the late Sterritt Woods. These men were large, fine physical specimens of men, social, and who were fond "of the chace dancing, fiddling and hospitality." Another old family were the Woods'. There was a large cluster of them in what is now the central portion of Dickinson Township. They owned large farms, probably in all about 1,000 acres. Of this family, within the recollection of men living, was Richard Woods, Squire, and Capt. Samuel Woods, who is said to have been the determined juror who was instrumental in acquitting Prof. McClintock when he was tried for inciting the riots in Carlisle. Capt. Woods was a large man, who weighed probably over 200 pounds, walked always with a stoop, was quiet, almost forbidding in his manner, but was in reality one of the most benevolent and kindest men that ever lived. Another, David Glenn, came from the north of Newville, and settled in this portion of the county in about 1825. He owned from the Walnut Bottom Road out to the Yellow Breeches Creek. He is described as a strict Covenanter.

Gen. Thomas C. Miller came (about 1830) and remained in the township until his death. He was the father of William H. Miller, Esq., a prominent

---

*The Lee family, of Dickinson Township, acquired the title to their lands by the old English ceremony of livery of seisen—or feudal investiture, the only instance of this kind which we know of in Cumberland County.

lawyer, still well remembered, of Carlisle. He had been a volunteer officer in the war of 1812, fought at Lundy's Lane and along the Canada border, after which he settled in Adams County, when he was elected to the Senate in the days when Thaddeus Stevens was a member of that body. He then came to Cumberland County and bought the Cumberland Furnace property, quite close to Huntsdale, just on the eastern border of Penn Township. He was a tall, venerable, fine looking man, proud, a good talker, and possessed of unusual ability. During the days of slavery, the South Mountain afforded a hiding place for colored people who attempted to escape from bondage, and Dickinson Township received its full share of these fugitives. In the year 1859, just before the breaking out of the Rebellion, occurred the last case of this kind. Three negroes, John Butler, wife and child, came in 1859 to reside in Dickinson Township, and lived in a small house near the Spruce Run. They had been slaves in Maryland, but had been manumitted by will at the death of their owner. The estate, as it turned out afterward, was insolvent, and the administrators sent their deputies to capture the human property, who were regarded as assets of the estate. At about midnight on the 12th of June, these negroes were stolen from their homes. Prompt measures were taken by the citizens of the township to discover the perpetrators of the crime, and among these, Richard Woods and John Morrison were particularly active. Myers, the principal kidnaper, was arrested just before reaching the Maryland line, and brought to Carlisle for trial.

This incident gave rise to an important case, in which the question was whether they had a right to invade the free soil of Pennsylvania for such a purpose. Judge Watts and A. Brady Sharpe were concerned with the district attorney for the commonwealth, while able counsel, among whom were Bradley Johnston and Johnston Meredith, represented the rights of the State of Maryland. Myers was convicted, but the sentence was suspended and the colored people returned, when they went back to Dickinson Township, where they have since lived. In a previous case, where the slaves of one Oliver passed through the township, one of its citizens was made to pay dearly for his having given them shelter during the night.

There are no villages in the township, and very little manufacturing, as its interests are almost purely of an agricultural character. There are stores at several points, and grist-mills and saw-mills sufficient to supply local demands.

The hotel known as the Stone Tavern was built by James Moore about 1788, and was at one time known, we are told, as the "Cumberland Hall Tavern."

CHURCHES.

There are but two churches in the township; one near Barnitz's Hills, which belongs to the *Methodist Protestant* congregation, and which was erected originally about 1844, but has since been rebuilt and improved; and another church located on Spruce Run. Most of the people of Dickinson attend services in the churches at Carlisle or in Penn Township.

After the Seceder Church was built in Carlisle in 1802, in which Rev. Francis Pringle, from Ireland, was pastor, the Woodburns, the Rosses, the Moores, and a number more of the most substantial and leading families of the congregation, lived at a considerable distance in the country, and for their convenience it was deemed expedient to provide a preaching place in the country, where public services could be occasionally held. Mr. Moore, of Dickinson Township, donated an acre from the corner of his farm, about six or seven miles from Carlisle, as a site for a meeting-house and grave-yard, and here, in

1809 or 1810, a stone church was built. We are informed it was nearly opposite the Stone Tavern. The building, which was but a preaching station does not now exist.

SCHOOLS, ETC.

The common schools, twelve in number, are well sustained and attended, and are taught by efficient teachers. Besides the regular terms of six months, private schools are also maintained in some of the districts during the summer months.

The postoffices in Dickinson Township are Mooredale, Barnitz and Uriah. There is one station on the Gettysburg & Harrisburg main line named Starners, and a station on the South Mountain Branch, called Henry Clay.

CHAPTER XXII.

EAST PENNSBOROUGH TOWNSHIP AND BOROUGH OF CAMP HILL.

EAST PENNSBOROUGH TOWNSHIP was originally a portion of Pennsborough Township, which, at that time, embraced nearly all of the territory which is now Cumberland County. As early as 1737 it began to be called east and west, and shortly afterward north and south parts of Pennsborough, but it was not until 1845, when the latter were dropped, that the division of the township into East and West Pennsborough seems to have been definitely recognized. The little fragment of it which now remains as the extreme northeastern portion of the county, and which still retains its maiden name, is bounded by the Blue or Kittatinny Mountains on the north, the Susquehanna River on the East, Lower Allen on the south, and on the west by Hampden Township.

EARLY HISTORY.

At a very early period the Shawanese Indians settled, with the consent of William Penn and the Susquehanna Indians, upon this west side of the Susquehanna River. They became disaffected, and under two chiefs, Shingas and Capt. Jacobs (killed afterward at Kittanning), they took up the hatchet against the whites, assigning as their reason for so doing that satisfaction had not been made to them for lands surveyed into the Proprietary's manor on the Conodoguinet Creek. About 1728 they removed to the Ohio River, and placed themselves under the protection of the French. The whites began to settle in this (Paxton) manor, which embraced all the portion of the township south of the Conodoguinet Creek, about 1730. Most, if not all of them, were Scotch-Irish, and after 1736, when this land was finally purchased from the Indians, the influx of immigrants was rapid. One year later (1736) the first road was begun westward.

On the west shore of the Susquehanna River one Kelso lived, and, in connection with John Harris, managed the ferry. The lots of the Paxton manor which lay within the township were:

No. 1, containing 500 acres. It first belonged to Capt. John Stewart; since to John Rupley, Jacob Rupley and Jacob Moltz; later to Halderman's, George Rupley's heirs and others.

No. 2, 267½ acres belonged to John Boggs; later to Christian Erb, Eichelberger and McCormick; 300 acres belonged first to Caspar Weaver, now owned by Eichelberger heirs, Eichelberger & Musser; 256 acres originally belonged to Col. John Armstrong, now to Hummel's estate and E. Wormley (they formed the present site of Wormleysburg); 227 acres belonged originally to James Wilson, and 227 acres to Robert Whitehill.

Tobias Hendricks had charge of Louther manor, and lived on it, in what is now East Pennsborough. He was the son of Tobias Hendricks, of Donegal, and hence their names have been confounded. He came into the valley at a very early period, possibly prior to 1725. In a letter to John Harris, bearing date May 13, 1727, he speaks of his father as "at Donegal," requesting Mr. Harris to forward a letter to him. He also alludes to "a trader" at the Potomac, of whom he bought skins, and of "the grate numbers coming this side of ye Sasquahannah." The valley was then being rapidly settled, for at this period the Scotch-Irish immigration had begun.

From another source we learn of the Hendricks family, as follows: "Scarcely," says the writer, "had the echoes of the thundering at Lexington, on the 19th of April, 1775, ceased reverberating, ere the brave sons of the valley, under the gallant Hendricks, were on the march to the relief of the beleagured city of Boston. Capt. William Hendricks was the grandson of Tobias Hendricks, an Indian trader, and possibly the first actual white settler in the valley, who located at what is now known as Oyster's Point, two miles west of Harrisburg. Here Tobias Hendricks died in November, 1739, leaving a wife, Catherine, and children, Henry, Rebecca, Tobias, David, Peter, Abraham and Isaac. William Hendricks was probably the son of Henry, who retained the "old place" where our hero was born. The company of Capt. Hendricks was raised in about ten days, and as soon as orders were received was on the march, reaching camp the first week in August, 1776. When the expedition against Quebec was decided upon, the company of Capt. Hendricks, of Pennsborough, was one which was detached from Col. Thompson's battalion of riflemen, and ordered to "go upon the command with Col. Arnold," better remembered now as Gen. Benedict Arnold. Capt. Hendricks fell in front of Quebec, and his remains were interred in the same inclosure with those of the lamented Gen. Montgomery. Many of those who went never returned. Some were killed and others were disabled by the severe exposure of that winter's march through the wilderness of Maine.

No. 17, 213 acres. First belonged to Robert Whitehill; afterward to Dr. Joseph Craine and Joseph Sadler.

No. 18, 311 acres. Belonged first to Philip Kimmel; now by numerous parties, and is the present site of the north part of Camp Hill.

No. 19, 267 acres. First owner, Andrew Kreutzer.

No. 20, 281 acres. First owner, David Moore.

Nos. 21 and 22, 536 acres. First owner, Edmund Physick.

No. 23, 282 acres. First owner, also Edmund Physick.

The following is a list of names of the original settlers on Paxton, or Louther, manor: Capt. John Stewart, John Boggs, Moses Wallace, John Wilson, John Mish, Richard Rodgers, Conrad Renninger, Caspar Weaver, William Brooks, Samuel Wallace, Christopher Gramlich, James McCurdy, Isaac Hendrix, Robert Whitehill, Philip Kimmel, Andrew Kreutzer, David Moore, Edmund Physick, Rev. William Thompson, Alexander Young, Jonas Seely, Jacob Miller.

Lands lying west of this had been settled still earlier than this manor, which had been reserved by the Proprietary Government as a special reservation for the Indians. John Harris had bought from the Penns, at an early date, seven or eight hundred acres of land on the west side of the Susquehanna River, and just north of the Conodoguinet Creek, which included the present site of West Fairview. In 1746 Michael Crouse also had purchased 435 acres from the Penns, lying north, in the great bend of the creek. North of this tract are the Rife farms, at the western boundary of which is Holtze's Run, a small stream which rises at the base of the Blue Mountains, and falls into the Conodoguinet Creek a short distance below, where Holtze's mill once stood.

To the north of the township, where the chain of the mountains is broken by the broad river, whose bright waters are studded with green islands, the scene is of surpassing beauty, and were it not for the many furnaces and forges along the river, which are marked by "a pillar of cloud by day, and of fire by night," we might almost expect to see some painted savage emerge upon its waters in his bark canoe. For there were Indian villages here in these lower parts of the county, which are still traditionally remembered; "on the banks of the Susquehanna, Yellow Beeches, Conodoguinet and other places." "There was an Indian town," says Rupp, "opposite Harris's, * * another at the mouth of the Conodoguinet Creek, two miles above."*

There are few families of the original Scotch-Irish settlers left. Four-fifths of the inhabitants of the township to-day are of German descent. Among them we find, as early as 1761, such names as Renninger, Kunckle, Bucher, Kast, Herman, Kimmel, Brandt, Kreutzer, Shoff, Coover, Ruff, Schneble and Kisecker, all of which are familiar names at the present day.

Among the prominent citizens of East Pennsborough Township may be mentioned ex-Gov. Bigler, of Pennsylvania, and his brother, John Bigler, once Governor of California. Both of them spent their boyhood in this township, and their father kept for many years what was known as the "Yellow Tavern," which has since been converted into a private dwelling.

VILLAGES.

The villages in the township are West Fairview, Wormleysburg, Whitehill and Bridgeport.

Fairview, now called "West Fairview," was laid out by Abraham Neidig, Esq., in 1815. It is pleasantly situated at the spot where the Conodoguinet Creek flows into the Susquehanna River. It has more than 300 houses, four schools, three churches, one hotel, and an extensive rolling-mill and nail factory, now owned by the heirs of James McCormick (deceased), which gives employment to many of the inhabitants of the town. In 1700 to 1720 the Indians had a village here. *West Fairview Lodge, No. 612, I. O. O. F.*, at this place has a membership of about fourteen.

Wormleysburg was laid out by John Wormley, Esq., after whom it is named, in the fall of 1815. It contains about forty dwellings, two schools and two churches. For years it was the center of a large lumber trade. The principal dwellings were erected by the proprietor and his sons. Mr. Wormley was for many years the proprietor of the ferry which bears his name, and which still stands.

Whitehill is a post village on the Cumberland Valley Railroad, one mile west of the Susquehanna River, and is called after Hon. Robert Whitehill, the original owner of the land upon which the town is built. After purchasing these lands from the Proprietaries, he erected, in 1771, the first stone house

---

*See Rupp's History, p. 352.

built in the manor of Louther. At this time there were but few houses in it. He was elected a member to the convention in Philadelphia in 1776, in which the Declaration of Independence was approved by Congress, and was a member of the convention which adopted the old constitution of Pennsylvania. For years he served as a representative of the people of Cumberland County, both in the State and in the National halls of legislation.

MISCELLANEOUS.

The postoffices in East Pennsborough Township are West Fairview, Wormsleysburg and Camp Hill. The Cumberland Valley Railroad crosses the southern portion of the township from east to west.

BOROUGH OF CAMP HILL.

Camp Hill is beautifully situated on the higher grounds just north of the Cumberland Valley Railroad, two miles west of the Susquehanna River. It is noted as the place where Tobias Hendricks had an Indian reservation as early as 1750. Four people were killed by the Indians near this place in July, 1757. From 1851 to 1867 the town was known as White Hall, from an academy of that name; but since 1867, when a postoffice was established at this place, it has been known by its present name. The "Soldier's Orphan School" is at this place. The town was organized as a borough in September, 1885.

CHURCH AND CEMETERY.

The first church erected in this lower portion of the county, about one mile north of Camp Hill, was a log one, erected in about 1765. It was two stories high, the lower portion being used as a school and residence of the teacher, and the upper story for religious worship. The old church was removed, and the present one, known as the Poplar Church, erected. There is an old grave-yard connected with the church, with partly obliterated inscriptions dating back to 1789.

CHAPTER XXIII.

FRANKFORD TOWNSHIP.

FRANKFORD TOWNSHIP, originally included in West Pennsborough, was formed in 1795. It lies in the northwestern portion of the county, bounded on the north by the North Mountains, east by North Middleton, south by West Pennsborough, and on the west by Mifflin Township. The Conadoguinet Creek forms the line of its boundary on the south, and the whole land of the township is intersected with small streams. The soil is of a slate and gravely character, but under improved methods of cultivation it produces good crops of cereals and fruit in abundance. The earliest settlers were principally Scotch-Irish. Among them were Allens, Armstrongs, Bells, Benders, Butlers, Browns, Dillers, Douglases, Ernsts, Espys, Galbreaths, Goods, Gillespies, Gettyses, Hayses, Leckeys, Logans, Lutzes, Lairds, McCommons, Mountzes, Nickeys, Powers, Sharps, Stoners, Woods, Wagners and Wards. Of these only the names of Douglas, Hays and Logan occur in the tax-list of West Pennsborough (which then included Frankford) in 1750. Butler and Brown and Woods occur in the list for 1762. When the Germans began to settle in Frankford is not known, but it was probably as early as the formation of the township.

THE BUTLER FAMILY.

Among the names which we have mentioned (many of which are not now represented in the township or county), there is one family of National fame, worthy of especial mention. Thomas Butler, and Eleanor, his wife, emigrated from the North of Ireland in 1740, and settled first in York County, subsequently removing to a tract of land "adjoining ye Blue Mountains," in West Pennsborough, now Frankford Township, Cumberland County. Here Thomas Butler died in July, 1791, and little more is known of him save that he was the father of a remarkable family of sons. For our account of them, which follows, we are indebted to an article on "The Butlers of the Cumberland Valley," by Rev. J. A. Murray, of Carlisle, published in the first number of the *Historical Register*.

There were five sons, all of whom so favorably distinguished themselves in the American Revolution that afterward Gen. Washington recognized them as "The Five Butlers, a gallant band of patriot brothers." They were generally called the "fighting Butlers." They claimed to be of noble blood, and traced their descent to the house of Ormond.*

These five sons of Thomas Butler were Richard, born April 1, 1743, fell in battle November 4, 1791; William, born in January, 1745, died May 16, 1789; Thomas, born May 28, 1748, died September 7, 1805; Pierce (sometimes Percival), born April 6, 1760, died September 9, 1821; Edward, born March 20, 1762, died May 6, 1803. There was also a daughter, Eleanor, born about 1754.

Richard Butler's first military experience was as an ensign of Capt. James Hendrick's company, First Pennsylvania Battalion, in Col. Bouquet's expedition of 1764. At the beginning of the Revolution he entered the Pennsylvania Line as major of the Eighth Regiment; was promoted lieutenant-colonel March 12, 1777, and was transferred to lieutenant-colonel of Morgan's rifle command June 9, 1777, whom he afterward succeeded. He was esteemed by Gen. Washington and Gen. Wayne as one of the ablest partizan officers of the Revolution and most familar with Indian life and affairs. He was also, it is said, familiar with a number of their dialects, and was requested by the commander to compile a vocabulary. He was sent with his rifle command to protect the flank and rear of Gates from the Indians under Brandt, and after fighting successfully at the battle of Saratoga (October, 1777) was ordered back to headquarters. He fought at Monmouth, was assigned as colonel of the Ninth Pennsylvania, with which regiment he took a prominent part in the capture of Stony Point, where, says St. Clair (in a letter to Reed, July 25, 1779) "my friend Col. Butler commanded one of the attacks and distinguished himself." After the revolt of the Pennsylvania Line, the Ninth Regiment generally re-enlisted under their old colonel in the Fifth Pennsylvania, who commanded in the campaign under Gen. Wayne in the South. In October following, in view of Col. Butler's valuable services prior to and at the capture of Yorktown, he was honorably designated to plant our flag upon the British works

---

*James Butler, Duke of Ormond, was the first of the Anglo-Irish family of Butlers on whom the ducal title was conferred. Lord Dunboyne, of the house next in remainder to that of Ormond, said: "I consider the five American Revolutionary Butler brothers as adding lustre to the Dunboyne peerage." (See account of Pierce Butler (as a delegate to the Constitutional Convention in 1787) in McMaster's History of the United States.

after the surrender of Lord Cornwallis. He detailed for this purpose his ensign, Maj. Ebenezer Denny, from Carlisle, but Baron Steuben unexpectedly appropriated this honor, for which reason Butler "sent the arrogant foreigner a message, as every one expected, and it took all the influence of Rochambeau and Washington to prevent a hostile meeting."

"On a plan of Carlisle, made in 1764, the Butler home is then and there indicated as being on Lot 61 West Main Street, north side, and third lot from Pitt Street." In 1789 Col. Butler removed to Pittsburgh, and much of his career follows. The first hotel and a street, at an early period in that city, were named after him, as were also the county and town of Butler, in Pennsylvania.

He was prominent in securing the formation of Allegheny County; was appointed to various positions; was commissioned one of the justices of the court of common pleas of Allegheny County November, 1788, resigned 1790, having been elected to the Assembly. He was commissioned (October, 1788) with Col. John Gibson (father of John Bannister Gibson, Chief Justice of Pennsylvania) to purchase Indian claims to the triangle on Lake Erie. He was appointed, after the failure of Gen. Harmer's expedition, major-general, and second in command (under Gen. St. Clair), and fell, when that army was defeated on the Miami, in the very bloody battle fought against the allied Indians under Brandt, on the 4th of November, 1791. Two of his brothers, Cols. Thomas and Edward Butler were also in this disastrous battle, and the first was severely wounded. "After Gen. Butler," says Dr. William Denny, in his memoir of his father, Maj. Ebenezer Denny, "had received his first wound, he continued to walk in front, close along the line, with his coat off and his arm in a sling, encouraging the men, and retired only after receiving a second wound in the side. The Commander-in-chief sent Maj. Denny with his compliments to inquire how he was. He found him in the middle of the camp in a sitting posture, supported by knapsacks; the rifle balls of the Indians, who now surrounded closely the whole camp, concentrated upon that point. One of the wounded General's servants and two horses were shot here. He seemed, however, to have no anxiety, and to the inquiry of the aid-decamp he answered that he felt well. Whilst making this reply, a young cadet from Virginia, who stood by his side, was hit on the cap of the knee by a spent ball, and cried so loudly with the pain and alarm that Gen. Butler actually shook his wounded side with laughter. This satisfied Maj. Denny that the second wound was not mortal–that the General being very fleshy the ball might not have penetrated a vital part. He always believed that he might have been brought away and his life saved. Probably his own aid-decamp, Maj. John Morgan, may have offered to bring him off, as was his duty, and the wounded General declined, conscious that his weight and helplessness would only encumber his brave young friend for no use, and hinder him from saving himself." "About the time to which reference is here made," says Dr. Murray, "it is reliably stated that the youngest brother, Capt. Edward Butler, removed the General from the field and placed him near the road by which he knew the army must retreat, and on returning to the field found his other brother, Maj. Thomas Butler, shot through both legs. He then removed him to the side of the General, who, learning that the army was in retreat, insisted on being left alone, as he was mortally wounded, and that he should endeavor to save their wounded brother. He consequently placed Thomas on an artillery horse, captured from a retreating soldier, and taking a sad leave of their gallant and noble brother 'they left him in his glory.'"

A letter from Edward Butler to his brother Pierce, who had moved to the

South, dated Fort Washington, November 11, 1791, says: "Yesterday I arrived here with our worthy brother, Major Thomas Butler, who is illy wounded, he having one leg broken, & shot thro' the other. * * * He has borne the hard fortune of that day with the soldierly fortitude you might have expected from so brave a man. We left the worthiest of brothers, Gen Richard Butler in the hands of the savages, but so nearly dead that I hope he was not sensible of any cruelty they might willingly wreak upon him." Chief Justice Hugh H. Brackenridge, who spent the last years of his life in Carlisle, where he died and was buried, wrote some lines on Gen. Wayne, in which the name of Butler occurs:

> "The birth of some great man or death
> Gives a celebrity to spots of earth:
> We say that Montcalm fell on Abraham's plains;
> That Butler presses the Miami bank;
> And that the promontory of Sigeum
> Has Achilles' tomb."

Gen. Richard Butler's will, dated September 29, 1785, is recorded in Book E, page 251, at Carlisle, and as it is curious and interesting we will quote some portions of it. It was evidently written in haste and before some dangerous expedition. It begins:

"It being proper for all men to consider the interest of their families, and to do justice to all people with whom they have had dealings, which can never be done to so much advantage to the parties conccearned as when men are in health and out of bodily pain—which I thank God is my present situation. Therefore, in the name of the great God of heaven, creator of the universe, before whom I believe all men will be judged for their conduct in this life, I, Richard Butler, being in perfect health and senses, think it my duty (as I am going far from my family and into some degree of danger more than generally attend at my happy and peaceful home) to make some arrangement of my worldly affairs as I wish and desire may take place in case of my death, which I hope for the sake of my family, the great and almighty God will avert."

The will speaks of his "much loved and honored wife Mary Butler" and children William and Mary. An inventory attached to the will shows his estate to have consisted of a house and lot in Carlisle, furniture, plate, etc.; tract of land in Westmoreland county, adjoining land of late Col. George Croghan; tract on Allegheny River, below and adjoining land of Col. Croghan; tract on Plumb Creek, including the large forks of Plumb Creek, etc.; two lots in town of Pittsburgh, adjoining the lots of William Butler; two lots in the town of Appley, on the Allegheny River, near the old Kittanning: "One thousand acres of land, being a donation of the State of Pennsylvania, and six-hundred acres of land, a donation of the United States in Congress—these donations are for my services as a Colonel in the United States;" various notes, etc. The testator wishes his executors to construe the will "in the most natural construction of the expressions, as I well know the writing is not done in the most methodical way, or form, not having time even to copy or correct it." The executors were his wife Mary, his brother William, his "respected friend Thomas Smith, Esq., attorney at law, Carlisle, and my friend John Montgomery"; date September 29, 1785.

Col. William Butler, second son of Thomas, was born in York County; served during the Revolution as lieutenant-colonel of the Fourth Regiment Pennsylvania Line, but acted as colonel, as the colonel of that regiment was a prisoner on parole.

Col. Thomas Butler was born May 28, 1748, in West Pennsborough, now Frankford Township, Cumberland County. He was an eminently brave soldier. In 1776 he was studying law with James Wilson, one of the signers of the Declaration, at Carlisle. He entered the war as first lieutenant of the Second Pennsylvania Battalion, under Gen. St. Clair, January 5, 1776; became captain in the Third Regiment in the line; fought in almost every battle in the Middle States, retiring from service January 1, 1781. At Brandywine (September 11, 1777) he received the thanks of the Commander-in-chief on the field of battle for his intrepid conduct in rallying a detachment of retreating troops, giving the enemy a severe fire. At Monmouth he received the thanks of Wayne for defending a defile in the face of a heavy fire, while his brother's, Col. Richard Butler's, regiment made good their retreat. After the war he returned to his farm, but left it in 1791 to fight the Indians on the frontier. He commanded a battalion in the disastrous battle of the 4th of November, in which his eldest brother fell. Though his own leg had been broken by a ball, yet, on horseback, he led his battalion to the charge. He was subsequently promoted as major (1792) and as lieutenant-colonel (1794); was in command of Fort Fayette (Pittsburgh) during the whiskey insurrection; was sent to Tennessee, 1797, to dispossess intruders on unpurchased lands and treat with Indians.

"Col. Butler," says Dr. Murray, "was subsequently quite well known for disobeying the order to cut off queues, the amusing history of which may be here stated. The Butlers were the stanch friends of Washington and his school, and not very partial to Wilkinson and his clique. The famous military order to cut off queues, issued by Wilkinson, was chiefly designed for Col. Thomas Butler, whose queue was dressed and head powdered (even during a campaign) before *reveille*. When the order reached the command, where it was especially intended, the subordinate officers, who generally wore the offensive appendage, called upon Col. Butler to get his advice and opinion for their guidance; and to the question 'What must we do?' he replied: 'Young gentlemen, you must obey orders.' And when asked if he designed cutting off his queue, answered: 'The Almighty gave me my hair, and no earthly power shall deprive me of it.' For this he was twice tried by court martial; first mildly reprimanded, and secondly suspended for one year, but before the sentence was pronounced he was gathered to his fathers (died at New Orleans September 7, 1805). And this gallant, sturdy, veteran son of Cumberland County died and was buried with his beloved queue." The most interesting fact is to come. The facts which we have briefly mentioned were "worked up with great humor by Washington Irving, in 'Knickerbocker's History.' Gen. Wilkinson being the original Von Puffenburgh, and Keldermeester (master of the cellar) being a Dutch translation of Butler." The passage in Irving is as follows: "The eel-skin queue of old Keldermeester," recounts Diedrich, "became instantly an affair of the utmost importance. The Commander-in-chief was too enlightened an officer not to perceive that the discipline of the garrison, the subordination and good order of the armies of the Nieuw Nederlands, the consequent safety of the whole province, and ultimately the dignity and prosperity of their High Mightinesses, the Lords States General, imperiously demanded the docking of that stubborn queue. He decreed, therefore, that old Keldermeester should be publicly shorn of his glories in presence of the whole garrison; the old man as resolutely stood on the defensive, whereupon he was arrested and tried by a court-martial for mutiny, desertion, and all the other list of offenses noticed in the articles of war, ending with a '*videlicet*, in wearing an eel-skin queue three feet long, contrary to orders.' Then came on arraignments and trials and pleadings, and the whole garrison was in a ferment about this unfortunate queue. As it is well known that the commander of a frontier post has the power of acting pretty much after his own will, there is little doubt but that the veteran would have been hanged or shot, at least, had he not luckily fallen ill of a fever through mere chagrin and mortification,

FRANKFORD TOWNSHIP.

and deserted from all earthly command with his beloved locks unviolated. He obstinately remained unshaken to the very last moment, when he directed that he should be carried to his grave with his eel-skin queue sticking out of a hole in his coffin."

The will of Col. Thomas Butler, filed in the records of the county, is dated September 20, 1787. It begins "I, Thomas Butler, of West Pennsborough Township, in the county of Cumberland and State of Pennsylvania, Gunsmith," etc. It bequeathes to his loving son, Richard Butler, and spouse, and to his loving son, William Butler, and spouse, certain property; to his wife, Eleanor, his personal property, with excepted legacies; to his daughter, Eleanor, one hundred pounds, "now in the hands of my son, Edward Butler," also fifty pounds, "now in the hands of my son, Pierce Butler." Also to said Eleanor Butler all claims of cow-cattle at the stand in the barn, and her riding horse, also five pounds a year while she remains single. To my "loving and worthy son, Capt. Thomas Butler, all my real estate in West Pennsborough, [now Frankford] Township," county of Cumberland, etc. To loving wife, Eleanor, twenty pounds yearly. To my loving son, Pierce Butler, the sum of one hundred and seventy-five pounds. To Edward Butler the sum of one hundred and seventy-five pounds. His wife, Eleanor, and sons, Thomas and Edward, executors.

Col. Pierce Butler was born April 6, 1760, in West Pennsborough (now Frankford) Township, Cumberland County. He served in the Pennsylvania Line of the Revolution; was with Morgan at Saratoga and at siege of Yorktown and other engagements. He moved from Cumberland County, after the war, to the South. He was adjutant-general in the war of 1812. He was the father of William Orlando Butler, who succeeded Gen. Winfield Scott in Mexico, and ran for Vice-President (Democratic ticket) in 1848.

Mr. McMaster, in his "History of the People of the United States," thus mentions Pierce Butler, in speaking of the delegates to the convention in 1787: "Another Irishman, Pierce Butler, was in the South Carolina delegation. Butler was a man of ability, and had attained to some eminence in his State; but no distinction was to him so much a matter of pride as his blood, for he boasted that he could trace unbroken descent to the great family of Ormond"; and in a note he adds: "Butler was often twitted in the lampoons of late years with noble descent. As one of the ten delegates who voted against Jay's treaty, he is described as

"Pierce Butler next, a man of sterling worth,
Because he justly claims a noble birth."*

Col. Edward Butler, youngest son of Thomas, was born (March 20, 1762) on the homestead in West Pennsborough, now Frankford Township, Cumberland County. He served as a valiant soldier in several regiments of the Pennsylvania Line. In the operations on the Miami, he was adjutant general under Wayne. He died in Tennessee in 1803. He was the father of Edward G. Washington Butler, of the Mexican war, who still lives, venerable in years (aged now, 1886, eighty-six), in Louisiana, and who married the daughter of Lawrence Lewis and Eleanor Parke Custis, of Virginia, then the nearest living relative both of Gen. and Mrs. Washington—her father being the son of Fielding Lewis and Elizabeth Washington, the General's only sister, and the mother being the daughter of Mrs. Washington's only son, John Parke Custis, and of Julia Calvert, granddaughter of Lord Baltimore. Such was one of the distinguished families, whose first American home was under the shadow of the North Mountains, in the county of Cumberland.

---
*The Democratiad—A poem. Philadelphia, 1795.

VILLAGE.

There is only one village in the township, Bloserville, called, like so many of the smaller towns of the valley, from a family who owned the land upon which it is built. The first house was erected at Bloserville in 1847. There is a postoffice here.

CHAPTER XXIV.

HAMPDEN TOWNSHIP.

HAMPDEN TOWNSHIP was formed from East Pennsborough Township in 1845. It is bounded on the north by the mountains which form the dividing line between Cumberland and Perry Counties; on the east by East Pennsborough Township; on the south by Upper and Lower Allen Townships, and on the west by Silver Spring Township.

The soil is well adapted for agriculture, and large crops of wheat and other cereals are raised annually. The Conodoguinet Creek here winds with more than its usual serpentine curvatures, from the center, but extending into the southern portion of the township, the land to the south being of the usual limestone formation, while that to the north is black, sandy loam land near the creek, and red slate farther away. Hampden Township lying near the Susquehanna River, was one of the first portions of the north valley into which white settlers began, about 1730 or 1731, to push their way. These were at first Scotch-Irish, and later Germans.

They began settling in that portion of the township north of the Conodoguinet, and also south of the creek and west of the road leading from the Conodoguinet to the Yellow Breeches, past "Frieden's Kirche" and immediately below Shiremanstown. The portion east had been reserved as a proprietory manor, and upon it, at this period, the whites were not allowed to take up land. The part west of the above road was called the "barrens," because it was poorly timbered.

Among the earliest of the Scotch-Irish settlers were two brothers, John and William Orr, who went from Scotland into Ireland and came from Parish Calade, County Antrim, Ireland, and settled in Hampden Township on the north side of the creek, as early as 1743. The north side was the only side of the creek that then had timber—fine large trees, consisting of hickory, white oak, black oak, walnut, poplar, beech, buttonwood, locust, swamp oak, chestnut and other varieties.* There were plenty of fish in the stream—plenty of shad and a great deal of game on the north side of the creek, because it was woodland, while on the south side it was low, marshy land and brush. There were deer on the south side. As late as 1785 there were plenty of shad, and parties would come to catch them with seines. The Youngs were also early settlers and lived in the next bend above the creek. Other names will be given when we speak of the lots of the Louther (then Paxton) Manor.

One of the earliest, evidently, of the German settlers in this township was Jonas Rupp. After having come from the fatherland, and, in order to become a "denizen," taken the prescribed oath—among other things, "of hav-

---

*Some sixty or seventy years ago, says the writer's informant, "Mr. James Orr," there were thirty-three varieties of timber, large and small, on "the Orr farms."

ing taken the Lord's Supper within three months before holding of the court."* (see Rupp's *Biographical Memorial, p. 35*)—he removed first to Lebanon and then into Cumberland County.

The pen picture of that early flitting we prefer to give in the language of one of his descendants: "The time of his removal" says I. D. Rupp in his biographical sketch, "had come. On a bright sunny morning the flitting moved orderly and slowly from the happy home, around which clustered hallowed memories, to be, for a while, cast among strangers beyond the Big River. The first place where they halted was at the newly laid out Fredericktown (Hummelstown), nine miles east from Harris' Ferry, to partake of provisions and to bait the horses and stock. The same day, just before nightfall, they reached Harris' Ferry, so named after John Harris, who settled here about 1718 and 1719. Here they tarried for the night. Early the next morning they forded the broad Susquehanna—for the water of the stream at this season of the year was shallow. Onward they went, five miles westward, when they reached, at high 12, the new home."

"Providence Tract" is the original recorded name of the tract or parcel of land which Jonas Rupp purchased from George Thawley. Part of this tract was taken up by William McMeans, Jr., December 10, 1742, and part thereof May 13, 1763. McMeans sold, October 4, 1768, 211 acres to George Thawley, who sold the same, in the fall of 1772, to Jonas Rupp, for £400.

"The improvements consisted of a log cabin, a mere apology for a log barn, and fifteen acres of cleared land, principally inclosed with a brush fence and saplings."

In the spring of 1773 Rupp erected a house one story and a half high, of hewn logs, close to a well which he had sunk. This house is still standing. In the course of ten years 100 acres were cleared and "his farm," says his descendant, "was soon distinguished from those of his Scotch-Irish neighbors."†

MILLS, BRIDGES, ETC.

Along the winding courses of the Conodoguinet Creek there are a number of flour and grist mills in the township. The first is Bryson's, situated in the extreme western portion of the township. It is on the south side of the creek and is supplied with water by the Silver Spring, which here empties into the Conodoguinet. It occupies the site of what was formerly known as "Briggs' mill." Further down, almost in the center of the township, on the north side and at the beginning of the great bend of the creek, is the Good Hope mill, now owned by J. B. Lindeman. It was built by Jonas Rupp about 1820. Across the creek from this mill John Whisler built a woolen factory, which is still standing, and which was once connected with an oil-mill. At an early date it seems to have been the habit of every householder living in the country to raise a patch of flax, and oil seems to have been one of the early products of this section.

Three bridges cross the Conodoguinet Creek in this township; one at Eberly's (built about 1842), one at Lindeman's (built 1823), and one in the southern section of the second bend, built, principally, by James Orr in 1834 and 1835. This latter is known as Orr's Bridge.

THE INDIANS.

The Indians had a number of villages in this lower portion of the county. They had a number of wigwams on the banks of the Conodoguinet Creek, north

---
*The certificate of the oath above alluded to is dated September 22, 1765.
†"A house built by the first Germans in Pennsylvania," says Rupp, "was easily distinguished from that of his Scotch-Irish neighbor's house, by its huge chimney, always in the center of the edifice."—*Biog. Mem.* p. 44.

of the turnpike three miles from the Susquehanna, on lands now owned, or lately owned by Albright, Rupp, Merkel, John Shoop and others. There were also several cabins half a mile north of Frieden's Kirche, in Hampden Township. "An aged aunt" says Rupp (History, page 352) "late of Hampden Township, informed me that she remembered well the evacuated Indian huts north of Frieden's Kirch. and those at Ruby's." The Indians had a path, crossing the Conodoguinet, near those wigwams toward Yellow Breeches.

PAXTON MANOR IN HAMPDEN.

A small portion of the manor of Paxton was embraced in Hampden Township. This, extending from the road past Frieden's Kirche, and between the two creeks to the Susquehanna, was reserved by the Proprietary government as a special reservation for the Indians, and consequently was not so soon settled by the whites as the adjoining lands. Of the twenty-eight lots or parcels of lots into which it was divided, some few fell in Hampden Township. These were:

Lot No. 23, called Westmoreland, containing 282 acres, 36 perches and allowance, a warrant for which was issued to Edmund Physick dated December 10, 1767; patent August 15, 1768; afterward owned in whole or parts by Hershberger, Funk, Nichols, Bollinger, Rupp, Ruby, Shopp, and lately by Albright, Rupp, Meckel, Shopp and others. The Indian wigwams "three miles from the Susquehanna," above alluded to, were on this tract.

Lot No. 24, 287 acres: Rev. William Thompson, Daniel Sherbahn, John Sherbahn; lately William Stephen, Samuel Eberly and others. The cabins "half a mile north of Frieden's Kirche," above alluded to, were on this tract.

Lot No. 25, 150 acres: Alexander Young, Robert Young, late Dr. Robert G. Young.

Lot No. 26, 209½ acres: for this tract, called "Manington," a warrant dated 17th of May, 1767, was granted to Jonas Seely, who conveyed, in December, the same year, to Conrad Maneschmidt, to whom a patent was issued August 15, 1774. Maneschmidt and wife conveyed, September 20, 1774, a portion of this tract to Ulrick Shopp, and it is still owned by his descendants.

Outside of the portion of the township which was embraced in this manor, John Wisler owned a large tract on the south side and within the first bend of the creek. About half a mile farther down and on the north bank was the residence of Daniel Basehore, who settled there about 1791, on what was then known as the Rye Gate Tract. It was while attempting to rob Mr. Basehore's house that Lewis, the robber, was taken prisoner, and lodged in the Carlisle jail. South of this Rye Gate tract there was another tract called "Steyning," containing 187 acres, which was surveyed to James McConnell by warrant January 15, 1763—for which a patent deed was issued January 16, 1808, to Jonas Rupp, which was afterward owned by David Rupp, Sherbahn, Early, and (now) the Erbs.

CHURCHES.

Frieden's Kirche.—The history of the old stone church known as "Frieden's Kirche" is as follows: A German Reformed congregation had been organized in the lower part of the county, and, in 1797, they agreed to build the house (now occupied exclusively as a schoolhouse) for the purpose of holding their religious meetings, and for school purposes until another structure should be built. This house was built of logs, with one portion designed for the teacher's residence. In this same year (May 26, 1797), the congregation purchased land connected with the schoolhouses from Henry Snively and Nicholas Kreutzer; and, in 1798, the stone church was erected under the supervision of a building committee, consisting of Frederick Lang, Jonas Rupp, Leonard Swartz, and Rev. Anthony Hautz, then stationed at Carlisle and Trindle Spring. Martin Rupp and Thomas Anderson were the builders.

A Lutheran and German Reformed Congregation had been organized in 1787 or 1788, who had a log house for public worship in Louther Manor, several miles northeast of Frieden's Kirche, known as "Poplar Church," so called because it stood in a grove of lofty poplar trees. In May, 1806, this congregation, on the payment of £405 17s. 3d. (being one-half of the cost of Frieden's Kirche, land, building of schoolhouse, and inclosing the grave-yard), became consolidated with the German Reformed congregation of Frieden's Kirche. At this time the following persons constituted the vestry of the congregations: German Reformed—Frederick Lang, Jonas Rupp, Frederick Schweitzer, Christian Swiler, Henry Manessmith and Martin Rupp; Lutheran—Nicholas Kreutzer, John Wormley, Christoph Eichelberger, Andrew Shuely, Christofel Gramlig and Daniel Scherban.

April 20, 1812, the joint congregations purchased five acres more on which the present dwelling house, contiguous to the church stands. In 1830 another small parcel of ground was purchased to enlarge the grave-yard. In 1864 about two more acres were purchased from Thomas Oyster for the same purpose.

St. John's Evangelical Lutheran Church.—In 1865 the Lutherans purchased from the German Reformed congregation their interest in a portion of ground near the old church, and commenced the erection of a new brick building, which, under the name of "St. John's Evangelical Lutheran Church," was completed and dedicated July 2, 1866. June 23, of this year, the German Reformed congregation held their last communion service in the old church, which still stands, after having withstood the storms of nearly ninety years, in a good state of preservation. It is used for a Sunday-school, and occasionally for funeral services, but it is now chiefly valuable as an antique relic of the past.

The other churches in the township are the Salem Church; Methodist, on the turnpike, about two and one-half miles north of Mechanicsburg, erected in 1825; the Good Hope Church (Church of God denomination), erected in 1843; and the Mount Zion Church, on the State road leading from the river to Sterritt's Gap, about four miles from West Fairview, which is a large frame building erected and dedicated in 1857.

HAMLETS.

There are two small places in the township. One is called Good Hope, which consists of a few dwelling houses, a wagon and blacksmith shop, a store, which has been kept there for sixty years, and a postoffice—the only one in the township—established about thirty-three years ago. Sporting Hill is a cluster of less than a dozen houses, one of which was formerly a store, and another a hotel. It is about five and a half miles west of Harrisburg, on the turnpike road leading to Carlisle. "During the French and Indian war," says Rupp, "a man was shot by the Indians near this place. Several persons met on public business at Mr. Wood's, late John Everly's; one of the company went down toward McMean's (Kreutzer's) spring, where he was shot and scalped."

MISCELLANEOUS.

Hampden is well supplied with good school buildings, five in number, and with numerous good roads in every portion of the township. The oldest of these date as follows: From Harris Ferry westward, November, 1734; from

Hoge's Spring to the Susquehanna River, October, 1759; from Trindle Spring to Kelso's Ferry, January, 1792.

The Cumberland Valley Railroad runs along the southern border of the township, dividing it from Upper Allen and Lower Allen Townships.

CHAPTER XXV.

HOPEWELL TOWNSHIP AND BOROUGH OF NEWBURG.

THE township of Hopewell, a twin sister of Pennsborough, was formed in 1735. These were then the only two townships in the North Valley, and this county was still a portion of Lancaster. They were divided by a line crossing at the "Great Spring," now Newville. Hopewell included then not only the corner of Cumberland, but most all of what is now Franklin County. Later (1741) this township of Hopewell was divided by a line "beginning at the North Hill, at Benjamin Moor's; thence to Widow Hewres' and Samuel Jamison's, and on a straight line to the South Hill," and it was ordered that "the western division be called Antrim, and the eastern, Hopewell." The territory of Antrim was nearly or altogether coincident with what was afterward the county of Franklin. Hopewell was gradually reduced to its present limits by the formation of Southampton, on the south, in 1791, and Mifflin, on the east, in 1797.

The land in the township is of a rolling character, of slate or dark slate formation, and, since lime has been freely used as a fertilizer, has become quite productive. The Conodoguinet Creek runs in a northeasterly direction through the southern portion of the township.

EARLY SETTLEMENT.

The early settlers of this upper portion of the county are invariably the Scotch or Irish, or the admixture of both, who, becoming dissatisfied and moved by the spirit of adventure, like Homer's heroes, passed

"The shadowy mountains and the roaring sea"

to found themselves new homes in the, then, almost unknown recesses of this North Valley.

> "Roll back the shadows of the crowning years,
> And, lo! a sylvan paradise appears!
> As bright and bounding then as now thy flow,
> Fair Susquehanna, ever murmuring low.
> But where the farm land basks, where busy town
> Beneath its guardian spires has nestled down,
> Stood darkling forests, then of sturdy oak,
> Tall pine and poplar, echoing to the stroke
> Of men by fever of adventure moved,
> Or dream of gain, to leave the fields they loved,
> And with fond wives and prattling children roam
> Far to these wilds to build anew a home."

As early as 1731 settlements were made along the Conodoguinet, within the limits of what is now Hopewell Township. There is good evidence that, as early as 1738, this section of the valley between Shippensburg and the North Mountain was as thickly settled as almost any other portion of it.*

---
*The number of freeholders in Hopewell in 1751 was 134.

HOPEWELL TOWNSHIP.

"There is a well authenticated tradition," says Rev. S. S. Wylie, in his address at the "historical exercises" at Middle Spring Church, in 1876, "handed down in the Johnson family of our church, that John Johnson, the grandfather of George Johnson, with his wife behind him, rode from his residence, three and one-half miles above Shippensburg, along a narrow bridle path, through almost continuous forest, passed the former residence of Wendel Foglesonger, crossed Middle Spring at the dilapidated Creamer Mill, and attended preaching in the woods in the vicinity of this church years before there was any house erected; and we know the first meeting-house was built in 1738."

George Croghan, the celebrated Indian interpreter, owned a large tract of land in Hopewell Township, a little north of Shippensburg. On or before 1730, one of the Chambers brothers (Robert), settled at Middle Spring. It is a matter of history that the first land taken up in this valley under the "Blunston license" was by Benjamin Furley, and afterward occupied by the Herrons, McCombs and Irwins, a large tract lying on the Conodoguinet Creek in the neighborhood of Orrstown. In evidence of the early settlement of this vicinity, at the house of Widow Piper in Shippensburg, as early as 1735, a number of persons from along the Conodoguinet and Middle Spring met to remonstrate against the road which was then being made from the Susquehanna to the Potomac, passing through the barrens, but wanted it to be made through the Conodoguinet settlement, which was more thickly inhabited. This indicates that at this time a number of people lived in this vicinity. Some of these, who settled here before the year 1738, were Robert Chambers, Herrons, McCombs (McCoombs), Youngs (three families), McNutts (three families), Mahans (three families), Scotts, Sterritts, Pipers; soon after the Brady family, the McCunes, Wherrys, Mitchells, Strains, Morrows and others. It was such pioneers as these who, with their children, made Shippensburg the most prominent town of this valley, prior to the year 1750.* Here, in this northwestern portion of the county, settled, prior to this time, besides the names which we have mentioned, the Quigleys, Laughlins, Nesbitts (Allen, John, and John, Jr.), Hannas, Bradys, Martins, and, if not so early, soon after, the Jacks, Hendersons and Hemphills. Many of these families were represented afterward in the Revolution, and after defending the frontier against a savage enemy, they turned to defend their country against a foreign foe. It may seem almost incredible, but it is known to be a fact, that of the members or adherents of the Middle Spring Church (now in Southampton, but then in Hopewell Township) there were five colonels, one major (James Herron), fifteen captains and twenty-eight privates. Their patriotic pastor, Robert Cooper, surcharged with patriotism, preached earnestly for the cause, and then, like Steel, King and Craighead, went as a chaplain to the field of actual conflict. (His commission is dated December 24, 1776.) He acted as a soldier, bore arms, marched and countermarched through the Jerseys on foot so long as he was able, and stood in the line of battle with the men at Trenton." Among the officers in the number to which we have alluded were Col. Benjamin Blythe, who lived at the head of Middle Spring, and was a noted Indian and Revolutionary soldier; Col. Robert Peebles, who lived on the farm since owned by Gen. David Middlecoff; Col. James Dunlap, who lived near Newburg. Among those also were Capt. Mathew Henderson, Capt. William Strain, Capt. Joseph Brady, Capt. Robert Quigley, and Capt. Charles Looper, killed at the battle of Crooked Billet, May 1778.

The Rev. Dr. Cooper, to whom we have alluded lived on and owned the farm a short distance south of Newburg now owned by David Foglesonger.

---
*See Rev. S. Wylie's historical discourse (1876) at Middle Spring.

This farm he purchased of John Trimble on the 7th of June, 1776. It contained about 207 acres. The stone end of the house, adjacent to the road, was built for him, it is said, by the congregation. Col. (then captain) Peebles marched with one of the earliest companies which was mustered into the field. It was in the battle of Long Island, August 27, when a portion was captured, and the remainder fought at Princeton, Trenton and White Plains. On his return from the war Col. Peebles resided on Peeble's Run near Newburg.

The Bradys.—Among the earlier settlers in this township was one, some of whose descendants were destined to become of historic interest. This was Hugh Brady, who emigrated from the North of Ireland about the year 1730, and settled first in the State of Delaware, but soon after in Cumberland County, on the banks of the Conodoguinet Creek, within five miles of where Shippensburg now stands.* At this time the county was settled only by a few Scotch and Irish emigrants, simple, religious and sincere. Here he raised a family of nine children: John, Joseph, Samuel, Hugh, William, Ebenezer and James; and daughters, Margaret and Mary.

Of these, John was the father of Capt. Samuel and Gen. Hugh Brady. He was born in Delaware in 1733, but came with his father when they founded their home in Cumberland County. In the quiet preceding the storm of the French and Indian war he followed the usual vocation of frontier life, the primeval forest yearly bowing to the settler's ax. John and his brother Hugh, we are told, studied surveying. His personal appearance has come down to us by tradition; he was six feet high, well-formed, had coal black hair, hazel eyes and was of rather dark complexion.

About the year 1755 he married Mary Quigley, of Hopewell Township, also of that Scotch-Irish extraction whose ancestors had read their Bibles by the camp fires of Cromwell's army, and, in the year 1756 his eldest son, the celebrated Indian fighter, Capt. Samuel Brady, was born in Shippensburg in the midst of the tempestuous waves of trouble that rolled in upon the settlements of this valley in the wake of Braddock's defeat.

During this critical period John Brady was very active against the Indians, and, as a reward for his services, was appointed a captain in the provincial lines, which, at that time, was a mark of no small distinction. In the *Pennsylvania Gazette* of April 5, 1764, there is an account of the Indian depredations in the Carlisle region on the 20th, 21st and 22d of March, "killing people, burning houses, and making captives;" adding, "Capts. Piper and Brady, with their companies, did all that lay in their power to protect the inhabitants. No man can go to sleep within ten or fifteen miles of the border without being in danger of having his house burned and himself or family scalped or led into captivity before the next morning. The people along the North Mountain are moving farther in, especially about Shippensburg, which is crowded with families of that neighborhood." John Brady's life was eventful. He served, as we have seen, in the French and Indian war; went as a private with Col. Armstrong from Cumberland County in his expedition against Kittanning; was commissioned July 19, 1763, as captain of the Second Battalion of the Pennsylvania Regiment; fought in the Revolution; was commissioned (October 12, 1776,) one of the captains of the Twelfth Regiment; was wounded at Brandywine (where his sons, Samuel and John,) the latter only sixteen, who was wounded, fought by his side) and, after leaving this county, he became one of the most prominent pioneers and defenders of the West Branch Valley.

When he left Shippensburg he located himself at the Standing Stone, a

---

*From a letter written by a descendant we learn: " He settled on the farm now (1869) owned by Joseph Whistler, adjoining the estate of the Smith heirs on the west." His name appears in the list of taxables for 1751.

celebrated Indian town at the confluence of Standing Stone Creek and the Juniata River. The present town of Huntingdon stands in part on the site of Standing Stone. From thence he removed to the west branch of the Susquehanna River, opposite the spot on which Lewisburg or Derrstown, in Union County, stands. He also resided near Muncy, where he erected, in the spring of 1776, the semi-fortified residence known afterward as "Fort Brady," near which place he was shot from his horse and killed by the Indians on April 11, 1779, a centenary celebration of which event was held at Muncy in 1879, at which time a monument was erected to his memory.

Capt. Samuel Brady, better known as "Capt. Sam," whose name is familiar in history and in fiction as an inveterate Indian killer and captain of the "rangers" or spies, was born in Shippensburg in 1756, and was the oldest of the five sons (James, John, Gen. Hugh and Robert Quigly Brady) of Capt. John Brady, whom we have mentioned.

He entered the Revolutionary Army at the age of twenty; was in the surprise at Paoli, where he narrowly escaped being taken prisoner; fought at Monmouth, and in 1779, at the age of twenty-two, was promoted to a captaincy by brevet.* He was afterward ordered to join the command of Gen. Broadhead and to march to Fort Pitt, where he remained until the army was abandoned. In 1778 his brother James was cruelly murdered and scalped by the Indians, and some time after this he began a career which, interwoven as it is with fiction, is certainly one of the most remarkable which can be found anywhere in the annals of Indian warfare. On the Susquehanna, the West Branch, Beaver's Creek, the Ohio and Alleghany, out as far as Sandusky (where he was sent with despatches by Gen. Broadhead), the stories of his adventures, bravery and hair-breadth escapes were told.† Says one (John Blair Linn, Esq.,) "When border tales have lost their charm for the evening hour, or when oblivion blots from the historic page the glorious record of Pennsylvania in the Revolution of 1776, then, and then only, will Capt. Samuel Brady of the rangers be forgotten."

Capt. Samuel Brady, the son of Cumberland County, is emphatically the hero of western Pennsylvania, around whom the concealment of romance has most been woven. The fact that his father and brother (who is described as a handsome and noble man) were both killed by the Indians, and that he is said to have sworn eternal enmity against them, has given rise to a popular but erroneous idea of his character. He has been considered as a devoted Indian killer, reckless of all sympathy and destitute of all humanity, whereas he was a gentlemanly, fine-looking man, "possessed of a noble heart and intellect of a high order." As Gen. Hugh Brady, his brother, said of him, "Never was there a man more devoted to his country," and few rendered her more important service. Active, vigilant, cool in the midst of danger, with deliberate courage and capacity for physical endurance, knowing all the wiles of Indian warfare, he followed and watched them until his name became a terror to his foes, but a comfort to those on the defenseless frontier who were in danger of their depredations. If he was vengeful, which is doubtful, he had cause. He was a patriot and a protector to the unprotected.

In appearance he was five feet, eleven and three-quarters inches in height, with a perfect form, lithe and active; somewhat reticent in conversation. His walk was peculiar, agile; his step light; his form erect, as was always his posture in sitting, he sat upright. His face was handsome, his manner quiet,

---
*The party from whom the writer obtained this information has this commission in his possession.
†See "Otzinachson," or History of the West Branch Valley, by J. F. Meginess, or the chapters relating to him in "Border Life."

and in speaking or turning he moved his head less than his eyes. His manner and conversation, as it has come down to the living from one who knew him, was, in their language, "that of as fine a gentleman as I ever met."

Of his brother, Gen. Hugh Brady, as he was but a descendant of a pioneer of Cumberland, we have naught to say, except that he was an educated kind-hearted gentleman and lion-hearted officer, who fought under the "mad" Wayne, and of whom his friend and admirer, Gen. Winfield Scott, said, "God never made a better man or a better soldier." The lines from the poem of Rev. George Duffield, of Carlisle, written on the occasion of his death, might apply equally to others of the family we have mentioned:

> "And manly eyes may weep to-day
> As sinks the patriot to his rest;
> The nation held no truer heart
> Than that which beat in Brady's breast."

Hugh Brady, one of the seven sons of Hugh Brady the elder, who emigrated from Ireland, married Jean Young, whose father and mother lived on and owned the plantation lately owned by the heirs of Alexander Kelso. They had nine children, one of whom, Hannah Brady, married Samuel McCune and another, Rebecca, married his brother Hugh McCune. Both had large families. James the eldest child of Samuel and Hannah (Brady) McCune, married John Sharpe, a son of Alexander Sharpe of Green Spring, members of an early and one of the most prominent families of that portion of the township now embraced within the bounds of Newton. Two of the sons, James and Joseph, settled in Northumberland County. The former was an eminent citizen of Greensburg, represented the county in the State Senate and was at one time secretary of the commonwealth.

From a letter written some few years ago we learn that Moses Hemphill bought the two farms of the Bradys on the Conodoguinet Creek. "These farms were bounded as follows: On the north by the Rev. Dr. Cooper, at the present time by D. Foglesonger; on the east by the Owens, at present by J. Filer and the Chamberlains; on the south by the Conodoguinet Creek and the Duncans; and on the west by Hendersons. The mansion farm of the Bradys is now owned by John Clippinger, and the Hugh (son of Hugh Brady, the original settler) Brady farm adjoining is now owned by Benjamin Newcomer. The farm owned by James Brady is now owned by Moses Hemphill." There are none now of this family remaining in the county, but we have thought it well to preserve this record of a family whose sons were worthy of their sires.

HOPEWELL ACADEMY.

A classical school, known as "Hopewell Academy," was founded by the learned and genial John Cooper (son of Rev. Robert Cooper, D. D., of the Middle Spring Church), about the year 1810, "which, notwithstanding," says Dr. Alfred Nevin, "the barren hill on which it stood, and its secluded surroundings, sent forth many from its unpretending portals to act well their part." The academy stood near Newburg. Its founder, who was also its only teacher, was a graduate of Dickinson College under Dr. Nesbitt. The name of the school was derived from the township in which it was located. The furniture consisted of a stove (manufactured by Peter Ege at the Pine Grove Furnace) a table, professor's chair and benches. It stood about 150 feet in the rear and to the east of the mansion house of the farm on which it was located. The road from Shippensburg to Newburg at that time ran directly by the academy building. The logs of the structure were used in the erection of a house near the spot on which the plain, substantial building so long stood.

The students of this academy came, many of them, from a distance, and others from the more immediate vicinity of the school.

Some came from Carlisle, others from Shippensburg or Newville, others from more distant points. Some, within a reasonable distance, came daily to the school on horseback. This "academy," like the much earlier "log college" in Buck's County, or the Academy of Blair, (founded by Rev. John Blair, afterward pastor at Middle Spring) at Fagg's Manor, was the last of these unpretentious schools which helped to lift the standard of education and sent men out into the world whose career afterward reflected honor upon these nests where they were fledged.

Among the students of Hopewell Academy, to prove that we have made no idle boast, were such names as Alexander Sharpe, D. D., a prominent Presbyterian divine; Rev. John Kennedy, at one time professor of mathematics and natural sciences at Jefferson College; John W. McCullough, D. D.; the three Williamson Brothers, James, Moses and McKnight, from the vicinity of Newburg, all of whom became clergymen; Judge William McClure, of Pittsburgh; H. M. Watts, minister to Austria; Bishop Samuel A. McCoskry of the Episcopal Church; Charles McClure, afterward secretary of the commonwealth; Com. Gabriel O'Brien, who was afterward lost at sea; John and Alfred Armstrong, from Carlisle; Isaac G. Strain, lieutenant in the United States Navy, who explored the Isthmus of Darien; Jack Hemphill, who studied law with Andrew Carothers, Esq., of Carlisle, but died at middle life in Newburg; the Revs. D. E. Nevin, Edward H. Nevin, D.D., and Alfred Nevin, D.D., LL.D., who was admitted to the bar at Carlisle, but entered the ministry, and who is still living and well known; Thomas McCandlish, who died and is still well remembered in Newville. These and many others whom we have not mentioned, were among the number known by the neighbors at that time as "Cooper's Latin scholars." The disipline of the school was not remarkable for strictness, but there were few temptations. The "entertainments" of the neighborhood were very few and simple. "Often in the evening," says Dr. Nevin, "some of the boys would be pitching iron rings by the roadside, near the gate, whilst others on the porch were playing checkers, and others still, with the violin and flute, were making sweet strains of music to float out upon the gentle breeze, over the quiet and beautiful landscape that lay beneath. Now and then a fishing in the creek was resorted to as an expedient for enjoyment. With well prepared torch-lights, nets and poles, all the students would march about dark to the Conodoguinet, and spend five or six hours wading in that beautiful stream, often returning with success, at midnight, to their homes, sometimes with no success, but always with glad hearts, making the surrounding woods echo with their songs."* Such were the harmless recreations, the simple amusements, at this primitive academy, in the township of Hopewell,—scenes such as some modern Goldsmith might delight to picture. The academy closed its existence about the year 1832.

MISCELLANEOUS.

There are, at present, six public schools in Hopewell Township; the time for the "log colleges," in remote places, away from the great thoroughfares of civilization, with the ceasing of their necessity, have passed away. In the mean time the township is noted only for its fine farms and industrious agricultural community.

*Dr. Nevin's address at Middle Spring, 1876.

BOROUGH OF NEWBURG.

Newburg is the only village in Hopewell Township. It is situated on slightly elevated ground on the main road leading from Carlisle to Roxbury, about one mile northwest of the Conodoguinet Creek. It was laid out in 1819 by Thomas Trimble. There were then but three or four houses in the place. One at the western end was Mr. Trimble's; another, at the eastern, was occupied by George McCormick; and a third by John Carson and Joseph Barr. In 1845 it is described by Rupp as "a post village in Hopewell Township; * * contains twenty or more dwellings, two stores and a tavern." It has now three churches, three dry goods stores, one drug store, one tavern, tannery and other shops, and a population of about 400. It was organized as a borough in 1861.

In 1858, a school known as "The Sunny Side Female Seminary" was begun at Newburg. It was regularly chartered by the Legislature and issued diplomas, but lasted only for a few years.

CHAPTER XXVI.

LOWER ALLEN TOWNSHIP AND BOROUGH OF NEW CUMBERLAND.*

LOWER ALLEN TOWNSHIP was formed by the division of Allen Township in 1850. It lies in the extreme southeastern portion of the county, and is bounded on the north by Hampden and East Pennsborough, on the east by the Susquehanna River, on the south by the Yellow Breeches Creek, and on the west by Upper Allen Township. The whole of the land of which this township is formed was, long before the formation of Cumberland County, a portion of the proprietary manor known as "Paxtang."

From a period unknown the Susquehanoc Indians inhabited the woods on the western shore of the river, and long before the first white man had crossed it, or the first ax had made the primeval forest ring, some sixty families of Shawanese, who had come from the far south, had settled here upon the river's border. There they remained until about 1727 or 1728, when they removed to the Ohio, and placed themselves under the protection of the French. They, and the Delawares, who also lived on this side of the Susquehanna, assigned as a reason for this course that satisfaction had not been made them for land surveyed into the proprietary manor on Conodoguinet. A number of Indian villages existed in this lower portion of the county, three in Lower Allen Township. One was a little north of the spot where the Yellow Breeches Creek empties into the Susquehanna (now New Cumberland) where James Chartier had a landing place; another Indian village was a short distance north of the house now occupied by William Kohler; and the third on an elevation in the neighborhood of Milltown, where there was an Indian burial place, the graves of which, it is said, were easily distinguishable in the early days of some of the present inhabitants.

Of the earliest white settlers who crossed over the river into the North Valley, we have no knowledge. They were probably "squatters," who settled on lands west of the Susquehanna prior to the final Penn purchase in 1736,

*For Borough of Shiremanstown see page 268.

and who have left no record of their names. On the west shore of the Susquehanna, at a very early period, one Kelso lived, and, in connection with Harris, managed a ferry. This building is the oldest of its kind in the Cumberland Valley. It was built prior to 1740, and possibly before 1730. In 1739 Alexander Frazier bought of the Penn heirs a tract of 200 acres on which the present mills and a part of the town of Lisburn are situated. The elder Harris, at his death, owned land in the Cumberland Valley, including Gen. Simpson's place below Yellow Breeches, extending to the South Mountain. Among the earliest settlers Isaac Hendrix lived upon the manor, as did also William Brooks, of Scotch-Irish origin, who purchased Lot No. 12 of the manor plot, situated on the Yellow Breeches Creek about three miles from the Susquehanna River, and erected thereon a grist-mill and saw-mill, which were very important at that early period. He was a Presbyterian and a very correct man in all his dealings.

In 1740, Peter Chartier, the Indian interpreter, who was of mixed French and Shawnee Indian blood, purchased from John Howard and Richard Penn, 600 acres, bounded on the north by Washington Kinster's and George Mumper's lands, on the east by the river, on the south by the Yellow Breeches, and on the west by property belonging to Andrew Ross and the Flickinger heirs. William Black, from Scotland, purchased property in 1773, now belonging to the above mentioned heirs; and John Mish, a native of Wurtemburg, in 1770, bought 283 acres, Lot No. 6 of the manor, where the Zimmermans live, and built upon the bank of the Yellow Breeches Creek a house and tannery, prior to the period of the Revolution. About this time (1770) John Wilson purchased 200 acres, Lot No. 5 of the manor, now owned by the heirs of Wm. Mateer, and extending from the Feeman to the McCormick farm. The land lying between this tract and the bridge at Harrisburg was purchased by Moses Wallis in 1768-70. It is Lot No. 4 of the manor, and is now owned by the McCormicks. Extensive quarries of limestone are on this land.

John Fleck, who died at the age of sixty-five, in the year 1795, was in his day the largest land-owner in this portion of the county, and must have settled there at a very early period. The great-grandfather of William R. Gorgas came from Holland near the beginning of the century, but did not settle in the valley and township till 1791. Michael T. Simpson, prominently connected with the war of the Revolution, established the Simpson ferry four miles below Harris', and was a prominent man of the times.

The pioneer settlers in the eastern portion of Cumberland County were principally from the North of Ireland, although some came directly from Scotland and some few from England.

After a time a number of German settlers mingled with them. The fertility of the soil and the beauty of the newly settled valley attracted them into it, where they established homes, and where, by their industry and frugality, they have increased in wealth and numbers, so that they have in a great measure displaced the descendants of the original Scotch-Irish.

The character of the soil in Lower Allen is principally limestone. In the neighborhood of Lisburn, on the Yellow Breeches Creek, the middle secondary red shales and sandstones pass across from York County, overlapping the limestone to a limited extent. The predominant interest is the agricultural, and fine farms, highly cultivated, are to be seen in every part of the township. Iron ore, of excellent quality, has been found in detached portions, and some 10,000 tons were taken from the farm of William R. Gorgas, to supply in part the Porter Furnace at Harrisburg prior to 1846. For various causes, however, we believe they have been long abandoned.

LISBURN.

Lying in a loop of the Yellow Breeches Creek, in the extreme south, is Lisburn, the oldest village in the township. The portion of it north of the public road was laid out 120 years ago by Gerard Erwin, and that part south of the road in 1785 by Alexander Frazer and James Oren. The mills, the old forge and a portion of the town are all located on a tract of land which was conveyed by the heirs of William Penn to William Frazer in 1739. The names "New Lisburn," "Lisborn" and "Lisbon" are found in various deeds and conveyances as far back as 1765, and in them lots are numbered to correspond with a plat of the town which had been made previous to that time. One is "From Ralph Whitsett (Whiteside) to William Bennett for a lot where Jacob Flickernell has built his brick house," which was possibly the first brick house erected in the township. The Lisburn Forge, near the present mill, was built in 1783. It is said of this town that fairs used to be held annually in it to which the people resorted, dressed in the fashions of the "old country." Among the more prominent men connected in early days with the history of this village were Alexander Frazer, the original proprietor, William Bennett, Ralph Whiteside (or Whitsett), James Galbraith, Adam Brenizer, Robert Thornberg, Michael Hart, Benjamin Anderson, Andrew Mateer, Peter McKane, J. Snyder and John McCue.

Of the above names, James Galbraith, the younger, settled in Donegal about the year 1719. He was an Indian trader, and commanded a company of rangers during the French and Indian war. He was also a member of the Assembly for a number of years. He moved to the Susquehanna, established a ferry below Paxtang, but shortly after purchased large tracts in Pennsborough (now Lower Allen) about the year 1761. He went into the Revolution, and was chosen lieutenant-colonel for Cumberland County, but on account of his great age was unable to continue active duty in the field. He died June 11, 1787, aged eighty-three years. He left to his son, Robert, a farm in Allen Township. His granddaughter by his son, Andrew, married Chief Justice Gibson.

MILLTOWN.

Another cluster of seventeen or eighteen houses in the township is known as Milltown or Eberly's Mills. It is pleasantly situated in a dell on the Cedar Spring, three miles southwest of Harrisburg. It is on land originally owned by Rev. William Thompson. Caspar Weaver (or Weber), who owned two lots of the original manor, erected a mill at this point more than a 115 years ago.

A grist-mill was erected by George Fahnestock in 1817, which is still standing. A building which was once a clover-mill was, years ago, fitted up as a machine shop, and in it worked Daniel Drawbaugh, who claims to be the original inventor of the telephone, a claim which, after very expensive and protracted litigation, has, either rightly or wrongly, been recently decided against him.

Of the other mills, a quarter of a mile east of Milltown stands the stone one erected by Henry Weber in 1817. The Lisburn Mills were probably first erected as early as 1751, for in that year a portion (some twenty acres) of the Frazer Tract was dedicated to that purpose, and a log mill erected on it. The property belonged to a son of the original proprietor until 1765. Garver's mill was built in 1826 by Jacob Haldeman, who owned it until 1863. The woolen factory on the creek, two miles northeast of Lisburn, was erected upon the site of an old oil, grist and saw-mill in 1857. The old Liberty Forge on the creek, one mile north of Lisburn, was erected some time during the last century. There are a number of other mills in the township, but the list which we have given embraces those which are the most ancient and interesting.

CHURCHES.

There are three churches in the township, the Mennonite, the Bethel at Milltown, and the Union Church ot Lisburn. The Mennonites began to come into the county about 1800, or shortly after, and held meetings at the Slate Hill, one mile south of Shiremanstown, in Allen Township. Their brick church was erected here about the year 1818. The church at Milltown was erected upon an eminence near that place in 1842, and the Union Church at Lisburn in 1829.

CEMETERIES.

There are a number of old burial places in the township. Of some of these no record of their origin remains. The one at Lisburn, on the southeastern slope of the high grounds near the creek, is probably one where the early settlers of this section deposited their dead. There is a public cemetery near the Stone Tavern, and a private one near Paul Gehr's residence; one on the farm of John Feeman contains the graves of the Black family, and must have been among the first established in the township. Another is on an eminence known as Bunker Hill, and contains the graves of the Miller family, also dating from the earliest settlement.

There is yet another grave-yard, the origin of which has passed away, seemingly, from the recollection of the living. For our information we are indebted to a note left by the late Dr. Robert Young, whose grandfather, Alexander Young, settled on a lot in Louther Manor in 1769. Says he: "The Scotch-Irish settlers at an early date, somewhere before 1740, and possibly prior to the location of the meeting-house at Silvers' Spring, had selected a burial place near to a beautiful spring, about two miles from the Susquehanna River, on the Simpson ferry road, on land long owned by Mr. George Rupp, an estimable citizen and minister of the old Mennonite Society." [It lies just south of the road and a little distance west of the Cedar Spring.] "This ground was brought to the notice of the writer, when quite young, by those who were then old men." At this period the stones had fallen to the ground, and long after, in 1875, the ground was covered with scrubby thorns, briars and long grass.

SCHOOLS.

John Black, one of the early settlers who came into the valley about 1773, erected a log schoolhouse within half a mile west of his residence, for the education of his own and his neighbor's children.

Another school was then, or afterward, where New Cumberland now is, and these were the only schoolhouses in the township until 1815, when the Cedar Spring Schoolhouse was built and maintained by private subscription until the introduction of the common school system. At this latter place, in 1850, a new and substantial building was erected, with a basement intended for a primary department. The schoolhouse, one mile northwest of New Cumberland, known as "Mumpers," was built in 1846, on the spot where a more substantial brick edifice was erected in 1864.

MISCELLANEOUS.

The Cumberland Valley Railroad runs along the entire northern boundary line of the township, and the Harrisburg & Potomac Railroad passes through the center portion. The postoffices are Shiremanstown, New Cumberland, Lisburn and Eberly's Mills.

BOROUGH OF NEW CUMBERLAND.

New Cumberland is beautifully situated on the west bank of the Susquehanna River and at the mouth of the Yellow Breeches Creek, in the extreme southeastern corner of the county. It was formerly known as Haldeman's town, after Jacob M. Haldeman, by whom it was laid out in 1814. As late as 1730 a Shawnee Indian village occupied the site where New Cumberland now stands. Here, also, was the landing place of Peter Chartier, a celebrated Indian trader, to whom a large grant of 600 acres, including the present site of New Cumberland, was made by the three Penns in 1739. He was of mixed French and Shawnee Indian blood, and many of these latter, over whom he had great influence, he persuaded afterward (1744) to join the French.

Some eight years before the town was laid out Mr. Haldeman purchased a forge at the mouth of the creek, added a rolling and slitting mill, and soon became one of the foremost iron men in Pennsylvania. The product of his forge, for many years, was sold to the Government for purposes at Harper's Ferry.

There was then no bridge over the creek at New Cumberland, and none over the Susquehanna at Harrisburg. The ferries were valuable properties, and their owners usually made historic names.

In the early history of the place, large quantities of coal and lumber were brought to New Cumberland, on the river, by means of rafts, which supplied Cumberland Valley and other territory; and flour, grain, iron and whisky were received in great quantities, and sent, by means of "arks," upon the river, to Port Deposit, Philadelphia and Baltimore.

A large grain depot was erected by Mr. Haldeman in 1826, which supplied a terminal market for the Cumberland Valley. Here the great teams which were used in those days might have been seen discharging their loads of grain, and reloading with lumber ere starting again upon their homeward trip. At this time the lumber trade was carried on extensively. Prior to 1814 there were two lumber yards, one just north of the town belonged to John Crist and Robert Church, and another, on the south side of the creek, to John Poist, who built and kept what was known as the White Tavern. Mr. Church married Miss Bigler, and their daughter Mary became the wife of Gov. Geary, and presided at the executive mansion during his term of office.

In 1831 New Cumberland was incorporated as a borough, and, about a year later, the turnpike road through the town was established, with its daily stages, to Washington and Baltimore. At this time no railroad had yet been built in this portion of the country, although the time was fast approaching when one of the first ones built in the United States was to extend through a portion of the Cumberland Valley. This, however, did not reach New Cumberland. The York & Cumberland Railroad was opened for business in 1851, and from that time the long line of teams gradually disappeared from the streets, the lumber was taken away by the cars, the hotels were no longer crowded with the boisterous raftsmen and teamsters, and many of them in the town and vicinity have since ceased to exist. The lumber business, with some periods of depression, continued steadily to increase, reaching its highest point in 1857, when seven firms were engaged in that business. From this time, however, there has been a gradual diminution in the trade, which is now represented by one firm.

New Cumberland has now about 140 dwellings, 2 churches, 2 hotels, a number of stores, 1 flour, 2 saw-mills, and a large planing-mill, while new homes are being yearly erected.

The first church was built in 1828, and was the only one in the town for a period of over thirty years. The present Methodist Episcopal Church was erected in 1858, and the United Brethren in 1873.

In the early days, about 1816, the Rev. Jacob Gruber, who is still remembered by many on account of his striking eccentricity, and Rev. Richard Tidings, both itinerant Methodist ministers, established an "appointment" in New Cumberland.

Many of the denizens of New Cumberland find steady employment in the Pennsylvania Steel Works, which are on the other side of the river, just opposite the town. They may be seen crossing it at almost all hours of the day or night.

Gen. Geary made this place his home during the period of the war, and lived in New Cumberland at the time he was elected Governor of Pennsylvania.

CHAPTER XXVII.

MIDDLESEX TOWNSHIP.

MIDDLESEX TOWNSHIP was formed from a portion of North Middleton, by a decree of the court, confirmed November, 1859.

It is bounded on the north by the North Mountains, on the east by Silver Spring Township, on the south by South Middleton Township, and on the west by North Middleton Township.

The Conodoguinet Creek flows, with a slightly southern bend, until it reaches Middlesex, where, suddenly taking an almost northerly direction, after several smaller bends, it leaves the township. The character of the soil is the same as that of North Middleton,—the slate land lying to the north and the limestone to the south, with the creek as the dividing line.

The Cumberland Valley Railroad runs through the southern and richer portion of the township.

EARLY SETTLERS.

The lands upon the creek were probably the ones where the early settlers founded their first homes. Where the Letort stream empties into it was a large tract, owned by Rowland Chambers, and back of him on the Conodoguinet was a settlement, where, some claims, the first mill in the county was erected. North of this, and beyond the creek, were lands of Joseph Clark and Robert Elliott, who came from Ireland about 1737. Soon after Abraham Lamberton settled on lands lately in possession of his descendants, north of the Rowland Chambers' tract, while still further north Thomas Kenny settled on a tract which is now principally in the possession of the heirs of John Wilson. East of them were John Semple, Patrick Maguire, Christopher Huston and Josiah McMeans. Other parties living in different portions of this neighborhood in 1793, were William Sanderson, Alexander McBeth, Robert Kenny, James Lamberton, David Elliott, Hugh Smith, Robert Morrison, Ralph Sterritt. We find the names also of James Giffen (Given) 1798; Robert Elliott, 1799; James Flemming, 1799; John McClintock, 1801.

Sterrett's Gap was originally called Croghan's Gap, after George Croghan, one of the Indian interpreters of these early days; but whether he ever resided there, or in any portion of what is now this township, we have not been able to determine.

The family of Clarks were early settlers in Middlesex, and owned a tract now owned by the Clendenin heirs, just above the Carlisle Sulphur Springs. The first brick house built in this part of the county, about one-half mile or more south of Sterrett's Gap, is said to have been built by Philip Zeigler, and is still in the possession of the descendants of that family. Near this, about one mile east, on the public road leading from the Sulphur Springs, was erected the old log house, still standing, with its loopholes through which its inmates watched the Indians. This Zeigler tract was originally owned by Mr. Kenny, who was, we are told, a man of considerable acquirements, and fond of hunting.

MIDDLESEX.

Middlesex, situated at the confluence of the Letort and the Conodoguinet, is one of the oldest settlements in the county. The name "Middlesex" was originally given to a tract of land containing abut 560 acres, located at the mouth of the Letort Spring, and afterward to the village which was built partly upon it. Some of the first buildings erected—several dwelling houses, a grist-mill saw-mill, fulling-mill and distillery—were on this tract. Others were built near it. All these, with the exception of the fulling-mill, were built prior to 1757; most, if not all of them, by John Chambers, Sr., the owner of the tract at that time.

Later, from the Chambers family, the Middlesex estate came into the possession of Capt. Robert Callender, one of the largest fur traders in Pennsylvania. He held a captain's commission in the French and Indian war; was a colonel during the Revolution; distinguished himself, it said, at Braddock's defeat; and was a liberal contributor to all the then improvements in Carlisle, a man well educated and highly esteemed. He was one of the justices of Cumberland County in 1764. He commenced to trade with the Indians at an early day, and built the large flouring-mill at the mouth of Letort Run, now Middlesex. In 1774 he was appointed colonel for Cumberland County; died in 1776, and is buried in the old grave-yard at Carlisle. Capt. Robert Callender married, first, a daughter of Nicholas Scull, surveyor-general of Pennsylvania from 1748 to 1759. His daughter Anne, by this wife, married Gen. William Irvine, of Revolutionary fame. His second wife was a sister of Col. Gibson, the father of Chief Justice John Bannister Gibson, by whom he also had a number of children.

In 1791 the Middlesex estate was purchased at sheriff's sale by Col. Ephriam Blaine, from whom it passed to his son, by whom it was conveyed (1818) to James Hamilton, Esq., and afterward (1831) to Hon. Charles B. Penrose, who erected the paper-mill there in about 1850. The first dwelling house stood near the present site of this paper-mill, and was still standing twenty years ago.

In 1846, according to Rupp, the village consisted of eleven dwellings, one of which was a tavern, a store, a saw-mill, a grist-mill, plaster and oil-mill and a woolen factory, at that time owned principally by Mr. Penrose. It is now a scattered village of about twenty-five or thirty houses.

We learn from Rupp that one of the first Indian tracts westward led past Middlesex. It extended from Simpson's Ferry (four miles below Harris') on the Susquehanna River, crossed the Conodoguinet at Middlesex, and thence over the mountain, by way of Croghan's, now Sterrett's Gap.

CARLISLE SPRINGS.

Carlisle Springs is the name of a postoffice village near the North Mountains, in the northwestern corner of the township. It was, for many years, one of the most popular watering places in the county. There is at this place a splendid spring of sulphur water, still flowing into its marble basin, in a now neglected grove. The first hotel, a small two-story frame building, was erected by Hon. William Ramsey, who was the owner of the land before 1830. In 1832 his executors conveyed this property to David Cornman, who continued to own it for a period of about twenty-one years, during which period it became a very popular summer resort.

A large hotel, which would accommodate several hundred boarders, was erected by Morris Owen and A. P. Norton about 1854, which was destroyed by fire about 1867. A small hotel, near the site of the former one, was built shortly afterward, but has since been converted into a private residence. From this place a small stream, known as the Sulphur Springs Run, flows in a southeasterly direction until it empties into the Conodoguinet Creek at Middlesex.

MISCELLANEOUS.

There are eight schools in the township, three bridges crossing the creek, good roads, and many fine farms, with substantial buildings, bearing evidence to the prosperity and thrift of its inhabitants.

CHAPTER XXVIII.

MIFFLIN TOWNSHIP.

MIFFLIN TOWNSHIP was formed from the eastern portion of Hopewell in 1797, and was called after Thomas Mifflin, then Governor of Pennsylvania. It is bounded on the north by the North Mountains and on the south by the Conodoguinet Creek, while Frankford Township lies upon the east and Hopewell on the west.

The soil is a mixture of clay, gravel and slate, such as lies along the base of the North Mountains, which has become fertile by cultivation. Four streams run from the mountains through the township, and empty into the Conodoguinet Creek.

From what we have said of Hopewell, in which Mifflin was included, it will be seen that this portion of the county was settled at a very early period. Before the time of the white settlers there was an Indian trail, of a local character, through Doubling Gap, and a more important one through the Three Square Hollow, in the northwestern corner of the township, which was a branch of the great trail leading from the Ohio to the Susquehanna. This trail came down through the Three Square Hollow, crossed the Conodoguinet Creek near the mouth of Brandy Run, passed along the Green Spring to the head of the Big Spring, and thence southeastwardly toward Monaghan (Dillsburg) and York. Along this trail, between the two branches in the fork of Brandy Run, it is said that evidence of an old Indian burial ground existed many years ago, and there are traditions that an Indian village existed in the same neighborhood, and that the peninsula in the long bend of the creek, now owned by Matthew Thompson, was used for raising the Indian corn which, in connection with game, constituted their food. In support of these traditions, says Rev. James B. Scouller, to whom we are indebted for the above, are the two facts that the first settlements made in Mifflin were along this trail, and all the massacres which took place during the old French war were in its vicinity.

The time of the first settlement in Mifflin is earlier than has been supposed.[*] We have in our possession a letter from Mr. W. C. Koons, a descendant, on the maternal side, of the Carnahans, who were among the earliest settlers in the township, which we will lay before the reader:

"The first settlers in Newton and Mifflin Townships, then included in Hopewell, were Robert Mickey, William Thompson and Andrew McElwain. They were brothers-in-law, and came at the same time to make their homes in this part of Cumberland Valley. Robert Mickey located near the source of the west branch of Green Spring, in Newton Township; William Thompson on the great bend in the Conodoguinet Creek, and Andrew McElwain (or McIlvaine) on the "Fountain of Health" farm, both in Mifflin Township. There is uncertainty as to the particular year of their settlement; but by receipts given to Robert Shannon by John Penn, dated respectively 1732, 1733, 1734, and a deed, on full payment, dated 1735, it is certain that their coming was not later than 1729, as they had preceded Shannon by three years. Still, as the papers indicate that it was not unusual for the settlers to occupy their lands for years before warrants or patents were issued, it is quite possible that the settlement may have been made several years previous to 1729. Soon after they were joined by Stevenson, Shannon, the Carnahans, Nicholsons, Williamsons and others. These were all Presbyterians, and during hostilities with the Indians, they were in the habit of carrying their fire-arms with them to church for protection in case of assault.

The Williamson Massacre.—"The Williamson massacre, as to date and details, is a matter of tradition, as far as known. We find it put down as having occurred in 1753 or 1754. The family lived on the farm adjoining the Andrew McElwain tract on the east side. The evening preceding the massacre several men from the Carnahan Fort were stopping at Andrew McElwain's, distant about three miles from the fort. About dusk Mrs. McElwain went out to look after some cattle. Nearing the stock-yard she heard the sound of footsteps, as of men getting over the fence at the opposite side. Believing them to be Indians she returned to the house and informed the inmates of what had occurred. The men from the fort remained keeping watch during the night. About daylight the sound of guns was heard from beyond the hill in the direction of the Williamsons, nearly a mile distant. Immediately all started for the fort, and after proceeding a little way it was discovered that a babe had been left in the cradle. Two of the men returned, brought the child away,[†] and all reached the fort in safety. Shortly after their arrival a number of men was sent out from the fort to look after the Indians. Reaching the Williamson farm they found that the whole family—some eight or nine persons, Mrs. Williamson excepted—had been murdered. I may add, that the only material difference between this and other versions of this bloody affair which have come to my notice, is, that Mrs. Williamson, carrying a child with her, escaped.

"Another incident connected with the strife between the hostile Indians and the early settlers I may mention, although not so fully informed as to its details. The Nicholsons lived near the Whisky Run, on what is probably best known as the farm once owned by Rev. John Snoke. The event is put at

---
[*] Rev. James B. Scouller, well versed in the local history of the township, places the date of the earliest settlers in Mifflin, in his sketch in Dr. Wing's History, at 1734-36, "because at the time the wave of population flowed up the valley on the north side of the Conodoguinet."
[†] "This rescued babe," says Rev. James B. Scouller, "was the grandmother of James M. Harlan, of Mifflin."

about 1755. During the night the Nicholsons were disturbed by the barking of their dog. The married brother opened the door to see what was the matter. Instantly he was shot by the Indians, fell dead at the door, was drawn inside and the door closed. The Indians made several attempts to get into the house, but in each case were successfully resisted. The unmarried brother, assisted by the dead man's wife, kept up a constant fire. They had three guns; the women, while the fight went on, made bullets and loaded the guns. The Indians retired, leaving no dead, but blood marks seen in several places on the ground the next morning proved that they had suffered severely.

"The brother and widowed mother each mounted a horse, the former carrying the body of the slain man before him, and the latter a child before her, and another behind, rode to Shippensburg, and buried him there."

Says the writer of the above: "I feel as if I ought to say that I have relied very much upon my own recollection of what I heard my mother, who was born in Mifflin Township in 1795, and her brother William, who was born ten years before, say in reference to the fort, the defense made by the Nicholsons and the Williamson massacre. I am indebted to Mr. Andrew McElwain, of Fannettsburg, Penn., for the names of the first three settlers.

"The places they had located I had known from my boyhood. My recollection of the Williamson affair is confirmed by Mr. McElwain's statements, and it is upon his say entirely that the number of the murdered is put at 'eight or nine.' I have a very clear recollection of mother's statement respecting the killing of Mr. Nicholson, the defense made by the brother, and heroism of the woman who assisted him in loading the guns and molding bullets while the fight went on. But as to the statement which I have added upon information obtained from other sources, in respect to carrying the dead body on horseback to Shippensburg for burial, my memory supplies nothing. I do not make this qualification, however, with a view to cast discredit upon the alleged fact, but simply to indicate that it is well nigh impossible that my mother ever told it to me. With this explanation before you [the township historian] it will be for you to judge of the authenticity and value of these reminiscences."

Besides the early settlers whom we have mentioned, the Laughlins Browns, McLaughlins, Agers, Bradys, were all probably settled in what is now Mifflin Township; before 1751 the names of all are found in the tax-lists of Hopwell (which then included Mifflin) of that year. To these we may add probably the Porterfields and Lightcaps. Seemingly at a later time came the McElhennys, Bells, Scoullers, Sterritts, Morrows, Lusks and others. Most of these families have departed. The Nicholsons were extensive slaveholders, and when Pennsylvania abolished slavery they removed to Kentucky. One of the descendants of the Shannon family has been Governor of Ohio. Of the Carnahans a descendant says: "I have no means of fixing the precise date of the Carnahan settlement, nor can I say that the two brothers, James and William, came the same year. Both, however, settled previous to 1740, and the probability is, that it was but a few years, at most, after the settlement of the first comers (1729). They were Scotchmen. James bought land in Newton Township, William in Mifflin. James and William Thompson joined lands on opposite sides of the creek, and William Carnahan located a little lower down the stream, the upper part of his tract, however, adjoining James', with a tract belonging to one of the Williamsons intervening between his and William Thompson's on the Mifflin side. James had two sons, Adam and James. The son, James, was a captain in the Revolutionary war. Joseph Koons has in his possession the sword which he carried during the war. Adam Carnahan died in 1800. His brother, James, and Robert Carnahan (son of William) were his executors, and at this death the name of the Carnahans disappears from Newton Township.* Robert only remained in Mifflin. He was married to Miss Judith McDowell, who was born in Philadelphia a few days after her parents landed (1763), and died May 24, 1835. They had four children—two sons, William and Robert, and two daughters, Margaret and Jane. William, the elder son, immigrated to Indiana in 1835 (died 1869, aged eighty-four). Robert went to Cincinnati (died ——). Margaret married Robert McElhenny. They moved to Columbus, Ohio, but, he dying soon after, she returned to the old home in Mifflin. Jane married Isaac Koons.

Block-Houses.—There was a number of smaller forts or block-houses in Mifflin Township. One, probably the oldest, built about the beginning of the French and Indian war, is said to have been located on the creek near the mouth of Brandy Run, on the Carnahan farm. (See sketch of Newton Township.) Others, some of them built at a later date, seem to have been located as follows: One on the Lusk farm, near Sulphur Spring; one at McComb's, near Doubling Gap; one on the old Knettle farm, near Center Schoolhouse, remains of which existed in 1809; and another on the old Zeigler farm, the chimney of which, it is said, is still standing, now the chimney of the house of James M. Harlan.

During the Revolution there lived, in the Brandy Run region, the celebrated Capt. Samuel Brady, the Indian fighter and commander of a company of rangers. He was the grandson of Hugh Brady, the elder, who settled in Hopewell Township, where we have given some account of Capt. Brady in connection with that family. There was also living in this section, it is said, one Joseph Ager (or Aiger, as we find the name in the early, 1751, tax list), more familiarly known as "Joe Aiger," who, returning one day to his home (about 1755), found his father and mother murdered by the Indians. Over their dead bodies, it is said, as of Brady, that he swore eternal enmity against all Indians, and that he would take a hundred of their scalps for each parent who had been murdered. Tradition states that he fulfilled his oath, and that he would wander through the wilderness as far west as the Allegheny River and the valley of the Ohio.

To return again to more certain ground. It can not now be told who settled first along the Big Run. The deed for a tract at its mouth from the Penns to John Scouller was given in 1762. A Mr. Thompson was located higher up, between the Big and the Back Runs, most of which land was sold, in 1765 to 1770, to the Fentons, Mitchells, Mathers, and possibly some others. John McCullough was still further north, near the mountain, on the headwaters of a branch of the Big Spring, on what was since known as the McDannell farm, partly owned by G. Stewart. Adam Bratton and his three brothers-in-law, James, Robert and Nathaniel Gillespie, all of whom had slaves, came into the township in 1776. Bratton lived on the farm owned by his grandson Samuel, James Gillespie lived partly in Frankford Township, Robert on the Wagoner farm, and Nathaniel on the Brown or Snyder farm, where he established the first tannery in the township.

In the records of the court for October, 1778, is the petition for a road from the dwelling house of Adam Bratton into the great road at William Laughlin's mill, leading to Carlisle. Viewers: James and George Brown, Robert McFarlane, James Laughlin, Samuel McElhenny and John Reed.

Another petition in 1781, from Newton (Mifflin had not yet been formed),

---

*Capt. James probably went to Westmoreland County. Of the Carnahans who went to Westmoreland at an early date comes the Rev. J. A. Carnahan, a pioneer preacher of Indiana, now deceased, and doubtless it is to the Carnahans of that county to which the parentage of Dr. Carnahan, of Princeton, can be traced.

MIFFLIN TOWNSHIP.

is for a road beginning at Hogg Ridge, at the foot of the North Mountain, thence to Col. Chambers' mill; thence to William Laughlin's mill on the Big Spring. Viewers: Hugh Patton, James Scroggs, William Hodge, Robert Sharpe, Robert McComb and Samuel McCormick. Another in 1781, is for a road from Laughlin's mill to James Irwin's mill; thence to John Piper's mill; thence to cross the spring at William Hodges; from thence, by Mr. McCracken's tavern, past John Johnston's, to Squire Charles Leiper's saw-mill. Viewers: Col. James Chambers, John Scouller, John Agnew, Allen Leeper, William McFarlane, James Laughlin. Another, still earlier, in 1772, is the prayer for a road from the Three Square Hollow, above Robert McComb's, to Chambers' mill, by John Piper's mill, to James Smith's Gap, in the South Mountain. Viewers: James Jack, Robert McComb, John Piper, John Irwin, Robert Bell, and James Carnahan. Another, in 1782, is for a road from the gap of the Big Run, above Samuel McCormick's, to John Scouller's mill; thence to William Laughlin's mill; thence to Thornberg's Furnace in South Mountain. Viewers: David Sterritt, Adam Bratton, William Hodge and others.

James McFarlan located about 1,000 acres just below Doubling Gap, and in this connection the following will be of interest: In the court records for April, 1791, is the prayer for a road "from Thomas Barnes' sulphur spring, in the gap formerly known as McFarlan's Gap," to Philip Slusser's mill; thence to Samuel McCormick's mill; thence to Carlisle. Viewers: John Moore, John Scouller, William Galbreath, and others. The above indicates to us, seemingly, the original name of Doubling Gap, or the name by which it was known prior to 1791.

McFarlan's land was divided between his two sons, John and William, and his two sons-in-law, Robert Galbreath and Samuel Mitchell. William McFarlan sold his to Samuel McCormick, who built a grist and saw-mill upon it.

All these early settlers before the Revolution, with the exception, possibly, of a few English, were Scotch or Irish. The Germans came into Mifflin at a later period, and probably not before 1782-83. From 1790 they came in rapidly; until, to-day, they have gradually supplanted many of the descendants of the original settlers.

SULPHUR SPRINGS, ETC.

Sulphur springs exist in various portions of the township. Of these the celebrated sulphur spring, in a beautiful grove in the midst of the mountains at Doubling Gap, is best known and most worthy of mention. The place has been a popular summer resort from the beginning of the present century, if not from a still earlier period. The hotel, also in a grove, with lofty mountains lifting their green tops to the blue sky on either side, is situated in a scene of special beauty. The hotel itself will accommodate more than 100 guests. In front of it, beyond the shadowy groves, which are separated by the road which winds through this bending gap, rises one knob of the mountains 1,400 feet, from whose lofty top, "Flat Rock," the whole beautiful valley, from the gleaming Susquehanna on the east to where the turning mountains seem like subsiding waves to the southwest, lies like a panorama at your feet.

About one-third of the distance, as you climb the ascending path, is the recess, under a shelving rock, known as the "Lewis' Cave," so called because that celebrated highwayman and robber once used it for some time as a resort and hiding-place from justice. This was probably about 1816 or 1820. Unlike the ordinary highwayman, "Lewis the Robber," is said to have stolen from the rich and given to the poor. This fact, in connection with his faculty of making friends, his love of fun and adventure, has caused him to be remembered as a sort of Robin Hood. One instance of rather humorous generosity is told, in which he loaned a widow money to save her property from the sheriff, but "recovered" the same from the sheriff himself in the evening as he was proceeding homeward to Carlisle. Some of the neighbors and Nicholas Howard, of Newville, who kept the hotel during those summer days, knew of his retreat, but were fast friends of the generous outlaw. When the coast was clear Howard would hang out a flag from an upper window, which could be seen from the "Cave," and Lewis would come down, and, with some trusted neighbors, have "a jolly night at the hotel." When danger was on his track, he kept concealed in his secret hiding-place, and was supplied with food. In a diary kept by Samuel J. McCormick, who lived two miles south of Doubling Gap, is the following: "On Tuesday, the 20th of June, 1820, the sheriff of Franklin County arrived with a party in search of David Lewis (the robber), and early the next morning proceeded to the mountain southeast of the Sulphur Springs, where they discovered a cave or den, where they found blankets and other articles known to belong to Lewis. But, according to the best information, the inhabitants had decamped on the Thursday before." This was only about three weeks before Lewis' death. It was known that Lewis had a cave somewhere in the mountain to which he fled from time to time, but its locality was not discovered before June, 1820. A confrere, who is described as being coarse and cruel, sometimes encamped with Lewis at this cave, but found no friends in the Gap. He was killed at the same time that Lewis was wounded unto death.

Whisky distilling was a prominent industry of Mifflin more than a century ago. Indeed so common was this habit of turning grain into this fluid form, that a distillery might be seen on almost every farm. From this, two streams, the Whisky and Brandy Runs, derived their names. The western stream is called after the Gap from which it flows, the triangular shape of which suggested, humorously, to some Irishman, its name, "The Three Square Hollow," a name by which it is still known.

CHURCHES.

Beside the early Presbyterians there were a few Covenanters in the township, the former attending service at Big Spring. When the German Reformed and Lutheran population came, they first erected a Union Church, in which the ministers of each would preach alternately. About 1790 ground was given by Jacob Zeigler, near Council Bluff Schoolhouse, for a church and grave-yard. Here a log church was erected, with a high goblet pulpit, on the projecting sides of which were painted the four evangelists. Long afterward, 1832, the Lutherans organized in Newville, erected a church, and soon absorbed the Mifflin membership, so that the old church was seldom used and was finally abandoned. Later it was altogether removed.

Some Menonnite families in the upper part of Mifflin erected a log meeting-house many years ago, which has since been turned into a private dwelling. There are other churches in Mifflin, but more modern, and which need no special mention.

MISCELLANEOUS.

There are eight schools in the township, quite a number of fine farms, and an industrious agricultural community. No railroad touches Mifflin Township, and it has but one postoffice, Heberlig.

CHAPTER XXIX.

MONROE TOWNSHIP.

MONROE TOWNSHIP was formed in 1825, from the western portion of Allen, which then extended to the Susquehanna River. It lies in the southern tier of townships, and is bounded on the north by Silver Spring Township, on the east by Upper Allen Township, on the south by York County, and on the west by South Middleton Township. The northern chain of the South Mountains extends over the southeastern portion of Monroe, bounding its fertile fields with the long line of its blue horizon, and inclosing within its deep recesses a number of valuable beds of iron ore, such as are to be found also in other portions of the township. Beyond the "Callaposink" or Yellow Breeches Creek, which flows in an easterly direction, not far from the base of these mountains, are the slightly rolling hills of the rich limestone and loam land, where fine farms and farm houses everywhere abound, whose fields, cultivated as they are by the industrious farmer, offer an abundant harvest.

The first settlers who came into what is now Monroe Township, when it was a portion of Allen, were evidently the Scotch-Irish, although there are few, if any, of the present inhabitants by whom their names are still remembered. They were here soon supplanted by the Germans, who came into this portion of the county (Allen Township) prior to 1775.

Of these earlier Scotch-Irish, whom seem first to have taken up the lands along the streams, we know, however, that somewhere east, upon the Yellow Breeches Creek, there was a settlement known as Pippin's tract, where Charles Pippin settled as early as 1742, and that, following the creek westward, were John Campbell, the owner of a mill, Rodger Cooke, David Wilson, John Collins, James McPherson, Andrew Campbell, Andrew and John Miller, Robert Patrick, J. Crawford, William Fear, John Gronow, Charles McConnel, Alexander Frazier, Peter Title, Arthur Stewart, Thomas Brandon, Abraham Endless, and, last, John Craighead, who, as we know, settled upon the stream to the west, in the adjoining township.

Of the Germans who came prior to 1775, all of whom we believe have descendants still living in the township, were John Brindel, Martin Brandt, Jacob Bricker, John and Jacob Cocklin, Samuel Niesley, Joseph Strack, Leonard Wolf, Gideon Kober (Coover), Jacob Miller and a number of others.

George Beltzhoover, Sr., the grandfather of George Beltzhoover, came into the township from York County at a much later period (about seventy-five or eighty years ago). Joseph Bosler now owns the George Beltzhoover, Sr., tract. His son John lived on the south side of the creek, on land now owned by his daughter, Mrs. Leidich, and his son, John Beltzhoover. The mill in that vicinity, now owned by the Shaffner heirs, was built by Michael G. Beltzhoover, Jr., upon the site of one bought of the Hopples, and the mill now owned by Mrs. Leidich, on the creek just below Shaffner's, was for many years known as Bricker's Mill—after Samuel Bricker, who was owner of it nearly a century ago. The lower part is stone and the upper part frame, which has been added within the recollection of the living. Even's Mill, on the creek still below, was known as Brandt's Mill, and Givler's, still further east, as Clark's. Some families, eighty or one hundred years ago, were large landowners in the township. The farms now belonging to David Niesley, Herman Bosler, of Carlisle, Mrs. Sample, and David K. Paul, were all owned by the Brickers—Joseph, William and Moses.

The farm at Lutztown, owned by Mr. Pressel, and the one owned by Samuel Cocklin were once, some three-quarters of a century ago, the property of Peter Bricker. The farms now owned by John Musselman, John Engle and Joseph Bosler were owned by George, Abraham, and Martin Brandt. Clusters of other family names can be found in the township, where the sons have often been born on the same homestead, have cultivated the same fields, and walked, almost literally, in the footsteps of their sires.

CHURCHES AND CEMETERY.

Of the Germans, many are Lutherans, but there are some German Mennonites, who have a house of worship west of Churchtown. There is also a Dunkard Church and cemetery on the Lisburn road, about one mile north.

SCHOOLS, INDUSTRIES, ETC.

There are twelve schools in the township, most of them substantial brick buildings. Besides the predominant agricultural interest and the iron ore, the burning of lime is also an industry, and quite a number of kilns can be seen in different portions of the township. The Harrisburg & Potomac Railroad passes through the township from east to west, and the Dillsburg & Mechanicsburg Railroad from north to south, through the eastern part. The postoffices are Allen and Brandtsville.

VILLAGES.

Churchtown (Allen P. O.), the most important village in the township, is situated near its center. It derived its name, about the year 1830, from an old Lutheran and German Reformed Church, which was erected just east of the present town about 1790.

About seventy years ago there was considerable woodland and only three houses in the immediate vicinity of Churchtown. The first town lots were sold by Peter Leivinger in 1830. He was owner of the land on the eastern side of Main Street, between Church and High Streets. The plat of the town contained eight lots east of and fronting on Main, five south and fronting on Church, and one lot north fronting on High Street. The old house which has for many years been occupied as a hotel, was erected by Jacob Wise about 1804, and was the first house built in Churchtown. The town has at present four churches: Mennonite, Lutheran, Bethel and United Brethren. It has two public schools. Some of the earlier residents were Peter Leivinger, Daniel and Rudolph Krysher, Adam Stemberger, David Diller, Jacob Ritner (son of ex-Gov. Ritner, of Pennsylvania), George Lutz, John A. Ahl, Samuel and John Plank.

It was at this place that Jacob Plank, the grandfather of A. W. Plank, now a justice of the peace, came at an early date from Lancaster County, and invented what was probably the first plow patented in Pennsylvania. One of these patents, about 1836, is entitled "J. Plank's improvement in the Plough," and bears the plain and characteristic signature of Andrew Jackson.

Allen Lodge, No. 299, K. of P., has here a membership of about 100. G. W. Eberly is R. & C. S.

Leidich's Station, on the Harrisburg & Potomac Railroad, about two and a half miles east of Boiling Springs, was called after George W. Leidich, who owned land in the vicinity, and was established in 1874.

The first grist-mill here was built by Mr. Wolf about ninety-seven years ago. The farm at this place, now owned by George Beltzhoover, was patented to Leonard Wolf the 19th of June, 1786, and was for a long time in the possession of his descendants. The farm on the south side of the creek, now owned by Jacob Hoffer, was part of this Leonard Wolf tract, owned afterward by his son Leonard Wolf, by whom it was sold to Michael Ege, from whom it was purchased by Samuel Hoffer, Sr.

Brandt's Station, on the Harrisburg & Potomac Railroad, about three miles east of Boiling Springs, was named after Michael G. Brandt, who owned the land on which it is located, and was established in 1874. This land has been in the possession of the Brandt family since 1765. Martin Brandt, grandfather of Michael, was the first of the family who owned it. A saw-mill and clover-mill were built here about 1828.

Worleytown is a small cluster of houses on the York road, not far from the Yellow Breeches Creek. It dates from about 1815, and was called after David Worley, who owned the land in the vicinity.

Roxbury is a small cluster of houses upon the line which separates Monroe and Silver Spring Townships.

CHAPTER XXX.

NEWTON TOWNSHIP AND BOROUGH OF NEWVILLE.

NEWTON TOWNSHIP, originally included in Hopewell, was formed in 1767. It is of a wedge-like shape, and is bounded on the north by Mifflin Township, the Conodoguinet Creek being the dividing line; on the east by West Pennsborough, Penn, and Cook Townships; its extreme point south touching the line of Adams County, while on the west lie the townships of Southampton and Hopewell.

In its southern portion, extending some two or three miles northward from the base of the South Mountains, are what are known as the pine lands, of a gravelly character, but which produce good crops of wheat. Then, through the center of the township, for the breadth of several miles, is the belt of the richer clay and limestone land, while to the north is found the slate formation which, under the improved methods of agriculture, has grown to produce yearly more abundant crops.

There are a number of small springs or streams in the northern and southern portions of the township. In the south, among the mountains, rises the Yellow Breeches Creek, which is here, however, only a small stream, the name of which is more properly Pine Run. On its northeastern boundary is the Big Spring, which empties into the Conodoguinet Creek, and near its western the Green Spring, in the northern portion of the township. The lands known as the "Barrens" lay near Oakville, a small region devoid of streams. The road from Carlisle to Shippensburg passes through them. When the township was first settled, the southern portion of it was covered with a dense growth of yellow pine, with undergrowth of oak, hickory and chestnut. The center—

that known as the "Barrens"—was without timber; but about the middle of the last century, small pine trees began to make their appearance on these barren lands, until, about 1800, they were covered with a thriving growth of valuable timber. Within the last half century much of this timber has disappeared and much of it has been needlessly destroyed.

In the early days, before the white settlers, there was an Indian pack trail through the township, extending along the Green Spring, thence over to the head of the Big Spring, and thence toward Dillsburg and York. There was also, at a later day, a fort known as "Fort Carnahan," or as it was sometimes called, "Fort Jack." It was built on the James Jack farm, now owned by James and Joseph Koons, situated in Newton Township near the Conodoguinet Creek, opposite the William Carnahan tract in Mifflin Township, now owned by Parker Q. Ahl. There is no doubt about this being the fact, says our informant, himself a descendant of the Carnahans. "The Carnahans," says he, "spoke of its location with the greatest certainty." As late as 1840, evidences of its foundations remained, and the channel cut from the Green Spring to supply the fort with water even then could be traced."

What a wonderful change has occurred since those days, seemingly so distant, of the Indian trail, or the log fort, not only here, but throughout this whole universally admired region! As strange, they are in reality, as are the sudden changes in a dream.

> "Look now abroad—another race has filled
> These populous borders; wide the wood recedes,
> And towns shoot up, and fertile realms are tilled;
> The land is full of harvests and green meads."

The earliest settlers in the township were, as everywhere in the county, the Scotch-Irish. Among them were the McCunes, Sharps, Sterritts, Fultons, Graceys, Mickeys, Scroggs, Kilgores, Beattys and others. Some of the descendants of these are still in the possession of the homes where their ancestors settled. Much of the land in Newton Township had not been taken up at the time of its formation in 1767. A tract of 100 acres, partly in Newton and partly in Mifflin Township, was taken up by Robert McCoome in 1746; one was located, of 100 acres, by John Herman in 1752; James Kilgore and Samuel Williamson also each took up a tract this year; John and Hugh Laughlin took up tracts, of 200 acres each, in 1766, and George Thompson 100 acres, while in the following year, 1767, when the township was formed, tracts were taken up by Samuel Bratton, Matthew Boyd, William Carnahan, Joseph Eager, Robert Mickey, William Nicholson and others.

By far the largest amount of land, however, seems to have been taken up in 1794, during which year twenty-five tracts of 400 acres each, aggregating 10,000 acres, were taken up by the following twenty-five persons: William Auld, Horace and John Bratton, Samuel Dickenson, Thomas Heeling, Josiah Lewis, Atcheson and John Laughlin, Adam and George Logue, James Lamberton, William and Henry Miller, James Moore, William McFarlan, Samuel McClintock, William McCracken, Mark and William McCasland, Benjamin, David, George and Alexander McCune and George Wilson.

David Rawlston also took up a tract of several hundred acres on the Big Pond during this year 1794.* Many tracts of land on the North Mountain, from Doubling Gap to Sterrett's Gap, were taken up by various parties in 1794. Nearly all of the early inhabitants of Newton Township were Scotch-Irish Presbyterians, and among those who came at about or before this time

*There were probably earlier warrants than we have mentioned, as of some known to have existed we can find no record.

was a minister, who settled at Big Spring, whose grandfather, John Brown, a pious carrier of Muir Kirk Parish, Scotland, was shot, in 1685, by Graham of Claverhouse. It was not until near the close of the last century that a few German families began to come into the lower portion of the township. They settled on the pine lands along the mountain. Before 1802 they had erected a small church, which was known as the Dutch Meeting-House. Among these were the Seavers, Thrushes, Frys, Brickers and others. Until after 1830 the German inhabitants of Newton constituted but a small portion of its population; to-day they own much of the most desirable land in the southern portion of the township.

Among the families still represented in Cumberland County by numerous descendants, were the Sharps, who settled in Newton Township at an early period. The ancestor was Thomas Sharp, but the first who came to America was his son Robert. He came over at a very early age, and soon returned to the North of Ireland, where they had immigrated at some previous period from Scotland, and persuaded his father to bring his family over. This was not later than 1746.* Thomas Sharp, the father, had married Margaret Elder, the daughter of a Scottish laird, by whom he had five sons and five daughters. All of these owned lands afterward in Cumberland County, in the neighborhood of the Big Spring. These were Robert, Alexander, Andrew (killed by the Indians), John and James. Of the daughters one married John McCune, another James Hemphill, another —— Fullerton, another John Smith of Lurgan Township, now Franklin but then Cumberland County, and another —— Harper, father of the late William Harper of Dickinson Township. All of these sons, except Andrew, and all the husbands of the daughters, lived and died in the neighborhood of the Big Spring. Their bones and those of their children, and many of their children's children are buried there, in the old grave-yard of the United Presbyterian Church at Newville. All of these sons of Thomas Sharp were, with the exception of Alexander, commissioned officers in the Indian war or the Revolution. Alexander went as a private. The children of Alexander, who married Margaret McDowell, were Andrew, Rev. Alexander Sharp, Dr. William M. Sharp, John, the father of Gen. Alexander Brady Sharpe, of Carlisle, known as "John Sharp of the Barrens;" Col. Thomas Sharp, elder, who died unmarried, aged nineteen, and Ellen, who married Samuel McCune. Rev. Alexander Sharp married Elizabeth Bryson, and his children were Dr. Alexander Sharp, who married Nelly Dent, a sister of the wife of Gen. Grant, and Andrew, who was the father of the late Hon. J. McDowell Sharp, born in Newton Township, one of the ablest lawyers in Pennsylvania, and one of the most prominent members of the Constitutional Convention in 1872–73. Rev. Alexander Sharp lived on the Green Spring, and was pastor of the church at Newville (Big Spring), from 1824 until the time of his death in January, 1857.

Alexander Sharp, the son of Thomas, the ancestor, was the largest land-owner in the township, his tract extending from near Newville to the turnpike above Stoughstown, a distance of about four miles in length and several miles in breadth, nearly all of which, variously divided, is in the hands of his descendants to this day. It bordered on the north on the headwaters of the Green Spring, the right to the watercourse of which stream was the cause of the long war between the Sharps and Kilgores. That litigation, after old Mr. Kilgore had been nearly impoverished by it, was brought to an end by the in-

_{*Two tracts, one of 200 acres another of 20, are found in the list of land warrants as taken up by Thomas Sharp in 1762, 1766. James Sharp, a brother of Robert and son of Thomas, is one of the signers of a petition from Cumberland County to Gov. Hamilton for aid against the Indians July, 1763. — See Rupp's History of Cumberland County, etc., page 68.}

tercession of Samuel McCune (father of the wife of John Sharp of the Barrens) who was known in the community as the peacemaker. Alexander Sharp had a tannery, distillery, mills, etc., and one of his apprentices at the tanning business, which he carried on extensively, was Robert Garrett, of Baltimore, father of John W. Garrett, former president of the Baltimore & Ohio Railroad, and grandfather of Robert M. Garrett, the present president of that road. He sent him, after his apprenticeship was over and before he was twenty years of age, to Baltimore, where he had never been, to begin life, secured for him a warehouse, turned much of the trade of the valley, then carried to Baltimore in wagons, to his place of business, and laid the foundation of the fortune of which he died possessed.

Andrew Sharp, the son of Thomas Sharp, the ancestor, was killed by the Indians at what is now Sharpsburg, a town which was called after him. He went from this valley to Indiana County in 1785, and located on Crooked Creek, eight miles west of Indiana, on the famous Indian trail known as the Kittanning Path, and which Gen. Armstrong followed in his expedition against the Indians at Kittanning in 1756. He took with him his only child, Hannah, born in Cumberland County February 14, 1784 (married in 1803 to Robert Leason), from whom we take the following account of the killing of her father, Capt. Sharp, which was given by her in a letter written to her grand-nephew, William Moorhead: "My father," says she, "was a militia captain, and served under Gen. Washington in the Revolution. He was married to my mother, Ann Woods, in their native place, Cumberland County, in 1783, and with a family of one child moved to Crooked Creek, in what is now Indiana County, Penn. This being a new country, there was no chance for schooling his children. My father, after living there ten years, was determined on having them schooled. He swapt his place for one in Kentucky, where my mother's friends lived. We started to move to Black Lick River, and got into our boat, but the water was low, and we had to land over a day and a night. We started the next. Father had a canoe tied to the side of the boat. It got loose. He went back for it. When he was away, there was a man came and told us the Indians were coming. By that time father got back. All the women and children were in the boat. The men went out to tie up their horses. The sun was an hour and a half high. Seven Indians fired upon them. They were hid behind a large tree that had fallen down. The first fire shot off my father's eyebrow. When he was cutting one end of the boat loose he got a wound in the left side. When he was cutting the other end loose they shot him in the other side, but he got the boat away before they could get in. He saw an Indian among the trees. He called for his gun. Mother gave it to him. He shot him dead. The boat got into a whirlpool, and went round and round for awhile, when the open side went toward land and the Indians fired at us. They followed us twelve miles down the river. They called to us to go out to them or they would fire again. Mrs. Leonner and her son wanted to go out to them. They said the men were all killed or wounded [*i. e.*, the seven who had gone ashore]. Father told him to desist or he would shoot *him*. The Indians shot him dead that minute. He fell across my mother's feet. There were two dead men and two wounded. One of them died the next morning. There was no woman or child hurt. There were twenty in all. They took my father's horses. The others got theirs. My mother worked the boat, and we got to Pittsburgh again by daylight. One man went on before us and had doctors ready. When we got to Pittsburgh there were a great many kind neighbors came to see us when we landed. We lived awhile in the boat. We moved up to the city before father's death. He lived forty days after he was wounded. There were three [wounds] in him, one on each side and one in his back.* He died the eighth day of July in the forty-second year of his age, in the year 1794. He was buried with honors of war in Pittsburgh."

His brother, Alexander Sharp, went from Cumberland County to see him, but Capt. Andrew Sharp had died before he arrived in Pittsburgh. "My uncle," the writer continues, "stayed with us till there were wagons sent for. We went over the mountains to Cumberland County, where our friends lived, and stayed there three years, where we went to school," when they moved back to their old home in Indiana County. "It was a party of twelve Indians that went to Pittsburgh to trade," we are further informed, "who killed Capt. Sharp. The people would not trade with them. They got angry and killed all they could that day. There were three men went down the river in a canoe before us, one of whom was shot dead; the other two were wounded. One of them died and the other got well. He lay in a room next to father's room. He could come to see father. This was the last war which was in that part of the country. It was in the year 1794 when all these things happened."†

We have given the above vivid account, not only because it concerns one of the early pioneers belonging to one of the largest families, or cluster of families, in Newton Township, but also as illustrative of the times, and as one instance of the trials and tribulations of the early settlers, who, impelled by the restless spirit of adventure which was in their blood, moved still farther westward, and were driven back to Cumberland County by the remorseless cruelty of the Indians.

Among the pioneers who settled at an early date in the upper portion of the county were the Moorheads, some of whom resided in that portion which is now Franklin. The name of John Moorhead is found in the tax list of 1750. One of the earliest of this family was Fergus Moorhead, who, impelled westward by the "Saxon hunger for land," left the county in 1769, the year in which the land office was opened for the sale of lands in the northwestern and southwestern counties of Pennsylvania, and purchased, of the Penns, a large tract, known in the patent, after the English fashion, as "Suffield," two miles west of the present town of Indiana, on the road to Kittaning. The smoke of Moorhead's cabin was the first that arose from the chimney of a legal landowner between the Conemaugh River and the old French fort at Le Boeuff. He, like his co-settlers in the Cumberland Valley, was a Scotch Presbyterian, who "carried his Bible in one hand and his rifle in the other."

Two of his brothers, Samuel and Joseph, accompanied him from their old home in Cumberland County, to help in bringing the wagons, live-stock and goods. On their trip they traveled partly on the road made by Gen. Armstrong and his men some twelve years before, when he led his expedition against the Indians at Kittanning. Here he lived until the outbreak of the Revolutionary war, when the Indians became hostile to the English. In 1775 he undertook to conduct a man, by the name of Simpson, from his home to Fort Kittaning. Simpson was the bearer of dispatches from the government to the commander of the Fort, who was Moorhead's brother. Near the Fort they were waylaid by the Indians, Simpson was shot, and Moorhead taken prisoner, carried to Quebec and sold to the British. When his wife had become convinced that some misfortune had befallen him, she started through the wilderness for Cumberland County, with one child in front of her on the

---

* It seems also from the letter that he was recovering, but that the cannons fired on the 4th of July caused his relapse.
† It was in August of this year (1794) that Gen. Wayne gained his decisive victory over the Indians.

HISTORY OF CUMBERLAND COUNTY.

horse and one behind her. She went by way of Fort Ligonier, and reached the Cumberland Valley in safety. Just one year after being taken prisoner, Moorhead returned to his father's home in Cumberland County from Quebec, he having been exchanged as a prisoner.

At Fort Shippen, in the Cumberland Valley, he and his brother Samuel (who also had gone away, built a grist-mill above Homer City, which was burned, and he driven back by the Indians) signed a petition to Gov. Penn, that means might be adopted to protect the frontier inhabitants. After the close of the war he returned again to his new home, near Indiana, which he found in ruins; but he soon built a stone house, which is still standing, and which has ever since been occupied by his descendants. It was said to have been built of memorial stones heaped by the Indians upon the graves of their dead. One son of Fergus Moorhead, Joseph, was wounded at St. Clair's defeat; another, James, was killed at Perry's victory, on Lake Erie; another, Fergus Moorhead, Jr., was the paternal grandfather of Silas M. Clark, of the Supreme Court.*

VILLAGES.

The township contains few villages. Jacksonville (Walnut Bottom P. O.), before 1825, consisted of but six log houses. One, a two-story house on the hill, was kept as a tavern by an Irishman named John McCaslin. Some distance east was another, known as the "Bull Ring" tavern, kept by Michael Hawk. The land on the north side of the road was the property of Peter Fry, and the village was at first called Frystown. It was afterward called Canada, and later Jacksonville. About 1820 the pine forest extended to the town.

Stoughstown, on the turnpike in the eastern portion of the township, was called after Col. John Stough, who kept a tavern there for many years, which tavern was also, prior to 1846, kept by his son. The town dates back to nearly the beginning of the century, and the tavern, for many years, was one of the most noted as a relay house for the teamsters and the stages on the road. Near Stoughstown is a large spring, from which a fine stream issues.

Oakville is a small post-village west of the center of the township and a station on the Cumberland Valley Railroad. Prior to the building of this road it had no existence.

MISCELLANEOUS.

There are small beds of iron ore at places, particularly in the southern portion of the township. The Big Pond Furnace was built some three miles southeast of Leesburg, or Lee's Cross Roads, about forty years ago, near the Big Pond, a deep and somewhat stagnant pool, from which seemingly there is no outlet, made by a mountain stream, on which are Seever's mill, Buchanan's mill, and, after the Three Springs flows into it, Oyster's mill. This furnace, however, at the Big Pond, was long ago abandoned.

The Cumberland Valley and the Harrisburg & Potomac are the two railroads which pass through Newton Township. The postoffices are Newville, Green Spring, Oakville, Big Spring, Stoughstown and Walnut Bottom.

BOROUGH OF NEWVILLE.

The borough of Newville is handsomely situated on the Big Spring, on the line of the Cumberland Valley Railroad, some twelve miles westward of

---

*As to the Moorheads settlement in Indiana County, see also the sketch of that county in Dr. Egle's History of Pennsylvania, p. 793. The date is there given as 1772, but as we have obtained our information from a descendant, who gives the date as 1769, we prefer to let it stand.

NEWTON TOWNSHIP.   323

Carlisle. It was first incorporated as a borough by an act of the Legislature on the 26th of February, 1817, but its inception as a settlement ante-dates the century, and carries us back to the days of our Colonial Government.

In the earlier part of the last century there was something of a settlement in the country surrounding the Big Spring, as a Presbyterian congregation was in existence at that place prior to 1737. A warrant for a tract of about ninety acres of land was issued by the provincial authorities on March 2, 1744, to four persons, namely: William Lamond, James Walker, Alexander McClintock and David Killaugh, in trust for the Presbyterian congregation at Big Spring, which had previously, about 1738, erected a house of worship.* Upon this glebe the congregation built a parsonage, which was occupied until after 1786, but prior to 1790 it was abandoned as a parsonage, and in 1794 laid out into village lots. A plan of the new town was drawn, which consisted of one (Main) street, extending from the spring westward, with Cove and Glebe Alleys running parallel on the north and south, crossed by Corporation, High and West Streets, the former two extending northward to the boundary of the glebe. The first lots were laid out upon these streets, and the remaining portion of the tract was divided into larger parcels of from two to five acres, for pasture or tillage.

The first sale of lots was September 9, 1790. Other sales occurred during the eight or ten years succeeding, until all were sold. They were not put up at auction, but were disposed of at fixed prices, most of them selling for $6 each.† The pasture lots were all sold April 9, 1795, at prices ranging from $24 to $27 per acre. About eight acres on the northeast corner of the glebe were reserved for a parsonage, and subsequently purchased by the pastor, Rev. S. Wilson. On all of these lots laid out for the new town, there was a reserved incumbrance, with an annual quit-rent of 6 per cent to the church, most of which annual quit-rents were extinguished in 1836.‡

FIRST HOTELS, STORES, ETC.

The first buildings were erected upon the eastern part of Main Street and on North Corporation. Robert Lusk was one of the earliest citizens, and is said to have been the first innkeeper in Newville. He built the third house from the spring on Main Street, in which he opened the first tavern. This was before 1792, for in the petition to the court for a license in August of that year he speaks of having kept "a house of entertainment in the house where he now lives the preceding year, and is desirous of continuing the same." Samuel McCullough, having provided himself with a house for keeping a tavern in the town of Newville, also prays the court to recommend him to the Governor for a license this same year. John Dunbar shortly opened a hotel in the third house above Corporation Street, but at what exact date is to us unknown.

The first store is said to have been opened on North Corporation Street, on the east side and north of Cove Alley. About 1797 Thomas Kennedy, father of the late Judge John Kennedy, of the supreme court of Pennsylvania, and of James Kennedy, for many years a justice of the peace in Newville, opened the second store upon the opposite side of Corporation Street, in what is known as the Woodburn row. "Stephen Ryan then opened where Morrow's brick house stands, and was succeeded by Christian Geese. Joseph Colbertson next

---

*This same tract was confirmed to the church, by another patent, under the State authority, in 1794.
†A few lots, on account of exceptional advantages, brought much higher prices; as Lot No 1, on account of water privileges, $213, bought by William Laughlin, and one opposite, $50, bought by George McKeehan.
‡The incumbrance on the front lots was $22.22 each, making the annual quit-rent $1.33; on the back lots $17.90 each, with quit-rent of $1.07, on billious at 3.00 per annum with quit rent of 90 cents. Owing to the annoyance of collecting these rents, the trustees of the church accepted, in 1836, the payment of the incumbrance on most of the lots, and granted to the owners titles in fee simple.

opened in the stone house on the southeast corner of Main and Corporation Streets, which Gen. Samuel Finley had built in 1799. Joseph Showalter, Alexander Barr, William McCandlish, John Johnson, James Huston and others followed." These were the early merchants of the town. The first resident physician was John Gedds. He came from Silver Spring, and settled in Newville about 1792, after having studied medicine with Dr. McCoskry, of Carlisle. Here he practiced until his death in 1840.

The village must have improved with tolerable rapidity, for in 1799, nine years after the sale of the first lots, there were five tavern-keepers in Newville. These were James Woodburn, Joseph Shannon, Thomas Clark, Thomas Martin and Philip Beck. Two years later, 1801, James Woodburn built the Logan House, which is still standing.

In the year 1800 the first postoffice was established. Before this time there were no offices nearer than Carlisle and Shippensburg. For about twenty years there was but one mail each way per week. Then there were two until the building of the railroad in 1838, when the daily mail and the daily papers first made their appearance. There is now Pullman cars and a variable number of daily mails each way.

Coming down to about 1806 and after, we find that the appearance of the town is within the recollection of the living. James Woodburn kept the hotel on the corner of Main and Corporation Streets. Up two or three lots, John Dunbar kept a hotel. The names of two of the sehotels were "The Indian Queen" and "The Eagle." Opposite was Samuel Crowell, on the corner of Main Street, not yet built up. Near the corner of Main and High, Philip Beck kept a tavern. On the extreme upper end of Main Street Patrick Dunfee and William MacMonagal had their inns. Besides these there were two on Corporation Street, Thomas Clark and Andrew Thompson. The area of these public houses embraced the extreme limits of the town. Few buildings had been erected west of High Street. Clusters of buildings afterward grew up on the western end of Main Street, and the two portions of the town gradually grew together. The original portion of the town, however, was that lying just north or slightly northwest of the old Presbyterian Church and cemetery.

INCORPORATION, ETC.

The town, which was first laid out in 1794, remained for more than twenty years a part of Newton Township. Dissatisfaction existed as to the proportionate assessments of property, and on application to the Legislature a borough charter was granted February 26, 1817. The town, however, continued to pay its proportion of road taxes to Newton Township until January sessions, 1828, when the borough was formed into a township by the court. To get rid of the inconvenience of two sets of officers—borough and township—a more comprehensive charter was granted by the court in 1869.

Since the building of the railroad, the track of improvement has turned south toward the depot, and westward along the line of the road, giving to the plan of the town quite an irregular form.

What was known as Newtown was laid out prior to the war by the McFarlan brothers, John and William Gettys, and some buildings erected. Shortly after the Ahl brothers laid out an addition to the borough, extending southwesterly toward the railroad, on the Jerry McKibbon land, which two portions of the town were taken into the borough of Newville in 1874, and now constitute the South Ward. Until this time the boundaries of the old glebe farm, which had been originally granted to the church, constituted the limits of the borough.

NEWTON TOWNSHIP.

Newville, in 1845, is described by Rupp as having about 100 dwellings, several mills, taverns and churches (two Presbyterian and one Lutheran), and three public schools. Previous to this, in 1840, it is described as having six stores and three taverns. Its population at various periods has been: In 1830, 530; 1840, 564; 1850, 715; 1860, 885; 1870, 907; 1880, 1,650.

The town was divided into the north and south wards by a decree of the court, confirmed July, 1874.

AN HISTORICAL CHARACTER.

One of the most interesting facts in connection with the history of the town of Newville, is that the artizan, William Denning, who succeeded in making the first wrought-iron cannon in America, lived, after the Revolution, in the neighborhood of Newville, and was buried in the grave-yard of the old Presbyterian Church at that place. No tombstone, however, marks the spot, although some of the older citizens claim to have located it. He died December 19, 1830. The following account is given of him in Hazard's Register, Vol. VII: "The deceased was an artificer in the Revolution. He it was who, in the days of his country's need, made the only successful attempt ever made in the world to manufacture wrought-iron cannons, two of which he completed at Middlesex, in this county, and commenced another and larger one at Mount Holly, but could get no one to assist him who could stand the heat, which is said to have been so great as to melt the buttons off his clothes. This unfinished piece, it is said, lies as he left it, at either Mount Holly or the Carlisle Barracks. One of those completed was taken by the British at the battle of Brandywine, and is now in the Tower of London. The British Government offered a large sum and a stated annuity to any person who would instruct them in the manufacture of that article, but the patriotic blacksmith preferred obscurity and poverty in his own beloved country to wealth and affluence in that of her oppressors, although that country for which he did so much kept her purse closed from the veteran soldier till near the close of his long life, and it often required the whole weight of his well known character for honesty to keep him from the severest pangs of poverty. When such characters are neglected by a rich government, it is no wonder that some folks think Republics ungrateful."

CHURCHES.

The First Presbyterian Church at Newville was erected about 1738. It was a log building, in the southern part of the grave-yard now used by the congregation. The present stone structure was built about 1790. It was a plain stone building, with three doors, and with the pulpit, on the north side. It had pews with high, straight backs. In 1842 it was handsomely remodeled in modern style, and is now one of the handsomest churches in the valley. It is built in a delightful grove near which, in the language of Dr. Nevin, "rolls gently along the clear and lovely stream from which it has received its name, and which for ages has been flowing on, apparently the same, whilst the crowds that have been weekly gathering on its brink have, one after another, lain down within the sound of its murmurs" to their long, last sleep. Thomas Craighead was the first pastor, installed in 1738. He died in the pulpit after the close of an eloquent sermon, while its last words were still upon his lips. His remains were buried where the church now stands, the only monument of his memory.

United Presbyterian Church.—This church, originally "Seceder," was built of logs, according to the inscription on it, in 1764. This was followed by a stone church about 1790, a brick 1826, a new brick in 1868. The present handsome brick church edifice was built in 1882. It is upon an elevation in a beautiful grove, and with its grave-yard just back of it. Upon a tablet in the church building is engraved the dates which we have given: "United Presbyterian Church. Founded A. D. 1764—Erected A. D. 1882."

First Methodist Church.—This was built in 1826. It was of brick and stood on the back part of the present lot on Main Street. The present one, of brick, was built in 1846.

First Lutheran Church.—This was built in 1832 on North High Street, and the present one in 1862 on West Main Street.

"Bethel" Church.—A Bethel Church was built in 1830, which is now occupied by a colored congregation. The present Bethel Church on Railroad Street was built in 1859.

United Brethren Church.—This is located on Fairfield Street, and was built of brick in 1867.

CEMETERY.

Owing to the necessity for new burial ground, the Newville Cemetery was organized a few years ago. It is beautifully situated west of the town.

EDUCATIONAL INSTITUTIONS.

For some years before and after the middle of the century, classical schools were established in Newville. In 1832, Joseph Casey, the father of Judge Casey, of the United States Court of Claims, opened a classical school, which lasted for a period of eight or ten years. He had received his education at Glasgow, and was a thorough Latinist. About 1843 another clasical school was opened, which included all the ordinary academic studies. This was established by R. D. French, who was succeeded, in 1846, by Mr. Kilburn; in 1849, by James Huston; in 1852, by W. R. Linn.

Rev. R. McCachren erected an academy building at about this time, where he and others taught until 1857, when it was succeeded by a normal school. The Rebellion broke this up; but even after the war a classical school was conducted by F. L. Gillelon, who was succeeded by Dr. Stayman and W. H. Thompson. At this time the academy building was used as a female school. Both succumbed, however, either to the growing favor for larger colleges or the public schools.

There are eight public schools in Newville, with fit buildings, one of which, a commodious brick structure with inclosed grounds, has been recently erected.

NEWSPAPERS.

The first newspaper published in Newville was in 1843, but it was a small sheet and of brief duration. *The Star of the Valley* was started in 1858 by J. M. Miller. *The Enterprise*, which had been established at Oakville, in May, 1871, by the Fosnot Bros., was moved to Newville in December, 1874, and the two papers were consolidated as *The Star and Enterprise*, under the management of J. C. Fosnot & Son, in January, 1886. It is an eight page weekly paper. *The Times*, which was begun at Plainfield, and known as the *Plainfield Times*, in the winter of 1881, was moved to Newville in the winter of 1885; it is a neat eight-page weekly paper, conducted by J. W. Strohm.

BANKS.

The first bank in Newville was the "Newville Saving Fund Society." It was organized March 9, 1850 and dissolved March 31, 1858. A private banking firm was started by Rea, Gracey & Co., in 1857, and was reorganized under the United States charter in August of 1863, as the First National Bank of

NEWTON TOWNSHIP.   327

Newville. It is in a handsome building on Railroad Street. Its capital is $100,000.

FIRE DEPARTMENT.

Friendship Fire Company, No 1, meets in the Council Room, East Main Street, on the second Tuesday evening of each month. J. C. Fosnot, president; J. M. Reed, secretary.

Washington Fire Company meets on second Friday evenings of each month. D. N. Thomas, president; Geo. L. Gussman, secretary.

SOCIETIES.

Big Spring Lodge, No. 361, A. Y. M., was instituted June 1, 1866, with the following named charter members: J. A. Kunkel, Harry Manning, W. B. Shoemaker, Peter A. Ahl, David Ahl, A. Byers, Samuel Byers, William Borland, James Elliott, George M. Graham, D. H. Gilmore, J. S. Hays, H. S. Ferris, G. H. Hammer, S. I. Irvine, William Klink, R. R. McAchlan, C. T. McLaughlin, James McCandlish, J. P. Rhoads, Henry Snyder, S. A. Sollenberger, J. A. Woodburn, M. Williams, S. C. Wagner. Number of members September 15, 1866, forty-four. Officers: Robert H. Stake, W. M.; G. A. Rea, S. W.; John E. Mickey, J. W.; A. Byers, Treasurer; S. G. Glauser, Secretary.

Conodoguinet Lodge, No. 173, I. O. O. F., was organized May 28, 1846, with the following named charter members: James F. Coxel, A. J. North, J. B. Myers, H. S. Ferris, Archibald Bricker, J. G. Kyle, Joseph Fry, Lewis Rhoads, George Blankney, E. E. Brady and John C. Kyser. Membership numbers sixty. Present officers are D. P. Sollenberger, N. G.; J. H. Ployer, V. N. G.; J. C. Fosnot, Secretary; B. F. Shulenberger, Treasurer.

Big Spring Encampment, No. 92, I. O. O. F., instituted February 23, 1855, has a membership of nineteen. Present officers are George Murphy, C. P.; D. P. Sollenberger, S. W.; G. B. Weast, J. W.; J. C. Fosnot, Scribe; B. F. Shulenberger, Treasurer.

Sawquehanna Tribe, No. 131, I. O. R. M., was instituted at Shippensburg June 21, 1870, with the following named charter members: J. Berr Reddig, William H. Lawrence, A. D. Rebok, O. M. Blair, Samuel S. Shryock and H. M. Ash. The tribe removed to Newville December 2, 1875. Its present membership numbers about twenty, and its officers are Joseph Jeffries, Sachem; Joseph S. Tolhelm, Senior Sagamore; J. W. Taylor, Junior Sagamore; J. C. Fosnot, Chief of Records; D. N. Thomas, Keeper of Wampum.

The *"I. L. C."* a social and literary club, meeting weekly, was organized June 24, 1884, with the following named members: W. B. Stewart, G. B. Landis and E. D. Glauser. Present membership numbers fourteen, and the officers are George Fosnot, President; George Landis, Vice-President; E. D. Glauser, Secretary; W. B. Stewart, Treasurer. This club has a library.

CHAPTER XXXI.

NORTH MIDDLETON TOWNSHIP.

NORTH MIDDLETON was originally a portion of Middleton until that township was divided into North and South Middleton, in 1810, when it became a separate township. It then embraced also Middlesex, which was formed from it subsequently.

It lies just north of Carlisle, bounded on the north by the Blue Ridge or the North Mountains, on the east by Middlesex, on the south by South Middleton, and on the west by West Pennsborough and Frankford Townships.

The Conodoguinet Creek flows, with very abrupt and irregular curvatures, through the southern portion of the township, the land lying on the south side being the usual limestone, and on the north slate, formation. There are very many fine farms in the township, and particularly on the south side of the creek.

EARLY SETTLERS.

This township, like all or most of the others in Cumberland County, was originally settled by the Scotch-Irish, but at a later period many Germans came into it, so that, to-day, very few of the descendants of the original settlers are left. In this sense it stands in marked contrast with some other sections of the county.

One of the very earliest settlers, not only in this township, but among those who first pushed their way into the North Valley, was Richard Parker, many of whose descendants are still living. He, with Janet Martha, his wife, emigrated from the Province of Ulster, Ireland, in 1725, and settled three miles from Carlisle, acquiring land by patent near the Presbyterian Glebe Meeting-House on the Conodoguinet Creek in 1730.

That the Parker family settled west of the Susquehanna in 1725 there is sufficient evidence in the land office, where, among the records, is the application of Richard Parker in 1734 (the year his tract of land was surveyed to him), for a warrant for the land on which he had "resided ye ten years past," which would carry the date of his settlement on the Conodoguinet Creek, near Carlisle, back to 1724. And indeed it is probable that even at this early period there were quite a number of settlers between this point and the Susquehanna. In 1729, when the county of Lancaster was organized, which then included Cumberland, there were "over Sasquehanna," Hendricks, Macfarlane, Silvers, Parker and others, who claimed a residence of from five to ten years, and possibly some periods which were still further back, but which are now unknown. Emigrants did not wait for the purchase of the lands by the proprietories from the Indians, especially the aggressive Scotch-Irish, who were "not wanted," where the lands had already been acquired, but were directed to push forward to the frontier.

Thomas Parker, the son of Richard, was also born in Ireland, but came over with his father. He died in April, 1776. A number of the members of this family served in the Revolution; and the widow of one, Maj. Alexander Parker, who laid out the town of Parkersburg at the mouth of the Little Kanawha, and who is buried at the Meeting House Springs, afterward married Charles McClure, near Carlisle, one of whose children, Charles, who was secretary of the commonwealth under Gov. Porter, married Margaretta Gibson, the daughter of Chief Justice Gibson, of Pennsylvania.

Comparatively few of the names of the early Scotch-Irish settlers in this township are within the recollection of the living. At an early period Patrick and William Davidson, William Gillingham, James Kilgore, Joseph Clark, Peter Wilkie and John McClure owned land near the proposed site of Carlisle, and portions of it had to be bought back by the Proprietaries. "William Armstrong's Settlement," on the Conodoguinet, was just below the Meeting House Springs. David Williams, a wealthy land-owner and the earliest known elder of that church, James Young and Robert Sanderson were probably included in that settlement. In following the creek, Thomas Wilson resided further to the east, near Henderson's mill, while adjoining him on the east was James Smith, and on the south Jonathan Holmes, by the spring and on the land now owned by Mrs. Parker. Turning westward again upon the creek, just one mile or more north of Carlisle, and just to the left of the "Cave" hill, was the home of Col. Ephraim Blaine,* an officer in the Indian war, a patriot in the Revolution, and the grandfather of the Hon. James G. Blaine, of Maine. Turning northeasterly from Carlisle, at some early period, Com. O'Brian owned a large tract of about 700 acres, including the tract upon which the almshouse stands and several farms. Mr. Stiles afterward came into possession of about 300 acres of this tract, where the almshouse now stands, and erected his home, which was known as "Clermont." It was afterward purchased by the county for its present purpose. On the glebe belonging to the Meeting House Springs, was the Rev. Samuel Thompson (1798), near which were lands belonging to John Davis, Esq., who at one time (1777) commanded the Second Battalion of Cumberland County troops in the Revolutionary war. Still further up the creek were William Dunbar and Andrew Forbes, near which place a mill was afterward erected by William Thompson.

Among the Scotch-Irish who, in the year 1793, lived in the surrounding neighborhood of the Meeting House Springs, were the following: James Douglas, John Dunbar, Alexander Blaine, John Gregg (died 1808 or 1809), Robert Sanderson, John Logan, James Milligan, Ross Mitchell, John Forbes; and at a still earlier period than this, Stuart Rowan, who died there. Other names we meet, with the dates, are as follows: William Parker and David Williamson, 1794; William Templeton, 1795; Alexander Logan, 1797; Andrew Logan, 1798; William Douglas and William Dunbar, 1799; George Clark, 1803; John Reid, William Dinney, James Cameron, 1805; Samuel McKnight, 1807.†

But there is a list of still older names of the "heads of families" in this section, for which we are indebted to a manuscript fragment, made by the Rev. Dr. Robert Davidson, who, in connection with Dr. Charles Nesbitt the first president of Dickinson College, was the first pastor over the United Presbyterian congregations of Carlisle. The manuscript is dated November 26, 1816, and is headed, "Names of the Heads of Families belonging to the different districts of the Presbyterian Church in Carlisle."‡ The list, which is possibly unfinished, is as follows: John Templeton, Andrew Logan, Matthew Agnew, Margaret Logan, David Parker, Andrew Gregg, John Forbes.

---

*He lived also in Carlisle, and, it is said, that it was at his house that Washington stopped during his brief visit at the time of the insurrection. The old stone homestead, just west of the Cave hill, is still standing.
†These dates, taken from authentic documents, indicate that the parties lived in these years, but how much earlier or later (often) we do not know.
‡All of these early Scotch-Irish were Presbyterians.

And these notes of a few families as they were then (1816) constituted: (1) John Templeton and Jane Templeton, May McKee and Sarah Kennedy. (2) Alexander Logan and Jane Logan, William, Alexander, John, Mary Jane and Elizabeth—three young children. (3) Margaret Logan, Margaret Davidson and Eleanor Logan, with black man Coesen. (4) Mathew Agnew and Rebecca Agnew—two small children.

Families living north in the township, in 1793, in the neighborhood, including Crane's Gap, were as follows: Richard Crane, William Clark, John Sanderson, John Templeton, Widow Stuart, Robert Chambers, Robert Patton, Widow Harper, William Fleming, Patrick Davidson, James Sanderson, Widow Randolph, Joseph Kennedy, William Davidson, Jr., James Douglas.

We meet the names with dates attached, as follows: Joseph Kennedy, 1795; Hugh McCormick, 1795; Thomas Guy, 1797; John Kincade, 1797; John Flemming, 1798; James Mooreland, 1799; James Flemming, 1801; John Stewart, David Williamson and Job Randolph, 1802; John Williamson and Robert Blaine, 1803; Davidson Williams,* 1804; Joseph Clark, 1805; John Goudy, 1805, Paul Randolph, 1806.

Some of these families consisted, in December of the year 1816, as follows: (1) Patrick and Ann Davidson—George, Patrick, John, James. Sarah, Eliza and two small children. (2) Richard Crain, Sr.—Elizabeth Crain, William Crain, Abner Crain and Maria Dill. (3) Joseph Clark and Mary W. Clark—Mary Clark, Ralph Simson, George Crain, and servant girl, Margaret. (4) Thomas and Sarah Guy. (5) Samuel and Elizabeth Guy—two children. (6) Paul Randolph—William, John, Ann, Susan. (7) James and Margaret Flemming—William, John, Margaret and a girl. (8) Rebecca Sanderson—Mrs. Simkins, Miss Sanderson, Mr. and Mrs. McMichael. (9) Richard Crain, Jr., and Sarah—Jane, Eliza Ann, Sarah, Richard. (10) Job Randolph—William, Sarah, Eliza Ann, Fanny, Paul and Job. (11) R. Clark and Ann—Alexander Gregg, Widow Crain, Margaret Crain, John. Robert, Ann and Margaret. (12) John and Deborah Kincade—Jane and Susanah, and Francis Kelly. (13) William Manwell and wife—Sarah, Jane, Elizabeth and Mary.†

THE CAVE.

One of the greatest natural curiosities in the county is "The Cave." It is just one mile north of Carlisle, on the Conodoguinet Creek, in a large limestone bluff, which is covered with evergreen trees. The entrance to it is a symmetrical, semi-circular archway, about eight feet high and ten feet wide, from which there is a nearly straight passage of about 270 feet to a point where it branches in three directions. The passage is high enough to admit the visitor erect until he reaches this point. The passage on the right is broad and low, but difficult of access on account of its humidity. It leads to a chamber of very considerable length, which is known as the Devil's Dining Room. The central one is narrow and tortuous, and can not be entered for more than a distance of thirty feet, when it terminates in a perpendicular precipice. The passage on the left, at a distance of three or four feet, turns suddenly to the right, and measures in length about ninety feet, with a sufficient opening to permit a small lad to creep along it, after which it becomes too narrow for further progress.

About seven feet from the entrance are several small pools, probably caused by the drippings from the roof, which are called the Seven Springs. Apart from the picturesqueness of the spot, traditions and legends have been asso-

*At this time deceased.
†Here ends the manuscript of Dr. Davidson; for which we are indebted to the Rev. Dr. Joseph Vance, the present pastor of the First Presbyterian Church in Carlisle.

ciated with it. It has been stated that human bones have been found in it. It was a place of retreat for Lewis the robber, and probably for Indians at a still earlier period. Several examinations have been made of it, and organic remains of many species of animals were found in it. Among the bones were found those of almost every species of mammals of the State, besides those of one or two species not now found in Pennsylvania, but known in regions not far remote. The bones seem to indicate that the size exceeded that of the same species of the present time. It is stated that, within the recollection of many living, the cave has grown smaller, probably on account of the accumulation of earth in it.

MEETING HOUSE SPRINGS.

About two miles northwest of Carlisle there is a beautiful spring of crystal water, which flows from under limestone rocks, at the bottom of a bluff on the south side of the Conodoguinet Creek.

Near this spot, on the high ground, the Presbyterians, about the year 1736, erected a log church in "West Pennsborough," as it was then called, by reason of which the place has ever since been known as the "Meeting House Springs." The church was one of the very earliest erected in the valley, and years before the formation of the county or the existence of Carlisle. No vestige of this building now remains, nor are there any of the oldest surviving inhabitants of the neighborhood who are able to give anything like a satisfactory account of it. All has passed away. The members of the large congregation which worshiped within its walls, have all, long ago, disappeared, and with them the memory of the venerable edifice and the interesting incidents which were, doubtless, connected with its history.

THE GRAVE-YARD AT MEETING HOUSE SPRINGS.

The old grave-yard, however, still remains, with its dilapidated and neglected tombs, needing the chisel of some modern antiquary to make plain their almost illegible inscriptions. Some of them which are still decipherable are dated as far back as 1736. On some there are armorial bearings, which indicate the fondness of our fathers for the family distinctions of their transatlantic home. Some families claim to know the spot where their ancestors are buried; such are the Agnews, Forbeses, Dunbars, Lairds, McAllisters, Greysons, Parkers, Youngs and others; but, in many cases, the inscriptions do not tell us who are buried here.

The place reminds us forcibly of the quaint words of an English writer: "Gravestones tell truths scarcely sixty years; generations pass while some trees stand, and old families last not three oaks."

As a matter of interest we may state that not more than sixty years ago there was a woodland which began within, probably, half a mile northwest of Carlisle, and extended all the way to Meeting House Springs.

This burial place is in a handsome grove of lofty trees, and is inclosed with a stone wall on the high ground of the almost precipitous limestone bluff which here rises above the creek. The tombstones are of an extraordinary character; one small one remaining, of dark slate, most of limestone or brown sandstone, with rude lettering, and some having upon them the rude sculpturing of animals, faces, Masonic emblems or coats of arms. Many are reclining, some lying down. In order that some who have lived and are buried here shall not wholly be forgotten, we have attempted, with considerable difficulty, to decipher some of the inscriptions.

On a leaning granite one, which stands alone in the northeast corner, in large, rude letters some nine inches long, we read: "Here lys the Boly of

John and Alexander McKehan." It has no date. Others are as follows: "Here lys ye Body of Janet Thompson, wife of ye Rev. Samuel Thompson, who deceased Sep. ye 29, 1744, aged 33 years." "Alexander McCulloch, who deceased January ye 15, 1746, aged 50 yrs." Another reads: "Here lies the body of James Young, seiner, who parted this life Feb. 22, 1747, aged 79 years." Another reads: "Here lys ye body of Meyr donnel, who departed this life Oct. 15, 1747, aged 64 yrs." On a small, dark slate stone, on which is sculptured a round, cherub face, we read in letters still distinct: "Thomas Witherspoon, who departed this life Mar. 22, 1759, aged 57." The flat tomb, which is without date, reads: "Sacred to the memory of Major Alexander Parker and his two children, Margaret and John."

Others are as follows: "Ronald Chambers, died Dec. 24, 1746, aged 60." "William Graham, died April 24, 1761, aged 67." "John Flemming, died Apr. 22, 1761, aged 39." "James McFarlan, born Dec. 24, 1685, died Oct. 31, 1770." "John Kinkead, died Aug. 4, 1772, aged 51." "Mary Kinkead [daughter], died Aug. 1758, aged 17." "James Weakly, died June 6, 1772, aged 68." "Jane Weakly [wife], died Nov. 30, 1768, aged 53." "James Weakly [infant son of Samuel and Hetty], died Sept. 4, 1777."

Besides these, of later date, we find the names of Drenna, Saunderson, Crocket and others who were well known.

The remains of an Indian, it is said, were discovered a few years ago in digging a grave near the stone wall in the western portion of this burial ground.

Among those buried in this grave-yard in the present century is Samuel Laird, Esq., who died in September, 1806, in the seventy-fourth year of his age. He was an associate justice in 1791, and one of the commissioners for the county to collect money which non-associators were expected to contribute in lieu of military service in 1778. Upon his tomb we read:

"Of simple manners, pure, and heart upright,
In mild, religious ways he took delight;
As elder, magistrate or judge he still
Studied obedience to his Maker's will.

A husband kind, a friend to the distressed,
He wished that all around him might be blessed:
A patriot in the worst of times approved,
By purest motives were his actions moved."

MISCELLANEOUS.

Col. Ephraim Blaine erected a mill, lately known as Henderson's mill, on the Conodoguinet Creek, about a mile north of Carlisle. Within the past year this mill has been taken down. On its corner-stone was the following mark:

$$\frac{\text{Er}}{\text{B}}$$
$$1772$$

which is construed to mean that it was erected by Ephraim Blaine, 1772.

There are six schools in the township, several mills, four bridges (one iron) over the creek, many roads, some of them in good condition. There is no town or railroad within the township, Carlisle and the Cumberland Valley Railroad lying just on its southern border; but there are fine farms everywhere, even on the rolling lands which extend back to the North Mountains. There is a postoffice in the township named Grissinger.

CHAPTER XXXII.

PENN TOWNSHIP.

PENN TOWNSHIP was formed from the western portion of Dickinson in 1860. Cook Township has since been formed from the southern part of Penn, reducing it to its present limits, and including nearly all of the mountain land which was formerly a portion of that township. It is bounded on the east by Dickinson Township, on the south by Cook Township, on the north by West Pennsborough Township, and on the west by Newton Township.

Its physical features, as thus reduced, are the same as those of the upper portion of Dickinson: On the north side of the Yellow Breeches Creek heavy limestone land, very fertile, and which yields to the labor of the husbandman abundant harvests; on the south side a gravely or sand formation, but which, when well tilled, is also well adapted to agriculture. Many excellent farms, in a high state of cultivation, are to be found in almost every portion of the township. This land is also well watered by numerous springs or streams, all of which empty into the Yellow Breeches Creek, which flows in an easterly direction through the township. Most of these have their source in the South Mountains; while, at a point where the Walnut Bottom road crosses the Newton Township line, are what are known as the Three Springs, the water flowing from under the limestone rocks at a distance of a few rods apart.

These springs are somewhat south of the Quarry Hill—a sandstone ridge which extends in an easterly direction through Southampton, Newton, and the northern portion of Penn Townships. Of late years they sometimes run dry in the summer months, but it may be interesting to state that before the time when so much timber had, sometimes needlessly, been destroyed, they were much larger and more copious streams. This fact is within the recollection of some who are still living.

The principal stream, however, is the Yellow Breeches Creek, which rises in the mountains and, small comparatively until it reaches this point, twice crosses the Walnut Bottom road—the second crossing being at the dividing line between Penn and Newton Townships. Its original Indian name was "Callipascink," meaning rapid or "horseshoe bends."*

We find it was known as the "Yellow Breeches," however, as early as 1740. How it derived this "uncouth appellation" is not now known. One explanation is that the words are a corruption of Yellow Beeches—a number of which once grew upon its banks. Another rather improbable account, but which has received some credit, is as follows: In speaking of the second crossing on the Walnut Bottom road, to which we have alluded, a resident of the township writes: "I was born and raised within 300 yards of that place, and from a boy have known the stream to be called Pine Run down to this second crossing, and from there down Yellow Breeches Creek. I have been told time and time again, in my boyhood days, that the name was given to it because a family living at that place (known as "Three Springs"), on a washing day,

---

*In "Trego's Geography, Geology, etc. of Pennsylvania," published 1843, he says (page 33) :"The present uncouth appellation given to this beautiful stream renders it very desirable that its original Indian name should be restored. This seems, however, now to be lost, for after the most diligent research we have been unable to discover it."

hung out a pair of leather yellow breeches, which were stolen by a roving band of Indians, after which, in speaking of certain places, this one was known as the place or creek where the Indians had stolen the yellow breeches, from which the creek itself, in time, derived its name—but above this point it is still known as 'Pine Run.'" We have thought it worthy to state this legend here, for, if it be true, then this stream derived its name from an incident which happened in Penn Township.

Iron ore, in detached quantities, is found in various portions of the township, while at Huntsville is the site of the old Cumberland Furnace, built by Michael Ege, but which has long since been abandoned. Grist-mills and saw-mills are along the streams, but for local uses only, while many of the older ones have disappeared.

The population of Penn is more dense than in Dickinson, but fewer of the descendants of the original settlers remain, and there is a larger infusion of the German element, which came into it at a later period. Michael Ege, at one time probably the most extensive land-owner and iron master in Pennsylvania, owned much of the land on the south side of the creek, which descended at his death to his daughter, Mrs. Wilson, and which extended also into Dickinson Township, in the sketch of which we have given an account of its division after protracted litigation. One of the Weakley families owned land in the neighborhood of the Dickinson Church, and up toward Centerville, some generations ago, and there were other family names which are the same as those which are found in Dickinson Township. As the pioneer settlers seemed always to have preferred the lands which lay adjacent to the springs or along the streams, there can be little doubt that such portions of this township as lay along the Yellow Breeches Creek or the Three Springs, were settled at a very early period.

Among the older families are the McCulloughs, and, as a matter of interest, we may mention that Alexander McCullough, who married Elizabeth McKinstry and was father of James, went to California in 1855, and joined the famous Walker's expedition, where he lost his life.

VILLAGES.

Small villages are numerous in Penn Township. Along the Walnut Bottom and the Pine roads are clusters of houses which have as yet no name, but along the former are Cumminstown, called after Rev. Charles Cummins, the second pastor of Dickinson Church; Centerville, so named, it is said, because it is midway between Carlisle and Shippensburg; and Hockersville, called after John Hocker, who owned a farm and tavern-stand some years ago at this place. On or near the Pine road are Huntsville, formerly Spring Mills, a station on the Harrisburg & Potomac Railroad; Brushtown, from the brush that surrounded it; and Milltown, a mile east, so called because of the number of mills (a fulling-mill, grist-mill, saw-mill, plaster-mill, clover-seed-mill and a whisky distillery), which were once in that immediate vicinity. Centerville is described in 1845, by Rupp, as "a small village on the Walnut Bottom road in a well improved, fertile region of the country; it contains a store and tavern." It has now a church, schoolhouse, postoffice, shops, and about 200 inhabitants.

CHURCHES.

There are six churches within the limits of Penn Township. Of these the oldest is what is known as the Dickinson Church, belonging to the Presbyterian congregation. As early as 1810 an application was made, subscribed by James Moore and Joseph Galbraith, for a pastor to supply what was called the

"Presbyterian congregation of Walnut Bottom," but it was not until 1823 that a congregation was organized in Dickinson Township, and not until 1826 that a call was given to Rev. McKnight Williamson, their first pastor, who continued to serve until October, 1834. He was succeeded, in the following year, by Rev. Charles Cummins, who served for a period of ten years, and after whom, as we have seen, the small village derives its name. The place is still better known, however, as the Dickinson Church. At the close of Mr. Williamson's pastorate, the session consisted of Samuel Woods, John Ross, William Woods, Jr., George Davidson and David W. McCullough; at the close of Mr. Cummins', the elders were William Woods, Jr., Robert Donaldson, William G. Davidson and Lewis Williams.

At first the congregation worshiped alternately in the stone church belonging to the Covenanters and in the log church of the German Reformed and Lutheran congregations, both of which were in Dickinson Township. Since the formation of Penn, the Dickinson Church is included in that township, although its name was derived from the one in which it was erected in 1829. It stands on a slight eminence, at a point where the road leading from Mount Rock to Spring Mills crosses the Walnut Bottom road, eight miles west of Carlisle. The lot of ground upon which it is erected was given for that purpose by William L. Weakley. The situation is a beautiful one, and the building itself, with its neat interior, does credit to the taste and liberality of the congregation. The Lutheran Church at Centerville is a handsome brick building, erected in 1852; while south of the Dickinson Church and near the creek is the church of the German Baptists—known as Dunkers—erected in 1863. The other churches of the township are smaller and have been more recently erected than those which we have mentioned.

SCHOOLS.

A private school or academy was begun at Centerville in 1856, by Robert Lowry Sibbet, a graduate of Pennsylvania College, in which were taught Greek, Latin, the natural sciences and higher mathematics. The school was for a time quite successful. Mr. Sibbet was succeeded by Rev. George P. Hays. After a few years, however, it ceased to exist. Of the students of this school two are ministers, one a missionary in Japan, three are lawyers living in Carlisle, one a physician, and several have been teachers. Of its teachers, Dr. Sibbet is now practicing medicine in Carlisle, and his successor was afterward president of Washington and Jefferson College.

At present there are ten public schools in the township, and although the school term is six months, in many of the districts they are kept open three months longer by subscription.

The Harrisburg & Potomac Railroad traverses through the center of the township. The postoffices are Dickinson and Huntsdale.

CHAPTER XXXIII.

SILVER SPRING TOWNSHIP.

SILVER SPRING TOWNSHIP was formed from East Pennsborough in 1757. It contains about thirty-five square miles, part slate and part limestone land, and is bounded on the north by the North Mountains, on the east by Hampden, on the south by Monroe Township and a small portion of Upper Allen and Mechanicsburg, and on the west by Middlesex Township. The township is named after Silvers' Spring, a limpid body of water which rises in it, and which was called after James Silvers, who, with his wife Hannah, came into this valley about 1730 or 1731. He took out a warrant in October, 1735, for a tract of land, containing 532 acres, which adjoins the old Silvers' Spring Church, and extends into the loop of the Conodoguinet Creek, embracing land now owned by Mr. Kauffman, Mrs. Briggs, Mr. Bryson and Mr. Long. Here Mr. Silvers settled and lived. But, although the springs was called originally after James Silvers, common consent seems to have changed the name both of the spring and of the township to the more appropriate designation of "Silver Spring." This spring is one of the most beautiful in the Cumberland Valley. It rises from out limestone rocks, spreads into a large and somewhat circular crystal sheet, and, after serving several mills, empties itself into the Conodoguinet Creek.

This Conodoguinet Creek flows just north of Hogestown, in such circuitous loops or bends, that, although the general direction of the creek through the township is east and west, it is often here more nearly north and south; and although the township is only five miles across, the course of the creek measures more than twice that distance. The windings of the creek enclose the farms of James McCormick, J. C. Sample and Samuel Senseman.

This portion of the township adjoining Silver Spring and Hogestown was settled at a very early period. About 1730 John Hoge bought a large tract of land, including that on which Hogestown stands, and settled upon it.

There were other settlers here in 1733, and the records show that the land between this and the river was, at least, partially occupied at this date. Most of these early settlers seem to have located on the slate land—on account of the spring, leaving the richer lands, called "barrens," unoccupied. These early settlers were all Presbyterians. The old church was erected here at about this time. The congregation is spoken of as "over the river." No road had yet been built. It was not until November 4, 1735, that the court of Lancaster County appointed a commission of six men, among whom was James Silvers, to lay out a road from Harris' Ferry toward the Potomac River. They reported February 3, 1736, but their view was opposed "by a considerable number of the inhabitants on the west side of the Susquehanna in those parts," and another commission of viewers was appointed, who reported May 4, 1736, that "they had reviewed the easternmost part of said road and found it very crooked and hurtful to the inhabitants, and therefore altered it and marked it. From the ferry near to a southwest course about two miles, thence westerly course to James Silvers', thence westward to John Hoge's meadow," etc.

This road was nearly identical with the turnpike, and as it passed James

Silvers' place, it would locate his house on Mrs. Brigg's farm, now occupied by George Messinger.*

ORIGINAL SETTLERS.

Of the early settlers of this portion of Silver Spring we have some interesting reminiscences. Two Loudon brothers, James and Mathew, came from Scotland; one settled in Sherman's Valley, but was driven out by the Indians. Mathew Loudon came to Silver Spring, married Elizabeth McCormick about 1760, and settled on the tract now occupied by the Cathcart heirs. The Hoges lived upon their property, but not where the town now stands, and the McCormicks, northeast of the town, on the Conodoguinet Creek. The Irwins also owned tracts just southwest of the present town. The McCormicks now own a large brick house, just east of town, which belonged to the Hoges. Of this latter family there were two brothers, David and Jonathan. David lived just across the spring south or southeast of the town; Jonathan, just across the run, northeast, along the pike. Of the Galbreaths there were also two brothers, Andrew and John. Andrew lived just below Bryson's (now Eberly's) farm, and John, up the creek, north of Bryson's farm. Mr. Oliver's family lived west of Hogestown, on the ridge, and were intermarried with the McCormicks. Wm. Walker owned two farms which joined the Oliver farms. He married Betsy Hoge. Reese also owned a farm beyond the ridge, joining the Loudon tract, which was purchased by Archibald Loudon in 1788. Immediately west of that was Mr. Christopher Herman's farm, while the Junkin tract (owned by Joseph and Benjamin) laid just south. The Irwins' lands near joined the Hermans', Loudons' and Armstrongs' tracts. There were four Irwin brothers, William, Armstrong and John Irwin, all of whose tracts joined, and James, who owned the land which now belongs to Mr. Huston, where the mill is on the Conodoguinet Creek. An old mill stood where the iron bridge now spans the creek, known originally as Kreider's mill, the farm of Kreider's brother was opposite. and the Coble tract, belonging to Daniel and David, lay just north of this latter. Below the iron bridge joining the Kreider farm was Ashleys, and just below it, down the creek, were the two Bell farms (David and Robert), now owned by Benjamin and Samuel Voglesong. Just north of Hogestown, on the road leading to Sterritt's (originally Croghan's) Gap, was the Trimble farm, while recrossing the iron bridge, just joining the Douglas farm, was the old Carothers' farm, belonging to John Carothers, who, with his wife and whole family, was poisoned by a jealous domestic, Sallie Clark.†
Of the four sons, John (who married Sallie Hoge) was afterward sheriff, and Andrew, who was crippled by the poisoning above mentioned, became one of the leading lawyers of Carlisle.

Martin Herman, a native of Germany, landed in Philadelphia July 12, 1752, and settled in Cumberland County on the 15th of April, 1771, on a tract of land called St. Martins, in Silver Spring Township, which farm has been in the possession of that family for a period of 115 years.

Besides the names of the early settlers whom we have mentioned, were the Walkers, Clendenins, Hustons, Trimbles, Semples. Fishers, Waughs, Mathers, Barnhills, Beltzhoovers, Hendersons and McHoes, and on the south side of the creek were the Trimbles, Longsdorfs, Kellers, Kasts, Kings, Slonechers, Junkins, Hoges and others.

SOME EARLY EVENTS.

During the Indian wars, from 1753 to 1758, there were many murders and depredations throughout the valley. In Rupp (p. 128) we find: "May 13,

---

*See Rev T. J. Ferguson's Historical Discourse on Silver Spring Church.
†This incident was made the subject of a poetical effusion by Miss Isabella Olliver, a volume of whose poems was issued from the press of Archibald Loudon, of Carlisle, in 1805.

1757, William Walker and another man were killed near McCormick's fort, at Conodoguinet." The following account, as it concerns Silver Spring, we take from a former sketch: "The early settlers were much annoyed by Indians, and consequently settled in groups as much as possible for self-protection. One of these was at a place called Roaringtown, on the bank of the Conodoguinet, where there is a very fine spring. It is on the farm now owned by Samuel Adams, two miles west of Hogestown. Mr. John Armstrong, one of the old citizens, born about 1760, whose wife was a daughter of Jonathan Hoge, frequently told us that he could see from his house, near the Stony Ridge, groups of Indians prowling about through the barrens several miles distant; also wild animals, which were another source of annoyance to anxious mothers, whose children would stray from home. An uncle of Judge Clendenin, late of Hogestown, went, in company with two others from his father's residence, in the northeast part of the township, where Emanuel Neidich now resides, to watch a deer lick, some two miles up along the mountain foot, on the farm where Michael Garman now lives, and whilst waiting, in the dusk of evening, for the deer to come down from the mountain to drink, and lick the salt placed there to attract them, they were fired upon by Indians in ambush, who severely wounded Clendenin. They fled for home, but his strength failing from loss of blood, his companions secreted him in the bushes and made their escape. He was found in the morning cold and lifeless."

It was one of the members of the Bell family, mentioned elsewhere, of whom the following is told: "Among the many achievements," says Loudon, "against the Indians in our wars with them, few exceed that performed by Samuel Bell, formerly owner of the noted farm on the Stony Ridge, five miles below Carlisle, which was as follows: Some time after Gen. Braddock's defeat, he and his brother, James Bell, agreed to go into Shearman's Valley to hunt for deer, and were to meet at Croghan's, now Sterritt's, Gap, on the Blue Mountain. By some means or other they did not meet, and Samuel slept all night in a cabin belonging to Mr. Patton, on Shearman's Creek. In the morning he had not traveled far before he spied three Indians, who at the same saw him. They all fired at each other; he wounded one of the Indians, but received no damage, except through his clothes by the balls. Several shots were fired on both sides, for each took a tree; he took out his tomahawk and stuck it into the tree, behind which he stood, so that, should they approach, he might be prepared. The tree was grazed with the Indians' balls, and he had thoughts of making his escape by flight, but, on reflection, had doubts of his being able to outrun them.

"After some time the two Indians took the wounded one and put him over a fence, and one took one course, and the other another, taking a compass, so that Bell could no longer secure himself by the tree; but by trying to ensnare him they had to expose themselves, by which means he had the good fortune to shoot one of them dead. The other ran and took the dead Indian on his back, one leg over each shoulder. By this time Bell's gun was again loaded; he then ran after the Indian until he came within about four yards from him, fired and shot through the dead Indian and lodged his ball in the other, who dropped the dead man and ran off. On his return, coming past the fence where the wounded Indian was, he dispatched him, but did not know he had killed the third Indian until his bones were found afterward."

HOGESTOWN.

This village is situated on a small stream known as "Hoge's Run," which rises at the Stony Ridge, and empties into the Conodoquinet Creek at a beautiful grove called "Sporting Green." It was called after John Hoge, who owned all the land on which the town is built and a large tract surrounding. The old stone tavern was for years the only house, and was owned by the Hoge family. The first house built after that was a small log one near the old road, and was erected about 1820. The McCormicks and the Hoges had a stockade at a very early date. John Hogue (or Hoge) married Guintheleum Bowen (said to have been a descendant of the royal family of Wales), who, after her marriage, still retained and was known by her maiden name. It is stated that it was the money obtained from the sale of her jewels which purchased their lands.

NEW KINGSTON.

New Kingston is a post village in Silver Spring Township, on the pike, six and a half miles east of the county seat. The Cumberland Valley Railroad runs within half a mile of the place.

The first owner of the lands upon which the town is built was Joseph Junkin, Sr. He came from Counties Down and Antrim, Ireland (his lands lying on both sides of the line), about 1736 or 1740. At Oxford, Chester County, he met and married a Scotch girl, Elizabeth Wallace, and soon after crossed Harris' ferry, into the wilderness of Cumberland (then Lancaster) County. He took up a tract of 500 acres, which includes the site upon which New Kingston is now built, and erected the stone house which still stands, east of the town, on what was afterward known as the Walker tract. He had a number of children, among whom were Joseph and Benjamin, who afterward owned a portion of this land. Joseph (born in 1750), built the house now owned and occupied by H. W. Kanaga, in 1775-77, in which he resided until he removed to Mercer County in 1806. He was a captain in the Revolutionary war, fought at Brandywine, and was wounded in a skirmish shortly after.

The date of the original patent of this land to Joseph Junkin, Sr., was about the year 1740, and, after his death it was divided into three parts.

One tract was owned by John Carothers, who in 1814 sold it to John King. In the spring of 1818 King laid out the village, which was called after him, Kingston, a name which it retained. A postoffice was established here in 1851, called New Kingstown.

The three stone houses were built long before the town was laid out, but in 1818 a number of dwellings were erected, probably six. by John Wynkoop, Henry Miller, George Williams, Thomas Ashley, Henry Monesmith and John Shoemaker, and possibly one other. These houses were all log buildings. The second tract was owned by Joseph Junkin, Jr., the son of the original patentee, who built the stone house above referred to, in the western portion of the town. The building of this, it is said, had been delayed on account of his absence as a captain in the Revolutionary war during the period of its erection. This tract and property he sold in 1805 to Joseph Kanaga, Sr., after whose death it descended to his son, Joseph Kanaga, Jr., who, after the town was laid out, built the first frame house for a store. It is now owned by Henry W. Kanaga, the grandson of the original purchaser. The brick house in Kanaga's addition was built by H. W. Irvin.

The third tract was owned by Benjamin Junkin, Jr., also a son of the original patentee, who is said to have built two other houses—the hotel, and the dwelling which he occupied until his death. Part of this tract came into the possession of John King, by whom it was conveyed (1830) to Peter Kissinger, who, in 1844, laid it out into the town lots which now compose the greater part of New Kingston.

The town is conveniently situated on the pike road which leads from Carlisle to Harrisburg, amid the cultivated farms of this beautiful portion of the valley, and is not distant from the railroad, which passes to the South. It has a hotel, postoffice, stores, three churches, schools and a population of between 300 and 400 inhabitants.

Silver Spring Lodge, No. 598, I. O. O. F., was organized April 20, 1867, with twenty charter members. Its present membership numbers about fifty, and the officers are now (September 15, 1886): R. E. Anderson, P. G.; J. D. Bishop, N. G.; H. W. Morrison, V. N. G.; W. H. Humer, Sec.; Jacob Mathias, Asst. Sec.; J. A. Senseman, Treas.

THE FIRST COVENANTERS' COMMUNION IN AMERICA.

Nearly all of the early Scotch-Irish who came into this valley were Presbyterians, reared in connection with the synod of Ulster, but there were some Covenanters among them, even at the early date. They were not numerous at this time in Ireland, where some secession churches were then being established.

In this valley there were only a few clusters of families scattered here and there in different in different localities, and at first without any fixed place of worship. Sometimes, without an ordained minister, they met at each other's houses. They could not and did not fraternize with the Presbyterianism around them. At about this time two places of worship were established—one at Paxtang, east of the river, and the other on the Stony Ridge, in Silver Spring Township. When the weather allowed they met in their "tent," as it was termed, and, when it was not propitious, in their cabins. This "tent" was pitched in a shady grove, and consisted simply of an elevated platform for the minister, a board nailed against a black oak tree to support the Bible, a few rude benches for seats, and some boards overhead to protect the speaker from the sun and rain. Thus accommodated they worshiped for hours at a time, and their communion services sometimes lasted nine hours. Rev. John Cuthbertson, a Scotchman by birth, from Ireland, preached for the first time in the valley on Wednesday, August 21, 1751 or 1752, at Walter Buchanan's, near the present New Kingston, midway between Carlisle and the river. His text was, Proverbs VIII, 4: "Unto you, O men, I call; and my voice is to the sons of man." He also baptized Joseph Glendenning, John M'Clelland and Jane Swansie, infant children of residents of that neighborhood. August 23, 1752, Mr. Cuthbertson held his first communion in America. It was at Stony Ridge, or the Walter Buchanan or Junkin "tent," in Cumberland County. The communicants came to the table singing the Twenty-fourth Psalm. About 250 persons communed, and this comprised very nearly all the Covenanters in this county, for the place was central, the season pleasant, and they gathered in from their different settlements, the Covenanters also of adjoining counties.

This was the first time that the followers of Cameron and Cargill ever gathered at the communion table in the new world or outside the British isles.

Their next pastor was Rev. Matthew Lind, of the Covenanter congregation at Aghadoe, near Coleraine. He came in December, 1773; locating at Paxtang, and assumed the pastorate of that church and of the Stony Ridge. Walter Buchanan was the only elder in Stony Ridge when Mr. Lind was installed. About that time Joseph Junkin was ordained. He lived upon the present Kanaga farm; built his present stone house, and had the "tent" upon it during his life time. Still later it was known as "Widow Junkin's tent." This little church was always a colony, surrounded by a population which had no sympathy with them. Later, when the Germans came in, they literally crowded out the Irish, and in a few years both congregations were completely exterminated—so completely that there is scarcely a tradition of their existence left among the present inhabitants.

The Bells, and the Swansies, and the Junkins attached themselves to the Big Spring congregation; but in time they, too, passed away, and not a single descendant of the original stock is now known to reside in the neighborhood.

The late Dr. Robert G. Young, of Mechanicsburg, in speaking, in a manuscript note in our possession, of some account of this Covenanters' "tent," says: "The description of this tent is strictly correct, as handed down to us, but there is inaccuracy in the location. The writer of this note, now in his sixty-seventh year, during his boyhood and youth was familiar with its location, and his recollection is corroborated by that of an old citizen, formerly a resident of that vicinity. Our statement is that 'Widow Junkin's tent' was about 300 yards from the turnpike road, near to the foot of the Stony Ridge, and almost directly opposite to an old stone house, at the time occupied and owned by Mr. Thomas Bell, in which he had for many years kept a hotel for the accommodation of the traveling public. The 'old citizen' above mentioned says that this 'tent' was an object of nearly every day observation while he resided in the vicinity of New Kingston, and that it disappeared about the year 1830. The recollection of the writer confirms his statement. My paternal grandfather attended divine services when held here, being a descendant of that branch of the Presbyterian Church familiarly called the Covenanters."

THE SILVER SPRING CHURCH AND CEMETERY.

The church at Silvers' Spring, now known as the "Silver Spring Presbyterian Church," was probably, in its inception, the first church established in the valley. The earliest mention made of this congregation, in which they are first spoken of as the "people over the Susquehanna," is in October, 1734. Later they are called "East Pennsborough," and finally "Silvers' Spring." The present stone church, which is built only a short distance from the spring, and is surrounded by a handsome grove of trees, was built in 1783. A wooden one had been erected here, according to Rupp, forty years before. Its inception was at a time when no public road had yet been made through the valley, but when the thoroughfares were the bridle-paths of the Indians. It seems that there was a still earlier building, but not upon the site of the present ones, for Col. A. Loudon Snowden states, in an address at the centennial anniversary, in 1883, that although the present church is now less than "a mile, in a direct line, from the creek, the original log structure in which our ancestors worshiped was much nearer the stream than the present building.* Indeed, the traditions which my father received from some of the old settlers, and gave me, make the location within a very short distance from the same, a little way above where Sample's bridge now stands."

The pastors of this church have been Revs. Samuel Thompson, 1739–45; Samuel Caven, 1749–50; John Steel, 1764–76; Samuel Waugh, 1782–1807; John Hayes, 1808–14; Henry R. Wilson, 1814–23; James Williamson, 1824–38; George Morris, 1838–60; Wm. H. Dinsmore, 1861–65; W. G. Hillman, 1866–67; W. B. McKee, 1868–70; R. P. Gibson, 1872–75; T. J. Ferguson, 1878.

---

*We have already entered into a period of fabulous antiquity. "The church edifice which preceded the present one," says Dr. Nevin, in his history of "The Churches of the Valley" [published in 1852], "and which was the first meeting-house at Silvers' Spring, was, we have been informed by one who learned it from his grandparents, a small log building, near the place where the present house stands. No record of the building of that house, or of the organization at it church in it, can be found; and, as the members of the congregation at that time are, of course, all dead and gone, it is impossible to tell with certainty when these things were done. It is, however, far more than probable, from the facts which we have already given, and from the epitaphs which are found in the cemetery, that the old log building, in which the first settlers in what is now the eastern part of Cumberland County, with its beautiful landscapes and thriving villages, assembled for the worship of God, was erected about one hundred and twenty years ago." [*Churches of the Valley*, p. 75.]

A burial place in the grove is connected with the church, and some of the inscriptions can be read with dates as early as 1747, if not earlier still. Within a few years past a handsome memorial gothic chapel has been erected in the grove by the McCormick family. The circular grove of trees in which these churches stand is one of the most beautiful which can be found in the valley, and we do not wonder that the beauty and the hallowed associations of this spot gave birth to the following poem, from the pen of an unknown author, which was published about thirty-five years ago in the *Gazette*, a paper published in Mechanicsburg:

SILVER SPRING.

'Twas on a quiet Sabbath,
  One warm midsummer day,
When first, with childish eagerness,
  I trod its moss-grown way;
Yet paused with every footstep,
  Lest my coming might intrude
On the spirit-haunted trysting-place
  Within its solitude.

For, where the grass grew tallest
  In a myrtle-covered dell,
And softest, deepest shadows
  From waving branches fell,
Lay, in unbroken stillness,
  Old Scotland's exiled dead,
O'er whose mysterious slumbers
  An hundred years had fled.

No pompous, proud mausoleum
  Or sculptured marble tomb
Threw round this spot a mockery
  Of dark, funereal gloom;
But through the tangled walnut boughs,
  Half veiled, but not concealed,
Like a sentinel on duty,
  An old church stood revealed.

A beaten, narrow, thread-like path
  Wound through the thick green wood,
And, following where it seemed to lead,
  I, in a moment, stood
Beside a rill so beautiful,
  Of coloring so rare,
I surely thought the sunshine
  Had been imprisoned there.

A ledge of gray, uneven rocks
  Rested against the hill;
And from their veins the water gushed
  With such a gleeful trill—
Such liquid, silver, soothing sounds—
  I almost held my breath,
Lest e'en a whisper might disturb
  The harmony beneath.

The quiet dead, the old stone church,
  And myrtle-covered dell,
Each had its tale of thankfulness
  For living love to tell;
What wonder, then, that pleasant
  Recollections always cling
Around the sunny Sabbaths
  I spent at Silver Spring.

MISCELLANEOUS.

The Cumberland Valley Railroad passes through the southern portion of the township, in a west by northerly direction from Mechanicsburg, till within a short distance of Middlesex Township line, when it takes a sudden southwesterly course.

The postoffices in Silver Spring Township are New Kingstown and Hogestown.

CHAPTER XXXIV.

SOUTHAMPTON TOWNSHIP.*

SOUTHAMPTON is the extreme southwestern township of the county, and is bounded on the north by Hopewell, on the east by Newton, and on the south and west by the lines of Adams and Franklin Counties. It was formed, originally, one year before the formation of Franklin County, from portions of Lurgan and Hopewell Townships, in October, 1783. At this session of the court a petition is presented praying the court to erect into one separate township such parts of the said townships of Hopewell and Lurgan as are included in the description given, and that it "be called henceforth by the name of Southampton," which petition was confirmed by the court.

In this petition complaint is made of the great length of the said townships—namely, Hopewell and Lurgan—"which at present extend from the North to the South Mountains at a distance of about fifteen miles." The creation of Franklin County, in September, 1784, disturbed the boundary of this township, so that another petition of a number of the inhabitants of Southampton Township is presented to the court in January, 1791, setting forth that the said township of Southampton was some years laid off from Hopewell and Lurgan Townships into a separate township by the name of Southampton; that, soon after that, the "said township of Southampton was cut in two by a line dividing Franklin from Cumberland County," etc., and states that at a meeting of the inhabitants of Hopewell and Southampton Townships it was agreed that "the future boundary between Hopewell and Southampton Townships begin at Capt. William Strains' mill-dam; thence along the southeast side of the laid out road leading from said Strains' mill to James Irvin's mill until it intersects the line between Newton and Hopewell," etc., and prays the court to grant relief by confirming the said boundary; which was done, so that "that part of the said township of Hopewell lying southeast of the road leading from Strains' to Irwin's mill shall be henceforth called Southampton."

CHARACTER OF SOIL, ETC.

The character of the soil in Southampton Township is, in the north, undulating limestone land, more or less rocky, but productive, and in which, at its settlement, was what was known as "barrens," a sort of prairie land where the Indians had burned the forests, which grew up afterward into brush; this limestone land containing oak, hickory, and several varieties of locust and walnut, while on the gravel land south there were large forests of yellow pine

---
*For borough of Shippensburg, see page 257.

extending from the base of the mountains three miles into the valley. This description is true of the whole south side of the upper portion of the valley until it reaches almost the center of the county. This land is well watered by numerous streams.

Some superior ore banks have been discovered in this township, and therefore it was that, long ago, furnaces were established. The first of these, built by John Moore, of Carlisle, in 1824, on the stream near the foot of the South Mountain, was one known as Augusta. Another, on the same stream, in the forest below, was known as Mary Ann. A third, still later, about four miles east of the latter, was called Big Pond. They have all long since ceased to be in operation. Other mills, and for other purposes, have since been built in the neighborhood of Middle Spring. Deposits of superior hematite iron ore are to be found at different places in the township, while fine farms abound on the limestone land.

One matter in connection with the township during the Revolution is of interest. Two powder-mills were erected, one near the foot of South Mountain, and the other about a mile northwest of Shippensburg. The former was but a short distance on the run above where the Mary Ann Furnace was subsequently built, and the other just below where the Zearfoss flouring-mill now stands. Both mills were blown up, at different times, and in both cases resulted in the death of the proprietors.

EARLIEST SETTLERS.

The southwestern portion of this township was settled at a very early period. Large tracts of land, lying between the southeastern boundary of the first purchase made by Edward Shippen and the base of the South Mountains, were owned by John Reynolds, Benjamin Blythe, Col. James Dunlap, John Cesna and others. John Reynolds' tract joined that of Mr. Shippens on its southeastern side, while south of the latter lay that of Mr. Blythe. Just southeast of the Blythe tract lies the one which was purchased by Col. Dunlap in 1767. East of this tract is the Cesna farm, upon which Dennis O'Neiden and John Kirkpatrick were killed by the Indians July 18, 1757. This farm was one of the first occupied in the township, and remained in the possession of the descendants of Mr. Cesna until about the year 1827. On the north and northwest of the second purchase of Mr. Shippen, were the Brumfields, Duncans, Wherrys, McCunes, Caldwells, Culbertsons, Morrows, Finleys, Montgomerys and others. These were among the earliest settlers in the valley, and most of them were men of intelligence and enterprise, constituting such a group of these hardy Scotch-Irish as will bear comparison with any which can be collected at the present day.*

VILLAGES.

There are three villages in the township, namely, Leesburg, Cleversburg and Middle Spring.

Leesburg is situated on the Harrisburg & Potomac Railroad, on the Walnut Bottom road, four miles east of Shippensburg, and was originally settled by Scotch-Irish families, such as the Maxwells, Highlands, Chestnuts and others, who lived upon the lands upon which it is built, or just adjacent. It contains at present a postoffice, a church, three stores, graded schools, and a population of about 300 inhabitants. The town was called from George Lee, who kept a tavern in a log house which stood on the south side of the Walnut

*The writer has to say that some of the above facts were obtained from the late Hon. John McCurdy who seems to have made a careful study of this portion of the county.

Bottom road. This house, a farm house of Mr. Adam Reese, and a house which stood on the north side of the road below that of Mr. Reese, were the only houses then standing within the present limits of Leesburg. The land to the south and west of Lee's house, we are informed, was then covered with heavy timber, consisting of yellow pine, white and black oak, and hickory, nor was there any cleared land on either side of the Walnut Bottom road from that point until within a mile of Shippensburg excepting two farms, the Beltz and Rebrick.

Cleversburg is situated just south of the center of the township, about one mile from the South Mountains, on land which originally belonged to George Croft, but which was purchased afterward by George Clever. The town was begun about 1860. It was called after George Clever, and was laid out upon the lands of George Clever and Wm. Sibbet and others. Up to this time (1860) there were but two houses, and a grist or flour-mill which is still standing. Clever owned the Gochenaur, or, originally, Croft, mill. The town contains a postoffice, a furnace, two churches, schools, a grist-mill, and a population of about 350. A branch railroad runs to the ore banks and furnaces from Cleversburg.

Middle Spring is located about two miles north of Shippensburg. It takes its name from the spring and the old church which stands there. There is here a store, postoffice, blacksmith's shop and a number of dwellings.

MIDDLE SPRING CHURCH AND GRAVE-YARD.

For some reason all the old Presbyterian Churches of the Cumberland Valley were erected near a spring or stream of water, and from their location they derived their names. Of these Middle Spring is one. Of the exact date of the origin of this congregation no record has been preserved; neither can it be ascertained from any other source. A log church, thirty-five feet square, was erected here about 1738, not far from where the present Middle Spring Church now stands. In 1765 a new structure was erected, and enlarged from time to time, which was succeeded in 1781 by the stone structure, which gave place, in 1847, to the new brick church, which has since been remodeled and improved.

Instead of, ourselves, attempting to describe these churches, we prefer to use almost *verbatim*, the words of one who is more familiar with them. "Those," says Dr. Nevin, "who are familiar with this locality, remember well the green slope to the right on which the building stands; the grave-yard in the rear; the beautiful wood stretching back, with its refreshing shadows; the old mill-dam to the left; the fountain of fresh water bubbling up close by; the murmuring stream, which rolls on under thick hanging foliage; and the "Lower Grave-yard" a little to the north, along which the stream flows in its course, chanting its sweet requiem for the dead." It was in this grave-yard that the first church in this region was built. This was about 1738. It does not now stand. It was demolished, and another log one built upon the spot. This was considerably larger, being about forty-eight feet long and forty-eight wide. In a little while this was extended, by removing three sides of the building then in use, and embracing a little more space on either side, which was covered with a roof, something in the form of a shed. Up the sides of these additions to the main edifice, and over the roofs, were erected wooden steps, by which access was gained to the gallery. This arrangement was made for want of room in the interior of the building for the construction of a stairway. About the year 1781, the old stone church was erected, whose site, as is well known, was just beside that of the present building. This was still larger than its predecessor, fifty-eight by sixty-eight feet, and at about this same time the grave-yard immediately in its rear was located. This was done, not only because the old one was already filled, but also because its soil was of a gravelly description, and its lower section, by reason of its nearness to the stream, was subject to frequent inundation.

The present brick church at Middle Spring was built, but seemingly, at least, not without poetic protest, in 1747-48, as in the volume from which we have quoted, among others, there appears this verse:

> "That old stone church! Hid in these oaks apart,
> I hoped the newer world would ne'er invade,
> But only time, with its slow, hallowing art,
> Would touch it, year by year, with softer shade,
> And crack its walls no more, but, interlaid,
> Mend them with moss. Its ancient sombre cast
> Dearer to me is than all art displayed
> In modern churches, which, by their contrast,
> Make this to stand forlorn, held in the solemn past."*

Of the list of persons, to show the warlike mettle of these men, members or adherents of this church, who took part in the Revolution, we may mention Cols. Benjamin Blythe, Isaac Miller, Robt. Peebles, William Scott, Abraham Smith; Maj. James Herron; Capts. William Rippey, Matthew Henderson, Matthew Scott, David McKnight, John McKee, William Strain, Joseph Brady, Robert Quigley, Charles Leeper (killed at Crooked Billet, May, 1778), Charles Maclay, Samuel Blythe, Samuel Walker, James Scott, Samuel McCune, Samuel Kearsley and Lieut. Samuel Montgomery (lost a leg at Crooked Billet); John Heap, Esq., Samuel Cox, Esq., Francis Campble, John Reynolds, Esq., Thomas McClellan, Joseph McKenney, James McKee, Robert Donavin, William Turner, Thomas McCombs, William Sterritt, John Woods, Esq., William Anderson, John Maclay, James Dunlap, Esq., James Lowry, Esq., John Maclay (mountain), William Barr, Archibald Cambridge, John Herron, David Herron, David Duncan. John McKnight, James McCune, David Mahan, John Thompson, Jacob Porter, Isaac Jenkins (one of five brothers who died in camp of contagious disease, all of whom are buried in the Lower Grave-yard), Samuel Dixon, John Grier. A number of the members of this church were present in the meeting held in the Presbyterian Church, in Carlisle, June 12, 1774, to protest against the closing of the port of Boston.

MIDDLE SPRING CHURCH LANDS.

The history of the lands which belonged to the Middle Spring Church is thus given by Rev. S. Wylie, its present pastor: "On the 27th of May, 1767, there was surveyed and sold to Francis Campble, Robert Chambers, William Duncan and John Maclay, the tract of land in Hopewell Township, Cumberland County, called 'Mount Hope,' very much in the form of a wedge, with the head extending along the Middle Spring, beyond the old grave-yard, and the sharp point reaching almost to Mean's Run in the direction of Shippensburg, containing 49 acres and 110 perches, for which they paid the State of Pennsylvania the sum of £9 and 16s. This land was patented by these men September 17, 1790, and in November, 1793, they deeded it to the trustees of the Middle Spring Church. On the 3d of December, 1813, there was sold of this land, at public auction, nine acres and nine perches, lying along and including the water-right of Middle Spring, to Samuel Cox, at $150 per acre. On the 10th of May, 1825, of the remainder twenty-four acres and fifty-three perches were sold to Mr. George Diehl for the sum of $486.62. There thus remains something above sixteen acres of these lands, which still belong to the church.

---

*From poem by Prof. W. M. Nevin: "The Guardian," May, 1852.

"The old grave-yard belonging to this church was used from its earliest history. The oldest records now legible, however, only date back to 1770. The oldest names appear to be the Wrights and Johnsons. The present stone wall was built before 1805. It had a shingle comb-roof and was painted red. The upper or new yard was inclosed in 1842."

MISCELLANEOUS.

Southampton Township is favored with two railroads, the Cumberland Valley and the Harrisburg & Potomac, the former running through the more northerly part of the township, and the latter through the center portion. The postoffices are Shippensburg, Middle Spring, Cleversburg and Lee's Cross Roads.

CHAPTER XXXV.

SOUTH MIDDLETON TOWNSHIP AND BOROUGH OF MOUNT HOLLY SPRINGS.

SOUTH MIDDLETON TOWNSHIP was originally a portion of Middleton, which was created from Pennsborough in 1750, but divided into its northern and southern townships in November, 1810. It lies just south of Carlisle, bounded on the north by North Middleton and Middlesex; on the east by Monroe; on the south by the counties of York and Adams, and on the west by Dickinson and a small portion of West Pennsborough. The character of the soil is not the same in all portions of the township. In its southern extremity the South Mountains slope gradually, like a great wave, broken into crevasses and smaller valleys, until it reaches the rich limestone lands below. There is a great contrast. The former is scrub pine and forest mountain land, and was long ago described as "a wild and desert region covered with forests, which yield fuel for furnaces in them or on their borders; but offering little attraction to any except the woodcutter and the hunter," while below the soil is of almost exceptional fertility, with highly cultivated farms, good buildings and large barns.

If one reaches the South Mountains he finds that the rocks are of a different character from those of the level region. Lying along this range he meets with compact white sandstone, some portions timbered, some barren, others with laurel undergrowth and brush. At Pine Grove, on Mountain Creek, there is a detached bed of limestone land, with brown argillaceous earth and hematite iron ore, which had always furnished a plentiful supply to the furnace of that place.

Among the numerous branches of the Cumberland Valley Railroad the South Mountain, originally built to Pine Grove Furnace for the transportation of the iron ores and manufactured products of that region, but now extended to Gettysburg, is exceedingly interesting on account of the wildness of the scenery. The view as you pass along over these mountains toward Gettysburg is varied by intervals of forest, rude rocks, abrupt or broken declivities, deep chasms, over which the road is supported by trestle work reminding one still of the unbroken and silent wilderness, but into which civilization is already pushing its way. These remarks apply only to the southern or mountainous portion of the township, for the greater part, the northern and limestone land consists, as we have said, of fertile fields and farms.

ROADS AND STREAMS.

Of the numerous roads which lead in every direction, and many of which are well macadamized, we may mention particularly the old Carlisle and Hanover turnpike, which was for many years the principal route to Baltimore, and which was laid out principally by parties who lived in South Middleton Township in 1812.

The streams by which the township is well watered are the Yellow Breeches Creek, Letort Spring, Boiling Spring and Mountain Run; the former flowing through nearly the center of the township, east and west, and the two latter nearly north and south.*

EARLY SETTLEMENTS.

This portion of Cumberland County, which is now South Middleton Township, was settled at a very early period. James Le Tort, a French-Swiss, and one of the old Indian interpreters, lived in the township at the head of the spring which bears his name, as early, it is said, as 1720. William Patterson afterward owned this farm at the head of the Letort, and Hugh Stuart, the grandfather of Jos. A. Stuart, also occupied this "Patterson tract." The earliest warrant of land which lay in what is now South Middleton, of which we have any knowledge, was one granted to George Brandon, in 1743, of a tract of land which lay on the York County line on the turnpike.

The Craigheads were among the earliest settlers on the Yellow Breeches Creek. Most, if not all, of these earlier settlers were Scotch-Irish. Such were the Craigheads, Stuarts, Pattersons, Mahaffeys, Eges, Grahams, Moores, Saundersons, McClures, Dennys, Holmes, and others, all of which names date back to the formation of the county. Among other old families, besides those mentioned elsewhere, are the Burkholders, Gliems, Myers, Zugs, Weakleys, Bradleys, Givins, Ritners, Searights, Ahls, Flemmings, Kauffmans (whose descendants laid out Boiling Springs), Peters, Goodyears, McFeeleys, Eisenhaeurs, and others.

The name "Trent" is found at a very early period, and the gap now known as Mount Holly was originally called Trent's Gap. Of the present families who live upon the lands originally settled, James B. Weakley occupies part of the original tract taken up by his grandfather, James Weakley; William Moore and the Craigheads also occupy a portion of the lands first settled by their families. The only land in the vicinity of Boiling Springs which is still in possession of (maternal) descendants of first settlers of it is that now owned by A. M. Leidich. Andrew Holmes owned a large tract in the township, upon a portion of which Mr. George W. Hilton now lives. The Pattersons were early settlers, and occupied a large tract on Letort. Stephen Foulk lived in the township, on a farm near the toll gate, now owned by Joseph Stuart. George A. Lyon, Esq., and James Hamilton, Esq., both lawyers of Carlisle, owned large farms in the township.

Above the Richard Peters' tract, west of Boiling Springs, large tracts were taken up at a very early period by Joseph Gaylie and Patrick Hasson. On the south side of the Yellow Breeches Creek large tracts, extending to the mountains, were taken up by Charles and Guian Mahaffey; while to the east of

---
*Letort Spring rises in the township, from a large fountain as its source, near Carlisle; Boiling Spring flows but for a short distance; Mountain Creek flows down through the winding gorges of the mountains, and, at a point near Craighead's Station, empties into the Yellow Breeches Creek.

SOUTH MIDDLETON TOWNSHIP.

Boiling Springs lands were taken up originally by James and Andrew Crockert. In the vicinity of Boiling Springs there are three tracts which are particularly worthy of mention: The ore banks, a large tract adjacent, and the land upon which the town of Boiling Springs is built. The three ore banks seem to have been taken up at a very early period, and afterward the large tract surrounding them. This latter is described as "one tract in Middleton [now South Middleton] Township, in the county of Cumberland, containing 1,644 acres, surveyed in the name of John Rigby & Co. on the 8th, 9th, 10th and 12th days of July, 1762," and which was returned in pursuance of certain warrants issued by the proprietaries of Pennsylvania, dated May 31, 1762, "to John Rigby, Francis Saunderson, and Joseph, Samuel and John Morris, Jr." This tract was divided into sixteen equal parts. John Armstrong and wife owned two in 1764, but re-conveyed them to Michael Ege in 1792. Two parts belonged to Robert Thornburg, and the rest remaining in the original owners or their descendants, the whole tract passed, by various conveyances, to Michael Ege, the elder. The earliest mention in these various deeds or conveyances of the Carlisle Iron Works is in 1765, but they had been evidently, at this period, for a number of years in existence. The probabilities are that they were started when this original grant was given, in July, 1762, if not at a still earlier period. At these works, it is said, the earliest cannon manufactured in the United States were made, one of which is said to have been captured during the Revolutionary war and removed to the Tower of London. The three ore banks were described as having about twenty acres each, but these tracts were embraced in an original sale of land made by William Penn to Adam Kroesen, then of Holland, by deed of 7th of March, 1682, the right whereof was afterward vested in Richard Peters, secretary in the land office in Philadelphia, who, in April, 1761, conveyed to Jacob Yoner, of Lancaster, 1,000 acres of the said land; but Jacob Yoner, in pursuance of a warrant from the proprietaries, dated April 16, 1761, caused to be surveyed to him, instead of the 1,000 acres, the three ore banks above mentioned. By deed of Jacob Yoner, 6th of November, 1761, these banks, were conveyed to John Rigby and Nathaniel Giles, and a patent of confirmation was granted, and by various conveyances they became vested in the firm known as Rigby & Co., which consisted of John Rigby, Francis Saunderson, and the Morrises, of Philadelphia. They afterward came into possession of Michael Ege, the elder, who was at this time one of the most prominent iron men in Pennsylvania, at one time owning the forges and furnaces at Pine Grove, at Mount Holly and at Boiling Springs.

The third tract was the one upon which the Carlisle Iron Works and the town of Boiling Springs is built. It is described as "a tract of 398 acres, 132 perches, and all called Boiling Springs, situated on the Yellow Breeches Creek, granted by the proprietaries of Pennsylvania to Richard Peters, by patent dated 13th of October, 1762."

A portion of this tract was granted to John Dickey, embracing the head of Boiling Springs; another portion to David Reed, embracing the upper or smaller spring, and about twenty-nine acres to Rigby & Co. for the Carlisle Iron Works. It was a portion of this tract of land, originally granted in October, 1762, to Richard Peters, which, after being owned by John Dickey and his descendants, came into possession of Michael Ege, the elder, and afterward, by deed dated April 4, 1808, became the property of John and Abraham Kauffman.

SOME EARLY REMINISCENCES.

The following letter, written by Thomas Craighead, Jr., in 1845, is full of interesting reminiscences: "John Craighead settled at an early date on the Yellow Breeches Creek, near Carlisle. * * * He married, spent the fortune, all but a few webs of linen, with which he purchased from the proprietor 500 acres of land on Yellow Breeches, which is now descended to the fifth generation by inheritance, and the sixth is born on it. * * * I have seen many a pack-horse loaded with nail-rods, at Ege's Forge, to carry out to Somerset County and the Forks of Youghiogheny and Red Stone Fort, to make nails for their log cabins, etc. I have known the farmers' teams to haul iron from the same forge to Virginia, load back corn for feed at the forge. All the grain in the county was not enough for its own consumption. I have known fodder so scarce that some farmers were obliged to feed the 'thatch' that was on their barns to keep their cattle alive. James Lamb bought land in Sherman's Valley, and he and his neighbors had to pack straw on horses across the mountains. He was on the top of the mountain waiting until those going over would get up, as they could not pass on the path. I saw the first mail that passed through Carlisle to Pittsburgh. * * * I happened, a short time ago, to visit a friend, Jacob Ritner, son of that great and good man, ex-Gov. Ritner, who now owns Capt. Denny's farm, who was killed during the Revolutionary war. The house had been a tavern, and, in repairing it, Mr. Ritner found some books, etc., which are a curiosity. Charge, breakfast, £20; dinner, horse feed, £30, and some charges still more extravagant; but we know it was paid with Congress money. So late as 1808 I hauled some materials to Oliver Evans' saw-mill at Pittsburgh. I was astonished to see a mill going without water. Mr. Evans satisfied my curiosity by shewing and explaining everything he could to me. He looked earnestly at me and said: 'You may live to see your wagons coming out here by steam.' The words were so impressed on my mind that I have always remembered them. I have lived to see them go through Cumberland County, and it seems to me that I may see them go through to Pittsburgh; but I have seen Mr. Evans' prophecy fulfilled beyond what I thought possible at that time; but things have progressed at a rate much faster than the most gigantic minds imagined, and we are onwards still."

Think of it! the old wagons, the thatched barns, the narrow roads, and we may form some faint conception of those times.

SCHOOLS.

This township is among the most advanced in the matter of education. There are nineteen schools, some graded, and with the schoolhouses in good condition, supported for six months in the year by public and for three months additional by private funds. So, here, as in every portion of the county, some contemplative Jaques can see

* * * "the whining school boy, with his satchel
And shining morning face, creeping like snail
Unwillingly to school."

RAILROADS AND POSTOFFICES.

The South Mountain Railroad, from Carlisle to Pine Grove Furnace, was built in 1869 and 1870 by the South Mountain Iron Company. In 1883 it was extended to Gettysburg and organized under the name of the "Gettysburg & Harrisburg Railroad." It now extends from its junction at Carlisle to Round Top, beyond Gettysburg, which is one of the prominent points of that famous field. J. C. Fuller was the first president; William H. Woodward, first superintendent, treasurer and secretary.

SOUTH MIDDLETON TOWNSHIP.   351

The *Harrisburg & Potomac Railroad*, which runs east and west, passing through nearly the center of the township, was incorporated in May, 1869, as the "Meramar Iron Company." Its name was afterward changed to its present one. Work was begun on the road in October, 1871, and that part which extends between Mount Holly Springs and the Dillsburg branch of the Cumberland Valley Road was completed before 1875. Daniel V. Ahl was the first president.

The *Cumberland Valley Railroad* runs partly along the northern border of the township, forming the greater part of the boundary line between it and North Middleton Township.

The postoffices in the township are Mount Holly Springs, Boiling Springs, Hatton and Hunter's Run.

BOILING SPRINGS.

This place was laid out by Daniel Kauffman, son of Abraham Kauffman, who owned all the land upon which the town is built, during the year 1845. The first survey of the town was made in the fall of this year by A. M. Leidich, who also purchased the first two lots, Nos. 1 and 2, where he now resides and the one adjoining. At this time there were but two buildings, the stone tavern built by Philip, and the stone farm house opposite, built by Frederick Brechbill. The village of Boiling Spring is beautifully situated in the rolling bluffs of rich land which lie almost at the foot of the South Mountain. The town is handsomely laid out, part of it fronting on the beautiful sheet of crystal water, from which the tract originally, and the town afterward, derives its name. Under this beautiful sheet of water there are subterranean springs, coming from cylindrical rocks, where the water is thrown perpendicularly upward from its rocky bed to the surface which it disturbs, at places, giving to them the appearance of water which is "boiling," thus suggesting naturally the name by which it is known. The largest of these outlets is said to have a capacity of about twenty hogsheads per minute. The main body of the water, however, has an untroubled surface, and is deep and clear. Handsome shade trees near it also enhance the beauty of this spring, the water of which flows into the Yellow Breeches Creek near Island Grove, a beautiful spot not far distant from the village. The town itself is laid out in wide streets, on which there are a number of handsome residences: First, Second, Third and Fourth Streets running east and west, and Front, Walnut and Cherry north and south. The town has many shady trees and, situated as it is upon the beautiful spring from which it derives its name, and with exceptionally beautiful scenery surrounding it, promises to become, if it is not already, as beautiful a town as can be found in the Cumberland Valley. It has postoffice, railroad, iron works and forge, three churches (one Lutheran, one Methodist and one Dunkard), one double and two single schoolhouses, many private dwellings, and a population of about 500.

The furnace which stands near the spring came into the possession of C. W. and D. V. Ahl, in 1859, from the assignees of Peter F. Ege. It was operated successfully until 1882, when a large anthracite furnace was erected by C. W. Ahl and son, which is still being operated under the firm name of C. W. Ahl's Son. There are ore banks near the town, which were leased in 1873 to the Pennsylvania & Reading Railroad Company, under the management of Asbury Derland, and other banks in the South Mountains, which are being successfully operated by J. C. Lehman, a citizen of Boiling Springs.

BOROUGH OF MOUNT HOLLY SPRINGS.

Lying almost within the shadow of the South Mountains and at the entrance to the gap from which it derives its name, is the beautiful borough of Mount Holly Springs. The town lies partly in the mountain gorge called Holly Gap, and partly in the mountains called Upper Holly, through which flows Mountain Creek. Holly was the name originally given to the gap at a very early period, on account of a large holly tree which stood where Upper Holly now is.

The borough now comprises what was formerly known as "Upper and Lower Holly," "Kidderminster" and "Papertown." In the original plan of the town, in 1815, it was also known as South Middleton.

It appears that prior to the year 1812 there were not over one-half dozen houses between what is now called Upper Holly and the present paper-mills of William A. and A. Foster Mullin. As to who built the first house we have no record, but it is certain that the oldest house of any importance erected within the present borough limits was the old stone mansion of Mrs. Jane Thompson, which stands back in a yard nearly opposite the present Holly Inn. and which was erected as early as 1812 or 1817. There was also, at a very early date, an old log tavern-stand belonging to Mrs. Thompson, on the site of the present Holly Inn, which was replaced in 1822 by a stone structure, which was then an inn, and which still stands as a portion of the present hotel. Mrs. Thompson was the mother of Elizabeth Thompson, who married the Rev. Jasper Bennett, who resided in the old stone mansion above mentioned till about 1857. Two small log schoolhouses occupied successively the lot where Mr. Simeon Fisk's residence now stands, which was built also for a schoolhouse in 1855, and afterward used as such until it was purchased by him and converted into a residence. A small story-and-a-half building stood near where the late Mr. Samuel Schriver's house now stands, and was purchased by him many years ago. It was then owned by Rev. Jasper Bennett, who owned all the land within the borough, from the present Holly Inn to where the Methodist Church now stands, including that lot on the east side of Baltimore Avenue, and most of the land on the west side. The Carlisle and Hanover Turnpike was then what is now called Baltimore Avenue. A small log house stood where William A. Mullin's house now stands, and another where Daniel Stees' house is erected, and these, with the old paper-mill of W. A. & A. F. Mullin, were the only buildings in the place in the year 1812.

EARLY SETTLEMENT AND INDUSTRIES.

Tradition has it that Elizabeth McKinney, grandmother of Mary Smith, was the first settler in Holly Gap. Their house stood on the present site of the old stone house adjoining the residence occupied some years ago by A. Mansfield. They moved out of the fort at Shippensburg which the people had erected to protect themselves against the incursions of the French and Indians. The building occupied by the McKinneys was a log structure, and was torn down by Mr. Foulk preparatory to the erection of the present stone building.

An early settlement of the lands around Mount Holly Springs was occasioned by reason of the large deposits of iron ore which were found in its vicinity. Furnaces were built there at a very early period, and the manufacturing of iron was for many years the sole employment of its inhabitants. The first furnace of which anything definite is known was built by Stephen Foulk and William Cox, Jr., about the year 1785. It was called the "Holly Iron Works," and was situated near the present site of the paper-mill at Upper Holly. It is quite probable that the first iron works were established at Mount Holly before the year 1765, and that these early works were frequently remodeled and rebuilt. Tradition says that there was a furnace at Upper Holly before the furnace built by Foulk & Cox, but nothing authentic on this subject can now be definitely ascertained. In the year 1803 this furnace of Foulk & Cox was sold at sheriff's sale, and was purchased by Michael Ege.

During the year 1812 George Ege, a son of Michael Ege, built a new furnace near the site of the former furnace erected by Foulk & Cox. It was known as the Mount Holly Furnace, and stood upon the site of the present paper-mills at Upper Holly. It is stated on good authority that prior to the erection of Holly Furnace, a forge for the manufacturing of cannon occupied the furnace site, that a mill for the boring of the barrels stood near the toll gate on the turnpike, and that the oldest cannon at present in the United States was manufactured at this forge. A former historian says: "The lumber used in building the Carlisle Barracks was sawed upon a mill erected in Holly Gap. The parties were Englishmen." More probably they were Hessians, captured at Trenton, who built the Carlisle Barracks.

At this time there was very little improved land between Mount Holly and Carlisle. In 1812 a paper-mill was erected by William Barber on or near the site of the mill now owned by the Mullin brothers. It was subsequently owned by Messrs. Barber & Samson Mullin, the grandfather of the owners of the present mill. It afterward passed into the hands of Messrs Knox and McClure, and was burned December 25, 1846. The present mill was then erected in the succeeding year by William B. Mullin, the father of the present owners. This earlier paper-mill was the first ever erected at Mount Holly Springs. Paper-making now became the chief industry of the place, so that the name Holly Iron Works was rarely applied to it, but it everywhere began to be known by the name of Papertown.

About the year 1827 that portion of Mount Holly Springs in the vicinity of the brick mills now owned by the Mount Holly Paper Company, was called Kidderminster, from a factory for the weaving of carpets there erected by Samuel Givin, near the present site of that paper-mill. It was a five-story brick building, and was afterward converted into a mill for the manufacture of paper by Robert and Samuel Givin, for which purpose it was used until its destruction by fire in 1864. The present paper-mill in Lower Holly, belonging to the Mount Holly Paper Company, and which was built near the site of the old Kidderminster factory, was erected in 1866.

The large mill at Upper Holly was built by the Mount Holly Paper Company at its organization in 1856. Its original incorporators were Samuel Kempton, of Baltimore, William B. Mullin, Sylvester Megargee, of Philadelphia, and Robert and Samuel Givin.

There was another old paper-mill to the north of the town, which was destroyed by fire, the ruins of which still stand.

The land belonging to the Mount Holly Paper Company, with many other tracts sold to private individuals, belonged originally to Charles McClure, who took out a patent in 1772. Later the Eges owned much of the mountain land. The Givins came into their estate by deed dated 1827, Mr. James Givin, of Ireland, being the original settler and grantee. The handsome residence of Robert Givin, which stood in the beautiful grove northwest of the brick mill, was consumed by fire in March, 1865.

WAR OF THE REBELLION.

Mount Holly Springs responded promptly to the proclamation of the President for troops to put down the Rebellion, so that many of its citizens are found in the various regiments. On the call for the State troops in 1862, one company (Company G, Twelfth Regiment), under the command of Capt. Charles H. Mullin, was raised entirely from the town.

If, in this connection, we may for a moment drop the dignity of the historian, we would like to picture a panic—one of those little comedies in the real tragedy of war, which occurred here in this part of the great world-stage, in the first act, in the year 1861. The object of history is not only to preserve dry skeleton statistics, but to present to the reader also panoramic pictures of the past; and whether they make us laugh or cry does not much matter, in this world where the two are kin, and both are brief. Well, the report reached here that the Confederate Army was advancing; that they were marching toward Holly Gap from Hanover Junction, that the Carlisle Barracks was one of their objective points, and that they were spreading desolation without delay and consternation with ruthless hands. A company, quickly organized, under Capt. Robert McCartney, of Carlisle, marched to protect the village. Upon reaching the town they took a fortified position in the Gap, ready to sweep like a besom of destruction upon the foe. To achieve this mighty victory (alas, the grandest scene of all the war was played within their hearing), and to immortalize themselves like those sturdy Spartans in a pass of old, they came with flint-lock muskets, many minus locks, and others armed with knives for closer conflict in the mountain passes. The company had come prepared to die in the last ditch, and many of the farmers joined to show "the mettle of their pasture;" but after holding peaceable possession of the Gap, they finally concluded that the reports which had disturbed them were untrue, and when the first rays of the morning sun had dispelled both the mists of the mountain and the fears of invasion, they departed, some of them, we have no doubt, reluctantly, to their homes, where some remained, having no doubt become unfitted to perform further military duty on account of disease contracted at the bloodless battle of Mount Holly Gap.

The signs of the severer conflict were to follow. In 1863 Gen. Ewell's corps passed through the town on their way to Gettysburg to reinforce Gen. Lee. Fitzhugh Lee's cavalry also passed through the town. Many of the Pennsylvania and New York militia marched through the streets on their way to Gettysburg. Taking the Confederate and Union soldiers together, not less than 40,000 men passed through Mount Holly Springs during the months of June and July, 1863.

INCORPORATION, ETC.

Mount Holly Springs was incorporated as a borough in 1873. It is a beautiful, clean town, with one long principal macadamized street, on which are a number of handsome residences. The place is not only noted for the manufacture of fine paper, but is an old and established summer resort, dating from a very early period. Its situation is delightful; protected by the mountains, cool in summer, particularly in summer evenings, it lies amid scenery which might afford an inspiration to an artist. The Mountain Creek, flowing rapidly down through the long gorge from its high recesses, here rests in wider crystal sheets, "where the green mountains bending hang their heads," and are reflected as in a mirror. These sheets, particularly the Upper Holly Dam, afford both boating and piscatorial sport, as well as ample motive power for the mills. From Upper Holly the stream runs in a deep bed beside the turnpike, and under the shade of many trees, and with the mountains on either hand. There are few more beautiful places in Pennsylvania; and it will, on account of its situation and scenery, its pure mountain air and summer climate, continue to attract the weary who are longing for recreation or rest, and the lover of nature who seeks to live where she lavishes her beauties.

SOUTH MIDDLETON TOWNSHIP. 355

The borough lies almost due north and south, and the longer streets, Walnut, Chestnut, and Baltimore Avenue, run almost parallel with the creek, in this direction. The streets running east and west are Butler, Pine, Harman and Railroad. The principal street is Baltimore Avenue, which consists of all that portion of the turnpike road embraced within the borough limits. It is a wide, level street, a mile or more in length, sixty feet in width, beautifully macadamized with fine gravel taken from the mountains. With the exception of our large cities, there can be found no finer street in the State.

Mount Holly Springs lies twenty miles southwest from Harrisburg, the capital of the State, and six miles south of Carlisle, the county seat. It is connected with Carlisle and Harrisburg by two railroads. A daily line of stages runs to York Sulphur Springs, Carlisle, and other points, so that its mail facilities are equal to those of any like inland town elsewhere. It is now a thriving and prosperous town, and bids fair to become a still more beautiful and important one in the future. The various paper-mills afford continual employment to hundreds of operatives, who, in their turn, contribute to the development of its resources.

CHURCHES, SCHOOLS AND NEWSPAPER.

The churches of the borough are the Evangelical Lutheran Church, on Baltimore Avenue, and the Methodist Episcopal Church, a commodious structure, erected in 1860, also on Baltimore Avenue. There are five schools—four white and one colored—in the borough. The press is represented by the *Mountain Echo*, a weekly paper, established by R. Melvin Early in 1872.

HOTELS.

The hotels in the borough for the accommodation of the public will compare favorably with those of larger towns and cities, and of these the "Central" and the "Holly Inn," which was for many years known as the "Mullin Hotel," but which has been remodeled and refitted, and is now under the charge of a stock company, are particularly worthy of mention.

SOCIETIES.

Holly Gap Lodge, No. 277, K. of P., was organized December 8, 1870, with the following named charter members: S. P. Goodyear, J. L. Wolf, Samuel G. Givin, T. J. Wolf, Jacob Hemminger, F. L. Goodyear, M. S. Goodyear, Chas. H. Mullin, J. L. McAllister. Number of present members, seventy-five. Present officers: Dr. R. B. Pollinger, V. C.; James A. Stees, P.; Lincoln Vinck, M. A.; S. P. Goodyear, K. of R. and S.; G. R. Klopp, M. of F.; Thomas Haycock, M. of E.; Thomas Wolf, P. C.

Mount Holly Lodge, No. 650, I. O. O. F., was organized November 17, 1868, with the following charter members: John Humes, N. G.; Chas. H. Miller, V. G.; James L. McAllister, Sec.; Henry Mullin, Asst. Sec.; Jacob Hemminger, Treas. Present officers are A. Simpson, N. G.; John A. Bosler, V. G.; S. P. Goodyear, Sec.; Edward C. Beach, Asst. Sec.; Thomas Wolf, Treas.

Canada Post, No. 490, G. A. R., was organized in August, 1885, with the following named charter members: Alexander Adams, W. H. Brinn, Jos. S. Early, N. J. Glass, John Goodyear, Geo. W. Kinter, John Cauffman, Jacob Hoffert, Wm. H. Hatz, A. Noffsinger, J. E. Mondorf, D. A. Nagle, A. T. Richwine, W. H. Ricker, Geo. Slusser, Milton Still, S. J. Sadler, Philip Snyder, James Snyder, Eli Toner, Silas Toner, Henry Wallet, John Ward, Moses Wagner, Benj. F. Wallet, Philip Harman, Augustus McGonigal. Present number of members, sixty-one. Present officers: Rev. J. Wise Shannon, C.; Augustus Miller, S. V. C.; Samuel Sadler, J. V. C.; Daniel Wallet, O. D.; Milton Still, O. G.; P. Herman, Q. M.; James Snyder, Q. M. S.; Wm. Goodyear, Adjt.; Benj. Wallack, S. M.; John Ward, Chaplain.

There are also *Patriotic Sons of America, Washington Camp, No. 181*, a *Building and Loan Association*, a *Literary Society*, a *Cornet Band*, etc.

CHAPTER XXXVI.

UPPER ALLEN TOWNSHIP.

ALLEN TOWNSHIP was formed from East Pennsborough in 1766. It then embraced what is now Monroe, Upper and Lower Allen Townships. Monroe was taken from Allen first in 1825, and in 1850 the remainder was divided into Upper and Lower Allen.

Upper Allen is bounded on the north by portions of Silver Spring and Hampden; on the east by Lower Allen; on the south, where the Yellow Breeches Creek is the dividing line, by York County; and on the west by Monroe Township.

EARLY SETTLERS, MILLS, MINES, ETC.

The earliest settlers were Scotch-Irish, principally from Lancaster County, of which this, then, was the frontier, although the Germans began to come into this lower portion of the county about 1760.

Among the earlier Scotch-Irish who settled here before the year 1762 were the Quigleys, Dunlaps, Rosebarys, Brysons, Trindles, McCues, Gregorys, and others.

The names of other early settlers were the Hunters, Musselmans, Switzers, Taylors, Harknesses, Brysons, Longneckers, Brenizers, Mohlers, Shelleys, Bitners, Rupps, Hecks, the Gorgas family, Cochrans, Coovers, Beelmans, Eberlys, the Eckels family, Browns, Myers, Lambs, and others.

The Pattersons were an old family, and lived on land since owned by Moses C. Eberly. The Grahams settled where James Graham owns; the Wertzes on the farm since owned by Milton Stayman; the Dunlaps on land since owned by Mrs. Coover, on the Lisburn road; and the Coovers, originally from Switzerland, on a place in the possession of their descendants. The Mohlers, Daniel and his uncle, Christian Mohler, purchased their land in Cumberland County in 1800.

The Cocklin farm, known as "Spring Dale," was purchased from the Penns in 1742 by Andrew Miller, who sold it in 1772 to Jacob Cocklin, who came in 1733 from the western part of Germany, and settled first in Lancaster, but afterward in Cumberland County. The Yellow Breeches Creek forms the southern boundary of the two Allen Townships. The first mill, it is said, was built of logs, and was owned by Richard Peters until 1746. It was torn down, and other mills (the last now owned, or lately owned, by Levi Lautz) have been successively erected upon its site. The farm on which this mill is located, 295 acres, including the mill, was once purchased by John Anderson from Richard Peters for £50. The Quigleys located close to what is now Bowmansdale and built a mill there, which was known as Quigley's mill. This was owned by Henry Quigley before 1818. The Bryson estate came in on the east, and on the west the Niesleys, who also erected a mill, now known as Hertzler's mill. About a mile and a half east of the Quigleys was the Switzers, and they also owned a mill on the site of what is now Gingrick's mill. The present one was erected in 1837. This mill (also known as Underwood's) was purchased from Richard Peters, between 1740 and 1750, by Frederick Switzer, who joined the army, and was absent during the Revolutionary war, and bequeathed it to his son, from whom it has passed through various hands.

Three prominent families which came into this section at a very early period were the Grahams, the Harknesses, and the Browns. The two latter estates reached almost from Mechanicsburg to the Yellow Breeches Creek. The Graham estate lay east of the Harknesses, and the Browns south.

Of this Harkness family, as we have material from a sketch of one of the Lamberton family, and as it contains points of general interest, we will here give an account.

William Harkness was born October 1, 1739, in the North of Ireland, and when quite a boy immigrated with his father, William Harkness, Sr., and settled among the Presbyterians of Donegal, in Lancaster. He married, in 1771, Priscilla Lytle, of the same Scotch-Irish stock, and living in the same settlement. After the close of the harassing Indian wars (by the treaty of Col. Bouquet) which ravaged the Cumberland Valley until 1764, William Harkness, Jr., bought of the proprietaries, on August 1, 1766, land now in Allen Township. The Indian titles having been extinguished, and the boundary difficulties with Maryland adjusted, the proprietor advertised that the office for the sale of lands west of the Susquehanna would be opened on August 1, 1766, the settlers prior to that holding their lands under license certificates. Judge Huston says the number of applications issued on that day was 669. The application of William Harkness was number thirty-eight. The survey was on January 24, 1767, and patent issued subsequently.

Prior to this he and his neighboring settlers were often engaged in defending their homes against a savage enemy, and in the work of the harvest-fields there, and in the Sherman's Valley, carried their rifles with them. They were armed agriculturists. The name of William Harkness is found on the list of taxables of Cumberland County as early as 1753. Later, in 1776, he entered the colonial service as an ensign, and together with Mr. Lytle, his brother-in-law, was amongst the conflicts at Brandywine and Germantown. At the latter place Mr. Lytle was killed by his side.

After the war Mr. Harkness, by purchase, added to his property until he possessed a large estate of some 700 or 800 acres. On it he erected a large stone dwelling house, among the first of that kind in the valley, and other buildings, and devoted himself to agriculture and other business pursuits. His house was famous for its hospitality.

At this time there was slavery in Pennsylvania. In the registry of the last 297 slaves registered under the requirements of an act to explain and amend a former "Act for the gradual abolition of slavery, etc., in Pennsylvania," passed the 1st of March, 1780, among the records of Cumberland County we find the well-known names of Armstrong, Buchanan, Butler, Carothers, Crawford, Clarke, Craighead, Bryson, Duncan, Blaine, Dunlap, Irvine, Galbreath, Gibson and others, and that William Harkness returns those born on his estate. Some who desired it he afterward manumitted at the age of twenty-one, seven years before the time fixed by law, having previously sent them to school and in other ways given them preparation for self-dependence. Others lived long afterward on his estate—the children of some until the death of his son, William Harkness, in 1851.

William Harkness died May 4, 1822; Priscilla, his wife, October 31, 1831. Both are buried in the old grave-yard at Silver Spring. Their daughter, Mary, became the wife of Major Robert Lamberton, of Carlisle.

Another family, the McCues, dating back of 1762, lived a short distance south of the Graham estate, and between them lay the large estate of the Poormans. Another family who were large land-owners were the Gregorys— also dating beyond 1762, and the last of whom (so far as we know). Walter Gregory, was buried in the Silver Spring grave-yard in 1730. They owned the estate part of which is now owned by Harry McCormick, where the bridge crosses the Yellow Breeches Creek, on the line of the State road leading from Harrisburg to Gettysburg. One Rosebary (probably Robert Rosebary) married one of the daughters, and built a mill, which for more than a century has been known as Roseberry's Mill. The bridge at that point was also known as Roseberry's Bridge. Another family who owned large landed estate was the Myers family, on the Trindle Spring, just above Mechanicsburg. Here, also, were the Trindles and the Lambs. The Trindles lived at Trindle Spring and, adjoining them on the southwest, the Lambs. Samuel Eckels settled in the township about 1809. He erected a house not far from what is known as Winding Hill, near the Mennonite Church, on the State road.

Besides the mills which we have incidently mentioned there were a number of carding and fulling-mills, a number of which are still in existence, and the business of raising wool was once an extensive industry in the Allen Townships.

The oldest buildings, according to an account given by Henry S. Mohler, are a log house and barn on the farm belonging to the Garrett heirs. They are supposed to be more than a hundred and thirty years old. On this farm, nearly sixty years ago, there were over 200 cherry trees, under which, in the season, used to be celebrated what was called "cherry fairs," when "cherry bounce" circulated freely, and when the owner derived more profit from the sale of his fruit than from his crops of grain. The first stone house in the township was on the farm now owned by H. G. Mosser, but it has since been replaced by a more imposing brick structure. The first stone house which is still in existence, was built on the farm now owned by Joseph Bosler, near the close of the Revolutionary war. Another was built in 1790 on the farm of H. M. Cocklin. The first stone barn was built in 1801, on J. W. Byer's farm, and the first of brick was in 1812, on the farm of Jacob Gehr, near Lisburn, but was destroyed by lightning in 1837.

Nearly half a century ago, a mine of hematite ore was discovered in Upper Allen Township, a short distance west of Shepherdstown, from which several thousand tons were taken, about 1848, for the iron works at Boiling Springs and for the Dauphin Furnace. Boulders containing iron ore have been found in other portions of the township. Rich deposits of magnetic ore were discovered in 1853, on several farms on the Yellow Breeches Creek south of Shepherdstown, while men were digging the foundation for a barn. There is little doubt that there are a number of places where iron ore can be found, and that they will be worked in the future, if the time arrives when it will prove remunerative. There is also much lime burned in Upper Allen, sometimes as many as fifty kilns being kept in constant operation.

The distilling of whisky was also, at one time, a prominent industry. When the railroads and canals were unknown most farmers converted their grain into this form, in order that it might be conveyed to market at the least possible expense. At this time such goods were sent to the large cities by means of the great Conestoga wagons, which traveled often in company and took a week or more to make their trip. At night the drivers would stop to rest and build their camp-fire on the road. Now that the reason has ceased, there is no distillery in operation in the township, although the remains of former ones can be seen at several places.

VILLAGES.

Of the villages in the township the first was known as Stumpstown, but it never had more than six houses, and, in 1810, a store, which has been abandoned.

Shepherdstown, near the center of the township, is a post village of about 175 inhabitants, three miles south of Mechanicsburg, on the State road. It was called after William Shepherd.

Kohlerstown.—In 1867 a small cluster of houses was built on the State road, half a mile from Mechanicsburg, which was called "Kohlerstown," after the family by whom it was originally settled.

Bowmansdale is another small village in the southern portion of the township, called after Jacob Bowman, a former sheriff of Cumberland County, and the principal proprietor.

CHURCHES, BURIAL PLACES, ETC.

The oldest church in the township, known as the "Western Union Church," on the Lisburn road, was erected in 1835, but the grave-yard connected with it has been used as a place of interment for more than a hundred years. Another Union Church was built at the eastern end of Shepherdstown in 1844, which was also used for school purposes. The Reformed Mennonites have a church, erected in 1851, on Winding Hill, so called because of the road which winds around it. Near it are the water works which supply Mechanicsburg. The "Mohler Meeting-House" is a large structure built by the German Baptists in 1861. On the farm of John Dunlap is a grove which has long been used for Methodist camp-meeting purposes, from 1820 until 1862, and twenty acres of which grove, at his death, were bequeathed to them for such purposes forever. The grounds are elevated, sloping toward the east. Of the grave-yards besides the one which we have mentioned, the oldest is on the farm of Henry Yost, and there are, at different points, three private ones, for the Zug, Lautz and Mohler families. The Chestnut Hill Cemetery, on a beautiful rounded elevation in this township, for the use of the people of Mechanicsburg and vicinity, is under the control of an association which was incorporated in 1852.

SCHOOLS.

The first schools of which we have any knowledge were taught in private houses. The first building erected for school purposes was built at a date unknown, but before 1800, on the farm now owned by David Coover. It was of logs, covered with thatched straw, with slabs or three-legged stools for seats, and no desk, save for the teacher. In 1805 another was built upon the same farm; in 1809, another on the farm of John Beelman, near Shepherdstown; and two years later, another on the farm of the late Judge Moser. These were the earliest schools of which we have any record.

For the following recollections of his school-boy days we are indebted to William Eckels, of Mechanicsburg, who was born in Upper Allen Township. It throws a gleam of light upon the primitive methods of education which were in vogue at the beginning of the century. "Of the places remembered most distinctly," says he, "beyond the home domicile, are the two schoolhouses situated about equal distance from the place of my birth and childhood days.

These structures were known as Bryson's and Taylor's schoolhouses. The former stood in a large piece of woodland, not far from the new barn recently erected by William M. Watts on the north side of his farm. It was a rude structure in every way, being lighted only by windows inserted between the logs on each side, ten inches high. But, with all its apparent discomforts, it served the double purpose of a place for preaching and school for many years, until accidentally burned down about fifty years ago.

"The other schoolhouse stood on the Taylor farm, now owned by Judge Moser, and is still standing and is used as a place of shelter for farming implements. This house was considered quite modern in its day, with its pyramid roof and its two square windows in front, with twelve lights, 8x10. Its present dilapidated condition is a sad and forcible reminder of the flight of time to those who, long years ago, came there to enjoy the benefits of the rude system of education which then prevailed in the county, and who often made the surrounding forest ring with the boisterous play and the merry laugh of childhood. Like the former, this, too, was a place for preaching, as well as for "school;" and of the ministers whom my earliest recollection recalls as being at the former place, was the eccentric Lorenzo Dow and the grave old Scotchman, Dr. Pringle, who was pastor of the Seceder Church, of Carlisle. Many quaint stories were related of Lorenzo Dow, which interested children and kept him in their memory at an early age. Dr. Pringle was noted mainly for the gravity of his manner of conducting the services of the house of worship, and his severe dignity at all times. Perhaps no two men were more unlike, in the same calling, than were Dow and Pringle." To such worthies (whose names, to the older inhabitants, are still "household words") these school boys, at the beginning of the present century, listened; characters whose severe earnestness and sinew—grit—made amends for culture, and was more fitting for the comparative wilderness in which they worked.

There are at present nine school buildings in the township, of which eight are of brick or stone, and all more or less fitted, according to our modern ideas, for their purpose.

MISCELLANEOUS.

The Cumberland Valley Railroad runs across the northern border of the township. The postoffices are Shepherdstown and Bowmansdale.

CHAPTER XXXVII.

WEST PENNSBOROUGH TOWNSHIP.

PENNSBOROUGH was one of the two original townships which were formed in the North Valley as early as 1735. This was fifteen years before the formation of the county. For some few years after it was divided, for purposes of convenience, in the early tax-lists, into north, south, east and west parts of Pennsborough, until, in 1745, it seems to have been definitely divided into East and West.

In the years which have intervened since its formation, West Pennsborough has been gradually reduced to its present limits. It first lost Newton, on the west, in 1767; then Dickinson, which included Penn, on the south, in 1785; and Frankford, on the north, ten years later.

FIRST SETTLEMENTS, ETC.

The names of the earliest settlers found on land warrants between the years 1743 and 1786, indicate that they were all of Irish or Scotch-Irish descent. Such are the names of Atcheson, McFarlane, Dunbar, McAllister, Dunning, Ross, Mitchell, Davidson, M'Keehan, and others. Not a single German name can be found until about 1790, when the German Mennonites began to move into Cumberland from Lancaster and Lebanon Counties. Some of these, as the Dillers and the Bears, not only purchased large tracts of land, but erected substantial stone dwelling houses and barns upon them, and began to improve their farms in such a manner as made them a worthy object of imitation to the earlier settlers. Some few of the Hessians captured by Washington at Trenton in 1777 settled in this township, and were represented by such names as Washmond, whose descendants lived until 1840, or later, on the farm now owned by Levi Clay, and the Rhines, who owned the property now belonging to William Kerr.

The earliest settlers here, as in other portions of the county, seem to have preferred the land upon the springs or along the streams in the various portions of the township. The lands, therefore, which lay upon the Big Spring on the west, the Conodoguinet on the north, the Mount Rock Spring on the south, or McAllister's Run, seem to be those which were first settled by the early pioneers.

"The earliest settlement," says Hon. Peter Ritner, "was made by a family named Atcheson at a place now owned by J. A. Laughlin, a descendant of the original settler, and at the 'Old Fort,' on land now in the possession of William Lehman, formerly of Abram Diller. This fort was built at an early day (perhaps 1733) to be a refuge from the Indians." It probably antedated the final purchase of Penn, for it was spoken of as "the Old Fort" in the original warrant for the 200 acres upon which it stood, which was taken out by James McFarlane in 1743. "One of the grandparents of the present generation of the Laughlin family was born in this fort. Abram Diller built an addition of stone to the original structure, covered the log portion with weatherboards, and occupied the whole as a dwelling house. In 1856 the entire building was accidentally burned. Adjoining the original tract on the eastward was another containing 400 acres, which was also taken up in 1743 by James McFarlane, and has since been known as the "New Farm." Both tracts were sold by him, in 1790, to Abram and Peter Diller, whose descendants are still in possession of a portion of the New Farm. None of the houses built by the original settlers are now standing, the log cabins of the Atchesons and Laughlins having long since given place to substantial stone dwellings."

The farm near Mount Rock which was purchased by ex-Gov. Ritner, and which is now the residence of his son, Peter Ritner, is on a tract for which a warrant was taken out in 1732. John Davidson had land patented on Mount Rock Spring as early as 1745, and the name of McKeehan is found as early as 1751. A place several miles east of Mount Rock, on the turnpike, belonging to J. Z. Paul, was settled by John Rhoads July 22, 1762.

The settlement commenced by James Chambers, whose residence was about three miles southwest of Newville, was one of the most thickly populated in the valley. It was as early as 1738 able to form a religious congregation and to call a pastor—the eloquent and celebrated Thomas Craighead. In each direction from the Big Spring the land was almost or entirely taken up before 1750, so that, says Dr. Wing, the people there presented strong claims to the county seat. Among the earliest of these settlers was David Ralston, on the road westward from the spring; Robert Patterson, on the Walnut Bottom road;

James McKeehan, who came from Lancaster County, for many years an elder in the church of Big Spring; John Carson, who lived on the property of Judge Montgomery; John Erwin, Richard Fulton, Samuel McCullough and Samuel Boyd. In the "reminiscences" of Rev. Dr. Junkin, first president of Lafayette College, whose father, Joseph Junkin, was one of the earliest settlers in Silver Spring Township, we find the following: "In the summer of 1799, my father lived on a farm, which he owned, two miles east of Newville, having removed to it for the purpose of making improvements, having meanwhile leased the homestead at New Kingston. That summer I went to school to William McKean in a log schoolhouse, near to one Myers' house, a tenant of Mr. Leipers. Joseph Ritner was then Myers' hired boy. I saw him many years afterward in Harrisburg, when he was Governor of Pennsylvania. My parents belonged to the Associated Reformed Church at Newville, of which, at that time, the Rev. James McConnel, a 'United Irishman,' was pastor." Joseph Ritner, the eighth and last Governor under the Constitution of 1790, was born in Berks County March 25, 1780. He was the son of John Ritner, who emigrated from Alsace on the Rhine. At the age of sixteen he came to Cumberland County, and was, for a time, a hired hand on the farm of Jacob Myers, which lay on the road leading to Mount Rock, one mile east of Newville. In the year 1800 he married Susannah Alter, of West Pennsborough Township. He then removed to Washington County, from which, in 1820, he was elected to the House of Representatives, and served six consecutive terms. In 1824 he was elected speaker of that body, and was re-elected the following year. In 1835 he was elected Governor of Pennsylvania. On the expiration of his term he purchased the farm now owned by his son, Peter Ritner, on Mount Rock Spring, where he resided until his death in October, 1869. Gov. Ritner was a great friend of the common school system, and his bold and unhesitating condemnation of slavery brought forth, in his message of 1836, in admiration of that "one voice" that had spoken, a patriotic poem of praise from the pen of Whittier:

"Thank God for the token! one lip is still free,
One spirit untrammeled, unbending one knee!
Like the oak of the mountain deep rooted and firm,
Erect when the multitude bends to the storm."

and in which, after using the name "Ritner," he pays a beautiful tribute to

"That bold-hearted yeomanry, honest and true,
Who, haters of fraud, give labor its due;
Whose fathers of old sang in concert with chime
On the banks of Swatara, the songs of the Rhine."

Jacob Alter, whose daughter Susannah became the wife of Gov. Ritner, came from Lancaster County, and settled on the Conodoguinet Creek, at Alter's mill, in 1790. His son, Jacob Alter, Jr., was elected to the Legislature in 1814, and was for quite a number of consecutive terms a member of that body.

In the January Court, 1789, viewers were appointed to lay out a private road from John Moore's house to his farm on the "Rich Lands," and from thence to Mount Rock, etc., in all a distance of two miles and 128 rods. The viewers were: George McKeehan, John Miller, James Heal, Joshua Murlin and Mathew Davidson. The road was confirmed.

The oldest-burial place in the township is supposed to be the one on the tract which was known as the New Farm, near the Old Fort, in the center of which there is a plat with graves, but nothing left to tell who lie below. In the later extension of it, there are more recent graves, on the three sides of the old plat, and on some of the older grave-stones inscriptions in the German language. These, however, do not date beyond the century, but there are others where the inscriptions are entirely obliterated.

The first flour-mill in the township of which we have any definite information, was built in 1770, and still stands at Newville on the old Atcheson tract. Piper's mill, on the Big Spring, also in the western portion of the township, was built in 1771. There was, however, an old mill built upon the Conodoguinet Creek at a very early date, which some claim to be the oldest in the township. It was once known as Alter's mill. The warrant of the entire tract now owned by the heirs of William Alter was taken out by Richard and John Woods, in 1786, who sold the land to Landis and Bowman the same year in which their patent was granted. The mill was in existence at that date, and in 1798, it is spoken of as "the Landis' mill, formerly Woods'." The present mill was built by William Alter in 1832. Other mills in the township are as follows: On the Big Spring. Manning's. above Piper's; Ahl's, formerly Irvine's, between Piper's and Laughlin's; and Lindsey's, formerly Diller's. On the Conodoguinet are King's, formerly Shellabarger's; McCrea's, formerly Alter's; Greider's, formerly Diller's, and Lindsey's, formerly Forbes'. Alter's mill was at one time, also a local trading-post, where sugar, coffee, salt, etc., were kept for the accommodation of the people. There was also a saw-mill, a clover-mill and a distillery on his property, but the flour-mill alone remains.

There was at one time quite a number of whisky distilleries in the township, such as Alter's, McFarlane's, one at Mount Rock, one at the spring where Peter Ritner lives, and another on the Weaver property, four and a half miles west of Carlisle. The first house of public entertainment is said to have been kept on the property of Henry Bear, about midway between Carlisle and Newville. The land was patented by a man named Mitchell in 1786, and the place was named Mitchellsburg. The house was known as the "Irish House," and was a place of extensive resort and drinking. It is said that a barrel of whisky was sometimes consumed in one day. No vestige of this house remains. Taverns were kept at a later day at Plainfield and on the main road leading from Carlisle. Philip Rhoads kept one three miles west of the latter place, and John Paul where John Z. Paul now lives. This last was a relay house, where the stages stopped. Mount Rock was a favorite stopping place also, for the heavy wagons then in use. Palmstown had a tavern. and Jacob Palm kept a relay house on the now Myers' farm. Since the introduction of the "iron horse," these teams and taverns are no longer on the turnpike; they have passed away with the necessities of the early days which gave them birth.

VILLAGES.

Small villages are numerous. On the Cumberland Valley Railroad, which runs through Pennsborough, the first station, seven miles west of Carlisle, was occupied in 1839 by John and David Alter, and was called "Alterton." It is now called "Kerrsville."

In 1856 John Greason laid out a station on his farm, now known as "Greason." The first house was built at this place some thirty-seven years ago, and the station has become the nucleus of a village. These are the only stations. The land on which Palmstown is located was surveyed in 1785, on a warrant granted to John Turner. In the patent it was called "Mount Pleasant." In 1800 the land was purchased by Jacob Palm, who kept a tavern in the first house erected at that place. The building has since received additions and is still standing, at present the property of Jacob Chiswell. The town has never been regularly laid out, but is simply a line of houses along the road.

The land where Springfield, at the Big Spring, stands, was patented to William McCracken and Samuel Finley at an early date, and the town was laid out probably as early as 1790. After building the first mill, Mr. McCracken sold out, in 1809, to Robert Peebles. The tract consisted of 130 acres "deeded in fee, except the part on which Springfield stands, for which the said Robert Peebles was to receive quit-rents." These quit-rents were extinguished only about thirty years ago. At one time, before the turnpike was constructed, Springfield was a more important place, and where more business was transacted than at present, there being in operation a flour-mill, three taverns, four distilleries, two stores, and the usual number of mechanic-shops. The first road laid out westward toward the Potomac crossed here at the Big Spring. There is now in the town two schools and a church belonging to the United Brethren. The situation is romantic, and the town has probably about 200 inhabitants.

The western part of the land on which Plainfield stands was patented to Jacob Alter in 1793; the eastern, at an earlier date, to Richard Peters, the secretary, under the Provincial Government, in the land office in Philadelphia. In Alter's patent the tract he purchased was called Plainfield. In 1794 forty-three acres of this tract were sold to Frederick Rhoadacker, who seems to have kept a hotel there, and to have made the first improvements. It was not, however, until 1812 that several parties—viz.: Jacob Weigel, blacksmith; Henry Weigel, wagon-maker; John Howenstein, cooper; and probably some others—purchased lots from the owners, and began to ply their respective trades. The place was then, or afterward, known as "Smoketown," because the blacksmiths, manufacturing their own charcoal, kept the atmosphere surcharged with smoke. This name is used as late as 1845, when the town consisted "of a few houses." When a postoffice was established at Plainfield its original name was restored.

Mount Rock, on a slight eminence, evidently so called from the large limestone rocks which protrude from the surrounding hills, is beautifully situated, seven miles west of Carlisle, near a large spring which issues from a limestone rock, the water from which, after flowing for a short distance, sinks again into the earth, and, passing under a hill, re-appears on the north side, and pursues its course to the Conodoguinet.

Here, some seventy years ago, were two Miller families, Presbyterians, intermarried with the McCulloughs and McFarlands. One, John, kept a hotel at Mount Rock. Here, also, were the McKeehans, who had lands adjacent to Mount Rock, and the Davidson family, who owned lands upon the spring—both descendants of the early pioneers who settled in this county. About a half a century ago the hotel at Mount Rock was the "Furgeson House," and among the families living there were the Millers, whose land lay principally in Dickinson, the Tregos, Bixlers, Spanglers, Zinns, and others. The township elections and the musterings and reviews of the old militia were also held there. Now, the old tavern has been turned into a private dwelling and the distillery into a warehouse. There is also a Union Church here, built sometime subsequent to 1846.

MISCELLANEOUS.

About 1845 the Legislature passed an enactment meant to divide the township, so that the eastern portion should be called "West Pennsborough Township," and the western "Big Spring Township." This, however, was opposed by the inhabitants, and the act was repealed in the succeeding Legislature.

The postoffices in the township are Plainfield, Big Spring, Greason, Kerrsville and Mount Rock. The Cumberland Valley Railroad passes from east to west through the township, almost dividing it in two.

James Moore

Biographical Sketches.

CHAPTER XXXVIII.

BOROUGH OF CARLISLE.

WILLIAM BARNITZ, president of the Farmers Bank, Carlisle, is a native of York County, Penn., born near Hanover, July 29, 1817. His great-grandfather, John George Carl Barnitz, born December 14, 1722, undoubtedly in France (now the Prussian provinces of Alsace and Lorraine), settled in York County, where his death occurred in 1796. His children were Jacob, Daniel, John and George (twins), Michael, Susan and Barbara. John was born in York County in 1758, and died April 16, 1828, after having served as captain in the Revolutionary war. At the age of eighteen years he became ensign of Capt. Stokes' company and Col. Swope's regiment of the famous "flying camp," and was wounded at Fort Washington. He was register and recorder of York County from 1785 to 1824. His wife was a daughter of Archibald McLean, of York County. (Charles A. Barnitz, a son of Jacob, was an eminent member of the bar of York County, and served as a member of the Twenty-third Congress.) Daniel was a major in the war of the Revolution; John was a colonel in the Revolution; George was an associate judge of York County; Michael located in Lancaster County; Susan married a Mr. Eichelberger, of Baltimore, Md.; Barbara married a Mr. Lauman, of York. Daniel Barnitz, the grandfather of the subject of this sketch, married Susan Eichelberger, and to them were born ten children—six sons and four daughters. Jacob was born April 6, 1777, and was married to Miss Mary G. Etzler, and settled on a farm near Hanover, which he purchased in 1800 (now owned by a son, Daniel), and in 1836 removed to Cumberland County, where he purchased mill property, located on Yellow Breeches Creek, of John Weakley, now owned by a son, Jacob E. He was a man of great energy, projected and held stock in the old Baltimore Turnpike, and took great interest in educational matters. His death occurred in 1863, aged eighty-six years. To Jacob and Mary G. (Etzler) Barnitz were born six sons and four daughters, namely: Henry, Charles, Mary (married Michael Carl, of Hanover), Susan (died unmarried), Jacob Elder, Daniel, Eliza (married Michael Bucher, of Hanover), William, Alexander, and Jane R. (died unmarried). Our subject was educated in Pennsylvania College, at Gettysburg, and Dickinson, at Carlisle. Subsequently he was for a time engaged in teaching schools at Frankford, Penn., and in Delaware; then returned to Carlisle, and in 1851 was married to Miss Caroline M. Wonderlich, who was born in Middlesex, Cumberland County, a daughter of John and Susannah (Hettrick) Wonderlich, old settlers of that county. Mr. and Mrs. Barnitz have three sons and one daughter: John A. H., clerk and book-keeper in the Farmers' Bank, a graduate of Dickinson College; Jacob E., a sketch of whom appears elsewhere; S. Marion, a student in the Moravian Female Seminary, at Bethlehem, Penn.; and U. Grant, attending Dickinson College. Mr. Barnitz was one of the original stockholders in the bank of which he is now president. He possesses a large farm in North Middleton Township, and is engaged in manufacturing tile. He is a plain and unassuming gentleman and a practical business man, enjoying the confidence and esteem of the community in general. He and his family are members of the Lutheran Church.

JACOB EDWIN BARNITZ, attorney, Carlisle, was born in that place November 9, 1854, son of William and Caroline M. (Wonderlich) Barnitz. He is a graduate of the high school and of Dickinson College—class of 1875. He began the study of law in the office of A. B. Sharpe, and was admitted to the bar in August, 1877, since which time he has been actively engaged in the practice of his profession. In 1884 he was a delegate to the Democratic State Convention, and has held several local offices of trust in Carlisle. He is a member of Cumberland Star Lodge, No. 197, F. & A. M., and K. of P., True Friends Lodge, No. 56.

BIOGRAPHICAL SKETCHES:

JACOB S. BENDER, M. D., Carlisle, was born at Bendersville, Adams County, Penn., September 21, 1844. His grandfather, Conrad Bender, a native of Germany, came to Pennsylvania when a young man, and settled at Hanover, in York County, and there married. He had two sons, Jacob and Henry, who laid out the town of Bendersville, and four daughters. Jacob married Miss Eva Schlosser, who died in 1859, upward of sixty years of age. Jacob's death occurred in 1865, aged eighty-four years; he was the father of eleven children, seven of whom are living: Conrad; Catherina, wife of Wilson Naylor; Elias, who is a farmer in Holt County, Mo.; Susan, wife of Tobias Schlosser, a dentist to Hagerstown, Md.; Hannah, wife of John Cullings, a farmer near Bendersville; John Wesley, a dentist at Shippensburg, Penn., and Dr. Jacob S. Our subject worked on his father's farm, attending school in the winter seasons until eighteen years of age; then entered Hagerstown Academy, where he pursued his studies for three years, and began to study medicine with his cousin, Dr. J. J. Bender, and was graduated from the Pennsylvania Homœopathic College of Medicine in the spring of 1862. Soon after his graduation he was appointed assistant surgeon (with the rank of first lieutenant) in the Twenty-ninth Regiment, Pennsylvania Volunteers, and remained in the service until the close of the war. He was with Sherman on his "march to the sea;" was at the battles of Gettysburg, Lookout Mountain, Marengo, Ga.; Resaca, Ga.; Pumpkin Vine Creek, Ga.; Peach Tree Creek, Kenesaw Mountain, and at the various other engagements and skirmishes in which his regiment participated. He was mustered out with the regiment at the close of the war; then went to Colorado and Nebraska, where for four years he was engaged in practicing medicine between Omaha and the Rocky Mountains. After this experience he located in Carlisle, where he has since practiced his profession. October 21, 1876, he was married to Miss Laura Conlyn, a native of Carlisle, and a daughter of Thomas and Esther (Barber) Conlyn. One child has been born to this marriage—Esther McKinley Bender. Dr. Bender is a member of Post No. 201, G. A. R., and he and wife are identified with the Presbyterian Church of Carlisle.

JOHN M. BENTZ, dentist, Carlisle, is a native of Cumberland County, born at Carlisle, September 24, 1854. He was graduated from the high school of that place at the age of seventeen, and soon thereafter began the study of dentistry at Carlisle. He subsequently entered the Pennsylvania Dental College, of Philadelphia, from which he was graduated in 1874, before he was twenty one years old. After his graduation he located in Altoona, Penn., and there remained one year, when he removed to Carlisle, where he has been quite successful in his business, increasing, from time to time, until he now has a large practice. November 11, 1884, he was married to Miss Lulie Norbeck, of Lancaster, Penn., a native of Gettysburg, Adams County. Dr. Bentz was elected a member of the council of Carlisle in 1883, and re-elected in 1886. He is a member of the I. O. O. F. and Carlisle Lodge, No. 91, I. O. H. The parents of our subject were William and Jane (Mell) Bentz, both natives of Carlisle; the former a dry goods merchant. To Mr. and Mrs. William Bentz were born the following children, Abner W., a printer by trade; Joseph G., a telegraph operator; Samuel, a hardware merchant; William, a farmer; John M.; George C., a druggist, of Leadville, Col., and steward of St. Luke's Hospital; Elizabeth, wife of R. L. Broomall, late counterfeit detector of the United States mint; and Mary M., who resides with her mother. The father (William Bentz) died in 1875, aged fifty-five years. He was a member of the I. O. O. F.. Carlisle Lodge No. 91. Weirich Bentz, the grandfather of our subject, was born at Ephratah, Lancaster Co., Penn., in 1788. He was a son of Jacob Bentz, a native of the same county, and he, too, a son of Jacob, who emigrated from Germany, and settled near Ephratah. Weirich Bentz learned the wagon-maker's trade in York County, and when a young man removed to Lebanon, Penn., where he married Elizabeth Zollinger, a native of Harrisburg, a daughter of Jacob Zollinger.

GEN. EDWARD M. BIDDLE, Carlisle, was born in Philadelphia. He is a descendant of William Biddle, who was a friend of William Penn, and one of the original proprietors of West Jersey, and who settled in that province in 1681, and under various purchases became entitled to 42,916¾ acres of land. He fixed his residence at what is now known as Kinkora, on the bank of the Delaware River, and took up an adjacent island of 278 acres, which is still known as Biddle's Island. William Macfunn Biddle, the father of the subject of this sketch, was a great-great-grandson of the early proprietor, and resided in Philadelphia. The mother was Lydia, youngest daughter of Rev. Elihu Spencer, D. D., of Trenton, N. J. She removed to Carlisle in 1827 and built the house in which her son, Edward M., still resides. Mr. Biddle, our subject, received a classical education, and graduated at Princeton College, with distinction, in the class of 1827. After graduating he removed from Philadelphia to Carlisle, his present residence, and here pursued the study of law under his brother-in-law, Hon. Charles B. Penrose, and in 1830 was admitted to practice in the several courts of Cumberland County. Subsequently he embarked in other business pursuits, and then, in connection with a partner, erected the Big Pond Iron Furnace, in Cumberland County, and for several years carried on its business. In 1836 Mr. Biddle was married to Miss Julia A. Watts, the youngest daughter of the late David Watts, Esq., of Carlisle, and sister of Hon. Frederick Watts.

They have had eight children, six of whom survived: David W., Charles P., Frederick W., Edward W., William M. and Lydia S. In 1839 Mr. Biddle was appointed secretary of the Cumberland Valley Railroad Company, and in 1840 was made treasurer and secretary, which position he has held continuously to the present time. In 1858 he was elected major-general of the volunteers of the Fifteenth Pennsylvania Division, composed of the counties of Cumberland, Franklin and Perry. In 1861, upon the breaking out of the Rebellion, he was tendered by Gov. Curtin, and accepted, the position of adjutant-general of Pennsylvania, and organized for service the earlier Pennsylvania regiments which were put into the field. At the expiration of a year he resigned, his personal business requiring his entire attention.

EDWARD W. BIDDLE, Carlisle, was born in Carlisle May 3, 1852, son of Edward M. and Julia A. (Watts) Biddle, natives, the former of Philadelphia, who, in 1827, came with his mother to Carlisle, and the latter a native of Carlisle, a daughter of David and Julia (Miller) Watts, she a daughter of Gen. Henry Miller, of Revolutionary war fame and from Cumberland County. The father of our subject has been secretary and treasurer of the Cumberland Valley Railroad since 1840. Our subject attended the public schools until twelve years of age, when he entered the preparatory department of Dickinson College, and two years later the college proper, from which he was graduated at the age of eighteen years, being a member of the class of 1870. He was then engaged in the surveying corps on the Dillsburg & Mechanicsburg Railroad for six months, when he began the study of law in the office of William M. Penrose, Esq., was admitted to the bar in 1873, and has since been occupied in the practice of law. He was attorney for the commissioners of Cumberland County during the years 1879-81. Mr. Biddle was married February 2, 1882, to Miss Gertrude D. Bosler, of Carlisle, a daughter of J. Herman and Mary J. (Kirk) Bosler, former of Cumberland County and latter of Mifflintown, Juniata Co., Penn. To Mr. and Mrs. Biddle two sons were born: Herman Bosler, born April 14, 1883, and Edward Macfunn, born May 29, 1886. Mrs. Biddle is a member of the Second Presbyterian Church.

ABRAHAM BOSLER (deceased) was born in Silver Spring Township, Cumberland Co., Penn. His paternal grandfather, John Bosler, when a young man, emigrated from Hanover, Germany, alone. He settled between Elizabethtown and Maytown, Lancaster County, Penn., in 1761, and there married Miss Longenecker and had a large family. His son John married Catherine Gish, of Lancaster County, and removed to Cumberland County, settling in Silver Spring Township in 1791. They had three sons and two daughters, viz.: Jacob D., M. D., who married Ann D. Herman; John, who was married twice (his first wife was a daughter of the Rev. Jacob Keller, and his second a daughter of George Webert); Nancy also married twice, her first husband being John Rife, and her second, Melchoir Webert; Catherine, who married Dr. Fahnestock; Abraham, whose portrait appears at the head of this sketch, was the youngest child of John and Catherine (Gish) Bosler. On February 20, 1830, he married Eliza Herman, of Silver Spring Township, who was a daughter of Martin and Elizabeth (Bowers) Herman. (See sketch of Hon. M. C. Herman, in this volume.) Abraham Bosler, early in life, engaged in merchandising at Hogestown, and a few years later formed a partnership with Francis Porter in the produce business, shipping largely in arks and boats on the Susquehanna River to Baltimore, Md. Mr. Bosler, in the spring of 1851, sold his property in Silver Spring and moved to South Middleton Township, where he purchased a farm, mill and distillery, and was here actively engaged in business until 1871, when he retired and moved to Carlisle, in which place he died December 21, 1883, in his seventy-eighth year. His wife survived him two years, and died in her seventy-sixth year. Early in life Mr. and Mrs. Bosler connected themselves with the Old Presbyterian Church at Silver Spring, and with certificates of dismissal from that church, upon their removal from Silver Spring, became members of the Second Presbyterian Church of Carlisle. They were both liberal supporters of this church and deeply interested in its prosperity. They had eight children, all born in Silver Spring Township: John Herman, James Williamson, Benjamin C., Joseph, Elizabeth Bowers, Mary Catherine, George Morris and Charles, the last dying in infancy.

JOHN HERMAN BOSLER, of Carlisle, is the oldest living representative of the family. He was born December 14, 1830. His early life was spent upon his father's farm. At the age of seventeen he went to Cumberland Academy, and from there entered Dickinson College. He left college to enter into a partnership with his father in the milling and distillery business, in which he remained for five years. He then withdrew to engage in the iron business in Huntington County, where he remained for two years, during which time he was married, on October 1, 1856, to Mary J., eldest daughter of James and Martha (Saiger) Kirk, of Mifflintown, Juniata Co., Penn. Shortly after his marriage he returned to Cumberland County, and from that time was engaged in the milling, distilling and produce business until 1870. In this year he and his youngest brother, George, established a cattle ranch on the plains of the great West, which they have continued to the present time. They were the pioneer representatives of this business from Cumberland County. Mr. Bosler is one of the most active and successful business men of Carlisle. He is at present president of the Carlisle Manufacturing Co., a director in the Carlisle

Deposit Bank, and director of the Ogallalla Land & Cattle Co. of Nebraska, as well as being engaged in other large western enterprises. Mr. and Mrs. Bosler are members of the Second Presbyterian Church of Carlisle. They have had ten children, six of whom are living, viz.: Gertrude D., wife of E. W. Biddle, attorney at law, of Carlisle; Herman E., who is a graduate of Dickinson College, and at present is manager of Snake Creek Cattle Ranch in northwestern Nebraska; Eliza McClellan, Jennie M., Fleeta Kirk and Kirk.

JAMES WILLIAMSON BOSLER (deceased), late capitalist, of Carlisle, is deserving of more than a passing notice in this work. He was born April 4, 1833. He assisted on the farm until he entered Cumberland Academy, at New Kingston. Two years later he entered Dickinson College and remained through his junior year. During vacation he conceived the idea of going West, which he did with the approval of his parents. He taught school at Moultrie, Columbiana Co., Ohio, during the winters of 1853-54. He then went to Wheeling, W. Va., where he read law and was admitted to the bar. He then moved to Sioux City, Iowa, where he formed a partnership with Charles E. Hedges, to engage in real estate business. They then established the Sioux City Bank, under the firm name of Bosler & Hedges, and later they engaged in furnishing goods, cattle and general supplies for the Interior and War Departments of the Government, on the north Missouri River. The partnership was dissolved in 1866, and Mr. Bosler continued the business until the time of his death. During his residence in Sioux City he was an active politician, and in 1860 was sent as a delegate to the Charleston Convention. Having, by dint of energy and business capacity, acquired a considerable fortune, he returned, in 1866, to his native county in Pennsylvania and built a beautiful home in the suburbs of Carlisle. Here he continued to reside until his death. He was a member of the Republican National Committee of 1880, and he, John Roach, ship builder, and Senator Chaffee, of Colorado, were a committee appointed in charge of the interest of Hon. James G. Blaine, at the Chicago convention in that year. For many years he was Mr. Blaine's warm personal friend. After the nomination of Garfield, he became one of his strong supporters. In 1882 he was nominated by the Republicans of the Nineteenth District for senator. This district had 1,800 Democratic majority and he reduced it to 130. He was at the time of his death, December 17, 1883, president of the Palo Blanco Cattle Company, of New Mexico, and of the Carlisle Manufacturing Company, and director of the Carlisle Gas and Water Company. No man was ever more generally beloved in a community than Mr. Bosler in Carlisle, for his benevolence was as broad as his means were great. With a strong intelligence and remarkable judgment he united great kindness of heart. In 1860 he married Helen, a daughter of Michael G. and Mary (Herman) Beltzhoover. They had five children, four of whom are living: Frank C., Mary Eliza, De Witt Clinton and Helen Louise. Mrs. Bosler and son, Frank, are members of the Second Presbyterian Church, of Carlisle.

BENJAMIN C. BOSLER, as his brothers did, passed his early years on his father's farm, attended Cumberland Academy for several years; then went to California, where he died in 1863 in his twenty-ninth year.

JOSEPH BOSLER was born March 23, 1838. He attended the common schools and the academy at New Kingston and the grammar school of Dickinson College. He also spent his early life on his father's farm, with the exception of several years passed with his brother James in Ohio. In 1863 he joined said brother in Sioux City, Iowa, and engaged with him in merchandising and Government contracting until 1866, when he returned to Carlisle and formed a copartnership with his brother, J. H. Bosler. This partnership lasted eight years, during which time they were interested in stock and real estate in the West. Joseph still continues this business. November 4, 1868, he married Sarah E., daughter of Thomas Newton and Margaret (Billmeyer) Lemen, of Berkeley County, W. Va. Mr. and Mrs. Bosler have had seven children, five of whom are living: Margaret, Joseph, Jr., Eliza Herman, Mary and Susan Lemen. Mrs. Bosler and daughter, Margaret, are members of the Second Presbyterian Church, of Carlisle.

ELIZABETH B. BOSLER is unmarried and is living in her father's home in Carlisle.

MARY C. BOSLER married Joseph R. Stonebraker, of Baltimore, Md., in 1874. They have had five children, four of whom are living: James Bosler, Harry, Joseph and Eliza Herman.

GEORGE MORRIS BOSLER was born May 14, 1846. After leaving the public schools he attended Tuscarora Academy, in Juniata County, Penn. He has been a partner of his brother, J. Herman Bosler, in the cattle business in the West for the past sixteen years, in the practical management of which he has taken an active part. In January, 1880, he married Martha J., daughter of George W. and Mary (Hedges) Robinson. Mr. and Mrs. Bosler have three children: Eliza Herman, Abram and George Morris, Jr. Mrs. Bosler is a member of the Second Presbyterian Church, of Carlisle.

JOHN B. BRATTON, retired editor, Carlisle, was born in Mifflintown, Juniata Co., Penn., and learned the art of printing in the *Juniata Free Press* office. He worked as a journeyman printer for three years, and in 1840, in connection with two partners, started the *State Capitol Gazette*, at Harrisburg. At the end of one year he bought out his partners; was elected State printer three times. In 1845 he sold the *Gazette* and bought the *American Volunteer*, of Carlisle, which paper he conducted ably for thirty-two years, when he sold out to S. M. Wherry. In 1848 he was a prominent candidate for the responsible office of canal commissioner, and came within a few votes of securing the nomination by the Democratic State Convention. He had carried the Southern tier of counties (Perry, Fulton, Franklin, Cumberland, Adams and York) without missing a delegate, but Simon Cameron (then a Democrat and a delegate to the convention) was hostile to Mr. Bratton and worked hard for his defeat. Seth Clover was nominated by a trifling majority. In 1867 Mr. Bratton was a candidate for State senator and carried his county. Cumberland, triumphantly. Four of his instructed delegates, however, voted for his competitor, Col. Chestnut, who was nominated and elected. In the year following Mr. Bratton was a candidate for Congress, and carried the county; but here again bad luck followed him, six of his instructed delegates forsook him and voted for Col. Haldeman, who was nominated by the skin of his teeth and elected. Two years later Mr. Bratton again contended against Haldeman and defeated him, under the Crawford County system, by 700 majority, but Haldeman was again nominated by receiving the votes of the six conferees from York and Perry to Bratton's three from Cumberland. In 1880 Mr. Bratton was again a candidate for Congress, but was defeated by F. E. Beltzhoover, who was elected and re-elected. Mr. Bratton was postmaster of Carlisle under Presidents Pierce and Buchanan, and of the latter he was a personal friend. He was a member of the town council, and for several years president of that body. He is at this writing a director of the Carlisle Gas and Water Company; is a member of the board of education of Carlisle and president of the body; a director in the Carlisle Deposit Bank; a director of the Carlisle Land Association and president of the body; also a director in the Hamilton Fund Association. Mr. Bratton has filled efficiently all offices of trust to which he has been called by his fellow-citizens, and has been elected to more non-paying offices than any man in Cumberland County, holding often, during the last thirty years, four, five and sometimes six of these thankless offices at the same time. He has been a strong and consistent Democrat, a recognized power in his party. As an editor he was trenchant, often bitter, and during the period of his greatest strength, when he was editor of the *Volunteer*, that paper was quoted from, editorially, in almost every State in the union. Mr. Bratton is now living in retirement in Carlisle.

WILLIAM H. BRETZ, proprietor of the livery stables, Carlisle, is a native of Cumberland County, born in Carlisle, September 2, 1832, a son of Jacob and Mary (Dipple) Bretz, former born in Harrisburg in 1806. Jacob Bretz, who was a coachmaker, came to Carlisle when a young man, was there married, and soon after went to Gettysburg, where he remained two years; then returned to Carlisle and engaged in the manufacture of coaches, which business engaged his attention until 1855 or 1856, and subsequently he was engaged in the manufacture of brick. He held the office of register of Cumberland County one term, and is now the court crier of that county. His wife was born in Carlisle, in 1809, and died December 25, 1883, a member of the Methodist Episcopal Church. They were the parents of eight children, who lived to be men and women, seven living: Eliza J., widow of Dr. J. F. Freichler; William H.; Mary A., wife of William H. Cornman, liveryman, Carlisle; Margaret A., wife of George G. Boyer, superintendent of car works of Harrisburg, and president of Harrisburg & Steelton Railway Company; George M., photographer, of Pottsville, Penn.; Laura C., widow of John T. Crozier, formerly chief clerk of Mount Holly Paper Mills; Fannie G., wife of Sylvester Garwood, manager for the Western Union Telegraph Company, Philadelphia. The subject of this sketch received instruction in the common schools of Carlisle and the preparatory department of Dickinson College, from which institution he withdrew, after having passed the examination for college, to enter a drug store, which business he learned, subsequently purchasing the store, which he carried on until 1856. In 1857 he went to Kansas, and there cast a vote to make that a free State; eight months later he returned to Carlisle, and for a period was engaged in the butcher's business. In 1866, he embarked in the livery business, with his brother-in-law, William H. Cornman, and four years later purchased Mr. Hilton's stable, on the corner Church Alley and Pitt Street. In 1874 he bought his present property on the corner of Main and Pitt Streets, where he has a building 90x60 feet, which he built, and where are kept twenty fine horses, a full line of buggies, carriages, omnibuses, coaches, sleighs, etc., and where he is fully prepared to accommodate the public. May 22, 1868, Mr. Bretz married Miss Martha Stumbaugh, who was born near Cashtown, Adams County, a daughter of Peter and Barbara (Keffer) Stumbaugh. Mr. and Mrs. Bretz are members of St. John's Episcopal Church. Mr. Bretz is identified with St. John's Blue Lodge, No. 260, Chapter 173, and Commandery No. 8, K. T. He started in life dependent on his own resources, and by industry and good management has acquired a competency, possessing, in addition to his stables, a farm of 104 acres in North Middleton Township, a nice residence on North Street, and other property in Carlisle.

HON. THEODORE CORNMAN, attorney, Carlisle, was born in that place May 11, 1836; attended the public schools of his native place, and served an apprenticeship at cabinet-making in the same town; and at the age of nineteen began teaching, and taught ten years in the public schools of Carlisle and two years in North Middleton Township, and during three years of that time read medicine in the office of Dr. S. B. Kieffer, and also, while teaching, studied law. In 1868 he was elected to the Legislature from Cumberland County, and was re-elected to the same in 1869. At the close of his second term he returned to Carlisle, and entered the law office of C. E. McLaughlin, with whom he furthered his studies, and was admitted to the bar in 1870, since which time he has been actively engaged in the practice of his profession. In 1881, he, in partnership with William Vance and Samuel Site, organized the Enterprise Manufacturing Company of Carlisle, under the firm name of Vance & Company, manufacturers of sashes, doors, blinds, etc. In 1884 he was elected a director of the school board of Carlisle, and is now serving in that capacity. In 1875 he received the nomination of his district for Congress, but withdrew in favor of Col. Levi Maish. December 20, 1859, Mr. Cornman was married to Miss Lydia Miller, a native of York County, and a daughter of Daniel and Eve Miller, old settlers of York County. Our subject and wife have had four children, viz.: George W., a tinner, who died in August, 1885, aged twenty-five years; Charles T., of the firm of Kissell & Cornman, dry goods merchants of Carlisle; Sarah E., who died young; and Theodore, a clerk and telegraph operator. The mother died in October, 1878, a member of the Reformed Church. In December, 1880, Mr. Cornman married Miss Annie E. Green, a native of Cumberland County, and a daughter of Thomas and Nancy (Parks) Green, also natives of Cumberland County. Mr. and Mrs. Cornman are members of the Reformed Church. Mr. Cornman has passed all the chairs in Masonry and all the chairs in the I. O. O. F., and is a member of the I. O. H. In politics he has always been a Democrat. John Cornman, the father of our subject, was born in North Middleton Township, this county, in 1788, and died in 1861. He was reared on a farm, but subsequently moved to Carlisle, where for years he was engaged in the hotel business. His marriage with Anna M. Wonderlich, of Cumberland County, was blessed with ten children, five now living: Ephraim, Ellen (who married Robert Harris), Frederick, Theodore, Joseph; those deceased are Daniel, Margaret (intermarried with John H. Fredrick), John, Alexander and Franklin. The father was a member of the Reformed Church, and the mother of the Lutheran. The father, John Cornman, was a son of Valentine Cornman, a native of Germany, who settled in Cumberland County in an early day and engaged in farming.

WILLIAM W. DALE, M. D., Carlisle, stands prominent among the city's public-spirited citizens. He was born in Lancaster, Penn., a son of Col. Samuel and Elizabeth (Gundaker) Dale, the former of whom (Judge Dale) was among the many worthy public men of that locality, having served with distinction (holding colonelcy) in the war of 1812; seven years as a member of the Legislature of Pennsylvania; for many years associate judge of Lancaster, and in other worthy local official positions. At his death he left five sons, who have borne important parts in the public, social, and industrial lives of their localities. They are Judge M. G. Dale, of Edwardsville, Ill.; Col. Samuel F. Dale, of Franklin; James Dale, druggist, who died in Mechanicsburg, Penn.; Charles, and the subject of our sketch, who completed a good literary training in Lancaster County Academy and Franklin College, and was graduated from the Jefferson Medical College, of Philadelphia, in 1838. He then came to this county, and, after spending some years at Mechanicsburg, and latterly at New Kingston, removed here in 1847, where he has contributed, in no small degree, to the advancement of professional work and to the development of the social and industrial life of Carlisle.

JAMES RAMSAY DIXON, sheriff-elect of Cumberland County, and a resident of Carlisle, was born in Mount Holly, April 11, 1834 a son of David and Christina (Young) Dixon, the former a son of Andrew Dixon, a machinist, and a native of Scotland who settled in Cumberland County, and who left two sons, David and James R. The subject of this sketch left his father's business (blacksmithing) to engage in butchering, with which he has since been successfully connected at this place. He married Mary J., daughter of Samuel and Charlotte Allgeir, the union being blessed with one son and three daughters: Ellen (deceased), Andrew (associated in business with his father), Laura (wife of Charles Meck, a merchant) and Ella. Mr. Dixon is a strong supporter of the Democratic party, and until the last convention, at which he was nominated and subsequently creditably elected to the sheriffalty of his county, he has always refused public office. He is a worthy Mason and a member of the Royal Arcanum.

DR. JAMES G. FICKEL, physician and surgeon, of Carlisle, has been identified with the city all his life. He was born at Petersburg, Adams County, September 14, 1853, and when three months old was brought by his parents, Benjamin F. and Lucy A. (Bender) Fickel, natives of Adams County, to York County. His father was a farmer and a miller, and his grandfather, Henry Fickel was born in England, and soon after came with his parents to Adams County, where he carried on farming. Benjamin F. Fickel moved to York County in 1853, and his death occurred in Adams County. He and his wife were members of the Lutheran Church. Four children—two sons and two daughters—were born to them, viz.: Dr. James G., Isabella, (wife of William Leer, a farmer in Latimore Township, Adams County), Henry F. (a farmer, who married Miss Christiana Shank, of York County, daughter of Jacob and Harriet (Ernst) Shank); Ann L. (wife of Louis Arnold, a farmer of York County.) Dr. James G. Fickel, the subject of this sketch, attended school

BOROUGH OF CARLISLE.   373

in York County until fifteen years old, when he went to New Berlin, Union Co., Penn., where he attended the Union Seminary for two years. Then he went to Philadelphia and entered the Hahnemann Medical College, from which institution he graduated in 1878. He then returned to Carlisle, where he has since been actively engaged in the practice of the profession. September 5, 1878, the Doctor was married to Miss Ella Arnold, who was born in York County, a daughter of Dr. George P. and Sarah (Law) Arnold. Mrs. Fickel died February 22, 1884, the mother of one child, Almeda J., and July 21, 1885, Dr. Fickel married Miss Mary A. Sierer, a native of Monroe Township, Cumberland Co., and daughter of Adam and Elizabeth (Niesly) Sierer. She is a member of the Lutheran Church. From time to time the Doctor's practice has steadily increased, and, although a young man, he now enjoys an extensive practice, having more than he can really attend to, the reward of study and honorable treatment of the people in general. He enjoys the confidence and esteem of the community at large, among whom he is gaining prominence as a physician.

ANTHONY FISHBURN, retired farmer, Carlisle, is a great-grandson of Philip Fischborn, born in Plannich der Churfatz, Hessen-Darmstadt, Germany, May 7, 1722 and who immigrated to America and settled in Derry Township, Dauphin Co., Penn., in 1749. He married Miss Catherine E. Bretz, whose birth occurred September 27, 1724, and to them five sons and four daughters were born: Margaretta, John Philip, Ludweg, Peter, Magdalena, Anthony, Dietrich, Catherine and Anna Maria. John Philip Fishburn was born in Derry Township, Dauphin Co., Penn., November 15, 1754, and was twice married; first, August 14, 1780, to Miss Barbara Greiner, who bore him six children, as follows: Catherine E., Magdalena, John, Anthony, Margaret and Anthony (second), two of whom only lived to maturity—John and Anthony (second). The mother died June 19, 1790. John Philip married, December 25, 1792, for his second wife Miss Anna M. Hack, who was born June 9, 1771, and became the mother of twelve children, ten of whom lived to be grown: Eve, Barbara, Jacob, Michael, Elizabeth, Benjamin, Jonas, Sophia, Thomas and Joshua. John, son of John Philip and Barbara (Greiner) Fishburn, was born in Derry Township, Dauphin Co., Penn., December 12, 1784; married Miss Catherine Carmana November 26, 1809, and to them were born six sons and four daughters (nine of whom lived to be men and women): Philip, John, Anthony, Barbara, Hannah C., Helena, Rudolph, Adam, Reuben and Maria. The father died April 11, 1861, and the mother, who was born April 9, 1791, died March 15, 1874. Anthony Fishburn, their son, and the subject of this sketch, removed with his parents from Dauphin County to this county in 1832, and settled in Dickinson Township. He was occupied at farming with his father until his marriage, February 15, 1842, with Miss Salome Ann Le Fevre, when he settled on his farm in Dickininson Township. She was born June 12, 1824, in West Pennsborough Township, being a daughter of Lawrence and Salome (Line) Le Fevre, the former of whom was born near Wrightsville, York Co., Penn., a son of George and Anna Barbara (Slaymaker) Le Fevre (the Slaymakers being of German and the Le Fevres of French descent). George Le Fevre was a grandson of Isaac Le Fevre, a French Huguenot, who immigrated to America to escape religious persecution. He landed in Boston in 1708, and settled in Lancaster County, Penn., in 1712, having been married in France to Miss Catherine Fierre, a daughter of Daniel and Maria (Warrenbuer) Fierre. Isaac Le Fevre, with his sons, came to Chester, now Lancaster County, and located near Strasburg, where some of their descendants still reside. Philip, Isaac Le Fevre's second son, born March 16, 1710, in Boston, had eight children: Isaac, George, Adam, Jacob, Catherine, Esther, Eve and Elizabeth. George married Anna Barbara Slaymaker, who bore him twelve children: Elizabeth, Lawrence, Isaac, Mary, Jacob, George, Adam, Peter, Anna Barbara, Samuel, John and Daniel. Lawrence was married twice; first to Miss Veronica Alter, in May, 1792, and they had the following named children: Margaret and George died young, Jacob, Elizabeth, John, Isaac, Fannie, Esther, David Alter and Joseph Ritner. The mother died October 15, 1817. Lawrence Le Fevre married for his second wife Miss Salome Line, October 29, 1822, and they had one daughter, Salome Ann, wife of Anthony Fishburn. To our subject and wife have been born three children: Philip H., born January 23, 1843, and died February 11, 1845; Anna Maria, born January 19, 1851, died March 3, 1855; and Louisa Elbe, born December 26, 1860, resides at home with her parents. Mr. Fishburn retired from the farm March 19, 1885, and built his present brick residence on the southeast corner of Pomfret and West Streets. He is one of the representative men of Cumberland County, with whose interests he has been identified since he was sixteen years of age, and stands high in the estimation of all as an upright citizen and Christian gentleman. He and his wife are members of the Lutheran Church.

ADAM FISHBURN, retired farmer, Carlisle, is a son of John and Catherine (Carmany) Fishburn, natives, the former of Dauphin County, and the latter of Lebanon County, Penn. Our subject is the fifth son, and eighth in a family of ten children, nine of whom lived to be men and women, and was born three miles east of Hummelstown, Dauphin Co., Penn., March 6, 1826. The family, in 1832, moved to this county, and settled on the farm in Dickinson Township now owned by Adam. Our subject remained on the homestead, attending school in the winter seasons, and at his father's death inherited the farm, where he remained until 1883, when he purchased his present property on

West South Street, Carlisle, building the house. Mr. Fishburn was twice married; first, January 26, 1854, to Miss Ellen J. Kenyon, a native of Dickinson Township, a daughter of Samuel M. and Sarah Jane (Kinkaid) Kenyon, and to this union was born, December 19, 1854, one son, Samuel K., now a resident of Dickinson Township, and engaged in farming on the old homestead. His marriage occurred April 15, 1879, with Miss Annie M. Lee, a native of Dickinson Township, and a daughter of Thomas and Elizabeth (Myers) Lee. Both are members of the church; he of the Lutheran, and she of the Episcopal. They have two children: Mary L. and Fred C. The wife of our subject died December 28, 1854, and Mr. Fishburn December 8, 1859, married Miss Catherine E. Heffelbower, a native of Newton Township, but reared in West Pennsborough Township, a daughter of George and Catherine (Au) Heffelbower, natives of Cumberland County. Two children were born to this union, both dying in infancy. Mr. Fishburn is one of the enterprising, representative farmers, business men and citizens of the county, and stands high in the estimation of all as an honest man and a Christian gentleman. Both he and his wife are members of the Lutheran Church.

JAMES K. FOREMAN, farmer and stock-dealer, Carlisle, is a native of Cumberland County, Penn., born in Southampton Township January 29, 1837, a son of Jacob W. and Catherine A. (Bughman) Foreman. Jacob W. was born and reared in Maryland, a son of Peter and Catherine (Heck) Foreman, who, too, were natives of Maryland, and all of whom settled in Southampton Township, Cumberland County, about the year 1829. Mrs. Jacob W. Foreman was a daughter of Henry and Catherine (Russell) Bughman, her father being one of the first Methodists in Southampton Township, and who assisted in organizing the first Methodist Episcopal Church in that section. He was of German parentage, and a native of Lancaster County. His wife, a native of Ireland, came to Cumberland County when a girl, with her brother, John Russell, and her sisters Polly and Martha. Jacob W. Foreman and wife had nine children: Catherine (deceased), married Benjamin Baxter; George Keyner, a farmer of Southampton Township; James Kelso; Rachael, wife of Jacob H. Rebuck; Samuel (deceased); Joseph W., who resides on the old homestead; Martha (deceased wife of Henry Hoch); Isabelle, wife of Calvin B. Little, stock-dealer in Southampton Township; Corilla, wife of Hiram Highlands, forwarding merchant and farmer of Leesburg. Our subject learned the carpenter's trade with his father, which he followed, contracting and building until 1870, when he was elected sheriff of Cumberland County, and moved to Carlisle. He performed the duties of his office three years, since which time he has been engaged in farming and dealing in stock. July 29, 1858, he was married to Miss Margaret Atherton, a native of Shippensburg, and daughter of Henry and Mary (Culp) Atherton, and granddaughter of Jacob Culp, and to them have been born eight children: Lilly, Nannie J., wife of Harry Spangler, an engineer in the United States Navy; Jacob H., a clerk in the Farmers Bank of Carlisle; Kattie, wife of Harry Hertzler, a liveryman of Carlisle; Vermont, M. Blanch, Frank (Miss) and Malon Sydney. Mr. Foreman is one of the representative citizens of Cumberland County, with whose interests he has been identified a lifetime.

FRANKLIN GARDNER, proprietor of the Letort Axle Works, Carlisle, was born in York County, Penn., December 11, 1820, a son of Martin and Mary (Thomas) Gardner, both of worthy German ancestry of York County. At the age of twenty Franklin came here, where he learned the business with which he has since been very worthily connected. He married, here, Sarah Jane, daughter of Jacob and Mary (Hager) Abrahims, who came from Lancaster County here, the union being blessed with five sons and five daughters: Carrie is the widow of William Maize, Esq., and has two sons and two daughters; Annie is the wife of H. L. Bowman, of Philadelphia, and has one son; Edward J. is superintendent of the Carlisle Manufacturing Company; Alice is the wife of Jacob R. Beetem, of Columbia, Penn.; John H. is associated in business with his father, and has a daughter; Laura, the youngest, is at home. They have buried William, Martin M., Sallie and Charles. Mr. Gardner has been a worthy member of the First Lutheran Church for over thirty-five years, and is at present a member of its vestry. He is an Odd Fellow, in good standing; is a member of the board of directors of the Gas & Water Company, of Carlisle, as also of the Carlisle Manufacturing Company. He has always led an honorable life in his business, and has the pleasure of seeing his children worthy members of society and well associated in business.

GEORGE GIBSON, third son of Chief Justice Gibson, of Pennsylvania, and grandson of Col. George Gibson, of Revolutionary fame, who was killed at St. Clair's defeat, was born at Carlisle, Penn., April 4, 1826, and received his education at Dickinson College, Carlisle, Penn. April, 1853, saw him appointed a military storekeeper in the Quartermaster Department of the Army, which position he retained until May, 1867, rendering service in the Quartermaster General's office at Washington, also at Albuquerque, New Mexico, Schuylkill Arsenal, Philadelphia, when he was appointed a captain in the Eleventh Regular Infantry, and assigned temporarily to duty in Washington as approving officer of requisitions made upon the clothing, camp and garrison equipage by the troops congregated about that city. June, 1863, saw him serving with his regiment in the field (Army of the Potomac), being shortly afterward assigned to duty with Gen. Sykes as commissary of musters and inspector-general of the Fifth Corps. He also served as acting assistant inspector-general of the provisional brigade at Gen. Meade's headquarters, rejoining his regiment at Richmond at the conclusion of the war, upon its being assigned to the duty of garrisoning that city. Here he was placed in charge of all matters pertaining to the colored people of that city and the adjoining county of Henrico, and shortly afterward was made acting assistant inspector-general of the Department of Virginia, under Gen. Terry, and of the First Military District of Richmond, Va., under Gen. Schofield. While serving in the latter capacity he was temporarily placed in command of the sub-district of Ft. Monroe, comprising that post, as well as Norfolk, Camp Hamilton and Yorktown. January, 1868, he was promoted major of the First Infantry, and placed on duty, by orders of the Secretary of War, in the War Department, as recorder of a board of claims. June, 1869, saw him assigned to the Fifth Infantry and command of Ft. Hays, Kas., being shortly afterward placed on duty at Ft. Leavenworth, under Gen. Pope, as acting assistant inspector-general, Department of the Missouri. From this place he was transferred, by orders of the War Department, to Memphis, Tenn., as a disbursing officer, under direction of the adjutant-general of the army, where he continued until July, 1876, when he was placed in command of the cantonment on Tongue River, M. T. (afterward known as Ft. Keogh), where he remained up until the time of his promotion as lieutenant-colonel of the Third Infantry (March 20, 1879), when he was assigned to the command of Ft. Missoula, M. T. Here he remained until his final promotion to the colonelcy of his old regiment, the Fifth Infantry, at Ft. Keogh, August 1, 1886, at which place he is now serving.

ROBERT GIVIN (deceased), late banker and manufacturer of Carlisle, was a native of Cumberland County, born at Carlisle June 11, 1810, son of James and Amelia (Steele) Givin, former a native of Coleraine, Ireland, and the latter of Cumberland County, Penn. James Givin was for many years a dry goods merchant of Carlisle. Our subject received his education in his native village, and January 13, 1841, was married to Miss Sarah H. Gibson, at Romney, W. Va., the place of her birth. Her parents were David and Eliza (Armstrong) Gibson, natives, he of Winchester, W. Va., and she of the vicinity of Romney, W. Va. David Gibson was a merchant and farmer. After the marriage of our subject and wife they moved to Mount Holly Springs, in Cumberland Co., Penn., where Mr. Givin, with others, had established the Mount Holly Paper Mills, of which company he was president from its organization until his death, which occurred February 9, 1879, at Carlisle, to which point he had previously removed. At the organization of the Farmers Bank, Mr. Givin became its president, and remained as such until his death. The children born to Mr. and Mrs. Givin were David Gibson Givin, who died when a young man; James (deceased); Samuel G. (deceased), who married Miss Ella Mark; Robert H., and Amelia S., who resides with her mother. Mr. Givin was an active, energetic business man and citizen, always taking special interest in anything that promised progress to his county. He was a man of the highest honor, enjoying the confidence and respect of all. As a friend, neighbor and citizen he possessed all the noblest qualities. His widow lives in her elegant residence in the Farmers Bank building. She and her daughter are members of the Second Presbyterian Church.

BENJAMIN K. GOODYEAR, deputy clerk and recorder, Carlisle, is a native of Cumberland County, born in Shippensburg December 25, 1836, a son of David and Anna (Kenower) Goodyear, both natives of South Middleton Township, Cumberland County; former a pump manufacturer, who, in 1840, moved to Adams County, where he opened a hotel at Graeffenburg Springs. They had nine children: Mary A., wife of Oliver P. Melhorn, an engineer, killed at Middletown by an explosion in tube works; Regina C., married to G. E. W. Sharretts, a clerk in the treasury department at Washington, D. C., since 1856; Benjamin K.; Naoma J., married Joseph S. Ewry, a business man of Lafayette, Ind.; Corella E., widow of Jacob Weigle, who was a blacksmith and machinist; Cordelia R., wife of William Wormley, a merchant of Lafayette, Ind.; Eliza, deceased; Hadessa, wife of William Barber, a farmer near Martinsburg, W. Va.; Henrietta F., unmarried, and residing at Shippensburg. Benjamin K., until sixteen years of age, attended school in Adams County and in the city of Lancaster; then spent two years in the preparatory department of Franklin and Marshall College, Lancaster. He then began the study of law in the office of Stumbaugh & Carlisle, at Chambersburg, and was there admitted to the bar in 1861. That same year he went to Carlisle, was admitted to the courts of the county in November, and continued practice until August, 1862, when he enlisted as a private in Company A, One Hundred and Twenty-sixth Regiment Pennsylvania Volunteer Infantry; was wounded at the battle of Fredericksburg, Va., December 13, 1862, by a gunshot in the right shoulder, which caused a compound fracture of the clavicle. He was sent to Point Lookout Hospital, Maryland, where he remained three weeks, and was two months at Stanton Hospital, Washington, D. C. In April, 1863, he was mustered out of the service and returned to Cumberland County, where he engaged in teaching school until the spring of 1864. He then assisted in raising Company G of the Two Hundred and Second Regiment Pennsylvania Volunteer Infantry, in which he enlisted in August, 1864 (refusing to accept a commission), and remained in the service until the close of the war. After that he was for a time engaged in teaching school at Shippensburg, and for three years acted as agent for the Adams Express Company at that place; then came to Carlisle, and was appointed deputy sheriff under James K. Foreman, serving as such until 1874. In that year he moved to Pine Grove Furnace, and took charge of the company's store for the South Mountain Iron Company, where he remained until the works closed in November of that year; then located in Shippensburg, and, in connection with his brother-in-law, Samuel R. Murray, established the *Democratic Chronicle*, which they conducted until 1878, when Mr. Goodyear purchased his partner's interest, and some two months later disposed of the paper to Alonzo P. Orr. From January 1, 1877, until January 1, 1880, Mr. Goodyear acted as deputy to D. H. Gill, then sheriff of the county; at the expiration of which time he took charge of the Antietam Iron Works near Sharpsburg, Md., serving in that capacity until April 1, 1884. He next took charge of the Codorous Flint Mill, in York County, until September 15, 1884, when the property changed hands, and he returned to Carlisle. January 5, 1885, he was appointed deputy clerk and recorder under John Zinn, which position he still holds. December 24, 1868, Mr. Goodyear was married to Cecelia F. Steinman, of Shippensburg, a native of that place, and a daughter of Adolphus Steinman. The children of our subject and wife are William A., Anna M. and Oro B. Mr. Goodyear is a member of Cumberland Lodge, No. 90, I. O. O. F., of Shippensburg, and a member of Capt. Colwell Post, No. 201, G. A. R. Mrs. Goodyear is a member of the German Reformed Church of Shippensburg. Our subject never identified himself with any Church.

HON. WILLIAM RITTENHOUSE GORGAS, now of Harrisburg, is a native of Cumberland County, born on the homestead in Lower Allen Township, May 8, 1806, a son of Hon. Solomon Gorgas, a native of Ephratah, Lancaster Co., Penn., born January 22, 1764, the eldest of three sons and one daughter, viz.: Solomon, Jacob, Joseph, and Maria, who married Hon. Charles Gleim, of Lebanon County, Penn. The father of Hon. Solomon Gorgas was Jacob Gorgas, a native of Germantown, Philadelphia Co., Penn., whose father, John Gorgas, emigrated from Holland about the year 1700, and located at Germantown. John Gorgas was naturalized by an act of the Legislature in about 1708 or 1709. Jacob when a young man located at Ephratah, where he married a Miss Mack, and to them were born the four children named above. He was a clock-maker and farmer. Solomon, his eldest son, who, too, was a watch and clock-maker, was married to Miss Catherine Fahnestock, a native of Chester County, Penn., and to them were born four sons and three daughters: Daniel F., born September 30, 1792, died January 17, 1848; Christina, born July 27, 1791, died September 21, 1804; Mary, born July 7, 1797, married to Peter Bernhart, and died June 17, 1875; Sally, born January 19, 1800, married to Samuel Bowman, and died in August, 1878; William R.; Joseph M., born June 12, 1809, and died May 13, 1852; and Solomon Perry, born August 31, 1815, now a resident of Mechanicsburg. The father, in 1804, removed to Cumberland County, locating in Lower Allen Township, and kept the first tavern and store in that section of the country. He was a man of sound judgment, and was practical, being self-made and self-educated. In 1821-22 he served as a member of the Legislature from Cumberland County, being a Democrat in politics. His death occurred September 21, 1838, and that of his widow August 9, 1853. Both were identified with the German Seventh-day Baptist Church. Our subject grew up on a farm and worked with his father until the latter's death, obtaining such schooling as the neighborhood afforded when he took charge of the farm. Beginning with the year 1836, he was three successive times elected a Democratic member of the Legislature from Cumberland County, being a member during the celebrated "Buck-shot war." In 1842 he was elected a member of the State Senate, and served for a period of three years, after which he returned to his farm. Mr. Gorgas was one of the original members and directors of the Merkel, Mumma & Co. Bank, which became a State Bank, and finally the present First National Bank of Mechanicsburg, of which he is still a director. Since 1845 he has been a director of the Harrisburg National Bank, and of the Harrisburg Bridge, Company. He is a director of the Harrisburg Market Company and the City Railway Company, and president of the Harrisburg Burial Case Company; and also president of the Allen and East Pennsborough Fire Insurance Company. In 1877 Mr. Gorgas moved to Harrisburg, and in 1882 he received the Democratic nomination, by his party in that city, as their representative to the State Legislature, and, notwithstanding the city was Republican by a majority of 500, he was only defeated by eighty-eight votes. March 5, 1840, Mr. Gorgas was married to Miss Elizabeth Hummel, of Harrisburg, a native of that city, and a daughter of David and Susan (Kunkel) Hummel, and to this union have been born eight children: David H., who died at the age of sixteen years; Kate F., unmarried; Susan K., who died at the age of five years; William L., now a clerk in the Harrisburg National Bank; Mary E., unmarried; Solomon R., a physician and surgeon, who graduated at Jefferson Medical College, and was resident physician at the Philadelphia Hospital eighteen months; Elizabeth E., who died at the age of nine years; and George, a druggist, of Harrisburg, and a graduate of the College of Pharmacy, Philadelphia.

JAMES HUTCHINSON GRAHAM, LL.D. The subject of this sketch was of Scotch-Irish descent. He was born September 10, 1807, on the paternal domain granted his great-grandfather Jared Graham, by Thomas and Richard Penn, in 1734. James Graham, the grandfather of James H., built the log house on the site of which the latter was born, and which was used as a refuge against the Indians by the early settlers. James Graham had five sons: Jared, Thomas, Arthur, Isaiah (the father of James H.) and James. Isaiah Graham was a man of very strong mind, a leading politician of the State, and for many years a ruling elder in Big Spring Church. He was elected to the Senate in 1811,and re-elected. He was appointed associate judge by Gov. Findlay in 1817, and filled the position until his death in 1835. James Hutchinson Graham received his preparatory training for college at Gettysburg Academy under Dr. McConaughy, entered Dickinson College as a member of the junior class and graduated with honor in 1827. He studied law with Andrew Carothers, Esq., then the leader of the Carlisle bar, and was admitted to practice in November, 1829. He was a careful and laborious student, patient and painstaking in his investigation of questions, and he soon acquired a large and lucrative practice. In 1839 he was appointed deputy attorney-general for Cumberland County, a position he filled for six years, declining a reappointment. In 1850 he was elected, on the Democratic ticket, president judge of the Ninth Judicial District composed of the counties of Cumberland, Perry and Juanita, and re-elected for a second term in 1860. His service on the bench during a period of great political excitement marked him as one of the foremost jurists of his State. In 1852 Dickinson College conferred on him the degree of Doctor of Laws, and he was chosen professor of law in that institution, a position he occupied at his death in 1882. Judge Graham was a very useful man in the community in which he lived. He was one of the earliest members of the Second Presbyterian Church of Carlisle, and was for many years president of its board of trustees. He was a director and president of the Carlisle Deposit Bank until his elevation to the bench, and filled many trusts with scrupulous fidelity and honor. The high esteem in which he was held by the bar is well expressed in the resolution presented by Hon. Lemuel Todd at the meeting of the bar on the occassion of his death: "That the purity and consistency of his life in all its relations, his firm and conscientious performance of all personal, professional and judicial obligations, and his modest and unpretentious conduct and deportment were so marked and real as to challenge and possess the respect and esteem of the bar and all who were associated with him." Judge Graham left a large family to survive him, among whom are Lieut. Samuel L. Graham, United States Navy, Frank Gordon Graham of the Kansas City *Times*, and Duncan M. Graham, Esq., of the Carlisle bar.

MARTIN GUSWILER, Carlisle, collector of internal revenue for the Ninth District, Pennsylvania (residence Mechanicsburg), is a native of Cumberland County, born in Mechanicsburg, December 31, 1846, a descendant of two of the oldest families of Cumberland County, and of the State. His great-grandfather, John Guswiler, immigrated to America from Germany at an early day and settled at Shireman-town, and his son, John, a farmer, was born in Cumberland County; married a Miss Rupp, and settled near Shiremanstown. He had two sons, John and Martin, the latter of whom was a physician and married Miss Mary Eberly, to whom was born one son, Van, who married a daughter of Judge Fisher, of York County. John Guswiler, father of the subject of our sketch, was a coach-builder in Mechanicsburg, and established the present coach and carriage works of George Schroeder & Sons, of that place. His death occurred in California, in 1849 or 1850, while prospecting. His wife was Miss Elizabeth Singiser, of Mechanicsburg, daughter of George and Mary (Halbert) Singiser. To them were born three sons, two of whom died young. After the death of Mr. Guswiler, the widow married Maj. Samuel B. King, of Mechanicsburg, late of the firm of Miller & King, manufacturers of sashes and doors. Our subject, who was about five years of age at the time of his father's death, was schooled in the place of his nativity, graduating at the high school when nineteen, and soon thereafter was engaged in a cigar manufactory in the same place, which claimed his attention until 1863. In that year he enlisted as a private in Company D, One Hundred and Twentieth Regiment Pennsylvania Cavalry, under Capt. Singiser. He was made sergeant of the company, and served with the command until the expiration of his term of service in 1864, when he returned to Mechanicsburg,and resumed his former business, which he followed until 1876, when he was elected register of deeds by the people of Cumberland County, carrying his town by over a hundred majority, notwithstanding he was a Democrat. This position he retained three years and returned to Mechanicsburg, where he was engaged in the wholesale tobacco business until January, 1882, when he became deputy sheriff of Cumberland County, under George B. Eyster, and served as such until July 4, 1885, when he was appointed collector of internal revenue for the Ninth District of Pennsylvania, which position he still retains. Mr. Guswiler was three successive times elected to the office of chief burgess of Mechanicsburg, notwithstanding the fact that it is Republican; he also held the offices of councilman and judge of elections. His marriage with Miss Eliza M. Allen took place at Mechanicsburg, in November, 1865. She was a native of Newberry, York County, a daughter of Michael and Margaret (Eply) Allen, natives of York County, and residents of Mechanicsburg (the father a retired shoe manufacturer). To our subject and wife five sons have been born: George M., John, Martin, Jr., Frank B. and Mervin. Mr. Guswiler is an active and energetic business man, and has the confidence and respect of the community at large. He has been a member of the Democratic standing committee of Mechanicburg since 1866, and was in 1879 and 1883 sent as a delegate to the State convention.

JOHN HAYS, president of the Carlisle Deposit Bank, and a prominent and successful member of the bar, is a descendant of the Hays and Blaine families, two of the oldest and most prominent in the State. His paternal great-grandfather, Adam Hays, was a descendant of a Holland family, who immigrated to America at an early day, and who became members of the Swedish settlement at New Castle on the Delaware. Adam Hays was born at New Castle, and immigrated to Cumberland County, Penn., and settled on the north bank of the Conodoguinet Creek, in Frankford Township, in 1730. His sons, Adam and Joseph (the latter the grandfather of our subject), were born in Cumberland County. Joseph married and had three sons: Adam, John and Joseph. John was born in August, 1794; was a farmer in early life, and at thirty years of age engaged in the iron trade. He married twice: first, Miss Jane Pattieson, of Cumberland County. They had one daughter, Annie E. (She also married twice: her first husband was Lieut. Richard West, a nephew of United States Judge Taney; her second husband was Lieut.-Col. J. W. T. Garder.) Mrs. Jane (Pattieson) Hays died in 1822 or 1823, and Mr. Hays married Mrs. Eleanor B. Wheaton, a daughter of Robert Blaine. She was a grand-daughter of Col. Ephraim Blaine, of Cumberland County, who was born in Ireland, and came with his parents to Cumberland County in 1745, when he was but a year old. Col. Ephraim Blaine was a prominent man and served his county and country. He was a friend and confidant of Washington, and was sheriff of Cumberland County in 1771, and during the Revolution was deputy commissary-general with the rank of colonel. Mr. and Mrs. John Hays were members of the Presbyterian Church. He died April 29, 1854, and she January 9, 1839. They had two sons and one daughter: Robert Blaine Hays, Mary Wheaton Hays (who married Richard O. Mullikin, of Baltimore), and John Hays, the subject of our sketch. The last named graduated from old Dickinson College in the class of 1857, and that year entered the law office of Hon. R. M. Henderson, and was admitted to the bar of Cumberland County in August, 1859. In 1862 Mr. Hays entered Company A, One Hundred and Thirtieth Volunteer Infantry; was promoted first lieutenant, then adjutant of the regiment, and then adjutant-general of a brigade. He was mustered out May 1, 1863. He was wounded in the right shoulder at Chancellorsville by a musket ball, and had seven other balls that cut his clothing and killed his horse under him. He was in the battles of Antietam and Fredericksburg. The Second Corps, of which his regiment was a part, lost 5,500 men at Antietam. The entire regiment was commanded by the gallant Col. H. I. Zinn, as the regiment was not organized at the time and had no field or staff officers. At Fredericksburg Col. Zinn lost his life. After his regiment was mustered out, Mr. Hays returned to Carlisle and formed his present partnership with his preceptor, Hon. R. M. Henderson. Mr. Hays married Miss Jane Van Ness Smead, August 8, 1865. She was born in the city of New York, a daughter of Capt. R. C. Smead and Sarah (Radcliffe) Smead. Her father was a graduate of West Point, and captain in the Mexican war. He died of yellow fever while on his way home at the close of the war. Capt. John R. Smead, brother to Mrs. Hays, was in command of a battery in the battle of the second Bull Run, where he was killed. Our subject and wife are members of the Presbyterian Church at Carlisle, and have two sons and three daughters: Anna A., Elizabeth S., George M., Raphael S. and Eleanor B. Mr. Hays is a prominent and successful business man. He is a Republican, and was a delegate to the National Convention in 1880. He was one of the original trustees and mainly instrumental in the management of the building of the Metzgar Institute of Carlisle, of which his uncle, George Metzgar, was the founder. Mr. Hays is a member of the board of directors of the Carlisle Gas & Water Company; vice-president and chairman of the executive committee for the Carlisle Manufacturing Company.

JACOB HEMMINGER, county treasurer, Carlisle, was born on the homestead farm in South Middleton Township, Cumberland County, July 1, 1838. His grandfather, John Hemminger, emigrated from Germany to Lancaster County, Penn., when a young man, and married Miss Barbara Rhemm, of that county, and to them were born three sons and one daughter: John, Jacob, Samuel and Nancy; the latter married to George Stubbs, of Cumberland County, in 1890. John, the eldest son of John and Barbara (Rhemm) Hemminger, married Miss Eliza Heagy, and settled on the old farm two miles and a half west of Carlisle, where were born their twelve children, viz.: Jane A., wife of Lafayette Pfeffer, of Dickinson Township; John a farmer near Waynesboro, Franklin County; Sarah (unmarried), of Carlisle; Samuel (deceased); Catherine, wife of J. E. B. Graham (they reside near Lincoln, Neb.); William, who died in 1873 (his widow resides in Newville); Joseph, who died in 1883 (his widow resides in Dickinson Township); Mary, the wife of William McCullough, a resident of near Shippensburg, Cumberland County; Hettie, wife of Joseph Beetem, of Carlisle; Jacob, of Carlisle; George, M. D., of Carlisle; and Susannah (unmarried), of Carlisle. Jacob Hemminger, when a youth, worked on his father's farm, and received such schooling as is generally given to farmers' sons. January 22, 1863, he was married to Miss Ellen Drawbaugh, a native of Cumberland County, and a daughter of George and Barbara (Bloser) Drawbaugh, old settlers of the same county.

BOROUGH OF CARLISLE. 379

Our subject was engaged in farming until 1868, when he opened a general store at Mount Holly Springs, and, in 1870, was elected auditor of Cumberland County. In 1872 he returned to his farm, and there remained, when he again removed to Carlisle, and engaged in merchant tailoring and general mercantile business, in connection with real estate and auctioneering; the mercantile business he closed out in 1881, and to the other department added fire insurance. In 1884 he was elected treasurer of Cumberland County. To Mr. and Mrs. Hemminger have been born four children: Sarah E., Wilmer A., Charles P. and John R. The parents are members of the Lutheran Church. Mr. Hemminger is a member of the K. of P.

GEORGE HEMMINGER, M. D., physician and surgeon, Carlisle, is a native of Cumberland County, Penn., born on his father's farm two and one-half miles west of Carlisle, September 8, 1840. His parents were John and Eliza (Heagy) Hemminger, the latter a daughter of John and Eliza Heagy. John Hemminger was also the name of the grandfather of the Doctor, and for his history, with that of his son John and family, the reader is referred to the sketch of Jacob Hemminger. Our subject grew up on the farm, and received the rudiments of an education in the neighborhood schools. In 1861 he entered Pennsylvania College as a freshman, and one year later passed examination for the sophomore class. In August, 1862, he, in company with seven of his classmates, went to Harrisburg, where, on the 16th of that month, they enlisted in Company B, One Hundred and Thirty-eighth Regiment Pennsylvania Volunteers. George was assigned to the Middle Department with duty at the Relay House, Maryland, where he remained until June 16, 1863. He was in the Second Brigade, Third Division and Corps (in June), escorting stores to Washington, D. C. From the 1st to the 5th of July he was at Wapping Heights, Va.; July 23, he was at Kelly's Ford; November 7, at Brandy Station; November 8, at Mine Run; from November 26 to December 2, at Locust Grove. In March, 1864, he was in the Sixth Corps, same brigade and division; May 5 and 7 he was at the battle of the Wilderness; at Spottsylvania, from the 12th to the 19th of May; Cold Harbor, 1st to 3d of June; at the Trenches, Bermuda Hundred, June 17; destruction of the Weldon Railroad June 22, 23; Monocacy, Md., July 9; February 17, 1865, in prison at Danville; next to Libby prison, Richmond, until March 25, when paroled and returned to the regiment April 10. He then marched to Danville, and thence with the army of Gen. Sherman to Washington, D. C., where he was in the grand review June 8, 1865. Returning to Carlisle, he entered Dickinson College, where he pursued his studies one year; then read medicine under Dr. J. J. Gitzer; later he passed one term in the medical department of the University at Ann Arbor, Mich., and entered the College of Medicine at Detroit, Mich., from which institution he was graduated in 1869. After his graduation he located at Newville, and there practiced his profession six years. From there he went to the city of Baltimore, Md., and formed a partnership with his old preceptor, Dr. J. J. Gitzer, with whom he remained until the fall of 1875, when he returned to Carlisle, and has here since been actively engaged in the practice of medicine. February 11, 1871, the Doctor married Miss Annie Powell, a native of Maryland, a daughter of Col. Samuel R. and Mary A. (Kelly) Powell, of Baltimore. To Dr. Hemminger and wife one son, George R., was born at Newville, Cumberland Co., Penn., April 25, 1872. Dr. Hemminger stands high as a physician and a citizen. He was a member of the Cumberland County Medical Society. He is a member of the A. F. & A. M.

HON. ROBERT M. HENDERSON, was born March 11, 1827, in the same house where his father was born, on what is now known as the McDowell or Miller farm, one mile east of Carlisle, Penn. In 1832 his parents moved to the old farm on which his father still resides, a part of which is now in the borough of Carlisle. Our subject worked on his father's farm, and was one of the first to graduate in 1838 from the high school of Carlisle under the present common school system. In 1845 he graduated from Dickinson College, studied law with Hon. John Reed, and was admitted to the bar August 25, 1847, and at once began the practice of his profession in Carlisle. In 1851 he was elected, by the Whigs of Cumberland County, a member of the Pennsylvania Legislature, and re-elected in 1852. He was appointed additional law judge of the Twelfth Judical District of Pennsylvania, in April, 1874, and was elected to the same office without opposition, in November of the same year. January 1, 1882, he became president judge of the district. In March, 1882, he resigned this position and resumed the practice of law in Carlisle. At the outbreak of the Rebellion he raised Company A, Seventh Pennsylvania Infantry Volunteer Reserves, and was elected and commissioned captain of this company, April 21, 1861. He served through the Peninsular Campaign, and was wounded in the left shoulder by a minie ball, at Charles City Cross Roads, Va., June 30, 1862. July 4, 1863 he was promoted lieutenant-colonel of the Seventh Regiment Pennsylvania Infantry Volunteer Reserves, and returned with his regiment from the Peninsula, when the reserves joined the Army of Northern Virginia under Gen. Pope. The regiment remained with that command, was engaged in the second battle of Bull Run, and during the battle, on the eve of August 30, 1862, while making a charge, Col. Henderson was shot through the body with a minie ball, and carried from the field. He rejoined his command January 2, 1863, at Belle Plain, and remained with his regiment until May 1, 1863, when he was appointed provost-marshal of the Nineteenth District of Pennsylvania, under an act of Congress, and held that position until the close of the war. March 13, 1865, he was made brevet colonel and brevet brigadier-general for services and gallantry on the Peninsula during the seven days fights and at the second Bull Run. Judge Henderson, as a soldier, judge and citizen always discharged the duties imposed upon him faithfully. He and his wife are members of the First Presbyterian Church, of which for many years he has been trustee. In 1871 he was elected ruling elder in the church, which position he still retains. Judge Henderson married June 7, 1853, at Baltimore, Md., Miss Margaret A. Webster, a native of Baltimore, a daughter of John S. and Elizabeth (Thornburg) Webster, natives of Maryland and of English descent. Mr. and Mrs. Henderson have five children: William M., a miller and merchant of Carlisle; John Webster, attorney and partner in the office of Henderson & Hays; Margaret T., residing at home with her parents; Elizabeth P., wife of H. C. McKnight, a wholesale merchant of Pittsburgh, and Rebecca, at home. William M. Henderson, father of the judge, was born May 28, 1795, and is still living at the advanced age of ninety-one years, possessed of all his faculties. He is a son of Matthew and Margaret (Miller) Henderson, natives of Pennsylvania. Matthew Henderson moved to Perry County, where he died near Gibson's Rock. William M. Henderson worked at milling and farming all his life. He married Elizabeth Parker of Cumberland County, a daughter of Andrew and Margaret (Williams) Parker, Scotch Presbyterians and early settlers of Cumberland County.

JUDGE MARTIN C. HERMAN, attorney at law, Carlisle, was born on the old family homestead near the village of New Kingston, Silver Spring Township, this county, February 14, 1841. This farm was purchased in 1771, by his great-grandfather, Martin Herman, who was born in Germany, and when a young man immigrated to America, landing in Philadelphia in 1754, where he remained a few years; then moved to Lancaster County, Penn., where he married Miss Anna Dorothea Boerst, and engaged in farming until 1771, when he purchased the old farm in Silver Spring Township, this county, where he died in 1804, aged seventy-two years. He and his wife, members of the Lutheran Church, had four sons and four daughters. The sons were Christian, John, Jacob and Martin. Christian was born in Lancaster County, Penn., October 20, 1761, and died October 23, 1829. He was a farmer; a soldier in the war of the Revolution, he fought in the army under Washington at the battle of Germantown, passed through the trials and sufferings at Valley Forge, and participated in the important engagements of this branch of the Continental Army up to the siege of Yorktown, being present at the surrender of Cornwallis. He married Miss Elizabeth Bowers, of York County, Penn., in 1793. They were members of the Lutheran Church; had a family of eleven children, eight of whom lived to be men and women and had families, the sons being: John, Jacob, Martin, Christian and David; the daughters were Mary (married to Michael G. Beizhoover); Anna (married to Dr. Jacob Bosler, of Dayton, Ohio), and Eliza (married to Abram Bosler, of this county). Martin Herman, by occupation a farmer, was born on the old farm in Silver Spring Township, this county, July 10, 1801, and inherited the farm by will from his father, Christian H rman, and died May 22, 1872. He married in February, 1827, Miss Elizabeth Wolford, who was born in 1802, in York County, Penn., a daughter of the Hon. Peter and Elzabeth (Albert) Wolford, former of whom was a prominent man of York County, Penn., having represented that county in the Legislature. Mr. and Mrs. Martin Herman were members of the Lutheran Church. She died July 30, 1852. They had six children: Margaret, wife of Ezra M. Myers, of Adams County, Penn.; Margery A., wife of the Rev. A. W. Lilly, of York, York Co., Penn.; Mary J., wife of Crawford Fleming, of Carlisle; P. Wolford, a farmer, who owns and resides on the old farm in Silver Spring Township, this county; Martin C., our subject; and David B., born December 29, 1844, killed by hostile Indians on the North Platte River, Neb., May 20, 1876, while he was in charge of a cattle ranch. He was a member of the Cumberland County bar, admitted in 1867. Judge Martin C. Herman, our subject, worked on the old farm with his father, and attended school during the winters, until the age of sixteen. He t en entered the academy at York, Penn., presided over by George W. Ruby, and remained there until the close of ther summer term of 1858. He then entered the freshman class of Dickinson College, in September, 1858, from which he graduated June 26, 1862. In his junior year at this institution he took the silver medal for oratory at the junior p ize contest, and on June 24, 1862, delivered the seventy-sixth anniversary address of the Belles-Lettres Society; but prior to this, in January, 1862, he registered as a law student in the office of B. McIntire & Son, at Bloom eld, P rry County, Penn. In April, 1863, he transferred his registry as a student of law to William H. Miller, of Carlisle; studied law with him, and was admi ted to the bar of Cumberland County, January 13, 1864; began the practice of law in Carlisle, and has been actively engaged in that profession ever since. He was elected by the people of Cumberland County president judge of the Ninth Judicial District, composed of the county of Cumberland, at the general election of 1874, at that time being not quite thirty-four years of age. He took the bench on the first Monday of January, 1875, and served for ten years until the first Monday of January, 1885. Was renominated by acclamation in August, 1884. He was married June 5, 1873, to Miss Josie Adair, a native of Cumberland

County, Penn., and a daughter of S. Dunlap Adair (deceased), at one time a brilliant and leading lawyer of the Cumberland County bar, and who married Miss Henrietta Gray, daughter of John Gray, of Carlisle. Mr. and Mrs. Herman have four children: Adair, Henrietta G., Joseph B. and Bessie H. Mrs. Herman is a member of St. John's Episcopal Church, and the Judge is one of the vestrymen. He is not only a representative of one of the oldest and best families of Cumberland County, with which he has been identified all his life, but is one of the self-made men, standing at the head of his profession, and having the confidence and esteem of all.

ALFRED J. HERMAN, M. D., physician and surgeon, Carlisle, was born near Pottstown, Montgomery Co., Penn., in May, 1845, a son of Frederick L. and Mary (Fite) Herman; former a native of Germany, latter of New Jersey. Frederick L., when a young man, was sent to America as a missionary of the Reformed Church, of which he was a minister. Eight sons and five daughters were born to Frederick L. and Mary Herman, Alfred J. being next to the youngest son. Our subject, until sixteen years of age, attended the college at Pottstown, which had been established by his father for the education of young men for the ministry; then began the study of medicine with Dr. David Rutter, of Pottstown, who, some two years and a half later, received a professorship at Chicago, and young Herman then accepted a partnership with Dr. Slemma, a physician of Kutztown, Berks County, Penn., and in 1846 was graduated from the University of Medicine at Philadelphia. He practiced medicine in connection with his partner at Kutztown until the fall of 1846, when he settled in Middlesex, Cumberland County, where he remained some four years; then located at Sterrett's Gap with the intention of establishing a hydropathic institution, but was kept too busy with his patients. In 1852 he located in Carlisle, where he has since followed his profession. At the organization of the Cumberland County Medical Society, Dr. Herman took an active part, and has since taken a deep interest in its success. He has served as its resident physician, and otherwise officiated in its meetings. In January, 1886, he was elected an honorary member of the society. He is also a member of the State Medical Society of Pennsylvania, and a life member of the American Medical Association, to the latter of which he has been three times a delegate. Dr. Herman stands high as a physician, and has enjoyed an extensive practice. He is a member of the Reformed Church.

CHRISTIAN PHILIP HUMRICH, attorney, Carlisle, was born in that place March 9, 1831, of parents John Adams and Mary Ann (Zeigler) Humrich. The former was born in Lancaster City, and the latter in Montgomery County, this State. John A. was a son Christian Humrich, a native of the Palatinate, in Germany, who came to America about 1800, and was naturalized in Lancaster County, Penn., on June 14, 1802. He was a saddler by occupation. He married in Lancaster City, and moved to Cumberland County in 1807, where he opened a hotel (now the Pennsylvania Inn; then the "Black Bear"), which he kept over thirty years. His death occurred in Carlisle in 1842, at the age of ninety-four years. His children were Philip, Maria, John, Catharine and John Adams. The last, too, was a saddler and harness-maker by trade and, later in life, farmed. He died in February, 1880, aged eighty years. John Adams and wife had four sons: Christian Philip, John A., Samuel K. and William A. John died in 1862. All the rest are living in Carlisle. The parents were members of the Lutheran Church. Christian P. attended the first common school in Carlisle (opening August 13, 1836), and at the age of sixteen years attended Dickinson College, graduating in 1852. He then began the study of law with Judge Robert M. Henderson, and was admitted to the bar November 14, 1854, since which time he has been actively engaged in the practice of law. He has been twice nominated district attorney by the Republican party, also received the nomination for Representative, but that party being in the minority, was defeated at the election. He has served as school director since 1857, and has been secretary of the school board since 1860. May 12, 1859, Mr. Humrich was married to Miss Amanda R. Zeigler, a native of Cumberland County, and a daughter of Jesse and Mary (A. Peffer) Zeigler, old settlers of that county. To our subject and wife have been born nine children, six of whom are living, namely: Charles F., insurance agent, Carlisle; Ellen K., Carrie A., Blanch Z., Mary A. and Christian P., Jr. The parents are members of the Lutheran Church. In politics Mr. Humrich was first an old-line Whig, and on the organization of the Republican party, espoused its principles, and has ever since been one of its strong supporters.

ADAM KELLER, cashier of the Carlisle Deposit Bank, Carlisle, was born in Philadelphia, December 9, 1842, a son of Adam and Mary (Loller) Keller, natives of Philadelphia. He graduated from the Central High School of that city, in 1861, and entered as a clerk, in Philadelphia, in a notary's office, where he remained until the spring of 1862, when he engaged in mercantile trade at Harrisburg until 1865, in which year he entered the law office of Col. William M. Penrose, at Carlisle, and was admitted to the bar of Cumberland County. He engaged in the practice of law until 1869, when he was elected cashier of the Second National Bank at Mechanicsburg. In February, 1877, he was elected cashier of the Carlisle Deposit Bank, of Carlisle, which position he has filled and continues to fill, to the present time, to the satisfaction of all. He married at Carlisle, Penn., December 9, 1869, Miss Katherine Wilkins Stevenson, who was born in Carlisle, a daugh-

28

ter of Dr. Thomas Collins and Eliza (Duncan) Stevenson. Dr. Thomas Collins Stevenson, an able practicing physician, was a son of Dr. George Stevenson, a very learned and courteous gentleman, at one time president of the old United States Bank, at Pittsburgh. He married a Miss Maria Barker, of Delaware, a granddaughter of Gov. Thomas Collins, of that State. Mr. and Mrs. Adam Keller are members of St. John's Episcopal Church, of Carlisle. He is treasurer of the parish and a vestryman. He and his wife have had three children; two daughters (now deceased), Bessie Duncan and Mary Loller, and one son, Thomas Collins Stevenson Keller, born July 2, 1884, who is living. Mr. Keller stands high in the estimation of all as a strict business man and an upright gentleman.

STEPHEN BARNETT KIEFFER, A. M., M. D., Carlisle, was born in Franklin County, Penn., and spent the earlier part of his life on his father's farm. He comes of a line of ancestors dating back through five generations, descending from Abram Kieffer, a French Huguenot, from Strasburg. He entered Marshall College as a student in 1844, and graduated with honor in 1848. He subsequently read medicine in Mercersburg, Penn., and graduated at the University of Pennsylvania in 1851, after which he immediately located, for the practice of his profession, in Carlisle. Since that time he has devoted all his energies to his profession, in which he takes a sincere interest. In his professional life Dr. Kieffer combined both medicine and surgery, and as a surgeon he has made some of the most interesting and difficult operations in this portion of Pennsylvania. Dr. Kieffer was honored with the degree of A. M. by his *alma mater* in due course of time; was president of the Medical Society of the State of Pennsylvania; is a member of the American Medical Association; and was a member of the International Medical Convention in 1876. Principally, in his life, he feels honored in having been largely instrumental together, especially, with Dr. R. L. Sibbet, in inaugurating the national movement, which has resulted in the establishment of the American Academy of Medicine, the grandest medical association of the United States. Besides, Dr. Kieffer has contributed frequently to the leading medical journals, both in the interest of medicine and surgery. He has frequently delivered orations before various medical associations, and a few years ago was chosen by his *alma mater* to deliver the address before the alumni of Franklin and Marshall College, where, taking for his subject, "The Relations of Science and Faith," he made a masterly philosophical oration. Large-hearted, sympathetic with suffering, social in instinct, he is popular as a citizen, and is, undoubtedly, one of the real leaders of his profession in Pennsylvania.

JOHN B. LANDIS, Carlisle, was born on his father's farm in Upper Allen Township, one mile south of Mechanicsburg, August 21, 1841. He worked on the farm and attended school until he was seventeen, when he began teaching, and taught in York and Cumberland Counties five sessions; then entered the select school of Prof. S. B. Heiges, where he completed his studies. In April, 1860, he began the study of medicine with Dr. R. H. Long, of Mechanicsburg, with whom he remained until August, 1862, when he enlisted as a private in Company F, One Hundred and Thirtieth Regiment Pennsylvania Volunteer Infantry, and was later made a corporal. He participated in the battles of Antietam and Fredericksburg, and in the latter received a shell wound in the neck and shoulder. He was sent to Point Lookout Hospital, Maryland, and on February 12, 1863, was discharged for disability, when he returned home. Subsequently he assisted in raising Company A, Two Hundred and Ninth Regiment Pennsylvania Volunteer Infantry, of which company he was made captain in September, 1864, serving as such until the close of the war. From September 29 until November 24, 1864, he was in command of Redoubt Carpenter on the Bermuda Hundred front, on the south bank of the James River. His regiment was next stationed in front of Petersburg, at Meade Station. He participated in the battles of Fort Steadman March 25 1865, and Petersburg April 2, 1865, besides various skirmishes, and was mustered out with his regiment May 31, 1865, and returned to his home in Mechanicsburg. In 1866 Capt. Landis was appointed military instructor for the White Hall Soldiers' Orphan School, and in April, 1867, received the appointment of deputy collector of internal revenue for the Fifteenth District of Pennsylvania, which he resigned September 30, 1876, to enter the Carlisle Deposit Bank, accepting the position of cashier. This position he held until February, 1877, when he resigned on account of impaired health, and after a year's rest began the study of law in the office of John Hays, Esq., of Carlisle. In 1881 he was admitted to the bar, and has since been actively engaged in the practice of his profession. The Captain was elected treasurer of the Carlisle Gas & Water Company July 1, 1882, and has been a member of the town council since the spring of 1881. On June 9, 1870, he was married to Miss Barbara H. Merkel, a daughter of Hon. Levi and Susannah (Martin) Merkel, former of whom was a banker of Mechanicsburg and the organizer of the present First National Bank there. To our subject and wife have been born four sons and two daughters: Victor (who died in infancy), Norman, Merkel, Naomi, Olive and Kenneth. Mr. and Mrs. Landis are members of the First Presbyterian Church, in which he is an elder and trustee. The father of Capt. Landis was Jacob Landis, a native of York County, a farmer and mill-wright, who married Miss Mary Mohler, of Cumberland County, a daughter of Daniel Mohler, of Lancaster County. Capt. Landis has the following brothers and sisters: Anna, wife of George Brindle, a retired farmer of Franklin County; Daniel, minister and farmer of York County; Mary, the wife of John Senseman, farmer of Cumberland County; Leah, wife of John Knisely, farmer in Upper Allen Township; David, a contractor and builder of Huntingdon, Penn.; Philip, a farmer of Osborne, Kas., and Susan, wife of Andrew Knoderer, a farmer of Upper Allen Township.

ALBERT ALLAN LINE, residence Carlisle, was born in Dickinson Township, this county, about five miles west of Carlisle, January 20, 1850, a son of Emanuel and Catherine (Myers) Line, the former born in Dickinson Township, this county, and the latter at Rossville, York County, Penn. Emanuel Line was a son of Emanuel, Sr., and Elizabeth (Myers) Line, both natives of Cumberland County. Our subject is the youngest of three children, and the only surviving one. He married October 12, 1876, Miss Mary L. Johnson, a daughter of Samuel A. Johnson of Philadelphia, Penn. Mrs. Line died December 25, 1877. Mr. Line's family is of Swiss origin, having immigrated to America and settled in Lancaster County, Penn., at a very early date. He is superintendent of the First Lutheran Church Sunday-school at Carlisle, secretary of the Cumberland County Sunday-school Association, secretary of the Cumberland County Temperance Alliance, director of the Farmers' Bank, Carlisle and a member of the directors of the Carlisle School Board, instructor at Mountain Lake Park, Maryland Summer School Amateur Photography. He is also a member of the board of managers for the Y. M. C. A., Carlisle, and chairman of committee on boys' work, Y. M. C. A.

WILLIAM H. LONGSDORF, M. D., Carlisle, was born in Cumberland County, Penn., March 24, 1834. His grandfather, Henry Longsdorf, was a native of Germany, and in an early day came to Cumberland County, where he purchased land from William Penn, and located two miles west of Mechanicsburg. Adam, a son of Henry, was born on this land in Silver Spring Township, and was occupied as a farmer; served three years as sheriff of the county from 1844, and died the year following. He married Mary Senseman, born in Cumberland County, her parents having removed thither from Lancaster County, and to this union were born four sons and three daughters, William H. being the fourth child and only one now living. Our subject lived on the old homestead until fifteen years of age, saving a residence of about five years in Carlisle, during his father's term of service as sheriff. At the age of fifteen years he entered Dickinson College, where he pursued a course of study for three years; then read medicine with Dr. Dale, and, in 1856, graduated from Jefferson Medical College, and in the spring of 1857 from the Pennsylvania Dental School, at Philadelphia. He then located in the practice of medicine at Bellevue, Neb., where he remained until the fall of 1858, when he went to Denver, Col., then a place of four cabins and forty men. Here he prospected and practiced medicine one year, and in July, 1857, returned to Cumberland County, where he continued practicing until August, 1861, when he was commissioned first lieutenant of Company I, Ninth Pennsylvania Cavalry Volunteers. He was subsequently promoted major of the regiment, and discharged January 19, 1864, with both legs broken at the ankles. Dr. Longsdorf participated in some eighty engagements, among which were the battles of Perryville, Ky., Chickamauga, Ga., Shelbyville, and siege of Knoxville, Tenn. The Doctor, on being discharged from the service returned to Cumberland County, and after a time resumed his practice, continuing until the fall of 1881, when he was elected treasurer of Cumberland County, the duties of which he performed for three years, when he again became engaged in the practice of his profession at Carlisle. April 7, 1857, he was married to Miss Lydia R. Haverstick, a native of Cumberland County, daughter of Benjamin and Lydia (Mylin) Harverstick, old settlers of that county, now residents of Mechanicsburg. To Dr. Longsdorf and wife have been born two sons and four daughters: Harold H., born in Nebraska, a graduate of Dickinson College, also of the College of Physicians and Surgeons, of Baltimore, Md., now practicing medicine at Centerville; John E., deceased at the age of twenty-one years; Zatae S., Hilda, Jessica, W. D., and Persis—the last five reside with their parents. Zatae and Hilda are attending Dickinson College, they being among the first female students admitted to the institution, and Zatae being the first female student to contend for the Pearson Oratorical Prize and took the first prize, the parents are members of the Second Presbyterian Church. Dr. Longsdorf is a Mason, and has passed all the chairs in the Blue Lodge, Chapter and Commandery of Carlisle. He ranks among the leading physicians and surgeons of Cumberland County, and is an esteemed and respected citizen. He is among the original members of the Cumberland County Medical Society.

JAMES ANDREW McCAULEY, D. D., LL. D., president of Dickinson College, was born near Elkton, Cecil Co., Md., October 7, 1822. His earliest educational advantages were had in the schools of the neighborhood; but the family removing to Baltimore, in his boyhood, his education was continued in the city. Quitting school at seventeen, he took a position in a business house, without, however, serious thought of adopting business as a life pursuit; for, thus early even, monitions of duty to preach had been, at times, distinctly heard. These monitions pervaded the years spent in business, acquiring, at length, a constancy and force, which, in the end, he came to feel it were a peril not to heed. Business was accordingly relinquished, and preparation for the ministry commenced. After a year of preparatory study he entered, in 1844, the freshman class at Dickinson, and, at the suggestion of the faculty, doubling work the second year, he graduated the second in scholastic rank in the class of 1847. The two years succeeding graduation were spent in teaching, as private tutor, in one of the old historic families of Maryland. Admitted to the Baltimore Conference in 1850, and assigned a charge adjacent to the city, he was, midway the year, transferred to the principalship of the Wesleyan Female Institute, a school of high grade for ladies, located at Staunton, Va., whose patronage the Conference had assumed. To the development of this new enterprise he gave unsparing labor, with the result of conspicuous success. The cares and labors incident to organization and constant supervision affected his health, and at the end of the third year, though in the midst of great prosperity, he was constrained to seek release. A period of rest and travel restored his health, and in the spring of 1854 he resumed the work of the pastorate. Except two charges in Virginia—Front Royal and Fredericksburg—his ministry, till 1872, was chiefly exercised in Baltimore and in the District of Columbia; from 1869, as presiding elder of the Washington District. In the summer of 1872 he was elected president of Dickinson College, which position he has since continuously held. His term of service here has witnessed great improvement in all the interests of the college. Besides the addition to its endowment of more than $100,000, and the thorough repair of its old buildings, three new structures have been erected, at an aggregate cost of $115,000. On two occasions—first in 1872, and again in 1884—he was chosen to represent his conference in the general conference, the highest council of the church. In 1872 he was designated by this body its fraternal messenger to bear the greetings of the American Church to that of Great Britain. In 1874, in association with Bishop Harris, he performed this duty, visiting the Wesleyan Conference, at Cambourne, Cornwall. On completing this service, various parts of England and the continent were visited, including the Universities of Oxford and Heidelberg. In 1868 his *alma mater* conferred on him the degree of D.D., and, in 1883, Lafayette College the degree of LL.D.

HON. CHARLES McCLURE (deceased) was a native of Cumberland County. His father, Charles McClure, was born in Cumberland County, 1789, and was the son of John McClure, of Scotland, who died in Cumberland County October 9, 1757, aged sixty one years. Charles McClure, the father, married Miss Mary Blair, who died without issue. He subsequently married Emelia Blair, cousin of his first wife, and by her had two children: John, a farmer and literary man, and Mary, who became the wife of Joseph Knox, a merchant of Carlisle. One daughter of John is now the widow of J. F. D. Lanier, who was a wealthy banker of New York City. Of Mary's children two are now living: George, an attorney of Philadelphia, and Rebecca Steele, wife of a prominent lawyer of Chicago. Charles McClure, Sr., was the third time married, his last wife being Mrs. Rebecca Parker, widow of Gen. Parker, of the war of 1812, the result of which union was two sons and two daughters: Charlotte, who married Dr. Adam Hays, of Carlisle; Rebecca, who married Elisha White, an attorney of Carlisle; Judge William McClure, of Pittsburgh, who married Miss Lydia Collins, and Charles McClure, the subject of this sketch. The latter was graduated from Dickinson College; read law in Carlisle, and was there admitted to the bar. He was elected a Representative to the State Legislature in 1834, and subsequently served two terms in Congress. His death occurred in 1846, at the age of forty-two years. His wife was Miss Margaretta Gibson, daughter of Chief Justice John Bannister Gibson, one of the most prominent and learned men of the State; born in Perry County, Penn., a son of Col. George and Ann (West) Gibson; she an intelligent and highly-educated lady for her time, a daughter of Francis West, the first magistrate of Cumberland County. Col. George Gibson was a native of Lancaster County, commanded a regiment through the Revolutionary war, and was killed at St. Clair's defeat, November 4, 1791. He was a great linguist and possessed much wit; was a splendid officer, and beloved by everyone for his jovial nature. His brother John, also an officer in the Revolution, was familiar with the customs of the Indians and their language, and it was he who translated and published the famous speech of the Indian chief Logan. Col. George Gibson and wife had four sons: Francis West, a farmer, who lived to be ninety years old; George, a commissary-general of the United States Army, who organized the commissary department of the army, for which purpose he was sent to Washington. He was the intimate friend and adviser of Andrew Jackson while President of the United States, with whom he had served, as his quartermaster-general, in the war of 1812, and by whom he was called "honest George Gibson." Gen. Gibson was a very generous warm-hearted gentleman, always remained a bachelor, and died in his eighty-seventh year, at Washington in 1861, in full possession of all his faculties. William, who died young, from yellow fever contracted in the West Indies; and Chief Justice John Bannister Gibson. The latter was a young child when his father died, and the mother being left in straitened circumstances, though possessing a farm in Perry County, inherited from her father, managed to keep her sons together and instructed them herself, to which training the Chief Justice said he was indebted for all that he was. Subsequently the mother moved to Carlisle, where John's education was furthered at Dickinson College through the efforts of his elder brother George. John read law with Judge Thomas Duncan, of Carlisle, who became one of the judges of the supreme court of the State; and was admitted to the bar in Cumberland County; was later appointed one of the judges of the Supreme Court of the State, and served on the bench with his preceptor. At the death of Chief Justice Tighlman, of Philadelphia, Judge Gibson was appointed to the position. President Jackson desired to appoint him to the supreme bench of the United States, and promised him the first vacancy; but owing to great political claims of Judge Baldwin, Chief Justice Gibson yielded to his appointment. The wife of Chief Justice Gibson was Miss Sarah Galbraith, of Cumberland County, and a daughter of Maj. Andrew Galbraith, an officer in the Revolutionary war, who was made a prisoner by the British. Chief Justice Gibson and wife had eight children, five of whom lived to be men and women: Mrs. McClure, widow of Charles McClure; Mrs. Roberts, wife of William Milnor Roberts, a distinguished civil-engineer, who died in Brazil, while acting as chief of the engineering works of Brazil; Sarah, wife of Capt. Richard H. Anderson, of the United States Army, of Charleston, S. C., afterward lieutenant-general in the Confederate Army; Col. George; and John Bannister, the latter a lieutenant in the United States Army, died from disease contracted in the Mexican war. Of these, George Gibson, colonel of the Fifth Infantry, United States Army, now stationed at Fort Keogh, M. T., and Mrs. Charles McClure are living. Our subject's widow has three sons: Charles, brevet-colonel, who served in the Union Army, during the war of the Rebellion, as captain, and until 1880 in the Regular Army, when he was appointed paymaster, with the rank of major, in the United States Army (married Miss Annie, daughter of Gen. George and Elizabeth (Graham) Getty; George Gibson, paymaster's clerk in the United States Army (he was for sixteen years in the Third National Bank of New York City); and William McClure, a banker and broker, New York City (married Miss Ella, daughter of Theo. Crane, a deceased merchant of New York City). Our subject was, and his widow now is, identified with the Episcopal Church.

LEWIS MASONHEIMER, prothonotary, Carlisle, was born in Waynesboro, Franklin Co., Penn., December 5, 1840. When he was seven years old his parents moved to Carlisle, where he attended school until fourteen, when he learned the confectionery business, and later engaged in the same, remaining until early in the war of 1861-65, when in August, 1862, he enlisted as a private in Company A, One Hundred and Thirtieth Regiment Pennsylvania Volunteer Infantry. After ten months' service he was discharged and returned to Carlisle, and for three years was engaged in the livery business. He next carried on a meat market for three years, when he began clerking in a dry goods and grocery store, which position he held until 1874 or 1875, when he opened a grocery, which he carried on for seven years. In January, 1882, he was appointed deputy clerk for the county prothonotary, and in November, 1884, was elected to his present office by the people of Cumberland County, without opposition. May 5, 1864, Mr. Masonheimer was married to Miss Eliza Wetzel, a native of Cumberland County, and daughter of John and Catherine (Wise) Wetzel, of the same county. Five children have been born to this union: Harry L. (died at the age of eight months), Kate M., John E., Laura E. and Wilbur. Mr. and Mrs. Masonheimer are members of the Reformed Church; he is a member of True Friends Lodge No. 56, K. of P. Our subject is a son of John and Elizabeth (Dysert) Masonheimer—former a native of Maryland, and a shoe-maker by trade; who was married in Adams County, Penn., and became the father of six children: George D., a boot and shoe-maker and dealer, in Boyle County, Ky.; Mary, a resident of Carlisle; Kate, wife of William B. Crouse, of Waynesboro, Penn.; James M., a resident of Brooklyn, N. Y.; John H., accidentally killed in Carlisle, at the age of twelve years, and Lewis. The mother and father were identified with the Reformed Church.

JACOB L. MELOY, grocer, Carlisle, is a native of Cumberland County, born one mile east of Carlisle October 15, 1843, a son of Samuel and Catherine (Haverstick) Meloy, also natives of Cumberland County; the former, by trade, a blacksmith. They wer· the parents of the following named children: George H. (now a farmer of Cumberland County), Jacob L., William M. (now a cigar-maker of Greason, Penn.), and Miss Mary E., of Carlisle. When our subject was six years of age his parents moved to Harrisburg, and when only nine, his father died, and at that early age Jacob L. began earning his own living. He worked for farmers in Perry and Cumberland Counties until April 1, 1860, when he went to Carlisle and lived with James Hamilton (deceased), with whom he remained one year, when he entered the sash and door factory of Frank Gardner, with the intention of learning the trade; but, on the breaking out of the war of the Rebellion, he left his employment and enlisted in Company A, which was organized at Carlisle, and tendered its services to the Government April 19, 1861, but which was not accepted, on account of the already full quota, until June 6 of that year. However, in the meantime the company was maintained, drilled and kept ready for service, and mostly, too, at the individual expense of the members; and when discharged, the men were credited with enlistment from April 21, 1861. Mr. Meloy served throughout the war, and was mustered out March 22, 1865, having participated in the following engagements, and been confined in the prison pens mentioned: The seven days' fight before Richmond; the battle of Charles City Cross Roads, where he was made a prisoner, June 30, 1862, and was confined at Richmond and Belle Isle, Va., until August 6, of the same year, battles of Gaines' Mill,

Bull Run, South Mountain, Antietam, in the pursuit of Stuart's cavalry, battles of Fredericksburg, the Wilderness, where he was taken prisoner and confined in the prisons at Lynchburg and Danville, Va., and at Andersonville, Ga., from May 22 to September 17, and at Florence, S. C., from September 24 to December 8, 1864. At the close of the war he returned to Carlisle, and entered the grocery store of William Blair & Son, as a clerk, April 1, 1865, and with them he remained until January, 1871, when he opened a store of his own, on Pitt Street, in the 16x20 room formerly occupied by Peter Faust. He started in a small way, with a stock of only $300, but, by close application to business and fair dealing, he won the confidence of the people, and some five months later bought the southeast corner lot, Pitt and South Streets, where he has his present store. His trade increased, from time to time, until he did a business of $38,000 a year. In 1879 he was appointed postmaster, which position he held nearly five years. In April, 1880, he sold his store to Mahon & Mundorf, but in 1886 repurchased. In 1882, at the organization of the Carlisle Manufacturing Company, he became one of its directors, and in 1884 was elected secretary of the board. Mr. Meloy was one of the original members of the Cumberland County Fertilizing Company, and on its organization as a company was elected its president, and has since remained as such. He is a member of the G. A. R., and was the first senior vice commander of Capt. Colwell Post, No. 201, and subsequently was elected commander of the post. November 16, 1866, he was married to Miss Martha B. Zimmerman, of Carlisle she being a native of the vicinity of Carlisle, and a daughter of Abraham and Keziah (Copperstone) Zimmerman; former of Schuylkill County, and latter of Adams County. Our subject and wife had born to them four sons: Andrew D., Thomas M., Charles L. and Harry W. Mr. Meloy is one of the self-made and successful business men of Carlisle. He was a member of the town council two terms, and took an active part in the organization of the Carlisle Board of Trade, and was elected its first secretary; but at the end of two terms declined re-election, on account of other duties. He is a member of the State Firemen's Association, and secretary of the Carlisle Firemen's Union, and vice-president of the Carlisle Live Stock Company, Wyoming Territory.

CAPT. WILLIAM E. MILLER. Abraham Miller came to this country in 1738, and settled in Lebanon County, Penn. He laid out what was formerly Millerstown, but is now known as Annville. During his residence there he was engaged as an iron master. He came to Cumberland County about 1765, purchased lands in Allen Township, along the Yellow Breeches Creek, where he built mills, and near which he resided. One of these, a fulling-mill, remains standing at the present day. He served as a soldier during the Revolutionary war. He married Rebecca Epwright, of Harrisburg, an English lady by birth, by whom he had six sons and one daughter. His sixth son, Abraham, was born at and became possessor of the homestead. His wife was Elizabeth Boyer, a daughter of Frederick Augustus Boyer, a German by birth, who took degrees at Heidelberg, and who also served as a soldier during the revolution. Abraham, the younger, had five sons and two daughters. Andrew G., the father of the subject of this sketch, was born at the old homestead in 1811. He became a merchant. During the years 1869-71, he served his district (the eighteenth) in the Senate of the State. He married Eleanor Umberger, whose paternal ancestor, John Leonard Umberger, came to this country in the ship "Hope" in 1732. He had six children: William E., Mary, John R., Ellen, Henrietta M. and Andrew G. Mary, died in infancy; John R. and A. G., both graduated at Princeton, and are now practicing lawyers at the Carlisle bar; Ellen, married H. Lee Snyder, an officer of the United States Navy, by whom she had two children: Richard Henry Lee and George McKnight; Henrietta, married George Bridges, of Shippensburg, Penn., and has one son—John; John R., married Caroline O. Rankin, a daughter of Dr. William Rankin, of Shippensburg, Penn., and had one daughter, who died in infancy, and one son—Hugh Rankin; A. G., married Jane Kennedy, a daughter of Joseph Kennedy, of Shippensburg William E., the eldest son, was born at West Hill, Cumberland County, February 5, 1836. He was reared on the farm, and owing to the limited means of his parents and to the fact that his father was a great invalid for many years, he received but a limited common school education. Young Miller showed a fondness for military life in his youth, and at the age of sixteen joined a military horse company, known as the "Big Spring Adamantine Guards," which company was organized in 1814, and when the war of the Rebellion broke out was among the first to tender its services to the Government, through the Governor of the State, A. G. Curtin. Cavalry was not included in the three months' call, so that the services of this company were not accepted until the later call for three years' troops was made. August 8, 1861, this troop left Newville, Cumberland County, for Washington, D. C., where, on the seventeenth of the same month, it was sworn into the United States service, in the yard in front of the war office, by Lieut. Elwood, and became Company H, Third Pennsylvania Cavalry. Up to this time William E. Miller served as a private, but was mustered into service as a second lieutenant. Owing to our limited space it is impossible to give a full account of the achievements of this officer, and we will, therefore, relate but a few of the more important events in his military career. He was one of the few officers that survived the rigid discipline at the training school of Camp Marcey during the winter of 1861-62, under Col. W. W. Averill, a graduate of West Point. In the spring of 1862 he accompanied his regiment to the Peninsula, and, upon the arrival of the army at Fortress Monroe, was assigned the advance to Yorktown, where he received his baptism of fire, on the same ground, where, nearly a century before, his great-grandfather closed his military career under Gen. Washington. A singular coincidence that his great-grandson should draw his sword in defense of the same Union,and on the same ground, where, nearly a century before, the great-grandfather had concluded fighting for its establishment. After leaving Yorktown Lieut. Miller's regiment again led the advance to Williamsburg, where it participated in the fight on the left under Gen. Heintzelman. Torrents of rain fell during this battle, and the night following was the essence of darkness, rainy and muddy. During this night, Lieut. Miller was summoned to Gen. Heintzelman's headquarters, and handed a dispatch with the following sententious order: "This dispatch is for Gen. McClellan. You may find him at Yorktown, or you may find him on the road between this and Yorktown, or you may find him anywhere along the line of this army, but you must find him, and a reply must be at these headquarters before daylight to-morrow." The task was accomplished, and Lieut. Miller received the congratulations of both Gens. McClellan and Heintzelman. So much, indeed, was Gen. McClellan impressed with this occurrence, that, though he never saw Miller until nineteen years afterward, he at once recognized him and recalled the circumstance. Lieut. Miller participated in all the sad scenes that followed on the Peninsula. He took an active part in the invasion of Maryland, and September 16, 1862, led Gen. Hooker's advance across Antietam Creek, and drew the first fire from the Confederate guns. During the 17th he was assigned an independent command, and acted under orders from Gen. Hooker direct. At a critical period in the battle, when Lieut. Thomas' battery was charged by Jackson's troops, Lieut. Miller came to the rescue and aided in saving the guns. For his gallantry on this occasion he was made captain, being promoted over all the first lieutenants of the regiment. In the campaign of 1863, Capt. Miller took a conspicuous part in the battles of Brandy Station, Aldie, Middleburg and Upperville; and at Gettysburg, on the 3d of July, won distinction by a gallant and timely charge, made in violation of orders, on Wade Hampton's flank, which contributed largely to the defeat of Stuart in his attempt to gain the rear of the Federal right flank. After participating in thirty-seven cavalry engagements, Capt. Miller, with his regiment, was mustered out of service August 24, 1864. In 1856 he was married to Elizabeth Ann Hocker, by whom he had two children: Caroline O. R. and Elizabeth. The latter died in the spring of 1862, while he was encamped in front of Yorktown, while the former grew to womanhood and married George K. McCormick, with whom she now lives at Knoxville, Tenn. In 1859 Mrs. Miller took malignant typhoid fever, and died. June 25, 1868, Capt. Miller was again married, this time to Anna De Pui Bush, of Tioga County, Penn., a daughter of J. S. Bush, a wealthy and retired lumber merchant. This lady is possessed of considerable literary attainments and position, and is the author of a reference book, "Who and What," and many minor stories. Since the war Capt. Miller has been engaged in the hardware business at Carlisle, Cumberland Co., Penn. He is social, but retiring and modest, firm in his opinions, and unchangeable in his convictions. He is highly esteemed by his neighbors and friends, as he was respected and admired by his comrades in arms. Some estimate may be formed of the man by the remarks made by his old commander, Gen. D. McM. Gregg, at the dedication of the cavalry shaft at Gettysburg, October 15, 1884: "Of course everybody expects to hear from Capt. Miller, whose name is so inseparably and honorably connected with our shaft. Possibly having built so well, on the very ground on which he fought so well, he will try to escape talking, which he can do well also. How pointedly he can write you can all attest." Capt. Miller takes an active part in all public enterprises; has served two terms as chief burgess of his town; was the original commander of Post 201, G. A. R.; is a member of the Military Order of the Loyal Legion of the United States, president of the Carlisle Board of Trade, and vestryman of St. John's Episcopal Church.

WILLIAM HENRY MILLER (deceased) was born near Millerstown, Adams Co., Penn., January 15, 1820. He attended the Pennsylvania College until about the age of eighteen, when his father moved to this county and bought the Cumberland Furnace, now owned by the Crane Iron Company. He soon after entered the law office of Judge John Reed, and was admitted to the bar. He married, May 30, 1843, Miss Jane Rebecca McDowell, who was born in Carlisle, Penn., a daughter of Andrew and Rebecca (Wilson) McDowell. Mrs. Miller is a member of St. John's Episcopal Church, of Carlisle. Mr. McDowell was born near Pittsburgh, and clerked in Philadelphia when a young man. He married in Perry County, Penn., and after that event came to this county. He was a son of Alexander and Nancy (Archer) McDowell, the former of whom was a civil engineer, and a son of Andrew McDowell, a Scotchman, who married, in Pennsylvana, Miss Sarah Shankland, of Port Lewis, Del. They settled in this county and became rich, owning iron works and a great many slaves. Rebecca Wilson, mother of Mrs. William Henry Miller, was a daughter of Maj. James Armstrong Wilson (a major in the Revolutionary war), a graduate of the Princeton College, who was admitted to the bar at Easton, Penn., where he afterward practiced. He was a large land owner and farmer of this county, where he was born. He married Miss Margaret Miller, a native of Carlisle, Penn., and a daughter of Robert Miller, a rich tanner. His wife was Elizabeth Calhoon, a native of Juniata County, Penn. Mr. William H. Miller died June 18, 1877, a member of the Second Presbyterian Church of Carlisle.

> "His place, in all the pomp that fills
> The circuit of the Summer hills,
> Is that his grave is green."

JOHNSTON MOORE, of Carlisle, is a descendant of James Moore, who came to America from Ireland in 1730, and purchased large tracts of land along the Yellow Breeches Creek. At the death of James Moore, which occurred about the close of the eighteenth century, he left four sons and three daughters. The third son, John, who was born August 29, 1740, and died October 18, 1822, married Eleanor Thompson, who was born in 1746 and died May 15, 1817. At their death they left five sons and two daughters. James Moore, Esq., the eldest son, born in 1765, was married January 28, 1808, to Nancy Johnston, of Antrim Township, Franklin Co., Penn., a daughter of Col. Thomas Johnston, a distinguished officer of the Revolution. (It may be mentioned here that these Johnstons are descendants of the celebrated Johnstons of Dumfriesshire, Scotland. James, the great-grandfather of Johnston Moore, came to America in 1735. They were also among the noted military families of Pennsylvania.) Dr. Robert, a brother of Col. Thomas Johnston, and who was an intimate friend of Washington and La Fayette and a member of the Society of the Cincinnati, joined the American forces before Boston, and continued with them until the surrender of Cornwallis, at Yorktown. James Moore, Esq., died in 1813, and his wife in 1823, leaving one son, Johnston Moore, born September 5, 1809. After the death of his parents he lived with his aunt, Elizabeth Johnston McLanahan, at her home, Prospect Hill, near Greencastle. He was educated a Dickinson College, Carlisle, and during this time lived with his guardian, Andrew Carothers, Esq. At the age of eighteen he took possession and management of his estate, including the original lands which had descended to him from his great-grandfather James, and which he still holds. On the 15th of July, 1836, he married Mary Veasey Parker, daughter of Isaac Brown Parker, of Carlisle. They had three sons and six daughters. All of these children are dead except three daughters. Johnston Moore's life has been passed quietly in the management of his estate and in pursuit of his favorite sports, hunting and fishing. He owns one of the finest trout preserves in the State, "Bonny Brook," one mile and a half from his home. He is a vestryman of St. John's Church, and has lived since his marriage at his present residence in Carlisle.

GEORGE MURRAY was born near Fort Pitt, western Pennsylvania, March 17, 1762, and was the only child of William and Susanna (Sly) Murray. He was left an orphan, and in early life settled in Carlisle, where he died May 6, 1855, in his ninety-fourth year. On the 21st of June, 1804, he was married, by the Rev. Dr. Davidson, to Mary Denny, daughter of William and Agnes (Parker) Denny, and sister of Maj. Ebenezer Denny, of Revolutionary fame, who was born in Carlisle March 5, 1778, and there died April 10, 1845, in her sixty-eighth year.

JOSEPH ALEXANDER MURRAY, the youngest son of George and Mary (Denny) Murray, was born in Carlisle October 2, 1815. His preparatory education had been obtained in his native place and elsewhere, and in August, 1837, he graduated from the Western University of Pennsylvania at Pittsburgh. In the autumn of the same year he entered the Western Theological Seminary in Allegheny, Penn., and from it graduated in the autumn of 1840. In October of the same year he was licensed to preach the gospel by the Presbytery of Ohio, which then embraced the churches in and about Pittsburgh. Soon after he received invitations to visit vacant churches, and accepted one to preach at Marion, Ohio. This church he supplied for six months, from December, 1840, to May, 1841, inclusive, but finally declined a unanimous call to become its settled pastor. He then visited his native place, and in October, 1841, received and accepted a call to the united congregations of Monaghan (Dillsburg) and Petersburg, and was ordained and installed pastor of the same by the Carlisle Presbytery in April, 1843. This relation happily and usefully subsisted for about eighteen years. During his pastorate the present church edifice was erected at Dillsburg. For years he served there also as school director, and was president of the board. During the same period he had received several invitations to churches at other places, which he declined. Finally, however, in consequence of impaired health, he resigned the charge. The pastoral relation was dissolved in October, 1858, and he then retired to Carlisle, but he often afterward ministered to the charge in Dillsburg, and supplied for years the church at Petersburg. His health never again permitted him to undertake the active work and assume the responsibilities of a settled pastor, though he has often filled vacant pulpits and assisted his clerical friends. Of all the members who belonged to the venerable Presbytery of Carlisle in 1841, when he joined it, he is now the only one who is still in connection with it. The body now numbers forty-two ministers and three licentiates, but only two are before him on the presbyterial roll, and because of their prior ordination, which was the basis for the reconstruction of the rolls in the union of the two branches of the church in 1870. On four different occasions he has been chosen by his presbytery as a commissioner to the General Assembly—in 1844, 1861, 1865 and 1875. On the last occasion he had also been chosen by his synod, with the Hon. H. W. Williams, to defend, if necessary, a decision of said body before the General Assembly, and in this highest church court he was appointed one of the judicial committee. In 1876 he was chosen, by acclamation, moderator of the Synod at Harrisburg. In 1869 his *alma mater* conferred on him the honorary degree of D. D. In 1870 he was elected a corresponding member of the Numismatic and Antiquarian Society of Philadelphia. In 1873 he was elected a member of the Historical Society of Pennsylvania. At a public meeting held in Carlisle in 1876 he was selected to prepare an historical address pertaining to Cumberland County, to be delivered on the 4th of July of said year, but circumstances prevented. In 1880 he was elected a member of the American Philosophical Society at Philadelphia. In 1886 he was elected a director of the Western Theological Seminary, in Allegheny City, Penn. In the same year he was appointed to furnish biographical sketches for the centennial anniversary of the Carlisle Presbytery, but declined in favor of his alternate. He is president of the Cumberland County Bible Society, also secretary of the Hamilton Library and Historical Association of Carlisle. Several of his discourses and addresses have been published. He frequently contributes to some of the periodicals of our country, literary, historical and religious, in which work he still continues, as well as preaches and mini-terially officiates when desired, and is able to do so. But in no instance would he accept of any work or position that would interfere with his high calling and character as a minister of the gospel of Jesus Christ. Dr. Murray has been twice married—first, April 25, 1843, to Miss Ann Hays Blair, of Carlisle, daughter of Mr. Andrew Blair, born May 6, 1819, and died September 14, 1875; secondly, October 2, 1879, to Miss Lydia Steele Foster, of Philadelphia, born March 9, 1836, in Carlisle, daughter of Mr. Crawford Foster, and niece of Dr. Alfred Foster, all natives of Carlisle. By the first marriage he had one child, born February 11, 1848; graduated in 1866 from the Mary Institute. Carlisle, then under the presidency of the Rev. Dr. Francis J. Clere, and in January, 1868, married Prof. Charles F. Himes, Ph. D., who has been an honored member of the faculty of Dickinson College since 1865.

GEORGE NORCROSS, D D., Carlisle, pastor of the Second Presbyterian Church, was born on his father's farm near Erie, Erie Co., Penn., April 8, 1838. His parents were Hiram and Elizabeth (McClelland) Norcross, the former of Erie County, and the latter of Crawford. George, our subject, is eldest in a family of five sons and one daughter: William C., an attorney, of Monmouth, Ill.: H. Flemming, attorney, of Chicago, Ill., Isaiah, a business man, of Monmouth; Thomas Rice, grain dealer, Liberty, Neb.; and Sarah, wife of Henry Beckwith, died in 1863, are the other children. The family removed from Erie County to Monmouth, Ill., in 1844. George graduated at Monmouth College in 1861, and the fall of that year entered the Northwestern Theological Seminary at Chicago, where he remained one year. Returning to Monmouth he was elected to a professorship in Monmouth College, which he held for two years, and during that time studied theology at the United Presbyterian Theological Seminary, Monmouth, and was licensed to preach by the Presbytery of Warren, in April, 1863; preached at North Henderson, Ill., where he remained three years, and during one winter of that time, attended the Theological Seminary at Princeton, New Jersey. In the spring of 1866 he was called to the Presbyterian Church at Galesburg, Ill., and preached there until January, 1869, when, having been called to the Second Church of Carlisle, he moved hither. During his ministry here the manse and new church building, corner of Hanover and Pomfret streets have been erected. His labors in this church have been very successful; from a membership of 230 it has grown to 400, and is entirely out of debt. He was married, in Monmouth, Ill., October 1, 1863, to Miss Mary S. Tracy, who died March 25, 1865; and on April 22, 1867, Rev. Mr. Norcross married Mrs. Louisa Jackson Gale, widow of Maj. Josiah Gale, of Galesburg. To this union five children were born (four now living): Delia Jackson, born in Galesburg; George born in Carlisle, where he died December 28, 1878, aged eight years; Bessie, Mary Jackson, and Louisa Jackson Norcross. In 1879 Princeton College conferred the degree of D. D. on Mr. Norcross.

JOSEPH WHEELER PATTON (deceased) was born at Bellefonte, Penn., December 22, 1803, the second child of three sons and two daughters, of Benjamin and Phœbe Patton. When a young man, Mr. Patton came to Harrisburg, and first clerked for Mr. Haldeman, an iron merchant, and later for a Mr. Espy, a dry goods merchant. Subsequently he rented the Mary Ann Furnace, located near Shippensburg with which he was identified until 1835, when he became superintendent of the Lancaster Railway, a position he held for six months, when he went to Maria Furnace in Adams County, Penn., where he was engaged in clerking for a short time, when he received, at the hands of Gov. Ritner, the appointment of superintendent of the Portage Railway, which he filled two years, residing at Carlisle, where he subsequently kept the Mansion House; thereafter went to Mount Holly Furnace of which he was manager for Robert Givin. Later he and Mr. Mullin bought the Mount Holly Springs Hotel, from which Mr. Patton retired in two years, returned to Carlisle, and kept the Mansion House, with the exception of a short time, until the war. He was then appointed provost-marshal under Col. R. M. Henderson. He also served as collector of internal revenue for the Fifteenth District of Pennsylvania for three or four years, after which he retired from active life. His death occurred October 30, 1880, and thereby the people of Cumberland County lost one of their prominent and useful citizens. Mr. Patton married, December 2, 1834, Miss Mary Noble, of Carlisle, who was born in the old Mansion House, Carlisle, March 12, 1814, a daughter of James Noble, who was born in Ireland, in December, 1775, and who at the age of twenty years came to America with his father, John Noble, who settled in Carlisle. James Noble married Miss Mary Cooper, of Carlisle. To the marriage of Joseph W. Patton and Mary Noble one child (deceased) was born. The widow is a member of St. John's Episcopal Church, of which Mr. Patton was treasurer for sixteen years, until his death.

THOMAS PAXTON, retired, Carlisle, was born on his father's farm near Cumberland, Allegany Co., Md., May 24, 1807. His father, Samuel Paxton, came from Scotland when a young man, with his brothers, Joseph and James. Joseph located in the western part of Pennsylvania, James somewhere in Virginia, and Samuel, the eldest of the three, in Bedford County, Penn., but afterward moved to near Cumberland, Md. Samuel Paxton was possessed of means, which, however, he lost before the birth of his youngest son. He was a captain in the Revolution. He was twice married, his first wife being a Miss Bageley, of Bedford County, Penn., who bore him three children: David and Joseph, who removed to Kentucky, and Prudence, who died unmarried; and his second wife was Miss Elizabeth Lesher, of English birth, who bore him four sons and five daughters: Nancy, Rachael, Mary, John, Joseph, Ellen, William, Susan, and Thomas. The latter was but an infant when his father died. He attended school until he was fifteen years of age, when he determined to become a business man. He secured employment on the Potomac, as chief clerk for Mr. George Hobbleson, who owned a line of produce boats. About this time our subject's old friend, Gen. Thomas Dunn, was appointed by Gen. Jackson superintendent of the Government works at Harpers Ferry, and young Paxton was employed as confidential clerk, in which capacity he remained until 1826, when Gen. Dunn was shot by an employe, whom he had discharged. Subsequently Mr. Paxton became superintendent for Gen. Ridgley's iron works, at Piney Woods, five miles south of Baltimore, and as such served until the death of Gen. Ridgley, one year later. Soon after this (in 1828) Mr. Paxton received a proposition from Adam Hauk, of Cumberland County, to build a forge on Yellow Breeches Creek, in Dickinson Township, which he complied with. April 30, 1838, he was married to Miss Galbraith, of Cumberland County, daughter of Samuel and Nancy (Moore) Galbraith, and he, after his marriage, purchased and operated Moore's mill on the Yellow Breeches for about five years, when he sold out, and began to build railroads, first building some two miles of the Cumberland Valley Railway, and graded six miles of the Baltimore & Ohio Road, between Martinsburg and Cumberland, Va. He next performed work for the Pennsylvania Railway Company for four consecutive years, when he became employed on the North Pennsylvania Railroad, grading up through the coal regions, remaining for two years, when he built the Mechanicsburg & Dillsburg road. Mr. Paxton owns a great deal of stock in various roads east and west. He, in company with Robert Givin, organized the Farmers Bank of Carlisle, and on the death of Mr. Givin, some years later, who was its president, Mr. Paxton was elected his successor, remaining president of the bank some years, when he resigned and retired from business. Mrs. Paxton died in 1848, the mother of two children: Ellen, who died at the age of nine years, and Annie M., widow of Park Moore, the eldest son of Johnson Moore, of Carlisle. October 18, 1859, Mr. Paxton was married to Mrs. Olivia Farnsley, of Evansville, Ind., who was born in that place January 23, 1834, daughter of John and Elvira (Riggs) Mitchell (a large property owner of Evansville, and for many years president of the Branch of the State Bank of Evansville, from its organization until his death), and grand-daughter of Joseph Mitchell and Elizabeth Campbell, the latter of whom was a direct descendant of the celebrated Rob Roy and also of the Laird of Glenfalloch. The first husband of Mrs. Paxton was Dr. David A. Farnsley, whom she married December 21, 1854, he being a native of near Louisville, Ky., son of David and Sarah (Merriweather) Farnsley. Dr. Farnsley died in April, 1855. Mrs. Farnsley had one daughter, Albertina Olivia, who was born October 2, 1855, now wife of Frank E. Bradner, attorney at law, Newark, N. J. To the last marriage of Mr. Paxton were born two children: Thomas, who died in infancy, and Josephine E., who resides with her parents. Mr. and Mrs. Paxton are members of St. John's Episcopal Church.

H. K. PEFFER, editor and proprietor of the daily and weekly *Sentinel*, is a native of Cumberland County, Penn. His parents were Adam and Mary (Kerr) Peffer, also natives of the same county. Adam Peffer was of German parentage; Mary Kerr of Scotch descent. He was born in South Middleton Township January 13, 1827; was raised on a farm; and at the age of twenty four immigrated, in 1853, to Warren County, Ill., where for ten years he was engaged in farming. At the expiration of that time he took up his residence in Monmouth, Ill., where he formed a law partnership with Col. James W. Davidson, which continued for three years. In 1862 he was elected to the Legislature as a representative from Warren County, and at the expiration of his term received the unanimous nomination of his party for State senator. He was also, at the same time, named as one of the presidential electors on the McClellan ticket in 1864. In the fall of 1865 he removed with his family to Carlisle, Penn., where, after spending a year in Texas and the Southwest, he permanently located. In 1871 he received the nomination of his party for State senator—the senatorial district then embracing Cumberland and Franklin Counties. In that year the Democracy was unsuccessful, the entire ticket, with one or two exceptions, being defeated. In 1872 he was admitted to the Carlisle bar, but shortly after took charge of the *Valley Sentinel*, which was then published at Shippensburg. In 1874 the *Sentinel* was removed to Carlisle, when he became sole owner of the paper. In 1881 the daily evening *Sentinel* was issued from the office of the weekly, and was the first daily paper ever issued in Cumberland County. In 1848 Mr. Peffer was married to Jane Mary, daughter of Nathaniel Weakley. His family consists of following: Mary, William, Charles, Adam and Kitty, all of whom are residents of the county.

WILLIAM GLANCY PEFFER, dealer in agricultural implements, Carlisle, and chief burgess of the city, was born in South Middleton Township, Cumberland County, November 11, 1833, a son of Adam and Elizabeth (Glancy) Peffer, the former of whom was a son of Henry, and he a son of Philip Peffer, a native of Germany. Mrs. Elizabeth (Glancy) Peffer was a daughter of William Glancy, a native of Ireland. William G. was reared on a farm, and with agricultural interests he has always been considerably identified; although he has carried on other lines of business, he has been ever active in the development of the social and industrial life of his locality. He has served with credit in official capacities in South Middleton Township, this county, and recently was elected to his present office. He married here Rebecca G., daughter of Andrew and Eliza Washwood, of Dickinson Township, to which union two daughters and one son have been born, viz.: Iva G. and Nettie, young ladies of clever literary and musical attainments, and Ambrose, a student of medicine. Mr. Peffer has always contributed liberally to measures tending to the welfare of his locality, and has drawn around him the respect of all classes through his benevolence and kindness. The family attend worship at the First Presbyterian Church.

WILLIAM McFUNN PENROSE (deceased) was born in Carlisle, this county, March 29, 1825, the eldest child of Hon. Charles Bingham and Valeria Fullerton (Biddle) Penrose. He graduated from old Dickinson College, Carlisle, and, in 1857 married Miss Valeria Collins Merchant, who was born in Pittsburgh, Penn., a daughter of Gen. Charles Spencer Merchant, a native of New York, and a grandson of Rev. Elisha Spencer. To Mr. and Mrs. Penrose were born four daughters: Sarah Merchant, Valeria Biddle, Ellen Williams and Jennie Anderson Merchant. They reside with their mother on High Street, Carlisle.

CAPT. WILLIAM MONTGOMERY PORTER (deceased), was born in Carlisle, August 5, 1808, and died July 27, 1873. His grandfather, Robert Porter, with his family, left Scotland and settled at Coleraine, Ireland. Robert Porter was stamp master of County Down until the Rebellion of 1798, when he took part as a "United Irishman," and was the friend of James Nappertandy, Thomas Sedley Birch, Robert Emmet, and Lord Fitzgerald, who were all "United Irishmen," and leaders in the Rebellion. He and his eldest son, William, the father of the subject of this sketch, were pursued by the king's troops and obliged to flee for their lives. They found their way to a seaport, got on board of a vessel bound for America, and after a three months' voyage, landed at Camden, New Jersey. They, with the rest of the family, soon afterward settled on a small stream in Lancaster County, called "Swatara," and after a time they moved to Perry County and finally to Carlisle. Sarah Montgomery Porter, the mother of William M. Porter, was born in Carlisle, near the close of the Revolution. Her family, the Montgomerys, were from Scotland. William M. Porter read law under Samuel A. McCoskry, afterward bishop of Michigan, and was admitted to the Carlisle bar in 1835. He practiced for a time, but from 1836 to 1839 was editor of the *Perry County Freeman*, and from 1856 to 1861 of the *Carlisle Herald*. In October, 1839, he was commissioned by Gov. David R. Porter as captain of the Carlisle Light Artillery. In 1841 he was appointed postmaster of Carlisle, and served four years under the administration of President Tyler. In October, 1862, he was commissioned by Gov. Curtin as captain of Company A, One Hundred and Thirtieth Regiment Pennsylvania Volunteer Infantry, and served until May 21, 1863, having been in the engagements at South Mountain, Antietam, Fredericksburg, Chancellorsville and Petersburg. Before this time, 1851, Capt. Porter had been elected treasurer of Cumberland County. He was a corresponding member of the Historical Society of Pennsylvania. His last position was under Gov. Hartranft, in the office of Secretary of the Commonwealth. Capt. Porter married Martha Vashon, by whom he had five daughters: Sarah J., now Mrs. Petinos; Fanny M., now Mrs. William Mullen; Mattie, now Mrs. Sellers; Ida H., now Mrs. Crook; and Minnie, now Mrs. Buckingham. As a husband and father Capt. Porter was kind, as an editor able, as a soldier brave, and as a citizen esteemed, quiet and unostentatious. He is among the number of the citizens of Carlisle, who have died within the memory of this generation, and who well deserve to be remembered.

CAPT. RICHARD HENRY PRATT, superintendent of the United States Indian Industrial Schools at Carlisle, to which position he was appointed in September, 1879, is a native of Rushford, Allegany Co., N. Y., born December 6, 1840, a son of Richard S. and

Mary (Herrick) Pratt. Richard S. Pratt, who was a contractor and builder of canals, constructed the Welland Canal, in Canada, and the Wabash Canal, in Ohio and Indiana. To Richard S. and Mary (Herrick) Pratt were born three sons, of whom Capt. Pratt is the eldest. In the summer of 1846, the family moved to Logansport, Ind., where our subject attended the common school and Logansport Seminary, and in 1857 he began to learn the tinner's and coppersmith's trades. He removed to Delphi, in 1858, where he remained working at his trade until the breaking out of the late Rebellion, when, on April 16, 1861, he enlisted in Company A, Ninth Indiana Infantry; was discharged July 29, 1861, and re-enlisted in Company A, Second Indiana Cavalry, September 18, 1861, and served as sergeant and first sergeant until April 19, 1864, when he was promoted first lieutenant of Company C, of the Eleventh Indiana Cavalry. September 1, 1864, he was promoted captain of this company, and May 29, 1865, was mustered out of the service. Capt. Pratt participated in the battles of Philippi, Va., June 3, 1861; Laurel Hill, Va., July 7; Belington, Va., July 10, and Carrick's Ford, Va., July 13 and 14; in 1862, Shiloh, Tenn., April 6 and 7; Pea Ridge, Tenn., April 15; Monterey, Tenn., April 17; several engagements around Corinth, Miss., April 30 to May 30; Tuscumbia Creek, Miss., May 31; McMinnville, Tenn., August 9; Gallatin, August 13 (where his horse was shot); engagements about Murfreesboro, Tenn., August 20, 25, 27, and September 7, New Haven, Ky., capturing the Third Georgia Cavalry in September; Perryville, Ky., and Crab Orchard, October 6, 7 and 8; Stone River, December 31 to January 3, 1863; in 1863, Murfreesboro, Tenn., March 10; Shelbyville Pike, June 6; Triune, Tenn., June 11; Shelbyville, Tenn., June 23; Tullahoma, June 25; Middletown, June 24; Grey's Gap, June 27; Elk River Bridge, July 2; Sparta, August 9; Chickamauga, Ga., September 19 and 20; Anderson's Cross Roads, and pursuit of Wheeler (fighting daily); in 1864, Huntsville, Ala., in October; Shoal Creek, Ala., November 9; Lawrenceburg, Tenn., November 22; Campbellsville, Tenn., November 24; Nashville, November 15 and 16 (where he had a horse killed); Hollow Tree Gap, Tenn., December 17; Linnville, Tenn., December 23; Pulaski, Tenn., December 25 and 26. At the close of the war the Captain returned to Delphi, Ind., and there worked at his trade until September, 1865, when he went to Bement, Ill., and one year later to Minnesota, where he remained for a few months, and then returned to Logan-port, Ind., and was tendered an appointment by Schuyler Colfax as second lieutenant in the Tenth Regular Cavalry, which he accepted, and joined his company at Fort Gibson, Indian Territory, in June, 1867, and July 31 of that year was promoted first lieutenant of the same company, which office he held until February 7, 1883, when he was promoted captain. April 20, 1864, Capt. Pratt was married to Miss Anna Laura Mason, of Jamestown, N. Y., a daughter of Belden B. and Mercy (Whitcomb) Mason, to whom have been born four children: Mason D., born January 23, 1865; Cora Marion, October 2, 1868; Nana Laura, July 27, 1871, and Richenda Henrietta, August 25, 1882. Capt. Pratt belongs to St. John's Blue Lodge, No. 260. The Indian Industrial School, of which he is at the head, and for whose improvement he has worked untiringly for years, owing to his good management is a successful institution.

CHRISTIAN REIGHTER, brick mason, contractor and builder, Carlisle, was born in that place January 10, 1820, son of George and Ann Catherine (Leibe) Reighter. George Reighter, a stone and brick mason, contractor and builder, and a native of Crawford County, Penn., removed to Berks County, and thence to Carlisle in 1813, where, in 1816, he was married to Miss Leibe, a native of Berks County, and a daughter of Christian and Catherine (Franklinberger) Leibe. He died April 7, 1836, aged about thirty-five years. His parents were Henry and Sarah J. (Sanders) Reighter, the former of whom, a native of Crawford County, came in 1813 to Cumberland County, and in 1835 moved to Pittsburgh. He was also by trade a brick and stone-mason. To George and Ann Catherine (Leibe) Reighter were born six sons and one daughter: George L., who served in the Eleventh Pennsylvania Volunteer Infantry, under Col. Coulter, and was killed at Fredericksburg; Christian; Henry B., who served in the Mexican war, and died from disease contracted therein; Charles O., who served in Company A, First Regiment Pennsylvania Veteran Reserve Volunteers, and was wounded at South Mountain, and died from the effects; John T., a painter in Philadelphia (Charles O. and John T. were twins); Mary C., who died in 1851, the wife of Henry McCord, a farmer of Ohio, and Andrew J., a brickmason, who also served in the First Regiment Pennsylvania Veteran Reserve Volunteers, and died in 1879. The parents were identified—the father with the Episcopal, and the mother with the Lutheran Church. Our subject, when young, learned the brick-mason's trade in Carlisle, which he has since followed. February 1, 1850, he was married to Miss Sarah Jane Dickinson, a native of Cumberland County, Penn., and a daughter of David and Christian (Yingest) Dickinson, and to this union have been born two children: Edward F., now engaged in the grocery business in Gettysburg, and Mary C., who resides with her parents.

WILLIAM F. REILY, physician, Carlisle, is a native of Cumberland County, Penn., born at Carlisle, December 2, 1851. His grandfather, James Reily, who was born in Ireland and there educated for the priesthood, when a young man emigrated to America and settled in Cumberland County, Penn., and was here married. William, a son of

James, married Miss Elizabeth Kernan and to them were born three sons and one daughter: Rev. Dr. Theo. M. Reily (professor of ecclesiastical history in the theological seminary at Nashotah, Wis.), Thomas A. Reily (late second lieutenant in the Fifth United States Infantry from 1867 to 1871, when he resigned and returned to Carlisle; also chosen captain of Company G, Eighth Regiment National Guard of Pennsylvania, at its organization, and subsequently made lieutenant-colonel of the regiment), Euphemia Parker Reily (who resides with her mother in Carlisle), and Dr. W. F. Reily. Our subject attended the common school of Carlisle until eighteen years of age, when he entered Dickinson College, and later entered the medical department of the University of Pennsylvania at Philadelphia, from which he was graduated in March, 1875. He then located at Carlisle, where he has since been actively engaged in the practice of his profession. He is a member of the Cumberland County Medical Society, and of the Medical Society of Pennsylvania. The Doctor and wife are members of the St. John's Episcopal Church, of which he is one of the vestrymen. Dr. Reily is a past master of St. John's Lodge, No. 260, F. & A. M. He has been physician to the county asylum since 1885.

HENRY M. RITTER, merchant tailor, Carlisle, was born in that place February 6, 1847. He attended the public schools of Carlisle until thirteen years of age, and then entered Dickinson College, where he remained one year. He next entered Eastman's Business College, at Poughkeepsie, N. Y., from which he was graduated in 1863. He then returned to Carlisle and embarked in his present business, succeeding his father. He carries a full and complete stock of fine imported and domestic goods. January 10, 1868, Mr. Ritter married Miss M. Maybury Hassler, of Carlisle, a native of Philadelphia, and a daughter of John P. and Amelia M. (Herr) Hassler. Mr. Hassler was a native of Franklin County, Penn., and for many years was cashier of the Carlisle Deposit Bank. Mrs. Hassler was a native of Franklin County, a sister of the Hon. A. J. Herr, U. State Senator, and a daughter of Daniel Herr, proprietor of the "Tremont," Philadelphia, and the "Lochiel," Harrisburg. Mr. and Mrs. Ritter have two sons: John E. and Harry G., both born in Carlisle. The mother is identified with the Reformed Church. The parents of our subject are Henry S. and Mary (Wonderlich) Ritter, natives, the former of Reading, Berks County, and the latter of Cumberland County. Henry S. Ritter, a merchant tailor by occupation, opened, in 1837, the first merchant tailoring establishment in Carlisle. He and his wife are members of the English Lutheran Church. To them were born three sons and five daughters, of whom two sons and two daughters are living: Mary E (wife of Robert McCartney, foreman of the printers in the office of the Mechanicsburg *Journal*), Fannie A. (wife of John H. Rheem, a piano and music dealer at Ottumwa, Iowa), Henry M., and Charles H. (tailor of Carlisle, who married Miss Anna Reep). Benjamin Crane, great-grandfather of Henry M. Ritter, was a native of England, and in an early day settled in Cumberland County, and was engaged in farming. Christiana Crane, his widow, a native of Berks County, died in Carlisle, at the advanced age of one hundred and four years, retaining her mind and being quite active to the last. Her death was caused by a fall and from fright during the bombarding of Carlisle by the rebels in 1863, a shell bursting in her room. The Ritters are of German descent. Samuel, the grandfather of Henry M., was born in Reading, Penn., of which city he was a merchant and served as postmaster for a period of twenty years. His wife was Katherine Kast, a native of Reading.

HON. WILBUR F. SADLER, Carlisle, was born in Adams County, Penn., October 14, 1840, his paternal ancestor being among the first settlers of Adams County. Richard Sadler emigrated from England about the middle of the last century and settled in that part of Pennsylvania now forming Adams County. In 1750 he took out a warrant for land which is still in the possession of some of his descendants. He was buried in 1764, at Christ Church, Huntington Township, of which he was one of the early members. His son, Isaac, married Mary Hammersly, and their eldest child was named Richard. He married Rebecca Lewis, and their second son, Joshua, became the father of Wilbur F. The subject of this sketch was brought by his parents to Cumberland County the year following his birth. After the completion of his education, in 1863, he enlisted in a cavalry company, which was mustered into the United States service for the "emergency" at the time of Lee's invasion of Pennsylvania. He was admitted to the Carlisle bar in 1864, and besides acquiring a large practice was actively connected with the educational and business interests of the place, serving as a director of the common schools, trustee of Dickinson College, director of several corporations, and president of the Farmers' bank. In 1869 he was nominated by the Republican party for the State Senate, in the district composed of York and Cumberland; was elected district attorney two years afterward, and president judge of the Ninth Judicial District of Pennsylvania in 1884, having been defeated for the same office ten years previous.

WILLIAM SADLER, Heidlersburg, Adams County, was born November 16, 1816. He is a son of William Sadler, who was born October 1, 1777, and died July 8, 1848. His grandfather was Isaac Sadler, and his great grandfather Richard Sadler, who was a native of England and settled near York Springs prior to 1750. His mother was Lydia Loase. Mr. Sadler has been a resident of Heidlersburg for many years. His energy, business foresight, facility of accumulation and wise investments have made his counsels valuable and much sought in financial matters. He is a director of the Dillsburg National Bank.

JOHN SCHMOHL, SR., baker, Carlisle, was born at Metzingen, Wurtemburg, Germany, November 16, 1824, a son of Jacob and Catharine Schmohl, who came to Cumberland County in 1846, former of whom died in 1868, and latter in 1859. The subject of our sketch learned his trade in the old country, and coming here embarked in the business with which he has since been successfully connected. He was married here to Elizabeth Fredericka, whom he buried in January, 1863, and who left him three sons and three daughters: Philip, Lena, Jacob, John, Catharine and Lizzie. Mr. Schmohl was again happily married, this time to Catharine Weidman, a native of Arnstaafer, Hessen-Darmstadt (the place of nativity of his first wife), and who came to America in 1838, a daughter of Jacob Weidman, who died here in 1869, his widow following him in September, 1885, aged eighty-seven years. Mr. Schmohl is one of Carlisle's public spirited citizens, and has contributed liberally to the support of the industrial interests of the place. He is a prominent Knight of Pythias, and has done much toward keeping alive the society here. The family attend services at the Lutheran Church.

ALEXANDER BRADY SHARPE, Esq., of Carlisle, son of John and Jane (McCune) Sharpe, was born in Newton Township, Cumberland County, on the 12th of August, 1827. His ancestors, paternal, and maternal, were among the first settlers in the upper end of the county. His great-grandparents on his father's side, Thomas and Margaret (Elder) Sharp, were Covenanters, who, because of their religious faith, were driven from Scotland to the province of Ulster in the North of Ireland, about or shortly after the middle of the seventeenth century, and resided near Belfast, in the County of Antrim, until about the year 1747, when they immigrated with their children, consisting of five sons and four daughters, to Cumberland County, Penn., and settled in Newton Township. His grandfather was Alexander Sharp, of Green Spring, the youngest of the five sons. His maternal great-grandparents were James McCune and Abigail, his wife, of Newton Township, whose son Samuel married Hannah Brady, a daughter of Hugh Brady the second, whose father, Hugh Brady, was an emigrant from Enniskillen, and one of the first settlers in that portion of the county now embraced in Hopewell Township. He began his studies preparatory to entering college with Joseph Casey the elder, father of Hon. Joseph Casey, at Newville, in 1839, and after his death continued them at Academia, Juniata County, and completed them with Vanleer Davis, at Chambersburg; entered the sophomore class at Jefferson College, Cannonsburg, Penn., in 1843, and graduated on the 23d of September, 1846, with the highest honors of his class. The college was then under the presidency of Rev. Dr. Robert J. Breckenridge, and two of his classmates were Hon. William H. West, of Ohio, and Hon. John M. Kirkpatrick, of Pittsburgh. On his return from college he commenced the study of law with Robert M. Bard, Esq., of Chambersburg, and completed his course with Hon. Frederick Watts, of Carlisle. Hugh Gaullagher, Esq., W. M. Biddle, Esq., and Hon. J. H. Graham, were the committee appointed to examine him, and on motion of the last named he was, on the 21st of November, 1848, admitted to practice. He remained with Judge Watts until the 1st of April, 1849, when he opened an office and has since been engaged in the practice of his profession, except during the years of the war of the Rebellion, when from the 21st of April, 1861, until the 28th of January, 1865 (less the period from the 27th of December, 1862, to the 28th of August, 1863), he was constantly in the service as a private or a commissioned officer. April 21, 1861, he enlisted as a private in Company A, Seventh Regiment Pennsylvania Reserve Volunteer Corps, and served as such until the 25th of September, when he was commissioned second lieutenant of Company E, and appointed adjutant of the regiment. On the 4th of December he was relieved from duty with his regiment, which was a part of the Second Brigade (Meade's) of McCall's division, and ordered to report to Brig.-Gen. Ord, commanding the Third Brigade, who had appointed him aide-de-camp. He joined Gen. Ord the same day and served on his personal staff until the General was wounded and disabled temporarily for field service, when he resigned. After Ord's recovery he was, at the General's instance, again commissioned a captain and assigned to duty with him, where he served until he resigned on the 28th of January, 1865. During the war he was in field service in the Army of the Potomac, of the Rappahannock, in the Army of the Tennessee, Army of West Virginia, Army of the Gulf, and in the Army of the James. He participated in the engagement at Drainesville, on the 20th of December, 1861; the battle of Iuka, September 18 and 20, 1862; Big Hatchie, October 5, 1862; Burnside's Mine Explosion, July 30, 1864; Battle of New Market Heights, or Chapin's Farm, and capture of Fort Harrison, September 9 and 10, 1864. He was brevetted and promoted to the rank of captain and aide-de-camp, United States Army, for gallant and meritorious service at the battle of Drainesville, and on the 13th of March, 1865 (on the recommendation of Gens. Ord, Meade and Grant) received the brevet ranks of major, lieutenant-colonel and colonel United States Volunteers for gallant conduct at Petersburg and the various affairs before Richmond, Va. On the 19th of December, 1854, Col. Sharpe married Katherine Mears Blaney, a daughter of the late Maj. George Blaney, Engineer Corps, United States Army. He never held an office, and never was a candidate for any, political, judicial or otherwise,

BOROUGH OF CARLISLE. 395

but he has political convictions coeval with the existence of his party, from which he has never turned away, a sense of professional and social duty which has never yet caused him to be ashamed, and an abiding faith in the doctrines of the church of his fathers.

DR. ROBERT LOWRY SIBBET, Carlisle, was born in Cumberland County, Penn. His paternal grandfather, Samuel Sibbet, and grandmother, Alice Lowry, with their brothers, John, James and Robert Sibbet, and three sisters, Mrs. Gourley, Mrs. McCann and Mrs. Copely, emigrated from the North of Ireland about the close of the last century His maternal grandfather, Timothy Ryan, and grandmother, Rachel Williamson, also emigrated from the North of Ireland about the same time. Samuel Sibbet was a man of decided political convictions, and on account of his pronounced sentiments 50 guineas were offered for his head. He was, however, not without friends, and after bidding farewell to his wife and three children—James, Robert and Thomas— set out for America. He reached Baltimore in the early part of 1800, in a concealed manner, being connected with the Order of Freemasons. A few months later his devoted wife, having disposed of their personal effects, ventured to cross the ocean with her three helpless children, and landed safely at the same port. Having heard of the Scotch Irish settlement in the Cumberland Valley, they proceeded at once to the head of the Big Spring where they were welcomed by their numerous Presbyterian friends. To their small family were here added Samuel, Margaret, Lowry and Hugh Montgomery. Thomas Sibbet was born in County Armagh, Ireland, in 1797. Catherine Ryan, whom he married, was born in Cumberland County in 1793, and by this union were born Rachel A., Dr. Robert L., Henry W., Rev. William R., Elder C., Joanna J. and Anna M. Sibbet. The subject of this sketch graduated in Pennsylvania College, Gettysburg, with the degree of A. B. in 1856. He afterward engaged in teaching a classical school, first in Centreville, and then in Shippensburg, in his native county, until 1862, when he began the study of medicine. He graduated with the degree of M. D. in the University of Pennsylvania, in 1866, and in the meantime the degree of A. M. was conferred upon him. He practiced his profession in Harrisburg and afterward in New Kingston. In 1870 he visited Europe, where he spent two full years in the universities and hospitals, being seven months in Paris during the entire siege, two months in Berlin, ten months in Vienna and two months in London. After returning from Europe Dr. Sibbet settled in Carlisle as a general practitioner, where he still resides. In 1873 the medical society of the State appointed him chairman of a committee on medical legislation, and it was mainly through his persevering efforts, in the midst of great opposition, that the passage of the present registration law was secured. In 1882, nine months after the law took effect, he collected statistics and made a report to the society, which shows that 6,492 practitioners had voluntarily complied with the law in the several counties, that 838 of these were practicing without graduation, and that 105 were females. At the same time he corresponded with a large number of prominent medical gentlemen in the United States, and in 1876 was instrumental in effecting the organization of the American Academy of Medicine, an association founded on protracted courses of literary and medical study with degrees corresponding thereto. As a recognition of these services he has recently been elected " vice-president of the section of obstetrics in the Ninth International Medical Congress, to be held in Washington, D. C., in 1887." He has been a frequent contributor to the literature of his profession, and has now in manuscript form, nearly completed, a series of chapters on the Franco-Prussian war and siege of Paris.

ALEXANDER D. BACHE SMEAD was born in Carlisle, March 24, 1848. He is the youngest child of Capt. Raphael C. Smead, Fourth United States Artillery. The latter was a New Englander by birth, descended from a family established in Massachusetts two centuries ago. His parents, Selah and Elizabeth (Cummings) Smead, removed to Genesee County, New York, and from there the son was sent to the West Point Military Academy in 1821, graduating four years later. In 1829 he married Sarah M. Radcliffe, daughter of John and Jane (Van Ness) Radcliffe, of Dutchess County, New York, a woman of beauty and talent and of remarkable force of character. He thus allied himself with several of the oldest colonial families of New York, which have furnished that State with some of her ablest judges, both for the supreme and inferior courts, as well as men prominent at the bar and in official life. Both of Mrs. Smead's parents were of Dutch extraction, some of her father's ancestors having emigrated from Holland to New Amsterdam as early as the year 1630, and their descendants intermarried with later English and Huguenot settlers. Capt. Smead passed unhurt through the Florida and the Mexican wars, but had barely reached American soil, on his return from the latter, when he fell a victim to yellow fever contracted at Vera Cruz. Having, in 1847, been sent North for a short time to Carlisle Barracks to recruit additional men for his regiment, he had left his wife and children in Carlisle when he himself rejoined Gen. Scott's army. Her husband's sudden death, in 1848, left Mrs. Smead among comparative strangers and in very straightened circumstances. But adversity could not overcome her energetic nature. Deciding to make Carlisle her home, she at once took up her increased burden of responsibility, and carried it to the end without flinching. She still (in 1886) resides in the town where she so successfully reared and educated her sons and daughters. Raphael C. and Sarah M. Smead had the following children: First—JOHN R. SMEAD. He graduated at West Point in 1854 and was commissioned lieutenant in the Second United States Artillery, spent a couple of years on the Indian frontier, acted as assistant professor of philosophy at West Point, and was on topographical engineer duty when the war of the Rebellion broke out. The disloyalty of the captain of the "National Rifles," of Washington, led to Capt. Smead's detail, by their request, to reorganize and command them until Northern troops could arrive for the defense of the Capital. With this company he led the first advance of the Union Army into Virginia. He was soon promoted captain in the Fifth United States Artillery, commanded his battery through the Peninsular campaign, and was killed in battle August 30, 1862. He married Annie B. Ege, of Carlisle, and left one child, Raphael C. Smead, now a civil engineer. Second—ELIZABETH C. SMEAD. She died in infancy. Third—ELIZABETH C. SMEAD. She has made music her profession. She has been a member of the faculty of "Metzger Institute" since its foundation, and has charge of the department of instrumental music. Fourth—JANE V. N. SMEAD. Since 1865 she has been the wife of John Hays, Esq., of Carlisle. Fifth—RAPHAEL C. SMEAD. He was book-keeper of the First National Bank of Carlisle, and died May 25, 1869, unmarried. Sixth—SARAH CORNELIA SMEAD. She resides with her mother in Carlisle. Seventh—A. D. B. SMEAD.

The latter graduated in 1862 from the public schools of Carlisle, then studied until 1863 at the preparatory school of Dickinson College, and in 1864 entered that college, from which he graduated June 25, 1868, with the first honors. In the spring of that year he was nominated by the President for a commission in the Regular Army, and passed an examination before a board of military officers convened for that purpose. On August 1, 1868, he was commissioned second lieutenant in the Third United States Cavalry. He was an officer of that regiment for over eleven years. He was stationed in Pennsylvania, New Mexico, Arizona, California, Nebraska, Wyoming, Dakota and Montana; was much on active duty in the field and occasionally engaged in Indian hostilities. He was promoted first lieutenant in 1874, and regimental adjutant in 1878. In 1879 he resigned from the army for the purpose of practicing law, to the study of which he had devoted much attention in connection with his military duties. His legal studies were completed in Philadelphia, and he was admitted to the bar of that city as well as to that of Cumberland County. He then settled in his native place for the practice of his profession. Mr. Smead has spent over two years in European travel and study. He has long been a member of the Second Presbyterian Church, of which he is also a trustee.

LEMUEL R. SPONG, register of wills, Carlisle, was born on a farm in East Pennsborough Township, Cumberland County, Penn., May 21,1855, a son of Joseph and Caroline (Marsh) Spong, the former a native of the same county and township and the latter of York County. Joseph Spong was a son of John Spong, also a native of East Pennsborough Township, and his (John's) father, John Leonard Spong, a native of Germany, who was married there, immigrated to America, and settled in East Pennsborough Township, this county. John Spong, father of Joseph Spong, married Barbara Dewerton, of Dauphin County, Penn., and had ten children. To Mr. and Mrs. Joseph Spong were born four children, all of whom are dead except Lemuel R. When our subject was six years of age his father moved to West Fairview, Cumberland County, where Lemuel attended school until he was thirteen years old, when he went to work for the Harrisburg Nail-works, with which he remained in the capacities of office boy, clerk and shipping clerk until 1873, when, in connection with the position he was holding, he acted as agent for the Adams Express Company, and later became freight agent for the Northern Central Railroad. From 1874 until 1885, during the fall and winter seasons, he was engaged in buying and shipping all kinds of produce. October 24, 1875, Mr. Spong was married to Miss Rosa Mann, a native of East Pennsborough Township, this county, and a daughter of George and Mary A. (Edinger) Mann, both of this county.

HUGH STUART was born in County Antrim, Ireland, June 23, 1758; came to America in 1784; and, in 1790, married Ruth Patterson and settled on the Patterson tract of land on the head of Letort Spring, in what is now South Middleton Township. Ruth Patterson was born in Scotland, in 1763. The children of this marriage were five sons: Hugh, William, John, James and Joseph. Hugh and William died in early life; John settled in this county; and James and Joseph went with their father to Bucyrus, Ohio, in 1821, where they were the first settlers. Hugh Stuart, Sr., died there in 1854, at the age of ninety-eight years. All of the family are now dead, except Joseph, who still lives in Bucyrus, now in his eighty-seventh year. John Stuart, the third son, was born at the head of the Letort, in October, 1794. January 4, 1816, he married Barbara Steen, a daughter of John and Elizabeth (Cairns) Steen, also of County Antrim, Ireland. Ten children were born to this union, eight of whom lived to maturity, the sons being Hugh, John, Joseph A., James T. and William P.; and the daughters: Amelia, married to Thompson Weakley; Elizabeth, married to William Wherry, and Martha A., married to George Searight. John Stuart, the father, after his marriage, lived in Carlisle, and was engaged in milling until 1827, when he moved to his farm in South Middleton. He was appointed associate judge of Cumberland County, under the Constitution, in 1835, for life. After the judiciary was made elective, he held the office by election until 1857. He died in 1870. His eldest son, Hugh, was born in the latter part of 1816; was a farmer; a member of the State Legislature during the two sessions of 1857 and 1858; in 1861 was elected associate judge, and held the office by re-election until 1871. He died in 1880. Joseph A., the only surviving son, was born in 1826, and still farms in South Middleton Township, this county. He was married, in 1850, to Mary A. McCune, whose grandfather, of Scotch-Irish parentage, settled near Shippensburg, on the farm where his descendants still live. Their children living are John T. and H. S. Stuart.

JOHN T. STUART, prosecuting attorney of Cumberland County, and of the firm of Stuart & Stuart, attorneys at law, Carlisle, was born in South Middleton Township May 23, 1851, son of Joseph A. and Mary A. (McCune) Stuart, worthy people of a very long line of descent in this locality. Mr. Stuart spent two years in Susquehanna College, and, after a short time at West Nottingham Academy, Md., entered Princeton in 1870, from which institution he was graduated in 1874. He then entered upon the study of law, and was admitted to the bar in 1876, and in 1883 was elected to his present incumbency, which he very creditably fills.

REUBEN SWARTZ, the general proprietor of the "Thudium House," Carlisle is a native of Cumberland County, born three miles north of Hogestown, in Silver Spring Township, February 11, 1845, a son of Peter and Catherine (Burtner) Swartz, both natives of Silver Spring Township, and descendants of old families of Cumberland County. When nine years old he went to live with his uncle at Bridgeport, this county, and remained with him five years. He then learned the plasterer's trade at Mechanicsburg, where he remained three years; then went to Canton, Ohio, and worked at his trade two years, when he returned to Pennsylvania and located at Titusville four years. He formed a partnership with Francis Le Rew, and they conducted the "White Hall Hotel," at Harrisburg, Penn. Two years later, Mr. Swartz engaged in buying and selling horses and clerking at the "White Hall Hotel." In the spring of 1878 he came to Carlisle and leased the "Thudium House," which he still conducts. In 1884 he formed a partnership with S. P. Jackson, and dealt in horses and general stock. March 11, 1878, he married Miss Alice Simons. She was born and reared in Landisburg, Perry County, a daughter of George and Catherine J. (Parkinson) Simons. Her father was in the Mexican war as a drummer-boy; also served in the civil war. He was a son of George Simons, a soldier in the war of 1812; both were blacksmiths. To Mr. and Mrs. Swartz two sons were born, one living, William L., born March 4, 1879. Mr. Swartz is a member of Cumberland Star Lodge, A. F. & A. M., Carlisle. He keeps a first-class house in every respect, neat and well furnished, and he and wife pay special attention to the comfort of their guests. They are justly popular and have hosts of friends. During the civil war, in 1864, Mr. Swartz drove a Government wagon one year.

FRANK E. THOMPSON, of the firm of Dale & Thompson, grain and coal merchants, Carlisle, was born in that place December 1, 1847, son of Joseph C. and Jane (Smith) Thompson, natives of Carlisle, where they now reside, respected citizens, latter a member of the Methodist Episcopal Church. Joseph C. Thompson is a printer by trade, having learned the business in the office of the *American Volunteer* and other papers of Carlisle, and for many years he was foreman in the office of the *Volunteer* and Carlisle *Herald*. They had four sons and five daughters, of whom three sons and three daughters are living: Annie, wife of A. J. Hecker, a carpenter and contractor, of Carlisle; Sallie S., unmarried; Frank E.; Harriet C.; J. Marlin, engaged in the transfer business, in Carlisle; John M., saddler of Carlisle, and Frank E. Our subject was educated at the schools of his native place, and at the age of seventeen years began clerking in a dry goods store for Leidich & Miller, of Carlisle, with whom he remained for a short time. He next worked for a brief period at the carpenter's trade, when he went to Harrisburg, where he clerked for three years and later engaged as clerk with G. B. Hoffman, in the grocery business, with whom he remained for a short time, when he was appointed agent at Carlisle for the Adams Express Company, which position he held for five years, when he resigned and bought the interest of Mr. A. Bosler, in the grain and coal house of A. Bosler & Dale, and the firm has since been Dale & Thompson. March 19, 1878, Mr. Thompson married Miss Annie S. Black, who was born in Carlisle, a daughter of Robert M. and Sarah (Barnhardt) Black, natives of Cumberland County, former an architect, contractor and builder, of Carlisle. Mr. and Mrs. Thompson have two children: Laura A. and Nellie. Mrs. Thompson is a member of the Reformed Church, and Mr. Thompson is a member of St. John Lodge, No. 260, F. & A. M., St. John's Chapter, No. 171, R. A. M., K. T., St. John Commandery No. 8; is a member of Carlisle Lodge No. 91, I. O. O. F., and a member of the I. O. H. He is among the enterprising and representative men of Carlisle.

ALEXANDER A. THOMSON, M. D., Carlisle, was born on the old family farm near Scotland, Franklin Co., Penn., February 11, 1841. His great-grandfather emigrated from Scotland to Franklin County, with his family of thirteen children, in 1777, and settled midway between Shippensburg and Chambersburg, at a point now called Scotland, in honor of his native place. His son, John, grandfather of our subject, married Hannah Rea, and six daughters and two sons were born to them. Nancy, married to John Runfrew; Eliza, married to William Agnew; Margaret, married to a Mr. Lusk; Hannah, married to Robert McKee; Sarah, married to Adam Brown; Ann, married to Dr. D. S. McGowan; Alexander, married to Margaret Kerr, and Samuel, the youngest, and father of subject, married to Miss Mary Kyner, a daughter of George and Chri-tina (Nye) Kyner. Samuel and Mary (Kyner) Thomson were members of the Reformed Presbyterian Church, and had nine children, three sons and three daughters living: Elizabeth, wife of John Wilson, a farmer, of Chester County, Penn.; Agnes, wife of George Dice, a grocer, of Shippensburg; John R., a farmer, of Franklin County; Alexander A.; McLeod W., superintendent of "maintenance of way" on the Pennsylvania Railway, at Altoona, Penn., and Miss Mary A., who resides with Alexander A. When Alexander A. was twelve years old his father moved to Fayetteville and bought an interest in the female seminary and the boys' academy, at Fayetteville, and managed the boarding house for this seminary for four years. Our subject took a four years' course in the latter institution, at the completion of which, in 1857, his father died, and Alexander A. was engaged the following winter in teaching school at Fayetteville, and in the spring began farming with his eldest brother on the old homestead near Scotland. He followed agriculture three years; then began the study of medicine with Drs. Stuart and Howland, of Shippensburg. Eighteen months later he went to Ann Arbor, Mich., and there attended a course of lectures; then read one summer with Dr. A. Harvey Smith, an eminent surgeon of Detroit, Mich. In the fall of 1863 he entered Jefferson Medical College, of Philadelphia, Penn., from which institution he was graduated in March, 1864, and the same spring located in the practice of medicine at Newburg, Cumberland County. Here he remained in practice several years and then moved to Cumberland, Md., where he, with his brothers, McLeod W., and William Paxton, built the Cumberland Steel Works, which they operated one year, when the Doctor sold out, and returned to Newburg and formed a partnership with John C. Elliott, under the firm name of Elliott & Thomson, in general merchandising for three years (until the fall of 1875). He was then nominated and elected, by the people of Cumberland County, Republican treasurer, which office he held three years, and in the fall of 1879 was elected by the same party sheriff of the county, filling the incumbency three years. In the spring of 1882 he engaged in the cattle business in Wyoming Territory, and the year following formed a partnership with James D. Greason in the same line. Two years later they formed the Carlisle Live-stock Company, of Wyoming Territory, of which Dr. Thomson was chosen president and manager, and he has since been engaged in this business. December 15, 1864, Dr. Thomson was married to Miss Susan Rosetta Frazer, a native of near Shippensburg and a daughter of Andrew and Annie (Wilson) Frazer, natives of Dauphin County, and who became a member of Middle Spring Presbyterian Church. Dr. and Mrs. Thomson have two children living: Frank Frazer, now attending Dickinson College, and Nellie E., attending school. Mrs. Thomson is a member of the Second Presbyterian Church, of Carlisle. The Doctor ranks among the leading successful business men of Carlisle, and, starting in life dependent on his own resources, he may be said to be a self-made man. As a public officer and business man, he has always had the confidence and respect of all.

JOHN R. TURNER, architect, contractor and builder, Carlisle, has been identified with the place since 1833, and is, perhaps, the oldest in this line at Carlisle. He learned his profession with Jacob Spangler, with whom he served a regular apprenticeship, since which time he has been actively engaged in his business. He was born at Franklin (four miles southwest of Shippensburg) March 6, 1815, a son of David Turner, who was born and reared near Mount Rock, Dickinson Township, this county, and of Irish parents, who settled in Cumberland County, and there died. When a young man David removed to Franklin County, where he was married to Miss Rebecca Rudisill, who was born in what is now Adams County, Penn., a daughter of Baltzer and Elizabeth (Schmidt) Rudisill. Mr. and Mrs. David Turner settled in West Pennsborough Township, Cumberland County, in 1823, and to them were born eleven children: Eliza (unmarried), Mary A. (married to John Cresler, a farmer near Shippensburg), Rebecca (widow of James Davidson, of Peoria, Ill.), John R., Susan (widow of John Keller), Jane (widow of Joseph Heister Gibson), Sarah (widow of Samuel Corl, of Bedford County), Lydia C. (wife Alpheus Hagan, resident of Brandonville, Va.), Margaret (widow of John R. Natcher, a contractor and builder of Pittsburgh), Caroline (wife of George Sulluff, a contractor and builder of Allegheny City), and Agnes (wife of Thompson Walker, a farmer of Cumberland County). The parents were members of the Presbyterian Church. John R. received his schooling mainly in West Pennsborough Township, and in the spring of 1833 went to Carlisle, where, September 6, 1838, he was married to Miss Catherine Halbert, a native of Carlisle, and a daughter of Joseph and Elizabeth (Du Boise) Halbert, former of whom came from England, and latter a native of Carlisle. The grandfather of Mrs. Elizabeth Halbert (Abraham Du Boise) immigrated to Holland, from France, during the French Revolution, and subsequently to America, settling in Montgomery County, Penn. To our subject and wife have been born three daughters: Virginia (wife of William D. Sponsler, a retired merchant of Carlisle), Belle (residing at home), and Kitty (deceased, aged thirty-five, and unmarried). The parents are members of the First Presbyterian Church. Mr. Turner is identified with St. John Lodge, F. & A. M., Carlisle, and the I. O. O. F., Carlisle Lodge, No. 91. He has been the architect and builder of many of the buildings in Carlisle and elsewhere; was the architect and builder of the court house, Cumberland County, Stevens' Hall, Gettysburg; architect for the Farmers High School Building, near Bellefonte, Penn. (now the Pennsylvania Farm School), architect of the market house in Carlisle, and was also architect and superintendent of the court house of Clarion County, Penn., and now, August, 1886, is engaged in superintending a first dwelling for H. Gould Beetem, having furnished the plans and specifications. Mr. Turner has long been one of the city's active and enterprising business men.

REV. JOSEPH VANCE. D. D., pastor of the First Presbyterian Church, Carlisle, son of Samuel and Mary Vance, of South Strabane Township, Washington Co., Penn., was born October 8, 1837. In 1853 he entered Washington College, now Washington and Jefferson, and graduated in September, 1858. In the same month he entered the Western Theological Seminary at Allegheny, Penn. He was licensed to preach the gospel by the Presbytery of Washington in April, 1860, and graduated from the seminary in 1861. His first charge was the Assembly Church, Beaver Dam, Wis., where he began his work in July, 1861. In June, 1862, he was ordained by the Presbytery of Winnebago. In January, 1865, he entered the work of the Christian Commission, and was sent to Vicksburg, Miss. In February he was appointed by Col. John Eaton assistant superintendent of the schools of the Freedman's Department in the district of Vicksburg, and served in that capacity until the 1st of July. He was called to the Second Presbyterian Church of Vincennes, Ind., in September, 1865, and continued as its pastor until it was united with the First Presbyterian Church in April, 1873. Accepting a call to the church formed by the union, he remained until July, 1874. During his pastorage in Vincennes he was stated clerk of the presbytery, permanent clerk of the synod and a trustee of Hanover College. In April, 1866, he was married to Mary Hay Maddox, of Vincennes. She died in July, 1871, leaving one child, Charles Thompson. During the summer of 1875 Dr. Vance supplied the pulpit of the First Presbyterian Church of Reading, Penn., in the absence of its pastor. The Rev. Dr. C. P. Wing having resigned the pastorate of the First Presbyterian Church, Carlisle, in October, 1875, Mr. Vance was, in November of the same year, invited to supply the pulpit, and on the 30th of April, 1876, was installed pastor by a committee of Presbytery, consisting of Rev. Drs. C. P. Wing, J. A. Murray and George Norcross, of Carlisle, and Thomas Creigh, of Mercersburg. In September, 1880, he was married to Sarah H. Maddox, of Vincennes, Ind. Miriam C. is their only child. In June, 1884, the degree of D. D. was conferred upon him by the Western University of Pennsylvania, and also by Washington and Jefferson College.

HON. FREDERICK WATTS, retired lawyer, Carlisle. An eminent minister of the gospel once said: "The leading lawyer is always the most prominent member of the community in which he lives." Whether this is always the case in large cities and commercial centers, or not, it is, no doubt, generally so in agricultural communities. That Judge Watts was the most prominent member of the community in which he lived for more than a quarter of a century is not questioned. As early as October, 1827, he practiced in the supreme court of this State, and as late as the May term of 1869, and all through that period of forty-two years (except the three years he was on the bench), there is not a single volume of reports containing the cases from the middle district in which his name is not found; to which add the fact that for fifteen years he was reporter of the decisions of that court, and during that period, and before and after it, he was engaged in a large office business, and in the trial of nearly all the important cases in the courts below, in his own county and the county of Perry. But this did not satisfy his love for labor. He was, during this period, president of the Cumberland Valley Railroad, and continued in that office for twenty-six years. To his professional duties, and those connected with the railroad, he added constant activity in agricultural pursuits, not only in managing his farms, but as president of the Cumberland County Agricultural Society, and an active projector of the Agricultural College of Pennsylvania, furthering the general agricultural interests of his county and State. Judge Watts was born in Carlisle, this county, May 9, 1801, and is a son of David Watts, one of the most distinguished lawyers of his day, and whose practice extended through all the middle counties of the State. His mother was a daughter of Gen. Miller, of Revolutionary fame, who afterward commanded the United States troops at Baltimore during the war of 1812. His grandfather, Frederick Watts, was a member of the executive council of Pennsylvania before the Revolution, and was one of the prominent men of the province and subsequent State. Our subject, having been duly prepared, entered Dickinson College, from which he was graduated in 1819. He passed the two subsequent years with his uncle, William Miles, in Erie County, where he cultivated his taste for agricultural pursuits. In 1821 he returned to Carlisle, and entered the office of Andrew Carothers, as a law student; was admitted to the bar in August, 1824, and soon acquired a lucrative practice. In 1845 he became president of the Cumberland Valley Railroad. It is to his energy and able management that the people of the valley are indebted for a road which, when he took hold of it, was in debt, out of repair, unproductive, and in a dilapidated condition, but which, through his energetic and economical management, has been brought up to a high state of prosperity, having paid all of its indebtedness and been made to yield handsome returns. March 9, 1849, Mr. Watts was commissioned by Gov. Johnston president judge of the Ninth Judicial District, composed of the counties of Cumberland, Perry and Juniata. He retained the office until 1852. In 1854 he was elected president of the board of trustees of the Agricultural College of Pennsylvania, in which capacity he still acts. During the year 1854 he projected the erection of gas and water works for Carlisle, and, having formed a company, was elected its president. He is a man of great force of character and abiding self-confidence. Whatever he has undertaken he has done with all his might, and whatever be his belief he believed implicitly. He never sat down at the counsel table to try a case that he did not impress the court and jury that he had perfect confidence that he would gain it. His temper was completely within his control; his equanimity was perfect, and he was ever ready to avail himself of any slip of his adversary. He had great powers of concentration, and always prepared his law points at the counsel table as soon as the evidence was closed. This he did with great facility, always directing them to the main points of the case. His power with the jury was very great. He was known by every man in the counties in which he practiced, and was regarded as a man of large intellect, sterling integrity, and unblemished honor. To these he added the impression of perfect belief in the justice of his cause, and this was effected by a manner that was always dignified, and in speech that was clear, strong, convincing, and never tedious. He despised quirks and quibbles; was a model of fairness in the trial of a cause, and always encouraged and treated kindly younger members of the bar that he saw struggling honorably for prominence, and when he closed his professional career he left the bar with the profound respect of all its members. In 1871 he was tendered the appointment of commissioner of agriculture, which he declined. The offer was renewed, and he finally accepted the appointment, and entered upon its duties August 1, 1871. An admirable system pervaded this department, and the three divisions were so arranged that the most detailed and accurate information could be obtained with the greatest facility. The country had not in its employ a more industrious, honest, faithful and large-hearted servant. He has ever since devoted himself assiduously to the practical development of the agricultural resources of the country.

EDWARD BIDDLE WATTS, attorney, Carlisle, son of Hon. Frederick and Henrietta (Ege) Watts, was born in Carlisle, September 13, 1851. In 1865 he entered Dr. Lyons' private school at West Haverford, ten miles west of Philadelphia, where he remained until 1868, when he went to Cheshire, and entered the Episcopal Academy of the State, and here pursued his studies until 1869, when, at the request of Dr. Horton, the principal of that institute, he accompanied him upon a tour in Europe. Immediately upon his return he entered Trinity College at Hartford, Conn., from which institution he was graduated in 1873. He returned to Carlisle and read law with John Hays, an attorney of the place, and was admitted to the bar of Pennsylvania, in 1875, and at once entered on the practice of his profession, at which he has since been engaged in his native town. In 1885 he was appointed attorney for the county commissioners of Cumberland County. Although a young man, Mr. Watts ranks high in his profession, in which he has thus far made a success. He is a member of the Eighth Regiment, National Guards of Pennsylvania, having served as captain of Company G (Gobin Guards) since February, 1885. He is identified with St. John's Episcopal Church.

HON. JOHN WISE WETZEL, lawyer, Carlisle, was born at that place, April 20, 1850, a son of George and Sarah E. (Shade) Wetzel. The subject of our sketch completed a good common school education, and took a preparatory course of study in Prof. Robert Sterrett's Academy here, and graduated from Dickinson College, in 1874. Meantime he had entered the study of law in the office of the late C. E. Maglaughlin, Esq., and was admitted to the bar a short time before receiving his decree from Dickinson College. After his admission he located in practice here, and has since been deservedly successful. He has always been an ardent Democrat, and has taken considerable interest in the placing of able men before the people for office. In 1876 he was elected as a representative to the Democratic State Convention from Cumberland County; in 1882 he was elected to preside as chairman of the county executive committee of his party for Cumberland County; and in 1884 was elected district attorney for the county. He married Lizzie, youngest daughter of John and Elizabeth Wolf, the union being blessed with a son, Frank. Mr. Wetzel has succeeded through life by his own exertions, being a self-made man. He gives liberally to all worthy objects, and is one of the active workers in the development of the social and industrial interests of Carlisle. He is a member of the Belles Letters, and Omega Chapter of the Chi Phi Fraternity of Dickinson College; is a member of the board of trustees of Franklin and Marshall College; solicitor for the Board of Trade and Building & Loan Association of Carlisle; solicitor for the Harrisburg & Potomac Railroad, etc., etc. He is a worthy Mason and a member of the K. of P. Mr. and Mrs. Wetzel are regular attendants of the services of the Reformed Church of the United States.

BARRENS SYLVESTER WILDER (deceased), late proprietor of the "Mansion

House," Carlisle, was a native of Ohio. He was born December 18, 1833, and was a son of Dwight and Harriet (Barrens) Wilder, the former a native of Massachusetts, and by occupation a farmer. To Mr. and Mrs. Dwight Wilder three sons and one daughter were born, of whom Barrens S., the subject of this sketch, was the second son and child, and when but a small boy his parents moved to this county, and settled on a farm, where Barrens grew up, attending school during the winters. December 29, 1859, he was married to Miss Elizabeth Gurtner, who was born in York County, Penn., July 22, 1843, a daughter of John and Susan (Wise) Gurtner, the former of whom was a blacksmith, a native of Germany, and who came to this country when a child, and whose father, George Gurtner, settled in York County, Penn. John and Susan (Wise) Gurtner were the parents of one son and three daughters: Mary, who married Hezekiah Williams; John; Harriet, who married John Barnet, and Elizabeth, the wife of our subject. Mr. and Mrs. Barrens S. Wilder soon after marriage engaged in the hotel business, taking charge of the "Railroad House," at New Cumberland, which they conducted for four years; then took the hotel at Bridgeport, Cumberland County, with which they were identified until 1876, when they removed to Carlisle, and took charge of the "Mansion House," where Mr. Wilder died March 17, 1884. He was prominently connected with Masonry, having passed all the chairs in the various degrees of the order to the thirty-second degree, and was also a prominent member of the I. O. O. F. He was a member of the town council of Carlisle for three years, and stood high in the estimation of all as an upright, honest citizen. To Mr. and Mrs. Wilder five children were born, of whom the following named are living: Clara, wife of John Klink, resident of Harrisburg, a telegraph operator by profession, but at present employed as a clerk and book-keeper for Cumberland Valley Railroad Company; Susie, Arabella and Robert A. All the children were born at New Cumberland, Cumberland County, and the youngest three reside with their mother.

CONWAY PHELPS WING, D. D., Carlisle, belongs to a family traceable through five preceding generations to a progenitor who came from England in 1632 and settled finally in Sandwich, Mass. He is the son of Enoch and Mary (Oliver) Wing, who went from Conway, Hampshire Co., Mass., to Ohio in 1796, and settled on the right bank of the Muskingum, twelve miles above Marietta. He was born there February 12, 1809, but removed with his father in 1813, to Phelps, Ontario Co., N. Y. At a very early age he left home to pursue study preparatory to his collegiate course in the neighboring town of Geneva, at an Episcopal academy, which soon afterward became Hobart College. After two years there he entered the sophomore class in Hamilton College, where he graduated in 1828. Nearly a year after this he entered a theological seminary at Auburn, where he enjoyed the instruction of Dr. James Richards and graduated in 1831. He was licensed to preach by the presbytery of Geneva, February 3, 1831, just before entering his twenty-first year, and commenced preaching at once in Sodus, Wayne Co., N. Y., where he was ordained and installed September 27, 1832. During the extraordinary revivals of religion which prevailed in that region about that period, he was one of its active and successful promoters. In 1836 he removed to Ogden, Monroe Co., N. Y., and in 1838 to the city of Monroe, Mich., where his vigorous health gave way under his protracted labors, and he was obliged to seek its restoration, first by a year's residence in St. Croix, West Indies, and then by a more protracted sojourn in the Southern States. For a year and a half he preached in Columbia, Tenn., and vicinity, and finding, on experiment, that he could not safely venture upon a settlement in the North, reluctantly yielded to the solicitations of his new friends in the South, and became pastor of a congregation in Huntsville, Ala. Though he frankly informed that people that he was opposed to slavery and should do all in his power wisely to abolish it they persevered in calling and sustaining him, believing that his prejudices would soon be removed. He continued in his pastorate there with great acceptance and usefulness until April, 1848. He twice represented his presbytery there in the general assembly of the Presbyterian Church, and earnestly resisted the attempts of a party in that body to withdraw all Christian fellowship from the Southern churches. He was the author of a long and elaborate report, adopted by the synod of Tennessee, in October, 1847, in reply to the objections of this party, and maintaining that, while humanity and religion might require that some, under favorable circumstances, should emancipate their slaves, many masters were so situated that such a course would be utterly inexpedient and unjust, and they were bound to retain them, and treat them with kindness and love. After two or three years of experience, however, he found that public opinion would not permit him to act up to his convictions of duty in the enforcement of church discipline, against those who were guilty of immoralities against their slaves, and that he was likely to be involved in complications which would be perilous. Though he urged upon the slaves the apostolic duties of ordinary forbearance and submission, instances sometimes came to his knowledge, in which a different course seemed to him quite justifiable, and where he could not withhold his views. Such expressions of opinion, though tolerated when uttered by native citizens, were not relished by those who were suspected of Northern proclivities. He, therefore, became satisfied that it was his duty to give up his pastoral relation, and although his own congregation expressed their unanimous resolution to sustain him, and offered him extraordinary inducements to continue with them, he saw no way of compliance consistent with a good conscience. Just as he had reached this conclusion, a call reached him from the First Presbyterian Church of Carlisle, which he immediately accepted. That people had heard him while on a visit north, in 1843, and now, on becoming destitute of a pastor, they invited him to settle among them. He arrived at Carlisle and commenced his ministrations there April 28, 1848, but was not installed until October 15, of the same year. His congregation, though not in ecclesiastical sympathy with the great majority of the Presbyterian Church in this region, grew in numbers and prosperity during his entire pastorate of more than twenty-eight years. He took a high rank as preacher in the synod of Pennsylvania, was more than once a candidate for the moderator's chair in the general assembly, and has served with acceptance on most of its important committees. He has been a member of eight general assemblies (besides two adjourned meetings), and has declined several invitations to prominent churches. He was especially active in efforts for the reunion of the two great branches of the Presbyterian Church, being a member of the convention of Presbyterians in Philadelphia in 1867, and of the assembly of reunion which met in New York and Pittsburgh in 1867. He was also a member of the joint committee of reconstruction for the organization of the synods and presbyteries of the reunited church. In addition to the ordinary work of a pastor, from the duties of which he has always been scrupulously careful that nothing should divert him, he has generally had in his hands such literary engagements as were consistent with it. He reads with a good degree of facility in seven different languages. In 1849, at the request of the faculty and students of Dickinson College, he supplied for one year the place made vacant by the transfer of William H. Allen, LL. D., to the presidency of Girard College, and in 1856, he, in connection with Prof. Charles E. Blumenthal, published a translation of Hase's History of the Christian Church (D. Appleton & Co., New York, pp. 720), in the composition of which he bore the largest share. For some years he contributed one article annually to the *Presbyterian Quarterly Review*, among which the most noted were two on "Abelard," two on the "Historical Development of the Doctrine of the Atonement," and one on the "Permanent in Christianity," and one article, in the *Methodist Quarterly* on "Miracles and the order of Nature." About a dozen sermons and discourses have been published by his people and his friends, as they were preached on special occasions. He was also the writer of two elaborate articles on "Federal Theology," and "Gnostics and Gnosticism," in McClintock & Strong's Encyclopedia, and in 1867 he contributed to Dr. Schaff's American edition of Lang's Commentary on the Bible, a translation with large additions of Kling's Commentary on Second Corinthians. Notwithstanding these engagements, Dr. Wing's health became so completely restored that, during his long pastorate, he lost on account of illness not more than six Sabbaths. In 1869, however, his congregation perceived such tokens of impaired energy, that they allowed him a suspension of labor for six months, during which time they employed an assistant for the performance of his work. On two different occasions after this, as he found his strength giving way, he requested either an entire or partial dissolution of his pastorate, but could not obtain the acquiescence of his people. It was not until July 18, 1875, that, after a laborious service as a commissioner to the general assembly, his congregation consented that he might henceforth take the place of Pastor Emeritus; but after some consultation and experience he repeated his request for a complete dissolution of the pastoral relation. This was finally acquiesced in by the people, October 17, 1875, and was complied with by the presbytery, October 23, 1875, though for some years a partial salary was continued to him. A severe illness in the autumn of that year proved that this action had been taken none too soon; but on his recovery his health began to improve, until, finally, he has been restored nearly to his earlier vigor. His subsequent life has been almost as active as at any other period. On the Sabbath he ordinarily preaches in some of the neighboring congregations, or in his former pulpit. He enters with ardor into most of the theological discussions and practical measures of the day, in which he almost uniformly advocates the side of real progress. He is especially fond of exegetical and historical investigations. He has in manuscript extended comments upon almost the entire Greek Testament, and has become thoroughly familiar with the "History of Cumberland Valley." In 1879 he contributed the principal part of the "History of Cumberland County" (published by J. D. Scott, Philadelphia, quarto, pp. 283), and recently he has published two editions of a historical and genealogical register of the Wing family in America. (Carlisle and New York, 8vo and quarto, pp. 332 and 500.)

CHARLES R. WOODWARD, of the firm of Woodward, Graybill & Co., millers. Carlisle, is a native of Pennsylvania, born in York, York County, December 8, 1844, a son of Capt. Robert C. and Sarah E. (Spangler) Woodward, the former a native of Newburyport, Mass., and a son of Capt. Salem Woodward, of that place, a sea-captain, who ran a line of ships from Charleston, S. C., to Liverpool, England. Robert C. Woodward sailed with his father for a number of years as a sea captain and as captain on the Mississippi River from New Orleans to Cincinnati. He located in York County, where he married Miss Sarah E. Spangler, and engaged in the grocery business at York until 1850, excepting three years spent in California, prospecting, just prior to 1850, when he came to Carlisle and formed the company of Woodward & Schmidt, forwarding and commission agents, and erected the building now occupied by his son, Charles R. Robert C. died at Carlisle in August, 1877, and his widow in November, 1885. Their five children were George (deceased), Ellen (deceased), Charles R., Robert S. (deceased); and Florence W., wife of the Rev. J. Hepbron Hargis, of Philadelphia. The parents were identified with the First Presbyterian Church. Charles R. was but six years old when his parents came from York. He attended the high school and Dickinson College, of Carlisle, assisting his father as clerk until 1864, when he became a partner of his father, with whom he remained until 1876, when he purchased his father's interest, and became associated with John G. Bobb, as a partner of the firm of Woodward & Bobb. This firm continued until 1882, when Mr. John Graybill became a partner in the business, and one year later the present firm was established (Mr. Bobb's interest being purchased by Woodward, Graybill & Co.). In April, 1870, Mr. Woodward married Miss Jessie V. Elliott, who was born in Wyoming Territory (the first white child born in that Territory), a daughter of Gen. W. L. and Hattie (Jones) Elliott, of Cincinnati, now living in San Francisco. To Mr. and Mrs. Woodward five children were born: Florence V., Jessie E., Robert C., Sarah E. and William G. The mother is a member of the Episcopal Church. Mr. Woodward is a member of Carlisle Council, No. 502, Royal Arcanum. He is a director of the Carlisle Deposit Bank, treasurer of the Carlisle Land Association, and is one of the enterprising business men of Carlisle. In 1882 he and his partner built the Carlisle roller flouring-mill, a three-story brick building, in which are fourteen pairs of rollers, being otherwise fully equipped.

WILLIAM H. WOODWARD, general superintendent of the Gettysburg & Harrisburg Railway, and treasurer of the South Mountain Railway & Mining Company, and of the South Mountain Iron & Mining Company, office at Pine Grove Furnace, and residence at Carlisle, is a native of Chester County, Penn. Soon after his birth the family moved to the city of Philadelphia, where he attended the public schools until thirteen years of age, when he began clerking in a drug store, in which he remained until fifteen; at that early age, September 3, 1861, he enlisted in Company A, Sixty-seventh Regiment Pennsylvania Volunteer Infantry; served through entire war, and was mustered out July 15, 1865, as sergeant-major of the regiment. The regiment to which he belonged was attached to the Second Brigade, Second Division, Sixteenth Army Corps of the command, most of the time. He was taken prisoner at Winchester, Va., June 15, 1865, from which time until August following he spent in Libby and Belle Isle prisons, when he was paroled and sent to Annapolis, Md., and soon after joined his regiment, this being his only absence from the regiment during the war. He was mustered out of the service at the close of the war, and returned to Philadelphia; then went to Plymouth, Luzerne County, where he became employed as book-keeper and paymaster for J. C. Fuller, of the Shawnee Coal Mines, which position he held until 1871, when he was elected treasurer, and subsequently, in 1877, general superintendent of the Gettysburg & Harrisburg Railway. In 1870 Mr. Woodward was married to Miss Emma McGee, of Philadelphia, who died in 1881, and to them were born one son and three daughters: Dora F., Bessie A., Harry F. and Emma E. B. In February, 1883, he then married Miss Annie M. Bixler, of Carlisle, a daughter of Joshua P. and Julia (Beetem) Bixler, former of the firm of Saxon & Bixler. Mrs. Woodward is a member of the Lutheran Church. Mr. Woodward is Past Master of Cumberland and Star Lodge, No. 97, Carlisle; Past High Priest of St. John's Chapter and St. John's Commandery, No. 3, Carlisle; is also a member of Capt. Colwell Post, G. A. R., of Carlisle.

JOHN ZINN, county clerk and recorder, Carlisle, is a native of Lancaster County, Penn.; was born in what is now Rhineholtz Station, February 26, 1830, a son of Isaac and Catherine (Spotz) Zinn, former born in Lancaster County, and latter born just across the county line in Berks County. Isaac Zinn in early life worked at coopering; in April, 1834, he, with his family, came to Cumberland County and settled on a farm near Barnitz Mill. in Dickinson Township. They were the parents of six children: John, the eldest; Eliza, wife of Jacob Hess, a resident of Penn Township; Hannah, deceased at the age of three years; Catherine, wife of William W. Spandler, a farmer of Mifflin Township; William, who married Jane Fickes, and resides in Cumberland County; and George, who married Lucy Straw, and resides on a farm near Centerville. John worked on the farm, attending and teaching school until his marriage, September 16, 1858, with Miss Mary R. Spangler, who was born at Mount Hope, Cumberland County, a daughter of William and Nancy (Sheaffer) Spangler. Mr. Zinn, after his marriage, settled on his father's farm in Penn Township, and engaged in agriculture for three years; then for four years was occupied in teaching school after which, for thirteen years, he was engaged as a farmer in Cumberland County. During two years he drove stage from Carlisle to Shippensburg, residing at Centerville. Subsequently, and until he was elected clerk and recorder of Cumberland County, in November, 1884, he was occupied in keeping a warehouse at Longsdorf Station one year and a half, farming four years, and carrying on a general store at Hockersville. To his marriage with Miss Spangler eight children were born: Anna M. C., wife of Parker H. Trego, of Carlisle; George B. McClellan, who married Alice Coover, and resides in Cumberland County; Philip S., who married Miss Sarah Barrick, and is a resident of Cumberland County: William I. N.; Thomas E. E ; John W., who died young; Harry C. S. and Edward C. S. The Zinns have been identified with this section of the county for many years. Jabob, the great-grandfather of John, was born in Lancaster County. His eldest son, Peter, married a Miss Swigert, and was the father of four sons and three daughters, of whom Isaac, the father of John, was one. Our subject in 1867 was elected a justice of the peace of Penn Township; was re-elected in 1872, and again in 1877, holding the office over thirteen years. He has discharged the duties of his present office with credit to himself, and to the satisfaction of his constituents. Mr. Zinn is a member of the Lutheran Church. Mrs. Zinn died September 6, 1885, a member of the Lutheran Church.

JACOB ZUG (deceased) was born near Elizabethtown, Lancaster Co., Penn., in 1793, and died March 25, 1877, aged eighty-four years, one month and thirteen days. He was a son of John and Margaret (Mohler) Zug, both of Lancaster County, Penn., and was a great-grandson of Ulric Zug, who, with his own and other Swiss families, immigrated to Pennsylvania from the Palatinate of the Lower Rhine, on the invitation of Queen Anne, renewed by George I, and encouraged by William Penn by the pledge of freedom of conscience, his ancestors having, at an early day, left Switzerland for the Palatinate on account of religious persecutions. He landed at Philadelphia September 27, 1727, and immediately settled in the northwest part of Lancaster County, in the township of Warwick, now called Penn. There he located, by warrant from the proprietary government, nearly 400 acres of land, where he and a number of his descendants lived and died. On this homestead was born, in 1731, John Zug, the fourth child of Ulric and the grandfather of Jacob Zug, the subject of this sketch. This John Zug died in 1821, aged ninety years. He was seventy two years a member, fifty-two years a minister, and forty-one years an elder or bishop in the Church of the Brethren, properly styled the German Baptist, and was one of the most faithful, devoted and honored ministers, a worthy man, highly esteemed by all who knew him. The father of Jacob Zug was the second son of the aforesaid John Zug, and was also called John. He was born on the same old homestead in Lancaster County in 1763, and died one mile east of Carlisle in 1824. In 1806 Jacob Zug came with his father to near what is now Mechanicsburg, at which time there were but three houses within the village. In 1814 they sold their farm and removed to the junction of Cedar Spring with Yellow Breeches Creek, where his father purchased a farm and mill, which property they exchanged for a farm one mile east of Carlisle. Here Jacob Zug started in life for himself, and in 1823 removed to Carlisle, where he lived until his death. He took a deep interest in politics, but was never from choice a candidate for office. In 1835, at the urgent request of some of his friends he was induced to accept the nomination for the office of county commissioner, to which he was elected at a time when his political associates were in the minority. Subsequently he was called by his fellow-citizens at different times to serve them as chief burgess and councilman. He was a man who made many warm friends, and was loved and respected by all for his manly qualities. He married Miss Elizabeth Kimmel, of Cumberland County, and to them were born five sons and one daughter, who lived to manhood and womanhood: Samuel, who resides in Detroit, Mich.; John, an attorney (deceased); Ephraim (deceased), late a merchant of Mechanicsburg; Elizabeth, now living in Carlisle; Augustus (deceased), aged twenty-seven years; Jacob T., who was a lieutenant in the Seventh Regiment Pennsylvania Reserves, and lost his right arm in the battle of Fredericksburg. The latter married Miss Annie E. Eberly, of Mechanicsburg, and to them the following children were born: Frank D., Augusta and Ray, who reside in Carlisle.

RECEIVED TOO LATE FOR INSERTION IN PROPER PLACE.

AMERICUS R. ALLEN, M. D., Carlisle, is a graduate of the University of Pennsylvania. He was born at Lee's Cross Roads, Cumberland Co., Penn., January 13, 1861, and is the eldest son of Wm. H. and Anna (Clark) Allen, who had a family of five sons and four daughters. Americus R. Allen worked at farming, and attended the common schools and the Normal at Shippensburg, Penn., until twenty-one years of age, when he was employed by the Bosler Cattle Company, and remained with this company, in Nebraska, one year. He then began the study of medicine, in the office of S. B. Keefer. A. M., M. D., Carlisle. After graduating at the university, he located in Carlisle, where he has since engaged in the practice of medicine, and enjoys the confidence and respect of all.

CHAPTER XXXIX.

BOROUGH OF MECHANICSBURG.

REV. AUGUSTUS BABB, retired clergyman, has been pastor of the Evangelical Lutheran Church, Mechanicsburg, for the past fifty-three years. His great-grandfather was born in Germany and came with his wife to America, settling in Berks County; they had four sons and three daughters, who lived to be men and women; his son, Mathias Babb, was the first to enlist in Gen. Heister's company (afterward governor of Pennsylvania). During the war of the Revolution he was a coppersmith and tinsmith; married Miss Rosanna Bierley, and had three sons and five daughters. John, the eldest, born in Reading, Penn., was also a coppersmith and tinsmith; married Miss Barbara Ann Henritze, a native of Reading, Penn. He was a member of the Lutheran, and she of the German Reformed Church. They had a family of three sons and four daughters: John, Mary, Barbara, Augustus, Sarah, Mathias and Roseanna, all born in Reading, Penn. Augustus, the subject of our sketch, was born January 19, 1810, and, when fourteen, was apprenticed to learn the cabinet-maker's trade until he was nineteen, when he entered the manual labor school at Germantown, Penn. Some fourteen months later he entered Gettysburg Gymnasium, which became a theological seminary; there he finished a regular course, and in May, 1833, was licensed to preach in Pendleton County, Va., and began his ministrations in Augusta County, Va. Four years later he came to Mechanicsburg, and two years later was appointed, by the West Pennsylvania Synod, missionary for Clearfield, Jefferson, Armstrong, Clarion and Venango Counties, holding that position four or five months, when, owing to a fall and subsequent ill health, he was appointed pastor of Blairsville, Indiana County, Church, where here mained until 1845; then returned to Mechanicsburg Church, remaining here until 1851, when he became agent for the Pennsylvania College at Gettysburg; a year later he resigned to accept the pastorship of Somerset Church, Somerset County, where he had four churches in charge. In 1856 he returned to this county and took charge of the church at Centerville until 1860, when he went to Turbotville, Northumberland Co., Penn., to preach in German and English. During a Thanksgiving sermon, after Lincoln's election, he gave offense to the Democratic brethren by saying that our form of government was a Republican form of government; so, in 1863, after the battle of Gettysburg, he took charge of his farm in Hockersville; this county, where he farmed, and preached at different places, until 1870, when he took charge of Blairsville, until 1875, when he returned to his farm, and two years later came to Mechanicsburg, where he has since resided. He married, June 27, 1833, Miss Mary A. Hoffman, a native of Franklin County, Penn., daughter of James Hoffman, a teacher. Mrs. Babb died August 11, 1838. Our subject was married, on the second occasion August 6, 1840, to Jane Logue, born in Carlisle, daughter of Joseph and Nancy Ann (Jumper) Logue, former of whom died at Fort Niagara in the United States service, September 19, 1813. Mrs. Babb died June 20, 1872. Our subject is one of the oldest ministers living. His life has always been one of activity, and through his efforts many have been brought to Christ; and his name will be handed down to posterity as one who did his duty as a Christian, a minister for the cause of Christ, and worshiper of God "who so loved the world that he gave his only begotten Son, that whosoever believed in Him should not perish but have everlasting life."

GEORGE BOBB, grocer, member of the firm of George Bobb & Son, Mechanicsburg, was born in Mechanicsburg, Penn., November 8, 1819, son of John and Margaret (Longsdorff) Bobb, old settlers of this place, where the former followed the trade of harness and saddle-making. They had eight children, four living. When George, the second child and eldest son, was thirteen years old, his father died, and his mother subsequently married Peter Baker, of Carlisle, Penn. Our subject worked during the summers, attending school winters, until he was sixteen, when he began to learn the stove and tinware trade with Jacob Rupley. Six years later he bought the tin and stove store of Robert Wilson, which he sold out in 1861 and opened a hardware store. In 1879 he sold out again and opened his present grocery. In September, 1843, Mr. Bobb was married to Miss Margaret Giffin, born in Middlesex Township, Cumberland County, daughter of Hon. James Giffin, ex-member of the Pennsylvania Legislature from this county. Mrs. Bobb died May 13, 1884, the mother of two sons, one living, James G., born in Mechanicsburg, this county, November 10, 1844, a partner with his father in the grocery store; was married to Miss Mary C. Quigley February 26, 1867, who was born May 21, 1848, in Beach Creek, Clinton

Co., Penn., daughter of Hon. Cline, ex-associate judge of Clinton County, Penn., and Agnes (Thompson) Quigley, old settlers of Clinton County, Penn. Mr. and Mrs. James G. Bobb have had six children, five living: Agnes Q., George W., Mary C., James G., Jr., and Anna M. The subject of our sketch was married on second occasion, November 16, 1884, to Mrs. O. Grace Schock, born in Knox County, Ill., in 1834, daughter of Dr. Charles and Eliza (Morris) Hansford, natives of Virginia. Mr. George Bobb was elected county treasurer by the people of Cumberland County in 1871 for one term. He has held various local offices of trust in Mechanicsburg. He and his son are members of Eureka lodge, No. 302, A. F. & A. M., Samuel C. Perkins Chapter, No. 209, and St. John's Commandery, No. 8, Carlisle; Mechanicsburg Lodge, No. 215, I. O. O. F.; and George Bobb is a member of Wildey Encampment, No. 29, Mechanicsburg. They are representative business men of this city, and carry a full and complete stock of fine groceries, glass, queensware and woodenware.

ELI B. BRANDT, physician and mayor, Mechanicsburg, was born on the old homestead farm of his father and grandfather in Monroe Township, five miles south of Mechanicsburg, April 16, 1829, son of George and Barbara (Beelman) Brandt, the former of whom was born on the old home farm in Monroe Township, and died in 1875, aged eighty-four; and the latter, born in Upper Allen Township, this county, died in 1835, a member of the Lutheran Church. They had a family of four sons and three daughters, of whom Eli B. is the youngest. Our subject worked on his father's farm, attending and teaching school during winters until he was twenty-one, when he began the study of medicine with Dr. L. H. Leaher, of Churchtown, Monroe Township, and graduated from the Jefferson Medical College, Philadelphia, Penn., in 1855. He located first at New Cumberland, this county, thence went to Shiremanstown and to Mechanicsburg in 1868, where he has since engaged in the practice of his profession. Dr. Brandt married at Harrisburg, Penn., February 12, 1856, Miss Margaret C. Mateer, who was born in Lower Allen Township, this county, daughter of William and Mary (Porter) Mateer, both born and raised in Cumberland County, Penn. Dr. and Mrs. Brandt have had seven children, two now living: Mary, wife of Oliver Yohn, dealer in pianos, organs and other musical instruments; and Arthur D., unmarried and remaining with his parents. Dr. Brandt enlisted as surgeon of the Thirty-first Pennsylvania Volunteers May 29, 1863, and was mustered out in August, 1864. He was elected president, in 1861, of the Allen and East Pennsborough Society for the recovery of stolen horses and mules and the detection of thieves; re-elected in 1869, and has held the office ever since. He is a member of the Cumberland County Medical Society, of which he has been president and secretary, and is also a member of the State Medical Society, and of the American Medical Association. He has lived to see Cumberland County and towns undergo many interesting and important changes. His grandfather, John Brandt, was among the earliest settlers of Cumberland County. The family is of German descent. The Doctor stands high in the estimation of all who know him. He was elected mayor in 1878-79-80, and again in 1884 and 1885. He was a delegate to the national convention at Chicago in 1868, and a delegate to Philadelphia in 1872. He was nominated Republican State senator of the Twentieth Senatorial District in 1874.

LEWIS BRICKER, retired farmer, Mechanicsburg, was born in Newville, this county, August 6, 1812, a grandson of David Bricker, a native of Lancaster County, Penn., who married a Miss Erbe and moved to Newville in 1806, where he kept a hotel and died. He had five children: Jacob; Elizabeth, wife of Henry Gebler; David; Mary, wife of Peter Dock; and John. Jacob, the eldest, was born in Cocalico Township, Lancaster Co., Penn., December 25, 1781, and married Miss Mary, daughter of Martin and Mary (Cap) Fry. He was a miller at Newville, and afterward built the Silver Spring mills, in Silver Spring Township; he died April 3, 1868; his wife was a member of the Lutheran Church. To this couple were born five children, one now living, Lewis. Lewis Bricker, the subject of this sketch, moved with his parents to Silver Spring Township, this county, when nearly a year old, and, when he was old enough, worked on his father's farm and in the mill here until his marriage with his first cousin, Miss Elizabeth Fry, who was born January 1, 1815, in Cocalico Township, Lancaster County, daughter of Peter and Sarah (Hauck) Fry. After his marriage, Lewis Bricker settled on his farm in Hampden Township, this county. Mrs. Bricker was a member of the Lutheran Church. Of the twelve children born to this union nine are living: Sarah, wife of John Smith, a baker and grocer of Princeton, Ill.; Martin, married to Miss Martha Mosser, resides on a farm near Camp Hill, this county; Mary, wife of George Martin, resides on a farm near Don Cameron, Perry Co., Penn.; Elizabeth, wife of Andrew Clark, on a farm in Silver Spring Township, this county; Jacob, married to Miss Susan Long (they reside on the old family farm in Hampden Township, this county); Theresa, wife of Franklin Fry, who works in the bessemer steel works at Steelton, Penn.; Clara, wife of Dr. John Sibert, of Steelton, Penn.; Ida, wife of Thomas L. Long, a brick manufacturer at Oskaloosa, Iowa, and Rebecca, wife of John Becker, dentist, Steelton, Penn. Mrs. Bricker died November 2, 1874, and Mr. Bricker then married for his second wife Mrs. Emeline Smick, widow of George Smick, a farmer, who died March 7, 1866. Mr. and Mrs. Smick had two children: one son, John W., born December 16, 1852, is a miller in Adams County, married to Miss Hannah H., daughter of Absalom and Sarah (Plank) Asper. Mr. and Mrs. Bricker are members of the Lutheran Church. He is one of the few old settlers remaining, and has lived to see this county undergo many interesting and important changes. He stands high in the estimation of all, and is a descendant of one of the oldest families in Pennsylvania.

ABNER C. BRINDLE, cashier of the First National Bank, Mechanicsburg, is a descendant of one of the oldest families of Cumberland County and Pennsylvania. His grandfather, George Brindle, who was born in Lancaster County, Penn., came to this county when a young man, and was married here to Miss Elizabeth Bricker. They had six children: Susan, John, George, Peter, Elizabeth and Solomon. John, the second born, married Miss Mary Baker. He and his wife were members of the Dunkard Church. They had a family of twelve children, eleven now living: John, Daniel (deceased), George, Elizabeth, Peter, Elias, Jesse, Mary, Leah, Rebecca, Susan and Abner C. The subject of our sketch, the youngest in the family, was born six miles southwest of Mechanicsburg, in Monroe Township, September 17, 1837. He worked on his father's farm, attending and teaching school, and acting as clerk in a store until 1863, when he was employed as clerk in a wholesale tobacco house in Philadelphia, remaining in the tobacco house and as clerk in a dry goods store until February, 1864, when he was appointed teller in the First National Bank at Carlisle, Penn., and in February, 1865, was elected teller of the First National Bank of Mechanicsburg. In November, 1868, he was elected cashier and he has held that position ever since. In 1862 he responded to a call from the governor of Pennsylvania, as a member of the Pennsylvania State Militia, and in 1863 enlisted in the Forty-ninth Regiment, Pennsylvania State Militia, under Col. John Murphy, and was mustered out at the expiration of the company's term of enlistment, at Philadelphia, in September, 1863. Mr. Brindle married, December 3, 1868, Miss Mary E. Egbert, born in Perry County, Penn., daughter of I. R. and Sarah (Carver) Egbert, the former a retired merchant, of Carlisle, both natives of Montgomery County, Penn. To our subject and wife have been born two children, one living, Charles E., born in Mechanicsburg September 30, 1870. Mrs. Brindle is a member of the Methodist Episcopal Church. Our subject is a great-grandson of Peter Bricker, born in Lancaster County, Penn., in 1735, and married to Miss Mary Barr; settled in Cumberland County, Penn., in an early day; he was a son of Peter Bricker, who came to this country from Switzerland in the early part of the eighteenth century.

JOHN COOVER (deceased) as one of the early settlers deserves more than a passing notice. Prominent in church, society and business, he and his descendants have always been people of note. He was one of the founders of Mechanicsburg, and was descended from the German family named "Kobar"—afterward changed to Coover—who immigrated to this country as early as 1760. Soon after this date his grandfather, Gideon Coover, bought a large tract of land, being of the "Manor on Conodoguinet," situated by the Cedar Spring, south of Shiremanstown, Cumberland Co., Penn. One of his sons, Hon. George Coover, was married October 22, 1764, to Elizabeth Mohler, by Rev. Nicholas Hornell, of York, minister of the High German Lutheran Church, of which both were members. They lived on the plantation at Cedar Spring, and had five sons and four daughters: George, Jr., Henry, Elizabeth, Susannah, Catherine, Anne, Michael, Jacob and John. The subject of this sketch was born February 22, 1787. His early life was spent on his father's farm, where he attended such schools as his day afforded. About 1816 or 1817 he came to Mechanicsburg, and, with Adam Reigel as partner (which partnership was subsequently dissolved), opened the first important store in that place, becoming thereafter a successful merchant; continuing therein engaged until 1849, when he disposed of his stock and retired from active business life, always, however, taking a keen and decided interest in the public affairs of the borough, State and Nation. Some years previous to this time he purchased a large tract of land, lying immediately south of the borough of Mechanicsburg—bounded by the middle of Simpson Street—which since his decease has been incorporated into the borough, and laid out by his heirs, into town lots, with fine wide streets, and being slightly elevated, is being rapidly built up, and bids fair to become the most beautiful part of the town. On February 4, 1819, he was married to Miss Salome Keller, who was born September 13, 1792, and was the daughter of Martin Keller, who landed in Baltimore, Md., in 1786, emigrating from the Canton of Basle, Switzerland. About 1800 he removed to Cumberland County and purchased a large tract of land in Silver Spring Township, known as "Barbace," situated one-half mile north of Mechanicsburg, which is still owned by his descendants. The children of John Coover were six in number—one son, who died in infancy, and five daughters: Susan K. (widow of Philip H. Long), Sarah (married to Ephraim Zug, who died in May, 1862, afterward married to William H. Oswald, who died in January, 1884), Marianne (wife of Richard T. Hummel, Hummelstown, Dauphin Co., Penn.; A. Elizabeth (married to Levi Kauffman, now deceased) and J. Emeline (widow of Daniel Coover). John Coover died May 13, 1862, and his widow January 3, 1883, and they were both buried in the old family grave-yard at Barbace, by the side of Martin Keller and Martin Keller's wife and mother. The old homestead built by John Coover, situated on the northeast corner of Main and Frederick Streets, Mechanicsburg, and in which he and his wife lived to the date of their death, is still occupied by one of his daughters. Mr. Coover was a quiet, unassuming man, one who made many friends, and of wide influence in his church and society. He was a great reader, and had a fine mind and tenacious memory. His name was a synonym for honesty and integrity, and from time to time he filled the various municipal offices; was for many years justice of the peace; and so great was the confidence reposed in him that he was constantly sought after to act as executor and administrator in settling the estates of decedents, and many were the children to whom he was guardian—as many as 100, it is believed. A consistent and leading member of the German Baptist or Dunkard Church, he was good to the poor, a kind husband and indulgent father. Generous to a fault, kind-hearted and true, he was beloved by all who knew him, and his memory is deeply cherished for his sterling worth and Christian character, of which his descendants may well be proud.

JACOB H. DEARDORFF, physician, Mechanicsburg, was born on his father's farm in Washington Township, York Co., Penn., February 4, 1846; son of Joseph F. and Lovinia (Hoover) Deardorff; the former, a farmer, born in Adams County; the latter a native of York County, Penn.; they were members of the Lutheran Church. Of their eight children (five sons and three daughters) Jacob H. is the youngest. He attended school during winter and worked on his father's farm in summer until he was eighteen, when he began teaching and at the same time attending school. He graduated from Fairbanks Business College and the Hahnemann Medical College of Philadelphia. March 9, 1876, he located in Middletown, Dauphin Co., Penn., and after two years and a half he came to Mechanicsburg, where he has practiced medicine ever since. The Doctor was united in marriage, December 26, 1867, with Miss Mary A. Stouffer, born near Andersontown, York Co., Penn., daughter of Washington and Sarah (Kline) Stouffer. The Doctor and wife have three children: Clarence M., born in York County, Penn.; Raymond P., born in Lisburn, this county; Gertrude F., born in Slatington, Lehigh Co., Penn. Dr. Deardorff is a member of the A. O. of M., Mechanicsburg. He has a first-class practice, and stands high in the estimation and confidence of all who know him. His success as a physician since he located in Mechanicsburg, has been most satisfactory to himself and his patients. The Doctor's great-grandfather and grandmother came from Germany to Pennsylvania. His father is still living at the advanced age of eighty-one and resides near East Berlin, Adams Co., Penn.

LEVI F. EBERLY, of Levi F. Eberly & Sons, wholesale and retail dealers in all kinds of lumber, sash, doors, blinds, etc., corner of High Street and the railroad, Mechanicsburg, was born on the old family farm in Upper Allen Township, Cumberland Co., Penn., May 6, 1818, son of David and Catharine (Frankenberger) Eberly, the former born in Lancaster County, Penn., November 9, 1781, and died in 1861; the latter born in this county in 1791, and died in 1869; both members of the Mennonite Church. They had three sons and six daughters who lived to be men and women. Levi F., the eldest son and fourth child, assisted his father on the farm until his marriage, October 24, 1839, with Miss Eliza Shuey, who was born in Lebanon County, Penn., daughter of Christian and Magdalena (Miley) Shuey, natives of that county. After his marriage Mr. Eberly engaged in farming in Lebanon County for five years, when he sold out and purchased a farm in Upper Allen Township, this county. In 1859 he came to Mechanicsburg, and in 1861 established his present business. Mr. and Mrs. Eberly are members of the United Brethren Church. They have four sons: W. Harrison, David H., Edward M. and Ira S. Of these, W. Harrison, born near Mechanicsburg November 16, 1840, at sixteen began teaching school, and two years later entered the Cumberland Valley Institute; remained here, and in the Otterbein University, at Westerville, Ohio, for two years; was then appointed teller of the Merkel, Mumma & Co. Bank, holding this position through the various changes of this bank until 1864, when he was appointed clerk in the quartermaster's department for the Government until the close of the war. In 1876 he was one of the projectors of the West End Railway, which owned and operated the narrow gauge railroad that ran outside of the Centennial grounds, so familiar to all visitors to that exposition. At the close of the Centennial, he and others established the "Dime Express" in Philadelphia, and in 1878 he sold out and engaged in his present business with his father and brothers. W. Harrison Eberly was married, May 25, 1863, to Mary C. Power, born in Perry County, Penn., daughter of John and Elizabeth (Barns) Power. David H. Eberly was born October 14, 1842; married Miss Kate A. Waidley, born in Cumberland County, Penn. Edward M., born April 1, 1845, married Miss Margaret Zacharias, also a native of this county. Ira S., born December 8, 1847, married Miss Laura Maloy. Levi F. Eberly & Sons do an average yearly business of $40,000. Our subject was one of the original members that organized what is now the First National Bank of Mechanicsburg, and is a director in the same. The family is of German descent, and came to Pennsylvania at a very early date.

SAMUEL EBERLY, retired lumber merchant, director of the First National Bank, Mechanicsburg, is a representative of one of the oldest families in Cumberland County. He was born on the old family farm in Monroe Township, February 24, 1822, son of Samuel and Elizabeth (Hocker) Eberly, former born on the same farm in Monroe Township, and latter born in Harrisburg, Penn.; she was a granddaughter of Andrew Sholl, who emigrated from Germany in 1745, and settled near Richland Station, in what is now Lebanon County, but was then (1745) Lancaster County. Samuel Eberly, Sr., father of our subject, was a farmer in early life, but later became a machinist and helped build the first Potter threshing machine in the year 1828 or 1829. He died in 1845, aged fifty-seven years; his widow died in 1861, aged seventy-five, a member of the German Reformed Church. They had eight children, four daughters and three sons living to be men and women. Samuel, who is the eldest son, attended school until he was twelve years old, when he engaged in farming until he was seventeen, when he came to Mechanicsburg and learned the carpenter trade, which he worked at here three years, afterward assisted his father in the manufacture of threshing machines until 1846, when he formed a partnership with Abraham Staufer and built a foundry. He engaged in that business until 1854, when he sold out to his partner and erected a saw-mill, soon after adding a planing-mill, forming a partnership with Frederick Seidle and Benjamin Haverstick, of Mechanicsburg. In 1862 he closed out the mill. Mr. Eberly then served in the army bridge corps as a carpenter in the Army of the Potomac for three months; then returned to Mechanicsburg and bought and sold old iron until 1870, when he and Samuel Hinkle engaged in the lumber business at Rowlesburg, W. Va. Five years later they bought a saw-mill at Rowlesburg, and took into partnership John M. Senseman, under the firm name of Eberly, Hinkle & Co., and this business they continued until November, 1884, when Mr. Eberly sold out his interest to Hinkle, Senseman and his nephew, John A. Hosteller. January 24, 1850, our subject married Miss Rebecca Brown, born in Adams County, Penn., but who moved to North Middleton Township, this county, with her parents, John and Susannah (Krysher) Brown. Mr. and Mrs. Eberly are members of the Church of God. They had one son, Albert, who died in infancy. Mr. Eberly is a member of the I. O. O. F., No. 215 Mechanicsburg Lodge. He has lived to see this county undergo many interesting and important changes; for when he came to Mechanicsburg, it was but a small place, and his foundry was the first manufactory here. He is purely a self-made man, learning early in life to depend on his own resources. His success has been the result of a long life of untiring energy and pluck, combined with strict integrity and honor.

AUSTIN G. EBERLY, of Eberly & Orris, manufacturers of wheels and wheel material, and all kinds of hardwood lumber, Mechanicsburg, is a native of this county, born in Hampden Township, three miles north of Mechanicsburg, February 1, 1850, son of John and Barbara (Shelly) Eberly, both natives of this county. John Eberly, a farmer, a member of the Methodist Church, died in 1883, aged seventy-one years; his widow, a member of Messiah Church, is still living; they were the parents of six children, five living: Benjamin, a traveling salesman, with headquarters at Mechanicsburg; Daniel W., a grocer of Mechanicsburg; Anna E., widow of Jacob T. Zug, residing at Carlisle, Penn.; Austin G., Lizzie B., wife of John B. Uhrich, died in 1880; John M., treasurer of the Columbus Wheel and Bending Works, Ohio. Austin G. Eberly remained on the farm, attending school winters, until he was sixteen, when he clerked for four years in the grocery store of his brother in Mechanicsburg, and then bought his brother out and conducted the business alone until 1880, when he formed a partnership with another brother, John M., in the wheel and wheel material manufactory; his brother sold out to Adam Orris in 1884, and the firm has since been Eberly & Orris. Austin G. Eberly married, October 5, 1876, Miss Lizzie A. Coover, a native of Dunkirk, N. Y., daughter of Jacob H. and Jane (Sarvent) Coover, the former a native of this county, the latter of Piermont, Rockland Co., N. Y. To this union have been born five children: Paul C., Austin C., Richard C., Olive C. and Ira C. Paul C., Richard C. and Olive C. died of scarlet fever in the winter of 1884-85. Mr. Eberly is a member of Eureka Lodge, No. 302, A. F. & A. M., Samuel C. Perkins Chapter, No. 209, R. A. M., St. John's Commandery, K. T., No. 8, at Carlisle. He has passed the chairs in both the Blue Lodge and Chapter. Mr. and Mrs. Eberly are members of the Church of God, Mechanicsburg. He is one of the enterprising representative business men of the place, and one of the leading manufacturers in the valley. His grandfather, Benjamin Eberly, a farmer, married Elizabeth Kauffman. They were of German descent, and early settlers of Pennsylvania.

WILLIAM ECKELS, retired postmaster, Mechanicsburg. The Eckels family is one of the earliest of those sturdy pioneer Scotch-Irish Presbyterians, who, driven by religious persecution from the North of Ireland, were among the first to seek new homes and freedom for religious worship in this valley. Francis Eckels, Sr., came at a very early date to this country, and settled in western Pennsylvania. Francis Eckels, Jr., his son, was born it is said, at sea, during the passage over. He married Mabel Flemming, of Cumberland County, and died in August, 1814, at the age of sixty-five. Samuel Eckels, his son, and father of our subject, settled in Allen Township, about three miles south of Mechanicsburg. He was twice married: first to Agnes Monasmith, by whom four children were born: Mary and Martha (twins), James and William. By his second wife, *nee* Mary Cooper, there were Robert, William, Nancy, Elizabeth, Samuel and Margareta. Willaim Eckels, the subject of this sketch, was born on his father's farm, in what is now Upper Allen Township, January 15, 1817. He learned the trade of cooper, and at twenty-five located at Cedar Springs, now Milltown, where he took charge of the cooper shops of George Heck, distiller and miller. In the spring of 1846 he came to Mechanicsburg. In 1853 he was appointed postmaster by President Pierce, which position he held for a period of five years. He afterward erected a number of houses in Mechanicsburg, where he is now living in retirement and comfort. December 24, 1846, he married Miss Sarah A. Proctor, born in Carlisle, this county, November 4, 1820, daughter of John and Mary H. (Officer) Proctor. Mr. and Mrs. Eckels had six children, three of whom are living: John P., married to Miss Anna Hurst, now in the hardware business in Decatur, Ill.; George Morris, physician, engaged with his brother, Walter L. (the youngest son) in the drug business in Mechanicsburg. George Morris Eckels, M. D., was born in Mechanicsburg, Penn., April 29, 1857. He graduated at the College of Pharmacy, in Philadelphia, in March, 1879; then returned to Mechanicsburg, where, in connection with his brother, Walter L., he purchased the drug store of his old employer, Mr. Bridgeford, and established the present firm of the Eckels Bros. In January, 1883, Dr. Eckels was elected transcribing clerk of the House of Representatives at Harrisburg, which position he held during the session. In September of that year he entered the medical department of the University of Pennsylvania at Philadelphia, from which he graduated May 1, 1885, and afterward commenced the practice of his profession at Mechanicsburg.

GEORGE MAFFLIN DALLAS ECKELS, teacher, Mechanicsburg, a member of the Pennsylvania Legislature, is a native of Cumberland County, born near New Kingston, December 23, 1844, son of Nathaniel H. and Margaret (Williams) Eckels, natives of this county and members of New Kingston Lutheran Church. Nathaniel H. Eckels, a farmer by occupation, taught school when a young man; served as county commissioner of this county, 1859-61. He is a son of Hon. Francis L. and Isabella (Clendenin) Eckels, the former of whom was elected, by the people of Cumberland County, representative to the Legislature in 1840; he was also a farmer and justice of the peace, and a descendant of the hardy Scotch-Irish Presbyterians who, driven from the North of Ireland by religious persecutions, sought homes in America and settled in Pennsylvania. The subject of our sketch is the second son and child in the family of five girls and two boys that lived to be men and women. His life, until sixteen, was passed on the farm, and in attending school, winters; he then entered Millersville Normal School, where he remained three terms; then taught school in this county for two winters, and was subsequently principal of the Wickersham Academy at Marietta, Penn., for a year, when he returned to Mechanicsburg, and taught in the public school here. In 1878 he formed a partnership with W. H. Humer, in a general store at New Kingston, but sold out his interest to his partner in 1882. He was elected Democratic representative to the Legislature by the people of Cumberland County March, 1882, re-elected in 1884, and is the present incumbent. He served on the committees of ways and means, general judiciary, education, constitutional reform, agriculture and elections. He has taught two terms in the Cumberland Valley State Normal School, located at Shippensburg, Penn., and at present holds the chair of pedagogics and general history in that institution. Mr. Eckels was married, June 6, 1871, to Miss Anna Humer, born in Silver Spring Township, this county, daughter of Daniel and Jane (Brownawell) Humer, also natives of Cumberland County. To this union have been born three children: Minnie G., George H. and Nathaniel O. Mr. Eckels and wife are members of the Lutheran Church, of the Sunday-school of which he has been superintendent for ten years.

WILLIAM H. ECKELS, Jr., proprietor of a general grocery and provision store on West Main Street, Mechanicsburg, was born on his father's farm, on the State road leading to Harrisburg, Silver Spring Township, this county, January 5, 1820. His grandfather, Nathaniel Eckels, a son of Francis Eckels, was born on the sea while his parents were coming to America; they were Scotch-Irish Presbyterians, who, on account of religious oppression, were driven out of the North of Ireland, and were among those hardy pioneers who sought homes in America; they landed at Baltimore, Md., and settled in western Pennsylvania. Nathaniel Eckels was born in 1744, and died in 1830, in the eighty-sixth year of his age; he had two sons: William and Francis, born near Carlisle, this county. William first married Miss Rebecca Huston, born in Silver Spring Township, this county, daughter of Jonathan and Margaret Huston, of Silver Spring Township, members of the old Silver Spring Church. Mrs. Eckels died in 1820, one hour after the birth of her son, William H., and she is buried on the Pine Hill, that being connected with Silver Spring. Mrs. Eckels, her father and mother have been taken to the Silver Spring grave-yard, where they now peacefully repose. Mr. and Mrs. William Eckels were members of the old Silver Spring Presbyterian Church; they had five children—three sons and two daughters—William H. being the only one living. Mrs. William Eckels, Sr., dying in 1820, aged thirty-three, Mr. Eckels then married Miss Jane Starr, by whom he had four children, one now living, James S., an attorney in Princeton, Ill. William Eckels, Sr., married on third occasion Miss Hannah Starr, by whom he had three children, one now living, John S., residing near New Kingston, this county. The subject of this sketch remained with his father, engaged in farming until his marriage, in January, 1844, with Miss Elizabeth Adams, a native of Hampden Township, this county, a daughter of Isaac and Jane (Anderson) Adams. Some two years after his marriage he engaged in mercantile business at Sporting Hill, Hampden Township, where he remained until 1862, when he opened a general store in Hogestown. His wife died in 1866, the mother of three children, one living: Agnes, wife of Samuel Sample, employed in steel works in Steelton, Dauphin Co., Penn. He and wife were raised in Silver Spring Township; the former was born in Hampden Township. Mr. William H. Eckels, after the death of his wife, retired from business and settled on a farm near Hogestown, now owned by Mrs. Gibble. He resumed business in Hogestown, three years later, with L. B. Ewalt, and also had a branch store, two miles north of Huston's mills in Silver Spring Township. In April, 1881, Mr. Eckels came to Mechanicsburg and formed his late partnership with Andrew O. Sample and established the business. This partnership was dissolved by mutual agreement, Mr. Sample taking the entire stock, and Mr. Eckels opening his present place of business, where he has succeeded in building up a fair trade. Mr. Eckels married, in June, 1881, Mrs. Jennie Armstrong, born in Silver Spring Township, this county, daughter of William and Rebecca Hershman, and to this union have been born three children: Minnie, Blanch and Olive. (Mrs. Eckels had two children by her first husband: Charles S., clerking for our subject, and Clara.) Mrs. Eckels is a member of the Evangelical Church. Mr. Eckels is an enterprising, representative business man and citizen. He has been a member of the board of trustees of the Presbyterian Church of Silver Spring Township for twenty-five years.

JOSEPH ELCOCK, retired merchant, Mechanicsburg, has been identified with Mechanicsburg since the fall of 1866. He was born on the old homestead farm of his father near the "Half Way House," in Warrington Township, York Co., Penn., November 13, 1813; son of Richard and Mary (Wagoner) Elcock. Richard Elcock was born in Ireland and came alone to America when nineteen years old, settling in York County, Penn.; was a weaver by trade, but followed farming in York County, where he was married, and lived to be seventy-two years old; his widow lived to be about seventy-four; they were Presbyterians. They had five sons and two daughters. Joseph, the youngest, attended school and worked on his father's farm until he was sixteen, when he went to what is now Franklingtown, York Co., Penn., where he learned the tailor's trade. Three years later he started West on foot, and was gone twenty weeks. Settlements were few and far between, and Mr. Elcock went as far as Oberlin, which was then a town three years old. To give some idea of his pluck as a boy, he cleared $9 a month while gone by working at his trade, buying and selling watches, etc. He returned home and worked at his trade in York and Cumberland Counties, but subsequently managed his father's farm until the spring of 1838, when he took charge of the "Half Way House," owned by his father, which stood on the old York road between York and Carlisle. Our subject was married here, October 10, 1838, to Miss Elizabeth Stroninger, who was born in York County, Penn., daughter of Daniel Stroninger. Mr. and Mrs. Elcock left the hotel in 1840, and moved to their farm near Mount Pleasant, where Mrs. Elcock died September 9, 1850. To this union were born six children: Mary A., wife of David Biddle, a merchant of Mechanicsburg, a member of the firm of T. J. Elcock & Biddle; Jacob R., who resides in Kansas, married to Miss Christianna, daughter of Daniel Kahm; John, engaged in the manufactory at Bement, Ill., married to Miss Ferrins; Theodore, unmarried, traveling in the West; Thomas J., of T. J. Elcock & Biddle, merchants, Mechanicsburg; Eliza J., wife of David Myers, a farmer residing near Mount Pleasant, York Co., Penn. On January 1, 1852, Joseph Elcock, our subject, married Miss Mary Branamon, born near Bowmansdale, Cumberland Co., Penn., daughter of Jacob and Mary (Ginter) Branamon. Mr. Branamon was a miller and farmer, and he and his wife were old settlers of York County, Penn., members of the Church of God. Mr. and Mrs. Elcock have had four children, two living: Lillie, wife of Samuel Hauck, a hardware merchant and manufacturer, a member of the firm of Seefert & Hauck, Mechanicsburg, Penn.; Samantha Lizzie, born February 20, 1854, died August 13, 1879; Sarah Ellen, born September 4, 1858, died March 29, 1881; and Anna F., residing at home with her parents. Mr. and Mrs. Joseph Elcock have been members of the Church of God for the past forty-four years. Our subject remained on his farm in York County, engaged in pottery manufacturing and farming until 1855, when he opened a store in Mount Pleasant, and ran this in connection with his farm and pottery until 1866, when he came to Mechanicsburg and engaged in mercantile trade. From 1875 to 1878 he conducted a furniture store. He engaged in the plow manufacturing business in 1878, and patented the Cumberland Valley Plow, and also the "Self-sharpening Cumberland Valley Plow," which business he continued until June, 1883, when he sold out to the present manufacturer, Robert Shapley. Mr. Elcock helped organize the Second National Bank of Mechanicsburg, and is still a director of this bank. He is purely a self-made, practical man, full of activity and life. He never used tobacco in any form, and was never under the influence of liquor. When a boy he drove teams from his father's farm, in York County, to Baltimore, Md., hauling flour to merchants in that city (this was before the railroads were built). Mr. Elcock is of Irish and German descent; his mother's people came from Germany to America in an early day.

JACOB EMMINGER, retired farmer, Mechanicsburg, was born near Quincy, Washington Township, Franklin Co., Penn., October 21, 1816, son of David and Magdalena (Miller) Emminger, natives of Silver Spring Township, this county, and Washington Township, Franklin Co. Penn., respectively, and parents of ten children. Jacob, the second son and third child, was ten years old when he came with his parents to Silver Spring Township, this county, where he worked on his father's farm, attending school during winters. He was married on the old farm, January 2, 1840, to Miss Sarah Lehn, a native of Silver Spring Township, this county, daughter of David and Christina (Barnhart) Lehn. After his marriage Mr. Emminger farmed in Silver Spring Township until 1861, when he bought his present place in Upper Allen Township, where he remained until 1869 and then moved to Mechanicsburg and purchased his home on the corner of Market and Green Streets. To Mr. and Mrs. Emminger were born six children, four now living: Susannah E. (wife of Jacob D. Ruffensberger, a music dealer in Mechanicsburg), Mary C. (wife of John C. Bowman, justice of the peace and merchant in Mechanicsburg), Naomi J. (wife of Henry Hertzler, a farmer in Upper Allen Township), Martin L. (who resides at Yonkers, N. Y., a grocer and merchant, married to Miss Mary J., daughter of Dr. Ringland). Mrs. Emminger died in March, 1874, a member of the Lutheran Church. Our subject is not only a representative of one of the oldest families of Cumberland County, but is one of the enterprising farmers and citizens. He stands high in the estimation of all who know him as an upright Christian gentleman. He is a member of the Lutheran Church.

SAMUEL N. EMINGER, ex-clerk to the county commissioners, Mechanicsburg, is a native of Cumberland County, born in Silver Spring Township, February 19, 1829. His grandfather, Andrew Eminger, born in Germany, but who came to this country at a very early date, was a soldier in the Revolutionary war; he married Miss Christiana Bruner and settled in Silver Spring Township, this county. Our subject's father, David Eminger, married Magdalena Miller, born in Franklin County, Penn., and had a family of seven boys and four girls. He was elected director of the poor in 1828, and afterward ran as a Masonic candidate for the Legislature, but was defeated in the anti-Masonic raid by twelve votes. Samuel N. attended the schools of Mechanicsburg and afterward at Eminger's schoolhouse, Silver Spring Township, and was one of the students in the first Cumberland Valley Institute, under Mr. Franklin Gillan, when it was opened on the Van Huff property, now opposite Eckel's drug store. He attended two years. In 1844 he learned the trade of coach-maker under his brother-in-law, George Hauck, and from 1849 to 1851 traveled in Virginia and the Carolinas, Tennessee and Florida. He returned to Mechanicsburg and bought the first patent and brought the first wire tooth sulky rake into Cumberland County about 1852, and started to manufacture them in company with George W. Miller, but subsequently sold his interest to Frederick Seidle who had then a factory in Mechanicsburg. In 1855 Mr. Eminger was nominated deputy sheriff under Sheriff Bowman. He resigned in the fall of 1856 and was elected register of wills in the fall of 1857, serving three years. He was appointed by Judge Graham jury commissioner, and served three years. In 1864 he was appointed special agent of the Treasury Department under Andrew Johnson. He resigned on the 1st of March, 1868, and his resignation was accepted in June following. From this time till 1873 he was with D. M. Osburn & Co., who were engaged in manufacturing reapers. From that time (1873) on, he was in the sheriff's office till 1877; served as deputy register under Martin Guswiler, and after, until elected clerk to the county commissioners in 1879, which office he filled until 1885. He married, September 4, 1856, Rachel, daughter of George and Mary (Halbert) Singheiser, by whom he had four children, three living: Arabella (married to D. A. Ulrich, of Upper Allen Township, this county); H. Foster, and Luella (a graduate of the high school). During the war Mr. Eminger enlisted in Company F, First Pennsylvania Volunteer Infantry, when they were called temporarily for the defense of Pennsylvania; was elected lieutenant and promoted to quartermaster. The company served only for a short time. Mr. Eminger is a member of Eureka Lodge, A. Y. M., Past Master by service, and also of the I. O. O. F., No. 215. In politics Mr. Eminger is a Democrat, and has for many years been strongly identified with the politics of the county. He has twice been chairman of the Democratic County Committee, and has been a delegate to many of the State conventions. In 1878 he was elected councilman of the North Ward and served three years, notwithstanding that this was a Republican ward.

DR. GEO. FULMER, born October 14, 1829, son of Christian and Sarah (Pifer) Fulmer, and the oldest practicing physician in Mechanicsburg, having located here as a physician in 1853, is a graduate of Jefferson College, Philadelphia. Christian Fulmer, a stonecutter by trade, died in 1841 aged fifty-three, and his widow in 1860 aged seventy-two. They had a family of three sons and two daughters, two living: Christian and George. The subject of our sketch attended school in Mechanicsburg, under Prof. John Hinkle, until he was sixteen years old, when he began teaching in this county, continuing in the profession until he was nineteen; then read medicine with Dr. P. H. Long, and in 1853 graduated from Jefferson Medical College, Philadelphia, after which he formed a partnership with his preceptor, Dr. Long, and continued that partnership until 1860, when they dissolved, since which time Dr. Fulmer has practiced alone. In 1861 he passed an examination at the

BOROUGH OF MECHANICSBURG.

State capital, Harrisburg, and received a certificate of examination from Surgeon-General Phellips, signed by Andrew G. Curtin, governor, and registered to hold himself in readiness for duty, and, in 1861, was assigned to a regiment, Chattanooga, Tenn., but on account of his practice and his family, he did not accept the commission. Dr. Fulmer was married, February 18, 1854, to Miss Susan Long, sister of Dr. P. H. Long and daughter of Philip and Elizabeth (Springer) Long. To this union have been born five children, three now living: Emma M. graduate of the Irving Female College, married to Dr. M. K. Bowers, Harrisburg, Penn.; Robert B. born in Mechanicsburg, Penn., September 18, 1865; and Bertie M., residing at home with her parents. Dr. Fulmer is a member of the Lutheran Church. He is one of the oldest practitioners of medicine in Cumberland County.

EUGENE C. GARDNER, editor and book-keeper for the "Thomas Printing House," and insurance agent, Mechanicsburg, was born at York Springs, Adams Co., Penn., July 16, 1847, son of Benjamin F. and Sabina (Moul) Gardner, old settlers of York Springs. The family consisted of four children, of whom Eugene C. is the only one living. Our subject was but ten years old when his father died. His mother resided with her father, Conrad Moul, proprietor of "York Springs Summer Resort" until 1858, when she located in Mechanicsburg. Eugene C. Gardner attended the common schools and the Cumberland Valley Institute. In 1865 he was employed as a "typo" on the *Cumberland Valley Journal*. In 1867 he was appointed local editor of the *Valley Democrat*, owned by Hon. T. F. Singiser. In February, 1871, Mr. Gardner, with R. H. Thomas and A. H. Brinks, purchased the *Valley Democrat* and changed the name to the *Valley Independent*, and a year later they purchased the *Cumberland Valley Journal* and consolidated the two papers into the present *Independent Journal*. In 1874 Mr. Gardner sold out his interest to H. C. Demming, of Harrisburg, Penn., and has since been engaged in the fire and life insurance business. In 1878 he accepted his present position as local editor of the *Independent Journal*. Our subject was united in marriage, June 5, 1871, with Miss Sue A., daughter of Robert and Sarah (Schock) Wilson. Mrs. Gardner is a member of the Lutheran Church. To this union have been born four children: Earl W., Pauline S., Bertha E. and S. Grace. Mr. Gardner is secretary of Integrity Council, No. 197, O. U. A. M.; secretary of W. C., No. 164, P. O. S. of A.; and is president of the Washington Fire Company, Mechanicsburg. In politics he is a strong supporter of the Republican party.

SOLOMON PERRY GORGAS, banker, Mechanicsburg, is one of the pioneer children of Cumberland County, born August 31, 1815, on the old homestead farm, in Lower Allen Township, the youngest in the family of four sons and three daughters of Solomon and Catharine (Fahnestock) Gorgas, natives of Pennsylvania, who were married in Lancaster County, Penn., and came to this county about 1803, settling on the old farm now owned by their son, William R., in Lower Allen Township. Solomon Gorgas, Sr., was a prominent man of his day; was elected by the people of this county to the Legislature two terms; he opened a store and hotel on his farm in Lower Allen Township (the only store and hotel in that part of the county for many years), and died here September 21, 1838, aged seventy-four years, seven months and four days. His widow died August 9, 1853, aged seventy-nine years, five months and six days. Both were members of the Seven Day Baptist Church. Solomon P. Gorgas married, May 8, 1845, Miss Elizabeth Eberly, born in Hampden Township, this county, March 31, 1822, daughter of Benjamin and Barbara (Kauffman) Eberly, natives of this county. Our subject farmed in Fairview Township, York Co., Penn., until 1850, when he came to Mechanicsburg, this county, and in 1855 purchased fifty-six acres of what is now a part of the east side of the city. In 1859 Mr. Gorgas, in company with Levi Merkel, Jacob Mumma, Jacob, Levi F. and Samuel Eberly, William R. Gorgas, John Nisley and John Brandt, formed a banking company, under the firm name of Merkel, Mumma & Co., with John Brandt, president, and Levi Kauffman, cashier. In 1861 the bank became the Mechanicsburg Bank, chartered under the State law, Levi Merkel, president. In February, 1864, the bank was chartered as the First National Bank, with Solomon P. Gorgas, president, and re-chartered in February, 1883. To our subject and wife have been born nine children, of whom one son and three daughters are living: Kate E., wife of Dr. J. Nelson Clark, of Harrisburg, Penn.; William F., formerly connected with the First National Bank, in Mechanicsburg, now residing in St. Louis, Mo.; Anna B., wife of Jacob H. Kohler, a member of the firm of J. B. Kohler & Co., manufacturers, Mechanicsburg, Penn.; and Mary E., wife of William C. Hicks, proprietor of the "Peoples Tea Store," at Harrisburg, Penn. Mr. Gorgas has been identified with this county for the past seventy years. He built the Irving Female College, of Mechanicsburg. He and his wife stand high in the estimation of all who know them. They reside in the house in which they were married forty years ago. Mrs. Gorgas is a member of the Methodist Episcopal Church. Our subject is not only one of our old settlers, but one of the honest, upright, solid business men. He has held various local offices of trust in his town, and has lived to see Mechanicsburg and Cumberland County undergo many interesting and important changes.

GEORGE HAUCK, county commissioner, member of the firm of Hauck & Comstock, machinists, etc., Mechanicsburg, is a representative of one of the old families of Cumberland County, born on the old homestead of his father and grandfather, in Meadow Valley,

414   BIOGRAPHICAL SKETCHES:

Lancaster Co., Penn., July 6, 1823. His parents, George and Hannah (Senseman) Hauck, were born in Meadow Valley, Penn. His father, who was a farmer, was a son of George Hauck, who came from Germany and settled in Meadow Valley, Lancaster Co., Penn., in 1760. He was a shoe-maker by trade, but followed farming. George Hauck was the fifth child and third son in a family of nine children, six of whom attained maturity. Our subject was but two years old when he came with his parents to Silver Spring Township, settling on a farm four miles northwest of Mechanicsburg, where George remained, attending school winters until he was seventeen years of age, when he began to learn wagon-making at New Kingston, this county. In 1843 he came to Mechanicsburg and finished his trade in the coach-making establishment of his brothers, and in 1845 bought a half interest in the business. His brother Adam dying in 1855, George Hauck bought out his interest, and later he and his brother Samuel bought out the half interest that their deceased brother owned in what is now the Hauck & Comstock foundry. In 1860 George Hauck sold out his coach-making establishment and that same year he and his brothers bought out the partner's (Jeremiah Senseman's) interest and ran under the firm name of S. & G. Hauck until 1880, when they sold a half interest to George S. Comstock, the business then being under the firm name of Hauck & Comstock. Mr. George Hauck has always been an active business man. He was elected county commissioner of Cumberland County in November, 1884; in September, 1885, he was elected director of the Allen and East Pennsborough Fire Insurance Company, and treasurer in October, 1885. Mr. Hauck has been director of the First National Bank since 1863, and has served as president and director of the Mechanicsburg Gas and Water Company since 1856. He is a self-made man, having learned early in life to depend upon his own resources, and stands high in the estimation of all as an honest citizen and gentleman. Although a commissioner of the county he is not a politician. Mr. Hauck is a Universalist in belief; his wife is a member of the Lutheran Church. They have ten children, four living: Sarah E. (wife of John A. Eberly, a land agent residing at McPherson, Kas.); David A. (married to Miss Mary Singiser, who died in 1884), is a foreman in the machine shops of Hauck & Comstock; Abner J. (married to Miss Anna Henry) is a car accountant in the car department of the New York, Philadelphia & Norfolk Railway at Cape Charles, Va.; Susan A. (wife of John A. Keesberry, chief clerk, car accountant's office of the Pennsylvania Railroad at Philadelphia). The Hauck family is of German descent.

GEORGE W. HAUCK, dealer in stoves, tinware and hardware, Mechanicsburg, was born in Mechanicsburg, Penn., May 6, 1841, son of Adam and Susannah (Wonderly) Hauck. Adam Hauck was an iron manufacturer and at one time a partner of Jeremiah Senseman, with whom he did business under the firm name of Senseman & Hauck, which afterward became S. & G. Hauck and is now Hauck & Comstock. Adam and Susannah Hauck had four children. George W., the second child and son, attended the common schools and Cumberland Valley Institute until he was nineteen. He began to learn the tinner's trade at the age of fifteen, and from nineteen until twenty-six worked at his trade in Cincinnati (Ohio), Rochester, Wabash (Indiana), Harrisburg and other places. In 1867 he formed a partnership with his uncle, F. Wonderly, and engaged in the stove and tinware business until 1869, when Mr. Hauck bought out Mr. Wonderly, and soon after formed a partnership with his brother S. F. Hauck, which continued until August, 1878, when he bought out his brother's interest and has since conducted the business alone. He and his brother, S. F. Hauck, and J. K. Seifert and S. H. Coover organized the Huston Net Company, afterward purchasing Mr. Coover's interest, and the net industry is now owned and conducted solely by G. W. and S. F. Hauck, doing business under the name of Huston Net Company. George W. Hauck, married, January 5, 1869, Miss Alice Starr, of Quaker descent, born in Lisburn, this county, daughter of Reuben T. and Elizabeth (Lloyd) Starr. Mrs. Hauck is a member of the Methodist Episcopal Church. To this union have been born three children, two now living: Walter L., born August 6, 1875, and E. Starr, born March 19, 1877. Mr. Hauck has one of the finest and most modern houses in the county, on South Market Street, where he and his family reside. He is one of the enterprising, responsible citizens and business men of Cumberland County. His family is of German descent, his ancestors having settled in Pennsylvania in a very early day. Mr. Hauck is a charter member of K. of P. Lodge and O. U. A. M., Mechanicsburg.

SAMUEL F. HAUCK, of Seifert & Hauck, wholesale and retail hardware merchants and fly-net manufacturers, Mechanicsburg, was born in Mechanicsburg, Cumberland Co., Penn., August 30, 1850; son of Adam and Susan M. (Wonderly) Hauck, also natives of this county, and who had three sons and one daughter. Samuel F., the youngest, attended school until he was sixteen, when he went to Harrisburg, Penn., and clerked for U. R. Buck & Bro., grocers; worked for them and at the tinner's trade until 1869, when he formed a partnership with his brother, George W., and opened a tin and stove store in Mechanicsburg. In 1872 he, in company with others, formed the Hauck Bros. & Co. Patent Faucet Company. In 1879 he sold out his interest in the stove and tinware business, formed his present partnership, and established his hardware trade. In 1881 he engaged in the leather fly-net manufacture under the present firm name of "The Huston Net Company." Mr. Hauck was married in December, 1870, to Miss Ella Hertzler, a native of near Shepherds-

BOROUGH OF MECHANICSBURG. 415

town, this county, daughter of C. D. Hertzler. To this union was born one son, Ralph S., who died aged eight months. Mrs. Hauck died in September, 1875, and November 4, 1880, Mr. Hauck married Miss Lou E. Elcock, born in Siddonsburg, York Co., Penn., daughter of Joseph and Mary (Breneman) Elcock, Mechanicsburg. Mrs. Hauck is a member of the Church of God. Mr. Hauck has a beautiful brick residence fitted up in the most modern style, where he and his family reside. He is a member of Eureka Lodge, No. 302, A. Y. M.; I. O. O. F. and I. O. O. H., Mechanicsburg. He is one of the leading enterprising representative citizens of Cumberland County, where he has been identified all his life. He has the confidence and respect of all and is known as an honest, upright business gentleman.

BENJAMIN HAVERSTICK, retired farmer, Mechanicsburg, was born on the Conostogo River within three miles of Lancaster City, Lancaster Co., Penn., March 2, 1801, son of Michael and Eve (Bender) Haverstick, natives of Lancaster County. Their parents came from Germany. They were members of the German Reformed Church. They had five children—three sons and two daughters: Michael, George, Maria (wife of Socrates Myers), Nancy (wife of Adam Kindig) and Benjamin. The subject of our sketch, the youngest, remained on the farm with his father until his marriage, November 28, 1824, with Miss Lydia Meylin, who was born four miles south of Lancaster, Penn., March 8, 1807, daughter of Abraham and Anna (Shank) Meylin, also natives of Lancaster County, and members of the old Mennonite Church. After marriage Mr. and Mrs. Haverstick moved to Cocalico Township, Lancaster Co., Penn., and engaged in farming until April, 1834, when they settled on a farm one mile west of Mechanicsburg, in Silver Spring Township, this county, and there followed agricultural pursuits until 1875, when the farm was rented. They have since resided in Mechanicsburg. They are members of the Methodist Episcopal Church. Of the ten children born to this couple, six survive: Anna M., born November 3, 1825, was married, December 29, 1846, to John A. Hensel, since deceased; Hiram A., born November 10, 1828, was married July 4, 1855, to Miss Nancy J. Johnson, and is a farmer in Marion County, Ind.; Benjamin, who married Mary L. Snavely, was a member of a Pennsylvania volunteer regiment under Col. Rush, was wounded and captured by the rebels, and died June 15, 1868, from exposure while in service; Martin M., married Miss Sarah Jane Wonderly, and residing on a farm in Vernon County, Mo.; Lydia R., married, April 7, 1857, to Dr. William H. Longsdorf, ex-county treasurer, and major of a Pennsylvania cavalry regiment from Cumberland County; Barbara Eve, born June 22, 1838, died December 30, 1839; Levi M., married to Miss Emma E. Frantz January 4, 1870, was captain of an infantry company under Col. H. I. Zinn, and was wounded at the battle of Antietam and at Fredericksburg, where his colonel was killed—his widow resides at Rock Island, Ill.; Mary E., married November 28, 1866, to John A. Longsdorf, resides in Mechanicsburg, Penn.; Fannie and Carrie (twins), the former, married to Edward Weibly, died September 30, 1882, aged thirty-six years, four months and four days; the latter, married to William Williamson October 14, 1869, resides in Mechanicsburg, Penn. Mr. and Mrs. Benjamin Haverstick have been married sixty-one years, and enjoy good health. They stand high in the estimation of all, and are among the few old settlers who have lived to see this county undergo so many interesting changes.

JESSE C. HAYS, retired merchant, Mechanicsburg, was born in Newberrytown, York Co., Penn., July 24, 1818. His grandfather, Jesse Hays, was born in Wales, and came alone to America when a young man, settling in Chester County, Penn., but afterward moved to York County, same State, and took up large tracts of land in Fishing Creek Valley. He married Miss Margarety Mills. Though Jesse Hays and his wife were at first Methodists, they subsequently became Quakers; their family consisted of three daughters and one son: Lydia, wife of Joseph Willett; Susan, married first to a Mr. Clark, and then to a Mr. Carskaddon; Hannah, a maiden lady, and Mills. Mills Hays, the last-named, was born in Newberrytown, York Co., Penn., and in early life followed coopering, but afterward taught school; served as justice of the peace for eighteen years, and was elected, later, to the office of associate judge of York County, Penn., filling this position for five years. He died in 1858, aged seventy-two years; he married Miss Eve Crull, of York County, and had two sons and three daughters, who lived to be men and women, and of whom two daughters and one son are now living: Sidney, widow of William Epley, resides in Newberrytown; Jesse C. and Jane, wife of Samuel P. Harmon; they reside in Newberrytown, York Co., Penn. Our subject attended school in Newberrytown until he was eighteen, when he began teaching, and after following this profession eight winters engaged in mercantile trade with his father. In 1848 he bought out his father's interest and engaged in business for himself until 1865, when he sold out. He was elected justice of the peace for Newbery Township in 1863, and held that office five years; was also postmaster eight years. In 1869 he came to Mechanicsburg, where he has since resided. Mr. Hays was married, May 13, 1852, to Miss Mary Miller, born in Newberry Township, York Co., Penn., February 15, 1827, daughter of Samuel and Mary (Reeser) Miller, old settlers of York County, and whose parents came from Germany. Mr. Hays attends the Presbyterian Church; Mrs. Hays is a member of the United Brethren Church. To them have been born two children: Mills M., born in Newberrytown, York Co., Penn., married to Miss Clara Bowers, is a cigar manufacturer, and Maine, at present attending Miss Woodward's school at Harrisburg. Mr. Hays is an enterprising business man and representative citizen of Mechanicsburg, where he has been a resident since 1869. He has a nice residence on West Main Street, where he and his family reside. In politics he is a Democrat.

SAMUEL F. HOUSTON, harness-maker, at present engaged in fly net manufacture, Mechanicsburg, was born September 13, 1833, in Silver Spring Township, this county, on his grandfather's (Michael Saxton's) farm; is a son of James (a farmer) and Mary (Saxton) Houston, also natives of this county, attendants of the Silver Spring Presbyterian Church. They had three sons and one daughter, Samuel F. being the second son and third child. His father dying when our subject was but four years of age, the latter was raised by Henry W. Irwin in Silver Spring Township until he was twelve years old, when he was apprenticed to Samuel Fisher to learn the harness-maker's trade, at New Kingston, where he served four years; then traveled west in Ohio, Indiana, Illinois, Iowa and Missouri; then returned to New Kingston and carried on a shop of his own six years (until 1859),when he located in Mechanicsburg, and engaged in the same business here until 1863; then acted as salesman for George De B. Keim, ex-sheriff of Philadelphia, in the hardware business until 1864; then clerked in a dry goods store at Harrisburg until 1866; then formed a partnership with George Beelman and engaged in the grocery business until the spring of 1871, when he sold out to his partner, and opened a grocery store in Mechanicsburg, continuing this till 1881. In 1882 he established his present net manufacture, where he employs from eight to ten hands, and manufactures over forty different kinds of leather nets. Mr. Houston owns the store building (occupied, the first floor by M. H. Spahr and John A. Kauffman; the second floor by Mechanicsburg Library and Literary Association, John L. Shelly and J. N. Young; the third being lodge rooms of P. S. A. and K. of G. E., respectively), some building lots and his house on Main Street, where he and his family reside. Our subject was married, December 26, 1865, to Miss Sallie A. Beelman, born in Monroe Township, this county, daughter of John and Susan (Coover) Beelman. To this union have been born three sons: J. Milton, born July 2, 1867; Glen R., born June 26, 1871, and George B., born November 26, 1874. Mr. Houston is a member and treasurer of Eureka Lodge, No. 302, F. & A. M., also a member of Grand Lodge of Pennsylvania, and member of Samuel C. Perkins Chapter, No. 215, R. A. M., and member of Grand Chapter of Pennsylvania. He has held various offices of trust in Mechanicsburg; was councilman one term, burgess three terms, and was treasurer of Mechanicsburg Loan and Building Association for nine years. The family of Houston is of Scotch-Irish descent, and our subject's ancestors were among the hardy Scotch-Irish people driven out of Ireland on account of their religion, seeking homes in America and settling in Pennsylvania.

GEORGE HUMMEL, grain and coal merchant, Mechanicsburg.

EDWIN W. HURST, leading merchant tailor of Mechanicsburg, was born in Philadelphia. Penn., December 31, 1829, son of Jacob Bricker and Susan (Hershfeldt) Hurst. Jacob B. Hurst was born near Dillsburg, York Co., Penn., son of John and Catharine (Cocklin) Hurst, who were the parents of three sons and four daughters: Edwin W., the eldest; Jacob, a merchant, of Mechanicsburg, Penn.; Lydia, wife of William Spahr, superintendent of the city railway stables, Harrisburg, Penn.; Ellen, wife of William Nelson, a farmer near Dillsburg, York Co., Penn.; Kate, wife of Robert Mateer, hardware merchant, Harrisburg, Penn.; Templeton B., who married Miss Jennie Lyman, a daughter of Col. Lyman, attorney at Lock Haven, Penn. (he, Templeton B., served all through the war of the Rebellion); Mellie, wife of George W. Hackett, a hardware merchant at Sunbury, Penn. Our subject, when an infant, was brought by his parents to Dillsburg, Penn., where his father engaged in the tailoring and merchant tailoring and was postmaster and who later opened a general store. Edwin W. assisted his father, learning the tailoring of him. He was married in August, 1851, in Newville, Penn., to Miss Sarah Miller, born in Fishing Creek Valley, York Co., Penn., daughter of Henry and Catharine (Roth) Miller; former a son of John Miller. In 1855 our subject went to Philadelphia, Penn., and worked at his trade some ten years, then came to Mechanicsburg and did the merchant tailoring for his father who had opened a dry goods store here. In 1872 he established his present business here. He and his wife are members of the Presbyterian Church. They have six children: Annie C., wife of John P. Eckels, of Decatur, Ill., a traveling salesman for Morehouse, Wells & Co., wholesale hardware dealers, Decatur, Ill.; J. Harry, born in Dillsburg, York Co., Penn., February 21, 1854, married December 23, 1879, to Miss Sarah A. Eberly, born in Upper Allen Township, daughter of Jacob and Mary (Hertzler) Eberly, (he, J. Harry, is a tailor of Mechanicsburg, has had two children, one now living: Hattie Maude Hurst); Ida, who died aged two years; Charles M., hardware merchant, junior partner in firm of Morehouse, Wells & Co., and who married Miss Rella Shockley, and resides at Decatur, Ill.; Maude, who died aged eight years; Robert T., born in Mechanicsburg, Penn., died in 1876, aged three years. Our subject is a member of Humane Lodge, 342, I. O. O. F., York County, Penn., and a member of the American Mechanics, and Knights of the Golden Eagle, and Commandery, and a member the G. A. R., Capt. Zinn Post, No. 415. He is an enterprising representative business man, and stands high in the estimation of all who know him.

BOROUGH OF MECHANICSBURG.   417

JACOB HURST (originally spelled Horsh), dry good merchant, Mechanicsburg, is a native of York County, Penn., born at Dillsburg August 13, 1832, son of Jacob B. and Susan (Herchfeldt) Hurst, former of whom born near Dillsburg York Co. Penn., January 7, 1808, was a son of John (who was a farmer) and Catharine (Cocklin) Hurst, who were the parents of four sons and three daughters, who lived to be men and women. Jacob B. was raised on a farm until he was fifteen, when he began to learn the tailor's trade with William Gilbethorp; four years later he went to Harrisburg and Philadelphia, and after working at his trade a number of years returned to Dillsburg and opened a tailor shop on his own account in 1831. He afterward (in 1855) opened a general store, and in the spring of 1866 came to Mechanicsburg and established the dry goods house of J. B. Hurst & Son. He was a director of the First National Bank and a man of high honor and sterling worth. He and his wife were earnest Christians and members of the Presbyterian Church, in which he was elder for a number of years. Jacob B. Hurst stood high in the estimation of all as an upright, honest Christian gentleman. He departed this life November 18, 1875; his widow is living in Mechanicsburg. This couple had seven children, three sons and four daughters: Edwin W., a merchant tailor of Mechanicsburg; Jacob, our subject; Lydia B., wife of William A. Spahr, a stock-dealer, residing in Harrisburg; Mary E., wife of William B. Nelson, resides on a farm near, Dillsburg, Penn.; Templeton B., of East Saginaw, Mich,, an ex-soldier from Company H Seventh Regiment Pennsylvania Reserves; Kate M., wife of Robert B. Mateer, a hardware merchant of Harrisburg, Penn.; Melizena M., wife of George W. Hackett, a hardware merchant of Sunbury, Penn. The subject of our sketch attended school until he was fifteen, then assisted his father in the merchant tailoring and general store at Dillsburg until the fall of 1865, when he came with his father to Mechanicsburg and formed a partnership with him, under the firm name of J. B. Hurst & Son. Three months after his father's death he purchased the entire stock and has since conducted the business alone; he now carries a full line of dry goods and notions, carpets, etc., valued at $17,000. September 5, 1872, Mr. Hurst married Julia Wilson, born in Carlisle, Penn., daughter of Robert and Sarah (Shock) Wilson. To Mr. and Mrs. Hurst have been born two children: Wilson and Corliss. Mrs. Hurst is a member of the Lutheran Church. Our subject is one of the leading business men of Cumberland County, and stands high in the estimation of all as an upright business man. The family is of German descent, and is one of the oldest in Pennsylvania.

E. RANKIN HUSTON, the leading painter of the eastern portion of Cumberland County, is a son of William Huston, who was a most excellent farmer and worthy citizen, and on his mother's side a direct descendant of the historic Enders family of Dauphin County. Samuel Huston, the paternal great-grandfather, emigrated from Scotland in the early part of the eighteenth century; was a farmer and settled in what was then East Pennsborough Township, but which is now included in the township of Silver Spring. The tract of land on which the original house was built has been known since as the Huston homestead, and occupies a pleasant site some three miles north of the village of Hogestown. His maternal great-grandmother was Isabella Sharon. Samuel Huston died in 1800, and his widow, Isabella, in 1804. Both are buried in the Pine Hill burying-ground. They had two sons: John and Jonathan. His paternal grandfather was Jonathan Huston, a farmer, whose wife was Margaret Rankin McIntire, a native of Ireland. They had eleven children: Rebecca Eckels, John, John, Samuel, Samuel, Isabella, Isabell (Shafer-King), William, Jane C. Talbert, Mary Swiler and Margaret Eckels. The father of this family died November 10, 1830, aged seventy years, and the mother, August 24, 1846, aged seventy-six years, and both are buried at Silver Spring. William Huston, the father of our subject, was born on the old homestead, on the original settlement, December 19, 1799. He spent his youth on the farm; learned the carpenter's trade, and for a number of years enjoyed quite a reputation as a bridge-builder in the western part of this State. March 29, 1838, he married Mary Ann, daughter of Peter and Catherine Phillips, *nee* Enders. William Huston was not only a model farmer and ingenious mechanic, but a gentleman of sterling character and great physical endurance. He was a descendant of that class of Scotch-Irish settlers who came into the Cumberland Valley from the eastward, and who have left everywhere the unmistakeable evidence of thrift and enterprise. Perhaps to them more than any other class this portion of the Cumberland Valley owes its superiority, its fine sense of right and high standard of moral excellence. He died April 29, 1883, and his remains repose by the side of his parents, in Silver Spring. Mary A., his wife, was born September 22, 1817. She was a member of Trindle Spring Lutheran Church, and her life bore the testimony of the sincerity of her profession. Gifted by nature with qualites which were rare and desirable, she was appreciated by all who knew her. She was amiable and kind, and in the consistency of her life an ornament to Christianity. She died October 7, 1881, and was buried at Silver Spring. They had one daughter, who died in infancy, and one son, E. Rankin Huston, who was born September 28, 1843, at the old homestead, and spent his earlier years on a small farm, one-half mile north of Mechanicsburg. During the winter season he attended the public school of the district until he had mastered all the branches embraced in its curriculum. He subsequently entered the Pennsylvania College of Trade and Finance, from which he graduated in the class of 1867. Afterward he gave himself up to the study of painting and decoration, and his marked success evidences the wisdom of his choice. December 4, 1873, he married Mary E., youngest daughter of Daniel and Margaret (Weibley) Walters, who was born January 22, 1850. Two children are the results of this union; Carrie I., born September 11, 1874, and Mary E., born August 10, 1878. Mr. Huston has resided in Mechanicsburg since 1872, and is held in deservedly high esteem by his fellow-townsmen. He is a member of Eureka Lodge, No. 302, F. & A. M.; treasurer of Samuel C. Perkins Chapter, No. 209, R. A. M., of Mechanicsburg; St. John's Commandery, No. 8, K. T., of Carlisle; Grand H. R. A. Chapter of Pennsylvania; Mechanicsburg Lodge, No. 215, I. O. O. F. His great-grandparents on his maternal side were Jacob and Mary Phillips, who were born in Germany and immigrated to Pennsylvania. Jacob Phillips was a soldier in the Revolutionary war three years; was wounded in the head and face, and died in 1783. Mary, his widow, died in 1807, and both are buried in the Catholic cemetery at Carlisle. Peter Phillips, his grandfather, was born in Cumberland County May 8, 1781. In his younger days he learned the carpenter's trade. He enlisted as a private in the war of 1812. His eminent qualities as a soldier were fitly recognized in his rapid promotion, having become, soon after entering the service, first lieutenant. He participated in the battles of Chippewa, Lundy's Lane, and various other engagements with the English and their Indian allies, narrowly escaping on several occasions from falling in the hands of the savage foe. He was wounded by Indians lying in ambush. Returning to his home in the fall of 1814, he again resumed his trade. April 6, 1806, he married Catharine, daughter of Philip C. and Anna Enders. She was born March 18, 1783, in Lancaster County, and died November 28, 1844, and is buried near Belleville, Ohio, leaving behind her tender memories of her kindness of heart and graces of character. Peter Phillips died October 5, 1860, and was buried at Trindle Spring Church. The Enders family, of which our subject is a lineal descendant, was quite distinguished in the part of Germany in which it resided. Philip C. Enders, the great-grandfather of E. Rankin Huston, was born July 22, 1740, in Braunsigweilen, Germany. After completing his education he entered the military service of his sovereign, and participated in numerous battles of the seven years' war. For gallantry and other soldierly qualities he was promoted to a captaincy in the royal cavalry. He resigned his commission, and on May 13, 1764, married Anna, a daughter of Conrad Degen, and a few months later came to America. His first settlement was in Philadelphia, and later he moved to Lancaster County. In 1788 he purchased a tract of over 1,300 acres in Upper Paxton, Dauphin County, and moved there with his family, where he continued to reside until his death, February 26, 1810. Anna, his wife, died in 1796. He was in many respects a remarkable man, and has left his mark on the subsequent history of Dauphin County. He was the founder of Fetterhoff's Church, erected the first sawmill in the valley, organized and taught the first school in that section of country, and was the leading spirit in all public enterprises. It is thus seen the family of which E. Rankin Huston is a representative, is one of the original and leading families of this part of the State, and closely identified with all movements of its general prosperity.

JAMES S. HUSTON, inventor, farmer and manufacturer, Mechanicsburg, is a great-grandson of Samuel Huston, who was born in Ireland, and came to America when a young man, settling in Pennsylvania, where he married. His son, Samuel, born in Cumberland County, Penn., in 1776, married Miss Nancy Clendenin, and had five sons: Samuel, Robert, William, John and James (twins). They were members of the old Presbyterian Church at Silver Spring. Of their children James was born in Silver Spring Township, this county, became a farmer, and in the course of time married Miss Mary Saxton, who bore him four children—three sons and one daughter: John, Sarah, Samuel F. and James S. The subject of our sketch, who is the youngest, was but two years old when his father died; he then went to live with his uncle, William Saxton, and remained with him working on the farm and attending school until he was sixteen, when he was apprenticed to the harness-making trade at New Kingston, this county, for three years; thence went to Hogestown, but after one year returned to New Kingstown, and two years later moved to Wooster, Ohio, but in a short time came to Mechanicsburg and opened a harness shop. In 1869 he invented the Huston fly net used by the Huston Fly Net Company of Mechanicsburg, and also invented the Huston Net No. 2, used by I. C. Deihl, of Shippensburg, Penn. He then engaged in the manufacture of fly nets until 1881, when he sold out and embarked in farming and milling, purchasing the Boucher Mill at Hogestown, which was burned in September, 1885. June 15, 1856, Mr. Huston married Miss Sarah Huntsburger, born in Lower Allen Township, this county, daughter of Jonas and Leah (Tyson) Huntsburger, and to this union have been born four children, one living—Arthur J.—born in Mechanicsburg May 25, 1865. They are members of the Presbyterian Church. Mr. Huston is an enterprising business man; starting in life without a cent he deserves much credit for his success. His grandfather, Samuel Houston (or Huston) and Samuel Houston, the founder of Houston, Tex., were cousins.

LEVI KAUFFMAN, deceased (see portrait). Prominent among the honored dead of Cumberland County there is none more worthy of representation than the subject of this sketch. His family have, from a very early date, been closely

BOROUGH OF MECHANICSBURG. 419

identified with the history of Pennsylvania. Christian Kauffman, his great-grandfather, immigrated to America from Germany about 1730, and settled in Manor Township, Lancaster Co., Penn., where he died March 1, 1799. He was married to Barbara Bear, whose death occurred January 12, 1801. They had six children, of whom Isaac, the second son and grandfather of the subject of this sketch, was born in Manor Township, Lancaster Co., Penn., in 1762, and died January 4, 1826. In the year 1786 he married Catharine Baughman, who died July 9, 1833. Their youngest son, the Hon. Andrew I. Kauffman, father of Levi Kauffman, was born August 24, 1802, at the old homestead in Manor Township, Lancaster County, and spent the greater part of his life in that township. He represented Lancaster County in the House of Representatives in the State Legislature, and was closely associated with Hon. Thaddeus Stevens and Hon. Thomas H. Burrows, in the establishment of our justly prized common school system. In 1850 he became a resident of Cumberland County, and in 1853 removed to Mechanicsburg, where he engaged in mercantile pursuits, and continued therein until his death, which occurred December 14, 1861. Andrew I. Kauffman was married, March 24, 1825, to Catharine Shuman, who was born July 16, 1806, and was the only daughter of Christian Shuman, of Manor Township, Lancaster Co., Penn. She died at Mechanicsburg May 18, 1875.

Levi Kauffman, their fourth son, the subject of this sketch, was born at Little Washington, Lancaster Co., Penn., September 13, 1833. At the age of thirteen he left home and entered the drug store of Dr. George Ross, at Elizabethtown, as an apprentice. At the end of four years he received, from Dr. Ross, a strong testimonial of his ability as a druggist, for aptness, intelligence and integrity of character. Mr. Kauffman remained in the drug business in Elizabethtown until April, 1854, when he removed to Mechanicsburg, and opened a new drug store in that place. A year or two later, in connection with his father, Hon. Andrew I. Kauffman and Henry G. Rupp, he entered the hardware business, connecting the drug store therewith, and continued therein until 1859, when he accepted the position of cashier in the banking house of Merkel, Mumma & Co., subsequently chartered as the First National Bank, of Mechanicsburg, Penn. This position he resigned in 1862, when he was appointed by President Lincoln collector of internal revenue for the Fifteenth District of Pennsylvania, comprising the counties of Cumberland, York and Perry. He held that position until September, 1866, when he resigned rather than endorse the odious policy, known as "My Policy," of President Johnson. His letter of resignation, published in the Philadelphia *Press* of that date, gave clear evidence of his sterling patriotism. Early in 1864 Mr. Kauffman assisted in organizing and became cashier of the Second National Bank of Mechanicsburg, and held that position until he resigned in the latter part of 1869. The *State Guard*, a daily newspaper, started at the State capital during 1867, was a project of Mr. Kauffman, and one in which he invested a large sum of money; not proving a financial success he abandoned its publication in 1869. From 1870 until the time of his death, which occurred February 10, 1882, Mr. Kauffman was engaged in the fire insurance business, having the State central agency of several large companies, his principal office being at Harrisburg, Penn. Mr. Kauffman never hesitated to perform any duty imposed upon him by his fellow citizens, his church or society. As burgess, town councilman, school director, and member of the board of trustees of Irving Female College, he was always on hand to take his full share of work and responsibility. He was noted for his public spirit and local pride in the town of his adoption, and many of the public and private improvements erected in Mechanicsburg were due to his foresight and energy. He was liberal to a fault. For more than thirty years he was a member of the Church of God, and faithfully filled the offices of superintendent of the Sabbath-school, deacon and elder. He frequently represented his church in the annual eldership of east Pennsylvania, and on several occasions was a lay delegate to the triennial sessions of the general eldership of the church. Mr. Kauffman was a man of strong will, great energy, dauntless courage, inflexible in the right, and afraid of nothing but of being wrong. Fond of the sports of his children, as they were of playing and being with him. While abounding in anecdote, jovial at table, with pleasant voice, it was in harmony with the nature and power of Mr. Kauffman, who was a hero in action in every condition of life, and possessed of a will and energy that fitted him to be a leader in every party to which he belonged. Politically Mr. Kauffman, like the others members of his family, was a Republican, and assisted in the organization of that party in Pennsylvania. He took a keen interest and active part in the primary and general elections, frequently participating as a delegate in the party conventions. In 1864 he was a delegate to the National Republican Convention at Baltimore, and assisted in the nomination of Lincoln and Johnson. His eldest brother, Hon. C. S. Kauffman, of Columbia, Penn., represented Lancaster County in the State Senate from 1878 to 1882. Lieut. Isaac B. Kauffman, his second brother, served faithfully in the war of the Rebellion in the Ninth Regiment of Pennsylvania Volunteer Cavalry, and died June 7, 1862, from disease contracted in the service. His brother, Andrew J. Kauffman, Esq., a member of the bar of Lancaster County, was appointed, by President Arthur in 1882, collector of internal revenue for the Ninth District of Pennsylvania.

Mr. Kauffman was married, February 5, 1856, to A. Elizabeth Coover, daughter of the late John Coover, Esq., of Mechanicsburg. (See page 407.) Mr. and Mrs. Kauffman had five children, two of whom—Harvey and Willie—died in infancy. Their eldest son, Percival C., was born in Mechanicsburg August 13, 1857. He is a graduate of the University of Pennsylvania at Philadelphia; studied law in the office of Hon. Wayne MacVeagh; was admitted to the bar in June, 1879, and is now the junior member of the firm of Troutman & Kauffman, attorneys at law, at Hazleton, Luzerne Co., Penn., representing, as counsel, many of the largest individual coal operators and companies in the anthracite region. Their second son, Walter Lee, was born in Mechanicsburg August 9, 1860. He attended Dickinson College, Carlisle, Penn., for several sessions, and is now assistant to the superintendent of the American Tube & Iron Co., and has charge of the offices of the company at Youngstown, Ohio. Miss Edith B. Kauffman, their only daughter, resides with her mother, at their residence on West Main Street. This family ranks among the first families in the county.

COL. DAVID H. KIMMEL, proprietor of restaurant and private boarding house, Mechanicsburg, is one of the pioneer children of Cumberland County and is a representative of one of its oldest families. His grandfather, Valentine Kimmel, born in Lancaster County, Penn., came to Cumberland County, Penn., when a young man. His father was a native of Germany and one of the earliest settlers of Lancaster County, Penn. Col. D. H. Kimmel, was born in Shippensburg, this county, March 15, 1835, the second son and seventh child in the family of two sons and seven daughters, of George and Mary (Swiler) Kimmel, natives of this county, members of the Church of God, in which the former was an elder and a deacon for forty-five years; he was a farmer by occupation. Our subject attended school winters and worked on his father's farm until he was seventeen, when he came to Mechanicsburg, and learned the tinner's trade with George Bobb and Robert Wilson. He worked at the trade seven years, then formed a partnership in the boot and shoe business with D. A. Holmes, under firm name of Kimmel & Holmes, for three years; then engaged at the tinner's trade until the breaking out of the Rebellion, when he was one of the first to shoulder a musket and enlist his services in defense of his country. He raised Company H, Sixteenth Pennsylvania Volunteer Infantry, commanded by Col. Ziegle, the first company organized for three years' service in the State of Pennsylvania. He was mustered out, by an order from the War Department, for the purpose of raising Company H, of the Ninth Pennsylvania Cavalry, and was elected captain, and subsequently major, then lieutenant-colonel, and latterly colonel, remaining until close of the war, his regiment being one of the last mustered out. He was in 104 battles, besides skirmishes; was with Sherman in his celebrated march to the sea. Col. Kimmel and his regiment composed of Cumberland, Dauphin, Perry, Lancaster and Schuykill County boys, made one of the grandest charges on record. This was at the battle of Reedyville, Tenn., September 6, 1864, when they charged Gen. Debarell, who had 1,800 men and Col. Kimmel 240. The Colonel charged the General eight miles, passing clear through the enemy's lines, capturing 400 horses and 200 men; of the Confederates there were 33 killed and wounded, while the loss in the Colonel's regiment was but 7 killed and wounded. A few days afterward Gen. Debarell sent Col. Kimmel word if he would meet him on an open field he thought that he (Debarell) and his 1,800 men could whip the Colonel and his regiment. The Colonel sent back word that he and his boys would meet him anywhere, and for him to appoint a place and date. (The Colonel's regiment rode gray horses, and was known as the "Gray Horse.") Strange as it may seem, the Colonel, though a large man, weighing 200 pounds, never received a wound, though he had a horse killed under him at Raleigh, N. C., when charging Johnston's rear. Of the original company of 106 men raised in Cumberland County, three-fourths were killed. The Colonel has complimentary letters from Gen. W. H. Sherman, Gen. Stanley, Gen. Kilpatrick, Gen. Gordon Granger, Gen. Jackson, and others. At the close of the war our subject returned to Mechanicsburg and formed a partnership with George Bobb, under firm name of Bobb & Kimmel, and engaged in the hardware business for three years; then opened his present hotel and restaurant. November 26, 1857, he married Miss Kate Hoover, a native of Mechanicsburg, Penn., daughter of John and Mary (Martin) Hoover, old settlers of Cumberland County. To this union have been born the following named children: Frank H., born March 3, 1859, a traveling salesman for Powell & Co. wholesale grocers, Harrisburg, married to Miss Mary Welzel, of Carlisle; Minnie E., residing at home with her parents; John G., born March 3, 1868, assists his father in business; Sarah B., residing at home. The Colonel is a member of Col. H. I. Zinn Post, No. 415, G. A. R. He has in his possession a Confederate flag, captured at the battle of Milledgeville, Ga. In his charge there he captured thirty-four guidons or small flags. The colonel stands high in the estimation of all, as a brave soldier, honest business man, and good citizen.

JONAS KOLLER, farmer, P. O. Mechanicsburg, was born in Shrewsbury Township, York Co., Penn., November 15, 1831, a son of Jacob and Elizabeth (Miller) Koller, also natives of York County, the former of whom, a mill-wright and farmer by occupation, died at the age of seventy-seven years and seven months, and the latter when aged seventy-one years. They were members of the Lutheran Church. They had five sons and four daughters. Jacob Koller had been previously married to a Miss Peterman, by whom he had two sons and two daughters. Jonas Koller, the subject of this sketch, is the youngest son and eighth child by the second marriage, and was but thirteen years old when his parents came to Cumberland County and settled near Oysters Point in East Pennsborough Township. In 1848 they moved to their farm near Shepherdstown, in Upper Allen Township, where Jonas attended school during the winters and worked at farming and the trade of wagon-making, until his marriage with Miss Catherine Bingaman, March 9, 1856. She was born in Shepherdstown, this county, October 26, 1831, a daughter of Charles and Susan (Keiper) Bingaman, natives of Lancaster County, Penn., who settled in Shepherdstown soon after their marriage. They were members of the Reformed Church, and had six daughters who grew up. Charles Bingaman, who was a contractor and builder, died in 1876, aged seventy-four years. After his marriage, Mr. Jonas Koller settled at Kollerstown one-half mile south of Mechanicsburg, where he and his father built the first of two houses and the town was named for them. In 1873, our subject moved to his present farm of fifty-five acres in the eastern part of Mechanicsburg, where he has a beautiful residence. Mr. and Mrs. Koller have had five children, four now living: James B., Mary H., Jacob H. and William M. The boys comprise the firm of J. B. Koller & Co., proprietors of the Cumberland Valley Spoke Bending, and Wheel Works. Mrs. Jonas Koller is a member of the Lutheran Church. Mr. Koller became a Mason in early life, and later a Knight Templar and a member of St. John's Commandery, No. 8, at Carlisle. He and his family stand high in the estimation of all. The family are of German descent, our subject's great grandfather having come from Germany and settled in York County, Pennsylvania, at a very early date.

ALFRED C. KOSER, proprietor of "Koser's City Market," near corner Main and Market Square, Mechanicsburg, a representative of one of the oldest families of Cumberland County, was born on Main Street, Mechanicsburg, Penn., May 12, 1847, son of John and Sarah (Rockafellow) Koser. John Koser, born in Mechanicsburg, Penn., was a butcher by trade. At the breaking out of the Rebellion, he was one of the first to shoulder a musket in the defense of his country, enlisting in the spring of 1861, in Capt. Dorsheimer's company of infantry for three months; returned home and re-enlisted, as sergeant of Company C. Ninth Pennsylvania Cavalry, and was among the killed or missing at the battle of Murfreesboro, Tenn., in the summer of 1863. He and his wife had four children. Alfred C., the only son and eldest in the family, was but fifteen when his father was killed, but at that early age he enlisted in Company A, Twentieth Pennsylvania Cavalry. He weighed 160 pounds and claimed he was eighteen, passed and was promoted to corporal, thence to commissary-sergeant, and remained with this company six months; re-enlisting, he served to the close of the war. War reports as follows: "Private Company C. Twentieth Pennsylvania Cavalry, One Hundred and Eighty-first Pennsylvania Volunteers; enlisted second lieutenant, January 28, 1864; enlisted at the age of fifteen years, transferred to Company A, promoted to corporal and commissary-sergeant. Service —Assigned to First Brigade, Second Division, Eighth Corps, March 20, 1864; engagement at Newmarket, Va., May 15; Harrisonburg, June 4; Piedmont, June 5; Buffalo Gap, June 6; Staunton, June 10; Midway, June 11; Rose Mills, June 12; Cedar Creek, June 12; Lexington, June 13; New Glasgow, June 14; Otter Creek, June 16; Quaker Church, June 17; Lynchburg, June 18 and 19; Liberty, June 20; Salem, June 21. Detailed to service in charge of orderlies at Harper's Ferry, July 3 and 18; Ashby's Gap, July 19 and 21; Winchester, July 20; Kernstown, July 23 and 24; Martinsburg, July 25 and 26. Second Brigade. First Cavalry Division—August 7; Berryville Pike, August 10; Fisher's Hill, August 15; Front Royal, August 16; Berryville, August 21, September 3 and 4; Smithfield, August 25, 26 and 29; Winchester, September 19; Fisher's Hill, September 22; Luray Valley, September 24; Brown Gap, September 26; Waynesboro, October 2; Tom's Brook, October 8 and 9; Cedar Creek, October 19; Nineveh, November 12; Roods Hill, November 22; Somerset, December 21; Gordonsville, December 23; Jack's Shop, December 23; Waynesboro, February 28, 1865; White House, March 27; Stony Creek, March 30; Dinwiddie Court House, March 31; Hatcher's Run, March 31; Five Forks, April 1; South Side Railroad, April 2 and 3; White Oak Road, April 4 and 5; Harper's Farm, April 6; Amelia Court House, April 6; Sailors Creek, April 7; Appomattox Station, April 8; Appomattox Court House, April 9. Mustered out, June 10, 1865. Had two horses shot under him —one killed at the battle of Lynchburg, Va., and the other had most of his neck shot away at Five Forks, Va." At the close of the war, July 1, 1865, he returned home and established his present business. Mr. Koser was married at Mechanicsburg, in December, 1868, to Miss Annie M. Markley, who was born at Shiremanstown, this county, daughter of Henry and Susan (Raudenbaugh) Markley, natives, respectively, of Cumberland and Lancaster Counties, Penn. Mr. and Mrs. Koser have one daughter: Grace Ella, born in Mechanicsburg, October 11, 1869, now attending school at Mechanicsburg. Mrs. Koser is a member of the Church of God. Our subject is a junior vice-commander of Col. H. I. Zinn Post, No. 415, G. A. R., Mechanicsburg. He has held various local offices of trust; was elected city councilman by the people of his ward for three years. In politics he is a Republican. His people are of German descent.

JOSEPH LEAS, justice of the peace, Mechanicsburg, was born on his father's farm in Greenwood Township, Perry Co., Penn., January 27, 1822, son of Benjamin and Jane (Mathews) Leas. Benjamin Leas, born October 21, 1759, was twice married; on first occasion to Miss Susannah Bowers, by whom he had thirteen children, seven sons and three daughters living to be men and women. His first wife died March 14, 1814, and he then married Mrs. Jane (Mathews) Purcell, who bore him three children—two sons and one daughter: George, who resides in Shirleysburg, Huntingdon Co., Penn.; Joseph, our subject, and Susannah, widow of Daniel Eshelman, residing in Greenwood Township, Perry Co., Penn. Benjamin Leas died February 21, 1828, and Jane, his second wife, died February 25, 1857. Joseph Leas began clerking in Millerstown in the spring of 1838. In 1841 he clerked in Frankstown, Blair Co., Penn., one year; then followed same occupation at Dillsburg, York County, two years. In 1844 he went to West Hill, Cumberland County, returning in 1845 to Dillsburg, and in October, 1847, he came to Mechanicsburg and clerked for his brother, a merchant and postmaster. In 1854 Mr. Leas was elected justice of the peace, and has held that office ever since. In May, 1865, he was elected borough treasurer, and has held the office ever since, except one year (1879). He is president of the Mechanicsburg Gas & Water Company, and is a director in the Second National Bank. He was married, in 1853, to Miss Sarah Shurr, born in York County, Penn., and who died, leaving one daughter, Laura R., who resides at home with her father. Mr. Leas married Miss Emmaline H. Gould, a native of this county, daughter of Henry and Elizabeth (Rice) Gould, and to this union were born three children: Harry G. (deceased), Fannie G. and Charles W. Mr. and Mrs. Leas are members of the Presbyterian Church. Our subject owns a house on North Market Street, where he and his family reside, and other property in Mechanicsburg. He was but six years old when his father died, and early started to earn his own way in life. At fourteen he drove horses on the canal line between Hollidaysburg and Philadelphia. His brother, Hon. George Leas, was elected a representative to the Legislature from Huntingdon County, Penn., and his half-brother, William B., was elected associate judge of Huntingdon County, Penn. The Leas are of German descent.

LEVI H. LENHER, physician, Mechanicsburg, is a native of Pennsylvania, born near Ephratah, Lancaster County, October 19, 1822, son of John and Mary (Hauck) Lenher, natives of Lancaster County, Penn., who had four sons and two daughters, who lived to be men and women. John Lenher, a machinist, was a member of the firm of Lenher & Pennel, Lancaster Locomotive and Machine Works, and built the first locomotive west of Philadelphia, called the "Hugh Keys." Levi H., the second child and eldest son, when fourteen years of age, entered the Franklin and Marshall Academy, at Lancaster. At sixteen he began to read medicine with Dr. John L. Atlee, and graduated at the Pennsylvania College, Philadelphia, in 1843. He then located at Ephratah, Lancaster Co., Penn., where he remained until October, 1847, when he moved to Churchtown, this county, where he resided until 1872, when he came to Mechanicsburg; went thence to Belmont, Wright Co., Iowa, where he remained three years; then to Harrisburg, Penn., for three and a half years; when he returned to Mechanicsburg and has here since resided. The Doctor was married September 25, 1845, to Miss Mary A. Martin, born in Lancaster County, Penn., daughter of William and Jane Martin. Mrs. Lenher died April 23, 1867, the mother of two children: J. W. Clarence, a clerk in the Pennsylvania Railway recorder's office at Philadelphia, and Mary, who resides at home with her father. January 28, 1869, the Doctor married Mrs. Susan Burnette, born near Lititz, Lancaster Co., Penn., and to this union have been born two children: Elsie Hortense and Victor. Dr. Lenher is a member of the K. P. Lodge, Churchtown, the I. O. O. F. and F. & A. M. He and his wife are members of the Presbyterian Church. The Lenher family is of German origin, and early settlers of Lancaster County, Penn. Dr. Lenher stands high in the estimation of all who know him as a physician and Christian gentleman. He is a member of the State Medical Society of Pennsylvania and the Cumberland County Medical Society.

WILLIAM PENN LLOYD, attorney at law, ex-United States collector of internal revenue, etc., Mechanicsburg, was born in Lisburn, Cumberland County, Penn., September 1, 1837, only son of William and Amanda (Anderson) Lloyd, both of Cumberland County, former of whom learned the trade of cabinet-maker, engaged in the drug business, and was postmaster of Lisburn for thirty years. William P. Lloyd worked on a farm and at cabinet-making, with his father, until his eighteenth year. He attended the public schools, Dickinson Seminary, Cumberland County Normal School, and Whitehall Academy—a single session at each of the last three-named institutions, amounting in all to about one year of academic instruction—teaching in the winter and attending school in the summer. At the age of eighteen he began teaching, and at twenty he began the study of law under Col. William M. Penrose, then a prominent lawyer at Carlisle, and continued teaching and studying until the outbreak of the Rebellion, when he raised a company for the three months' service, but the quota of the State being filled before it was ready to be mustered in, it was disbanded, and in August, 1861, he enlisted in Company G, First Pennsylvania Reserve Cavalry. He served sixteen months as a private, was promoted to hospital steward of the regiment, then to first lieutenant of Company E, and next to adjutant of regiment, acting as assistant adjutant-general of brigade. In this capacity he served until September 9, 1864, when the regiment was mustered out at expiration of its three years' term of service. He was engaged in the battles of Drainsville, Harrisonburg, Cedar Mountain, Gainesville, Second Bull Run (both days), Fredericksburg, Brandy Station, Aldie, Gettysburg (second and third days), Shepherdstown, New Hope Church, Todd's Tavern, Childsberg, Richmond Heights and Meadow Bridge, Haws Shop, Cold Harbor, Barker's Mill, Trevillian Station, White House, St. Mary's Church, and a score or more of skirmishes. Col. Lloyd returned home to Lisburn, and on the organization of the State Guards, under Gen. Hartranft, was appointed inspector-general, with rank of lieutenant-colonel. He resumed teaching and the study of law until April 18, 1865, when he was admitted to the bar of Cumberland County. A year later, regaining his health, which had suffered the courts of Dauphin, York and Perry Counties, the supreme court of Pennsylvania, and district court of the United States. September 16, 1866, he was appointed collector of internal revenue for the Fifteenth Congressional District of Pennsylvania, comprising the counties of York, Cumberland and Perry. The important and responsible duties of the position were discharged by Collector Lloyd in such a manner as to win the unqualified approval of the General Government, and was made the subject of highly commendatory remarks by Gen. Cameron in the United States Senate. He resigned the collectorship August 1, 1869, to accept a position in the Dauphin Deposit Bank at Harrisburg, remaining nearly fifteen years, and until January, 1884, when he quit the bank and went to work on his farm near Mechanicsburg. A year later, regaining his health, which had suffered from confinement in the bank, he opened his present law office (January 1, 1885). He is one of the executors and trustees of the estate of the late Hon. Henry G. Moser, a director of Harrisburg Bridge Company, and of the Mechanicsburg & Dillsburg Railroad Company. He has been commander of Col. H. I. Zinn Post, No. 415, G. A. R., since its organization, March 4, 1884. He is the author of the "History of the First Pennsylvania Reserve Cavalry," a very complete work, giving a graphic history of the three years' service of this regiment during the late Rebellion, etc. Mr. Lloyd was married, May 23, 1865, to Miss Anna H., daughter of Israel L. and Margaret (Moser) Boyer, and their family consists of three children: Weir B., Mary E. and George E. Col. Lloyd is a Mason, a member of Eureka Lodge of Mechanicsburg, and a Knight Templar, St. John's Commandery, No. 8, Carlisle. His family is Welsh and English on the father's side, and Scotch-Irish on the mother's side. He himself is known extensively as a prompt and capable business man and a genial and affable gentleman.

THOMAS H. MAUK, undertaker, Mechanicsburg, was born within eight miles of Stuttgart, at Lauffen, on the River Nager, Wurtemberg, Germany, December 22, 1833, a son of Gottleib and Gottleiben (Metzler) Mauk. The former was a cabinet-maker and undertaker, and the father of two girls and two boys: Gottleiben, Dorothea C., Thomas H. and Jacob. The last named resides at Broken Bow, Custer Co., Neb. Dorothea C. is the widow of Christian Metzgar, and resides in Philadelphia. Gottleiben resides in Germany. Thomas H. was but seven years old when his father died. He attended the common schools until fourteen; he then learned the cabinet and undertaking trade until he was seventeen at Lauffen; then went to Stuttgart and worked until 1852; when he came with his brother Jacob to America, landing in New York after a voyage of eight weeks. Later he came to Philadelphia, where Thomas worked at his trade two years; then moved to Churchtown and remained eight months, after which he came to Mechanicsburg and worked for Samuel Worst, cabinet-maker and undertaker, three years. He then went to Shiremanstown and opened a shop of his own, and while there was married to Miss Elizabeth Houmburg, May 3, 1856. She was born in Hessen-Cassel, a daughter of Beltzer and Charlotte (Holts) Houmburg. In 1859 Mr. Mauk came to Mechanicsburg and worked for Samuel Worst until 1865, and in 1866 formed a partnership with William S. Diehl in the furniture and undertaking business. In 1882 Mr. Mauk sold his interest in furniture but retained the undertaking business, which he has since continued. He has the leading establishment of the kind in this part of the country. He is a member of Shiremanstown Beneficial Society. He and his wife are members of the Bethel Church. They have had ten children, viz.: John J. married Miss Malinda Myers, and is engaged in the undertaking, cabinet and furniture business at Mechanicsburg, Ohio; Thomas M. married Miss Louisa Walker, of Bendersville, Adams County, and is engaged in the cabinet and furniture business at Mechanicsburg, Penn.; Charles H. is engaged in the undertaking and cabinet business at York Springs, Adams Co., Penn.; Kate S. resides with her parents, as do Mary E., Edward G., Samuel T. and Elizabeth C.

JAMES McALLISTER RALSTON, retired, Mechanicsburg, is a descendant of the Ralstons and McAllisters, two of the oldest families of Cumberland County and Pennsylvania. Among those hardy Scotch-Irish Presbyterians who, on account of religious oppression, sought homes in western Pennsylvania, was Andrew Ralston, who located at Big Spring, near Newville, this county, as early as 1728. He was a native of County Armagh, Ireland, and came over to America at the outset of the Scotch emigration. Shortly after the opening of the land office he applied for a warrant, stating that he had occupied the land "ye past eight years." A license was directed to be issued, and below is given a verbatim copy, as in the original, in this connection: "Lancaster Co S S, by order of the proprietary—these are to license and allow Andrew Ralston to continue to improve and dwell on a tract of 200 acres of land on the Great Spring, a branch of the Conedogwainet, joyning to the upper side of a tract granted to Randel Chambers for the use of his son James Chambers, to be hereafter surveyed to the s'd Ralston on the common terms other lands in those parts are sold, provided the same has not been already granted to any other person, and so can be had without prejudice to other tracts before granted. Given under my hand this third day of January Ano: Dom: 1736-7—SA: Blunston. Pensylvania, S. S. "Endorsed:" License to Andrew Ralston—200 acres—this land was subsequently surveyed to him by the surveyor of Lancaster County, Samuel Blunston." There is no date of the death of Andrew Ralston. He left three daughters and two sons. One of his daughters married one Hayes, another married one Mickey. David Ralston, the eldest son, remained at Big Spring on his father's farm. He was twice married, first to a Miss Scott, secondly to a Miss McClintock; both wives died at Big Spring. He removed to Westmoreland County, Penn., in 1806, and died there, in 1810, near Greensburg. By his first wife David Ralston had the following named children: Elizabeth, married to Thomas Jacob; Jane first married to a Mr. Donald and second time to Mr. Taylor; Eleanor, married to Mr. Miller; James, married to Ruth Carson; Andrew, married to Miss Kirkpatrick. By his second wife David Ralston had the following named children: Agnes, married to Mr. Allsworth; Margaret, married to Mr. Moorhead; Ann, married to Mr. Banks; Mary, unmarried; Sarah, unmarried, and David, Jr. His son, David Ralston, was born at Big Spring, near Newville, this county, September 26, 1784; married Miss Lacey McAllister; he and his wife were members of the Presbyterian Church; they had four children: James McAllister, born near Newville, this county, January 14, 1823; David, Andrew, Mary E., wife of David Line. The father of these children died March 8, 1849, and the mother in 1863 in her seventy-third year. James McAllister Ralston, the eldest child, was raised on a farm, and when in his seventeenth year (in 1839) moved with his parents to the old farm (now owned by him) four miles west of Carlisle, and which was located by his great-grandfather, Archibald McAllister, 1728, who purchased over 1,000 acres of land on both sides of McAllister Spring from William Penn. The old foundation of the second mill built west of the Susquehanna River 120 years ago is on the above tract. He, Archibald McAllister, married Miss Jean McClure, near Carlisle, and their children were as follows: Daniel, who settled in West Virginia; John and James, who went to Savannah, Ga., and settled where Fort McAllister now stands; Richard, who laid out the town of Hanover, York Co., Penn., which was called McAllister until changed to Hanover, about 1825; Archibald, settled at Fort Hunter above Harrisburg, in Dauphin County, now called Rockville about 1750; Mary, married to Mr. McKnight; Jean, married to Mr. Ormsby, and settled in what is now Pittsburgh; and another married Mr. Williamson, and Andrew. The last named, Andrew McAllister, was born in the old McAllister farm in 1731. He married Miss Margaret Young, a daughter of James Young, and both husband and wife died in 1804, aged seventy-three and sixty-one, respectively. The children of Andrew and Margaret (Young) McAllister were: Elizabeth, wife of James Parker and who moved to Lexington, Ky., in 1800; Jean, married to Joseph Pierce, they settled in this county; Mary, married to Thomas McIntire; Archibald, unmarried; Margaret, who went with her eldest sister to Lexington, Ky., and married a Mr. Calhoun; James, unmarried, who resided on the old farm; Sarah, who died unmarried; Eleanor, unmarried; Lydia, married to Joseph Jacob; and Lacey, the youngest, who, as above stated, married David Ralston, the father of James McAllister Ralston, the subject of this sketch. During the last three days of June, 1863, Johnston's division of Gen. Ewell's corps of the Rebel Army encamped on the McAllister (now J. Mc. Ralston's) farm, and was then ordered to proceed directly twenty-five miles south, to participate in the battle of Gettysburg. Ewell's division contained the "Louisiana Tigers," and also the Virginia artillery.

LEVI MERKEL (deceased) founder of the First National Bank, Mechanicsburg, is deserving of more than a passing notice in this work, as a man of noble principles, one who stood high in the estimation of all, a good neighbor and friend, and an upright, honest business man and Christian gentleman. He held many important trusts during life, and was the financial counselor of the widow and orphan. The inexperienced sought his advice, for he was kind-hearted and true, and had the entire confidence and respect of all. Upon the organization of the common school system he became its warm friend, and held the position of school director for many years. In the constitutional convention of 1838 he voted against the use of the word "white" in the constitution, for which he was much censured at the time, but lived to see the signature of the President of the United States appended to the emancipation proclamation. In the same convention the resolution restraining the power of the banks was fought step by step by the adherents and tools of the United States Bank, which had become a Pennsylvania State institution, and they left no stone unturned to secure its defeat or postponement. It passed by the deciding vote of Mr. Merkel, who voted against his own political partisans—principle with him was everything, policy nothing. The wisdom of this vote was soon demonstrated in the history of the bank. Among his effects is a book containing the signatures of every member of the convention, with marginal notes, showing the age and birthplace of each, his business or occupation, etc. His prominent characteristic was his rigid adherence to principle and to his convictions of what was right. On this ground he judged men, on it he made his friends. Deception was not in his nature, in business he was exact; in judgment clear and sound, in language always chaste, in habits frugal, in affection strong but undemonstrative, in religion firm in faith in an all-ruling Providence. He wrote frequently for publication in religious papers, and his articles were full of strong argument and beautiful thoughts. He was born near Ephrata, Lancaster Co., Penn., May 2, 1803, the only child of Jacob and Mary (Carpenter) Merkel, natives of Lancaster County, Penn., descendants of two of the oldest families of that county, and died at Carlisle, Penn., on September 20, 1876. He was but four years of age when the family moved to what is now Lower Allen Township, where he remained on the farm, attending school and teaching until his marriage, on November 27, 1828, with Miss Susanna Martin, who was born on October 13, 1810, on her father's farm near Shiremanstown (which adjoined that of her husband's father). She was the daughter of David and Barbara (Hessin) Martin. They remained on the farm until the spring of 1858, when they moved to Mechanicsburg. To this union were born five sons and four daughters, of whom five children are living: David R., a professor of music (at present engaged in farming on the old homestead farm in Lower Allen Township), married to Miss Sarah Eberly; Mary C., wife of C. B. Niesley, a produce and grain merchant, Mechanicsburg; Barbara H., wife of John B. Landis, Esq., at Carlisle; Naomi S., who resides at the home of her mother; James Weir, a banker, married to Miss Lilla A. Irvine, of Elmira, N. Y. The daughters are all members of the Presbyterian Church.

JOSEPH MILLEISEN, coal and lumber dealer, Mechanicsburg, was born in Lower Paxton Township, four miles east of Harrisburg, Dauphin Co., Penn., September 19, 1813, on the old homestead of his father, where he remained until his marriage, in February, 1844, with Miss Barbara, daughter of Christian and Mary (Brookhart) Martin, of Cumberland County. Mr. Milleisen, in February, 1845, came to Mechanicsburg, where he engaged in the grain and produce trade until 1859, when he established his present coal and lumber business. Our subject has been actively identified with the best interests of Mechanicsburg. He, with Dr. Ira Day, Jacob Mumma, S. P. Gorgas, John Brandt and George Bilner organized the water and gas company which supplies the town. He was elected and served as treasurer of the Gas and Water Company for three years, when, retiring, his son, John, was elected in his stead. He has also held other local offices of trust in Mechanicsburg, and is a director of the Mechanicsburg & Dillsburg Railroad. The Milleisens are, as the name indicates, of German descent, and are members of the Reformed Church at Mechanicsburg. To our subject and wife were born seven children, four of whom are living, and all were born in Mechanicsburg: George C., John J., Alfred W. and Martin. George C., born January 24, 1847, married Miss Mary, daughter of John and Frances (Bowman) Baker, who was born near Churchtown, this county, and to this union were born two children: Fanny and Joseph. George C. lost his first wife by death in 1872, and November 29, 1874, he married Miss Emma, daughter of Conrad Kime, of Cumberland County. He is now in partnership with his father in the lumber and coal business, under the firm name of Milleisen & Son. He is a member of the I. O. O. F., Mechanicsburg Lodge, No. 215, Wildey Encampment, No. 39, and a member of the Improved Order of Heptasophs, J. H. Conclave, No. 105 Mechanicsburg. John J., second son of our subject, learned the druggist business, but was afterward appointed station agent at Mechanicsburg for the Cumberland Valley R. R., which position he filled for three years, when, after a short time passed in Shippensburg, he engaged in mercantile business at Topeka, Kas., and in 1881 was persuaded by Mr. Talmadge, general manager of the Wabash & St. Louis Railroad, to accept a position on this road, with headquarters at Jacksonville, Ill.; he married Miss Jennie, daughter of John Thompson. Alfred W., of the firm of Milleisen & Keefer, is engaged in the hardware business here; is a mason and member of the I. O. O. F. and Heptasoph societies; he married Miss Ida, daughter of Henry G. Rupp, of Mechanicsburg. Martin is first teller in the Second National Bank of Mechanicsburg. Joseph Milleisen is one of the active and energetic business men of Cumberland County, with which he has been identified for a period of nearly half a century. In politics he was first a Whig, but on the rise of the Republican party became a Republican, and has since given that party his support. His brother Jacob is still living (the third generation of this family) on the old homestead in Paxton Township, Dauphin Co., Penn.

DAVID MILLER, grain and coal merchant, Mechanicsburg, was born May 14, 1825, on the old homestead farm of his father in Windsor Township, fourteen miles north of Reading, Berks Co., Penn. His parents, George and Mollie (Raver) Miller, natives of Berks County, were members of the Lutheran Church; they had a family of eight children—five sons and three daughters. David, the second son and child, worked on his father's farm, attending school during the winters, until he was seventeen, when he went to Leesport, Berks Co., Penn., and began to learn the trade of miller. After remaining here three years and three months he attended school at Reading six months. He then rented a water-mill on Maiden Creek, Maiden Creek Township, Berks Co. (before he was twenty-one), and operated the mill three years; then he returned to Leesport and here formed a partnership with William Major and bought the steam-mill (in which Mr. Miller learned his trade) some twelve months later. Mr. Miller sold his interest to his partner, and in the fall of 1853 came to Mechanicsburg, this county, and built the steam flouring-mill now owned by the Cumberland Valley Railroad Company, and used as a warehouse. Mr. Miller operated this mill some seven years, in partnership with E. Zook two years; then Mr. Zook sold his interest to Moses Eberly, and in 1861 Mr. Eberly purchased Mr. Miller's interest. Our subject then engaged in the grain business, and some four years later began to handle coal in connection with same. Mr. Miller was married, October 18, 1852, to Miss Leah Forney, born in Berks County, Penn., daughter of John and Lydia (Hartzler) Forney, natives of Pennsylvania. Mr. and Mrs. Miller are members of the Lutheran Church. They have had seven children, three now living: Samuel F., clerking for his father, married to Miss Sallie Landers; Lillie, residing with her parents; Annie M., wife of John Planck, dry goods merchant of Carlisle. Mr. Miller is a member of Eureka Lodge, No. 302, F. & A. M.; is one of the directors of the Second National Bank, and is one of Mechanicsburg's enterprising representative business men, and stands high in the estimation of all who know him as an honorable citizen and Christian gentleman. He is of Scotch and German descent; his great-grandfather came from Scotland. Mr. Miller now owns and runs a flour-mill two miles south of Shermanstown, York County (it is a mill of fifty barrels per day capacity), and a farm of fifty acres—the mill stands in the center of the farm—and a dwelling-house in Mechanicsburg, and a warehouse for handling grain.

DAVID R. MILLER, proprietor of Miller's Sash, Door and Blind Factory, Mechanicsburg, was born on the old family farm in Silver Spring Township, this county, July 15, 1829, son of Abraham and Elizabeth (Shupe) Miller, natives of Silver Spring Township, this county, and Dauphin County, Penn., respectively. Abraham Miller, who was a farmer and distiller, a son of John Miller, was born in Germany, and came to Lancaster County, Penn., and afterward to Silver Spring Township, this county. He and his wife were members of the Lutheran Church. They had five sons. David R., the eldest, remained on the farm and attended school during the winters until he was apprenticed three years to learn the carpenter's trade, and contracting and building, in which he continued until 1848, when he began to work in the sash, door and blind factory of Seidle & Eberly. Soon afterward he became foreman, and remained with this company until 1852. He then worked at his trade in Franklin, Cumberland and Dauphin Counties until 1863, when he, with F. Seidle, Samuel Eberly and others commenced bridge-building for the Government. Then he worked in George Frullinger's factory, Harrisburg, and at carpentering in Mechanicsburg until 1867, when he, with three others, built a sash, door and blind factory. A short time after, Mr. Miller and S. B. King formed a partnership, purchased the factory, and continued doing business under the firm name of Miller & King until March, 1884, when James Fulton purchased Mr. King's interest, and soon after Mr. Miller purchased Mr. Fulton's interest, and has since conducted the business alone. In May, 1852, Mr. Miller married Miss Frances Brownewell, a native of Roxbury, Silver Spring Township, this county, daughter of Henry and Barbara (Baker) Brownewell, natives of Silver Spring Township, this county, and Adams County, respectively. Mr. and Mrs. Miller are members, the former of the Lutheran and the latter of the Reformed Church. They have three children: John H., assisting his father in the factory; Barbara E., at home with her parents; and David J. L. Mr. Miller has been elected councilman by the people of Mechanicsburg two terms. He is a member of the Mechanicsburg Lodge, No. 215, I. O. O. F. He is a self-made man, and learned early to depend on his own resources for a living. He started without a cent, but went bravely to work, and by hard work, honest dealing and close application to business has made life a success.

JEREMIAH H. MORRET, proprietor of the "National Hotel," Mechanicsburg, is a native of Cumberland County, born in Churchtown, Monroe Township, June 20, 1837, and is a descendant of one of the oldest families in Pennsylvania. His grandfather, Michael Morret, born in this county, was a blacksmith of Newburg, where he died; he was the parent of four sons and three daughters: William, the third son, was born in Newburg, learned the blacksmith trade and when a young man moved to Churchtown and opened a shop there; he married Miss Sarah A., daughter of Adam and Polly Diller, and had two sons and three daughters: Alfrida A., wife of Jacob Beistline, a farmer at Oaks' Point, this county; Jeremiah H.; Hezekiah, married to Angeline Harmon, lives in Franklin County, Penn.; Lucilla, widow of Edward Westhaver, is a milliner at Mechanicsburg; Mary J., wife of John Slonaker, an employe of the Cumberland Valley R. R. Company. Mr. and Mrs. William Morret were members of the Lutheran Church. When Jeremiah H. Morret was but three years old he moved with his parents to a mile north of Locust Point, where he learned blacksmithing of his father, and there remained until November, 1862, when he became a member of Company A, One Hundred and Fifty-eighth Pennsylvania Volunteer Infantry. Ten months later he was mustered out and then returned to his home near Locust Point. In the spring of 1863 he went to New Kingston and there learned the painter's trade; three years later he moved to Carlisle, Penn., and clerked in the "Thudium House" until December, 1867, when he clerked for John J. Ringwalt in the "American House" until March 1, 1868, when he went to New Kingston and ran a hotel, eating-house and livery stable. Five years later he came to Mechanicsburg and here clerked for Mr. Ringwalt in the "American House," until July, 1884, when he opened his present hotel, on Main Street, a three-story brick building containing twenty-six rooms, fine large drawing-room, parlor and sample rooms. Mr. Morret was married, March 16, 1874, to Miss Rachael Daugherty, born in Upper Allen Township, this county, daughter of George and Mary (Stallsmith) Daugherty. To this union have been born two sons and one daughter: Jennie, William and Herman. Mr. Morret is a member of H. I. Zinn Post, G. A. R., No. 415, Mechanicsburg. Politically he is a Democrat. He is a perfect gentleman and an admirable host. His hotel is a model of neatness.

HON. HENRY G. MOSER (deceased), late member of the Legislature, and associate judge of Cumberland County, and whose portrait appears in this volume, was born in Berks County, Penn., February 22, 1813. His family was one of the oldest and most prominent in Berks County. His father, Jacob Moser, born in that county, a farmer by occupation, married Miss Elizabeth Gresh, of Berks County, a daughter of George Gresh. Jacob and Elizabeth (Gresh) Moser were of German descent, members of the Lutheran Church. Their family consisted of four sons and seven daughters, Hon. Henry G. being the eldest. Our subject worked at farming, attending school in the winter in Amity Township, Berks County, and it is said that his desire for knowledge was so great that he would carry a slate and pencil to the field, and there sit on his plow, while resting, and would figure out some difficult problems. In this manner he obtained his education, and at the age of seventeen or eighteen he began teaching school in Berks County, a profession he followed until 1835, when he became manager and clerk for the Glasgow Iron Works (consisting of forge, furnace, mill and farm, near Pottstown, Montgomery Co., Penn.,) continuing there until 1837, when he came to this county and took charge of the Iron Works, known as Liberty Forge, near Lisburn, and was one of those who purchased the works. In 1846 he became sole owner of this property. In 1852 he sold a half interest to I. L. Boyer, his brother-in-law, and in 1852 sold out his interest to Mr. Boyer; but in 1858 he became a partner with him, continuing in that relationship until 1864, when he again sold out to Mr. Boyer, and retired from business. In 1865 he removed to Mechanicsburg, where he died May 20, 1884. In 1853 Mr. Moser was nominated and elected a Democratic representative to the Legislature by the people of Cumberland County; was also elected and served as associate judge of this county five years, and was the last associate judge of the county under the Constitution of 1837. He held various other offices of trust. He was for a number of years a director of the Harrisburg Bridge Company; a director of the First National Bank of Mechanicsburg, the Gas & Water Company, and the Mechanicsburg & Dillsburg Railway Company; was also president and treasurer of the Allen and East Pennsborough Society for the Recovery of Stolen Horses and Mules, and the Detection of Thieves. He was a recognized leader, and his judgment at all times was fair and impartial. A man of great natural ability and force of character, he had the confidence and respect of all, and his opinion was greatly sought and much valued; he was practical, self-reliant, cautious and slow at arriving at conclusions, but prompt and energetic in the execution of his designs. Mr. Moser came to this county a young man with very limited means, but at his death was one of the wealthiest men in his county, having accumulated a fortune, not by speculation, but by careful business habits, wise investments and strict economy. While he was an active and successful business man, he did not permit these relations to crowd out his duties as a citizen and a Christian. He was warmly attached to the Lutheran Church, as were his ancestors, and to it he was a liberal and generous contributor both of his means and influence, as well as to such other religions and social movements as met with his approval. Our subject was married twice; first, November 6, 1838, to Miss Ester Ann Lorah, of Amity Township, Berks Co., Penn., a most estimable, Christian lady, to whom, as a helpmate, Mr. Moser attributed much of his success in life. She died February 10, 1876, having had no children. His second marriage was June 13, 1878, with Miss Margaret J. Urich, who was born in Upper Allen Township, this county, daughter of Jacob B. and Sarah (Ayers) Urich, old settlers of Cumberland County. Mr. and Mrs. Moser had two children: Ruth, born October 13, 1879, and Margaret, born November 13, 1881. They reside with their mother in Mechanicsburg. Mrs. Moser is a member of the Presbyterian Church of Dillsburg.

JACOB MUMMA, retired farmer, Mechanicsburg, was born six miles east of Harrisburg, in Swatara Township, Dauphin Co., Penn., September 14, 1809. His parents, John and Elizabeth (Frantz) Mumma, were natives of Pennsylvania, and members of the Mennonite Church. They had a family of four sons and two daughters. Jacob, the second son and third child, remained on the farm with his father until his marriage, January 19, 1832, with Miss Elizabeth Nissley, born in Dauphin County, Penn., daughter of Martin and Elizabeth (Kreider) Nissley. Mr. and Mrs. Mumma moved to Lancaster County, Penn., in 1835, and engaged in farming until 1839, and there Mrs. Mumma died March 20, 1836. The family consisted of two sons and one daughter: Martin, who resides on the old homestead farm of his father, one-half mile north of Mechanicsburg; John, who resides on a farm a mile south of Mechanicsburg, and Anna, wife of Levi Musselman, resides on a farm three miles southeast of Mechanicsburg. In the spring of 1839 Jacob Mumma came to Cumberland County and bought a farm in Monroe Township, afterward purchasing the old homestead farm in Silver Spring Township. Our subject was married on second occasion December 1, 1836, to Mrs. Catharine Rupp, born in Cumberland County, daughter of John and Anna (Snavely) Eberly, and who died May 1, 1861, the mother of six children, four living: Jacob E., farmer and stock dealer; Amos, a miller in Upper Allen Township; Eli, farmer in Upper Allen Township; Eliza, wife of Christian Hertzler, a farmer in Hampden Township. Mr. Mumma married September 25, 1862. His present wife, Mrs. Mary Hertzler was born in Lancaster County, Penn., daughter of Henry and Elizabeth (Kauffman) Schoph. To this union has been born one daughter, Emma, who resides with her parents. Mr. and Mrs. Mumma are members of the Mennonite Church at State Hill. Mr. Mumma is one of the founders of what is now the First National Bank of Mechanicsburg (the others are Levi Merkel, deceased, who had established a private bank, John Brandt, John Sadler, Levi Eberly, Samuel Eberly, Jacob Eberly, John Niesley, Solomon P. and William R. Gorgas). Mr. Mumma is one of the solid retired business men whose life has been one of interest and success, and has been identified with the county since 1839. He is of German descent and his ancestors were among the earliest pioneers of Pennsylvania, his great-great-grandfather having come from Switzerland to this country to settle in Lancaster County, Penn., as early as 1731.

CHRISTIAN B. NIESLEY, wholesale and retail coal and produce merchant, Mechanicsburg, engaged in agricultural and horticultural pursuits, was born on the old family farm in Middlesex Township, Cumberland Co., Penn., August 15, 1834. He attended school and assisted his father on the farm until he was seventeen, when he taught school winters and studied with a private tutor, and one year in the academy of Juniata County, Penn. At twenty-one he went to Osborn, Ohio, and taught school there one year; then engaged as manager and salesman for the Neff & Carson Nursery Company, of Dayton, Ohio, one year; then took charge of the nursery business himself for several years, extending his trade into the Southern States. Having been successful he returned to Cumberland County, purchased the farm his father had selected for him, and soon after settled in Mechanicsburg. He was married here, November 12, 1861, to Miss Mary C. Merkel, born in Lower Allen Township, this county, daughter of Levi and Susan (Martin) Merkel. Mr. Merkel, who was one of the first bankers in Mechanicsburg, organized what is now the First National Bank. Since his marriage Mr. Niesley has been engaged in commercial, agricultural and horticultural pursuits. Mr. and Mrs. Niesley are active members of the Presbyterian Church. He was sent as commissioner to the last General Assembly at Minneapolis. They had two children, one son living—Charles Merkel, born in Mechanicsburg August 9, 1865, graduate of Lafayette College, Pennsylvania, class of 1886. Mr. Niesley takes a lively interest in common schools, and has been director for many years; is chairman of the Pennsylvania State Sabbath-school Association, and he was one of the organizers of the Cumberland County Sabbath-school Association, organized at Carlisle, September 13, 1873; was elected chairman of the executive committee; then president, serving three successive years, and has been associated with it officially ever since; and, seeing the great need of better preparation by the Sunday-school teachers for their responsible position, he was one of the leading spirits in establishing and conducting the Cumberland Valley Sunday-school Assembly at Williams' Grove, where some of the best normal and primary instruction was given and some of the most noted lecturers of the age were heard. Our subject is a son of Jacob and Mary (Miller) Niesley, natives of Lancaster County, Penn., the former of whom was born in Donegal Township November 8, 1797, and died March 13, 1869; the latter, born July 21, 1802, died August 8, 1877; they were members of the Mennonite Church; had four sons and two daughters, of whom Christian B. is the youngest. Our subject's great-grandfather, Christian Niesley, came from Switzerland, during the religious persecutions, with two brothers, and settled in Lancaster County, Penn. Christian B. Niesley's maternal grandfather came to Lancaster County, Penn., from Switzerland. The subject of our sketch is one of the enterprising business men and representative citizens, and stands high in the estimation of all as an upright, honest, Christian gentleman. He has one of the most beautiful residences in Mechanicsburg, situated on Main Street, where he and his family reside.

LINDSAY PITTS O'NEALE, physician, Mechanicsburg, was born on his father's plantation, in Essex County, Va., October 11, 1838. His parents, Albert G. and Anna (Wearring) O'Neale, were both born in Essex County. Albert G. O'Neale was a captain in the war of 1812, and his father, Thomas O'Neale, who was born in Dublin, Ireland, was a merchant in that city until he joined the rebellion against England, and after it was quelled he immigrated to Essex County, Va., where he was married to Miss Elizabeth Pitts, of English descent, and to this union were born two sons and three daughters: Albert G., Elizabeth, Mary, Johnson and Emeline. Albert G. married Anna Wearring, and had two sons: Thomas J. and Lindsay Pitts. During the late war of the Rebellion the father lost all of his property. At the age of sixteen Lindsay P. O'Neale struck out for himself; went to Baltimore, Md., and clerked in a grocery and drug store until 1858; he then ran a stitching machine in his brother's boot and shoe factory, studying medicine in the meantime, until the fall of 1860, when he entered the York Academy, and here remained until the spring of 1861, studying medicine until the fall of 1861, when he entered the medical department of the United States Army. In 1864 he entered Washington Medical College, of Baltimore, and studied and attended lectures until March, 1865, when he located in York, York Co., Penn., where he practiced medicine until 1870, when he settled in Mechanicsburg, Cumberland Co., Penn., and here he has since been actively engaged in the practice of his profession. Dr. O'Neale was married here November 26, 1868, to Miss Margaretta W. Eckels, who was born near Mechanicsburg, Penn., daughter of Samuel and Mary (Cooper) Eckels. Mrs. O'Neale is a member of the Presbyterian Church. Dr. O'Neale is a charter member of the Eclectic Association of the State of Pennsylvania, and was president of this association two terms. He is also a member of the National Eclectic Medical Association of the United States.

ADAM ORRIS, of Eberly & Orris, manufacturers of patent and wood-hub wheels, etc., Mechanicsburg, is a representative of one of the oldest and best families of Cumberland County. He was born on the old homestead of his father, in Silver Spring Township, this county, two miles north of Mechanicsburg, March 31, 1838. His father, David Orris, was of English descent, born in this county; first married Miss Susan Eichelberger, also a native of this county, daughter of Adam Eichelberger, who was of German descent, and by this union had eight children, of whom three are living: John, a retired carpenter and hotel proprietor, residing in Mechanicsburg; Susan M., wife of William E. Beistline, a boot and shoe manufacturer, of New Kingston, this county, and Adam. Mrs. Susan Orris died in 1840, a member of the Lutheran Church. David Orris married, for his second wife, Miss Susan Senseman, and by her had ten children, of whom the following survive: Elizabeth, Catharine, wife of Eli Dunkelberger; David; Samuel; Jennetta, wife of Samuel Kast, and Levan H. David Orris died in 1869. The mother is still living. She and her husband were always members of the Lutheran Church. Adam Orris, subject of our sketch, attended school during winters, working on his father's farm in summer time until he was sixteen, when he clerked in a general store at Hogestown until he was twenty. He then clerked at New Kingston until 1862, when he entered the army, serving as sergeant-major of the One Hundred and Fifty-eighth Regiment Pennsylvania Infantry. At the expiration of his term of service he was mustered out and returned to New Kingston, where he bought a half interest in the store of David Strohn, and one year later purchased his partner's interest and conducted the business alone some two years, when H. H. Lamb was admitted as a partner. In 1870 Orris & Lamb sold out to J. A. Heagy, and Orris formed a partnership with Capt. Samuel J. Shoop. They purchased 2,000 acres of timber land in Franklin County, Penn., erected saw-mills and engaged very extensively in the manufacture of lumber, etc. In May, 1885, Mr. Orris formed his present partnership with A. G. Eberly. Our subject was united in marriage, March 1, 1864, with Miss M. Isabella Fought, born in Silver Spring Township, this county, daughter of Peter and Margaret (Armstrong) Fought, natives of Cumberland County. Mr. and Mrs. Orris are members of the Lutheran Church. They have two children; Talbert D., the eldest, attended the high schools of Mechanicsburg, Chambersburg Academy, and graduated from the Harrisburg Business College in 1883. In March, 1884, he went to Philadelphia, and was employed as salesman in the wholesale wall paper house of Elder & Bentley until July, 1885, when, at his father's request, he became assistant and traveling salesman for Eberly & Orris. Miss Maggie M. Orris resides at home with her parents. Adam Orris is one of the energetic, enterprising men and leading manufacturers of Mechanicsburg, and stands high in the estimation of all as an upright, representative citizen and Christian gentleman.

FREDERICK K. PLOYER, bank cashier, Mechanicsburg, of German-American descent, was born at Jackson Hall, near Chambersburg, Franklin Co., Penn., December 21, 1844, son of Jacob and Sophia (Kissell) Ployer, natives of Pennsylvania, who moved to Cumberland County about the year 1856, and settled on a farm near Newville. They were members of the German Reformed Church. Of their family of seven children, Frederick K., the eldest of six sons, remained on the farm with his father, attending school during the winters until he was eighteen, when he began teaching in Cumberland County, continuing in the profession until the breaking out of the late war of the Rebellion, when he, with his father and brother John H., enlisted their services. Frederick K., the subject of this sketch, enlisted in Company D, One Hundred and Eighty-seventh Regiment of Pennsylvania Volunteers February 4, 1864, and served with his regiment in the field from May, 1864, to October, 1864, participating in the battle of New Cold Harbor, and all engagements of the Fifth Army Corps at and during the siege of Petersburg in the summer of 1864, most important of which were at Petersburg & Norfolk Railway, June 18 and 19; Jerusalem Plank Road, June 20; Weldon Railroad, August 18, 19 and 20. His regiment having been ordered to Philadelphia for duty, Private Ployer was detailed for special duty at headquarters Department of the Susquehanna, and was ordered to report to Capt. Francis H. Wessels, judge-advocate of the department of Harrisburg, Penn., where he was engaged in clerical work with the military commission in the trial of the Columbia

County conspirators. From the conclusion of this work until the muster out of his regiment at the close of the war, he continued as record clerk in the judge-advocate's office, headquarters District of Pennsylvania. In August, 1865, Mr. Ployer returned to Newville, this county, and taught school until June, 1869, when he was appointed assistant assessor of internal revenue of the Fifteenth Congressional District of Pennsylvania and continued in that position for four years; then located in Altoona, Blair Co., Penn., where he was employed as assistant shop clerk of the Altoona machine shops of the Pennsylvania Railroad Company, and continued there until February 1, 1878, when he was appointed teller of the Second National Bank of Mechanicsburg, Penn., and January 1, 1880, was appointed to his present position as cashier. Mr. Ployer was married, January 18, 1870, to Miss Sarah R. Lloyd, of Welsh descent on her father's and Scotch-Irish on her mother's side, born November 16, 1844, at Lisburn, this county, daughter of William and Amanda Lloyd. Mr. and Mrs. Ployer have one daughter, Nellie M., born December 12, 1872, now attending school at Mechanicsburg. Mr. and Mrs. Ployer are members of the Presbyterian Church. Mr. Ployer is a member of Big Springs Lodge, No. 361, F. & A. M., at Newville; St. John's Chapter R. A. M., at Carlisle, Penn.; and is a Past Commander of St. John's Commandery, No. 8, K. T., Carlisle; is also a member of Col. H. I. Zinn Post No. 415, G. A. R., Mechanicsburg. He is one of the leading business men and is a representative citizen of Mechanicsburg and Cumberland County.

REV. SAMUEL W. REIGART, pastor First Presbyterian Church, Mechanicsburg (called from the church of Sunbury, Penn.), entered upon his pastoral duties October 25, 1868, although, at his own request, his formal installation by the presbytery was deferred until June 15, 1869. He was born at Lancaster, Lancaster Co., Penn., July 29, 1837; son of John Franklin and Caroline (White) Reigart, natives of Pennsylvania. J. Franklin Reigart held various public appointments in Lancaster, Penn., including State offices. He and his wife were members of the Presbyterian Church; they had three sons and two daughters. Samuel W., the eldest, graduated at the Lancaster High School and afterward at "Franklin and Marshall College," in 1859, and took the second honor in his class; was appointed principal of Lancaster High School in 1860, and held the position five years. While teaching he read theology, under the direction of the Rev. Walter Powell; received his degree of A. M. in 1862, and was licensed to preach the gospel by the presbytery of Donegal (now Westminster) October 4, 1864, and the next year was called to the pastorate of the church of Sunbury, and was ordained and installed as pastor of the church by the presbytery of Northumberland, Penn., October 17, 1865, which position he held until 1868, when he was called to the church at Mechanicsburg, and here preached his introductory sermon October 25, 1868. He was married, December 31, 1860, to Miss Anna E. Hodgson, born in Columbia, Lancaster Co., Penn., daughter of the Rev. Francis Hodgson, D. D., and Agnes (Long) Hodgson, the former of whom was for many years a prominent minister and residing elder in the Methodist Episcopal Church, his field of labor being principally in Philadelphia and New York. To Mr. and Mrs. Samuel W. Reigart have been born five children, four now living: John Franklin, Agnes H., Caroline W. and Mary H. Our subject's labors have been very successful building up a strong church from a weak one and increasing its membership over 300 souls. Mr. Reigart is a descendant of one of the oldest families in the State, who settled in Lancaster County, coming from Germany, more than 100 years ago.

JOHN RIEGEL, retired merchant, secretary of Allen and East Pennsborough Mutual Fire Insurance Company, member of the Mechanicsburg Gas and Water Company, Mechanicsburg, is the oldest native born resident of Mechanicsburg, where he first saw the light of the day, August 14, 1818. His parents, John Adam and Esther (Brandt) Riegel, were born and raised in what is now Dauphin County, Penn. John Adam Riegel came to Mechanicsburg, this county, in 1816, formed a partnership with John Coover, and opened a dry goods and general store, the first one of any importance in the town. Mr. Riegel was elected city burgess by the people of Mechanicsburg and held other offices of trust, including that of trustee of the Union Church. He died January 11, 1851, aged fifty-six years and some months. His wife was a member of the Dunkard Church. They had three sons and five daughters, of whom two sons and four daughters are now living: Levi; John; Margaret, wife of Daniel Ulrich; Sarah, wife of John Stine, a retired Methodist Episcopal minister of Mechanicsburg; Eliza, widow of Dr. J. B. Herring; Mary, wife of George Zacharias, residing in Mechanicsburg. Catharine, wife of Christian Brandt, died in 1878. John, the second son and child, attended the schools of Mechanicsburg, and clerked for his father until 1848, when he engaged in business for himself, and, at the death of his father, succeeded him. In 1867 he closed out his business, retaining the property which included the building occupied by the Second National Bank and his residence, adjoining which is the old homestead once owned by Adam Riegel (deceased). Mr. Riegel married at Lebanon, Lebanon Co., Penn., September 5, 1843, Miss Susan A iams Ingol, who was born in Baltimore, Md., April 28, 1826, only daughter of Samuel and Susannah (Moulton) Ingol, natives of England and Newburyport, Mass., respectively; they were members of the Congregational Church. Mr. and Mrs. Riegel are members of the Lutheran Church (general council). They have had two children: Sarah Gertrude, wife of Rev. Johnson R. Groff, a Lutheran minister of Danville, Penn., and Nellie, born in 1847, first wife of Maj. Azor H. Nickerson and who died, in 1867, at Fort Boiscé, Idaho. Mr. Riegel is one of the pioneers of Cumberland County, and stands high in the estimation of all as an upright business man and Christian gentleman. He held an office in the school board twenty-one years. He has lived to see the borough undergo many interesting and important changes and can remember when there were but twelve houses, of which but one is now standing—the building on the northeast corner of Federal and Main Streets, where he was born. Mr. Riegel is a grandson of John Adam Riegel, who came with his brothers, Abraham and Samuel Riegel, from Germany and settled near Hummelstown, Dauphin Co., Penn.

JESSE W. RINGROSE, proprietor of the Ringrose Fly-Net and Collar Manufactory, Mechanicsburg, was born on the old homestead farm of the family, two miles northeast of Berwick, in Luzerne County, Penn., August 30, 1847. E. Aaron Ringrose, his father, was born in Northamptonshire, England, but came to this country while still a young man, and settled in Luzerne County, where he engaged in buying and selling stock. He married Miss Catharine, daughter of William E. Fowler, one of the old settlers of Columbia County, Penn. The family consisted of eight children, of whom four sons and three daughters are still living, of whom Jesse W. is the youngest. Our subject attended school until he was fourteen years of age, when he began clerking in a grocery at Lock Haven, which position he continued to hold until he was twenty, when he entered Andalusia College, Andalusia, Penn., where he remained three years; he next engaged in a flour, bread and cracker manufactory, in which business he remained for a period of about fifteen months. He then sold out his interest in that business, and entered the Pennsylvania University of Medicine, at Philadelphia, where he remained for a period of two years, until, his health failing, he went south to Martinsburg, W. Va., and opened a general grocery store, in which business he continued until the death of his father-in-law, Henry W. Irvine, in 1877, when he came to Mechanicsburg, and soon after invented a leather net. Mr. Ringrose was married, January 28, 1875, to Miss Dessie A. Irvine, a daughter of Col. Henry W. and Mary (Kanaga) Irvine, and born at New Kingston, this county, where both the Irvine and Kanaga families are well known. Mr. Ringrose is a successful business man. He first established his fly-net and collar factory at Mechanicsburg in 1881, since which time his business has continually increased, and his facilities have been greatly enlarged, until, to-day, he has one of the largest manufacturing establishments of this kind in the United States. Mr. Ringrose is the patentee of most of the improved machinery used in the manufacture of his nets, and which he will not sell or lease, it giving him an immense advantage over other manufacturing establishments of the same kind. To give some idea of the rapid growth of this business: Mr. Ringrose starting unaided (or with the help at first of only one man); now uses steam-power, gives direct, permanent employment to from 75 to 100 workmen, and employs three traveling salesmen. From a small beginning the business amounted last year to $60,000, and has extended from a small field to a territory which covers nearly the whole of the United States.

JOHN J. RINGWALT, Mechanicsburg. The jolly, large-hearted, whole-souled proprietor of the "American House" was born near Carlisle, this county, March 21, 1838; son of Cyrus and Anna (Shaffer) Ringwalt, who were born in Lancaster County, Penn., and came to Cumberland County, settling near Carlisle; both were members of the Episcopal Church; they had a family of ten children, eight of whom are living: George, Kate, Mary, John J., Lydia, Cyrus, Emma and Lew. Our subject remained with his father on the farm until 1868, when he took charge of the "Locust Point Hotel" between Mechanicsburg and Carlisle. One year later he took charge of the "American House," and three years later of the "Bentz (now the "Florence") House," and in the spring of 1881 became proprietor of the "American House" in Mechanicsburg. Our subject was married here August 25, 1884, to Miss Maezey Wilson, born at Bridgeport, Cumberland Co., Penn., daughter of Robert and Sarah (Schock) Wilson, old settlers of this county. Mr. Wilson is ex-associate judge and clerk of Cumberland County courts.

LEW RINGWALT, brother of John J., was born in Monroe Township, this county, April 3, 1851, and is now serving as clerk for his brother at the "American House," Mechanicsburg. He was united in marriage with Miss Fannie, daughter of Theodore Chew, a farmer near Barnesboro Station, N. J., and to this union was born a son who died in infancy. Mrs. Lew Ringwalt died in New Jersey, in 1872, a member of the Methodist Episcopal Church.

JOHN L. SADLER, lumber manufacturer, Mechanicsburg, is a native of Cumberland County, Penn., born on the old family farm near Cummingstown, Penn Township, this county, November 16, 1842. His grandfather, Richard Sadler, had moved from Adams County to Centre County, Penn., when twenty-one years old; married Miss Rebecca Lewis, of Centre County, by whom he had five sons and three daughters. Joshua, the second son of this couple, born in Centre County, married Miss Harriet Staley, of Adams County, and in 1841 moved to the old farm adjoining Cummingstown, and settled in the woods where he cleared a farm, and died in December, 1862, aged sixty-two years; his widow died in January, 1868, aged fifty-two. They were members of the Methodist

Episcopal Church, parents of three sons and one daughter, two sons living: Wilbur F., president judge of Cumberland County, and John L. In 1866 Mrs. Sadler moved to Carlisle. Our subject early went to Martinsburg, Va., and engaged in the manufacture of lumber, and has followed this industry ever since at Hagerstown, Md., and New Cumberland, this county. He moved to Mechanicsburg in the spring of 1880. He was married, November 7, 1873, at Hagerstown, Md., to Miss Louisa F. Smith, daughter of John L. and Magdalena (Hershey) Smith. Mr. Smith, a retired merchant, was elected associate judge of the orphans' court of Washington County, Md., serving for three terms. To Mr. and Mrs. Sadler have been born one son and one daughter: John and Harriet. Our subject is a F. & A. M. and a member of the I. O. O. F. and K. of P. He started in life with limited means, conducting the farm for his mother four years after his father's death, and at twenty-two struck out for himself. He has made life a success, and stands high in the estimation of all as an upright, honest business man. He is of Scotch-Irish descent on his father's side, and German on his mother's side, her family having settled in Lancaster County, Penn., at an early day.

JOHN O. SAXTON, retired farmer, of Silver Spring Township, Mechanicsburg, is a representative of one of the oldest families in Cumberland County, born July 3, 1833, on the old homestead farm, in Silver Spring Township, near the town of New Kingston, son of John and Nancy (Saxton) Saxton. John Saxton was born in Silver Spring Township, this county, and in early life engaged in farming, which he continued until his death; he died in 1843, aged thirty-six years; his widow is still living in Mechanicsburg, with her daughter, Miss Mary E. Saxton. Mr. and Mrs. John Saxton had three children. John O., the eldest in the family and only son, worked on his father's farm, attending the common schools until he entered Dickinson College, where he remained three terms; then taught school four years in Harrisburg, Penn.; then engaged in farming in Silver Spring Township. November 15, 1866, he married Miss Ellen Dunlap, born in Lower Allen Township, this county, daughter of James and Margaret (Mateer) Dunlap one of the oldest families of Cumberland County. After this marriage Mr. and Mrs. Saxton moved to Mechanicsburg. To this union were born six children, one son and two daughters living: Carrie S., born October 3, 1872; Lynn M., born December 4, 1874, and Maggie D., born October 13, 1878. John O. Saxton is president of school board of directors, was in town council several terms, and has held various local offices of trust. In 1880 he was a Democratic elector for president from the Nineteenth Congressional District of Pennsylvania. He is one of the board of managers for the Cumberland County Agricultural Society; is past high priest of Mechanicsburg Chapter R. A. M. past officer of the I. O. O. F. Lodge and Encampment, and has been district deputy grand master for Cumberland County two terms. Has been treasurer of the Mechanicsburg Bible and Tract Society since its organization in 1871. He owns a farm in Silver Spring Township, this county, of 145 acres; and Mrs. Saxton is owner of a farm in Lower Allen Township, this county, of over 200 acres, besides a fine residence on corner Main and York Streets, Mechanicsburg. Mr. and Mrs. Saxton are members of the Presbyterian Church, in which he has served as secretary of the board of trustees. Mr. Saxton's family is of English and his wife's people are of Scotch-Irish lineage, and they are among the oldest families in the county. Gov. Pattison appointed him a delegate from the Nineteenth Congressional District to the Farmers' National Congress held at St. Paul, Minn., in August, 1886.

JNO. SCHERICH, a justice of the peace, fire and life insurance agent, Mechanicsburg, born near Lisburn, this county, April 7, 1812, is a representative of one of the old families of Cumberland County, Penn. He is the only son of Christian and Anna (Spitzer) Scherich, natives of Lancaster County Penn., the former of whom, a farmer, came with his father, Christian Scherich, to this county, when he was young. Jno. Scherich, the eldest of four children, worked on his father's farm near Lisburn until he was sixteen, when he was apprenticed to the carpenter's, cabinet-maker's and painter's trades, at New Cumberland and Shepherdstown, and at twenty years of age had learned his trade; having aptness and energy soon became one of the first mechanics of his day. He then located near Lisburn, where he carried on his trade. He superintended one section of the first railroad bridge across the river at Harrisburg. He quit his trade about 1850, bought a tract of land west of Lisburn, erected commodious brick buildings, and soon became one of the first farmers of the county. In connection with farming he extensively carried on the brick-making business for many years. In 1875 he came to Mechanicsburg and continued in the insurance business, in which he had been engaged for more than forty years. He was married, November 30, 1832, to Miss Rachael Millard, born near Lewisburg, York County, March 14, 1814, daughter of Jonathan and Phœbe (Thornburg) Millard, old settlers of York County. Mr. and Mrs. Scherich have been members of the United Brethren Church for the past forty years. While at Lisburn their home was the home for all Christian workers, always active in the cause of morals and religion. They have seven children living: Christian, a carpenter, but engaged in the agency business at Lisburn, married to Miss Eliza A. Floyd; Ann Jane, wife of Elias Rhiver, a puddler at West Fairview; Jno. Andrew, a farmer near Lisburn, married to Miss Margret J. Hickernell; Phœbe Samantha, wife of Geo. Forry, a farmer near Mechanicsburg; Jonathan H. Clay (married to Rebecca Kerr), a farmer residing in Clay County, Nebraska; Rachael Ellen, wife of Geo. Levingston, carpenter and farmer, at West Fairview; Winfield Q. (married to Miss Mary A. McClure), a farmer near Churchtown. Mr. Jno. Scherich's great-grandfather, Christian, came from Switzerland and settled in Lancaster County, Penn.; he had two brothers, one of whom settled in Canada, and from these come all the Scherichs in the United States and Canada. The subject of this sketch died March 27, 1886, at the age of seventy-four years, and it can be justly said, that, for enterprise, energy and ability, he was unsurpassed. Not only being a practical mechanic and farmer, but also a close Scripture student, and notwithstanding his great asthmatic affliction, his place was seldom vacant at church or Sabbath-school. He took an active part in the politics of the day, and, with his great memory, could give statistics and could refer to most of the important actions Congress and of the State Legislature for the past fifty years.

GEORGE SCHROEDER, carriage manufacturer, firm of G. Schroeder Sons & Co., Mechanicsburg, has been identified with this county since May 1, 1833. He was born at East Berlin, Adams Co., Penn., January 22, 1816, son of Henry and Elizabeth (Bowers) Schroeder, the latter a sister of Judge Mart Harmon Bowers, and a descendant of the Harmons, one of the oldest families of Cumberland County. Henry Schroeder, a tailor by trade, was born near Berlin, Germany, and came to America and alone to Pennsylvania when eighteen years old. He located in East Berlin, Adams Co., Penn., where he married Miss Malon, who died some four years after without issue. He was married on the second occasion to Miss Elizabeth Bowers, of Adams County. He and his wife were members of the Lutheran Church. They had a family of three sons and two daughters, of whom two sons and one daughter survive. When George, the second son and child, was about twelve years old, his parents purchased a farm near Conowago Creek, four miles north of Gettysburg, and here our subject remained until he was seventeen, when he came to Mechanicsburg and worked in Henry Kimmel's blacksmith shop one year; then bought out Thomas Harris and carried on a blacksmith shop and engaged in coach-making, plating, etc. In 1845 he established his present business which he has increased from time to time until now he has the largest carriage and buggy manufactory in the valley, giving employment to from twenty-five to thirty men. He has over $45,000 invested in this business. Mr. Schroeder was married at Lititz, Lancaster Co., Penn., September 13, 1834, to Annie Buch, daughter of Henry Buch, a weaver by trade. To this union were born five children: Luzetta (wife of James Irvin, a coach-maker, member of the firm), Harry B. (also a member of the firm; married to Miss Susan Wicks, of Brockport, N. Y.), William (also a member of the firm; married to Miss Mary Gesamon, and after her demise to Miss Laura Wise, of Mechanicsburg, this county), Mary (widow of Simon Bowman; is a clerk in the Treasury Department, Washington, D. C.), Ellen (wife of Theodore Singeiser, member of Congress from Idaho Territory). Mrs. Schroeder died in March, 1865, a member of Bethel Church. In 1867 Mr. Schroeder married Mrs. Martha Leas, born in this county, daughter of Robert Galbreath a descendant of James Galbreath, Jr., the founder of the family in Pennsylvania, and who was of Scotch-Irish stock, having immigrated to Pennsylvania, settling in 1712, at Donegal, in what is now Lancaster County, where he bought large tracts of land from William Penn. He married, in 1735, Elizabeth Bertram, who, with her father, Rev. William Bertram, came from Edinburgh, Scotland—all these people were Presbyterians. James Galbreath, Jr., was elected sheriff of Lancaster County in 1742 and judge of common pleas in 1745, and for many years served as justice of the peace. He removed to Cumberland County in 1760, and in 1763 was appointed judge of Cumberland County. He took an active part in the French and Indian war of 1755-56, and during the Revolution, in 1777, was appointed a colonel in this county, being at that time seventy-three years of age. Mrs. Schroeder died in November, 1881, a member of the Methodist Episcopal Church (she was the mother of two children by her first marriage, one living, Dr. Harry Leas, of Mechanicsburg). Mr. George Schroeder is not only one of the old settlers, but is an enterprising representative business man, standing high in the estimation of all who know him. He is a purely self-made, self-educated man. Early learning to depend on his own resources, he went bravely to work, and by close application to business, honest dealing and hard work, has made life a success. He owns six houses and lots, besides his own residence and shops. Mr. Schroeder has three grandsons and two grand-daughters, children of his son, Harry B.

FREDERICK SEIDLE, proprietor of F. Seidle's Wheel, Spoke and Bending Works, Mechanicsburg, was born in Philadelphia, Penn., October 16, 1825, son of Frederick and Magdalena (Bergner) Seidle, natives of Wurtemberg, Germany, who came to Philadelphia in 1825. Frederick Seidle, Sr., engaged in the produce business in Philadelphia and Lancaster until 1836, when he purchased the old farm in Silver Spring Township, Cumberland Co., Penn. He and his wife were members of the Mennonite Church; they had two sons and four daughters. Frederick, Jr., the eldest son and second child, remained on the farm until he was eighteen, when he came to Mechanicsburg and served an apprenticeship at the carpenter's and cabinet-maker's trade. He was married, in November, 1850, to Miss Elizabeth Stevenson, born in this county, near Harrisburg, daughter of David and Leah (Shriner) Stevenson, natives of Pennsylvania. Mr. and Mrs. Seidle attend the Presbyterian Church. They had three children, two living: Albert E., married to Miss Marie Rogers, and William D. They assist their father in the management of his business. Mr. Frederick Seidle's life has been one of activity and toil. He started with a very small capital, but by hard work, good management and honest dealing has made life a success. He attended the Paris Exposition, receiving the Paris medal, and traveled over France, Germany, England, Belgium, Holland, Switzerland, visiting many carriage manufacturing establishments, and took enough orders to keep his manufactory running over a year. In partnership with Mr. Samuel Eberly he engaged in the building business with all its kindred branches and established the spoke and bending business, where he also carries on the manufacture of the Seidle & Eberly hay rake, invented and patented by himself, and which has a large sale throughout the entire West. In 1860 they closed their business and engaged as bridge builders for the Government. After a year Mr. Seidle returned to Mechanicsburg and resumed the hay-rake business until 1865, when he re-entered the spoke and bending industry, which has since grown to its present great proportions.

RUFUS E. SHAPLEY, jeweler, Mechanicsburg, was born in Hummelstown, Dauphin Co., Penn., December 23, 1840, son of Edmunds and Eliza (McElrath) Shapley, whose family consisted of eight children, four sons and four daughters. Edmunds Shapley, a cabinet-maker by trade, lived for a time in Carlisle, and died in Mechanicsburg in May, 1876, in the sixty-fifth year of his age. Rufus E., the eldest son, attended school in Hummelstown until, when twelve or thirteen years of age, he moved with his parents to Uniontown, Carroll Co., Md., where he attended school until he was eighteen, when he began to learn the trade of cabinet-maker with his father. This was of brief duration, however, as he commenced an apprenticeship to the jeweler's and watch-maker's craft in Uniontown in 1859, at which he remained until, while on a visit to Hummelstown, he enlisted in Company C, One Hundred and Twenty-seventh Pennsylvania Volunteer Infantry, in 1862. While a volunteer in Pennsylvania he was also drafted in Maryland, and although himself a soldier and not able to be in two places at the same time, was compelled to pay $300 commutation on account of the Maryland draft. After ten months' service, on the disbandment of his company, he was mustered out, receiving honorable discharge, and in 1863 located in Shippensburg, where he first engaged in the jewelry business upon his own account. Two years afterward he came to Mechanicsburg, and here, after a brief partnership of two years with the late J. W. Swartz, an old resident jeweler of the place, he established his present business in April, 1867. Our subject was married February 14, 1864, to Emma E. Landis, born in Cambridge, Lancaster Co., Penn., daughter of Isaac and Catharine (Wademan) Landis, both of Pennsylvania. To this union were born two children: Laura C., born May 8, 1865, and Edith R., born January 8, 1874. Mr. Shapley is a member of Eureka Lodge, No. 215, F. & A. M., Lodge No. 215, I. O. O. F., Col. H. I. Zinn Post, No. 415, G. A. R., Mechanicsburg. He is one of the enterprising representative citizens of Mechanicsburg. The family, of English and Irish descent, is among the oldest of the early settlers of the county.

ROBERT N. SHORT, physician, Mechanicsburg, was born on the Cumberland River, Pulaski Co., Ky., September 6, 1831, the eldest son in the family of eight children of Milton and Mary (Tate) Short. When our subject was seven years of age his parents removed to Lawrence County, Ind., where he worked on the farm, attending school during winters. This and two years at Spring Creek Academy, and private tutorship under Prof. E. F. Eaton, constituted his school advantages. In 1850 he began the study of medicine, graduating from the Southern Medical College in 1853. He then attended a full course of lectures at St. Louis University Medical Department, session of 1853–54, and subsequently graduated from Miami Medical College in 1871; practiced medicine in Jefferson Parish, La., about two years; went thence to Palestine, Crawford Co., Ill., two years; later to Springville, Lawrence Co., Ind., in partnership with his brother, Wesley Short, M. D., in 1861; moved to Centreville, this county, in October, 1861, devoting his time to the practice of medicine and surgery until October, 1865, when he located at Mechanicsburg, Penn., where he has since been actively engaged in the practice of his profession. Dr. Short married, April 12, 1860, Miss Anna E., daughter of Robert and Sarah (Schock) Wilson, and to this union were born the following named children: Sarah T., born December 11, 1861, died August 7, 1882; Robert W., born September 22, 1863 (a graduate of Mechanicsburg High School, at present attending the Pennsylvania College at Gettysburg). Dr. Short is a member of Eureka Lodge, No. 302, F. & A. M., Samuel C. Perkins Chapter, No. 209, R. A. M., and St. John's Commandery, No. 8, K. T., and Mechanicsburg Lodge, No. 215, I. O. O. F.; has been a member of Cumberland County Medical Society since its organization (1866), and was its president from 1876 to 1877. He has been a member of the State Medical Society since 1867, and of American Medical Association since 1880. He was appointed United States Examining Surgeon July 31, 1885.

JAMES A. SIBBETT ex-prothonotary, auctioneer, Mechanicsburg, is a representative of one of the old families of Cumberland County, Penn. His grandfather, John Sibbett, born near the city of Armagh, County Armagh, Ireland, was a shoe-maker by trade; he and his brother Robert were the only sons of their father. Robert Sibbett was one of

BOROUGH OF MECHANICSBURG. 435

the "united men" in the rebellion against England, but did not come to America; his brother, John, when a young man, came to America and settled in Chester County, Penn., in 1788; was married here to Miss Bridget Montague, and came to Cumberland County, Penn., in the spring of 1823 or 1824, locating at Churchtown; a short time thereafter he moved to Mount Holly Springs; he was a member of the first Presbyterian Church of Carlisle. To Mr. and Mrs. John Sibbett were born three daughters and seven sons: John and James (twins), Robert, Samuel, Andrew, Thomas, Aaron, Molly, Jane and Elizabeth. John, the eldest, born near West Chester, Chester Co., Penn., in 1792, married Miss Annie Lightfoot, who was born in Maryland in 1801, and who moved with her parents to this county about 1807; he came to this county about 1817, and, being a shoe-maker, made the first pegged shoes in Cumberland County, making his own pegs. He died August 7, 1832. His widow died February 4, 1857. They had seven children, two living: Elizabeth, born August 20, 1820, residing in Mechanicsburg, is a member of the Church of God, and James A., the youngest, born in what is now Jacksonville, Cumberland Co., Penn., March 7, 1832. He worked on the farm, attending school winters, until he was eighteen, when he began to learn the tailor's trade at Churchtown; was married, May 29, 1856, in Mechanicsburg, to Mrs. Jane Stroop, who was born in New Bloomfield, Perry County, May 20, 1834, daughter of Conrad and Sophia (Shober) Roth, old settlers of Perry County. Mr. and Mrs. James A. Sibbett are members of the Church of God. They have had six children: Robert E., an employe of the Cumberland Valley Railroad at Bridgeport, Penn.; Charles L., who died, aged twelve months; Curtis A., a painter of Mechanicsburg, married to Mrs. Mary Koser; Harry L., Kate A. and Lizzie. At the breaking out of the late war of the Rebellion our subject became a member of Company A, One Hundred and Fifty-eighth Pennsylvania Volunteer Infantry, and remained in the army until honorably discharged in October, 1863, when he returned home, and in the spring of 1864 came to Mechanicsburg, soon after being employed in the quartermaster's department at Harrisburg, under Maj. Richenboch until the close of the war. He then engaged with W. Y. Johnson & Bro., forwarding agent, who owned individual cars, for two years; then resumed his trade of tailor until 1880, when he was appointed census enumerator for the Third Ward of Mechanicsburg, by Hon. J. Simpson Africa. In 1881 Mr. Sibbett was nominated and elected, by the people of Cumberland County. prothonotary of the county for three years, since which time he has been engaged as auctioneer. He is a member of the I. O. O. F. and the Encampment; a member of Capt. Colwell Post, No. 201, G. A. R., Carlisle. In politics he is a Democrat. He has a nice residence on North Market Street, Mechanicsburg. where he and his family reside.

PETER SIPE, cooper, proprietor of flour and feed store, corner of Chestnut and Simpson Streets, Mechanicsburg, was born in Franklin Township, York County, in September, 1829; son of Martin (a cooper) and Mary (Freisinger) Sipe, also natives of York County, and parents of twelve children, of whom Sarah, Jake, Lydia, Peter, Leah and Maria are now living. Mr. and Mrs. Martin Sipe, were members of the Lutheran Church. The subject of this sketch, who is the third child, was but eight or ten years old when his father died, and at that early age started out to make his own way in life. He went to live with Peter Wolford, who is now a capitalist in Minneapolis, Minn., and worked with him at farming in York and Franklin Counties until he was fourteen years old, when he came to Churchtown, this county, and worked on a farm for Henry Lutz, four years; then went to work for Hon. William R. Gorgas, in Lower Allen Township, and while farming for him was married, February 29, 1848, to Miss Caroline Wilson, born in New Cumberland, this county, daughter of Jacob and Sarah (Warts) Wilson. After his marriage, Mr. Sipe learned the cooper's trade, under George Chapman, at Eberly's Mills, Milltown, Lower Allen Township, and there remained until 1865, when he moved to Harrisburg, where he worked at his trade two or three years, and then removed to Wheeling, W. Va. One year later he went to New Orleans, but after a short time returned to Harrisburg, and six months later came to Bryson's Mills, Silver Spring Township, this county, and there remained until 1879, when he moved to Mechanicsburg, where he has since resided. He and his wife have had seven children, six now living: Mary, wife of Charles Murdock, a machinist, Mechanicsburg; Sarah, wife of John Strasbauch, a butcher, Mechanicsburg; Clara, wife of Joseph Bricker, a retired farmer; Barbara, wife of Sterling Glace, of Mechanicsburg; Ella, wife of Peter Stone, a tailor, of Mechanicsburg; and David L., a cooper, residing with his parents. Wm. Henry Sipe, the oldest son, was killed at Fort Harrison, in the late war, in 1863. Mr. Sipe is a representative of one of the oldest families in the State.

FRANCIS H. STRICKER, founder and rector of St. Luke's Episcopal Church, Mechanicsburg, is a native of Germany, born in Rothenfelde, near Osnabruck, Province of Hanover, November 24, 1845; son of Frederick W. and Charlotta (Nollmann) Stricker, the former a merchant and manufacturer, of Rothenfelde; they were members of the Lutheran Church; they had four sons and four daughters. Francis H., the second son and third child, was educated in Germany until he was eighteen years old, when he came to New York City, and in June, 1864, entered the Classical Institution at Gambier, Ohio, for two years; thence went to the Divinity School in Philadelphia, until 1871, when he entered the General Theological Seminary of the Episcopal Church, in New York City, whence he graduated in 1873, and the same year was ordained by Bishop Horatio Potter, and went as a missionary to Hankow, China, where he remained two years, learning the language in six months, so that he could read the service, and subsequently learned the language sufficiently to preach to the people. At the close of his labors at Hankow he traveled in China, visiting Shanghai and Hong Kong; from here, in February, 1876, he went to Saigon, Anam; thence to Singapore; thence to Ceylon; thence across the Indian Ocean to Aden, Arabia; thence up the Red Sea to Suez, and through the Suez Canal, to Port Said, where he remained a short time; then crossed the Mediterranean to Naples, where he also remained a short time; then went to Marseilles, France, traveling overland through France to Lyons and Belford, where he visited the celebrated fortifications; thence to Strasburg, Germany; thence to Mainz; thence to Coblentz and Cologne; remained in Germany visiting Munster and Osnabruck. (It was in these two cities the peace of Westphalia was negotiated.) He traveled over Germany, France and Switzerland, visiting many of the important and historical cities. In August, 1876, he came to the Centennial at Philadelphia, Penn., and in October, same year, was given charge of St. David's Mission Church, under Bishop Stevens, at that city, remaining there until July, 1878, when he came to Mechanicsburg, and founded his present church. There was no church when Mr. Stricker came here and only eighteen members, but he went bravely to work, and with the assistance of these members, he has built up his present congregation, and in 1880 they erected their elegant stone church, corner of Keller and Market Streets. The church has a fine organ, presented by Mrs. William Watts, of Mechanicsburg. The edifice was opened in October, 1880, and consecrated free of debt, in April, 1881. It is not only out of debt but has a surplus in the treasury of several hundred dollars. Much credit is due Mr. Stricker for his untiring energy and successful labor.

JOSEPH STROCK, retired, Mechanicsburg, was born near Churchtown, this county, September 15, 1805, son of Jacob and Elizabeth (Wise) Strock, natives of this county; they were members of the Reformed Church first, and latterly joined the Church of God. Jacob Strock, who was a farmer, was accidently killed when aged seventy-three; his widow lived to be nearly eighty years. They had five sons and four daughters, all of whom attained maturity, and three sons and two daughters are now living: Mary, wife of John Zimmerman, a farmer and justice of the peace, Smithville, Wayne Co., Ohio; Joseph; George, a retired farmer, Churchtown, Penn.; Rachael, wife of Jacob Coover, residing on a farm near Shepherdstown, this county; and David, a farmer in Clarke County, Ohio. Joseph, who is the eldest son, worked on his father's farm, attending the old log schoolhouse in Churchtown until he was eighteen years of age, when he began the trade of cabinet-maker in New Cumberland, and there remained two years. He then worked in Carlisle, New Cumberland, Baltimore, Md., York, York Co., Penn., and Harrisburg, Penn., until the fall of 1829, when he came to Mechanicsburg. He was married December 24, 1829, to Miss Margaret Neagley, born in Silver Spring Township, Cumberland Co., Penn., daughter of Daniel and Elizabeth (Stoner) Neagley, natives of Lancaster County, Penn. After his marriage Mr. Strock worked at his trade in Mechanicsburg two years, then moved to Trindle Spring, where he purchased a farm. He came to Mechanicsburg in 1871 or 1872, and purchased his present home property. Mr. and Mrs. Strock had nine children, seven now living: Daniel N., born November 18, 1830, married to Miss Mary Rathburn, they reside in Princeton, Ill., where he and his brother have a planing mill; Ann E., born November 20, 1832, married first to Dr. Samuel Long, second to P. Vanest, of Ohio, and third to John Mumper, her present husband (they reside on a farm in York County, Penn.); Mary A., born April 28, 1835, wife of William J. Shearer, a lawyer of Carlisle; William E., born November 16, 1836, unmarried, resides in Jackson County, Miss.; Sarah R., born July 26, 1838, married John C. Reeser, of Monroe Township; Jacob N., born June 13, 1841, married Miss Hettie Brandt, and after her death Miss Sarah Gibler, they reside on the farm of his father at Trindle Spring; Joseph H., born August 9, 1844, married first to Miss Etta Glime, and after her death to Miss Lizzie B. Mumert, they reside in Princeton Ill. The mother of these children died May 29, 1852, she was a member of the Church of God. Mr. Strock married March 1, 1859, for his second wife, Mrs. Eliza Bigley, born in North Middleton Township, daughter of Frederick and Catharine (Snyder) Wonderly. Mr. Strock and wife are members of the Church of God. Mr. Strock is one of the old settlers and enterprising citizens of Mechanicsburg.

R. H. THOMAS was born in the city of Philadelphia January 28, 1834. His ancestry on his father's side descended from the Welsh-English, and on his mother's side from the Scotch-Irish. He was educated in the public schools of Lancaster City, where his father Rev. E. H. Thomas had the pastoral charge of a large congregation. At the age of fourteen years he apprenticed himself to the business of house and sign painting, and wall decorating, which he followed during the summer months for some years, teaching school during the winter season. Impaired health caused him to relinquish this occupation and turn his attention to mercantile pursuits. In 1851 he took up his residence in Mechanicsburg, Cumberland County, and, in 1854 was united in marriage with Miss Annetta, daughter of Henry Kimmel, Esq., one of the old and prominent families of the Cumberland Valley. Two children: R. H. Thomas, Jr., editor of the *Saturday Journal*, and Miss Estelle Thomas, a prolific and entertaining writer, are the results of this union. In 1859 he became a Freemason, a member of the Grand Lodge of Pennsylvania, in 1863, and an officer of the same in 1864, serving for thirteen consecutive years as district deputy grand master. In 1862 he was appointed deputy collector of internal revenue for the Fifteenth District of Pennsylvania, and continued in that office until 1866. During the civil war he served, on several occasions, in different emergency regiments, resuming his duties at home as soon as the exigency which called him to the field had subsided. On Monday, June 30, 1863, he was appointed a special aid-de-camp by Gov. Curtin, with the rank of colonel, and assigned to duty in the department commanded by Gen. Smith, who, at that time had his headquarters at Fort Washington, near Harrisburg. When the Confederate forces were driven south of the Potomac, and peace again reigned in Pennsylvania, he retired from military duty and entered upon business pursuits. In 1870, he purchased the *Valley Democrat*, and changed the name of the paper to the *Valley Independent*. In 1872 he bought the *Cumberland Valley Journal*, a rival newspaper, and consolidated the offices and papers under the name of the *Independent Journal*. In the fall of 1872, he espoused the cause of the Patrons of Husbandry, an order then coming into prominence in this state, and during the following summer organized a large number of subordinate granges. Upon the organization of the State Grange, at Reading, in 1873, he was elected secretary, and has acceptably filled that position ever since. On January 1, 1874, he began the publication of the *Farmers' Friend and Grange Advocate*, the organ of the Patrons of Husbandry, and an agricultural journal of high charcter, extended circulation, and great influence. Impressed with the idea that there ought to be a better understanding between the farmers and the manufacturers of the country, he in 1874 originated and organized the Inter-State Picnic Exhibition, at Williams' Grove, Cumberland Co., Penn., which has, from the date of its inception, steadily grown in magnitude and importance until it stands almost unrivaled in the history of agricultural exhibitions in this country. The subject of this sketch filled the office of president of the State Editorial Association, and is now, and has been for several years past, its secretary and treasurer. He is also one of the officers of the International Editorial Association. He was the commissioner from Pennsylvania to the World's Industrial and Cotton Centennial Exposition, held at New Orleans during 1884 and 1885, and was likewise appointed a commissioner to the American Exposition to be held in London, England, in May, 1887. In all the varied positions he has been called upon to fill, R. H. Thomas has retained the full confidence of the general public, and esteem and respect of all with whom his official duties brought him into relationship.

CHRISTIAN H. TITZEL, furniture dealer and undertaker, Mechanicsburg. Prominent among the leading business men of Cumberland County is the esteemed citizen, Christian H. Titzel, who was born on the old family farm in Upper Allen Township, one mile east of Mechanicsburg, July 7, 1845, a descendant of two of the oldest families of Pennsylvania. The name is of German origin and his ancestors were among the first to immigrate to Pennsylvania. Christian H. is a son of Christian and Polly (Rupp) Titzel, the latter of whom subsequently married John Wonderlich and had eleven children. Christian Titzel, father of our subject, was born in Tyrone Township, now in Perry County, Penn., July 28, 1800, the only child born to John and Mary Magdalene (Heckendorn) Titzel. He was a skillful mechanic, and for many years pursued his trade of house carpentering and bridge building; in 1827 he began merchandising, and in 1835 purchased a farm one mile east of Mechanicsburg; he served his fellow-citizens in various capacities, settling up estates, and acting as guardian for children; was county commissioner of Cumberland County from 1843 to 1846; he took a great interest in educational matters and in everything pertaining to his church (Reformed); he died on the old farm December 25, 1861; his widow died October 1. 1883, a member of the Reformed Church. To this couple were born seven children—four sons and three daughters: John Martin Titzel, D. D., born at Mechanicsburg, Penn., March 19, 1832, is pastor of the Reformed Church at Lancaster, Penn. (he is a graduate of Franklin College, Lancaster, Penn., and in 1857 received from the theological seminary at Mercer, Penn., the degree of A. M. from his *alma mater*); Benjamin, born October 13, 1833, is a farmer in Silver Spring Township, this county; Anna; Mary Elizabeth resides in Mechanicsburg; George W., born October 11, 1842, died August 1880; Christian Heckendorn and Salome Frances. Christian H. Titzel's early life was spent on the farm with his father and in attending school winters until he was eighteen years old, when he served a two and a half years' apprenticeship with Samuel Werst. He then purchased a shop in company with his brother and carried on business under the firm name of Titzel & Bro. for three years, when he bought his brother's (George H.'s) interest, and has since conducted the business alone. Our subject commenced with small capital, but by hard work, close application and honest dealing has increased his business until he now has the largest and most complete stock of domestic and imported furniture, etc., in Mechanicsburg. He also, in connection with the furniture business, established an undertaker's establishment, and stands at the head of his profession in this line. Mr.

Titzel married, November 9, 1860, Miss Clarissa M. Comfort, a native of Adams County, Penn., daughter of Daniel and Elizabeth (Brugh) Comfort. Mr. Comfort was a dry goods merchant of Mechanicsburg for many years. Mr. and Mrs. Titzel have one son, Daniel Comfort, born August 29, 1867, now attending the high school in Mechanicsburg; he is possessed of a fine talent for music, which he cultivates; he assists his father in business. Mr. C. H. Titzel is a grandson of Martin Rupp, born in Lancaster (now Lebanon) County, Penn., September 15, 1769, married in 1797 to Anna Schnebele; he died July 18, 1843. Mr. and Mrs. Titzel are members of the Reformed Church.

COL. JOSEPH TOTTON, proprietor of the oldest and most reliable livery, feed and sale stables, Mechanicsburg, one of the representative men of Cumberland County, was born in Dillsburg, York Co., Penn., July 8, 1823, son of John and Hattie (McClure) Totton. John Totton, by trade a shoe-maker, was born in Portadown, Ireland; enlisted in the English Army and had served nine years (during the French war) when he was brought to America in the war of 1812, but refused to fight the Americans and became a citizen, settling in Dillsburg, York Co., Penn., where he was married. He died in Dillsburg in 1847, aged sixty years, and his widow died in 1849, aged fifty-eight, a member of the Presbyterian Church. The family consisted of six children—two sons and four daughters. Joseph, who is the eldest, acquired an education in a little schoolhouse in Dillsburg, and then learned shoe-making, and remained in his native town until 1854; then went to Shippensburg, but in 1857 located in Mechanicsburg, where he engaged in the manufacture of boots and shoes until the breaking out of the late war of the Rebellion, when he raised the Cumberland Guards, which became Company H, Seventh Pennsylvania Reserves, and Mr. Totton was elected captain, and subsequently lieutenant-colonel. He remained with the regiment one year, when, being compelled to resign owing to impaired health, he received an honourable discharge. He came home, and a year later opened a livery stable and established his present business. In 1873 he was elected sheriff of Cumberland County, and resided in Carlisle three years during his term of office, since which time he has resided in Mechanicsburg. Mr. Totton married at Dillsburg, June 8, 1848, Miss Lydia Wagoner, who was born in East Berlin, Adams Co., Penn., daughter of Samuel and Lydia (Oiler) Wagoner, the former a blacksmith, born in Adams County, and the latter born in Hanover, York Co., Penn. Mr. and Mrs. Totton have had eleven children, nine now living: David E., born in Dillsburg, York Co., Penn., October 30, 1849; James M., born in Monroe Township, this county, September 25, 1851 (he assists his father in the livery business); George B., born in Dillsburg, York Co., Penn. (is a farmer in Silver Spring Township); Ellen, born in Shippensburg, Penn. (is the wife of Talbot Crain, and resides in Hogestown, this county); Anna M. (resides with her parents); Maggie (with her parents); Joseph, Jr. (book-keeper for C. N. Owen, Mechanicsburg); John and Frank (who both assist their father in the business). Mrs. Totton is a member of the Presbyterian Church. Mr. Totton is a member of Mecanicsburg Lodge, No. 215, I. O. O. F., and of Wildey Encampment, Mechanicsburg, and is the oldest member of the I. O. O. F. in the town, having been connected therewith forty-one years; is a member of the G. A. R., Carlisle Post, No. 201. Mr. Totton is one of the leading business men of the place. He is of Irish descent on his father's side, and Scotch on his mother's side.

ALEXANDER UNDERWOOD, retired, Mechanicsburg, proprietor of Mount Hope Magnet Ore Mine, near Dillsburg, York Co. Penn., was born on his father's farm in Washington Township, August 16, 1813, son of Amos and Lydia (Bales) Underwood, natives of York County, and who had a family of eight children—six sons. Alexander, the second born, when nine years old, went to live with a friend of his father, James S. Mitchell, ex-congressman from Pennsylvania, and remained with him, attending school, until he was sixteen, when he was apprenticed to learn the saddle and harness-maker's trade with Stephen Packer at York Springs, Adams County. Three years later he returned home, and assisted his father (who was a farmer) until his marriage, November 30, 1837, with Miss Matilda Mumper, who was born in Carroll Township, York Co., Penn., daughter of Abraham and Mary (Lerew) Mumper, natives of York County. After marriage, Mr. Underwood worked at his trade in York Springs, Adams County for three years, then located on a farm fourteen miles west of Baltimore, Md., where he remained five years; then returned to York, York Co., Penn., and engaged at his trade until 1868, when he bought 215 acres in Carroll Township, York County, where he has his mine. He employs from twenty-five to thirty men. He also has a mine which he leases to Augustus Longenecker. Mr. Underwood located in Mechanicsburg in 1871. He owns a fine two-story brick building on Main Street, where he resides; a two-story frame residence and store on Main, near corner of High; a two-story brick house on Main Street, near the female college; three building lots on the corner of Market and Keller Streets; 240 acres farm land in Russell County Kas., and 640 acres in Ida County, Iowa. Mr. Underwood started without the aid of any one, but by hard work, close application to business and honest dealing, has made life a success. His great-grandfather, Alexander Underwood, a Quaker preacher, came from England and settled in York County, Penn. Mr. Underwood has in his possession a cannon ball, a relic of the Revolution. He and his wife are members of the Lutheran Church.

GEORGE WAGONER, of George Wagoner & Sons, leading dry goods merchants,

Mechanicsburg, was born near East Berlin, Adams Co. Penn., July 17, 1818. His great-grandfather, Mathias Wagoner, a native of Ruthesheime, Hohenzollern, Prussia, had two sons who came to America: Jacob, who settled in Virginia, and Peter, who settled in what is now York County, Penn. The latter's son, Peter, a farmer and hotel keeper, married Miss Mary Arnold, and had six sons and seven daughters. Of these children, Samuel, born in York County, Penn., a blacksmith by trade, married Miss Lydia Oiler, of York County, and had three daughters and three sons, of whom George is the eldest. They were members of the Lutheran Church. Our subject, when some seven years of age, went with his father to East Berlin, Adams Co., Penn., and there learned blacksmithing of his father. December 24, 1839, he married Miss Ann Smith, born near East Berlin Adams County, daughter of Martin B. (a miller), and Mary (Swigert) Smith. Her grandfather, Abraham Swigert, was born in Alsace, France (now Germany), April 12, 1748, and died February 24, 1813, son of Jacob Swigert, one of the old French Huguenots. Mrs. Wagoner's grandmother, Eleanor Housel, born April 21, 1764, died August 14, 1828. After marriage, George Wagoner moved to York Springs, Adams Co., and worked at his trade one year; then located between Dillsburg and Petersburg, York County, where he worked at his trade one year; then located at Dillsburg, where he remained engaged at his trade and in merchandising, until 1872, when he moved to Mechanicsburg, and here he has since resided. He and his wife had five sons, two living, Samuel M. and Edward S. Samuel M., born in Dillsburg, York Co., Penn., November 15, 1844, married, April 9, 1871; Miss Anna Shriver, of Adams County, Penn., daughter of Benjamin and Maria (Forry) Shriver (have two daughters: Cora M. and Florence K.). Samuel Wagoner, one of the firm of George Wagoner & Sons, is a member of Mechanicsburg Lodge, No 215. I. O. O. F.; Wildey Encampment, No. 29, Mechanicsburg; Treasury Integrity Council, No. 197, O. U. A. M., of Mechanicsburg. Edward Wagoner, born in Dillsburg, York Co. Penn., in July, 1847; married Mrs. Maria H. S. Dyson, a native of Dillsburg, York Co., Penn., daughter of Dr. George L. and Eliza (Eichelberger) Shearer (have one daughter, Maria S). Mrs. Edward Wagoner is a direct descendant of John Daniel Duenkle, chief justice of the courts of Strasburg, Germany. Edward Wagoner is a member of the Lutheran General Synod, and his wife of the Presbyterian Church. He is a member of the firm of George Wagoner & Sons and is also passenger agent for the Baltimore & Ohio Railroad Company. George Wagoner, subject of our sketch, is a member of Humane Lodge, No. 342, I. O. O. F., York County, Penn., and Berlin Beneficial Society, East Berlin. He and his sons are enterprising, representative citizens of Mechanicsburg. They carry a stock of $15,000, and stand high in the estimation of all as upright business men.

HON. WILLIAM MILES WATTS (deceased) was born in Carlisle, Cumberland Co., Penn., August 1, 1809, and received his elementary education at Dickinson College, Carlisle. Before maturing he immigrated to Meadville, Crawford Co., Penn., and studied medicine under Dr. Beemus. Finding this profession unsuited to his taste, he entered the office of John S. Riddle, Esq., a distinguished lawyer of Meadville, and was there admitted to the bar. He commenced the practice of law in Erie City, Erie Co., Penn., and was elected district attorney of that county; was a member of the State Constitutional Convention of 1837, and also represented the county of Erie in that body. In 1838 he was elected to the Legislature by the people of that county as their representative. The session of the Legislature, during the winter of 1838 and 1839, was made memorable by the extraordinary political excitement throughout the borders of Pennsylvania, by the outgoing of the Ritner administration and the incoming of the Democrats. There was an angry and vehement contest in both the Senate and House of Representatives for the political control, and it was boldly asserted by the Democrats that gross frauds had been perpetrated by the Whigs in the elections to the Senate and the House. Charles B. Penrose, Jesse Borden, Thomas Cunningham and others, who had been elected to the Senate by the Democrats, had, in consequence of their support of the rechartor of the Bank of United States, and the improvement and educational law, been drawn from their party into the ranks of the opposition, and encountered its fierce displeasure. Thaddeus Stevens, the reporter and advocate of the obnoxious bill, William B. Reed, George Sharswood, Henry Spackman, Joseph Fisher, George W. Tyson and others, representatives from Philadelphia, were alike offensive, and thus originated the Buckshot war, which the Governor was induced to resist by calling out the militia force of the State. At this fearful crisis, Mr. Watts, being of athletic frame, undoubted courage and patriotic impulses, was selected to prevent the forcible demonstration of Henry Spackman, who had been chosen speaker of the House by the Whigs. He encountered vigorous attacks, and firmly defeated all efforts to remove the speaker. His personal and political affiliations were with such intellectual and reliable men as Joseph Clarkson, William B. Reed, Edward Olmstead, Joseph Fisher, George Sharswood, Frederick Fraley, Jacob Gratz, Henry Carey, Joseph McIlwaine and others, who laid the foundation of the Pennsylvania system of internal improvements, of finance and the higher departments of collegiate and common schools. To the intellectual force and earnest efforts of such Philadelphians, and other conspicuous citizens of the State are we indebted for our present prosperity and State prominence. Mr. Watts, after relinquishing his official connection with the State, returned to his birth-place and purchased one of the oldest iron-works in the State, belonging to the family of Peter Ege, on the southern boundary of Cumberland County, called "Pine Grove," and containing 20,000 acres. Here for many years he operated a forge, furnace, grist-mill, and carried on other industrial pursuits. During the civil war, this domain, lying northeast of South Mountain, between Carlisle and Gettysburg, became the track of the armies of the North and South, and was thus desolated by both. Mr. Watts cheerfully surrendered the contents of his mill, the provisions and shelter of his house to the Northern Government, and never claimed, or allowed others to claim any compensation from either the Federal or State Governments for the large losses he sustained. During the administrations of Gov. W. F. Johnston and A. G. Curtin, Mr. Watts was an intimate friend of both, and enjoyed their implicit confidence and affection. Each relied much upon the political sagacity of Mr. Watts, and many things which led to important results were advised by him. He was unswerving in his attachment to men whom he believed to be lovers of the country, and firm adherents of its Republican institutions and the true policy of Pennsylvania, and was never remiss in his extraordinary influence to define them against an assailant. Mr. Watts married Miss Anna M. Reed, at Carlisle, June 28, 1847. She was born at Carlisle May 30, 1836, a daughter of Judge John and Sarah A. (McDowell) Reed. The former was born at Millerstown, Adams County, this State, in June, 1786, and was appointed judge, under Gov. Findlay, of Cumberland, Franklin and Adams Counties, and held that office for many years. He died January 19, 1850, at Carlisle. His wife was born at Fort Harmer, May 21, 1787, a daughter of Dr. John and Margaret Sanderson (Lukens) McDowell. Dr. McDowell was a surgeon in the Revolutionary war. Mr. and Mrs. Watts had two sons and two daughters, viz.: Sarah R., wife of William J. Rose, of Harrisburg; Julia, wife of George S. Comstock of Hauck & Comstock, manufacturers, Mechanicsburg; David Watts, engaged in iron at Harrisburg, Penn., married to M. B. Cameron; and Reed Watts, who died at the age of eleven years. Hon. William Miles Watts was more than ordinary, both mentally and physically. His mind was cultured by extensive reading and reflection, and his heart endued with all the graces of affection and charity.

ALEXANDER WENTZ, postmaster, Mechanicsburg, was born in Jefferson, York Co., Penn., only son and youngest child of Jacob B. and Catharine (Troxel) Wentz, the former a native of Pennsylvania and the latter of Maryland, who died at the age of ninety-one. Jacob B. Wentz was a merchant, farmer and miller in the towns of York and Jefferson, York Co., Penn., and for some time in the city of Baltimore, Md. He was a member of the Masonic lodge at York, where he resided until his death. He died at the age of seventy-five years, his widow at the age of ninety-one. Alexander Wentz, the subject of this sketch, remained with his father in York County, Penn., for some years and was there elected county treasurer. In 1882 he opened a general store at Dillsburg, but soon after located at Shepherdstown, this county. In April, 1868, he moved to Mechanicsburg, where he still resides. He was employed in the internal revenue office for two years, and on the 1st of July, 1885, was appointed postmaster of Mechanicsburg, which position he now holds. Mr. Wentz has held various local offices of trust in Mechanicsburg, all of which he has discharged faithfully and to the satisfaction of the public. He aided in forming Mechanicsburg Lodge, I. O. O. F., and is a member of York Lodge, F. & A. M. at York, Penn. He married Miss Isabella, daughter of David Stuart, of Maryland, and to them were born two sons, one living, Annan, born July 14, 1877. Mr. and Mrs. Wentz are members of the Presbyterian Church. He has been long known and highly esteemed as an honest citizen and business man.

ROBERT WILSON, retired, Mechanicsburg, who has been identified with Mechanicsburg since the fall of 1830, was born in Baltimore, Md., November 29, 1810, only child of Robert and Susan (Armstrong) Wilson. When our subject was but three years of age his father (a native of Maryland) died, and after his death Robert, with his mother, moved to Harrisburg, Penn., where she subsequently married John Wright, a tinner by occupation, by whom she had one son and two daughters. Robert Wilson learned the tinner's trade with his stepfather. In the fall of 1830 he came to Mechanicsburg and opened a tin and stove store. He was married here, December 22, 1831, to Miss Sarah Schock. Mrs. Wilson still enjoys good health and is as lively as many young ladies are; she was born in Berks County, Penn., August 6, 1811. To this union were born eight children, seven living: George W. (married to Miss Susan Hoover, they reside in Mechanicsburg), Elizabeth (wife of Dr. Robert N. Short, Mechanicsburg), William H. (baggage master on the Cumberland Valley Railroad), Julia (wife of Jacob Hurst, a merchant here), Mary (wife of John Ringwalt, proprietor of the "American House," Mechanicsburg), Ida (who resides with her parents), and Susan (wife of Eugene Gardner, local editor of the *Independent Journal*, Mechanicsburg). Robert Wilson is a self-made, self-educated man; his life has been full of activity and enterprise. He was elected by the people of this county, in 1842, county recorder and clerk of the courts for three years, discharging his duties faithfully and to the entire satisfaction of all. He has filled various local offices of trust in Mechanicsburg, and at one time was postmaster. In 1847 he, with Peter Ritner (son of ex-Gov. Ritner, of Pennsylvania), were appointed collectors and general agents for the

Cumberland Valley Railroad. At that time business on this road was conducted in a very different manner than now, there being no station agents, and Messrs. Wilson and Ritner were both freight and passenger agents, collecting, as conductors, for passengers and freight. In 1869 Mr. Wilson retired from active business life, since which time he has been acting as administrator for various estates. He has lived to see this county undergo many interesting and important changes, and his life is an example to our young men, who know but little of the difficulties and trials that the pioneers of this county had to contend with. Mr. Wilson was a Whig in his younger days, but since the organization of the Republican party has been one of its strong supporters. He and his wife are members of Trinity Lutheran Church.

FREDERICK WONDERLICH, dealer in stoves and tin-ware, Mechanicsburg, was born four miles northeast of Carlisle, Cumberland Co., Penn., July 13, 1828, son of Frederick (a farmer) and Catharine (Snyder) Wonderlich, also natives of this county, and members of the Lutheran Church; they had a family of three sons and three daughters, of whom Frederick and William (twins) are the youngest. When Frederick was two years old his parents moved to Carlisle and kept hotel, and two years later (1833) came to Mechanicsburg and opened a hotel. Our subject attended school and assisted his father in the hotel until he was seventeen, when he began to learn his trade with George Bobb, and two years later worked as journeyman at Carlisle, Churchtown; Landisburg, Perry Co.; Petersburg, Adams Co.; Columbus, Lancaster Co.; Allentown, Lehigh Co.; Catasauqua, Lehigh Co., Penn.; Staunton, Va.; then returned to Mechanicsburg, in 1852, and that year formed a partnership with his brother, William, and engaged in the stove and tinware business until 1860, when he sold out to his brother and went to Mount Pleasant, Iowa; four months later he went to Rochester, Fulton Co., Ind., where he purchased a farm and engaged in agriculture until 1865, when he returned to Mechanicsburg, but that summer worked at his trade in Harrisburg, Penn. In 1868 Mr. Wonderlich formed a partnership with George Hauck in the tinware and stove business, but at the expiration of two years sold out and formed a partnership in the same business with his brother George, who died in August, 1885. Mr. Wonderlich was married, in 1852, to Miss Catharine Hartman (who died in 1858), a daughter of John and Susannah (Messinger) Hartman. To this union were born two children: Harry H., married to Miss Amelia Gross (is a butcher at Liberty Mills, Ind.); and George A., who died, aged four months. In 1860 our subject married, for his second wife, Miss Jane Hartman, sister of his first wife, and they have two daughters: Susan L., wife of George A. Edleblut, a painter, of Mechanicsburg; and Dora C., wife of James Koller, a manufacturer, member of the firm of J. B. Koller & Co. Mr. Wonderlich is a member of the American Mechanics Association and Shiremanstown Benefit Association; his wife is a member of the United Brethren Church. He is an enterprising business man and stands high in the estimation of all who know him. His family is of German descent, his ancestors coming from Germany and settling in what was then Lancaster County, Penn., at an early date.

CAPT. EDWARD P. ZINN, dentist, Mechanicsburg, was born in East Berlin, Adams Co., Penn., August 3, 1827, son of John and Anna Mary (Beitzel) Zinn, the former of whom, born near Dover, York County, a miller, shoe-maker and butcher by occupation, was a son of Jacob Zinn, of York County, Penn. John and Anna Mary Zinn had thirteen children—seven sons and six daughters—two sons and three daughters now living, Edward P. being the fifth son and ninth child. Our subject was some five years old when his parents moved to a farm near Dover, York County, and in 1840 he came to the vicinity of Churchtown, this county, where he farmed until 1843; then moved to Churchtown, and worked at shoe-making until 1846, in which year he went to New Bloomfield, Perry Co., Penn., where he opened a shop of his own. He was there married, January 1, 1848, to Miss Caroline Sophia Klinepeter, who was born in New Bloomfield, Perry Co., Penn., daughter of Samuel Klinepeter. She died January 1, 1852, the mother of two children: One daughter, who died in infancy, and one son, William B., who died aged thirty-one years. In 1853 Mr. Zinn went to Philadelphia, New York, and Savannah, Ga., traveling until the fall of 1853, when he located at Newburg, and worked at dentistry two years; then began practicing in Churchtown, where he remained until the fall of 1855, when he l cated in Mechanicsburg. Mr. Zinn was here married, January 1, 1856, to Miss Margaret J. Pisle, a native of Hopewell Township, this county, a daughter of Peter and Elizabeth (Lesher) Pisle. Mr. and Mrs. Zinn have had five children (four now living): Anson B., born in Mechanicsburg, December 5, 1856, now proprietor of Zinn's bakery and confectionery; Ida E., born in Mechanicsburg November 18, 1860; Annie M., born in Mechanicsburg June 8, 1864, died June 5, 1874; Harry I., born in Mechanicsburg October 10, 1866, at present engaged in the bakery business; Minnie B., born in Mechanicsburg February 16, 1871. Anson B. and his brother, Harry I., are members of P. O. S. of Washington Camp, No. 164, Mechanicsburg. Edward P. Zinn is a member of Eureka Lodge, No. 302, A. Y. M., and Post No. 58, G. A. R., of Harrisburg, Penn. In politics he is a Republican. Mrs. Zinn and her daughter, Ida E., are members of the Lutheran Church.

HENRY ZINN, manufacturer of and dealer in boots and shoes, Mechanicsburg, was born in York County, Penn., April 25, 1828, son of Jacob and Lydia (Newman) Zinn, natives of York County, Penn., parents of nine children, seven living: George, David, Henry (our subject), Lydia, Mary, William and Daniel. They were members of the Evangelical Church. The mother dying, the father then married Mrs. Mary Greenwalt, by whom he had one child, now living. Our subject remained on the farm in his native county until he was eighteen, when he was apprenticed to learn to shoe-maker's trade at Manchester; thence came to Mechanicsburg, in 1852, and established his present business. Mr. Zinn was married here in December, 1853, to Miss Sarah Leidig born in Mechanicsburg, Penn., daughter of Jacob and Catharine (Ritner) Leidig, natives of this county. Mr. and Mrs. Zinn are members of the Methodist Episcopal Church. They have had six children, three now living: Laura, wife of Samuel Coover, a stock-dealer of La Cygne, Kas., and Emma and Joseph, both attending school. Our subject is a grandson of Jacob Zinn, who was born in Lancaster County, Penn., and settled in York County, Penn., at an early day. The family is one of the oldest in Pennsylvania. His father's people are German, and his mother's English. Mr. Zinn is not only one of our leading business men, but is also an honest, Christian gentleman, who enjoys the confidence and respect of all.

CHAPTER XL.

BOROUGH OF SHIPPENSBURG.

J. C. ALTICK, druggist, Shippensburg, was born in Shippensburg, Penn., November 18, 1832, son of John and Elizabeth (Byerley) Altick, natives of this county, former of whom was a manufacturer of wagons, plows and farming implements, in which branch of industry he was engaged in Shippensburg for many years; he died in 1882. J. C. Altick, the fourth in a family of ten children, grew to manhood in Shippensburg, chose the drug business for his occupation, and has been engaged in that line in Shippensburg for over forty years. He is a Republican in politics, and has been burgess for two terms. He is a prominent member of the I. O. O. F.; is also a Master Mason.

JOHN L. BARNER, Shippensburg, was born in Juniata County, Penn., July 16, 1844, son of George and Lydia (Lehr) Barner, natives of Pennsylvania, and of German descent. His maternal grandfather, Peter Lehr, was a soldier in the War of 1812, and his paternal grandfather, Henry Barner, was a farmer. George Barner was a carpenter in early life, and in later life was justice of the peace in Juniata County, Penn., in which capacity he served for thirty years. He was a prominent and influential citizen. Of his nine children, John L. is the youngest. Our subject was reared in Juniata County, Penn., and attended the common school. At the age of twenty-three years he came to Shippensburg, this county, and engaged as clerk in the dry goods store of George H. Stewart, where he remained for nearly two years, when Mr. Stewart sold the store. Mr. Barner then accepted a clerkship in the Cumberland Valley freight office of J. B. Hurs & Co., remaining with them nearly two years; was then appointed freight and ticket agent for the Cumberland Valley Railroad Company, which position he filled until August, 1881, since which time he has been engaged in settling the estate of Ira Long (deceased), and also doing business for his father-in-law, C. Long, a wealthy citizen of Shippensburg. Mr. Barner was married, in 1871, to Mary Ella, daughter of Christian and Hannah Ellen (Atkinson) Long, and to them was born, October 6, 1878, one son—George Stewart, named in honor of our subject's first employer in Shippensburg. Mr. and Mrs Barner are members of the German Reformed Church. He has served four years as justice of the peace in Shippensburg. In politics he is a Democrat.

J. D. BASHORE, dentist, Shippensburg, was born in Franklin County, Penn., October 25, 1859, son of Emanuel and Elizabeth (Rebuck) Bashore, natives of Pennsylvania, and of German descent. Emanuel Bashore was a tanner by occupation for nearly forty years, and still resides in Franklin County, Penn. Of his five children Dr. J. D. is the youngest. Our subject was reared on the farm, and received his schooling in Franklin County, Penn. At the age of nineteen years he commenced the study of dentistry, and afterward attended the Baltimore College of Dental Surgery, where he graduated in 1880, and the same year he commenced the practice of his profession in Shippensburg, where he has met with marked success. He was married, in 1883, to Madge L. Hartley, and they have one child, E. Gorgas. The Doctor and wife are members of the Reformed Church in Shippensburg, of the Sunday-school of which he is treasurer.

CAPT. WILLIAM BAUGHMAN, grain dealer, P. O. Shippensburg, was born in this county May 22, 1829, son of William and Mary E. (Fosnaughet) Baughman, natives of this county, and of German descent. Of their family of six children, the subject of this sketch is the fifth. Capt. William Baughman was reared on the farm, and acquired his education in the common schools. He followed agricultural pursuits until the breaking out of the war of the Rebellion; then enlisted, in August, 1861, in Company H, Third Pennsylvania Volunteer Cavalry, and was elected first lieutenant. After the battle of Fredericksburg he was appointed captain of Company E, and served in that capacity until the expiration of his term of service in 1864. At the close of the war Capt. Baughman returned to Shippensburg, embarked in the grain business, and has remained here since. The Captain was united in marriage, in 1852, with Mary C., daughter of Frederick Hepfer, and of German descent. Their children now living are Mary Irene, wife of W. J. Angle; Ida Ann, widow of Walter F. Singmaster; Lilly May, wife of Edward Fenstermacher, and Cora Burd, wife of William Mifflin. Capt. Baughman and wife are members of the Church of God. In politics he is a Republican. He has been assistant burgess, and has also served as chief burgess of Shippensburg for two years. He is a member of the order of K. of P.; is also a F. & A. M., and a member of the G. A. R.

B. D. BIGGS, produce dealer, Shippensburg, was born in Frederick County, Md., May 7, 1830, son of Benjamin and Delila (Groff) Biggs, natives of Maryland, of German and English descent. Of their family of ten children B. D. is the fifth. Benjamin Biggs was a farmer all his life. Our subject was reared on the farm, and followed agricultural pursuits for some years with success. He was married, in 1854, in Adams County, Penn., to Charlotte A. Chamberlin, daughter of David Chamberlin, and of German and English descent. They have one child, Milton, now a young man, still at home. Mr. Biggs has resided in Shippensburg since 1855, and for several years has been engaged in dealing in produce. He is a liberal buyer and has met with success in his business. Mr. and Mrs. Biggs are members of the Methodist Episcopal Church in Shippensburg. He has held most of the church offices; has been Sabbath-school superintendent, and is an earnest Christian worker. In politics he is a Republican.

O. M. BLAIR, general agent and dealer in agricultural implements, also plumber and insurance agent, Shippensburg, was born in York County, Penn., March 1, 1848, son of Thomas P. and Rebecca (Ferree) Blair, natives of Pennsylvania, former of Scotch-Irish descent, and latter a descendant of the Huguenot stock. Thomas P. Blair was a farmer by occupation, and a dealer in grain. He was a prominent man, and at one time served as associate judge of Cumberland County, Penn. He died in Washington County, Md., in 1877, where he had resided only two years. His family consisted of six sons, four of whom are still living, O. M. being fifth in the family. Our subject was reared on the farm and received a common school education in Cumberland County, Penn. At the early age of fourteen years he took charge of his father's farm and followed agricultural pursuits for ten years. In 1867 Mr. Blair accepted an agency for agricultural implements, and continued that in connection with his farming until 1872, when he engaged in his present business. He was married, in 1872, to Nannie Gish, daughter of John Gish, and of German descent. Mr. and Mrs. Blair are members of the Presbyterian Church. In politics he is a Democrat.

REV. W. B. CRAIG, Shippensburg, was born in Dauphin County, Penn., June 22, 1827, son of Hugh and Rachel (Boyd) Craig, natives of Pennsylvania and of Scotch-Irish descent, former of whom was a successful farmer. Of their two sons our subject is the elder. Rev. W. B. Craig was reared on the farm, but had the advantage of a regular college curriculum; he graduated at Jefferson College in 1853, and in 1856 graduated at the Western Theological Seminary, Allegheny City, Penn. He then accepted a united call from the churches of New Bloomfield, Sherman's Creek and Mouth of Juniata, Perry County, Penn., remaining in his first charge nearly eleven years; he was then transferred to Congruity, Westmoreland Co., Penn., where he remained five years; and in 1880 came to Shippensburg, Penn., and here he has passed the early years of his life, where his parents had resided for many years. He was married, in 1859, to Catherine H. Singer, a lady of German descent. Of their five children four are now living: Hugh, reading law in Pittsburgh, Penn.; Samuel, attending school in Philadelphia, Penn.; Catherine and Rachel, attending the State Normal School at Shippensburg, Penn. Mrs. Craig is a lady of culture, a member of the Presbyterian Church. In politics Rev. W. B. Craig is a Republican, and during the late civil war was untiring in his devotion to the Constitution, the Union and Freedom.

WILLIAM FENSTERMACHER, carriage manufacturer, Shippensburg, is a native of Pennsylvania, born in 1824 in Schuylkill County, son of John and Elizabeth (Kutz) Fenstermacher, natives of Pennsylvania, former a farmer by occupation. Of their fifteen children, thirteen of whom grew to maturity, William is the ninth child. Our subject was reared on the farm until eighteen years of age; then commenced learning the coachmaker's trade, which he has followed for over forty years. He makes the manufacture of coaches and buggies a specialty, and, since 1866, has also conducted a livery stable. Mr. Fenstermacher was married, in 1847, to Maria Kreider. Of their ten children four are now living: Cyrus, a coach maker; Elizabeth, wife of George Finston; Edmon S. and Emma. Mrs. Fenstermacher is a member of the Methodist Episcopal Church. Our subject is a Republican in politics, and has been a member of the town council two terms.

JOHN J. GETTEL, merchant, Shippensburg, was born in Franklin County, Penn., June 19, 1857, son of Miley and Mary (Wengert) Gettel, natives of Pennsylvania, of German descent. Miley Gettel was a carpenter in early life, but later became a farmer. Of his family of six children, five of whom are now living, John J. is the fourth. Our subject was reared on the farm, and acquired a common school education. He worked on the farm until he was sixteen years of age; then clerked in a store for about three years, all of which were spent in Shippensburg, and in 1876 he embarked in business, in Shippensburg, as a general merchant. He has met with marked success, and carries an extensive stock for a town of the size. Mr. Gettel was married, in 1879, to Zora L. Hollar, daughter of Henry Hollar. They have three children: Raymond, Velva and Harold. Mr. and Mrs. Gettel are members of the Church of God, in which he is deacon and also assistant superintendent of Sabbath-school. In politics he is a Republican; has been assessor for two years.

C. R. HARGLEROAD, butcher, Shippensburg, was born in Franklin County, Penn., November 14, 1847, son of Jacob and Elizabeth (Retter) Hargleroad, natives of Franklin County, Penn., former of German and latter of English descent. Our subject's grandfather, John Hargleroad, a cooper by trade, was also born in Franklin County, Penn. Jacob Hargleroad, father of our subject, in early life followed milling; at present he is the proprietor of the National Hotel at Shippensburg. Of his ten children C. R. is the third. Our subject was reared on the farm, and attended the common school, and also academy. He assisted in his father's mill, learning the milling trade, and operated the mill for eight years. In 1875 he purchased the Clifton Flouring Mill in Franklin County, Penn., and after running it for three years, sold it and came to Shippensburg and here dealt in horses. In 1880 he imported horses from Canada (it is said that these were the first horses ever brought from Canada to the Cumberland Valley), and continued in this business for two years; was also engaged in importing sheep, which branch of business he still continues. His plan of operating is to import sheep and allow the farmers here to raise them on shares, and in this way he has done much to improve the stock of sheep in this vicinity. Since 1883 he has also done an extensive butchering business. Mr. Hargleroad has been successful, financially, ever since starting in business for himself. He was married, in 1865, to Julia, daughter of Benjamin Kyle, and of German descent. Their children are John A., Bernice, Nellie, Bruce and Clara. Mrs. Hargleroad and the eldest child are members of the Methodist Episcopal Church. In politics Mr. Hargleroad is a Republican. He is a member of the town council of Shippensburg.

JOHN J. KOSER, M. D., Shippensburg, was born in Franklin County, Penn., June 5, 1857, son of Jacob and Elizabeth (Wingert) Koser, natives of Pennsylvania, former of French and German and the latter of German descent. Originally the Kosers descended from the Huguenots. Jacob Koser is a retired farmer and now resides in Shippensburg, this county. Of his two children our subject is the eldest. The Doctor was reared on the farm, and attended the common and State normal schools. His medical education was obtained in the University of Pennsylvania, where he graduated with the degree of M. D., in 1881, and the same year he commenced the practice of his chosen profession in Shippensburg, this county, and has met with more than average success. Dr. Koser is a member of Cumberland County Medical Society, also of the State Medical Association, and is greatly attached to his profession.

WILLIAM A. LUTZ, Shippensburg, traveling salesman for Lewis Kraemer & Co., manufacturers of cotton and woolen goods, Reading, Penn., was born in this county October 1, 1857, son of David and Elizabeth (Brant) Lutz, natives of Pennsylvania, of German descent. David Lutz, who was a farmer all his life, died in 1877; his father, John Lutz, was also born in Franklin County, Penn., and his grandfather, Bernard Lutz (great-grandfather of our subject), a native of Germany, came to America, being among the early settlers of Lancaster County, Penn., William A. Lutz, the subject of this sketch, is the eldest of a family of seven children, six of whom are still living, three boys and three girls. He resided on the farm in Southhampton Township, this county, until he was eighteen years of age, and acquired his education in the common schools. Not liking farm-life, however, he obtained a position as clerk in a dry goods store in Carlisle, Penn., in 1875, where he remained two years, and since then has been engaged as traveling salesman. He has been successful in business, and at present is the owner of three houses and lots in Shippensburg. He was married, December 5, 1883, to Miss Laura A., daughter of Henry C. and Catherine Beidle, and of German descent. Mr. and Mrs. Lutz are members of the United Brethren Church, of which he is trustee. In politics he is a Republican.

REV. WILLIAM A. McCARRELL, pastor of the Presbyterian Church in Shippensburg, was born in Greene County, Penn., August 20, 1846, son of Rev. Dr. Alexander and Martha (McLain) McCarrell, natives of Washington County, Penn., of Scotch-Irish descent. The Rev. Alexander McCarrell, D. D., was pastor of the Presbyterian Church at Claysville, Washington Co., Penn., for thirty-five years. His children now living are: S. J. M., an attorney at law; Rev. J. J., a Presbyterian minister; Rev. William A.; and Thomas C., a Presbyterian minister. The subject of this sketch acquired his education at Washington and Jefferson College, where he graduated in 1868. He then accepted a position at Harlem Springs (Ohio), in Harlem Springs College, as professor of Greek and Latin, and mental and moral science. Remaining there one year, he then entered the Theological Seminary at Allegheny City, Penn., from which he graduated in 1871, and in the same year accepted a call to the churches of Gravel Run and Cambridge, Crawford Co., Penn., where he remained until 1875, when he accepted a call from the Presbyterian Church in Shippensburg. In 1876 he wrote a very creditable history of the Presbyterian Church of Shippensburg, which has since been published. He is a frequent contributor to the newspapers of articles on religious and moral topics. He was married, in 1871, to Martha, daughter of Benjamin Means, and a native of Washington County, Penn., of Scotch-Irish descent. Their children are Martha E., William Alexander, Margaret and Ella R.

JOAB MARTIN, dealer in grain, coal and fertilizers, Shippensburg, was born in Shippensburg, Penn., November 17, 1828, son of Paul Martin and Mary Fry Martin. Paul Martin was the son of Thomas Martin. Thomas Martin was the son of Paul Martin, one of eight brothers who came to this country from the North of Ireland in the year 1725, and settled in Delaware County, Penn.; in 1730, a part of the family of eight brothers moved into Cumberland Valley. Four of the eight brothers were Presbyterian ministers, and in about the year 1727 left Delaware County, Penn., and settled in North and South Carolina, where they were inter-married with the Preston family. Our subject's great-grandfather, Paul Martin, and his grandfather, Col. Thomas Martin, were both soldiers in the Revolutionary war; and his father, Paul Martin, was a soldier in the war of 1812. Joab Martin was married to Lucinda O. Hostetter, of Lancaster County, Penn., in 1863, and they have six children: One son, Thomas Paul, studying medicine at the College of Physicians and Surgeons, of Baltimore, and five daughters, of whom Mary O. is a graduate of the State Normal School and his other four attend the borough schools. In politics, Mr. Martin is a Republican. Mr. and Mrs. Martin and their two eldest daughters are members of the Presbyterian Church of this place.

JAMES B. MARSHALL, physician, Shippensburg, was born near Fairfield, Adams Co., Penn., January 1, 1856, son of Thomas and Jane Ann (Kyner) Marshall, natives of Pennsylvania, and of Scotch-Irish descent. Thomas Marshall was a farmer all his life, and was also a prominent Democratic politician. Dr. James B. Marshall is the fourth in a family of five children. He acquired his education in the common schools and in the Normal School at Shippensburg, this county, and at the age of eighteen years he commenced the study of medicine in the office of Dr. Alexander Stewart & Son. In 1877 he entered Bellevue Medical College, New York, where he graduated with the degree of M. D. in 1879, and the same year commenced practice in Shippensburg, this county, where he still continues. The Doctor is a member of Cumberland County Medical Society. In politics he is a Republican.

DR. ALEXANDER STEWART, retired physician, Shippensburg, Penn., was born in Frederick County, Md., September 28, 1809, son of John and Rosana (Sheeler) Stewart, natives of Maryland, and of Scotch-Irish descent. He is the eldest of a family of nine children—only two of whom survive—and bears the name of his grandfather, Alexander Stewart, who emigrated from the County Antrim, Ireland, in 1773, and settled in Frederick County, Md. His father, John Stewart, was an only son and became a successful business man and farmer. Through a long life he enjoyed the respect and esteem of his community. Himself a man of more than ordinary acquirements, he gave to his children whatever educational advantages he could command. Dr. Stewart was educated at Mount St. Mary's College, and at the age of nineteen years commenced the study of medicine at Emmittsburg. His professional course was completed at Washington Medical College, Baltimore, Md., from which institution he was graduated in 1831. The same year he began the practice of his profession in Shippensburg, where he has continued to reside uninterruptedly until the present time. His skill as a physician was early recognized and appreciated and he soon acquired an extensive practice. For nearly half a century he devoted himself untiringly, or, to a large degree, unselfishly, to the most exacting of all professions. During all these years, his was a familiar and welcome presence in most of the homes in Shippensburg and the surrounding country, in many cases through several successive generations. It was only when impaired vision interfered with the active discharge of his professional duties, that he ceased from his labors. To his medical skill he added a personal character which made him conspicuous and beloved, and now in the retirement of a serene old age he enjoys the affectionate regard of his fellow-men. Dr. Stewart was married, in 1832, to Miss Margaret Grabill, of Frederick County, Md., who died in May, 1835, without issue; he then married in 1836, Elizabeth Hamill, daughter of Capt. George Hamill, of Shippensburg. She died April 24, 1853. By this marriage there were seven children, six of whom survive: George H. (who resides in Shippensburg and is engaged in business as a grain merchant), John (an attorney at law, residing in Chambersburg), Alexander (farmer and grain dealer of Scotland, in Franklin County), Robert C. (a practicing physician in Shippensburg), Mary Augusta (wife of James E. McLean of Shippensburg), and Charlotte Louisa (wife of John H. Craig, of Reading, Penn). In 1858, Dr. Stewart was married to Miss Eunice G. Wilson, of Vermont, his present wife. Because of advanced age he has renounced all business cares and responsibilities except the presidency of the First National Bank of Shippensburg, which position he has held for twenty-one years, being the first and only president.

GEORGE H. STEWART, dealer in grain and real estate, Shippensburg, was born in Shippensburg, Penn., December 29, 1837, eldest son of Dr. Alexander Stewart, of same town. George H. attended the schools in his native town, and also Millinwood Academy, Shade Gap, Huntingdon Co., Penn. From boyhood he had a strong desire to become a business man. His first important business venture was in 1857, when he embarked in the dry goods business, and met with more than average success. He also became interested in tanning and in buying and selling real estate. His business outside of the store grew so rapidly that in 1868 he sold his store, and devoted his time to dealing in real estate and to the leather trade. In 1869 he became interested in the warehouse and grain trade at Shippensburg, since which time he has done a large grain business, and dealt extensively in real estate. His residence stands on the site of the old Stone Tower Hotel, near the Branch, where Gen. Washington stopped when passing through Shippensburg, during the whisky insurrection of 1794. Mr. Stewart is a thorough business man, a generous and courteous gentleman, and is a liberal contributor to moral and Christian enterprises. He married, in 1862, Mary C., daughter of William McLean, of Shippensburg, Penn. She died in 1884, a faithful member of the Presbyterian Church.

DAVID KNIGHT WAGNER, of the firm of D. K. & John C. Wagner, publishers, Shippensburg, was born in Shippensburg, this county, February 6, 1832, son of David and Catharine Elizabeth (Gessner) Wagner, former a native of Cumberland County, of German descent; latter born in Hanover, Germany. David Wagner was a wagon-maker, and carried on this business extensively in Shippensburg for many years, but after the Cumberland Valley Railroad was built to this place he embarked in the grain and produce business, owning his own cars. He was twice married, and had eleven children; he died here in November, 1845. Our subject (child by second wife) received his education in the public schools of his native town, and early in life was employed as salesman; subsequently learned the printing trade, and, in 1851, formed a partnership with J. Bomberger in the publication of the Shippensburg *News*, but in 1856 he sold his interest, and, until 1861, was employed a part of the time as traveling salesman. In the fall of 1861 he enlisted in the Seventh Pennsylvania Reserves as a member of the regimental cornet band, and served until it was honorably mustered out of service, in 1862. He then worked at printing in Bedford County, Penn., until 1866, when he purchased the Fulton *Republican* at McConnellsburg, Penn., which he sold out in 1867, and the same year the present firm was formed, and purchased and are publishing the Shippensburg *News*. They established the News, book and stationery store in Shippensburg. Mr. Wagner was married, in 1869, to Susan, daughter of Mr. John Gish, late postmaster at Shippensburg. Mr. Wagner is a Republican in politics. He served as member of the school board for several terms, and is its late secretary. He is a member of Colwell Post, No. 201, G. A. R.; of the Grand Lodge of Odd Fellows of Pennsylvania, and also of the Masonic order.

JOHN CAREY WAGNER, of the firm of D. K. & John C. Wagner, and brother of D. K., was born July 31, 1838, in Shippensburg, this county, and is the youngest member of the family. He received his education in the public schools and academy in Shippensburg, and in 1853 learned the printing trade. In the fall of 1856 he went to Knoxville, Tenn., and worked in the office of *The Knoxville Whig* (the editor at that time being Parson Brownlow), remaining there until 1860, when he went to Newville, and engaged in publishing *The Star*, in company with James M. Miller. In 1861 he enlisted in Company H, Third Pennsylvania Cavalry, serving as sergeant until discharged at the expiration of his term of enlistment. In 1864 he was detailed into the United States Telegraph Corps (having learned telegraphy before he enlisted), and served in that capacity until 1866, when he took charge of the Bankers' and Brokers' Telegraph Line, at Somerville, N. J., where he remained until 1868, when he returned to Shippensburg and took his present position. He was married, December 29, 1869, to Miss Emma, daughter of John S. and Rachael (Talbott) Morrow, of Newville, this county, of Scotch-Irish descent. They have five daughters living: Ella F., Mary T., Blanche G., Isabella M. and Katharine A. Mr. Wagner is a member of Conedoguinet Lodge, No. 173, and Valley Encampment, No. 4, I. O. O. F., and of the Grand Lodge and Encampment of I. O. O. F. of Pennsylvania; also a member of Colwell Post, No. 201, G. A. R. In politics he is a Republican.

WILLIAM M. WITHERSPOON, physician and surgeon, Shippensburg, was born in Franklin County, Penn., October 17, 1844, son of William Noble and Mary Ann (Lytle) Witherspoon, natives of Pennsylvania, former a farmer of Scotch descent, latter of Irish descent; their family consisted of seven children, four of whom are now living. William M. being the third. Our subject was reared on the farm and attended the common school, also the academy at Chambersburg, Penn., and afterward taught school for one term. He commenced the study of medicine, in Chambersburg, Penn., under the eminent physician Dr. J. L. Suesserott, remaining with him one year and a half, and then entered the medical department of the University of Pennsylvania, from which he graduated in 1869, and has been in active practice in Shippensburg ever since. He was married, in 1881, to

Flora, daughter of John Bridges, a lady of Scotch descent. The Doctor and wife are members of the Presbyterian Church. He is a member of Cumberland County Medical Society. In politics he is a Republican.

CHAPTER XLI.

BOROUGH OF NEWVILLE.

JOHN ALEXANDER AHL, M. D. (deceased), was a grandson of John Peter Ahl, who came to this country about the beginning of the Revolutionary war, and soon entered the Continental Army as surgeon; at its close he began practicing in Rockingham County, Va., but some years later was ordained in the Lutheran Church, preaching in it up to the time of his death, which occurred in Baltimore at the advanced age of ninety-six years. John Peter Ahl had four sons and two daughters, his son John being father of Dr. John A. Ahl. He was also a physician in Rockingham, where he married Nancy Ellen Vaughan, and removed to Franklin County, Penn. Ten years later he came to Shippensburg, this county, staying but a few months; thence moved to Newville, where he practiced until his death, which occurred April 9, 1844. He had five sons. John Alexander Ahl was born in Strasburg, Franklin Co., Penn., August 13, 1813, and subsequently determined to follow his father's profession, reading in his father's office and attending lectures in the University of Maryland and in Washington Medical College in Baltimore, obtaining his degree there in 1838. He practiced in Centreville, Penn., for ten years, then moved to Churchtown, same State, where he obtained a lucrative practice, thence he went to Brandtville, Penn., practicing and milling and grain-dealing for about six years, when he came to Newville, this county, engaging in paper manufacturing, and shortly thereafter associating with him in the business his sons John S. and Q. P. Ahl. He was also extensively engaged in forwarding business and in real estate with his brothers. A stanch Democrat, not having held office before, he, in 1856, was elected to Congress by 1,561 majority over Gen. Lemuel Todd, who had carried the district two years before by a large majority. He served his constituents admirably, and on his return devoted himself with characteristic energy to his large business interests, in which he was eminently successful, acquiring a large estate. He was a presidential elector in 1860. On April 22, 1845, he was married to Elizabeth, daughter of James Williams, by whom he had eight children: John Sherrod, Q. Parker, Abram Williams, Elizabeth W., Laura Bell, Emma Louisa, Frank Woodard and Augusta Vaun. Q. Parker, the second son and only child living, was born July 19, 1847; is unmarried and lives with his mother in Newville. Dr. John Alexander Ahl died April 25, 1882. An energetic and upright man, who often helped the deserving, he was a credit to his family and name, and when he died left to his widow and son the priceless heritage of a good name.

PETER AUGUSTUS AHL and DANIEL VAUGHN AHL. The paternal ancestors of these gentlemen were originally from Berlin, Prussia. The grandfather, Dr. John Peter Ahl, came to America about the opening of the Revolution and settled in Bucks County, Penn. He entered Washington's army as surgeon, and remained as such until the close of the war. After the restoration of peace, he settled in Rockingham County, Va., where he practiced medicine for a number of years. Abandoning medicine, however, he was ordained a minister of the Lutheran Church, his field of labor being Baltimore, where he remained in pastoral work until the time of his death, at an advanced age. He had four sons and three daughters. John, one of the sons, adopted medicine as a profession, and graduated from the schools of Baltimore; began his practice in Rockingham County, Va., where his father had practiced before him. There he married Miss Nancy Ellen Vaughn, and shortly after removed to Strasburg, Franklin County, this State. He remained here about ten years, and then removed to Shippensburg, and thence to Newville, Penn., following his profession in each of these places. He died at Newville in 1844, and his remains rest in the old church-yard of the Presbyterians at that place. He left five sons and three daughters: Samuel Snyder, Carey Watkins, John Alexander, Peter Augustus, Daniel Vaughn, Catharine Washington (married Rev. Jacob Newman, a minister of the Lutheran Church), Martha Jefferson and Mary Etta, all of whom were reared and educated in Newville. Samuel followed the occupation of hatter, and carried on the manufacture of hats largely and profitably in his native place until his death. Carey engaged in school-teaching, subsequently following the mercantile business, besides dealing in real estate, and finally became a well known and successful iron master. John adopted medicine as his profession, practicing successfully in Centreville, Churchtown and Newville.

He was also interested in the manufacture of flour and iron. Engaging in politics, he represented the interests of the Democratic party of the congressional district composed of the counties of York, Cumberland and Perry, during the administration of President James Buchanan. Peter Augustus, one of the subjects of this sketch, was born in Strasburg, Franklin County, this State. He secured a good education, and chose the occupation of druggist. At an early age he entered upon his studies under the direction of Samuel Elliott, a practicing druggist of Carlisle, remaining with him about two years. He then abandoned the profession and engaged in mercantile pursuits. Daniel Vaughn, the other subject of our sketch, and the youngest of the family, was born in Strasburg. He early evinced a natural business talent and a speculative turn of mind, and at the age of fifteen he was employed as clerk in the store of his brothers, Carey and Peter, at Churchtown, remaining several years as salesman in their stores in Churchtown, Shepherdstown and Shiremanstown, in their native county. In this business he continued until the death of his brother, Samuel, who requested that his brother Peter and himself return to Newville and reside with their mother and sisters, Martha and Mary. They complied with his request, made their home with them, and cared for them during their lives. From this time the history of the two brothers is identical. Together they remained, being unmarried, and together they engaged in a great many large, varied and successful enterprises, which gained for them a celebrity throughout the State. Originally without capital and entirely self made, they were characterized by a boldness in their financial undertakings and a public spiritedness in their enterprises which won for them a wide reputation for daring, energetic and successful speculators, railroad and iron men. Daniel, the younger of the two, early displayed an inclination for stock-dealing and speculating in venturesome enterprises. Their first large and successful dealings in stock was in connection with Charles Beltzhoover, of Boiling Springs, Penn., with whom they carried on an extensive business as dealers and shippers of horses and mules. They continued the business themselves, after the retirement of Mr. Beltzhoover, their retail sales of mules alone amounting to as many as 600 head annually. Their stock was principally purchased in the States of Kentucky, Missouri, Indiana and Illinois. In 1856, at the outbreak of the Mormon war, they secured a contract from the Government for the delivery, at Fort Leavenworth, Kans., of 1,500 head of broken mules, for the transportation of the troops from that place to Salt Lake City. These mules were nearly all purchased in the State of Pennsylvania, and delivered at the required point, a distance of nearly 2,000 miles, in sixty days. This was their first Government contract. They also, during the same year, furnished 200 head of mules at Pike's Peak, for the Pike's Peak Overland Stage Company.

They continued in the mule trade until the breaking out of the civil war, amassing a considerable fortune, having, in the meantime, entered into the iron trade, by the purchase of the "Carlisle Iron Works," and acquiring, besides, a large amount of real estate, consisting of mills, farms and mineral lands. The Carlisle Iron Works property comprised some 10,000 acres of valuable timber and mineral lands. The furnace had fallen into disuse before their purchase of it from Peter F. Ege, its former owner. They rebuilt the works, in connection with their brother, Carey, who held an interest in the property, and the manufacture of iron was carried on by them largely and profitably for many years. They also purchased the abandoned "Big Pond Furnace" property in Cumberland County, rebuilt it and established the manufacture of charcoal iron at that place, and continued its manufacture until the sale of the property, with their developed ore lands adjoining, to the Philadelphia & Reading Coal & Iron Company. Daniel also held, at this time, an interest, in connection with Hon. Thaddeus Stevens, in the Caledonia Iron Works, Franklin County, and rebuilt it, after its destruction by Gen. Lee's army, during the memorable invasion of 1863. The Mount Pleasant Iron Works, located at Richmond, Penn., now known as the Richmond Furnaces, and the Beaver forges and furnaces, located at Fort Loudon, in the same county, were purchased and rebuilt by them. After developing large quantities of iron ore on these properties in connection with these works, they agitated and, with other capitalists, carried to completion the construction of the Southern Pennsylvania Railroad, having its terminus at Mount Pleasant, near Cowan's Gap, and connecting with the Cumberland Valley Railroad at Chambersburg. This short line was a link of the great route projected by them through the southern portion of the State, from Harrisburg westwardly, connecting with the Connellsville Road, and its western terminus being Pittsburgh. It was originally known as the Miramar Railroad & Iron Company, with Daniel as its president. The undertaking was abandoned, on account of the antagonism of its rival, the powerful Pennsylvania. The abandoned line had been well chosen, as it was practically the same route adopted and located by the present South Pennsylvania or Vanderbilt Trunk Line. At these places they were large manufacturers of iron for a number of years, but they finally disposed of the works, with a large amount of ore lands, to the Southern Pennsylvania Railroad & Iron Company, Daniel being one of its officers. They also acquired and rebuilt the old Gov. Porter Furnace, in the city of Harrisburg, now owned by the car manufacturing company of that city. The Antietam Furnaces, in Maryland, formerly known as the "Brinn" Iron Works, were purchased and rebuilt by them during the war, and were profitably operated for a number of years. They also acquired

BOROUGH OF NEWVILLE. 449

large holdings of valuable ore lands adjoining these works in the States of Maryland and Virginia, which they operated in connection with the mineral lands purchased of the United States Government, at Harper's Ferry, the whole comprising about 2,500 acres. The "Mammoth" Ore Banks, at Cleversburg, and many other rich and valuable lands were owned and controlled by them during their active operations in the iron trade in that locality, the development of which led to the organization of the Caledonia Iron Land & Railroad Company, and subsequently merged into the Harrisburg & Potomac. Daniel was its principal projector and its president, while to Peter belongs the honor of its construction, the road being practically owned and controlled by them. Upon the completion of the railroad, their various ore lands in its vicinity became very valuable, and large quantities were disposed of to the Philadelphia & Reading Coal & Iron Company, and to the Crane Iron Company, of Catasauqua, Penn. The road was eventually absorbed by the Philadelphia & Reading, and is now owned and operated by that company, with Daniel as one of its directors. In connection with railroads they have also the honor of being the projectors of the York Springs Railroad, and of exerting a considerable influence in the location and construction of the Western Maryland extension into the Cumberland Valley, which adds so materially to the manufacturing interests of Waynesboro and the prosperity of the other towns and the valley through which it passes.

During the war they furnished large supplies of various kinds to the Government, and, in connection with William Calder, of Harrisburg, large numbers of horses and mules, at one time furnishing a number of horses to Gen. Averill's command, while engaged in active operations on the field at Culpeper C. H., Va. This achievement gained for Daniel the title of colonel, by which he was ever after familiarly known. During the darkest days of the Rebellion, when the integrity and financial condition of the Government was in doubt, and when other prominent and leading contractors refused, they undertook and furnished the army 1,000 horses and 1,000 mules in less than thirty days' time. Being of a speculative nature, possessing unusual sagacity, shrewdness and foresightedness in their enterprising projects, they secured and controlled large quantities of real estate in the counties of Cumberland, Franklin, Adams, York, Huntingdon, Clinton, Fulton and Perry, and the adjoining States of Maryland and Virginia, also valuable lands in Minnesota. They were extensively engaged in the manufacture of straw board paper, and possessed large milling interests in various parts of the country. The "Tyboyne Tannery," in Perry County, is owned and was operated by them a number of years quite profitably. The famous Doubling Gap, White Sulphur and Chalybeate Springs in Cumberland County, owned by them, is a popular summer resort, largely patronized on account of the natural beauty of the surroundings and its healthy and delightful location. They also have obtained control of the Cumberland Valley Fruit Farm adjoining, which has been beautified, the buildings repaired and is a valuable acquisition and desirable annex to these springs.

Newville, the place of their early home, their residence now and during their remarkable business career, has not escaped their enterprising spirit. The old hotel property at the railroad station, with the land adjoining, was purchased by Peter. He rebuilt, remodeled and enlarged it, and made it as commodious as any in the valley. The lands between the station and the town were laid out in lots; and a beautiful street, with shade trees planted along its sides, and adorned by large and spacious mansions and the neat and attractive residences of the town business men and a stately church edifice. This most beautiful town now takes the place of what was before broken hills and pasture lands. Warehouses and dwellings were erected by them around the railroad station, and their numerous farms surrounding the town were all handsomely improved by the remodeling and construction of elegant residences and large and commodious barns. Their enterprising spirit yet manifests itself, for, having attained to that age that they should cease their labors and rest upon the fruits of their achievements, yet their active minds will allow of no rest, and even now they are engaged in projecting a railroad from Perry County, via Doubling Gap Springs, to connect with the Cumberland Valley, Western Maryland and the South Pennsylvania Railroads. Notwithstanding the occupation of their minds in so many worldly enterprises, gigantic in their nature and wonderful in their results, and the continued strain upon them in these undertakings, a reflection on their mortality has not escaped them nor been forgotten. A large, beautiful and costly monument, of elaborate design, surmounted by a figure of Faith, pointing heavenward, has been erected by them in the old Presbyterian church-yard, underneath which lie the remains of their beloved parents, a loving brother and two affectionate sisters, and where, in due course of time, they also hope to repose in peace beneath it, a fitting monument to their genius and ability and a commemorative history of the lives of these two enterprising and remarkable men.

JOHN BLAIR DAVIDSON, bank cashier, Newville. The great-grandfather of this gentleman, John Davidson, was one of the first to take up land in West Pennsborough Township, this county. His farm is still in possession of a descendant, James A. Davidson. He was born in 1743 and died in 1823. His son, John, was born in 1772; was married to Elizabeth Young, and died in 1810, his widow dying in 1877; they had five children: Eleanor, John Young, Samuel, Nancy and William. Of these, Samuel was born April 20, 1804, and after getting such education as the schools of that day afforded he went to Carlisle, learning the trade of a tanner with Andrew Blair. Mastering the trade he came to Newville, and worked in a tannery, which he soon bought, and ran for a number of years. An upright, generous man he often helped others to his own detriment. October 19, 1830, Samuel Davidson married Catherine Leckey, born May 21, 1807, daughter of Alexander Leckey, of West Pennsborough Township, this county. To this union were born three children: Alexander Leckey (deceased in 1852); John Blair; and Elizabeth A. (residing in Newville). Mr. Davidson died in August, 1880, his wife in April of the same year. For forty-four years he was an elder in the Big Spring Presbyterian Church. John Blair Davidson was born December 24, 1833, in Newville, Penn. He completed his education at Jefferson College, Washington County, Penn., graduating in 1852, and taught school for ten years, at the end of which time he went into the quartermaster department, at Washington, for five and a half years, where he learned those methodical habits which have done so much to make him successful. In 1869 he returned to Newville, and entered the First National Bank, and in 1882 was promoted to the responsible position of cashier. In October, 1857, he married Margaret Ellen, daughter of William Burnside, of Centre County, Penn., one of which family, Thomas, was judge of the Supreme Court of Pennsylvania. They have one son, Samuel A., born in October, 1869, who lives with his parents. The family are all members of Big Spring Presbyterian Church. Mr. Davidson is characterized by straightforward, unremitting attention to his responsible duties, which he discharges in a manner eminently satisfactory to the directors and to all with whom he is brought into contact.

WILLIAM M. DAVIDSON (deceased) was a descendant of the Davidson family who settled in West Pennsborough Township, this county, where they took up a tract of land in 1750, still owned by A. Davidson. John, grandfather of William M., was born in 1743 and died in 1823. He married, when quite young, a Miss Graham, who died, leaving four children. His second wife was Mrs. Lacey Sterrett, who had been a Miss Laughlin, of an old and widely known family. They had five children, one of whom, named William, was the father of the subject of this sketch. William Davidson was born December 23, 1788; was married November 3, 1814, to Miss Mary Miller, born November 19, 1791, and had the following children: John Laughlin, born November 10, 1816, died February 8, 1837; Eleanor, born September 27, 1818, died September 2, 1838; Mary Jane, born May 9, 1823, died in June, 1845; William Miller, born November 19, 1820, died March 8, 1863. William Miller Davidson was married October 28, 1845, to Miss Margaret Eleanor, daughter of Dr. William M. [see sketch of Alexander Brady Sharpe, page 394] and Jane (Wilson) Sharp, the latter a daughter of Rev. Samuel Wilson, pastor of Big Spring Church, Newville, for fifteen years, and who died, while pastor, March 4, 1799. Dr. William M. Sharp was born July 23, 1798, died August 20, 1835; his widow was born December 3, 1794, and died June 27, 1876. Besides Margaret Eleanor Mr. and Mrs. Sharp had three sons: Samuel Wilson, born March 27, 1822, died December 6, 1877; Alexander Elder, born March 27, ——, died December 13, 1860; Joshua Williams, born May 24, 1831, died in Jaffa, Palestine, April 7, 1881, and was buried in the Protestant Cemetery there. William M. Davidson and wife had three children, all now living: Jane Wilson and Mary Miller, who live with their mother and Oliver Cromwell, who was born January 27, 1856, married in November, 1879, to Miss Mary C., daughter of William Mills Glenn (have one child), and live in West Pennsborough Township, just east of Newville. After her husband's death Mrs. William M. Davidson continued to live on her farm until 1889, when, with her two daughters, she came to Newville.

J. C. FOSNOT, editor *Star and Enterprise*, Newville, is a son of Jacob and Mary Fosnot, natives of Cumberland County, and who had twelve children: William C., J. C., Peter T., Joshua V., Edward W., Lewis C., Henry J., Elizabeth A., Mary Jane, Margaret E., Sarah C. and Martha M. Our subject was born October 3, 1831; learned the trade of a weaver, and later clerked in his uncle's store in Newburg. In 1856 he bought the Oakville store, which he kept for eighteen years, at the same time—three years, from 1866 to 1869—being engaged in business in Baltimore. In May, 1874, in order to give employment to two brothers, he started the *Oakville Enterprise*, which, in December, 1874, he removed to Newville, and has since then devoted himself assiduously to it with gratifying results. Instead of a six-column, four-page, it is now a seven column, eight-page paper, the largest in the whole Cumberland Valley. January 1, 1885, he bought the *Star of the Valley*, which his son George B. McC. conducted for one year, when Mr. Fosnot united it with the *Enterprise* under the name of the *Star and Enterprise*. The double paper is achieving a rare success. October 3, 1855, Mr. Fosnot was married to Elizabeth Ferguson, who has borne him six children: Laura Belle, Maggie R., Lou Ella, George B. McC. and William J., and another daughter who died when six years old. Lou Ella is the wife of Abraham J. Myers, farmer of Mifflin Township, this county. The rest are single, and living with their parents, respected by the community among whom they live.

JOHN GRAHAM, tanner, Newville. This gentleman is of Scotch-Irish descent, his great-great-grandfather, Jared Graham, having emigrated from the North of Ireland in the eighteenth century, locating in Lancaster County, Penn. His descendants have in their possession a deed from "Thomas and Richard Penn, proprietaries of the Province of Pennsylvania," dated March 13, 1734, to Jared Graham, of Salisbury Township, Lancaster County, for a tract of land in the Manor of Maske, West Pennsborough Township, Cumberland Co., Penn., on the south side of the Conodoguinet Creek. He never lived on this land, but continued to reside in Lancaster County, where he died. About 1745 his son James removed to this tract, at that time called the back woods, which was conveyed to him in 1762. His cabin was about thirty miles west of the Susquehanna. He died in 1807, aged eighty-two, leaving five sons: Jared, Thomas, Arthur, Isaiah and James. Thomas was the grandfather of our subject. On the death of his father Jared removed to Ohio. James was educated at Dickinson College, Carlisle, where he graduated, and, having studied theology under the learned Dr. Cooper, was licensed as a Presbyterian minister, and received a call from the congregation of Beulah, eight miles east of Pittsburgh, where he remained thirty-eight years, until his death in 1844. On the death of his father the land was divided between Thomas, Arthur and Isaiah. The two latter resided on the land, and Arthur's portion is yet held by his descendant, Robert Graham. Isaiah's descendants are represented by Duncan M. Graham, Carlisle. Thomas was married to Mary McKeehan, who was born in December, 1778, and died January 23, 1842. They had but one child—George, father of John Graham—who was born December 24, 1802, a short time before the death of his father. He inherited the farm, on which he lived until 1866, when he removed to Newville, having sold the farm. He died March 20, 1870. February 3, 1830, he was married to Miss Eliza Alter, who was born January 16, 1805, and died February 26, 1870. They had nine children, three of whom, Laura, George and Jane, died in infancy, and two, Lizzie and Mary, when nearing maturity. The others were George W., born December 6, 1840, who enlisted in his brother's Company F, Thirteenth Pennsylvania Cavalry, and was killed at Ashby's Gap, Va., May 16, 1863; Thomas J. was born November 25, 1830, and has been living in Colorado for twenty-six years past; Jacob A., born September 30, 1832, went into the army from Kansas, and afterward was captain of the company of which George W. was a member when killed. John, the subject of our sketch, was born August 4, 1843, on the homestead, attended district schools, and received a commercial education at Eastman's College, Poughkeepsie, N. Y. After a few months spent in the West he returned to Newville, this county, bought a store, which he sold two years later, to become book-keeper in the First National Bank in 1870, and resigned in 1876 when, in company with Joseph B. Hurst, he bought the Big Spring tannery, which they still own, and is also engaged in other business enterprises. November 10, 1870, he married Miss Harriet McKee, of Newville, who died eleven months later. June 12, 1878, he was married to Miss Isabella Sterrett, an amiable and accomplished lady, daughter of Brice Innis Sterrett, of West Pennsborough Township, this county. In 1882 Mr. Graham was elected to the Pennsylvania Legislature, and re-elected in 1884. He is now serving his second term with eminent satisfaction to his constituents. The people among whom his life has been spent speak of him in terms of highest praise, and none grudge him the honorable position he has achieved. He and his wife are members of Big Spring Presbyterian Church, of which he was trustee. In politics he is a Democrat.

JOHN HURSH, grain dealer and forwarder, Newville, is a grandson of Henry Hursh, who was a farmer in Lancaster County, Penn., afterward living in York County some time before the Revolutionary war; he died in 1837. His wife was Susanna Rudesil. They had three sons: John, Joseph and Henry. Joseph, married to Mary Fisher, retained the homestead, in which he died in 1849. Henry took a farm a few miles off, on which he died in 1840. John was born in York County, Penn., in 1799, and lived on the farm until his marriage with Barbara Bruckhart; he died in 1880, his wife two years before. They had nine children: Henry, Susan, Daniel, Mary, John, Joseph B., Elizabeth, Abraham and David. Susan, Daniel and Mary are deceased. Henry is married to Cassandra Dietz, and lives in Hopewell Township; Elizabeth is the widow of Christian Rupp, and lives in Mechanicsburg; Abraham is married to Fanny Frantz, and lives in Steelton; David is married to Catharine Hale, and lives in Newville. John was born January 19, 1824, on the farm in York County, where he lived until twenty-four years old, at which time he went to Manchester, York Co., Penn., and engaged in dry goods business with his brother, Joseph B., and when the latter went to Virginia he took the business alone. In 1854 he removed to Mechanicsburg, Penn., and January 1, 1856, to Newville, where he has since resided, engaged in forwarding and dealing in grain, flour, salt, fish, coal, lumber, etc., etc. Until 1870 he was in company with Joseph B., but since then has been alone. At that time they had an interest in the flouring-mill of D. Shipp & Co., of Tamaqua, which in the division his brother assumed, John retaining the business here, including the milling business on Big Spring. He and Joseph own together one-half interest in the Mount Vernon Mill on the Conodoguinet. In 1850 Mr. Hursh was married to Miss Sarah A., daughter of George Livingston, of York County, Penn., and born in 1823. They had five children, one of whom, John, born May 10, 1857, died young. Those living are Daniel G., born June 24, 1851, who was married December 17, 1874, to Annie C. Bert, of Newville, and is his father's book-keeper; Sheua, born October 17, 1852, is the wife of W. B. Oyler, of Newville; Sarah, born August 3, 1855, is the wife of Erwin C. Glover, of Detroit, Mich., and James, born July 23, 1860, is married to Annie C. Kratzer, of Newville. Mr. Hursh has held many township offices, and is now and has been, for several years, treasurer of Newville Cemetery. He and his wife and son Daniel, and daughter, Susan, are members of the United Brethren Church, and in all the relations of life he has ever shown himself to be a man of probity.

ROBERT McCACHRAN, attorney at law, Newville, is a representative of an old Scotch family, who came to this country early in the last century, at which time his great-great-grandfather emigrated, with his wife, three sons and one daughter. His son, James, married Mary Ralston, whom he had known in the old country, and they had three sons: James, John and Robert. In 1790 they purchased a farm on the Brandywine from the Penns, and here they lived until, on the death of his wife, the father, having made other arrangements for his youngest son, divided the farm between James and John, with whom he lived until his death, September 22, 1822, aged eighty-seven. John, the grandfather of Robert McCachran, was born about 1763, and in 1794 or 1795, was married to Isabella, daughter of John Cunningham, who enlisted in the Revolutionary war, and was never again heard of. John McCachran died February 8, 1808, aged about forty-five, leaving five children. His widow died February 12, 1851, at the residence of her son John, near Newville, aged eighty-six. Their children were James, Elizabeth, Robert, John and Isabella. Robert, father of our subject, was born in 1798. He had an ardent desire for a liberal education, which he procured under great difficulties in various places, finally completing the three years' course at the Theological Seminary at Princeton, N. J. He was licensed to preach in 1827 and given a charge at Middleton, Penn., also attending to the religious wants of the community for miles around. He was ordained May 19, 1829. In 1830 he took a journey in search of health, and in Newville was invited to preach in the Big Spring Church, then without a pastor. This resulted in his becoming pastor of that church in which he labored for twenty-one years, resigning in 1851. In 1834, he married Jane, daughter of Atcheson Laughlin, head of one of the oldest and most widely known and respected families of this region. She was born in 1799. They had two children: Robert, born October 6, 1835, and Mary born in 1837 (wife of James Oliver); she died in 1875. Robert McCachran, Sr., died at Newville, February, 15, 1885, aged eighty-five years; his wife died in 1872. Until 1853, young Robert attended a classical school taught by his father. He then went to Jefferson College, and graduated from Lafayette College, Easton, Penn., the following year. He engaged in teaching and read law in the office of Judge Frederick Watts, of Carlisle, and was admitted in 1857, but did not practice for some years, having the management of his father's property. Having prepared himself for the profession, he, in 1870, became civil engineer on the Harrisburg & Potomac Road, and, in 1872, took a similar position on the Pennsylvania Railroad, resigning in 1875, to look after his father's interests. In 1883 he began practicing as an attorney. In December, 1874, he married Martha McCandish, born in 1847, daughter of Thomas McCandish, of an old Scotch family, who have been in this neighborhood since early in the last century. To this union were born six children: Thomas, born February 16, 1876; Mary, born September 11, 1877; Jane. born October 28, 1878; Margaret, born December 21, 1879; Robert, born November 28, 1881 (deceased) and Russell Atcheson, born March 1, 1886. Mr. McCachran was a member of the Legislature four years, elected in 1878, and again in 1880, and is attorney for the borough. He is a K. T. He is a man of unswerving honesty and is in every way trustworthy.

J. NORRIS and THOMAS E. MYERS, merchants, Newville, are grandchildren of John Myers, an old and respected citizen of Georgetown, D. C., who died there in 1853. He, John Myers, had seven children: John H., a prominent citizen of Lexington, Va., where he died; Charles, a merchant of Georgetown, where he lived all his lifetime; Thomas, the father of our subjects; Edward and William E., who were in business as partners in Georgetown for several years (the former died recently in Brooklyn, N. Y., and the latter, some years ago at sea, while on a health trip); Louisa (deceased in 1873), was the wife of Joseph Libbey, a prominent and wealthy merchant of Georgetown, and Catharine S., unmarried, lives in Georgetown. Thomas Myers was born in 1813; in 1835 he entered the Baltimore Conference of the Methodist Episcopal Church; in 1843 and 1844, was stationed on the Carlisle Circuit and lived in Mechanicsburg, where he is well remembered. In March, 1885, he preached by special request, before the Conference, his semi-centennial sermon, in the Eutaw Street Church, Baltimore, Md. He has, for the past three years, been stationed at Woodberry, Md., and is now agent of the Maryland Bible Society, at Baltimore, Md. His remarkable tact and business ability have caused his being sent on several occasions to struggling parishes to build new churches and parsonages, in which he has always succeeded. Now, in his seventy-fourth year, he is as hale and vigorous as many men of twenty years his junior. His deceased children are Lottie. a young lady, who died in 1876, and two other children who died in infancy. The living are J. Norris, Mary L., Thomas E. and James R. Mary L. is the wife of John J. Frick, teller in First National Bank, York, Penn. James R. is married to Laura V. Murray, and is in commission business in Baltimore, Md. J. Norris was born in Lewistown, Penn., November 17, 1842. He at-

BOROUGH OF NEWVILLE. 453

tended the grammar school at St. John's College, Annapolis, Md., and completed his education in Newton University, Baltimore. In 1858, he went into the hardware store of Duer, Norris & Co., in that city, which he left, in 1866, to engage in business under the firm name of Ullrich & Myers, giving up, several years after, on account of his health and engaging as a commercial traveler. In 1879, with his brother, Thomas E., he came to Newville, this county, and established the firm of Myers & Bro., which was dissolved in 1882, when he returned to Baltimore. While confidential clerk for a large importing house, his health was impaired by overwork, and by his physician's advice he removed to the country, and in February, 1886, the firm of Myers & Bro. was revived by his purchase of the interest of his brother's partner. In 1876 he was married to Laura V., daughter of William M. Starr, of Baltimore, a man of brilliant attainments, who has occupied many positions of honor and trust. He was a son of the wealthy Wesley Starr, who built the Starr Methodist Protestant Church in that city and endowed its parsonage. Mr. and Mrs. Myers have three children: William Starr, John Norris and Thomas Miller. Mr. Myers is welcomed back to Newville by all who know him. He and his wife are communicants of the Methodist Episcopal Church and command universal respect. Thomas E. Myers, our other subject, was born in Cumberland, Md., in 1850, and was educated mainly in Baltimore. In 1866 he went into his brother's store there, and remained until 1872, when he became book-keeper in the largest retail hardware store in Baltimore, remaining until 1878. In 1879 he came to Newville, as stated above, and on the dissolution of the firm, in 1882, formed a partnership with John M. McCandlish, which was dissolved the following year in consequence of the failing health of his partner, who went West. He then formed a partnership with James S. Brattan, under style of Myers & Brattan, which continued until the purchase of his partner's interest by his brother, J. Norris. He was married, in 1882, to Miss Emma J., daughter of Rev. Thomas M. Reese, one of the oldest members and a leading one of the Central Pennsylvania Methodist Episcopal Conference, who died in March, 1882. To this union two children have been born: Lottie Reese and Elizabeth Parrish. He and his wife are members of the Methodist Episcopal Church, and, as an upright Christian business man, he bears an enviable reputation.

ROBERT S. RANDALL, bank teller, Newville, is a grandson of George and Margaret (Steinbeck) Randall, natives of Philadelphia, Penn., whose parents came from Germany. George Randall died in 1812 or 1813, and his widow in 1856; they had thirteen children, five of whom died young. The others were John, David, George, Joseph S., Lawrence H., Sarah, Catharine and Mary. Lawrence H. Randall was born October 14, 1810, learned the trade of a tailor, and came to Newville, this county, in 1833, where he carried on the business until 1875. He is a director of the First National Bank, of which he was an incorporator. In 1833 he was married to Miss Mary Jane Dunlap, of Harrisburg, and on October 14, 1883, they celebrated their golden wedding, in company with twenty six of their descendants and a large number of other friends, receiving many expressions of esteem and good-will. They had twelve children: Margaret, Scott, and William, deceased; and Mary, wife of W. R. Tittler, of Newville; Sarah A., wife of Albert H. Newman, of Catasauqua, Penn.; Edmund, married to Maria E. Williams and living in Catasauqua; William L., living in Altoona; Laura, Marian J., Eva K., and Joseph S., living with their parents; and Robert S., who was born June 21, 1840, and learned his father's trade, and lived with his parents until 1862, when he enlisted at Chambersburg, in Company A, One Hundred and Twenty-sixth Pennsylvania Volunteers, for nine months. He was in the battles of Fredericksburg and Chancellorsville, where he was captured and taken to Belle Isle, at Richmond. He was one of the 5,000 prisoners paroled by the rebels, who were afterward exchanged and were sent to Camp Parole, at Annapolis, Md., thence to Harrisburg, where he was honorably discharged with his regiment in May, 1863. On his return he entered a commercial college in Philadelphia to acquire a business education, and then was in business with his father for ten years. In 1875, he went to Catasauqua, Penn., where, with his brother Edmund, he published *The Catasauqua Dispatch*, still conducted by his brother. Two years later he returned to Newville, this county, and bought the Lewis Sumac and Bark Mill, which he ran for three years, when he accepted the position of teller of the First National Bank, which he retains. In 1868, he was married to Florence, daughter of George Bricker, Sr., of Newville, who died in 1871, her two children having preceded her to the grave. Mr. Randall re-married in 1882; his wife is Maimee, a daughter of Maj. Edmund Hawkins, of Catasauqua, Penn. They have two children: Ernest H., born October 18, 1883, and Lawrence E., born June 12, 1885. Mr. Randall belongs to Colwell Post, No. 201, G. A. R.; has once been councilman, and is now school director. He and his wife are members of the United Presbyterian Church. As a man of character and probity he has no superior in the community in which he lives.

JOHN W. STROHM, editor *Times*, Newville, was born in this county December 6, 1855, son of George and Eliza Strohm, of Plainfield, Penn. George Strohm was one of four brothers who came to this county from Lebanon County prior to 1838, in which year he was married. He engaged in wagon and cabinet-making, and amassed a comfortable competency. He has had nine children: Benjamin F., married to Annie Grove; Mary A., widow of Dr. Wilmer James, a prominent homœopathic physician; Sarah J., wedded to Robert E. Myers, living in Ohio; J. Silas, married to Catherine Bear; George W., married to Cathrine Faust, of Carlisle; David E. married Sadie E. Paul; Horace L. married Clara Jacoby; Lizzie G. is the wife of John Paul, and John W., our subject, was married, March 23, 1880, to Alice, daughter of David and Rachael Sanderson, of this county. One son, Orie Curtis, has blessed this union. Prior to his marriage, John W. Strohm was engaged in mercantile business at Plainfield, this county, where, on May 11, 1882, he began the publication of the *Plainfield Times*, purchasing a complete outfit, including steam press, and has made the paper a pronounced success, its popularity growing with each issue. In November, 1885, he removed it to Newville, and called it *The Newville Times*. It has a large circulation. In August, 1883, he started a matrimonial paper called *Cupid's Corner*, which has proven a profitable venture. Mr. Strohm has evinced his ability, and is a man of rank in journalism.

JOHN WAGNER, bank president, Newville, is the representative of the Wagner family, from whom Wagner's Gap, in the Blue Ridge, took its name. His great-grandfather immigrated in 1740, and his grandfather, Jacob Wagner, whose father and mother both died on the ocean while on their way from Switzerland, first settled in Rock Hill Township, Bucks County, Penn., afterward removing to this county, where he took up a tract of 700 acres on what is known as Wagner's Road, leading from Carlisle to the Gap. He died there in 1809. The farm is still owned by members of the family. His wife was Mary Cathrine Bauer. They had nine children: John, Jacob, George, Abraham, Philip, Catherine, Mary, Margaret and Henry. Jacob, father of John Wagner was born in 1760, and on his father's death inherited half of the land where he lived all his days. In 1806 he married Christiana, daughter of Nicholas Ferdig, of North Middleton Township, Cumberland County. They had four children: John, Jacob, George and Elizabeth. Of these Jacob, who succeeded to the mansion farm, married Ann, daughter of John Lane, Esq., and died near Carlisle in 1884; George married Sarah Strohm, and lived near Carlisle, where he died in 1880, his widow is still living; Elizabeth (deceased in 1853) was the wife of Peter Lane, a brother of Ann Lane (Mrs. Jacob Wagner); John, the only survivor, was born April 30, 1808, in North Middleton Township, Cumberland County, Penn., and when eighteen years old he went to Perry County, Penn., to learn the tanner's trade; thence to Buffalo, N. Y., for a year, and then back to the farm. The following year he worked in a tannery, which he subsequently bought in 1850, and ran until 1878, since which time he has leased it. In January, 1871, he was elected president of the First National Bank of Newville, an office which his associates have since insisted on his retaining. In 1836 he married Jane, daughter of George Klink, of Newville. They celebrated their golden wedding June 2, 1886. To this union nine children have been born. The deceased are Mary Ellen, who became wife of John Curn, of California, and died in 1877; Jacob A. and Eva F. died after reaching their majority. The living are John P., a contractor living in Iowa; Samuel C. of whom a sketch appears below; Annie E., wife of S. I. Irvine, now living in Sioux City, Iowa; Sarah J., wife of Thomas N. Henderson, merchant of Germantown, Md.; and Lydia, wife of Joseph S. Henderson, a farmer near Germantown (the Hendersons are sons of the former pastor of Big Spring Presbyterian Church in Newville); Rebecca K. lives with her parents. Mr. Wagner has on many occasions held the office of burgess, town councilor, and was school director for nearly forty years. He and his wife are members of Big Spring Presbyterian Church, of which he is an elder, and for thirty years he was superintendent of the Union Sabbath-school. He and his wife are now enjoying the fruits of a long unblemished life, with all the comforts that ample means can procure and with the good-will of every member of the community.

SAMUEL C. WAGNER, grain and flour dealer, and State Senator, representing the Cumberland and Adams District, Newville, a son of John and Jane (Klink) Wagner, was born August 9, 1843, and was educated at schools and academies in the county, afterward getting a business education at the Iron City Commercial College, Pittsburgh, Penn. In 1859 he kept books in a wholesale dry goods house in Leavenworth, Kas., for a few months, when he returned to Newville, this county, and worked in the tannery of his father until August 8, 1861; when, just eighteen, he enlisted in Young's Kentucky Cavalry, afterward the Third Pennsylvania Cavalry. He has a most brilliant record as a soldier. Six months after his enlistment the young man was promoted to regimental commissary sergeant, and in a few months more was promoted again to second lieutenant of Company I. In a short time he was again promoted to first lieutenant and regimental commissary. On the reorganization of the cavalry, under Gen. Pleasanton, he was assigned to the staff of Gen. J. B. McIntosh, commanding the First Brigade of Gregg's division of the Cavalry Corps of the Army of the Potomac. He was afterward assigned to fill a vacancy caused by the disability of Capt. Pollard, of Gen. Gregg's staff, at Warrenton, Va., in the winter of 1863. In the spring of 1864, when Gen. Grant began his movement toward Richmond, he was ordered to report to Gen. Patrick, provost-marshal-general of the Army of the Potomac, as commissary to prisoners, in which he remained until mustered out in the fall of 1864, in front of Petersburg, where he was brevetted captain for gallant services. He took part in the battles of Savage Station, White Oak Swamp, Charles City Cross Roads, Malvern Hill (where he was one of the last officers to leave the

Hill), Antietam, Kelly's Ford, Stoneman's cavalry raid in rear of Lee's army, the cavalry fight at Culpeper, where he had a narrow escape. He was on the left of the skirmish line, when he was ordered by Col. Horace Binney Sargent, in command, to give report to two officers on a hill, a short distance away, whom he supposed to be Gens. Gregg and McIntosh. Young Wagner told the colonel they were rebel officers, but was not believed, the colonel sending his own orderly after him. On reaching and saluting the group he found his suspicions verified, and was ordered to dismount, but instead he struck spurs to his horse, threw himself flat on the animal's back, and galloped back amid a shower of bullets. The orderly, who was behind him, sat erect, and was literally riddled with bullets. The next fight he was in was at Sulphur Springs; then Auburn, Bristow Station, Salem, Upperville, and in all the cavalry skirmishes on the march to Gettysburg, at which place he was wounded by a piece of rebel shell while fighting the rebel cavalry under Wade Hampton and Fitzhugh Lee. On recovering he rejoined his command, near the Rappahannock, and was in the advance when Grant crossed the Rapidan, and then took part in all the fights in the Wilderness, at Spottsylvania, North Anna River, Cold Harbor, and the different skirmishes in front of Petersburg. He was with the Army of the Potomac until mustered out, as stated, by expiration of term, when he returned home, a veteran, barely twenty-one years of age, having seen more service than fell to the lot of many a soldier. He was then elected book-keeper of the First National Bank of Newville, which he resigned July 1, 1868, to engage in the grain and lumber business. This he disposed of in July, 1884, when he bought the "Keller Mill," at the head of Big Spring, which he remodeled, making it one of the most complete roller flour-mills in the State. This he is still engaged in. In 1882 he was a candidate for nomination for State Senator in the district composed of Cumberland and Adams Counties, under the Crawford County system, against two veteran journalists of the county, when he received 600 more votes than both combined, and was elected after a memorable contest over James W. Bosler. His term will expire January 1, 1887. In 1866 Mr. Wagner married Laura E., daughter of John M. Woodburn, of Newville. They have eight children: Charles W., Jennie E., Annie L., Sallie G., George B., Walter E., Samuel C., Jr., and Thomas H., in ages from eighteen to four years. Mr. Wagner is a Knight Templar, belonging to St. John's Commandery of Carlisle, and to Big Springs Lodge, No. 361, of Newville. He is also a member of Cavalry Post, No. 35, G. A. R., of Philadelphia. A gallant soldier, a pure politician, and an upright business man, he deserves the honors put upon him by his neighbors. In politics he is a Democrat.

MUHLENBERG WILLIAMS, attorney, Newville, is a son of John Williams, who was born in Middlesex Township (then North Middleton) in May, 1808, and who was a son of Henry Williams, of Lebanon County, but who removed to North Middleton some years after his marriage. He had ten children, viz.: Henry, who was married to Elizabeth Zook, and who died in North Middleton, leaving no issue; David, who lived all his life on part of the old homestead, married and died there; Frederick, who was a farmer, inherited a part of the old farm, married Susan Rheem, and died, leaving a son, Thomas, who is farming the same place; Rudolph, who is now a druggist in Columbia, Penn.; Jacob, who was a cripple, was never married, and died on the farm; Thomas, who died before attaining his majority; Samuel, who lived on the old homestead, which he afterward sold, and then removed to North Middleton, where he died in 1885; Catherine, widow of Michael Wise, of North Middleton, and now living in Carlisle; Elizabeth, wife of George Hetrich, of Franklin County, where she died; and John, the youngest of the family and father of our subject, who learned the drug trade and went into business at Newville, where he continued a number of years. He afterward gave this up, and bought a farm close to the borough, on which he has since lived. In 1832 he was married to Susan R., daughter of George Wise, farmer of North Middleton Township, whose connection is very large. They had twelve children, viz.: David W., who is married to Miss Adeline Knettle; Muhlenberg, our subject; Eleanor, unmarried and living with her parents; John, who died in infancy; Mary, wife of Jonas D. Huntzberger, of Newville; Catherine, wife of George Lehman, of West Pennsborough Township; Susan R., wife of Samuel E. Heberlig, of West Pennsborough Township; Jennie, wife of John D. Brehm, living in Newton Township; Martha, wife of David S. De Haven, living in Newville; Rudolph, married to Charlotte S. Faber, and living in Newville; Lucretia, unmarried, living with her parents; Maggie N., wife of J. Hess, residing in Osborne, Mo. In his youth, Muhlenberg worked on his father's farm in summer, going to school during winter, until twenty-one years of age, and the last two winters he attended the academy in Newville, of which Rev. Robert McCachran was principal. He then taught school three sessions, and studied law in the office of William H. Miller, Esq., of Carlisle, where he was admitted to the bar November 14, 1860, being examined and recommended by Hon. Frederick W. Watts, Lemuel Todd and A. B. Sharpe, Esqs. After he was admitted he began the practice of his profession at Newville, where he has remained. May 23, 1872, he was married to Miss Lydia E., daughter of William M. Scouller, of Mifflin Township, and has five children, viz.: John, Nellie, William Scouller, Lydia Belle and May. Mr. Williams has been identified largely with the politics of his township, borough and county. He has been school director of the township three years, and of the borough nine years; auditor three years. In 1866 he was appointed assistant assessor of Division No. 10, of the Fifteenth Collection District of Pennsylvania, which office he held during the Johnson administration, and was elected to the Legislature in 1872. He bears the reputation of being a skillful, adroit practitioner, who has the interest of his clients very much at heart. He is rated as one of the ablest members of the bar of Cumberland County.

CHAPTER XLII.

BOROUGH OF SHIREMANSTOWN.

JOHN R. BAKER, carriage-maker, Shiremanstown, was born October 20, 1845, and is a son of John S. Baker, now living near Shepherdstown, Upper Allen Township, where John R. was born. The elder Baker was born in York County, Penn., in 1813, where he lived with his parents, until he came to this county, over forty years, settling on the place where he now lives. The family consists of the father (the mother is but a few months deceased), three sons and two daughters. John R., who is the second son, lived at home until he was ten years of age, when he went to his grandfather's for three years. There he was hired out until he joined the Union Army in the spring of 1862, when but sixteen years of age, a volunteer in the Eighty-seventh Regiment Pennsylvania Volunteer Infantry, in the Army of the Potomac, in which he saw a great deal of service. He participated in the battle of Winchester, the battles in the Wilderness, Mine Run, Spottsylvania Court House, Cold Harbor, the capture of the Weldon Railroad, the battles of Cedar Creek and Monocacy River, the siege and capture of Petersburg and the final fight at Appomattox. His time had expired a few days before this last event, but he preferred to stay and see the war out. Though but a boy he became a veteran, and in spite of the many battles in which he participated, beside skirmishes innumerable, he never received a wound. On the field of Appomattox he got his well-earned honorable discharge, and afterward, with the rest of his comrades of the historic Army of the Potomac, was mustered out of the service at Washington. On his return home he apprenticed himself to John Palmer, of Mechanicsburg, to learn carriage painting. In 1872 he and his brother Henry established a carriage factory at Camp Hill, in East Pennsborough Township. Here they remained for eight years, when John R. bought Henry's interest, and after staying there one year more, removed to Shiremanstown, where he has been engaged in the business ever since, building up a large and constantly increasing trade by honest work. He was married, in 1867, to Annie, daughter of Simon Dean, of Mechanicsburg, and they have seven children—two boys and five girls. Mr. Baker is a member of the Winding Hill Reformed Mennonite Church, and among his fellow-men bears a well-deserved reputation as a man of probity whose word can always be relied upon, for what he promises he will perform. Yet a young man, a long and honorable career lies before him.

DR. W. SCOTT BRUCKHART, Shiremanstown, was born March 10, 1848, near Columbia, Lancaster Co., Penn. His father was born on the same farm, and his grandfather in the same neighborhood. His great-grandfather was one of a colony which came to this country from Switzerland early in the last century, coming directly to Philadelphia, Penn. From there the party went to Virginia, but shortly after returned to York and Lancaster Counties, where many of their descendants are yet to be found; here he engaged in farming, as did his son, the father of our subject, latter acquiring a competence by his industry. Our subject's father and mother still live on the original farm; he is also interested in mining enterprises in Chestnut Hill District; his wife was Catherine Habecker, of the same place; they have seven boys living, of whom the Doctor is the eldest. Our subject stayed on the farm until he was sixteen years of age, then taught school for three winter terms, attending the normal school at Millersville in the summers. In 1868 he began the study of medicine with Dr. A. K. Rohrer, of Mountville, one of the most prominent physicians in that part of the State, regarded as high authority on the treatment of typhoid fever. Here Dr. Bruckhart stayed for two or three years, taking at the same time a full course of lectures in the Jefferson Medical College, Philadelphia, where he graduated in March, 1870, at the early age of twenty-two years. The following month he removed to Mount Joy, Lancaster County, and commenced the practice of his profession. In February, 1874, he came to Shiremanstown, where he has ever since devoted himself to the practice of his profession. During this time several other physicians have located in the borough, at different times, but all have retired from the field in turn, leaving Dr. Bruckhart the sole practitioner in the neighborhood, in which he has, by his skill and knowledge of his profession, as well as by his other good qualities, acquired the confidence and esteem of his neighbors. In December, 1872, he married Attilla, daughter of John Strickler, of Mount Joy, a retired farmer. They had three children, of whom only one, Paul Holmes, survives. The Doctor is a member of Columbia Lodge, No. 286, F. & A. M., and Corinthian Chapter and Cyrene Commandery, No. 34, all of Columbia. He is also a member of Irene Lodge, No. 425, K. of P., of Shiremanstown, and is likewise president of the Beneficial Society of Shiremanstown, an incorporation of residents of the vicinity for mutual aid. Dr. Bruckhart has held the office of school trustee ever since the second year of his residence in the borough, and has during all that time been secretary of the board. He also served two years as burgess, and, as will be seen by the above, is one of the most active members of society in this part of the county. He has, in a very marked degree, the confidence and esteem of his neighbors, who will probably call upon him to serve them in a higher capacity. He is well qualified to adorn any position for which he may be chosen.

CHRISTIAN HESS, retired farmer, Shiremanstown, a son of Christian and Elizabeth (Martin) Hess, natives of Lancaster County, who were married in 1808, and in 1811 removed to Fairview Township, York Co., Penn., to a farm owned by the Rev. Samuel Hess, his father. Christian Hess was born November 28, 1779, in Elizabethtown, Lancaster Co., Penn. They reared eight children: Samuel, the eldest son, born in Lancaster County, died at the age of fifteen; the other children, Nancy, Barbara, George, Christian, Elizabeth, Henry and Susannah were born in York County. Our subject was married, in 1840, to Judith, daughter of Peter and Esther (Martin) Zimmerman, Rev. John Mumma performing the ceremony. After marriage Christian Hess assumed charge of his father's farm, working it on shares until 1857, when he purchased the homestead, paying for it in installments. The children, eight in number, were all born on the homestead in York County, viz.: Elizabeth, Peter, Hetty (the two latter twins), Barbara, Mary, Rebecca, Samuel and Catharine. Of these, Samuel is a minister of the Mennonite faith, and served a congregation at State Hill, Lower Allen Township; Peter married Lydia Brechbill, of Lancaster County; Hetty married Jacob M. Zimmerman, of the same county; Barbara, Elizabeth and Mary are housekeepers for their parents, and Rebecca, wife of George F. Umberger, died a few years ago. The Rev. Samuel Hess, above mentioned, wedded Annie Metzler, of Lancaster County, Penn. In 1875 Mr. and Mrs. Christian Hess removed to State Hill, where a nice farm was purchased, and which will probably be their home in the future. The church near by makes it convenient for these aged Christians who, for more than half a century, have gone hand in hand to the house of God, setting noble examples for their children, who, without exception, follow in their footsteps.

DAVID R. MERKEL, farmer (son of Levi Merkel, whose sketch see), P. O. Shiremanstown, was born in the year 1835, on the farm on which he now lives, and which was purchased and occupied by his grandfather, Jacob Merkel, in 1804, and has been in the family ever since. Jacob Merkel built a house on the opposite side of the road to that on which D. R. Merkel's new residence stands, and in 1812 built a stone barn, which is still in use and in perfect condition. With the exception of the time spent in school, D. R. Merkel lived on this farm until 1866, at which time he removed to the borough of York, Penn., where he was professor of music in the Cottage Hill Female College for five years. His health failing he returned to the farm, remaining three years. He then went to Elmira, N. Y., and engaged in music-teaching for the succeeding six years, after which he returned to the farm, which he now owns, and which he is making a model place. He is a progressive gentleman, quick to adopt the best methods of obtaining desirable results, and his success is evidenced by his surroundings. He was married, in 1857, to Miss Sarah J., daughter of Samuel Eberly, formerly of Hampden Township, this county. They have one child, Romaine, married to M. W. Jacobs, Esq., attorney and counselor, of Harrisburg, Penn. D. R. Merkel has never held any office except that of school director, which was forced upon him. His whole time and attention is given to agricultural pursuits, for which he has a genuine love. In personal character Mr. Merkel stands high, and shows himself a worthy son of his illustrious father.

HENRY S. RUPP, nurseryman, Shiremanstown, was born in Lower Allen Township, this county, in 1826, and is the son of George Rupp, a native of Lancaster County, Penn., where his father settled about 1790, when he emigrated from Germany. Henry S. lived on his father's farm, in Lower Allen Township, until he was twenty-four years old, when he removed to where he now lives, buying the farm in 1855. He married, in 1852, Nancy, daughter of Joseph Hursh, of York County, Penn. They have a family of four sons and two daughters, one, Lizzie, being married to Amos Landis, of Upper Allen Township; the others are unmarried. Henry S. Rupp gave his attention to farming until 1865, when he embarked in the nursery and florist business. He has at present over 5,000 square feet under glass, and forty acres of his farm of 100 acres are devoted to this business, in which his sales are constantly increasing. His flowers and plants go all over the country; his trees are sold mainly in southern Pennsylvania and Maryland. A special feature of his business is the growing of primrose seed for the trade, of which seed he is the largest grower in the country, most of the seed hitherto used having been imported.

He has now many customers for this seed among the florists, and the demand for it is rapidly increasing. Two of his sons are associated with him in the nursery business: John F. and David C. Mr. Rupp has never given much attention to politics, and could hardly be induced to hold office of any kind. His neighbors speak of him as a man of strictest probity in all his dealings.

JOHN K. TAYLOR, dealer in sundries, Shiremanstown. Since March, 1846, J. K. Taylor has been a resident of Cumberland County, and during the intervening years has been one of the representative business men. He was born in Newberry Township, York Co., Penn., in 1826, a son of Libni and Mary (Krieger) Taylor, who, for nearly fifty years, lived on the farm which was improved by them. He comes from English ancestry, of the Puritanical type, on the paternal side, and his maternal ancestors were natives of Germany. Libni and Mary Taylor reared a family of seven children, of whom three sons are living: Jacob K., John K. and Benjamin K. Upon arrival in Allen Township, in 1846, John K. Taylor became an apprentice to and learned the trade of blacksmith with, Ezekial Worley, whose shop stood near the present site of Mr. Taylor's smithy. After completing his trade our subject went to Milltown, and engaged for nine years in smithing. He then purchased his Slate Hill property, and since that time has conducted a shop, and has also engaged largely in dealing in meats, etc. In 1850 he was married to Elizabeth Arter, of York County, Penn. They have no children, but their home is made happy by their affection for each other, and the comforts which are always found in the home of the prosperous man. John K. Taylor, who has always been a representative man in his township, by dint of energy and business qualifications has accumulated considerable property. He is one of the self-made men of Cumberland Valley, and has filled nearly every official position in the township with honor.

CHAPTER XLIII.

COOK TOWNSHIP.

DANIEL KING, superintendent of South Mountain Mining & Iron Company, P. O. Pine Grove Furnace, was born in Queen's County, Ireland, January 1, 1844. His parents, William and Catherine King, immigrated to Pennsylvania in 1841, but returned, in 1843, to Ireland, where they still reside. Daniel King, after receiving a classical education in Ireland, came to America in the early part of 1862, and in August of that year enlisted in the One Hundred and Sixteenth Pennsylvania Volunteers. He was honorably discharged in 1863, on account of disabilities incurred in the line of duty. After recovery, in the same year, he re-enlisted and served sixty days in the Fifty-second Pennsylvania Militia (raised during Lee's invasion) and on the disbandment of same again entered the service of his adopted country, this time in the Naval branch, and served until 1865 in the North Atlantic blockading squadron. After leaving the public service Mr. King engaged in the study and practice of mechanical engineering at Paterson, N. J., Baltimore, Md., and Jersey City, N. J. In April, 1871, he located at Pine Grove Furnace, in this county, as assistant superintendent of the South Mountain Iron Company, where he remained until 1873, when he entered the service of McCormick & Co., of Harrisburg, Penn., as furnace and mine superintendent, a situation he held until 1876, during which time he developed and operated several valuable mining properties in this and the adjoining counties of York and Adams. From that time until 1879 he was exclusively engaged in mining iron and copper ores in Sussex County, N. J., and Carroll County, Md. In October, 1879, he again accepted the superintendency of the South Mountain Mining & Iron Company, which position he has continuously held since. Our subject is a gentleman, studious and active, conversant with all the details of his calling, and is recognized among the business men of his acquaintance as a skillful metallurgical chemist and scientific and practical mining engineer. In 1865, Mr. King was married to Miss Alice Fuller, of Paterson, N. J. They have one son living—Charles King.

DANIEL LEEPER, superintendent of the wood and coal department of the South Mountain Mining & Iron Company, was born in Dickinson (now Penn) Township, this county, July 24, 1819. His father, James Leeper, of Lancaster County, Penn., came to this county about the year 1812, and here married Eliza Fort, who was born in New Jersey, and came as far as this county with her parents, on their way to Ohio. Her mother took sick on the way and died at Centreville, and her father remained here some years, and finally returned to New Jersey. After living in this part of the State for a time,

James Leeper and wife finally located near Mount Union, Huntington Co., Penn., where they passed the remainder of their lives, and now lie buried at Mapleton. Daniel Leeper has made his home principally at Pine Grove since 1839, and has followed the occupation of charcoal-maker during most of these years. In 1870 he was appointed superintendent of the wood and coal department of the South Mountain Mining & Iron Company, which responsible position he has ever since held. March 21, 1844, he married Nancy Warren, a native of Adams County, Penn., but a resident of this county at the time of her marriage. Their children are Mrs. Anna Eliza Helm, John, Mrs. Mary E. Sheaffer, Amanda, Mrs. Susan Hewitt, Daniel, Mrs. Sallie Danner, David and U. S. Grant Leeper. Our subject enlisted, October 16, 1862, in the One Hundred and Sixty-fifth Regiment Pennsylvania Volunteer Infantry, and was assigned to the Army of the Potomac. He was in many engagements around Suffolk, Va., and received an honorable discharge July 28, 1863. Mr. Leeper is a stanch and life-long Republican, and takes a deep interest in public affairs. He and his worthy wife are members of the Methodist Episcopal Church. He has been a class-leader for many years, and an exhorter. He is one of the old pioneers of this locality, a worthy and upright citizen, highly respected by the entire community.

COL. J. D. NORTH, merchant, P. O. Pine Grove Furnace, is a native of Ontario County, N. Y. In early manhood he engaged in the wholesale dry goods business in New York City, and, after spending two years in California, re-engaged in the same enterprise. He located at Hastings, Minn., in 1855, in merchandising and in the grain and commission business, and while there he built the largest grain elevator, at that time, in the State. In 1863 he sold out, and embarked with his brother in the wholesale glove and mitten trade. In 1869 he became largely interested in farming lands in North Carolina, where he resided, as a planter and fruit culturist, until 1878. In that year he accepted an invitation from the South Mountain Iron Company to locate with them. He has entire charge of their extensive farms and mill, and also carries on the store in their building. He also holds the appointment of postmaster of Pine Grove Furnace. Col. North first married Miss Henrietta E. Claflin, of Buffalo, N. Y., and, she dying a short time thereafter, he subsequently married Miss Elizabeth B. Mulford, of New York City, who died at Pine Grove Furnace January 9, 1881, leaving one daughter, Henrietta E., now attending school at Canandaigua, Ontario Co., N. Y.

CHAPTER XLIV.

DICKINSON TOWNSHIP.

DAN HENRY AMES, farmer, P. O. Mooredale, was born in Cincinnati, Ohio, May 11, 1860. His father, Dr. Fisher W. Ames, was a native of Cincinnati and a graduate of Ohio Medical College, and was for many years a very successful medical practitioner in Cincinnati. Dr. Ames rendered valuable services to the Government, as surgeon of the Sixth Regiment Ohio Volunteer Infantry, during the war of the Rebellion. During President Grant's administration, the Doctor held the position of United States Consul at St. Domingo, for about six years, and then resigned on account of ill health; he died in 1876. His wife, Catherine (Hendricks) Fisher, died in 1872. Dan Henry Ames, after attending the Cincinnati High School, completed his education at Buchtel College, Akron, Ohio. He purchased a farm near Abilene, Kas., where he located in 1879, and while there he married, December 9, 1880, Cyprianna Hutchison, a native of Dickinson Township, this county. Her parents, William A. and Elizabeth Hutchison, now reside in Huntsdale, this county. In March, 1881, Mr. and Mrs. Ames came to this county and located permanently in Dickinson Township, where they have a fine farm of 100 acres of land, on which they have erected an elegant brick residence and substantial farm buildings; they also own another farm of 97 acres in same township. To Mr. and Mrs. Ames has been born one son, Kenneth Fisher Ames. In politics Mr. Ames is a Republican. He is a gentleman of upright character and of modest demeanor, a man of excellent influence in the community.

RUDOLPH FISHBURN, P. O. Greason or Carlisle, was born in Dauphin County, Penn., April 3, 1824. His parents, John and Catherine (Carmany) Fishburn, natives of Pennsylvania, settled in Dickinson Township, this county, in 1832. Their children were: Philip (deceased), John, Anthony, Mrs. Barbara Myers, Mrs. Helena Myers, Rudolph, Adam, Reuben and Mrs. Maria Lee. The parents of these children acquired a fine estate of over 500 acres of land in this county. The father died in April, 1861, aged seventy-seven years, and the mother in April, 1875, aged eighty-three years. They were upright pioneer people, and their memory will long be cherished by those who knew them. Rudolph Fishburn, the subject of this sketch, married, November 17, 1857, Mary Magdalena Lehman, a native of South Middleton Township, this county, born near Mount Holly Springs. Her father, Adam Lehman, a native of Tolpenhocken, Berks Co., Penn., came to this county when a young man, and married here Miss Magdalena Burkholder, a native of South Middleton Township, this county, and they lived long and active lives in that township, until his death, May 25, 1845. His widow passed her last days with her daughter, Mrs. Fishburn, dying March 21, 1871, in her eightieth year. She and her husband were members of the Lutheran Church at Carlisle. They acquired an estate of three farms, and were among the prosperous and influential residents of this county. Of their ten children six are living: Daniel, David, Mrs. Fishburn, Mrs. Sarah Sener, Mrs. Margaret Wolf and Samuel. Those deceased are John, Elizabeth, Adam and William. Since their marriage Mr. and Mrs. Fishburn have resided on their present farm in Dickinson Township, where they have 110 acres of fine land, well improved, on which is an elegant stone residence. Mr. Fishburn is a member of the Lutheran Church. He is a man of frank and generous nature, and has many friends. In politics he is a Republican.

SAMUEL GALBRAITH (deceased), of Scotch descent, was born in County Antrim, Ireland, in 1767, and came to the United States while quite a young man. There were four brothers—Robert, Samuel, Joseph and John. The subject of this sketch was a contractor on public works, and as such was closely connected with the early development of the country. In 1794 he settled in Cumberland County, buying, with his brother Robert, a tract of land in Dickinson Township, to which he moved when he retired to private life. He married a daughter of Squire Moore (John Moore), who died in 1813, leaving six children—John, Eleanor, Samuel, Maria, Matthew and Thompson Moore. He died in January, 1851.

THOMPSON MOORE GALBRAITH (deceased), youngest son of Samuel Galbraith, was born November 10, 1813. He left school at fifteen years of age and at once commenced work on his own account. Like his father, his first ventures, even before reaching manhood, were on public works, being engaged at various times on the Erie Canal, Baltimore & Ohio Railroad, Cumberland Valley Railroad (the heavy cut at Newville), the Pennsylvania Railroad, at Perrysville, Mifflin, Huntington and Greensburgh, and the North Pennsylvania Railroad. He returned to the Cumberland Valley, and commenced farming at the old homestead in the spring of 1854, where he remained until the time of his death, December 28, 1863. A modest, gentle, generous, unassuming, able man, he made many friends, and had few, if any, enemies. The soul of honor himself, his charity and generosity were at all times being exercised in behalf of his fellow-men. He was married, October 10, 1848, to Elizabeth Woods, of Salem, Ohio, a daughter of Robert H. Woods, a Scotch-Irish Presbyterian, who came to America in 1818. Four children survived him—William W., Emma W., Lois C. and Annie M., the eldest child, a son, dying in infancy. Of these, Emma W. died March 25, 1871, as she was verging on womanhood; Annie M. chose the study of medicine, and graduated with great credit at the Woman's Medical College of Philadelphia, taking a post-graduate course, lasting two years, under some of the most eminent specialists of Vienna and Munich; whilst Lois C. more modestly sought happiness in the beaten paths.

WILLIAM WATTS GALBRAITH was born September 30, 1851, in Dickinson Township, this county. After receiving a common school education he went to the Pennsylvania State College, graduating in the scientific course. In 1871 he commenced farming at the old homestead, but quit in 1873 to go to West Point. Graduating there in 1877, he was appointed second lieutenant in the Fifth Artillery, and served successively in Charleston, S. C., Atlanta, Ga., and Fort Schuyler, N. Y., until May, 1882, when he was ordered to the artillery school, where he graduated in April, 1884, and was ordered to Governor's Island, N. Y. In July of that year he was detailed professor of military science and tactics—serving also as professor of mathematics—at the Pennsylvania Military Academy, from which he was relieved, at his own request, July 1, 1885. Being again ordered to Governor's Island, he was detailed to go with his battery to Mount McGregor at the time of Gen. Grant's death, and served with the Guard of Honor from July 28 until the interment, August 8. Promoted to a first lieutenant in the same regiment, and ordered to Fort Hamilton September 23, he served with the guard at Grant's tomb from December 15, 1885, to February 15, 1886. Serving, August 26, 1886, at Fort Hamilton, N. Y., in command of Battery M, Fifth Artillery.

HARRY HANCE, miller, P. O. Huntsdale, was born in Frederick County, Md., February 26, 1849. His parents, John and Sarah (Eicholtz) Hance, were natives of York County, Penn., and removed to Maryland, where they remained until their death; he died July 10, 1867, and his widow May 9, 1872. Of their ten children our subject is the third. At the age of sixteen years Harry Hance came to this county, and began learning the milling business at Bridgeport, which he has since followed at various places on the Yellow Breeches Creek, with the exception of two years (from 1879 to 1881) spent at Wilson, Ellsworth County, Kas. He located at Huntsdale, this county, in the spring of 1882, and here he is interested in the production of the Cumberland Mills (formerly known as Chambers'

Mill). Harry Hance, who is sole manager and operator, is a skillful and scientific miller, and his products have a first-class reputation among his patrons. He married, December 27, 1874, Jennie E. Swigert, of Mount Holly, this county, and to them have been born four children, Nora Edi h, Theodore, Blanche and an infant (deceased). Our subject is a life-long Republican, and is now serving his township as school director. He is an upright and worthy citizen and an enterprising and successful business man.

REV. JACOB HOLLINGER, minister and retired farmer, P. O. Mooredale, was born in Monroe Township, this county, August 22, 1827. His great-grandfather came from Switzerland to America in a very early day, and his grandfather, Jacob Hollinger, was born in America. Daniel Hollinger (father of our subject), a native of York County, Penn., married Catherine Dillinger, also a native of York County. Immediately after marriage they settled in Monroe Township, this county. Of their eleven children nine grew to maturity and six are now living: Daniel, in Plympton, Kas.; Jacob; John, in Russell, Kas.; Mrs. Elizabeth Hutchison; Mrs. Catherine Eckert; and Mrs Rebecca Martin. The father of these children departed this life in 1859, and his widow survived until 1872. He was a life-long minister of the German Baptist Church, and five of his sons, following in their father's footsteps, became ministers of the gospel. He was an upright pioneer, and his memory is cherished and honored by all who knew him. Rev. Jacob Hollinger, the subject of this sketch, was married, October 4, 1849, to Mary A. Sheaffer, a native of Monroe Township, this county, where her parents, Jacob and Elizabeth Sheaffer resided until their death. After their marriage, Rev. Jacob Hollinger and his wife settled in Dickinson Township, this county, and in 1852 they moved to South Middleton Township, where they resided until 1861, then returned to Dickinson Township, and have since resided here. By industry and good management they have acquired a fine farm of 130 acres of well improved farm land, and also own thirty-five acres of timbered land on South Mountain. To them have been born eleven children, seven of whom are now living: John Edward, George William, Mrs. Florence Hertzler, Mrs. Elizabeth Myers, Jacob S., Mrs. Anna Mary Cooper, and Alice Eva. Our subject united with the German Baptist Church in 1854, and was chosen a minister in the church in 1869, which relation he has sustained ever since. He is a man of firm principles and strict integrity, a worthy citizen, highly respected by the entire community.

ABRAM L. LINE, farmer, P. O. Mooredale, was born in Dickinson Township, this county, March 2, 1841. George Line, great-grandfather of our subject, emigrated from Switzerland to America with his parents, about 1710, when a young boy; they settled in Pennsylvania, where he grew to manhood, and married, in Lancaster County, Salome Zimmerman; and in 1778 they came to Dickinson Township, this county, and purchased land. Of their children, David remained in Lancaster County; John, William, Abraham, Elizabeth, Susanna and Salome settled in this county. John married Anna B. Le Fevre, and they remained on the family homestead until their death; their children were John, George L., Mrs. Catherine Tritt, Mrs. Mary Coulter and Salome. George L. married Maria Line, and succeeded his parents on the family homestead, and to him and his wife were born four children: Mrs. Elizabeth Hemminger, John A., Emanuel C., and Abram L. George L. Line was a very prominent man in public affairs, and was colonel of a regiment in the old State militia; he died in 1885; his wife departed this life in 1869. Their son Abram L. Line, the subject of this sketch, married, October 21, 1863, Sarah H. McMath, a native of Carlisle, and daughter of the well-known merchant, James McMath, of Scotch-Irish descent. Since their marriage, Mr. and Mrs. Line have resided on their present farm, which descended to him from his mother's branch of the Line family, and has been in the possession of the family for the last fifty years; it is a fine property of 120 acres of fertile and well improved land, and includes one of the finest picnic grounds in the county. To our subject and wife have been born two children: George L. and Laura Augusta. Mr. Line enlisted, in July, 1862, in Company A, One Hundred and Thirtieth Regiment Pennsylvania Volunteer Infantry. He was assigned to the Army of the Potomac, and served in the historic campaigns in Virginia and Maryland; he took part in the hard-fought battles of South Mountain, Antietam, Fredericksburg and Chancellorsville; he received a slight wound at Antietam, and was honorably discharged in May, 1863, after having risen, by promotion, to the rank of fourth sergeant. Mr. Line was for many years a Republican in politics, but is now an earnest Nationalist. He takes great interest in public affairs, especially in the cause of education, and has been called upon to serve his township as school director. He is a man of genial, social disposition, an upright and worthy citizen, highly respected by the community in which he lives.

DAVID LINE, farmer, P. O. Carlisle, was born in Dickinson Township, this county, May 4, 1830, son of David, who was a son of William, who was a son of George Line, the founder of the Line family in this county. Our subject attended the schools of the home district, and completed his education by a course in Burns Academy at Good Hope, Penn. Seven years of his early manhood were spent principally in Washington County, Iowa, during which time he returned home to attend school for one winter. He married, November 30, 1864, Mary E. Ralston, a native of this county, a daughter of David and Lacey (McAllister) Ralston, and soon after marriage they located where he now

33

resides, in Dickinson Township, where he has a fine farm of 173 acres, being part of the homesteads of both families. On this farm David Line has erected a handsome brick residence and very complete and substantial farm buildings. To our subject and wife were born five children: James Edwin, William D., Samuel A., Marion Myers, and Sarah Ella. Mrs. Line died November 12, 1876. She was a sincere Christian, a devoted wife and mother, and her death was mourned by a large circle of friends. She was a member of the Presbyterian Church. Mr. Line and all his sons are members of the First Presbyterian Church at Carlisle, Penn. Our subject devotes a great deal of attention to the education of his children, and takes a deep interest in all enterprises for the mental and moral improvement of the community. In politics he is a Republican.

EMANUEL C. LINE, farmer, P. O. Carlisle, was born on the farm where he now resides, in Dickinson Township, this county, May 8, 1837. His father, Geo. L. Line, was a son of John Line, and a grandson of George Line, the original founder of the family in this county. John Line married Barbara Ann Le Fevre, and to them were born five children, viz.: George L., John (deceased), Salome (deceased), Mrs. Catherine Tritt (deceased), and Mrs. Mary Ann Coulter. George L. Line married his second cousin, Miss Maria Line (daughter of Emanuel Line, and granddaughter of William Line), and they settled on the family homestead, which was purchased, in 1778, by George Line (grandfather of George L.) from Gen. John Armstrong, and has been in the possession of the family for four generations. The old mansion residence, built of stone, was erected by Gen. Armstrong, in 1768, and is still occupied. Here Mr. and Mrs. George L. Line resided until their death. Their children are as follows: Mrs. Elizabeth M. Hemminger, John A., Emanuel C. and Abram L. Mrs. George L. Line died November 27, 1869, and Mr. Line died November 5, 1885, aged eighty years, ten months and ten days. He was a useful and highly respected citizen, and the memory of this couple is cherished by a large circle of relatives and friends. Emanuel C. Line remained on the mansion farm, and took care of his parents in their old age. He now owns here a fine property of 101 acres of well-improved land.

JACOB ZITZER LINE, farmer, P. O. Carlisle, was born in Dickinson Township, this county, September 22, 1854. His father, George Line, a son of Abraham and grandson of George, was born March 5, 1801, and married Miss Rebecca Myers, daughter of Jacob and Susan Myers, and to them were born, Abram (deceased), George (deceased), Mrs. Rebecca Long (Rebecca's twin sister died in infancy), Jacob Zitzer, Mrs. Anne Lindsey, William, Mrs. Agnes Allen, and Mollie (deceased). The father of these children died September 9, 1877, and the mother now resides in Carlisle, Penn. Jacob Zitzer Line married, December 28, 1876, Jane Margaret Lindsey, a native of West Pennsborough Township, this county, and a daughter of John F. and Rachel (Woodburn) Lindsey, and after their marriage they settled on their present farm, where they have 108 acres of fertile and well improved land. To them have been born the following children: Mervin Lindsey, George Valentine and Leroy Zitzer. Mr. Line is a member of the Evangelical Association, his wife being a member of the First Presbyterian Church at Carlisle. She is earnestly devoted to the cause of literature and education, and is a member of the "Pansy" class of the Chautauqua Literary and Scientific Circle. In politics he is a Republican, with strong temperance principles.

JAMES V. LINE, farmer, P. O. Carlisle, was born on the farm where he now resides, in Dickinson Township, this county, February 14, 1851. His grandfather, Abraham, son of the well-known pioneer George Line, married Christina Eby, and their children were as follows: Abram, William, Gabriel, George, Henry, Mrs. Ann Carothers, Mrs. Sarah Kurtz, Mrs. Susan Tritt and Mrs. Betsy Le Fevre. William became the founder of Linesville, Crawford Co., Penn., Henry married Francis Donor, and reared a family of four children: Mrs. Frances Peffer, Mrs. Jane Myers, James V. and Laura; his wife died April 19, 1875, and he followed her May 19, 1879. Henry Line was an influential citizen; he acquired an estate of 522 acres of land, in four farms. James V. Line, the subject of this sketch, married, January 20, 1874, Catherine Spotts, a native of Dickinson Township, this county; her parents, Abram and Mary Spotts, now reside at Battle Creek, Ida Co., Iowa. Since their marriage Mr. and Mrs. Line have resided on the old homestead of his father, and here he has a fine farm of 150 acres of fertile and well improved land. To our subject and wife have been born two children: James Harvey and Millicent May. Mrs. Line is a member of the Lutheran Church. Mr. Line is a life-long Republican. He is an enterprising and successful farmer, and enjoys the respect of the entire community.

SAMUEL C. LINE, farmer, P. O. Carlisle, was born in Dickinson Township, this county, October 2, 1840. His great-grandfather, George Line, a native of Switzerland, came to this county from Lancaster County, Penn., in 1778, and purchased 540 acres of land from Gen. John Armstrong, and resided here until his death. His sons and daughters were: William, David, Abraham, John, Mrs. Elizabeth McFeely, Mrs. Sarah Houk and Mrs. Susanna Smith. William, a soldier in the Revolutionary war, married a Miss. Bear, and they ended their lives in Dickinson Township, this county; their children were: George, Nancy Musselman, Catherine Eby, Mary Spangler, Emanuel, Sally Tritt, Rachel Snyder, Susanna Myers, David, Rebecca Givler, and Lydia Myers. David was born

August 30, 1792; he married Miss Sarah Myers, and they located on the family homestead, where they erected the present commodious mansion, and reared a family of eight children: Mrs. Mary Ann Greason (deceased), Dr. William Line, George, Mrs. Matilda Huston (deceased), David, Mrs. Sarah Jane Huston, Frances R. (deceased), and Samuel C. The subject of this sketch, after attending the district school, completed his education at Burns Academy, Good Hope, this county. He married, February 23, 1871, Miss Emma Myers, who was born in Carlisle, Penn., while her father, John Myers, was holding the office of sheriff of this county. John Myers came from Lancaster County, Penn., to Dickinson Township, this county, with his parents, when he was four years of age; married Miss Elizabeth Fishburn, and to them were born thirteen children, eleven of whom grew to maturity, Emma (wife of our subject) being the youngest. Mr. Myers located, with his family, in McCutchenville, Wyandot County, Ohio, in 1845; there purchased the hotelstand, and remained during the remainder of his life; many of his descendants now reside in that locality. Mr. and Mrs. Samuel C. Line are now residing on the mansion farm, which has been in the possession of the family for four generations. He has here a fine place of 140 acres of fertile and well improved land. He is a life-long Republican in politics. His wife is a member of the First Presbyterian Church at Carlisle.

JOHN MORRISON, retired farmer, P. O. Barnitz, was born in Dickinson Township, this county, July 1, 1818. His father, William Morrison (a native of Ireland) immigrated to America, when a boy, with his parents, and came to this county when a youth, where he was engaged for many years as door-keeper at the jail in Carlisle. About 1805 William located in Dickinson Township, he being then twenty-one years of age, and here he married Sarah Wolf, a native of this county; her father, William Wolf immigrated to this country from Germany, when seven years of age, and resided in this county until his death; both he and wife are buried at Boiling Springs. William Morrison died in 1834; his widow survived him many years, and resided with her son John until her death; she died February 20, 1872, aged eighty years; her children were Margaret, Mrs. Ann Knopp (deceased), John, William (deceased), Samuel, and James (deceased). John Morrison, the subject of this sketch, passed his early life on the farm in this county. He married, February 24, 1842, Jane Lockhart, daughter of Samuel and Catherine Lockhart, natives of this county, latter of whom died in 1876 at the advanced age of ninety years. Mr. and Mrs. Morrison have resided in Dickinson Township, this county, ever since their marriage, and located on their present farm in 1853; they own here a fine place of 130 acres of well improved land, besides a tract of fifty acres of timbered land on South Mountain. They have reared nine children: Mrs. Grizelle Hollinger (deceased), Winfield Scott, Mrs. Caroline Stouffer, William H., Mrs. Sarah Catherine Martin, Mrs. Anna Mary Martin, Frank G., John S. and Martin L.

WINFIELD SCOTT MORRISON was born May 12, 1844. He enlisted, August 11, 1862, in the One Hundred and Thirtieth Regiment Pennsylvania Volunteer Infantry, and after taking part in the battles of Antietam, Fredericksburg and Chancellorsville, received his discharge May 23, 1863, and afterward enlisted in the one-hundred days' service. He married in December, 1865, Della Frehn, and to them were born Harry Grant, Charles Monroe, Stella Blanche, and Arthur Ray. Winfield Scott now holds the position of school director. On the premises now occupied by him stands a willow tree, said to measure nine feet in circumference, which sprang from a switch that was stuck in the ground by his sister Sarah in 1863. John Morrison, the subject of this sketch, is a life-long Republican. He and his wife and five of their children are members of the Methodist Episcopal Church. Personally, John Morrison is a man of robust physique, and has a very social disposition. He is an upright and worthy citizen, enjoying the respect and esteem of the entire community.

JACOB MYERS, farmer, P. O. Greason, was born in Dickinson Township, this county, May 13, 1823. His grandparents, George and Maria Myers, located in this county, coming from one of the lower counties, in very early times, and resided here until their death; their son Jacob was reared here and married Susanna Line, daughter of William Line, the fruits of which marriage were as follows: Mrs. Maria Line, David (deceased), Mrs. Rebecca Line and Jacob. The father of these children was accidently killed by a wagon running over him, while making a trip to Baltimore, Md., in 1824. His widow survived him until February 9, 1873, when she died in her eighty-fourth year. The subject of this sketch, Jacob Myers, resided with his widowed mother until he reached manhood. He married June 4, 1846, Eliza E. Worley, a native of Adams County, Penn., born in March, 1825; her father, George Worley, died in Adams County, Penn., and her mother afterward married John Paxton, and located in this county, where she resided until her death. Mr. and Mrs. Jacob Myers located on the present family homestead in 1847, and here, by industry and good management, have acquired a fine farm of ninety-one acres of fertile and well improved land, on which they have erected a fine residence and made other valuable improvements. They own another farm of eighty-six acres, also in Dickinson Township. To Mr. and Mrs. Myers have been born nine children: John T., Benjamin F., George M., Jacob F. (accidently killed by the caving in of an ore bank, November 11, 1871), Washington Emory, David H. (deceased August 7, 1878), William L., Ida B. and Jennie E. Mrs. Myers died February 7, 1881. She was a devoted wife and mother, an earnest Christian, and her death was mourned by a large circle of friends. Mr. Myers now resides on the homestead with his daughters. He is a member of the German Baptist Church. He has devoted a great deal of attention to the education of his children; his son David was for many years before his death a very successful and much loved teacher in this county. Jacob Myers is a useful and worthy citizen, universally respected wherever he is known. He filled the office of school director for many years. In politics he is a Democrat.

GEORGE W. PAXTON, postmaster of Hunters Run, was born in Carroll County, Md., in 1849. Being abandoned by his mother when he was an infant, he was brought to Hunters Run, in this county, when he was nine months old, and was reared in the family of Godfrey Fenner, one of the first residents of this part of the county. Our subject spent his boyhood on a farm, cutting wood and doing the general work of a farmer's boy in this mountain community. He attended the primitive schools of those times, and has since acquired a good education by private reading and study. From his twelfth to his twentieth year he worked with Mr. Philip G. Howe. In 1873 he engaged in merchandising at Gardiner's store, South Mountain, locating in 1876 in Myerstown in his own building, which he had erected for that purpose in the spring of that year. In addition to this enterprise he opened another store, in 1880, at Hunters Run Station, and also dealt in coal and grain, and acted as freight agent for the South Mountain Railroad Company, and also for the Adams Express Company. From 1873 till 1882 he was extensively engaged in the manufacture of charcoal, selling to the South Mountain Mining and Iron Company, at Pine Grove Furnace, Cumberland Co., Penn., and to C. W. Ahl & Son, of Boiling Springs, Cumberland County, the contract for coal running as high as 150,000 bushels per year, giving employment at certain times to 100 men in cutting cordwood, coaling, hauling, etc. The amount paid for labor, for four years, ranged from $5,000 to $7,000 annually, the most extensive work done and the greatest number of laborers employed having been during the four years mentioned, the year 1882 representing the maximum. In 1881 he sold his store at Myerstown, but still retained ownership of the building, and continued business at Hunters Run until March, 1885. He began the manufacture of lumber, near Hunters Run, in 1872 and continued it until 1885, when he sold the mill, which has since been removed. In addition to all these business enterprises Mr. Paxton has done a very extensive business in real estate, handling more real estate than any other ten men in his vicinity. Mr. Paxton married, July 1, 1875, Anna M. Myers, a native of this county and daughter of David and Julia Myers, and to them have been born four children: Ellis M., Morris T., Jessie Armeda and Irvine (latter deceased). Mr. Paxton is a Democrat in politics. He was appointed postmaster at Hunters Run January 23, 1883, which office he still holds. He took a very active and energetic part in the encouragement and construction of the Gettysburg & Harrisburg Railroad, from Hunters Run to Gettysburg, which was built and formally opened for travel in the early part of 1884. Our subject has led a very active and successful business life, and has acquired a handsome estate. He and wife are members of the Lutheran Church.

DR. J. H. SMITH, physician and surgeon, Mooredale, Penn., was born in Middlesex Township, this county, October 26, 1854. His parents, George O. and Susan (Stickle) Smith, moved to near Plainfield, West Pennsborough Township, this county, when he was but two months old, and there our subject was reared on his father's farm, and attended school. The Doctor early engaged in teaching, and taught for four terms. He completed his literary education in the State Normal School, at Shippensburg, this county, and in the fall of 1875 he took up the study of medicine, under Dr. A. J. Harmon, of Carlisle. He entered Jefferson Medical College, Philadelphia, in 1877, and graduated therefrom March 13, 1880. November 12, 1880, he began the practice of his chosen profession at Whitehouse (now Mooredale), Dickinson Township, this county, where he has built up an extensive practice. Dr. Smith married, September 19, 1884, Miss Ella M. Zeigler of East Berlin, Adams County, Penn. The Doctor is recognized as a skillful and scientific physician, and enjoys the confidence and esteem of the entire community. In politics he is a Republican.

JOHN SOURS, farmer, P. O. Barnitz, was born September 23, 1828, son of Samuel and Sarah Sours. March 6, 1862, he married Agnes Caroline Donaldson, a native of Franklin County, Penn., born in 1828; she came to Dickinson Township, this county, in 1830, with her parents, Robert and Jane (Huston) Donaldson. Her father died February 12, 1867, aged eighty-seven years, and her mother departed this life July 30, 1872, aged eighty-eight years. Mr. and Mrs. John Sours have resided in this neighborhood ever since their marriage. They now own the family homestead of 104 acres of well improved land. They are members of the Methodist Episcopal Church. Mr. Sours is a man widely known for his wonderful memory of local historical events; he retains in his memory, the exact day of most events which have taken place within his lifetime. He is a worthy descendant of one of the oldest pioneers of this county. In politics he is a Democrat.

WALTER STUART, farmer, P. O. Mooredale, was born in Dickinson Township, this county, January 27, 1824. His grandfather, Samuel Stuart, one of the sturdy Scotch-

Irish race, a native of Donegal, Ireland, came to America when a young man, and married Miss Margaret Reed of this county. They located in the then village of Carlisle, and there conducted a tavern for several years, and afterward retired to a farm in Dickinson Township, this county where they resided until their death. Their children were: Samuel (father of our subject), James, Walter, Mrs. Polly Greer, Ann, and Margaret. Samuel married Nancy Donaldson, a native of Dickinson Township, this county, and they resided on a farm in this township, until their death; she died June 22, 1866, and he died May 2, 1873, in his eighty-fifth year. Their children were: Samuel (deceased), Mrs. Eliza Jane Hays, and Walter. The subject of this sketch remained with his parents during their life and took care of them in their old age. He married, February 18, 1869, Julia Ann Spangler, and they lived on the old homestead until 1879, when they moved to the farm on which they now reside; they have here a property of 180 acres of fertile and well improved land, besides the old homestead farm, and a tract of thirteen acres of timbered land on South Mountain. To them have been born nine children: Samuel, Walter, Anna May, Hays (deceased), Nancy Jane, Margaret Ramsey, John Knox, Ella M. and George Spangler. Our subject has been a Republican ever since President Lincoln's second term. He takes a deep interest in public affairs, especially in the cause of education. He and his worthy wife are members of the Presbyterian Church at Dickinson. He is a worthy descendant of one of the oldest pioneer families of this county, an upright citizen, enjoying the respect and esteem of his fellow-townsmen.

JOHN L. WILLIAMS, merchant and postmaster of Mooredale, this county, was born in Leesburg, this county, February 18, 1847, son of the well-known and successful merchant, Joseph Williams. Our subject received his education in the schools of the home district, and, having been engaged in his father's store from childhood, he was employed, at fourteen years of age, for William H. Allen, as clerk, until 1864. He next clerked for Peter Garber, at Centreville, for one year, and after that he clerked for five years at Chambersburg. In March, 1872, he established a general store at Mooredale, which he still continues, under the firm name of Williams & Co.; they keep a very complete line of dry goods, groceries and provisions, boots and shoes, hats and caps, clothing, hardware, queensware, notions, and an assortment of such other articles as are needed to supply the wants of a country community. Mr. Williams has, by courtesy and strict business principles, built up a large and prosperous trade, and has made himself popular with all classes. He married, November 13, 1868, Susan Garber, daughter of Peter Garber. They have four children: Harry J., Samuel G., Sarah B. and Catherine E. Mr. Williams was appointed postmaster of White House in 1872 (the name of the office was changed to "Mooredale" April 1, 1885), and he still holds the office by re-appointment. He and his worthy wife are consistent members of the German Baptist Church. He is a man of strict integrity, and an upright citizen, respected by the entire community. In politics he is a Republican.

CHAPTER XLV.

EAST PENNSBOROUGH TOWNSHIP AND BOROUGH OF CAMP HILL.

ROBERT C. BAMFORD, heater, P. O. West Fairview, is a native of Wheeling, W. Va., born November 4, 1849. His father, Henry A. Bamford, was born at Antietam, Md., and his grandfather, also named Henry, emigrated from Belfast, Ireland, when sixteen years old. The father of Robert C. was a horseman in Antietam, afterward removing to Birmingham, Allegheny Co., Penn., and later to Sharpsburg, returning to Antietam. He entered the Union Army, and was wounded at Harper's Ferry; recovered at Sandy Hook Hospital, and was discharged for disability in 1863; then rejoined his family, who had removed to West Fairview, this county, after the battle at Antietam, their house having been used as a hospital, and when one morning nineteen Union soldiers were found dead in their house, they left it. Henry A. Bamford was married to Maria Williams, a native of Wales, and they had the following named children: William S., Robert C., Henry A., George B., Annie Ann, Virginia (living), and Sarah and Ann Sophrona (deceased). Robert C. Bamford was thirteen years old when his parents removed to West Fairview, this county, and he at once went to work in the nailsmill here, where he is now a heater. In 1872 he was united in marriage with Mary J., daughter of George B. Brown, of Baltimore, Md. They have four children living: Robert C., Mary Bessie, George Coleman and Alvah. Five are deceased: Edwin A., Clarence B., Walter, Millie S. and Millie Maria. Mr. Bamford is one of the crack shots of the county, having taken part in contests with Bogardus and other well-known shots. He is a member of the I. O. O. F. His wife is a member of the Methodist Episcopal Church and is known as a Christian lady.

HENRY BENDER, plate-roller, West Fairview, who has resided here since 1851, was born in Lancaster County, Penn., March 6, 1844, where his father and grandfather lived, the former having a farm near Elizabethtown, Penn. In 1851 Leonard Bender, the father, went on a farm in East Pennsborough Township, this county, where he died in 1858, his wife and son dying the same year. At this time Henry, our subject, was seven years old. For five years he lived with Joseph Huntsberger, of this township, going to school. After he left here he worked in a number of places, at various occupations, until 1864, when he was employed in the plate-mill in West Fairview, where he has since remained. In 1871 he was married to Sarah, daughter of George Mann, of this township; she died in 1876 without issue, and in 1878 Mr. Bender married Miss Annie M., daughter of William H. Rice, then of Mechanicsburgh, Penn. She was born at Bendersville, Adams Co., Penn., in 1868, whence, on the death of her mother, she went to live with her aunt in Franklin County, Penn., staying ten years, attending school. From there she came to Mechanicsburg, where her father was living. Shortly after the family removed to near West Fairview, where she was married. They have had twin girls, who died in infancy. Mr. and Mrs. Bender are members of the Lutheran Church. She is an accomplished lady, highly respected by all, while Mr. Bender stands as high in the estimation of the community as any person in it—a result due to his uniform good principles.

JOHN D. BOWMAN, M. D., Camp Hill, is a son of John Bowman, and was born, in 1832, in the house where his father and brother, H. N. Bowman, now live. With the exception of the time spent in school and in Jefferson Medical College at Philadelphia, Penn., of which he is a graduate, our subject remained at home until his marriage, in 1858, with Elizabeth B., daughter of David G. Eyster, of Camp Hill. They had seven children, only two of whom were alive when their mother died in 1870. One is Florence E., wife of J. W. Baxter, of Harrisburg; the other is Joanna, attending Metzgar Institute, at Carlisle, Penn. In 1871 the Doctor married Margaret A. Kisecker, of Franklin County, Penn., and they have one son and four daughters, all quite young. After his graduation, in 1856, Dr. Bowman established himself in practice at Camp Hill, remaining over sixteen years, and in 1872 removed to Harrisburg, where he built up a large practice, which he kept up until, his health failing, he removed, in August, 1885, to his old home, where he is rapidly recuperating, and where he expects to again resume his profession. In 1863 he was elected to the House of Representatives, and cast a vote to give soldiers in the army the right to vote. In 1864 he was re-elected, and served his constituents faithfully, when he abandoned politics and devoted himself to his profession. He is prominent in Masonic circles, a member of Eureka Lodge, No. 302, and Samuel C. Perkins Chapter, No. 209, of Mechanicsburg, and of Pilgrim Commandery, No. 11, of Harrisburg. He and his wife are members of the Church of God. He is yet in the prime of life, and has plenty of time to add to his already honorable career. His old friends and neighbors hope that now he has returned to them, he will spend the rest of his days among them.

H. N. BOWMAN, justice of the peace, Camp Hill, is a native of Camp Hill, born in 1840. His father, John Bowman, now eighty-one years old, lives with him in the house in which he was himself born in 1805—probably the only person of his age in the county living in the house in which he first saw the light. He is in perfect possession of all his faculties, and can narrate many interesting reminiscences of the place, in which he has lived all his life. H. N. Bowman lived at home until his marriage, in 1866, with Miss Jennie M. Kline, of Lower Allen Township, this county. A year after that, in company with Peter Nicholas, he built and stocked a general store at Camp Hill, which he subsequently owned and conducted alone for two years, when he sold it to Sadler & Bowman. Our subject is a Democrat, the town being strongly Republican, but in 1880 he was elected justice of the peace by a majority of twenty-eight, and re-elected in 1885 by seventy-one, showing the estimation in which he is held by his neighbors. In 1882 he was a candidate for nomination in the Legislature, receiving 1,630 votes to 1,800 for G. M. D. Eckels, the successful man in the race (in which were seven candidates, Mr. Bowman being second). In 1862 he enlisted in the First City Troop of Harrisburg, taking part in the battle of Antietam and minor engagements. He is a member of Post No. 58, G. A. R. In 1878 he became connected, as one of the proprietors, with the White Hall Soldiers' Orphans School, acknowledged the best of the many admirable schools sustained by the State for the education and care of the orphans of her soldiers. Mr. and Mrs. Bowman have buried two daughters, and have three sons and one daughter living: Harry, Allie, Jessie and Addison M. He and his wife are members of the Church of God, at Camp Hill. He is also prominent in the Masonic fraternity, being connected with Eureka Lodge, No. 302, and Samuel C. Perkins Chapter, No. 209, of Mechanicsburg, and Pilgrim Commandery, No. 11, of Harrisburg. He takes a leading part in all enterprises tending to the advancement of his native place, where he bears, deservedly, a very high character as an honorable man and good citizen, in the first rank among the best men in the community in which he lives.

SAMUEL C. CRAWFORD, painter, Camp Hill, has lived eight years in Camp Hill, East Pennsborough Township, carrying on the business of house painting. He was born in Lancaster County, Penn., in 1838. His father, William Crawford, a farmer, and his mother, Elizabeth (Cunningham) Crawford, were also natives of Lancaster. His grandfather, Thomas Crawford, immigrated to this country from Cork. Ireland, many years ago, and bought a farm in Lancaster County, near Good Hope Furnace, where his family were all born, and where he himself died. They were John, James, Robert, Thomas, William, David, Jane, Eliza and Maggie. William, father of Samuel C. Crawford, lived on the farm, which he managed until his death; he died in 1840, aged thirty-seven. His widow still survives him. They had three sons: Jeremiah, William, and Samuel C., the only survivor. He was less than two years of age when his father died, but he continued to live on another farm, with strangers, until he was fourteen, when he went to Lancaster, Penn., to learn the trade of a painter. He served three years and removed to Columbia, where he worked until 1856; thence he went to Cross Creek and remained a year; then to West Middleton, and later to New Orleans. At the outbreak of the Rebellion he was in Nashville, Tenn., where he enlisted in the Union Army, and served until the close of the war, when he returned to Pennsylvania, arriving in Harrisburg in August, 1865, and there he stayed nine years. In September, 1870, he was married to Miss Sarah A., daughter of John Stouffer, of Oysters' Point. They have had four children: Maggie W. (deceased), Albert B., Philip S. and Saidee E. Mr. and Mrs. Crawford are members of the Church of God, in Camp Hill. He is an intelligent gentleman, whose travels have enlarged his ideas, and he bears, among all who know him, an admirable reputation.

MRS. ANNIE E. ESHELMAN, Camp Hill. This lady is the widow of John Eshelman, who was a farmer, and one of the best-known residents of this part of the county. He was a son of Samuel Eshelman, who died in the old homestead, near Camp Hill, twenty years ago. Samuel Eshelman had five daughters and one son—John, born in 1821, on the farm on which he spent his entire active life. The latter, when twenty-five, married Susanna Wolff, who died in 1881, leaving no children. January 9, 1883, he was married to Mrs. Annie Grissinger, and died October 6, 1885, leaving no issue. Some years prior to his death he rented his farm and bought a fine brick residence in Camp Hill, where his widow now lives. He left behind him an honorable reputation. His widow, born July 14, 1842, is a daughter of Josiah and Elizabeth Nelson, of Upper Allen Township, this county, where they still live. She lived with her parents until 1865, when she was married to Jacob H. Grissinger, of Upper Allen Township, a farmer, justice of the peace and surveyor, an honored citizen, who died December 3, 1881, leaving three children: Homer Nelson, born in 1871; Bertha N., born in 1872; Bessie N., born in 1876, living with her mother. One died young. After her husband's death Mrs. Grissinger went with her children to live with her relative, Mr. Robert Cornman, of Silver Spring Township. A year later she married Mr. Eshelman and removed to her present residence. With ample means and a family of affectionate children, she is happily situated. She is a member of the Presbyterian Church. As a conscientious, Christian lady she well deserves the esteem in which she is held.

DAVID G. EYSTER, farmer, Camp Hill, is a great-great-grandson of George Eyster, who immigrated to this country in the seventeenth century, locating in Berks County, Penn., where he prospered. One of his sons married there, and was the father of Jacob, who became the husband of Magdalene Burkhouse, and they were the grandparents of David G. They lived in Abbottstown, York Co., Penn., and had three sons and one daughter. His wife having died, Jacob Eyster, about the year 1780, leaving his oldest son (who was a hatter) and his daughter in Abbottstown, took his two young boys to relatives at Adamstown, Lancaster County, and started for Virginia to buy a farm, intending to return for the boys and his girl, but was never after heard of. At this time a man was robbed and killed on the Baltimore road, on which he was traveling, and his family supposed him to be the murdered man. The boys stayed at Abbottstown for awhile, Abraham learning the trade of a tailor, and George (father of David G.) going to his grandfather Eyster, in Berks County, and afterward to Wolferts Mills. As soon as he was able he took up the occupation of driving team on the Pittsburgh and Harrisburg road, which he followed for eight years. He then went for four years into the milling business, during which time he was married to Elizabeth, daughter of Nicholas Kelsicker, of Berks County, Penn. Subsequently he bought the farm of 250 acres in East Pennsborough Township, which is still owned by David G., who is an only child. George Eyster died in 1846, and his widow a few years later. David G. Eyster, who was born in 1808 at Milltown, Allen Township, Cumberland County, three miles from Harrisburg, spent all his life as a farmer until, in 1859, he retired from active duties, renting his farm and building the house in Camp Hill, in which he lives. In 1838 he married Miss Hannah Bechtel, who lived near Reading. To this union seven children were born, three of whom are now living. The eldest, George B., is sheriff of Cumberland County; David is on a cattle ranch in Texas, and the daughter, Magdalene, lives with her father. The mother died in 1875. Mr. Eyster is liked in the community for his strong upright character, which commands universal respect.

H. M. GLESSNER, merchant, West Fairview, is a son of John Glessner, who emigrated from Mecklenburg, Hessen-Cassel, Germany, in 1833, when sixteen years old, and remained in Philadelphia three years, working as a shoe-maker; then he went to Lancaster City, where he was married, in May, 1841, to Margaret Berg, a native of Darmstadt, Germany. In October, 1844, John Glessner removed to West Fairview, Cumberland Co., Penn., where he carried on his business until 1861, when he established the grocery business in the building, corner of the square, which has been carried on by his son, H. M., since 1874. At one time he held the position of postmaster. He accumulated considerable means, buying the store property and another near the river. After his retirement he was in ill health, and died of apoplexy, August 26, 1876, aged fifty-nine years. His widow still lives in their old home with her two youngest children. They had nine children: H. M., born February 7, 1847; William, born May 6, 1856, living with his mother; Jennetta, born March 7, 1842, wife of F. G. Sparrow, of Sharpsburg, Md.; Elizabeth, born February 28, 1844, wife of George Rowan, of Bellefonte; Elonora, born August 20, 1853, wife of C. C. Montelle, of Norristown, Penn., and Margaret, born February 16, 1861, single. Those deceased are: John, Reuben E. and Margretta. H. M. Glessner attended school until 1861, when he went into the nail factory, working as a feeder until the burning of the mill, when he worked on the premises until March, 1867, when for five months he attended the business college at Harrisburg; then clerked for his father until he succeeded him. In 1879 he failed in business and compromised with his creditors for 40 per cent, but has since, like an honorable man, paid every dollar of his indebtedness in full. This indicates his sturdy integrity, and is a record he and his family may justly be proud of. In 1871 he married Margery Armstrong, of Mechanicsburg, this county, who died in 1873, leaving a son, John A., now fourteen years old, and in 1877 Mr. Glessner married Emma L. Eckman, of Columbia, Lancaster Co., Penn., and they have had five children, two of whom died within a few days of each other. The living are Thomas C., born in 1878; Milton F., born in 1882, and an infant daughter. Mr. Glessner well merits the regard shown him by his neighbors. He is a member of the United Brethren Church.

JOHN B. HECK, surveyor, P. O. Wormleysburg, is son of John K. Heck, who was born in Lower Allen Township, this county, in 1799, and who married Miss Sarah Bechtel, born near Reading, Penn., in 1811, a descendant of the Adams family, who are so numerous and influential in Berks and Lancaster Counties, Penn. For twenty-two years John K. Heck followed distilling, when he inherited a farm near Oyster's mills, in East Pennsborough Township, this county, to which he removed and on which he lived until his death, in 1877. He had an extraordinary strong constitution, but had a stroke of paralysis in 1852, and numerous others, until one finally terminated his life. His widow is still living. They had three sons and four daughters. The living are John B., Bella, Sarah, wife of D. W. Sheetz, M. D., of Northumberland; Hannah, wife of Wilson Miller, of Shiremanstown, and William H., a practicing physician in Philadelphia. John B. Heck was born at his grandfather's, near Oyster's mills, this county, April 3, 1840. When but twelve years of age he took the oversight of both his father's farms; when thirteen he went alone to Bloomfield, paid the taxes on some unseated lands, and redeemed them. Because of disease in his joints, in his fourteenth year he gave up school, but received private instruction at home, and obtained his higher education at Mount Pleasant College, Westmoreland County. In 1855 he studied surveying, and the following year did some public work in Perry County, and has continued the profession to the present time. The same winter and for six consecutive years he taught school, at the same time overseeing his father's farms. In 1869 he married Miss Sarah J., daughter of William F. Martin, of Fairview Township, this county. They have one son, John F., thirteen years old, and one daughter, Elizabeth Helen, aged ten. Mr. Heck was twice a candidate for the nomination to the Legislature, but, running solely on his merits, he was defeated by corrupt combinations. In 1869, in a total vote of over 4,000 he was barely defeated by twelve votes. In 1875, a combination on the judicial nomination again defeated him. For several years after his father's death he carried on the farm (which belongs to the estate still) together with doing some surveying. He also has charge of the Bridgeport warehouse. He is a member of Eureka Lodge, F. & A. M., and of Samuel C. Perkins' Chapter, of Mechanisburg, and of St. John's Commandery, of Carlisle. An incident of his career is especially worthy of mention. His father and neighbors felt the need of a bridge across the Conodoguinet, and got a grant for one from the court, but for twenty years the commissioners refused to build it. Our subject went quietly to work, and by his energy and shrewdness got it built in 1868. It is known as Heck's bridge. But for him, it is safe to say this great public convenience would not yet be built. He is public spirited and enterprising, and has the respect and confidence of his fellow-citizens, and deserves the success he has achieved. Mrs. Heck is a member of the Methodist Episcopal Church.

JACOB L. HEYD, farmer, P. O. Camp Hill, was born in 1832 in Upper Allen Township, this county, son of George Heyd, who died in Mechanicsburg in 1876, aged eighty-two. His mother was Leah, daughter of Jacob Grass, of Adams County, Penn. His paternal grandfather, George Heyd, emigrated from Germany in 1760, settling in Lancaster County, afterward moving to York County, Penn., and subsequently to Cumberland County, where he died, and is buried not far from where his grandson lives. The father of Jacob L. was born in Lancaster County, and went with his parents to York County, staying there six years, when he came to Cumberland County, and here lived more than fifty years. Our subject lived with his father until, at the age of twenty-three, he was married to Miss Catharine, daughter of Jacob Coover, who lived near Dillsburg, York County, Penn. His father gave up the farm to him, and he cultivated it for three years, when he removed to his father-in-law's farm, in York County, and there lived three years; then bought a small farm in Upper Allen Township, this county, which he owned for fifteen years, selling it in 1877 and buying the fine 100-acre farm on which he now lives. He has taken great pains to beautify his place and make it a comfortable home, as is evinced by its surroundings, which are greatly superior to those usually found on a farm. He has two sons living: Clinton G., twenty-two years old, book-keeper for a wholesale hardware house in Harrisburg, and Coover W., fourteen years of age, attending school. Mr. Heyd has three brothers and three sisters living: H. G., of Philadelphia; George W., belonging to the Baltimore Conference, and E. D., who lives in Dakota. Of his three sisters, Elizabeth is a widow of Henry Krell; Rebecca is wife of Michael Myers, of Carlisle, and Mary is wife of Jacob Brant, of Upper Allen Township. Mr. Heyd was justice of the peace in Upper Allen Township; he is now school director. He takes a warm interest in educational matters, and was prominent in the movement to have Camp Hill made a borough, to give its people increased school facilities. He and his wife are communicants of the Methodist Episcopal Church in Mechanicsburg. In all the relations of life he is known as a man of sterling character, whose uprightness and probity are well spoken of by every person to whom he is known.

HENRY HOLLER, farmer, P. O. Camp Hill, is a grandson of Francis Holler, who was born on the Atlantic Ocean in 1777. His parents settled in Lancaster County, Penn., on a farm, where they lived for some time, afterward removing to Manchester Township, York Co., Penn., where Francis was married and lived until his death in 1861. He had two sons and five daughters. One of his sons, Philip, removed to Huntingdon County, and died there. The other, Francis, lived at home until about 1855, when he removed to a farm in Fairview, York County, where he is still living, aged seventy-seven. He, Francis, married Annie Cook, and had a family of thirteen children, of whom eleven are still living: Sarah, wife of Jacob Bardhardt; Jacob, married to Susan Coleman; Samuel Manassas, married to Rebecca Rawhouser; Francis; Annie, wife of Henry Mesias; and William (all of whom live in York County); Catharine, wife of David Strine, of Williamsport, Penn.; Charles, and Leah, wife of John Yetter (both of whom live in Dauphin County); and Henry, the subject of our sketch, who was born on the homestead in Manchester Township, York Co., Penn., in October, 1832, and lived there until his marriage, in 1854, with Miss Mary, daughter of Daniel Dreyer, of Fairview, York County. He then began housekeeping, but worked on his father's farm for another year. For a year following he farmed for John Horn, and then rented a farm in Silver Spring Township, this county, where he stayed four years, and thence, in the spring of 1865, moved to the farm on which he now lives. He has five children living (one died young), viz.: William, married to Jennie, daughter of Stephen Simmons, of Hampden Township (he farms in East Pennsborough); Ellen, A. Lincoln, Charles and Daniel living at home. Mr. Holler was drafted for nine months, in 1862, but sent a substitute for three years. He has been a school director for six years, but never held any other office. He and his wife are members of the United Brethren Church. He has proved himself a good citizen and a man of uprightness and honor.

WILLIAM L. LANTZ, merchant, P. O. West Fairview, is a son of Philip Lantz, whose father came from Germany and settled in the vicinity of West Fairview, Cumberland Co., Penn., many years ago. Philip Lantz was born in East Pennsborough Township and lived there all his lifetime. His father had six children: Jacob, a farmer in East Pennsborough Township, this county; Catharine, wife of Jacob Bretz, of Hampden Township, this county; Mary, unmarried, living in West Fairview, and Philip and two daughters, deceased. Of these, Philip was born on the farm in 1820, and lived there until his death in 1854; he married Catharine Sheetz, by whom he had five children; Jesse, Catharine, William L., Joseph and one daughter, who died young. Philip Lantz's widow lives in West Fairview. William L., our subject, was born April 30, 1850, and went to school in West Fairview, this county, until he was eleven years old, when he was appointed a page in the State Legislature, holding the place seven years, attending school in the intervals of the sessions. During the summer of 1865 he was a messenger in the Quartermaster Department at Washington. In 1868 and 1869 he was in the office of Jay Cooke & Co., New York, and in 1870 returned to West Fairview, this county, and built the store he now occupies, a dwelling opposite, and, with his mother, the residence in which he now lives. In 1874 he married Henrietta, daughter of Henry Glessner, then residing in Lancaster County, Penn., where she was born March 10, 1852. They have five children: Harper, William, Harry, Carrie and Charles. Mr. and Mrs. Lantz are members of the Lutheran Church. His practical experiences peculiarly fit him for business, in which he has been eminently successful.

GEORGE B. LONGENECKER, postmaster, West Fairview, was born in this township, near West Fairview, and is a great-great-grandson of Abraham Longenecker, who came here from Lancaster County in 1772. He located near the mountain, on the farm now owned by John Roth. He paid $8.50 an acre for his land, while that in Mechanicsburg and Shiremanstown could be bought for $1.25. When he moved in, the huts, formerly owned by the Indians, were still standing on the banks of the small stream on which he located. His son, Isaac, was the great-grandfather of our subject. He was born in 1788, and on the death of his father, in 1819, he with a younger brother inherited the farm. Isaac purchased his brother's interest, and worked the farm until shortly before his death in 1849. Jacob, grandfather of George B., was born and lived here until he was twenty-three years of age, when he married Miss Christiana Kuntz. They had five children, viz.: George W., Benjamin F., Jacob, Catherine and Maria. The last three died when quite young. Benjamin F., by trade a carpenter, is a resident of Marysville, Perry County. George W., a farmer by occupation, is the father of George B.; he was born November 19, 1834, and always lived in the vicinity of West Fairview until the spring of 1885, when he removed to Marysville, from which place he went to Illinois in the spring of 1886. February 11, 1862, he married Miss Elizabeth Brenner. To this union five children were born, viz.: Laura E., Lilly D., Alice M. and Dora C., who are with their parents in Illinois. George B. is the eldest in the family. He was born May 4, 1863, in this township, and when only three years of age was taken by his grandparents, with whom he continued to live until the death of his grandmother in May, 1885. He attended common schools, and when sixteen years old began working in the nail factory in his native town, where he remained until November, 1885, when he was commissioned postmaster of West Fairview. Mr. Longenecker is an ambitious young man and a fine penman. He is one who has the confidence and esteem of all who know him, and is looked upon as one of the rising young men of the place. Of irreproachable character and habits, he deserves the success he is achieving.

FRANKLIN MARTIN, contractor, West Fairview, is of the Scotch-Irish race who settled the western part of the county. His grandfather, John Martin, who came to this country many years ago, married, in 1800, Elizabeth Mencough, and settled near Gettysburg, Penn., where they lived many years, afterward removing to Dauphin County, and later to East Pennsborough Township, this county, settling near West Fairview in about 1830. John Martin died in 1841, aged sixty-two; his wife died in 1839, aged fifty-eight. They had three sons and two daughters: Robert, born November 30, 1808, died November 1, 1830; Sarah, born February 23, 1810, wife of Henry A. Gross, of Buck Lock, Dauphin County, Penn.; Nancy, born September 14, 1811, died January 11, 1881; John, born October 5, 1814, died December 9, 1885; and William, born June 23, 1817, died August 23, 1877. Of these, William had only three months' regular schooling, but so well improved his spare moments that he became one of the best informed men in the region, assisted by a remarkably tenacious memory. He learned his trade in a nail factory, and in February, 1844, was married to Miss Elizabeth Starr, of near Lewisberry, York Co., Penn., having the year previous built and furnished the house on Main Street. West Fairview, where he lived until his death in 1877. His wife was born December 29, 1821, and died February 20, 1884. They had seven children: Franklin, born in the house where he now lives, November 3, 1843; Jane M. and John A. (twins), born April 7, 1847, both of whom died in infancy; Sarah J., born September 5, 1848, wife of John B. Heck, of Wormleysburg, this county; Elizabeth A., born April 23, 1851, wife of Silas W. Gleim, of Harrisburg, Penn.; Sylvania, born September 23, 1853, died December 6, 1877; Susan A., born October 23, 1858, died January 13, 1863. Franklin attended public schools until 1860, when he went to White Hall Academy, at Camp Hill, this county. In September, 1862, he enlisted in the "Emergency Men," and was in the battle of Antietam. Returning a few days later, he re-enlisted, before he was eighteen years old, for three years, or during the war, in the Third Pennsylvania Heavy Artillery. While garrisoning Fortress Monroe he was promoted to second lieutenant, and later to first lieutenant, in which rank he served until mustered out at Philadelphia, November 9, 1865. Although a veteran he was not yet twenty-one years old, and he again went to White Hall Academy for a term, subsequently teaching for three years. In April, 1867, he married Laura C., daughter of John Bowman, of New Buffalo, Perry Co., Penn. They had seven children: Sarah Alice, born June 13, 1868; Martha Bowman, born August 4, 1870, died August 18, 1872; William F., born October 6, 1872; John B. F., born June 4, 1875, died May 20, 1881; Elizabeth Sylvania, born July 16, 1878; George Warren, born April 6, 1880, and an infant but a few months old. In 1868 Mr. Martin engaged in lumber business in West Fairview, Penn., with H. M. Rupley. Their mill burned in December, 1868, but they continued dealing in lumber, and rebuilt in 1869. Our subject sold his interest in 1870, and for three years was cashier of a bank in West Fairview, and subsequently superintendent of Isaac Frazier's two mills and planing-mill at Goldsboro. He returned to West Fairview at the end of three years, and bought the business from his former partner, running it until September, 1881, when he sold the mill to the Harrisburg Nail Works, and entered into contract with them to furnish their kegs, operating the mill here as well as another owned by them in Perry County. He is also engaged in the business of fire insurance. He and his wife and eldest daughter are communicants of the Methodist Episcopal Church, and he deservedly stands high in the community.

DANIEL G. MAY, contractor, West Fairview, is a grandson of Joseph Gingrich, who lived near Middletown, Dauphin Co., Penn., in the latter part of the eighteenth century, and later removed to near Mifflin, in Juniata County, Penn. Joseph Gingrich was twice married, having four children by his first wife and six by his second. One of the first wife's daughters, Magdalena, married, in 1820, Frederick May, of Middletown, Dauphin Co. Penn., a farmer, born in that county. They had nine children: Joseph, Daniel G., Catharine, Elizabeth, John, Jacob, Frederick, David and Barbara. They removed to Lancaster County, and later to West Fairview, this county, where Mr. May built the house in which our subject now lives, buying a farm of nearly one hundred acres, a large part of which is now occupied as town lots. Besides farming he engaged in cabinet-making, following these occupations until his death in 1856. His widow died in 1870, aged seventy-three years. At this time but four of their children were living: Joseph, in Philadelphia, Penn; Catharine, wife of Samuel Butner, of East Pennsborough Township, this county; Jacob, in West Fairview, and Daniel G. The latter was born, February 2, 1825, in Lancaster County, Penn. John Frederick, Barbara and Elizabeth are dead. Another son, David, was captain of Company K, Seventh Pennsylvania Cavalry, and was killed while leading a charge at the battle of Chickamauga, in October, 1863. His men were greatly attached to him, and, making three successive charges, recovered his body, which is interred in the National Cemetery, at Chattanooga. Daniel G. worked for his father until he was twenty-one, when he married Mary, daughter of John Rupley, of East Pennsborough Township, this county. To this union five children were born: Luther, accidentally killed in his twelfth year; Joseph, Harry, Susan and Rebecca, who died in infancy. In 1858 Mr. May married ——Eshelman, by whom he has two daughters, Ellen E. and Fanny, living in Fairview, Penn. After his first marriage he moved to a farm owned by his wife, but in 1863 came back to the homestead, which he took at the appraisement, and has lived there since. At various times he was engaged in brick-making, lumber-dealing, and in grocery business, but subsequently adopted carpentering, which he now follows exclusively. He is a self-made man. Without the advantages of school education he has raised himself to an honorable position, and is high-minded and honorable—a man who was never known to violate his promise.

THEODORE M. MOLTZ, merchant, West Fairview, is a native of Cumberland County, as was his father, who was a son of Jacob Moltz, who was born in Manor Township, Lancaster County, March 4, 1784, and died of paralysis in West Fairview, this county, in 1838. Jacob Moltz was a son of George Moltz, who emigrated from near Wurtemberg, Germany, and settled in Lancaster County, Penn. Jacob Moltz removed to East Pennsborough Township, this county, where he married Catharine Olewine. George, their son, was born here in 1809, and in 1831 was married to Catharine Gehr, of Lisburn, Penn., born April 30, 1811. For some years after marriage George Moltz lived at various places, and in 1836 moved to what is known as the Haldeman farm. While on the old homestead two children were born: Theodore M., born August 19, 1832, and Cyrus, born February 2, 1834, died, in 1865, from disease contracted while in the army. On the Haldeman farm three more children were born: Ann Eliza, born January 1, 1837, died young; Margaret Jane, born July 16, 1840, died in infancy, and George, born October 8, 1842, now auditor of the United Pipe Line Company, at Oil City, Penn. July 23, 1855, George Moltz, the father, was accidentally drowned in the Conestoga Canal, in Lancaster County, Penn. His wife died August 17, 1850. Theodore M. lived with his grandfather until the latter's death, when he returned to his father's farm until 1844, when his parents removed to West Fairview, this county. The following summer he went to work in the nail factory, going to school three winters. At the age of sixteen he became a feeder and nailer, which occupation he followed for twenty-five years. March 6, 1862, he married Florinda Susan, daughter of Thomas McClune. They have two sons: George Thomas, born December 8, 1862, and Gouverneur Warren, born February 6, 1864. George Thomas, after getting a common school education, went in 1878 to Millersville State Normal School for two and a half years, and then for eighteen months to the Central State Normal School, at Lock Haven, where he graduated in July, 1883. On his return he was made teacher in one of the six schools in West Fairview, and January 1, 1885, was appointed to the responsible position of principal over all. For so young a man this is a high testimonial to his worth and ability, and shows the estimation in which he is held by those who have known him from childhood. In addition, he gives lessons to pupils on the piano and organ, in which he acquired proficiency while in the normal schools. Gouverneur Warren attended common school until he was eighteen, when he went for a year to Seiler's Academy, at Harrisburg, after which he undertook the practice of photography, under the teaching of Hon. D. C. Burnite, of Harrisburg, where he is now living with his parents. In January, 1869, Mr. Moltz established his grocery and notion store on Main Street. In May, 1869, he was made postmaster under Grant's administration, holding the position until December, 1885. In addition to the performance of these varied duties, he studied the art of photography, which he still carries on. It was here his son, G. Warren, got his first lessons in the art. Mr. Moltz has also for twenty years been extensively engaged in bee culture, and in all his undertakings has won that success which is assured by industry and intelligent application. He is a member of Eureka Lodge, No. 302, F. & A. M., of Mechanicsburg. He is a member of the Lutheran Church, in which he has been chorister for nearly twenty years. His wife and younger son are also members, the son being one of the deacons. A strictly trustworthy Christian, he will leave to his family the priceless heritage of a good name.

JOSEPH ADDISON MOORE, late principal White Hall Soldier's Orphan School, Camp Hill, is deserving of more than a passing notice. He is a descendant of Robert and Margaret Moore, who emigrated from the north of Ireland early in the seventeenth century. One of Robert Moore's sons, William, with his sister Ann, the noted Quaker preacher of that day, settled at Ringgold Manor in Maryland. In consequence of religious persecution, after the settlement of that country by Lord Baltimore's colony, they abandoned their claim rather than violate their principles by litigating it. Another son of Robert Moore, named James, married Jane Caughran, and settled in Adams County, Penn., at a place now known as Bendersville. He gave his life for his country, being killed at the battle of Brandywine. He left a son, who became Maj. John Moore, born in February, 1761, who married Rebecca Curran, and lived in Juniata County, Penn. He also was a Revolutionary soldier. He died in 1853 at the advanced age of ninety-two years. His son, James, born in 1789, in Juniata County, Penn., was the father of our present subject. He lived on the farm until he was twenty years old, when he began to read medicine with Dr. McDonald, of Thompsontown, Juniata Co., Penn., and Dr. Cunningham, of Concord, Franklin Co., Penn. In 1813 he began practicing in Shirleysburg, Huntingdon Co., Penn., where he continued over thirty years at his profession, having a large practice and acquiring the reputation of a very skillful physician. In 1816 he was married to Harriet Barton. He afterward removed to Wells Valley, Fulton Co., Penn., where he continued to practice his profession until within eight years of his death, which occurred March 27, 1872. His wife died in September, 1864, while all of her eight sons were in the Union Army. The family is an extraordinary one, comprising eight sons and three daughters, all now living. They are Kimber A., residing in Nebraska; Rebecca A., wife of J. B. Alexander, of Fulton County, Penn.; John C., living at Camp Hill, Penn.; Charles W., who is a practicing physician in Sterling, Neb.; Julia A., wife of William A. Gray, of Adams, Neb.; Harriet L., of Sterling, Neb.; Joseph Addison, our subject; and James M., B. Frank, William H. and Curran E., all of whom are residents of Nebraska.

JOSEPH ADDISON MOORE was born in Shirleysburg, Penn., August 26, 1833. As said above, the eight sons were all in the Union Army at the same time, two of them being seriously wounded. Their record is not surpassed by that of any other family in the country, and is one of which they and their children may be justly proud. This remarkable family was represented in nearly all the great battles of the war, and the fact that all are alive and well to-day is very remarkable. Immediately after the firing on Fort Sumter, our subject enlisted in Company D, Fifth Pennsylvania Infantry for three months, and was made first sergeant. At the expiration of his time, he raised Company O, Twenty-eight Pennsylvania Infantry, and in August, 1861, took the field as first lieutenant under colonel (afterward general and governor), John W. Geary, under whom he served all through the war, at one time for seven months on his staff as division commissary. At Antietam, while as first lieutenant, in command of his company, two of his men captured two rebel flags. Here his command suffered severely, one-third of his company being killed and wounded. Four color-bearers belonging to his company were shot. His company was shortly after transferred to Company B, One Hundred and Forty-seventh Pennsylvania Infantry, and in February, 1863, he was commissioned captain, commanding at Cedar Mountain, Chancellorsville and Gettysburg in the East, and at Lookout Mountain, Mission Ridge, Taylor's Ridge, Wauhatchie, Chattanooga, Cassville, Rocky Face Ridge. Dug Gap, Resaca and New Hope Church in the Southwest. He was severely wounded at New Hope, and in consequence was incapacitated for further active service, and was transferred to the barracks at Madison, Wis., until the end of his term of service, October 28, 1864. He was later brevetted major for gallant and meritorious service. At the close of the war he resumed mercantile pursuits in Pittsburgh, Penn., but in 1867 he was called by his old commander, then governor of the State, to take charge of the White Hall Soldiers' Orphan School at Camp Hill, which under his management became the leading school of the State, reflecting great credit on his ability as a manager. He continued in charge of the school until September 1, 1886, when, having leased the same, he retired from the responsible position which he had so long and faithfully filled. In 1869 he was married to Miss Lizzie, daughter of Jacob Kline, of Lower Allen Township, this county. They have one son, Joy Addison L., now nine years old. Maj. Moore enjoys the unbounded respect of every one who knows him, and in the community of which he is a leading member, no man stands higher in character or is more deservedly respected.

HENRY D. MUSSER, merchant, West Fairview, was born near New Cumberland, in York Co., Penn., December 20, 1828. His grandfather, Dr. John Musser, a native of Lancas-

EAST PENNSBOROUGH TOWNSHIP. 473

ter County, Penn., where he practiced medicine, but who later removed to York County, where he bought a farm, was a noted physician and acquired a reputation for the treatment of white swellings and kindred disorders; his wife was Elizabeth Neff, of Lancaster County, Penn. Their children were Benjamin, Henry, John, Elizabeth, Mary, Susan, Martha and Nancy, now the wife of Joseph Bowman, of Lancaster County, Penn. Benjamin Musser, father of Henry D., born February 22, 1801, married Frances Snavely, of Hampden Township, this county, who bore him thirteen children: Elizabeth, John S., Henry D., Catharine, Annie, Joseph R. and Josiah, living; and Benjamin, David, Jacob, Levi, Daniel and Sarah, deceased. Benjamin Musser had charge of the farm until his father's death, when it was sold to Mr. Garner, father of the present occupant. He then removed to Hampden Township, Cumberland County, staying there three years, when he went West to prospect, but returned and bought a farm and mill property near Millersburg, in Dauphin County, Penn., where he lived seventeen years, when he sold out and returned to Cumberland County, to the farm now occupied by John N. Musser, stayed a year, and then removed to near Fairview, Penn., where he died in 1854. His widow died a few years later at White Hall, Penn. Henry D. attended common school, and qualified for teaching at White Hall Academy. At eighteen years of age he began teaching, and taught for six terms. On his father's death he took charge of the farm for a year, when, his mother selling out, he began farming for himself in 1856, continuing until 1865, when he and his brother Joseph engaged in mercantile business, in Fairview, for a year and a half, during which time he also held the position of postmaster. He then retired until 1873, in which year he again engaged in business where he now is. May 16, 1855, he married Mary E. Rupley, born December 19, 1832, daughter of George and Magdalena Rupley, of East Pennsborough Township, this county, and who on the death of her parents became possessed of one-half of their farm, which she and her husband still hold. They have two children living: Charles Emery, born November 30, 1859, and Harry Clinton, born August 14, 1861. Three are dead: George, Whitfield and an infant daughter. Mr. and Mrs. Musser are prominent members of the United Brethren Church. Mrs. Musser is president of the Mite Society, and her husband has been superintendent of the Sunday-school for twenty years. They are known as sincere Christians, whose character commands the respect of the community.

AUSTIN TAYLOR PALM, teacher of mathematics, Camp Hill, is a son of Peter and Maria Palm, natives of Cumberland County, and now residents of Chicago, Ill. (Mrs, Palm's maiden name was also Palm, but she is no blood relative of her husband's family), five of whose children are deceased. Those living are Austin T.; Warren, married and living in Chicago; Sharon, married and living in Goldsboro, Penn.; Milton, married and living in Springfield, Ohio; Eudora E. and Carondelet B. living with their parents. Austin T. was born in West Pennsborough Township, this county, in June, 1835. He remained at home working for his father, as a carpenter, until twenty years of age, when he began teaching district school, for which vocation he had qualified himself by study and attending normal school. He continued in this profession until 1876, during a part of which time he was principal of the high school at Mechanicsburg, and was also principal of public schools of Columbia, Lancaster Co., Penn. In 1876 he was elected professor of mathematics in the State Normal School at Shippensburg, Penn. In 1883 he taught in normal school in Morris, Ill., and in the fall of that year went into the public schools of Harrisburg, but resigned in 1885 to take the position of professor of mathematics and of music in the White Hall Soldiers' Orphan School, at Camp Hill. Mr. Palm was married, in 1859, to Miss Maggie A. Machlin, of York County, who died in November, 1885, leaving no family, her five children having preceded her to the grave. Mr. Palm is known as a gentleman of spotless integrity, frank and outspoken, and has an excellent reputation as a teacher, excelling in discipline and in the gift of being able to impart what he knows.

HENRY M. RUPLEY, merchant, West Fairview, is a great-grandson of Johann Jacob Rupley, who emigrated from Unter Waslingen, Germany, in 1743, bought 600 acres of land in East Pennsborough Township, this county, near what is now West Fairview, and died June 12, 1793. Jacob, son of Johann J. Rupley, married Anna Maria Rupp, and died in 1806; she in 1827. They had four sons and two daughters. Of these, George was born February 6, 1803, and lived all his life on the farm, dealing largely in stock. In 1830 he married Magdalena Musser, of Marsh Run, York Co., Penn., and died December 26, 1842, leaving one son and one daughter. His widow is still living in West Fairview. He was school director, constable and supervisor, and many stories are yet told of his remarkable marksmanship. His daughter, Mary Ellen, married Henry D. Musser, of East Pennsborough Township, this county. His son, Henry M., was born December 7, 1838, and November 21, 1861, married Mary M., daughter of John K. Heck, of East Pennsborough Township, this county. She was born September 30, 1842, and died September 13, 1864, leaving a son, George H., born September 1, 1862, who, after going through the common school, went to Selinsgrove for two years, and then to Ann Arbor (Mich.) Academy, subsequently serving a time in the Harrisburg Machine Shops; he is now a draughtsman in the Carlisle Manufacturing Works, and is a young man of excellent character and prospects. December 5, 1867, Henry M. Rupley was married again, this time to Miss Phœbe A., daughter of George W. and Elizabeth Ringwalt, of near Carlisle. She was born April 20, 1845. They have three children living: Arthur R., born November 13, 1868; Lucy Ellen, born August 26, 1872, and Mary Magdalena, born December 12, 1882. One son, Max Roland, born July 14, 1877, is dead. Arthur Rupley attends the normal school at Shippensburg; the rest are at home. Until he was seventeen years old our subject attended school winters, working on the farm other seasons. At that age he went to White Hall Academy, Camp Hill, for two years. In January, 1865, he rented his farm and came to West Fairview, buying, in 1867, a half interest in the steam saw-mill there, which was burned a few months later, and rebuilt in 1869. On first coming to West Fairview he was engaged in furnishing men for the last draft of the war; after that in a grocery, which he gave up for the mill, and was in the lumber business until 1884, selling his interest in the mill in 1882, on account of ill health. In 1868 he sold his farm. In 1884 he built his present residence and place of business, where he conducts a general store. He has been township auditor, judge of election, inspector, school director, constable, and is now serving his second term as justice of the peace. He is prominent in town affairs, and is universally esteemed.

WILLIAM SADLER, farmer, P. O. Camp Hill, is a grandson of Jacob Sadler, who came to this country many years ago, and settled in York County, Penn., near the Maryland line, where he married, and had a family of eight sons and five daughters. He died near Pittsburgh. Our subject's paternal ancestors were among the first settlers west of the Susquehanna River. William Sadler died in 1765; he was one of three brothers who came from England prior to 1750, and settled in that part of York County which is now included in Adams County, near York Springs. William Sadler had a son, Jacob Sadler, who, in his early life, resided in York County, near the borough of Little York. Jacob Sadler had thirteen children—eight sons and five daughters—one of whom was Joseph Sadler. Joseph, the father of our subject, was born in York County in 1782, and when he was quite young his parents removed to Allegheny County, Penn., where he stayed until twenty years old; then he went to Lancaster County, and in two years after to East Pennsborough Township, this county, where, in 1807. he was married to Mary Gabel, of the same place. He then entered into farming and distilling. and had also what is known as the "Pitt" wagons, carrying goods to Pittsburgh, Baltimore and Philadelphia. He accumulated property, part of which was the farm afterward the property of his son William. His family consisted of six sons and two daughters: Jacob, John, Samuel, Joseph, William, George, Susan and Mary. The three survivors, Jacob, William and George, all live on the turnpike, at Camp Hill, within a quarter of a mile of each other. William Sadler was born October 6, 1824, and worked on the home farm until he was of age, when he was married to Mary, daughter of George Beidelman, of East Pennsborough Township. He then hired his father's farm until the latter's death, in the summer of 1858, when he bought it from the estate. In 1882 he sold the farm and moved to Camp Hill, where he stayed two years; then he bought the property known as "Oyster's Point" and a small farm adjoining. Mr. and Mrs. Sadler have had the following named children: Jacob, George and Austin, the two latter dying young, and Jacob, in 1880, at age of thirty-three years, up to which time he had lived at home, except a short period spent in business in New Cumberland; one daughter, Ellen, likewise died young. The living are Laura B., wife of Jacob Worst, of Upper Allen Township; Alice C., married to James E. Martin, of Hampden Township; Annetta; Emma M. and Effie M., who live at home. Mr. Sadler has been county commissioner, school director for twenty-one consecutive years, assessor, supervisor, judge and inspector of elections, and has discharged all the duties intrusted to his care with a fidelity which has elicited the commendation of his fellow-citizens. He and his family have the entire respect of all who know them.

WILLIAM H. SHAULL, carpenter and contractor, P. O. West Fairview, was born in Hamden Township, this county, in 1838. His father, Henry Shaull, a native of Lebanon County, born about the year 1811, was a son of John Shaull, who lived and died in York County, leaving seven children. On his father's death Henry Shaull was bound out to John Benson, of Colebrook Furnace, to learn blacksmithing, working there until after he became of age. At twenty-three he was married to Catharine, daughter of John Garrett, of Lebanon County, Penn., and for five subsequent years worked at Colebrook Furnace, when he removed to Hampden Township, Cumberland County, and engaged in business on his own account. Here he remained until his death; he died in 1877, at the age of sixty-six, leaving a family of five sons and two daughters: William H.; Sarah, wife of Samuel Shaumberger; Levi; George F.; Elizabeth, wife of John Basehore, of Hampden Township; Charles H.; and Martha E. now deceased. William H. worked two years at his father's trade, but at the age of eighteen went to Sterrett's Gap to learn carpentering. When his time was up he moved to Hogestown to work, but in August of the same year (1862) he enlisted in the One Hundred and Thirtieth Pennsylvania Regiment for nine months, and a few weeks after was in the battle of South Mountain, and then in Antietam, where he was struck in the head by a glancing bullet, which, fortunately did not penetrate the skull. His regiment was removed to Harper's Ferry, and afterward sent up the Shenandoah Valley to Warrington Junction and thence to Fredericksburg to take part in the fight there, in which they lost their commander, Col. Zinn. From Fredericksburg they went to Chancellorsville, in which three day's fight they bore an active part. Thence they were sent to Acquia Creek, and home to Harrisburg, where they were mustered out, after an active campaign. Mr. Shaull re-enlisted in the Two Hundred and First Pennsylvania Regiment for one year, but the regiment was most of the time employed guarding railroads, supplies, etc., and at the end of the term was mustered out at Harrisburg. After this Mr. Shaull worked at his trade for six years, when he established himself in his present business as carpenter and contractor, at West Fairview. He was married, in 1863, to Miss Mary E. Bowers, of East Pennsborough. They have six boys and two girls: Martha E. is married to George H. Shaeffer, of Baltimore; Harry, aged eighteen, works with his father; William, Tillie, Franklin, Albert, Ira and Nelson are at home. Mr. Shaull is a member of Post No. 58, G. A. R. He and his wife belong to the United Brethren Church, and he is held in esteem by all who have been in any manner associated with him as a man of honesty and worth.

LESLIE H. SINGISER, hotel-keeper, P. O. Wormleysburg, is a grandson of George Singiser, for many years a forwarder in Mechanicsburg, Penn., and one of the first contractors on the Cumberland Valley Railroad. George Singiser was well known and much liked, beloved and respected for his probity and generous impulses. An enterprising man, he took part in every movement calculated to advance the interests of the valley. He died in 1854. His wife was Mary Halbert, of Carlisle, a Christian lady and fit companion for such a man. She died in 1884, at Altoona. They had four sons and five daughters. One of the sons, Andrew, succeeded his father, in 1863, and later engaged in the grocery business in Mechanicsburg. He is a straightforward man, and is always willing to help the struggling, which he has often done to his own detriment. Andrew Singiser married Miss Annie Wyle, of Mechanicsburg, Penn., who wears woman's highest crown of a good wife and mother. They have four sons and one daughter: George, Leslie H., Harry, Willie L. and Alberta. Leslie H. was born in 1852. He lived with his parents until his twenty-first year, when he was married to Miss Sallie, daughter of George Winemiller, of Upper Allen Township, this county. He then carried on the green-grocery and general dealing business for six years, when he gave it up to take position in the Cumberland Valley Railroad office, which he held for three years, relinquishing it to engage in the livery, and afterward in a restaurant business, which he sold in November, 1884; in April following he rented the hotel at the end of the bridge from Harrisburg to Bridgeport, where he is doing a good business, as such a kind friend and generous man must. He is ably assisted by his wife, who takes charge of the interior management. She is a prominent member of the Reformed Church. They have two sons: George Alfred, aged eleven, and Murray, nine years old. All who know this worthy couple are pleased with their success and wish them long life and continued prosperity.

WILSON P. WALTERS, farmer, Camp Hill, is the grandson of John Walters, a native of the county, whose father settled here after his immigration from Germany. His farm was in what is now Hampden Township, near the mountain. His son John inherited the farm, on which he died. He had four sons: John, Daniel, Joseph Henry and Jacob. Daniel Walters, the father of our subject, was married to Margaret Weibby, of Carlisle. He took the home farm, but some years after sold it, and bought another near Mechanicsburg, where he died about 1872, in his seventy-seventh year; his widow died in 1876, aged seventy-five. Their children were Levi, Jacob, Margaret, Wilson P., John H., David, Mary and Sarah and Ephraim, who both died young. Levi died in Hampden Township in 1885; Jacob died in 1858; Margaret is the wife of Jacob A. Basehore, of Hampden Township; John H. is married to Miss Jennie Ziegler, and is now burgess of Mechanicsburg. Wilson P., was born September 8, 1836. He worked at carpentering for seven years, when he hired the Simon Oyster farm, which he worked for nineteen years, at which time he bought from his father-in-law, Jacob Sadler, the one on which he now resides. November 17, 1859, he married Miss Mary Sadler, who was born on the farm they now own. They have two children, Julia A., born January 18, 1861, now the wife of A. O. Sample, merchant of Mechanicsburg; and William Franklin, born December 2, 1863, who is single and living with his parents. Mr. Walters has never held office, but gives his entire time and attention to his farm. He is a member of Eureka Lodge, No. 302, A. Y. M., of Mechanicsburg, and bears a high character for honesty and uprightness.

CHARLES F. WILBAR, mail-carrier, West Fairview, was born in Wareham, Mass., October 2, 1833. His father, Charles Wilbar, was born in that State, and there lived until 1837, when he came to West Fairview, this county, to take charge of the nail factory of J. Pratt & Son, the senior member of which firm was a brother of Mrs. Wilbar. On the sale of the works to James McCormick, Mr. Wilbar retired from active life. He died in 1865. He was twice married; first to Miss Lydia Pratt, by whom he had one daughter, Jane P., who died in Boston in 1883. His second wife was a sister of his first, Agatha B. Pratt, who died in Fairview in 1880. They had seven children, of whom one son and one daughter are deceased. Those living are Lydia Ann, wife of Rev. S. Dasher, of Harrisburg, Penn.; Charles F.; Elizabeth, wife of Solomon A. Alexander, of York, Penn.; Josiah P., book-keeper at the nail factory, and Bethiah, wife of George Schutt, of Fairview. Charles

F. Wilbar was educated in the public schools, and at eighteen began working in the keg shops attached to the nail works, of which he was afterward foreman for twenty-three years, retiring in 1881. Since July 1, 1885, he has carried the mail between Fairview and Harrisburg. In 1862 he married Eliza, born in 1834, daughter of John Holtz, of Fairview, Penn. To this union the following-named children have been born: Charles Edward, born November 7, 1865, now teaching in the village; Emma Loretta, born August 18, 1868; Lily Viola, born January 30, 1872—all living at home; and Harry F., who died September 29, 1864. Mr. and Mrs. Wilbar, son and eldest daughter are members of the Lutheran Church. An estimable couple, with a fine family, a pleasant residence and the respect of their neighbors, they are happily situated.

HENRY K. WITMAN, contractor, Wormleysburg. John Witman, the grandfather of our subject, was a native of Lancaster County, Penn. Although a farmer, he carried on the business of weaving, operating four looms. He married Mary Yontz, also of Lancaster County, and had eight children: Elizabeth, Mary, Catharine, Anthony, John, Joseph, Jacob and Paul. Of these, John was born in 1799, and came, in 1809, to Londonderry Township, Dauphin Co., Penn., with his parents, who had purchased a farm there, upon which they resided until they died. John Witman learned the trade of weaving, which he followed for many years. His wife was Mary Irwin, by whom he had eleven children: Henry K., John, William, Paul, Joseph, Catharine, Lydia, Mary, Elizabeth, Sarah and Phianna—all born and reared on the homestead. Henry K. Witman, the only one of the family residing in Cumberland County, acquired a practical education early in life, and when twenty-two years old was made foreman by a contractor grading the Lebanon Valley Railroad through Dauphin County. He afterward superintended the grading of the Northern Central in Northumberland County, and the Huntingdon & Broad Top Railroad, in Huntingdon County, Penn. January 1, 1860, he superintended a "floating gang" on the North Central. In this year he was married to Mary J. McCanna, of Chester County, Penn., and began housekeeping in Bridgeport, Penn. He became foreman on the North Central Railroad, holding that position until 1879, when he opened a stone quarry on the McCormick estate, which he still works. In a wreck on the road, in 1862, he lost his right arm, but with indomitable will kept his position and made a success in life. In 1864 he purchased a residence in Wormleysburg, Penn., which he sold in 1875, engaging in mercantile business in Bridgeport until 1881, when he bought his present home. No more desirable place could be had. It overlooks the broad Susquehanna and the flourishing city of Harrisburg. He has four children: John, Harry, Lydia and Naomi, who may feel a just pride in bearing a name that knows no stain. A competence, honorably acquired, and a good income, enables him to surround his family with all the comforts of life. Books, music, etc., make cheerful their happy home, and he well deserves the esteem accorded him by his neighbors.

CHAPTER XLVI.

FRANKFORD TOWNSHIP.

M. F. ANTHONY, farmer, P. O. Bloserville, is a grandson of John Anthony, who was brought to this country an infant, about 130 years ago, from Germany. His parents settled in Adams County, near Hanover, where he lived until his death. He married Margaret Huffman, and they had six children: Michael, Elizabeth, Margaret, Catherine, Lena and John. Of these, John, the sole survivor, married Margaret Shaeffer, of North Middleton Township, and lives a few miles from Carlisle. Michael, father of our subject, was born June 23, 1791, and died October 5, 1859. His wife was Eva Doyhl, who was born June 1, 1792, and died January 15, 1864. They had six children, one dying in infancy. The others were: Catharine, wife of Henry Neff, of Newville; Margaret, wife of John Fenton, of Newville; Sarah, wife of Joseph McDermond, of Mifflin Township; John, who died when fifteen years old, and Michael F., who was born January 2, 1826, two miles from Carlisle, in North Middleton Township. He worked as a weaver for fifteen years, when he began farming, first in Mifflin Township, for two years, then in Newton Township eight years; lived a year in Newville, and then returned to North Middleton, where he resided eight years, when he came to the farm which he and his wife own in Frankford Township. In 1854 he married Miss Sarah Asper, who was born April 15, 1831, and died January 15, 1864, the mother of one child, who died young. January 9, 1872, Mr. Anthony married Mrs. Mary Ann Allen, widow of George Allen, who was a Miss Barley.

They have two children: Sarah Catharine, born August 3, 1872, and David Edward, born March 1, 1880. Mr. Anthony is a member of the Lutheran Church, a man of high character and probity.

MRS. NANCY DRAWBAUGH, Bloserville, is descended from one of the old families of the county, as was her husband, John Drawbaugh, whose grandfather came from York County a great many years ago and settled in what is now Lower Allen Township. One of his sons, George, was the father of John, the husband of Nancy. George was born in 1801 and died March 10, 1866. He was married, in 1822, to Barbara Bloser, of North Middleton Township, where he was then living. She died in June, 1885. He was a wagon-maker and a farmer in Frankford Township, but sold out and moved to another place, which he owned, in South Middleton, near Carlisle. By careful management and industry he acquired a competence. He was enabled to give his later children a start in life, and at his death left a fine estate. He had seven children: John (husband of our subject), born November 26, 1823; William, married to Margaret Ebright, who died, leaving six children, and he then married Mrs. Maria Elliott, who has one child—they live in this township; Elizabeth, wife of John Bowman, who lived with her father until his death; Alexander Cornman, married to Emma Roberts, living in West Virginia; George B., married to Eliza Basehore, living in West Pennsborough Township; David Porter, who died unmarried; and Ellen, wife of David Hemminger, county treasurer. In early life John worked on his father's farm, and three years after his marriage moved to a farm in West Pennsborough Township, where they lived eleven years, when he bought a farm in North Middleton Township. Here they lived four years, and selling this property removed to a farm owned by his father, in West Pennsborough Township, where they lived three years, and then bought and removed to the farm, where he died, October 7, 1882, and where his widow and surviving children now reside. He was an honest hard-working man, who provided well for his family, and lived and died with the respect of the entire community. January 25, 1844, he married Miss Nancy Ziegler, born July 15, 1819, a daughter of William and Margaret (Adams) Ziegler, of this township and Mifflin. They were an old and well-known family, many of whom are to be found all over the county. Mr. and Mrs. Drawbaugh had nine children: Ezemiah C., born June 25, 1845, the wife of Solomon W. Lehn, living in North Middleton Township, this county; Anna Maria, born August 15, 1847, living with her mother; Catherine Agnes, born October 28, 1849, and died December 6, 1864; Samuel Wilson, born December 18, 1852, married to Sarah Barrick, and died October 9, 1882; Margaret Grizel, born December 9, 1853, wife of Martin Foos, and living in Harrisburg; William Edgar, born November 3, 1855, and married to Isabel Sharp, and living in Newton Township; George Albert, born July 2, 1857, and died November 6, 1882; John Freeman, born February 13, 1860, and died October 4, 1882; and David Porter, born August 23, 1862, unmarried and living with his mother (he teaches the school at Bloserville, and is a young man of exemplary habits and character.) The history of this family contains a sad record of the ravages of death; the father, John, the sons, John Freeman and Samuel Wilson, dying within one week, and another son, George A., following them to the grave in less than a month. The widow lives in retirement with her unmarried son and daughter in a new house on a part of the farm, which she has rented, and in the evening of her days is enjoying a well-earned rest from active cares. She is a member of the Lutheran Church.

JOHN JACOB ERFORD, farmer, P. O. Carlisle, is a grandson of John Erford, who emigrated from Germany, and took up a large tract of land in East Pennsborough Township. He had seven children—three sons, John, Jacob and Benjamin, and four daughters. Jacob, father of our subject, was born in 1806, and lived on the home farm, where he died in 1855. His wife was Susanna, daughter of John Hoover, of South Middleton Township, who died in 1858. They had five children: Julia Ann, born February 8, 1837 (she became the wife of John Givler, who was killed in the army, and after his death married John Kiehl), and died in 1881; John Jacob, our subject, born July 5, 1839; Elizabeth, born December 3, 1842, is the wife of John Myers, and lives in West Fairview; Mary Matilda, born November 4, 1845, is the wife of David Wolf, of this township; Sarah Sophia, born August 30, 1849, is the widow of Joseph Hess, and lives in East Pennsborough. John Jacob worked on his father's farm until eighteen years of age, when he attended the normal school in Newville, and afterward taught for two winters. He then returned to farming. In 1862 he enrolled as a soldier, serving over ten months, and was then honorably discharged, when he again returned to farming, also raising and dealing in poultry, in which he is yet engaged. In 1867 he removed to West Pennsborough Township, where he stayed five years. He has since made several changes, but for five years past has lived on his father-in-law's farm in this township, renting his own farm. January 1, 1861, he married Rebecca, daughter of John Darr, who died on the farm now occupied by Mr. Erford. They have had ten children, one of whom, John Wesley, died in infancy; Mary Elizabeth is the wife of Elias E. Hoover, of this township. The rest are living at home, and are named as follows: Sarah Ann, born October 8, 1861; Emma Catherine, born February 25, 1866; Joseph Sylvester, born October 24, 1869; William Francis, born March 6, 1872; Ida Jane, born January 16, 1874; Clara Eleanora, born Feb ruary 21, 1879; Ella May, born May 27, 1881, and Martha Blanche, born January 17, 1885. Mr. Erford has been a justice of the peace for nine years; is assistant assessor of the township, and is justly held in high esteem as a man whose word is as good as any man's bond.

FRANCIS MENTZER, lumberman, Bloserville, one of the enterprising citizens of the township, who has done much to develop the resources of the section in which he lives, was born in the township he has lived in all his life. His ancestors on the paternal side came from Hungary, and on the maternal from Germany, before the Revolution. His great-grandfather, John, was twice married. This branch of the family is descended from the second wife, whose name was Christiana Wasinger. One of their sons, also named John, grandfather of Francis, was born in Lancaster County December 15, 1780, and died in this township February 5, 1861, aged eighty-one years. His wife was Elizabeth Ernst, a daughter of John Ernst, who came from Germany when eighteen years old. She was born March 14, 1793, and died July 6, 1880, aged eighty-seven years. They had nine children: Frederick, father of our subject; John, born November 12, 1818, married Eliza Seitz, and after her death Eva Householder, and died in 1879; Henry, born July 29, 1820, married Polly Lemon, of West Pennsborough Township, where they are living; Simon, born October 2, 1829, married Barbara Radabaugh, of this township, and lives here; David, born November 24, 1832, married Ann Fry, and lives in West Pennsborough Township; George, born February 27, 1835, married Harriet Oiler, and lives on the Bloser mansion farm; Barbara is the wife of John D. Snyder of this township; Catherine was the wife of William Kost, and both are deceased; and Sarah, who is unmarried, lives with her brother George. Frederick, father of Francis, was born August 31, 1813. He lived on his father's farm until after his marriage, when, after many changes, he bought the Laied farm, now owned by his son, Francis. In 1864, he retired and bought a small place south of Bloserville, removing to the village two years later, and died July 7, 1874. He was a thorough-going man, pretty sure to accomplish whatever he undertook, and enjoyed the confidence of his fellow-citizens, and was several times elected to responsible township offices. He was a religious man, a member of the Lutheran Church. January 26, 1837, he married Martha Bowman, of this township, whose father was born December 11, 1788, and died April 21, 1846. Her mother, Martha, also was a widow, a Mrs. Messner, and originally a Miss Bloser, who died January 26, 1856, at the advanced age of ninety-seven years. They had six children: William, born July 15, 1838, married Ellen De Sanno, and died February 28, 1865 (his widow, now the wife of William Lucas, resides in Peoria, Ill.); William was a practicing physician in Carlisle, a graduate of Jefferson Medical College, and had visited the medical schools of the principal European cities; John was born May 29, 1842, married Annie Keck, of Perry County, and was accidently drowned in the Conodoguinet Creek, (his widow and family still reside on his farm in West Pennsborough Township); Abraham, born July 14, 1844, married Sarah, daughter of Hezekiah Koch, of Mifflin, and is now living on Francis' farm; David, born April 4, 1847, married Mina Chronister, of Adams County, and is living on the homestead farm, also owned by our subject; Mary Elizabeth, born July 8, 1849, is the wife of A. P. Schimp, and is living in South Middleton. Francis, who is the second son, was born February 4, 1845. He lived at home until his marriage, when he began farming on two or three farms, finally removing to Mount Rock, Penn Township, where he stayed seven years, and in 1870 came back to the old farm which he had bought from his father two years before. Here he remained six years, then in Bloserville eighteen months, during which time he went West; on his return he went back to the farm and remained there until the spring of 1885, when he removed to the place where he now resides. In 1884 he had bought an interest in the business now carried on under the name of Stambaugh & Mentzer, which he sold in the spring of 1886 to his son Frederick. November 22, 1860, he married Mary, daughter of William Drawbaugh, of this township; she was born February 28, 1840, and died November 11, 1881, accidentally burned to death by her clothing taking fire from an exploded lamp. They had following named children: Abner D., born September 13, 1862; Frederick, born March 18, 1865, who has taught school and now succeeds his father in mercantile business at Bloserville; Martha E., born May 14, 1867; William H., born May 21, 1870, and died July 15, 1870; Harvey, born December 17, 1871; Francis, born December 31, 1873; and Minnie Catherina, born September 30, 1876, all living at home. December 21, 1882, Mr. Mentzer married Kate D. Mentzer, a cousin, a daughter of John Mentzer, and born February 8, 1851. They had one child, Mamie, born May 19, 1884, who died May 4, 1885. Mr. Mentzer has always been an active man. He has built many houses and barns, is now engaged in the lumber business with his brother-in-law, Joseph Drawbaugh, in Mifflin Township, has taken an active part in the affairs of the townships, and has held several offices. He and his wife and several members of the family are members of the Evangelical Association. Mr. Mentzer is universally esteemed as an upright, trustworthy man and a consistent Christian.

WILLIAM JACKSON WALLACE, farmer, P. O. Newville. The grandfather of our subject settled in this township some time after his immigration from Ireland, on land of which the farm of William J. was a part. He was married here and reared a family. Those who arrived at maturity were: James, who was married to Susan McCrea, and lived on the homestead, where he died; Thomas, who went to Ohio when young, married a Miss Watt, and died there; John, who lived on a farm adjoining the homestead, married a Miss Mary Thompson, removed to Newville, and died there in 1876; Jane, who married a Mr. Shoemaker, went to Monmouth, Ill., where he died; Margaret, who died unmarried; Nancy, the wife of Thompson Mathers, of Mifflin Township, this county, where she died; William, the youngest son, who was born in 1800, and lived on the farm, until a few years before his death, at Newville, in 1874. He married Miss Mary Wherry, of Hopewell Township, and had nine children: John W., who died at home unmarried, aged about twenty-two; James M., who also died single; Margaret, the eldest of the girls, who died young; Agnes S., living in Newville; Lizzie E., killed by a train at Harrisburg; Anna Mary, who died after reaching maturity; Ida X. and Laura M., twin sisters (the former died when a young lady, the latter is living at Newville), and William Jackson, the youngest of the sons. Our subject was born March 20, 1839, and worked on the farm until his marriage, when he removed to the farm, which he had previously purchased. The homestead became his on his father's death. December 27, 1870, he married Miss Mary G., daughter of Rev. James Shield's, of Juniata County, who was born, September 11, 1843. Mr. and Mrs. Wallace had one son, James Shields, who was born September 8, 1873, died July 11, 1886. He had been school director for nine years, and was justice of the peace for the five years previous to his death. He was a member of and ruling elder in the United Presbyterian Church at Newville. He had the reputation, in his community, of being a conscientious man, and a good citizen. His widow is a member of the United Presbyterian Church at Newville.

CHAPTER XLVII.

HAMPDEN TOWNSHIP.*

ABRAM A. BOWMAN, farmer, P. O. Mechanicsburg, is a son of Abram Bowman, now of Upper Allen Township, formerly of Fairview, York Co., Penn., where our subject was born November 27, 1851, and where he lived until 1878, when he removed to a farm owned by Samuel Eberly, nearly adjoining his present residence. In 1881 Abram A. and his father purchased a fine farm, on the road known as "Brandy Lane," from the heirs of J. Best, and in 1884 the former bought the old Barnhart mansion farm, and now farms both places, living on the first mentioned property. In January, 1875, he married Elizabeth, daughter of Samuel Eberly (one of the best known residents of Hampden Township), and they have one son, Samuel A. Although Mr. Bowman is still quite a young man, yet he has already achieved a good measure of success. What property he has acquired has been by his own unaided exertions, and, should his life be spared, the energy and business capacity he has already exhibited, will undoubtedly place him in the front rank of the citizens of this county.

DAVID DIETZ, farmer, P. O. Shiremanstown, is a native of York County, Penn., born in 1826, son of Daniel and Lydia (Stoner) Dietz. His grandfather was George Dietz. His father and his grandfather were born on the same farm, making two generations born on the same property. In 1837, when David was eleven years of age, his parents removed to East Pennsborough Township, this county, buying the place known as the "Carothers' farm," which has been in the possession of the Carothers family for one hundred years. Here the father, Daniel Deitz, died in 1860, aged sixty years; his widow died in 1866. David worked on his father's farm until his marriage, in 1850, with Caroline, daughter of Christian Sheely, of Hampden Township. A year later his father gave the management of the farm to him, and he lived there until 1869, when he bought the place on which he now resides, in Hampden Township, about one mile north of Shiremanstown. He, however, still owns the old homestead, which is farmed by his son, Daniel. David Dietz has had nine children, two of whom are deceased. Daniel is the eldest living, and is married to Susan, daughter of William Mechling, and carries on his father's farm; Simon, his second son, is married to Barbara, daughter of Jacob Eberly, and carries on farming. Three daughters are married: Mary Ellen, wife of John H. Smith, of Mechanicsburg, Penn.; Annetta, wife of Jonas C. Rupp, of Monroe Township, and Carrie M., who married Frank S. Hertzler, of Lower Allen Township; the two younger daughters are at home. Mr. Dietz was elected county commissioner in 1869, serving his

*See also borough of Shiremanstown, page 456.

term of three years to the great satisfaction of his fellow-citizens. He has been school director also for many years, the last three as secretary of the board. He has also been assessor several times, besides filling several minor offices. In every position to which he has been called he has discharged its duties with credit to himself and satisfaction of his constituents. He and his wife are prominent members of St. John's Lutheran Church. David Dietz is universally esteemed by all who know him, and bears a well-deserved reputation as a man of upright character and the most unblemished integrity.

CHRISTIAN DIETZ, farmer, P. O. Good Hope, is the younger son of Daniel and Lydia (Stoner) Dietz, and was born in York County, Penn., on the same farm where his father and grandfather were born. He is fifty-three years of age, having been born in October, 1832. His parents came to this county in 1837, buying the well-known "Carothers' farm," which had been owned by that family for 150 years. Here Christian lived until the spring of 1851, when his father turned the farm over to his elder son David, himself and family removing to a house he had built on that part of his own farm lying in the then new township of Hampden. Here Christian lived until his marriage, in 1856, with Elizabeth, daughter of John Wilt of East Pennsborough Township, he then removed to a farm bought by his father, in 1852, from Anderson and William Orr. Here he stayed until the spring of 1882, when he removed to a new house which he built at the lower end of his farm, to which he had added fifty acres bought from James Orr, and this, with the original Orr Farm of 160 acres, which he got from his father's estate, and ninety-five acres which he purchased from Susan Sierer, gives him a fine farm of 305 acres in one tract, making him about the largest land-owner in Hampden Township, and one of its heaviest taxpayers. He has five children: George W., married to Lillie C., daughter of Eli C. Shuman (he farms his father's upper farm); Alice J., wedded to Frederick Mumma, grocer, of Mechanicsburg; Rebecca E., Milton C., and Katie N., who are unmarried and live at home. Mr. Dietz has held several township offices, and has been school director for eighteen years, assessor two terms, county auditor, and held several minor offices. He has worthily discharged the duties of every position, and should his fellow-citizens call him to a still higher post of honor, which seems probable, his life and charater, which are open and known to all men, are a guarantee that he will faithfully discharge the trust committed to his care.

SAMUEL EBERLY, retired farmer, P. O. Shiremanstown, is a native of this county, born near Mechanicsburg in 1820, son of John Eberly who came to Hampden Township from Lancaster County, with his father, when a young boy. John Eberly's father bought a farm of 288 acres of land (a part of which is now owned by the subject of this sketch), where he lived, and on his death his son John inherited that part of the land, which, on his (John's) death, was inherited by Samuel, and on which the latter has since resided. In 1843 Samuel Eberly married Susan, daughter of Christian Garver. She died in 1851, leaving one son and three daughters, of whom one has since died. The following year Samuel Eberly married Frances, a sister of his first wife, and in this year he retired from active farm labors, which he has never resumed. He built for himself, in 1877, a substantial and commodious brick residence on the Pittsburgh & Harrisburg Turnpike, which intersects his farm. The house denotes that he is a man of taste and refinement, being much superior in appearance and internal arrangement to the majority of the houses in the valley. His family consists of his wife; his son, Simon, now forty years of age, who married Ellen, daughter of Samuel Bashore, an old settler and near neighbor; Sarah A., wife of John Strong, residing on a farm in Silver Spring Township, owned by Mr. Eberly; Mary, wife of Benj. F. Zimmerman, who also lives on a farm, owned by her father, in Hampden Tp.; these are the children by his first wife, as was also Frances, who married J. B. Lindeman (he built a house immediately adjoining Mr. Eberly's, and they had just moved into it when Mrs. Lindeman died). By his second wife, who died February 22, 1886, Mr. Eberly has five daughters: Elizabeth, wife of Abram A. Bowman of Hampden Township; Kate, wedded to Jacob S. Miley, of Silver Spring Township; and Ellen, Emma, and Ida, living at home. Mr. Eberly has accumulated large means. He owns five farms: The one on which he lives contains 176 acres, for which he gave $12,000 to his father's estate; one in Silver Spring Township, 126 acres, which cost $10,775; one of 128 acres in Hampden Township, for which he gave $14,000; one of 105 acres, in Silver Spring township, cost him $13,573; and another in Silver Spring Township, costing $18,000. Besides these, he bought, in 1869, a farm on the turnpike, of 132 acres, which cost him, including improvements, over $30,000 (this latter farm he subsequently deeded to his son Simon, for much less consideration). He has also property of other kinds. Since 1851 he has been largely engaged in the business of settling estates, having been administrator, executor, trustee, guardian, or agent for no less than fifty-two estates, few of which are now unsettled. He has also written twenty-nine wills, his neighbors knowing his sterling worth, good judgment, and strong common sense, insisting on him acting for them. He has written, since 1861, 1,762 letters, of which he keeps a record. Mr. Eberly is practically a self-made man. Starting in life with scarcely any education, he is a bright example of what may be accomplished by rigid adherence to truth, justice and right, backed by industry. First, a poor and comparatively uneducated lad, to-day no man in the community stands higher among all classes of people. That he may long be spared to his family, and for the benefit of the people who depend so largely upon his family, is the sincere wish of all who know him.

BENJAMIN ERB, farmer, P. O. Mechanicsburg, is the youngest son of Benjamin and Susan (Sadler) Erb, born in 1843, on his father's farm, a part of which he now owns and lives upon; it embraces most of the land between two bends of the Conodoguinet Creek, which bounds it on three sides. After his father's death Benjamin's elder brother, Joseph, bought the farm from the estate, and two years later sold seventy-seven acres on the point to Benjamin. Here Benjamin erected a new brick house and barns. His father was a native of East Pennsborough Township, this county, and lived in Wormleysburg; he bought a farm in that township, which he afterward sold. He then removed to the farm now occupied by his sons. Benjamin, the subject of this sketch, lived at home until he was twenty-six years of age, when he married Mary, daughter of Amos Hicks, of Mechanicsburg, Penn.; she died in 1876, leaving a son, Benjamin, Jr., now fifteen years old. In 1881 our subject was again married, this time to Miami, daughter of Peter Plank, of Mechanicsburg, Penn. They have one child, Charles, now three years old. After the death of his father, Mr. Erb farmed his father's farm for two years, and then removed to Shiremanstown; two years later he came back to his farm, and, after remaining here two years, he removed to Mechanicsburg, where he resided for six years. After his marriage with Miss Plank he came back to his farm and has since resided here. He is justly proud of his farm, as well as of his fine stock. Mr. Erb has never held office, and could scarcely be induced to accept any, but his neighbors may not be disposed always to acquiesce in that decision. Should he be induced to accept a public position, his character is sufficient guarantee that he will worthily fill it.

CHRISTIAN HERTZLER, farmer, P. O. Mechanicsburg, was born April 30, 1833, near Millersville, Lancaster Co., Penn. His father, likewise named Christian, was also born in Lancaster County, where he lived until our subject was four years old, when he removed to Monroe Township, this county, where he resided until his death, about twelve years since. On this farm young Christian worked until he was twenty-four years of age, at which time he married Eliza, daughter of Jacob Mumma, of Mechanicsburg, and took a farm of his father's, which he worked successfully for nine years, when he resold it to his father and bought his present farm of 110 acres, adding largely to the buildings and making it one of the best in the township, showing every evidence of thrift and comfort. To Christian Hertzler, Jr., and wife have been born nine children, who are now living, and two who died while quite young. The names and ages of those living are Anna Mary, twenty-five, wife of Elias Shelley, of Upper Allen Township; Martin Wilmer, twenty-three; Alice Jane, twenty-two; Ira Mumma, twenty; Cora May, fifteen; Christian Elmer, thirteen; Ella Eliza, eleven; Jacob Ray, nine; and Ada Grace, four. The last named five attend the Pike School. Mr. Hertzler has not been an office seeker, and has never held an office, except that of school trustee. In politics he is, like all the Hertzlers, a staunch Republican. He and his wife are members of the Slate Hill Mennonite Church, near Shiremanstown, and live up to their professions of religion, enjoying the confidence and esteem of all who know them.

JOHN LININGER, farmer, P. O. Good Hope, was born near where he now lives, in 1837, a son of Jacob and Eliza (Monasmith) Lininger, both natives of this county. His grandfather was born in Franklin County, whence he came to this county, where his son, Jacob, was born and reared, but about thirty-five years ago he removed to Iowa, where he still lives. At the age of four years John was adopted by John Basehore, who owned the farm where Mr. Lininger lives. John worked for his foster father until 1854, when he went to Mechanicsburg to learn the trade of carpenter. At this he worked for four years, when he married Miss Mary Jane Basehore, a niece of his foster father. John then took charge of the farm until Mr. Basehore's death, in 1870, when the farm was bequeathed him for a consideration. He has had three children, of whom one is now living: John B., now (1886) twenty-six years of age, who is married to Susan, daughter of Henry O. Booser, of East Pennsborough Township. Mr. Lininger has, for the past twenty years, had to contend against the misfortune, which then happened to him, of losing his right hand in a threshing machine. Five years ago Mr. Lininger was duly elected and ordained a minister of the River Brethren, and is also actively engaged in the management of his farm: on Sundays officiating in his ministerial capacity wherever services are held, the Brethren having no church edifice in the district, services being mainly held in the residences of members, and sometimes in edifices owned by other denominations. Mr. Lininger is regarded, not only by members of his own church, but by all who know him, as a man of strictest probity and integrity.

WILLIAM B. LOGAN, farmer, P. O. Good Hope, was born near where he now lives, in 1845, son of William Logan, a native of Lebanon County, Penn., who came to this county in 1842, and died in 1878. His grandfather, likewise a native of Lebanon, named William, died during the war of 1812. Our subject lived on the home farm until 1867, when he married Mary J., daughter of Christian C Rupp, of Silver Spring Township, this county. They have seven children: Abner C., Dessie Kate, John D., Frances Lizzie

Blanche, Ira N. and Mary. Two other children died in infancy. Mr. Logan taught school from 1861 until 1883. On the death of his father, in 1878, he purchased his present farm from the estate, remodeling the dwelling, building a new barn, etc., and then rented it until 1882, when he occupied it himself, combining farming with school-teaching. In 1884 he was elected county auditor, which position he now holds. He and his wife are communicants of Salem Methodist Episcopal Church. Mr. Logan is still a young man, with every prospect of a useful and honorable career before him, and is universally esteemed. He will fill, with credit to himself and satisfaction to his constituents, any position to which he may be chosen. In politics he is a Democrat.

JAMES E. MARTIN, farmer, P. O. Good Hope, lives on the farm on which he was born in October, 1851, on the banks of the Conodoguinet Creek, near Lindeman's mill. His father, James Martin, is also a native of this county, and formerly cultivated the farm on which his son James E. now lives, but retired in 1871, and now lives with his daughter, Elizabeth, wife of William Sherban, in Mechanicsburg, Penn. Our subject's mother was Caroline, daughter of Peter Fessler, of Harrisburg, Penn. James E. Martin lived with his father until the latter gave up the farm; then our subject went to live with Mr. Sherban, at Oyster's Point. In 1881 Mr. Martin married Miss Alice, daughter of William Sadler, of Camp Hill, East Pennsborough Township, this county, and they have one child, Willie, a particularly bright little boy of three years. After their marriage Mr. and Mrs. Martin removed to the farm. Mr. Martin has, besides Mrs. Sherban, another sister, Jennie, wife of John Funk, of Springfield, Ohio. Mrs. Martin has four sisters: Nettie, Laura, Emma and Effie. Laura is wedded to Jacob Worst, of Upper Allen Township, this county. The others are unmarried and live at home. Mr. Martin, it will be seen, is quite a young man, who, it is to be hoped, has a long and useful career before him. He is industrious and careful, and a gentleman of excellent character, and deserves success.

JOHN M. RUPP, farmer, P. O. Mechanicsburg, is one of the descendants of John Jonas Rupp, who came to this county from Reihen, Grand Duchy of Baden, in 1751, and first located in Lancaster County, or what is now known as Lebanon County. He was the progenitor of the numerous family of Rupps which are found scattered all over this part of the country. From Lebanon he came to Cumberland County, and built the stone house now occupied by the subject of this sketch, and lived there until his death. One of his sons was Martin, grandfather of John M., who lived for a time on a farm near the stone church, of which he was one of the principal builders. He afterward removed to the Samuel Eberly farm, where John, father of our subject, was born January 17, 1801. The following April John Jonas Rupp died, and Martin took possession of the house, and at his death, in 1843, left it to his son John, who had married, in 1840, Anna, daughter of John Markley, who kept the old Trendle Spring tavern. Mr. and Mrs. John Rupp had a family of three sons and four daughters, all of whom died young, except Mary, wife of Charles Hertzler, and John M. The subject of this sketch was born in March, 1844. He and his sisters inherited the house and farm on the death of their father in 1872. Mr. Rupp is thus the direct representative of the original founder of the family in this county. In October, 1873, he married Ellen, daughter of Jacob Spidle, of Hampden Township, and they have two boys and two girls: John M., Jr., Jacob S., Maggie E. and Naomi; all attending school. In early life Mr. Rupp dealt in patent rights; was also engaged in mining enterprises, but now gives his attention and entire time to his farm, which affords him ample occupation. His farm comprises 117 acres, and is one of the most fertile in the valley. He is a member of the Allen & East Pennsborough Society for the Recovery of Stolen Horses and Mules, and the Detection of Thieves. He is also a life member of the Horticultural Fair Company of Mechanicsburg, where he makes yearly exhibits. Among other curiosities which he has shown there is some soap made by his great-grandfather, and a specimen of the first apple-butter ever made in the county. He is a member of the Dunkard Church in Upper Allen Township, and is a man of excellent report among his neighbors.

JOHN SHAEFFER, farmer, P. O. Good Hope, is a native of Hampden Township, this county, born on the old Shaeffer farm, at the foot of the Blue Mountains, in 1829. His father, John Shaeffer, was born on the same place, which his grandfather bought shortly after arriving in this country from Germany. This property is still held by the family, being now in the hands of John and his two brothers. At the age of twenty-one years John Shaeffer went West, but returned two years later, and engaged in the profession of school-teaching for the ensuing twelve years, farming in the summers. In 1862 he married Elizabeth A., daughter of Christian C. Rupp, of Silver Spring Township, this county. In 1864 he gave up school-teaching and gave his whole time to farm work. In 1871 he again began teaching, and taught for three years in Hampden, and one year in Hogestown. Then he again farmed for two years in Silver Spring Township, and while a resident of New Kingston, in that township, he was elected clerk of the courts and recorder, which position he filled for three years. On the expiration of his term of office, he bought the farm on which he lives, and now gives his attention exclusively to it. He has three daughters: Flora Jane, Bertha Frances and Alta Mary, who live with their parents. In his official position Mr. Shaeffer made many friends by the thorough and conscientious

HAMPDEN TOWNSHIP.

manner in which he performed his duties, and should he again be called to serve his fellow-citizens, which is likely, he will bring to the discharge of his duties the same sterling qualities which have distinguished his past career. He is one of the citizens of the county who must inevitably take a leading part in the administration of its affairs. He and his wife and two elder daughters are communicants of Salem Methodist Episcopal Church in Hampden Township.

ANDREW SHEELY, farmer, P. O. Mechanicsburg, is one of the oldest residents of the county, having been born near where he now lives, March 16, 1806. His father, John Sheely, was also born on the same farm, and died before the war of the Rebellion. Our subject's mother died while the Confederate forces were at Chambersburg, and, as Andrew Sheely says, was buried somewhat hastily for fear of a raid. Our subject's grandfather, also a resident of this county, when a young man went to Germany in search of a fortune said to have been left to him, but returned without it, and settled down to farming, in which he was successful, owning four farms at the time of his death. Andrew Sheely has seven children living—four daughters and three sons. His eldest son, William, in 1861, at the age of twenty-one years, enlisted in the Twentieth Regiment Pennsylvania Volunteer Infantry, and three months afterward, while carrying dispatches, attempted to ford the Potomac River on horseback, at a place known as "Sir John's Run," and was drowned; his body was recovered by his comrades, was sent home and was buried in the cemetery attached to St. John's Lutheran Church, near by. He was one of the first of Cumberland County's heroes to give up his life for his country. One daughter of our subject is also deceased—Fanny, wife of Martin Wise. The children now living are Catherine (wedded to Solomon Beck, farmer, of Hampden Township), Elizabeth (wife of William Koser of Mechanicsburg), Susan (wife of John Blair, of East Pennsborough Township), Samuel (married to Margaret Bosley), Mary Ann (keeping house for her father), John (residing in Shiremanstown and married to Becky, daughter of Benjamin Spong), Levi (married to Sarah, daughter of David Sheaffer). Until he was about twenty-five years of age, Andrew Sheely lived with his father. He then married Fanny, daughter of John Eichelberger, of Lower Allen Township, and moved to the farm he now occupies, and on which he has ever since resided. His wife died in 1884. Although in his eightieth year, Mr. Sheely carries on his farm himself, and is hale and hearty. He is a consistent member of the Lutheran Church and enjoys the respect and esteem of the entire community.

JOHN SHOPP, retired farmer, near Shiremanstown, was born July 6, 1794, on the place where he now resides. His farm is one of the original tracts, called "Manington," for which a warrant was granted May 17, 1767, by Thomas and John Penn. After but two intermediate transfers, it was purchased, September 20, 1774, by Ulrich Shopp, grandfather of our subject, and has continued in the ownership of the family ever since. Ulrich Shopp left, *inter alia*, a son John, who married a Miss Annie Hershey, and they had eleven children: Elizabeth, Magdalena, Christian, John (our subject), Sarah, Samuel, Jacob, Annie, Fannie, Catharine and David. They were a long-lived family. Magdalena died when a child, David in his seventieth year, and the others at ages ranging from eighty to eighty-nine years. John is the sole survivor. He was born in the small log schoolhouse which now stands near St. John's Church, one-fourth mile from his farm, but which at that time was near the site of his present residence. He followed farming until about twenty years ago, when he retired, and has since been engaged in no special active business. He has long been an active member of the United Brethren Church, the first edifice belonging to that denomination in the neighborhood having been built on land which he gave for that purpose, together with sufficient ground for a grave-yard. In January, 1841, he married Nancy, daughter of Martin and Fannie Nissley, of Dauphin County. She died July 7, 1841. March 16, 1843, he married Louisa, daughter of Rev. John Crider, who was born October 11, 1806, near Chambersburg, Penn. They had two sons, one of whom died in infancy; the other is J. H. Shopp, Esq., of Harrisburg, who was born January 20, 1850. He was educated at Dickinson College, from which he was graduated in 1872. Afterward he read law, and was admitted to the bar of Dauphin County, February 9, 1878. In 1881 he entered into partnership in the practice of law with Hon. David Mumma, one of the prominent citizens of that place. April 8, 1884, Mr. Shopp married Alice M., daughter of George Cunkle (deceased), formerly of Hurrrisburg. The elder Mr. Shopp has a singularly bright recollection of matters pertaining to the early history of this section of Cumberland County, covering the greater part of the present century, and communicates his recollections in a clear and entertaining manner. Throughout his long life he has ever borne the reputation of a man of unblemished character, and has had in a large degree the esteem and respect of his neighbors, who hope to see him live to the full measure of a century.

ELI C. SHUMAN, farmer, P. O. Good Hope, is a native of Manor Township, Lancaster Co., Penn., born January 1, 1830; his father, Jacob B. Shuman, and his grandfather, Christian Shuman, were also natives of Lancaster County, as were also his mother and grandmother. His mother's maiden name was Fanny Urban, and his grandmother's name was Anna Brenneman. In 1851 he married Elizabeth, daughter of Bernard Mann, of the same place, and continued to live on his father's farm until 1860, when his father bought the farm in Hampden Township, where they still live. He has a family of seven daughters and two sons. His daughter Laura is married to Jacob Bretz, son of Jacob Bretz, Sr., a farmer, of the same township; Elizabeth is the wife of George Dietz, son of Chrn. Dietz, of the same township; Catharine is the wife of David V. Kapp, son of Wm. Kapp, of Silver Spring Township, this county; the other children are unmarried, their names are Maggie, Harriet, Ida, Fannie B., B. Frank and Albert N. Mr. Shuman devotes his whole time to farming. He and his wife and two of the daughters are members of the Methodist Episcopal Church, at Salem.

GEORGE W. SHUMBERGER, teacher and merchant, P. O. Good Hope, is a well known young man in Hampden Township, this county, where he was born and raised. Both his parents are natives of this county and live in Hampden Township, where his father carries on the tailoring business. George W. was born in 1855; remained at home working for his father on a farm he was cultivating, until twenty years of age, when he engaged in the profession of teaching, for which he had qualified himself by persistent study, having attended normal school but one term. In 1878 he married Sallie, daughter of John Simmons, of Silver Spring Township This union has been blessed with four daughters. Our subject continued teaching until 1883, when he purchased the general store at Good Hope, this county (formerly conducted by Samuel McGaw), and the same year he was appointed postmaster. The following year he resumed teaching, which he still continues, his wife assisting him in his other business. Mr. Shumberger has been twice elected justice of the peace, but would not serve; he has been township clerk and auditor, and inspector of elections, the duties of which positions he performed with fidelity and care. He is emphatically a self-taught and self-made man, universally esteemed for his exemplary conduct and character. Both he and his wife are consistent members of the United Brethren Church, of which he is an elder.

AMOS C. WERTZ, fence builder, P. O. Good Hope, is a native of this county, born in Monroe Township in 1840. His father, Samuel Wertz, still lives, aged eighty years. His mother, nee Elizabeth Fry, died six years ago. Both parents were natives of York County, Penn. The father of Samuel Wertz was a native of Baltimore, Md., and died in York County, Penn., when Samuel was but six years old. Samuel learned the trade of shoe-making, and, notwithstanding his advanced age, still carries it on in Silver Spring Township, his son Adam doing the more active part of the work. Amos C. Wertz, when eleven years old, hired out on a farm until he was eighteen years of age, when he went to Ohio, where he stayed four years, and from there enlisted, in 1862, in the Ninety-fourth Regiment Ohio Volunteer Infantry. Six weeks later he was captured and sent to the Confederate prison at Versailles, Ky., where he was soon paroled, and, after experiencing many hardships, made his way to Columbus, Ohio. He soon re-enlisted in the general mounted service of the Regular Army, and his record is a brilliant one. In August, 1865, he received his discharge (as sergeant), and on the back of it the officer mustering him out has put a list of the battles and skirmishes in which our subject took part, numbering thirty-five. This splendid record is one to which he can point with just pride. He received several wounds, but fortunately has not been permanently disabled, although he will always feel their effects. In 1869 Mr. Wertz was married to Rebecca, daughter of William Miller, of Hampden Township, this county; they have no children. Mr. Wertz has been school director and secretary of the board for four years, auditor six years and collector two years. In every position to which he has been chosen he has faithfully discharged its duties. An intelligent and upright man, a brave soldier and a good citizen, he has always borne himself with honor, and has acquired the respect of all who know him.

GEORGE WILT, farmer, P. O. Good Hope, is a native of East Pennsborough Township, this county, as was also his father, John Wilt. His grandfather came from Germany many years ago. Our subject was born in 1822, and ten years later his father died on the farm where our subject now resides, to which he had removed two years previously (it belonged at that time to the estate of George Mann). At his death he left four children: George; Catherine, wife of Samuel Newcomer, of Mechanicsburg; Mary, who died a few years after the death of her father; and Elizabeth, wife of Christian Dietz. After the death of his father George continued to live on the farm, which was rented to Frederick Muma, who farmed it for seven years. About four years after her husband's death, Mrs. Wilt bought the farm at an appraised valuation, and at the time specified took charge of it herself, and with the aid of her son conducted it for twenty-nine years; she then rented the farm until her death in 1874. George bought his sister's interest in the farm, and became sole owner. He has never married, is no politician, and has never held any office, except that of school director, his farm of 156 acres demanding his whole time and attention. He is spoken of by all who know him as a man of the highest character.

CHAPTER XLVIII.

HOPEWELL TOWNSHIP AND BOROUGH OF NEWBURG.

ZACHARIAS BASEHORE, farmer, P. O. Newburg. Of the remote ancestry of this branch of the Basehore family but little data can be obtained, but it is probable that they were natives of Lebanon County, Penn., as William, the father of our subject, came from that county. He was married in Cumberland County, Penn., to Susannah Orris, about 1837, and had probably been a resident here as early as 1830. By trade he was a shoe-maker, and soon after marriage settled in Lizertsburg, North Middleton Township. His wife was born in this county, a daughter of Christopher and Margaret (Bistline) Orris, who for many years were residents of Cumberland Valley. Zacharias, the eldest son, was born in 1840, and later other children followed, viz.: Isaac, Maria, and one that died in infancy. In 1849 the death of the father occurred, and in 1854 the mother was laid to rest in the village cemetery. The children were thus separated—Isaac was taken care of by William Lutman, of Perry County; Maria resided with Alexander Corman, of North Middleton Township, with whom she found a comfortable home until her marriage with George Drawbaugh, a member of one of the old families of this county. Our subject had to earn his own living from the age of nine. He was first put in charge of an uncle, Christopher Orris, and two years later was indentured to Jacob B. Hoover, who was to find him suitable clothing in return for his work, and to give him a good freedom suit at the age of fourteen. When our hero arrived at that age he found himself a lusty lad with a suit worth 75 cents on his back, not a dollar in his pocket, but with the world before him. His first venture was an engagement to Jacob Nickey for $6 per month; that winter he also attended school, and he had previously managed to pick up a fair education. From this date he received better wages, and after his marriage commenced farming on his own account. August 15, 1860, he was wedded to Sarah, daughter of Jacob and Julia Christlieb, and a member of one of the most important families in Mifflin Township, this county. Their domestic life was commenced on the John Ahl farm, in Mifflin Township, and four years later Mr. Basehore sold his stock and engaged in different lines of trade, rapidly accumulating money until his purchase of his present farm in 1879. The children born to Mr. and Mrs. Basehore are Mina J, George B. Mc., Sarah E., Laura J., John C., Jacob C., Carrie M., Elizabeth and William. Mina J. is the wife of Daniel Mowery, and Sarah E. is the wife of George Laughlin. The others still remain under the paternal roof. Our subject is a self-made made, and is not only one of the wealthy and influential men of the township, but is allied to a family which for more than a century has been of note and importance in the business and political world.

ADAM HEBERLIG, farmer, Newburg, is a great-grandson of Rudolph Heberlig, who came from Switzerland before the Revolutionary war and settled in Berks County, between Reading and Adamstown, Penn. He was twice married, and by the first wife had four children: John and Rudy, and two daughters whose names are unknown. Of these, John was married in Berks County, Penn., to Martha Schoenhour, and had six sons: Rudy, John, Jacob, Samuel, Benjamin, Joseph, and two daughters, Mary and Elizabeth. In 1811 the family immigrated to this county and settled at Glenn's mill, near Newville, where they both resided until their death. John Heberlig, the father of our subject, was married to Barbara Failor, December 20, 1821, who bore him four children: Jane John, Joseph and Christopher. She died December 11, 1827, and January 29, 1829, he was again married, this time to Margaret Failor, a sister of his first wife, and to this union were born seven children: Adam, Benjamin, Margaret, Elizabeth, William, Mary J. and Benjamin F. (the first son bearing the name dying in infancy). John Heberlig purchased 314 acres of land in Hopewell Township, this county, in 1829, and in 1854 he bought the farm now owned by his sons Adam and Benjamin F., and in 1864 the farm where he now resides. He has been noted during his long life for energy and perseverance, and, perhaps, no man has done more for the improvement of this township—purchasing tract after tract of land, making substantial improvements and erecting fine residences on each. His second wife died December 17, 1867, since when he has resided with his daughter, Elizabeth, widow of Benjamin Hefflefinger. He was born February 23, 1795, has been a farmer all his life, and when the writer called was shoveling snow with the ease of a man fifty years of age. Of his immediate family only himself and one sister, Elizabeth Lehman, now a widow of eighty-seven years, are living. Adam, eldest son of John Heberlig by second wife, was born October 16, 1829. He was reared on the homestead farm, and his education was obtained in the common schools of this township, and until his marriage he remained with his father. In 1854 he engaged with his brother Joseph in farming. April 17, 1856, he was united in marriage, by Rev. David Hefflefinger, with Elizabeth, daughter of John and Jane (Beatty) Schulenbarger, of Mifflin Township, this county. In October of that year he brought his young wife to the pleasant home they now occupy, and here were born their children: Margaret J., Mary A., Martha E., George B. Mc., Myra B., William M. and Annie L., all living except the eldest, who died November 19, 1861. Our subject has been one of the most successful farmers of his township. He is known as a leader in politics in his neighborhood. His well-known business qualifications were early recognized by the people, and, in 1861, he was elected assessor, and with but short intervals has been an official to date. In 1883 he was elected director of the poor, which office he still holds. He has filled every office within the gift of the people of his township, except three minor offices, which of itself is proof of his popularity.

JOSEPH F. HEBERLIG, farmer, P. O. Newburg, is the second son of John and Barbara (Failor) Heberlig; was born October 12, 1825 in the old stone house near Glenn's mill in Newton Township, this county, on the place his father first settled after coming to Cumberland County. Until he was twenty-three years of age our subject worked for and made his home with his father. His first business experience for himself was in 1852, when he farmed the homestead on shares, and the next year in partnership with his brother Adam. December 7, 1853, he was united in marriage with Catharine A., daughter of Peter and Margaret Myers, of Adams County. Their married life was begun in the house which he purchased in 1858, and there his children were born: John C., Margaret J. (married to Samuel G. Lehner, December 18, 1877), Peter H. (deceased) Andrew R. (married Emma Spangler, December 26, 1882), Jeremiah H. (deceased) and Mary A. (deceased). Mr. Heberlig has been quite a prominent man in the township from the beginning of his business life. In recognition of his capabilities and worth he has been repeatedly elected to office, and several terms has served as inspector, school director, judge of election, and two terms as supervisor. As an enterprising agriculturist his farm gives the best evidence. As a man the voice of his neighbors tell the story; as an official his re-election verifies all that has been said.

BENJAMIN F. HEBERLIG, farmer, P. O. Newburg, is the youngest son of John Heberlig; was born in 1844 on the ancestral farm. He remained with his father until his marriage, in 1868, with Miss Harriet L., daughter of Henry and Catherine Holby, at that time residents of Hopewell Township, this county. The ashes of both now mingle with the silent dust, their demise occurring at the home of Mr. Heberlig. The home life of the young couple was begun on the farm which is now their residence, and which was a part of the third tract purchased by his father. Seven children have blessed their union, of whom Albert E., Anna J., Charles F., John W. and Bessie May, are living. In 1880 Mr. and Mrs. Heberlig removed to Hedgesville, W. Va., remaining there four years, and while a resident there Mr. Herberlig was honored by being elected mayor, and since his return to Pennsylvania he has served as judge of election. While in Virginia Mr. Heberlig was engaged in the lumber business, of which he made a success. He owns and operates a saw-mill near his present residence and within a few rods of the old site of a mill built by his father in 1853. In 1869 he purchased his present farm, and which will probably be his home for years.

DAVID HEFFLEFINGER, cooper, Newburg. It can positively be asserted that Philip Hefflefinger was a resident of Cumberland County as early as 1780, and prior to coming here, was a resident of Lebanon County, Penn., where he was married to Catharine Eichholtz. He was a fifer during the Revolutionary war and participated in the battles fought in that struggle. It is stated that on one occasion after his return home he asked his mother to bake some cakes, such as soldiers made by cooking their dough in the ashes. "Hunger is the best cook, my son," said his kind old mother, "but I will bake you some." After Philip Hefflefinger came to Hopewell Township, this county, he purchased a farm, which for many years has been known as "Sodom," in consequence of two distilleries and a tannery located there. On this farm Philip and his wife reared the following children: Philip, Jacob, Samuel, John, William, David, Thomas, Mary, Elizabeth and Catharine, of whom William is the only one now living. Thomas, the youngest son, the father of our subject, was a farmer, but devoted part of his time to getting out coopers' supplies and lumber of all kinds, from the fine timber which then abounded here. He was born in 1804; was married in 1827, to Agnes Watson, born August 31, 1803, daughter of William and Susannah (Weicklein) Watson, residents of Newton Township, where some of the descendants yet reside. Thomas Hefflefinger purchased a small farm, half a mile east of the paternal homestead, and in 1840 bought the Boyd farm in the same vicinity, and on this farm lived until his death. His first wife died in 1868, and January 18, 1870, he wedded Mrs. Martha Dougherty, of Roxbury, the ceremony being performed by Rev. William Krouse. Mrs. Martha Hefflefinger's maiden name was Shoemaker, and she was descended from old Roxbury ancestry. On the first farm were born William, David, Thomas, Alexander, Joseph, John and a daughter (deceased). On the Boyd farm were born Benjamin, Ann E., Agnes, Sarah J., Philip (deceased) and Adahzillah. The father

HOPEWELL TOWNSHIP.

died in 1878 and his widow in 1880. David, our subject, was born September 5, 1829. His boyhood was passed on the farm and his education was gained in the common schools. He remained at home until of age, and in 1851 went to Orrstown, Franklin Co., Penn., and there learned brick-making. In the autumn of the same year he commenced the cooper's trade in Greenwood. He was married, in 1855, to Elizabeth J., daughter of Cornelius and Mary (Mumper) Baker, of Perry County, Penn. Henry Mumper was a prominent distiller and farmer, wagoned on the road and so on to Baltimore, residing near Germantown, Penn. Of the ten children born to this union seven are living: Mary E. A., Sarah A., William A., Annie L., John C., Thomas M., and Elice E. Frank H., an infant, and David C., are deceased. Mary E. A. is the wife of George H. McCoy; Sarah A. wedded Jacob A. Burkholder, and William A. married Emma Clippinger. In 1856 our subject established a shop in Mifflin Township, this county, and also made bricks at the same time in Perry, Franklin and Cumberland Counties. In 1860 he came to Newburg, and has continued brick-making and coopering in the village to date. In all his undertakings he has been successful and has accumulated a competence.

JOHN HENSEL, retired, Newburg, was born July 28, 1821, in this county, on a farm (now his property) which has been in possession of the Hensel family for sixty-seven years. Christian Hensel, his father, was born January 15, 1794, and came from Saxony, settled there in 1816, and was married in 1820 to Mary Shoemaker, born March 17, 1785. He had nothing when he came to this county; was a baker in Saxony and learned to still in America, and before his marriage had saved $200, which he invested in 200 acres of land. He built a distillery on the farm and for many years worked at his trade. John, his eldest son, relates that when a small boy he attended the still sometimes during the afternoons, and although a man sixty-five years of age has never tasted a drop of liquor, has never used tobacco, and has never sworn an oath in his life. The land was very poor at that time, but it has been brought up to a high state of cultivation and now brings large returns. To Christian Hensel and his wife were born three children, of whom John, born in 1821, and Elizabeth, born in 1823, reached adult age. The mother died in 1851 and the father in 1867. John Hensel was one of the few children anxious for the welfare of their parents, and remained with his father until he died, and was forty-five years of age before celebrating his marriage, October 22, 1874, with Sophia Nicholas, who secured a husband noted alike for his honesty and kindness. This union has been blessed with two sons: Charles C. and John H.; the former born October 4, 1875, and the latter April 28, 1879. Mrs. Hensel is thirty-eight years of age, and perhaps no better mated couple can be found in the township. She was a daughter of Charles Nicholas, who is now in the West. John Hensel succeeded to his father's estate, to which he has added by good management. The Hensels have ever been noted for their liberality, and many poor people of Hopewell have cause to remember their many acts of kindness.

HENRY HURSH, hotel proprietor, Newburg. Henry Hursh, grandfather of our subject, was born in Pennsylvania 143 years ago, and from the most authentic information to be obtained was a resident, from the time of his birth, of Fairview Township, York County. His father had three children: Abraham, Henry and Susan, each of whom inherited large farms in that neighborhood. Henry was married as early as 1793, but to whom can not be learned, and three children were born: John, Joseph and Henry. Of these, John, the eldest, was born in 1794; married Barbara Brookart about 1817, and commenced married life on a part of the grandfather's homestead, to which was added, by subsequent purchase, the Asten farm; and on this land were born nine children; Henry, our subject; John, married to Sarah Livingston; Joseph, married to — Hogan; Abraham, married to — Frank; Elizabeth, widow of George Rupp, and David, married to — Hale, are residents of Cumberland County. The deceased are Daniel, Susan and Mary. Our subject was born May 17, 1819, and remained with his father until his marriage, in 1841, with Catharine, daughter of Henry Deitz, of York County, Penn. His father owned a distillery, which Henry managed from the time he was old enough to attend to the business until after his marriage, when he tried farming on his own account. In 1843 he and his brother purchased the farm now owned by the Westhafer heirs. Farming was too dull for Henry Hursh, however, and he erected on this farm a hotel, which was known as the "Bulls Head," and was a great resort for cattle drovers, then very numerous in this county; he was a popular landlord, and made money in the business. In 1852 he left the "Bulls Head," and became proprietor of the "Big Springs Hotel," where he established a fine reputation for the hostelry. This place had been a losing investment for its former proprietors, but the cordiality and good business qualifications of the new host brought its usual reward, and he reaped a golden harvest. He also engaged in the stock business about the year 1855, with Col. Gracy and John Brown as partners. Later he purchased the "Black Horse" hotel in Shippensburg, which he conducted for a number of years, and then engaged in selling farming implements and cattle. Nothing proved so congenial to him, however, as hotel life, and again he took possession of the "Big Spring Hotel," and later the "Union Hotel," in Shippensburg. The next year he engaged in the wholesale and retail liquor business, in which he continued till the local option law was passed, when he removed to Hagerstown, Md. After the repeal of that law he returned to Shippensburg, where he carried on the same business two years more. Again the hotel business was an inducement to him, and for the third time he became proprietor of the "Big Spring Hotel;" and after his two years' lease had expired he took charge of a new hotel at Shippensburg, Penn., and three years later he took charge of the "Exchange," at Newburg, and he has lost none of his popularity as caterer to the tastes of the public. Three children were born to Mr. and Mrs. Hursh: Adaline (deceased), Daniel and Ann, who is housekeeper for her father.

FREDERICK B. LEBERKNIGHT, physician, Newburg. The great-grandfather, Leberknight, came from Germany; his son, Frederick, resided in Lightersburg Md., and was the father of seven children, of whom Daniel (the father of our subject) was by trade a weaver, an occupation he followed in the village of Green Castle for forty years. He was sober and industrious, and was not married until the age of forty, when he won the affections of Mrs. Susan (Kuhn) Reymer, a widow, and at that time the mother of seven children. To this union were born the following children: Daniel C., Frederick B., John and Adam. John died when twenty years of age. The father concluded to rear his large family on a farm, and, after a few moves, settled on the Wilson farm, at Back Creek, on the Loudon road, Franklin County, Penn., and there all were taught to work and were given a practical education at the common schools. The mother of these children died in 1854, and Mr. Leberknight married Mrs. Elizabeth Holland, who had at that time one son—Koser. The fruit of this union was James G., Maggie, Martha, Sarah, and Susan. In this large family, comprising four sets of children, the utmost harmony prevailed. The last wife died in 1885, and the aged father is still living at Cheesetown, eighty-one years old. Of the four sons by the first marriage, three were graduates of Jefferson Medical College, of Philadelphia, Penn.; Adam K., is practicing at Orrstown, Penn.; Daniel, at Lemaster's, Franklin County; and Frederick B., at Newburg. Our subject, prior to his graduation, taught school, and afterward studied medicine with Drs. Richards & Montgomery, of Chambersburg. He entered Jefferson College in 1871, and after taking two full courses, went to Lathrop, Mo., where he practiced one year. Returning in 1873, he completed his course and graduated with honor. He then located in Newburg, this township. In 1874 he was married to Sarah, daughter of Andrew and Charlotte A. Elder, of Chambersburg, Penn. After a four years' practice at Newburg he went to Bellevue Hospital Medical College, New York, and graduated there in 1879. Since that date his practice has been an uninterrupted one in this village. The Doctor and his wife have had two children: Bessie, born six years after their marriage, died six weeks after birth, and Vernon B., born in 1882. The Doctor was the preceptor of all his brothers, and in connection with his fine literary attainments, is a graduate of two of the best Eastern medical colleges. His popularity is only equaled by his success as a physician.

JOSEPH McELWAIN, retired, P. O. Newburg. The remote ancestry of this family in this country dates back much more than a century, for Ebenezer (father of subject) was born to Joseph McElwain, near Eckhard's mill, about 1717. His parents had resided in this country prior to that date. Although the territory on this side of Conodoguinet Creek then belonged to the Indians, a number of whites were living on it, and sometimes when a quarrel would arise the settlers would fly for safety across the creek, which was considered the boundary line. A building was burned near the residence of the McElwains about 1720, and the occupants (Mr. White and family) were all murdered, except a little child, who was rescued. Jean, a daughter, was born in 1802 (to Joseph McElwain), followed by Mary, Joseph, Andrew, William, Elizabeth and Ebenezer. Ebenezer McElwain was married, September 24, 1801, to Elizabeth Crow and after their marriage they settled near "Three Square Hollow," and there their children were born. Our subject learned the trade of miller, and for many years operated a saw and grist mill erected by his father in an early day. He was married, in May, 1848, to Elizabeth, daughter of James and Elizabeth Cook, of Perry County, Penn. This union has been blessed with nine children, six living: Sarah J., wife of John Mowery; Amanda, wife of Thomas Diven; Margaret, wife of Ira Fylar; Mary, wife of Allen Kuhn; Joseph A. and Laura B. All were born on the homestead, near the mill, where so many of their name have been born and reared. Joseph McElwain has always been an exceptionally prosperous man, and during the years spent in the Hollow amassed a nice competency. In 1875 he disposed of the mill and purchased the fine farm on which he now resides. The log house was erected more than a century ago, but it contains a family who have long been noted as among the best in the land. Four generations have been born in Cumberland County bearing the name of McElwain.

WINFIELD SCOTT McGAW, liveryman, Newburg, was born in the family homestead in Mifflin Township, this county, October 13, 1837, son of Samuel and Elizabeth McGaw. His father was, undoubtedly, the most popular man of his day, in Mifflin Township, and was elected county commissioner by an immense majority; and at the expiration of his term (so well were his duties discharged) his constituents were almost a unit in favor of his re-election. It had been an axiom, however, with the Democratic party that a man should only serve in this position one official term, and the dissatisfaction ensuing by putting forth another candidate caused a disruption of the party which

HOPEWELL TOWNSHIP. 489

was not healed for many years. Finely educated, possessed of a brilliant mind and unquestionable honesty, Samuel McGaw was intrusted with the settlement of more estates than any other man in the history of his township. In fact he allowed his own business to suffer in consequence of his faithfulness to the interests of others. Too much can not be said in his praise, or in that of his son George, who, as mentioned elsewhere, was a brave soldier, and enacted the story of Damon and Pythias, for, in attempting to make the last moments of a dying soldier (David Carl) comfortable, he was taken prisoner, when by leaving him to die alone he could easily have escaped, but true to the vow they had made to each other before leaving home, his life paid the forfeit, for he starved to death in Libby Prison, leaving a record of honor and courage. Our subject was educated in the public schools, and remained with his father until the spring of 1861, when he took a lengthy trip through the Western States. Returning in the autumn of the same year, he made arrangements for commencing business. February 13, 1862, he was married to Sadie A., daughter of Samuel and Barbara (Bear) Stevick, of this county. Their married life was commenced on the J. V. Bowman farm, in Whisky Run District. To this union have been born six children: David S., Minnie B., Frank L., Joseph C., Mable G. (living) and Thomas E. (deceased). Our subject continued agricultural pursuits, in Mifflin and West Pennsborough Townships, until 1873, when he removed to the pleasant village of Newburg, and for eight consecutive years carried the United States mail from Newburg to Newville, since which time he has had the passenger route between Newburg and Shippensburg. He is the only liveryman in Newburg, and is as full of enterprise as were his ancestors in the early days of this county's history. Perhaps no sketch will give greater interest to this section of the county than that of the McGaw family, who, from first to last, have been among the most honorable and enterprising men.

JOHN and SAMUEL H. MITCHELL, farmers, Newburg. John Mitchell, the grandfather, came from County Antrim, Ireland, about 1760, and settled on the farm, now the property of our subjects. At that time the lands in this neighborhood were nearly all subject to pre-emption, and he received a warrant for about 300 acres. At that date his uncle, Samuel Mitchell, resided on the tract now owned by Joseph Heberlig, but just when Samuel Mitchell came to this country can not be ascertained. John Mitchell was married, after locating his land, to Miss Mary Irwin, about 1773. The young couple went to work with a will, and ere long a log house and log barn were erected, both of which are yet standing, in a good state of preservation, and in the barn loft is still hay and straw which were placed there before the Revolutionary war. The historian learns of no buildings ante-dating them in the county that are still serviceable. The land was then in its primitive state, but with combined energy and muscle John Mitchell soon had a few acres cleared and ready for the plow. With prosperity came also a number of children to gladden their home in the wilderness: Margaret, William, Mary, Martha, Jennette and Elizabeth. Through his wife (Mary Irwin) John Mitchell acquired quite a considerable fortune, as the Irwins were a wealthy and noted family of Scotch origin, who resided near Middle Springs, Franklin (then known as Lancaster) County. Of John Mitchell's children the only son, William (father of our subjects), was born September 2, 1777. He was reared and educated under the old roof tree. During his younger days he was a lieutenant in the militia formed to protect the State and county from invaders; he was one of the most lithe and active men of his times, and enjoyed a great reputation as a runner, and he was as fearless as he was fleet. He was married, about 1817, to Letty McCune, being at that time about forty years of age. Her death occurred as early as 1819, and in 1822 he was married to Mary Hanna. The death of John Mitchell occurred prior to the second marriage of his son, his widow having preceded him a number of years. William Mitchell purchased his sister's interest in their father's estate, and with his last wife began a happy domestic life under the roof which had sheltered the family so many years. Aside from his home duties William was quite a noted politician and swayed a power in his neighborhood, and he was courted alike by Democratic and Republican friends, for as "Billy" voted so voted a majority of his neighbors, and numerous candidates for office owed their election to his earnest support. Of the children born to this good man six are deceased and five living: Elsie J., widow of John Gilmore; John; Mary; Samuel; Elizabeth, wife of John Swartz. Samuel was married, in 1866, to Margaret, daughter of Abraham and Elizabeth Wingert, and on the ancestral farm their married life commenced, and there were born their children: Minerva J., Elizabeth M., Annie M. and William W. (the latter was born in September, 1877, and his grandfather, William Mitchell, in whose honor he was named, in September, 1777). John and Mary Mitchell have never married, and make their home with their brother Samuel and his pleasant family, who revere the spot where for more than a century the family have lived and where their father and grandfather died.

ANDREW MOWERY, farmer, P. O. Newburg, was born in 1829. His grandfather, Andrew Mowery, came from Germany, and settled more than a century ago at the foot of the North Mountain, where Philip Miller now owns land. Prior to coming to this county he located in York County, and there was married to Kathrina Bauder. He was a widower at this time, and by his first wife had three sons: Michael, John and Peter; the latter, who was a soldier, was killed in the war of 1812. His second wife bore him the following named children: Andrew, Jacob, Adam, Solomon, Elizabeth, Magdalena and Catharine. By trade Andrew Mowery was a shoe-maker, and many a pair of shoes did he make for the Indians. At the time he was living in York County the Indians became very troublesome, and killed a number of white settlers, among whom were several women and children. Andrew Mowery was one of a party of whites who undertook to punish the murderers, made a raid into an Indian camp and killed a number of savages. He died in 1806, and his widow in 1826. Solomon Mowery, the father of our subject, was married to Catharine Carper in 1813, and commenced domestic life in Hopewell Township, where his half-brother Michael had a distillery. He was employed at this business for a number of years. To Solomon Mowery and wife were born these children: Mary, John, Elizabeth, Adam, Sarah, Margaret, Catharine, Andrew, Samuel C., David C.; the first death in the family being that of John in 1885. The father died in 1870, and the mother in 1871. Our subject worked for his father until twenty-three years of age, then rented the farm where he now resides, and a year later moved to a farm near Newburg. In 1859 he purchased the farm on which his first money was earned after he began business. Until 1875 his sister Mary was his housekeeper. June 14, 1875, he was united in marriage with Annie M. C. Dunlap, of Mifflin Township, this county. Her parents, James and Elizabeth (High) Dunlap, were married in Cumberland County in 1852, and still reside in Mifflin Township. To this union were born David E., James F., Harry E. M. and John C. In 1858 Andrew Mowery was elected supervisor, and he has also served as an official of the public schools. His acts, both in public and private, have been heartily indorsed by those who know him. His aged sister, Mary, makes her home with the family, and she surely could not find one more suited to her domestic tastes.

SAMUEL DALLAS MOWREY, justice of the peace, Newburg. The original Mowrey in this county, came from Berks County, Penn., and settled in Hopewell Township, near the foot of the Blue Ridge Mountains; his name is supposed to have been Andrew, and his youngest son, Adam, was the grandfather of our subject. Adam Mowrey was reared and received his education in this township. He enlisted in the war of 1812, under Col. Fenton, the regiment being armed with rifle, scalping knife and tomahawk, and adopted nearly the same tactics employed by the Indians. He was in several noted battles: Fort Niagara, Chippewa, Lundy's Lane and Fort Erie. After the war was over Adam Mowrey returned here, and was soon afterward married to Mary Horting, of Berks County, Penn. He brought his young bride to Hopewell Township, this county, and remained here during the balance of his life. Three children were born and reared here: David, Christian and Lavinia, wife of Mr. Givler. Christian was accidentally killed in a gold mine in California in 1854. David married and reared a family in his native place. Adam Mowrey was twice married; on second occasion to Mary Finkenbinder. He died in January, 1874, and his widow in 1882. Samuel D. was born in Newburg, this county, in 1849, and was reared and educated by his grandparents. At the age of fifteen he enlisted in Capt. Lambert's company of Independent Scouts, in the 100-days' service, and after his return learned the harness trade, but later engaged in teaching school in Newburg and adjoining townships. Abandoning the profession, in 1879, he was elected justice of the peace, and re-elected in the spring of 1884. November 27, 1879, he established a weekly publication, known as *The Telephone*, and until January 1, 1884, was editor and proprietor. Then purchased the business, and continues its publication. Mr. Mowrey has mastered the science of civil engineering, which might now be appropriately termed his business. For three years he was in the employ of the South Pennsylvania Railroad as assistant "right of way" agent of the second, third and fourth divisions, and his field of operation was from Newville to the Allegheny Tunnel. In 1869 he married Melissa Jane, daughter of J. A. and Elizabeth Rea, of Cumberland County. Three children have blessed this union: Archie B., Carrie E. and Moss M. In a home made bright with books, music, and surrounded by the comforts which come to the energetic business man, and under the care of highly educated parents, these children will surely do honor to the family name which for so many years has been well known and honored among the old families of Hopewell Township.

FERDINAND REINHARDT, tanner, Newburg, was born in Strehla, Saxony, in 1826, and is the only one of the family bearing the name residing in the country. He emigrated from Hamburg to America in 1854, coming in a sailing vessel. He had served eight years as a soldier, and one year was yet due the crown, but he was allowed to depart unmolested. His father was a tanner, and taught his son the business. The children of that country are obliged to attend school eight years, consequently he obtained a comparatively good education prior to learning his trade. The father of our subject, John Gottfried Reinhardt, was first married to Christiana S. Pfitzer, of Strehla, and of the children born to this union, Christiana, now the widow of Ernst Schuettze, resides with her brother, coming from Saxony in 1876 (her husband for nearly fifty years was a school teacher in Germany). The first wife of John Reinhardt died in 1823, and the next year he wedded Christiana S. Hensel, by whom he had six children: Harriet S., Ferdinand C., Amelia, Augusta, Ernst E. and Wilhelmina, all of whom came to Cumberland County, Penn. Ferdinand landed in New York City April 14, 1854, and his uncle, Christian Hensel, residing near Newburg, procured him a situation in the tannery at that village, and in April, 1856, in partnership with his brother Edward, leased the tannery and embarked in business for themselves. In 1859 they purchased the tannery where our subject now does business. In 1871 the death of Edward occurred, and Ferdinand secured his interest. In 1873 our subject was married to Mary J., youngest daughter of John Heberlig. They have three children: Minnie S., John E. and Mary E., a bright and interesting trio. The business of Mr. Reinhardt has been a prosperous one during his residence in America, for he had not a dollar in his pocket when he landed at Newburg. His well known business qualifications and unswerving integrity have made him a man of mark in the community.

GEORGE H. RUSSELL, editor, merchant, farmer, inventor and author, Newburg, Penn. Was born April 27, 1835, at Laughlinstown, Westmoreland Co., Penn. His father, Dr. Alexander H. Russell, was a distinguished physician of Westmoreland and Cumberland Counties. On his father's side his ancestry was Irish, and on his mother's it was German. Our subject's education was not higher than that obtained at an academy. While going to a select school in Newville, taught by John Kilbourn; the scholars played a trick on their teacher with his (Russell's) dog. The teacher took the school to an account about it; and they all denied it except "the boy," G. H. Russell, and instead of a whipping he got a Washington monument; printed in acrostic form of letters, to commemorate him as a second Washington for truthfulness. The acrostic was copyrighted. In 1857, 1858 and 1859 Mr. Russell engaged in the ice trade in Baltimore. While in this business he was the first man in the United States to introduce the "new idea" of delivering ice on Saturday evening for use over Sunday. The idea became popular, and was adopted in other cities and towns. In the year 1860 he removed to Cumberland County, and engaged at country store-keeping at Huntsdale, and subsequently in farming at North Newton. While engaged in farming in the year of 1871, he called several meetings of the farmers at Oakville, and lectured upon the necessity of farmers organizing against the encroachments of monopolies and middlemen. These advanced ideas were printed in *The Enterprise*, published at Oakville, and reprinted in other papers. It is alleged by some that these ideas took shape and action in the organization of the Grange, or Patrons of Husbandry. In 1875 Mr. Russell engaged in tanning leather at Newburg. In 1882 he called the attention of the craft, through their trade organ, the *S. and L. Reporter*, to a new method in leaching and steaming bark; upsetting old theories and producing great savings. These ideas were hooted at, but subsequent tests proved Mr. Russell to be correct; and some of the leading factories adopted his plans; which will no doubt become universal. Mr. Russell's political views were reformatory and independent, and of the common sense kind. Not a communist—he took sides for labor, and was identified with the Greenback Labor Party from its first inception, and was always a member of its State Committee. In 1859 he invented and patented a fire-place heater, among the first of its class. He subsequently obtained patents for a fruit can, a washer; and stove drum. In 1884 he became the editor and proprietor of the *Newburg Telephone*, and became noted as a writer of force and wit. In 1882 he wrote his new discoveries in physiology on the "Functions of the Spleen." In 1883 he wrote his new discoveries in physiology on the "Ductless Organs and Their Functions." In these works he claims to have discovered the functions of these organs, which had previously been unknown. He claims, as his discovery; that the functions of these organs are to regulate the circulation of the blood; and that they are the cause of suspended animation of life; and that they act as a positive and negative for the purpose of electrifying the blood, producing human electricity; besides many other ideas that are new in physiology. Colleges, physicians and schools of medicine have received these ideas and theories in astonishment; and while none have yet been able to controvert them, some have admitted to him that pathological tests and observation proves his theory to be true; and that they must stand until proven false. He says he desires to be the "chosen vessel," to make these discoveries for the use of mankind, and esteems them to be "the crown," the glory and the honor of his life! In a later work on physiology he explains the cause of fever heat, which had previously been unknown. He takes a deep interest in common and Sunday-schools. In religion he holds that those Christians who settle disputes by fighting are frauds, and that baptism, as taught by most churches, is idolatrous.

ENOCH STAVER, wagon-maker, Newburg. John Staver, the grandfather of our subject, emigrated from Germany as early as 1795, in company with two brothers, and all settled in Lancaster County, Penn. One was a minister, another a lawyer, and the third, John, was a farmer. He was married probably a few years after his arrival. For his son John was born in 1797 and Samuel in 1799, following whom came Solomon, Emanuel and two others. Of these, Samuel married Elizabeth Rudy, in 1821, by whom he had ten children: Matilda, Lydia, Sophia, Lucy, Nancy, Fanny, Rudy, Enoch, Samuel and John, all of whom were born and reared in Lancaster County, Penn. In 1841, Samuel Staver sold his farm and came with the most of his family to Cumberland County, settling near the line of Franklin County, on the farm now owned by Andrew Gross. Later he disposed of that tract and moved to Newburg, remaining there until his death in 1864, his wife preceding him four years. Enoch, son of Samuel Staver, was born in 1831; learned the wheelwright's trade in Orrstown, Penn., with Solomon Bashore, commencing in 1847. He was married to Susannah, daughter of Adam Hamshoer, of Franklin County. Their married life was commenced in the village of Newburg, and continues to this date in the same social manner as when their troth was plighted. They have had six children: Alonzo, James, Harvey, Cora and Charles are living, and Mary died in childhood. Alonzo married Bertie Baucher, James married Fanny Glosser, Harvey married Sallie Lautsabaugh. For thirty-three years Mr. Staver has been a coach and wagon maker in Newburg, his brother Felix being a blacksmith next door. He has in his possession a brass kettle which had been the property of his grandmother, and has been an heirloom in the family for 153 years. Our subject has been several times elected to official positions in the village and township, in all of which he has well discharged his duties.

CHAPTER XLIX.

LOWER ALLEN TOWNSHIP AND BOROUGH OF NEW CUMBERLAND.*

JACOB BARBER, farmer, P. O. Lisburn. The many reminiscences of the early days in the history of the various townships are replete with interest, and none more so than that of the Barber family, which, since 1790, has been well known in this and adjacent counties. The father of George C. Barber resided at Boiling Springs, Monroe Township, before George was born, which event occurred in 1794. There were eight children in his family: George C., Joseph, David, James, William, Mary, Elizabeth and Margaret. George C., the father of our subject, left home at the age of eighteen and went to York County, the next year was married to Barbara Rinehart, of that county, and in 1839 removed to New Cumberland, and in 1840 purchased the farm on which his son now resides. To George C. and Barbara Barber were born nine children: William, Jacob, John, Nancy, Martha, Elizabeth, Barbara, Susan and Sarah (the last named is the only one who was born in Cumberland County). George C. Barber, by trade a mason, continued in that calling until 1840 and scores of buildings remain as monuments to his skill in this and Dauphin Counties. In 1870 he died at the ripe age of seventy-six years, having had the satisfaction of seeing his children grown to be useful men and women. Jacob Barber was born in 1828; at the age of twenty-one he went to California, sailing from Baltimore on the clipper "Flying Cloud," the journey taking one year and nine months. When he arrived at Fiddletown, near Sacramento City, Cal., he purchased the necessary tools and commenced digging for gold, and from the first was quite successful. Having formed an attachment for Miss Elizabeth Hoff, of York County, Penn., prior to his Western trip, Mr. Barber returned to his native State in 1857, and in December of the same year the marriage ceremony was performed by Rev. Mooney, of Harrisburg. They commenced home life on the Barber homestead, and have reared a family of four children: Mary E., Harry, George C. and Charley. The well-known business qualifications of Mr. Barber early brought him forward as a candidate for official honors and he was first elected supervisor, which position he filled for three terms; three years he served as an official in the public schools, and in 1873 he was elected county commissioner, re-elected in 1875, and again in 1878, for a term of three years. During all these years of public service Mr. Barber was never known to do a thing that would detract from his good name.

COSMUS S. CLENDENIN, postmaster, Eberly's Mills, was born in Lebanon County, Penn., in 1833, son of William and Mary (Snoke) Clendenin, who had three children: William, Cosmus S. and Mary A. Our subject learned the trade of shoe-making with his father, and continued in the business for a number of years. In 1856, he was married to Lucinda W. Fox, and worked at his trade in his native county for twelve years before removal to York County, Penn., where a farm was purchased and trade discontinued. Mr. and Mrs. Clendenin have six children living: Clara A., Emma M., William H., John M., Lizzie M. and Ellen G. James O. died in infancy. All the children, except James O. were born in Lebanon and Dauphin Counties, Penn. Our subject has been a successful business man and has given his children the benefit of a liberal education. William H., a merchant of Milltown, having the only store in the village, married Hattie, daughter of Eli and Elizabeth Coxen, of York County; Clara is the wife of H. W. Zimmerman; Emma

*For borough of Shiremanstown, see page 456.

is the wife of Wilson B. Kauffman; John M. married Phœbe Womer. In 1878 Mr. Clendenin disposed of his farm and came to Milltown and, in 1880, established himself in mercantile business. The same year he was appointed postmaster, a position he has since held. The mercantile business was transferred to his son, W. H., January 1, 1886, and Mr. Clendenin will hereafter live a retired life, having no need to care for aught but the duties of the postoffice. He was a member of the German Reformed Church for twenty-six years, and then united with the United Brethren denomination. Politically he has trained with the Republican party from its organization, but has no aspirations for official honors.

DANIEL DRAWBAUGH, machinist, Eberly's Mills. From a German ancestry on both sides has emanated a man whose name will not only become famous throughout the civilized world, but from the obscurity in which his talent had been for so many years hidden it comes with an intensity which brightens the pages of Cumberland County records and forever perpetuates the name of one of her most talented sons, who was born and reared in Lower Allen Township. He is a son of John and Leigh (Blozier) Drawbaugh, and was born July 14, 1828. His father was a blacksmith and also engaged in the manufacture of edge tools and gun barrels. Daniel Drawbaugh was put to work at an early age, for boys then were supposed to be worth only what they could earn—education was a secondary thought, and his father paid no attention to matters of this kind. The genius of his son was developed at an early age, and he became quite expert with a jack-knife, fashioning a clock, etc., and many inventions made in his younger days were never patented. At seventeen he learned coach-making with his brother, J. B. Drawbaugh, and while thus engaged largely improved the machinery used in that work. At fifteen he had made a steam engine, which he disposed of only a few years ago. He also displayed great talent for drawing from nature, and his portfolio is full of fine sketches. He also improved the methods of photographing on paper in an early day, but only engaged in that business experimentally; wood engraving was also one his fortes. January 1, 1854, he was married to Elsetta J., daughter of John and Mary (Thompson) Thompson. Mr. Thompson was for several terms a member of the State Legislature, and was also commander of a company of men during the Buckshot war. Daniel Drawbaugh and his young wife commenced housekeeping in the house where he was born. They had eleven children, of whom Emma C., Laura V., Iola O., Bella B., Maude C. and Charles H. are living, and Dovan T., Naomi E., Emma C., Ida M. and Harry W. S., are deceased. The long and useful life of Mr. Drawbaugh promises to become of especial interest. Naturally of an inventive turn of mind, he has perfected and had patented more than fifty useful appliances and instruments. His crowning success in life was the invention of the telephone, which has been claimed and for a time awarded to A. G. Bell, but a suit at law will determine his right to such invention. There is no doubt but that the principles of that medium were first put in operation in the little workshop in the hamlet of Milltown. Should this suit be decided in his favor, Mr. Drawbaugh at once becomes the most noted man in Cumberland County; should the decision be adverse he is none the less a talented gentleman and has earned for himself a high place in the inventive fraternity. Our subject employs a number of men and operates quite a large factory in which electrical and other apparatus form the basis of experimentation. His family has been reared in a style of modern elegance and their education carefully looked after.

JOSEPH FEEMAN, retired, New Cumberland. In 1790, Adam Feeman, the grandfather of Joseph Feeman came from Lancaster County, Penn., and purchased the farm now the property of John Feeman, and here reared a family of four children: Valentine, the youngest son, born in 1783 and died in 1843, married Margaret Shafer, by whom he had eight children, of whom six reached adult age: John, Adam, Elizabeth, Joseph, Valentine and Susan. Of these, John, who has remained a bachelor, owns the homestead; Adam married Nancy Kirk; Elizabeth is the wife of Rudolph Martin; Joseph married, in 1840, Eliza Prowell, who bore him six children, only one now living—Susan, wife of Charles Hoot, and a resident of Harrisburg (Mrs. Joseph Feeman died in 1880, after forty years of happy domestic life); Valentine married Matilda Lutz, of Harrisburg, Penn., and Susan is the wife of James Eckels, of this county. The old homestead has been made a beautiful farm by three generations of Feemans, who have converted it from a dense woodland into a fertile tract of land. The old house, which was erected prior to the purchase by Adam Feeman, has undergone extensive repairs; beneath its hospitable roof three generations have been born and reared. Comparatively few of the race now remain who can hand down a name that for 136 years has been familiar in the history of the township. The two brothers, John and Joseph, live a retired life in the village of New Cumberland, and are both easy in a financial way, having lived an economical and unostentatious life.

OWEN JAMES, retired, P. O. New Cumberland. It was with the greatest reluctance that Mr. James allowed this brief sketch to appear. His modesty and good deeds are so proverbial, however, that common report would furnish a voluminous history, did he not seriously object. He was born in Lower Allen Township, on the old Peter Zimmerman farm, March 15, 1815. His parents, Thomas and Hannah James, moved to the old home stead, in Fairview Township, York County, two weeks after his birth, and from that date Owen James resided there until he was twenty-two years of age. There were ten children in the family: Lewis, Jane, Owen, Mary A., Eliza, William, Hannah, Thomas, Sarah and Harriet. Their grandfather, Owen James, was a soldier in the war of 1812, serving until the close of that campaign, and, upon his return home, in 1815, he was taken sick, and died at Painted Post, N. Y. Thomas and Hannah James then took charge of the two grandmothers, and with their ten children resided on the farm until the death of Thomas James in 1843. In 1858 Mrs. James left the farm and came to New Cumberland, all the children having married, and made her home until death, in 1876, at the ripe age of eighty-six years, with a sister, Mrs. Hannah Lee. Owen James for a time worked with his father on the farm. In 1830 he was driving a team freighted with iron and nails between New Cumberland and Duncannon. In 1833 he carted stone for the turnpike between York Haven and Harrisburg. The next year he hauled lumber from York Haven for the Cumberland Valley Railroad bridge at Harrisburg. In 1837 Owen James left his home, and without a dollar engaged as mason's helper at 50 cents per day. He engaged later in the stock business, on a small scale, in which he prospered until 1840, when, aided by Messrs. B. H. Mosser and George Crist, he engaged in the butcher's trade. From this time he prospered, everything he touched seemingly turning to gold. In 1843 he was married to Esther Prowell, of York County, Penn., daughter of James and Rebecca Prowell. Their housekeeping was commenced across the street from their present residence in New Cumberland. In 1849 Mr. James formed a partnership with B. H. Mosser & Son, continuing in same until 1864, when ill health caused his retirement. Since then, with the exception of four years (1867 to 1871), Mr. James has done no active business, confining himself to settling estates and managing farms for other parties. He still owns the farm which belonged to his grandfather, the deed bearing the date 1783 for 100 acres and allowances. Mr. and Mrs. James have never had any children, but their good and kindly acts have endeared them to all who know them. Mr. James is the last of his name in this State, but his fame as a man, a neighbor and a Christian are proverbial. He and his wife have, for nearly half a century, been members of the Methodist Episcopal Church. They have had the pleasure of seeing the borough transformed from a stage of comparative vice to one of the most moral places in the valley, made so by the continuous vigilance on the part of the Christian people among whom they are numbered. From the first half-dollar earned by the sweat of his brow Mr. James has accumulated a handsome fortune, not one dollar of which was dishonestly earned, nor to increase his gains was the poor man ever oppressed. He is one of the few men in Cumberland County who has seen six generations come here, and is still hale and hearty, although his locks are as white as the driven snow.

HENRY R. MOSSER, dealer in lumber, P. O. New Cumberland. From a line of ancestry that came from Switzerland as early 1734 and settled in Lancaster County, Penn., comes the subject of our sketch. The most reliable information obtainable of this family begins with Dr. Benjamin Mosser, who purchased a large tract of land in Fairview Township, York Co., Penn., upon which three sons and a married daughter subsequently settled. The sons, John, Henry and Christian, were all prominent men in the neighborhood. The eldest, John, practiced medicine for many years in the village of Newmarket, and his descendants are numerous in Cumberland County at the present time. The daughter, Barbara, above referred to, married Michael Kauffman, and they, too, have many descendants in Cumberland and York Counties. Henry, one of the three sons, married Susannah Neff, an orphan, reared and educated by William and Deborah Wright, of Columbia. The Wrights were Quakers, and gave Susannah an education far superior to that of the women of her day. Her father owned the Wrightsville ferry when Washington's army encamped at Valley Forge; and when Congress assembled at York, Susannah was six years of age, and Washington stopped at the Wrights' for breakfast. While waiting for the repast the General lifted her upon his lap and entertained her with some of his droll stories, and, although so young, she well remembered the circumstance, and was fond of relating it to her grandchildren, of whom Henry R. was the second born. Henry and Susannah (Neff) Mosser had a family of five children: Benjamin H., father of our subject; Dr. Daniel Mosser, who for many years was bishop in the Reformed Mennonite Church in the United States and Canada, the author of most of the religious works of that denomination; Rev. Joseph Mosser, of Salem, Ill., for many years traveling agent for the Illinois Bible Society; John N., a farmer in Cumberland County; Magdalena, now the widow of George Rupley. Benjamin H. Mosser was married to Elizabeth Rupley, of Cumberland County, Penn., daughter of John and Barbara (Stine) Rupley, of Berks County, Penn. John Rupley, Esq., was quite a prominent man in his time, and was not only a noted justice of the peace, but also served as sheriff of this county. There were two children born to Benjamin H. and his wife, viz.: Susannah, wife of Dr. Augustus H. Vanhoff, a noted physician of Mechanicsburg, and also an honored representative from this county to the State Legislature. Henry Rupley Mosser, the only son, was born in York County in 1828, and until twelve years old remained on the farm, obtaining the rudiments of a practical education in the common schools. Later, he attended the Strasburg Academy, in Lancaster County, and the old York County Academy, from which he went, in 1848, to take charge of the books and business of his father, in the village of New Cumberland, who had established a lumber trade in that place in 1839. In 1850 Henry R. Mosser was admitted as partner in the lumber and grain business, Owen James being also asssociated, and from that date the firm was known as B. H. Mosser & Co. In 1857 the senior member of the firm retired, and in 1864 Mr. James also retired, leaving Henry R. Mosser sole proprietor. The firm is now Mosser & Sadler, the latter being Judge Sadler, of Carlisle, Penn. With the exception of a few years, Mr. Mosser has always been connected with the lumber trade of Dauphin and Cumberland Counties, but has also a large saw-mill and lumber establishment in Tioga County, in which he has associated with him Julius B. Kauffman, who for many years was his confidential clerk and book-keeper. The firm of Mosser & Sadler employ forty men, and their business is the leading enterprise in the village. Henry R. Mosser was married to Margaret A. Yocum, in 1852, a daughter of Jacob and Henrietta (Duncan) Yocum, of York, York Co., Penn. To this union were born two children: Nettie E. and Rev. Benjamin H. Mosser, of Mechanicsburg. In 1859 Mrs. Mosser died, and in 1863 Mr. Mosser married R. Jennie Miller, of New Cumberland, this county, by whom he has two children: Annie, a graduate of Dickinson Seminary, Williamsport, and John C., who is preparing for college under the tutelage of Prof. Seiler, of Harrisburg, Penn. Mr. Mosser has lived a long and useful life, and perhaps no man living in the village has done more to advance its interests. For many years he has been an active Republican politician in State and National affairs. In theological matters he stands very high, and for more than twenty years has been superintendent of the Methodist Episcopal Sabbath-school, and for six years president of the famous Cumberland Sabbath-school Assembly, now a part of the Chautauqua system, located at Mountain Lake Park, on the summit of the Alleghenies, Maryland. He has been president of Cumberland Valley Camp Meeting Association, and represented the Central Pennsylvania Conference of the Methodist Episcopal Church, at Baltimore, in 1876, and also at the Centennial Conference, at Baltimore, in 1884, and which was the most noted Conference ever held by that body, in which all the branches of the church and Sabbath-school work were represented. For more than a quarter of a century he has officiated as trustee, steward and class-leader of the Methodist Episcopal Church in New Cumberland, and was the first president of the Y. M. C. A. of this village. He is also treasurer of the Conference Education Society, in which capacity he has served since the organization of this commendable enterprise to assist young men to obtain an education.

GEORGE W. MUMPER, farmer, P. O. New Cumberland, was born in Carroll Township, York Co., Penn., in 1828, son of John and Jane (Beelman) Mumper, who were the parents of twelve children, nine of whom are living: Elizabeth, widow of Jacob Heiges, of Dillsburg; Christina, widow of Daniel Bailey, Esq.; Michael, married to Eliza A. Coover; Maria, widow of Maj. Jacob Dorsheimer; Margaret, widow of Col. S. M. Bailey, a noted man in the military and civil history of Pennsylvania; John; Catharine residing with her brother John; Samuel married to Mary King, of York County; George W.; Ann (deceased); Mrs. Lydia Porter (deceased). November 2, 1854, our subject married Miss Mary J. Mateer of Dillsburg, a daughter of William and Mary A. Mateer, who were the parents of three daughters: Ann E., residing with Mr. Mumper; Margaret C., wife of Dr. E. B. Brandt, of Mechanicsburg, and Mary J. Her parents were among the early settlers in Lower Allen Township, and all the daughters were born on the farm now owned by Mr. Mumper; this property has been in possession of the Mateers for more than sixty years, and has been the home of Mr. and Mrs. Mumper since their marriage, he at that time purchasing the interest of the other heirs. To Mr. and Mrs. Mumper have been born six children: The two eldest are deceased; Lulu B. (as was her mother before her) is a graduate at Lititz; George B. is a graduate of Dickinson College; Samuel completed his course at Collegiate Institute at York, and Mary A. graduated from Wilson College at Chambersburg. Mr. Mumper is prominent in political circles, both National and local, and was one of the first Representatives elected under the new Constitution in the county of Cumberland. He has for eighteen years served on the school board, of which he has continuously been president, and has taken a prominent part in everything that advances the business, social moral and educational interests of his chosen county.

LEVI MUSSELMAN, farmer, P. O. Shiremanstown, is the only representative of this family in this county, and which came originally from Germany, but at what date the first one settled in Lancaster County nothing is known. Christian Musselman was born in Lancaster County in 1796; came to Cumberland County in 1820, and took service with Christian Hurst on the farm now owned by Mrs. Musselman. After the death of Mr. Hurst Mr. Musselman married his widow, and by her had three children—two sons and one daughter: One son died in infancy; Levi, and Elizabeth, now the wife of Peter Musselman, of Adams County, Penn. Levi Musselman was born, in 1827, on the Hurst farm, and has always followed the occupation of farming. In 1849 he was married to Annie, daughter of Jacob and Elizabeth (Nisley) Mumma, whose family history forms an important record. Their married life was commenced on the farm, now the homestead, and there John the eldest son was born. A few years later Mr. Musselman moved to the Hurst farm, and there Elizabeth and Fanny were born. Of the other children, Kate was born on the Christian Mumma farm, and Samuel, Jacob, Christian, Martin, Harry and Edward on the Musselman homestead. Kate and Elizabeth are deceased, the former in her seventeenth and the latter in her twenty-fourth year. John married Annie Zimmerman; Samuel married Annie Hess; Jacob married Grace Hartman; Fanny is the wife of Jacob Bucher. The married life of Mr. and Mrs. Levi Museleman has been an unexceptionally pleasant one. They have prospered financially, and have educated their children in that practical manner which makes the men and women of Cumberland County famous.

GEORGE N. RUPP, gentleman, P. O. Shiremanstown, is a grandson of George Rupp, who was born in Lancaster County, Penn., May 21, 1772. May 6, 1800, he married Christina, daughter of Daniel and Annie M. (Wolff) Boeshor, and in 1802 came to Cumberland County, and with his brother, Martin, purchased the farm now owned by John M. Rupp. The children reared were George (father of our subject), Daniel, Jonas, Mary, Elizabeth, Jacob G., Martin G., John G., Jane, David G., Henry G. and Francis. George Rupp, the eldest son, was born in 1802, and in the course of time married Mrs. Catharine (Schopp) Neidig, who was born December 9, 1803. Previous to his marriage George Rupp was a teacher in this county, and having a fine education became one of the most useful men in the neighborhood, settling many estates, collecting taxes and other business of importance was done by him in a manner which gained for him the greatest respect and confidence of all who knew him; he died May 29, 1849. Our subject, the only child born to his parents, inherited his grandfather's patronymic, and might be termed George the Third; he was born March 1, 1847. His education was acquired in the schools of his native county, and from his youth he has been a practical farmer and successful business man. February 28, 1871, he married Elenora G. Sadler, born December 13, 1850, daughter of Joseph and Annie (Grove) Sadler, of New Kingston. By this union are two children: George S., born March 31, 1872, and Joseph P., born February 7, 1875. The married life of Mr. Rupp was commenced on the farm, so many years the Rupp homestead, and which was his by inheritance in 1868. Their circumstances from the first were auspicious, the farm being one of the finest, the buildings the most commodious, and the situation unsurpassed by any in the valley. To this was added the enterprise of the young couple, both having received a practical training, and they have followed in the footsteps of their ancestors—financially, socially and morally.

JOHN SHEELY, farmer, P. O. Shiremanstown. The grandparents of our subject were Andrew and Barbara (Barnhort) Sheely, the former born August 11, 1752, the latter November 6, 1753, and were married August 31, 1777. Andrew Sheely was a soldier in the Revolutionary war, and helped to fight the battles which gained the American people their independence. Their children were Adam, John, Andrew, Ann M., Michael, Christian, Frederick, Barbara, and another son Frederick (both of the name died during boyhood). Of this honored family a number yet represent the name in this county. On our subject's maternal grandparents' side was John P. Cromlich, born in 1797, and his wife, Margaret Sipe, born in 1807, who had ten children: John, Frederick, Susannah, May, David, Catharine, Elizabeth, William H., Jacob and Samuel. The father of our subject, John Sheely, was born on the farm now owned by David Oyster in 1781. He was married to Elizabeth Cromlich, probably in 1804, as the first child, Andrew, was born in 1806; the other children were Frederick, Barbara, Elizabeth, John, Benjamin, Samuel, Susan, Annie and Catharine. About the time of his marriage John Sheely's father, Andrew Sheely, purchased and presented him with the fine farm on which his grandson now resides, and on which all his brothers and sisters were born. The Sheelys were all men of herculean frame, and have been noted agriculturists from the date of their coming, and have been very prosperous, each of the brothers now residing in the county counting their wealth by the thousands. John, Jr., has remained a bachelor, not from lack of personal charms, but because he was so wedded to his agricultural pursuits that matrimony was forgotten until his habits were so firmly fixed that he had no wish to become a benedict. The home farm is owned in partnership by himself, Benjamin and the heirs of Samuel Sheely, whose widow, Mary (Cromlich) Sheely, and sister-in-law, Catharine, are housekeepers, the farming being managed by John Sheely and the two sons of his brother, John H. and Jacob M. The finest steer in Cumberland County is now their property, and special attention is given to the breeding of fine stock and poultry. The Sheelys are noted as money-makers and savers, and are withal men of the strictest integrity and uprightness.

JOHN UMBERGER, farmer, P.O.Lisburn. As early as 1770 the name Umberger was known in this county, and, though the family is really of Scotch and Irish nativity, the name is unquestionably German. Leonard was the first one of the family to come to Lancaster County, Penn., which then included this territory. In Rupp's History mention is made of Leonard Umberger purchasing Rupp's great-grandfather at public sale, the custom in those days, the vessel owners having the right to dispose of their passengers, in this way to obtain their passage money. Leonard Umberger was the great-grandfather of our subject, as he begat Adam who begat David, the father of John. Adam Umberger settled in "Path Valley," now in Franklin County, in 1770, and by his wife, Catharine, had three children: David; Elizabeth, married to Mr. Heckart of Dauphin County; John who engaged in mercantile business in Harrisburg, but died while a young man. Adam Umberger, who was a millwright, was preparing to build a mill near his home when he died; his family then returned to Dauphin County and settled near Linglestown. David, the eldest son, was born in 1775, and was indentured to Mr. Berry, in 1791, to learn the blacksmith's trade (his mother about that time married Michael Umberger, a brother of her first husband, and moved to York County, near Lisburn). About 1796 David Umberger came to Lisburn, purchased property and established himself in the blacksmith's trade. In 1798 he married Dorothy Maish, of York County, Penn., by whom he had a large family; the oldest child, Mary, was born in Lisburn in 1799, and a few years later David Umberger (in 1809) sold his Lisburn property, moved to Warrington Township, York County, and there purchased a farm and carried on an extensive smithy. On this farm were born Ann, Elizabeth, Catharine, David and Rebecca (twins) and Sarah. About 1812 he purchased the Daniel Kahm farm, near Lisburn (where he resided until his death), and here were born Ellen, John, Jane, George and Esther. John Umberger, our subject, was born in 1816; in 1841, he married Susan Miller, of York County, Penn., daughter of Jacob and Susan Miller, and they commenced married life on the paternal homestead, and their two children were born: David M., in 1843, and Eliza J., in 1845. In the spring of 1846, our subject, with his family, came to this county, purchasing the farm, now his homestead, and which has been made beautiful by his own industry; every fence, the handsome stone house, commodious outbuildings, etc., were erected since the purchase, and the nice orchard was planted by the hands of himself and wife, and they have lived to see their labors crowned by beautiful harvests, which have filled their purse. Rachael E., John, Jr., Agnes J., George F., Lewis C., William M., Franklin P., Lilly E., Charles E. and Clarence S. were born on this farm. Always popular among the people, Mr. Umberger has been foremost in promoting every important feature of educational and social life. A lifelong Democrat, he has lived to see the rise and decline of numerous political parties, and to-day hails with delight the supremacy his chosen party occupies. For nearly half a century he and his wife have belonged to the Church of God, and have reared their family in that faith. Rich in experience, ripe in years, they remain as they have lived, beloved by all who know them.

GEORGE WALKER, retired, Lisburn. More than a century ago Benjamin Walker, and his wife, Sarah (Morris) Walker, came from Wales to Chester County, Penn.; later removed to York County, finally settling near Rossville, and there purchased a farm and erected commodious buildings. They were members of the society known as "Friends;" and the church now standing, although more than a hundred years old, was the house in which they worshiped, and from its sacred desk William Penn has preached to the pioneer Christians. On the farm their family of seven children was reared; Isaac, the youngest son, married Mary Cramer, and their home was made during the early years of wedded life at the mansion of his father. The subject of this sketch was born in York County, Penn., another son, John, and a daughter, Mary A., now the wife of Samuel Gehr, of Camp Hill, were born in Cumberland County, after the removal of their parents to this county in 1825. Isaac Walker (father of our subject) died in 1839, and his widow in 1864. Lewis, an elder brother of Isaac Walker, worked for forty years in Harrisburg, married Mary A. Hull, of Lisburn, in 1845, and had two children: Clara and Jacob M. In 1884, an unfortunate accident caused the death of Mrs. Walker, since which time Lewis Walker has made his home with his brother George. Our subject was one of the most enterprising young men in this county. Choosing in early life the trade of shoe-making, he established himself at Lisburn. His mother, younger brother and sister lived together until the marriage of the sister, in 1853, with Samuel Gehr, by whom she has two children: Geo. W. and John A. His aged mother made her home with him until her death. With untiring energy he persevered in his work until a handsome competence was accumulated, consisting of a fine farm and the best residence property in the village. In 1866 Mr. Walker was married to Elizabeth Reiff, of York County, and two children were born, who died in infancy. After ten years of pleasant married life Mr. Walker was left a childless widower, and, in company with his brother Lewis, his days are passed in the quiet home at Lisburn. But for an accident, in 1885, Mr. Walker would be as hale and active as a man of fifty. In forty years he has not experienced an attack of sickness. He has a cheery home, surrounded by all the comforts wealth brings to intellectual minds, and has a record without a stain.

EMANUEL ZIMMERMAN, retired, P. O. Eberly's Mills, the only son of Peter Zimmerman, now living in Cumberland County, was born on the homestead, in this county, December 8, 1818. His father was born in 1776, in Lancaster County, Penn., and there married Esther Martin, also born in the same year. When the Zimmerman family came to Cumberland County there was no bridge across the Susquehanna, and trains were forded, and goods carried over in boats. The land now owned by the family was then unimproved, and the fine houses and barns, with the exception of Henry Zimmerman's stone house, have been erected since their coming. Of their twelve children, Emanuel is the youngest and the second one born in this county. October 22, 1844, he was married to Susannah, daughter of Christian and Elizabeth Hess, born in York County, Penn., March 4, 1825. They commenced housekeeping on State Hill, in an old tenant house, now the property of J. C. Comfort. In 1859 Emanuel Zimmerman made his first purchase of land,

and every thing in the way of improvements has been done by him. The fine house and extensive barns were erected in 1860, and are models of architecture. Mr. and Mrs. Zimmerman are parents of five sons and four daughters: Joseph, George, Elizabeth, Anna, Jonas, Mary, Rebecca, Levi and Isaac. Joseph Zimmerman married Mary J. Blair, George married Adaline Crisinger, Elizabeth is the wife of Rudolph Hartzler, Annie is the wife of John Musselman, Jonas wedded Susanna Shoop, Mary is the wife of David C. Blair, and Isaac married Agnes Huston. Nearly half a century ago Mr. and Mrs. Zimmerman were made members of the Mennonite Church; that was before their marriage, and their love for their Creator has never been dimmed nor their family circle broken by death. They have now seventeen grandchildren and a family of whom any parents may feel proud.

HENRY W. ZIMMERMAN, farmer. P. O. Eberly's Mill. The history of the Zimmermans in this county dates back more than a century. The grandfather of our subject, Peter Zimmerman, came from Lancaster County, Penn., in 1814, and purchased the farm now the property of Emanuel, Henry, Solomon and brothers. The original tract comprised 300 acres, on which was a stone house, now the residence of Henry Zimmerman, and which was built in 1781 by the Meisch family. Peter Zimmerman married Esther Martin, by whom he had twelve children: Christian, Henry, Peter, Samuel, Martin, Emanuel, Esther, Mary, Barbara, Annie, Julia and Elizabeth. This large family was reared on the the farm, and all the sons adopted agriculture as their vocations. Peter Zimmerman, Jr., married Magdalena, daughter of Henry and Magdalena Weaver. Mr. Weaver built the stone mill now owned by Calvin Etter, and which will no doubt remain a monument to his enterprise for many years to come. Peter Zimmerman and his wife commenced their married life in York County, opposite the homestead, and when that place was sold he purchased it, and his son Henry and sister Magdalena have managed the farm since. Peter Zimmerman, Jr., and wife had six children: Esther, Moses, Mary, Henry, Peter and Magdalena. The loving wife and mother died in 1840, and four years later Mr. Zimmerman was married to Barbara Hess, by whom he had six children: Samuel, Christian, Amos, David, Benjamin and Elizabeth. The death of the father of this large family occurred in 1874. Henry W. Zimmerman worked for his father until he was thirty-five years years old. In 1875 he was married to Clara A., daughter of Cosmus and Lucinda Clendenin. In 1875 our subject purchased the ancestral home, where his grandfather had reared a family of noble sons and daughters, and who rank among the leading farmers in Lower Allen Township. Henry W. and Clara A. Zimmerman have had four children born to them: Cosmus (deceased), Harry, Elmer and Howard. In a comfortable home, and encouraged by fond parents, they will no doubt do honor to the family name.

CHAPTER L.

MIDDLESEX TOWNSHIP.

WILMOT AYRES, M. D., is a descendant of English and Scotch-Irish ancestry, and was born in York County, Penn., September 25, 1847. His father, Samuel A. Ayres, married Emily Robinson, of Baltimore. He entered the army during the civil war, and died while being a second time a prisoner in the hands of the Confederates. Wilmot is the eldest son, and graduated April 12, 1883. He immediately began the practice of medicine in Middlesex and surrounding country. He succeeded no one, but built up an independent practice of his own, and has been highly successful as a practitioner. He is a member of Cumberland County Medical Society.

HENRY C. BABBLE, proprietor of the Carlisle Springs. P.O. Carlisle Springs, was born in York County, Penn., May 15, 1829. In 1837 he moved to Cumberland County, and hired out on a farm until 1850, when he began to learn the tanner's trade, at which he remained three years. He then married, March 16, 1853, Phœbe Worts, who bore him ten children, nine now living: Emma L., Margaret J., Mary A., Sarah C., Clara E., Susie E., William H., Samuel C. and Tolbert Mc. After marriage he came to Middlesex Township, this county, and worked four years on a farm. In 1857 he bought an old tannery at Sportsburg, Silver Spring Township, this county, and conducted it for twenty-six years. October 3, 1882, he moved to Carlisle Springs, and bought the tannery from Samuel Sample, which he has since conducted. He tore down all the old buildings and erected new ones. He also runs a chopping-mill, and corn and rye mill in connection, the machinery being all operated by steam power, the engine being an eight horse-power of the Geiser manufacture. He also owns the building in which he resides, a large two-story frame structure. His first wife died October 26, 1873, and March 2, 1876, he married Elizabeth Swartz. Mr. Babble made his start in life by gathering chincapins, a small nut growing like chestnuts, when a boy in York County, and selling them in Dover. He owns seventeen acres in Silver Spring Township, and thirty-six acres (and ten unseated) where he lives at Carlisle Springs. He has labored hard, and can now boast of having as much as the average man. He and his wife are members of the Reformed Church. Mr. Babble also owns two residences in the village of Carlisle Springs. He turns out of his tannery, on an average,each year 1,300 hides,which are shipped in the rough, principally to Philadelphia and Boston. The tannery is 36x51 feet, two stories in height, with an L 30x14 feet; the bark-shed is 24x50 and the mill-room 24x22, and the engine-room 16x18 feet; leach-room, 16x24; new bank barn, 36x50, 16 feet 2 inches in the square; scale-house, 16x22 feet.

DAVID P. BRINDLE, farmer, P. O. Carlisle Springs, was born on his father's farm September 30, 1832. George, his father, settled upon this farm at an early date, and married Elizabeth Dewey, daughter of Peter Dewey, a Revolutionary soldier, who died in the old house which is still standing on the farm. George was the father of six children, three of whom are living, viz.: Capt. Peter Brindle, of Carlisle, Margaret and David P. The last named married Sarah Barr, of Middlesex Township, Cumberland County, December 13, 1856, and by her has three children, viz.: Amelia, Samuel and George W. William Drennan originally took a large tract of land in this northern portion of what is now Middlesex Township, but was then North Middleton, which included a part of the whole of the farm now owned by Mr. Brindle. But that family, with the other early Scotch-Irish settlers of this northern part of Middlesex, are extinct, and it has been the later German settlers who, by their toil, have made the border of our valley "blossom like the rose."

CHARLES CLENDENIN, merchant, Carlisle Springs, was born in New York City May 30, 1858, and is a son of James and Barbara (Keiffer) Clendenin, natives of Pennsylvania and of English descent. James Clendenin was in the patent-right business in his younger days, and later engaged in the tanning business, at Hogestown, Penn., for several years. He then moved to Cumberland County and engaged in the same business, erected all the buildings necessary for a tan-yard, and followed the trade until 1878, when he sold out to Samuel Sample, and then engaged in mercantile business, at Carlisle Springs, until the time of his death, November 19, 1885. He was the father of three children, viz.: Ida C., wife of W. E. Reddig, of the firm of J. & J. B. Reddig & Sons, of Shippensburg; Charles, a merchant of Carlisle Springs, and James B., who resides in Carlisle Springs. His brother John was elected judge of the county, but died before taking his seat. James Clendenin owned a large tract of land at the time of his death. He was a Democrat and took a great interest in politics, being the leader in his vicinity. He was a member of the I. O. O. F. lodge, at New Kingston. Charles, our subject, was reared to the tanning trade and was in the business with his father until the latter's death, after which he bought the store and has since been engaged in commerce at Carlisle Springs. He carries a general line of merchandise, such as will supply the country trade, his stock being valued at $2,000, which is fully insured. March 24, 1881, Mr. Clendenin married Julia F., daughter of John and Elizabeth Cameron. Our subject and wife are the parents of two children: William and Elsie Clendenin. His wife is a member of the Lutheran Church. James R., our subject's brother,went to Shippensburg, in 1878, where he engaged in merchandising for three years, and then went west, to Holden, Mo., and spent five years in the same occupation. Mr. Clendenin is also postmaster at Carlisle Springs, having been appointed under the present administration. His father was also postmaster for a number of years before his death.

CHRISTIAN R. GLADFELTER, miller, was born in York County in 1838. He moved first to Silver Spring Township, this county, and later to Middlesex Township, and when a boy attended the schools of the time. He afterward followed farming until three years ago, when his father, Moses, purchased the grist-mill at the confluence of the Letort and Conodoguinet Creeks. Moses Gladfelter is descended from men of Revolutionary fame. Three brothers came from Germany, two of whom served in the Revolutionary war. Moses is the son of George, and married Miss Ruhl, of Cumberland County. To them two sons and one daughter were born, of whom Christian is the eldest. The mill which Christian now operates is of historic interest. In 1756 it was conveyed by John Chambers to his sons, Randle and William. Just prior to the Revolution it was sold to Robert Callender, an Indian trader, and a man of education and influence in those times. In 1792 it passed into the hands of Ephraim Blaine, grandfather of Hon. James G. Blaine, of Maine, from whom it has descended down, through various parties and by various conveyances, to the present owners, who have remodeled and greatly enlarged it, so that it is now one of the largest and most successful roller-mills in the county. Mr. Gladfelter also purchased the handsome residence adjoining.

GEORGE W. JACOBS, farmer, was born on his father's homestead, on the northern border of Middlesex Township, October 29, 1832. Jacob Jacobs, the grandfather, came from Germany and settled first in York, then in Perry County, Penn. Henry, his son, and the father of George W., moved into Cumberland County, and was the first of the family to settle on the farm in Middlesex. George W. Jacobs married Phœbe Wetzel, of Cumberland County, December 25, 1855, by which marriage there were eight children, six of whom are still living on the homestead farm.

DAVID MILLER, farmer, was born in Lancaster County, September 18, 1825. He is the third son of David, Sr., and Mary (Eshelman) Miller, who moved to Cumberland County from Lancaster in 1833. He attended the country schools of the day, followed farming with his father, and engaged for many years in the nursery business on the large farm at the Middlesex Station. He married Elizabeth Stouffer, a lady of refinement, and the daughter of Jacob Stouffer, of Franklin County, Penn. About the same time, Mr. Stouffer purchased the Middlesex estate from the Blaine and Penrose heirs. He was for a time in partnership with Mr. Stouffer in operating the old paper-mill at that place, and in the lime-burning and coal business. Mr. Stouffer's son Benjamin had supervision of the flour-mill. A financial reverse crippled this estate; some branches of its business were closed, while the rest passed into other hands. Mr. Miller is a man of large reading and judgment, and fond of books, but with little time to cultivate his taste in that direction. His family consists of two sons and three daughters. He is now living on and has charge of the "Indian Farm" for the training in agriculture of the Indian youths at the training school, Carlisle. The farm lies just at the edge of the village of Middlesex.

ROBERT S. WITMER, farmer, P. O. Carlisle, was born near Shippensburg, Cumberland County, Penn., December 9, 1850, and is a son of Jacob and Hannah (Senseman) Witmer, natives of Cumberland County, Penn., and of German descent. His grandfather Joseph was born in Lancaster County, but came to Cumberland County when a boy, and was one of the early settlers of the county. He settled near Middlesex Station, where he lived until his death, in about 1854. He was a farmer, and owned a large tract of land. Jacob, subject's father, was born on the homestead in 1814; was a farmer, and a consistent member of the Lutheran Church. He died, in 1874, on the farm now occupied by Robert S. Our subject was reared on a farm, and remained with his father until his death. Mr. Witmer is one of the substantial and successful farmers of the county. He owns 163 acres of good land. His mother is now in her sixty-eighth year, is yet living, and resides with him. She is a consistent member of the Lutheran Church. Mr. Witmer is a member of the I. O. O. F. Lodge, No. 91, Carlisle. He is a prominent man, intelligent and enterprising; politically he is a Republican.

SAMUEL WITMER, farmer, P. O. Middlesex, was born in Cumberland County March 4, 1825, and is a son of Joseph and Catharine (Eberly) Witmer, natives of Lancaster County, Penn., and of German descent. His grandparents came to Cumberland County in 1791, and settled in Middleton (now Middlesex) Township, where they owned a good tract of land, and the house, erected by the grandfather when he first came to the county, is still standing. The grandfather was at one time quite wealthy, but his wealth was considerably reduced on account of the excise tax, which he was obliged to pay on whisky in which he dealt at that time. He lived on the old homestead until his death. Joseph Witmer was born in 1785, and died in 1853. He was one of the successful farmers of the day, made his own way in the world, and at his death owned 315 acres of valuable land. He was a member of the Mennonite Church, the father of nine children, three of whom are living: Mrs. Elizabeth Givler, Samuel and Mrs. Daniel Kutz. Samuel was reared on the farm, and when twenty-nine years of age started in life for himself. In partnership with his brother, Abraham, he farmed the homestead for fourteen years, and in 1868 sold out his interest to his brother, and bought 94 acres of land, where he now lives. His farm is well improved with good buildings, and he now owns 460 acres, also a house at Middlesex Station, which was erected in 1874. It is a large, two-story brick grain warehouse, and affords a commodious store-room and a good shipping point for the vicinity. Mr. Witmer is ticket agent, freight agent and postmaster of the station, the postoffice of which was established in 1878. November 5, 1863, he married Clarissa, daughter of Samuel and Catherine (Waggoner) Williams, and to them six children were born, three of whom are living: Annie M., Joseph and Abram. Mrs. Witmer is a member of the German Reformed Church of Carlisle. Politically Mr. Witmer is a Republican. His mother was one of twelve children, all of whom lived to be married and have families.

JOHN WOLF, farmer, P. O. Middlesex, was born on the farm where he now resides July 6, 1834, and is a son of David and Anna (Corman) Wolf, natives of Pennsylvania and of German descent. His grandfather John was reared in this county, and in 1803 bought the farm where our subject now lives, consisting of 160 acres, on which he made all the improvements. He built a barn 100 feet long, which was destroyed by fire in 1819, and the same year he erected the stone one, 72x45 feet, which is still standing. He also operated a distillery for a number of years on this farm, and hauled the whisky to Baltimore. His wife was a very strong, healthy woman, being able to lift the barrels onto the wagon. He was very successful in life. He died in 1822. David Wolf, his son, was reared on the homestead, and later bought two farms. He owned 376 acres in this county, and 48 acres in Perry County. He served as lieutenant of a rifle military company for many years; also held the office of director of the poor of the county for nine years; was also school director for a number of years; was in politics a Democrat. He died in 1878. Our subject was reared on the farm, and remained at home until twenty-three years of age. January 8, 1857, he married Margaretta Wert, by whom he had one child—Joseph P.—who died at the age of ten years. Mrs. Wolf died October 15, 1862. After his first marriage he settled on the farm now occupied by his brother Joseph. Here his wife died, and after her death he went back to the homestead and remained some three years, when, November 10, 1864, he married Catherine Wetzel, who bore him six children: David H., Raymond S., Anna C., Mary E., Charles H. and Cora E. After his second marriage Mr. Wolf located in Silver Spring Township, where he farmed three years; then moved to his father's farm in West Pennsborough Township, and remained four years. In 1873 he bought the old homestead, where he has since lived. In 1878 his house was totally destroyed by fire, and in the same year he built a large two-story brick residence, at a cost of over $3,000. It has a 14-inch wall, and contains 67,000 brick. It is a beautiful structure, and kept in neat order. Mr. and Mrs. Wolf are members of the Reformed Church. He has held the office of school director; is a member of the I. O. O. F. Lodge, No. 598, of Silver Spring; has held all the offices in his lodge,and is now filling the chaplain's chair. At present he owns 125 acres. On his farm there is a sand bank which yields very fine sand.

JACOB SWILER ZEARING, county commissioner, P. O. Middlesex, is a native of Cumberland County, born in Shiremanstown, January 18, 1843. He attended school and clerked in a general store until eighteen years of age, when he began clerking in the drug store of Dr. C. W. Reiley, president of the Harrisburg Bank. For 8 years he was located in Mechanicsburg, engaged in the drug business for himself. His present fine farm of 100 acres, beautifully situated in Middlesex Township, he purchased in 1875. Mr. Zearing was elected auditor, by the people of Cumberland County, in November, 1882, which office he held three years, when he was elected to his present office of county commissioner. Mr. Zearing is a son of Jacob and Eliza (Swiler) Zearing, both natives of Cumberland County. The old gentleman died December 25, 1885, but his widow is still living, a member of the Bethel Church. Mr. and Mrs. Jacob Zearing had two sons: Jacob S., and Henry M., who resides at Shiremanstown. Our subject married, January 16, 1873, Miss Kate Witmer, daughter of Jacob and Hannah (Senseman) Witmer, both natives of this county, and to this union were born two children: Robert W. and Katie H. The mother died February 2, 1881, a member of the Lutheran Church. Mr. Zearing is one of our leading representative citizens, and stands high in the estimation of the people of Cumberland County, among whom he has lived all his life.

ABRAM J. ZEIGLER, farmer, was born on the old Zeigler homestead, November 5, 1842. His father, Abram Zeigler, Sr., was born in Montgomery County, and came to Cumberland County in 1801. He settled on the farm not far from the North Mountains, in Middlesex Township, now occupied by our subject. The father married Elizabeth Horner, of Cumberland County, and the son, in 1867, married Barbara Rebbert, of the same county. The family consists of five children, all of whom are living on the homestead. This farm was once a portion of a tract owned by one Kenney, an early Scotch-Irish pioneer. From him it descended to the Zeigler family, the representatives of which now own a number of fine farms in the northern portion of Middlesex Township.

HENRY H. ZEIGLER, farmer, is a representative of one of the old German families which, at an early date, settled among the slate hills which extend for some miles in from the North Mountain. He was born on the old homestead, in this portion of Cumberland County, in 1843. Philip Zeigler, the grandfather, was the first pioneer. He settled on the farm where Abram Zeigler now resides. Samuel, the father of Henry H., was born there, and the old log building, part of which was built by David Elliott, with its large chimney in the center, its small, one-pane window, and loop-holes through the logs for rifles, is still standing. Philip Zeigler had a large family. Samuel, his son, was the father of eight children, of whom four, two boys and two girls, are living. Of these, Henry, our subject, is the eldest of the boys. Henry H. married the daughter of Jacob Wagner, of North Middleton Township, Cumberland County, in 1870. His family consists of two sons and three daughters, all of whom are living on the homestead. The farm where our subject resides was originally the property of ¡David Elliott, a man of wealth, and the owner of slaves in the early days. It was also subsequently owned by the Saundersons, who were connected with the Elliotts. Both of these families are now extinct, but their large tract has been but little subdivided.

CHAPTER LI.

MIFFLIN TOWNSHIP.

ALFRED CARL, farmer, P. O. Newville. George Carl and his wife (who was a Heckadorn) came from Berks County, and settled near the Canigagig Ridge, in Perry County, prior to 1809. They reared a family of children: George, Christian and Isaiah (twins), John, Adam, Daniel, Eliza, Rachael and Fanny. Of this family, George learned the blacksmith's trade, came to this county about the year 1834, and was married the same year to Margaret Kulp, a native of Columbia, Lancaster Co., Penn., but who was a resident of White Hill when the nuptials were performed; she, as well as Mr. Carl, is of German descent, her parents coming from Germany. The married life of the young couple was commenced near the village of Loysville, Perry County, but they moved to White Hill later, and in 1843 came to Mifflin Township, this county, locating at the McCormick Mill, in Doubling Gap, where George Carl built and conducted a smithy for twenty-one years. Of his children, Alfred, Mary A., Elizabeth E., and Margaretta, were born at White Hill; David R. was born on the McCalister farm, and Francis E. and Julia A. on the homestead near the mill. Of these, Alfred Carl was born in 1834, learned the trade with his father, and October 14,1856, was married to Elizabeth L., daughter of John and Catharine Oiler, Rev. Hefflefinger, of Newville, performing the ceremony. Andrew and Susannah (Sweetwood) Oiler, grandparents of Mrs. Carl, were residents in this county from 1792; reared a family of twelve children: William, Andrew, John, George, Daniel, James, Margaret, Maria, Catharine, Elizabeth, Susannah and Letitia. Of these, John (father of Mrs. Carl) for many years was a teacher in Frankford and Mifflin Townships. He married Catharine Hefflefinger in April, 1834, and this union was blessed with six children, all born in this county: Elizabeth, John, Catharine, William, George and Mary B. Alfred Carl and his wife commenced married life at West Hill, West Pennsborough Township, where he engaged in blacksmithing. From there they removed to Plainfield, thence to Newville, and, in 1864, to the mills in Mifflin Township, where he purchased the smithy of his father, who bought himself a nice farm near by. For twenty-one years our subject carried on business there, earning his money by the sweat of his brow. In 1885, he purchased his father's farm, and now resides on it. To Mr. and Mrs. Alfred Carl have been born eleven children: Mary E. (wife of Henry H. Hoover), Kate B., Margaret L., Lizzie D., Lottie T., George, Clara A., Albert I., Charles T., Millie A. and Morris R. This large family, with the exception of Letitia, Lottie and Morris R., who are deceased, are now residing beneath the paternal roof. Especial attention has been paid to their education, and all will surely follow the good example showed them by their parents.

SAMUEL CHRISTLIEB, retired, Newville. In the year 1765 Frederick Carl Christlieb (grandfather of Samuel) emigrated, with his wife, sons Frederick Carl and Jacob and step-son George Buck, from Durkheim, Rhenish Bavaria, to America, landing at Baltimore, Md. The sons, who were in their minority, located near the boundary line between Pennsylvania and Maryland and close to the Susquehanna River, where they remained for several years. The parents, soon after their arrival in Baltimore, found their way to Newville, this county, and were among the earliest German settlers in this locality. The mother died in a few years, and her remains were interred in the Big Spring burial-grounds. A few years later the father died while en route to a physician's home in Virginia, where he hoped to get relief from the disease which caused his death. The family did not become permanently settled for several years after their arrival in America. Charles Christlieb and his step-brother George Buck came to Mifflin Township, and their brother Jacob settled in Virginia. Charles Christlieb was born in Germany in 1750. After his marriage with Catharine Umberger, of Lebanon, Penn., about 1780, he settled in Mifflin Township, this county. To this union were born six sons and one daughter: John, Charles, Solomon, George, Sarah (married to a Mr. Koutz), Isaac and Jacob (twins), who were born in 1791. Charles Christlieb died in 1837, aged eighty-seven, and his widow a few months later, aged ninety-three. Jacob, the father of our subject, was married, April 13, 1824, to Julia Ann Morritt, by whom he had ten children: Samuel, Mary J., Ann, Elizabeth, Nancy, Sarah, David, Lavina, Levi and Ellen (twins). Jacob Christlieb was a quiet but enterprising farmer, and was noted for his liberality and Christian spirit. He was for almost three-quarters of a century a communing member of the Lutheran Church, and from 1833 he was a member of Zion Church at Newville. He died at the residence of his son Samuel, May, 9, 1884, aged ninety-three years, one month and twenty-one days. His funeral sermon was preached by the Rev. S. A. Diehl, from a text selected by himself, viz.: "Daughters of Jerusalem, weep not for me, but weep for yourselves, and for your children." Luke xxiii, 28. He came "to the grave in a full age, like as a shock of corn cometh in its season." Three sons, seven daughters, forty-eight grandchildren and sixteen great-grandchildren yet remain to do honor to his good name. Our subject was born on the homestead October 10, 1826. In 1851 he married Matilda Hershey, of Mifflin Township, and their wedded life was commenced on her father's farm, where they remained twelve years. Their children, Esemiah C., Ida M. and William A., were born on that farm; thence Mr. Christlieb moved to a farm near Newburg, remaining there two years, when he returned to his father's homestead, where he remained until 1882, when he purchased a neighboring farm and erected an imposing residence, a large barn and commodious out-buildings, taking possession the same year. The eldest daughter is the wife of Henry J. Whistler; the other children reside at home with their parents. Mr. and Mrs. Christlieb are a model couple and are reverenced in their neighborhood.

ALBERT S. GILLESPIE, farmer, P. O. Newville, born September 13, 1846, in Frankford Township, this county, is a great-grandson of William Gillespie, a native of Scotland, who immigrated to America about the year 1700, and settled in Cecil County, Md., where he lived until the year 1766. He then sold his plantation there and purchased a large tract of land in what is now known as Frankford and Mifflin Townships, Cumberland County. His family consisted of ten children: Robert, Margaret, Samuel, Eloner, James, Nathaniel, George (who died in infancy), Ann, William and George. Of these, the youngest son, George, married Sarah Young, of Cumberland County, and they reared a family of ten children, all of whom were born in Frankford Township this county. Their names are William, Elizabeth, Eloner, Mary, Nelly, Margaret, Ann, James, Samuel and George. Of these the youngest son, George, the only one living, married Lucinda B. Stewart, by whom he had eight children: Sarah B., Thomas G., Robert, Albert S. (our subject), James, Elizabeth J., Samuel B. and Mary E. This large family was reared on the farm, still George Gillespie's property, though a few years since he moved to Newville, where he lives a retired life. His wife died in 1875, having lived to see her children comfortably settled and the beautiful Cumberland Valley transformed into a miniature paradise. Albert S., our subject, was married September 19, 1878, to Amelia, daughter of James T. and Martha Stuart, of this county, Rev. Erskine, a Presbyterian divine, performing the ceremony. The housekeeping of the newly wedded couple was commenced on the farm since purchased by them, and which is now one of the most attractive in the valley. The neat brick residence, fine barn and commodious out-buildings are situated within a valley flanked on three sides by the Blue Mountains, which is picturesque either in summer or midwinter. Their children, three in number are Joseph S., M. Jane S. and George Y. Mr. and Mrs. Gillespie are members of the Presbyterian Church, having remained true to the faith of their ancestors. He has refused to fill official positions in the township, which, by reason of good judgment and a practical education, he is eminently qualified for, but always lends his influence toward the advancement of the business, social and educational interests of the township. The Gillespies were among the first settlers in this part of the county.

JACOB HEMMINGER, retired, Newville, was born in Mifflin Township, this county, March 16, 1810. His parents, Jacob and Susan (Ramp) Hemminger, were both born in Berks County, Penn., and with their two children, John and Elizabeth, came to Cumberland County in 1804, remaining the first year with Mr. Hemminger's brother near Carlisle, Penn. About 1806 he purchased the farm where our subject now resides and on which he was born. Two children, Mary and Catharine, were born on this farm prior to Jacob, and Benjamin was born afterward. Catharine married Jacob Bowman and, with her brother (of whom we write), represents the entire Hemminger family of the original stock. The house now owned by our subject was built prior to the purchase of the farm by his father, but has since been repaired and is yet a handsome substantial dwelling. Jacob Hemminger, Sr., was a prominent man in the Lutheran Church; he cared little for politics. He was a tailor by trade, which occupation he followed in the winter, devoting the summer to farming. He died in 1830 and his widow in 1862. Jacob Hemminger, Jr., purchased the homestead in 1838, and in 1844 wedded Mary, daughter of Henry and Elizabeth (Sensabaugh) Brehm, of this township, Rev. John Heck performing the ceremony. On the farm where he was born and reared, Jacob and his young wife commenced their domestic life, and there were born their six children: John D., Samuel H., Susan M., Elizabeth, Mary and Annie M. John D. married Maria Fry and, after her death, Mrs. Elizabeth Green; Samuel H. wedded Martha J. Lenny; Susan M. and Elizabeth reside with their father; Annie M. is the wife of Samuel J. Zeigler; Mary married John E. Lehman. Our subject learned the wheelwright's trade of John Albert, who, in 1830, had a shop near Conodoguinet Creek. A few years later Mr. Hemminger established a shop on his own farm, and has carried on the business steadily for more than half a century. He has been a successful business man, and has reared a family who do credit to the old name they bear. The death of Mrs. Hemminger occurred in 1857, since which time the daughters mentioned above have been housekeepers for their father. Our subject voted for Gen. Jackson and Martin Van Buren, but after that time was a Whig, and since the formation of the party has been an ardent Republican. He is one of the oldest living residents of Mifflin Township, and bears a reputation for honesty and uprightness. Eight grandchildren look up to the venerable man, and it is hoped that his last days will be pleasantly spent on the ancestral manor amid peace, comfort and plenty.

W. H. McCREA, teacher, Newville, is a grandson of William McCrea, who left County Tyrone, Ireland, for this country, in June, 1790, bringing with him his wife, Margaret (Ballentine), daughter, Sarah, and an infant son, Walter, who died on shipboard and found a grave in the broad Atlantic. They settled the same year near Newville, in West Pennsborough Township, this county, and after residing there several years moved to the vicinity of Bloserville, in Frankford Township. William McCrea was a weaver by trade and followed this occupation until his death. To him and his wife were born eight children, all natives of this country but the two already mentioned: Sarah, wife of James Wallace; Walter (deceased); Martha, wife of Alexander Logan; Catharine, wife of Robert Giffin; Margaret, wife of James Hume; Jane, wife of Robert Fenton; William, married to Mary, daughter of Henry and Elizabeth (Mentzer) Snyder, and John. Of these John was born May 28, 1803, and followed the occupation of farmer until his fifty-first year. June 15, 1854, he married Barbara M. Snyder (sister of his brother William's wife), the Rev. Joshua Evans, a Lutheran divine, performing the ceremony. Several years prior to his marriage, John McCrea had purchased the mill property and farm formerly owned by Samuel J. McCormick, at sheriff's sale. Mr. McCormick was a noted man in the valley in his day, his ancestors being among the first settlers of Doubling Gap. For a quarter of a century the mills were operated under the supervision of Mr. McCrea, who disposed of the property, in 1868, to Maj. Henry Snyder, but it is still known as the McCrea Mills. Two children were born to John McCrea and wife: W. H. and Mattie E., who became the wife of H. M. Koser, in 1882. John McCrea died March 19, 1879, at the ripe age of seventy-six. He was born and reared amid the privations attending a pioneer's life, but in his last years witnessed the substantial development of his beloved county. His first ballot was cast in 1824 for Gen. Jackson, and from that date he never swerved from the Democratic party, in fifty-five years never missing an election, either special or general. W. H. McCrea, his son, was born January 13, 1856, in Mifflin Township. From his early childhood he showed a fondness for books, and at an early age was sent to the brick schoolhouse near the mill, and William M. Hamilton, who was for a number of years an able instructor, gave him his first start. As our subject increased in years and knowledge a desire came to him to impart his information to others, and he taught his first term in the Blean Schoolhouse, Mifflin Township. The following year he received a course of instruction at the normal school in Shippensburg, after which, for five consecutive terms, he taught in the Blean School. He accepted a position in the grammar school at Newville in 1880, and two years later was promoted to the position of principal, in which he has since continued. As a practical educator he has but few equals and no superiors in the county. Courteous, social, talented, and coming from ancestors noted in this county as honest and practical men, the people of Mifflin Township have reason to be proud of W. H. McCrea who was born, bred, reared and educated in their midst, and here has developed into one of the most widely-known educators in the county.

LEWIS C. MEGAW, farmer, P. O. Newville, is a grandson of James and Sarah (Murrell) McGaw, who were married in West Chester, Chester Co., Penn., November 27, 1804. James McGaw was a native of Belfast, Ireland, whence he emigrated in consequence of participating in a rebellion against the crown of England. In 1817 he came to Mifflin Township, Cumberland Co., Penn., with his wife and one son, Samuel, settling on the John Cutshall farm. He also owned the farm, now the property of John Hurst, which remained in the McGaw family from 1817 to 1882. He was in his day a prominent local Democratic politician, and, although not a member, he was an ardent supporter of the Presbyterian Church, contributing largely to the Big Spring Church. His son Samuel was born April 17, 1807; was married about 1826 to Elizabeth Gurrell, who was born in Newville, Penn., and whose entire life was passed in Cumberland County. Their domestic life was commenced on his father's farm, where their children—Sarah, James, Belle, Jane, Mary and Scott—were born. When Samuel McGaw came to the farm where our subject now lives, he was accompanied by his mother, who made her home with him until her death. On this farm were born the other children of Mr. and Mrs. Samuel McGaw: John, George, Lewis C. and Ellen. All of the ten children reached adult age. George enlisted in Company F, Seventeenth Pennsylvania Cavalry, in 1861; was captured at Brandy Station in 1863, and confined in Libby Prison, from whence, a few months later, the gallant soldier was carried an emaciated corpse. Lewis C. Megaw, our subject, was born February 24, 1845. Leaving home in 1870 he began lumbering in Clinton and Potter Counties, Penn., and Allegany, N. Y. Returning to this county in 1876 he was married to Miss Julia, daughter of George and Margaret (Kulp) Carl. Mr. Megaw and his young wife commenced housekeeping on the farm where he was born and reared, and here four children were born to them: Samuel, George, Florence and Grace. Mr. Megaw has been an enterprising and prosperous farmer, and, like his ancestors before him, has taken

MIFFLIN TOWNSHIP.

an active part in local politics. He has been elected an official of the township several terms, which of itself is sufficient proof that he has served his constituents faithfully and well. Coming from a family of the highest respectability and having a wife belonging to a family that for more than a century has been identified with the growth and prosperity of Cumberland County, it is with pleasure that a place is given them in the history. The name was McGaw originally, but the children have by common consent changed it to Megaw, but it still shines as brightly now as did that of James McGaw, who had to flee for his life from the isle of Erin.

JOSEPH MINNICH, farmer, P. O. Newville, is a son of Daniel Minnich, who came with his parents from Perry to Berks County, Penn., in 1808. There were a number of sturdy sons and daughters, and a farm was purchased, on which not only the grandparents but also the parents of our subject lived and died. Daniel Minnich (son of George Minnich) was married to Mary Kozer, in 1823, and about that date purchased the homestead in this county. Their children were as follows: Jeremiah, John, Eliza, Daniel, William, Joseph, David, George, Andrew and Columbus. Of these, Eliza is the wife of Daniel M. Derr, and she and our subject reside in this county; William was a soldier during the late war of the Rebellion, the others remaining on the farm. Joseph Minnich was married, May 18, 1865, to Catharine A., daughter of Samuel and Mary Collor, of Perry County, Penn., the ceremony being performed by the Rev. Peter Song, a Lutheran divine. They commenced house-keeping, in 1869, on the Westhafer farm, near Green Spring. The first years of wedded life were spent on the farm with his parents, and there Ida E. and Annie M. were born. The only son, Daniel, was born on the Woodburn farm near Newville. In 1880 Mr. Minnich purchased a nice farm near the pleasant village of Newville, and he is considered one of the prosperous farmers of Mifflin Township, ranking high in the estimation of the public as a good business manager. The home is made pleasant by the comforts which come to those who make their money honestly, and by the good taste of mother and daughters. The parents are worthy members of the Lutheran Church and have reared their children in that faith.

MICHAEL SHAMBAUGH, farmer, P. O. Newville. It is safe to say that George Shambaugh, the grandfather of Michael, came to Cumberland County prior to the year 1790. His parents, of whom no history can be obtained, had two sons and several daughters, but only the sons, George and Philip, can be located, both of whom settled in Frankford Township, this county, and George's youngest son, John, born in this township, and now ninety-two years of age, resides in Harrison County, Ohio. His sons were named Jacob, George, John and Philip, and there was one daughter, Catharine, who married Jacob Holtz, of Richland County, Ohio. Philip, the youngest son, married Elizabeth, daughter of Adam and Mary Kessler, of Perry County, who was born in Frankford Township, this county, in 1798. At the time of his marriage Philip Shambaugh resided in Perry County, and he commenced housekeeping in Toboyne Township, where he afterward purchased a farm. To him and his wife were born seven children, of whom John, Sarah, Mary and Michael are living. Michael, the last named, was married, in the autumn of 1851, to Mary A., daughter of Daniel and Esther Cutshall, of Toboyne Township, Perry Co., Penn. They commenced wedded life on the paternal homestead with but little of this world's goods ($80), but they went to work with a will, and he soon purchased an interest of one of the heirs, and when the place was sold, after the death of his father, he owned half the proceeds. Four children were born on the homestead—the first died in infancy; then came Lavina J., Josiah and Isaac. Josiah married Bessie Kremer, Isaac married Rebecca Dewalt, and Lavina is the wife of John Hoover. All have done well, and Mr. and Mrs. Shambaugh may congratulate themselves on having such representatives. In 1866 our subject and his family came to Mifflin Township, this county, and after renting his farm for one year, purchased it, and has since, by economical habits and industry, earned enough to pay for the splendid tract, and on this farm the youngest son, John F., was born. For an upright, conscientious man Mr. Shambaugh ranks high in the estimation of his neighbors, and those who know him best testify to his mental and moral worth. He has a fine farm and comfortable home, and has never made a dollar dishonestly.

CHAPTER LII.

MONROE TOWNSHIP.

GEORGE BELTZHOOVER, farmer, Boiling Springs. The grandfather of the subject of this sketch, George Beltzhoover, the first of this name of whom we find any record, served in the war of 1812; moved from York County to this county, and here bought land. He was the father of eight children by his first wife: Catharine, Michael, George, Elizabeth, Jacob, John, Rachael and Sarah; by his second marriage with a Mrs. Gross he had one son, Daniel, who lived to be over seventeen years of age. His son, John, was born in York County, Penn., in 1798, came to this county with his father when a boy, and became a farmer. He married Margaret Smith, in 1822, and had three children: George, Anne and Mahala. Mr. and Mrs. John Beltzhoover were members of the Lutheran Church; in politics he was a Republican. He was a land-holder (part of the estate is still in the family), and lived on his farm near Boiling Springs over fifty years. His house was the scene of one of the most cowardly and brutal robberies ever perpetrated. At the time (July 29, 1878), his household consisted of his aged wife, over seventy-six years of age, a female servant, sixty years old, and himself, about eighty. The old gentleman and lady slept down stairs and were awake at the time the robbers effected an entrance, who bound him and his servant with a cord from the bed, after beating Mr. Beltzhoover with a club until his head was cut open. The old lady, though treated roughly, was not injured severely, and was forced to act as their guide. Bureau drawers were ransacked and were "thrown on her feet so that the nails came off her toes," and their contents scattered on the floor: the house was thoroughly searched for about two hours and over $100 in silver coin and greenbacks secured. The alarm was given by the servant, who worked herself loose and made her escape while the robbers were in the house, and saved the house from fire and probably the lives of the aged couple, by bringing timely assistance. Word was sent to all the different places in the county and a reward of $100 offered for their arrest. Constables Johnston and Altland, of Dillsburg, got on their trail the morning after the robbery and tracked them to a barn about six miles below Dillsburg, where they were secreted in a hay-mow. On going in one entered on his toes and the other on his heels. In the morning the constables searched the hay-mow but failed to find them, but in the evening the barn was again visited, and on hearing a slight noise in the mow they proceeded to the spot and probed with a pitchfork, when one of them said he would come out. Two rough looking men crawled from their hiding place, and were immediately taken before Mr. and Mrs. Beltzhoover, who identified them as being the party who twenty-four hours before had disturbed their quiet home by cowardly ill-treating and robbing them. J. C. Lehman, Esq., of Boiling Springs, before whom they were next taken, then committed them to jail. One of the men came from Pottsville and the other from Harrisburg, and their names were John Lemon and John Myers, both of whom were recognized by the jail officials as tramps, both being young men not over twenty-one years of age, heavy set, but not tall. On being searched the money taken from Mrs. Beltzhoover was recovered, also a watch and chain, two revolvers and a razor. The money was equally divided between them. Mr. Beltzhoover paid the reward at once. The prisoners were sent to the penitentiary. Mr. Beltzhoover lived to be nearly eighty-four years of age, considered one of the best citizens of the county, and always contributed largely of his means to build up the township. George Beltzhoover, son of the above, was born in Monroe Township, this county, in 1823, on his grandfather's farm. He married, in 1846, Miss Maria C. Niesley, of this county, daughter of Jacob Niesley, and this union was blessed with six children: Mary E., John A., Margaret A., Maria C., Clara E. and Monroe C. Mr. and Mrs. George Beltzhoover are members of the Lutheran Church. In politics he is a Republican.

JOSEPH BERKHEIMER, farmer, P. O. Mechanicsburg, was born in York County, Penn., July 14, 1833. His grandfather, Valentine Berkheimer, was born in same county, and was a fuller by trade. He married Elizabeth Lauchs, of York County, and had eight children: John, Samuel, Henry, George, Andrew, Elizabeth, Catharine and Leah. He was a member of the Lutheran Church; in politics, a strong Democrat. John Berkheimer, our subject's father, a shoemaker by trade, was also born in York County in 1803; was married to Miss Lydia, daughter of John and Elizabeth (Sifert) Slothower. To this union were born the following children: Joseph, Henry, Catharine, Susan, Elizabeth, Leah and Rebecca. He was a member of the Lutheran Church; in politics, a Democrat. He was honest and industrious, a kind father and husband, and died in his seventy-sixth year. Our subject, who learned carpentering, came in 1851 to this county, and followed his trade. In 1853 he married Miss Catharine, daughter of Jacob and Fannie (Musser) Eckert. This union has been blessed with seven children: John, Agnes, Alice, Joseph, Margaret, Jacob and George. Subject and wife are members of the German Reformed Church. In 1882 he moved with his family to his present residence. Politically, like his father, Mr. Berkheimer is a Democrat. In 1864 he enlisted at Carlisle in Company F, Two Hundred and Ninth Regiment, Pennsylvania Volunteer Infantry, for one year; went with his company to Baltimore; and thence to City Point; from there to Point of Rocks, where a severe battle was fought; thirteen were killed or taken prisoners from Company F alone. Mr. Berkheimer was in another battle at Mead's Station, where the regiment suffered severely, Company F losing fourteen men—seven killed and seven taken prisoners—including Henry Lee, of Carlisle, who was badly wounded. The war closing, Mr. Berkheimer returned to Harrisburg, where he was mustered out in 1865. When he went to war Mr. Berkheimer left a family consisting of his wife and five small children, who may now point with pride to their father's record as a soldier. Mrs. Berkheimer's great-grandfather Eckert came from Germany when a young man, and settled in York County, Penn., over a hundred years ago, and followed the business of a real estate dealer, but subsequently moved to Lancaster County, Penn., and there died. Of his four children, two were sons: Michael and Philip. Michael was born in York County, a wagonmaker by trade; married Catharine Young, of York County, and had the following named children: Henry, John, Jacob (father of Mrs. Berkheimer), George, Henry, Mary and Elizabeth. Michael Eckert was a member of the German Reformed Church, a sober, industrious man, always attentive to his business. Jacob Eckert was born in York County in 1803; learned wagon-making; married Miss Fanny Mercer, of York County, and had a family of six children: Michael, John, Joseph, Catharine (Mrs. Berkheimer), Susan and Fannie. In 1833 Mr. Eckert moved to this county, and in 1878 to his present farm, and is now a venerable gentleman, who has lived an honorable and valuable life.

GEORGE M. BRANDT, manufacturer and postmaster, Brandtsville. Martain Brandt, the great-grandfather, who emigrated from Hummelstown, Dauphin Co., Penn., to Cumberland County, Penn., in 1773, built a stone house in 1776, a barn in 1777, and a large mansion in 1779. The two houses are in good condition to-day, and are now owned by Henry Hesey. He was a large land-holder, owning about 1,000 acres of land. He had six children: Catherine, Martain, Betzy, Adam, David and Henrietta. Martain Brandt, Sr., departed this life March 26, 1835, aged eighty-five years, five months and fifteen days. Barbra Brandt, wife of Martain Brandt, departed this life February 26, 1855, aged seventy-nine years, eleven months and sixteen days. Martain Brandt, Jr., grandfather of Geo. M. Brandt, was born on the homestead, in this township, inherited from his father and which has been in the family since 1773. He was also a manufacturer, and built a saw-mill and a clover-mill. He married Miss Catherine Beltzhoover, of this county, October 16, 1810, who bore him six children: Rachel, Michael G., Samuel, George, Henry and Sarah. He met his death by an accident, caused by a runaway team, and died July 24, 1833, in his forty-ninth year. His widow lived to be eighty-four, and was remarkably well and active up to her last day. Michael G., the oldest son of this couple, born in the old homestead August 23, 1816, was a farmer and manufacturer, carrying on the business of his father. He married, April 5, 1846, Miss Eleanor, daughter of Jacob Emmett, of York, York Co., Penn., and to this union were born seven children: Henrietta E., George M., Jennie M., Jacob E., Samuel H., Lydia E. and Annie K. He erected the homestead, workhouse, and, in fact, most of the buildings on the property. He manufactured both red and yellow ocher and lumber. He was a very prominent man, and did a large business in iron ore and other enterprises, among which was buying and selling stock. He and his wife were members of the Lutheran Church. In politics he was a Republican. He was a liberal man and did a great deal for the poor, and some of the neighbors depended on him for any aid they might require, and he acted as bondsman for many men. When the railroad was built through Brandtsville, he assisted the enterprise in every way. He is well remembered for his mild and pleasant ways and honorable dealings. George M. Brandt, our subject, was born on the old homestead July 2, 1848, and passed his early days assisting his father. June 20, 1872, he married Miss Mary C. Lehman, of this county, and to this union were born seven children: Bertha G., Ellen E., Eva R., Laura E., Mary C., Michael E. and Marcy G. Mr. Brandt lives with his large family on the old homestead, and on land which has been in the family for 113 years. He carries on the manufacture of lumber and red and yellow ocher, and conducts a coal yard and warehouse besides two farms. He is postmaster of Brandtsville. In politics he is a Republican. He is a man of most excellent reputation and standing as a business man.

DAVID L. CLARK, farmer, P. O. Mechanicsburg, Penn. The family originated in England. John Clark, the grandfather of David L., was born there in 1727, and came to America when a young man; he married in this county, and became the father of seven children, four sons, John, Thomas, James and William, and three daughters. John Clark, Sr., entered 300 acres of land, and built the first flouring-mill in this county on the

Yellow Breeches Creek; lived to be nearly seventy-nine years old, and was greatly respected for his sterling worth. William Clark, the father of our subject, was born in Cumberland County, Penn., October 12, 1768; married Sarah Lamb, March 5, 1798, and had eleven children—nine sons and two daughters. He inherited half of his father's property (150 acres of land and the mill), and was a prominent man in the community, serving as justice of the peace for more than twenty years. One of his sons, Richey Clark, of Dillsburg, Penn., inherited 72 acres of the original tract, and which has thus remained in the Clark family for more than 140 years. David L. Clark, the present representative of the family in this county, was born June 13, 1808, on the banks of the Yellow Breeches Creek, at Clark's mill, this county. He married Elizabeth Mumper May 1, 1828, and to this union were born four sons and four daughters: William, John, Andrew A., David R., Sarah A., Margaret J., Hannah C. and Mary E.—all living but one that died in infancy. Our subject lived one year at the mill after marriage, and then began farming on his father's farm, near Mechanicsburg, where he remained eighteen years, and at his father's death the farm became his by inheritance. He has resided, in all, thirty-four years on this one farm. In 1862 he built his present residence at the Trindle road. Mr. Clark has been a consistent member of the Presbyterian Church for nearly fifty years, an elder in it for the past twenty-five years, and is now the oldest male member of the Mechanicsburg Church. Never an office seeker, he has held some minor offices, being a strong Republican in a Democratic county. That Mr. Clark has always been true to his convictions, and had full faith in the Government in the dark days of its trials in 1863, is shown by the fact that though while he was building his present substantial brick residence the great battle of Gettysburg was being fought about 25 miles away, yet he continued his building at the time of Gen. Lee's invasion of Pennsylvania.

CYRUS DORNBACH, farmer, P. O. Mechanicsburg. The Dornbach family is of German origin, and came to this country at a period long antedating the Revolutionary war. The great-grandfather of our subject was born in Lancaster County, Penn., and was the first of the name of whom we have any record. George Dornbach (grandfather of Cyrus) was also born in Lancaster County, Penn., married Mary Brenicer, of the same county, and had the following children: John, Jacob, Elizabeth, Annie, Catharine and Sarah. Mr. and Mrs. George Dornbach were members of the German Baptist Church. Their son, John, was born on his father's farm, in Lancaster County, Penn., in 1799; was a miller by trade. In 1829 he married Miss Sarah Mohler, of same county, and this union was blessed with two children: Levi M. and Cyrus. In 1832 John Dornbach removed with his family to this county, and settled on the farm now owned by his son Cyrus. He was a German Baptist, as was also his wife. In politics he was a strong Republican. He was a thorough-going business man, honest and upright in all his dealings, and at his death owed no man a dollar. He was universally respected by his friends and neighbors, being a kind hearted, generous man. Cyrus Dornbach, Jr., was born on his father's farm, in this county, in 1835, and has passed his entire life on the same land. In 1861 he married Miss Sarah Mater, of this county, and to them were born Ulysses G., John V., Alice S., Sarah M., Cora E., Mabel D., Noah and Rosa C. Mrs. Dornbach is a member of the United Brethren Church. Cyrus Dornbach is a Republican in politics.

CHRISTIAN FULMER, farmer, P. O. Mechanicsburg. Christian Fulmer, the grandfather of our subject, was born near Strasburg, Germany. He was the father of two sons: Christian and one who was killed in the French Army under Napoleon Bonaparte in the war for religious freedom which was waged against the Pope of Rome. Christian Fulmer was born in 1791; married Sarah Peifer and had six children: Elizabeth, Christian, Charles, George, Barbara and Leah. About 1830 he moved to this country with his family, the mother wishing her sons to escape the rigid military regulation of that country, where all males of proper age are subject to enrolment. The family landed in Baltimore, and, finding relatives, came by their advice to Mechanicsburg, this county, where Mr. Fulmer found work at his trade. He later removed to Pittsburgh, Penn., remaining but a short time, however. He died March 19, 1842. He was a very pious man, a member of the Lutheran Church. Christian Fulmer, our subject, was born, (as was his father before him) near Strasburg, Germany, and came to this country with the family when a lad of eleven years. He underwent great privations when young, and could go to school but little. His father being sick and very poor, young Christian early began to assist the family by hard work and perseverance, helping his parents greatly until their death. Among our subject's earliest remembrances is the time when he was with the other children at his mother's knee, listening to the lessons taught by Christ in the New Testament. Mr. Fulmer greatly reveres his mother's name, for it was she who taught him the principles of honesty, saying that "An honest heart will prevail." In early life our subject learned the trade of carpenter. In 1844 he married Miss Catharine Myers, and to them were born four children: Edmond, Christian, Susan and Catharine. After marriage Mr. Fulmer lived a short time in Mechanicsburg and then moved to his present residence. At that time the farm was small, but, by diligence, hard work and economy, more land was gradually bought and the farm increased. He is a man who loves honesty and carefulness, and teaches his children the principles of truth and uprightness. His son Edmond married Miss Mary Plough, of this county, and has two children: Mary A. and Sarah S. His daughter Susan married John Warner, of this county, and has two children: F. Christian and Blanche. Mr. Fulmer is a member of the Lutheran Church, and is a very religious man. He has had many sorrows, but puts his trust in Him who doeth all things well for his final reward.

JOHN B. GARVER, German Baptist minister, P. O. Allen, is a grandson of Benjamin Garver, who was born in Lancaster County, Penn., about the year 1771, his ancestors having emigrated from Germany at an early date. Benjamin Garver was a farmer and landholder, and moved from Lancaster to Franklin County, Penn., at an early date, where the following named children were born: John, Daniel, Samuel, Benjamin, Joseph, Susan and Sarah. He lived to be sixty-five years of age. His son Benjamin, father of our subject, was born in 1810 in Franklin County, Penn., and began life for himself as a teamster. In 1836 he married, and in 1837 bought a farm in Franklin County, Penn. He was the father of eleven children: Elizabeth, John B., David, Levi, Benjamin, Samuel, Daniel, Christian, Amanda, William and Abraham. Benjamin Garver moved to Huntingdon County, Penn., in 1851; was a member of the German Baptist Church. He was a sober, industrious man, noted for his energy and honesty. John B., our subject, was born October 11, 1840, on his father's farm in Franklin County, Penn. He received his education in the common schools and at the academy at Shirleysburg, Penn. At the age of twenty-two, becoming interested in religion, he joined the German Baptist Church. The next year he was elected minister by the congregation. He began preaching immediately in Huntingdon County, Penn. In 1863 he married Miss Sarah S., daughter of Samuel Loutz, of Huntingdon County, Penn. To them were born two children: Ira A. and Loretta A. In 1870 his wife died, and in 1872 he married Miss Sarah D., daughter of George and Sarah (Baker) Brindle, of Cumberland County, and by her he has two children: Lizzie B. and Paulina E. In 1875 Mr. Garver moved to this county and began preaching. He and his wife are beloved by their congregation and the people for their Christian worth and high character. Mrs. Garver is a member of one of the oldest families in Monroe Township, her great-grandfather emigrating from Germany years ago, and was subsequently drowned while crossing the ocean, on a visit. George Brindle (Mrs. Garver's grandfather) was born in Cumberland County, Penn., and was a farmer, land-holder and distiller in Monroe Township. He married Elizabeth Bricker, of this county, by whom he had six children: John, George, Peter, Solomon, Elizabeth and Susan. He was a member of the German Reformed Church. George Brindle (father of Mrs. Garver) was born in this township in 1796; married Sarah Baker, daughter of Daniel and Barbara (Keller) Baker, of Lancaster County, Penn., by whom he had seven children: Cyrus, Elizabeth, Amos, Barbara, Rebecca, George and Sarah D. (twins). Mr. George Brindle was a very prosperous man, a member of the State Legislature, and held other offices of trust. He was administrator of a number of estates and guardian of several families of children. He lived to the patriarchal age of eighty-five, respected by all, and his death was deeply lamented by his many friends.

JOHN HERTZLER, farmer, P. O. Allen. The grandfather of the subject of our sketch, a farmer during his lifetime, was born in Lancaster County, Penn., in 1773, and married Miss Mary Brubaker, of same county, by whom he had nine children: Annie, Jacob, Mary, Christian, Elizabeth, John, Barbara, Abraham and Rudolph. He was a respected member of the Mennonite Church. Abraham, the father of our subject, was born in Lancaster County, Penn., in 1812, and passed his early life on his father's farm. In 1837 he married Miss Mary Bender, of Lancaster County, Penn. To this union were born nine children: Rudolph, Christian, Michael, Charles, John, Elizabeth, Daniel, Mary and Amos. Abraham Hertzler moved to Cumberland County in 1852, and is now a venerable gentleman, the snows of many winters having whitened his hair and beard. He is a devout Christian and a member of the Mennonite Church. John Hertzler, our subject, was also born in Lancaster County, Penn., in 1846, and came to this county with his father when a boy. In 1876 he married Miss Martha Bowman, of York County, Penn., daughter of Christian and Susan Bowman, parents of the following children: John, Jacob, Calvin, Samuel, Martha and Jane. Mr. Bowman is a member of the German Reformed Church, and is still living in York County at the age of seventy-five years. Mr. and Mrs. John Hertzler have two children; Earle B. and Elva Margaret. Mrs. Hertzler is a member of the German Reformed Church. In politics our subject is a Republican. By his unaided efforts he has accumulated enough to buy a good homestead, pleasantly situated. Mr. Hertzler holds to the principles taught him by his father—honesty, industry and carefulness. His children may well be proud of these traits in the family character.

JACOB M. HERTZLER, farmer, P. O. Allen, is a grandson of —— Hertzler, who was born in this country, and came to Lancaster County, Penn., when a young man, settling on a farm; he was the father of six children. Christian Hertzler, his son, born in Lancaster County, Penn., in 1806, was a farmer by occupation; married Miss Barbara Myers, and to this union were born eight children: Abraham, Mary, Christian, Samuel, Elias, Barbara, Jacob M. and Benjamin, all now living, except Abraham. Christian Hertzler moved to this county in 1839, and bought a farm in Monroe Township, which is now owned by his son Elias. Mr. and Mrs. Christian Hertzler were members of the

Mennonite Church. In politics he was a Republican. He was a kind, pleasant man, governing his family more by love than fear, and was known for his honesty, industry and generosity to the poor. He died in this county in his sixty-seventh year. Jacob M. Hertzler, his son, was born in this county in 1848, and received such education as the public school then afforded. In 1873 he married Miss Emma, daughter of George Beltzhoover, of this county, and the union was blessed with four children: Barbara R., James W., Emma L. and Jacob B. Mr. and Mrs. Hertzler are members of the Lutheran Church, in which he has served as deacon three years. He renders all the assistance in his power to his church and the cause of Christ.

ELIAS HERTZLER, farmer, P. O. Williams Mill. The founder of this family came to this county from Germany at early day. The great-grandfather was born in Lancaster County, Penn., on a farm. Christian Hertzler, the father of our subject, was born in Lancaster County, Penn., in 1806, and was a farmer by occupation. He married Miss Barbara Myers, and to this union were born eight children: Abraham, Mary, Christian, Samuel, Elias, Barbara, Jacob and Benjamin. Christian Hertzler moved to this county in 1837, and bought a farm in Monroe Township, which is now owned by his son Elias. Mr. Hertzler and wife were earnest members of the Mennonite Church; he was an energetic and upright man, accumulated a good deal of property, and gave each of sons a good farm. Elias Hertzler was born on the old homestead in 1837, and has spent his entire life on the old farm. In 1865 he married Miss Sarah J., daughter of Jacob Lehman, of this county. This union was blessed with seven children: Clara Agnes, Sarah Jane, Albert Alcidor, David Lehman, Catharine Barbara, Alice Gertrude and Edna. Mr. and Mrs. Hertzler are members of the Mennonite Church. They met with a sad misfortune in the death of three of their children in the fall of 1884, by diphtheria, in the short space of a few weeks. This great affliction caused great sadness to their hearts, but, with trust in Him who doeth all things well, they have borne their great burden with Christian patience and resignation.

E. J. HOOVER, druggist and farmer, P. O. Williams Mill. The great-great-grandfather of the subject of this sketch came to this country a great many years ago, and settled in Dauphin County, Penn. His son Christian Hoover was born in Dauphin County, married Susan Spidle, of Cumberland County, and had six children: John P. D., Christian, David, Elizabeth, Catharine and Susan. Christian Hoover and his wife were members of the Lutheran Church. They first settled in Cumberland County, but later moved to Franklin County, where Mr. Hoover died at fifty years of age. John P. D., one of the sons of this couple, was born in Dauphin County, Penn., in 1789; married Hester Myers, and had six children who attained maturity: Henry, Elizabeth, John, Mandilla, George and Christian. John P. D. Hoover was a member of the Lutheran Church; in politics he was a Democrat. John Hoover, the son of J. P. D. Hoover, was born in Franklin County, Penn., in 1815; married Eliza Yessler, of Lancaster County, Penn., and this union was blessed with two children: Susanna and Elijah J. He is a Republican in politics. Elijah J. Hoover was born in 1844, in this county, learned the profession of druggist, and when Abraham Lincoln made his first call for 300,000 men, was among those who responded, enlisting, August 8, 1862, in Company F, One Hundred and Thirtieth Pennsylvania Volunteer Infantry. This was the original company raised by Col. H. I. Zinn. He was in the battles of Antietam and Fredericksburg (where Col. Zinn was killed) and Chancellorsville. He was mustered out in May 21, 1863. He re-enlisted January 4, 1864, as a veteran, in the Third Pennsylvania Artillery, and was stationed at Fortress Monroe. Here he was detached from his company and was put on the medical staff and served as acting steward in fort dispensary, Fortress Monroe, and prison hospital, Newport News, and in medical purveyor's office, Department of Virginia and North Carolina, Richmond, Va. He was mustered out by special order, November 14, 1865. He then served under chief medical officer of B. R. F. & A. L. State of Virginia. He served until July, 1866. Returning home he married, in 1868, Miss Martha Crist, of this county. To them were born two children: Anna O. and Lizzie R. Mr. Hoover had the misfortune to lose his wife in 1873, and in 1877 he married Miss Kate Stambaugh, of this county, and commenced farming. He is a member of Post 415, G. A. R. He is a member of the German Reformed Church; in politics a Republican. Few men in this county have such a record as Mr. Hoover, and he justly deserves a place in its history for his patriotism.

JOHN HUTTON, farmer, P. O. Williams Mill. The Hutton family is of German origin. The great-grandfather, a farmer, lived in York County, Penn.; his son, John, who was born in that county was the father of four children: Elija, Jacob, John and Eliza. Jacob, the second son (father of our subject), was born in York County, Penn., in 1813, and was a farmer; in 1840 he married Miss Jane Strominger, and to this union were born eight children: Rachael A., Andrew, Jacob, Daniel, Lucinda, John, Alice J. and Paris. Jacob Hutton, Sr., was a Democrat in politics until the war, when he became a Republican. He has always remained at home, and, although living within six miles of a railroad, never rode on a train until about four years ago, when he took a short trip with his son. He is a man of great will power and stern determination, and is much respected in the community in which he lives, an upright and temperate man. Our sub-

MONROE TOWNSHIP. 511

ject was born in York County, Penn., in 1851, and passed his early life on his father's farm. At the age of fourteen, he became patriotic, and would have enlisted if not prevented by his father on account of his youth. At the age of eighteen young Hutton and two companions were stricken with the California fever. He took French leave, well knowing that his father would oppose the project, and with a few cents in his pocket managed, by working among the farmers, to get as far as Columbus, Ohio. He went thence to Burlington, Iowa, but becoming tired of his own daring, returned home, after an absence of nearly a year, but, unlike the prodigal son, came back in good health, well dressed and supplied with money. In 1876, he married Miss Catharine E. Reiff, of this county, daughter of John K. Reiff, and a descendant of a very old family, of German origin. The great-grandfather, Henry Reiff, who came to York County from Lancaster County, Penn., and formerly from Germany, was the father of two sons: Daniel and Henry (the latter the grandfather of Mrs. Hutton), and tradition says brought a stocking full of gold, with which to buy the property, now the old homestead, originally comprising 300 acres of fine timber land. Henry Reiff (grandfather of Mrs. Hutton) married Catharine Kilmore, of York County, Penn., and over fifty years ago built the mill now called Williams' Mill and the buildings on the old homestead. John K., the father of Mrs. Hutton, was also born in York County, and came to this county with his father, married Catharine Dick, of York, York County, and had three children: John H., Catharine E. and Frances M. D. John K. Reiff was a member of the German Reformed Church, and died January 3, 1874, when forty-seven years old. When Gen. Lee's army invaded Pennsylvania, a detachment of troops took breakfast at the old homestead; they were polite, paid for their entertainment with Confederate scrip, and were very gallant to the ladies, giving them as mementoes buttons cut from their uniforms. This is the third generation which has lived in the old residence inherited from her father by Mrs. Hutton and conveyed by her to her husband. Mr. Hutton has been quite an extensive traveler, visiting sixteen States, Washington and the Gulf of Mexico, Luray caverns, Natural Bridge, Va., Mount Vernon, etc. He is a Republican in politics, a member of the State Grange, and one of the managing committee of the Granger's Picnic Exhibition, which is annually held at Williams' Grove, this county. He comes of a large and robust race, stands six feet and two inches in height, and weighs 210 pounds, the picture of stalwart manhood.

G. W. LEIDIGH, farmer, P. O., Allen. The founder of this family came from Germany to America long before the war of the Revolution. Adam Leidigh, the first of the name of whom there is any record, bought land in Monroe Township, this county, in 1791; he was a farmer and manufacturer. In politics he was an old line Whig; in religion a member of the Lutheran Church. By industry, he accumulated a handsome property, and gave each of his sons a farm. He was the father of four sons: David, George, Jacob and John. He was a prominent man in the community, and trustee for at least one estate. From all that can be learned of him, he was a good business man and honorable in all his dealings. Jacob Leidigh, his second son, was born in Cumberland County, Penn., January 15, 1788; was a farmer all his life, inheriting his land from his father. He married Miss Sarah, daughter of Michael Leidigh, of this county, January 14, 1821 (she was of no blood relationship) and to this union were born five children; Mary A., Sarah, Catharine, George and Samuel. Mr. Leidigh was a member of the Lutheran Church; in politics, an old line Whig; he died August 13, 1832. His widow, who lived for many years, afterward married Henry Gross, of this county, by whom she had one daughter: Eliza A. Mrs. Leidigh died in her eighty-first year. G. W. Leidigh was born in this county July 13, 1828, and, his father dying when he was only five years old, John Brindle became his guardian. At twenty he learned the miller's trade of Jacob Goodyear, his brother-in-law. In 1851, he married Miss Mahala, daughter of John Beltzhoover, of this county, and this union was blessed with three sons: John B. (married to Miss Mattie A. Bowers, daughter of Jere Bowers, of this county), George M. (married to Gertie R., daughter of L. V. Moore, of this county), and Harry M., an attorney. In 1881, our subject bought the Junction Flouring Mill, one of the oldest on Yellow Breeches Creek, being built in the last century, rebuilt in 1828, and again rebuilt by Mr. Leidigh, in 1865. The structure bids fair to stand for many years to come. Mr. Leidigh has followed the business of a miller for thirty-three years on the same creek, and for thirty-five in the old mill which he now owns, and this makes him the oldest miller on Yellow Breeches Creek. During the war of the Rebellion, when Gen. Ewell was stationed at Carlisle, a picket line was formed near Mr. Leidigh's residence, and Gen. Ewell sent him a very stern order to the effect that if any goods were smuggled or removed from the mill, he would burn the building to ashes. It is singular that although the neighbors, who were more or less remote, were plundered, not a single thing was taken from Mr. Leidigh's premises. Mr. and Mrs. Leidigh are members of the Lutheran Church. In politics he is a Republican. He is a hale, stalwart man, wearing his years lightly. Has done a large milling business—probably more than any other miller on the creek. He still continues active labor and lives in the same township where he was born and reared.

GEORGE B. LUTZ, farmer, P. O. Allen. The great-grandfather of our subject was born in Switzerland, and immigrated to this country, on account of religious persecutions, about the year 1772, and settled in Lancaster County, Penn. George Lutz, his son, was born on board ship, while on the passage to this country. He early learned the wagonmaker's trade, and came to this county about 1790, and began the business which his son and grandson have since followed, in the same shop, for nearly one hundred years. George Lutz married Miss Wolf, of this county, and to this union were born nine children: Samuel, George, Baltzer, John, Henry, Philip, Catharine, Mary and Rosanna. He was a member of the German Reformed Church, an old-line Whig, and lived to the patriarchal age of eighty-eight years. He was a remarkably hale and hearty man in his old age, and retained his full vigor to his last day. He was respected by all who knew him. John Lutz, his son, born in this county, followed the trade of his father. He married Catharine Miller in 1830, and had ten children: Samuel W., Henrietta E., William H., Catharine, Emeline, Mary, John, George B., Chester C. and Myra. John Lutz was a member of the German Reformed Church; in politics a Republican. It could well be said of him that his word was as good as his bond. He was a good financier and, although money came slowly in his day, he accumulated a handsome property. George B. Lutz was born in Cumberland County, Penn., in 1848, and learned his father's trade, which he now follows. In 1868 he married Miss Sarah, daughter of Henry Breebill, of this county. This union was blessed with five children: Cora K., John C., George O., Franklin B. and Edna G. By energy and industry our subject has accumulated a fine property, largely increasing the business left him by his father. He is a practical mechanic and understands every detail of his business. He can make, with his own hands, every part of a buggy, including the wood-work, trimming and iron-work. He is a prompt, reliable business man; in politics a strong Republican.

JACOB M. NIESLEY was born in Monroe Township, Cumberland Co., Penn., in the year 1851. He was married, in the fall of 1872, to Mary E. Pressel, of the same township. Having been reared a farmer, he followed this occupation for several years, when, on account of ill health, he left the farm and turned his attention to clerking, moving to Churchtown and working for his uncle, George Brindle, in Boiling Springs, in whose employ he remained several years. He then clerked for J. Frank Moist, in Churchtown, in J. N. Plank's building, and now in the same store, with A. G. Burtner as proprietor. He now fills the important office of director of schools in his native town, following in the footsteps of his grandfather, George Brindle, who once helped to direct the affairs of the State, as Legislator, in 1843-44.

GEORGE O'HARA, farmer and teacher, P. O. Allen. Stephen O'Hara, the grandfather of our subject, immigrated to this country and settled in Philadelphia, Penn., many years ago. He married a Miss Fruger, of Lancaster County, Penn., and was the father of five children, the sons being James and Henry. James O'Hara, son of the above and father of our subject, was born in Philadelphia, Penn., October 15, 1799. He went with his mother to Churchtown, Lancaster Co., Penn., after the death of his father, which occurred when James was very young. He passed his early life on a farm and always followed that occupation. About the year 1830 he married Miss Anna M., daughter of George and Elizabeth Youndt, who were descended from the first settlers of Ephratah, Lancaster Co., Penn. The original deeds to their lands bear the signature of one of the Penns. They had six children: Leah, George, Jessie, Henry, Charles and Anna. Mrs. O'Hara is a member of the Lutheran Church, and is still living at the advanced age of eighty-two. Mr. O'Hara was a strong supporter of the Republican party, making political speeches on many occasions. He was a well-read man, although he acquired his education in the common schools and by his own unaided efforts. In 1857 he moved to Cumberland County, Penn., and purchased land. He died at the age of seventy-six years. He was generally respected as an honorable business man. He brought up his family to believe and practice the principles of truth and justice. George O'Hara, our subject, was born in Lancaster County, Penn., in 1835; passed his early life on the farm of his father, and when about eighteen year of age began teaching school, and taught continuously for twenty-five winters, following farming during the summer. His education was gained at White Hall Academy and Mount Pleasant College. In 1869 he married Miss Anna C. Jacobs, of Cumberland County, and their union was blessed with five children: James, Mary, Horace, Stuart and Charles. In 1880 he bought his present farm and residence. Mr. and Mrs. O'Hara are members of the Lutheran Church. Politically he is a Republican. He is very much interested in the temperance question, took an active part in favor of local option, and now votes the Prohibition ticket. Mr. O'Hara frequently made addresses in the temperance cause, which he firmly believes will ultimately prevail.

DAVID K. PAUL, farmer, P. O. Allen, was born in this county in 1840. His father, Henry Paul, was born in York County, and in the course of time learned the miller's trade; he married Rachael Heikes, of Cumberland County, Penn., and to this union were born six children: Catharine, John, David K., Henrietta, Anna and Emma. In politics he was an old line Whig, but afterward a Republican. He was a man of mild disposition, and while strict in his family was always kind and generous. Prompt in all his business dealings, he had the confidence of all who knew him. It could truly be said of him that his word was as good as his bond. He was a man of few words, and not given to idle

MONROE TOWNSHIP. 513

talk. He died, aged seventy-six years, after accumulating a handsome property, which he left to his children, one of whom now owns the original homestead. David K. Paul passed his early life with his father. He married Miss Lucy Strickler, of Cumberland County, daughter of Joseph Strickler, and to this union were born five children, all living: Cora E., wife of William Givler, of this county; Emma N., Ida R., Henry S. and J. Frank. Mr. Paul is a Republican in politics. In 1876 he bought his present homestead, which is pleasantly situated, and the buildings are substantial structures, bidding fair to last for many generations. Mr. Paul is regarded as a careful, honorable man by the community.

JACOB PLANK, the veteran plow-maker, was born within four miles of Reamstown, in the northeastern part of Lancaster County, October 15, 1792. Here his father, Nicholas Plank, who was one of five brothers and four sisters, was possessed of a small tract of land, thirty acres in extent, and followed the occupation of a weaver. His grandfather came from Switzerland. When Jacob was in his fifteenth year his father died at the age of forty-five years. In 1809 Jacob engaged himself with Fred Gerhart to learn the business of wheelwright or wagon-making. He set in on his apprenticeship on Christmas day, 1809. In the summer of 1810 Mr. Gerhart sold his property in Lancaster County, and moved to Cumberland County, which then bore the same relation to Lancaster County as the far West does to Pennsylvania now-a-days. Mr. Gerhart bought a property lying along the road leading from Mechanicsburg to Williams' Grove, in the lower part of what is now Monroe Township. Jacob Plank was induced to accompany Mr. Gerhart to Cumberland County by a promise that three months should be taken off his term of apprenticeship, making the term two years and three months. Mr. Gerhart, while yet in Lancaster County, made old-fashioned wooden plows, and a Mr. Zeigler, a blacksmith, left the same neighborhood in Lancaster County, and came to Cumberland a year prior to Mr. Gerhart's coming, made known the fact that Mr. Gerhart, "a good plow-maker," was coming to set up business near his (Zeigler's) shop. Mr. Gerhart brought with him, besides Mr. Plank, a Mr. Burkhalter, a journeyman, who assisted in making plows. After arriving, the demand for plows was so great that Mr. Gerhart prevailed upon Mr. Plank to stop working at wagon-making and assist at plow-making. In the spring of that year George Lutz, a wagon-maker, who then lived a short distance west of where Churchtown now stands (the same place at which George B. Lutz, son of John, and grandson of George Lutz, is extensively engaged in the business of manufacturing wagons and buggies, etc.), hearing that Mr. Gerhart had brought some journeymen with him from Lancaster County, came to see if he could not employ the services of some. Mr. Plank then had eleven months to serve before his term of apprenticeship would expire, and consequently could not go, but Mr. Lutz stipulated with him that he should go as soon as his apprenticeship was completed. The following April, 1812, he was free, and on Easter Monday he set out on foot to find Mr. Lutz's workshops, passing what is now Churchtown, which at that time was a place without a name, and consisted only of one house and a blacksmith shop, standing where the hotel is situated, and a log house standing where the store property of John N. Plank, son of Jacob Plank, is at present situated. Mr. Plank helped to build another log house in this same village. It was erected by Judge William Line, and two days were required for the raising of it. The time, however, was mostly occupied at playing "long bullets," a game that was very popular in those early days, and consisted in casting a bullet weighing a half or three-quarters of a pound, the man throwing it the farthest winning the game. The first work that Mr. Plank engaged at with Mr. Lutz was to make a a new wagon, for which he received the sum of $9. In the year 1813 he made his first grain cradle without any instructions from any one, merely using another cradle for a pattern, after improving it to some extent. He sold this cradle for $7, which was considered a big price. The year following he made two more, and the next year he made four. He remained with George Lutz over three years, and left him July 4, 1815, to enter the employ of Adam Stoneberger, who lived eight miles above Carlisle, in Frankford Township. Mr. Stoneberger's business was principally that of making wagons, but he also made wooden plows and grain cradles, and had Mr. Plank work at the latter. He worked with Mr. Stoneberger until 1817, when he went to the south side of the county and worked several months at plow-making for Mr. Adam Heensey, after which he returned to Mr. Stoneberger's, and remained until February, 1818. He then went to Mount Rock, to work for Mr. Samuel Spangler at plows, and remained until the following August. November 28, 1818, he married Mary Reifsnyder, whose parents lived on the State road, one mile east of Newville. The next day he rented a house with the privilege of erecting a house on the property for his use. That same fall he built his shop, and in the spring of 1819 moved to his new home and engaged in the business of plow-making in his own name, having made a reputation as a plow-maker for himself while with Mr. Spangler at Mount Rock. He made 106 plows here, but remained only a year, as he bought a property, containing 100 acres, near the ridge in South Middleton Township. Here he moved in the spring of 1820, built a large shop, and carried on the business of plow-making extensively. In 1835 he applied for a patent on his invention of a plow, which was granted June 2, 1836, and upon it are to be found the autographs of Andrew Jackson, then President of the United States; John Forsyth, Secretary of State; B. F. Butler, Attorney-General, and as witnesses the names of William P. Elliott and John Goodyear, Jr., the latter being at one time prothonotary of Cumberland County. This is a rare old document, and one which he prized very highly, and in order that it might be cared for, a few weeks prior to his death in 1879, he presented it to his grandson, A. W. Plank, the inventor of the celebrated Plank, Jr., plows. Mr. Plank continued in the plow business until 1844, when he bought a farm in the lower end of Monroe Township. His son Samuel had a shop on the same place; owned and carried on the business of wagon-making and plow-making. Samuel Plank remained on the place until the year 1852, at which time he bought the property in Churchtown, built a large shop, and carried on plow-making successfully until 1879, when he retired from active business. During the time he manufactured plows he invented the Plank Shifting Beam Plow, which has plowed more acres in the Cumberland Valley than any other plow manufactured in the State. He made other valuable improvements in the plow, and retired from the business. He was succeeded by his son, A. W. Plank, who continued to manufacture the shifting beam until he found it necessary to get up a new plow, which he did on four different patents, each plow proving a success. These plows are noted for being easily conducted and turning all kinds of soil. Jacob Plank lived to be eighty-seven years old, and was highly successful, and was pleased to see his son and grandson successful in their plows. It will be fifty years June 2, 1886, since his plow was patented, and there are at this time many of the Plank Coulter Plows in use in this county. No farming implement has ever gained a stronger and more lasting reputation in the Cumberland Valley.

GEORGE W. PRESSEL, retired farmer, Boiling Springs. The great-grandfather of the subject of this sketch, John Valentine Pressel, came from Prussia to America September 18, 1733, and settled in Lancaster County, Penn., but later moved to York County, Penn. The grandfather of our subject was born in that county in 1766; married Miss Mohler, of Cumberland County (whose family is one of the oldest and best in the county), and to this union were born four children: Michael, John, Joseph and Susanna. Mr. Pressel, a farmer and land-holder, accumulated considerable property which he left to his children, and some of this land has remained in the family for more than a hundred years. He was a member of the German Baptist Church, known as Dunkards. John Pressel, his son, born in York County, Penn., November 29, 1798, in course of time became a farmer, inheriting his land from his father. He married Miss Abigail, daughter of Valentine Paup, of York County, Penn., who came from Wales about the year 1789, and settled on the south side of Conowago Creek; he was a weaver by occupation, a Quaker in faith, and a very kind father and husband. By this union John Pressel has four children: Eliza J., George W., Lewis J. and Henry W. He was a Lutheran in religion and a Democrat politically. He was a very hardworking, industrious man, and owned at least 400 acres of land. After 1831 he passed his life on same farm. He was a kind husband and loving father. He assisted his son to buy farms, and was noted for his honesty and morality. He died September 29, 1883, at the patriarchal age of eighty-five years. His widow, who is still living, is in her eightieth year. George W., son of John and Abigail Pressel, was born in York County, Penn., November 27, 1827, in the old homestead built by his grandfather. August 30, 1849, he married Miss Eliza A. Reed, who died May 10, 1862, and to this union were born three children: Samuel A., a farmer; Mary E., and John La Fayette (died October 30, 1862). Mr. Pressel, the second year of his marriage, moved to his present farm and homestead in this county. He was married, on second occasion, October 27, 1863, to Mrs. Catharine (Corman) Huchinson, and this union was blessed with four children: George Brinton McClellan (died October 1, 1870), Penrose W. M., Charles H. and Orrin A. Of Mr. Pressel's children, Mary E. is the wife of Jacob M. Niesley, and Penrose W. M. is teaching in South Middleton Township, this county. Charles H. and Orrin A. are going to school. Mrs. Pressel is a member of the German Reformed Church. Our subject is a well educated man and has taught school. Mr. Pressel intends giving his children good education. He is a surveyor and has studied civil engineering; has filled many local offices promptly, but never desired them; has been on different committees, to draft constitutions for Sabbath-schools, the "Northern Sunday-School" and the "Mount Zion Sunday-School" at Churchtown. Since the late Rebellion of the South he is very independent in politics and in religious views very strong in faith with the Friends or Quakers.

JOHN F. SENSEMAN, farmer, P. O. Williams Mill. The great-grandparents of our subject were born in Germany, and his grandfather was born in Lancaster County, Penn., and worked at his trade, that of a miller, near Ephratah. He was the father of eight children: John, Joseph, William, Samuel, Daniel, Rebecca L. and Hannah. Samuel, the fourth son (father of our subject), was born in Ephratah, Lancaster Co., Penn., in 1796, and in early life learned carpentering. He married Miss Elizabeth Haines, also a native of Lancaster County, and ten children were born to them: Susan, Jeremiah, John, Harriet, Lydia, Samuel, David, Adam, William and Sarah. Samuel Senseman, Sr., moved to this county in 1828, and bought a farm in Silver Spring Township. He and his wife were members of the Lutheran Church. In politics he was a Democrat. The confidence of the people in his integrity and ability is shown in the fact that in settling many estates every dollar was strictly accounted for and the estates wisely administered. John F. Senseman was born in Lancaster County, Penn., in 1822; he came with his father to this county and passed his early years on the farm. In his life he had many experiences, having traveled a great deal through his native country, engaged in different mercantile pursuits. In 1854 he married Miss Mary L. Landis, of this county. He then began agriculture, near Mechanicsburg, and remained thirty-two years on the same farm. To our subject and wife were born five children: Charles, George W., Harry, Anna and David E. In 1878 Mr. Senseman traveled in Europe, visiting its principal cities and the Paris Exposition. In 1885 he purchased his present homestead, which is pleasantly situated, with fine, substantial buildings. Mr. Senseman is a self-made man in every sense of the word, and has secured his property by industry. His life is a good illustration of what can be attained by energy and perseverance.

GEORGE W. SOUDER, farmer, P. O. Allen. The great-grandfather of this gentleman came from Germany at an early day, settling in Perry County, Penn., and there his son George was born. He was an agriculturist, and his farm at Shermansdale is still owned by a lineal descendant, having been in the Souder family for more than a century. He (grandfather of subject) was a soldier in the Revolutionary war; married a Miss Sheivly, of Perry County, Penn., and was the parent of four sons: Jacob, Henry, John and George. Of these John was born on the old homestead, in this county, in 1811. He, too, was a farmer; he married, in 1837, Miss Sarah A. Fenical, of Perry County, Penn.; moved to Cumberland County in 1838; and to this union were born the following named children: George W., Susan, Margaret, Henry, Caroline, Elizabeth, Sarah, and Mary. After marriage, in 1837, John Souder moved to Cumberland County and settled on a farm in South Middleton Township. In 1850 he removed to Silver Spring Township, and there (from 1859 to 1865) purchased four farms, comprising 500 acres. His first wife died, and, in 1885, he married Mrs. Dunkeberger, of Perry County, Penn. He is now a hale, strong man of seventy-four years, and is well known for his great energy, perseverance and industry. George W., his son, was born in Perry County, Penn., in 1838, and was brought to this county by his parents when an infant. He lived with his father on the farm until twenty-four years of age, and greatly assisted him in accumulating property. In 1862 George W. Souder married Miss Emma E. Shoop, of this county. This union has been blessed with seven children: David L., Amy B., George O., Cora L., John V., Jacob J. and Bertie I. D. L., the oldest son, a teacher by profession, acquired his education in the common schools and at State normals. He has been teaching near Fortress Monroe, Va. After marriage our subject farmed a farm owned by his father, where he remained five years, when he bought a farm near Mechanicsburg, and there he lived thirteen years. In 1881 he purchased his present farm and homestead, which is pleasantly situated near Churchtown. Mr. and Mrs. Souder are members of the Lutheran Church. In politics Mr. Souder is a Republican. The entire family is well known for respectability and worth.

GEORGE W. STROCK, farmer, P. O. Allen, was born in Cumberland County, Penn., in 1854. His great-grandfather came from Germany, when a young man, and settled near Churchtown, Cumberland Co., Penn., and bought 300 acres of land. He was the father of two children: Joseph and Jacob. The date of his coming to this county is lost, but the second home that he built here has the date 1775. Jacob Strock, his son, born in the old homestead, married Elizabeth Wire, of this county, and to this union were born nine children: Joseph, George, Jacob, David, John, Mary, Elizabeth, Rachel and Rebecca. Of these, John was born in this county in 1823; learned the trade of saddler, and was a farmer and land-holder. He married Elizabeth Stephenson, of this county, and to this union were born six children: Clara K., Howard K., George W., Mary, Alice and Laura A. Mr. and Mrs. Strock were members of the Winebrennerian Church. He was a Republican in politics. George W. was born in this county in 1854. In 1880 he married Miss Barbara A. Herman, of Churchtown, Penn., daughter of George T. B. and Barbara (Brindle) Herman. Mr. Herman was for many years a merchant in Churchtown, but has now retired from business. He is a member of the Lutheran Church. Politically he is a Democrat. Mr. Strock and wife have but one child, John Roy. In 1884 our subject bought his present home, which is pleasantly situated near Churchtown. He and his wife are members of the Lutheran Church. Politically he is a Republican.

JAMES WILLIAMS (born October 28, 1775) was the youngest son of John Williams, who immigrated to this country from England many years before the Revolutionary war. John Williams married Mary Wilson, and settled on the Yellow Breeches Creek, on the farm now owned by his grandson Abram. He was one of the earliest settlers in the Cumberland Valley. He became a large land owner, and was one of the good men of his day. He had ten children. At his death, part of his land became vested in his three sons: Abraham, David and James. His youngest son James, succeeded him upon the old homestead. He, like his father, was a farmer by occupation. He was married August 25, 1808, to Elizabeth Myers, and had eight children: David M., Mary, Catharine, John, Elizabeth, James, Abram and Henry H. He was a man of strong convictions, dignified in appearance, and noted for his kindliness, honor and charity, and never had a law-suit. He lived to be eighty-two years of age. Some years before his death he divided a part of his real-estate between his four surviving sons. Abram succeeded his father on the mansion-farm. The Williams family have always settled their own business, and there has never been a public sale on the mansion farm. In religion they have been Presbyterian, and liberal and earnest supporters of their church. In politics they have been Democrats, but would never accept office.

THOMAS U. WILLIAMSON, farmer, P. O. Allen. The Williamsons were among the very oldest settlers of this county, and are of the hardy Scotch-Irish stock, which first settled in Silver Spring Township. The great-grandfather of our subject was the first of this name to settle in Cumberland County, buying a large tract of land from the Indians, for which he gave a web of cloth and $200. He was a Scotch Presbyterian. His son Thomas was three years old at the time of the settlement, and at the death of his father he inherited land and lived on the old homestead all of his life. Thomas Williamson kept the tavern on the Trindle Spring Road near the west end of the township, for many years. He married a Miss Anderson, of Silver Spring Township, this county, and had three children: James, Samuel and Susan. Thomas Williamson's first wife died, and he subsequently married a Miss Brown, of this county, by whom he had three children: Rebecca, Elizabeth and Thomas. He was also a Presbyterian. Of his children, James was born on the old homestead, and there lived nearly all his life. He married Miss Mary, daughter of Thomas Ulric, of this county, who bore him one son: Thomas U. This wife died, and he married Miss Catharine, daughter of Joseph Kanaga, of this county. To this union nine children were born: Susan R., Anna M., James A., John J., William S., Samuel H., Catharine A., Elsetta J. and Rebecca E. In political opinions James Williamson was a staunch Democrat. He held several township offices. He was colonel of a regiment at the time of the old militia, and lived to the good old age of eighty years. Thomas U., his son, was born on the old homestead bought by his great-grandfather from the Indians. In 1855, he married Miss Maria E., daughter of John and Elizabeth (Beltzhoover) Herman. This union has been blessed with eight children: Mary E., Thomas U., James W., Jennie L., C. Herman, Cora M., Lillie G. and Linda F. Mr. Williamson began farming in South Middleton Township, where he remained twelve years, and then bought a portion of the old tract owned by his great-grandfather, where he lived for seven years; then moved to his present residence in Monroe Township. Our subject served for ten months as a member of Company A, Fifty-eighth Regiment Pennsylvania Volunteer Infantry, under Col. D. B. McKibbin, and was honorably discharged at Chambersburg, Penn., August 10, 1863. Politically Mr. Williamson is a Democrat. He and his wife are members of the Lutheran Church.

JONAS B. ZIMMERMAN, farmer, P. O. Allen. The great-grandfather of the subject of our sketch came from Germany and settled in Lancaster County, Penn. He was a Mennonite, and fled, with his family, from religious persecution, leaving everything, good homes and wordly possessions, to come to the land of William Penn, for they had heard that in Pennsylvania every man could worship God after his own conscience. These peaceful men underwent terrible persecutions for Christ's sake, and fled to a wilderness that they might be at peace with all men. Mr. Zimmerman had four sons: Peter, John, Christian, and Jacob, a bishop. Of these, Peter was born in Lancaster County, Penn.; was a farmer and land-owner; married a Miss Martin, of the same county, and to this union were born twelve children: Christian, Peter, Henry, Martin, Samuel, Mannol, Esther, Mary, Judah, Barbara, Anna and Elizabeth. Peter Zimmerman was a deacon in the Mennonite Church, in this county, to which he had come in 1814 with his family. He was a very honorable man, and brought up his family in strict religious principles. In disposition he was very cheerful and happy, of a very friendly nature. It is said of him that he never turned a wayfarer from his doors. He left 300 acres of land to his sons, all of which is still in the Zimmerman family. The father of our subject was born in Lancaster County in 1810, and came to this county with his father when he was only four years of age. In 1836, he married Miss Susannah Plough, of York County, daughter of John and Susan Plough, and to this union were born eleven children: Anna, Jonas, Sarah, Mary, Samuel, Esther, Martin, Leah, John and Sarah. Mr. Zimmerman was ordained to the ministry in 1861, and preached sixteen years, and in 1877 died of typhoid fever. He was a farmer, a strong, hearty man and could endure a great amount of labor, and of great frankness and gentleness of manner. The church of which he was preacher flourished, and he made a great many converts to the cause of Christ, and his memory is yet green among the people, for he was a peace-maker and possessed loving and gentle ways that won their love and respect. Jonas B. Zimmerman was born in 1838, and remained with his father until he was twenty-nine years of age. In 1867, he married Miss Annie, daughter of Jacob and Mary Hege, of Franklin County, Penn. This union has been blessed with seven children: Ira H., Annie M., Samuel J., Benjamin J., Jacob H., Susan E. and Martha R. Mr. and Mrs. Jonas B. Zimmerman are members of the church of their fathers. Our subject, in 1879, bought his present home. He was a member of the committee that built the new Mennonite Church.

CHAPTER LIII.

NEWTON TOWNSHIP.*

JONATHAN BARRICK, farmer, P. O. Newville, is descended on his grandfather's side from an old resident of Perry County, Penn., and on his grandmother's side from an old Cumberland County family. George Barrick, the father of our subject, was born in Mifflin Township, this county, where he became a farmer, also carrying on weaving. His wife was Mary, daughter of Philip Heckman. They had nine children: Andrew, who married Rebecca Shover, living in Hopewell Township; Daniel, married to Elizabeth Robinson, living in Newton Township; George, married to Catharine Whistler, living in Ohio; John, who died in Illinois; David L., married to Margaret Whistler; Jonathan; Henry, married to Margaret Gilbert; Elias, married to Elizabeth Failor; Elizabeth, who is the wife of Isaac Hershey. David L., Henry, Elias and Elizabeth are living in Mifflin Township. Jonathan, who is the sixth son, was born March 15, 1836, his father dying before he was six years old. He lived out until his majority. April 5, 1857, he was married to Nancy Whistler, of Mifflin Township, and began farming on the place now owned by his brother David; subsequently moving to a large farm, and again to a still larger, until, in the fall of 1873, he bought a farm in Mifflin Township, on the creek, on which he lived a year, when he removed to the John R. Sharp farm in this township, where he has since lived. In January, 1882, he bought a farm on the opposite side of the creek from his first purchase—the two aggregating 350 acres. He also owns thirty-six acres of timber land on the North Mountain. He has had thirteen children, of whom six died in infancy. The living are Alfred, born October 5, 1859, married to Elizabeth Jones, and living on his father's farm in Mifflin Township; Emma, born September 9, 1861, wife of Robert Lytle, of Newton Township; Sarah J., born September 24, 1862, wife of Philip Zinn, of Penn Township; Naome Catharine, born April 26, 1865, wife of Josiah Baum, and living in Fayette County, Penn.; George Parker, born January 16, 1867; Annie A., born September 16, 1870; and Charles E., born March 6, 1875, the last three living at home. Mr. and Mrs. Barrick are members of the United Brethren Church. Starting humbly in life, he has, by his correct habits and sterling character, acquired a fair share of this world's goods and the confidence and respect of his fellow-men.

W. LINN DUNCAN, farmer, P. O. Oakville, is a grandson of John Duncan, of Southampton Township, Cumberland County, who died there many years ago, and who had eleven children: William, John, Alexander, Samuel, David D. G., Mary, Jane, Theresa, Eliza, Sarah and Rebecca. Six of these are still living. David D. G., known all over the county as D. D. G. Duncan, is W. Linn's father, and is living in West Pennsborough Township, this county; his wife, Grizelda (Linn), was a native of Southampton Township, Franklin Co., Penn., a daughter of William Linn, a prominent citizen and leading elder in the Middle Spring Church, and well known in political affairs, in which took an active part. Mr. and Mrs. D. D. G. Duncan also had eleven children: W. Linn, Samuel A., David Glenn, John Knox, James Patterson, Mary Gilbreath, Emma Jane, Elizabeth Ann, Sarah Ann, Flora and Eva. W. Linn, the eldest, born December 5, 1845, in Southampton Township, this county, was raised on the farm on which his father now lives, on the Big Spring. Getting his education in the public schools, he acquired a business training in the Iron City College, Pittsburgh, and then lived on the farm until he was twenty years of age, when, for a year, he was in the railroad office at Bergettstown, Penn.; then returning to Cumberland County and buying a farm in Newton Township, near Newville, where he stayed until 1871, when he rented it and traveled in the West for three years, then returning to Bergettstown, where, for four years, he was assistant secretary and treasurer of the savings bank at that place. In 1879 he bought the old John Gracey farm on the Ridge road, and has settled down as a farmer. This farm has been in only three names since it was patented, and the papers relating to it are now in Mr. Duncan's possession. December 19, 1867, he married Arabella Davidson, of West Pennsborough Township, who died January 15, 1872, leaving three children, one of whom died in infancy. The living are Hugh Linn, born October 25, 1868, and Hudson Davidson, born February 9, 1870. September 21, 1876, Mr. Duncan was married to Miss Lydia Belle Tritt. They have three children living. James Linn Patterson, born June 10, 1877; David Daniel Glenn, born July 29, 1879; and Charlotte Grizelda, born November 27, 1882. One child,

---
*For borough of Newville see page 447.

518   BIOGRAPHICAL SKETCHES:

Matthew B. Boyd, born October 26, 1880, was instantly killed by the sudden starting of a horse on which he was sitting with an older brother. Mrs. Duncan is a great-great-grandchild of Isaac LeFevre, who fled from France late in the seventeenth century, to escape the persecutions inflicted on the Huguenots, landing in Boston. His son, Philip, was Mrs. Duncan's great grandfather, and Philip's daughter Elizabeth was her grandmother. She (Elizabeth LeFevre) married Peter Tritt, and her son Christian (Mrs. Duncan's father) was born July 25, 1796, in West Pennsborough Township, where they had come many years before, and where the family owned a farm for over a hundred years. Christian Tritt was married to Lydia Stough and had twelve children. After her death he married Mrs. Frances Charlotte McCulloch, and had one child, Mrs. Duncan, who was born August 16, 1854. Her father died January 10, 1871; her mother is now living in Florida. Mr. Duncan has held many township offices. In politics he is a Democrat. He and his wife belong to Big Spring Presbyterian Church. He is a member of Big Spring Lodge, No. 363, A. Y. M. He is known as an upright man and enterprising citizen.

ABRAHAM ERNST (deceased) was a native of York County, born June 4, 1838. His father was also born in that county, and died there in April, 1885. He had lived several years in Perry County and in Mifflin Township, this county, where Abraham was principally reared until he was thirteen years old, when he came to Jacksonville, Newton Township, and worked for James Kyle in the winter in the store and in the summer on his farm, and part of the time engaged in other business. December 27, 1860, he married Tabitha Ewing, who was born April 8, 1839. Her father, George Ewing, died on his farm in this township in 1849. After their marriage Mr. and Mrs. Ernst farmed in Mifflin Township for a year and in Franklin County for three years. In August, 1864, he and George Clever, of Cleversburg, bought the store in Jacksonville (to which he moved the following spring), and in 1867 built the new brick store, in which he carried on business until his death. In 1874 he built a fine brick residence adjoining, in which he died March 5, 1882. While living here he also bought a farm at Jacksonville. He and Mr. Clever also bought a store and dwelling in Milltown, Dickinson Township, still owned by Mrs. Ernst; also had stores at White House, Centreville, Lee's Cross Roads, and Morversville, Mr. Clever being partner with Mr. Ernst in all business transactions up to the latter's death. Mr. and Mrs. Ernst had eleven children, four of whom died in infancy. Those now living are George Ewing, born June 19, 1861, who conducts the store, and is universally known as an energetic, pushing and rising young merchant of excellent habits and character; Anna Ella, born November 21, 1862, wife of Dr. H. H. Longsdorf, of Centreville; Lincoln Williams, born December 3, 1865, working his mother's farm; Bradford Patterson, born February 20, 1868; Alice Belle, born May 25, 1862; Conrad Clever, born May 27, 1874, and Oren Roscoe, born May 26, 1880. Mr. Ernst, though taking much interest in political affairs, never held office. He was a regular attendant at the United Presbyterian Church at Newville, of which his widow is a member. He left to her and his children not only a competence, but the better heritage of a good name.

DANIEL HEBERLIG, farmer, P. O. Newville, is a great-grandson of Rudolph Heberlig, the founder of the Heberlig family in this country, who came from Switzerland before the Revolutionary war, and settled in Berks County, Penn., between Reading and Adamstown. Rudolph Heberlig was twice married, having by his first wife two sons, John and Rudolph, and two daughters names unknown. His second wife had no children. John (grandfather of Daniel) was born in Berks County, Penn., and married Martha Schoenhouer; they had eight children: Rudolph, John, Jacob, Samuel, Benjamin, Joseph, Mary and Elizabeth, all born in Berks County, Penn. In 1811 they removed to this county and settled on a farm at Glenn's Mills, near Newville, where both the parents died. Rudolph (father of Daniel) married Susan Hard, of Berks County, and had ten children: John, Jacob, Daniel, Rudolph, Samuel, Catharine, Susan, Elizabeth, Martha and Mary. The father of this numerous family died in 1863, the mother the year previous. Our subject was born May 30, 1812, and lived at home until his marriage, in March, 1836, with Miss Sarah, daughter of Peter Utley, of Frankford Township, and who was born in 1818 and died April 9, 1863. They had twelve children: Samuel, born January 17, 1838, living in West Pennsborough Township, this county; Mary Jane, born September 28, 1840, married to John Heberlig, of Newville, Penn.; Margaret, born August 25, 1842, living with her father; Rebecca, born May 28, 1844, died April 24, 1867; William, born July 9, 1846, died November 28, 1851; David Porter, born June 28, 1848, died May 13, 1850; Susanna E., born February 11, 1850, died December 2, 1850; Sarah Belle, born December 2, 1851, died December 14, 1857; Anna Martha, born January 14, 1854, living at home; Daniel, born July 21, 1856, died February 6, 1857; Nancy Ellen, born August 7, 1858, died May 26, 1861, and John Edwin, born September 27, 1861, living at home. Mr. Heberlig was married to his second wife, Mrs. Rebecca E. Dobbs, December 11, 1879. They have no children. After his marriage our subject farmed in Frankford Township, this county, for a year, in West Pennsborough Township for a year, then in Frankford Township again for ten years, and then removed to the Samuel W. Sharp farm, in Newton, where he lived for eighteen years. In 1866 he bought the farm on the State road, on a part of which he now lives retired, having built a new house on it. He has never held public office, but

NEWTON TOWNSHIP. 519

is satisfied with the reputation of an honest, well-to-do farmer. He and his wife and all the family at home are members of the Lutheran Church in Newville.

ROBERT HAYS IRVINE, farmer, P. O. Newville, is a great-grandson of William Irwin (as it was then spelled), one of the first settlers on the "Walnut Bottom," whose widow, Eleanor, in 1745, left the farm, now owned by our subject, to her son Samuel, who was a major in the famous "Light Horse Troop" during the Revolutionary war, and was for years, before and after, a justice of the peace in Middlesex Township. He married Mary, daughter of Samuel Miller, a wealthy settler in that township, whose will, on file in Carlisle, is a curiosity. One of their sons, also named Samuel, was the grandfather of Robert Hays. He married Isabella Kilgore, of Green Spring, in Newton Township, and lived in the house now occupied by his grandson adjoining the Irvine Mill, on the Big Spring. Here the father of our subject, as well as he, was born, and here the father of Samuel first lived for many years, but afterward removed to Newville, where he engaged in mercantile business for thirteen years. His wife was Maggie, daughter of R. M. Hays, then of Oakville, now of Newville. They had two children, of whom one died an infant; the other is Robert Hays, who was born February 11, 1862. The elder Irvine returned to the farm in 1876, and here his wife and younger son died. Later he was married to Annie, daughter of John Wagner, of Newville, and a year after removed to that place, where he again engaged in business. In the fall of 1884 he sold out and went to Sioux City, Iowa, where he now resides. In 1880 Mr. Irvine took the farm, which he has since carried on. He is a member of Big Spring Presbyterian Church, an upright and thrifty man and a good citizen.

DANIEL KENDIG, retired farmer, P. O. Newville, is a native of Lancaster County, Penn., where his father and grandfather were both born. His father, Tobias Kendig, was born about 1770, and died in this township in 1855. He was united in marriage with Mary Bowman, of Lancaster County, Penn., and had eight children: Abraham, who died in Ohio, nearly thirty years ago; Henry, who died in Newville in 1875; Elizabeth, widow of Peter Rowe, of Newton Township; Rudolph, who died in 1880; Emanuel, who died in 1866; Tobias, who died before the family came to the county; Jacob, who lives in Franklin County, and Daniel, who was born June 6, 1806. Our subject learned the trade of shoe-making, and followed it for ten years, when he became a drover, stock-dealer and farmer on the farm he now owns across the road from where he lives. About twenty-three years ago he retired, renting his farm. December 10, 1833, he married Susanna Ruth, who was born July 29, 1805, and died April 18, 1872. They had three children: John Francis, born December 4, 1837, who lives in this township; Daniel Bowman, born June 30, 1840, who died February 16, 1861, and William Henry, born September 10, 1841, living on the next farm to his father. May 1, 1873, Mr. Kendig married Elizabeth (Scheffler) Jacoby, widow of Peter Jacoby, by whom she had two sons and one daughter: William, Maria and David. Mr. and Mrs. Kendig have no children by their second marriage. Mr. Kendig has been supervisor, road-master, etc., in this township. He and his wife are regular attendants of the Church of God, Green Springs. He is known as a shrewd, careful and honorable man.

HENRY KILLIAN, farmer, P. O. Newville, is a son of John Killian, a native of Lancaster County, Penn., whose father settled there on his emigration from Europe. In 1823 John Killian came to Mifflin Township, this county, where he stayed seven years; then in West Pennsborough Township for a year; in Mifflin Township again for three years; thence moved to Newton Township, where he lived eleven years on the Sharp farm. In 1845 he bought a farm on the creek, to which he removed the following spring, and where he died. He married Elizabeth Long, of Lancaster County. They had nine children: Chrisdtina, who was twice married and is now the widow of John Mellinger; Lydia, widow of Samuel Geese; Charles, deceased; Abraham, married to Susan Sigler, and living in Newville, Penn; Eliza (deceased) was the wife of Elias Diehl; John, married to Catharine Iry, died in Illinois; Margaret, who died in her brother Henry's house December 29, 1884; Susan, also married to Elias Diehl (after her sister Eliza's death), and after his demise married to William Shaeffer, and died in September, 1884, and Henry. Our subject was born November 2, 1813, in Lancaster County, Penn. December 20, 1836, he married Ann Eliza Jones, a native of Silver Spring Tp., this county. For a year after, he lived in Franklin County, Penn., and then for a year on a farm adjoining where he now lives. Thence he went to the farm of Robert McFarland, staying fourteen years, when he and William McFarland bought a farm on the Big Spring, on which the latter erected a paper-mill. A few years later Mr. Killian bought his partner's interest in the farm, to which he removed, selling it three years later and buying the McKinney farm, on which his son John now lives. Here he farmed nineteen years, when he retired and moved to his present residence, which he had previously built. He is the father of eight children: John, born November 11, 1837, married to Wilhelmina Heberlig; Catharine, born April 3, 1840, widow of Henry Livingstone; Samuel, born March 20, 1842, married to Mary Jane Drake, of Stroudsburg, who died in Kansas (he returned to Newville, and is now husband of Alice Staples, also of Stroudsburg, Penn.); Jacob, born October 15, 1844, married Susan M. Brehm, and lives on a farm of his father; Eliza, born May 28, 1847, died December 28, 1855;

Lucetta, born December 2, 1849, wife of G. Allen Brehm; Henry, born April 5, 1852 married to Jane E. Westafer, living on another of his father's farms; and Lydia Belle, born October 30, 1854, wife of David A. Cromleigh, now of Mechanicsburg. Mr. Killian has been school director, appraiser, and has held many other township offices. Beginning life without any advantages, he and his wife have, by industry and thrift, accumulated a competence, now owning four farms. They have reaped the fruits of a well spent life, and in the evening of their days are enjoying its comforts. Both are devout members of the Lutheran Church.

WILLIAM CARNAHAN KOONS, farmer, P. O. Newville, is a grandson of Isaac Koons, who came from Lancaster County, where he was born in 1760; his wife was Margaret E. Swartz, also of Lancaster. About the close of the Revolutionary war they settled at a place called "Thunder Hill," three miles northwest of Newville. He died August 15, 1830, in his seventy-first year, and his widow April 11, 1833, in her sixty-second year. Their children were David, Isaac, John, Jacob, Adam, George, Philip, Joseph, Elizabeth, Catherine and Mary. They are all deceased. Isaac was the father of William Carnahan Koons, and was born in 1792. His wife was Jane Carnahan. They had nine sons and one daughter, Margaret, who died young. The sons were Robert Carnahan, Isaac, John McDowell, William Carnahan, Alexander Sharp, Thomas Sharp, Adam, James and Joseph. Robert C. and Isaac went to Indiana, where they both died; Thomas S. died on the old homestead; John McD. is living in Indiana; Alexander S. is living in Nebraska; William C., Adam, James and Joseph live in Newton Township. The father of this family, Isaac, was a farmer and tanner on the Green Spring, in Newton Township, near Conodoguinet Creek, where he purchased a farm in 1826, on which he built the house in which his son Joseph now lives. Here he died November 19, 1874, aged eighty-two. He was a plain man, kind, contented, outspoken, determined and preserving. His integrity was unswerving, and his character above all suspicion of reproach. He began life a poor boy, but by thrift and careful habits accumulated a considerable property, which, with the heritage of a good name, he bequeathed to his children. His wife was born in 1795, and died August 11, 1866, in her seventy-first year. She was a daughter of Robert Carnahan, a son of William Carnahan, who came to Mifflin Township soon after the first settlement, which was made in 1729 or 1730. Robert Carnahan was married to Judith McDowell in 1784. Their children were William, Robert, Margaret and Jane. William went to Indiana in 1835, and died there in 1879, aged eighty-three. Mrs. Koons was a quiet, patient, industrious, kind-hearted woman, and much of her husband's success in life was due to the constant care which she exercised in the affairs of the house. William Carnahan Koons was born February 27, 1827, and with the exception of attendance at the common schools and two sessions at the Big Spring Academy, he had no other facilities for acquiring an education. He worked on the farm until 1857, when, January 22, he was married to Mary Jane, daughter of James Stewart, of Mifflin Township, where she was born August 20, 1821. They had five children, three dying in infancy, and a son, William Carnahan, born December 23, 1857, died June 24, 1875. The surviving son is James Stewart, born December 7, 1859, who is unmarried and living with his parents. For four years after his marriage Mr. Koons farmed on shares, and in April, 1861, removed to the farm he now owns, but which then belonged to his father. Here he has since remained, attending strictly to his own affairs. When not at work he was busy with his books and papers. A desire to maintain right and oppose wrong sums up and explains the rest.

JAMES McCULLOCH, farmer, P. O. Big Spring, is a great-grandson of John McCulloch, who emigrated from the North of Ireland, and settled in what is now Mifflin Township, but afterward removed to a farm near Newville, which is still owned by and in possession of some of his descendants. He had three sons: John, William and James; and five daughters: Susanna, married to Ezekiel Mitchell, who in an early day emigrated to Kentucky; Elizabeth, married to Robert McCormick, of Path Valley; Margaret, married to James Hill, who also went West; Sarah, married to Richard Patton, and Jane, married to James McKinstry. James was the grandfather of the subject of this sketch. He was born in 1761 or 1762. Though quite young at the time, he drove a team in the army of the Revolution. In or about the year 1790 he purchased 600 acres of land bordering upon and extending back about one mile from Big Spring, near its source, nearly all of which is still owned by some of his descendants. He was married June 7, 1792, to Mary Henderson, daughter of Thomas Henderson, whose wife's name was Wharton. From this union eight children were born, viz.: John, Thomas and William, each of whom owned and occupied a portion of the home farm during life; James, once register of wills of this county and afterward a physician, who died at Muncie, Ind.; Sarah, married to James Huston; Eliza, married to Andrew Coyle; Mary Jane, married to Samuel Piper, and Margaret Anne, married to David Jackson McKee—of whom Mrs. Coyle, Mrs. Piper and Mrs. McKee are the only survivors. Thomas McCulloch, the father of James, was born April 2, 1797, on the farm where he spent most of his life, and where he died February 16, 1868. April 3, 1823, he was married to Isabella Blean, daughter of Robert Blean, an only son of David Blean, who settled, in an early day, upon the farm on Big Spring, now owned by David Duncan. Robert Blean married Mary Craig, and had ten children, nine

NEWTON TOWNSHIP. 521

of whom reached mature age, viz.: John, David, Robert, William, Isabella (wife of Thomas McCulloch), Grizelle (wife of James Fulton), Mary (wife of Alexander Thompson), Jane (wife of George McBride) and Margaret (wife of John Work). Of Thomas and Isabella were born seven children, viz.: James, born January 5, 1824; Robert Bleau, born May 12, 1825, now living in Peoria, Ill.; Thomas Henderson, born September 1, 1827, for many years a resident of Monmouth, Ill., but now of Omaha, Neb.; John Craig, born October 28, 1829, who died August 24, 1850; David, born January 25, 1832, now an attorney in Peoria, Ill., where for eight years he was judge of the circuit court, and six years of that time assigned to duty as one of the justices of the appellate court of the State; Mary Ellen, wife of William S. Morrow, living in Chambersburg, and Isabella, who died in infancy. James owns and lives upon the farm owned by his father in his lifetime, having never left the place of his nativity. February 4, 1847, he was united in marriage with Miss Martha Brown, daughter of Joseph Brown, Esq., of West Pennsborough Township. To this union three children were born, viz.: Isabella Craig, born November 5, 1848, wife of J. Sharp Hemphill, now living on part of her father's farm; Nancy Jane, born May 30, 1850, living with her father, and Mary Grizelle, born June 20, 1852, died September 26, 1881, who was the wife of Prof. John C. Sharp, a noted worker in educational matters. Mrs. McCulloch died April 10, 1854, and is buried in the United Presbyterian Cemetery at Big Spring, of which church both she and her husband were members. He is one of the most prominent citizens of this township, a self-made man who, without the educational facilities of the present day, has, by force of character, observation, reading and good judgment, became one of the best informed men of this part of the county, and whose opinion has weight among his neighbors. In politics he is a Democrat.

HUGH McCUNE, farmer, P. O. Oakville, is a grandson of Robert McCune, who came from Ireland about the middle of the last century. The latter's son, Hugh, father of our subject, was born in this county in 1772, and died in 1828. His wife was Rebecca (Brady) McCune. Their children were as follows: Isabella, born April 18, 1797, wife of William Duncan, now deceased; Jane, born April 26, 1799, wife of James Boyd, and also deceased; Hannah, born August 9, 1802, deceased; Robert, born September 28, 1804, married Nancy Gibb, and died in Illinois; John, born May 24, 1807, married Jane Henderson, and died in Hopewell Township; James, born February 5, 1809, married Matilda Williams, and lives in Westmoreland County, Penn.; Samuel, born April 2, 1811, deceased; Elizabeth, born May 13, 1811, deceased; Joseph, born March 17, 1818, married Sallie Crider, and died on the home farm, and Hugh, our subject, born December 15, 1815, on the place where he now lives, in a brick house built by Hugh and Joseph. The property has never since been out of the family. His father's farm is now owned entirely by our subject, who has never left it, and who is now recognized as one of the industrious and thrifty farmers of the neighborhood, who have done much to develop the agricultural resources of the county. By his strictly temperate, industrious and upright habits he has accumulated a competence, and enjoys in a high degree the confidence and esteem of all. Though of strong political convictions, he has never sought office, preferring to aid his party without self-seeking. An old line Whig, he is now a Republican. He is a member of Big Spring Presbyterian Church, and takes a warm interest in temperance matters and all other good works.

SAMUEL ALBERT McCUNE, retired farmer, Oakville, is a great-grandson of James McCune, who came here about the middle of the last century, with his brother Robert, from Ireland, and jointly took up a tract of 437 acres of land, where his descendants now live, and which is now in their possession. The subject of this sketch has a receipt dated April 7, 1824, from the State Treasurer, for patent fees for 135 acres of the original tract, and it states that it is surveyed on two warrants to Robert and James McCune, one dated May 13, 1763, and the other October 20, 1766. James' son Samuel was Samuel Albert's grandfather. He was born where his grandson now lives, in 1770, and died November 16, 1813. His wife was Hannah Brady, born January 1, 1776, and died May 16, 1847. They had eleven children, of whom two died in infancy. The others were Jane, born October, 1795, who became the wife of John Sharp; James, born January 22, 1799; Addie, born December 9, 1798; Margaret, born April 9, 1801, was the wife of Moses Kirkpatrick; Rachel, born July 27, 1803; Hugh Brady, born October 11, 1805; William, born January 23, 1807; Rebecca, born October 8, 1811, and Samuel, born April 9, 1814. Of this numerous family but one remains—Rebecca, single, and living in her nephew's house. Hugh Brady, father of Samuel Albert, lived all his life on the farm. Starting poor he acquired a farm and other property in the West. He died in September, 1881. His wife was Isabella Jane Kirkpatrick, who is now living with her daughter, Hannah M. Their ten children were Jane Elizabeth, Eleanor Culbertson, Rebecca Shields, Hannah Malvina, Margaret, Samuel Albert, William Alexander, John Kirkpatrick, Cyrus Brady and James Henderson. Hannah M. is the only daughter living. She is the wife of Robert Fulton, of Big Spring West Pennsborough Township. The sons are all living, except William A., who died May 31, 1860. Samuel A. was born May 18, 1842. After leaving school he attended Duff's Commercial College, in Pittsburgh. During school intervals he worked on the farm, and the habits of industry acquired were strengthened by the strict religious training of God-fearing parents. August 2, 1862, he enlisted in Company E, One Hundred and Thirtieth Pennsylvania Volunteers, and on the following 18th of September, in the great battle of Antietam, received two wounds—one from a musket ball in his right arm, and another by being struck in the right side by a piece of rebel shell. He was sent to the hospital, and, when nearly convalescent, was attacked with typhoid fever, and his health being thus seriously impaired he received an honorable discharge. His uncle Samuel, on his death, in February, 1881, left him the farm, on which he has had a tenant three years past. Mr. McCune has been a member of the executive committee of the Cumberland County Temperance Alliance since its organization, and was one of the standing committee of the Prohibition party in the last State election. He has been for several years a ruling elder in the Big Spring Presbyterian Church, and has, ever since its organization, been a teacher in the Sabbath-school at Oakville. He is known as an upright Christian man of blameless life and character.

HENRY MANNING, merchant, Oakville. This gentleman is descended on the paternal side from the family of the name who originally came from England, and who are related to the same family of whom the celebrated Cardinal Manning is the representative head. The great-grandfather of our subject emigrated and settled in Lancaster County, Penn., before the war of the Revolution. He married a lady of German extraction, and both died there. His son George (Henry's grandfather) was born in Manor Township, Lancaster Co., Penn., about 1788 or 1790, and died a few years ago, aged ninety. His wife was Mary Kendig, member of a family still among the leading citizens of that place. Their children were John, Christian, Martin and Elizabeth, all now living. John (father of our subject) was born in 1813, in Dauphin County, Penn., to which his parents had removed. In 1832 he married Miss Lydia Culp, of Lancaster County, Penn., and continued to live on his father's farm until 1837, at which time he moved to Silver Spring Township, Cumberland Co. Mrs. John Manning, on her mother's side, was of the Boughter family, who were prominent in that region in the war of the Revolution, and of whom many anecdotes are told in that locality; she died in 1864. To John and Lydia (Culp) Manning were born six children: Henry, born October 29, 1834; Abraham, born in 1839, married to Miss Emma Leeds, of Carlisle, and now living at Mount Joy, Lancaster County; John, born in 1842, married to Emma Sanderson, of Newville, and is now living in Chambersburg; Sarah, born in 1846, is wedded to William Hauck, of Silver Spring Township, this county; Lillie, born in 1852, is the wife of Levi Baer, of same township; and Anderson, born in 1856, is single, ticket agent at Oakville; Henry was born at Middletown, Dauphin County; the rest in Silver Spring Township, this county. When sixteen years of age Henry Manning left home to learn the milling trade, serving a two years' apprenticeship, when he went to Ohio for a year; then worked a year for I. B. Buyson of Hampden Township, this county, after which he began the business on his own account at the old Silver Spring mill in that township. At this time he was but twenty years old. He carried on this mill successfully until 1862, when he entered into partnership with J. H Singiser, of Mechanicsburg, Penn., and bought the mill at the head of the Big Spring. Mr. Manning sold his intetest to his partner in 1867 and purchased the warehouse property in Oakville, where he carries on the grain and forwarding business. February 18, 1862, he was married to Maggie, daughter of George Beistline, of Silver Spring Township, born May 19, 1839. They have one son now living: Edgar Stuart, born October 8, 1865, who lives with his parents. Another, George, born November 20, 1862, died October 20, 1865. Mr. Manning has always taken an active interest in political affairs; but was never an office seeker. Of late his growing business interests do not admit of much outside matters. He and his wife are members of Big Spring Presbyterian Church at Newville, and he is known as an active business man and upright citizen.

ROBERT MICKEY, farmer, P. O. Oakville, is a great-grandson of Robert Mickey, who came from Ireland and settled in what is now Newton Township, being one of the first settlers in the valley, and he and his wife, Agnes, are both buried in the Big Spring cemetery, at Newville. One of their sons, also named Robert, was grandfather of our subject. He inherited that part of the original tract on which his grandson now lives, and to which he added largely. He was born in 1746, and lived all his life on the farm, where, in 1767, he built the stone house in which our subject was born. His wife was Ezemiah Kelly, of York County. He died December 22, 1828, aged eighty-two years, and his widow December 8, 1830, aged seventy-five years. Their children were Andrew, Thomas, John, James, Mary, Agnes and Margaret, all now deceased. James, the father of Robert, was born February 15, 1795, became a farmer, and never removed from the house in which he was born. He died in the year 1835. April 15, 1818, he married Lucetta Carothers, of Silver Spring Township, who was born August 11, 1801, and died March 20, 1862. They had six children, two of whom died young. One daughter, Ezemiah, born April 26, 1820, became the wife of Joseph Moody, removed to Ohio, and died there. The living are Mary Ann, born February 19, 1828, wife of William W. Frazer, and living in Missouri; Hays, born August 6, 1833, married to Elizabeth, daughter of John Kelly, Esq., of York County, and now residing in California; Robert, the eldest son, born January 14, 1823, until three years ago, lived in the house built by his grandfather, but, in 1880, built his present house, across the road from his birthplace. For several years before his death his father's farm was rented, but when Robert was eighteen years of age he took a part of it into his own hands for his mother, and a few years later bought the shares of his two sisters, giving him three quarters of the mansion farm. He also owns the adjoining property, known as the Thomas Mickey farm. In November, 1846, he was married to Elizabeth, daughter of John McCulloch, of this township. To this union thirteen children have been born, three dying young. The living are Sarah Belle, wife of James Hemphill, living in Kansas; John E., merchant of Oakville (see sketch below); Lucetta Ellen, wife of William Park, of Franklin County; Mary Elizabeth, wife of John Witherspoon, of Franklin County; Robert Austin, married to Mary Belle McCoy, and living on his father's farm; James Ira, married to Sarah Hood, and now with the Carlisle Manufacturing Company, of Carlisle; Andrew Elmer, Eugene Sherman and Helen, all living at home. Quinn Thornton is a student at Lafayette College. Mr. Mickey has never filled office. He and his wife belong to Big Spring Presbyterian Church, and as one of the leading citizens of the township is held in high esteem.

JOHN E. MICKEY, merchant, Oakville, is a son of Robert Mickey, and was born August 2, 1848, in the old stone mansion house; went to the district school, and worked on his father's farm until 1876, when he engaged in the mercantile business in Oakville, in the store formerly owned by his wife's father, J. K. Beidler. He has since conducted a general store business, and, in connection therewith, for two years successfully carried on the sewing machine trade, which he recently relinquished, his increasing store business demanding his entire time and attention. May 4, 1875, he married Miss Elizabeth M., daughter of J. K. Beidler. To this union three children have been born, viz.: Rosie Berenice, born May 31, 1876; John Roy, born August 25, 1878; and Ruth B., born December 16, 1882. Mr. Mickey is a member of Big Spring Lodge, No. 361, A. Y. M., of Newville; of St. John's Chapter, No. 171, and St. John's Commandery, No. 8, both of Carlisle. Mr. Mickey has never held office, but takes a warm interest in political affairs. He and his wife are members of the Big Spring Presbyterian Church, of Newville, of which he is a trustee. He has also been superintendent of the Sunday school at Oakville for two years past, and the testimony of all who know him is that he is one of the best citizens of the place, a rising, pushing and energetic young man, perfectly trustworthy in all his dealings. For his ancestral history, see sketch above.

J. D. REA, retired farmer, P. O. Newville, is a son of George and Isabella (Dunlop) Rea, former of whom was reared in Bedford County, Penn., and came to this county about 1830. To them were born four sons and three daughters, all now deceased, except J. D. Our subject received a good academical education and then chose the occupation of a farmer. Soon afterward he married Elizabeth McCullough, and by this union were born three children: G. Arthur, a farmer, now cultivating the mansion farm; Charles E., arrived at manhood's years, and contemplates following the calling of his brother; and Mary, finishing her education. Mrs. Rea dying in 1871, after a few days' illness, Mr. Rea married, in 1874, Miss Annie H. Hall, of Jersey City, of which union there is now living one son, Dudley Hall, now (1886) a lad of nine summers. This wife died in 1883, and our subject married, in 1885, his present wife, nee Annie E. Sheller, daughter of Dr. Adam Sheller, a prominent physician of Mount Joy, Lancaster Co., Penn. Mr. Rea still resides on the home farm where he was born, and though he has ceased to perform the mechanical part of agriculture, he retains the management and direction of his farms. He has traveled considerably, both through the United States and over the continent of Europe. The family are members of church.

THOMAS SHARP, farmer, P. O. Newville. The grandfather of this gentleman, Robert Sharp, came from Ireland before the Revolution, when quite a young man; afterward returning and bringing with him the rest of the family, and locating between the forks of the Delaware. He married a Miss Margaret Boyd, and a sister of his married a Hemphill. He and his brother Alexander were wagoners in the Continental Army. After the war Robert came to Cumberland County. He had five children: James, John, David, Thomas, and Margaret, who was married to John Smith and lived in Franklin County, Penn. John Sharp, the father of our subject, was born on a farm adjoining where Thomas lives, in the latter part of 1773, and died July 12, 1863. His wife was Martha Huston. They were married in 1814, and had seven children: Andrew, born August 25, 1816, and died in infancy; Margaret, born April 18, 1818, never married, and died January 27, 1870; Andrew (second) born March 19, 1820, married Eliza Jacobs, and died November 13, 1865; Martha, born May 12, 1822, died September 27, 1861; Robert Boyd, born November 10, 1824, married Mrs. Carothers, and died March 30, 1874; Franklin, born January 3, 1831, married Paulina Jamieson, and is now a resident of Columbia City, Ind.; Thomas, born May 29, 1827, on the mansion farm, of which his present farm was then a part. He lived there until 1864, when he took his present place from his father's estate, and has since resided on it. In December, 1863, he was married to Margaret Jane Jacobs, of Mifflin Township, this county, and who died April 2, 1873, aged forty-seven years and twenty-five days. October 26, 1876, he married his second wife, Jennie E. Maclay, of Franklin County, Penn., who died April 1, 1882, leaving no issue. Mr. Sharp never held office, is a member and trustee of the United Presbyterian Church in Newville, and is regarded as a man of good sound judgment, ripe experience and unblemished character.

R. L. SMITH, of Oakville, is a son of David Smith and a great-grandson of Baltzer Smith, who came from Germany about the middle of the last century, and settled in Lancaster County, where he was married and had a family of twelve children. Of this numerous family William, grandfather of our subject, alone survives. The family is somewhat remarkable for the advanced age to which some of its members attain. Baltzer Smith died when eighty-six years old, and several of his descendants lived to be over ninety. William, grandfather of R. L., was born July 1, 1806, near Oakville. In the fall of 1830 he was married to Miss Susan Forebop, who died in 1879, and April 6, 1880, he married Rebecca, widow of Thomas Heffelfinger, of Frankfort Township. His children are all by the first wife. One died in infancy. The others are Samuel, David, William, Mary, Susan and Elizabeth. The elder Smith bought his father's farm in 1839, and lived on it for twenty-eight years after that, when he removed to Oakville, where he now lives. David, father of R. L., cropped his father's farm for seven years, and then bought it from him in 1873, and has since lived in Oakville. R. L. is the only child. He is studying medicine in the office of Dr. Israel Betz, of Oakville, and is intending to enter the profession as soon as practicable. He is a studious and capable young man.

H. A. T. STROHM, merchant and justice of the peace. P. O. Walnut Bottom. The grandfather of this gentleman came from Germany about the close of the Revolutionary war, and settled in Lancaster County, removing fifteen years later to this township. He afterward sold his farm here, and went to Ohio, where several of his children had located, and there he died about twenty-five years ago. He had nine children: David, Samuel, Peter, Mary and Rebecca, deceased; and Levi, Philip, Henry and Elizabeth, living. Levi, father of our subject, was born in 1820, and was married, in 1851, to Julia A. Coffey. For twenty years he was a merchant, having four stores in Leesburg and in the adjoining townships, and was also engaged in other enterprises. In 1877 he gave up merchandising and retired to his farm in Southampton Township, where he now lives. He is an active and prominent citizen of the township; he and his wife are members of the Methodist Episcopal Church. They had ten children, four of whom, Nora, Agnes, Flora and Mary, are deceased; the others are James J., married to Maggie Baker, and living in Leesburg; William B., married and living in Chambersburg; Wallace L., single and living at home; Abby A., wife of Rev. S. M. Mountz, of Centre County; Clara, living with her parents; and Henry A. T., who was born June 13, 1852, who went into his father's store when quite young, and stayed there until he was twenty-five. In 1877 he began business for himself at Rehoboth, and in 1879 removed to Jacksonville. October 22, 1878, he was married to Martha M., daughter of Thomas Price, merchant of Lykers, Dauphin County, a coal miner and operator, also, in Somerset County, and a prominent man. Mrs. Strohm was born in 1854. They have had three children: Martha, born October 8, 1879, died in infancy; Lottie Esther, born June 6, 1882, and Charles O., born November 24, 1884. Mr. Strohm is a Democrat in politics, in which he takes an active interest, and is now justice of the peace in Jacksonville. He is spoken of as an enterprising, active and trustworthy man, who must rise in the community.

CHARLES TRONE, superintendent of the Big Pond Furnace estate, Lee's Cross Roads, is a grandson of John Trone, a native of York County, whose father was from Germany, and who was married to Polly Clay, of that county. They had the following named children: Jacob, George, Conrad, William, Charles, Henry, Catherine, Elizabeth, Polly, Rebecca and Lydia. Our subject's father, George, was born March 6, 1795, and followed the occupation of a carpenter and cabinet-maker. In 1818 he married Susanna Carl, of Hanover. They had ten children: Charles, who was the eldest, was born January 29, 1819; Abdel, born January 14, 1823, was a member of Company H, Third Pennsylvania Cavalry, and was wounded at Warrenton, Va., and died from the effects at Brandy Station, Va., January 18, 1864; Reunem F., born June 14, 1831, married and living in Columbus, Ohio; George, born February 6, 1840, married Margaret Lee, of Shippensburg, now living in Cincinnati; Anna Maria, born September 11, 1820, wife of David Reese, of Newton Township; Amanda C., born October 29, 1824, widow of Peter D. Hendricks, and living in Michigan; Lucinda, born September 9, 1827, was wife of John Stough, of Newville, and died in December, 1878; Emma, born April 26, 1835, is the wife of John D. Laverty, of Philadelphia; Catherine L., born March 26, 1833, wife of John W. Donovan, living in Ohio; Elizabeth, born in 1838, became the wife of John D. Cole, of Shippensburg, and died in Middletown, Md. When Charles was twelve years old his parents came to what is now known as Cleversburg, Southampton Township, to a farm which his father sold in 1845, engaging in business and afterward at his trade in Shippensburg, retiring some years after, and died in Charles' house, July 18, 1876, aged eighty-one. His wife died March 29, 1874. Charles remained on the farm until his marriage, when he taught school for two years; then was clerk at Mary Ann Furnace, later going to Shippensburg until 1855, when he came to the Big Pond Furnace, bringing his family in 1864. At the time he came it was owned by Schoch & Sons, who sold it, in 1869, to P. A. Ahl & Bro., who disposed of it, in 1872, to the Philadelphia & Reading Coal & Iron Company, who are still its proprietors. It was idle for several years, and in 1879 was leased by C. W. Ahl & Son, who put it in running order, and would have had it in operation in a few days, when, unfortunately it took fire. and the greater part was consumed. The property then reverted to the Coal and Iron Company, and has never been rebuilt. In all these changes Mr. Trone has been, and is now in charge of the property. November 2, 1843, he was married to Anna Sierer, of Southampton Township, who died June 26, 1874. They had four children: Annetta; George, who died in infancy; Mary Ellen, deceased; and Leila, wife of George D. Clever, of Cleversburg. Mr. Trone is a member of Rehoboth Methodist Episcopal Church, of which he is steward, and bears a high character for intelligence and integrity.

CHAPTER LIV.

NORTH MIDDLETON TOWNSHIP.

REUBEN FISHBURN, retired farmer and stock-grower, P. O. Carlisle, was born in Dauphin County, Penn., June 5, 1828, son of John and Catharine (Carmony) Fishburn, natives of Dauphin County and of German origin John Fishburn was a farmer all his life. Our subject is the eighth born in a family of ten children, nine of whom grew to manhood and womanhood. He was reared on the farm and received his education in the common school in Dickinson Township, this county, where his parents had moved in 1832 and spent the remainder of their days. Reuben wisely chose the occupation of his father as his own, and has succeeded in accumulating a fine share of this world's goods. His farm consists of 150 acres of land, mostly under a high state of cultivation and with first-class improvements. On this farm is situated the meeting-house and Spring Grove grave-yard, said to be the oldest burying-ground in Cumberland County. Mr. Fishburn retired from the active pursuits of life in 1881, but still resides on the farm. He has been twice married, on first occasion, in 1855, to Rebecca Myers, who died in the same year. In 1859 he married his present wife, whose maiden name was Sarah Elizabeth Peffer. and who is of German origin. Mr. and Mrs. Fishburn have two daughters: Anna and Edna, residing at home. He and his wife are members of the Lutheran Church, in which he has been deacon for four years. In politics he is a Republican. He has served as school director in this township.

GEORGE GETTER, farmer and stock-grower, P. O. Carlisle, was born in Germany December 27, 1819, son of George and Elizabeth (Zimmerman) Getter, also natives of Germany, and who had a family of fifteen children, twelve of whom attained maturity. Our subject's father, by occupation a farmer and carpenter, served as a soldier under Napoleon Bonaparte, and after his discharge from the army worked at farming in Germany until 1828, when he came to America, and being a poor man it took the most of what he had accumulated to move his large family to Baltimore County, Md. He was very devoted to his family, and the anxiety for their welfare, the sea voyage and exertion of traveling so far, proved almost too much for him; but he was energetic, and soon obtained a position on the Baltimore Railroad. He was accidentally killed nine weeks thereafter, and the children were thus thrown on their own resources in a strange country. Our subject, the tenth born, was one month in the poor house and while there attended school. He was then bound out till he was twenty-one to a man living at Newville, this county. After serving his term of service he hired out to the same man three years longer. He was married, in 1841, to Miss Mary, daughter of Henry Kendig, also of German origin. Of the twelve children born to this union seven are living: Nancy Ellen, Henry K., David. Philip R., Weine, Leo and Jennie. Mr. and Mrs. Getter are members of the Church of God, in which he is elder, trustee and deacon. In business Mr. Getter has met with marked success, and by his own exertions has acquired the well improved farm where he now resides. Politically he is a Republican.

GEORGE B. WAGGONER, farmer and stock-grower, Carlisle, was born in Perry County, Penn., July 4, 1845, son of Peter and Mary (Snider) Waggoner, natives of Pennsylvania and of German origin. Peter Waggoner, who has made merchant milling the occupation of his life, has met with marked success; he moved to Missouri in 1868, where he resides at the present time, and is engaged extensively in the milling business. George B., the sixth in a family of seven children, grew to manhood in Cumberland County, and learned milling of his father. When troops were called for during the late civil war he enlisted in Company E. One Hundred and Thirtieth Pennsylvania Volunteer Infantry, and at the expiration of his time re-enlisted in an independent regiment which was raised in Cumberland County, and in which he served until the close of the war. He was in several battles and skirmishes, among which may be named Fredericksburg and Chancellorsville. After the war he went to Missouri, where he followed farming for two years, but on account of ill health he returned to Pennsylvania, and then entered the employ of C. W. Ahl, for whom he worked eleven years in the iron ore mines, being foreman for five years. In 1886 he bought his present farm of 120 acres in North Middleton Township, where he now resides. In 1868 he married Mary A., daughter of Simon B. Mountz, and of German origin. The children born to this union, now living, are William, Minnie, Maud, Charles, George, Mary and Grace. In politics Mr. Waggoner is a Republican.

HENRY F. WAGGONER, carpenter, P. O. Carlisle, was born in Perry County, Penn., January 8, 1841, son of Henry W. and Elizabeth (Wagner) Waggoner, natives of Pennsylvania and of German lineage. His father in early life was a carpenter, but in later years followed farming. Henry F., the sixth in a family of twelve children (eleven of whom attained maturity), was reared on the farm, attending the common school. He worked with his father on the farm until he was eighteen, when he learned the carpenter's trade, and followed this occupation until 1872, when he bought the farm of 97 acres well improved land, in this township, from which he lately retired to follow his trade, his sons carrying on the farm. The Waggoner family is prominently identified with the history of this county, the grandfather, Abram Waggoner, being an early settler and widely known; he served as a soldier in the war of 1812. During the late Rebellion, Henry F. Waggoner entered the army, in 1862, as a teamster in Col. Hunt's reserve heavy artillery, and served all through the Peninsular campaign, and until after the Pope campaign; then returned home to assist on his father's farm, while his brothers were serving as volunteers in the Army of the Potomac; then, in 1863, his brother B. F.'s term having expired, the latter took the place, at home, of our subject, who enlisted in the army and served to the close of the war. He was in the Two Hundred and Ninth Regiment Pennsylvania Volunteer Infantry, and participated in the battles of Fort Steadman and Petersburg. In politics Mr. Waggoner is a Democrat. He has been inspector and constable of this township four years. He was married, in 1868, to Rebecca, daughter of Phelix and Margaret (Minich) Swigart, and this union has been blessed with eight children: Angeline C., Elmer K., Estella J., Ida M., Loris F., Alvin B., Cora Ellen (deceased), and Althea Idene.

WILSON J. WAGNER, farmer and stock-grower, P. O. Carlisle, was born in North Middleton Township, this county, October 20, 1850, son of George and Sarah (Strohm) Wagner, whose ancestors came from Switzerland. His father, who was a farmer all his life, died in this county in 1877 at the age of sixty-six years; he was a thorough business man, and met with marked success at farming, being at the time of his death worth about $75,000, most of which he had made by his own exertions. He was a Democrat in politics, but no office seeker and could not be induced to hold any official position. His name was originally spelled Waggoner, but he instructed his sons to spell their name Wagner. Our subject, the second in the family of seven children (five of whom are still living), was reared on the farm and received his schooling in North Middleton Township. He has made agriculture his business, and is the owner of a farm of 127 acres with first class improvements. Our subject has been twice married, first, in 1877, to Emma, daughter of William Jacoby, who died in 1880, leaving two children: George and Sidney. Mr. Wagner was married on the second occasion, in 1883, to Anna, daughter of John Armstrong. Politically he is a Democrat.

CHAPTER LV.

PENN TOWNSHIP.

JOHN SAMUEL BURKHART, tinner, P. O. Dickinson, was born in Newville, this county, March 8, 1839. His father, Jacob, son of Jacob and Elizabeth Burkhart, residents of this county from childhood, married Martha, daughter of John and Elizabeth Diller, who were also children of early settlers of this county. The ancestors on both sides were of the old Mennonite faith. After attaining his majority our subject moved, with his widowed mother and half brother, to Selins Grove, Snyder Co., Penn., where he entered a missionary institute, to prepare for the ministry; he taught in the intervals and had the care of the family. In August, 1862, Mr. Burkhart enlisted in the One Hundred and Thirty-first Regiment Pennsylvania Volunteer Infantry. He took part in the battles of Fredericksburg and Chancellorsville, and was discharged in May, 1863, with the rank of orderly sergeant, leaving a record as a brave and faithful soldier. Returning to Snyder County, Penn., he was compelled to give up his course for the ministry, on account of an

PENN TOWNSHIP.   527

affection of the throat contracted while in the army. In 1865 he purchased a tin and stove store, which was destroyed by fire February 25, 1872. Our subject married Miss Elizabeth A. Schock, February 25, 1868, and they returned to this county in May, 1872. After devoting some years in looking after the interests of his mother's farm, and two years (1876-78) in teaching, he established his shop in the village of Centreville, this county; he does a general business, roofing, spouting, repairing and dealing in stoves, tinware, etc. Mrs. Burkhart died April 29, 1882, a devoted wife and mother, an earnest Christian, and her death was mourned by a large circle of friends. Of her eight children only three are now living: Mary Emma, Miriam May and Samuel Bruce. Mr. Burkhart is a life-long Republican; an earnest member of the Lutheran Church. He is an upright and worthy citizen, highly respected.

SAMUEL CAROTHERS, farmer, P. O. Dickinson, was born March 10, 1839, in Penn (then Dickinson) Township, this county. His father, John M. Carothers, came from York County, Penn., in early manhood, with his parents. Samuel and Jane (Nesbet) Carothers, and married Miss Sarah Jane Carothers, a very distant relative, a native of Huntingdon County, Penn. She died in 1842, and John M. Carothers again married, in Adams County, Penn., moved to Franklin County, and finally to this county, where he died. Our subject, Samuel Carothers, was reared by his paternal grandfather, in Penn Township, this county, and began life farming his grandfather's place. He married, December 24, 1859, Miss Rebecca Carl, daughter of Peter and Eliza Carl, early settlers of this county, he from Perry County and she from Lancaster County, Penn. Since their marriage, Mr. and Mrs. Carothers have resided in Penn Township, this county, where they have a pleasant and comfortable home and a tract of about 19 acres of fertile and well improved land. The widowed mother of Mrs. Carothers now resides with them. To our subject and wife have been born two sons: Samuel Henderson and James Elder, who have both made thorough preparation for the profession of teaching, and are doing useful service in that noble profession, giving excellent satisfaction as faithful and efficient educators. James E. is a graduate of the State Normal School at Shippensburg. Samuel Carothers is a life-long Democrat. He has served his township as assessor one year, and also as school director and as supervisor. He and his worthy wife are consistent members of the United Brethren Church. He is an upright and worthy citizen, respected and esteemed by all who know him.

JACOB G. CROMAN, merchant, residence South Fairview, P. O. Dickinson, was born October 9, 1843, in Penn Township, this county. His father, Jacob Croman, a native of Berks County, Penn., came to this county when a young man, and married Margaret Vance, a native of this county and daughter of John and Susan (Glenn) Vance, who resided in Penn Township, this county, until their death. Our subject's father was among the early settlers of Brushtown District (now South Fairview), Penn Township, and built the fifth house in the neighborhood. He was the father of seven children: Mrs. Sarah Neff, John W., Mrs. Eliza Sellers, Mrs. Ellen Cooper, Mrs. Susan Schroyer, Jacob G., and Isabelle (deceased). Jacob G. Croman enlisted, September 15, 1862, in the Seventeenth Pennsylvania Volunteer Cavalry, and was assigned to the Army of the Potomac, serving in the historic campaigns of Virginia; he took part in the hard fought battles of Chancellorsville, Beverly Ford, Alldee and Upperville, in Virginia; Gettysburg, Penn.; Boonsboro, Md.; Williamsport, Brandy Station, Culpeper, Stephensburg, the various battles in the Wilderness, Civilians Station, Winchester, Cedar Creek, Rock Fish Creek, Five Forks and various other engagements up to Appomattox, where he personally witnessed the surrender of Gen. Robert E. Lee. He was wounded while on picket at Garrisonville, Va., and he also received a life-long injury by the fall of his horse at the same place. He received his discharge in June, 1865, and left a record as a brave and faithful soldier, always ready for the call of duty. Returning home he married Miss Mary A. Rexroth, July 20, 1865; her parents, Henry and Mary Rexroth, natives of Saxony, came to this county in 1843, and resided many years in Pine Grove, Cook Township, where she was born: they afterward resided in Penn Township until their death; the mother died in 1875, and the father January 1, 1884, in his eightieth year. Mr. and Mrs. Croman have resided in South Fairview, Penn Township, this county, ever since their marriage. He followed shoe-making for three years; then established a store, which he still carries on. His children are William Glenn, Anna M. C., Henry Carol, Rosa Maud, Jacob Herman and Grace. In politics our subject is a Republican. He and his wife are members of the Disciples Church. Mr. Croman is a man of upright principles, a worthy citizen, respected by all who know him.

JAMES DUNLAP, farmer, P. O. Newville, was born in Penn (then Dickinson) Township, this county, February 20, 1819, son of William and Elizabeth (Sproat) Dunlap, both natives of this county, and who resided here until their death; he died in October, 1826, and she in 1820. Of their children, six grew to maturity, three of whom are now living: William, in Urbana, Ohio; James and Miss Nancy E., residing in Newville, this county. The subject of this sketch has resided on the old homestead farm of his great-grandfather Sproat all his life. He married Miss Lucetta Hays February 26, 1846. They have a fine farm of about 200 acres of fertile and well improved valley land, besides a farm of 145 acres in Newton Township, this county. To Mr. and Mrs. Dunlap have been born nine children, two of whom died in infancy. Those now living are: William S., Robert Hays, Mrs. Margaret Jane McCullough, John Armstrong, Lillie Belle, Fred S. and James Wallace. Our subject is a life-long Republican. He and his worthy wife are members of the United Presbyterian Church at Newville, this county. Mr. Dunlap has taken a deep interest in the education of his children, and they are taking a high position in business and social circles. He is a man of firm principles, an upright and worthy citizen, a liberal patron of useful public enterprise, and is respected and esteemed.

ELIAS B. EYSTER, P. O. Walnut Bottom, was born in Columbiana County, Ohio, July 16, 1809, son of John and Susan (Booz) Eyster, natives of Berks and Adams Counties, Penn., respectively, who, after their marriage, moved to Columbiana County, Ohio, where they remained until their death. They were among the earliest and most respected pioneers of Ohio. Elias B. Eyster left Ohio when he was twenty-one years of age, and came to Berks County, Penn. He there married, December 5, 1835, Miss Helena Dresher, and in 1837 they came to Oyster Point, this county, within two miles of Harrisburg. They kept the "Oyster Point Hotel" for five years, and then moved to the Cumberland Valley to the place where they now reside, in Penn Township, this county. They purchased "Long Meadow Hotel," and conducted it for a period of forty years (the house was built in 1780 and is still standing and occupied). Elias B. Eyster was a genial and popular landlord, and his house was a favorite resort for travelers seeking entertainment, good-cheer and rest, in the good old days long past. In 1855 Mr. Eyster purchased the mill on Yellow Breeches Creek, since known as Eyster's Mill, which he still owns, and in addition he has acquired here five farms, aggregating over 500 acres of fertile and well improved land, much of which he has given to his children. September 20, 1878, Mrs. Eyster departed this life, aged sixty-six years, six months and eight days. To our subject and wife have been born the following named children: Thomas Jefferson (deceased), Angelina, Elias G., Helena Jane, Mrs. Sarah Ann Moore, Charles J. (deceased), Mrs. Frances Josephine Myers, Laura Elizabeth (deceased), Margaret M. (deceased) and William L. Mr. Eyster is a life-long Democrat. He has filled most of the township offices at various times, and has held the position of director of the poor for one term (1870-73). He and his family attend the Lutheran Church. His wife has been a member of that church nearly her entire life. Mr. Eyster has led an active and useful life, and is honored and respected by his descendants and his fellow-citizens of this county.

ELIAS G. EYSTER, farmer, P. O. Walnut Bottom, was born March 27, 1840, at Oyster Point, this county (near Harrisburg). He was brought to Penn Township, this county, with his father's family when he was two years of age, and has resided here since. His school course was interrupted in May, 1861, by his offering his services in defense of the Government, in response to President Lincoln's first call for troops. His company was not accepted at that time, but was afterward, at the first call for three years' troops, in August of the same year. Mr. Eyster was assigned to the Army of the Potomac, and took part in the historic campaigns in Virginia, Maryland and Pennsylvania. He was present at the active engagements of Williamsburg, Malvern Hill, Antietam, Fredericksburg, Gettysburg, Mine Run, and the various battles of the Wilderness, up to Petersburg, besides a large number of severe skirmishes. He received a gunshot wound through the neck in a skirmish at Hartford Church February, 1863, which laid him up for six months and caused his absence from the battle of Chancellorsville. He was taken prisoner on the last day of the battle of Gettysburg, and was confined for one month in Libby Prison and Belle Isle. He received an honorable discharge from the army August 6, 1864, leaving a fine record as a brave and faithful soldier.

LEWIS GOODHART, farmer, P. O. Dickinson, was born April 15, 1822, in Penn (then Dickinson) Township, this county. His father, Isaac, was a son of Jacob Goodhart, who married Mary W. Shafner and settled in this county with his young family in very early times. The valley was then new and wild, and they cleared up their own farm. Our subject's father, Isaac Goodhart, married Miss Mary Magdalene Palm, daughter of Jacob and Mary (Bishop) Palm, who came from Lancaster County, Penn. Mr. and Mrs. Isaac Goodhart reared a family of ten children: Mrs. Eliza Gibbler (deceased), William, Beckie, Lewis, Mrs. Mary Piper, Mrs. Ann Bishop, Martin Alex P., Cyrus A. (deceased), Marion Anson, and Mrs. Agnes Druzilla Hess. Lewis Goodhart was educated in the schools of the early times. April 11, 1844, he married Miss Charlotte Farner, who was born in Franklin County, Penn., and came to West Pennsborough Township, this county, in girlhood, with her widowed mother, Mrs. Elizabeth Farner, her father, David Farner, having died in Franklin County, Penn. Mr. Goodhart has resided in Penn Township, this county, since his marriage. He owns a fine farm of 143 acres of fertile and well improved land in the valley, and a fine tract of timber on South Mountain. To Mr. and Mrs. Goodhart have been born ten children: Two died in infancy, and one, Frances Emma, died at the age of thirteen years; those now living are Marion Anson, Mrs. Mary Elizabeth Mitten, Mrs. Agnes B. Brandt, Calvin, Theodore, David G. McClellan and Clarence Eugene. Two of the sons, Marion Anson and David G. McClellan, have prepared themselves for the profession of teaching, and are now successfully engaged in that noble work. Our subject and wife and four of their children are members of the Presbyterian Church. He is a Democrat in politics, and has served his township in various official capacities. Mr. Goodhart is one of the self-made men of Penn Township. Unaided, and under adverse circumstances, step by step, he has built himself up to his present position in life, and is known and recognized as an upright man, enjoying the respect and esteem of all who know him.

JACOB N. HERMAN, marble cutter and dealer, residence Hockersville, P. O. Dickinson, was born in Straban Township, Adams Co., Penn., March 4, 1843. His parents, Col. Jacob and Sophia Herman, moved to York County, Penn., in 1864, where they resided until their death; the former died in 1875, and the latter in 1876; they had a family of ten children, five still living: George, in Sheridan, Nev.; David, in Adams County, Penn.; Mrs. Irene Knaub, in York County, Penn.; Mary, in Jacksonville, and Jacob N., our subject. Mrs. Herman was a daughter of Jacob and Margretta Gilbert, whose residence was near Arendtsville, Adams Co., Penn. Col. Herman's occupation was house carpenter and undertaker, which he carried on quite extensively. He was formerly an active officer in the militia service of the State, having received four different commissions from the commonwealth of Pennsylvania. He served one year as lieutenant, seven years as captain, seven years colonel, three years as brigade-major of the Second Brigade of the Fifth Division, composed of the militia of the counties of York and Adams, Gen. Craig Miller being commander of the Second Brigade of the Fifth Division. J. N. Herman entered upon an apprenticeship with Micah Arnold, of York County, August 7, 1865, remained there until the spring of 1866, when his employer bought out an establishment in Mechanicsburg, where our subject finished his trade as marble cutter August 7, 1868. Mr. Herman worked for Mr. Arnold from 1865 until the spring of 1877, with the exception of a short time in Lancaster City and Glen Rock, Penn. His recommendation from his employer, Mr. Arnold, reads as follows: "Mechanicsburg, April 6, 1877. This is to certify that J. N. Herman has served three years apprenticeship with me at marble-cutting, and afterward has been foreman in one of my shops for about seven years, and I can recommend him as a first-class workman and a reliable man. (Signed) M. Arnold." (This is quite a compliment to Mr. Herman's integrity and judgment as a skillful artist.) In the spring of 1878 Mr. Herman moved to Middletown, Dauphin Co., Penn., to engage in the marble business with S. A. Landis, of Mechanicsburg, as partner, but remained only there until October 1, same year, at which time J. N. Herman moved to the upper end of this county, to a place known as Big Spring; remained there one year and then moved to Jacksonville, this county, which is on the line of the Harrisburg & Potomac Railroad, and finally settled in Hockersville, this county, in 1883. Here he has carried on a shop ever since, and has an influential patronage in the surrounding community. Mr. Herman married Miss Maggie Harper, a daughter of the Hon. William Harper of Penn Township, who died March 3, 1873, a strong supporter of the Democratic party, and by that body was elected two terms as member of the Legislature; his wife, Isabella Harper, died March 13, 1863. J. N. Herman gave his services in defense of the government in September, 1864; he was a member of Company I, Two Hundred and Ninth Regiment Pennsylvania Volunteers; served in the Army of the Potomac, and took part in the memorable battle known as Fort Steadman.

SAMUEL F. HUSTON, farmer, P. O. Mooredale, was born in Penn Township, this county, February 17, 1859. His parents, James S. and Mary Jane (Brown) Huston, resided in Penn Township until the death of the former in 1865; the latter died in 1876. Of their children, Joseph B. died January 1, 1883; Mrs. Anna M. Caldwell, resides in Newton Township, this county; John R. and Samuel F. reside in Penn Township, this county. Our subject's grandparents, Samuel and Anna Huston, were natives of this county and descendants of early settlers. Samuel F. Huston, the subject of this sketch, completed his education in the schools of the home district, and, at the age of twenty-two years, engaged in teaching. He taught for three terms, giving excellent satisfaction as a faithful and efficient educator. November 1, 1883, he married Miss Maggie B. Sharpe, a native of Newton Township, this county, daughter of Samuel M. Sharpe, and they have one son, Samuel Sharpe Huston. Our subject is a life-long and enthusiastic Democrat. He and his worthy wife are members of the United Presbyterian Church, at Newville, Penn. Mr. Huston is an intelligent and enterprising young farmer, an upright and worthy citizen, highly respected by the entire community.

RT. REV. DANIEL KELLER, bishop or elder of the German Baptist Church, and farmer, P. O. Huntsdale, was born in Lancaster County, Penn., September 23, 1813. His father and grandfather were also born in that county, his great-grandfather, a native of Switzerland, having established the family in America. Our subject's mother, Elizabeth Hershberger, was also descended from a Swiss grandfather, who came to this country, and the two families have branched out far and wide in the New World. Elder Keller's father, John Keller, died July 27, 1876, at the age of nearly ninety-one years—all passed in this State. Elder Keller married, December 31, 1838, Miss Catherine Kline, of Lancaster County, Penn., born November 4, 1813, and they came to Centreville, this county, in 1845. In 1878 they moved to a farm near Milltown (now Huntsdale), and in 1869 located where they now reside, at Huntsdale, this county. Elder Keller has followed farming all his life, and has been uniformly successful. He has dealt largely in farm property, and was one of the first to establish the custom of liming the soil in this valley, by which course the value of the land in this county has been greatly increased. Elder Keller now owns a fine farm of 160 acres of fertile and well improved land in Penn Township, 320 acres in Russell County, Kas., and a large grist-mill on Yellow Breeches Creek, at Huntsdale, this county, also five dwelling houses and lots in Huntsdale. To Elder Keller and wife have been born thirteen children, nine of whom are living: Benjamin, in Shamokin, Penn.; Mrs. Catherine Brandt, near Centreville, this county; Daniel Jr., in Ellsworth County, Kas.; Mrs. Susanna Russell, in Newburg, this county; Henry, in Wilson, Ellsworth Co., Kas.; Mrs. Hedassah Coover, in Green Vale, Russell Co., Kas.; Samuel, in Bourbon, Marshall Co., Ind.; Jacob, in Plympton, Dickinson Co., Kas., and Mrs. Sarah Myers, at Huntsdale, this county. Nearly all of Elder Keller's family are members of the German Baptist Church. He joined the church in 1848, was chosen preacher in same in 1850, and ordained bishop in 1861. He is an influential member and a pillar of the church. In all his dealings Elder Keller has been upright and straightforward, generous to those in need and liberal toward public enterprises. He is a worthy and highly-respected citizen, and his name will long be honored by succeeding generations in Cumberland County. Following the non-resisting policy of the church, the Elder takes no part in politics, but is disposed to favor the Republican party. Elder and Mrs. Keller, in their course of life, have thus far experienced much joy, and also much sorrow.

REV. DAVID LEFEVER, minister of the Christian Church and farmer, P. O. Huntsdale, Cumberland County, was born March 5, 1823, in West Pennsborough Township, this county. In the year 1708 a Dr. Lefever came from France and settled in Boston, Mass., and from him, probably, sprung all of the Lefevers in the United States. He was one of the famous Huguenots who fled from religious persecution to find a refuge in the New World. The line from him down is Philip, George, Lawrence, John and David. Lawrence moved from York County, Penn., to this county, with his father, in 1785, and resided here until his death. His wife was Veronica Alter, of the well-known Alter family. (She was sister of the wife of Gov. Joseph Ritner.) Their son John married Miss Rebecca Rine. He was a farmer by occupation, but took an active part in public affairs. Being one of the few native citizens who could speak the German language fluently, he was appointed associate judge by Gov. Ritner about 1835, and, after rendering distinguished services, he retired from the position with honor. He was a man of very correct and methodical habits and kept an accurate diary for forty years. He was converted at the age of forty years, and at once rode 51 miles to Beaver Creek, Washington Co., Md., to be immersed. He did active duty in the Christian Church, as a preacher, until his death, which occurred September 13, 1864. His widow died in December, 1875. Rev. David Lefever is the eldest of their seven children, of whom he and Mrs. Maria Myers, of Adams County, Penn., are the sole survivors. Our subject married, December 29, 1847, Miss Matilda Cunningham, a niece of Gov. Ritner, and they at once settled in Penn Township, this county, and began to develop a home. They continued in a successful course until they acquired 3 fine farms, comprising 375 acres of fertile and well improved valley land, besides a tract of 115 acres of timber land on South Mountain. Mr. Lefever bought a foundry, on the edge of Shippensburg, Penn., in 1870, which he still owns. He carried it on for several years, residing in Shippensburg from 1876 to 1878. Mr. Lefever's wife departed this life January 8, 1885. She was a devoted wife, the mother of nine children, seven of whom are now living: Henry Rine, David Landis, Joseph C., Mrs. Margaret Smith, Matilda, Mrs. Clarinda Eyster, and Fannie. Our subject united with the Christian Church at the age of nineteen years; was chosen elder in 1855; began preaching in 1864, and has continued in the work of the gospel ever since. He built, almost entirely unaided, a handsome stone church on his land, and deeded it to the congregation. He has been a Republican most of his life. In 1885 he espoused the cause of the Prohibition party, and has devoted himself actively during the campaign, delivering lectures on the subject of temperance. He is a speaker of great force and energy, and wields a great influence for good among a large circle of friends and acquaintances.

MICHAEL LONG, farmer, P. O. Walnut Bottom, was born February 7, 1831, in Lancaster County, Penn. His father, John Long, died in that county, and his mother, Mary Long, came to Franklin County, Penn., where she remained until her death. Michael Long married Miss Rebecca Geesaman, of Franklin County, Penn., February 1, 1854, and they moved to Penn Township, this county, in the spring of 1857, locating at once on the place they at present occupy, in the valley of Yellow Breeches Creek; here they have a farm of 91 acres of valley land and 37 of timbered land on South Mountain. Their children are Alfred Claton, William Joseph, Daniel Abram, Aaron Albion, Franklin Clarence and Anna Belle. Mr. Long and his son established a store at Centre Valley in 1880, and moved it to Bendersville in 1883, where it is at present located. They do a general merchandising business, and are building up a prosperous trade. Our subject and wife and all their children, except the youngest, belong to the United Brethren Church. Mr. Long is very active in his devotion to the interest of the Church, and has been a class-leader for

PENN TOWNSHIP. 531

many years. He is a man of generous impulses, a liberal patron of public enterprises, and is one of the leading citizens of Cumberland County.

WILLIAM ALEXANDER McCULLOUGH, farmer, P. O. Newville, was born December 2, 1834, in West Pennsborough Township, this county, and is a son of Alexander and Elizabeth McCullough. December 27, 1866, subject married Miss Martha L. Clark, and they located where they now reside in 1874. Here they have a fine farm of 121 acres of land, also have a farm of 91 acres in Southampton Township, and a tract of 8 acres of timber on South Mountain. Their children are James Clark, Berdie and John Bruce. Our subject is a life-long Republican. He and his wife are members of Big Spring Presbyterian Church.

JOHN THEODORE McCUNE, retired farmer, P. O. Dickinson, was born April 9, 1844, in Southampton Township, this county, third child of Samuel and Mary Eleanor (McClay) McCune. Our subject's paternal grandfather, Samuel McCune, entered land in Hopewell Township, this county, which has been occupied by the family for three generations. John T. McCune, the subject of this sketch, enlisted August 12, 1862, in the One Hundred and Thirtieth Regiment Pennsylvania Volunteer Infantry. He was present at the battles of Antietam, Fredericksburg and Chancellorsville. After the expiration of his term of service, in 1863, he attended school at Academia, Juniata Co., Penn., for four months, and then re-enlisted in the Thirty-fourth Regiment Pennsylvania Volunteer Militia. After serving six weeks he was honorably discharged, leaving a good record as a faithful soldier. He next spent two years traveling in the stock business through the Northwestern States with his uncle, A. S. McCune, of Van Buren County, Iowa. Returning to this county, Mr. McCune married Miss Bethsheba Mahaffy December 4, 1866, and after spending four years in Virginia they have resided in Centreville, Penn., ever since. They have a fine farm of 102 acres adjoining the village. They have one daughter, Lillie M. Mr. McCune is a life-long Republican. He is a man of generous disposition, upright character, respected by a large circle of friends.

HENRY K. MILLER, grain dealer, agent for the Harrisburg & Potomac Railroad, etc., and postmaster of Huntsdale, was born August 18, 1849, in Middlesex Township, this county, son of Joseph and Susanna (Kaufman) Miller. After attaining his majority he spent about four years traveling through the Western States, visiting Missouri, Illinois, Iowa, Nebraska, Kansas and Ohio, and in the spring of 1877 he formed a partnership with his brother, D. H. Miller, in a grain warehouse at Huntsdale, he, Henry K., being the principal manager. In May, 1885, our subject bought his brother's interest, and has been carrying on the business since. He does a general commission and forwarding trade, dealing in grain, coal, flour, seeds, salt, etc., and by strict attention to business has built up a large and flourishing trade. In 1880 the postoffice Ernst was established, with Henry K. Miller as postmaster, and in November, 1882, the name of the office was changed to Huntsdale. In 1882 our subject was appointed agent for the Adams Express Company, and in October, 1885, agent for the Harrisburg & Potomac Railroad Company, all of which positions he now holds. January 20, 1879, Mr. Miller married Miss Anna Eliza Hastings, of Penn Township, this county. Our subject and wife are consistent members of the German Baptist Church. He is a life-long Republican, and takes a deep interest in public affairs. He is an enterprising and successful business man, a liberal patron of public enterprises, respected and esteemed by all who know him.

JAMES MOORE, retired farmer, Walnut Bottom, Cumberland County, was born December 10, 1805, in Dickinson Township, this county, and early began an apprenticeship at the blacksmith trade in Latimore Township, Adams County, with John Miller. He followed his trade as a journeyman for several years through Cumberland and Adams Counties. He married Miss Elizabeth Ripton January 20, 1831. He carried on a shop at the turnpike and Stone Tavern, in Dickinson Township, for fourteen years, in Cumberland County. His first wife had three children, all girls: Elizabeth, Isabella and Nancy. Elizabeth died when eighteen years old; Isabella married Mr. Kurtz, and Nancy married Mr. Miller. In April, 1844, Mr. Moore removed to the place where he now resides, in Penn Township, at once locating here, and has been engaged in farming. He has acquired a fine farm property of 131 acres of land in the valley, with two sets of buildings, and 200 acres of timber land on the side of South Mountain; and has also purchased 120 acres of land in Clinton County, Ind. His first wife died January 29, 1836, leaving the three daughters above mentioned, and our subject then married Miss Jane Smith, January 18, 1839. She gave birth to seven children four sons, (William, James, John and David), and three daughters (Margaretta J., Mary and Anna G. Moore). His second wife died in 1855, leaving four living children of her own: James, in Clinton County, Ind.; Anna G. Mitten, Margaretta J. Utley, and David, who was a soldier in Company H, One Hundred and Ninety-fourth Regiment Pennsylvania Volunteer Infantry, and died at Camp Mankinswood, Maryland, August 19, 1864, Mrs. Margaretta J. Utley died, leaving two children, a son and daughter; the son is still living, and resides with our subject. This leaves two children by the first wife, Isabella and Nancy, and two by the last wife, James and Anna G. Mitten, still living; the other three of the last wife's children died — William, at the age of one year and one month; John, at the age of five years and two months; Mary, at the age of four years and two months. James was in Boyd's cavalry in Virginia.

HENRY T. MYERS, tanner and currier, was born in the Kingdom of Bavaria, Germany, in the year 1836. He immigrated, with his parents, two brothers and one sister, to America in 1853, all landing at Boston, Mass. From there the family separated, going to remote sections. Our subject, Henry T., was apprenticed at Cape Cod, West Brewster, Mass., with Mr. William Winslow, one of the descendants of the noted Pilgrims that came over in the "Mayflower," to learn the tanning and currier trade, for a term of three years. After serving his apprenticeship he worked as journeyman at the same place for nearly another year. He then, on account of the business panic which occurred in 1857, came to Carlisle, this county, namely, Cumberland. Business being very dull, the first job he got was to saw and split two cords of hickory wood for a doctor, James Irvin, the stipulated sum being $1.50 for the job. He was paid $1 in gold and the half dollar in silver. He lost the gold dollar before he got to his place of abode, and never could be persuaded to take another job of that kind. However, not discouraged, he soon got employment at his chosen avocation, namely, finishing leather. Two years later, March 15, 1859, he married Miss Victorene Williams, a native of North Middleton Township, this county, two children being born to them. He enlisted in 1862 in Company E, One Hundred and Thirtieth Regiment, Pennsylvania Volunteers, then organizing in Newville for the United States service for the term of nine months, the official record of that regiment, the One Hundred and Thirtieth, being 409 men killed and wounded in action. He was discharged by reason of having served his time, May 21, 1863, and he again re-enlisted in 1864, "the breakfast job now being over," for another year. Discharged again in 1865, he at once located in Centreville, Penn Township, where he still lives, doing a good business in the way of tanning. He had also carried on the harness trade for seven years, which he relinquished in 1880. His son, George M., having learned the harness trade, is now carrying on that branch. To Mr. and Mrs. Myers have been born nine children: John H., George M., Mrs. Annie E. Stouffer, Willis K., Agnes C., Alex. C., Daniel K., Laura J., and Henry T. (deceased). Mr. Myers has been a life-long Democrat; has been a member of the school board of education for three years, and president for one year. He was appointed by the Hon. Postmaster-General, William F. Vilas, postmaster of Dickinson postoffice, on July 18, 1885, in which capacity he is serving the public at present. Being well educated in the German language, he has acquired a good education in the English by private study in his adopted country. Mr. Myers and his worthy wife have ever encouraged education, and are consistent members of the German Baptist Church. He is an active business man, and an honest and upright citizen.

JOHN F. MYERS, farmer, P. O. Dickinson, was born in Penn Township, this county, November 20, 1845. His father, James Myers (a native of this county, a son of Abraham Myers, and grandson of Abraham, one of the early pioneers of Dauphin County, Penn.), married Miss Barbara Fishburn, a native of Dauphin County, Penn., who came to this county with her parents when thirteen years of age. After their marriage Mr. and Mrs. James Myers located in Penn Township, this county, on the Chambersburg Pike, and here they reared their family of ten children: Mrs. Catherine A. Leidigh, Sarah E., Abraham George, John Fishburn, Mrs. Barbara Elizabeth Keller, James P., William Albert, Charles Calvin, Mrs. Annie B. Caldwell and Edwin E. The father, Jamer Myers, departed this life in June, 1879. John F. Myers, the subject of this sketch, married, December 27, 1870, Miss Fannie Eyster, and they located permanently were they now reside; they have here a fine farm of ninety-three acres of fertile and well-improved land, with a handsome residence, and good, substantial farm buildings thereon. Their children were Laura H., Nora E. (accidentally killed in 1875, aged two years and ten months), William Oliver, Josephine C., Nettie May, Harold E., Frankie (deceased) and John C. Mr. Myers is a life-long Democrat. He and his wife adhere to the Lutheran faith. He is an enterprising and successful farmer, an upright and worthy citizen, highly respected by all who know him.

WILLIAM ALBERT MYERS, farmer, P. O. Huntsdale, was born in Penn Township, this county, July 5, 1851. His father, James Myers, was a son of the well-known pioneer, Abraham Myers, who came from York County, Penn., to this county, and married Barbara Fishburn, settling on the line of the Chambersburg Pike, where they resided until his death, which occurred June 20, 1879; his widow now resides at Newville, Penn. William Albert Myers, the subject of this sketch, married, December 18, 1879, Sadie Keller, daughter of Daniel Keller, and born in Penn Township, this county. Mr. and Mrs. Myers have one son living, Daniel Keller Myers. They are owners of a fine farm in Brushtown District. Mrs. Myers is a member of the German Baptist Church. Our subject is a life-long Democrat, an enterprising and successful farmer, and an upright citizen.

SAMUEL PIPER, farmer, P. O. Newville, was born August 12, 1819, in West Pennsborough Township, this county. His grandfather, James Piper, came to America, from Ireland, with two brothers, and settled at Middle Spring, Franklin Co., Penn., in 1767, and about two years later they located at Big Spring, this county. They followed the usual course of pioneers in the wilderness and located along the principal streams. James Piper's only son, James, Jr., father of our subject, adopted the calling of a miller and carried on Piper's mill, which had been established by his father; this mill burned down,

PENN TOWNSHIP. 533

and, in 1826, James Piper, Jr., built, on the same site, the mill which is still standing there James Piper, Jr., married Miss Catherine Irvine, a native of Stony Ridge, east of Carlisle, this county, and they reared six children: Mrs. Mary Dunlap, Jane (deceased), John. Samuel, Mrs. Elizabeth Mallory (deceased) and James; the parents resided at Piper's mills until their death; she died July 7, 1844, and he January 1, 1846. Samuel Piper, the subject of this sketch, engaged in teaching early in life, and followed that profession for about six terms. October 12, 1848, he married Miss Mary Goodhart, and, after spending two and a half years at the old family homestead, they resided for fourteen years on an adjoining farm; in 1868 they located where they now reside; they have here a fine farm of 39 acres of fertile and well-improved valley land. To our subject and wife have been born three children: Samuel, who died in infancy; Mrs. Sevilla Goodhart, who died at Bowman's Dale March 29, 1885, and Lina, residing with her parents (she made thorough preparation for the profession of teaching—graduated from the State Normal School at Shippensburg, Penn., and is now successfully engaged in teaching). Mr. and Mrs. Piper have also reared in their family his brother John's son. John Jr., who has also been teaching in Penn Township for thirteen years. Mr. Piper is a life-long Republican. He and his worthy wife are consistent members of the Presbyterian Church. He is a man of firm principles, one of the leading and influential citizens of this county. By appointment of Gen. E. M. Gregory Mr. Piper took the ninth annual census in Penn and Dickinson Townships, this county.

HENRY C. RICE, mail contractor. P. O. Dickinson, was born June 19, 1844, near Landisburg, Perry Co., Penn., where his parents, Zachariah and Nancy (Landis) Rice, resided until their death. Our subject enlisted in the One Hundred and Fifty-eighth Regiment Pennsylvania Volunteer Infantry, October 16, 1862; took part in the campaign in North Carolina, and was engaged in the battle of Kingston, that State; was discharged in August, 1863, and re-enlisted August 31, 1864, in the Ninth Pennsylvania Volunteer Cavalry, serving under Gen. Kilpatrick; went through with Sherman to the sea, taking part in many historic engagements in Georgia and North Carolina, and was honorably discharged May 29, 1865. Mr. Rice married, November 13, 1866, Miss Catherine Zeigler, of Chambersburg, Penn., daughter of Jacob and Lydia (Turner) Zeigler, who resided near Carlisle, this county. Jacob Zeigler died April 18, 1882, at Greenview, Ill.; his widow died at Carlisle Springs, Penn., November 5, 1885. Mr. and Mrs. Rice are rearing, in their family, Gouverner and Lutie L. Natcher, children of Mrs. Rice's sister, Julia, deceased wife of J. A. Natcher. Mr. Rice belongs to a family of extensive mail contractors. His father was engaged for twenty-six years in that service. The mail route from Landisburg to Newport has been in the hands of the Rices for the last thirty-three years, and our subject has controlled the route from Carlisle to Dickinson for eighteen years, and the route from Carlisle to Landisburg for seven years. He has at this time seven routes under contract, and an interest in thirty-one routes. In politics Mr. Rice is a Republican. He and his wife are members of the Lutheran Church.

SIMON SNYDER, grain dealer, P. O. Dickinson, was born October 24, 1819, in Frankford Township, this county. His remote ancestors were of German origin, but his parents, Henry and Elizabeth (Mentzer) Snyder, were natives of Manor Township, Lancaster Co., Penn. They came to this county in early life, after having spent some years in Dauphin County. They were residing in Mifflin Township, this county, at the time of their death. The father died March 29, 1847, the mother in December, 1868. Their children were George (deceased), Mrs. Elizabeth Failor (deceased), Mrs. Catharine A. Camrey (deceased), Mrs. Mary I. McCrea (deceased), Mrs. Barbara M. McCrea, Simon, Henry (a major in the militia, died December 10, 1883), Mrs. Sophia Wise, and Mrs. Ellen N. Jacoby. Simon Snyder was reared on his father's farm, and enjoyed as good educational advantages as the school system of those days afforded. He early engaged in the profession of teaching, which he followed while completing his educational course at Pennsylvania College, Gettysburg, several terms, at Bloomfield Academy, two sessions, and at Washington College, Washington, Penn., where he graduated with the degree of A. B., September 24, 1846. After completing his course he went South, engaging in the profession of teaching. He had charge of the academy at Newburg, Jefferson Co., Ky., several years; next he was connected for several years with the Clinton Seminary, at Clinton, Ky.; was then chosen principal of the Columbus Masonic Seminary, Columbus, Ky., for three years. Returning to his native county, he engaged with his brother Henry, for several years, in mercantile business, near Newville. He then accepted a position as cashier and book-keeper for a large milling firm, Smith & Smyser, of Louisville, Ky., where he remained during the war of the Rebellion. Returning to this county, he was engaged from 1864 to 1874 with his brother in the grain business at Newville, and in the latter year established in the same line of business, on his own account, on the Harrisburg & Potomac Railroad and was located at Barnitz nearly four years, at Jacksonville six years, and came to Dover's Station, his present location, in May, 1884. He does a general commission business, dealing in grain, coal, etc. Simon Snyder has, by industry, acquired an independent competence. He began his life as a citizen by voting for Gen. Harrison in 1840, and has supported the Whig and Republican parties ever since. He has enjoyed the friendship of many men eminent in public life. He was class-mate of the celebrated Prof. James E. Murdock, and a fellow-student of James G. Blaine and of ex-Secretary Benjamin F. Bristow. Mr. Snyder still retains their friendship, and he has the respect of every community in which he has lived.

PETER TRITT, manufacturer, P. O. Huntsdale, was born June 24, 1821, in Penn (then Dickinson) Township, this county, son of Christian and Lydia (Stough) Tritt, former of whom was a son of Peter and Elizabeth (Le Fevre) Tritt, early settlers in this county, coming from Lancaster County, Penn.; they resided in Penn Township, this county, until their death; the mother died in 1849, and the father in 1871. Peter is the eldest of their fourteen children. June 10, 1845, the subject of this sketch married Nancy Nickey, a native of Perry County, Penn. Mr. Tritt followed farming for nine years after his marriage, and in March, 1855, located a saw-mill on Yellow Breeches Creek, below Milltown. Penn Township, this county, and to this he has added a shingle-mill, planing-mill and sash, door and blind factory, and is doing a large and prosperous business. To Mr. and Mrs. Tritt have been born seven children, five of whom are now living: John A., Samuel J. (the present county surveyor), Mrs. Lydia J. Shafer, Mrs. Elizabeth Feree and Peter Stough. In politics Mr. Tritt is a Democrat. He and his wife are members of the Lutheran Church. Mr. Tritt is a man of correct business habits, upright and straightforward in his dealings. He is a worthy citizen, highly respected by those who know him.

JOHN A. TRITT, lumberman, P. O. Huntsdale, was born in Penn Township, this county, September 23, 1847. His father, Peter Tritt, reared him to the lumber business. Our subject married, in January, 1869, Miss Jennie E. Tobias, of Carlisle, this county, and they have resided on their farm near Mount Rock, Penn Township, this county, for a period of nine years since their marriage. To Mr. and Mrs. Tritt have been born five children: Alice E., Edgar P., Florena E., Maud J. and Melvin J. Mr. Tritt owns a circular-saw mill, connected with his father's general lumber manufacturing establishment, at Huntsdale, this county. In politics he is a Democrat. He has filled the office of assessor for one term. At present he is school director.

DAVID P. TRITT, farmer, P. O. Dickinson, was born in Penn (then Dickinson) Township, this county, August 20, 1830. His grandfather, Peter Tritt, born March 5, 1755, died February 24, 1839, came from Lancaster County, Penn., about 1775, and was, it is thought, from Spain; he carried on the business of wagon-making in West Pennsborough Township, and served some time in the Revolutionary war, and was the founder of the Tritt family in the Cumberland Valley. Our subject's grandmother, Elizabeth (LeFevre) Tritt, was born December 8, 1751, and died February 7, 1835. Her grandparents, who were French, landed in Boston in 1710, went to Newburg, N. Y., thence to Lancaster County, Penn., and came to this county in 1775. Peter and Elizabeth Tritt had thirteen children: Barbara, born May 10, 1778, died young; Jacob, born January 18, 1780, died December 17, 1856; Peter, born January 28, 1782, died January 24, 1860; Elizabeth, born January 18, 1784, died October 17, 1831; Joseph, born January 16, 1787, died May 30, 1873; Barbara, born March 19, 1789, died young; George, born November 3, 1791, died October 4, 1882; Catharine, born July 5, 1794, died January 9, 1871; Christian, born July 25, 1796, died January 10, 1871; Anna, born November 21, 1798, died January 1, 1837; John, born January 18, 1801, died in September, 1884; Samuel, born September 14, 1803, died February 22, 1873; William, born May 26, 1807, died February 7, 1855. One of the sons, Christian, married Lydia Stough, and they resided on a farm in Penn Township, this county; she died June 9, 1849, and in 1853 he married Mrs. Francis Charlotte McCullough. David P. Tritt, the subject of this sketch, the third son of Christian Tritt, attended the schools of the home district and finished his course by a two years' attendance (1853–55) at Pennsylvania College, Gettysburg. He was then appointed general agent for the Cumberland Valley Fire Insurance Company, which position he held for four years. In 1858 he located on a farm on which he now resides. He has acquired a fine farm of 120 acres as a homestead, besides other property elsewhere. He married Miss Mary L. Fisher, of Hogestown, Silver Spring Township, this county, December 14, 1858, and she died February 7, 1862, leaving two children: Charles Edgar and Mary Ellen. December 25, 1865, Mr. Tritt married, for his second wife, Miss Sarah Ann Harper, daughter of William Harper, and their children are Edwin Greer and Lulu P. Mr. Tritt takes a deep interest in the cause of education, and has given his children excellent advantages, both literary and musical, and they are taking fine positions in school and society. Mr. Tritt is a life long Democrat, and in former years was quite active in public affairs, but now prefers to lead a private life. He and his wife are members of the Dickinson Presbyterian Church, of which he has been ruling elder for over fifteen years. He is a worthy descendant of one of the oldest pioneer families, and is one of the leading and influential citizens of Penn Township, this county.

CHAPTER LVI.

SILVER SPRING TOWNSHIP.

GEORGE W. BEST, farmer, P. O. Mechanicsburg, was born in 1850, in Monroe Township, this county. His father, John Best, of German origin, a resident of Monroe Township, was born in Lower Allen Township, Cumberland County, Penn. He was united in marriage with Miss Anna Bitner, a native of York County, Penn., who bore him thirteen children: Catharine, Elizabeth, Susan (deceased), Anna M., Joseph, Sarah (deceased), Margaret (deceased), George W., Samuel, Martha, Agnes and two who died in infancy. John Best who was a prosperous man. owning three farms, died at the age of sixty-five years. He was a member of the United Brethren Church; in politics a Republican. His son, George W., received his education in the common schools, and, in 1875, married Miss Clara L., daughter of Jacob H. and Rachael (Strock) Coover, who were the parents of six children: Elizabeth, Francis E., Catharine A., Mary Z., Clara L. and John A. Jacob H. Coover was born in Upper Allen Township, this county, and lived on his farm there for many years; politically he was a Republican. He was business manager of the East Pennsborough Fire Insurance Company and a good business man. He and his wife were members of the Bethel Church. Mr. Best is a Republican in politics.

JOHN BOBB, farmer, P. O. Mechanicsburg, is a grandson of Nicholas Bobb, who came from Germany and settled in this county about the year 1795, and owned two farms. Nicholas Bobb was the father of nine children: John, Daniel, Michael, George, Catharine, Mary, Barbara, Elizabeth and Margaret. Of these, John came to this county with his father when a young man. He was a carpenter by trade and afterward became a farmer. He married Miss Elizabeth, daughter of Martin Longsdorf, of this county, by whom he had four children: George, Margaret, John and Elizabeth. In 1800 Mr. Longsdorf built the brick house at Trindle Springs, called the "Trindle Springs Hotel." It is of interest that two of John Bobb's brothers married wives whose Christian names were Elizabeth and had the same complement of children as himself—two sons and two daughters. He was a member of the Lutheran Church. In early life he worked at the carpenter and cabinet-maker's trade, and erected several of the old buildings still standing in Silver Spring Township. John Bobb, Jr., his son, was born in the township August 26, 1813. He learned the trade of carpenter. In 1836 he married, Miss Margaret, daughter of Henry and Mary Nagle, and to this union were born three children: Elmira M., Henry M. and Anna E.; Henry M. the only one living. John Bobb, Jr., bought land near New Kingston, this county, in 1837, where he lived for seven years. He then moved to the Sailor farm, which he purchased April 1, 1847, and there resided until 1875, when he bought his homestead on Trindle Springs road and erected his present substantial buildings. The house is pleasantly situated, and is likely to remain in the family for many generations. Mr. Bobb is a strong Democrat, and in past years worked hard for his party. He has filled township offices, such as collector, assessor and school director, and has also been county commissioner. He has been administrator, executor and assignee for several estates, etc., and has settled all these matters with wisdom and without the loss of a dollar. That he deserves the respect and confidence of the community is beyond a question.

HENRY M. BOBB, the son of above, is an engineer. In May 1860, he married Miss Margaret J. Armstrong, of Mechanicsburg, Penn. To this union were born seven children: Ella S., wife of Charles Waggoner, of this county (have two children: Luella M. and Mary A.); Minnie E.; John M. married to Emma Chapman, of Mechanicsburg; James A.; Henry A.; George F. and Maggie M.

JOHN BRICKER, farmer, P. O. Hogestown. The Bricker family, which stands among the first families of Cumberland Valley, sprang from strong German stock, who settled in Lancaster County at an early date. Jacob Bricker, the grandfather of our subject, was born in Lancaster County. He married Miss Mary Fry, of the same county, and a few years later moved with his family to Cumberland County, and settled in Silver Spring Township (this was about the year 1812). He soon bought the Silver Spring Mill, prospered in business, and by his energy and thrift, accumulated $80,000, which he left at his death to his two sons. The estate consisted of six farms, embracing over 900 acres of land, the mill property, and a house in Mechanicsburg. His wife bore him two sons: Lewis and Peter. A very stout man, he was very active and industrious and noted for his thrift and strong common sense. He lived to the patriarchal age of eighty-four years.

Peter Bricker, the eldest son, was born in Lancaster County, Penn. He married Miss Kate Buttorf, of Cumberland County. To this union were born six children: George, Peter, Jacob, Samuel, Mary and Susan. His father gave him a farm which he had purchased of George Bobb in 1829, and here he settled after marriage, and in the old house built by Mr. Bobb in 1817 all his children were born. His wife died, and he then married Miss Mary Bricker, of Cumberland County. To them were born ten children: David, Lewis, Joseph, John, Levi, Christine, Eliza, Catharine, Clara, and Ella. Peter Bricker continued to reside on the same farm until 1860, when he moved to another of his farms, now owned by Jacob Meily. By perseverance, prudence and energy, Mr. Bricker accumulated property which, at his death, was valued at $162,000, which was legally divided among his children. John Bricker, our subject, was born in the old homestead July 11, 1848. In 1871 he married Miss Sarah M. Gross, of this county. They have been blessed with eight children: James, Peter, Lemuel, Clarence, Lawrence, Naomi, Bertie, and Mary. At his father's death he went to live with his family in the old homestead, where twenty-nine members of the Bricker family first saw the light of day and passed out to fight the battle of life. Since 1829, when Jacob Bricker bought the old homestead, none but Brickers have tilled the soil of the old farm. It is the cradle of the descendants of Peter Bricker. Like his father before him, John is a prosperous man, and well known for his industry, thrift, and honesty.

LEVI BRICKER, farmer, P. O. Hogestown, is a grandson of Jacob Bricker, who was born in Lancaster County, Penn. The family is of German origin, his ancestors settling in this country in a very early day, and Brickersville, in Lancaster County, was named for the great-grandfather. Jacob Bricker, already mentioned, married Miss Mary Fry, of Lancaster County, and had two children: Lewis and Peter. In 1812, when the latter was about six years of age, his father moved to this county and settled in Newville, where he followed milling. A few years later he purchased the Silver Spring Mill, which he owned for over forty years. He removed to Mechanicsburg a few years before his death, which occurred in 1867. He was a Republican in politics, a very sociable, prosperous and reliable man, and left a large property at his death. Peter Bricker, his son, was born in Lancaster County in 1807. He too, learned the miller's trade. He married Miss Kate, daughter of George Buttorf, of this county, and to this union were born six children: George, Peter, Jacob, Samuel, Mary and Susan. His wife died, and he married Miss Mary Bricker, of this county, daughter of David Bricker. To this union were born ten children: David, Eliza, Kate, Lewis, Joseph, John, Levi, Clara, Christian and Ella. Even with such a large family, Mr. Bricker contrived, by energy and prudence, to accumulate a large property, consisting of nine farms and the mill property in Silver Spring Township, estimated to be worth $162,000. In politics he was a Republican. Our subject was born on the old homestead, in this county, September 29, 1850, and passed his early life on the farm. In 1874 he married Miss Bella, daughter of George Breistline, of Cumberland County, and has two children: Mary and Willie. After marriage Mr. Bricker began farming on his own account. Like his father before him, he is a Republican in politics. He is a reliable, honorable business man.

JESSE BUCHER, farmer, P. O. Mechanicsburg. According to tradition the great-grandfather of this gentleman and his two brothers emigrated from Germany to America at an early date, and from them sprang the Buchers of Pennsylvania. Christian Bucher (grandfather of subject), was born on the farm where his father originally settled, near Union Station, Lancaster Co., Penn. His son, Christian Bucher, was born on the old homestead, which had then seen three generations of this family within its walls. He learned the trade of miller, which he followed in Lancaster County thirty-two years. In 1835 Christian Bucher married Miss Leah, daughter of George Youndt, of Lancaster County, Penn., who bore him six children: Jesse, Lydia A., Elizabeth, John, Isaac and Henry (all born in Lancaster County). In 1857 he moved with his family to Cumberland County, and bought a farm of 216 acres, where he remained so long as he lived. He and his wife were members of the Lutheran Church. He was a man of remarkable force of character and will-power; beginning life with nothing, by thrift and industry he accumulated a handsome property and was enabled to assist all his children to start in life. Jesse Bucher, his son, was born in Lancaster County, Penn., in 1836, and came to this county with his father when a young man. He learned the trade of a miller, and followed it until he came to this county. In 1863 he married Miss Mary, daughter of Jacob and Elizabeth (Kanogy) Crow, of Perry County, Penn. This union has been blessed with three sons: Albert H., Henry W. and Stewart E. After marriage Mr. Bucher bought, in 1865, his present homestead, which is a fine farm of 137 acres. The sons, now young men, are all at home, and the entire family is noted for thrift and those qualities which go to make up a successful life.

GEORGE CLEPPER, farmer, P. O. New Kingstown, is a grandson of Joseph Clepper, of German descent, who lived in Lancaster County all his life. Joseph, his son, was born in that county in 1817, and when only three years old was brought by his step-father, Jacob Holdemon, to Cumberland County, Penn. Joseph Clepper learned the miller's trade of Mr. Holdemon and afterward the millwright's trade. In 1844 he married Miss

Lydia, daughter of George and Hannah (Senseman) Hauck, of this county. To them were born five children: George, Lydia A., Lucetta, Hannah J. and Joseph. In 1852, Joseph Clepper entered agricultural pursuits, and passed the remainder of his life on the farm. He died in 1873 at the age of fifty-six. He was a man of excellent moral principles, highly esteemed by all who knew him. George Clepper, his son, was born in South Middleton Township, this county, in 1849. When about twenty-two years of age he visited the principal Western States and cities. He returned after two years and a half to this township, having had a varied experience as a traveler. He began farming in 1882 near New Kingston, this county, on 213 acres, which, by industry and energy combined with the skill of a practical farmer, he has converted into a model farm. The larger proportion of his stock is improved breeds. It is his custom during the fall to buy young Western cattle, which he fattens for market, and he has now thirty-two head of steers in splendid condition, stall-fed and ready for market. This farm deserves more than a passing notice, as it is an example of what can be accomplished in this county by industry, intelligent methods and skill. Mr. Clepper is an upright man and thoroughly understands his business.

ROBERT CORMAN, manufacturer, P. O. Mechanicsburg. Prominent among the capitalists and manufacturers of Cumberland Valley stands the name of Robert Corman. Beginning life as a poor boy, in this county, he, by his own industry and self-denial, has risen step by step to his present position of wealth and honor. His grandfather, Ludrick Corman, lived in Lebanon County, Penn., and was of German descent: he married a Miss Nimomaker, also of Lebanon County, Penn., and had nine children: George, John, Jacob, Abraham, Philip, Henry, Catharine, Mary and Eliza. He was a farmer by occupation; in political opinions a Democrat. He enlisted in the Revolutionary war, serving under Gen. Washington, and was one of the soldiers who passed the severe winter at Valley Forge, and, shoeless, ragged and hungry, braved almost death itself for the cause of freedom. A proud spirited gentleman of the old school he refused a pension for his services, as he thought it unbecoming in a patriot to take money from his (at that time) poor country. Many years thereafter he was unfortunate, and a pension was applied for, his name was found on the roll, but so much time had elapsed that all who knew him as a soldier were dead, and he could not be identified. Thus the soldier and patriot was not rewarded in his old age by the Government his services had helped to create. John Corman, his second son, was born in Lebanon County, Penn., April 9, 1778, and learned the trade of cooper. He married Elizabeth Campbell, born in Cumberland County, Penn., June 14, 1788, a descendant of the famous Campbells of Scotland, a branch of which had settled in Ireland, and our subject is therefore of German and Scotch-Irish descent. To John and Elizabeth Corman were born nine children: William, Robert, John, Agnes, Joseph, Charles, Eliza, George and Campbell--all dead but Robert and John. Of these, George was captain in Company F, Fifty-sixth Regiment Pennsylvania Volunteer Infantry, and lost his life in the second battle of Bull Run. His remains were not recovered, although his brother Robert went to the battle-field to obtain them, but rest on Arlington Heights, in the great tomb, with over 2,000 unknown soldiers. Our subject's father was an old-line Whig; he was a man of wonderful memory, and some remarkable incidents are yet remembered of this faculty. He was a quiet man, and a very honorable, good citizen. Robert Corman's mother had great influence on his character, and when young taught him to be self reliant, honest and industrious. He assisted her all he could, and she would say, "Robert, the good Lord will reward you." In after years her words came true; for, relying on her advice, he amassed a fortune, and can well thank her for her part in his success. Robert Corman was born March 30, 1810, near Warm Springs, Perry Co., Penn. At the age of four years he came with his father to Cumberland County. He lived with his parents on the farm until about nineteen, when, becoming discontented with farm life, he told his father he must make more money. Robert Bryson had offered to teach him tanning, and he went to live with him as an apprentice, possessing nothing in the world but an extra suit of clothes. He served three years with Mr. Bryson, and at the end of this time the latter offered him $11 a month and board. He continued to work for him for seven years as journeyman tanner, and during this time his wages were increased to 50 cents per day. Even with these small wages young Robert had, by strict economy, saved $700, which had been invested with Mr. Bryson on interest at 6 per cent. Becoming discontented at not getting along faster, Robert started for Cincinnati, then a young and growing city of 42,000 inhabitants, the journey thither being made by rail, steam-boat and stage. Still looking for work he went to Covington, Ky., and applied to a Mr. Grant, who ran a tannery there. Mr. Grant told him he could not give him employment as he had only a small tannery, but few vats, and he and two little sons did all the work; one ground the bark and the other handled the hides. The power was furnished by an old horse. Mr. Grant spoke very kindly to Robert Corman, who was a little discouraged, and bade him be of good cheer, that work would soon be found. This Mr. Grant was the father of Ulysses S. Grant, and it is very possible that Gen. Grant himself was one of the little boys helping his father at this humble occupation. Mr. Corman soon obtained work at his trade, and at the end of two years and a half had saved $ 75 in gold. He next went to Kittanning, Penn., and worked there at his trade, and in about eighteen months had saved

$700. Mr. Bryson, his old friend and employer, became embarrassed in business, and wrote him, offering a one-third interest in his tannery, which was accepted, and Mr. Corman retained this interest eleven years, working industriously, and during this time saved $12,000, bought 28 acres of land and built himself a fine house. October 2, 1849, he married Miss Elizabeth, daughter of John and Ann (Blair) Bailey. To this union was born one daughter—Laura—November 28, 1856; since married to Harry C. Gross, of Harrisburg, son of Dr. Daniel Gross. In 1853 Mr. Corman's partnership with Mr. Bryson was dissolved by mutual consent. Mr. Corman then rented his residence for a number of years to a nephew of Mr. Bryson, and hiring an old tan-yard at Trindle Spring, engaged in the tanning business for seven years, and while thus engaged built what is known as the "Florence House," in Carlisle, and which was the first four-story house in the city. He erected this building in ninety days, driving from the tannery to Carlisle each day. During these years Mr. Bryson had again been unfortunate, and assignees were chosen. His property consisted of a steam tannery in full operation, well stocked with about $40,000 worth of bark and hides, over 200 acres of land, a fine mansion and other buildings. This large property was bought by Mr. Corman at the assignees' sale for $18,000; the war being in full progress no one would bid any higher. At the end of three years Mr. Corman wound up his business, and sold the property and stock for $59,000, making a clear profit of $41,000. He then moved to Mechanicsburg and invested in 7-30 United States bonds, by which he largely increased his wealth. In 1866 he went on a pleasure trip overland to California, in company with Col. McCormick and John Haldmon, of Harrisburg, Penn. He visited Chicago, Denver, Salt Lake City, Idaho, Nevada, Oregon and California, and at San Francisco took steamer for New York. His wife died in March, 1867. He then bought an interest in the Trindle Spring paper-mill, which enterprise proved unfortunate to the stock-holders, but no one else lost a dollar. Mr. Corman then bought the property and converted it into a tobacco warehouse, buying three adjoining farms, which he cultivated and commenced raising tobacco. December 11, 1884, he was married to his second wife, Miss Eliza, daughter of Peter Bricker, of Silver Spring Township, this county. Mr. Corman is remarkably strong and active, and seems younger than most men of fifty. He has had a varied career, and is a man of mark. During his life he has taught sixteen youths the art of tanning, and in his many business enterprises has employed a large number of men. To Robert Bryson and his family Mr. Corman attributed much of his success, for they gave good counsel, encouragement, and were kind to him in the dark days of adversity, treating him like a son. Four principles to success are shown in our subject's active life—energy, industry, economy and honesty; and the young men of to-day may well emulate his example.

ZACHARIAH DEITZ (deceased). The family of Deitz originated in Germany and came to America in an early day. Daniel Deitz came from York County to Cumberland County, Penn., and settled in Hampden Township. He married Lydia Stonner, of York County, who bore him six children: David, Christian, Zachariah, Nancy, Mary and Betsey. Daniel Deitz was a member of the Lutheran Church. He was a large land-holder, and at his death left his property to his children. Zachariah Deitz, his son, was born in York County, Penn., February 24, 1828, and came to this county, with his father, when a small boy, and here passed his early life on his father's farm. March 11, 1862, he married Miss Anna Roth, of Cumberland County, daughter of Ferdinand and Anna (Seifert) Roth. This union was blessed with six children: John E., Norma A., Minnie C., Clayton Z., Ferdinand R. and Harry E. After marriage our subject came to Silver Spring Township and bought the present homestead where all the children were born. Here he lived happily for twelve years, blessed with good health, a comfortable home, loving wife and a fine healthy family of children, when suddenly, by a sad accident, all was changed, and the strong man and loving father was stricken to the earth, and, after a lingering illness, died in great suffering, leaving his wife to the task of bringing up and educating his young children. This great labor she has performed with true fidelity and courage, and now sees them nearly grown to manhood and womanhood as a reward for her trouble.

JOHN E. GIBBLE, farmer, P. O. Hogestown. This family originated in Germany and came to this county at an early date. The grandfather of this gentleman was born in Lancaster County, Penn.; was a farmer and the father of five children: Samuel, Christian, John, Fannie and Mary. He was a member of the German Baptist Church, commonly called Dunkards. He died in Lancaster County. Samuel, his son, was born in 1809, in Lancaster County, Penn.; he married Miss Nancy Eshleman, daughter of John Eshleman, of Lancaster County, Penn. To this union were born five children: Curtis, Catharine, Fannie, Salinda and John E. In 1844 Samuel Gibble moved, with his family, to this county and settled in Silver Spring Township. He was a very religious man, a member of the German Baptist Church; in politics a Republican; he died aged fifty years, greatly respected by all. John E. Gibble, our subject, was born in July, 1852, and passed his early life on his grandfather's farm. In 1885 he was united in marriage with Miss Mary A., daughter of Daniel Trortle, of Cumberland County. In political opinions he is a Democrat. He resides on a good farm, pleasantly situated near Hogestown, where he lives quietly with his wife and aged mother. He is a reliable man and a good farmer.

GEORGE F. HAILMAN, farmer, P. O. Mechanicsburg. This family originated near Heidelberg, Germany, and immigrated to America more than one hundred years ago, settling in Lebanon County, Penn. John F. Hailman, the grandfather of the subject of our sketch, was born in Lebanon County, Penn., and went to Dauphin County when but a boy, with his father. He, John F., married Miss Elizabeth Miller, of Franklin County, Penn., who bore him ten children: Sarah, Rebecca, Lydia, Susan, Elizabeth, Mary A., Mary J., David, Jonathan and Benjamin M., all born and reared on the old homestead, which was owned by the family for more than one hundred years, and consisted of a fine farm and residence, located within a mile and a half of Harrisburg. Benjamin M. Hailman was born on the same old homestead August 19, 1800, and lived on the old farm thirty-eight years. In 1834 he married Miss Jane, daughter of George and Christianna Rupp, of Cumberland County, Penn., and a descendant of John Jonas Rupp, the founder of the Rupp family. (I. Daniel Rupp, the historian, was Mrs. Hailman's brother.) This union was blessed with four children: Elizabeth, Christianna, George F. and John C. In 1838 Benjamin M. Hailman moved to Silver Spring Township, this county, and settled on the farm belonging to Mrs. Hailman's father, where they lived until 1849, when they moved to the present homestead. Mr. Hailman was a Lutheran, but always attended the Church of God, of which his widow is a member. In politics he was a Democrat until the war, when he became a Republican. He died at the age of seventy-nine. His widow is now living on the homestead, pleasantly situated, and in her old age is surrounded by her children and grandchildren. George F. Hailman, the son of this estimable couple, was born in Silver Spring Township, this county, in 1840. In 1879 he married Miss Julia, daughter of Henry and Caroline Kornbrust, a native of Germany. They are the parents of two children: John G. and Carrie E. In political opinions our subject is a Republican. He is a prominent farmer in his township, and desires no better reputation than that of being a skillful farmer and an upright man.

JOHN E. A. HERMAN, farmer, P. O. Middlesex. Cumberland Valley has no name of more antiquity and honor than that of Herman, and among the sons are men of high rank and great ability. Martin Herman, a native of Germany, landed in Philadelphia, Penn., July 2, 1752, and on the 15th of April, 1771, settled on a tract of land called "St. Martin's," in Silver Spring Township, this county, and this land, where he lived and died, has been in possession of his descendants one hundred and fifteen years. He had two sons: Christian and Martin. Of these, Christian was born on the old homestead, and in the course of time became a large land-holder and prominent farmer, owning 640 acres of land. He married Miss Elizabeth Bowers, and to them were born ten children: John, Jacob, Mary, Ann, Martin, Christian, David, Elizabeth, Benjamin and Joseph. He was a short, strong man physically, and died at the age of sixty-one years. John, the eldest son of Christian Herman, was born on the old homestead in 1797, and passed his early life on the farm; was married, in 1818, to Miss Elizabeth, daughter of George and Rachel (Leidigh) Beltzhoover, who bore him ten children: Christian, Rachel A., Henrietta, Manasseh, George T. B., John E. A., Margaret, Elizabeth, Joseph L. and Benjamin F. In 1821 he, John Herman, bought his father's farm, in Silver Spring Township, this county. He was a member of the Lutheran Church, serving as deacon and elder for many years. He died aged sixty-three. His son John E. A. Herman was born on the old homestead in March, 1836. In 1859 he married Miss Eliza J., daughter of Daniel Fought, and to this union were born two children: Mary E. and Bertha J. Mrs. Herman died in 1868, and March 13, 1873, our subject married Miss Lizzie A., daughter of Abraham and Elizabeth (Horner) Zeigler, of this county. In 1865 he purchased a farm in Monroe Township, this county, where he lived three years. In 1870 he purchased his present home in Silver Spring Township, a fine farm, pleasantly situated. Mr. and Mrs. Herman are members of the Lutheran Church. He is a man of excellent business habits, energetic and upright. In politics he is a Democrat.

MANASSEH HERMAN, farmer, P. O. New Kingstown, was born in 1829, on the old homestead, which has now been in the Herman family four generations; the farm is called "Maple Hall," and on it Mr. Herman has passed his entire life. He was educated at the common schools, and later took an academic course at New Kingston. He then went West, and on his return, in 1859, married Miss Mary E. Meily, daughter of Jacob and Mary (Fry) Meily, of Cumberland County. To them have been born five children: Warren S., A. Lorena, Mary E., Rachael A. G. and Manasseh H. After marriage Mr. Herman and wife went to housekeeping on the old homestead, and here they have reared their family. Mr. and Mrs. Herman are devout members of Trinity Evangelical Lutheran Church, Mechanicsburg; the children are all members of the same church, with the exception of the youngest. In politics Mr. Herman is a Democrat, as was his father before him. Mrs. Herman was one of the first graduates of the Irving Female College, Mechanicsburg. The eldest son is a graduate of the Carlisle High School, of the class of 1882. Mr. Herman is a careful farmer and a reliable man. (For early history of the family see sketch of John E. A. Herman).

JOHN W. HERSHMAN, farmer, Hogestown. The great-grandfather of this gentleman settled in Franklin County, Penn., more than 100 years ago, and his son, Frederick, was born in that county in 1777. Frederick Hershman was twice married, and was the father of five children by his first wife: John, Jeremiah, William, Daniel and Mary. His wife died, and he married Miss Sarah Ackerson, of Franklin County, Penn., and to this union were born four children: Joseph, Logan, Sarah J. and Annie. In 1835 Frederick Hershman moved to Cumberland County, where he owned a good farm near Shepherdstown. He died in Silver Spring Township, aged ninety-four years. He was a man of easy disposition, honest and upright; in politics a Democrat. William Hershman, his son, was born in Franklin County, Penn., October 7, 1802, and learned the trade of a miller; married Miss Rebecca, daughter of George Willson, of Franklin County. Penn., and this union was blessed with eighteen children: Elizabeth, Jeremiah W., John W., Catharine, Sarah, Isabella, Margaret, William, Armstrong J., Mary, Rebecca, Henry I., Angelina, Martha, Laura, Agnes, Nancy J. and one who died in infancy. In 1833 Mr. Hershman moved to this county. He was a Democrat politically. He and his wife are members of the Evangelical Church. He was well known as a man of integrity. John W., his son, was born in this county February 11, 1834, and learned the trade of carpenter, which he followed for twenty-five years, and was the architect and builder of several of the principal buildings in Mechanicsburg, Penn., viz.: Market house, Methodist Church, "American House" and "Merchants' Hotel." In 1858 he married Miss Mary Arbegast, of this county, by whom he has nine children: Raymond L., reading law in the office of William Penn Lloyd; William M.; Elmer O., married to Miss Mary Lichtenberger; Anna E., Minnie K., Harry N., Sarah J., Carrie E. and George W. In 1878 Mr. Hershman commenced farming, an occupation which he has since followed. Politically he is a Democrat.

SAMUEL HESS, farmer, P. O. Mechanicsburg. The Hess family, who originally came from Germany, settled in this country at a very early date. The Christian name of the grandfather is not known, but he was a substantial farmer in Lancaster County, Penn. He had two sons, Michael and Christian, and he went to York County and bought each of these sons a fine farm. Michael (father of our subject) was born in Lancaster County, Penn.; married Barbara Leib, of the same county, and after marriage moved to the farm in York County, which had been the gift of his father. To this couple were born five children: Abraham, John, Samuel, Michael and Annie. Mr. Hess was a careful farmer, and owned one of the finest farms in the whole county; he was accidentally killed. Samuel Hess, his son, was born in York County, Penn., August 11, 1818. He was very young when his father died, and lived with his mother until his marriage, March 20, 1845, with Miss Catharine Bitner, of York County, daughter of Samuel and Annie (Mish) Bitner. This union was blessed with three children: Annie, Henry and Barbara. Mr. Hess bought his present homestead about the year 1858. In 1876 Henry Hess, his son, married Miss Annie M., daughter of Daniel and Elizabeth (Morrett) Bobb, and to this union have been born three children: Amos E., Berttie M. and Lizzie R. The entire family have won the respect of their friends and neighbors for sterling worth, industry and honesty.

DR. MICHAEL L. HOOVER, P. O. Mechanicsburg. The grandfather of the subject of this sketch lived in this county in an early day, and was a farmer and land-holder. He married Miss Catharine Wonderlick, of Cumberland County, and had five children: John, Elizabeth, Annie, Mary and Catharine. He was a member of the Lutheran church. John Hoover, his son, was born in this county in 1787, and married Lydia Leidig, of Lebanon County, Penn. He was a farmer, a member of the Lutheran Church, and lived in the old homestead until his death, which occurred in his thirty-fourth year. His widow lived to be seventy-seven. To them were born four children: Michael L., John L., Sarah A., and Sarah E. Our subject, who was born in 1820, on the old homestead in this county, when young, learned the carpenter's trade. In 1844 he married Miss Mary, daughter of John W. and Catharine M. Millisen, of Dauphin County, Penn., and after marriage he began farming. To this union were born ten children: Anna C., Myers J., Eva J., Adam A., Sarah E., Margaret A., Laura V., John W., Clara A. and George M. Mr. Hoover had sad trouble in raising his children, eight having sickened and died in early life. The physicians employed were powerless to save them, and this determined Mr. Hoover to study medicine himself, to save the remainder of his family, if possible. He bought medical books and studied hard, and in his own family became successful. His friends and neighbors then pressed him to treat them, and gradually he gained a regular practice. He never attended a medical school, though after he attained success he was urged to do so, and was offered a diploma if he would attend medical lectures for a short time. Having gained his medical knowledge by his unaided efforts he preferred to continue in his own way, as he was uniformally successful. The people had confidence in him, and his success justified his ideas. His son, John W., married Miss Alice L., daughter of Isaac Sadler, of Carlisle, Penn.; Laura V. married George W. Hoover, of Churchtown, son of Jacob Hoover (have two children: Guy H. and Frank J.); the youngest son of our subject, George M., is a student at Franklin and Marshall College, Lancaster, Penn.

JOHN JACOBS, farmer, P. O. New Kingstown. Among the prominent families of Cumberland County is that of Jacobs, of Scotch-Irish descent. The grandfather of our subject, who settled in York County, Penn., came from Ireland and was a blacksmith by

SILVER SPRING TOWNSHIP.

trade. He was the father of four children: David, Elizabeth, Joseph, and one son who died young. Joseph Jacobs, his son, was born in York County, Penn., in 1798, and came to Cumberland County when a lad of about twelve years. He was a carpenter by trade. He married Miss Elizabeth, daughter of Philip Duey, of Cumberland County, Penn., and to them were born three sons: David, Ephraim and John. Joseph Jacobs was a Democrat in political opinions, was a member of the Lutheran Church, and died at the early age of thirty-seven. John, his son, was born in this township in 1830, and was but four years of age when his father died. By good management his mother secured a home, and gave her son all the advantages in her power. In 1864 our subject was elected sheriff of Cumberland County. In 1865 he married Miss Mary, daughter of Michael and Salome (Senseman) Kost, of this county. This union has been blessed with two children: Salome E. and Thomas Ralph. In 1866 Mr. Jacobs entered into partnership with Moses Bricker in the Letort Forge, in which he was engaged ten years. He then moved to his present farm and homestead. Mr. Jacobs is a stanch Democrat and has held several township offices. He is a stalwart man of fifty-six years and of easy and dignified manners. He takes life philosophically, and is one of the farmers who spend their evenings with the newspapers. He is well known throughout the county as a man of character and ability.

JOHN P. KAST, teacher, P. O. Mechanicsburg. Among the prominent families of Cumberland Valley and the earliest settlers appears the name of Kast, of hardy German stock; the family retain many of the characteristics of the stalwart pioneers who first settled in this beautiful valley. Michael Kast, the great-grandfather of our subject, emigrated from Germany in 1761, and bought land of the proprietary government about six miles west of Carlisle, in South Middleton Township, this county. Here he settled and remained until his death. He was the father of two sons, of whom, George, was born, lived and died on his father's homestead. He, George Kast, was the father of four sons: George, Philip, John and Jacob. Of these, Jacob was born in 1792, on the original homestead, where three generations of Kasts had now been born. In 1820, Jacob Kast married Miss Margaret, daughter of Benjamin Swartz, of Cumberland County, and to this union were born nine children: Catharine I., J. Benjamin, Jacob K., Margaret, Samuel J., David E., John P., Sarah and J. Theodore. Jacob Kast bought a farm in Silver Spring Township, where he settled and lived until his death. He was a Lutheran in religious belief; in politics a stanch Democrat. He was a man of strong determination and great will power, but though always strict with his family he kept his promises and was kind and gentle to all. John P. Kast, his son, was born on his father's farm, in this county, in 1831. He acquired his education in the common schools and at the Cumberland Valley Institute, Mechanicsburg. He began teaching at nineteen. In 1856 he went to Nebraska, then a Territory and considered in the far West, where he located land (which he still owns), taught school, and subsequently was elected county superintendent of schools of Sarpy County, and later passed his time farming and surveying. In 1859 he returned home and resumed school-teaching. In 1865 he married Miss Sarah C., daughter of George and Eliza (Hacket) Longsdorf, of this county. This union has been blessed with six children: Ella L., George A., Laura M., Charles L., Foster F. and Wilber B. Mr. Kast has taught school in all twenty-nine years, a record only equaled in this county by his brother, David E., who has been engaged in school work for thirty-eight years, and the number of pupils who have been instructed by the two brothers number thousands.

CURTIS KOST, justice of the peace, P. O. New Kingstown. Among the prominent families of Cumberland County and the very earliest settlers appears the name of Kost. They are of German descent. The great-grandfather, John George Jacob Kost, early settled in this township, buying land of the Indians, and part of the old mansion place, so called from being the old family residence, was bought from the Indians for three yards of calico per acre. John George Jacob Kost, the son of above, was born in the old log house which bears the date 1776 over the mantel. He married Miss Catharine Howk, and to them were born two children: Michael and a daughter that died in infancy. Michael, born January 14, 1807, married Miss Salome Senseman, of this county, and to this union were born six children: Jacob, John, Mary, Adeline, Daniel and Curtis. Michael Kost was a successful man and increased the paternal estate to 600 acres. In politics he was a stanch Democrat. He was county commissioner for three years and held various township offices. Of a mild and pleasant disposition, he was beloved by all his family, and in personal appearance his son Curtis greatly resembles him. He lived to the age of seventy-four years. He was a member of the Lutheran Church, as is also his widow, who is now aged seventy-eight years. Curtis Kost was born May 10, 1838, on the old homestead, where he remained until his marriage with Miss Margaret Amstrong, to which union were born three children, all of whom died young. The mother died September 14, 1863. November 20, 1870, Mr. Kost was again married, this time to Miss Nancy, daughter of John and Nancy (Boyer) Losh, of Perry County, Penn. To this union have been born eight children: Elsetta A., Abbie S., George L., Emma E., Cora E., Robert R., Maggie E. and Rebecca W. Mr. Kost followed agriculture until 1884 on the farm inherited from his father, and which has been in the family four generations. In 1885 he was elected justice of the peace, and is now living in New Kingston. Mr. Kost is also a stanch Democrat and has stood by his party in the dark days of defeat and in the bright sunshine of victory. He is a prominent man in the community and is well known throughout the county. He has the reputation of being a sensible and gentlemanly business man.

JOHN M. LOUDON, farmer, P. O. Mechanicsburg. The great-grandfather of this gentleman was the first of the name of whom there is any record. He was of English origin, and settled on the State Ridge, in Silver Spring Township, this county, and when he died his farm was left to his children, but was afterward bought by his son, James, who later sold it. In these early times the Indians were very numerous, and their depredations troublesome. At one time when some children were going to school they saw a party of Indians, and on reaching the schoolhouse told their teacher, who did not seem to fear any trouble, for he told them to recite one lesson, and then he would let them go home. In a few moments the "red-skins" were upon them, and, though the teacher begged for mercy for the children, they were all mercilessly killed and scalped but one, who escaped to tell the horrors of the tale. At this time Silver Spring Township was covered with small oak scrubs. The first settlements were made on the ridge, on account of water being easy to reach there. James Loudon, grandfather of our subject, was born on his father's farm. He married Mary Pinkerton, and by her had one son—Mathew—who was born in 1812, on the old homestead. He (Mathew) married Catharine Myers, of Monroe Township, this county, and to this union were born John M., Albert J. and Elizabeth. After his marriage Mathew Loudon began farming near Trindle Spring, where he remained for about seven years. He then bought a farm in Silver Spring Township, where he reared his family. He and his wife were members of the Lutheran Church. In politics he was a Republican. In 1881 he bought the present homestead, then called the Longsdorf farm. He was a careful, honorable man, and attended strictly to his business, rearing his family to the principles of industry and truth. John M. Loudon, his son, was born on the old homestead May 27, 1841, and passed his early life on his father's farm, gaining his education in the common schools. In 1875 he was united in marriage with Miss Eliza, daughter of Thomas and Margaret (Jones) Ellis, English people, who first settled in Tennessee. This union has been blessed with four children: Margaret E., Mary C., John Matthew and Lillie E. In politics Mr. Loudon is a Republican. He owns one of the best farms in this township, and the entire family have the respect of the community.

GEORGE MESSINGER, farmer, P. O. Hogestown. The grandfather of this gentleman, John W. H. Messinger, a tailor by trade, immigrated to this country about 1765, when a young man of twenty, to make a home in the wilderness, settling in York County, Penn., where he bought a farm. He married Miss Catharine, daughter of John Goswiler, of Cumberland County, Penn., and to them were born ten children: Mary, Henry, John, Jacob, William, Catharine, Susannah and Bostorra (twins), Daniel and Margaret. In 1804 John W. H. Messinger moved to this county, and settled in Silver Spring Township, on the farm now occupied by John C. Ropp; after ten years he moved to Perry County, Penn., and bought a farm, where he lived until his death; he died at the age of seventy-five years. He was a member of the Lutheran Church. Jacob Messinger, his son (father of our subject), was born in Cumberland County in 1804, and when but a lad went with his father to Perry County, Penn. He married Miss Susannah, daughter of Abraham Jacobs, of Perry County, and two children were born to them: Mary and George. Jacob Messinger was reared a farmer, but later kept a tavern at Shermansdale, where he died, aged thirty-three years, a member of the Lutheran Church. George Messinger, his son (subject of this sketch), was born in Perry County, Penn., June 21, 1825. As his father died when he was but a small boy he early endured the hardships of having to live among strangers. At the age of eighteen he learned carpentering. In March, 1847, he married Miss Elizabeth, daughter of George and Elizabeth (Fenical) Albright, of Perry County. This union has been blessed with the following named children: Mary, William, Henry, Henrietta, James D., Anna C. and Jeremiah A. Mr. and Mrs. Messinger had a sad loss in the death of three of their children: Mary, the wife of John A. Kimkle, and the mother of five children at her decease; Henrietta, who died at the early age of ten years; and Amos C., who was stricken down just as he was entering manhood. These great trials have been met with patience and Christian resignation. In 1868 Mr. Messinger moved to this county, where he has since lived. He is a member of the Lutheran Church, and his wife of the German Reformed. In politics he is a Democrat. He is an industrious, careful farmer and an honest man. The Messingers still retain many of the characteristics of the hardy stock from which they sprang.

JOHN M. SHOEMAKER, music teacher and farmer, P.O. Mechanicsburg. The great-grandfather of this gentleman, Henry Shoemaker, emigrated from Germany to America at the age of seventeen, and settled in Berks County, Penn. His son Henry was born in Berks County, Penn., about the year 1751, and in the course of time became owner of a fine farm in that county; he was a soldier in the Revolutionary war; was thrice married, twice in his native county, and by his first wife had two sons: Henry and Samuel. After she died he married a Miss Staumbugh, of Berks County, Penn., and to this union were born two sons: Jacob and John. (All the children were born in Berks County.) In 1807

SILVER SPRING TOWNSHIP. 543

Henry Shoemaker moved, with his family, to Perry County, Penn., where he bought two farms and a distillery. He was a very intelligent man, well educated for that day, and the people were accustomed to look to him for advice on general subjects. By diligence and thrift he accumulated a large property. He was a Democrat politically; a member of the Lutheran Church. John Shoemaker, son of Henry, and the father of our subject, was born in 1803, and came with his father to Perry County, Penn., when but four years of age. In 1825 he married Miss Elizabeth Bower, of Perry County, and to them were born six children: Susanna A., Anna E., Sarah J., William H., John M. and Elvina C. He began farming in Perry County, but in 1858 moved to Cumberland County, where he had bought a farm, and remained the balance of his life. He was a Lutheran in religious belief. He died at Mechanicsburg in 1880, at the age of seventy-seven years. He was a man of intelligence and probity. John M., his son, was born in Perry County, Penn., in 1845, and came to this county with his father when twelve years of age. He was a farmer until he was twenty-six years old, when he went West and taught music, for which he always had a talent. He was agent for the Estey organ, in which he was successful. At the end of two years he returned to Cumberland County, and has since sold organs, taught music and farmed. In 1885 he was united in marriage with Miss I. Lillie, daughter of Harrison and Rachel (Herman) Bowman, of this county. Mr. and Mrs. Shoemaker are members of the Lutheran Church at New Kingston, in which he has been organist for many years. In 1881 our subject bought the old homestead, where he has settled down to married life. His brother William H. owns an extensive organ factory at Harrisburg. The family comes of good stock and are people of sterling worth.

CHARLES SHREINER, cabinet-maker and farmer, P. O. Mechanicsburg. His grandfather, ——— Shreiner, a farmer by occupation, was born in Lancaster County; married Miss Barbara Fahreintrin, by whom he had four sons: Adam, Michael, Jacob and John. Of these sons, John was born in Lancaster County, Penn., September 26, 1775; in early life he learned cabinet-making, and he married Miss Rosanna Grosh, of Lancaster County, who bore him eight children: Samuel, Mary, Sarah, Elizabeth, Margaret, Catharine, Charles and Martin. In 1828 John Shreiner moved, with his family, to this county, settling in Silver Spring Township. He lived to the age of seventy years, and was respected by all for his sterling worth. Charles Shreiner was born in Lancaster County, Penn., January 19, 1815, and came to Cumberland County with his parents. He too learned the cabinet-maker's trade, which he followed for several years. He then worked at housecarpentering twenty-two years, building a large number of barns, etc. in this part of the valley. October 31, 1839, he was united in marriage with Miss Elizabeth, daughter of John and Elizabeth (Longsdorf) Bobb, of this county. This union has been blessed with five children, all now married: Margaret (wife of A. C. Miller, of Harrisburg, Penn.), John (married to Miss Elonora Morrett, of Hogestown, have five children: Charles T., D. Morrett, Mary E., Clara M. and Clarence M.), Catharine (wife of John Beck, of Mechanicsburg), Samuel (married to Mary Porter, of Middlesex; have three children: Bessie M., Edith P. and Roy P.) and Martin (married to Emma LeReu, of Plainville, N. J.). Mr. and Mrs. Charles Shreiner are members of the Lutheran Church, as were all his ancestors before him. In politics Mr. Shreiner is a stanch Democrat. In 1872 he purchased his present residence, which is pleasantly situated near Mechanicsburg. He is a man of strict principles and bears the reputation of being very reliable and honorable.

JOHN SIMMONS, farmer, P. O. Hogestown. The Simmons family originated in Germany, and immigrated to this country at an early date. George Simmons, a farmer by occupation and the father of John, was born near the line of Dauphin and Lebanon Counties, Penn. He married Miss Elizabeth Eckert, daughter of John Eckert, of the same locality. To them were born six children: Catherine, John, Jacob, George, Samuel and Elizabeth. About 1824, the father moved to and settled in this county. He was a Republican in political opinions; a hardworking and upright man. John Simmons, our subject, was brought to this county by his parents when he was a child. He grew up on the farm, and received a common school education. In 1851 he went to Illinois, but did not remain long. He married Miss Sarah Stine, daughter of Frederick and Elizabeth (Croll) Stine, of Dauphin County. This union was blessed with three children: J. W., John F. and Sarah E. His wife died, and Mr. Simmons then married her sister, Miss Mary Stine, who has borne him two children: Samuel and Emma C. In 1856, Mr. Simmons moved to his present residence in this township. In political opinions he is a Republican. He is considered a reliable and upright man.

ABRAHAM SOLLENBERGER, farmer, P. O. Mechanicsburg. The founder of the American branch of this family came from Germany and settled in Lancaster County, Penn., at an early day. John Sollenberger (grandfather of our subject) moved to Cumberland County, with his wife and two sons, in 1795, and bought a farm in Monroe Township. His wife was a Miss Barbara Yockey, of Lancaster County. She bore him ten children: John, Michael, David, Joseph, Samuel, Elizabeth, Barbara, Sarah, Catharine and Abraham. They all married and were the parents of children. Mr. and Mrs. John Sollenberger were members of the German Baptist Church. He was well known for his honesty, and lived to the patriarchal age of eighty-four years. John Sollenberger, his son, was born in Lancaster County. Penn., and came with his father to Cumberland County when but an infant. In 1818, he married Miss Hettie Scott, of Franklin County, daughter of William and Hannah (Howard) Scott. To them were born six children: Annie, Catharine, Abraham, John, Samuel and Joseph. In 1856 Mr. Sollenberger bought the old homestead where he lived until his death. He died, aged eighty-four years and ten months. He was a man of excellent moral character. Abraham Sollenberger, our subject, was born on the old homestead, which has now seen three generations at one time under its roof. In 1850 he married Miss Anna Seidle, a native of Lancaster County, Penn. To them was born one son, who died when but five years of age, a great misfortune, as they have since been childless. They adopted a friendless little child, however, whom they have tenderly cared for and educated, and who is now ten years old and is of a cheerful disposition and of more than ordinary intelligence. They have named her Annie May Sollenberger. In 1855, Mr. Sollenberger purchased his present homestead, which is a fine farm near Mechanicsburg. He and his wife are members of the church of his ancestors (German Baptist) and are well known for their kindness and good moral principles.

CAPT. J. S. SPONSLER, farmer, P. O. New Kingstown. The Sponslers, of Scotch-Irish origin, first settled in New Jersey. The great-grandfather of the subject of this sketch came to Cumberland County at a very early date, and his son George was born in this county in 1785, and owned a farm in North Middleton Township, on the Harrisburg Pike, two miles east of Carlisle. George Sponsler married Miss Jane Mortier, of this county, by whom he had six children: George, Jane, Margaret, Oliver, Jesse and Alexander. His wife died, and he afterward married her sister, Mrs. Margaret Ruperd, a widow, and to this union were born three children: Sarah, Frank and Alfred. After the decease of his second wife Mr. Sponsler married Miss Susan Harman, of this county. He was a Presbyterian in religious belief; in politics an old-line Whig. He was a man of strict business habits, and bore an excellent reputation. His son George (father of our subject) was born on the old homestead in 1810; married Miss Sarah Coover, of Mahoning County, Ohio. To them were born five children: Eliza, William, Joel S., Harriet, Marilla. When a young man of but sixteen, George Sponsler went to Ohio, and returned to Cumberland County when about forty years of age. He is a member of the Evangelical Church; in politics a Republican. Our subject was born in Mahoning County, Ohio, in 1837, and came with his parents to Cumberland County when a lad of ten years. He received a common school education, and in 1856 married Miss Annie, daughter of John and Mary (Gruver) Dull, of Franklin County, Penn. This union was blessed with six children: John O., William S., Annie K., Robert P., George F. and Julia M. In September, 1862, Mr. Sponsler enlisted in Company F, Seventeenth Regiment Pennsylvania Cavalry. He left his quiet home, wife and family of small children to fight the battles of his country, went to the front, and served with honor to the close of the war. His regiment, the famous Seventeenth Pennsylvania Cavalry, was one of those which won imperishable renown, and its gallant deeds are memorialized on every field of battle, from the Rappahanock to the James, and in all the battles (57) in which this regiment engaged Mr. Sponsler was present, among which Chancellorsville, Gettysburg, Winchester, Appomattox and the Wilderness were the most prominent. He was promoted for gallant services from private to first sergeant, second lieutenant, lieutenant and captain. He was mustered out June 20, 1865. After the close of the war Capt. Sponsler returned to Cumberland County and settled down to the peaceful pursuit of farming in Silver Spring Township, and here has remained on the same farm twenty years, and is well known throughout the county as an honorable and industrious man. He is a Republican in politics.

SAMUEL VOGLESONG, farmer, P. O. New Kingstown. The grandfather of this gentleman immigrated to this country and settled in York County. John Voglesong, his son (father of subject), was born in York County about 1783. He was a farmer and landholder, and married Miss Mary Lichty, of York County. To them were born ten children: Henry, John, David, Samuel, Elizabeth, Susan, Benjamin, Sarah, Thomas F. and Mary F. (twins.) About 1809, John Voglesong moved to this county and settled in Silver Spring Township. He died in 1849 at the age of sixty-four years. Samuel Voglesong was born in 1819, on his father's farm in Silver Spring Township. He remained at home after the death of his father until he was thirty-two years of age. In 1851 he married Miss Elizabeth Hartman, daughter of Christian and Annie (Gontz) Hartman. Both Mr. and Mrs. Voglesong are devout members of the Lutheran Church. In politics he is a Democrat. By industry and thrift he has accumulated a handsome property, consisting of 279 acres of land in this township, and is greatly respected by all who know him.

HENRY ZIMMERMAN, farmer, P. O. Mechanicsburg, Cumberland Co., Penn. The ancestors of this gentleman emigrated from Switzerland on account of religious persecution, and were glad to seek an asylum in the land of William Penn, where they could worship God after the manner of their own conscience. These Mennonites Penn received kindly, allowing them full liberty, and land to settle on in Lancaster County, Penn. Christian Zimmerman, the great-grandfather, was a powerful man physically, and weighed over 400 pounds. His son, Peter, married a Miss Martin, and had twelve children: Christian, Henry, Peter, Esther, Mary, Barbara, Annie, Martin, Samuel, Yontz, Elizabeth and

Emanuel. In 1812, Peter Zimmerman moved to Cumberland County, buying 300 acres of land in Lower Allen Township. He died, aged eighty-six years. Christian Zimmerman (father of our subject) was born in Lancaster County. He came with his father to this county when a lad of thirteen years. He married Miss Lizzie Weaver, of this county. The Weavers came from Switzerland at the same time as the Zimmermans, and were noted for their longevity. To Christian Zimmerman and wife were born nine children: Henry, Peter, Christian, Isaac, Solomon, Elizabeth, and three who died in infancy. Mr. and Mrs. Christian Zimmerman were devout members of the Mennonite Church. He died at the age of seventy-two years, respected by all as an upright, honorable man. Henry Zimmerman, our subject, was born in Lower Allen Township, this county, February, 17, 1824, and lived with his father until he was thirty years old. In January, 1855, he was married to Miss Mary Ann, daughter of William and Mary (Houst) Tate, and to this union was born one son, David L., who remains with his parents. Mr. Zimmerman began farming on one of the McCormick farms, and remained there for twenty-five years, and in 1879 he bought his present homestead. The family is well known for industry and honesty, and need no higher praise.

CHAPTER LVII.

SOUTHAMPTON TOWNSHIP.*

JEREMIAH ALLEN, Sr., retired farmer, P. O. Shippensburg, was born in Lehigh County, Penn., April 4, 1818, son of Americus and Rachel (Swigert) Allen, natives of Massachusetts and Pennsylvania, respectively. His grandfather, Jeremiah Allen, was a captain in the artillery during the Revolutionary war, and received a slight wound at the battle of Bunker Hill. Our subject's father, who was a farmer, and came to Pennsylvania in an early day, enlisted in the war of 1812, but was never called into active service. Jeremiah Allen is the second child in a family of eight, seven of whom survive. His elder brother, Samuel, is a farmer in Southampton Township, this county, and is three years, three months and three days older than Jeremiah. Our subject was reared on the farm, and attended the common school in this county. He chose farming as his occupation, and is now owner of 133 acres of well improved land, on which he resides. He was happily married, in 1844, to Angeline, daughter of Jacob and Lydia (Line) Myers, who were of English descent, former of whom, a farmer, was born and reared in this county. To our subject and wife were born eight children, seven of whom are now living: Eveline, wife of James Waddle; Americus M., a farmer, and married; Isabella M., widow of Ira Long (deceased); Margaret E., wife of Cyrus Railing; Jacob, married and a farmer; William L., married, and manages the home farm; and Jeremiah F., married and a farmer. In 1844 our subject and wife united with the Lutheran Church at Newville, Penn. He takes an active interest in the Sabbath-school, and has been superintendent, and for many years he was deacon and trustee of the church. He has served nine years as school director. In his younger days he took an active interest in the I. O. O. F. He was a member of the old-fashioned State militia, and has taken part in many parades, sometimes using a cornstalk as a substitute for a gun.

WILLIAM H. ALLEN, dealer in horses, P. O. Lee's Cross Roads, was born near Carlisle, this county, February 14, 1834, son of Americus and Rachel (Swigert) Allen; former, a native of Massachusetts, of English descent, and latter a native of Lancaster County, Penn., of Dutch and Welch descent. Americus Allen, who was a farmer, came to this county in an early day. He was a captain in the war of 1812, but was never called into active service. His parents were Capt. Jeremiah and Abigal (Putnam) Allen (Gen. Putnam, of Revolutionary fame, was her great uncle), former of whom was a captain in the Heavy Artillery, under Gen Putnam, during the Revolutionary war. The maternal ancestors of our subject were generally farmers, and his paternal ancestors were generally active and successful business men. Our subject's uncle, Samuel R. Allen, was a trader, and dealt largely in merchandise in the West Indies islands; he was a native of Massachusetts, and at the time of his death was a wealthy citizen of Boston. William H. Allen, the subject of this sketch, the youngest in a family of eight children, was reared on the farm, in this county, and attended the district school, also the academy at Shippensburg. He has resided on the farm all his life, but his principal business has been dealing in horses. He has bought, imported, shipped and sold, and traded in horses very extensively for a number of years, and is an excellent judge of such stock. William H

*For borough of Shippensburg, see page 442.

Allen was married, October 14, 1859, to Anna, daughter of William Clark, and of Irish and English descent, her grandfather, James Clark, was a wealthy pioneer farmer of this county, owning several hundred acres of land at the time of his death. To Mr. and Mrs. Allen have been born nine children: Americus R., Abigal P. (wife of James Lamond), William C., Albert E., Emma C., Daniel L., Annie A., Nellie and J. K. F. Mr. Allen is a Democrat in politics; has been school director of his district.

G. EDGAR BEATTIE, farmer and stock-raiser, P. O. Oakville, was born in Newton Township, this county, January 17, 1852, son of Samuel and Lucinda (Allen) Beattie, natives of this county and of Scotch-Irish descent. Our subject's grandfather, James Beattie, came from Ireland in an early day and settled on a farm.

HON. JAMES CHESTNUT, farmer, P. O. Cleversburg, was born in Southampton Township, this county, September 30, 1818, son of John and Charity (Kelley) Chestnut, natives of Pennsylvania, and of Scotch-Irish and English descent. John Chestnut came from Philadelphia, Penn., to this county, in 1766 and settled on a farm in what is now Southampton Township, and here passed the remainder of his days. Hon. James Chestnut, the youngest in a family of eight children, was reared on the farm, attended the common school, and afterward the Washington Medical College, at Baltimore, Md. He practiced medicine for two years in this county, but, on account of his business relations, he gave up his profession and devoted most of his time to farming and other business. He is well known as "Col." Chestnut, having been elected colonel of militia, when quite a young man, and served as such for six years. He is a member of the I. O. O. F. In politics he is a Democrat; has served as school director in his district, and justice of the peace in his township, and has represented this district (comprising Cumberland and Adams Counties) in the State Senate for two terms, from 1876 to 1880. In 1846, our subject married Anna Eliza, daughter of George Maxwell, and a native of this county, of Scotch-Irish descent. Of nine children born to our subject and wife eight are now living —two boys and six girls.

GEORGE CLEVER, farmer, P. O. Cleversburg, was born in this county January 4, 1819, son of Conrad and Catherine (Walters) Clever, natives of Lancaster County, Penn., of German descent. Conrad Clever was brought to this county when he was six years of age, and was raised here. He chose farming and lumbering as his occupation, and was very successful. He died in 1861, at the advanced age of eighty-one years. He had filled most of the town offices. He was a man of large stature and noted for his great strength, a man of unblemished character. Of his four sons George is the youngest. Our subject was brought up on the farm; has made farming and lumbering the principal business of his life, and has also engaged largely in the manufacture of iron and in shipping iron ore. In 1850 George Clever laid out the town of Cleversburg, this county, and in the same year he embarked in mercantile trade, in connection with his other business. He now owns several stores in different parts of Pennsylvania, and also several farms, as well as real estate in Cleversburg and other places. Mr. Clever was married, in 1845, to Miss Isabella Kelso, a sister of Maj. Kelso, of Shippensburg, Penn., and a daughter of Samuel and Catherine (Stough) Kelso,who were of Scotch-Irish descent. To Mr. and Mrs. Clever have been born eight children, of which four are now living: Conrad, a minister of the Reformed Church, in Baltimore, Md.; Samuel K., residing at home; George G., married and a resident of Southampton Township, Penn.; and Jennie S., residing at home. Our subject and wife are members of the Reformed Church, Shippensburg, in which he has been deacon and trustee for many years. In politics he is a Republican, but not a politician. He has served one term as jury commissioner.

GEORGE H. CLEVER, retired farmer, P. O. Cleversburg, was born in this county on the farm where he now resides, son of George and Elizabeth (Hippenstell) Clever, natives of Southampton Township, this county, of German descent, former a farmer. Our subject now owns the farms where his parents were born. Our subject's father was born in 1790, and his mother in 1800. His grandfather, Barnhart Clever, was an early pioneer farmer of this county, and the deed given him by William Penn, in 1788, is now held by George H. Clever. At the time this deed was made our Southampton Township was called Hopewell Township. Our subject, the fourth child and only son in a family of six children, has followed farming as an occupation, and now owns 624 acres of land. He was married, in 1849, to Sarah, daughter of Adam Warner, who was a farmer and of German descent, a native of Pennsylvania. The children of this marriage are Elizabeth, wife of George Miller; Cyrus, a farmer in Franklin County, Penn.; Emily, wife of William B. Bowers; Susan, wife of John C. Raybuck (he is a farmer in Franklin County, Penn.); Henry E., married and a farmer, and Samuel A., attending school. Mr. and Mrs. Clever are members of the United Brethren Church, of which church he has been class-leader and trustee and has been superintendent of the Sabbath-school. He has also been an exhorter for several years. Mr. Clever is an earnest advocate of the cause of Christ, and has done much good. He votes the Democratic ticket, and has served his township as justice of the peace for fifteen years.

JOSEPH CLEVER, farmer, P. O. Lee's Cross Roads, was born in Shippensburg in October, 1835, son of Henry and Elizabeth (Buchman) Clever, natives of Southampton

SOUTHAMPTON TOWNSHIP.

Township, this county, and of German descent, the former a farmer by occupation. Joseph's grandfather, Barnhart Clever, was an early pioneer of this county. Our subject, the third in a family of thirteen children, eleven of whom grew to maturity, received his education in Southampton Township, this county, and has made agriculture his business. He has resided on his present farm since he was two years of age, and is now the owner of 182 acres of land. Mr. Clever was married, in 1859, to Georgianna, daughter of James and Elizabeth (Dice) Waddle; the former was a farmer by occupation, and both of Irish descent. Mr. and Mrs. Clever have eight children: Clara E., John D., Martha C., Julia E., Harry W., Franklin E., Charles C. and Nellie M. Our subject and wife are members of the Reformed Church. In politics he is a Democrat. He has served nine consecutive terms as school director in his district.

JOHN COFFEY, farmer, P. O. Shippensburg, was born in Southampton Township, this county, February 9, 1830, son of James and Mary (Highlands) Coffey; former a native of Delaware County, Penn., of Irish descent, latter of this county, of Scotch-Irish descent. James Coffey, a farmer by occupation, served as a soldier in the war of 1812. He was a strict Presbyterian Church member, a man of large stature, and was noted for great strength. He lived to the advanced age of eighty-four years, dying in 1879. He was three times married, and reared a family of ten children, our subject being by the second wife. John Coffey was reared on the farm; a strictly self-made man. He only attended school six weeks in his life, and chose farming for his occupation. When first starting out for himself he rented a farm, and has since resided on the same for thirty-two years. He was married, in 1854, to Elizabeth Rank, daughter of Samuel Rank, of German descent. Mr. and Mrs. Coffey have five children: Ella, wife of George A. Reese; J. B. and W. J., partners, carrying on a clothing store in Shippensburg, this county; Della C. and Charles. Mr. Coffey is a Democrat in politics; is the present assessor of Southampton Township, a highly-respected citizen.

G. W. CRESSLER, farmer and stock-grower, Shippensburg, was born in Southampton Township, this county, February 22, 1844, son of John H. and Elizabeth (Clippenger) Cressler, natives of this county and of German descent. John H. Cressler was a blacksmith by trade, but in later life followed farming, in which latter occupation he met with marked success and owned, at the time of his death, which occurred in 1885, nearly 300 acres of valuable land in Southampton Township, this county (his widow still resides on one of the farms). He was a member of the Lutheran Church, and a captain in the old-time militia of Pennsylvania. His family consisted of seven children, four now living, G. W. being the fourth. Our subject was reared on the farm, and attended the common schools in Southampton Township, this county, and has made agriculture the principal business of his life. He was married, in 1869, to Henrietta, daughter of Isaac Hannah, and a native of Canada, of English descent. Mr. and Mrs. Cressler have five children: Charles E., John H., Clarence C., Myrtle and an infant not yet named. In politics Mr. Cressler is a Democrat.

D. S. CROFT, retired merchant, P. O. Lee's Cross Roads, was born in Southampton Township, this county, October 7, 1816, son of George and Susan Croft, natives of Pennsylvania and of German descent, the latter of whom (whose maiden name was Susan Ruply) was the widow of Dr. Fahnestock, of Carlisle, Penn., at the time of her marriage with Mr. Croft. George Croft was a saddler by trade, but in later life he followed the occupation of farmer. He was three times married, and reared nine children, D. S. being his sixth. Our subject was reared on the farm and attended the common school; in early life he accepted a clerkship in the iron works, and, afterward, taught school for several terms; then obtained a position as clerk in a store in 1838, and was employed in that capacity until 1852, when he embarked in business for himself, in Leesburg, this county, where he kept a general store until 1857, when he was elected clerk of the county courts, and served in that capacity until 1861, and was then appointed deputy clerk, a position he filled for five years. Returning to Leesburg in 1866, he carried on the general store until 1885, when he sold out and retired from active business. Mr. Croft is a highly respected citizen and has many warm friends. He was married, in 1841, to Jane, daughter of George Maxwell, and of Irish descent. Mr. and Mrs. Croft are members of the Presbyterian Church. He is a Democrat in politics, and has been school director.

HIRAM HIGHLANDS, grain and coal dealer, and ticket agent for the Harrisburg & Potomac Railroad Company, at Lee's Cross Roads, was born in Southampton Township, this county, November 12, 1850, son of William and Maria (Clever) Highlands, natives of this county and of Scotch-Irish descent, former of whom was a farmer all his life, and died in 1866. Of their family of nine children, eight of whom are still living, Hiram is the eldest. Our subject was reared on the farm, attended the common school, and followed agricultural pursuits until 1884. He is owner of a well improved farm of sixty-four acres. Mr. Highlands embarked in his present business in 1884, and is an energetic, successful business man. He was married in 1873, to Cora Foreman, daughter of Jacob Foreman, a prominent farmer in Southampton Township, this county. Our subject and wife have five sons now living: William, Milton, Joseph, Calvin and Jacob. Mrs. Highlands is a member of the Evangelical Association. In politics Mr. Highlands is a Republican.

WILLIAM D. McCUNE, retired farmer, P. O. Middle Spring, was born in Southampton Township, Cumberland Co., Penn., December 19, 1823, son of John and Sarah A. (Duncan) McCune, natives of Pennsylvania, of Scotch-Irish descent. John McCune was born on the farm where his son William D. now resides, which farm was purchased in an early day by John McCune's father. John McCune, our subject's father, was a soldier in the war of 1812, and was a farmer of Southampton Township, this county. William D. McCune, the eldest in a family of nine children, was reared on the farm, received a common school education, and has made farming his business. He is owner of 200 acres of land. In politics he is a Republican. He is a member of the Presbyterian Church, and has been elder and trustee and for many years a teacher in the Sabbath-school.

SAMUEL TAYLOR, retired farmer, P. O., Lee's Cross Roads, was born in Franklin County, Penn., October 15, 1815, son of John and Mary (French) Taylor, former of whom was born in Adams County, Penn. His grandfather, John Taylor, a native of northern Ireland, immigrated to Pennsylvania and was the first settler in Southampton Township, he served in the war of the Revolution. Our subject's father was a cabinet-maker by trade, but his later years were passed in farming. He reared nine sons and two daughters, all now living except two. Samuel Taylor learned the wagon-maker's trade, in Franklin County, Penn., and followed it for forty-five years. In 1835 he was married, and by this marriage had five children: John (deceased) was a practicing attorney in Pittsburgh, Penn.; Philip L. married and a farmer; Ringold, married (he is a carpenter and resides in Columbus, Ohio); Francis A., a wagon-maker by trade, is married; and George E., a wagon-maker. Mr. and Mrs. Taylor are members of the Methodist Episcopal Church, of the Sabbath-school of which he has been superintendent, and has been class-leader in the church for twenty-two years. He is a Republican in politics; has served six years as school director. Mr. Taylor is a kind-hearted gentlemen, always ready to assist those who are in sickness.

WHERRY. The origin of this family in America was Samuel Wherry, who emigrated from County Antrim, Ireland, in April, 1762; settled in what is now known as Hopewell Township, Cumberland County, Penn., and married Elizabeth Ewing in 1776. Both were Scotch-Irish. Samuel Wherry died in 1825, and Elizabeth (Ewing) Wherry died in 1779, leaving one child, John Wherry, who was born July 2, 1777, married Margaret Mitchell in 1801, and died April 8, 1827. Margaret (Mitchell) Wherry, his wife, died June 23, 1837. These last-named left offspring: Samuel, born July 22, 1804; John Mitchell, February 10, 1806; Isabella Mary, April 7, 1808; William, February 11, 1810, and Elizabeth Wherry, July 22, 1813.

HON. SAMUEL WHERRY was the first child of John Wherry and Margaret (Mitchell) Wherry, born July 22, 1804; married Margaret McCune February 9, 1832, and died April 2, 1861. Margaret (McCune) Wherry died May 23, 1877. Mr. Wherry was a man of marked nobility. His distinguishing qualities were purity, truthfulness, unaffected simplicity, clearness of intellect with unbiased judgment, decision of character beneath the mildest manner, modesty scarcely to be paralled, charity that knew no bounds but prudence, a lifetime integrity without one stain, Christianity, not of sentiment merely, but of the highest practical type, and conscientiousness in the discharge of duty that often brought him the deepest pain by exposing him to the censure of men who were not worthy to loose the latchet of his shoes. He was a notable farmer. He took a deep interest in education, public and private. All his children received a thorough seminary and collegiate education. He filled a large space in his church (Presbyterian). In 1853 he was elected to a three-year term in the Senate of the State, and filled the office with credit to the district and honor to himself. In 1860 Gov. Packer appointed him to the bench at Carlisle, to fill a vacancy caused by the death of Judge Woodburn. While yet holding that commission he died, in his fifty-sixth year, leaving children: Eleanor S., Margaret J., Rev. John, Samuel M., Alexander S., Robert S. and William R. Wherry.

HON. S. M. WHERRY, the fourth child of Hon. Samuel Wherry, born January 5, 1839, graduated from Princeton June, 1860; completed the usual course of legal studies in the office of Judge Watts, Carlisle; relinquished his chosen profession from necessities growing out of his father's death; became a practical farmer April 1, 1863; married Esther A. Stuart, daughter of Hon. Hugh Stuart, of Carlisle, January 27, 1864, and still resides at the homestead. S. M. Wherry is best known as a progressive and successful farmer, as the instigator and promoter of many educational schemes, as the quiet benefactor of many who came to him in their distress, as the unseen helper of youths of both sexes, who, without money or friends, were also without hope of a fair start in life. He was elected to the Constitutional Convention of 1872–73, from the district of Cumberland and Franklin Counties, served through the entire term of that distinguished body, and has left his record in its printed debates.

REV. SAMUEL S. WYLIE, pastor of Middle Spring Presbyterian Church, was born in Washington County, Penn., December 2, 1844, son of David and Harriet B. (Simison) Wylie, of Scotch-Irish descent, latter a native of Ohio. David Wylie, a native of Pennsylvania, was a Government officer in early life, and in later life became a farmer; their family consisted of six children, Samuel S. being the fifth. Our subject was reared on the farm, and attended the common school until he was sixteen years of age; afterward he entered Washington and Jefferson College, from which he graduated in 1867. He entered the theological seminary at Allegheny City, Penn., in 1867, and graduated at that institution in 1870. He was licensed to preach in 1869, by the Pittsburgh Presbytery. After graduating in his theological course, in 1870, he spent one year in teaching and as supply preacher, in Indiana County, Penn. He then went to Scotland, where he entered the Free Church Theological College at Edinburgh, and remained one year. On his return to America he was ordained, and accepted a charge at Middle Spring, this county, where he has remained for the past fourteen years. Rev. Samuel S. Wylie is a thorough scholar and an accomplished gentleman, and his efforts in his profession have been attended with marked success in winning souls to his Master and gathering in his church and Sabbath-school many individuals and families. He has written a very authentic history of the Presbyterian Church at Middle Spring, this county. This church was one of the first established in the Cumberland Valley. Our subject was married, November 24, 1874, to Miss Jane M. McCune, daughter of John McCune, and of Scotch-Irish descent. They have been blessed with three children: Two daughters, Harriet and Eva Theressa, and one son, Samuel D. Mrs. Wylie is a member of the Presbyterian Church.

CHAPTER LVIII.

SOUTH MIDDLETON TOWNSHIP AND BOROUGH OF MOUNT HOLLY SPRINGS.

C. W. AHL (deceased) was born in Franklin County, Penn., February 22, 1811, son of Dr. John Ahl, an eminent physician in that county, and who moved to Newville, this county, where our subject received his education and, when but seventeen years of age, obtained a certificate to teach, which profession he followed five years; then commenced farming and dealing in real estate. He was a man of great executive ability and was very successful. In 1859 he embarked in the iron business, opening mines on his lands in Pennsylvania, Virginia and Maryland, all of which proving successful he bought extensive tracts of land, and, at his death, in 1885, was owner of prosperous mines, iron furnaces and valuable town property and 10,000 acres of land. Mr. Ahl was a man of more than the ordinary ability. He was elected president of the Harrisburg & Potomac Railroad in 1879. He was married, in 1839, to Catharine, daughter of James Williams, and of English origin, and to this union were born six children, four of whom are living. Mr. Ahl, a Democrat in politics, was an enthusiastic politician but would never accept office. The responsibility of conducting his large property was confided to his son Thomas W., five years before Mr. Ahl's death, and he succeeded to the presidency of the Harrisburg & Potomac Railroad. Thomas W. Ahl, was born in 1848, in Churchtown, this county, and is the next to the eldest in his father's family; he received his education in Dickinson College, Carlisle, whence he graduated in 1867; then embarked in the iron-manufacturing business at Boiling Springs, and has proved himself to be a thorough business man. In politics he is a Democrat.

GEORGE BISHOP, farmer and stock-raiser, P. O. Carlisle, was born in Monroe Township, this county, October 5, 1831, son of Jacob and Margaret (Swisher) Bishop, who were also natives of this county and of German descent. (Jacob Bishop was a tailor in early life but in later years a farmer.) They reared a family of eight children—four boys and four girls. Our subject, the third born in the family, was reared on the farm, acquiring a common school education in his native county. He chose farming as his avocation, has met with more than average success, and is the owner of a well improved farm, on which he now resides. He was married, October 18, 1855, to Elizabeth H., daughter of James and Sarah Armstrong, natives of Pennsylvania and of English and German origin. The marriage of Mr. and Mrs. Bishop was blessed with two children, both of whom are now deceased: Margaret A., wife of Daniel B. Hoerner (had one child also deceased) and Sarah Jane, who died at the age of two years and ten months. Mr. and Mrs. Bishop are members of the Church of God, and they are numbered among the best citizens of the township. In politics Mr. Bishop is a Democrat. He has served as school director.

H. E. BRECHBILL, farmer, Boiling Springs, was born at Boiling Springs, Cumberland Co., Penn., April 29, 1836, the eldest son in the family of five children of Philip and Clarissa (Gitt) Brechbill. The former, a native of Lebanon County, Penn., was of German origin, and the latter, born in Adams County, Penn., was of English descent. Philip Brechbill, who spent most of his life in Cumberland County, was a farmer by occupation and one of the first residents of what is now known as the village of Boiling Springs. Our subject was reared on the farm and received a good English education. In early life he clerked in a dry goods store, and also farmed for a time in South Middleton Township; in later years he engaged in farming and milling, and was at one time a merchant. Mr. Brechbill has been financially successful, and at the present time is owner of a flouring-mill in South Middleton Township and of a farm and considerable real estate in Boiling Springs, where he still resides. He was united in marriage, in 1866, with Martha J., daughter of Joseph and Mary Brandt, a native of Pennsylvania and of German and Irish origin. They have two children: Philip, in school, and Mary Emily Brandt, attending the female seminary at Hagerstown, Md. Mr. and Mrs. Brechbill are consistent members of the Lutheran Church, in which he has been elder and Sabbath-school superintendent since its organization, in 1873, and was one of the prime movers in organizing the society, taking an active interest in the church at Boiling Springs. He is a Republican in politics. He is of a literary turn of mind, and supplies himself and family with the best literature of the day.

ELI BUSHMAN, farmer and stock-raiser, P. O. Carlisle, was born in Carroll County, Md., January 19, 1826, son of Henry and Mary (Starr) Bushman, natives of Adams County, Penn., and Maryland, respectively, and of English origin. Henry Bushman, who is a farmer, resides on a farm, near Carlisle, and is eighty-five years old. He reared two children: Eli and Louisa, wife of Mr. Lepperd. Our subject received his education in the common school, and early in life learned the blacksmith's trade, at which he worked, however, but two years; since when he has devoted himself to agriculture, and now owns a farm of over 103 acres, on which he resides. Eli Bushman was married, in 1847, to Eliza Jane Adams, of Irish origin, and this union has been blessed with ten children, all of whom are living: Theodore (a farmer, is married), Harry, Rebecca, John Scott, Sarah Ann, George, Mary, Kate, Ida and Calvin. Mrs. Bushman is a member of the Lutheran Church. In politics Mr. Bushman is a Republican.

G. A. BUSHMAN, farmer and stock-grower, P. O. Carlisle, was born in South Middleton Township, this county, January 21, 1860, son of Eli and Sarah (Stevick) Bushman, natives of Pennsylvania and of German origin. Eli Bushman, who was a farmer, a member of the Lutheran Church, died in 1880. Of the family of eight children born to this couple G. A. is the fifth. Our subject was reared on the farm, receiving a common school education, and wisely chose the occupation of his father, that of agricultural pursuits, though he spent two years working on the railroad, with headquarters at Grand Rapids, Mich. He was married, in 1884, to Gertrude, daughter of John Park, of German descent. Mrs. Bushman is a member of the Lutheran Church. Our subject is owner of 107 acres of land, on which he resides; his mother, who is still living in Carlisle, is also a member of the Lutheran Church.

ISAAC A. CHRONISTER, farmer and stock-grower. P. O. Uriah, was born in Adams County, Penn., but grew to manhood in York County, same State, and there acquired his education in the common schools. His parents, Levi and Catharine (Asper) Chronister, were natives of Pennsylvania and of German origin; the former a blacksmith in early life, and in later years a farmer. Isaac A. Chronister, the third in a family of seven children, learned the carpenter's trade, at which he worked several years, but now devotes his time to agriculture. He owns the farm on which he resides in this township. He was united in marriage, in 1875, with Leah, daughter of Joel Griest, a farmer and miller by occupation, and of English origin. To Mr. and Mrs. Chronister have been born three children: Charles, Della and George Levi. Mr. and Mrs. Chronister are members of the Lutheran Church.

JAMES COYLE, farmer, P. O. Carlisle, was born in South Middleton Township, this county, July 13, 1822, son of Joseph and Calista (daughter of Thomas Thompson) Coyle, of English and Irish origin, and who were the parents of three children. Joseph Coyle, a farmer, an early settler of Cumberland County, died in 1832. James, the eldest of the children, was reared among strangers, in South Middleton Township, this county, and here received a common school education. At the age of seventeen he commenced to learn carpentering, and soon became a thorough mechanic; he has followed the business of carpenter and contractor for forty-five years, building bridges, houses and barns, and it is safe to say that he has erected more houses than any other man in this county. He has now retired from active labor and resides on a fine farm of 100 acres. He is a self-made man in every sense of the word, having acquired, not only his worldly possessions by his own exertions, but his education. He states he has never drank any intoxicating liquors nor used tobacco in any form. He is a remarkably well preserved man for his age. Our subject was married, in 1846, to Mary Ann, daughter of Benjamin and Rebecca (Dixon) Johnson, natives of Pennsylvania and of English descent. Mr. and Mrs. Coyle have five children living: Jennie A., William G. (a contractor and builder), Rebecca (wife of Christian Leib), James A. and Charles T. The sons are all carpenters and farmers, and all the children have been given the benefits of good schools. Mr. Coyle and his wife are members of the First Presbyterian Church in Carlisle, in which he takes an active interest, and for years has been ruling elder. Our subject, in politics, is a Democrat; has been auditor and supervisor, also school director in the township, and, in 1885, was elected by a large majority a director of the poor in this county. He is a member of one of the oldest families here, his great-grandfather, Thomas Thompson, having enlisted in the Revolutionary war from Cumberland County.

J. C. DAVIS, M. D., Mount Holly Springs, was born in Cumberland County, Penn., April 16, 1848, son of John P. and Catharine (Shipp) Davis, also natives of this county. John P. Davis, a farmer by occupation, at present resides in Penn Township, this county; his family consists of four children. J. C., the eldest, was reared on the farm and attended common school in his native county and Pennsylvania College at Gettysburg, Penn., and after graduating taught school three sessions. He commenced the study of medicine in 1873, afterward attended the Jefferson Medical College, and graduated thence in 1875. Since completing his medical course the Doctor has built up a large and extensive practice. He was united in marriage, in January, 1879, with Ella C., daughter of Benjamin K. Peffer, and of German origin. To this union have been born two children: Anna Zoe and John Keller. Dr. Davis and wife are members of the Lutheran Church. The Doctor, who is a Republican in politics, has served eight years as school director in Mount Holly Springs, and while a member of that body was instrumental in getting free text-books introduced into the public schools at Mount Holly. December 2, 1885, the Doctor was called before the Teachers' Institute of Cumberland County, Penn., and delivered an address in favor of introducing free text-books in all the public schools in the county. He is a member of the K. of P.

CAPT. CHARLES S. DERLAND, merchant, Boiling Springs, was born in Blair County, Penn., October 16, 1840, son of John and Mary (Harpst) Derland, natives of Pennsylvania and of German origin. John Derland was a book-keeper by occupation, and was engaged nearly all his life in the employ of iron manufacturing companies. His family consisted of three children, of whom Charles S. is the youngest born. Our subject was reared and educated in his native county. In 1861 he enlisted, at Carlisle, in what is known as "The Anderson Body Guards," and was successively promoted to be corporal, sergeant, orderly sergeant, second lieutenant, first lieutenant and adjutant, and afterward captain, in which capacity he served until the close of the war, receiving an honorable discharge in November, 1866. His military record is truly a noble one; he participated in several noted battles, the most severe one being that of Pittsburg Landing. Returning home, after the war, Capt. Derland embarked in his present business. He was married, in 1864, to Sarah, daughter of John Embick and a native of Franklin County, Penn., of German origin. To this union have been born two children; Mary and Blanche. The family are all members of the Presbyterian Church. Mr. Derland is a Republican in politics.

SOLOMON DEWALT, retired farmer, P. O. Carlisle, is a native of Perry County, Penn., where he was born May 12, 1818. His father, John Dewalt, a prominent farmer, was a native of the Keystone State and of German origin. His mother, Margaret (Beard) Dewalt, was a native of this county and of English lineage. They reared six children, of whom Solomon is the second born. Our subject grew to manhood in his native county, acquiring his education in the district school. At the age of eighteen years he commenced to learn the tanner's trade, and in 1842 embarked in business, having for a partner Hon. Jesse Miller, who was then Secretary of State of the State of Pennsylvania. This partnership continued for three years, when Mr. Dewalt sold out and followed farming in Perry County, Penn., until 1866, when he came to this county, where he has since resided and is owner of a fine farm. Mr. Dewalt has been twice married; first to Jane McKinley, who lived only one year and died in 1842, leaving one child, Mary Isabella, now the wife of John W. Lindsey; and he was married, on second occasion, in 1845, to Susannah, daughter of George Shibley, and of German origin. Of the five children born to this union three are now living: Joseph A., a farmer; John S., a carpenter; Eliza Jane, wife of M. B. Ocker; and George S., and Harry E., deceased. Mr. Dewalt is a Democrat in politics; has been assessor and supervisor of North Middleton Township four years. He was first lieutenant of the Landisburg Guards, of Perry County, Penn.

R. M. EARLEY, editor, publisher and proprietor of the *Mountain Echo*, Mount Holly Springs, was born in Leesburg, Penn., February 11, 1846, son of Robert and Jane (McCormick) Earley, natives of Pennsylvania and of English descent; former a blacksmith by trade, in later life a farmer. R. M. Earley, next the youngest in a family of six children, received his education in the Williamsport Seminary, and then taught school for one year. In 1871 he established his present enterprise in Mount Holly Springs, and in the same year married Martha Fishburn, of German lineage, and daughter of Philip Fishburn, a farmer. To this union have been born two children: Frank Norman and Barton. Mr. and Mrs. Earley are members of the Methodist Episcopal Church. In politics he is a Republican.

H. M. EVANS, freight agent for the Harrisburg & Potomac Railroad Company, Boiling Springs, was born in Carroll Township, York Co., Penn., December 31, 1851, son of John and Elizabeth (Miller) Evans, also natives of York County. Our subject's mother was of German descent; his father, of Welsh lineage, was a land surveyor, and for many years followed his profession in York County. He, John Evans, moved to Newville, Cumberland County in 1863; was justice of the peace, and held several other offices of trust. He died in 1883. H. M. Evans' paternal grandfather was an officer in the war of 1812. Our subject is the elder in a family of two children, and grew to manhood in Cumberland County, attending the school in Newville and afterward Dickinson College, whence he graduated in 1874. He then studied surveying, and worked at it with his father for a time, but at the age of twenty-three accepted the position of freight agent, and has served in that capacity ever since. He was married, in 1881, to Laura E., daughter of John Beetem, and a native of this county, of German origin. To this union has been born one child: Maud Elizabeth. Mrs. Evans is a member of the Lutheran Church. In politics Mr. Evans is a Democrat.

W. F. GARDNER, merchant, P. O. Uriah, was born in South Middleton Township, this county, September 15, 1856, son of Barney and Agnes (Day) Gardner; the former of German origin, born in Adams County, Penn., in 1810, the latter also a native of Pennsylvania, of English lineage. They were married in Adams County, Penn. Barney Gardner, who was a farmer and merchant and successful business man, lived to be seventy years old, his life being mostly spent on the line between Adams and Cumberland Counties. He died in 1880. He was a Democrat politically. His widow still resides in South Middleton Township. Our subject is the youngest of three children (John, Uriah and William F.), and grew to manhood on the farm, receiving his education in the common school. Mr. Gardner has been conducting a general store in the southern part of South Middleton Township since 1875. He was married, in 1880, to Florence Mortorff, of English origin, and daughter of Israel Mortorff, who was a successful business man. Politically our subject is a Democrat.

SAMUEL GIVIN, president of the Mount Holly Paper Company, Mount Holly Springs, was born in Cumberland County, Penn., July 6, 1804, son of James and Agnes (Steel) Givin; the former a native of Ireland, the latter of Pennsylvania. James Givin came to this county in 1790, and for many years was a merchant in Carlisle and a prominent man. In early life he was a Democrat in politics, but in later years became a Republican. He was a member of Carlisle Town Council. Of the eleven children born to James and Agnes Givin seven attained maturity. Samuel Givin, the seventh born, grew up in Carlisle and there received his education, and early in life embarked in mercantile business, in which he continued until 1828, when he built a mill at Mount Holly Springs, near the site of the brick mill now owned by the Mount Holly Paper Company, and there for several years manufactured carpets, whose beauty in design and texture are said to have equaled the celebrated carpets of Kidderminster, England. In 1865 the paper company was incorporated, with a cash capital of $200,000, and Mr. Robert Givin was elected president, acting as such until his death in 1878, when Samuel Givin was elected president, which office he still holds. He is a Republican in politics, and has served as president of town council. He is a member of the Presbyterian Church.

P. HARMON, dealer in coal, grain and lumber, and agent for the Harrisburg & Potomac Railroad Company, Mount Holly Springs, was born in South Middleton Township, this county, December 13, 1848, son of George (a farmer) and Julia (Baker) Harmon, natives of York County, Penn., and of German origin; their family consisted of eight children. Our subject, the fifth born, was reared on the farm and attended the schools of his native county. Early in life he left the farm and clerked in a store in Mount Holly Springs; then embarked in mercantile trade, keeping a general store for fifteen years, most of the time in company with his brother, though he conducted business alone for six years. In 1877 our subject embarked in his present enterprise. He was married, in 1872, to Emily L., daughter of Stephen F. Weakley, and of Irish descent. Her father was a farmer, and was a strong Abolitionist in those days when it cost something to be an advocate of that doctrine. The children of Mr. and Mrs. P. Harmon are Bessie, Percy and Helen. Mrs. Harmon is a member of the Methodist Episcopal Church. Mr. Harmon is a Republican in politics; has served in the town council, and for three years was secretary of the school board. During the late war of the Rebellion he enlisted, in 1865, in Company H, One Hundred and First Pennsylvania Volunteer Infantry, serving until the close of the war.

E. F. HASKELL, farmer and proprietor of the Wood View Nursery, P. O. Uriah, was born in Massachusetts May 27, 1810, son of Charles H. and Demaris (Flagg) Haskell, natives of Massachusetts and of English origin. Charles H. Haskell was a farmer and manufacturer of woolen goods. Our subject, the third in a family of ten children, after receiving his education in the academy of his native State, at the age of seventeen learned the trade, with his father, of manufacturing woolen goods, which he followed seventeen years, a part of the time being in business in Delaware County, Penn. He also managed the carpet manufacturing business at Mount Holly Springs, this county, for five years, and afterward became general manager of the Pine Grove Iron Works, where he remained for eight years, when he engaged as superintendent of the Ahl Iron Works for a year. After this he moved on his farm, consisting of 205 acres, which he had purchased in 1850, and

SOUTH MIDDLETON TOWNSHIP.

embarked in the nursery business, selling trees in New York and the Western States extensively, meeting with more than average success. Our subject has been twice married; first in 1832, and, this wife dying in 1835, he was married, on the second occasion, in 1840, to Miss Eliza Watsbaugh, of German and Irish origin, and their three children are Amanda, wife of John Peters; Almira, wife of E. J. Hartzel; Harrison, who is married and farming the home place. Mrs. Eliza Haskell died in 1867. She was a member of the German Reformed Church. Mr. Haskell was a member of the Presbyterian denomination, but now has his membership with the Lutheran Church. He has always taken an active interest in his church, serving as elder and deacon. Mr. Haskell has lived in Cumberland County since 1838, and for a number of years has been a member of the school board.

GEORGE W. HEAGY, farmer and stock-grower, P. O. Carlisle, was born near Newville, Cumberland Co., Penn., September 24, 1837, son of John and Mary (Hemminger) Heagy. The former a native of Adams County, of English origin, was a farmer; the latter, born in Cumberland County, was of German lineage. George W. is the youngest in a family of seven children. His father died in 1856 in Cumberland County, where he had resided since he was a young man. Our subject attended common school and farmed until 1861, when he enlisted in Company H, Third Pennsylvania Cavalry, and served as a non-commissioned officer; was in several hard-fought battles, had two horses shot from under him, and was wounded while charging a rebel battery at the battle of Gettysburg, but served his full time, and was honorably discharged. Since the war Mr. Heagy has followed agricultural pursuits, and now owns 118 acres of land. He was married, in 1866, to Annie E. Stuart, of English descent, daughter of John Stuart, a farmer. The children born to this union are Mary, John, Robert, Minnie, Clark, Bessie, Florence, Maud and Annie. Mr. Heagy is a member of the Reformed Church, and his wife of the Presbyterian denomination. Mr. Heagy is a Democrat in politics; has served three years as county auditor and three years as overseer of the poor, and several years as school director.

C. K. HERR, farmer and stock-raiser, P. O. Hatton, was born in Lancaster County, Penn., February 19, 1834, the third in the family of five children of Christian and Mary (Meyers) Herr, also natives of that county and of German origin. Christian Herr, a farmer and minister in the old Mennonite Church, moved to this county in 1834, and settled on a farm in South Middleton Township, where he died in 1865. Our subject was reared on his father's farm, and received his education in the district school. In the course of time he chose agriculture as an occupation, and is now the owner of a farm of 102 acres, where he resides. He was married, in 1856, to Catharine, daughter of Jacob Spangles, and of German descent. To this union have been born ten children, nine of whom are now living: Emeison, Barbara, Jacob and Harry (twins; they have a stove and tinware store in Boiling Springs), Abraham, Christian, Mary, George and William. Mrs. Herr dying in 1878, Mr. Herr married, in 1881, Sallie S., daughter of John Kauffman. Mr. and Mrs. Herr are members of the United Brethren Church, of which he is a trustee. In politics he is a Republican.

DAVID HOERNER, retired manufacturer, Hatton, was born in Dauphin County, Penn., May 24, 1811, the third born in the family of twelve children of John and Magdalena (Ebersole) Hoerner, natives of Pennsylvania, and of German origin, and grandson of Andrew Hoerner, a soldier in the Revolutionary war. John Hoerner was a major in the war of 1812, and lived to the advanced age of ninety-one years. Our subject was a major in the State militia, and had two sons, who lost their lives in the late Rebellion; David, Jr., starved to death in Andersonville prison, and Thomas, killed in front of Petersburg. David Hoerner, Sr., received his education in Dauphin County, Penn., and at the age of eighteen commenced to learn the manufacturing of woolen goods, which business he followed forty-five years. In 1847 he bought the woolen mills in South Middleton Township, which he successfully operated until 1874, since when the business has been conducted by his son, Daniel B. Our subject was married, in 1831, to Barbara Hoover, of German descent, and of the nine children born to this union the following named are living: John H., the owner of 1,200 acres of land, a wealthy, influential merchant in Loudon, Penn.; Mary E., wife of Samuel Shelly; Sue B., who is living with said David Hoerner, and William H., living in Central City, Col.; Barbara M., wife of J. K. Graybill; Magdalena, wife of Rev. John P. Smith, a Methodist minister, and Daniel B., a manufacturer of woolen goods. Mr. Hoerner is a member of the Lutheran Church, Mrs. Hoerner of the United Brethren denomination. He is owner of a woolen-mill and a farm of sixty acres, on which he resides in South Middleton Township. In politics Mr. Hoerner is a Republican. During the late war of the Rebellion, in 1863, he went to Harrisburg to inform Gen. Smith that the rebel general, Fitzhugh Lee, was in this vicinity. On his return he states that he found himself in the midst of the enemy, and saw Gen. Lee sitting on a fence resting, and that the General, when he saw him, said: "Come, let us have a talk." Mr. Hoerner accepted the invitation, climbed up on the fence, and for half an hour argued the political questions of the day, all the time with a pass from Gen. Smith in his pocket, which, if found, would have condemned him as a spy. When he returned toward home three of the rebels accompanied him (as they said, to get something to eat), but Mr. Hoerner threw them off the scent by stopping at a farm house three miles from home, and asking for a piece of bread and butter, and when they saw him beginning to eat they left; so, by shrewdness and courage, he escaped.

D. P. HOOVER (deceased) was born in York County, Penn., February 13, 1825, son of John (a farmer) and Julia Ann (Livingston) Hoover, natives of Pennsylvania and of German lineage; they raised a family of nine children, eight of whom grew to maturity. Our subject, who was the seventh born, attended the district school, and at the age of nineteen learned blacksmithing, and after serving his apprenticeship followed his trade two years. He came with his parents to this county in 1833, and had therefore resided here for over a half century. He made farming the main business of his life and met with more than average success. Mr. Hoover was married in 1845, to Sarah, daughter of Jacob and Esther (Gline) Burkholder, the former of whom, a farmer, was of German origin. The union of Mr. and Mrs. Hoover was blessed with twelve children, eight of whom grew up and seven are now living: William M., Caroline Amelia (wife of William E. Reed), I. Willis, Anna, Esther, Samuel Philip, Matilda Clarissa. Mr. Hoover died July 24, 1886, a member of the Evangelical Chuch in which he had held most of the offices, having served as superintendent of Sabbath-schoool, class-leader and trustee; and had been a member of the church council. He served his township as school director. Politically he was a Democrat. His widow is a member of the Evangelical Lutheran Church.

ISRAEL HULL, farmer and stock-grower. P. O. Mount Holly Springs, was born in Lancaster County, Penn., February 23, 1821, son of Peter and Anna (Metz) Hull, also natives of Lancaster County and of Holland-Dutch descent. Peter Hull was a farmer by occupation; his father Peter Hull, Sr., served as a soldier in the Revolutionary war. Israel Hull, the fourth in a family of six children, attended the common school and worked on the farm until he was seventeen years old; then learned wagon-making, which occupation he followed until he attained his majority; he then, for several years, traveled extensively, going over the road between California and Pennsylvania eight times (working in the mines in California), and sailed on the ocean, visiting the Sandwich Islands, working in the shipyards there for ten months; he next embarked for San Francisco, Cal., arriving there a few months previous to the discovery of gold. In 1850 he came to New York, and in the same year to Mechanicsburg, Penn. Mr. Hull was married, in 1850, to Hannah, daughter of John and Hannah (Orth) Ricker, also natives of Pennsylvania and of German origin. To this union were born two children: Clara Jane and Margaret M. Mrs. Hull died in 1857. In politics our subject is a Republican. He is a member of Chico Lodge, No. 113, I. O. O. F., of California. In business he has been successful and is the owner of a well improved farm near Mount Holly Springs.

BENJAMIN KAUFFMAN, retired farmer, Boiling Springs, was born in Lancaster County, Penn., August 7, 1805, son of Christian and Maria (Miller) Kauffman, natives of Pennsylvania and of German origin, and who were the parents of eight children, of whom Benjamin is the youngest and the only surviving member of the family. Our subject was reared on the farm, attended the subscription school in his native county, chose the vocation of his father (who was a farmer all his life), and has met with marked success. He came to Cumberland County, Penn., in 1834, and settled in South Middleton Township on the farm where he now resides, and which now numbers 261 acres. He was married in 1828, to Martha, daughter of Jacob Bassler, also a native of Lancaster County and of German origin. Of the eleven children born to this union seven attained maturity: Maria, married to Charles Miller (both now deceased); Ann (deceased wife of John Bremer); Benjamin (deceased), was married, a farmer; Tobias, married, resides in Iowa (he enlisted at the breaking out of the war of the Rebellion in the Two Hundred and Ninth Pennsylvania Volunteer Infantry, was promoted to captain and subsequently to colonel; was taken prisoner by the enemy and suffered all the horrors of Libby prison); Sarah, at home; Martha, wife of John Strickler; Elizabeth, wife of Elias Moutz; Susan, wife of William Ely. Mr. Kauffman is a member of the new Mennonite Church.

WILLIAM KLEPPER, farmer and stock-grower. P. O. Mount Holly Springs, was born in Adams County, Penn., March 31, 1834, son of Adolphus and Susan (Kime) Klepper. His mother was a native of Adams County, Penn., and of German origin. His father, who was born in Germany, was a type-setter by trade, an occupation he followed in early life, but later was a farmer. Adolphus and Susan Klepper reared a family of nine children, of whom William is the eldest. Our subject acquired his education in the common schools of his native county, chose farming as his vocation, and is now the owner of 150 acres of land, on which he resides and which he has acquired by his own exertions. He was married, in 1863, to Mary Jane, daughter of John and Mary (Brame) Weigle, and a native of Adams County, Penn., of German descent. To this union were born the following children: Sarah Alberta, Anna Minerva (a teacher in South Middleton Township, Penn.), John Adolphus, William Henry, Maggie V., Jacob Emery, Emma Jane, Rebecca Irene and Clarence Reynolds. Mr. and Mrs. Klepper and two eldest daughters are members of the Lutheran Church, in which he has been deacon. In politics Mr. Klepper is a Democrat. He has served as school director three years; township assessor, and as judge of the primary election, three times.

SOUTH MIDDLETON TOWNSHIP.

D. P. LEHMAN, farmer and stock-grower, P. O. Boiling Springs, was born near the village of Newville, Cumberland Co., Penn., June 26, 1839, son of Jacob and Catharine (Givler) Lehman, natives of this county and of German origin. Jacob Lehman died in 1870. Our subject is the eldest of five children who grew to manhood and womanhood. He was reared on the farm and received a common school education in his native county. Wisely chosing farming as an occupation, he has met with more than the average success, and is now owner of 140 acres of land, with first-class improvements and well stocked. Mr. Lehman has been twice married; on first occasion, in 1863, to Elizabeth Burn, who died in 1872, and by this union has the following children: Dora (wife of John S. Keenport), Jacob, Ida, Clara and Minnie. In 1874 Mr. Lehman married his second wife, Mrs. Elizabeth Moore, daughter of Philip Maul, and of German origin, and by her he has two children: David and Charley. Mr. and Mrs. Lehman are members of the Lutheran Church, in which he has served as deacon and Sabbath-school superintendent. Politically our subject is a Democrat; he has served as school director and assessor of his township.

J. C. LEHMAN, justice of the peace, Boiling Springs, was born in Cumberland County, Penn., May 15, 1842, son of Jacob and Catharine (Givler) Lehman, also natives of this county and of German origin. Jacob Lehman, who was a farmer and stock-dealer, died December 26, 1870; his widow still survives. Their family consisted of seven children—two sons and five daughters. The sons are J. C. and D. P., a prominent farmer in this township. Our subject, the second born in the family, was reared on the farm, receiving a common school education. His first business transaction was dealing in stock. In 1876 he built the business room now occupied by Capt Derland and conducted a store three years. In 1880 he bought twenty-eight acres of land, where he thought he discovered indications of iron ore, developed it far enough to find his surmises were correct, and then quietly (through an agent) bought more, and at the present time owns 3,000 acres. He has an ore lead nearly three miles long on his land, which is being extensively developed by wealthy iron companies, among which may be mentioned the well-known Pine Grove Company (working J. C. Lehman, No. 2), and the Crane Iron Company, of which he is land agent for Cumberland County, (working J. C. Lehman No. 8). Mr. Lehman's lands bid fair to prove first-class in every particular. Our subject was married, in 1871, to Lyde C. (daughter of Wilson Fleming), a graduate of the State Normal School, who lived only one year after marriage; she was a member of the Presbyterian Church in Carlisle. Mr. Lehman is a liberal contributor to the church in Boiling Springs and is trustee of the Methodist Church in this township. He is a Democrat in politics and is serving as justice of the peace, being elected the third time.

CHRISTIAN LEIB, retired farmer, P. O. Boiling Springs, was born in South Middleton Township, Cumberland County, Penn., February 4, 1816, son of John and Mary (Wise) Leib, the former born in this county in 1781, a farmer by occupation. Our subject, the eighth born in a family of twelve children, received his education in the subscription school; chose farming as his occupation, and has met with average success, retiring from business and living on his little farm, comprising 38 acres, for which he paid $200 per acre, and on which he has a neat, substantial residence. Christian Leib was married, in 1836, to Nancy, daughter of Jacob Walter. This union was blessed with eight children, three of whom survive: Mary, Christian W. (a farmer) and Charles H. (a merchant). Mr. Leib's son, John, was a soldier in the Union Army, a member of the Two Hundred and Ninth Pennsylvania Volunteer Infantry, Company A, and was killed at the battle of Petersburg. Mr. Leib and wife are members of the Methodist Episcopal Church, in which he has been steward, class-leader and Sabbath-school superintendent. Politically Mr. Leib is a Republican. He is a descendant of one of the oldest families of Pennsylvania, and he and his wife have the respect and esteem of their many friends.

A. M. LEIDICH, surveyor and merchant of Boiling Springs, was born at "Leidich's oil-mill farm," in Monroe Township, Cumberland Co., Penn., on the 18th of October, 1822. He is a son of John and Mary (Diller) Leidich. His grandfather, Adam Leidich, was of German lineage, and died at the "oil mill-farm" in 1828. His mother was a daughter of Martin Diller, an early settler of this county and of German origin. John and Mary Leidich had two children: Adam, the subject of this sketch, and D. J., a prominent merchant of Carlisle, Penn. John Leidich died in 1826, and Mary Leidrich died in 1886. A. M. Leidich commenced the study of surveying at fifteen years of age, and two years later began the practice of his profession. He engaged in keeping a general store at Boiling Springs in 1845, and continued in that business until 1874, with only an interruption of two years. In 1845 he laid out the town of Boiling Springs for Daniel Kauffman, who owned the land on which the the town was built. The same year, he bought the lot on the corner of Main and Front Streets—the first lot that was sold in this town—paying the then enormous sum of $200 for it, and built the brick store which is still standing. Boiling Springs was so named as early as 1762. Our subject was married in 1847, to Regina, daughter of Capt. George McGowan and great-granddaughter of Andrew Crocket, who was prominent in the early history of this county. Mrs. Leidich's ancestors were early settlers of Pennsylvania, of Scotch-Irish origin. The children born to this union are Stewart M., an attorney at law, in Carlisle, Penn.; Mary, wife of R. Craighead; Margaret, wife of Dr. Houk, of Boiling Springs, this county, and Emma J., at home. Mrs. Leidich died in 1873; she was a member of the First Presbyterian Church of Carlisle. Mr. Leidich is a member of the same church. In politics he is a Republican. He was the first postmaster of Boiling Springs, appointed by President Pierce, the mail then being carried to Boiling Springs from Allen postoffice by Henry Erbin, who walked with it on his shoulder, or, more frequently in his pocket. He continued postmaster until the election of Abraham Lincoln.

M. H. LINDSAY, farmer and stock-grower, P. O. Carlisle, was born in Cumberland County, Penn., June 23, 1837, son of Alexander and Eliza (Wilt) Lindsay; the former of Scotch and the latter of English origin. Alexander Lindsay, who was a successful business man, died in 1875. The family of Alexander and Eliza Lindsay consisted of ten children, eight of whom grew to manhood and womanhood, and seven are now living. Our subject, the second born, was raised on the farm, in South Middleton Township, this county, and there attended the common schools. Since he reached his majority he has engaged in farming, and is now the owner of the home farm, consisting of something over eighty-two acres. He was married, December 19, 1867, to Miss Elmira, daughter of Jacob Hartman, and to this union were born two children: Rebecca (deceased) and Alice M. Mrs. Lindsay is a member of the Lutheran Church. In politics Mr. Lindsay is a Republican.

J. W. LINDSEY, farmer and stock-grower, P. O. Carlisle, was born in Cumberland County, Penn., December 21, 1835, son of Alexander and Eliza (Wilt) Lindsey, natives of Pennsylvania and of Scotch descent. They reared a family of ten children, eight of whom grew to manhood and womanhood, and seven are now living. Our subject, the eldest, was reared on the farm, received his education in the common schools in South Middleton Township, and has made farming his business in life. His father, who was a successful farmer, died in 1875. Mr. Lindsey, who has met with good success as an agriculturist, has lately built himself a neat, substantial residence on his farm, which consists of 88 acres. He was married in 1883, to Mary Bell, daughter of Solomon Dewalt, a prominent farmer of this township. The union of Mr. and Mrs. Lindsey has been blessed with one child: Bessie Wilt. Mrs. Lindsey is a member of the German Reformed Church. Politically Mr. Lindsey is a Republican.

D. A. McALLESTER, merchant, Mount Holly Springs, was born in Perry County, Penn., August 13, 1841, son of Alexander and Elizabeth (Baughman) McAllester, natives, respectively, of Dauphin and Perry Counties, Penn.; the former of Scotch-Irish and the latter of German origin. Alexander McAllester, who was a blacksmith by trade, in later life a farmer, died in Perry County, Penn., in 1880. Our subject is the seventh born in a family of nine children, seven of whom grew to manhood and womanhood. He was reared on the farm, receiving his education in the common school and in Bloomfield Academy. His first business venture was as a clerk in a dry goods store in Logansport, Ind., where he remained six years; he then went East and clerked for two years; subsequently embarked in mercantile trade at Mount Holly Springs, where he has since successfully conducted a general store. D. A. McAllester was married, in 1868, to Emma, daughter of Jacob Steel, and of German origin. They have five children: C. J., Steel, William, D. A. and Marie. Mr. McAllester is a Democrat in politics. He was appointed postmaster in 1885, and has served as treasurer of Mount Holly Springs. He is a member of the K. of P.

A. MANSFIELD, superintendent of the paper-mills of the Mount Holly Paper Company, Mount Holly Springs, was born in Berkshire County, Mass., March 26, 1825, son of William and Martha (Granger) Mansfield, also natives of that State and of English descent; they were parents of two children. Albert, the eldest, received his schooling in his native county, and for a time was employed in his father's store; afterward he learned to manufacture paper in his father's paper-mill, and in 1859 came to Cumberland County, Penn., accepting the superintendency of Mount Holly Paper-mill, which position he still fills with honor to himself and credit to his employers. He was united in marriage, December 3, 1850, with Miss Harriet E. Munson, born in Connecticut and of English origin. This union has been blessed with one child, Eva D., now the wife of Clarence J. Reddig, a merchant in Shippensburg, a graduate of Eastman National Business College, Poughkeepsie, N. Y., and a member of the class of 1877 of Pennsylvania College, Gettysburg, Penn. He is well known throughout the State as a Sabbath-school worker. Mr. Mansfield is a Republican in politics.

A. R. MAY, veterinary surgeon, P. O. Boiling Springs, born in York County, Penn., December 27, 1838, son of Daniel and Barbara (Rider) May; the former of whom was born in York County, Penn., in 1795, and lived to be seventy-eight years old; the latter, born in York County, Penn., in 1801, still residing with our subject at Boiling Springs. Daniel May was a miller in early life, but in later years a farmer. He was a very strong man, and during the time he was milling for Mr. Frick at the Big Conowago, in York County, Penn., he carried nine bushels of wheat up two flights of stairs at one time. A. R. May, the sixth born in the family, was reared on the farm, and received his education in the common school. He subsequently studied medicine, commenced to practice as veterinary surgeon in York County, Penn., and, in 1873, came to Boiling Springs, where he has been very successful, and is as well known as any veterinary surgeon in the county. The Doctor usually passes for a "Dutchman," and though his parents and grandparents were Americans, raised in York County among the Pennsylvania Dutch, he now speaks the English language with difficulty. He is a Republican in politics. For several years Mr. May has served as constable, and he has been mentioned as a candidate for sheriff of Cumberland County.

JACOB H. MEIXEL, farmer and stock grower, P. O. Boiling Springs, was born in South Middleton Township, Cumberland Co., Penn., January 22, 1846, son of George and Catharine (Hoover) Meixel, natives of Pennsylvania and of German origin. George Meixel was born in this county, and is a farmer by occupation, but in early life was a freighter; he now resides at Boiling Springs; he was a deacon in the Church of God. He raised three sons and one daughter: Jeremiah F., a minister in the Church of God; Jacob H., Zachariah T., teaching in the high school, Hanover, York Co., Penn.; and Sally, wife of Charles W. Otto. Our subject was reared on the farm, receiving his education in the township schools, the Iron City Commercial College, and at the Commercial College of Philadelphia, Penn. He is a first-class penman, and traveled through the West teaching penmanship. He was married, January 11, 1876, to Crara, daughter of Peter Bricker, of German origin. To this union were born four children, three now living: Jacob B., Rolland H., George G., and Christ. Mr. Meixel is a Republican in politics. He enlisted when he was eighteen years old, in Company I, One Hundred and Ninety-fifth Pennsylvania Volunteer Infantry, served his term of enlistment, and then re-enlisted in the One Hundred and Forty-ninth Independents, and became a non-commissioned officer. Mr. Meixel has traveled in two-thirds of the States of the Union. He is owner of 214 acres of land, is a first-class farmer, and raises thoroughbred chickens, turkeys, hogs and cattle.

ROBERT H. MIDDLETON, superintendent of the Harrisburg & Potomac Railroad, Boiling Springs, was born in Mifflin Township, Cumberland Co., Penn., January 25, 1845, son of Andrew M. and Nancy (Elliott) Middleton, also natives of this county and of Scotch-Irish origin, and who reared a family of five children. Our subject, the second born, lived on a farm until fifteen years old, attending the common school. His father, who was a farmer, then moved to Newville, Penn., where Robert H. attended the academy. In 1863 he went to Baltimore and attended the Commercial College, graduating the same year. He then obtained a position with P. A. Ahl & Bro. as book-keeper, remaining with them until 1865, when he went to Wabash, Ind., as book-keeper for his uncle, Thomas J. Elliott, and there remained until 1868. On returning to Newville, he was again employed as book-keeper for Ahl & Bro. until 1875, when he accepted a position on the engineer corps of the Harrisburg & Potomac Railroad, was made road-master in 1876 and in 1877 was appointed to his present position. Our subject was married, May 10, 1870, to Elizabeth A., daughter of Isaac Vanloan, of New York City; their children are Thomas E. and Robert H., Jr. Mrs. Middleton is a member of the Presbyterian Church and is of Huguenot origin.

WILLIAM MOORE, farmer and stock grower, P. O. Mount Holly Springs, was born in South Middleton Township, this county, November 28, 1835, in the house where he now resides. His parents, William and Catharine (Reighter) Moore, were also natives of this county and of Scotch-Irish descent. His father was a farmer and miller, and his grandfather, William Moore, also a farmer, was an early settler of this county. William Moore is the youngest in a family of six children, of which he and his sister Mary Ann (now the wife of John Craighead) are the only ones now residing in the county. Our subject was reared on a farm, acquired a common school education, and farming and milling have been his chief business. He is owner of 174 acres of land. Our subject has been twice married; first in 1858, to Catharine, daughter of Jacob Ritner and granddaughter of ex-Gov. Joseph Ritner of Pennsylvania. To this union were born the following named children: Robert, a cattle-dealer in Wyoming Territory; Emily and Bertha. Mrs. Moore died in 1866, and in 1869 Mr. Moore married, for his second wife, her sister Mary, and by this union has four children: Jessie, Minnie, Norris and Hugh. Mrs. Moore's father was a land surveyor and farmer, and his daughter Mary, being endowed with artistic taste, drew the drafts of the tracts of land for him; she is a member of the Presbyterian Church. Mr. Moore is a Democrat in politics.

ELIAS MOUNTZ, farmer and stock-raiser, P. O. Hatton, was born in Frankford Township, this county, August 13, 1840, son of John and Susanna (Knisly) Mountz, natives of Cumberland County, Penn., and of German descent; the former born in 1812, and the latter in 1814. Our subject's grandfather, Martin Mountz, and his great-grandfather, Lazarus Mountz, were tillers of the soil, as was also his father. John Mountz served, at one time, as captain in the militia; he died in 1879, his widow still survives him. Their family consisted of ten children, eight of whom grew to manhood and womanhood. Elias Mountz is the eldest in the family that attained maturity, and was reared on the farm, attending the normal school. At the age of seventeen he commenced teaching, and followed this vocation for ten years in this county, teaching in the high school at Mount Holly Springs and six terms in South Middleton Township; since he abandoned school-teaching he has devoted his time to farming. Mr. Mountz is one of the few farmers who keep a correct book account of all he buys and sells on his farm. He has been a very successful farmer, and is one-half owner of a well improved farm, on which his brother now resides. Mr. Mountz, in politics, is a Democrat; has served as school director in this township for nine years; in 1866 he was elected county auditor, and served in that capacity for three years. Our subject was married, February 23, 1865, to Eliza B., daughter of Benjamin Kauffman, and this union has been blessed with thirteen children, ten of whom are now living: Cicero K., Viola K., Elias K., Harry K., Olive K., Charles K., Minnie K., Elsie K., Stella K. and Annie K. Mr. and Mrs. Mountz are members of the United Brethren Church, in which he is class-leader and assistant superintendent of the Sabbath-school.

CHARLES H. MULLIN, Mount Holly Springs, is secretary and treasurer of the Mount Holly Paper Company, established in 1856, who do an extensive business in the manufacture of fine letter and writing papers; they make the commercial safety paper for checks, drafts, etc. He was born in South Middleton Township (now Mount Holly Springs), this county, October 31, 1833, son of William B. and Eliza (Lightcap) Mullin, natives of Cumberland County, and of Irish and English descent, respectively. Our subject's great-grandfather, who came from the North of Ireland to America in 1760, and settled in Cumberland County, Penn., was a farmer by occupation, and served as a soldier in the Revolutionary war, and his grandfather, who was a paper manufacturer in Franklin County, Penn., came, in 1819, to what is now Mount Holly Springs, and bought the paper-mill built in 1812 by William Barber and I. Knox, and which he carried on until 1838, when his son, William B. Mullin (subject's father), took charge of the business, and continued it until his death, which occurred in 1869. In politics Mr. Mullin is a Republican. He was one of the electors on the Republican ticket that elected Gen. Grant President his first term; he was delegate to the National Convention in 1876, and has also been delegate to all important State conventions since 1872, always taking a prominent part. He is a member of the I. O. O. F., K. of P., and is a Knight Templar. During the late war of the Rebellion our subject enlisted, in 1861, in the Seventh Pennsylvania Reserves. Mr. Mullin takes an interest in every thing that pertains to the welfare of Cumberland County. In 1872 he was elected president of Cumberland County Agricultural Society, which office he still holds.

WILLIAM A. MULLIN, of the firm of W. A. & A. F. Mullin, manufacturer of book paper, Mount Holly Springs, Penn., was born at that place August 18, 1833, the second child of William Barbour and Eliza (Lightcap) Mullin, natives of Cumberland County. Upon leaving school he associated himself with his father, and became a partner in the business. May 1, 1869, the father died, and since 1872 the firm has been known as W. A. & A. F. Mullin. William A. has paid much attention to the breeding of fine horses and Jersey cattle. The Mullins have all been and are active business men. William A. married, in October, 1862, Miss Fannie Porter, a daughter of Capt. and Martha I. (Hall) Porter. Mrs. Mullin is a lady of rare attainments, and is both an artist and poet. They are the parents of two daughters: Helen Hall and Nora Montgomery Mullin. Mrs. Mullin is a graduate of Irving Female College.

A. F. MULLIN is a member of the firm of W. A. & A. F. Mullin, manufacturers of book and printing paper, Mount Holly Springs. The mill operated by this firm is one of the oldest in the State, the business having been established by the grandfather and granduncle of our subject. The mill was burned down in 1846, and the ground was then purchased by W. B. Mullin (subject's father) who, in 1847, erected a larger building, introducing modern machinery, and conducted the business until his death in 1869, since when it has been operated by the present firm. A. F. Mullin was born at Mount Holly Springs, this county, in the house where he now resides, September 14, 1837, son of William B. and Eliza (Lightcap) Mullin, and is third in a family of eight children—five of whom are still living. Our subject attended school at Mount Holly Springs until he was sixteen, when he entered Dickinson College, Carlisle, Penn., where he graduated in his twenty-first year. He then accepted the position of principal of the Cumberland Valley Institute (1858–60); was principal of Dickinson College grammar school from 1860 to 1862, and then went into the paper manufacturing business with his father, in which he still continues. Mr. Mullin was married, in 1869, to Martha E., daughter of John S. Sterrett, and a native of Pennsylvania, her parents having been among the pioneers of the State. Mr. and Mrs. Mullin have three children: Lillian Sterrett, Charles L. and John Sterrett. Mrs. Mullin is a member of the Presbyterian Church. In politics Mr. Mullin was formerly a Republican, but now casts his vote with the Prohibition party. He was a member of the town council, and is now of the school board. In 1876 he was a candidate for State Senator on the Republican ticket, and, though defeated, ran 1,000 ahead of his ticket. Although not an office seeker he is now (1886) a candidate for the Legislature on the Prohibition ticket.

JACOB NOFFSINGER, farmer and stock-grower, Mount Holly Springs, was born in Berks County, Penn., May 24, 1834, son of Jacob and Catherine (Stahl) Noffsinger, natives of Pennsylvania, and of German and English origin, who came to Cumberland County soon after their marriage, and settled on a farm in South Middleton Township. Their family consisted of seven children, Jacob being the third born and the only member of the family residing in Cumberland County. Our subject attended the schools in this township; chose the occupation of his father (farming), and is the owner of the farm where he now resides. He was united in marriage, in 1859, with Annie E., daughter of Thomas and Anna (Shuck) Bradley, the former of whom was of Scotch-Irish origin, the latter a native of Switzerland. Mr. and Mrs. Noffsinger are parents of two children: Emma C. and Anna E. The family are members of the Lutheran Church. Politically Mr. Noffsinger is a Republican. He is a member of the A. O. U. W., and has been through the subordinate lodge of the I. O. O. F. Mrs. Noffsinger's ancestors were Dunkards, and were prominent members of the River Brethren Church—in fact were the originators and organizers of that society.

SIMPSON OTT, farmer and stock-grower, P. O. Carlisle, was born in Southampton Township, near Shippensburg, this county, in September, 1840; son of Jacob and Susan (Barmaster) Ott, of German and English origin, and who reared a family of eleven children. Our subject, the second born, was reared on his father's farm, receiving a common school education in South Middleton Township. At the age of seventeen he commenced the blacksmith's trade, serving a regular apprenticeship of three years. He was married, in 1862, to Mary daughter of Israel Kertz and of German origin. The children born to this union are William, Carrie, Florence and James. Mr. and Mrs. Ott are members of the Evangelical Association, in which he has been Sabbath-school superintendent and is now Sabbath-school teacher. He has been a school director for years. Politically he is a Democrat. Mr. Ott has been successfully engaged in agricultural pursuits since 1862, and is owner of a farm of forty-eight acres near Carlisle, on which he now resides.

GEORGE OTTO, farmer and stock-raiser, P. O. Boiling Springs, was born at Carlisle, Cumberland Co., Penn., March 11, 1822, son of John and Susannah (Smith) Otto, natives of Pennsylvania and of German descent; former a blacksmith by trade. They reared a family of seven children. John Otto was a soldier in the war of 1812, going from Carlisle in 1813, and his son, John, was in the late war, enlisting in 1861 and serving three years. George, the second born, attended the common school in Carlisle, Penn., and at the age of ten years commenced to work on the farm, and has made agriculture the business of his life. In early life he frequently worked as a farm-hand for 40 cents per day, and also for $5 per month, but by industry and economy he has succeeded in accumulating a handsome fortune, being now the owner of 260 acres of land. He was married, November 12, 1850, to Henrietta, daughter of Adam Bitner, and of German descent. They have five children living: Alphus S., a farmer; Charles W., a farmer and school-teacher (he taught school fifteen years); Lewis C., who is teaching school; Anna Maria and George B. In politics Mr. Otto is a Democrat; has served as school director. He is a member of the society of American Mechanics, the K. of P., I. O. O. F., and is a F. & A. M.

ABRAM PHILLIPS, retired farmer, P. O. Carlisle, was born in Carlisle, Cumberland Co., Penn., son of Patrick and Catharine (Williams) Phillips, natives of Ireland. Patrick Phillips emigrated from his native country to America when he was sixteen years old, chose farming as an occupation, and in 1803 received his naturalization papers at Carlisle, where he had settled, and the house which he built in 1812 is still standing. He was a successful business man, and at the time of his death, in 1849, owned a well improved farm. Abram and his sister Martha where the only children born to their parents. Our subject was reared on the farm, acquired a common school education, and has made agriculture his principal occupation. He is owner of the 100 acres of land where he now resides. In politics our subject is a Democrat. He holds to the religion of his father (Roman Catholic), and is a good neighbor and respected citizen. Mr. Phillips and his sister are both single, and reside together on the farm.

D. S. RICE, farmer and stock-grower, P. O. Barnitz, was born in Adams County, Penn., January 5, 1836, son of Peter and Elizabeth (Plank) Rice, natives of Pennsylvania and of German origin. Our subject's paternal grandmother was born on the ocean while her parents were coming to America from Germany. His paternal grandfather was a soldier in the Revolutionary war. Peter Rice, who was a farmer by occupation, was twice married and had four children by his first wife and eight by his second (of the latter David S. is the third born). Our subject was reared on a farm in his native county, receiving a common school education. At the age of sixteen he commenced to learn the blacksmith's trade, which he followed until 1862, when he enlisted in Company F, Fifteenth Pennsylvania Cavalry, served as a non-commissioned officer, and was honorably discharged at expiration of term of service. Since the war Mr. Rice has devoted his whole time and attention to farming and stock-raising, and is owner of 96 acres of land on which he now resides. He was married, in 1865, to Mary C. daughter of Benjamin Royer, a farmer. Her parents were natives of Pennsylvania and of German origin. The children born to this union are Benjamin Elmer, Emma Eva Alma, Seth Edwin and Robert. Mrs. Rice is a member of the Lutheran Church. In politics Mr. Rice is a Republican.

DANIEL RUDY, farmer and proprietor of the Sunnyside Dairy, P. O. Carlisle, was born in Dauphin County, Penn., December 8, 1837, son of Jonas and Frances (Hoffman) Rudy, natives of Pennsylvania and of German origin, and who reared a family of nine children, of whom Daniel is the third born. Four of the sons—Joseph, Levi, Jonas and

Frederick—served in the late war of the Rebellion, and all returned home but Joseph, who died at Andersonville, after an incarceration of one year and five days, in rebel prisons. Our subject was reared on his father's farm and, with his parents, moved to South Middleton, Township in 1838. He acquired a common school education in his native county, and at the age of twenty-two, attended the State Normal School. He then commenced to teach, with the intention of following the profession, but, at the expiration of four years, his father died (in 1861), and, being appointed administrator to the estate, he came home and took charge of the farm. Mr. Rudy is owner of 103 acres of well improved land, and has operated the Sunnyside Dairy since 1878, keeping from fifteen to twenty cows. In 1871 he married Elizabeth Ernest, of German descent, daughter of Jacob and Sarah Ann (Batterman) Ernest, and their living children are William Jonas, Jacob E. and Sallie A. Mr. and Mrs. Rudy are members of the Reformed Church. He has held most of the township offices.

SAMUEL SCHELL, carpenter, P. O. Boiling Springs, was born in York County, Penn., July 9, 1830, son of Andrew and Anna Mary (Koontz) Schell, natives of Lancaster County, Penn., and of German origin (his father was a carpenter and contractor by occupation). Andrew Schell and wife had a family of ten children, and of their six sons five were carpenters and the other a farmer. Our subject, who received his education in the common school, early learned the carpenter's trade with his brother, he being the youngest son, and has made that the principal business of his life. He was married, in 1855, to Mary Magdalena, daughter of Jacob and Mary (Givler) High, who were also of German origin. Her father was a doctor. Mr. and Mrs. Schell have two children: Adella, wife of Lewis Zeigler, of Pittsburgh, Penn., and Jacob Franklin, who was born in York County, Penn., August 30, 1858. At the age of sixteen he entered the Naval Academy as cadet in the engineer corps at Annapolis, Md., and thence graduated in 1878, and was then sent to sea and sailed in the ship which conveyed Gen. Grant in his trip around the world. At present Jacob F. Schell is instructor in the engineer department of the Naval Academy, Annapolis, Md. Mr. Schell and wife are members of the United Brethren Church. Politically he is a Democrat.

WILLIAM SENSEMAN, miller and dealer in coal, Boiling Springs, was born in Cumberland County, Penn., September 20, 1837, son of Samuel and Elizabeth (Haines) Senseman, natives of Lancaster County, Penn., of German origin. Samuel Senseman, a carpenter in early life but in later years a farmer, came to this county at an early date, and settled in Silver Spring Township. William Senseman, the ninth born in a family of ten children, lived on the farm and acquired a common school education, and has had to paddle his own canoe since he was fourteen years of age. When he reached his majority he went to Illinois, where he remained three years; then, in 1863, returned to this county. He was married, in 1865, to Hattie, daughter of Benjamin Shuh, and of German origin. In 1878 Mr. Senseman embarked in milling, which he continued for two years. From 1880 to 1884 he dealt in horses in company with A. R. May. In 1884 he again leased the mill at Boiling Springs, and has since conducted his present business. Mrs. Senseman is a member of the Lutheran Church. Our subject and wife have reared two orphans, giving them good educational advantages: John Cunningham, unmarried, and residing at Tecumseh, Neb., and Sadie Dean, now wife of Charles Rider.

ABRAHAM STRICKLER, farmer and stock-grower, P. O. Carlisle, was born in Middlesex Township, Cumberland Co., Penn., July 15, 1834, son of Ulrick and Catharine (Hatzler) Strickler, of German origin, natives of Lancaster County, Penn., and Cumberland County, Penn., respectively. Our subject, the eldest of two children born to his parents, lost his mother when he was but four years of age, and his father, who never remarried, carried on the farm and kept house with hired help for eighteen years; he was a successful farmer and business man, and succeeded in accumulating a goodly share of this world's goods, and gave his children a good start in life. He died in 1871. Our subject, who was reared on the farm, receiving his education in the district school, has made farming his principal business, and has met with marked success, being the owner of a well improved farm of 200 acres. Abraham Strickler was married, in 1867, to Barbara Herr, of German origin, and a daughter of Christian Herr, who was a farmer and Mennonite clergyman. The children born to this union, living, are Jacob E., Mary and Emma (twins) and Barbara. Mrs. Strickler is a member of the Mennonite Church. Mr. Strickler is a Republican in politics. He takes an active interest in educational matters, and has served for ten years as school director, and has been treasurer of the board.

R. M. STUART, farmer and stock grower, P. O. Mount Holly Springs, was born in South Middleton Township, Cumberland Co., Penn., October 19, 1849, son of John and Jemima (McCune) Stuart, natives of Carlisle and Shippensburg, Penn., respectively. John Stuart, a farmer by occupation, was twice married, and has five children now living. Our subject's grandfather, John Stuart, and his uncle, Hugh Stuart, were associate judges of this county. R. M. Stuart, the eldest child by his father's second marriage, was reared on the farm, receiving his education in the common schools and at the academy in Philadelphia, Penn., where he graduated in 1869. He was married, in 1870, to Jennie H., daughter of William McCune, of Scotch-Irish origin, who was accidently killed by the cars in 1878. To Mr. and Mrs. Stuart have been born the following named children: Mary

Louisa, Mima Rosalie, John William, Robert Bruce, James Brady and Frank Hays. The parents are members of the Presbyterian Church at Carlisle. Mr. Stuart is a Democrat in politics; for four years was school director in the district where he now resides. He is owner of a well improved farm of 140 acres.

SAMUEL B. SWIGERT, superintendent of machinery and paper-maker in Mount Holly Paper Mills, Mount Holly Springs, was born in Cumberland County, Penn., February 23, 1839, son of Joseph and Elizabeth (Sours) Swigert, natives of Pennsylvania, the former a butcher by occupation, born in Lancaster, and the latter in Cumberland County, of German origin. They reared a family of nine children, Samuel B. being the second. Our subject was reared in South Middleton Township, this county; was educated at the common school, and, after working at his trade six years, engaged with the Mount Holly Paper Company, with whom he has since continued. He is an energetic man, the owner of a neat, substantial residence in Mount Holly, where he resides. Our subject was married, in 1860, to Anna C., daughter of Joseph Decker, and by her he has six children: Minnie, Clara, Reed, Annie, Samuel and Benjamin F. Mr. Swigert is a Democrat in politics, and has served as school director and as member of the town council. He is a prominent member in Grand Lodge of the K. of P. at Mount Holly.

J. H. SWILER, merchant, proprietor of general store in Hickorytown, P. O. Carlisle, was born in Silver Spring Township, this county, July 22, 1835, son of John and Isabella (Eckels) Swiler, natives of Pennsylvania, of English origin, and who were the parents of three sons. In early life John Swiler was a teacher, in later years he was a farmer; he died in 1839. Isabella (Eckels) Swiler died May 20, 1858, aged forty-seven years and twenty-eight days. Our subject, the second child, was reared on the farm, received his education in the common schools, and worked on the farm until he was seventeen years old, when he entered a store at West Fairview, this county, and clerked for one year, for George W. Fessler. He then went to York County, Penn., and was there employed as a clerk, in all, about five years. In 1859-60 he clerked for Joshua Culp and J. J. Coble, in Hogestown, Cumberland Co., Penn. In 1861 Mr. Swiler established his present industry, and by strict attention to business and honest dealing with his customers has succeeded well. He keeps a much larger stock than is usually carried in country stores. He was married, January 9, 1861, to Martha E., daughter of George Beistline, and of English origin. Their children are Sadie I., wife of Christian Bricker, and Maggie Florence. Politically Mr. Swiler is a Democrat. He has been school director for nine years. He is a member of Silver Spring Lodge, No. 598, I. O. O. F.

GEORGE TANGER, farmer and stock-grower, P. O. Hatton, was born in Lancaster County, Penn., October 30, 1824, son of John and Ann (Cochnouer) Tanger, natives of that county and of German lineage, both born in the year 1803, former of whom died in 1830 and latter in 1876. His father, who was a weaver by trade, died in 1830. Our subject, the eldest of three children, acquired his education in his native county, where he resided until he was sixteen years of age, then came to this county and worked on a farm for 40 cents per day, and in this way got a start in life; he is now the owner of 502 acres of land, on a part of which he resides. He was married, in 1851, to Magdalena, daughter of Christian Herr, and of German origin. To George Tanger and wife have been born twelve children, eleven still living: Barbara, wife of Daniel B. Hoerner; Mary and Anna (twins), were married the same day, Mary to William H. Kenkel, and Anna to Jacob C. Baker; Jacob (deceased); John, a farmer, married to Mary C. Carman; Susan, wife of Jacob M. Keller; Martha, wife of John W. Miller; George, at home; Christian, married to Clara K. Gleim; Emma M., Abraham and Harry. Mr. Tanger is a member of the Church of God; was formerly a Republican in politics, but is now a Prohibitionist.

B. F. THOMAS, farmer and veterinary surgeon, P. O. Mount Holly Springs, was born in Adams County, Penn., June 30, 1832, son of Conrad (a millwright and carpenter) and Mary (Irvin) Thomas; the former of whom, born June 14, 1800, lived to be seventy-five years old; the latter, born June 7, 1804, is still living; they were natives of Pennsylvania and of English and German origin. Our subject, the fourth in a family of eight children, received his education in the district schools of his native county, and at twenty was apprenticed to the blacksmith's trade, which has since been his principal occupation. He came to this county in 1865, settled in South Middleton Township, and successfully followed his trade until 1884. He is owner of the farm where he now resides, and is at present following agricultural pursuits. B. F. Thomas was married, in 1854, to Margaret, daughter of Ferdinand and Eve (Weigle) Meals, natives of Adams County, Penn., and of German origin. The living children of Mr. and Mrs. Thomas are William H., a blacksmith here; Mary E., wife of W. H. Keeny; George B McClelland, Harvey Edgar and Harry Meals. Mr. and Mrs. Thomas are members of the Lutheran Church. Our subject, a Democrat politically, has been township auditor. He is a member of the I. O. O. F.

JAMES B. WEAKLEY (deceased) was born November 16, 1819, in South Middleton Township, this county, on the farm where he died, and which has been in the possession of the family since 1710. His father Nathaniel Weakley, and his grandfather, James Weakley, were both farmers. Our subject, the second born in a family of five children, made farming the business of his life, and met with marked success. He was married, in 1854, to Martha Eliza Bell, a native of Adams County, Penn., of Scotch-Irish origin, and who died in 1881, leaving an only child, Martha J. (now the wife of Thomas M. Craighead), who was born and reared in this township. Mr. and Mrs. Craighead have one child, James Bell Weakley Craighead, who was his grandfather's pet. Mr. Craighead's ancestors were among the early settlers of Pennsylvania and prominent people. Mr. and Mrs. Craighead are members of the Presbyterian Church. Mr. Weakley died February 28, 1886, a member of the Presbyterian Church, in which he took an active interest, and of which, at the time of his death, he was trustee.

THOMAS WOLF, boss in the finishing department of the Mount Holly Paper Manufacturing Company, Mount Holly Springs, was born in Mount Holly January 3, 1848, son of George and Nancy (Wolf) Wolf. George Wolf was born in Germany, and there married his first wife; his second wife (our subject's mother) was born in Cumberland County, Penn., and was of English origin. George Wolf was a millwright by trade, and, after coming to America, worked considerably at his trade in Cumberland County, and also for the Mount Holly Paper Company. Our subject, the eldest of a family of three children, received his education in his native place, and in early life commenced work in the finishing department in the Mount Holly Paper Mills, and, with the exception of two years that he spent in Massachusetts, engaged in same kind of work, he has since been constantly employed there, and now has full charge of the finishing room. Thomas Wolf was married, in 1869 to Annie M., daughter of Isaac and Susan (Sheffler) Fleming, and of English descent. The children born to this union are Grace A., Mary and George R. Mrs. Wolf is a member of the Methodist Episcopal Church. Politically Mr. Wolf is a Democrat. He is a member of Mount Holly Lodge, No. 650, I. O. O. F., and a member of Holly Gap Lodge, No. 277, K. of P.

CHAPTER LIX.

UPPER ALLEN TOWNSHIP.

JOSEPH R. BALSLEY, farmer, P. O. Mechanicsburg, a native of this county, is a son of George Balsley, who was born in Harrisburg, Penn., in 1806, and came to this county in 1812. The father of George Balsley died when the children were quite young, so he was early forced to earn his own living. As he grew older he worked on a farm for two brothers named Long, taking his wages out in flour, which he carried to his mother, who kept a little bakery in Harrisburg, thus enabling her to maintain herself and children. Her maiden name was Elizabeth Atick. From this period in his life George Balsley gradually accumulated and stored his earnings until his first purchase of land, in about 1843. He learned the trade of coach and wagon-making with George Drawbaugh, in Frankford Township, this county, and after his apprenticeship was ended established a manufactory of his own at Milltown, Lower Allen Township, later, he purchased land on Cedar Springs Run, near Milltown, erecting a large manufactory, and had an extensive trade. George Balsley married Miss Margaret Ressler, and reared a family of three children: Catharine, Marian and Joseph (Elizabeth died in infancy). Catharine became the wife of John Hickernell, of this county; Marian is the wife of William Westhafer; Joseph enlisted in Company D, Twentieth Pennsylvania Cavalry, June 23, 1863, and, although not participating in any of the great battles, was in a division that guarded outposts, acted as scouts, and did other duties equally arduous, as will be seen by the records of the Virginia campaign. After his term had expired, Mr. Balsley returned to Cumberland County. In 1866 he was married to Miss Mary M., daughter of John and Anna (Stambaugh) Gleim. Her parents, for sixty years prior to her marriage, have been residents of this county, and reared a large family of children, nine of whom still survive. Mr. and Mrs. Balsley have resided on the farm which has been under his management for seventeen years. He is a large shipper of stock, and has done extremely well, being a careful buyer of cattle, sheep and hogs. Of the children of Joseph R. Balsley and wife, Annie, the eldest daughter, was born at the Balsley homestead, now the Hartzler property, August 22, 1867; was married December 19, 1884, to W. Harlacher, a York County gentleman, well known as a commercial salesman; Maggie was born in 1868, and died in 1871; Lillie was born in 1871; Ella was born in 1873, and Edna was born in 1880. Mr. Balsley is a self-made man, generous, public spirited, and foremost in all that advances the business and social prosperity of the of the public.

CHARLES BARNES, manufacturer, P. O. Mechanicsburg, is the son of Philip and Eliza (Thompson) Barnes, of York County, Penn., descendants of the first settlers of that

UPPER ALLEN TOWNSHIP.

county. Enoch Thompson, grandfather of our subject, served as a soldier in the war of 1812; the company of which he was a member, after enlistment, marched from York to Baltimore. He served during the entire war, and was a pensioner in the latter years of his life; his wife, Catharine, was the mother of a large family, and died at an advanced age. William Barnes, the paternal grandfather of Charles, was married to Mary Whitcome, of York County, and also had a large family, of whom Philip, the youngest, by trade a tanner, was the father of our subject. Philip and Eliza Barnes had ten children: Alexander, Catharine, Albert, Elizabeth, William, Amanda, Charles, Jennie, Margaret and Frank. Of these, Alexander was the first man to enlist from Warrington Township, serving until the war closed; Albert, who also enlisted early in the campaign, was killed by guerrillas while skirmishing in Virginia; William also served until the war closed. Charles Barnes, our subject, was born February 20, 1850, in York County, Penn., and was apprenticed to learn the whip trade. He served his apprenticeship, and continued ten years longer with the firm of A. & J. E. Wells. July 31, 1870, our subject was married to Miss Mary E. Burns, daughter of William and Evaline Burns, of Warrington Township, York Co., Penn., and to this union were born two children: Clara M. and Harry. Three years after marriage Mr. Barnes came to Mechanicsburg and established a small business, manufacturing whips on a $25 capital. He hired one man, and when a small lot of whips was finished, peddled them through the country. During his first year he used only 250 sides of leather, now he averages 2,000 per annum. The goods manufactured are solid leather whips, and his is the only industry of the kind in the State. He has been very successful, and now owns an attractive residence, besides his manufactory, which is run by steam, and furnishes employment for twelve hands.

JACOB BOWMAN, farmer, P. O. Bowmansdale, was born in Lancaster County, Penn., in 1814. His widowed mother, Margaret (Barkey) Bowman, came to Cumberland County the following year; she subsequently married Dr. Jacob Bowman, of Lancaster County, and after his death came to Mechanicsburg, and afterward married John Karns, by whom she had eight children. Our subject learned the blacksmith's trade with David Sponsler, Sr., completing same in 1820. In 1842 Jacob Bowman was elected captain of Mechanicsburg Volunteer Infantry. Another company was formed in 1849, known as the "Quitman Guards," which was attached to the First Battalion, Cumberland County Volunteer Infantry. The captain received a major's commission, bearing the signature of William F. Johnston, governor of Pennsylvania. The next official recognition received by Maj. Bowman was his election as sheriff of Cumberland County. His commission bears date October 31, 1855, and the autograph of Gov. James Pollock. After serving his term faithfully and well, Sheriff Bowman was again elected to a military position as captain of the "National Blues," a volunteer company formed at Mechanicsburg April 17, 1859. He was the best drill master in this region, as is attested by his numerous commissions. No braver, better, or more patriotic man ever graced the soil of Cumberland County. For seven years Jacob Bowman was one of the directors of the Harrisburg & Potomac Railroad. He has built a fine warehouse, and has done much to further the interests of the village of Bowmansdale by liberal subscriptions of money and donation of valuable time. As a public-spirited citizen, ex-Sheriff Bowman has few equals and no superiors in this county. He was married, in 1842, to Elizabeth, daughter of Jacob and Nancy (Haymaher) Reeser, and to this union were born nine children: Alfred, Annie, Elizabeth, Sarah, Laura, Alice, Clara, William P. and Raymond. Mr. Bowman is the second oldest ex-sheriff living in the county, and is highly revered and universally beloved by her people.

DAVID BOWMAN, farmer, P. O. Mechanicsburg, is a son of Daniel and Mary (Smith) Bowman, who were long residents of Pennsylvania; Daniel being born in Lancaster County, and his wife in Germany, from which country she came with her father and step-mother at an early day. After their marriage Daniel Bowman and his wife settled near Lancaster, in Lancaster County, Penn., but ten years later moved to Cumberland County, and settled four miles southeast of Carlisle, and here two daughters, Ann and Mary, were born (Benjamin, David and Abraham were born in Lancaster County). The family subsequently moved to York County, just across the line, and there the parents lived and died, leaving a large family, of whom Mrs. Annie Weaver, Mrs. Mary Mohler, Mrs. Lydia Smith, Daniel and David are yet residents of the county. David Bowman married, September 19, 1865, Miss Rebecca Miller, who was born in this township, on the farm now owned by Israel Miller. Her parents, Peter and Catharine (Weltmer) Miller, came to the county in 1832. They had seven children: Elizabeth, Susan, Daniel, Mary, Peter, Rebecca and Israel (by a former marriage with Elizabeth Weltmer, Peter Miller had three children: John, Catharine and Abraham). Our subject enlisted in Company K, Ninth Regiment Iowa Volunteer Infantry, September 2, 1861; participated in twenty-three engagements, among which were the battles of Lookout Mountain, Missionary Ridge, Jackson, Atlanta and Raleigh. In these battles he never received a scratch, and, for meritorious conduct, was promoted from the ranks to first lieutenant of the company in January, 1863, and served faithfully until mustered out July 18, 1865. Mr. and Mrs. Bowman's only child, Frank, was born October 11, 1866, and will complete his education soon, and then probably follow in the footsteps of his father as an agriculturist. In 1871 Mr. Bowman purchased his farm of fifty-three acres in this township.

BIOGRAPHICAL SKETCHES:

HENRY M. COCKLIN, retired, P. O. Bowmansdale. In 1772 Jacob Cocklin came to Cumberland County, Penn., and purchased the Spring Dale farm. Previous to his settlement here, however, he had been a resident of Lancaster County, Penn., going there from Germany in 1733. He had two sons (Jacob and David) and two daughters. Jacob Cocklin, Jr., was the father of Michael, Jacob, David, Catharine, Margaret, Mary and Christiana (his wife was Margaret Hoover, of Lancaster County, Penn.). Michael, the eldest son of Jacob, Jr., and Margaret (Hoover) Cocklin, rose to great prominence in the history of this county, by reason of his erudition and merit. Reared on a farm, with but the limited facilities for obtaining an education in the district schools, it is indeed remarkable that this man should become so noted and gain such a reputation among the people of his county and State for his wisdom, honor and public spirit. He was not married until his thirty-third year, engaging in farming until that event. His marriage with Elizabeth Hopple was celebrated in 1828, and their housekeeping was commenced on the Spring Dale farm, which he then owned. Five children were born on the homestead which had been so long in the possession of their ancestors, viz.: George, Mary, Henry M., Andrew J. and Sarah E. In 1832 Michael Cocklin was elected a member of the General Assembly, and in 1834 was re-elected. Having long noted the inefficiency of the school system then in vogue, he, with other members of the Assembly, promulgated a plan which was carried into successful operation, and the creation of a free school system was the result. After his second official term had expired he resumed farm life. Twenty-two years later, and much against his desire, the people of Cumberland County nominated and elected him associate judge (in 1856), which position he so satisfactorily filled that he was again elected in 1861, and served another term of five years with equal honor to himself and his constituents. The position was again tendered him, but was firmly refused, as his business affairs demanded his entire attention. Retiring from the bench at the age of seventy-one years with an unimpeachable record, Judge Cocklin found the old home farm a haven of refuge and rest from the cares and annoyances of public life. He was always an indefatigable worker, and was administrator of many valuable estates. The management of the farm was given to his son Henry at the time he was elected judge, and this continued until 1884. In 1879 the death of Judge Michael Cocklin occurred, and his remains were interred with due solemnity in the cemetery near the Union Church. His aged widow still resides on the old homestead with her daughter, Mrs. Sarah E. Crist. Henry M. Cocklin, our subject, was married, in 1857, to Elizabeth, daughter of George and Elizabeth (Linebach) Himes. To this union were born six children: George M., Clara A., Mary J., Emma E., Andrew R. and William H. Mrs. Cocklin died in 1869, and in 1870 Mr. Cocklin was married to Mrs. Caroline F. (Gardiner) Cocklin, widow of Andrew J. Cocklin, by whom she had three children: Adda L., Michael G. and Lura M. By Mr. Cocklin's second marriage he has one child—Nevin Harbaugh. All the children reside in this county; the three children by Mrs. Cocklin's first marriage residing in a home by themselves at Mechanicsburg. Our subject has been an active agriculturist for many years, and is one of the originators and charter members of the Grange movement in this county. Naturally of a retiring disposition he has persistently refused the official honors which have been frequently offered him, and only by great persuasion was he induced to become a trustee of the theological seminary of the Reformed Church located at Lancaster.

JACOB C. COCKLIN, farmer, Shepherdstown, is one of the few persons in this township who have in their possession the original title deeds bearing the signature of John, Thomas and William Penn. In the document in Mr. Cocklin's possession, it is stated that the transfer of 249 acres was first made to Andrew Miller for the sum of £38 12s. This transfer was made January 14, 1742. The property first came into the possession of John Cocklin in 1763. At the death of John Cocklin the farm was willed to Deterich Cocklin, his son, who married Catharine Coover, and had five children, of whom Samuel, Maria and Jacob C. are now living. There were only a few acres cleared of the original tract purchased from William Penn, and where the cemetery is now located two children were buried. All the forests have since been cleared away, and the beautiful farm in the valley was made so by the hard toil of generations of Cocklins now passed away. Jacob C., the youngest son of Deterich and Catharine (Coover) Cocklin, has always been a farmer, and resided with his parents until their death; the father died in 1846 and the mother in 1861, both living long enough to reap the reward of their early labors, and died full of years and good deeds. Jacob C. Cocklin was married, May 31, 1846, to Elizabeth, daughter of David and Elizabeth (Keller) Nisewanger. They commenced housekeeping on the farm so long in the possession of the Cocklins, and have, from their earliest married life, been both prosperous and contented. They are the parents of five children, of whom Kate, John, Edward and Lizzie are living. John is married to Agnes Trimble. Edward married Hettie Myers, and Lizzie is the wife of John Zeamer. The old home is one of the most cheerful in the valley, and the family rank among the best and most highly respected in the land. Mr. Cocklin has always been noted for his enterprise, and his children may feel pardonable pride in not only his good record but also that of past generations of Cocklins.

JACOB H. COOVER, retired farmer, Shepherdstown. For more than a century the name of Coover has been familiar in this county. The great-great-grandfather came from

UPPER ALLEN TOWNSHIP.

Coburg, Germany, with four sons: Dederich, Gideon, George and Michael. They were a long-lived race, and all reared large families. Michael Coover was a member of the first State Legislature, serving two terms. Dederich was the grandfather, and his son Dederich, the father of Jacob H. Coover, the subject of this sketch. Dederich Coover, Jr., was born on the farm of his father, who, at that time, owned a section of land which included the greater part of what is now the site of Shepherdstown, but which was then a wild waste of land, for the pioneer's ax had made but few inroads in the great forests, and only log houses were to be seen, few and far between. Dederich Coover, Jr., married Catharine Cocklin, who bore him seven children: John B., David, Jacob H., William, Levi, Frances and Catharine. Our subject's paternal grandparents' family consisted of seven sons and three daughters, all of whom were born in this township, and which, up to date (1885) has been the birthplace of five generations of Coovers. The name was originally spelled Kobar, but later was written and used by the descendants "Coover." Dederich Coover, Jr., was a prominent personage in the county at an early date, being not only a large farmer and land-owner, but also a distiller. He operated a still where Ira D. Coover now lives, nearly a century ago, and, later, one where his son William now resides; a part of the latter building is still standing. He was an active man, both in business and politics; was an old-line Whig of the strictest type, and during the career of that party filled a number of offices in the township. Conscientious in all things, strictly honest and a God-fearing man, he possessed great popularity among the people. Jacob H. Coover, our subject, was born within one mile of where he is now living, February 3, 1808; early attended school, and acquired an excellent education. His first schooling was obtained on the Ira Coover farm, in a house furnished for school purposes by his father. He taught school seven years prior to his marriage, and several terms afterward. March 1, 1836, our subject married Rachael, daughter of Jacob and Elizabeth Strock, of Churchtown, and commenced housekeeping on the farm which he had previously purchased, and which is still in his possession, and there resided until within the past four years. Here were born Emma, Elmira E., Catharine, Mary, Clara and John A. Jacob H. Coover has been one of the foremost citizens in furthering the business and social interests of the community. For more than forty years he has been one of the directors, and for the past two years vice-president of the Allen & East Pennsborough Fire Insurance Company. (Of the original officers, only one other—William R. Gorgas—is now living.) He has settled numerous estates, and has always been noted for his integrity and fairness. To his children he will leave an unsullied reputation and a name ranking among the oldest in the county.

WILLIAM COOVER, farmer, P. O. Shepherdstown, was born, in 1818, on the Coover homestead, in this county, and is the fourth son of Deitrich and Catharine (Cocklin) Coover. Dederich Coover, the grandfather of our subject, was born in Lancaster County, Penn., August 20, 1745; was a blacksmith by trade; and in 1772 engaged in business in Upper Allen Township, and for many years did a large credit business, as is attested to by the ledger in possession of William Coover. The first entries in this book were made in May, 1772. All the accounts were closed and the book balanced in 1791, at which time he was expecting to reap a large reward for his labors, but, unfortunately, he received his pay in Continental money, which was carefully treasured up until it became worthless, and his prospects for a competence were rudely swept away. Dederich Coover's first marriage, June 2, 1768, was with Maria Hauk, and his second union, February 12, 1822, was with Salome Horning, who lived almost a century. At the time of the Whisky Insurrection in Pennsylvania, Deitrich (William's father) was working at the forge in Harrisburg, and Gen. Washington, who, with a detachment of cavalry, was passing, stopped to have some horses shod.

SAMUEL R. COOVER, postmaster, Shepherdstown. There are numerous men in this township bearing the name of Coover, but the branch of the family to which our subject belongs is composed of himself and his brother George. Of the remote ancestry of our subject but little is known. His father, George Coover, was born in Cumberland County, Penn., in 1808, and while yet a young man learned the trade of furniture-making, carrying on a manufactory in New Kingston for a long while. His success in business warranted him in taking a wife, and, about 1831, he was married to Catharine Reeser, a representative of one of the old families in this county. They commenced housekeeping in New Kingston, and reared five children: Sarah, Mary, Elmira, George and Samuel R., all of whom now live in this county. In 1859 the subject of this sketch was apprenticed to John Brownwell, at Roxbury, to learn the trade of shoe-making, which he completed. In 1863 he enlisted in Company D, Twentieth Pennsylvania Cavalry, serving until the expiration of his term; then enlisted for 100 days in Company I, One Hundred and Ninety-fifth Pennsylvania Infantry; re-enlisting for one year, at the expiration of the 100-days' service, in Company B, One Hundred and Ninety-fifth Independent Battalion, Pennsylvania Volunteer Infantry, in which he served until the close of the war. He was engaged in numerous skirmishes, but never wounded; most of his service was in the Virginia campaign. His brother George was also a soldier, and served during most of the war. After our subject returned home he worked for several years at his trade. In 1867 he was married to Mary E., daughter of David and Mary (Zering) Worst, old residents of the county. Soon after his marriage Mr. Coover commenced business for himself in Shepherdstown, and is now conducting the only shoe store in the village, which might be properly termed the pioneer store. To Mr. and Mrs. Coover were born five children, of whom three are deceased, and two living: Samuel R., Jr., and Emma M. Mr. Coover has always been a conservative man politically, but is a conscientious Republican, always voting with that party. By reason of his well-known ability as a business man, he was commissioned postmaster at Shepherdstown in 1870, and has filled that position for fifteen consecutive years. This office, notwithstanding the change in governmental policy, remains in his undisturbed possession, which well bespeaks the confidence of his political opponents in his ability and fitness for the position. He is a member of Post No. 415, G. A. R.; is a member of the United Brethren Church.

SAMUEL CRIST, farmer, P. O., Shepherdstown. The voluminous family history of the talented Judge Michael Cocklin will be found elsewhere in the series of biographical sketches, and to avoid repetition mention is not here made of it in this connection, except in so far as it may relate to his daughter Sarah E., the wife of the gentleman whose name heads this sketch. Samuel Crist was born in Holtswamp, Adams Co., Penn., May 5, 1825. His parents, John and Eve (Strayer) Crist, were natives of that county, the mother being born near Dover. The father was for many years a mason, and numerous houses and barns in Adams County yet remain as monuments of his skill. The children of John and Eve Crist were ten in number: Andrew, Elizabeth, Sarah, Henry, Leigh, Lydia, Samuel, Catharine, Susan and John. Our subject learned the trades of mason and plasterer of his father, with whom he worked until 1855. In 1851 he was married to Henrietta C., daughter of Dr. Joseph Bauman, of Ephratah, Lancaster Co., Penn., who for many years was both clerk and physician at the Pine Grove Smelting Works, being well known in Lancaster and Cumberland Counties. By this marriage Mr. Crist was father of five children, all now deceased: Elmira L., Annie M., Joseph M., Samuel and Clarence May. The death of Mrs. Crist occurred March 25, 1863. In 1866 Mr. Crist came to Mechanicsburg, and for one year engaged in the retail grocery trade. February 17, 1867, our subject married Sarah E. Cocklin, the cermony being performed by the Rev. John Ault, at the Reformed Church in Mechanicsburg. Soon after their marriage, Mr. and Mrs. Crist went to the home farm of Judge Cocklin in this township, and here Mr. Crist was duly installed as a farmer. Judge Cocklin and his wife were living a retired life on the Spring Dale farm, and the paternal roof since then has given them shelter. There the children, Andrew M., Caroline E., Henry D. and Ida M. were born. Mr. Crist has for forty years been an active member of the Reformed Church, serving it in various official capacities. He was also engaged in teaching for eighteen consecutive years, and has for six years served on the school board, and at different dates has served as assistant assessor in his township. October 16, 1862, Mr. Crist was drafted and served for nine months in Company I, One Hundred and Sixty-sixth Pennsylvania Militia, doing duty at Suffolk, Va., and though he engaged in numerous skirmishes escaped the dangers of the most memorable battles of the war. Our subject is one of the pioneer Grangers in this county, and is now a member of Monroe Grange, No. 362.

HENRY FORRY, farmer, P. O. Mechanicsburg, was born in York County, Penn., in 1823, and has been engaged in agricultural pursuits since a mere lad. His parents, Ulrich and Susannah (Low) Forry, of German origin, reared a family of three children: Maria, Elizabeth and Henry. Henry Forry came to Cumberland County in 1871, and, having lived near the line for twenty-six years, is as well acquainted with the people as a native. He married, in 1844, Miss Matilda Shearer, of York County, and by her has three children living: George, Henry and Susannah, all of whom were born in York County, and are now married and doing well. Susannah is the wife of Samuel Burkheimer, and resides on the old homestead, near her parents. Henry owns a farm in York County, Penn., and George follows agriculture near Mechanicsburg. Mr. Forry purchased his present farm in 1870, and has added largely to its improvements as well as to the original tract, and now owns 100 acres of the finest land in the Cumberland Valley, which cost him $280 per acre. Mr. and Mrs. Forry live quite a retired life, renting the farm to Mr. Burkheimer, the income maintaining them in elegant style, and their last days are pleasantly spent. They are both members of the Mennonite Church, and have hosts of friends who well know their worth.

JAMES FULTON, mechanic, P. O. Mechanicsburg, was born in Dillsburg, York Co., Penn., in 1832. His parents, Alexander and Mary (Deardorf) Fulton, reared a family of nine children: John, Mary A., Jane, Thomas, William, Catharine, David, James and Calvin. Of these Thomas was a Methodist minister, stationed at Sinnamahoning, Clinton Co., Penn., and while in that wild and unimproved country induced his brother David A., who was a carpenter, to join him, as there was great need of mechanics to erect homes for the pioneers then rapidly settling in the neighborhood. James, who was then fifteen, accompanied his brother, with whom he learned the carpenter's trade. Fully one-half the distance traveled was on foot, through a country without roads and very mountainous. Little thought the lad that the uninviting forest to him, at that time, would be his home for many years, but though his labors at first brought him but a small income yet he became satisfied with the wild life led in that rapidly improving country, and almost before he realized it had attained his majority and found himself the husband of a young wife, Margaret, daughter of Henry and Jane (Mason) Shaffer, one of the most prominent pioneer families in that region. Her grandfather, James Shaffer, a Revolutionary soldier, died at the ripe age of eighty years. Two years later James Fulton and his brother purchased a tract of land and erected a hotel at Wykoff's Eddy, then a great lumber center where all the supplies were brought in by boats from Lock Haven, 50 miles distant. He was proprietor of this hotel for ten years, during which time the P. & D. Railroad was completed. Selling his hotel property Mr. Fulton again commenced his trade, continuing same until 1883, when he came to Mechanicsburg and purchased a half interest in Miller & King's planing mill. In October of the following year he disposed of his interest in the mill. Mr. Fulton and wife have seven children: Mary J., Eliza A., William A., Nancy E., Kate, John H. and Alice, the last two mentioned being deceased. Our subject, a self-made man, acquired his money by honest toil and good business management. He commenced working at his trade for $4 per month, increased the second year to $6, and the third to $18 per month. He has accumulated a considerable fortune and is a liberal, enterprising man. His pleasant home is situated near the borough limits, convenient to business, on a site overlooking the mountain range and the beautiful borough of Mechanicsburg.

ABRAM E. GARRETT, stock dealer, P. O. Mechanicsburg. On what was formerly known as the old Bullinger farm, but which has been in the possession of the Garrett family for sixty-five years, resides Abram E. Garrett, one of the most widely known men of the township. He was born on this farm in 1842. His grandfather, John Garrett, came with his family from Lancaster County, Penn., in 1820, and purchased quite a large tract of land. At his death the estate was divided among his children: Frederick, Jacob, John, Andrew, Ann and Susan, of whom Andrew and Ann are now living. Frederick Garrett, the father of our subject, inherited the homestead, and subsequently married Harriet, daughter of Abraham and Susan Lobaugh, of Adams County, Penn. They commenced housekeeping on the Reeser farm, but a few years later moved on the farm where a son now resides, and which was noted in an early day for its immense cherry orchard. The neighbors from adjoining villages and the city of Harrisburg came by scores to secure the luscious fruit. (This was before the farm came into the possession of the Garretts.) Frederick Garrett and his wife were the parents of eleven children: Anna, Catharine, William, Susan, Elizabeth, Harry, Abram E., Amos, Lucy, Margaret and Emma, of whom Abram E. and Lucy are the only ones living in the county. The death of Frederick Garrett occurred in 1873, and that of his widow in 1882. Our subject received a practical education in the schools of his district, and has been quite a noted man in the township and county since the commencement of his business life. At the age of nineteen years, August 23, 1861, he enlisted in Company I, Eleventh Pennsylvania Cavalry, and served three years, mostly in the Army of the Potomac. He was engaged in some of the most memorable battles of the war, beginning with the Seven Days' fight, in which the Union Army was driven back from Richmond to the James River; the battle of Kelly's farm in which 104 men of his regiment were killed or wounded in a four hours' skirmish; the Blackwater River, Petersburg, Malvern Hill and Reame Station, where nearly half the men were lost. Where the bullets were thickest there was found this brave soldier, who seemed to bear a charmed life. Once only did he feel a bullet, which just grazed his throat as he was taking the saddle from a horse killed by a shot aimed at his rider. He was honorably discharged August 23, 1864. In December, 1866, Mr. Garrett was married to Mary J. Karns, a daughter of Henry and Sarah Karns, of this county, and who was born and reared at Roxbury, her family being one of the old and prominent ones in that part of the county; her father served as county commissioner and in other official positions, and was a prominent local politician. Mr. and Mrs. Abram E. Garrett were parents of seven children, six now living: Harry G., C. Frederick, Iola E., Andrew K., Ruth L. and Eli M. The business life of our subject has been confined to farming and stock dealing, and for years he has been one of the principal shippers at this point. His political influence in the township has been felt for years, and many who have filled official positions owe their election to his able management. He has, since his return from the army, been connected with the affairs of his township in an official capacity, and no man has served with greater zeal. For twelve years he has been secretary of the school board, and has been a director in the schools for almost twenty years. He is a prosperous business man, a kind father and generous provider for his family, and one of the most popular men in the township.

JAMES GRAHAM, farmer, Mechanicsburg. In presenting the name of this gentleman it can be pointed with pride to his long line of ancestry who have been for so many years identified with the business interests of the county and township, whose titles to lands bear the signature of William Penn, and have never changed ownership, save as they have descended from father to son, and from uncle to nephew. His great-great-grandfather, James Graham, settled on the farm now owned by our subject in 1685, having emigrated from Ireland. James Graham, the grandfather of our subject, was the eldest son, and married Miss Lytle, of Lancaster County, Penn., who bore him five children, and of whom John, the father of our subject, was the second son. John Graham was married, in 1811, to Miss Helen Taylor, of Halifax, Dauphin Co., Penn., and two sons and four daughters blessed their union, but all left home in the course of time except James Graham, Jr., who was presented by his uncle, James Graham, Sr., with the farm on which he has lived for so many years. He (James Graham, Jr.) was born June 25, 1823; was married, in the autumn of 1849, to Miss Louisa S. Sidier, of Bedford County, Penn., and has three daughters living: Ella, married to Martin L. Granville; Louisa married to A. B. Clarks, of the United States Navy, and Burdetta; three daughters are deceased. Mr. Graham has served as assessor, and has acceptably filled other township offices. He and his wife have always been ardent members of the Presbyterian Church. They are hale and hearty, and expect to enjoy many years of happiness.

HENRY HERTZLER, farmer, P. O. Shepherdstown. In 1850 Rudolph and Mary (Shupp) Hertzler came from Lancaster County, Penn., and settled one mile north of Givler's mill, in Monroe Township, this county. They had five children: Henry, Mary and Elizabeth (twins), Esther and Levi. Rudolph Hertzler died September 4, 1855, and in 1861 his widow married Jacob Mumma. Our subject spent his boyhood days on a farm, and when twenty-one years of age began clerking in a grocery store in Indianapolis, Ind., where he had gone on a pleasure trip. When he returned to Cumberland County he accepted a position with J. A. Kauffman, in Mechanicsburg, continuing in that position until his marriage, January 7, 1873, with Naomi J., daughter of Jacob and Sarah (Zane) Emminger, of this county. Mr. and Mrs. Hertzler the next year commenced housekeeping on her father's farm, remaining there nine years. In 1882 Mr. Hertzler made his first purchase of land, buying what was then known as the Milton Stayman tract, and which was finely improved and located near schools and churches. Although a young man our subject has for a number of years been officially connected with the schools in his township. Mr. and Mrs. Hertzler have four children: Hugh L., born October 9, 1876; Frank Revere, born July 16, 1878; Paul Mervin, born November 2, 1882, and Mary E., born July 10, 1884. Coming from such an honored ancestry on both sides the parents of these children have reason to feel proud of their lineage, and the completeness of their family history equals, perhaps, that of any in the land.

MRS. ELIZA HORST, P. O. Shiremanstown, who for thirty years has been a resident of this township, is a native of Lancaster County, Penn. Her parents, Henry and Anna (Landis) Mohler, had nine children, of whom she is the eldest daughter. After the death of her father our subject came to this county, and January 30, 1849, while *en route*, was married to Rev. David Horst, a worthy man, who was born on the farm now owned by his widow. Their married life was commenced under favorable auspices, and for a number of years they lived in supreme happiness. No children came to cheer their home, but two girls were adopted: one, Annie Mohler, a niece of Mrs. Horst, and the other, Kate Callar, who was born in this township. Both are still living with Mrs. Horst, who has been to them a loving mother and careful instructor from their early childhood. Rev. David Horst continued as pastor of the Lower Cumberland Brethren congregation until his death, September 15, 1863. He was renowned for his upright life and endeavors to benefit his brethren in this community. He was an active worker for Christ's cause, and large accessions were made to the church through his ministrations. Perhaps no man has lived in the township whose death was more regretted or loss more deeply felt. He left a competence for his widow, who still entertains with that old-time hospitality for which her nationality and faith are so noted. While this sketch was being written a number of friends and relatives were visiting her, and, previous to their departure, engaged in song and praise to that Power who keeps them in existence and sustains their faith firmly in the hope of a blessed future. No more fitting tribute can be given to the departed husband than to say "He hath done what he could." His widow is a personification of all the graces and attributes of a true Christian.

ANDREW C. KNODERER, farmer, P. O. Shepherdstown, was born September 22, 1833, in Hellam Township, York Co., Penn. His grandparents, Andrew C. Knoderer and wife, came with their three children, Harriet, Emma and Charles A., from France, and settled in York County, Penn., and there one daughter, Sophia, was born. By trade the grandfather of our subject was a weaver, an occupation he followed in the village of York until his death. Charles A., the only son, was married to Magdalena Scherrer, in 1825; and by her had ten children: David, Leah, Sophia, Henrietta, Maria, Andreas and Abraham (twins), Daniel, Charles and Lucy A. Of these, six are yet living, and five are residents of Cumberland County. Andrew C. Knoderer is by trade a carpenter, which he worked at for some time before coming to this county. In 1857 he married Elizabeth Phillips, of Adams County, Penn., who bore him the following children: John, Jacob and Maggie. The mother died in 1861, and on August 4, 1864, Mr. Knoderer was married to Susan Landis of this county. Her father was a man widely known and highly respected for his many virtues, and his children are now received among the first families in the land. The first purchase of land made by Mr. Knoderer, in this county, was in 1867, when he bought his present farm, and which was enlarged from the York County farm, as Mrs. Knoderer received from her father's estate a nice sum of money, which has been judiciously invested with that of her husband, and their lands have become very valuable. To Mr. and Mrs. Knoderer have been born four children: I. Romaine, D. Frank, Milton A. and Annie L. Frank is a carpenter, and works with his father, who is still an active business man. During Mr. Knoderer's business career he has built thirty-two bank barns in this and York Counties, which will, no doubt, remain as landmarks years after his sphere of usefulness has passed.

GEORGE H. MILLER, retired, Shepherdstown, one of the best known citizens of this township, is the son of Adam Miller, who came to this county as early as 1805, being then a mere boy; was employed in various pursuits and all the time accumulating money. Later in life he went to Dauphin County, Penn., and there learned the shoe-maker's trade, after which he returned to Upper Allen Township, this county, and opened a shop on the Samuel Mohler farm and prospered financially. March 14, 1817, he was married to Sophia, daughter of Henry Hann, of York County, Penn., and housekeeping was commenced on the Mohler farm, and there was born Ann, now the wife of John Graybill, of Indiana. In 1818 Adam Miller moved to the Eberly farm, near Shepherdstown, where he conducted business for thirty-six years, and there were born and reared following named children: George H., Catharine, Christiana, Sarah, Jacob, Eliza and Mary E. He purchased another farm later, and moved on it about 1854, but afterward sold it and went to live with his son, George, at whose home he and his faithful wife spent the remainder of their days. George H. Miller was born July 22, 1819; was married, September 24, 1843, to Susannah, daughter of Nicholas Urich, one of the pioneers of the Cumberland Valley. In 1844 George Miller and his young wife commenced on the farm, where for six years their life was one of domestic peace and prosperity, and on this farm their children, George W., Susan E. and Adam U., were born. The death of Mrs. Miller, in 1849, was the first sorrow that came to this household. Mr. Miller then moved, and September 9, 1851, married Sarah Ann Beelman, who bore him the following children: Laura E., Matilda C., Sarah H., Elmer E. and Ida C. George W., Mr. Miller's son, enlisted in the Two Hundred and Second Regiment Pennsylvania Volunteer Infantry, and served during the late war of the Rebellion as first sergeant; his death occurred in February, 1870. Our subject remained on the farm until 1884, when he removed to Shepherdstown, which he will probably make his home the balance of his life. He has ever been a man on whom the people could look with confidence. He has reared a family which do him honor, and has given his children liberal educational advantages, and George and Laura have been teachers. Politically Mr. Miller has always been a Democrat, and has held many official positions of trust in the township, and of him it may be said that he is a fit representative of that intrinsic worth which distinguished the families of a century ago.

HARRY J. MILLER, farmer, P. O. Mechanicsburg, one of the prosperous business men whose family history can be traced back for two centuries, is of German origin, his great-great-grandparents coming from Switzerland to Pennsylvania in 1732. George Miller, the great-grandfather of our subject, was born in Switzerland in 1722, and with his father, Michael, settled near Elizabethtown, in Lancaster County; united with the church and was the first minister of the Big Swatava German Baptist Church. He died in 1798, leaving ten children, of whom Henry begat Moses, who married Hannah Mohler, and by her had six children: Sarah; Amos, died in infancy; infant daughter deceased; Harry J., born June 26, 1848; Solomon and Mary. On the great-grandmother's side George Klein, the first minister at North Kill (now Little Swatava), was born at Zweibrucken, Germany, in 1715, and settled at North Kill in 1750. Elizabeth, the daughter of George Klein, was the mother of Moses Miller, who was the father of Harry J. Miller. Moses died June 26, 1885, aged sixty-five years, two months and twenty-nine days. Our subject has traveled over much of the Western country, and has ever been a close observer of the methods and manners of the people. He received a liberal education, adopted the vocation of a teacher, and for several terms taught in this township, near his boyhood's home, where he gave satisfaction. In 1869 he formed the acquaintance of Miss Martha C. Hutton, of Adams County, Penn., who was later married to Harry B. Palmer. After Mr. Palmer's death, in September, 1880, Mr. Miller renewed the acquaintance, and November 11, 1883, they were married (Mrs. Miller had three children by her first husband: Edgar, Bertha and Lillie, the latter died in 1880). To Mr. and Mrs. Miller was born, August 18, 1884, a daughter, Orca Z. They reside on a handsome farm near Shepherdstown, which was willed to Mr. Miller by his father at the death of his mother, who still lives in Mechanicsburg. In politics Mr. Miller is a Republican. He has done effective work for his party in this neighborhood, though he has never held or desired office for himself.

SOLOMON MILLER, farmer, P. O. Mechanicsburg, was born in the house in which he resides, in this township, May 18, 1850, the son of Moses and Hannah (Mohler) Miller, who were residents of Cumberland County fifty-eight years. His great-great-grandfather, Ludwick Mohler, came, with his family, from Switzerland in 1730, settling near Germantown, and was the father of Henry, the father of John, the father of Daniel, who was the father of Hannah Miller, the mother of our subject. On the father's side the great-grandfather, Michael Miller, also came from Switzerland, and settled in Lancaster County, Penn., in 1722. He begat George, who begat Henry, who begat Moses Miller, the father of our subject. George Klein, the great-great-grandfather on the father's side, was a native of Zweibrucken, Germany, born October 9, 1715. The Mohlers were one of the first families in this county, and many of the residents of this township trace their origin to this name. Solomon Miller, our subject, married Miss Hettie Hertzler, a daughter of Rudolph and Mary (Shoop) Hertzler, both born in Lancaster County. [For a sketch of Rudolph and Mary Hertzler, see sketch of Henry Hertzler, page 568.] On her twenty-second birthday, October 16, 1873, the ceremony was performed by the groom's father, Moses Miller, an elder in the German Baptist Church. Two sons, Clarence H. and Elmer R., have blessed their union. Since their marriage Mr. and Mrs. Solomon Miller have resided on the farm where he was born.

DAVID S. MOHLER, farmer, P. O. Mechanicsburg, is a grandson of Christian and Magdalena (Springer) Mohler, who were born in Cumberland County, Penn., the latter March 7, 1780, and after their marriage resided in this county, mostly in this township. They were the parents of sixteen children, of whom Samuel, the father of our subject, was the eldest son, and only one, Mrs. Esther Hoover, is now a resident of this county. Samuel Mohler married Miss Rachael, daughter of Henry Miller, of this county. Three of Mrs. Mohler's brothers and one sister reside in Cumberland County. Four daughters and two sons of the family of Samuel Mohler are now residents of this county. David S. Mohler, the subject of this sketch, was united in marriage, June 19, 1860, with Miss Mary Bowman. October 15, 1862, he enlisted in Company C, Third Regiment Pennsylvania Artillery, and served as a musician during his term of enlistment, being stationed at Fort Monroe, Va. He was honorably discharged, on account of disability, February 20, 1864. After farming for seven years he engaged in mercantile business until 1879, at Shiremanstown, this county, since when he has resided on the farm upon which he was born. Mr. and Mrs. David S. Mohler have two children living: Ida M. and Myrta V.; the second born died at his birth. Our subject has served his township as supervisor and for five years as school director. For many years he was engaged in teaching vocal and instrumental music, and for seven years had charge of the Harmonic Society of Shiremanstown, an organization noted throughout this and adjoining counties.

LEVI MOHLER, farmer, P. O. Mechanicsburg, a representative of one of the first families that settled in this township, was born August 20, 1845, on the old homestead, the second son of Samuel and Rachael (Miller) Mohler, who were for many years residents of this beautiful valley. Their children, ten in number, were all born on the old homestead, and Elizabeth, David, Mary, Priscilla, Levi and Hetty are still living in this county. Mrs. Mohler died February 8, 1870, and Samuel Mohler June 1, 1885. Both were for many years devout members of the German Baptist Brethren Church, and their children were reared in that faith. The parents of Samuel Mohler, Christian and Magdalena (Springer) Mohler, came from Germany to this county, and early settled on the farm now owned by our subject, and which has been in possession of the Mohlers over three-quarters of a century. They reared a family of fourteen children, who are now scattered over the States and Western Territories. Levi Mohler was educated in the common schools and adopted farm life. He married, July 4, 1869, Miss Fanny Beelman, of York County, Penn., daughter of Rev. Adam Beelman, who for thirty years was a minister in that county. The first year of Mr. and Mrs. Mohler's wedded life was spent with her parents, since which time they have resided on the Mohler homestead. They are the parents of five children: Harry B., Martha, Mary, Clara and Annie. The remote ancestors of Mrs. Mohler were from Germany, but her father, Rev. Adam Beelman, was born in this county, and her mother, Mattie (Hurst) Beelman, was a native of York County, Penn. This aged and worthy couple are living, and Rev. Beelman supplies a pulpit, being the oldest minister in the Lower Cumberland District of the Middle District of Pennsylvania. George and Eve (Metzgar) Beelman, grandparents of Mrs. Mohler on the father's side, were the parents of six children: George, Adam, John, Fanny, Sarah and Joseph. On the mother's side her grandparents were Abraham and Elizabeth Hurst, who reared a family of nine children: Christian, Fannie, Abram, Henry, Maria, Eliza, Nancy, Martha and Hetty.

AMOS MUMMA, grain dealer, P. O. Shepherdstown. One of the first and most prominent families in this county is that of the father of Amos Mumma, and a lengthy history of Jacob Mumma, the grandfather of our subject, appears in the borough history of Mechanicsburg, and different branches of this family are represented in the several townships in which they reside. Our subject is a son of Jacob and Catharine (Eberly) Mumma. His mother's first husband, Mr. Rupp, a farmer, died soon after the birth of her third child, when she became the second wife of Jacob Mumma, and bore him the following children: Eli, Jacob, Amos, Fanny, Eliza and Samuel—all of whom were born in Cumberland County, and living at this time, except Samuel and Fanny. Amos Mumma was married, November 17, 1868, to Marion E., daughter of Christian and Lydia (Miley) Herman, also of this county. The Hermans were among the first settlers near New Kingston, coming in 1771, and the representatives of this family celebrated their centennial in 1871, children of the sixth generation being present on that occasion. The original farm is now owned by Wolford Herman, and the land has been in possession of the name since the

UPPER ALLEN TOWNSHIP.

first purchase by the great-grandfather. Of the immediate family of Christian Herman are three children: Jacob, John and Marion. Amos Mumma and his wife have four children: Herman J., Alberta J., Levi H. and Lydia H. These children, as they grow older, can read with pride the history of their lineage, which extends back from both branches more than a century. Mr. Mumma has always been one of the most energetic and impulsive of men, brave and intrepid. He twice tried to enlist in the army during the late war of the Rebellion, but his youth prevented the accomplishment of his intention. As a man, a neighbor, and a citizen, Mr. Mumma has no superior, and is in all respects worthy to bear the name of his illustrious ancestors.

JOHN MUMMA, farmer, P. O. Mechanicsburg, the second son of Jacob Mumma, was born in Lancaster County, Penn., in 1836, and resided with his father until 1863, when he commenced business for himself on a farm near Mechanicsburg. Nine years later he was united in marriage with Miss Elizabeth, daughter of Rudolph and Mary (Schopf) Hertzler, old residents of Cumberland County, but natives of Lancaster County, Penn. To Mr. and Mrs. John Mumma have been born six children—all living: Charles H., Mary A., Grace E., Blanche V., Jacob R. and John I. Our subject first purchased land in 1865, which he still owns. He bought the present homestead fifteen years later. This farm is very attractive, and its comfortable surroundings and fine improvements make it indeed an elegant home. Mr. Mumma, one of the representative men of the township, is a member of one of its oldest families, and merits the greatest confidence reposed in him by the public.

ELI MUMMA, farmer, P. O. Mechanicsburg, was born, in 1850, on the old homestead in Silver Spring Township, this county. His father, Jacob Mumma, has been so liberal with his money and enterprising in spirit that he has stood at the head of the business industries and substantial improvements for fully half a century. Eli Mumma, the youngest son of Jacob and Catharine Mumma, received a practical education in the common schools, and has thus far passed his life on the farm, preferring agricultural pursuits to either a trade or profession. November 25, 1873, he was married to Annie B., daughter of Joseph and Sarah E. (Fritchey) Eberly, of Hampden Township, this county. To this union were born two sons and five daughters: Thomas C., Wilbur A., Annie B., Mary E., Martha F., Sarah E. and Emma J.—all of whom reside in the county. The death of Joseph Eberly, the father of Mrs. Mumma, occurred April 5, 1885, at the age of sixty-five years and seven months. The married life of Eli Mumma and his young wife was commenced on his father's farm under the same favorable auspices which have continued to this day. In 1875 they moved to the farm on which they now reside. One child—Joseph E.—was born on the grandfather's homestead; Mabel G. and Harry H. were born on their father's farm in this township. Politically and socially Mr. Mumma is of that liberal class whose object is to further the business and social interests in the community. Possessed of abundant means, a fine farm and happy family, he is surrounded by everything to make him happy.

H. O. SHELLEY, miner, P. O. Shepherdstown, was born in Lancaster, Penn., but later went to Dauphin County, where he owned a farm. In 1869 he commenced mining iron ore in York County, Penn., where he continued until 1878, opening a mine on Dan Landis' farm in 1874, and which he sold in 1875, but in 1883 again leased and has operated since. An analysis of the ore from this mine, in 1874, gave sixty-two per cent in the furnaces. The analysis made in 1884 showed fifty two per cent of the mixed oxides. In 1855 H. O. Shelley was married to Fanny Nisley, daughter of Henry and Mary Nisley, and who was born on the island bearing that name in the Susquehanna below Middletown. In 1867, our subject came to Upper Allen Township, this county, and purchased a farm, on which he moved in 1868, and which he has since operated in connection with mining. The children of Mr. and Mrs. H. O. Shelley are five in number: Samuel married Ella Coover, a daughter of one of York County's first families; Elias wedded Annie, daughter of Christian Hertzler, of this county; David, Lizzie, wife of William Nisley, of Mechanicsburg, and Annie. Mr. Shelley has repeatedly been solicited to become a candidate for official positions, but has always declined, preferring to manage his own business affairs and thus keep aloof from such annoyances as small offices provoke. He is one of the most highly respected men in his neighborhood, and lives in a style becoming a man of education and refinement.

JACOB F. STAUFFER, contractor and builder, Shepherdstown, was born in York County, Penn., in 1841, son of Frederick and Maria (Orry) Stauffer, who were probably married in 1830, and were the parents of nine children, of whom Jacob F. is the eldest son; then followed Susan, Moses, David, Samuel, Joseph, Maria, Frederick and Lydia. Our subject learned his trade in his native county and followed the business for twelve years previous to coming to Cumberland County. He was married December 2, 1860, to Sarah, who was the youngest of the ten children of Michael and Lydia Shellenberger, old residents of York County. The children of Mr. and Mrs. Jacob F. Stauffer are David; Ellen, wife of George Cromlich; Melinda, wife of Calvin Weaver; Lilly and Sally (born in York County), and Harry, Benjamin F., Walter, Maggie, Birdie and Lydia who were born in this township. In 1871 Mr. and Mrs. Stauffer came to this township and the farm where they now reside was purchased. Since coming here, however, our subject has given but little attention to farming, devoting all of his time to his trade. He built several large edifices, which will stand for years, monuments to his skill and industry, notably the Mennonite Church on Slate Hill; a fine residence for Samuel Eberly, also one for Daniel Ebersole; a residence for George Hummel, and has recently completed a nice church for the Mennonite congregation at Churchtown. By strict attention to business Mr. Stauffer has prospered financially, and is recorded as one of the substantial men of the Cumberland Valley.

JOHN SWARTZ, tailor, Shepherdstown, was born in Silver Spring Township, this county, and from the age of fourteen years has been a resident of Shepherdstown. His parents, John and Nancy (Mohler) Swartz, lived near the tan-yard in Silver Spring Township. John Swartz, Sr., learned the carpenter's trade of John Snavely (who died in 1849) early in life, and worked on the State House at Harrisburg. John Swartz, Sr., was born in this county in May, 1791, and died in August, 1866. His wife, Nancy Mohler, was born in September, 1799, and died in December, 1846. They had seven children, of whom John, Jr., is the fifth born. At the age of fourteen our subject came to Shepherdstown and became an apprentice to his uncle, Michael Hoover, who carried on a tailor shop in that village. When his trade was completed, in 1848, John Swartz, Jr., assumed control of the shop, and from that day to this has conducted business for himself. February 8, 1855, our subject married Magdalena Hetrich, born in East Hanover Township, Lebanon Co., Penn., June 25, 1834, daughter of Isaac and Sarah (Urich) Hetrich. Mr. and Mrs. Swartz commenced house-keeping where they now reside and there their children were born, viz.; Sarah A., born September 14, 1856; Albert H., born June 17, 1859; William S., born April 8, 1864, died October 30, 1864; and Harry C., born September 9, 1867. The children received liberal educations and Albert has chosen the profession of teaching. Harry follows in the footsteps of his father and is a tailor; Sarah, is the wife of A. H. Mohler, doing business at Shepherdstown. Mr. Swartz was drafted during the late war of the Rebellion, but furnished money to procure a substitute, as he was a man of peace and not in favor of war. He has filled numerous township offices with credit; has been a member of No. 215, I. O. O. F., since 1851. During a residence of forty-three years Mr. Swartz has not been absent from Shepherdstown for two weeks at one time. His business, his family and his home are located there, and no man in the valley is more contented.

HIRAM WATTS, farmer, Shepherdstown, is the only one of his immediate relatives who came to th s county, but his name is well known in this and adjacent counties. He was born in York County, Penn., January 21, 1824, and is second son of Andrew and Elizabeth Watts, who resided on a farm in Newberry Township, that county, and were the parents of two sons and seven daughters. Our subject came to Upper Allen Township, this county, in 1846, engaging with George Nebenger to work on a farm. December 3, 1848, he was married to Sarah A., daughter of Charles and Susan (Keiper) Bingaman, formerly of Lancaster County, but who came as early as 1820 to Shepherdstown (then known as Jennystown). Of the two sons and six daughters of Mr. and Mrs. Bingaman, Mrs. Eliza A. Morrett, Mrs. Catharine Kohler, Mrs. Rebecca Blosser and Mrs. Watts are still living. The year after their marriage Mr. and Mrs. Watts commenced housekeeping near Shepherdstown, and afterward built tnemselves a cottage in the village. For eleven years he worked at the carpenter's trade, earning the money which gave him a start in the business world, and in 1855 commenced farming. He prospered, and, in 1876, purchased the nice farm on which he now resides, and there were born his children: Lewis, Charles, Lizzie, Ira and Clara. Lewis married Mary Miller, and resides at Dillsburg; he is engaged in the drug trade. Charles is employed in the office of the Cumberland Valley Railroad at the same place. All the children are finely educated, and well fitted to attend to any business or grace any position in society. The parents live on the farm, surrounded by their children, and enjoy the comforts which come to those who have lived long, useful lives. When it is taken into consideration that Mr. Watts left the parental roof at the age of eight years, made a living, accumulated a fine property, and, besides, has maintained and educated a family that ranks second to none in the land, he certainly deserves great credit. He was judge of elections in 1857, and for many years served in an official capacity on the school board.

WILLIAM WESTHAFER farmer, P. O. Mechanicsburg, is of German ancestry. His grandfather, Abram Westhafer, who settled in Lancaster County about 1792, was married to Catharine Eschleman, and reared a family: George, Jacob, Peter, Susannah and Rebecca. Peter Westhafer married Maria Baker, a resident of York County, Penn. (where he was then living), and who died three years later. August 20, 1829, he married Annie M Stave. In 1860 Peter Westhafer and wife came to this county and settled near the Chestnut Hill Cemetery, on the Bosler farm. Their children, Jacob, William, (four deceased,) Leigh, Lucy A., Catharine, John, Edward, Eli, Abraham. Susannah and Maggie, were all born in York County. Of this family William, Lucy, Leigh and Kate live in Cumberland County at the present time. Most of Peter Westhafer's time was spent in farming, although he was by trade a shoe-maker; he, also kept the National Hotel in Mechanicsburg at one time, and afterward owned and operated a dry goods and grocery store. He was considered one of the most enterprising men in the county, and always did his share to advance the business and social interests of the community. He died greatly regretted; his widow still resides in Mechanicsburg. William Westhafer was married, in 1861, to Miss Marian, daughter of George A. and Margaret (Ressler) Balsley, one of the oldest and most highly respected families of the county. George A. and Margaret Balsley were married February 19, 1832, by the Rev. Nicholas Stroh, and were the parents of seven children, only three of whom are now living: Joseph, Mrs. Westhafer and Catharine. Our subject commenced farming for himself in the spring of 1861, on the old Bosler farm, and from the start has been very successful; everything he touched prospered, and his profits accumulated until he bought a couple of lots and erected a house at the corner of Marble and York Streets in 1865. His next purchase of real estate was on the opposite side of the street and a lot of twelve acres near Mechanicsburg which he still owns. In 1878 he moved to the Levi Eberly farm, and is now making money as easily as he did in his younger days; besides his farm interests he is also an extensive dealer in live stock. To Mr. and Mrs. Westhafer have been born three children: George E., born in 1863, and William B. and Grant S. (twins), born October 5, 1871. All are active promising young men, who have received a practical education, and are worthy to bear their father's name. Mr. and Mrs. Westhafer have been consistent members of the United Brethren Church since 1873. Politically our subject is a Republican.

SARAH WORLEY, Shepherdstown, is a daughter of George and Anna M. Daugherty, one of the old and prominent families of York County, Penn., where they were born and bred, and reared a family of nine children: Sarah, Ann, Maria, John, George, William H., Emma J., Rachael E. and Thomas L. Though these children were all born in York County, all live in Cumberland County except Emma and Thomas L. Our subject was born April 23, 1828. March 26, 1854, she was married to William W. Kline, a son of William and Jane (Goudy) Kline. They commenced housekeeping near Siddensburg, where Mr. Kline, a millwright by trade, worked at his business for some time. They came to Shepherdstown in 1855 and took charge of the only hotel in the place, and they prospered. To Mr. and Mrs. Kline were born five children: Mary H., born January 28, 1855, is the wife of John E. Acker, of Mansfield, Ohio; Benjamin, married to Ella T. Brubaker, manages a hotel at Hogestown, this county; Jane A., William R. and Ella M. W. W. Kline entered the army in 1861, served nine months, and then re-enlisted in Company A, One Hundred and Ninetieth Regiment Pennsylvania Volunteer Infantry. He participated in the thickest of the fight at the bloody battle of Gettysburg, and in many a hotly contested skirmish of the Virginia campaign. While his regiment was guarding the railroad at Weldon, N. C., it was captured by the rebels and the men confined in Libby prison, the name of which is yet spoken of with horror by every one who was unfortunate enough to experience the sufferings entailed upon the miserable victims confined within its walls. Three months after his captivity, November 25, 1864, the veteran soldier, kind husband and loving father was borne from that miserable place an emaciated corpse. Death had released him from suffering further privations; hunger, thirst and cold were remembered no more; of wife and children were his last thoughts. In 1868 Mrs. Kline was again married, this time to J. B. Worley, a well known business man of this county, and after their marriage again engaged in hotel business in New Cumberland, and prospered. No children were born to this union. In 1875 Mr. Worley died, leaving his widow and step-children well provided for. The mother of Mrs. Worley, who still lives with her son George, has attained the ripe old age of eighty years.

DAVID W. WORST, justice of the peace, Shepherdstown, was born October 2, 1839. His father David Worst, who was born in Frankford Township, this county, December 26, 1797, was a carpenter by trade, and carried on business in this county, many substantial buildings still standing as monuments to his industry. He also went to Cuba and erected a large number of sugar houses for planters on that island. January 30, 1834, he was married to Mary Ann Zearing, who was born November 7, 1814, and was a lineal descendant of the celebrated Rupp family. David and Mary Ann Worst were the parents of the following named children: Jacob, Sarah A., Daniel. David W., Eliza A., Susan A. Sarah A., Jacob H. and Mary E., all of whom were born in Mechanicsburg, Penn., David Worst, Sr., died in 1850, and his widow subsequently married John Lininger December 29, 1851, and bore him three children: Catharine, Elizabeth and Alice V. David W. Worst, our subject, at the age of eleven years was turned out to shift for himself, and was engaged by John Houser on a farm. At the age of eighteen he commenced a clerkship with Messrs Goswiler & Zook, in Shepherdstown, continuing with them a number of years. May 31, 1866, he was united in marriage with Annie M., daughter of ex-Sheriff Bowman, and by this union are the following named children: Carrie I., Annie G., Mary E., Edith G. and Martha W. All are making rapid progress with their education and form a pleasant family circle, where books, music, etc., are prominent features. Mr. Worst's popularity in his county is shown in the fact of his being elected prothonotary of Cumberland County in the autumn of 1872, which position he held three years with honor to himself and credit to his constituents. The people residing in his township nominated him justice of the peace in 1877, and re-elected him in 1882, his official term expiring in 1887, and during his public life he bears a clean record. He is a straight Democrat and one of the most prominent local politicians in his township. Liberal in every thing which advances the interests of society, he is ranked among the best citizens and most public spirited men of the county in which he has for a number of years been a central figure.

CHAPTER LX.

WEST PENNSBOROUGH TOWNSHIP.

JONATHAN BEAR, farmer, P. O. Plainfield, was born July 4, 1819, in West Pennsborough Township, Cumberland Co., Penn. His father, Samuel, a son of John Bear, married Miss Sarah, daughter of Philip Zeigler, and settled in what is now known as Bear's District, West Pennsborough Township, and here resided until his death, which occurred April 30, 1855, in his sixty-eighth year; his widow died in Plainfield December 26, 1871, aged eighty years and five months. They reared eight of their ten children: Mrs. Catharine Steiner, Jonathan, Mrs. Mary Seitz, Rebecca, Elizabeth, John (deceased), David and Philip (deceased). January 11, 1849, our subject married Miss Maria, daughter of Henry and Polly (Bear) Bear, from Lancaster County, Penn. They resided on the farm near Conodoguinet Creek until August, 1884, when they moved to their present residence, and now own a fine farm of 132 acres, besides a beautiful home of six acres where they reside. To them have been born nine children, of whom the following are now living: Abner, Mrs. Mary Eppley, Sarah and Lizzie. Ellen died at seventeen years of age, Emma when fifteen, Samuel when nineteen years old, and Refeea and Catharine when small. Mr. Bear and family belong to the Reformed Mennonite Church. He takes great interest in the education of his family and has given them good opportunities.

HENRY BEAR, retired farmer, Plainfield, was born March 17, 1824, in West Pennsborough Township, this county. About 1690 Michael Bear, a Mennonite minister, of Switzerland, fled from persecution to accept the generous offer of William Penn of a home in Pennsylvania. He settled in Berks County and has a large number of descendants. Michael, his son, had a son, Henry, who came to West Pennsborough Township, this county, in 1804, with his sons, Michael, John and Samuel. Of these, Michael was twice wedded, and by his first marriage (with Miss Esther Alter) had two children: Benjamin, who died in Summit County, Ohio, and Mrs. Esther Stephens, who died in this county. His second wife, Hannah Wax, was a daughter of Peter Wax, a Revolutionary soldier, who settled in Frankford Township, this county, coming from Schuylkill County, Penn., and lived to be ninety-four years of age; his wife died aged eighty-seven. Mr. and Mrs. Bear settled near Plainfield. To them were born seven children, five of whom attained maturity: Henry, Mrs. Margaret Greason (deceased), Maria, Maurice (deceased) and Mrs. Rachael LeFevre, of Carlisle. Mr. Bear was a very effective local preacher of the United Brethren faith; he died very suddenly December 16, 1849, while officiating in the pulpit, being striken down by apoplexy. He was a very active man, and exerted a wide influence for good. Henry Bear, who has lived on the home-farm all his life, owns a fine farm of eighty acres besides his handsome residence and farm of four acres where he resides. He was married, February 3, 1848, to Miss Margaret LeFevre, who died about two and a half years afterward. He next married, May 15, 1856, Miss Catharine Longnecker, and by her has one daughter, Mary. Mr. Bear, of Federalist descent, was formerly a Whig, afterward a Republican. He takes a deep interest in public affairs, and has rendered important services as a campaign orator. As a speaker he is clear, logical and forcible, and carries the weight of his own convictions in his addresses. He is one of the leading influential citizens of Cumberland County.

JOHN K. BEIDLER, merchant, Plainfield, was born April 2, 1828, in Lebanon County, Penn., son of John and Anna (Kaufman) Beidler, the latter of whom died in that county. His father, who afterward married again, located in West Middleton Township, this county in 1840, and now lives a retired life in Plainfield, this township, aged eighty-three. Our subject married, in November, 1851, Miss Sophia Zeigler, of Middlesex Township, this county. He enlisted, in August, 1862, in Company F, Seventeenth Regiment Pennsylvania Volunteer Cavalry; was assigned to the Army of the Potomac under Gen. Hooker, and took part in many of the historic engagements of the Virginia campaigns. He received an honorable discharge in 1863, on account of disabilities received in the service. He left a fine record as a brave and faithful soldier, always ready for the call of duty. In 1866 Mr. Beidler established, and for three years carried on, a general store at Sterrett's Gap, Perry County; three years conducted business in Plainfield, this county; then for three years at West Hill, and then purchased property at Oakville and built a fine store building. There Mrs. Beidler died in March, 1877, leaving one daughter, Mrs. Lizzie M. Mickey, now living at Oakville. In the fall of 1877 Mr. Beidler again located at West Hill. He was married, on second occasion, December 6, 1877, to Miss Anna M. Matthews, of Berks County, Penn., and by this union has one son, Earl J. Mr. Beidler owns a fine business property in Plainfield and carries a complete stock of dry goods, groceries, hats, caps, boots, shoes, hardware, notions, and a full line of general merchandise. By strict attention to business principles and courtesy to all, he has built up a large and flourishing trade. Personally Mr. Beidler is a man of portly build and fine physique; genial and social in his disposition, he makes friends wherever he goes. He is recognized as one of the leading business men and influential citizens of Cumberland County.

WILLIAM BLOSER, retired, Plainfield, was born December 11, 1818, in West Pennsborough Township, this county. Henry Bloser came, with his family, from Lancaster County, Penn., to Frankford Township, this county, in very early times. His son, Daniel, was twice married; on the first occasion to Eve Keihl, a native of this county, and settled near Hays Mill, this township. Mrs. Daniel Bloser died in 1824, and he subsequently married Sarah Rex, and moved to Richland (now Crawford) County, Ohio, in about 1840, where they resided until she died, when he lived a retired life with his son until his death. Our subject, the second born by the second marriage, and only one living of his mother's five children, received his education in the schools of the home district and early apprenticed himself to the carpenter's trade, which he has followed nearly all his life. He married, February 14, 1851, Miss Sarah Waggoner, a native of Frankford Township, this county, and to this union were born nine children, five of whom are living: Mary, Mrs. Kate Corman, Elizabeth, Mrs. Alida Smith and Anna. Mrs. Bloser died November 5, 1866, and Mr. Bloser subsequently married, April 7, 1868, Miss Mary A. Kendig, a native of this township, and who moved to Franklin County, Penn., at six years of age, with her parents, Emanuel and Anne (Bowers) Kendig, natives of Lancaster County, Penn., but residing in Cumberland County from childhood. They resided at Orrstown at the time of their death; Mr. Kendig dying April 11, 1863, and his widow, February 3, 1869. To Mr. and Mrs. Bloser were born one son (William Edward) and one daughter (Nora, deceased). Mr. Bloser has been industrious and successful in life and has acquired a fine farm of 204 acres in Frankford Township. In addition to this he owns a fine home in Plainfield and a handsome plat of four acres, on which is established the Plainfield Cemetery, located in 1867. Mr. Bloser and his worthy wife and family are members of the Church of God, and he has been an elder ever since the church was established. He is a life-long Republican and an earnest advocate of the principles of temperance.

WILLIAM C. BRADLEY, retired, P. O. Newville, was born near West Chester, Chester Co., Penn., in 1813, son of Joseph and Hannah (Carpenter) Bradley, who were the parents of eight children, of whom William C., Jason, Thomas, Caroline and Emmor are living. Our subject received a liberal education, and his first venture in a business way was with Robert Coleman, at Martick Forge, in Lancaster County, in 1836. At that time the Colemans were the best known iron manufacturers in the State, and from a small beginning the business has grown, until now their interests are second to none in the United States. For a number of years our subject was book-keeper, and afterward managed the business at Lebanon, Speedwell and Martick Forge. From Speedwell he went to Oregon, Baltimore County; from there to Columbia, Lancaster County; and thence to Harrisburg, where he took charge of Mr. McCormick's iron works, and, later, was interested in the manufacture of iron near Harper's Ferry on the Potomac. At numerous places in the Cumberland Valley and along the Potomac, he has managed the business of Hon. Thaddeus Stevens. Mr. Bradley has chiefly been interested in the iron trade, and is well known by all the manufacturers. He was married, in 1840, to Harriet Thomas, and this union was blessed with eight children, of whom five are living: Sallie (wife of T. C. Babb, of Philadelphia, Penn.), Susie (wife of George C. Kelly, of Lewisburg), Caroline, Albina and Harriet, who reside with their father in the pleasant mansion near the borough of Newville. Mrs. Bradley died in 1879, and the daughters now make the old home pleasant for their father; and amid the many comforts which surround men of wealth and refined tastes, his days are serenely passed. Our subject's life has been an active one, but his step is still elastic, though his hair is white as snow. He has now retired from active business and bears a name never smirched with dishonor.

FRANKLIN PIERCE BREHM, manufacturer, Plainfield, was born September 20, 1853, in Frankford Township, this county, where his father, Henry Brehm, still resides. Our subject followed farming until he was twenty-one years of age, when he began learning coach-making under George Strohm, of Plainfield, this county, completing his apprenticeship in three years, and then worked four years for Mr. Strohm. He located at Good Hope, this township, in 1880, and established a general coach house, which he continued until he built his present large and commodious establishment in the fall of 1885, into which he moved in the first week of December following. He has a large three-story building, 45x60 feet, well fitted up, where he carries on a very extensive business, manufacturing buggies, carriages, spring wagons, sleighs, etc., employing from nine to twelve hands. His goods have an excellent reputation, and besides supplying the home demand, he has quite a large shipping trade throughout the East and West. In addition to his business property, Mr. Brehm has built himself a very handsome residence not far from the station. He married, February 7, 1872, Miss Katie A. Beidlow, and has two children: Bessie Maude and Harry LeRoy. Mr. Brehm is an enterprising business man and an upright and useful citizen. He is a member of the Lutheran Church, and has been for seven years superintendent in the Sabbath-school at Plainfield. In politics he is a Democrat.

DAVID BRICKER (deceased), a native of Lancaster County, Penn., was a son of David Bricker, who immigrated to that county from Germany with his brother Christopher before the Revolutionary war. He raised his family in that county, and there resided until his death. He had a son—Christopher—who was a soldier in the Revolution. David Bricker, our subject, married a Miss Erb; came to Newville, Cumberland Co., Penn., in 1794, and acquired an estate of over 400 acres, including a part of the town of Newville. He lived to be nearly ninety years of age, his wife having died about four years before his death. They raised a family of six children: Levi (died in Westmoreland County, Penn.), John, Jacob (died in Mechanicsburg), David, Mrs. Mary Dork and Mrs. Margaret Ann Heffleman, all died at Newville, this county. The second son, John, married Miss Eliza House, and settled in the Cross Roads District, in West Pennsborough Township, and here resided until his death. He died February 16, 1875, at the age of eighty-four years; his widow now resides in Newville. They raised a family of five sons: John H.; William H., of Beaver Falls, Penn., the present register of Beaver County; P. D., an attorney at Jersey Shore, Penn.; Samuel, of North Vernon, Ind.; George S., of Newville.

JOHN H. BRICKER, farmer and nurseryman, P. O. Newville, was born March 13, 1836. He married Miss Catharine Shannon June 8, 1858, and after living in Monroe Township about four years, settled on the present home farm. Mr. Bricker enlisted, in August, 1861, in the Third Regiment Pennsylvania Cavalry; was assigned to the Army of the Potomac, and took part in the Virginia campaigns of that year, receiving disabilities in December necessitating his discharge. Returning home he has devoted himself to the arts of peace. He established a nursery on his farm in 1867, and now does a large and successful business, supplying the large home trade and shipping to the West and South. Mrs. Bricker died February 18, 1873, leaving two children: William, of Williamsport, Penn., and Mary. Mr. Bricker afterward married, in September, 1875, Miss Julia Bolen, and to this union have been born two children: John F. and Ellen. Mr. Bricker is a supporter of the Republican party; takes a deep interest in the cause of education, and has served his township as school director for about twelve years; is an upright and useful citizen, and enjoys the respect of the community.

HENRY J. BRINKERHOFF, merchant and postmaster, Mount Rock, was born November 19, 1855, in Gettysburg, Adams Co., Penn. His father, John J. Brinkerhoff, a native of same county, and a descendant of one of the oldest families in the county, married Miss Sophia Saltzgiver, of the same county. He was a merchant; died in 1855, leaving a daughter (now Miss Clara Grammar, of Altoona), and a son (Henry). Mrs. Brinkerhoff afterward married John Peoples, and now resides at Lisburn, Penn. Our subject was brought up in the family of his uncle, M. G. Saltzgiver, in Cumberland County, principally in Dickinson, Monroe and Newton Townships. When about seventeen years old he began clerking in a general store in Leesburg, afterward carrying on a store for three years, at Huntsdale, for Mr. Ernst. In 1878 he embarked in business for himself at Barnitz Station, this county. In March, 1883, he established himself at Mount Rock, under firm name of Brinkerhoff & Co., and here keeps a full stock of dry goods, groceries, boots, shoes, hats, caps, notions and a complete line of articles necessary to supply the wants of the community. By his courtesy to customers and strict attention to business he has built up a large and flourishing trade. He was appointed postmaster of Mount Rock at the time he took charge of the store; was also instrumental in establishing the postoffice at Barnitz, which he held during the time he lived there. Mr. Brinkerhoff was married, in 1875, to Miss Anna M. Watson, of Stoughstown. To this union have been born three children: George Erskin, William Henry and Sallie Bertha. Our subject is an earnest Republican, and takes a deep interest in public affairs. He is an enterprising and successful business man and an upright, useful and respected citizen.

THOMAS R. BURGNER, miller, P. O. Plainfield, was born July 14, 1833, in Lebanon County, Penn., son of Jacob and Anna Maria (Raub) Burgner (the latter was a member of an old and influential family in this county). They located on the old homestead of Mr. Burgner's family, where Mrs. Burgner still resides at an advanced age, but in robust health. Mr. Burgner died July 13, 1886, aged seventy-four years. Our subject, the eldest in a family of ten children, learned the miller's trade in 1854; enlisted, October 17, 1862, in the Third Pennsylvania Artillery, and was assigned to the Army of the James. Early in 1863 he was recommended, and passed an examination, for the position of military librarian, and had charge of the historical collections and artillery-school stores at Fortress

WEST PENNSBOROUGH TOWNSHIP.   577

Monroe, Va., until the expiration of his term, and during this time he also held the position of reporter for general courts-martial and military commissions. He was discharged October 17, 1865, bearing an excellent military record. Our subject was married, December 1, 1857, to Miss Lizzie Eckert, of Newville, this county, a daughter of John Eckert, who was born near Carlisle, this county, moved to Virginia in 1860, and died in 1880 at the age of eighty years. The children of Mr. and Mrs. Burgner were Mary Agnes, John E., of Nebraska, Alice C., Francis Henry (deceased). Lizzie A., Emma C., Ida Margery, Beckie Ray, Thomas U. S., Carrie Lucretia and Arthur LeRoy. Mr. Burgner has spent three years in the nursery and mercantile business at Shiremanstown, six years in the employ, as miller, of T. B. Bryson, of Mechanicsburg, and for the past twelve years has been engaged in milling on Conodoguinet Creek, this township. He was elected auditor of Cumberland County, on the Republican ticket, in 1875; re-elected in 1878, and during his term of service many reforms were accomplished in county affairs, due to his energy and interest in the welfare of the people. Personally Mr. Burgner is a gentleman of portly and commanding physique, genial and courteous disposition, and has a host of warm friends in Cumberland County.

HENRY CARL, postmaster and mechanic, Plainfield, was born April 14, 1836, in Spring Township, Perry Co., Penn. His father John Carl, a native of same county, married Miss Elizabeth Smee; was a carpenter and weaver, and resided in this locality until his death in 1880, when seventy-three years of age. His widow, who survives him, resides on the same place, and is seventy-six years old. Of their children. Mrs. Catharine Snyder, Mrs. Sarah Ellen Hood, Mrs. Jane Sponsler and John A. reside in Carlisle; Emanuel lives in Landisburg; Mrs. Amelia Fenicle and Adeline are still in Perry County. Our subject came to Cumberland County at sixteen years of age. He was married February 23, 1860, to Miss Sarah A. Watson, and after farming for twelve years moved to Plainfield in 1872, and here he has followed his trade, that of a carpenter and joiner, ever since. He was appointed postmaster of Plainfield October 1, 1885, and at the time established a confectionery in the same room. He has been industrious and successful in life, and has accumulated a comfortable home property in Plainfield. To Mr. and Mrs. Carl were born four children: Charles Edwin, William W., Anne E. and Effie M. Mr. Carl has ever been a Democrat. He has served this township three years as school director. He and his worthy wife are members of the Church of God.

WILLIAM CAROTHERS (deceased) was born January 12, 1789, in West Pennsborough Township, this county, son of Andrew and Margaret (Geddes) Carothers, early settlers of Cumberland County. Our subject was twice married; on first occasion to Miss Ann, daughter of Abraham Line, one of the sons of the original George Line. They settled at once on the family homestead, on the Chambersburg Pike, and here Mrs. Carothers died in 1838. To this union were born four children—two of whom died in infancy, Ann Rebecca died soon after her marriage with James M. Carothers, and Margaret Jane. Mr. Carothers, who afterward married Miss Esther McFeeley, died March 9, 1870, in his eightieth year, his widow following him January 19, 1873, in her eighty-ninth year. Mr. Carothers, who was an enterprising and successful farmer, acquired a fine farm of 200 acres, on which he had a handsome residence and substantial farm buildings. He was a conscientious member of the Presbyterian Church. Miss Margaret Jane Carothers, the daughter who survives, now owns the family homestead, where she resides, and is also the possessor of a fine farm of 184 acres of fertile, well-improved land. She is a consistent member of the Evangelical Association, and is a lady of estimable Christian character, having the respect of the community.

JAMES M. CAROTHERS, farmer, P. O. Plainfield, was born August 4, 1829, in the house where he now lives, in West Pennsborough Township, this county. His father, William M., a son of Armstrong Carothers, and also a native of this township, married Miss Fanny, daughter of George Clark, of Frankford Township. Cumberland Co., Penn., and granddaughter of William Clark, a colonel in the Continental Army during the Revolution. About 1828 William M. Carothers and family located in the McAllister District, West Pennsborough Township, this county, and here resided until his death. Their children are as follows: George, in Frontier County, Neb; Jane; Armstrong, who died in Wood County, Ohio; William W., in Big Spring, this county; Mrs. Martha Eliza Duffy, in Mount Holly Springs, this county; Rev. Martin J., a presiding elder in the Evangelical Association at Milton, Northumberland Co., Penn.; Mary (deceased) and James M. William M. Carothers ended a useful life July 21. 1864, and his esteemed widow followed him November 29, 1872, at the advanced age of eighty-three years. They were an upright pioneer people, and their memory will long be honored. Our subject completed his education under Prof. R. K. Burns, at Plainfield Academy, this county, and early adopted the profession of teaching, which he followed for six years, leaving an honorable record as a faithful and efficient teacher. He remained at home and took care of his aged parents until their death. He has purchased the interest of the other heirs in the homestead, and owns a fine farm of fifty-two acres of fertile and well-improved land. Mr. Carothers was married March 30, 1866, to Miss Ann Rebecca, daughter of William and Anne (Line) Carothers, and who died October 14, same year. She was a lady of estimable Christian character, and her early death was mourned by a large circle of friends. Mr. Carothers was married on second occasion February 23, 1871, to Isabel J. Kernan, of this township, and has one daughter, Mary J. Mr. Carothers is a life-long Democrat, with strong temperance principles. He and his worthy wife are consistent members of the Evangelical Association, in which he is class-leader.

JAMES A. DAVIDSON, farmer, P. O. Kerrsville, was born July 11, 1827, in West Pennsborough Township, this county, son of Alexander Davidson. He was brought up on his father's farm, and received his education principally in the schools of the home district. September 1, 1853, he married Miss Nancy C., daughter of William Nettle, of this township, and they have resided on the family homestead here ever since. To them were born ten children, seven now living: Mrs. Jane Ellen McKeehan, Lucy Cordelia, Mary Alice, Mrs. Nannie Merrette Green, William Alexander, Anna Amelia and Carrie Robecca. Mr. Davidson is a life-long Republican, and takes a deep interest in public affairs. He has served his township acceptably as school-director, assessor, and in other capacities, and is a highly respected citizen.

JOHN S. DAVIDSON, farmer, P. O. Kerrsville, was born March 2, 1829, in West Pennsborough Township, this county. His father, Alexander Davidson, also a native of this county, and a son of John Davidson, married Miss Jane, daughter of John and Jane Woodburn, of Dickinson Township, this county, and settled on a farm in the Kerrsville District, where they acquired an estate of about 500 acres of farm land. In 1858 they retired from active labor and located in Newville, where they resided until their death, Mr. Davidson dying October 19, 1865, aged seventy-eight, and his widow August 19, 1879, aged eighty-years and eight months. To them were born eight children. Our subject completed his education in the academy at Lititz, Lancaster Co., Penn.; was engaged in mercantile business in Plainfield, this township, from 1851 to 1859, and while there, January 1, 1856, was married. In 1859 he retired from mercantile business and located on the farm of 150 acres, where he now resides, and which, in early times, was owned by Rev. Joshua Williams, a Presbyterian minister, who built the handsome residence in which he resides. Mr. Davidson is a director in the First National Bank of Newville, as was also his father before him. He is a Republican in politics, and takes a deep interest in public affairs. He has served the township many years in the school board, and was appointed government assessor of internal revenue for Dickinson, West Pennsborough and Frankford Townships.

HENRY DONER, retired farmer, Plainfield, was born August 4, 1818, in West Pennsborough Township, this county. His parents, Daniel and Elizabeth Doner, of Lancaster County, Penn., located in Frankford Township, Cumberland County, Penn., in 1805, and after four years finally settled in West Pennsborough Township, where they took up a new farm, which they cleared and developed. They raised a family of ten children, all of whom married: Mrs. Elizabeth Hale died at Upper Sandusky, Ohio; Abraham (deceased); Daniel died in Johnson County, Iowa; John, in Pennsborough Township; Nancy Waggoner, of Newville; Jacob; Mrs. Fannie Line (deceased); Mrs. Maria Rudy, of Dauphin County, Penn.; Henry and David. Mr. Doner died February 25, 1853, in his seventy-second year; his widow followed him March 7, 1875, at the advanced age of ninety-six years, two months and twenty-six days. They were industrious pioneers, and their memory will long be honored. Our subject was brought up on the farm on which he now resides, and received his education in the schools of the home district. August 3, 1848, he married Miss Mary Ann Leidick, of Silver Spring Township, this county, where she was born March 2, 1830, daughter of John and Margaret (Albert) Leidick, natives of this county, where they passed their entire lives. Mr. and Mrs. Doner have resided on the homestead farm ever since their marriage, and own a fine farm of 135 acres of fertile and well improved land, with elegant residence and out-buildings. To them were born four children: Elizabeth Ann, who died at seven years of age; Mrs. Margaret Ellen Bear, living on the homestead; Henry Calvin, who died in his twenty-second year, and Mrs. Laura May Moyer, who died in her twenty-first year. Mr. and Mrs. Doner are consistent members of the Lutheran Church. Mr. Doner is a Republican in politics. He is an upright, useful citizen, a man of firm principles, and enjoys the highest respect and esteem of the community.

DAVID DONER, farmer, P. O. Kerrsville, was born April 6, 1820, in West Pennsborough Township, Cumberland Co., Penn., son of Daniel and Elizabeth Doner. He was brought up on his father's farm, and received his education in the schools of the home district. He married, October 26, 1845, Miss Susan Miller, who was born in York County, Penn., and moved to Mifflin Township, this county, in girlhood, with her parents, Henry and Elizabeth Miller. After living eighteen years on their farm on the banks of the Conodoguinet Creek, this township, Mr. Doner finally located on the State road, where he now resides and owns a fine farm of 114 acres, with handsome residence and farm buildings, besides another place of 106 acres on the creek. To Mr. and Mrs. Doner were born four children: Daniel Henry, who died in childhood; Joseph, who died at twenty-four years of age; Mrs. Elizabeth Bear, living on the home place, and Alfred M., of Plainfield. Mrs. Doner died April 5, 1885. Mr. Doner is an earnest Republican. He has lead an active industrious life, devoting himself mostly to the management of his farm. He is an upright man of strict integrity, highly respected by the whole community.

ROBERT H. FULTON, farmer, P. O. Newville, is the grandson of Francis Fulton, who was born June 21, 1765, and with his parents came from Scotland and settled in Juniata County and had a large family of children. Francis Fulton was married to Sarah McKinstry, born March 17, 1768, and they settled at "Quarry Hill," now in Penn Township, this county. "At that time the Indians, who claimed a large part of this county, were very troublesome, and they captured grandfather's father and mother and all the rest of the family, except grandfather, and burned the house and killed one little boy. Grandfather was pursued, but he wrapped his clothes in a bundle, placed it on his head, and swam the Juniata River and crossed over to Cumberland County. The rest were taken to a French settlement and sold, and after some time were released and settled where the city of Cincinnati now stands. Grandfather never knew what became of some of his brothers." On the Quarry Hill farm were born twelve children: Jennie, the eldest, born July 13, 1786, followed by Mary, John, Elizabeth, James, Sarah and Annie, all born prior to 1800; Nancy, born January 16, 1802, now the widow of John Duncan, and resides at Peoria, Ill.; Francis H. Isabella; Keziah, and Matilda. All this family lived and died in this valley except Nancy Bell and John. James (father of our subject) was born October 10, 1795; was married to Grizzella, daughter of Robert Blean, of this county, and commenced domestic life on his wife's father's farm, and there the first daughter, Mary, was born. In 1834 James Fulton purchased the Duncan tract, purchased in 1788 of James Irwan and Isabella, his wife. On this farm was born Sarah (the first of the children married), wedded Robert Hood; Mary Craig, is the wife of Rev. John S. McCullough; Francis, married Mary Jury; David B. died unmarried; Martha, unmarried, is a resident of Springfield, and James married Kate Bistline. Our subject, who was reared on the farm and educated in the Big Spring Academy, enlisted, in 1862, in Company C, One Hundred and Fifty-eighth Regiment Pennsylvania Volunteers, under Col. D. B. McKibben. Most of Mr. Fulton's service was in North Carolina, but the regiment also did duty in front of Richmond. He was promoted from corporal to sergeant of his company, and received his discharge August 18, 1863. November 26, 1863, his marriage with Minnie H. McCune occurred, and the young bride was taken to the old stone mansion, so many years in the possession of the Fultons, and which to-day is one of the oldest inhabited houses in the Cumberland Valley, and as substantial as ever. Robert Fulton and wife had following named children: Hugh Brady McCune (born November 14, 1864), Ellie Blean, Jennie Belle, Albert William, Robert Howerd, Orthelia, Mary Bell and James Bruce (Jennie B. and Orthelia are deceased). This interesting family are the representatives of the grand old name they bear. Mr. Fulton and wife are members of the Presbyterian Church at Newville, in which he has been a trustee for a number of years.

ROBERT M. GRAHAM, farmer, P. O. Plainfield. The Graham family is one of the oldest and most reputable in the county. Four of its members have been associated with the legal profession for more than three-quarters of a century, serving also continually in official positions. William Graham (father of subject) was born in 1811, in Frankford Township, this county, son of Arthur and Nancy (McClure) Graham, and was married, in 1836, to Nancy Davidson, who bore him six sons: Robert M., John D., James M., William F., Arthur H. and Alfred M. All the sons, excepting Alfred M. (deceased), married and reside in Cumberland County. The eldest son, Robert M., was born November 12, 1837, and, from eleven years of age, resided with his uncle, Robert M. Graham. He received a liberal education in the schools of his township, and when twenty-one commenced teaching school and for seven years followed this profession in Frankford Township, this county (F. K. Ployer was one of his pupils). Having been raised on a farm, and preferring agriculture to a professional life, he subsequently took charge of his uncle's farm. In 1868 he was married to Rebecca J. McKeehan, whose ancestry dates back more than a century. She is a daughter of Joseph and Jane M. (Skiles) McKeehan. The married life of Robert and his young wife was commenced on his uncle's homestead, which has descended from father to son since the days of William Penn, from whom they have the original grant. On this farm were born their children, Joseph M., William F. and Clemens McFarland. Our subject's present home was the paternal homestead of Mrs. Graham, to whom it descended by inheritance. The first official term served by Robert M. Graham was commenced in the autumn of 1878, when he was elected prothonotary and retained as deputy by his successor and still continues in this office. In 1884 he was elected justice of the peace in this township, and as a conscientious official, public-spirited citizen and good business man, he has few equals, and his neighbors unite in saying of him that "truly he is a man of the times."

JAMES D. GREASON, farmer, P. O. Greason, was born April 2, 1822, in West Pennsborough Township, this county. His father, James Greason, born November 25, 1776, in this county, was a son of William and Agnes (Waugh) Greason. James Greason, Sr., completed his literary course in Dickinson College, Carlisle, graduating in 1795, being a school-mate of President Buchanan. After graduating he pursued a legal course at Carlisle, and was admitted to the bar. He married Miss Mary Carothers, of this county, about the latter part of the year 1804, and at once retired to a farm in Silver Spring Township, but soon moved to a farm in West Pennsborough Township (a portion of the Carother's estate), to which he added, until he finally possessed about 800 acres in the Greason School District. He erected buildings on most of the farms during his life. He died July 4, 1855, his wife having preceded him in 1854. Our subject completed his education in the academy at Shippensburg, and, in the spring of 1843, opened a drug store in that town, where he continued until 1845, when he established himself in the same line of business at Nashville, Tenn. He returned from there in December, 1847, and has lived in Cumberland County ever since. January 10, 1854, he married Miss Elmira J. Bitner, and located at once on the family homestead, where they now reside, and where his father lived from 1826 until his death. They have here a fine farm of 150 acres, on which they have erected a fine residence, and also own 110 acres adjoining, and also 135 acres from his father-in-law's estate. To Mr. and Mrs. Greason have been born two children: Henry Bitner (deceased in infancy) and Ralph. They have also brought up in their family Miss Grace Eppley, Mrs. Greason's cousin.

JOHN GREIDER, retired farmer, Plainfield, was born October 1, 1812, in Silver Spring Township, Cumberland Co., Penn. His parents. Jacob and Anna (Bowers) Greider, natives of Lancaster County, Penn., were among the early settlers of Silver Spring Township, this county. Jacob Greider was stricken down with apoplexy in 1827; his widow survived him until 1858, and was nearly eighty-five years old when she died. Of their nine children three are living: Henry, of Kosciusko County, Ind.; Mrs. Anna Railing, of Des Moines, Iowa, and John. Our subject was brought up on his father's farm, and attended the schools of the home district. He was married, September 4, 1834, to Miss Catharine, daughter of John and Catharine (Keiser) Heikes, the former a native of York County, and the latter of Perry County, Penn., and who settled in West Pennsborough Township, this county, in very early times, and now lie buried on the farm. Of the six children of Mr. and Mrs. Heikes all lived to an advanced age: Mrs. Rachel Paul, George, Mrs. Elizabeth Leas, Mrs. Catharine Greider, David, Mrs. Rebecca Weisley—all now deceased but Catharine. Mr. Greider, after farming for three years, kept store three years at West Hill and in 1844 located on Conodoguinet Creek, and has resided here since that year. They possessed a fine estate of 300 or 400 acres at one time, most of which they have divided among their children, but still own the West Hill Mill, which is a fine property. To Mr. and Mrs. Greider have been born eight children—six of whom are now living: Mrs. Rachel Zolen (of Steele City, Neb.), Jacob, John, David and Mrs. Anna Diller (twins, now living near Steele City, Neb.) and George (of Belle Plain, Kas.). Mr. Greider, though a Republican in politics, has not cast a vote since he voted for Henry Clay, in 1844. He was an acquaintance and admirer of Bayard Taylor. He has been a man of very active life and industrious habits; has been a careful and extensive reader, a close observer of men and affairs, and being a natural orator has been called to preach at funerals, etc., for the past twenty-five years. His children, all well educated, are taking a high position in business and society.

GEORGE GROVE, physician Big Spring, has been one of the most active members of the medical profession, and is to-day the oldest practicing physician in the Cumberland Valley. He was born August 11, 1811, in Chambersburg, Franklin Co., Penn., son of Jacob and Elizabeth (Welsh) Grove, three of whose daughters, all widows, are still living: Mrs. Nancy Seibert, of Chambersburg; Mrs. Jane Pfeffer and Mrs. Mary Jeffries, of Philadelphia. Our subject received his scholastic education in Chambersburg; graduated with honor, in 1836, at the Jefferson Medical College, of Philadelphia, Penn., his diploma bearing the signatures of some of the most noted men in the State: Granville S. Pattison. M. D.; George McClellan, M. D., father of Gen. George B. McClellan, and also of Samuel McClellan, M. D., who is one of the finest obstetricians in the United States. Dr. Grove was married, April 6, 1837, to Miss Louisa Horn, of Hagerstown, Md., who bore him four daughters and two sons (both named George, the first of whom died in infancy, and the second enlisted in Company D. Seventy-eighth Pennsylvania Volunteer Infantry, when only seventeen, and died a few weeks later in the hospital at Nashville, Tenn.). The daughters are Josephine, Mary, Elizabeth and Emma L. Josephine and Emma are living, and in every respect inherit the noble qualities of their mother, who died October 27, 1847. Dr. Grove subsequently married Mrs. Martha Burkhardt, who bore him one son, Diller, now a resident of Carlisle. The Doctor's third wife was Mary A. E., daughter of John and Louisa Trego. He was an iron manufacturer and merchant of Cumberland Valley. After fifty years of active practice the Doctor is still hale and vigorous, his hair is raven black, and his step is as sprightly and elastic as that of a youth of twenty. Possessed of a liberal education and brilliant mind, he has for many years been considered an authority on medical matters in this and neighboring counties, and his position is a really enviable one among the faculty in the State. His daughters have also received a liberal education, and their accomplishments afford additional pleasure to their father, who has devoted so much of his valuable time to them.

JOHN C. KEISER, merchant, Plainfield, was born September 29, 1833, in Perry County, Penn., son of Jacob and Catharine (Ritter) Keiser, natives of that county, who

WEST PENNSBOROUGH TOWNSHIP. 581

located in West Pennsborough Tp., Cumberland Co., Penn., in early times, but afterward moved to Perry County, and there resided until their death. Our subject, the youngest in a family of four sons and three daughters, at ten years of age entered the store of his brother-in-laws, D. & J. Kochendofer, at Loysville, Perry County, and there remained until he was twenty years old. He spent four years in the West, engaged in mercantile pursuits in Rock Island, Ill., and Davenport, Iowa. He came to Cumberland County and established a general store at Greason, in 1859, which he has carried on ever since, locating at different times at West Hill, Good Hope, Mount Rock, Heberlig and Plainfield. He settled down permanently at his present stand in Plainfield in the spring of 1885, and here keeps a full stock of dry goods, groceries and general merchandise. He has built himself a fine residence and store building, and has, besides, a farm of eighty acres in Benton County, Minn. By strict attention to business Mr. Keiser has built up a large trade with the surrounding community. He married Miss Sarah Elizabeth Humer, of Carlisle, Penn., in 1860, and they have had five children: David K., Mrs. Cora C. Smith, Mary E. (deceased), Anna R. and Grace R. Mr. Keiser is a Republican in politics. He held the appointment as postmaster at Plainfield from 1875 to 1877; Mount Rock from 1878 to 1880; Heberlig in 1881. Mr. Keiser is one of the active enterprising business men, and is respected by all who know him.

WILLIAM KERR, a native of Huntingdon County, Penn., was born October 30, 1791, and came to West Pennsborough Township, Cumberland Co., Penn., in 1825, and on June 26, the same year, married Miss Eliza Belle, daughter of David and Isabel Sterrett, natives of this county and very prominent pioneers. Mr. and Mrs. Kerr lived one year in Huntingdon County after their marriage, and then settled permenently in West Pennsborough Township, this county, in 1826, and here acquired a fine estate. Mr. Kerr was a very active, public spirited citizen, devoting most of his attention to the management of his estate. He was one of the original founders and a member of the board of directors of the banking house of Kerr, Brenham & Co., since known as the First National Bank of Carlisle. His useful life ended September 20, 1874, his wife having preceded him December 23, 1844. Of their children four attained maturity: Elizabeth Jane and Mary Isabel (both deceased), William A. and David S., living.

WILLIAM A. KERR, farmer, P. O. Kerrsville, was born November 30, 1829; acquired his education in the academies of Huntingdon, Mount Joy, Lancaster County; Juniata County, and Good Hope, of this township. He married, January 10, 1854, Miss Elizabeth B. Orr, of Franklin County, Penn., and then settled down where they now reside. To this union have been born two children: Mary Eliza and William Orr.

DAVID STERRETT KERR, farmer, P. O. Kerrsville, was educated in common school and Mount Joy Academy, and has resided on the homestead farm all his life. These gentlemen have made many valuable improvements in the estate handed down from their ancestors.

T. FRANK KING, proprietor of Valley View Mills, P. O. Newville, was born April 19, 1836, in Georgetown, now a part of Washington, D. C. His father, John H. King, a native of the eastern shores of Maryland, was a son of a sea captain, and his mother was born in the Carlisle Garrison, this county. John H. King early engaged in mercantile business at Georgetown, and there married Miss Ellen Harriet, who was born in Monroe Township, this county. Her parents were also natives of this county. After a long and prosperous business career, Mr. King retired to Georgetown Heights, where he resided until his death, about 1855; his esteemed widow survived him until March, 1885, dying while on a visit to her daughter, Mrs. Dr. Anna Ingraham, of Palmyra, Wayne Co., N. Y. Our subject received his education in the academies and colleges of Washington City; came to Carlisle, this county, at about nineteen years of age, and learned his profession at Henderson's Mills. He married Miss Anna C. Bowers, a daughter of Daniel and Margaret Bowers, of Carlisle, the ceremony being performed December 17, 1857, by Rev. C. P. Wing. After living at Georgetown three years; at Seneca Mills, Md., about two years; near Spring Mills, this county, two years; Bucher's Mills, Silver Spring Township, two years; Newville, two years; and two years at Roxbury, Franklin County, they purchased the Shellaberger Mills on the Conodoguinet Creek, West Pennsborough Township, this county, in 1873, and have resided here ever since. Here they own a fine mill with four run of burrs, doing a fine trade with the surrounding community, and shipping to more remote points. Mr. King is also deeply interested in the culture of bees, and has an extensive apiary of fifty hives, from which he realizes from one to two tons of honey annually. To Mr. and Mrs. King have been born two children: Mrs. Margaret Mentzer and Harry M. Our subject has been successful in life, and has acquired a fine property in residences and lots in Newville, besides the mill and farm where he resides. He is past master in the F. & A. M., and a member of the Improved Order of Red Men.

GEORGE LANDIS, farmer, P. O. Newville, a son of George and Elizabeth Landis, was born in Franklin County, Penn., January 30, 1826, his father dying a few days before. Our subject came with his mother and other children (Jacob and Anna) to Mifflin Township, this county, in February, 1826. They were quite poor, and after coming to Mifflin Township the mother supported her family by the labor of her own hands until they were able to care for themselves. Mrs. Landis was married to John Negley about 1831, and by him had one son; John, now a resident of South Middleton Township, this county. George Landis remained with his step-father, working for his board and clothes, until he was thirteen years of age, when he was indentured to Andrew Snoke to learn the blacksmith's trade, which apprenticeship he completed in four years, and then found himself the possessor of $100, having received $25 per year for his services, he furnishing his own clothes. He worked the next year for his brother Jacob, for $5 per month, nearly all of which he saved, and then for five years worked in Newville, saving during that time enough money to establish himself in business. Having won the affection of Elizabeth H. Hoover, they were married, February 17, 1848, and in the spring moved to Mifflin Township, this county, where Mr. Landis worked four years at his trade, and then purchased the farm now owned by George Hosler. Full of enterprise, he rapidly improved his farm, for which he paid $1,800, and a few years later sold it for $6,000. Since then he has purchased other farms, and now owns not only his fine homestead in this township, but another farm in Mifflin Township. Nine children have been born to Mr. and Mrs. Landis, eight now living: Margaret E., widow of John Lay; Eliza J., wife of P. A. Ployer; Levi F., married to Mary A. Brehm; William H., married to Elizabeth Brehm; George A., married to Ella Strohm; John M.; Harvey and Samuel (the last three named are still single). The success of Mr. Landis has been phenomenal. He still does his own smithing, has followed the trade in all forty-seven years, and is one of the oldest blacksmiths in the county.

JOSEPH A. LINDSAY, miller, P. O. Newville, is a great-grandson of Samuel Lindsay, of Scotch origin, who early settled in this township and married Jane Martin, about 1766, and by her had five children: William, Robert, Jane, Margaret and Nancy. Robert Lindsay, who was a noted teacher in this county, married Elizabeth Conley, February 21, 1797, and was father of the following named children: Nancy, Joseph C., Samuel and Lacy. Of these children Joseph C. (father of our subject), was born in West Pennsborough Township, this county, in 1802; learned the miller's trade at the Shellabarger Mills (with the owners of that mill), and during his life-time followed that occupation and at the time of his death had engaged forty years continuously in the business. He (Joseph C.) was married December 24, 1829, to Elizabeth Shellabarger, born September 15, 1809, by whom he had five children: Ann M., John, Lacy, Mary J. and Robert (the latter was burned to death in the Hays Mill in Frankfort Township, this county, March 2, 1849). The death of Joseph C. Lindsay's first wife occurred February 19, 1841, and September 20, 1845, he married Mrs. Barbara (Bear) Stevick (who by her first husband was the mother of David B. and Sarah A., wife of W. Scott McGaw; David B. Stevick married Ellen Black and resides in Carlisle). Mr. Lindsay's second marriage was blessed with one child: Joseph A., born June 27, 1846. The second wife died in 1885. Our subject learned his trade with his father and, after the death of the latter, purchased the mill, in 1880. He was married, in 1867, to Clara, daughter of John and Rebecca Rhodes, residents near Middle Spring, Franklin Co., Penn. Of the five children born to this union two are living: Ralph and Laura.

GEORGE LINE, farmer, P. O. Greason, was born July 6, 1826, in Dickinson Township, this county, son of David Line and grandson of William and great-grandson of George Line, which William Line served as a minute man in the Revolutionary war. He was in the service at the time of the Trenton and Princeton battles, and to his lot it fell to take some of the Hessian prisoners as laborers on the farm. His sword is still held as a relic of the family. William Line married Maria Bear, and their children were Emanuel, George, David, Mrs. Mary Spangler, Mrs. Catherine Eby, Mrs. Nancy Musselman, Mrs. Sarah Tritt, Mrs. Susan Myers, Mrs. Rebecca Givler, Mrs. Lydia Myers and Mrs. Rachel Snyder. David, son of William Line, married Miss Sarah Myers, who bore him the following children: John (deceased), Dr. William Line (of Nebraska City, Neb.), George, David, Samuel C., Mrs. Mary A. Greason (deceased), Mrs. Matilda Huston, Mrs. Sarah Jane Huston and Frances (deceased). David Line died January 31, 1864; his widow followed him June 1, 1882, aged eighty-one years. George, the son of David and Sarah (Myers) Line, married, November, 1851, Mrs. Isabella W., daughter of Jonathan and Amy (Spear) Huston, the former of whom, a native of this county, was a son of John and Margaret (Huston) Huston; the latter, a native of Maine, came here with her mother and stepfather, Mr. Wheeler, who went the next year to Morgan County, Ohio. After living in South Middleton Township, this county, until 1872, Mr. and Mrs. George Line settled permanently in West Pennsborough Township, this county, where they now reside and have a fine farm of 136 acres, besides 100 acres in South Middleton Township, which 100 acres is a part of the tract purchased from Gen. John Armstrong in 1778. Their living children are Arthur Wing and Dionysius Page; four died of diphtheria within two weeks, in October, 1862. Mr. Line has lived a long and useful life in this county; is a Republican in politics with strong temperance principles; is an upright, useful citizen.

JOHN A. LINE, farmer, P. O. Greason, was born April 9, 1834, on the homestead farm, Dickinson Township, this county. During the time when the French Huguenots were settling in Switzerland, George Line, a native of Switzerland, sailed, with his wife and son, for America, but died on ship-board, and his widow located in Lancaster County,

WEST PENNSBOROUGH TOWNSHIP. 583

Penn., where the young lad George grew up, and in course of time married Salome Zimmerman. He was for many years proprietor of the famous Green Gardens, in Lancaster County, purchasing the property of Gen. John Armstrong, in Dickinson Township, this county, and settling here in 1778. He paid £9,000 Continental currency for the farm. Of George and Salome Line's sons, George L. died November 5, 1885, David died in Lancaster County, and William, Abraham and John lived in Dickinson Township, this county. John married Miss Anna Barbara Le Fevre, and had three daughters: Salome (deceased), Mrs. Catharine Tritt (deceased), and Mrs. Mary Coulter, now living in Vermillion, Marshall County, Kas.; and three sons: George L., Daniel, burned to death in childhood, and John, who settled in Warren County, Ill. George L. Line married Miss Maria Line, daughter of Emanuel Line and granddaughter of William Line, and to this union were born four children: Mrs. Elizabeth M. Hemminger, John A., Emanuel C. and Abraham L. Mrs. Line died November 27, 1869. John A., the eldest son, completed his education by taking a short course at Good Hope Academy and in White Hall Academy, near Harrisburg, Penn. He married, December 29, 1868, Miss Mary B. Bowman, and March 30, 1869, they settled where they now reside, in West Pennsborough Township, this county, and have a fine farm of 82 acres of fertile and well-improved land. Their children are Miriam (deceased), Herman Bowman, Charles Eugene and John Raymond. Mrs. Line is a consistent member of the Lutheran Church. Mr. Line, formerly a Republican in politics, is now a Prohibitionist. He has served his township in various official positions. He took a thorough course in civil engineering and does a large business as surveyor in this county.

JOHN K. LONGNECKER, farmer, P. O. Plainfield, was born September 29, 1839, in West Pennsborough Township, this county. His father, Benjamin Longnecker, a son of Isaac Longnecker, a native of Lancaster County, Penn., and an early settler in the lower part of Cumberland County, was born near Fairview, this county, and there married Miss Mary Reif, a native of Middleton, Dauphin Co., Penn., and settled permanently in Plainfield in 1833, where they died—Mr. Longnecker March 11, 1869, and his widow in 1885, aged eighty-five years. They reared nine of their eleven children: Mrs. Nancy Howenstine, of Decatur, Ill.; Mrs. Mary Bear, of Wichita, Kas.; Mrs. Catharine Bear; Mrs. Eliza Strohm; Mrs. Susan James (deceased); Mrs. Rebecca Carl (deceased); Sarah; Benjamin F., of Decatur, Ill.; and John K. At nineteen our subject engaged in teaching, and after following the profession four years, completed his education in the State Normal School, at Millersville; then continued teaching at Plainfield seven years, making eleven years in all in the place. He enlisted October 16, 1862, in the One Hundred and Fiftieth Regiment Pennsylvania Volunteer Infantry; served under Gen. Foster, at Middlebury, N. C., being detailed as clerk in the quartermaster's department during the entire term of service. He married Miss Sarah Belle Peffer, of Dickinson Township, this county, January 5, 1865, and then settled where he now resides, on the old family homestead. They own here a farm of 70 acres, with handsome residence and buildings, all of which they have acquired by their own industry. To them have been born four children: Benjamin H., Mary R., Myrtle B. and Willie P. (deceased). Mr. Longnecker is a Republican in politics. He has served as school director five years and takes a deep interest in the cause of education.

BENJAMIN McKEEHAN, farmer, P. O. Kerrsville, is a grandson of Benjamin McKeehan, a native of County Antrim, Ireland, whose first settlement in Cumberland County, Penn., was near the Conodoguinet, in what is now West Pennsborough Township. At that time he was only eleven years of age, but three brothers came with him: John, James and Alexander; they were the possessors of plenty of ready money, for an immense tract of land was purchased, extending from within a half mile from Newville to Mount Rock. Benjamin McKeehan was a Revolutionary soldier, and after the close of the war returned to this township; a few years later he married Margaret Wilson, and their first daughter, Mary, was born June 15, 1782, followed by the birth of Chrissy in 1784, Jane in 1787, John in 1789, William in 1793, and Margaret in 1797. This pioneer couple died, the father October 23, 1814, and the mother April 24, 1829. The youngest son (father of our subject) was married, in 1833, to Rebecca, daughter of James McManes, who came from Ireland when a young man, and settled near Plainfield; was married to Ann Holtsoppel, and had the following children: Irvin, Esther, Rebecca and John. To William McKeehan and wife six children were born: Margaret, Benjamin, Thaddeus S., Grizzell, Rebecca C. and Jane M. Thaddeus S. was a volunteer in Company E, One Hundred and Thirtieth Regiment Pennsylvania Infantry, and fell in the memorable battle of Antietam, upon which bloody field he was buried. William McKeehan lived a long and useful life, and died in April, 1871. His good widow finds a pleasant home with her son and daughter in the old mansion where her married life has been spent, and has passed her eighty-first birthday, having lived to see Cumberland Valley transformed from a forest into elegant farms, dotted with fine residences and prosperous villages. The children are of that intelligent class that may be expected from those who carry in their veins the blood of a Revolutionary soldier.

JOHN D. MAINS, farmer, Newville, was born in 1852, at Shippensburg, within a short distance of the Cumberland County line. His great-grandfather, Marshall M.

Mains, came with his family from Bucks County, Penn., almost a century ago, and of his children Marshall M. (grandfather of subject) married, and had the following children: Marshall M., William, Griselda and Sarah; of these William and Marshall inherited the large farm near the then village of Shippensburg. The elder son married Sarah M. Bell, by whom he had five sons and two daughters: Thomas B. (enlisted in the Second New York Cavalry, and, for bravery, was promoted first lieutenant of a colored regiment, and met his death while gallantly fighting in the battle of the Wilderness), William J., James M., John D. (our subject), Robert K., Jane M. and Margaret S. On the maternal side Mrs. Mains was a direct descendant of the Dunlaps, who for more than a century lived in West Pennsborough Township, and in their day were a numerous and influential family. John D. was in his third year when his mother died, and he then came to reside with John. Sarah. Nancy and Mary Dunlap, who lived in Mr. Mains' present residence, and here he was reared and educated. Sarah Dunlap, who was born in the old log house that stands near by, in 1792, died at the patriarchal age of ninety-three. John D. Mains became heir in part to the original Dunlap estate. Our subject chose farming; was married, December 1, 1875, to Emma J., daughter of David G. and Griselda (Linn) Duncan. Their married life has been passed on the fine farm previously mentioned, and their children—Glenn D., Sarah G., Robert M. and Thomas B.—were the first born in a house that for three quarters of a century has been occupied by a renowned family.

ALEXANDER S. MONTGOMERY, farmer, P. O. Newville, is a grandson of James Montgomery, who was married, April 30, 1812, to Elizabeth, daughter of Alexander and Sarah Scroggs, who, at that date, owned all the land on both sides of the spring in the neighborhood where our subject resides. Alexander Scroggs, who, in an early day, always carried his trusty rifle on his back while plowing, one day discovered what he thought to be a painted savage following him while at work. The sharp crack of the rifle announced the shot that laid the marauder low, and after washing off the paint, Mr. Scroggs found that a white man instead of an Indian had attempted to murder him. On this farm bushels of arrow-heads have been unearthed, which were probably made and hidden by the Indians in an early day. Alexander Scroggs died in 1826, aged nearly seventy-seven years; his wife died in 1864. They reared a numerous family, the descendants of whom are all now deceased but our subject, who is also the last of the Montgomery family. James Montgomery and wife had two children: Robert and Sarah J. (married to A. L. Irvin in 1839). Robert was born September 12, 1814, and married, in 1847, Rachael Thompson, who was born in 1813, and to this union were born Elizabeth, Alexander S. and Jane. The eldest daughter is the wife of S. M. Skinner, with whom Jane resides. All were born in the ancestral Scroggs mansion, which, in an early day, was used as a fort in which the family were frequently sheltered from the Indians. Robert Montgomery, the father, died April 11, 1879, and his wife October 20, 1862. Alexander S., the only son of this couple, was born March 17, 1851; was married November 14, 1877, to Clara, daughter of John and Maria Elliott, residents at that time of Plainfield, this county. The union of this young couple was blessed with three children: Sarah J., Rachael M. and Clara E., all of whom were born on the homestead, where four generations of the family have been born, and of which Mr. Montgomery is sole heir, who, no doubt, will, in his turn, transmit it to his children. In 1872 Robert Montgomery was elected associate judge, serving out his term with distinction. As a man and jurist he occupied the highest place in the estimation of the public, for his official life was characterized by many acts of kindness and public spirit.

MRS. EMILY W. MYERS, P. O. Newville, was born near Big Spring, Cumberland County, Penn., July 12, 1849, youngest daughter of Joseph and Mary S. (Woodburn) McKee, and was married, July 31, 1872, to John B. Myers, son of John B. and Eve (Bower) Myers, and born October 21, 1834. The original John B. Myers was of German descent; came to this county from Lancaster County, Penn., more than a century ago. He was the father of the following named children: John B., William A., Samuel, Catharine, Anna, Elizabeth, Maria, Sarah and Agnes. He purchased a farm (a part of the original Schuyler tract), and was one of the few who were able to withstand the terrible financial depression following the Revolutionary war, when the Continental money became worthless, and men holding thousands of dollars were reduced to poverty by the depreciation of this currency. Full of enterprise Mr. Myers pushed bravely on, and instilled in his son the same enthusiasm characteristic of his race and name, and succeeded in holding the property and becoming quite wealthy. After the marriage of John B. Myers, Jr., and wife, they commenced their domestic life on the pleasant homestead where the widow still resides. Up to the age of forty-five years he had long resisted the match-making mammas, but the many charms of Miss McKee won him from the ranks of batchelordom, and to the time of his death occasion never arose for regret that he had formed this alliance with a daughter of one of the oldest and most noted families in Cumberland Valley. Mr. Myers was a successful farmer. He and his wife, devout members of the United Presbyterian denomination, were prominent in church work. Retiring in manner Mr. Myers had great love for home, his wife and his children—Mary E., Harriet J., Joseph Mc. John B., Sarah J. and Maggie Y., all living but John B. and Maggie. March 21, 1884, the death of the kind husband and father occurred, since which time Mrs. Myers has managed the farm, her husband having such confidence in her ability that she was left sole executor, and well does she preform her trust. Her home is neat, cheery and attractive, and the bright children evince a careful training.

In connection with this sketch Mrs. Myers says: "I consider it very important in writing the biography of the lives of different persons to know for what purpose they have lived, whether the life of each has been a success or a failure, a blessing or a curse. In writing my own history, I would, in the spirit of meekness and deep humility, say that my object in life has not been to accumulate riches, neither have I coveted the honors and emoluments of this world, nor was it any good in me but through the free grace and loving kindness of our Heavenly Father. I was led in very early life to accept the Savior, and ever since my heart's desire and prayer have been that I might be instrumental in leading precious souls to Christ, independent of rank or station, color or nation. Much of my time and means has been employed in devising ways by which the cause of missions might be more rapidly advanced, thereby bringing glory to God and so rescue the perishing. And last, not least does my soul go out to the glorious temperance cause, and oh! how I long to be helpful in emancipating the millions of precious souls who are held captive under the terrible curse of the rum traffic, and which is sweeping over our beloved land like a mighty flood; the sin, if not being repented, will bring down the vengeance of an offended Deity, and cause this great Nation to be obliterated from the face of the earth. I would add, in conclusion, when we were married my husband was not a Christian. I officiated as priest at the family altar and at the family board, and, having grace administered to discharge my duty faithfully, I soon had the sweet consciousness of being the feeble instrument in my husband's conversion, and had his dying testimony as I saw his spirit leave the clay tabernacle to that 'house not made with hands, eternal in the heavens.' These few facts I have hastily penned, in the hope they may be productive of good as a stimulus and encouragement to some devoted wife who has an unregenerate husband,and as a legacy to my children to follow in my footsteps only in as far as I have followed Christ, and my earnest desire has been that each of their lives may be one constant sacrifice to labor for the Savior who has bought them at such an immense cost, even the shedding of His own precious blood."

BENJAMIN MYERS, retired, P. O. Big Spring, was born April 8, 1816, on the homestead owned by John Armstrong. Rev. Abraham Myers was the first of the Myers family to come to this county, probably in 1760, and was the first minister of the United Brethren faith in this locality. He subsequently married a Miss Baker, who bore him three sons: Abraham, Benjamin and John. The reverend gentleman not only engaged in farming, but for many years rode over a large territory while preaching, and his own house was one of the regular appointments. He died about 1825. Abraham, the eldest son, was born in 1789 on the farm now owned by Mrs. James Greason. He was married to Nancy Myers, whose parents were also early settlers in the valley. Mr. and Mrs. Abraham Myers settled on the farm now owned by John Armstrong, and there reared a family of seven children: Samuel, James, Benjamin, Abraham, William G., Mary A. and Elizabeth. Of this family, William G., an M. D., practiced medicine for many years in this county, and now resides near Carlisle with his daughter, Mrs. Joseph Hosler. The other sons were farmers, but Benjamin is the only one residing in this township. In 1847 our subject married Mary, daughter of Jacob and Rebecca Raber, of York County, Penn. (both now deceased), and to this union were born Samuel, George, Alfred, Joseph, John, Benjamin, Abraham, James, Ellen, Annie, Concordia W and Flora. Mr. Myers' married life was begun on his father's homestead, but three years later he purchased an adjacent farm, and in 1855 bought his present home, where for so many years he has lived and prospered. Some of the children are in the West, doing well, and those remaining with the parents make joyous the old home hallowed by so many pleasant memories.

LEVON H. ORRIS, farmer, Newville, was born October 10, 1834, in Lizertzburg. His great-grandparents, with their children, were forced to fly from Ireland, leaving behind them a large estate. When Christopher Orris (grandfather of subject) was a mere lad he came to North Middleton Township, this county, and remained in the employment of Abraham Wagner until his marriage with Anna M. Bistline. John, the eldest son, was born in August, 1809, followed by Elizabeth, Margaret, Maria, Christopher, Sarah A., Catharine, Susan, George B. and Zacharias. When the war of 1812 broke out Christopher Orris started to Carlisle, intending to volunteer, but the tears and entreaties of his wife and young children caused him to relinquish the idea. He was a good man and reared his family in the Lutheran faith of which church he was a member. John Orris was married October 10, 1833, to Elizabeth Koser, whose people were among the first settlers in the neighborhood, and many of the relationship are yet residents of Cumberland County. Levon H., Margaret and Rebecca were born prior to their parents' removal to Frankford Township, near the Lutheran Church, where the other children were born: John, Eliza J. and Sylvester, all now deceased, Sylvester dying in defense of his country at Alexandria, Va., during the late Rebellion. Levon H. Orris learned the tailor's trade with his father, working for him until 1855, when he married Nancy A., daughter of Moses and Maria (Sullenborger) Whistler, when he began farming in Mifflin Township on his wife's land. In 1859 he purchased a nice farm in Frankford Township, this county, residing there twenty-one years, during which time John S., Harvey H., Levon H. and Nannie M. were born (the birth of the first child occurring ten years after marriage). Mr. Orris has not only been a very enterprising man, but a liberal one, and many have had cause to remember him with gratitude. Mr. Orris has filled many offices of trust, and was chosen to represent the Democratic party as treasurer from a list of twenty-two candidates, was elected by a good majority in 1873, and served his official term with credit. In 1881 he purchased his present farm near Newville, and pays attention entirely to agriculture and stock-raising.

MERVIN LINDSEY RALSTON, farmer, P. O. Carlisle, was born in West Pennsborough Township, this county, February 15, 1857. His father, Andrew Ralston, a son of David and Lucy (McAllister) Ralston, was born in Mifflin Township, this county, October 6, 1827, and was married February 26, 1852, to Jane E. Lindsey, a native of West Pennsborough Township, this county, and daughter of James Lindsey. She died February 26, 1857. Of their children, Mervin L., the subject of this sketch, is the only survivor. After the death of his first wife, Andrew Ralston married Miss Anna B. McElwaine, who died, leaving three children: Joseph B., Ella N. and Harry M. Andrew Ralston departed this life July 1, 1885. After the death of his mother Mervin L. Ralston was reared in the family of his uncle, James M. Ralston, in Dickinson Township, this county, until he was nine years of age; since then he has resided on his father's old farm, which he now owns, having purchased the other heirs' interest in the same. He has here a fine farm of 102 acres of fertile and well improved land. March 15, 1883, Mr. Ralston married Josephine Duffy and they have one daughter: Florence I. Our subject is an enterprising, successful young farmer, an upright and useful citizen, highly respected by the community in which he lives.

JOSEPH RITNER (deceased), ex-governor of Pennsylvania, was born where the city of Reading, Berks Co., Penn., now stands, March 25, 1780. His grandfather, John Ritner, a descendant of one of the noble families of Silesia, located for some time in Alsace, then a part of France, but afterward came to America and settled in Berks County, Penn.; his son, Michael, who was a soldier of distinction in the Revolution, serving until its close, swam Long Island Sound, being one of the very few that escaped by that route, and he was in the service at the time of the birth of his illustrious son. He followed the trade of weaver, locating in turn at Lancaster, Carlisle and York, where he died. Our subject, at twelve years of age, was hired out by his father to Jacob Myers, a farmer near Churchtown, this county, but who afterward moved to near Newville, and there Joseph Ritner lived until his marriage, May 26, 1801, with Miss Susan, daughter of Jacob Alter. In 1803 they moved to Westmoreland County, Penn., with her father, of whom Mr. Ritner bought a tract of land in Washington County (about six miles west of Washington and three north of Taylorstown), and there devoted himself to the development of his estate; he served under Gen. Harrison in the war of 1812; was nominated to the Legislature, without his knowledge, in 1821, on the Democratic ticket, and triumphantly elected. He was re-elected six consecutive terms, serving as speaker three terms, being unanimously elected the last time—the only instance on record in this State. He was a candidate of the Democratic Anti-Masonic party for governor in 1829, 1832 and 1835, being elected the last time. The acts of his administration were in the highest degree beneficial to the people of Pennsylvania. It was during this time (in 1836) that the present efficient school law was finally enacted and the State debts reduced over $100,000, a striking contrast to the administration immediately preceding and succeeding. He took a decided stand against the formation of monopolies in coal, land and railroads; opposed re-chartering State banks, then making application, and pointed out the evils that would result if they were successful. His veto was disregarded, and the evils he predicted speedily followed, causing general financial distress throughout the State. The great statesman, Thaddeus Stevens, was his intimate friend, and the plans marked out by Gov. Ritner were generally followed by Mr. Stevens. Of the circumstances of his last race, in 1838, it is sufficient to say that had there been a more fair and honest election the State might have been spared the unfortunate administration of Gov. Porter. At the close of his term Mr. Ritner purchased the bank farm, formerly owned by Gen. Foster, at Mount Rock, West Pennsborough Township, this county, where he resided the remainder of his life. He was an intimate friend of Gen. Harrison, who favored him whenever the opportunity offered. He devoted his attention to managing his estate until his retirement in 1848, continuing to take an active interest in public affairs. He lived a temperate and regular life, enjoying robust health. Personally he was of medium stature and portly build, weighing about 240 pounds during the latter half of his life. He passed away painlessly, through natural decay, ending his eventful and useful life October 19, 1869, in his ninetieth year. Gov. Ritner was a man of clear, quick perceptions, strong and persevering will, and of unimpeachable honesty, ever interested in the welfare of the people. He was opposed to the institution of slavery, a foe to secession, and at the decline of the Whig party became a Republican. During his service in the Legislature he was cotemporary with Dr. Jesse R. Burden, William M. Meredith, Joel B. Sutherland, Jonathan Roberts, James L. Gillelen and other illustrious men, from among whom he was chosen to the highest positions and received the most distinguished honors. Gov. Ritner's beloved wife died in 1853. They reared nine children, all of whom reared families but one—Joseph, a graduate of the United States Military Academy at West Point, but who resigned from the army, married, and took a professorship in Washington College; afterward received a commission as first lieutenant in the army, but died at home, in 1833, before assuming his duties; he had served with great distinction in the Black Hawk war. Abraham, a conductor on the Cumberland Valley Railroad, died at Chambersburg, Penn., in 1852; Henry was killed by a railroad accident at Burlington, Iowa, in 1863; Michael died in Bloomfield, N. J., in 1872, was a civil engineer on the Morris & Essex Railroad; Jacob, a farmer, died in South Middleton Tp., this county, in 1871; Mrs. Susan Kreichbaum died in 1854; Emma died in 1876; Mrs. Margaret Alter is now living at Kirkwood, Mo.; and Peter, the only surviving son, and who was born September 13, 1818, in Washington County, Penn., completed his education under Prof. Alfred Armstrong, of Harrisburg, Penn., came to West Pennsborough Township, this county, with his father, in 1839, and here cast his first vote for Gen. Harrison in 1840, and has supported the Whig and Republican parties ever since. He remained on this farm with his father, which place he purchased in 1856, and still owns, having here a fine farm of 156 acres. He married, February 16, 1843, Miss Mary Jane, daughter of William Davidson, and who died June 5, 1845, leaving one son, William D., now a clerk in the Treasury Department at Washington, D. C. Mr. Ritner married, in 1848, Miss Amelia Jane, daughter of Alexander Davidson, and she died October 18, 1870, leaving four children: Anna M., Mary D., Walter Clark and Joseph Alexander, having lost three in infancy. Mr. Ritner subsequently married, November, 1872, Mrs. Jane Mary McKeehan. Mr. and Mrs. Ritner and daughters are members of the Presbyterian Church. He is a worthy descendant of a noble father, a man of education and wide influence.

JACOB G. SHAW, farmer, P. O. Newville, was born in Penn Township, this county, July 10, 1838. His grandfather came to Cumberland County in 1792, emigrating from Ireland, was married to Hannah Rippet in 1802, and had the following children: John F., Isabella, Mary A., James R., Alexander, Joseph and Benjamin. (The last named was killed by Indians while trading between Fort Leavenworth and Santa Fe.) James R., subject's father, a native of Penn Township, this county, married Catharine Goodheart, after attaining his majority, and had four children: Hannah A., Mary M., Jacob G. and Joseph A. (he was one of the brave soldiers who fell during the civil war; he enlisted in 1862, and after his term had expired re-enlisted for three years in Company D, One Hundred and Eighty-seventh Pennsylvania Volunteer Infantry, and in 1864 met his death at the battle of Weldon Railroad, Va.) Jacob G. was reared on a farm, attended the public schools, completing his education in the normal school, and for twelve years engaged in teaching in this county. December 21, 1871, he was united in marriage with Miss Jane M., daughter of William and Rebecca McKeehan, of West Pennsborough Tp., this county, and who were among the most prominent of the pioneer families in Cumberland Valley. To this union have been born the following named children: Ira E., Ralph Mc. and Jesse H. One term of school was taught after Jacob G. Shaw's marriage, when his inclination turned to agriculture, and he purchased the handsome farm on which he resides, and in 1872 donned the habiliments of a granger, and with the energy characteristic of his people has made this business a success. He is now serving his third term as an official in the public schools of this township.

ISAAC D. STEINER, farmer, P. O. Plainfield, was born July 26, 1845, in Upper Allen Township, this county, son of Dietrich and Mary (Kaufman) Steiner, natives of York County, Penn., who located in Upper Allen Township, this county, about 1830, and here resided until their death, Mr. Steiner dying in 1863, and his widow in 1864; they reared seven of their eleven children. Our subject, the next to the youngest, was brought up on his father's farm and attended the schools of the home district. He followed lumbering six years in Cameron, Elk and Clearfield Counties, Penn., and one year in northern Michigan. Returning to Cumberland County, he married, December 28, 1875, Miss Rebecca Jane Waggoner, of North Middleton Township, this county, daughter of the well-known Jacob Waggoner. Since their marriage Mr. and Mrs. Steiner have resided in Middlesex Township six years and in West Pennsborough Township eight years. Their children are Anna Mary, Robert W. and Clara Blanche. Mr. Steiner is a Republican in politics and takes a deep interest in public affairs. He has served his township in various offices of trust.

GEORGE STROHM, manufacturer, Plainfield, was born September 18, 1815, in Lebanon County, Penn., son of George and Mary (Nipe) Strohm, natives of the same county, and who settled in Frankford Township, this county, in 1819, where they spent the active part of their lives, but afterward moved to North Middleton Township, where George Strohm, Sr., died January 6, 1864, in his eighty-second year, and his widow February 5, 1866, in her seventy-fifth year. They were the parents of the following named children: Mrs. Susan Shaw (deceased), George, Mrs. Mary Wagner, William, Mrs. Sarah Wagner, Mrs. Eliza Wagner, Mrs. Anna Wetzel, John (died at Decatur, Ill.), Mrs. Catharine Priest (deceased), Mrs. Leah Barnetts (of Decatur, Ill.), Mrs. Rebecca McKeehan (deceased) and David (died at Decatur, Ill.). Our subject was united in marriage, February 1, 1838, with Miss Eliza Longnecker, and resided on the farm until 1848, when he followed fence-making for several years. About 1854 Mr. Strohm began wagon-making at West Hill, this township, gradually enlarging his business (by making buggies, sleighs, carriages, etc.), and in 1869 established his present coach shop at Plainfield, this county, purchasing a farm, adjoining, of 36 acres, to which he has since added 27 acres more. His trade has steadily increased, so that he is now occupying three buildings and employing from eight to ten hands. He has admitted into partnership his son, David, who has worked in the establishment for twenty-one years, since he was twelve years old. They do a large business, making carriages, buggies, spring wagons and sleighs, and keep a complete line of light vehicles. Their goods have an excellent reputation for first-class material and superior workmanship, and they supply a large domestic trade for Cumberland Perry and Adams Counties, besides shipping to the East and West. To Mr. and Mrs. Strohm were born nine children: Mrs. Mary Ann James, Benjamin (of Battle Creek, Iowa), Mrs. Sarah Jane Myers (of Carey, Ohio), Joseph Silas, George (of Battle Creek, Iowa), David E., John W., Horace L. (of Anthony, Kas.) and Mrs. Lizzie G. Paul (of Wellington, Kas.). Mr. and Mrs. Strohm are members of the Church of God. He is an upright, useful citizen, and enjoys the respect and esteem of the community.

JOSHUA E. VAN CAMP, physician and surgeon, Plainfield, was born February 22, 1814, in Perry County, Penn., son of William and Melvina (Huffman) Van Camp, natives of the same county. Among the Holland settlers in Delaware was a family of Van Camps. Three of the sons. William, Maj. Moses and Jacobus, were farmers, and were among the Indian fighters of the early colonial wars and also of the Revolution. Their history is very fully depicted in Dr. Egle's History of Pennsylvania. William, above mentioned, was the great-grandfather of our subject through his son Andrew and grandson William, who all lived in Perry County, Penn., and the original estate is still in possession of the family. The property is on the Juniata, within four miles of Newport. There our subject was brought up among the wild beauties of one of nature's most charming spots. After completing the course the schools of the home district afforded him, he took a literary course at the Pennsylvania College, Gettysburg. He took up the study of medicine in the spring of 1867, under Dr. J. E. Singer, of Newport, and graduated from the Michigan University, with the degree of M. D., March 30, 1870. After practicing two years in Markelsville, Perry Co., Penn., he located in Plainfield, this county, in 1872, and practiced his chosen profession. He has made a fine reputation as a skillful and scientfic physician, and has built up a large and influential practice. In the fall of 1880, the Doctor established a drug and grocery store, which he still carries on. He was married, November 3, 1870, to Miss Rachael M., daughter of David Keiser, of Middlesex Township, this county, and to this union have been born three children: David W., Anna M. and Rosa Alberta. During the late war, Dr. Van Camp enlisted, in August, 1862, in Company H, One Hundred and Thirty-third Regiment Pennsylvania Volunteer Infantry, and participated in the battles of Fredericksburg and Chancellorsville; re-enlisted in September, 1864, in Company E, Two Hundred and Eighth Regiment Pennsylvania Volunteer Infantry, and took part in the battles of Hatcher's Run, Fort Steadman, Black Water and the final charge on Petersburg. He was honorably discharged at the close of the war, with rank of sergeant.

RICHEY WOODS, the first of this name to locate in this neighborhood, came from Scotland, more than a century ago, and took up the lands on which the family still resides. Richey Woods remained a bachelor; his nephew, Nathan Woods, married Jean Means and reared five children: Nathan J. Ramsey, Richard C., Joseph McCord, Martha J. and Margaret R. Of these Nathan J. Ramsey married Charlotte H., daughter of Jonathan and Eliza Holmes, of this county, and granddaughter of Commodore Richard O'Brien, a man, the merits of whose public services were acknowledged by four successive Presidents. He died February 16, 1824. Nathan J. Ramsey Woods engaged in teaching school at Huntingdon, Penn., but after his marriage came to the ancestral home of his father and engaged in farming. On the manor farm have been four generations of the Woods, the last being the children of our subject: Nathan, Holmes, Elizabeth, Jennie, James, O'Brien and Lottie, of whom James, O'Brien and Lottie survive. Nathan J. Ramsey Woods was an ardent Democrat, a Presbyterian by faith, and a practical business man. He died January 28, 1866. The massive stone structure in which the family reside was completed in 1812, and in all possibility will remain a landmark and as a monument to uncle Richey for a century to come.

ANDREW YOUNG, farmer, P. O. Plainfield, is a native of York County, where he resided until 1852. His father, Abraham Young, who resided in York County during the war of 1812, married Miss Elizabeth Glessing and reared six children, five of whom are living: Mrs. Lydia Yinger, John, Joshua, Andrew and Mrs. Catherine Ward. Mr. and Mrs. Young located in West Pennsborough Township, this county, in 1852, and here resided until their death, the former dying in 1871, and the latter in June, 1878, each about eighty years of age. Our subject remained on the family homestead, taking care of his aged parents. In the fall of 1867 he was united in marriage with Miss Matilda Warner, of this county, who died February 14, 1874, leaving three children: Charles Edwin (deceased), an infant son and Addie Justina. Mr. Young was again married, March 19, 1878, this time to Miss Eliza Jane, daughter of George C. Carothers. The children born to this union are Pearlie Catharine and an infant, latter deceased. Mr. Young owns the homestead farm consisting of seventy acres of well improved land. He is a life-long Republican. Mrs. Young is a member of the Evangelical Association.

INDEX TO

HISTORY OF CUMBERLAND COUNTY

This is an index to the principal person in each biography.

Index to subject of biography (not everyname)

-A-

AHL, C. W., 549
  Daniel Vaugh, 447
  John Alexander, 447
ALLEN, Americus R., 404
  Jeremiah, 545
  William H., 545
ALTICK, J. C., 442
AMES, Dan Henry, 459
ANTHONY, M. F., 476
AYRES, Wilmot, 498

-B-

BABB, Augustus, 405
BABBLE, Henry C., 498
BAKER, John R., 456
BALSLEY, Joseph R., 562
BAMFORD, Robert C., 465
BARBER, Jacob, 492
BARNER, John L., 442
BARNES, Charles, 562
BARNITZ, Jacob Edwin, 367
  William, 367
BARRICK, Jonathan, 517
BASEHORE, Zacharias, 485
BASHORE, J. D., 442
BAUGHMAN, William, 442
BEAR, Henry, 574
  Jonathan, 574
BEATTIE, G. Edgar, 546
BEIDLER, John K., 574
BELTZHOOVER, George, 506
BENDER, Henry, 466
  Jacob S., 368
BENTZ, John M., 368
BERKHEIMER, Joseph, 506
BEST, George W., 535
BIDDLE, Edward M., 368
  Edward W., 369
BIGGS, B. D., 443
BISHOP, George, 549
BLAIR, O. M., 443
BLOSER, William, 575
BOBB, George, 405
  John, 535
BOSLER, Abraham, 369
  Benjamin C., 370
  Elizabeth B., 370
  George Morris, 370
  James Williamson, 370
  John Herman, 369
  Joseph, 370
  Mary C., 370
BOWMAN, Abram A., 479
  David, 563
  H. N., 466
  Jacob, 563
  John D., 466
BRADLEY, William C., 575
BRANDT, Eli B., 406
  George M., 507
BRATTON, John B., 370
BRECHBILL, H. E., 549
BREHM, Franklin Pierce, 575
BRETZ, William H., 371
BRICKER, David, 576
  John, 535
  John H., 576
  Levi, 536
  Lewis, 406
BRINDLE, Abner C., 407
  David P., 499
BRINKERHOFF, Henry J., 576
BRUCKHART, W. Scott, 456
BUCHER, Jesse, 536
BURGNER, Thomas R., 576
BURHMAN, Eli, 550
  G. A., 550

BURKHART, John Samuel, 526

-C-

CARL, Alfred, 502
  Henry, 577
CAROTHERS, James M., 577
  Samuel, 527
  William, 577
CHESTNUT, James, 546
CHRISTLIEB, Samuel, 502
CHRONISTER, Isaac A., 550
CLARK, David L., 507
CLENDENIN, Charles, 499
  Cosmus S., 492
CLEPPER, George, 536
CLEVER, George, 546
  George H., 546
  Joseph, 546
COCKLIN, Henry M., 564
  Jacob C., 564
COFFEY, John, 547
COOVER, Jacob H., 564
  John, 407
  Samuel R., 565
  William, 565
CORMAN, Robert, 537
CORNMAN, Theodore, 371
COYLE, James, 550
CRAIG, W. B., 443
CRAWFORD, Samuel C., 467
CRESSLER, G. W., 547
CRIST, Samuel, 566
CROFT, D. S., 547
CROMAN, Jacob G., 527

-D-

DALE, William W., 372
DAVIDSON, James A., 578
  John Blair, 449
  John S., 578
  William M., 450
DAVIS, J. C., 551
DEARDORFF, Jacob H., 408
DEITZ, Zachariah, 538
DERLAND, Charles S., 551
DEWALT, Solomon, 551
DIETZ, Christian, 480
  David, 479
DIXON, James Ramsay, 372
DONER, David, 578
  Henry, 578
DORNBACH, Cyrus, 508
DRAWBAUGH, Daniel, 493
  Nancy, 477
DUNCAN, W. Linn, 517
DUNLAP, James, 527

-E-

EARLEY, R. M., 551
EBERLY, Austin G., 409
  Levi F., 408
  Samuel, 408
  samuel, 480
ECKELS, George Mafflin Dallas, 410
  William, 409
  William H., 410
ELCOCK, Joseph, 411
EMMINGER, Jacob, 411
  Samuel N., 412
ERB, Benjamin, 481
ERFORD, John Jacob, 477
ERNST, Abraham, 518
ESHELMAN, Annie E., 467
EVANS, H. M., 551
EYSTER, David G., 467
  Elias B., 528

Elias G., 528

-F-

FEEMAN, Joseph, 493
FENSTERMACHER, William, 443
FICKEL, James G., 372
FISHBURN, Adam, 373
  Anthony, 373
  Reuben, 525
  Rudolph, 459
FOREMAN, James K., 374
FORRY, Henry, 566
FOSNOT, J. C., 450
FULMER, Christian, 508
  George, 412
FULTON, James, 566
  Robert H., 579

-G-

GALBRAITH, Samuel, 460
  Thompson Moore, 460
  William Watts, 460
GARDNER, Eugene C., 413
  Franklin, 374
  W. F., 552
GARRETT, Abram E., 567
GARVER, John B., 509
GETTEL, John J., 444
GETTER, George, 525
GIBBLE, John E., 538
GIBSON, George, 374
GILLESPIE, Albert S., 503
GIVIN, Robert, 375
  Samuel, 552
GLADFELTER, Christian R., 499
GLESSNER, H. M., 467
GOODHART, Lewis, 528

GOODYEAR, Benjamin K., 375
GORGAS, Solomon Perry, 413
  William Rittenhouse, 376
GRAHAM, James, 567
  James Hutchinson, 376
  John, 450
  Robert M., 579
GREASON, James D., 579
GREIDER, John, 580
GROVE, George, 580
GUSWILER, Martin, 377

-H-

HAILMAN, George F., 539
HANCE, Harry, 460
HARGLEROAD, C. R., 444
HARMON, P., 552
HASKELL, E. F., 552
HAUCK, George, 413
  George W., 414
  Samuel F., 414
HAVERSTICK, Benjamin, 415
HAYS, Jesse C., 415
  John, 378
HEABY, George W., 553
HEBERLIG, Adam, 485
  Benjamin F., 486
  Daniel, 518
  Joseph F., 486
HECK, John B., 468
HEFFLEFINGER, David, 486
HEMMINGER, George, 379
  Jacob, 378, 503
HENDERSON, Robert M., 379
HENSEL, John, 487
HERMAN, Alfred J., 381
  Jacob N., 529
  John E. A., 539
  Manasseh, 539

Martin C., 380
HERR, C. K., 553
HERSHMAN, John W., 539
HERTZLER, Christian, 481
  Elias, 510
  Henry, 568
  Jacob M., 509
  John, 509
HESS, Christian, 457
  Samuel, 540
HEYD, Jacob L., 468
HIGHLANDS, Hiram, 547
HOERNER, David, 553
HOLLER, Henry, 469
HOLLINGER, Jacob, 461
HOOVER, D. P., 554
  E. J., 510
  Michael L., 540
HORST, Eliza, 568
HOUSTON, Samuel F., 416
HULL, Israel, 554
HUMMEL, George, 416
HUMRICH, Christian Philip, 381
HURSH, Henry, 487
  John, 451
HURST, Edwin W., 416
  Jacob, 417
HUSTON, E. Rankin, 417
  James S., 418
  Samuel F., 529
HUTTON, John, 510

-I-

IRVINE, Robert Hays, 519

-J-

JACOBS, George W., 499
  John, 540

JAMES, Owen, 493

-K-

KAST, John P., 541
KAUFFMAN, Benjamin, 554
  Levi, 418
KEISER, John C., 580
KELLER, Adam, 381
  Daniel, 529
KENDIG, Daniel, 519
KERR, David Sterrett, 581
  William, 581
  William A., 581
KIEFFER, Stephen Barnett, 382
KILLIAN, Henry, 519
KIMMEL, David H., 420
KING, Daniel, 458
  R. Frank, 581
KLEPPER, William, 554
KNODERER, Andrew C., 568
KOLLER, Jonas, 420
KOONS, William Carnahan, 520
KOSER, Alfred C., 421
  John J., 444
KOST, Curtis, 541

-L-

LANDIS, George, 581
  John B., 382
LANTZ, William L., 469
LEAS, Joseph, 422
LEBERKNIGHT, Frederick B., 488
LEEPER, Daniel, 458
LEFEVER, David, 530
LEHMAN, D. P., 555
  J. C., 555

Index to subject of biography (not everyname) 5

LEIB, Christian, 555
LEIDICH, A. M., 555
LEIDIGH, G. W., 511
LENHER, Levi H., 422
LINDSAY, J. W., 556
   Joseph A., 582
   M. H., 556
LINE, Abram L., 461
   Albert Allan, 383
   David, 461
   Emanuel C., 462
   George, 582
   Jacob Zitzer, 462
   James V., 462
   John A., 582
   Samuel C., 462
LININGER, John, 481
LLOYD, William Penn, 422
LOGAN, William B., 481
LONG, Michael, 530
LONGENECKER, George B., 469
LONGNECKER, John K., 583
LONGSDORF, William H., 383
LOUDON, John M., 542
LUTZ, George B., 511
   William A., 444

-M-
MCALLESTER, D. A., 556
MCCACHRAN, Robert, 452
MCCARRELL, William A., 444
MCCAULEY, James Andrew, 383
MCCLURE, Charles, 384
MCCREA, W. H., 504
MCCULLOCH, James, 520
MCCULLOUGH, William Alexander, 531
MCCUNE, Hugh, 521

   John Theodore, 531
   Samuel Albert, 521
   William D., 548
MCELWAIN, Joseph, 488
MCGAW, Winfield Scott, 488
MCKEEHAN, Benjamin, 583
MAINS, John D., 583
MANNING, Henry, 522
MANSFIELD, A., 556
MARSHALL, James B., 445
MARTIN, Franklin, 470
   James E., 482
   Joab, 445
MASONHEIMER, Lewis, 385
MAUK, Thomas H., 423
MAY, A. R., 556
   Daniel G., 471
MEGAW, Lewis C., 504
MEIXEL, Jacob H., 557
MELOY, Jacob L., 385
MENTZER, Francis, 478
MERKEL, David R., 457
   Levi, 424
MESSINGER, George, 542
MICKEY, John E., 523
   Robert, 522
MIDDLETON, Robert H., 557
MILLEISEN, Joseph, 425
MILLER, David, 425, 500
   David R., 426
   George H., 569
   Harry J., 569
   Henry K., 531
   Solomon, 569
   William E., 386
   William Henry, 387
MINNICH, Joseph, 505
MITCHELL, John, 489
   Samuel H., 489
MOHLER, David S., 570

Levi, 570
MOLTZ, Theodore M., 471
MONTGOMERY, Alexander S., 584
MOORE, James, 531
   Johnston, 388
   Joseph Addison, 472
   William, 557
MORRET, Jeremiah H., 426
MORRISON, John, 463
   Winfield Scott, 463
MOSER, Henry G., 427
MOSSER, Henry R., 494
MOUNTZ, Elias, 557
MOWERY, Andrew, 489
   Samuel Dallas, 490
MULLIN, A. F., 558
   Charles H., 558
   William A., 558
MUMMA, Amos, 570
   Eli, 571
   Jacob, 427
   John, 571
MUMPER, George W., 495

MURRAY, George, 388
   Joseph Alexander, 388
MUSSELMAN, Levi, 495
MUSSER, Henry D., 472
MYERS, Benjamin, 585
   Emily W., 584
   Henry T., 532
   Jacob, 463
   John F., 532
   Thomas E., 452
   William Albert, 532

-N-

NIESLEY, Christian B., 428

Jacob M., 512
NOFFSINGER, Jacob, 558
NORCROSS, George, 389
NORRIS, J., 452
NORTH, J. D., 459

-O-

O'HARA, George, 512
O'NEALE, Lindsay Pitts, 428
ORRIS, Adam, 429
   Levon H., 585
OTT, Simpson, 559
OTTO, George, 559

-P-

PALM, Auston Taylor, 473
PATTON, Joseph Wheller, 389
PAUL, David K., 512
PAXTON, George W., 464
   Thomas, 390
PEFFER, H. K., 390
   Willliam Glancy, 391
PENROSE, William McFunn, 391
PHILLIPS, Abram, 559
PIPER, Samuel, 532
PLANK, Jacob, 513
PLOYER, Frederick K., 429
PORTER, William Montgomery, 391
PRATT, Richard Henry, 391
PRESSEL, George W., 514

-R-

RALSTON, James McAllister, 423
   Mervin Lindsey, 586

RANDALL, Robert S., 453
REA, J. D., 523
REIGART, Samuel W., 430
REIGHTER, Christian, 392
REILY, William F., 392
REINHARDT, Ferdinand, 490
RICE, D. S., 559
  Henry C., 533
RIEGEL, John, 430
RINGROSE, Jesse W., 431
RINGWALT, John J., 431
  Lew, 431
RITNER, Joseph, 586
RITTER, Henry M., 393
RUDY, Daniel, 559
RUPLEY, Henry M., 473
RUPP, George N., 496
  Henry S., 457
  John. M., 482
RUSSEL, George H., 491

-S-

SADLER, John L., 431
  Wilbur F., 393
  William, 393, 474
SAHULL, William H., 474
SAXTON, John O., 432
SCHELL, Samuel, 560
SCHERICH, John, 432
SCHMOHL, John, 394
SCHROEDER, George, 433
SEIDLE, Frederick, 433
SENSEMAN, John F., 514
  William, 560
SHAEFFER, John, 482
SHAMBAUGH, Michael, 505
SHAPLEY, Rufus E., 434
SHARP, Thomas, 523
SHARPE, Alexander Brady, 394

SHAW, Jacob G., 587
SHEELY, Andrew, 483
  John, 496
SHELLEY, H. O., 571
SHOEMAKER, John M., 542
SHOPP, John, 483
SHORT, Robert N., 434
SHREINER, Charles, 543
SHUMAN, Eli C., 483
SHUMBERGER, George W., 484
SIBBET, Robert Lowry, 395
SIBBETT, James A., 434
SIMMONS, John, 543

SINGISER, Leslie H., 475
SIPE, Peter, 435
SMEAD, Alexander D. Bache, 395
SMITH, J. H., 464
  R. L., 524
SNYDER, Simon, 533
SOLLENBERGER, Abraham, 543
SOUDER, George W., 515
SOURS, John, 464
SPONG, Lemuel R., 396
SPONSLER, J. S., 544
STAUFFER, Jacob F., 571
STAVER, Enoch, 491
STEINER, Isaac D., 587
STEWART, Alexander, 445
  George H., 446
STRICKER, Francis H., 435
STRICKLER, Abraham, 560
STROCK, George W., 515
  Joseph, 436
STROHM, George, 587
  H. A. T., 524
  John W., 453
STUART, Hugh, 396

John T., 397
R. M., 560
Walter, 464
SWARTZ, John, 572
Reuben, 397
SWIGERT, Samuel B., 561
SWILER, J. H., 561

-T-

TANGER, George, 561
TAYLOR, John K., 458
Samuel, 548
THOMAS, B. F., 561
R. H., 436
THOMPSON, Frank E., 397
THOMSON, Alexander A., 397
TITZEL, Christian H., 437
TOTTON, Joseph, 438
TRITT, David P., 534
John A., 534
Peter, 534
TRONE, Charles, 524
TURNER, John R., 398

-U-

UMBERGER, John, 496
UNDERWOOD, Alexander, 438

-V-

VAN CAMP, Joshua E., 588
VANCE, Joseph, 399
VOGLESONG, Samuel, 544

-W-

WAGGONER, George B., 525
Henry F., 526
WAGNER, David Knight, 446
John, 454
John Carey, 446
Samuel C., 454
Wilson J., 526
WAGONER, George, 438
WALKER, George, 497
WALLACE, William Jackson, 478
WALTERS, Wilson P., 475
WATTS, Edward Biddle, 400
Frederick, 399
Hiram, 572
William Miles, 439
WEAKLEY, James B., 561
WENTZ, Alexander, 440
WERTZ, Amos C., 484
WESTHAFER, William, 572
WETZEL, John Wise, 400
WHERRY, S. M., 548
Samuel, 548
WILBAR, Charles F., 475
WILDER, Barrens Sylvester, 400
WILLIAMS, James, 515
John L., 465
Muhlenberg, 455
WILLIAMSON, Thomas U., 516
WILSON, Robert, 440
WILT, George, 484
WING, Conway Phelps, 401
WITHERSPOOON, William M., 446
WITMAN, Henry K., 476
WITMER, Robert S., 500
Samuel, 500
WOLF, John, 500
Thomas, 562
WONDERLICH, Frederick, 441
WOODS, Richey, 588
WOODWARD, Charles R., 402
William H., 403
WORLEY, Sarah, 573

WORST, David W., 573
WYLIE, Samuel S., 548

-Y-

YOUNG, Andrew, 588

-Z-

ZEARING, Jacob Swiler, 501
ZEIGLER, Abram J., 501
  Henry H., 501
ZIMMERMAN, Emanuel, 497
  Henry, 544
  Henry W., 498
  Jonas B., 516
ZINN, Edward P., 441
  Henry, 441
  John, 403
ZUG, Jacob, 404

www.ingramcontent.com/pod-product-compliance
Lightning Source LLC
Chambersburg PA
CBHW070004010526
44117CB00011B/1420